Beatson, Matthews and Elliott's

ADMINISTRATIVE LAW

Beatson, Matthews
and Elliott's

ADMINISTRATIVE LAW

Text and Materials

THIRD EDITION

Mark Elliott
(Consultant Editors:
Jack Beatson and
Martin Matthews)

OXFORD
UNIVERSITY PRESS

OXFORD
UNIVERSITY PRESS

Great Clarendon Street, Oxford OX2 6DP

Oxford University Press is a department of the University of Oxford.
It furthers the University's objective of excellence in research, scholarship,
and education by publishing worldwide in

Oxford New York

Auckland Cape Town Dar es Salaam Hong Kong Karachi
Kuala Lumpur Madrid Melbourne Mexico City Nairobi
New Delhi Shanghai Taipei Toronto

With offices in

Argentina Austria Brazil Chile Czech Republic France Greece
Guatemala Hungary Italy Japan South Korea Poland Portugal
Singapore Switzerland Thailand Turkey Ukraine Vietnam

Oxford is a registered trade mark of Oxford University Press
in the UK and in certain other countries

Published in the United States
by Oxford University Press Inc., New York

First published 1983
Second edition 1989

British Library Cataloguing in Publication Data
Data available

Library of Congress Cataloging in Publication Data
Data available

ISBN 0–19–926998–X   978–0–19–926998–3

10 9 8 7 6 5 4 3 2

Typeset by RefineCatch Limited, Bungay, Suffolk
Printed in Great Britain
on acid-free paper by
Ashford Colour Press Limited, Gosport, Hampshire

CONTENTS—SUMMARY

17 Delegated Legislation

18 Inquiries

19 Statutory Tribunals

20 Ombudsmen

DETAILED CONTENTS

3   The Status of Unlawful Administrative Action

4   Discretionary Power: An Introduction

5   The Scope of Public Law Principles

6 | Retention of Discretion

7 | Legitimate Expectations

8 Abuse of Discretion I

9 Abuse of Discretion II

10 The Rule Against Bias

11 Procedural Fairness

12 Giving Reasons For Decisions

13   Remedies

14   The Judicial Review Procedure

15 Restriction of Remedies

16 Liability of Public Authorities and Crown Proceedings

Delegated Legislation

18 Inquiries

19 Statutory Tribunals

20 Ombudsmen

PREFACE

Since the last edition of this book was published in 1989, English administrative law and the landscape in which it operates have changed very substantially indeed. Administrative (and even legislative) power is wielded by an increasingly diverse range of bodies as a result of such developments as devolution and the transfer of powers from monolithic Whitehall departments to government agencies; and the involvement of the private sector in the delivery of public services, and sometimes the exercise of executive power, has accelerated, as 'government by contract' has become a reality.

The relationship between the citizen and the state has altered, too. The enactment of the Human Rights Act 1998 is the most prominent, but far from the only, example of this change. English courts, in their on-going development of administrative law, have articulated with increasing boldness the standards of good government to which citizens are entitled to expect public institutions to adhere. This can be seen in the growing emphasis placed by courts on the need for public authorities to respect individuals' human rights — as a matter of general administrative law, not simply under the 1998 Act; in the growth, since the last edition of this book, of the notion of substantive legitimate expectations, and the greater prominence of legitimate expectation theory generally; in the English courts' increasing enthusiasm for a duty upon administrative bodies to give reasons for their decisions; and in countless other areas which are traced in this volume.

Not only have the duties owed by public bodies to individuals changed substantially over the last 16 years. The scope of administrative law — in particular, the extent to which the principles of good administration may be applied outwith the traditional confines of statutory power — has been re-thought, too. In 1989, cases such as *Council of Civil Service Unions* v. *Minister for the Civil Service* [1985] AC 374 and *R v. Panel on Takeovers and Mergers, ex parte Datafin plc* [1987] QB 815 had only recently liberated English administrative law in this respect, clearly establishing that judicial review could extend to the mode of use of the royal prerogative, and to the exercise of certain so-called *de facto* powers. Such propositions are today regarded as axiomatic. There have been important changes, too, in the political climate in which administrative law exists. In 2005, in a political landscape dominated by such governmental and popular concerns as immigration control and counter-terrorism, the hallowed principles of administrative justice such as the right to a fair hearing, and ultimate jurisdiction of the High Court to see that such principles are respected, find themselves under increasing pressure.

As indicated by the change of title to *Beatson, Matthews and Elliott's Administrative Law: Text and Materials*, the format of the third edition of this book is somewhat different from that of its predecessors. As with the first two editions, however, the aim has been to make accessible to those studying administrative law key extracts from primary materials — not just cases, but also academic articles, official publications, and so on.

It is convenient, at this stage, to explain various practical matters concerning the presentation of material in the book which may be of help to readers. In addition to the various substantive changes to administrative law which have occurred since 1989, some of which were briefly traced above, there have been a number of procedural changes. One consequence of these has been a series of changes in terminology. For example, whereas 'applicants' used to issue 'applications for judicial review', 'claimants' now issue 'claims for judicial review'; 'respondents' are now known as 'defendants'. Meanwhile, the prerogative remedies '*certiorari*', '*mandamus*' and '*prohibition*' have been renamed 'quashing orders', 'mandatory orders' and 'prohibiting orders'. In this book, whenever reference is made to any of these matters in the text, the new nomenclature is used; however, in excerpts from materials published prior to these changes, the original language is retained. A further development since the last edition is the advent of neutral citation. Whenever neutral citations are available, they are given in this book in order to assist readers who wish to look up cases using electronic resources rather than conventional law reports. To the same end, where reference is made to particular passages of judgments or other materials, paragraph numbers (indicated by the use of square brackets) are always given in preference to page numbers (indicated by the absence of square brackets). The final practical matter to which attention should be drawn is that footnotes are always omitted from excerpts; however, where footnotes are considered to be essential, they (or their gist) are set out in square brackets in the excerpts.

I have attempted to state the law as of November 2004, which is when the majority of the manuscript for this book was submitted to the publisher. It has, however, been possible to include some more recent developments, and I am grateful to Oxford University Press for facilitating that. Although it was not possible to rewrite relevant sections of the book — in particular, parts of chapter 9 — in the light of the House of Lords' decision in *A* v. *Secretary of State for the Home Department* [2004] UKHL 56 [2005] 2 WLR 87, which was handed down in December 2004, an appendix has been added to the end of the book summarising the case and briefly explaining its significance to the principles of administrative law considered in this volume.

Inevitably, the writing of this book has been a long process, during which I have received a great deal of help and support from colleagues, friends and family. I am particularly grateful to Jack Beatson and Martin Matthews, the authors of the first two editions of this book and now its consultant editors, both for entrusting the new edition to me in the first place, and for their invaluable guidance, advice and comments, from which I have benefited immensely. I am also grateful to Martin for undertaking the majority of the work on chapter 16. I wish to thank various friends and colleagues — in particular Christopher Forsyth, Tom Hickman, Clive Lewis, Trevor Allan and Amanda Perreau-Saussine — who either commented on draft chapters or, more generally, discussed with me ideas relevant to the book. At the stage of completing the manuscript, I was fortunate to secure the excellent research assistance of two of my former students, Simon Atrill and Katherine Apps, whose help proved invaluable. I would also like to thank Oxford University Press for their assistance; particular thanks are due to Kate Whetter, Christina White (who was at OUP when this edition was commissioned), Jasmin Naim, Gabriella La Cava and Dan Leissner. Finally, I wish to record how grateful I am to my wife, Vicky, for her patience when the process of completing the manuscript consumed inordinate amounts of my time, and for her unstinting support throughout the course of this project.

Mark Elliott
Cambridge, March 2005

ACKNOWLEDGEMENTS

Grateful acknowledgement is made to all the authors and publishers of copyright material which appears in this book, and in particular to the following for permission to reprint material from the sources indicated:

Crown copyright material is reproduced under Class Licence Number C01P0000148 with the permission of the Controller of HMSO and the Queen's Printer.

Harry Arthurs for extract from H W Arthurs: 'Rethinking Administrative Law: A Slightly Dicey Business' (1979) 17 *Osgoode Hall Law Journal* 1.

Blackwell Publishing Ltd for extracts from *Modern Law Review:* Kate Malleson: 'Judicial Bias and Disqualifications after *Pinochet (No 2)*' (2000) 63 *MLR* 119; John Laws: 'Judicial Remedies and the Constitution' (1994) 57 *MLR* 213.

Butterworths Division of Reed Elsevier (UK) Ltd for extracts from *All England Law Reports* [All ER] and *Butterworths Medico-Legal Reports* [BMLR].

Cambridge University Press and the authors for extracts from Carol Harlow and Richard Rawlings: *Law and Administration* (1997), and Mary Seneviratne: *Ombudsmen: Public Services and Administrative Justice* (2002); previously published by Butterworths now part of the Law in Context series published by Cambridge University Press.

Canadian Bar Foundation extract from John Willis: '*Delegatus non potest Delegare*' (1943) 21 *Canadian Bar Review* 257.

Cambridge Law Review and the authors for extracts from *Cambridge Law Journal*: T R S Allan: 'The Constitutional Foundations of Judicial Review: Conceptual Conundrum or Interpretative Inquiry?' (2002) *CLJ* 87; Paul Craig: 'Ultra Vires and the Foundations of Judicial Review' (1998) *CLJ* 63; Bruce Harris: 'Judicial Review, Justiciability and the Prerogative of Mercy' (2003) *CLJ* 631; Clive Lewis: 'The Exhaustion of Alternative Remedies in Administrative Law' (1991) *CLJ* 138; and Joanna Miles: 'Standing under the Human Rights Act 1998: Theories of Rights Enforcement and the Nature of Public Law Adjudication' (2000) *CLJ* 133.

Tom Cornford for extract from T Cornford: 'The Freedom of Information Act: Genuine or Sham?' [2001] 3 *Web JCLI*.

Hart Publishing Ltd for extracts from M Elliott: *The Constitutional Foundations of Judicial Review* (Hart 2001); V R Aronson: 'A Public Lawyer's Response to Privatisation and Outsourcing' and M Hunt: 'Constitutionalism and the Contractualisation of Government in the United Kingdom' in M Taggart (ed): *The Province of Administrative Law* (OUP, 1997); and T Tridimas: 'Proportionality in Community Law: Searching for the Appropriate Standard of Scrutiny' in E Ellis (ed): *The Principle of Proportionality in the Laws of Europe* (OUP 1999).

The Incorporated Council of Law Reporting for extracts from *Appeal Court Reports* [AC], *Chancery Reports* [Ch], *Queen's Bench Reports* [QB], *King's Bench Reports* [KB] and *Weekly Law Reports* [WLR].

Oxford University Press for extracts from D J Galligan: 'Procedural Fairness' in P Birks (ed): *The Frontiers of Liability* Volume 1 (OUP 1994); Peter Cane: *Administrative Law* (OUP 2004); Christopher Forsyth: 'The Metaphysic of Nullity: Invalidity, Conceptual Reasoning and the Rule of Law' and S Sedley: 'The Crown and its own Courts' in Christopher Forsyth and Ivan Hare (eds): *The Golden Metwand and the Crooked Cord: Essays in Public Law in Honour of Sir William Wade QC* (OUP 1998); D J Galligan: *Discretionary Powers* (OUP 1986) and *Due Process and Fair Procedures* (OUP 1996); Jeffrey Jowell: 'The Rule of Law Today' in Jeffrey Jowell and Dawn Oliver (eds): *The Changing Constitution* (OUP 2004); S Schønberg: *Legitimate Expectations in Administrative Law* (OUP 2000); and William Wade and Christopher Forsyth: *Administrative Law* (OUP 2004).

Oxford University Press Journals and the author for extract from T R S Allan: 'Procedural Fairness and the Duty of Respect' (1998) 18 *Oxford Journal of Legal Studies* 497.

Sweet & Maxwell Ltd for extracts from *European Human Rights Reports* [EHRR]; from *Public Law*: P Cane: 'Standing, Legality and the Limits of Public Law' (1981) *PL* 322; P P Craig: 'Competing Models of Judicial Review' (1999) *PL* 428; Gavin Drewry: Judicial Inquiries and the Public Reassurance' (1996) *PL* 368; M R Freedland: 'The Rule against Delegation and the *Carltona* Doctrine in an Agency Context' (1996) *PL* 19; C Hilson: 'Judicial Review, Policies and the Fettering of Discretion' (2002) *PL* 111; Dawn Oliver: 'Common Values in Public and Private Law and the Public/Private Divide' (1997) *PL* 630 and 'Functions of a Public Nature under the Human Rights Act' (2004) *PL* 329; Abimbola A Olowofoyeku: 'The *Nemo Judex* Rule: The Case Against Automatic Disqualification' (2000) *PL* 456; Konrad Schiemann: '*Locus Standi*' (1990) *PL* 342; A P Le Sueur and Maurice Sunkin: 'The Requirement of Leave' (1992) in *PL* 102; and from *Law Quarterly Review*: William Wade: 'Unlawful Administrative Action: Void or Voidable? Part II' (1968) 84 *LQR* 95.

Thomson Legal and Regulatory Ltd for extracts from *Commonwealth Law Reports* [CLR], copyright © Lawbook Co, part of Thomson Legal and Regulatory Ltd, *www.thomson.com.au*.

Every effort has been made to trace and contact copyright holders prior to going to press but this has not been possible in all cases. Although we are continuing to seek the necessary permissions up to publication, if notified, the publisher will undertake to rectify any errors or omissions at the earliest opportunity.

TABLE OF CASES

*Page references in **bold** indicate that the item is given particular prominence in the text.*

TABLE OF STATUTES

*Page references in **bold** indicate that the item is given particular prominence in the text.*

TABLE OF STATUTORY INSTRUMENTS

*Page references in **bold** indicate that the item is given particular prominence in the text.*

TABLE OF EUROPEAN LEGISLATION AND INTERNATIONAL TREATIES AND CONVENTIONS

*Page references in **bold** indicate that the item is given particular prominence in the text.*

LIST OF ABBREVIATIONS

AC	Law Reports, Appeal Cases
Admin LR	Administrative Law Reports
All ER	All England Law Reports
ALR	Australian Law Reports
App Cas	Law Reports, Appeal Cases
BMLR	Butterworths Medico-Legal Reports
CBNS	Common Bench Reports, New Series
Ch	Law Reports, Chancery Division
CLJ	*Cambridge Law Journal*
CLP	*Current Legal Problems*
CLR	Commonwealth Law Reports
CMLR	Common Market Law Reports
CPR	Civil Procedure Rules
Crim LR	*Criminal Law Review*
DLR	Dominion Law Reports
EC	European Community
ECHR	European Convention on Human Rights
ECtHR	European Court of Human Rights
Ed CR	Education Case Reports
EHRLR	*European Human Rights Law Review*
EHRR	European Human Rights Reports
EMLR	Entertainment and Media Law Reports
Env LR	Environmental Law Reports
EU	European Union
EuLR	European Law Reports
EWCA Civ	[Neutral citation for Court of Appeal (Civil Division) decisions]
EWHC	[Neutral citiation for High Court decisions]
EWHC (Admin)	[Neutral citiation for Administrative Court decisions]
Ex	Exchequer Reports
Fed LR	Federal Law Reports
FLR	Family Law Reports
FSR	Fleet Street Reports
HC	House of Commons papers
HL	House of Lords papers
HLC	Clark & Finnelly's House of Lords Reports New Series
HLR	Housing Law Reports
HRA	Human Rights Act 1998

ICR	Industrial Cases Reports
ILJ	*Industrial Law Journal*
INLR	Immigration and Nationality Law Reports
IRLR	Industrial Relations Law Reports
JPL	*Journal of Planning & Environment Law*
JR	*Judicial Review*
Jur Rev	*Juridical Review*
KB	Law Reports, King's Bench
Law Com	Law Commission papers
Ld Raym	Lord Raymond's King's Bench and Common Pleas Reports
LGR	Local Government Reports
LQR	*Law Quarterly Review*
LR HL	Law Reports, English & Irish Appeals
LS	*Legal Studies*
LSG	*Law Society's Gazette*
LT	Law Times Reports
MLR	*Modern Law Review*
NILQ	*Northern Ireland Legal Quarterly*
NZLR	New Zealand Law Reports
OJLS	*Oxford Journal of Legal Studies*
P	Law Reports, Probate
Parl Aff	*Parliamentary Affairs*
P & CR	Property & Compensation Reports
PL	*Public Law*
Pub Admin	*Public Administration*
QB	Law Reports, Queen's Bench
RSC	Rules of the Supreme Court
S Ct	Supreme Court Reporter
SIAC	*Special Immigration Appeals Commission*
SJLB	*Solicitors' Journal Law Brief*
SR (NSW)	New South Wales State Reports
Stra	Strange's King's Bench Reports
TLJ	*Torts Law Journal*
TR	Taxation Reports
UBCLR	*University of British Columbia Law Review*
U Chi LR	*University of Chicago Law Review*

UKHL	[Neutral citation for House of Lords decisions]
UKHRR	United Kingdom Human Rights Reports
UKPC	[Neutral citation for Privy Council decisions]
UTLJ	*University of Toronto Law Journal*
VR	Victorian Reports
Web JCLI	*Web Journal of Current Legal Issues*
WLR	Weekly Law Reports

 # INTRODUCTORY MATTERS

1.1 Administrative Law

To many, if not all, readers of this book, *private law* will be a familiar notion. Private law refers to such branches of the law as contract and tort, and is concerned principally with the duties and obligations which individuals owe to one another. Now, it is, of course, possible for government and other public bodies to enter into contracts and to engage in conduct which may be tortious; when they do, they are, quite rightly, in general regulated by the same body of private law as citizens. However, it is clear that, in addition to doing things, such as breaching contracts and carelessly causing injury, that can readily be dealt with by private law, government and public bodies commit a wide range of acts that cannot meaningfully be so regulated. Consider, for instance, the position of an individual whose house is to be compulsorily purchased and demolished by government to make way for a new airport, or an asylum-seeker who is told that he must leave the country. Many of the issues which arise in such circumstances cannot adequately be regulated private law. Does the government, in the first place, possess the legal power to order the purchase and destruction of the house? Would it make a difference if the government had decided to site the airport in a particular location for self-serving party political reasons — *eg* to create jobs in a nearby marginal constituency? Should the asylum-seeker have been given an opportunity — and, if so, what sort of opportunity — to plead his case before the decision to deport him was taken? Can the asylum-seeker be deported to a particular country if there is evidence to suggest that he would be treated inhumanely or tortured upon arrival there? Questions such as these are peculiarly relevant to the type of powers exercised by government and public bodies, and a separate body of law to regulate the exercise of such powers — *administrative law* — is therefore required.

1.2 How is Good Administration to be Secured?

There can be little doubt that the central purpose of administrative law is to promote good administration. For example, administrative bodies should act efficiently and honestly to promote the public good; they should listen to individuals likely to be affected by their decisions, taking their views into account; and they should operate in a fair, transparent, and unbiased fashion, seeking always to serve the public interest while, at the same time, respecting the rights of individuals.

However, while it is uncontroversial that administrative law's central purpose is to secure good government along these lines, the same cannot be said of the methodology by which that objective is to be secured. For instance, should *courts* bear primary responsibility for ensuring good administrative conduct, or can this better be secured in some other way? And is it appropriate to borrow from the private law model of adjudication, under which courts seek to resolve disputes after they have arisen, so that administrative law operates retrospectively to correct misuses of public power, or should it be regarded as a template of good administrative practice which primarily exists not to punish or correct misuses of power, but to promote an environment within which such misuses are, in the first place, rare? Differing answers to these questions are supplied by the 'red light' and 'green light' models of administrative law.

1.2.1 Red Light Theory

The red light view — like its green light counterpart, to which we turn below — comprises a number of different threads, and is elaborated at length by Harlow and Rawlings, *Law and Administration* (London 1997), ch 2. They identify a strand of literature (*op cit* at 37) which reveals a 'preference for a minimalist state' in which 'the primary function of administrative law should be to control any excess of state power and subject it to legal, and more especially judicial, control'. They cite the following passage from Wade and Forsyth's *Administrative Law* (Oxford 1994) at 4–5 (which also appears in the most recent edition, published in 2004, at 4–5) as a paradigm example of this red light tradition:

A first approximation to a definition of administrative law is to say that it is the law relating to the control of governmental power. This, at any rate, is the heart of the subject, as viewed by most lawyers. The governmental power in question is not that of Parliament: Parliament as the legislature is sovereign and, subject to one exception [*viz* European Community law], is beyond legal control. The powers of all other public authorities are subordinated to the law, just as much in the case of the Crown and Ministers as in the case of local authorities and other public bodies. All such subordinate powers have two inherent characteristics. First, they are all subject to legal limitations; there is no such thing as absolute or unfettered administrative power. Secondly, and consequentially, it is always possible for any power to be abused. Even where Parliament enacts that a Minister may make such an order as he thinks fit for a certain purpose, the court may still invalidate the order if it infringes one of the many judge-made rules. And the court will invalidate it, *a fortiori*, if it infringes the limits which Parliament itself has ordained.

The primary purpose of administrative law, therefore, is to keep the powers of the government within their legal bounds, so as to protect the citizen against their abuse. The powerful engines of authority must be prevented from running amok. 'Abuse', it should be made clear, carries no necessary innuendo of malice or bad faith. Government departments may misunderstand their legal position as easily as may other people, and the law which they have to administer is frequently complex and uncertain. Abuse is therefore inevitable, and it is all the more necessary that the law should provide means to check it . . .

As well as power there is duty. It is also the concern of administrative law to see that public authorities can be compelled to perform their duties if they make default . . . The law provides compulsory remedies for such situations, thus dealing with the negative as well as the positive side of maladministration.

This passage exhibits two features which are characteristic of the red light model: it is the *courts* which are centrally charged with securing good administration, while the emphasis is on administrative law as a *control* upon government — an external fetter upon the freedom of public authorities, a corrective to be invoked when power is abused. Within this tradition, courts and public authorities are ultimately regarded as combatants, the former invoking the weapon of administrative law against the latter as part of an ongoing fight against the abuse of governmental power.

1.2.2 Green Light Theory

A different approach is proposed by green light theorists, as Harlow and Rawlings (*op cit* at 67–74) explain:

[We turn now to] an alternative tradition, which we have called 'green light' theory. In using this metaphor, we do not wish to suggest that green light theorists favour unrestricted or arbitrary action by the state. What one person sees as control of arbitrary power may, however, be experienced by another as a brake on progress . . . Where red light theorists favour judicial control of executive power, green light theorists are inclined to pin their hopes on the political process . . .

New accounts of administrative law . . . began to appear in England. These were *administration centred* — the role of administrative law was not to act as a counterweight to the interventionist state but to facilitate legitimate government action — and *collectivist* in character, advancing the claim to promote the public interest or common good . . .

Because they see their own function as the resolution of disputes and because they see the administrative function from outside, lawyers traditionally emphasise external control through adjudication. To the lawyer, law is the policeman; it operates as an external control, often retrospectively. But a main concern of many green light writers was to *minimise* the influence of courts. Courts, with their legalistic values, were seen as obstacles to progress, and the control which they emphasise as unrepresentative and undemocratic. To emphasise this crucial point, in green light theory, decision-making by an elite judiciary, imbued with a legalistic, rights-based ideology and eccentric vision of the 'public interest' — Griffith's phrase [see *The Politics of the Judiciary* (London 1991) at 274–300] — was never a plausible counter to authoritarianism.

If, as green light theorists maintain, the courts' influence should be minimized, how *should* good administration be pursued? We return to the explanation of Harlow and Rawlings (*op cit* at 75–78):

Griffith set out his personal creed in 'The Political Constitution' [(1979) 42 MLR 1]. Dismissing the recently fashionable constitutional device of a Bill of Rights, justiciable and enforceable in the courts to enshrine and protect individual 'rights', Griffith argued for the collectivist view of 'rights' as group interests or 'claims' to be evaluated through the political process. Griffith emphasised the need for access to information, open government, a free and powerful press, and ultimately expressed faith in decentralisation through local government and a strengthened Parliament. On the other hand, he prescribed a reduced role for the judiciary and a diminution in the amount of discretionary power at its disposal. Policy-making and accountability, in short, are political functions . . .

If the model of law is to be abandoned, then many feel that something other than the traditional model of government must take its place. Few administrative lawyers — or, indeed, citizens — would wish to set sail in a barque as frail as that of ministerial responsibility. Because it revealed the inadequacies of ministerial responsibility, Crichel Down is often described as the beginning of modern administrative law. Very briefly, Crichel Down had been acquired before World War II by the

Air Ministry as a bombing range. Subsequently, when no longer required for these purposes, it was transferred to the Ministry of Agriculture. Later, a dispute arose when the Ministry, wishing to dispose of the land, tried to let it as a single unit to a new tenant instead of allowing its original owners to buy it back. Fierce objections from the latter forced a public inquiry, which established the responsibility of civil servants both for the policy and also for its execution. Controversially, the Minister, Sir Thomas Dugdale, resigned . . .

Crichel Down exposed a world of administrative policy and decision-making apparently immune from political and parliamentary controls. In Griffith's phrase, 'the fundamental defect revealed was not a failure in the constitutional relations of those involved nor the policy decisions nor even the length of the struggle [the complainant] had to wage. It was in the method and therefore in the mental processes of the officials' [(1955) 18 MLR 557 at 569]. But content to rely on 'that personal integrity which is so much more than an absence of corruption', Griffith concluded that the civil service must be left to put its own house in order. Here we find the characteristic reliance of green light theorists on political and administrative institutions. For those who were less trusting, yet did not wish to tip the balance too far in the direction of judicial control, the challenge was to provide alternatives. In the aftermath of Crichel Down, this was to become a major preoccupation of administrative lawyers . . .

[The authors noted that they had used the word 'control' without stopping to consider its meaning, and continued:] Control can be symbolic or real; it can mean to check, restrain or govern. Griffith and Street [*Principles of Administrative Law* (London 1973) at 24] clearly sense latent ambiguities. They say: 'A great deal turns on the meaning which is attached to the word "controls". Banks control a river; a driver controls his car. The influence of a parent over a child may be greater than the power of a prison guard over a convict.' If we try applying these metaphors to the administrative process, we will see that the 'controls' are direct and internal rather than indirect and external. To extend our metaphors, a river bank may be inspected by an officer of the catchment board (today more probably the official of a privatised water authority) to see that it is in good repair; a policeman may stop the driver and caution him for speeding; a health visitor may advise the child's parents to exert a different kind of influence; and the prison guard may be questioned by the board of visitors. These are all controls, but they are external . . .

Dicey's controls were *external* . . . Obviously, however, the first control of administrative activity is *internal*: hierarchical and supervisory. Consider the doctrine of individual ministerial responsibility central to the argument over Crichel Down. One function of the doctrine is to provide internal control because the Minister must, as head of his department, supervise the activities of his subordinates by establishing policies and checking the way in which they are implemented. The doctrine also provides for external control through responsibility to Parliament, but this is envisaged as a last resort. And Griffith hints at the superiority of internal control when he prescribes as a remedy for Crichel Down 'more "red tape" not less'.

A second distinction is between *prospective* and *retrospective* control. Judicial review of administrative action is primarily retrospective, although it can possess a prospective element if the administration accepts that judicial precedent establishes the limits of its future conduct. Legislation is primarily prospective. Like the banks of the river, legislation controls administrative activity by prescribing its limits. When an administrator asks, 'May I do X?', the lawyer replies 'if the law permits'. He knows where to find the law: statutes, regulations, precedent etc, and he knows how to rank it when it has been found. Lawyers like to assume that administrators approach the law in the same way . . .

Generally speaking, [however,] neither administrators nor politicians seek their mandate in law but in policy; they are, in other words, policy-orientated. Administrators see law positively as a set of pegs on which to hang policies; viewed negatively, the law may be a series of hurdles to be jumped before policy can be implemented, in which sense it acts as a control . . .

As prevention is proverbially better than cure, so fire-watching can be seen as more 'efficient' than fire-fighting . . . [For this reason,] the notion of legislative control has widened. Rule-making has developed into a primary technique for control of bureaucracies. And . . . the trend of post-war public administration generally has been to put in place controls which are internal and prospective.

Alongside the new internal controls we find new fire-watchers added. The Council on Tribunals [see ch 19 below] was installed in the 1960s essentially to carry out fire-watching functions; the ombudsmen [see ch 20 below] were primarily used for fire-fighting. There is an irony here, in that the introduction of this new, external machinery for control had been heavily promoted by lawyers. Yet the agencies, although external, were often only semi-autonomous. In consequence, the developments were frequently misunderstood by lawyers who, using the courts as their paradigm, doubted the independence and integrity of the new institutions. Again, because they lacked some of the compulsive attributes of law, relying on negotiation rather than command/control, they were often described as 'toothless watch-dogs' . . .

This extract captures the essence of the green light view, and the way in which it contrasts with its red light counterpart. The former downplays the role of the judiciary as an agency which exerts external control over administrative bodies, and instead prefers to place greater trust in the political process — not only through the somewhat fragile doctrine of ministerial accountability, but also by means of more robust techniques of internal administrative regulation. This, in turn, re-characterizes administrative law itself: it shifts from being an external restriction upon state power which is largely concerned with righting wrongs occasioned by maladministration, and is instead conceived of as a framework which facilitates good government by providing a template of good practice, and practical mechanisms which permit the administration to regulate itself.

QUESTION

- Is the red light or green light theory preferable in your view? Why?

1.2.3 Why is Theory Important?

The red and green light theories of administrative law are presented here as polar opposites in order that their differences might be drawn out. In reality, most administrative systems reflect aspects of both traditions, relying upon a combination of external, court-based control, and internal regulation of the administrative process. Harlow and Rawlings (*op cit* at 127) acknowledge that reality presently lies somewhere between the pure red and green light models, in an 'amber light theory' which recognizes both the ' "fire-watching" and "fire-fighting" functions of administrative law, finding solutions outside as well as inside courts'. Indeed, notwithstanding Harlow and Rawlings' characterization of Wade and Forsyth's approach in red light terms, the latter (*Administrative Law* (Oxford 2004) at 7) recognize that judicial intervention does not have to be characterized in wholly combative terms, observing that the judge-made body of administrative law may serve as a template of best practice for administrators. The role of the courts thus transcends that which is ascribed to them by red light theory: in the words of Sir John Donaldson MR in *R* v. *Lancashire County Council, ex parte Huddleston* [1986] 2 All ER 941 at 945, 'a new relationship [has emerged] between the courts and those who derive their authority from the public law, one of partnership based on a common aim, namely the maintenance of the highest standards of public administration'.

While the position is therefore more complex than choosing *either* a red *or* green light approach, this discourse remains useful because it forces us to confront fundamental questions about the purpose of administrative law. This is valuable not only in relation to big picture issues such as the respective roles of judicial and other mechanisms, but also because it provides a theoretical framework in which to address more specific issues. For instance, to the extent that we are prepared to concede judicial oversight of the administration, should courts confine themselves to resolving disputes which have *already* arisen, or should they act pre-emptively, seeking to clarify the extent of administrators' powers even if no specific dispute has yet occurred? We explore this issue below at 15.5, where we consider what role is, and should be, played by 'advisory declarations'; here, we simply observe that reliance upon theory is imperative if coherent answers are to be supplied to this question and many others like it.

1.3 The Changing Face of Judicial Review

In light of the foregoing, it will come as no surprise that English law adopts a combination of judicial intervention and other approaches in an attempt to ensure good administrative practice. In chs 18–20, we consider extra-judicial methods of regulating government action, such as ombudsmen, inquiries, and tribunals. We begin, however, with judicial review, the principal court-based mechanism by which the legality of public authorities' actions may be addressed.

1.3.1 The Scope and Intensity of Review

One of the dominant themes which will be apparent throughout this book is that judicial review has changed rapidly in recent years. For instance, as we explain in ch 5, the scope of judicial review has expanded radically, now extending well beyond the sphere of statutory powers to include diverse forms of 'public' power in response to the changing architecture of government. Not only has judicial review grown wider in scope; its intensity has also increased. It is, however, central to received perceptions of judicial review that courts may not interfere with exercises of discretion merely because they disagree with the decision or action in question; instead, courts intervene only if some specific fault can be established — for example, if the decision was reached procedurally unfairly. Such judicial recognition of the so-called distinction between appeal and review has fundamentally shaped judicial review, and requires further explanation.

Sometimes, legislation specifically states that if an individual is not content with a particular administrative decision or act, then a right of *appeal* lies to a tribunal, court, or Minister. The general principle is that bodies with appellate jurisdiction can make up their own mind about the merits, substituting their view for that of the original decision-maker. The central question for appellate bodies, therefore, is whether they think the original decision was right or not. Where legislation does not provide for appeal, the decision will still be open to *judicial review* (unless this is specifically excluded). Reviewing courts, however, are concerned with the *legality* of the decision, not with its *correctness* or *merits*; intervention is therefore possible only if the administrator has exceeded the legal limits of its powers. Those limits are considered in detail elsewhere in this book, and we will not attempt to summarize them here. For the time being, the key point is that review has traditionally been understood in much narrower terms than appeal, as Laws J explained in *R* v. *Somerset County Council, ex parte Fewings* [1995] 1 All ER 513 at 515:

. . . [I]n most cases, the judicial review court is not concerned with the merits of the decision under review. The court does not ask itself the question, 'Is this decision right or wrong?' Far less does the judge ask himself whether he himself would have arrived at the decision in question . . . [T]he task of the court, and the judgment at which it arrives, have nothing to do with the question, 'Which view is the better one?'

A number of reasons underlie the courts' willingness to accept these limits upon judicial review. Appellate bodies can afford to adopt a bold approach because they are specifically given the power to reopen issues on appeal, whereas the power of reviewing courts, as we will see below, depends upon a constitutional assumption and is not explicitly conferred. In the light of this, reviewing courts confine themselves to questions of legality and avoid substituting their view for that of the decision-maker on the merits in order to avoid usurping the powers of the latter. Indeed, at the most fundamental level, the appeal/review distinction is keyed into the doctrine of parliamentary sovereignty: if the sovereign legislature has given power to a particular administrative body from which it has created no right of appeal then, the argument goes, the courts have no business interfering with the body's decisions (other than by making sure that it has acted lawfully). For these reasons, the courts have consistently accepted the appeal/review distinction, confining themselves to questions of legality — which, in practice, has led to a focus on the *procedure* by which decisions are made, and a tendency to eschew scrutiny of their *content*, for fear that this might lead to consideration of the merits.

QUESTION

- Are courts right to display reticence when asked to review the content, or merits, of administrative decisions?

In recent years, however, this line has become increasingly difficult to maintain. In a variety of contexts, the intensity of judicial review has increased, and the distinction between appeal and review has come under pressure. We will see this phenomenon time and again in this book — from the expansive approach to jurisdictional review (ch 2) which all but eliminates the distinction between appeal and review as far as questions of law are concerned, to the adoption of principles such as substantive legitimate expectation (ch 7) and proportionality (ch 9) which require the courts to look at the content of administrative decisions more closely than they have traditionally. Because we consider these developments in detail in subsequent chapters, it would be fruitless to attempt to summarize them here. It is important, however, to bear in mind the traditional distinction between appeal and review — and the rationale upon which it is based — when considering these developments, since this provides us with a useful benchmark by which to measure the development of judicial review, and to evaluate its legitimacy.

1.3.2 Why is Judicial Review Expanding?

Possible reasons for the growing prominence of judicial review were addressed by Lord Mustill in his dissenting speech in *R* v. *Secretary of State for the Home Department, ex parte Fire Brigades Union* [1995] 2 AC 513. The case concerned a challenge to the Home Secretary's refusal to exercise his discretion under s 171(1) of the Criminal Justice Act 1988 to bring into force a new scheme for compensating victims of crime. The majority concluded that, by introducing an alterative (cheaper) scheme and indicating that the statutory scheme would not be brought into force, the Home Secretary had acted unlawfully by breaching the duty (held to be implicit in s 171(1)) to keep under active consideration the implementation of the statutory compensation scheme. Lord Mustill, however, was against judicial intervention, arguing that, since the case essentially concerned legislation not yet in force, the matter was one which should have been resolved by Parliament and the executive. In developing this argument, his Lordship (at 567) made the following comments about the development of judicial review:

It is a feature of the peculiarly British conception of the separation of powers that Parliament, the executive and the courts have each their distinct and largely exclusive domain. Parliament has a legally unchallengeable right to make whatever laws it thinks right. The executive carries on the administration of the country in accordance with the powers conferred on it by law. The courts interpret the laws, and see that they are obeyed. This requires the courts on occasion to step into the territory which belongs to the executive, to verify not only that the powers asserted accord with the substantive law created by Parliament but also that the manner in which they are exercised conforms with the standards of fairness which Parliament must have intended. Concurrently with this judicial function Parliament has its own special means of ensuring that the executive, in the exercise of delegated functions, performs in a way which Parliament finds appropriate. Ideally, it is these latter methods which should be used to check executive errors and excesses; for it is the task of Parliament and the executive in tandem, not of the courts, to govern the country. In recent years, however, the employment in practice of these specifically Parliamentary remedies has on occasion been perceived as falling short, and sometimes well short, of what was needed to bring the performance of the executive into line with the law, and with the minimum standards of fairness implicit in every Parliamentary delegation of a decision-making function. To avoid a vacuum in which the citizen would be left without protection against a misuse of executive powers the courts have had no option but to occupy the dead ground in a manner, and in areas of public life, which could not have been foreseen 30 years ago. For myself, I am quite satisfied that this unprecedented judicial role has been greatly to the public benefit. Nevertheless, it has its risks, of which the courts are well aware. As the judges themselves constantly remark, it is not they who are appointed to administer the country. Absent a written constitution much sensitivity is required of the parliamentarian, administrator and judge if the delicate balance of the unwritten rules evolved (I believe successfully) in recent years is not to be disturbed, and all the recent advances undone.

QUESTIONS
- What sort of 'sensitivity' might Lord Mustill have had in mind?
- How, in practical terms, can the three branches of government display such sensitivity?

These comments reveal an important tension in our administrative order. One the one hand, Lord Mustill reminds us that the desirability of expanding judicial review must always be tested by asking whether the subject-matter of the administrative act is one upon which judges may legitimately adjudicate (a matter which we consider below at 5.3.3, 9.3.5, and 9.3.6). On the other hand, the doctrine of ministerial accountability, which has traditionally played a fundamental role in securing good administration, has in recent years been severely weakened by (*inter alia*) the stranglehold which the governing party (and hence, in practice, the executive) now has over Parliament as a result of rigid party discipline (see further Scott [1996] *PL* 410; Lewis and Longley [1996] *PL* 490; Woodhouse [1997] *PL* 262). Hence, as Lord Mustill puts it, the courts — by developing their powers of judicial review — have stepped in to fill the 'dead ground'.

This account should not, however, be accepted unquestioningly. After all, judicial review and ministerial accountability to some extent offer *complementary*, not *alternative*, mechanisms for ensuring good administration. Whereas the latter is focussed largely upon broad issues such as policy and the management of government departments, the former provides an apparatus whereby individuals may pursue specific grievances concerning legality against administrative bodies. In truth, the growth of judicial review must be located in a wider setting, prominent features of which are the increasing trend to resort to litigation (in both public and private law spheres) and the associated rise of a rights-based culture (see, *eg*, Irvine [1998] *PL* 221) which emphasizes the entitlements of the individual *vis-à-vis* the state. The most obvious evidence of this trend in the United Kingdom lies in the enactment of the Human Rights Act 1998, the impact of which on administrative law will be seen throughout this book. Understood in this broader perspective, judicial review's evolution is the product of a complex web of political and philosophical changes concerning the state, the individual, and their relationship with one another.

1.3.3 Is (More) Judicial Review a Good Thing?

The expansion of judicial review is not universally welcomed; green light theorists, for instance, remind us that extensive judicial regulation of the administrative process is by no means the only way in which good government might be pursued. Scepticism about judicial review is stimulated by a broad range of concerns — some pragmatic, others ideological.

The court-oriented model of administrative justice, which places judicial review centre-stage, is closely associated with the Diceyan conception of the rule of law which emphasizes the primacy of 'ordinary law' administered by courts of general jurisdiction. This tradition, which is antagonistic to the idea of a separate body of administrative law applied by specialized tribunals, was epitomized by Dicey's famous condemnation, in his *Introduction to the Study of the Law of the Constitution* (London 1959), ch 12, of France's *droit administratif*. Arthurs (1979) 17 *Osgoode Hall Law Journal* 1, in common with many commentators, strongly disputes Dicey's account. Many of Arthurs's concerns are practical in nature. For example, he observes (at 25) that, in addition to courts, there are many other agencies which might play a role in overseeing the administration, such as ombudsmen, the legislature, and tribunals, all of which are 'more likely than the courts to address the substance, rather than the technicalities, of discretion abused'. Rather than leaving everything to the courts, Arthurs prefers a pluralistic approach which recognizes that some regulatory tasks can more appropriately be performed by other institutions. Informed, at least in part, by a functional perspective — according to which the 'legal-administrative response' should be shaped by the demands of particular contexts, leading to the emergence of 'largely autonomous systems in various sectors of administrative activity' (*op cit* at 29) — Arthurs concludes (at 43–45) that judicial review should play a decidedly modest role:

> . . . [It is necessary] to distinguish Law — "Rule of" variety [meaning Dicey's "ordinary law", applied by traditional courts] — from law — administrative variety — in the conviction that the latter, much more than the former, is capable of vindicating essential democratic values in a modern state. It is true that some [of my] proposals, such as the considerable restraint on judicial review, may be seen as potentially depriving aggrieved individuals of recourse, but this is to assess the proposals only in terms of pathology.
>
> Constructive measures to enhance the original quality of decisions will not result in perfection, but they will, in the aggregate, ensure greater justice for more people than could possibly benefit from any system of judicial review. Such measures would include clearer statements of legislative purpose, better defined and more open procedures to ensure participation, more careful training of administrative decision-makers, systems of internal appeal, and external, but largely nonjudicial, accountability.
>
> In matters of policy formulation and institutional design, the legislature should clearly have, and periodically utter, the last word. Assessments of administrative professionalism and performance (including excessive zeal and sloth) should be confided to higher administrative bodies, and ultimately to authorities who are politically accountable. Remedies for patent injustice and violations of administrative law should be sought from a senior administrative tribunal or, in its absence, an ombudsman.
>
> What, then, of judicial review? I suggest that the focus of judicial review should shift to more authentic concerns from its present preoccupation with commanding adherence to "ordinary" law, often couched in the spurious language of "jurisdiction" and "error of law" and analogies to traditional court practices misdescribed as "natural justice". There are three main functions for judicial review: ensuring that tribunals (and other bodies) perform tasks of the sort generically confided in them, protecting transcendent constitutional values, and enforcing fidelity to the distinctive "law" of the tribunal . . .
>
> . . . [T]here is no reason why [judges] should not give full recognition to the distinctive legal systems which have emerged in various tribunals, no reason why they should not abandon the effort to evaluate these distinctive systems according to the inappropriate criteria of "ordinary" law. If they did so, they would not merely be acknowledging the reality of pluralism, which seems always to have been an important feature of the English legal system. They would, as well, be promoting the development of an authentic, indigenous administrative law, which is the citizen's best protection against abuse.

Scepticism about judicial review stems not only from practical concerns, such as those of Arthurs. Some writers also object to judicial review — or to an expansive form of review, at any rate — on ideological grounds. Griffith's doubts about judicial review reflect his wider concerns about judicial power. In *The Politics of the Judiciary* (London 1997), he argues that judges cannot be politically neutral because they are forced to make political choices that are inevitably affected by the rather narrow social, educational, and ethnic backgrounds from which the judiciary is presently drawn. In the public law sphere, this leads Griffith to declare himself 'very strongly against any further judicialisation of the administrative process' ((1979) 42 *MLR* 1 at 19). Criticizing Sedley's argument that an enhanced judicial review jurisdiction provides the best safeguard for individual liberty (see Sedley ((1994) 110 *LQR* 270, [1995] *PL* 386 and Nolan and Sedley (eds), *The Making and Remaking of the British Constitution* (London 1997)), Griffith (2001) 117 *LQR* 42 at 63 argues for a much more limited conception of judicial review, contending that 'the review of substantive policy decisions made by public authorities acting within the four corners of their statutory or prerogative powers should be out of bounds to the courts'. Griffith was therefore against the incorporation of the European Convention on Human Rights, arguing that its vague language gives judges too much latitude when reviewing government conduct, thereby affording them room to make political decisions which could more legitimately be made by elected politicians.

This is not to say that those who are sceptical about the courts' role in judicial review — and, more broadly, in enforcing human rights (see Campbell, Ewing and Tomkins (eds), *Sceptical Essays on Human Rights* (Oxford 2001)) — necessarily dispute the *norms* which underpin the principles of administrative justice or human rights. The key issue, as Griffith (2001) 117 *LQR* 42 at 64 puts it, is 'whether in a Parliamentary democracy particular decisions are best taken by the courts or by the Government'. As we will see, this creative tension lies at the heart of judicial review and has fundamentally shaped it.

1.4 The Constitutional Basis of Judicial Review

Although there is disagreement about the legitimate extent of judicial review, few commentators doubt that the courts should play some role in securing lawful administration. How is such judicial oversight of the administration to be justified constitutionally? In the absence of a written text, obvious starting points include constitutional axioms such as the separation of powers and the rule of law (which, as Jowell observes (see Jowell and Oliver (eds), *The Changing Constitution* (Oxford 2004), ch 1) provides the normative foundation for the specific principles of good administration enforced by way of judicial review). Although the precise relationship between judicial review, administrative autonomy, and parliamentary intention has been the subject of much academic disagreement (see generally Forsyth (ed), *Judicial Review and the Constitution* (Oxford 2000)), the inadequacy of the doctrine of *ultra vires* — the traditional constitutional justification for judicial review with which we begin — is widely accepted. It should be noted at this point that, although it makes sense to deal with these questions of justification at the outset, some of the issues raised in the following discussion inevitably anticipate matters covered later in the book; it may, therefore, be useful to refer back to this section once you have read later chapters concerning the nature and grounds of judicial review.

1.4.1 The *Ultra Vires* Doctrine

Understood in its traditional form, the *ultra vires* doctrine — the 'central principle of administrative law', according to Wade and Forsyth, *Administrative Law* (Oxford 2004) at 35 — may be stated with disarming simplicity. Courts may intervene whenever a decision-maker acts '*ultra vires*' — 'beyond the powers' conferred by legislation — while *intra vires* administrative acts are lawful and unimpeachable. The central idea here is that, in reviewing governmental action, the courts are merely doing Parliament's bidding by enforcing the limits upon power which are found (expressly or impliedly) in statute. *Prima facie*, this theory provides a powerful justification for the exercise of supervisory jurisdiction; as Baxter, *Administrative Law* (Cape Town 1984) at 303, explains:

. . . [T]he logic behind the doctrine provides an *inherent* rationale for judicial review . . . The self-justification of the ultra vires doctrine is that its application consists of nothing other than *an application of the law itself*, and the law of Parliament to boot.

This logic is particularly compelling in a legal system, like that of the United Kingdom, which embraces the principle of parliamentary sovereignty, for if judicial review can be characterized simply as the implementation of the legislature's unimpeachable intention, the courts find themselves on solid ground.

However, the assumption that, when courts review executive action, they are merely enforcing parliamentary intention — acting as 'modest underworkers' who 'fulfil Parliamentary sovereignty', as Cotterell (in Richardson and Genn (eds), *Administrative Law and Government Action* (Oxford 1994), at 16) puts it — is highly problematic. Although there certainly are situations in which the courts enforce limits upon statutory power which bear a clear relation to the words or policy of the statute — Forsyth and Elliott [2003] *PL* 286 at 299–303 point to *Lloyd* v. *McMahon* [1987] AC 625, *R* v. *Secretary of State for the Home Department, ex parte Venables* [1998] AC 407, and *Padfield* v. *Minister of Agriculture, Fisheries and Food* [1968] AC 997 as leading examples of this phenomenon — there are many others in which the courts enforce principles of good administration which bear no obvious relation to the statute. Laws [1995] *PL* 72 at 78–79 comments that:

In the elaboration of [principles of judicial review] the courts have imposed and enforced judicially created standards of public behaviour . . . [T]heir existence cannot be derived from the simple requirement that public bodies must be kept to the limits of their authority given by Parliament. Neither deductive logic nor the canons of ordinary language . . . can attribute them to that ideal, since . . . in principle their roots have grown from another seed altogether . . . They are, categorically, judicial creations. They owe neither their existence nor their acceptance to the will of the legislature. They have nothing to do with the intention of Parliament . . .

Laws therefore concludes that the *ultra vires* doctrine is a 'fig-leaf' which simply covers the 'true origins' of judicial review, while Woolf [1995] *PL* 57 at 66 makes the same point by means of a different metaphor, characterizing the doctrine as a 'fairy tale'. Similarly, Forsyth [1996] *CLJ* 122 at 136 remarks that '[n]o-one is so innocent as to suppose that judicial creativity does not form the grounds of judicial review'. The shortcomings of *ultra vires* do not, however, end there, as the following excerpt indicates.

....

Craig, 'Ultra Vires and the Foundations of Judicial Review' [1998] CLJ 63

. . . [T]he orthodox justification for the controls which exist on discretion makes little if any sense when we consider the development of these controls across time. The constraints which exist on the exercise of discretionary power are not static. Existing constraints evolve and new types of control are added to the judicial armoury. Changes in judicial attitudes towards fundamental rights, the acceptance of legitimate expectations, and the possible inclusion of proportionality as a head of review in its own right are but three examples of this process. These developments cannot plausibly be explained by reference to legislative intent. Let us imagine that, for example, the UK courts were to decide in 1998 that proportionality was an independent head of review. Can it plausibly be maintained that this is to be justified by reference to changes in legislative intent which occurred at this time? Would the legislature in some manner have indicated that it intended a new generalised head of review in 1998 which had not existed hitherto? The question only has to be posed for the answer to be self-evident . . .

A further problem with the ultra vires doctrine is that it is beset by internal tensions. These are most apparent in the context of statutory provisions which seek to exclude the courts from judicial review through the presence of preclusive or finality clauses [see below at 15.6]. If the rationale for judicial review is that the courts are thereby implementing legislative intent this leads to difficulty where the legislature has stated in clear terms that it does not wish the courts to intervene with the decisions made by the agency. As is well known such clauses have not in fact served to exclude judicial review. The courts have used a number of interpretative techniques to limit the effect of such clauses, most notably in *Anisminic* v. *Foreign Compensation Commission* [1969] 2 AC 147 [see below at 15.6.4] where their Lordships held that the relevant provision did not serve to protect decisions which were nullities.

Various attempts can and have been made to square such decisions with the orthodox ultra vires principle. It might be argued that Parliament really did not intend such clauses to cover decisions which could otherwise be rendered null. It might alternatively be contended that Parliament acquiesced in the actual decision reached by the courts in the instant case. It might further be argued that in the future Parliament would know that any such clause would be interpreted in this manner and that it signalled its consent in this respect by its willingness to include such clauses in legislation while being fully cognisant of their limited legal effect.

While such arguments can be made they are susceptible to two complementary objections, one substantive, the other formal.

In substantive terms, arguments of this nature should not be allowed to conceal the reality of what the legislature was attempting to achieve, nor should it be allowed to mask the judicial response. Such clauses were clearly designed to exclude the courts. This might be for a "legitimate" reason, in the sense that the legislature was merely trying to signify that it preferred the view of a specialist agency to that of the reviewing court. It might be for a more "dubious" reason, as where the legislature was merely seeking to immunise the decisions of a Minister from any challenge. We should be equally honest about the nature of the courts' response. Although it is capable of being reconciled with orthodoxy in the above manner, the reality is that the courts were reaching their decision by drawing upon a constitutional principle independent of Parliamentary intent. The essence of this principle was that access to judicial review, and the protections which it provides, should be safeguarded by the courts, and that any legislative attempt to block such access should be given the most restrictive reading possible, irrespective of whether this truly accorded with legislative intent or not.

The other objection to the arguments made above is more formal in nature. Even if one believes that the decisions in this area can be reconciled with ultra vires orthodoxy this reconciliation is only bought at a price. The price in this instance is the straining of the ultra vires doctrine itself. The malleability of the doctrine allows it to be formally stretched in the above manner. Yet the more contrived the search for the legitimation of legislative intent, the more strained and implausible does the whole ultra vires doctrine become . . .

For all its difficulties it is at least plausible to think of the ultra vires principle as being the basis for judicial review in relation to those bodies which derive their power from statute. The courts have, however, expanded the principles of judicial review to cover institutions which are not public bodies in the traditional sense of the term, in circumstances where these bodies do not derive their power from statute or the prerogative [see below at 5.4]. This trend has been more marked as of late because of reforms in the law of remedies. It would none the less be mistaken to think of this as a recent development. The courts have applied public law, or analogous principles to such bodies for a very considerable period of time, irrespective of whether this was in the context of an action for judicial review as such. Trade associations, trade unions and corporations with *de facto* monopoly power have, for example, been subject to some of the same principles as are applied to public bodies *stricto sensu.*

It is difficult to apply the ultra vires principle to such bodies without substantially altering its meaning. These bodies do not derive their power from statute and therefore judicial control cannot be rationalised through the idea that the courts are delineating the boundaries of Parliament's intent. The very language of ultra vires can only be preserved by transforming it so as to render the principles of judicial review of generalised application to those institutions which wield a certain degree of power; these principles are then read into the articles of association or other governing document under which the body operates. While this step can be taken it serves to transform the ultra vires doctrine. It can no longer be regarded as the vehicle through which the courts effectuate the will of Parliament. It becomes rather a juristic device through which those private or quasi-public bodies are subject to the controls which the courts believe should operate on those who possess a certain type of power.

QUESTIONS

- Do you find these criticisms of the *ultra vires* doctrine convincing?
- How powerful is the point that judicial review now extends beyond statutory power?
- Must review of the exercise of statutory and non-statutory powers rest on the same constitutional foundation?

1.4.2 The Common Law Theory

In light of the problems highlighted above, all commentators are in agreement that the *ultra vires* doctrine, understood in its traditional form, is unsatisfactory. So what should replace it? Oliver [1987] *PL* 543, concerned particularly with the last of the issues mentioned by Craig, noted the increasing prominence of bodies performing public functions but not created by statute or exercising statutory powers. Since judicial review of such bodies plainly cannot be justified by reference to the *ultra vires* doctrine, Oliver proposed that the fiction of parliamentary intention should be dispensed with, and that we should instead acknowledge that there exists a set of principles of good administration which the courts have developed and which they apply to a range of decision-making functions and powers. On this view, the content of those principles and the situations in which they are applicable fall to be determined not by reference to some notional parliamentary intention, but instead by recourse to openly normative factors concerning the appropriateness of judicial supervision.

Oliver's influential paper laid the foundation for what is now known as the common law theory of judicial review, a theory which commands the support of (*inter alios*) Craig (see [1998] *CLJ* 63; [1999] *PL* 428; [2001] *PL* 763) and Laws (see [1995] *PL* 72 and Supperstone and Goudie (eds), *Judicial Review* (London 1997), ch 4). The common law theory is explained in the following terms by Craig [1999] *PL* 428 at 429:

It is . . . self-evident that the enabling legislation must be considered when determining the ambit of a [statutory] body's powers. This is not, however, the same thing as saying that the heads of review, their meaning or the intensity with which they are applied can be justified by legislative intent. The central issue is therefore how far these relevant legal rules and their application can satisfactorily be explained by reference to legislative intent. Proponents of the common law model argue that the principles of judicial review are in reality developed by the courts. They are the creations of the common law. The legislature will rarely provide any indications as to the content and limits of what

constitutes judicial review. When legislation is passed the courts will impose controls which constitute judicial review which they believe are normatively justified on the grounds of justice, the rule of
law, etc. They will therefore decide on the appropriate procedural and substantive principles of
judicial review which should apply to statutory and non-statutory bodies alike. Agency action which
infringes these principles will be unlawful. If the omnipotent Parliament does not like these controls
then it is open to it to make this unequivocally clear. If it does so then the courts will then adhere to
such dictates. If Parliament does manifest a specific intent as to the grounds of review the courts
will also obey this, in just the same way as they will obey such intent in other areas where the
primary obligations themselves are the creations of the common law. There is, in this sense,
nothing odd or strange about a set of principles derived from the common law, which are then
supplemented or complemented by specific legislative intent if and when this is to be found. This is
indeed the paradigm in areas such as contract, tort, restitution, and trusts.

The common law theory successfully resolves many of the problems encountered by the
ultra vires doctrine. First, and perhaps most significantly, the implausible assumption lying
at the heart of the latter — that the principles of judicial review are somehow intended, yet
never actually articulated, by Parliament — is replaced with open acknowledgment that the
judiciary has largely created such principles, just as common law principles of tort, contract,
and so on have been fashioned by judges. Viewed in this way, the justification for enforcing
principles of review lies not in some notional parliamentary intention that they should be
enforced, but in the fact that such principles are desirable in a normative sense, since their
application helps to secure good government. This approach helpfully clears the way for
open discussion of the principles of judicial review applied by the courts: judges can no
longer hide behind the 'fig-leaf' of supposed parliamentary intention, and must instead be
willing to defend the principles of administrative law for whose development they are
acknowledged to be responsible. Not only is this more coherent and more believable than
the account furnished by the *ultra vires* doctrine; its transparency also rightly and construct-
ively exposes administrative law to the same critical scrutiny as other judge-made bodies of
common law.

As a result of this openness, the common law model can also comfortably accommodate
the changing content of administrative law — *eg* the emergence of new principles of review
— which, as Craig notes above, cannot plausibly be explained away, under the *ultra vires*
doctrine, on the basis of changing legislative intention. Within the common law theory,
it can simply be acknowledged that the nature and level of judicial control of the
administration varies over time, as circumstances change.

It has, however, been doubted by some commentators whether the common law theory
resolves all of the difficulties encountered by the *ultra vires* doctrine. One of those problems
is that *ultra vires* is a highly formal doctrine which is devoid of any real content. As Laws (in
Supperstone and Goudie (eds), *Judicial Review* (London 1991), at 52) puts it:

[The *ultra vires* doctrine has] nothing to say as to what the court will *count* as a want of power in the
deciding body; and so of itself it illuminates nothing. It amounts to no more than a tautology, viz that
the court will strike down what it chooses to strike down.

Adopting a similar position, Craig [1998] *CLJ* 63 at 66–67 (expressing a view shared by
Beatson (1984) 4 *OJLS* 22 at 24–29) remarks that the *ultra vires* doctrine is 'indeterminate',
meaning that it is so flexible that it can be used to justify any kind of judicial intervention
under the guise of implied legislative intention, but cannot 'provide any independent *ex ante*
guidance' as to the grounds on which the court should intervene. The very flexibility of the
doctrine therefore undermines its usefulness, since it provides no practical assistance to a

judge who is seeking to work out whether he should intervene in a particular situation. But is the common law model actually any less 'indeterminate' than *ultra vires*? Not according to Allan [2002] *CLJ* 87 at 100, who suggests that the specific principles of good administration are themselves so general as to be almost meaningless. (The term meaning of the term 'jurisdiction', which Allan uses in the following passage, is explored in ch 2.)

Could the ultra vires defenders not bring their own similar charges [of indeterminacy] against the common law school? Is not their reliance upon such open-ended categories [of judicial review] as "procedural impropriety", "illegality" and "irrationality" [as set out by Lord Diplock in *Council of Civil Service Unions* v. *Minister for the Civil Service* [1985] AC 374 at 410], in stressing the basis of the court's jurisdiction in the common law, not quite as futile and self-serving as the ultra vires defenders' invocation of legislative intent? Does anyone really imagine that such labels do more than announce the *conclusions* of legal analysis — an analysis that must focus on all the pertinent details of the particular case, including the statute that confers the administrative power?

If it is true, as is claimed [by critics of ultra vires], that enabling legislation will often afford "scant guidance" about which considerations are properly relevant to the exercise of discretion and which are not, it is equally true that no sensible conclusions could be drawn without close attention to the statutory scheme. As Elliott [in Forsyth (ed), *Judicial Review and the Constitution* (Oxford 2000) at 350–351] observes, it is the enabling statute that inevitably defines the "jurisdiction" of the public agency, in the narrow sense of its proper sphere of action. (And this is so even if it is also true that it may be controversial whether any particular statutory requirement should be treated as a jurisdictional condition.) And he is also right to insist that the other grounds of review — those that determine the agency's jurisdiction in its broader sense — cannot be applied without regard to legislative intention, even if such intention must be collected from a sense of the overall statutory scheme or purpose. Legislative intention — at least in the broad sense that the courts must be faithful to the statutory scheme as a whole — is plainly relevant to the *application* of the various grounds of review, even if it is thought irrelevant to their abstract formulation and intellectual defence.

This passage underlines two related points. First, it reminds us that although the *ultra vires* doctrine is problematic in that it views parliamentary intention as a panacea which can explain judicial review in its entirety, it is wrong to overlook the fact that such intention is part — albeit not the whole — of the explanation. Secondly, while the remainder of the explanation for the content of administrative law principles must be found elsewhere, this demand is not necessarily met by the common law theory. As Allan points out, it is all very well to invoke concepts such as fairness and reasonableness, and to argue that their normative weight justifies their application via judicial review. Such concepts, however, are undeniably vague; one person's conception of fairness might differ quite radically from another's. Craig [2003] *PL* 92 at 95 retorts that there may well exist a developed and thoroughly-worked out underlying theory which informs concepts such as fairness, giving them real depth and meaning; however, unless that theory is articulated and shared by the judges who apply the principles of review, the common law model does not constitute much of an advance on the *ultra vires* doctrine. The notion of implied parliamentary intention (under *ultra vires*) and generalized concepts such as fairness and reasonableness (at common law) are both able to be stretched to mean more or less anything, and both are therefore equally capable of forming a smokescreen behind which judicial policy preferences may be advanced, unarticulated and largely unseen.

1.4.3 Must Judicial Review be Related to Legislative Intention?

In spite of these difficulties, it is clear that the common law theory of judicial review is, in many respects, a significant improvement upon the *ultra vires* doctrine. The debate has not, however, stopped there. In addition to the criticism made by Allan, above, other writers have attacked the common law model on other grounds. Elliott (see (1999) 115 *LQR* 119; [1999] *CLJ* 129; *The Constitutional Foundations of Judicial Review* (Oxford 2001)) and Forsyth [1996] *CLJ* 122 have argued that, while the *ultra vires* doctrine, as traditionally understood, is indefensible, recognition of some form of relationship between parliamentary intention and judicial review remains essential. This has led them to develop a modified version of the *ultra vires* theory. The nature of that theory is considered below; first, however, it is necessary to consider why the relationship between legislative intention and review is considered so important by the *ultra vires* school. Forsyth and Elliott [2003] *PL* 286 at 288–289 advance two reasons. The first relates to practical considerations concerning ouster clauses and collateral challenge, matters which we consider in chs 15 and 3 respectively. For the time being, we focus on the second strand of the argument which favours the retention of some form of *ultra vires* theory. The essence of this part of the argument is that the courts' supervisory jurisdiction and the sovereignty of Parliament can *only* be reconciled by means of (some version of) the *ultra vires* doctrine. Forsyth [1996] *CLJ* 122 at 133–134 explains the reasoning behind this proposition as follows:

Suppose that a Minister in the apparent exercise of a statutory power to make regulations, makes certain regulations which are clearly so vague that their meaning cannot be determined with sufficient certainty. Classic [*ultra vires*] theory tells us that Parliament never intends to grant the power to make vague regulations — this seems an entirely reasonable and realistic intention to impute to Parliament — and thus the vague regulations are *ultra vires* and void; there would be no difficulty in the court striking down the regulations. But [within the common law model] classic theory has been abandoned: the grounds of review [including that which requires regulations to be clear, not vague] derive, not from the implied intent of the legislature, but from the common law. It follows that although the regulations are *intra vires* the Minister's powers, they are none the less invalid because they are vague.

The analytical difficulty is this: what an all powerful Parliament does not prohibit, it must author-ise either expressly or impliedly. Likewise if Parliament grants a power to a Minister, that Minister either acts within those powers or outside those powers. There is no grey area between authorisa-tion and the denial of power. Thus, if the making of vague regulations is within the powers granted by a sovereign Parliament, on what basis may the courts challenge Parliament's will and hold that the regulations are invalid? If Parliament has authorised vague regulations, those regulations cannot be challenged without challenging Parliament's authority to authorise such regulations . . .

The upshot of this is that . . . one is led inevitably to the conclusion that to abandon *ultra vires* is to challenge the supremacy of Parliament.

This argument reduces to the proposition that when statutory power is conferred, every-thing which is purportedly done under (and therefore made lawful by) that grant of power is actually either done within the scope of the power (and is therefore lawful) or outside the scope of the power (and is therefore unlawful). It must be one thing or the other; and while courts can strike down acts in the latter category, they cannot, if Parliament is sovereign, strike down administrative acts in the former, since Parliament has authorized them. There-fore, the argument runs, only an *ultra vires* doctrine will do: the courts are only consti-tutionally able to upset administrative action which lies outside the power conferred by Parliament, but have no business imposing common law restrictions on discretionary power which bear no relation to the scope of the power actually conferred by Parliament. To do so may involve removing from administrators power which Parliament conferred, thereby setting the courts and the legislature on a collision course.

QUESTION

• Is Forsyth's analysis of any relevance to judicial review of the exercise of *non-statutory* powers?

This analysis has been attacked on a number of grounds, three of which merit particular attention. First, the conclusion itself has been challenged by a number of writers, Endicott (2003) 53 *University of Toronto Law Journal* 201 and Laws supplying especially detailed critiques. The latter, writing in Supperstone and Goudie (eds), *Judicial Review* (London 1997) at 4.13–4.14, says that:

I think [Forsyth's] reasoning as to the "analytical consequences" of the abandonment of *ultra vires* is faulty. I do not accept that "what an all powerful Parliament does not prohibit, it must authorise either expressly or impliedly" . . . The absence of a legislative prohibition does not entail the exist-ence of a legislative permission . . . Forsyth's argument is vitiated by an implicit mistake: the mistake of assuming that because Parliament can authorise or prohibit anything, all authorities and prohib-itions must come from Parliament. It is a *non sequitur*. It neglects what logicians call the "undistrib-uted middle" — an obscure, but useful, academic expression, meaning that although X and Y may be opposites, like praise and blame, they do not cover the whole field; there might be Z, which involves neither. Thus Forsyth mistakes the nature of legislative supremacy, which is trumps, not all four suits; specific, not wall-to-wall. How could it be otherwise? A legislature makes and unmakes laws when it thinks it needs to; the fact that in England the common law allows it to make or unmake any law it likes confers upon it no metaphysic of universality.

On this view, Parliament might not have any intention at all about whether certain limits — *eg* a duty to act fairly — ought to exist in relation to a given power. This legislative vacuum can be filled by common law principles of fairness: no risk arises of contradicting Parliament because it has no relevant intention capable of contradiction. However, this assumption that Parliament is neutral about some or all of the conditions which attach to the exercise of discretionary power does not fit comfortably with broader ideas about the relationship between legislation and the rule of law. Although it is widely accepted that Parliament is sovereign, and can therefore, at least in theory, do as it pleases, the reality is that a high level of protection is conferred upon the rule of law by means of statutory interpretation. Leading examples of this technique are furnished by *Anisminic Ltd* v. *Foreign Compensation Commis-sion* [1969] 2 AC 147 (on which see below at 15.6.4) and *R* v. *Lord Chancellor, ex parte Witham* [1998] QB 575 (noted by Elliott [1997] *CLJ* 474), in which the courts went to considerable lengths to find interpretations of statutory provisions which were consistent with the constitutional principle of access to justice.

In neither of these cases did the courts doubt the sovereignty of Parliament; instead, they invoked the widely-held assumption that, as Lord Steyn put it in *R* v. *Secretary of State for the Home Department, ex parte Pierson* [1998] AC 539 at 587, 'Parliament does not legislate in a vacuum. Parliament legislates for a European liberal democracy founded on the principles and traditions of the common law. And the courts may approach legislation on this initial presumption.' It is the use of such presumptions which allows Allan [1985] *CLJ* 111 at 112 to conclude that the British constitution 'possesses its own harmony, in which the protection of individual liberties can coexist with recognition of the ultimate supremacy of the democratic will of Parliament'. Laws's suggestion that we should suppose Parliament to be agnostic about the principles of administrative justice, relying upon the courts *unilaterally* to impose standards of good administration, chafes awkwardly against the well-established tradition to which Allan refers, and which rightly advances a vision of the constitution within which courts, administrators, and the legislature are *collectively* engaged in the co-operative endeavour of promoting good governance.

The second criticism levelled at the defence of *ultra vires* focusses upon its consequences. Craig [1999] *PL* 428 at 433–434 writes that if the logic of the argument is extrapolated, then surprising — indeed absurd — results are produced. For example, Craig says that, on Forsyth's analysis, if Parliament passes a statute which gives power to a particular public body, then we would not be

entitled to impose any limits on the way in which that power is exercised unless we can find justification in terms of legislative intent. If therefore we wish to argue that the public body should be subject to rules of [for example] contractual, tortious or restitutionary liability then the requisite legislative intent must be found. There may be some specific legislative intent that we can point to, but this will often be absent, since Parliament will not have the necessary expertise, time, etc, to manifest a specific intent on the matter. So we have to fall back on some general legislative intent . . . If no such intent can be found then the existence and applications of such principles [of civil liability] cannot be justified. If we are satisfied that the requisite intent can be found then we can and must say that the "central principle" of this area of the law is legislative intent. We must, moreover, say this notwithstanding the fact that the principles of civil liability which are thus applied to public bodies have a normative force of their own which warrants their application to public bodies and to private parties where there is no relevant background statute.

This analysis is largely correct. If Forsyth's logical point is accepted, then any limits upon statutory power must somehow be related to the statutory scheme. It therefore would, as Craig suggests, be necessary to find some sort of legislative intention to the effect that the principles of civil liability should restrict the decision-maker's power, if such principles are to be operative. However, Craig's implicit assertion that this is ultimately absurd, because it is inconsistent with the fact that the principles of civil liability have a 'normative force of their own', conflates two separate issues — *viz* the *existence* and *application* of those principles. It is self-evident that they have largely been authored by judges; no-one disputes the fact that the judiciary is responsible for their *existence*. Correctly understood, Forsyth's argument is simply that when such principles are applied to — and are therefore restrictive of — statutory power, some legislative permission to this effect must exist if the *application* of the principles of civil liability is not to cut across the scheme laid down by the sovereign legislature. This argument denies neither the normative force nor the judicial authorship of those principles.

Craig goes further, arguing (*op cit* at 434–435) that if Forsyth's analysis is pressed to its ultimate conclusion, then much of private law would have to be justified by reference to parliamentary intention. For example, employment law is founded upon the common law of contract, but some aspects of it are regulated by statute (*eg* minimum wage legislation). Craig suggests that, on Forsyth's logic, once Parliament has passed legislation dealing with some aspects of the employment relationship, *all* of employment law must be characterized as the express or implied creation of Parliament, even though we know that much of it was created by judges using the traditional common law method. 'If this is true,' says Craig, 'then writers in areas as diverse as labour law, company law, commercial law and tax will have a good deal of re-writing to do.' However, Forsyth's argument relates only to circumstances in which Parliament has conferred a *power* upon a public body to do a certain thing, the limits of which must, he says, somehow be determined by reference to the statute. This is of no relevance whatever to areas such as employment law which regulate the *liberty* of private parties to enter into contracts and so on. When employers and employees relate to one another, they are not exercising a statutory power the limits of which must be determined by reference to the statute which created it, but are instead exercising their freedom to do as they please, subject to any relevant legal rules. Those legal rules may be created by the common law, by legislation, or by both.

The third, and strongest, criticism of the *ultra vires* school is advanced by Allan, although we should begin by noting that (in common with Dyzenhaus (see Forsyth (ed), *Judicial Review and the Constitution* (Oxford 2000) at 153–154) Allan [2002] *CLJ* 87 at 90 accepts the logic of the argument that judicial review may be reconciled with parliamentary sovereignty *only* through some form of *ultra vires* doctrine (the 'modified' version of the theory to which he refers is explained below):

Despite their protestations to the contrary, the common law theorists cannot reasonably object to *ultra vires*, in its very modest 'modified' version, while continuing to accept absolute parliamentary supremacy. In that sense Christopher Forsyth was right to maintain that 'weak' critics of *ultra vires* — those who do not explicitly challenge the sovereignty of Parliament — are 'whether they intend it or not . . . transmuted into "strong" critics' [who do challenge the supremacy of Parliament]. In so far as the common law basis for judicial review is offered as a viable and genuine alternative to legislative intent, broadly understood, it entails at least a limited qualification of legislative power . . .

Allan therefore attacks not the *logic* of *ultra vires*, but rather the *premise* upon which that logic is based. Allan's position reduces to the view that the *ultra vires* doctrine would be imperative *if* Parliament were sovereign — but that Parliament is *not* sovereign. This is an entirely logical position: *ultra vires* only makes sense if Parliament is sovereign, since its purpose is to reconcile judicial review and legislative supremacy. If Parliament is not sovereign, then *ultra vires* becomes unnecessary; more precisely (see Elliott (1999) 115 *LQR* 119), if the principles of administrative justice are constitutional fundamentals which, perhaps along with other values such as substantive human rights, form a higher-order of law which constrains Parliament, then parliamentary intention — and therefore *ultra vires*, as traditionally understood — becomes irrelevant. On this view, discretionary power is subject to the principles of administrative justice not because Parliament so intends, but because those principles are fundamentals which will *always* apply, irrespective of legislative intention.

However, while Allan's view is internally consistent, it rests on the highly controversial premise that Parliament is not, contrary to received wisdom, sovereign. This is a view which Allan has elaborated at length (see, *eg, Law, Liberty, and Justice* (Oxford 1993) and *Constitutional Justice* (Oxford 2001)). It is primarily informed by his opinion that legislative power must be understood in relation to the rule of law, and that the latter embodies principles — including those of administrative justice — whose fundamentality is such as to preclude their displacement by legislation. Allan is certainly not alone in expounding this view of the British constitution (see, *eg,* Laws [1995] *PL* 72; Woolf [1995] *PL* 57), and it is undeniable that the concept of parliamentary sovereignty finds itself under increasing pressure as a result of the momentous constitutional changes of recent years (see Elliott (2002) 22 *LS* 340). A further hardening of attitude in this area is evident from the fact that the government was, in effect, recently forced to withdraw a provision in what became the Asylum and Immigration (Treatment of Claimants etc) Act 2004 that would have excluded judicial review of certain asylum decisions (see further below at 15.6.4). Nevertheless, the concept of legislative supremacy is still accepted by the courts (see, *eg*, Thoburn v. *Sunderland City Council* [2002] EWHC 195 (Admin) [2003] QB 151) and most commentators (for detailed discussion, see Goldsworthy, *The Sovereignty of Parliament* (Oxford 1999)), and the *ultra vires* school contends that, so long as sovereignty remains the orthodoxy, some form of *ultra vires* doctrine will need to be retained in order to confer legitimacy upon judicial review.

QUESTIONS

- Do you agree?
- If Parliament is sovereign, must some form of *ultra vires* doctrine be retained?
- Conversely, if Parliament is not sovereign, is the *ultra vires* doctrine necessarily irrelevant?

1.4.4 The Modified *Ultra Vires* Theory

We saw above that the traditional *ultra vires* theory is riddled with problems. This led to the articulation of a 'modified *ultra vires* theory'. It is based upon what might be called constitutional interpretation, and draws heavily upon the tradition, described above and epitomized by the celebrated *Anisminic* decision (see below at 15.6.4), under which the courts approach statutory texts on the assumption that Parliament legislates consistently with a tradition of respect for fundamental constitutional values. That is a category which undoubtedly includes the principles of administrative justice which are vindicated through judicial review, and the characterization of those principles as the fruit of a process of constitutional interpretation is therefore unproblematic. This theme is developed in the following extract.

....

Elliott, *The Constitutional Foundations of Judicial Review*
(Oxford 2001)

. . . Just as the courts' construction of legislation dealing with, say, personal liberty is rationalised in terms of a legislative endeavour that is fundamentally shaped by constitutional principle, so the courts' approach to legislation which creates discretionary powers may be conceptualised as an interpretative process which is normatively premised on those values which make up the rule of law.

Consequently, when Parliament enacts legislation which (typically) confers wide discretionary power and which makes no explicit reference to the controls which should regulate the exercise of the power, the courts are constitutionally entitled — and constitutionally right — to assume that it was Parliament's intention to legislate in conformity with the rule of law principle. This means that Parliament is properly to be regarded as having conferred upon the decision-maker only such power as is consistent with that principle. It follows from this that, in the absence of very clear contrary provision, Parliament must be taken to withhold from decision-makers the power to treat individuals in a manner which offends the rule of law: for this reason, the competence to act unfairly and unreasonably should be assumed to be absent from any parliamentary grant. However, the task of transforming this general intention — that the executive should respect the rule of law — into detailed, legally enforceable rules of fairness and rationality is clearly a matter for the courts, through the incremental methodology of the forensic process. Parliament thus leaves it to the judges to set the precise limits of administrative competence. It is, therefore, the simple and plausible assumption — which is widely made in other contexts — that Parliament intends to legislate in conformity with the rule of law which bridges the apparent gulf between legislative silence and the developed body of administrative law which today regulates the use of executive discretion.

Hence, on this view, there is a relationship between parliamentary legislation and the grounds of review. However, whereas the traditional ultra vires principle conceptualises the relationship as direct in nature, the present approach maintains that the relationship exists in indirect form. While the details of the principles of review are not attributed to parliamentary intention, the judicially-created principles of good administration are applied consistently with Parliament's general intention that the discretionary power which it confers should be limited in accordance with the requirements of the rule of law. Thus it is possible to acknowledge the role of judicial creativity while ensuring that the limits which the judges impose on administrators can be reconciled with the intention of Parliament.

. . . [O]nce legislation which creates discretionary power is located within its proper constitutional context, it becomes clear that the rule of law must operate to limit and control the exercise of that power. Since the rule of law is a pervasive constitutional principle which shapes both the environment within which Parliament legislates and the context within which statutes are interpreted, the courts rightly impute to Parliament an intention that the rule of law should be upheld. In this manner the courts' vindication of the rule of law is of a piece with Parliament's will, and judicial review comes to rest on a secure constitutional foundation which acknowledges both its normative roots and its relationship with legislative intention.

. . . [T]here is nothing in this approach which denies that those constitutional principles to which judicial review gives effect possess an inherent normative value which exists independently of legislative intention. Indeed, one of the purposes of the modified theory is to permit open acknowledgement of the intrinsic worth of the principles on which administrative law is founded. Holding that Parliament's intention is consistent with respect for those constitutional principles does not, therefore, rob them of their autonomous normative resonance. Rather, it simply recognises that the constitutional order itself locates the legislature and the legislation which it passes within a framework which is founded on the rule of law, and which therefore attributes to the legislature an intention to act consistently with that principle. Far from denying the inherent normative worth of constitutional principles, such an approach recognises the pervasiveness of the values on which the constitution is founded, such that judicial vindication of the rule of law through judicial review is seen to fulfil, rather than conflict with, the endeavours of the legislature . . .

Supporters of the modified *ultra vires* theory claim that it overcomes the failings of its traditional counterpart, while preserving what they contend to be the all-important link between the principles of review and the enabling legislation. Most significantly, the modified version of the *ultra vires* doctrine jettisons the implausible assumption that Parliament directly intends the myriad principles of judicial review, openly acknowledging that those principles are normatively rooted, being developed by judges seeking to give meaning to the rule of law within, and subject to, specific statutory frameworks. The modified theory is also able to account for the evolution, over time, of administrative law, since it is self-evident that judges will draw upon contemporary notions of constitutionalism and the rule of law in developing the principles of administrative justice. An obvious criticism of the modified *ultra vires* doctrine is that it is weakened by its reliance upon the rule of law, because of the vagueness of that concept. However, while it is undeniable that, like the principles of good administration championed by common law theorists, the content of the rule of law — as it relates to administrative justice, as in all other contexts — is a matter of considerable debate (see, *inter alios*, Allan, *Constitutional Justice* (Oxford 2001) and Craig [2003] *PL* 92), the modified *ultra vires* theory, unlike its traditional counterpart, allows that debate to take place in the open, rather than attempting to conceal it behind an unconvincing façade of implied legislative intention.

1.4.5 Conclusion

Although some writers (notably Allan [2002] *CLJ* 87) regard the debate about the constitutional foundations of judicial review as largely sterile, Craig [2003] *PL* 92 at 93 denies that it is an

exercise in arid formalism. It is substantive and principled, and would be so regarded in any legal system, civil or common law. It speaks to the respective powers of courts and legislature in a constitutional democracy. It reflects contending views as to the autonomy of courts when developing judicial review. It encapsulates differing views about the relationship between the rule of law and Parliament.

Indeed, while considerable disagreements remain, the debate has clarified much. The traditional *ultra vires* doctrine is widely regarded as untenable; the role of judicial creativity in the development of the modern law of judicial review is openly acknowledged; and it is accepted on all sides that the principles of administrative justice are rooted in the constitutional bedrock of the rule of law. The principal difference between the two modern theories — common law and modified *ultra vires* — lies in what role, if any, is ascribed to legislation. The former characterizes the principles of judicial review as wholly independent, unrelated to any form of parliamentary intention, while the latter holds them to be the product of a process of constitutional interpretation of legislation.

Does this remaining difference really matter? Yes. If proponents of the modified *ultra vires* doctrine are to be believed, then that theory is key to the legitimacy of judicial review because, they contend, only an interpretative model can be truly consistent with parliamentary sovereignty. Moreover, the two models reflect very different views of the relationship between courts, administrators, and the legislature. The common law model envisages the pursuit of administrative justice as the sole preserve of the courts, with principles of good administration unilaterally imposed by the judiciary upon administrators, independently of legislative intention. In contrast, the modified *ultra vires* doctrine presents administrative law as a co-operative endeavour, in which shared and pervasive constitutional values are given concrete meaning and effect by the judicial branch. Properly understood, then, the *ultra vires* debate is much more than a discussion about how judicial review should be justified: it is a debate about the very nature of the British constitution, and of the courts' role within it.

1.5 Administrative Power in the Modern Constitution

When considering administrative power — the proper use of which is, as we have seen, administrative law's central concern — we tend to think principally of the familiar model of central government: of Ministers of the Crown (and their departmental officials: see below at 6.2.4) exercising powers conferred upon them by statute (or occasionally the prerogative: see below at 5.3) taking decisions for which they are legally accountable to the courts and politically accountable to Parliament. In fact, administrative power in the United Kingdom is wielded by an increasing diversity of institutions in a growing variety of ways.

1.5.1 Devolution

The Scotland Act 1998, the Government of Wales Act 1998, and the Northern Ireland Act 1998 established new seats of government in Edinburgh, Cardiff, and Belfast, devolving different amounts of legislative and administrative power to them. In this section, we highlight the main features of the Scottish and Welsh arrangements (devolution in Northern Ireland is, at the time of writing, suspended) to the extent that they illuminate changes in the locus of administrative power in the UK.

The Scottish and Welsh models are significantly different from one another. The former constitutes a system of administrative *and* legislative devolution. The Scottish Parliament now assumes legislative responsibility over a wide range of matters in respect of which the Westminster Parliament formerly legislated for Scotland. This is effected by s 28 of the Scotland Act which vests a general legislative power in the Scottish Parliament, subject to a (long) list of 'reserved matters' upon which it may not legislate (see s 29(2)(b) and sch 5). Some of these are defined in general terms, such as 'international relations' and 'defence of the realm', while others are set out more specifically, *eg* by reference to the subject-matter of particular acts, such as the Official Secrets Acts 1911 and 1989.

The Scottish Parliament therefore has wide-ranging, but not unlimited, legislative competence. The limits on that competence consist not only in reserved matters; the Parliament is also incompetent to (*inter alia*) modify certain (provisions of) specific Acts of the Westminster Parliament (see s 29(2)(c) and sch 4) and, by virtue of s 29(2)(d), to legislate incompatibly with the rights scheduled to and given effect by the Human Rights Act 1998 (which the Westminster Parliament is capable of contravening) and European Community law (from which the Westminster Parliament is apparently capable of specific derogation: *Thoburn* v. *Sunderland City Council* [2002] EWHC 195 (Admin) [2003] QB 151; cf Elliott (2003) 54 *NILQ* 25). The Scottish Parliament's legislative authority is non-exclusive, in that the Westminster Parliament explicitly (see s 28(7) of the Scotland Act) retains competence to legislate for Scotland on any issue. Its sovereignty therefore remains intact in theoretical terms, but the true position is more complex: by convention, it has already been established (see Burrows [2002] *Jur Rev* 213) that Westminster should not unilaterally legislate for

Scotland on non-reserved matters; indeed, viewed through the prism of political reality rather than legal theory, the notion that the Westminster Parliament may ride roughshod over the devolution settlement is an increasingly fanciful one (see further Elliott (2002) 22 LS 340).

In contrast to the Scottish model, the Welsh system is one of exclusively *administrative* devolution. By s 21 of the Government of Wales Act, the powers exercisable by the National Assembly for Wales are limited to those which were formerly exercisable by Ministers of the Crown in relation to Wales and which have been specifically transferred to the Assembly (see SI 1999/672, National Assembly for Wales (Transfer of Functions) Order, and SI 1999/2787, National Assembly for Wales (Transfer of Functions) (No 2) Order)) or otherwise conferred upon it. The Welsh Assembly therefore exercises, in relation to Wales, many discretionary powers which were formerly exercised by Ministers of the Crown. It is also able to make subordinate legislation (on which see ch 17) where appropriate powers have been transferred to or conferred upon it. Self-evidently, however, a power to enact such legislation is only as extensive as the parameters laid down in the relevant primary legislation. Therefore, as Barendt (in Feldman (ed), *English Public Law* (Oxford 2004) at [1.61]) notes, it is only when Westminster enacts 'framework' legislation that leaves much of the detail to be filled in by secondary rules that the Welsh Assembly is able, to any meaningful extent, to pursue a distinct legislative approach in Wales. To this end, the Richard Commission, established by the Welsh Assembly Government to review the devolution settlement in Wales, recently recommended the greater use of such framework legislation; the Commission also recommended that, in the longer term, devolution in Wales should be constituted along lines similar to the Scottish model.

Administrative authority is also enjoyed by the Scottish Executive in relation to devolved matters although, in contrast to the Welsh model, the administrative competence conferred upon the Scottish Ministers (as members of the Executive are known) is a general one, subject (as with the Scottish Parliament's legislative competence) to reservations (see ss 52–54 of the Scotland Act). The Scottish Executive, like the Welsh Assembly, exercises both discretionary and rule-making authority. The effect of s 53 is that such powers as are conferred upon Ministers of the Crown by pre-devolution Westminster legislation are now, so far as they are exercisable within devolved competence, to be exercised instead by the Scottish Ministers. Further provision is made in ss 104–107 of the Act for the making by the Scottish Ministers of subordinate legislation. It is also possible for Acts of the Scottish Parliament, within devolved competence, to confer administrative powers upon Scottish Ministers.

Just as the work of central government departments is scrutinized by the Westminster Parliament — by means of parliamentary questions, the work of select committees, and so on — so the Scottish Executive is accountable to the Scottish Parliament. There are, however, important differences. In particular, Members of the Scottish Parliament are elected, in part, by a system of proportional representation, thereby rendering coalition government more likely than at Westminster (where MPs are elected by a first-past-the-post system that tends to produce an overall majority for one political party). As Burrows, *Devolution* (London 2000) at 106–112, notes, when the executive consists of members of more than one party, the doctrine of collective responsibility — according to which all Ministers take joint responsibility for government conduct and policy — cannot work in the usual way. Moreover, the Westminster convention that if the government suffers a vote of no confidence Parliament will be dissolved and an election called is inapplicable, since the Scottish Parliament sits for fixed periods. The position in Wales is different again since, in the case of executive devolution, the traditional model of an administration answerable and accountable to a legislative body is inapt.

Exercises of legislative power by the Scottish Parliament and of administrative power by the Scottish Ministers and Welsh Assembly are subject to judicial review. The former proposition is noteworthy: because, as noted above, the Scottish Parliament, unlike its Westminster counterpart, has limited powers, the possibility arises that its enactments, or parts thereof, may be struck down as *ultra vires*. It is also significant that judicial scrutiny is possible *before* a Scottish Bill has become an Act of the Scottish Parliament and, similarly, *before* an administrative decision or piece of subordinate legislation has actually been made by the Scottish Ministers or the Welsh Assembly. Pre-enactment scrutiny of Scottish Bills is provided for by s 33 of the Scotland Act, which makes the Lord Advocate, the Attorney General, and the Advocate General competent to refer to the Judicial Committee of the Privy Council the question whether a Bill or any provision of a Bill would be within the legislative competence of the Scottish Parliament. Once this step has been taken, s 32 provides that the Bill may not be presented for Royal Assent — and therefore cannot become law — until the matter is determined by the Privy Council and unless it decides that the provisions in question are *intra vires*.

Of greater interest from a purely administrative law perspective are the arrangements for pre-emptive scrutiny of *administrative* decisions and legislation. By paras 33 and 34 of sch 6 to the Scotland Act, the Lord Advocate, the Attorney General, the Advocate General, or the Attorney General for Northern Ireland may refer to the Privy Council any 'devolution issue', whether or not it is already the subject of proceedings. Devolution issues, according to para 1 of the same schedule, include questions as to whether the purported or proposed exercise of a function by a member of the Scottish Executive is, or would be, within devolved competence or compatible with the rights scheduled to the Human Rights Act 1998 or with European Community law. Schedule 8 of the Government of Wales Act makes similar provision: the relevant law officers, or the Assembly itself, may refer devolution issues to the Privy Council irrespective of whether it is already an issue in proceedings (paras 30 and 31). Here, something is a 'devolution issue' if it involves a question as to whether 'a purported or proposed exercise of a function by the Assembly is, or would be, within the powers of the Assembly'.

These provisions give rise to a novel jurisdiction. As we explain below at 15.5.4, the courts have traditionally been reluctant to offer judicial opinions in advance of the taking of administrative action. The specific provisions in the devolution legislation permitting such matters to be referred to the Privy Council, if used appropriately, may allow the courts to carve out a new role for themselves which, by allowing involvement at an earlier stage, situates them nearer to the heart of the administrative process.

QUESTION

- How does the pre-emptive role ascribed to courts by the devolution legislation relate to the 'red light' and 'green light' models discussed at 1.2.1 and 1.2.2 above?

1.5.2 Local Government

Although devolution is a recent and stark example of the dispersal of administrative (and legislative) power, it would be wholly wrong to suppose that, prior to devolution, administrative authority was concentrated solely in central government. No attempt will be made here to list all the powers possessed by the institutions of local government, but it should be noted that they wield substantial administrative powers in certain fields (planning and licensing being prime examples) including legislative powers to enact byelaws (a form of secondary legislation).

The Local Government Act 1972 is the foundation of the contemporary system of local government. It envisaged a two-tier structure. Each metropolitan area had a metropolitan county council, but was also subdivided into districts, each with a metropolitan district council. Similarly, non-metropolitan areas were divided into counties, each with a county council, but also subdivided into districts, each with a district council; a similar structure applied in Wales. Meanwhile, London was divided into a number of boroughs, each with its own council, but there was also a city-wide authority, the Greater London Council. The organization of local government has changed somewhat since 1972.

Four main developments should be noted. First, the Greater London Council and metropolitan county councils were abolished by the Local Government Act 1985, and many of their functions transferred to London borough councils and metropolitan district councils. Secondly, this shift to a unitary model of local government is gradually being rolled out in non-metropolitan areas. The Local Government Act 1992 makes provision for the creation of unitary authorities which discharge the functions traditionally allocated to district *and* county councils. The decision whether to retain the two-tier structure or shift to a unitary authority is taken by central government in light of advice tendered by the Boundary Committees of the Electoral Commission. Thirdly, two-tier government has been reintroduced in London: the Greater London Authority Act 1999 created a new, city-wide Greater London Authority, comprising an elected mayor and elected members of the new Assembly. Fourthly, the Local Government (Wales) Act 1994 replaced two-tier government with unitary authorities in Wales. These radical, albeit somewhat piecemeal, changes to the structure of local government within a relatively narrow time-frame demonstrate the rather precarious constitutional position of local government.

This is evident in relation not only to the structural changes just described, but also to two more recent reforms concerning the role and operation of local government. As to the former, a radical change in emphasis — partly influenced by ideological considerations about the role and scale of the 'state', partly motivated by more prosaic concerns about efficiency — was effected by the Conservative government in the 1980s. The Local Government, Planning and Land Act 1980 and the Local Government Act 1988 required many services (*eg* housing management; refuse collection) previously provided in-house by councils to be put out to competitive tender (albeit that the local authority could itself bid for the work). In such spheres, the role of local government has been transformed as the fulfilment of its duties has increasingly been realized through recourse to contractual arrangements with private sector service providers.

The compulsory competitive tendering regime established by the Conservative government (for discussion of which see Greenwood and Wilson (1994) 47 *Parl Aff* 405) was abolished by its Labour successor because, according to a consultation paper published by the (now defunct) Department for the Environment, Transport and the Regions, *Improving Local Services through Best Value*, 'service quality [was] often . . . neglected and efficiency gains [were] uneven and uncertain'. However, this disaffection with compulsory competitive tendering did not herald a return to a monolithic system of service provision exclusively by local government. Instead, the Local Government Act 1999 introduced a new system known as 'best value', the central principle of which is that local authorities — and many other bodies, such as police authorities and National Park authorities — are duty-bound to make arrangements to secure continuous improvement in the way in which their functions are exercised, having regard to a combination of economy, efficiency, and effectiveness. There is no longer any requirement that service provision should be put out to tender, but it is envisaged that private sector provision should be chosen if that is the best option, applying the 'best value' criteria.

A more recent, but equally radical, programme of reform concerns the internal operation of local government. The traditional *modus operandi* of local authorities was described — and criticized — in Cm 4298, *Local Leadership, Local Choice* (1999) at [1.9]–[1.10]:

Traditionally councils carry on their business by, formally at least, taking decisions in sizeable committees and sub-committees having the same political balance as the full council. The council, its committees and sub-committees are advised by professional officers.

This committee system, designed over a century ago, does not work today. It is inefficient, opaque, and weakens local accountability. It is no system for the modern council which needs to give effective leadership to its local community, and to take decisions in a faster moving world to deliver quality local services. People are not well served by it.

The Local Government Act 2000 introduced new arrangements for the operation of local authorities, involving the creation of executive bodies within councils. Three models are set out in s 11 (although s 11(5) allows other models to be created by regulations): an executive consisting of an elected mayor and two or more additional councillors chosen by the mayor; a councillor elected as 'executive leader' by the authority, plus two or more additional councillors chosen by either the executive leader or the authority; or an elected mayor plus a 'council manager' — a council officer chosen by the authority. Those functions of local authorities which can be discharged by the executive are determined by s 13 and by regulations (see SI 2000/2853, Local Authorities (Functions and Responsibilities) (England) Regulations; SI 2001/2291, Local Authorities Executive Arrangements (Functions and Responsibilities) (Wales) Regulations) made thereunder. (For instance, functions relating to such matters as town and country planning, byelaws, elections, and health and safety cannot be discharged by executives.) By s 24 of the Act of 2000, the usual requirements (under s 15 of the Local Government and Housing Act 1989) as to political balance in local government do not apply to executives, meaning that all members of an executive can be drawn from one political party. Local authorities must consult their electorates before proposing to adopt one of the executive models (s 25(2)) and, in the case of models involving an elected mayor, a referendum must be held in the relevant area (s 26(2)). The division drawn by all of these models, between the executive and the council generally, is reflected in the requirement that at least one overview and scrutiny committee must be formed to hold the former to account (s 21). The ethos of these new arrangements is described, and cautiously welcomed, by Leigh, *Law, Politics, and Local Democracy* (Oxford 2000) at 246:

The argument that the roles of both backbench councillors and of the political elite should be strengthened by more clearly separating them appears compelling . . . The arrangements both for [overview and scrutiny] committees and for the institutional division of powers between elected mayors and their councils attempt to create a working tension within institutions in the hope of generating public interest in local democracy and producing greater openness. Whether this succeeds may ultimately depend on factors beyond the reach of the law and, especially, on whether the political parties genuinely work to change the political culture and climate within which the new legal regime will operate.

In spite of the raft of recent reforms, central government had intended to introduce further changes in England. It has been argued (see Cm 5511, *Your Region, Your Choice* (2002), ch 1) that English regions are acquiring their own identities through the creation of (*inter alia*) Regional Development Agencies, which have responsibility for the development of economic policy at a regional level, and Government Offices for the regions, which seek to improve the implementation of government policy in the English regions and facilitate a policy-making approach that is more sensitive to regional needs. Elected regional assemblies were proposed as a means of introducing political control over and accountability of these growing forms of regional government; however, following clear rejection of this proposal at a referendum in north-east England in November 2004, plans for elected regional assemblies have (at least for the time being) been abandoned.

1.5.3 Agencies and the Private Sector

Over the last 25 or so years, the role of government in Britain has been radically reconceived as a result of three interrelated innovations introduced by the Thatcher administration and pursued with varying degrees of enthusiasm by its successors. These changes reflect a critical view of the role of the state, and a willingness to question whether in-house provision by government is necessarily the best way of delivering services.

First, the landscape of the 'state' has been transformed by the *privatisation programme* instituted, and prosecuted with particular zeal, in the 1980s by the Thatcher government. Functions which had been performed by the state — most notably the provision of utilities such as electricity, water, and gas — were henceforth to be discharged by the private sector (albeit subject to state regulation). These changes were radical, and represented an entirely new view of the function of government; in particular, they reflected a vision of 'smaller' government, and the notion that many things hithertofore done by the state were not government functions properly so-called.

The other two key changes in this sphere were different in type, but no less radical. The *contracting out* of service provision (an example of which we have already encountered in relation to local authorities) and the introduction of *executive agencies* represented a new approach to the discharge of those functions which, within the new landscape, remained government functions. As we will see, these two developments are related, and share some common features; let us begin, however, with contracting out.

'Contracting out' should be distinguished from two other contexts in which contractual or similar principles operate. First, the Citizen's Charter scheme, launched by the Major government and retained, with modifications, by the Blair administration, encourages public bodies to set out clear standards which individual citizens are entitled to expect. This approach, considered below at 20.1.3, has a contractual flavour to the extent that it invokes notions of obligation and entitlement as part of a mechanism for promoting effectiveness and accountability in the public sector. Secondly, it has always been the case that government — central and local — has had to enter into contracts with the private sector in order to procure goods and so on. For instance, in discharging its functions with respect to the penal system, central government must purchase supplies for the purpose of building and maintaining prisons. However, within the traditional model, the function itself — in our example, the running of prisons — is discharged directly by government. Contrary to this tradition, contracting out involves fulfilling government functions by engaging private sector organizations: within this model, therefore, the government function of running prisons may be (and, in some instances, is) discharged by means of contractual arrangements with private sector security firms which are engaged to operate particular institutions.

The legal framework for contracting out is found in Part II of the Deregulation and Contracting Out Act 1994. The effect of s 69 is that Ministers may make provision for private sector organizations to exercise their statutory functions. Similar arrangements are made by s 70 in respect of functions of local authorities. By s 72, acts and omissions of the private sector body 'shall be treated for all purposes as done or omitted to be done' by the Minister, office-holder, or local authority, as the case may be. Although this appears to preserve the ultimate responsibility of government, two problems arise. First, there is a question mark over the extent to which Ministers can be held politically accountable for the actions of private sector bodies. Freedland [1995] *PL* 21 at 26 writes that he is

apprehensive that the effect of providing that public duties may be entrusted on a day-to-day basis to private contractors cannot fail to be the erosion of the responsibilities of the state to its citizens at quite a fundamental level. The state comes to look more like the sleeping trustee and less and less like the active trustee for the public good.

On the other hand, as Craig, *Administrative Law* (Oxford 2003) at 132, notes, 'it can be argued that these very contracts, like the framework documents used in agency creation [discussed below], sharpen accountability by defining goals, setting targets and monitoring performance'. The second issue concerns legal accountability. Existing case law shows that courts are reluctant to subject contracted out service providers to judicial review, and that such providers are also unlikely to be bound by the terms of the Human Rights Act 1998. This creates a risk that the use of contractual arrangements may defeat the protections to which individuals are usually entitled under public law; although the contracting-out public authority remains subject to public law, this may be of little practical utility where the complaint relates to the conduct of the private sector body. These issues are fully considered below at 5.4.4 and 5.5.

Like contracting out, the growing use of executive agencies (see generally Drewry (1994) 47 *Parl Aff* 583) represents a major change in the way in which government functions are discharged — Oliver and Drewry, *Public Service Reforms: Issues of Accountability and Public Law* (London 1996) at 39, suggest that it might 'well be regarded as "a revolution in Whitehall" '. Agencies which exist outside the departmental structure of central government are hardly an innovation. However, a new breed of such bodies was ushered in following a report, *Improving Management in Government: the Next Steps*, commissioned by the Prime Minister and published in 1988. The report concluded that many of the administrative tasks carried out by central government departments could be performed more efficiently by separate agencies; Ministers and civil servants would concentrate on policy strategy and formulation, while agencies, headed by chief executives, would implement policy and deliver services. Drewry (*op cit* at 589) explains that the Next Steps programme is premised on 'institutionalising the crucial but elusive distinction between ministerial support and policy functions on the one hand (performed by . . . civil servants, working in close proximity to ministers) and executive or service delivery functions on the other'. (It is, however, clear that some agencies *do* have responsibility for policy (*eg* the Pesticides Safety Directorate) or at least what is referred to in HM Treasury/Office of Public Services Reform, *Better Government Services: Executive Agencies in the 21st Century* (2002) (hereinafter the 'Treasury Review') at 10, as 'operational/process policy' (*eg* the Prison Service).) The present government (*loc cit*) considers that '[t]he agency model has been a success', transforming 'the landscape of government and the responsiveness and effectiveness of services' delivered by it. A number of reasons for this have been identified (*op cit* at 17–18), including agencies' 'clarity and focus on specified tasks', their 'culture of delivery' and their 'accountability and openness'.

There are now over 100 so-called 'Next Steps agencies', handling matters as diverse as child support and benefits payments, the running of the royal parks and the maintenance of highways. The appropriateness of 'hiving off' functions to agencies was considered by the Treasury Review (at 16):

In the majority of situations, executive services within departments are not highly politically sensitive and it is neither realistic nor appropriate for Ministers to take personal responsibility for the day-to-day running of the function. In this case an agency will be the best solution. The agency model is sufficiently flexible and accountable to make it the best choice for delivering most central government services.

However, there are still a small number of executive functions delivered internally within departments. The Immigration and Nationality Directorate . . . is one example of a large executive function that is not an agency. Agency status was thought inappropriate for a number of reasons, including a link between policy and operations, [and the] political sensitivity [of the work involved] . . .

This issue is intimately connected with that of the relationship between departments and agencies — a matter considered by Freedland [1994] *PL* 86 at 88:

When an executive agency is created by separation from its parent department, the relationship between the two is governed by a so-called Framework Document, which defines the functions and roles of the agency, and the procedures whereby the department will set and monitor the performance targets for the agency. Although it is asserted that the framework documents are not strictly speaking contracts, it is increasingly accepted that they are contracts in every sense but the technical one, so much is the nature of these arrangements like that of the contracts whereby activities are contracted out to the private sector.

It is evident, therefore, that framework documents can permit Ministers to hold agencies and chief executives to account, by making provision for appropriate oversight in terms of performance, service delivery, the attainment of targets, and so on. However, the Treasury Review highlighted some concerns in this regard. It noted (at 28) that framework documents need to be regularly reviewed in order to ensure that the governance of agencies and their relationships with departments are appropriate to contemporary circumstances. More generally, the Review found (at 10) that '[s]ome agencies have . . . become disconnected from their departments', giving rise to a 'gulf between policy and delivery'. In light of this, the Review reconsidered how departments and agencies should relate to one another, concluding that a rigid distinction between policy and operations is problematic because questions of effective delivery of services must feed into the departmental policy-making process. The Review therefore recommended (at 25–30) closer co-operation and better communication between agencies and departments.

In constitutional terms, the growing role of agencies poses challenges to the operation of the principles of ministerial accountability and responsibility. To what extent can, and should, Ministers be answerable to Parliament for functions that are performed by agencies, at arm's length from government? The difficulties which arise in this context are partially addressed by the Cabinet Office's guidelines on *Departmental Evidence and Response to Select Committees* at [43]:

Where a Select Committee wishes to take evidence on matters assigned to an Agency in its Framework Document, Ministers will normally wish to nominate the Chief Executive as being the official best placed to represent them. While Agency Chief Executives have managerial authority to the extent set out in their Framework Documents, like other officials they give evidence on behalf of the Minister to whom they are accountable and are subject to that Minister's instruction.

In light of this, the current arrangements are described by Drewry (in Jowell and Oliver, *The Changing Constitution* (London 2004) at 296) as follows:

In recent years, governments have sought to address the tricky problem of how to maintain some credibility for the classical doctrine of ministerial responsibility . . . by claiming . . . that there is a clear distinction between *responsibility* ([which lies in respect of] the job one is charged with doing) and *accountability* (the duty to explain, or render an account of what has or has not been done). Thus, in the present context, ACEs [Agency Chief Executives] are *responsible* for the operational performance of their agencies (and liable to shoulder the blame when things go wrong); ministers are *responsible* for the for the policy framework within which agencies operate and — in accordance with the rules of ministerial responsibility — *account to* Parliament and the electorate both for that policy and for matters that fall within the responsibility of the ACE.

The difficulty, of course, is that the distinction between policy and operations — and, therefore, between matters for which ACEs and Ministers are accountable/responsible (on which see further Oliver and Drewry, *Public Service Reforms: Issues of Accountability and Public Law* (London 1996) at 6–13) — is far from clear; it is, consequently, open to manipulation by Ministers wishing to evade responsibility for failures in areas in which agencies are involved. Although the direct responsibility of ACEs to Parliament is a necessary and desirable response to changing administrative architecture, the fact that — as the excerpt above from the Cabinet Office guidelines indicates — ACEs give evidence 'on behalf of' the relevant Minister, and 'subject to [his] instruction', has the potential to muddy the waters considerably (see further Oliver and Drewry, *op cit* at 5–6). We explain below at 6.2.4 that these problems of political accountability (for detailed discussion of which see Woodhouse [1997] *PL* 262 at 272ff) in turn raise legal difficulties.

1.6 Concluding Remarks

The location and nature of administrative power in the UK are increasingly diverse. Such power is today wielded by central and local government; by government agencies and devolved administrations; and by resort to novel contractual arrangements. These changes pose considerable challenges to administrative law, as it seeks to ensure that the enormous administrative powers wielded today are exercised lawfully and fairly. In the remainder of this book, we explore the principles applied to this end by courts of law, as well as extra-judicial methods of promoting good administration and dealing with abuses of power.

FURTHER RESOURCES

Allan, 'Constitutional Dialogue and the Justification of Judicial Review' (2003) 23 *OJLS* 563

Burrows, *Devolution* (London 2000)

Cabinet Office, *Departmental Evidence and Response to Select Committees www.cabinet-office.gov.uk/central/1999/selcom/index.htm*

Craig, 'The Common Law, Shared Power and Judicial Review' (2004) 24 *OJLS* 237

Craig and Rawlings (eds), *Law and Administration in Europe* (Oxford 2003), ch 7 (Freedland)

Forsyth (ed), *Judicial Review and the Constitution* (Oxford 2000)

Harden, *The Contracting State* (Buckingham 1992)

Jowell and Oliver (eds), *The Changing Constitution* (London 2004), ch 12

HM Treasury/Cabinet Office, *Better Government Services: Executive Agencies in the 21st Century www.pm.gov.uk/files/pdf/opsr-agenciesm.pdf*

Leigh, *Law, Politics, and Local Democracy* (Oxford 2000)

Oliver and Drewry, *Public Service Reforms: Issues of Accountability and Public Law* (London 1996)

Report of the Richard Commission on the Powers and Electoral Arrangements of the National Assembly for Wales (Cardiff 2004) *www.richardcommission.gov.uk/content/finalreport/report-e.pdf*

Web site of the Cabinet Office Team on Agencies and Public Bodies *www.cabinet-office.gov.uk/agencies-publicbodies*

Web site of the Local Government Association *www.lga.gov.uk*

Web site of the National Assembly for Wales and the Welsh Assembly Government *www.wales.gov.uk*

Web site of the Office of Public Service Reform *www.pm.gov.uk/output/Page249.asp*

Web site of the Scottish Executive *www.scotland.gov.uk*

Web site of the Scottish Parliament *www.scottish.parliament.uk*

2 JURISDICTION

2.1 Introduction

2.1.1 What is 'Jurisdiction'?

All administrative power is limited by (i) the express terms of the statute which confers it, (ii) the implied terms of that statute, and (iii) general principles such as natural justice and reasonableness. (We know, from ch 1 above, that *ultra vires* theorists consider that there is no distinction between (ii) and (iii).) Decision-makers act lawfully only so long as they do not transgress these limits on their powers. The central concern of the courts, on judicial review, is to identify whether the decision-maker has acted (or is proposing to act) outwith those limits. In this sense, all of judicial review is about jurisdiction: is the action under scrutiny within or outside the powers of the decision-maker? Provided that the decision-maker remains within the limits of his jurisdiction, the courts have no business interfering: if, however, the decision-maker exceeds his jurisdiction (or power), the courts have every right to strike down the resulting decision.

A simple example will help to illustrate the point. Assume that immigration legislation confers upon the Home Secretary a discretionary power to detain 'illegal entrants'. Adopting the most likely construction of this statutory power, it may be reformulated in the following manner: *if* the person concerned is an illegal entrant, *then* the Home Secretary may decide whether to detain him. Faced with such a power, it is probable that a Home Secretary would, in individual cases, address two major issues. *May* the power be exercised in respect of the individual in question? If so, *should* the power be exercised in respect of that person?

The answer to the first question depends upon whether the individual concerned is an illegal entrant. The Home Secretary must therefore seek to work out whether that person is an illegal entrant in the statutory sense. If the answer to that question is 'no', then it is clear that the person cannot be detained under this power. The person's status as an illegal entrant is a jurisdictional condition: only if it is met is it possible for the Home Secretary to proceed. The defining characteristic of jurisdictional matters is that they cannot conclusively be determined by the decision-maker. Of course the Home Secretary must himself try to work out whether the person is an illegal entrant — he has to do this in order to deduce whether he can go on to consider detaining him — but the Home Secretary's decision on the jurisdictional matter is not conclusive; because it represents a limitation upon his power, he cannot be the final judge of it. It follows that, if the person concerned is not shown to be an illegal entrant to the satisfaction of the reviewing court, then any purported exercise of the discretion to detain him will be struck down: there was no power to act because a jurisdictional condition was not met. Characterizing a particular matter as jurisdictional is therefore highly significant: the decision-maker's conclusions on such a matter are never conclusive, because it is open to the reviewing court to decide the matter for itself, substituting its opinion for that of the decision-maker. Jurisdictional questions — *eg* 'is this person an illegal entrant?' — have only one correct and lawful answer: the answer favoured by the reviewing court.

What if the Home Secretary decides (correctly) that the person concerned *is* an illegal entrant? He then moves on to address the second issue mentioned above: given that the power *may* be exercised in respect of that person, *should* he exercise it? Such questions are sometimes said to go to 'the merits of the case' or to the 'discretion of the decision-maker'. In other words, they are not jurisdictional questions *per se*. In our example, whether a given illegal entrant should be detained is the very issue which Parliament intended the Home Secretary to determine: that is why, after all, it gave the power to him. It is therefore for the Home Secretary to exercise his judgment in deciding whether to detain any particular illegal entrant. The court's view as to whether a particular illegal entrant should be detained is not determinative: it is for the decision-maker, not the court, to decide whether the power should be exercised in respect of any illegal entrant.

Thus far, the position may appear relatively straightforward. 'Jurisdictional questions' must be answered correctly, in the view of the reviewing court. 'Merits questions', meanwhile, are for the decision-maker. However, the picture is, in fact, more complicated. Even if the decision-maker correctly decides that the person under consideration is an illegal entrant, such that the power *may* be exercised in relation to him, it is wrong to suppose that the decision-maker, at that point, clears a single jurisdictional hurdle which gives him access to discretion that is otherwise unlimited. The decision-maker has cleared *a* jurisdictional hurdle: after all, if the person had not been an illegal entrant, that would have been the end of the matter. However, once the decision-maker clears *that* hurdle, the decision-maker must still remain within the scope of his power. The crucial point is that, even after the decision-maker has correctly decided the initial jurisdictional issue ('is this person an illegal entrant?') and has begun to address the 'merits question' ('should this person be detained?'), his power remains limited: issues will therefore arise *in the course of answering the merits question itself* which, if incorrectly determined, will send the decision-maker outside his jurisdiction.

This can be illustrated by returning to our example. Having correctly decided that a particular person is an illegal entrant, it is, as we know, for the Home Secretary to decide whether that person should be detained. However, in the course of reaching a final decision on that 'merits question', the Home Secretary must be careful to remain within his legal power. Two examples will serve to illustrate this point. First, let us assume that the person concerned approaches the Home Secretary and asks for an opportunity to present his case — that is, to put arguments before the Home Secretary as to why he should not be detained (*eg* that he is not a risk to national security, or that he has dependant relatives whom he must look after). Must the Home Secretary grant him such an opportunity — a 'hearing', as administrative lawyers would call it — or not? Although the ultimate question ('should this person be detained?') is a 'merits question', and therefore for the Home Secretary, this specific question ('must this person be given a hearing?') is a jurisdictional one. As we will see in ch 11, administrative law prescribes the circumstances in which individuals must be given a hearing: the duty to comply with what are known as the principles of natural justice therefore represents a limit on the Home Secretary's power. Ultimately, therefore, whether or not the illegal entrant must be given a hearing is a matter that the court can decide for itself:

if the Home Secretary incorrectly decides that no hearing should be afforded, the court can simply strike down the decision. Secondly, assume that the person concerned has attracted public attention (*eg* because he has expressed controversial and unpopular views on some matter of current interest) such that public opinion strongly favours his detention. May the Home Secretary take this consideration into account when deciding whether to detain the individual concerned? As with our first example, although the ultimate question ('should this person be detained?') is for the Home Secretary, this specific question ('may public opinion be taken into account?') is a jurisdictional one. As we shall see in ch 8, whether or not any particular factor may be taken into account by a decision-maker is regarded as a jurisdictional issue: either it may or may not be taken into account, and it is ultimately for the court to decide into which of those categories any particular factor falls.

This takes us back to the (disarmingly) simple proposition with which we began this chapter: that 'all of judicial review is about jurisdiction'. The one and only ground upon which the courts may intervene is that the decision-maker has 'acted *ultra vires*' or 'exceeded the limits of his power' or has 'exceeded his jurisdiction' (all three expressions mean the same thing). However, a practical distinction may be drawn, which reflects the way in which we tend to think about jurisdictional issues. As is apparent above from our example of the Home Secretary's power to detain illegal entrants, most statutory powers can be expressed in the terms, '(i) *If* [a particular condition is met, or a particular state of affairs exists (*eg* that the person concerned is an "illegal entrant")], (ii) *then* [the decision-maker may exercise discretion by choosing whether to, say, carry out some prescribed activity (*eg* detaining that person)].' This sort of formulation reflects the two-stage analysis which decision-makers, faced with a statutory power, will tend to adopt: (i) *may* it be exercised (a jurisdictional question); (ii) if so, *should* it be exercised (a merits question)? When the decision-maker addresses the first matter, he enjoys no discretion: either the power can or cannot be exercised in the circumstances of the particular case. This is a jurisdictional matter pure and simple. In contrast, when the decision-maker addresses the second question, it is ultimately for him to answer it; however, in the course of doing so, he will have to confront a number of subsidiary matters — whether a fair hearing must be given, whether certain information may be taken into account, and so on: these are jurisdictional questions which, if answered incorrectly, will cause him to exceed his power, and thereby to act unlawfully, just as though he had, at the first stage, erroneously concluded that he had the power to act. It follows that, in answering the ultimate question — in our example, 'should this person be detained?' — the decision-maker must clear a number of hurdles. Some of these, typically because they are explicit in the statute, naturally fall into the first part of our '*if . . . then*' formulation. It is jurisdictional questions of this type with which we are centrally concerned in this chapter. Others, typically because they are not explicit in the statute, tend to arise as sub-issues once the decision-maker has moved on to address the second question (given that the power *may* be exercised, *should* it be exercised?); such jurisdictional limits derive from general principles of administrative law such as natural justice and reasonableness, and are discussed in later chapters.

2.1.2 Distinguishing Jurisdictional and Non-Jurisdictional Matters

How do we know whether a given matter is jurisdictional? This is crucial since, as we have seen, the consequences of placing a particular matter in either the 'jurisdictional' or 'merits' category are considerable. If a particular matter (*eg* 'is this person an illegal entrant?') is regarded as a jurisdictional question then it is ultimately for the court to determine. Contrariwise, if a matter (*eg* 'should this illegal entrant be detained?') is regarded as a merits question, then it is ultimately for the decision-maker.

How, then, do we distinguish between jurisdictional and merits questions? There is, unfortunately but perhaps not unsurprisingly, no simple answer to this question. Indeed, the remainder of this chapter is largely devoted to addressing it. It is true that some situations are straightforward. Our example, for instance, is relatively simple: 'The Home Secretary may detain illegal entrants.' Working on the assumption that Parliament must have specified the category of persons capable of detention under this power for a reason — *viz* to ensure that the power can be used *only* in respect of such persons — it is fairly uncontroversial that a particular individual's status as an illegal entrant should be regarded as a jurisdictional limit upon the Home Secretary's detention power.

However, if we modify the example slightly, then the 'jurisdictional or merits?' question becomes more difficult. Assume now that our imaginary statutory power provides that, 'The Home Secretary may detain dangerous illegal entrants.' Is the dangerousness of an illegal entrant a jurisdictional matter? Did Parliament intend that the Home Secretary should be able to choose which, out of a group people who are 'dangerous illegal entrants', should be detained? If so, then we should treat dangerousness as a jurisdictional matter — something of which the court must ultimately be satisfied. Or did Parliament — perhaps because it felt that determining 'dangerousness' is a more impressionistic enterprise than deciding whether someone is an 'illegal entrant' — intend that the Home Secretary should decide which 'illegal entrants' are dangerous (and whether he should detain any of them)? If so, then we should not treat dangerousness as a jurisdictional matter; instead, it should be regarded as a 'merits question' because, on this view, the dangerousness of a particular illegal entrant is matter for the Home Secretary to decide.

These questions do not invite simple answers, although we explain later in this chapter that there are some general principles that can be applied in analysing such issues. For the time being, we merely note that the location of the line between factors upon which the decision-maker's jurisdiction depends and matters which are regarded as ultimately for the decision-maker is crucial, because it determines the scope of the relevant power. The greater the number of factors which are regarded as jurisdictional, the smaller the decision-maker's discretion. If this approach is carried too far, then that discretion vanishes: everything becomes a question of jurisdiction over which the reviewing court has the final word. There are, however, risks in the other direction, too. If jurisdictional limits are drawn too loosely, thereby making (nearly) everything a question for the decision-maker to determine on the merits, then it effectively becomes a law unto itself: it can decide the scope and limits of its own powers, and there is no (adequate) opportunity for objectively checking that the decision-maker is acting in accordance with the terms of the statute which, in the first place, conferred power upon him. This raises serious problems with respect to the rule of law.

Nevertheless, a very limited view of what matters should be counted as jurisdictional was famously championed by Gordon in a series of articles (see (1929) 45 *LQR* 459; (1931) 47 *LQR* 386 and 557; (1960) 1 *UBCLR* 185; (1966) 82 *LQR* 263 and 515). He argued that questions of jurisdiction depend on the nature of the facts into which a decision-maker has to enquire, not on the truth or falsity of those facts. On this view, returning once again to our example of a power to detain illegal entrants, the Home Secretary would be permitted conclusively to decide that someone was an illegal entrant *even if they were not actually an illegal entrant.* Any error which the Home Secretary made (*eg* by deciding that the person was a US citizen when in fact he was a UK citizen) in determining whether the person was an illegal entrant would be an error *within* jurisdiction. On this approach, judicial intervention on jurisdictional grounds would be confined to circumstances in which the Home Secretary formulated the question incorrectly (*eg* by asking whether the person was an 'undesirable character' rather than an 'illegal entrant').

Although this formalism may purchase certainty, by avoiding the need to make fine distinctions between jurisdictional and non-jurisdictional matters, it almost eviscerates jurisdictional control, in effect permitting the decision-maker to determine the extent of its own powers. In fact, such an approach is not adopted by English law which, as we explain below, characterizes a wide range of issues as jurisdictional, thus giving reviewing courts extensive powers in this context, and departing radically from the limited model of jurisdictional review advanced by Gordon.

2.2 Errors of Law

2.2.1 Introduction

In considering the courts' approach to questions of jurisdiction, we need to distinguish between a number of issues which can, again, be illustrated by reference to our example of a power to detain illegal entrants. We have already seen that the power of the decision-maker arises only if the individual is, in the first place, an 'illegal entrant'. The existence of an illegal entrant is therefore a jurisdictional requirement: it is something upon which the decision-maker's power depends. But what does this mean? The analysis of whether a particular individual is an illegal entrant can be broken down into at least three stages. First, some meaning must be attributed to the statutory term 'illegal entrant'. Most issues of this nature are characterized as *questions of law*. Secondly, the decision-maker must make certain findings of fact about the individual concerned: for instance, in what circumstances did he enter the United Kingdom? These are *questions of fact*. Thirdly, the decision-maker must apply these findings of fact to the legal definition of 'illegal entrant', in order to determine whether the person concerned is or is not an illegal entrant over whom relevant statutory powers of detention may be exercised. This involves *questions of both fact and law*. Are all of these issues jurisdictional? Can the court substitute its opinion in relation to all of these matters?

Before addressing these questions, we need to note that underlying this area which resounds with argument couched in *conceptual* language is a *policy* debate about how best to draw the line between judicial supervision and agency autonomy. This is clear from the following remarks of Farina (1989) 89 *Columbia Law Review* 452 at 452–453:

Assume . . . that Congress enacts legislation which establishes a system of rights and responsibilities for "employees" and creates an agency to administer that system. Should the court or the agency decide whether the critical statutory term "employees" encompasses persons who would be considered independent contractors under the common law, or workers who are foremen and so, at least arguably, part of management? To determine "what the law is" in the context of an actual controversy that turns on a question of statutory meaning is the quintessential judicial function. At the same time, however, such questions are so bound up with successful administration of the regulatory scheme that it may seem only sensible to give principal interpretive responsibility to the "expert" agency that lives with the statute constantly. And if this challenge of mediating between principle and practicality were not difficult enough, there are other pieces to the puzzle. At times, the consequence of adopting one interpretation of the statute over another is to subject an individual to civil or criminal penalties for her past behavior. Fundamental fairness to someone threatened with sanctions might require that the decisive legal standard be interpreted by a decision maker whose life tenure and salary protection promote impartiality, objectivity and insulation from political pressure. Finally, the legislature that enacted the statute may have had an intention about apportioning interpretive responsibility between court and agency. Determining how to "retrieve" such an intention after the fact and deciding whether, once retrieved, it is dispositive, present additional complications.

QUESTIONS

- Are the criteria suggested by Farina helpful?
- What factors do you think should be taken into account in identifying the dividing line between jurisdictional and non-jurisdictional matters?

2.2.2 Jurisdictional and Non-Jurisdictional Errors of Law

Until comparatively recently, some errors of law were regarded as jurisdictional, while others were not. A decision-maker could make a 'non-jurisdictional error of law' while remaining within jurisdiction; only a 'jurisdictional error of law' would take it outside jurisdiction. The point was explained in the following terms by Denning LJ in *R* v. *Northumberland Compensation Appeal Tribunal, ex parte Shaw* [1952] 1 KB 338 at 346:

No one has ever doubted that the Court of King's Bench can intervene to prevent a statutory tribunal from exceeding the jurisdiction which Parliament has conferred on it; but it is quite another thing to say that the King's Bench can intervene when a tribunal makes a mistake of law. A tribunal may often decide a point of law wrongly whilst keeping well within its jurisdiction.

There are, however, two difficulties with this approach. First, if a decision-maker is able to make a particular error of law while remaining within jurisdiction then, in the absence of a right of appeal, the error will stand: the decision-maker's conclusion is final, and the reviewing court cannot intervene. Different decision-makers may therefore attach different meanings to the same legal provision, with the result that the scheme laid down in the relevant legislation is interpreted and operated in different ways.

Secondly, the distinction between jurisdictional and non-jurisdictional questions was notoriously difficult to draw. It was said to turn upon matters which were collateral to the jurisdiction of the decision-maker — and upon which its jurisdiction therefore depended — and matters which the decision-maker itself was empowered to decide. Although it was generally held that such matters were to be resolved by recourse to the relevant legislation, in practice the statute was likely to provide little guidance. This gave rise to the strong impression that the courts manipulated the distinction for instrumental purposes, choosing to find that a particular issue was jurisdictional if they wanted to intervene, and non-jurisdictional if they did not.

We will see, in the following section, that the problematic distinction between jurisdictional and non-jurisdictional errors of law is now almost completely redundant. First, however, we should note one other issue. We have, thus far, assumed that jurisdictional errors of law were reviewable but that non-jurisdictional errors were not. However, some non-jurisdictional errors were reviewable under the doctrine of error on the face of the record, which Denning LJ revived in *R v. Northumberland Compensation Appeal Tribunal, ex parte Shaw* [1952] 1 KB 338 at 346–347:

> . . . [T]he Court of King's Bench has an inherent jurisdiction to control all inferior tribunals, not in an appellate capacity, but in a supervisory capacity. This control extends not only to seeing that the inferior tribunals keep within their jurisdiction, but also to seeing that they observe the law. The control is exercised by means of a power to quash any determination by the tribunal which, on the face of it, offends against the law.

The effect of this doctrine was to permit any error of law disclosed on the face of the record of the proceedings to be quashed, irrespective of whether it was categorized as a jurisdictional error. This provided the courts with a useful tool by which to expand the scope of review for error of law, free from the restrictions which would otherwise have been imposed by the distinction between jurisdictional and non-jurisdictional errors of law. However, the contemporary irrelevance of that distinction in practice, to which we now turn, has made the doctrine of error on the face of the record largely, if not wholly, superfluous.

2.2.3 The *Anisminic* Decision

The decision of the House of Lords in *Anisminic* is one of the most celebrated cases in modern administrative law for two (intimately connected) reasons. (For comment, see Wade (1969) 85 *LQR* 198; De Smith [1969] *CLJ* 161; Gould [1970] *PL* 358; Schwartz (1986) 38 *Administrative Law Review* 33.) First, it demonstrated an extremely robust judicial approach to a statutory provision which seemed to exclude the courts' supervisory jurisdiction; this aspect of the case is considered below at 15.6.4. Secondly, this bold interpretation of the statute was facilitated by the underlying view of jurisdiction adopted by their Lordships: although they did not actually abolish the distinction between jurisdictional and non-jurisdictional errors of law, they laid the foundation for such a step to be taken. It is this aspect of the case which is of present interest.

Anisminic Ltd v. *Foreign Compensation Commission* [1969] 2 AC 147
House of Lords

The claimant, an English company, had owned property in Egypt worth about £4.4m which the Egyptian authorities sequestrated in 1956. In 1957 the claimant sold the property to TEDO, an Egyptian organization, for £0.5m. By a treaty between the United Arab Republic and the United Kingdom, £27.5m was paid over to the latter as compensation for property confiscated in 1956 and the claimant sought to participate in this fund by applying to the Foreign Compensation Commission. The Commission's provisional determination was that the claimant had failed to establish a claim under the Foreign Compensation (Egypt) (Determination and Registration of Claims) Order 1962 on the ground that its successor in title was a non-British national and consequently it did not comply with the terms of Article 4(1)(b)(ii) of the Order (which is set out below in the excerpt from Lord Reid's speech). The claimant sought a declaration that the provisional determination was a nullity, contending that the Commission had misconstrued the Order. The Commission denied this and also contended that the court was precluded from considering whether the determination was a nullity because of the presence of an ouster clause in the Foreign Compensation Act 1950, on which see 15.6.4 below.

Lord Reid

. . . It has sometimes been said that it is only where a tribunal acts without jurisdiction that its decision is a nullity. But in such cases the word "jurisdiction" has been used in a very wide sense, and I have come to the conclusion that it is better not to use the term except in the narrow and original sense of the tribunal being entitled to enter on the inquiry in question. But there are many cases where, although the tribunal had jurisdiction to enter on the inquiry, it has done or failed to do something in the course of the inquiry which is of such a nature that its decision is a nullity. It may have given its decision in bad faith. It may have made a decision which it had no power to make. It may have failed in the course of the inquiry to comply with the requirements of natural justice. It may in perfect good faith have misconstrued the provisions giving it power to act so that it failed to deal with the question remitted to it and decided some question which was not remitted to it. It may have refused to take into account something which it was required to take into account. Or it may have based its decision on some matter which, under the provisions setting it up, it had no right to take into account. I do not intend this list to be exhaustive. But if it decides a question remitted to it for decision without committing any of these errors it is as much entitled to decide that question wrongly as it is to decide it rightly. I understand that some confusion has been caused by my having said in *Reg. v. Governor of Brixton Prison, Ex parte Armah* [1968] A.C. 192, 234 that if a tribunal has jurisdiction to go right it has jurisdiction to go wrong. So it has, if one uses 'jurisdiction' in the narrow original sense. If it is entitled to enter on the inquiry and does not do any of those things which I have mentioned in the course of the proceedings, then its decision is equally valid whether it is right or wrong subject only to the power of the court in certain circumstances to correct an error of law. I think that, if these views are correct, the only case cited which was plainly wrongly decided is *Davies v. Price* [1958] 1 W.L.R. 434. But in a number of other cases some of the grounds of judgment are questionable.

I can now turn to the provisions of the Order under which the commission acted, and to the way in which the commission reached their decision. It was said in the Court of Appeal that publication of their reasons was unnecessary and perhaps undesirable. Whether or not they could have been required to publish their reasons, I dissent emphatically from the view that publication may have been undesirable. In my view, the commission acted with complete propriety, as one would expect looking to its membership.

The meaning of the important parts of this Order is extremely difficult to discover, and, in my view, a main cause of this is the deplorable modern drafting practice of compressing to the point of obscurity provisions which would not be difficult to understand if written out at rather greater length.

The effect of the Order was to confer legal rights on persons who might previously have hoped or expected that in allocating any sums available discretion would be exercised in their favour. We are concerned in this case with article 4 of the Order and more particularly with paragraph (1) (*b*) (ii) of that article. Article 4 is as follows:

> "(1) The Commission shall treat a claim under this Part of the Order as established if the applicant satisfies them of the following matters:— (*a*) that his application relates to property in Egypt which is referred to in Annex E; (*b*) if the property is referred to in paragraph (1) (*a*) or paragraph (2) of Annex E — (i) that the applicant is the person referred to in paragraph (1) (*a*) or in paragraph (2), as the case may be, as the owner of the property or is the successor in title of such person; and (ii) that the person referred to as aforesaid and any person who became successor in title of such person on or before February 28, 1959, were British nationals on October 31, 1956, and February 28, 1959; (*c*) if the property is referred to in paragraph (1) (*b*) of Annex E — (i) that the applicant was the owner on October 31, 1956, or, at the option of the applicant, on the date of the sale of the property at any time before February 28, 1959, by the Government of the United Arab Republic under the provisions of Egyptian Proclamation No. 5 of November 1, 1956, or is the successor in title of such owner; and (ii) that the owner on October 31, 1956, or on the date of such sale, as the case may be, and any person who became successor in title of such owner on or before February 28, 1959, were British nationals on October 31, 1956, and February 28, 1959 . . ."

The task of the commission was to receive claims and to determine the rights of each applicant. It is enacted that they shall treat a claim as established if the applicant satisfies them of certain matters. About the first there is no difficulty: the appellants' application does relate to property in Egypt referred to in Annex E. But then the difficulty begins.

Annex E originally only included properties which had been sold during the sequestration, so the person mentioned in Annex E as the owner is the person who owned the property before that sale, and his claim is a claim for compensation for having been deprived of that property. Normally he will be the applicant. But there is also provision for an application by a "successor in title." The first difficulty is to determine what is meant by "successor in title." Before the Order was made the position was that former owners whose property had been sold during the sequestration had no title to anything. They had no title to the property because it had been sold. And they had no title to compensation. All they had was a hope or expectation that they might receive some compensation. They had no legal rights at all. It is now common ground that "successor in title" cannot mean the person who obtained a title to the property which formerly belonged to the applicant. The person who acquired the property from the sequestrator was generally an Egyptian and he could have no ground for claiming compensation. So "successor in title" must refer to some person who somehow succeeded to the original owner as the person now having the original owner's hope or expectation of receiving compensation. The obvious case would be where the original owner had died. But for the moment I shall leave that problem.

The main difficulty in this case springs from the fact that the draftsman did not state separately what conditions have to be satisfied (1) where the applicant is the original owner and (2) where the applicant claims as the successor in title of the original owner. It is clear that where the applicant is the original owner he must prove that he was a British national on the dates stated. And it is equally clear that where the applicant claims as being the original owner's successor in title he must prove that both he and the original owner were British nationals on those dates, subject to later provisions in the article about persons who had died or had been born within the relevant period. What is left in obscurity is whether the provisions with regard to successors in title have any application at all in cases where the applicant is himself the original owner. If this provision had been split up as it should have been, and the conditions, to be satisfied where the original owner is the applicant had been set out, there could have been no such obscurity.

This is the crucial question in this case. It appears from the commission's reasons that they construed this provision as requiring them to inquire, when the applicant is himself the original owner, whether he had a successor in title. So they made that inquiry in this case and held that T.E.D.O. was the applicant's successor in title. As T.E.D.O. was not a British national they rejected the appellants' claim. But if, on a true construction of the Order, a claimant who is an original owner does not have to prove anything about successors in title, then the commission made an inquiry which the Order did not empower them to make, and they based their decision on a matter which they had no right to take into account. If one uses the word "jurisdiction" in its wider sense, they went beyond their jurisdiction in considering this matter. It was argued that the whole matter of construing the Order was something remitted to the commission for their decision. I cannot accept that argument. I find nothing in the Order to support it. The Order requires the commission to consider whether they are satisfied with regard to the prescribed matters. That is all they have to do. It cannot be for the commission to determine the limits of its powers. Of course if one party submits to a tribunal that its powers are wider than in fact they are, then the tribunal must deal with that submission. But if they reach a wrong conclusion as to the width of their powers, the court must be able to correct that — not because the tribunal has made an error of law, but because as a result of making an error of law they have dealt with and based their decision on a matter with which, on a true construction of their powers, they had no right to deal. If they base their decision on some matter which is not prescribed for their adjudication, they are doing something which they have no right to do and, if the view which I expressed earlier is right, their decision is a nullity. So the question is whether on a true construction of the Order the applicants did or did not have to prove anything with regard to successors in title. If the commission were entitled to enter on the inquiry whether the applicants had a successor in title, then their decision as to whether T.E.D.O. was their successor in title would I think be unassailable whether it was right or wrong: it would be a decision on a matter remitted to them for their decision. The question I have to consider is not whether they made a wrong decision but whether they inquired into and decided a matter which they had no right to consider.

. . . In themselves the words "successor in title" are, in my opinion, inappropriate in the circumstances of this Order to denote any person while the original owner is still in existence, and I think it most improbable that they were ever intended to denote any such person. There is no necessity to stretch them to cover any such person. I would therefore hold that the words "and any person who became successor in title to such person" in article 4 (1) (b) (ii) have no application to a case where the applicant is the original owner. It follows that the commission rejected the appellants' claim on a ground which they had no right to take into account and that their decision was a nullity. I would allow this appeal.

Lord Pearce

. . . Lack of jurisdiction may arise in various ways. There may be an absence of those formalities or things which are conditions precedent to the tribunal having any jurisdiction to embark on an inquiry. Or the tribunal may at the end make an order that it has no jurisdiction to make. Or in the intervening stage, while engaged on a proper inquiry, the tribunal may depart from the rules of natural justice; or it may ask itself the wrong questions; or it may take into account matters which it was not directed to take into account. Thereby it would step outside its jurisdiction. It would turn its inquiry into something not directed by Parliament and fail to make the inquiry which Parliament did direct. Any of these things would cause its purported decision to be a nullity . . .

Lord Wilberforce

. . . I must first say something as to the legal framework of this appeal: for though, in my opinion, the solution of this case is to be looked for in the thickets of subsidiary legislation, it is useful to be clear as to the general character of the argument. I do not think that it is difficult to describe this and I shall endeavour to do so, initially at least, in non-technical terms, avoiding for the moment such words as "jurisdiction," "error" and "nullity" which create many problems.

The Foreign Compensation Commission is one of many tribunals set up to deal with matters of a specialised character, in the interest of economy, speed, and expertise. It has acquired a unique status, since it alone has been excepted from the provisions of section 11 of the Tribunals and Inquiries Act, 1958. It is now well established that specialised tribunals may, depending on their nature and on the subject-matter, have the power to decide questions of law, and the position may be reached, as the result of statutory provision, that even if they make what the courts might regard as decisions wrong in law, these are to stand. The Foreign Compensation Commission is certainly within this category; its functions are predominantly judicial; it is a permanent body, composed of lawyers, with a learned chairman, and there is every ground, having regard to the number and the complexity of the cases with which it must deal, for giving a wide measure of finality to its decisions . . .

In every case, whatever the character of a tribunal, however wide the range of questions remitted to it, however great the permissible margin of mistake, the essential point remains that the tribunal has a derived authority, derived, that is, from statute: at some point, and to be found from a consideration of the legislation, the field within which it operates is marked out and limited. There is always an area, narrow or wide, which is the tribunal's area; a residual area, wide or narrow, in which the legislature has previously expressed its will and into which the tribunal may not enter. Equally, though this is not something that arises in the present case, there are certain fundamental assumptions, which without explicit restatement in every case, necessarily underlie the remission of power to decide such as (I do not attempt more than a general reference, since the strength and shade of these matters will depend upon the nature of the tribunal and the kind of question it has to decide) the requirement that a decision must be made in accordance with principles of natural justice and good faith. The principle that failure to fulfil these assumptions may be equivalent to a departure from the remitted area must be taken to follow from the decision of this House in *Ridge v. Baldwin* [1964] A.C. 40. Although, in theory perhaps, it may be possible for Parliament to set up a tribunal which has full and autonomous powers to fix its own area of operation, that has, so far, not been done in this country. The question, what is the tribunal's proper area, is one which it has always been permissible to ask and to answer, and it must follow that examination of its extent is not precluded by a clause conferring conclusiveness, finality, or unquestionability upon its decisions . . .

The separate but complementary responsibilities of court and tribunal were very clearly stated by Lord Esher M.R. in *Reg. v. Commissioners for Special Purposes of the Income Tax* (1888) 21 Q.B.D. 313, 319, in these words:

> "When an inferior court or tribunal or body, which has to exercise the power of deciding facts, is first established by Act of Parliament, the legislature has to consider what powers it will give that tribunal or body. It may in effect say that, if a certain state of facts exists and is shown to such tribunal or body before it proceeds to do certain things, it shall have jurisdiction to do such things, but not otherwise. There it is not for them conclusively to decide whether that state of facts exists, and, if they exercise the jurisdiction without its existence, what they do may be questioned, and it will be held that they have acted without jurisdiction."

That the ascertainment of the proper limits of the tribunal's power of decision is a task for the court was stated by Farwell L.J. in *Rex. v. Shoreditch Assessment Committee, Ex parte Morgan* [1910] 2 K.B. 859, 880 in language which, though perhaps vulnerable to logical analysis, has proved its value as guidance to the courts:

> "Subjection in this respect to the High Court is a necessary and inseparable incident for all

tribunals of limited jurisdiction; for the existence of the limit necessitates an authority to determine and enforce it: it is a contradiction in terms to create a tribunal with limited jurisdiction and unlimited power to determine such limit at its own will and pleasure — such a tribunal would be autocratic, not limited — and it is immaterial whether the decision of the inferior tribunal on the question of the existence or non-existence of its own jurisdictions is founded on law or fact."

[Although Lord Wilberforce did not set it out in his speech, it is worth noting that this passage is immediately preceded by the following: "No tribunal of inferior jurisdiction can by its own decision finally decide on the question of the existence or extent of such jurisdiction: such question is always subject to review by the High Court, which does not permit the inferior tribunal either to usurp a jurisdiction which it does not possess, whether at all or to the extent claimed, or to refuse to exercise a jurisdiction which it has and ought to exercise."]

[Lord Wilberforce went on to cite the words of Denning L.J. set out above at the beginning of section 2.2.2 above, and continued:] These passages at least answer one of the respondents' main arguments, to some extent accepted by the members of the Court of Appeal, which is that *because* the commission has (admittedly) been given power, indeed required, to decide some questions of law, arising out of the construction of the relevant Order in Council, it must necessarily have power to decide those questions which relate to the delimitation of its powers; or conversely that if the court has power to review the latter, it must also have power to review the former. But the one does not follow from the other: there is no reason why the Order in Council should not (as a matter of construction to be decided by the court) limit the tribunal's powers and at the same time (by the same process of construction) confer upon the tribunal power, in the exercise of its permitted task, to decide other questions of law, including questions of construction of the Order. I shall endeavour to show that this is what the Order has done.

The extent of the interpretatory power conferred upon the tribunal may sometimes be difficult to ascertain and argument may be possible whether this or that question of construction has been left to the tribunal, that is, is within the tribunal's field, or whether, because it pertains to the delimitation of the tribunal's area by the legislature, it is reserved for decision by the courts. Sometimes it will be possible to form a conclusion from the form and subject-matter of the legislation. In one case it may be seen that the legislature, while stating general objectives, is prepared to concede a wide area to the authority it establishes: this will often be the case where the decision involves a degree of policy-making rather than fact-finding, especially if the authority is a department of government or the Minister at its head. I think that we have reached a stage in our administrative law when we can view this question quite objectively, without any necessary predisposition towards one that questions of law, or questions of construction, are necessarily for the courts. In the kind of case I have mentioned there is no need to make this assumption. In another type of case it may be apparent that Parliament is itself directly and closely concerned with the definition and delimitation of certain matters of comparative detail and has marked by its language the intention that these shall accurately be observed . . . The present case . . ., as examination of the relevant Order in Council will show, is clearly of the latter category.

I do not think it desirable to discuss further in detail the many decisions in the reports in this field. But two points may perhaps be made. First, the cases in which a tribunal has been held to have passed outside its proper limits are not limited to those in which it had no power to enter upon its inquiry or its jurisdiction, or has not satisfied a condition precedent. Certainly such cases exist (for example *Ex parte Bradlaugh* (1878) 3 Q.B.D. 509) but they do not exhaust the principle. A tribunal may quite properly validly enter upon its task and in the course of carrying it out may make a decision which is invalid — not merely erroneous. This may be described as "asking the wrong question" or "applying the wrong test" — expressions not wholly satisfactory since they do not, in themselves, distinguish between doing something which is not in the tribunal's area and doing something wrong within that area — a crucial distinction which the court has to make. Cases held to be of the former kind (whether, on their facts, correctly or not does not affect the principle) are

Estate and Trust Agencies (1927) Ltd v. Singapore Improvement Trust [1937] A.C. 898, 915–917;
Seereelall Jhuggroo v. Central Arbitration and Control Board [1953] A.C. 151, 161

> ("whether [the board] took into consideration matters outside the ambit of its jurisdiction and beyond the matters which it was entitled to consider");

Reg. v. Fulham, Hammersmith and Kensington Rent Tribunal, Ex parte Hierowski [1953] 2 Q.B. 147. The present case, in my opinion, and it is at this point that I respectfully differ from the Court of Appeal, is of this kind.

Lord Wilberforce went on to agree with Lord Reid's analysis of the statutory provisions and was in favour of allowing the appeal. Lords Morris and Pearson delivered speeches in favour of dismissing the appeal. Appeal allowed.

Three issues should be noted about this landmark case. First, a *broad concept of jurisdiction* was recognized, such that a decision-maker may commit a jurisdictional error either by embarking upon an unauthorized inquiry or, once having begun its decision-making process, by exercising its powers in an unauthorized manner, for example by breaching the rules of natural justice. This is particularly clear from the extract from Lord Pearce's speech above.

Secondly, the concept of jurisdiction which was embraced in *Anisminic* was central to *the impact of the 'ouster clause'*. The clause in the Foreign Compensation Act which prevented 'any court of law' from calling into question the Commission's 'determination' appeared to preclude judicial review. However, the House of Lords concluded that a determination made outwith jurisdiction was not a 'determination' in the statutory sense: it was merely an invalid attempt to reach a determination. When this interpretation of the ouster clause was linked to their Lordships' view of jurisdiction, it became clear that the impact of the ouster clause would be minimal. (In fact it only precluded review on the peculiar ground of non-jurisdictional error of law on the face of the record, all other grounds being jurisdictional and therefore unaffected by the ouster.)

The third major point which emerges from *Anisminic* concerns the concept of *jurisdictional error of law*. As the extract above shows, the claimant's complaint was that the Commission had made such an error by misconstruing the Foreign Compensation (Egypt) (Determination and Registration of Claims) Order 1962, leading it to conclude erroneously that the claimant was ineligible for compensation. The majority adopted a robust approach to errors of law, holding that the provision which the Commission had misinterpreted was a factor upon which its jurisdiction depended. This meant that the Commission's interpretation of the term was not conclusive: because, according to the House of Lords, Parliament had intended the term in question to delimit the Commission's power, it would be nonsensical to suggest that the Commission could itself authoritatively determine its meaning. *Anisminic* did not, however, render *all* errors of law jurisdictional. For instance, Lord Wilberforce concluded that a decision-maker might be permitted to decide some questions of law conclusively for itself, while other statutory provisions may constitute jurisdictional limits the interpretation of which is for the decision-maker in the first instance but ultimately for the reviewing court. His Lordship acknowledged that it may be difficult to distinguish between these categories, but suggested that adequate guidance would often be found if not in the specific words of the legislation, then in its 'form and subject-matter'. Moreover, Lord Wilberforce considered it desirable that some questions of law should be left to the decision-making body, bearing in mind that it may possess legal expertise.

QUESTIONS

- Do you agree with Lord Wilberforce? Should some questions of law be capable of being conclusively determined by the decision-maker?
- If so, can you suggest any more specific criteria which should inform the distinction between matters of law lying within the jurisdiction of the decision-maker, and those upon which its jurisdiction depends (and which are therefore ultimately open to interpretation by the reviewing court)?

2.2.4 The General Principle: Errors of Law as Jurisdictional Errors

In the years following *Anisminic*, the courts struggled to understand precisely what its implications were. In particular, there was disagreement about whether the concept of non-jurisdictional error of law survived, a proposition which is usefully illustrated by *Pearlman* v. *Keepers and Governors of Harrow School* [1979] QB 56. A county court judge decided that a tenant who installed central heating in a house which he held on a long lease had not carried out a 'structural alteration' and was not therefore eligible for certain benefits under the Leasehold Reform Act 1967. The tenant argued that the judge had misinterpreted the term 'structural alteration' and that this mistake of law constituted a jurisdictional error. Geoffrey Lane LJ, dissenting, strongly disagreed with this contention. In a passage which was later endorsed by the Privy Council in *South East Asia Fire Bricks Sdn Bhd* v. *Non-Metallic Mineral Products Manufacturing Employees Union* [1981] AC 363, he said (at 76):

I am, I fear, unable to see how that determination, assuming it to be an erroneous determination, can properly be said to be a determination which he was not entitled to make. The judge is considering the words in the [legislation] which he ought to consider. He is not embarking on some unauthorised or extraneous or irrelevant exercise. All he has done is to come to what appears to this court to be a wrong conclusion upon a difficult question. It seems to me that, if this judge is acting outside his jurisdiction, so then is every judge who comes to a wrong decision on a point of law. Accordingly, I take the view that no form of [quashing order] is available to the tenant.

The two majority judges held that a jurisdictional error had been committed, but they each reached this conclusion by distinct processes of reasoning. Eveleigh LJ accepted (at 77) that a distinction remained between jurisdictional and non-jurisdictional errors of law, concluding that the error in this case fell into the former category because the existence of a 'structural alteration' was a matter which was collateral to the county court's jurisdiction (that is, a factor upon which its jurisdiction depended and on which it could not therefore have the final word):

. . . [A] tribunal cannot give itself power to decide a question that Parliament has not empowered it to answer . . .

In the present case, before the tribunal could embark upon its inquiry, it was necessary for it to decide the meaning of the question it was required to answer. This was a collateral matter. It had nothing to do with the merits of the case . . .

It is not for the judge of the county court to decide, ie, to lay down, what structural alteration, etc means, although of course he has to comprehend what it means before he can answer the question he is empowered to decide under [the legislation] . . . Parliament determines what structural alteration means. If the judge proceeds to answer the question having wrongly comprehended its meaning his decision is a nullity.

The analysis of Lord Denning MR, at 69–70, was more radical:

. . . [T]he distinction between an error which entails absence of jurisdiction — and an error made within the jurisdiction — is very fine. So fine indeed that it is rapidly being eroded. Take this very case. When the judge held that the installation of a full central heating system was not a "structural alteration . . . or addition" we all think — all three of us — that he went wrong in point of law. He misconstrued those words. That error can be described on the one hand as an error which went to his jurisdiction. In this way: if he had held that it was a "structural alteration . . . or addition" he would have had jurisdiction to go on and determine the various matters set out in [the legislation]. By holding that it was not a "structural alteration . . . or addition" he deprived himself of jurisdiction to determine those matters. On the other hand, his error can equally well be described as an error made by him within his jurisdiction. It can plausibly be said that he had jurisdiction to inquire into the meaning of the words "structural alteration . . . or addition"; and that his wrong interpretation of them was only an error within his jurisdiction, and not an error taking him outside it.

That illustration could be repeated in nearly all these cases. So fine is the distinction that in truth the High Court has a choice before it whether to interfere with an inferior court on a point of law. If it chooses to interfere, it can formulate its decision in the words: "The court below had no jurisdiction to decide this point wrongly as it did." If it does not choose to interfere, it can say: "The court had jurisdiction to decide it wrongly, and did so." Softly be it stated, but that is the reason for the difference between the decision of the Court of Appeal in *Anisminic Ltd.* v. *Foreign Compensation Commission* [1968] 2 Q.B. 862 and the House of Lords [1969] 2 A.C. 147.

I would suggest that this distinction should now be discarded. The High Court has, and should have, jurisdiction to control the proceedings of inferior courts and tribunals by way of judicial review. When they go wrong in law, the High Court should have power to put them right. Not only in the instant case to do justice to the complainant. But also so as to secure that all courts and tribunals, when faced with the same point of law, should decide it in the same way. It is intolerable that a citizen's rights in point of law should depend on which judge tries his case, or in which court it is heard. The way to get things right is to hold thus: no court or tribunal has any jurisdiction to make an error of law on which the decision of the case depends. If it makes such an error, it goes outside its jurisdiction and [a quashing order] will lie to correct it. In this case the finding — that the installation of a central heating system was not a "structural alteration" — was an error on which the jurisdiction of the county court depended: and, because of that error, the judge was quite wrong to dismiss the application outright. He ought to have found that the installation was an "improvement" . . ., and gone on to determine the other matters referred to in [the legislation].

Lord Denning's dissatisfaction with the distinction between jurisdictional and non-jurisdictional errors of law rested upon two distinct foundations. First, he considered that the distinction could not be drawn in any principled fashion, and that in reality the courts manipulated it for instrumental purposes. Secondly, he felt that consistency required that the same meaning be attributed to legal provisions by all decision-makers and that, to this end, the High Court should be able to furnish *conclusive* interpretations of legislation.

QUESTIONS

- Which of the three judges in *Pearlman* do you agree with?
- Do you find Lord Denning's arguments in favour of treating all errors of law as jurisdictional convincing?

Some clarity was brought to this situation by the remarks of Lord Diplock in *In re Racal Communications Ltd* [1981] AC 374 and *O'Reilly* v. *Mackman* [1983] 2 AC 237 (see below at 2.2.5); in the latter, he suggested that, as a general principle, all errors of law should be regarded as jurisdictional. All of the judges in the following case subscribed to this view, although it was Lord Browne-Wilkinson who addressed the matter in most detail.

R v. *Lord President of the Privy Council, ex parte Page* [1993] AC 682
House of Lords

The facts, which are unimportant for present purposes, are set out below at 2.2.5.

Lord Browne-Wilkinson

. . . In my judgment the decision in *Anisminic Ltd. v. Foreign Compensation Commission* [1969] 2 A.C. 147 rendered obsolete the distinction between errors of law on the face of the record and other errors of law by extending the doctrine of ultra vires. Thenceforward it was to be taken that Parliament had only conferred the decision-making power on the basis that it was to be exercised on the correct legal basis: a misdirection in law in making the decision therefore rendered the decision ultra vires . . . [I]n my judgment the decision of this House in *O'Reilly v. Mackman* [1983] 2 A.C. 237 establishes the law in the sense that I have stated. Lord Diplock, with whose speech all the other members of the committee agreed, said, at p. 278, that the decision in *Anisminic*:

> "has liberated English public law from the fetters that the courts had theretofore imposed upon themselves so far as determinations of inferior courts and statutory tribunals were concerned, by drawing esoteric distinctions between errors of law committed by such tribunals that went to their jurisdiction, and errors of law committed by them within their jurisdiction. The break-through that the *Anisminic* case made was the recognition by the majority of this House that if a tribunal whose jurisdiction was limited by statute or subordinate legislation mistook the law applicable to the facts as it had found them, it must have asked itself the wrong question, ie, one into which it was not empowered to inquire and so had no jurisdiction to determine. Its purported "determination," not being "a determination" within the meaning of the empowering legislation, was accordingly a nullity."

Therefore, I agree with [counsel for the claimant] that in general any error of law made by an administrative tribunal or inferior court in reaching its decision can be quashed for error of law.

At this point I must notice an argument raised by Mr. Beloff for the university. He suggests that the recent decision of this House in *Reg. v. Independent Television Commission, ex parte T.S.W. Broadcasting Ltd.* [reported at [1996] E.M.L.R. 291], has thrown doubt on the proposition that all errors of law vitiate the decision. In my judgment this is a misreading of that authority. This House was asserting that the mere existence of a mistake of law made at some earlier stage does not vitiate the actual decision made: what must be shown is a relevant error of law, *ie*, an error in the actual making of the decision which affected the decision itself. This is demonstrated by Lord Templeman's quotation from the well known judgment of Lord Greene M.R. in *Associated Provincial Picture Houses Ltd. v. Wednesbury Corporation* [1948] 1 K.B. 223 (including the passage, at p. 229, "a person entrusted with a discretion must, so to speak, direct himself properly in law") and the manner in which thereafter he applied those principles to the facts of the case before the House . . .

This case is highly significant because it recognizes as a general principle that errors of law are jurisdictional. It is not, however, a panacea. What counts as an error of law is not always clear; we will see below that the fact/law distinction is malleable, and may be used by courts to manipulate the extent of judicial supervision. Moreover, the basic proposition that only courts should be able conclusively to determine questions of law is not itself uncontroversial. That view was famously rejected by the US Supreme Court in *Chevron USA Inc* v. *National Resources Defense Council Inc* (1984) 467 US 837, in which it was held that courts should substitute judgment on the meaning of statutory terms only if it is apparent that the legislature had a specific intention as to meaning; otherwise, agencies should be allowed to adopt any rational interpretation. Whether this represents a better division of competence between courts and agencies is a highly divisive question. For some writers, including Craig, *Administrative Law* (Oxford 2003) at 518, *Chevron* focusses on the key question: 'whose opinion on the existence and function of a statutory term should be accepted, that of the agency or that of the courts?' There are, however, two objections to the *Chevron* approach. First, even if we accept that there may be occasions on which it is appropriate to respect agencies' interpretations of the law, it is unclear that the *Chevron* reasoning correctly identifies those occasions. Reliance on (no doubt hard to discern) legislative intention is a poor substitute for engaging with a richer set of concerns relating to justiciability and relative institutional competence (on which see further Hare (in Forsyth and Hare (eds), *The Golden Metwand and the Crooked Cord* (Oxford 1998) at 138–139). Secondly, others — including Farina (1989) 89 *Columbia Law Review* 452 at 498 — attack not the methodology of *Chevron* but its fundamental premise:

Chevron's assumption that deference is necessary to avoid judicial usurpation of power Congress wished to place elsewhere fundamentally misperceives the separation of powers [doctrine], . . . [adherence to which implies] that much more is at stake than simply discerning and respecting the will of a coordinate branch. If Congress chooses to delegate regulatory authority to agencies, part of the price of delegation may be that the court, not the agency, must hold the power to say what the statute means. In other words, Cass Sunstein's pithy criticism of deference according to *Chevron* — "foxes shouldn't guard henhouses" — is a counsel not merely of prudence, but of constitutional necessity.

2.2.5 Exceptions to the General Principle

Characterizing errors of law as jurisdictional implies a hard-edged review whereby the court will substitute its view for that of the decision-maker. However, there appear to be some situations in which courts will not intervene whenever they disagree with the decision-maker's conclusion on a point of law. One such situation arises where the decision-maker in question is interpreting not the general law of the land, but some special system of rules — for example, one which applies only in relation to a specific institution, such as the statutes and ordinances of a university.

. . . .

R v. *Lord President of the Privy Council, ex parte Page* [1993] AC 682
House of Lords

The claimant was appointed to a lectureship at the University of Hull in 1966. His contract of employment provided that either party could terminate the appointment by giving three months' notice and was subject to the university statutes, which provided that lecturers had to retire at the age of 67. In addition, s 34(1) of the statutes stated that members of staff who, like the claimant, had been appointed to the retiring age could be removed 'for good cause', and s 34(3) provided that, subject to their terms of appointment, such individuals could not be removed save for good cause. The university purported to terminate the claimant's contract in 1988 on grounds not of good cause, but of redundancy. The claimant sought a declaration from the university visitor, whose role is explained below by Lord Browne-Wilkinson, that the dismissal was contrary to s 34 and therefore beyond the university's powers. The defendant, acting on behalf of the visitor, refused to grant such a declaration. The claimant sought judicial review, and the Divisional Court granted a declaration; however, the Court of Appeal decided that, while the visitor's decision was subject to judicial review, the university had not exceeded its powers in dismissing the claimant. The claimant appealed against the Court of Appeal's interpretation of the statutes; the university and the visitor cross-appealed against the Court of Appeal's decision that the visitor's decisions were subject to judicial review.

Lord Browne-Wilkinson

. . . It is established that, a university being an eleemosynary charitable foundation [that is, one "founded for the purpose of distributing the founder's bounty": *Thomas* v. *University of Bradford* [1987] AC 795 at 827, *per* Lord Ackner], the visitor of the university has exclusive jurisdiction to decide disputes arising under the domestic law of the university. This is because the founder of such a body is entitled to reserve to himself or to a visitor whom he appoints the exclusive right to adjudicate upon the domestic laws which the founder has established for the regulation of his bounty. Even where the contractual rights of an individual (such as his contract of employment with the university) are in issue, if those contractual rights are themselves dependent upon rights arising under the regulating documents of the charity, the visitor has an exclusive jurisdiction over disputes relating to such employment . . .

Under the modern law, [a quashing order] normally lies to quash a decision for error of law. Therefore, the narrow issue in this case is whether, as Mr Page contends and the courts below have held, [a quashing order] lies against the visitor to quash his decision as being erroneous in point of law notwithstanding that the question of law arises under the domestic law of the university which the visitor has "exclusive" jurisdiction to decide . . .

[Lord Browne-Wilkinson reviewed the authorities and continued:] In my judgment this review of the authorities demonstrates that for over 300 years the law has been clearly established that the visitor of an eleemosynary charity has an exclusive jurisdiction to determine what are the internal laws of the charity and the proper application of those laws to those within his jurisdiction. The court's inability to determine those matters is not limited to the period pending the visitor's determination but extends so as to prohibit any subsequent review by the court of the correctness of a decision made by the visitor acting within his jurisdiction and in accordance with the rules of natural justice. This inability of the court to intervene is founded on the fact that the applicable law is not the common law of England but a peculiar or domestic law of which the visitor is the sole judge. This special status of a visitor springs from the common law recognising the right of the founder to lay down such a special law subject to adjudication only by a special judge, the visitor . . .

[His Lordship considered general developments in the law of judicial review, in the terms set out above at 2.2.4, and continued:] Although the general rule is that decisions affected by errors of law made by tribunals or inferior courts can be quashed, in my judgment there are two reasons why that rule does not apply in the case of visitors. First, as I have sought to explain, the constitutional basis of the courts' power to quash is that the decision of the inferior tribunal is unlawful on the grounds that it is ultra vires. In the ordinary case, the law applicable to a decision made by such a body is the general law of the land. Therefore, a tribunal or inferior court acts ultra vires if it reaches its conclusion on a basis erroneous under the general law. But the position of decisions made by a visitor is different. As the authorities which I have cited demonstrate, the visitor is applying not the general law of the land but a peculiar, domestic law of which he is the sole arbiter and of which the courts have no cognisance. If the visitor has power under the regulating documents to enter into the adjudication of the dispute (*ie*, is acting within his jurisdiction in the narrow sense) he cannot err in law in reaching this decision since the general law is not the applicable law. Therefore he cannot be acting ultra vires and unlawfully by applying his view of the domestic law in reaching his decision. The court has no jurisdiction either to say that he erred in his application of the general law (since the general law is not applicable to the decision) or to reach a contrary view as to the effect of the domestic law (since the visitor is the sole judge of such domestic law).

. . . Mr Burke [for the claimant] urged that the position of a visitor would be anomalous if he were immune from review on the ground of error of law. He submitted that the concept of a peculiar domestic law differing from the general law of the land was artificial since in practice the charter and statutes of a university are expressed in ordinary legal language and applied in accordance with the same principles as those applicable under the general law. He pointed to the important public role occupied by universities and submitted that it was wrong that they should be immune from the general law of the land: "There must be no Alsatia in England where the King's writ does not run:" *per* Scrutton L.J. in *Czarnikow v. Roth, Schmidt & Co.* [1922] 2 K.B. 478, 488. He further suggested that to permit review of a visitor's decision for error of law would not impair the effectiveness of the visitor's domestic jurisdiction.

I accept that the position of the visitor is anomalous, indeed unique. I further accept that where the visitor is, or is advised by, a lawyer the distinction between the peculiar domestic law he applies and the general law is artificial. But I do not regard these factors as justifying sweeping away the law which for so long has regulated the conduct of charitable corporations. There are internal disputes which are resolved by a visitor who is not a lawyer himself and has not taken legal advice. It is not only modern universities which have visitors: there are a substantial number of other long-established educational, ecclesiastical and eleemosynary bodies which have visitors. The advantages of having an informal system which produces a speedy, cheap and final answer to internal disputes has been repeatedly emphasized in the authorities, most recently by this House in *Thomas v. University of Bradford* [1987] A.C. 795: see *per* Lord Griffiths, at p. 825D; see also *Patel v. University of Bradford Senate* [1978] 1 W.L.R. 1488, 1499–1500. If it were to be held that judicial review for error of law lay against the visitor I fear that, as in the present case, finality would be lost not only in cases raising pure questions of law but also in cases where it would be urged in accordance with the *Wednesbury* principle (*Associated Provincial Picture Houses Ltd. v. Wednesbury Corporation* [1948] 1 K.B. 223) that the visitor had failed to take into account relevant matters or taken into account irrelevant matters or had reached an irrational conclusion. Although the visitor's position is anomalous, it provides a valuable machinery for resolving internal disputes which should not be lost.

I have therefore reached the conclusion that judicial review does not lie to impeach the decisions of a visitor taken within his jurisdiction (in the narrow sense) on questions of either fact or law. Judicial review does lie to the visitor in cases where he has acted outside his jurisdiction (in the narrow sense) or abused his powers or acted in breach of the rules of natural justice. Accordingly, in my judgment the Divisional Court had no jurisdiction to entertain the application for judicial review of the visitor's decision in this case . . .

Lord Slynn

. . . With deference to the contrary view of the majority of your Lordships, in my opinion if [a quashing order] can go to a particular tribunal it is available on all the grounds which have been judicially recognised. I can see no reasons in principle for limiting the availability of [quashing orders] to a patent excess of power (as where a visitor has decided something which was not within his remit) and excluding review on other grounds recognised by the law. If it is accepted, as I believe it should be accepted, that [a quashing order] goes not only for such an excess or abuse of power but also for a breach of the rules of natural justice there is even less reason in principle for excluding other established grounds. If therefore [a quashing order] is generally available for error of law not involving abuse of power (as . . . I consider that it is) then it should be available also in respect of a decision of a visitor.

Lords Keith and Griffiths agreed with Lord Browne-Wilkinson. Lord Mustill agreed with Lord Slynn, who concluded that although review could lie for error of law, no such error had occurred. Appeal dismissed.

As well as the fact that the visitor was applying a body of 'domestic' law, Lord Browne-Wilkinson was influenced by practical considerations, such as speed and cost. The general principles articulated in *Page* therefore extend beyond the visitorial jurisdiction, and suggest that the general approach, which holds that errors of law are jurisdictional, may (exceptionally) yield in the face of practical considerations. For example, in *R v. Registrar of Companies, ex parte Central Bank of India* [1986] QB 1114 at 1175–1176, concerning the Registrar's power to register a charge, Slade LJ said that there was no absolute and unqualified rule that where an administrative authority has made an error of law its decision is inevitably *ultra vires*. On this view, considerations of commercial certainty as well as a statutory 'conclusive evidence' clause sufficed, it would seem, to show that the decision to register a charge was *intra vires* although in reaching it an error of law had been made.

The following case evidences further circumstances in which errors of law may not be reviewable on jurisdictional grounds.

....

In re Racal Communications Ltd [1981] AC 374
House of Lords

The Director of Public Prosecutions applied for an order to inspect the company's records and papers under s 441 of the Companies Act 1948, which provided for such an order if there was reasonable cause to believe that any officer of the company had committed 'an offence in connection with the management of the company's affairs'. The grounds for this application were that a departmental manager sent fraudulent statements to the company's customers claiming more money than the company was owed. Vinelott J dismissed the application on the ground that s 441 only applied to offences committed in the course of the internal management of a company. Nevertheless, despite the provision in s 441(3) that the decision of a High Court judge on an application under the section 'shall not be appealable', he gave leave to appeal. The Court of Appeal, relying on the *Pearlman* case (see above at 2.2.4), allowed the appeal on the ground that the judge had misconstrued s 441 and, in refusing jurisdiction as a result of this misconstruction, he had made an error of law going to his jurisdiction. An appeal by the company to the House of Lords was allowed on the ground that appeal to the Court of Appeal was barred by s 441(3), and that it could not entertain any original application for judicial review. This extract is solely concerned with the scope of judicial review.

Lord Diplock

. . . Parliament can, of course, if it so desires, confer upon administrative tribunals or authorities power to decide questions of law as well as questions of fact or of administrative policy, but this requires clear words, for the presumption is that where a decision-making power is conferred on a tribunal or authority that is not a court of law, Parliament did not intend to do so. The break-through made by *Anisminic* [1969] 2 A.C. 147 was that, as respects administrative tribunals and authorities, the old distinction between errors of law that went to jurisdiction and errors of law that did not, was for practical purposes abolished. Any error of law that could be shown to have been made by them in the course of reaching their decision on matters of fact or of administrative policy would result in their having asked themselves the wrong question with the result that the decision they reached would be a nullity. The Tribunals and Inquiries Act 1971, which requires most administrative tribunals from which there is not a statutory right of appeal to the Supreme Court on questions of law, to give written reasons for their decisions, now supplemented by the provisions for discovery in applications for judicial review under Ord. 53 of the Rules of the Supreme Court, facilitates the detection of errors of law by those tribunals and by administrative authorities, generally.

But there is no similar presumption that where a decision-making power is conferred by statute upon a court of law, Parliament did not intend to confer upon it power to decide questions of law as well as questions of fact. Whether it did or not and, in the case of inferior courts, what limits are imposed on the kinds of questions of law they are empowered to decide, depends upon the construction of the statute unencumbered by any such presumption. In the case of inferior courts where the decision of the court is made final and conclusive by the statute, this may involve the survival of those subtle distinctions formerly drawn between errors of law which go to jurisdiction and errors of law which do not that did so much to confuse English administrative law before *Anisminic* [1969] 2 A.C. 147; but upon any application for judicial review of a decision of an inferior court in a matter which involves, as so many do, interrelated questions of law, fact and degree the superior court conducting the review should not be astute to hold that Parliament did not intend the inferior court to have jurisdiction to decide for itself the meaning of ordinary words used in the statute to define the question which it has to decide. This, in my view, is the error into which the majority of the Court of Appeal fell in *Pearlman* [1979] Q.B. 56. The question for decision by the county court judge under paragraph 1 (2) of Schedule 8 to the Housing Act 1974 was whether the installation of central heating in a particular dwelling house amounted to a "structural alteration, extension or addition." If the meaning of ordinary words when used in a statute becomes a question of law, here was a typical question of mixed law, fact and degree which only a scholiast would think it appropriate to dissect into two separate questions, one for decision by the superior court, *viz.* the meaning of those words — a question which must entail considerations of degree; and the other for decision by the county court, viz. the application of the words to the particular installation — a question which also entails considerations of degree. The county court judge had not ventured upon any definition of the words 'structural alteration, extension or addition.' So there was really no material on which to hold that he had got the meaning wrong rather than its application to the facts. Nevertheless the majority of the Court of Appeal in *Pearlman* [1979] Q.B. 56 held that Parliament had indeed intended that such a dissection should be made and since they would not have come to the same conclusion themselves on the facts of the case they inferred that the judge's error was one of interpretation of the words "structural alteration, extension or addition." This was in the face of a powerful dissent by Geoffrey Lane L.J. Notwithstanding that on the facts of the case he too would have reached a different conclusion from that of the county court judge, he was of opinion that the statute conferred upon the judge jurisdiction to decide finally and conclusively a question which did involve interrelated questions of law, fact and degree, and that the Supreme Court had no jurisdiction to interfere with his decision by way of judicial review. For my part, I find the reasoning in his minority judgment conclusive.

There is in my view, however, also an obvious distinction between jurisdiction conferred by a statute on a court of law of limited jurisdiction to decide a defined question finally and conclusively or unappealably, and a similar jurisdiction conferred on the High Court or a judge of the High Court acting in his judicial capacity . . . There is simply no room for error going to his jurisdiction, nor . . . is there any room for judicial review. Judicial review is available as a remedy for mistakes of law made by inferior courts and tribunals only. Mistakes of law made by judges of the High Court acting in their capacity as such can be corrected only by means of appeal to an appellate court; and if, as in the instant case, the statute provides that the judge's decision shall not be appealable, they cannot be corrected at all . . .

Lord Edmund-Davies

. . . My Lords, like the Judicial Committee of the Privy Council in a recent decision to which I was a party (*South East Asia Fire Bricks Sdn. Bhd. v. Non-Metallic Mineral Products Manufacturing Employees Union* [1981] A.C. 363), I have to say respectfully that the existing law is, in my judgment, to be found in the dissenting judgment of Geoffrey Lane L.J. in *Pearlman* and that the majority view was erroneous.

Lord Keith agreed with Lord Diplock. Lords Salmon and Scarman delivered speeches in favour of allowing the appeal. Appeal allowed.

The point decided by this case was that the *High Court* could not commit jurisdictional errors of law for the reason given by Lord Diplock above; however, his *obiter* comments are of considerable interest. He opined that the general presumption is that *tribunals and administrative bodies* have no authority to determine questions of law conclusively: in the absence of clear contrary provision, any error of law which they make will constitute an excess of jurisdiction. However, no such presumption applies to *inferior courts of law*, since it is readily conceivable that Parliament may intend respect to be given to their views on certain points of law. Whether this is so is a matter of statutory construction; if it is, then those points will be non-jurisdictional, and the inferior court will be able to determine them conclusively (subject to the possibility of review for error on the face of the record).

Lord Diplock's comments in *Racal* beg two questions. First, do they accurately describe the current position? We should note in passing that Lord Diplock himself cast doubt on these comments in the later case of *O'Reilly* v. *Mackman* [1983] 2 AC 237 at 278 (quoted by Lord Browne-Wilkinson in *Page*: see the extract at 2.2.4 above), in which he appeared to suggest that the distinction between jurisdictional and non-jurisdictional errors of law had become redundant in respect of both tribunals *and* inferior courts of law. It would, however, be wrong to attach too much weight to these remarks, which were made in passing. The position in relation to inferior courts of law is not, unfortunately, placed beyond doubt by *Page*. Lord Browne-Wilkinson's leading speech sent mixed signals in this regard. On the one hand, he relied upon Lord Diplock's comments in *O'Reilly* in which no distinction was made between courts of law and tribunals, leading Sir Donald Nicholls V-C to assume (*obiter*) in *R* v. *Visitors to the Inns of Court, ex parte Calder* [1994] QB 1 at 37 that no such distinction was to be drawn. On this view, it seems that there is a presumption applying to all bodies that errors of law are jurisdictional. On the other hand, in the following passage ([1993] AC 682 at 703) Lord Browne-Wilkinson, in advancing a reason for recognizing the special position of visitors in addition to that set out in the excerpt from his speech above at 2.2.4, accepted (see also Lord Griffiths at 693–694) that it may sometimes be appropriate to acknowledge that an inferior court of law is capable of conclusively determining certain questions of law, thereby implicitly suggesting that the presumption that errors of law are jurisdictional applies in respect of tribunals and other administrative bodies but not to inferior courts (in respect of which, on this view, reviewing courts should be open-minded, looking to relevant contextual factors for guidance as to the weight to be attached to any particular inferior court's views on points of law). His Lordship stated:

In *Pearlman v. Keepers and Governors of Harrow School* [1979] Q.B. 56 a statute provided that the decision of the county court as to whether works constituted an "improvement" within the meaning of the Act should be "final and conclusive." A tenant claimed that the installation of a central heating system constituted an "improvement." The county court judge ruled that it did not. The tenant then applied to the Divisional Court by way of judicial review to quash the judge's decision. The majority of the Court of Appeal held that it had jurisdiction to quash the judge's order. However, Geoffrey Lane L.J. dissented. He held that the judge had done nothing which went outside the proper area of his inquiry. The question was not whether the judge had made a wrong decision but whether he had inquired into and decided a matter which he had no right to consider. Therefore he held that the court had no jurisdiction to review the decision of the county court judge for error of law.

This dissenting judgment of Geoffrey Lane LJ has been approved by the Privy Council in *South East Asia Fire Bricks Sdn. Bhd. v. Non-Metallic Mineral Products Manufacturing Employees Union* [1981] A.C. 363, 370e–f and by a majority in this House in *[In re Racal Communications Ltd]* [1981] A.C. 374, 384b–d and 390f–391d. In the latter case, Lord Diplock pointed out, at pp 382–383, that the decision in *Anisminic Ltd. v. Foreign Compensation Commission* [1969] 2 A.C. 147 applied to decisions of administrative tribunals or other administrative bodies made under statutory powers: in those cases there was a presumption that the statute conferring the power did not intend the administrative body to be the final arbiter of questions of law. He then contrasted that position with the case where a decision-making power had been conferred on a court of law. In that case no such presumption could exist: on the contrary where Parliament had provided that the decision of an inferior court was final and conclusive the High Court should not be astute to find that the inferior court's decision on a question of law had not been made final and conclusive, thereby excluding the jurisdiction to review it.

In my judgment, therefore, if there were a statutory provision that the decision of a visitor on the law applicable to internal disputes of a charity was to be "final and conclusive," courts would have no jurisdiction to review the visitor's decision on the grounds of error of law made by the visitor within his jurisdiction (in the narrow sense). For myself, I can see no relevant distinction between a case where a statute has conferred such final and conclusive jurisdiction and the case where the common law has for 300 years recognised that the visitor's decision on questions of fact and law are final and conclusive and are not to be reviewed by the courts.

In *R v. Bedwellty Justices, ex parte Williams* [1997] AC 225 at 233, Lord Cooke noted these comments in *Page*. However, there was no finality clause in the statute which was at stake in *Williams*, and Lord Cooke offered no guidance as to what approach would have been adopted had such a clause existed.

Given the state of the case law, it is appropriate to ask whether it makes sense to distinguish between inferior courts of law and other decision-makers in the manner suggested by Lord Diplock. The constitutional principle of the separation of powers (whose application in this context is considered by Hare (in Forsyth and Hare (eds), *The Golden Metwand and the Crooked Cord* (Oxford 1998)) suggests that the willingness of reviewing courts to overturn others' conclusions on questions of law should be affected by the ability of the latter to determine such questions. This effectively reduces to an argument of relative institutional competence. However, while this sort of thinking appears to underlie Lord Diplock's remarks in *Racal*, his proposed distinction between inferior courts of law and other decision-makers is too crude. Whether or not the label 'court' is attached to a body should hardly be the issue. For instance, although not called courts, some specialized tribunals have considerable expertise of the particular area of law with which they routinely deal (see, *eg, Chief Adjudication Officer v. Foster* [1993] AC 754 at 767, where Lord Bridge noted the 'great expertise' of the Social Security Commissioners in the 'somewhat esoteric area' of social security law). It is therefore wrong to assume that 'courts' possess legal expertise while 'tribunals' and other bodies do not. The decision whether to recognize that a particular body may conclusively determine some questions of law should not be made by reference to crude assumptions based on labels. (For further comment on this matter, see Beatson (1984) 4 *OJLS* 22 at 37–39.)

Finally, it is necessary to consider the following case.

....

R v. *Monopolies and Mergers Commission, ex parte South Yorkshire Transport* [1993] 1 WLR 23
House of Lords

The first claimant was a company which provided public transport services in South Yorkshire, and was owned by the second claimant, South Yorkshire Passenger Transport Authority. When the first claimant acquired a number of bus companies operating in South Yorkshire, the Secretary of State for Trade and Industry, acting under s 64 of the Fair Trading Act 1973, referred the matter to the defendant Commission, which could investigate the matter if (*inter alia*) the area concerned was 'a substantial part of the United Kingdom'. The Commission considered that 'substantial' meant 'something real or important as distinct from something merely nominal', and that although the area in question comprised only 1.65 per cent of the total geographical area of the UK, the statutory requirement was met because of the important part which the region played in the 'economic development and growth, and cultural life of the country'. In light of this the Commission recommended that the first claimant should be required to divest itself of the acquisitions in question. The Secretary of State adopted the Commission's conclusions and recommendation. The claimants sought judicial review, arguing that the requirement that the matter concerned a 'substantial part' of the UK was a jurisdictional precondition, and that the Commission erred in its interpretation of the Act in this respect. They succeeded at first instance. Having appealed unsuccessfully to the Court of Appeal, the defendants appealed to the House of Lords.

Lord Mustill

. . . [N]o recourse need be made to dictionaries to establish that "substantial" accommodates a wide range of meanings. At one extreme there is "not trifling." At the other, there is "nearly complete," as where someone says that he is in substantial agreement with what has just been said. In between, there exist many shades of meaning, drawing colour from their context. That the protean nature of the word has been reflected in the decided cases is, I believe, made quite clear by the judgment of Otton J. [at first instance], in which the authorities are so thoroughly discussed as to make it unnecessary to go through them again. It is sufficient to say that although I do not accept that "substantial" can never mean "more than *de minimis*", . . . I am satisfied that in section 64(3) the word does indeed lie further up the spectrum than that. To say how far up is another matter. The courts have repeatedly warned against the dangers of taking an inherently imprecise word, and by redefining it thrusting on it a spurious degree of precision. I will try to avoid such an error. Nevertheless I am glad to adopt, as a means of giving a general indication of where the meaning of the word in section 64(3) lies within the range of possible meanings, the expression of Nourse L.J. [1992] 1 W.L.R. 291, 301g "worthy of consideration for the purpose of the Act." . . .

Thus far, therefore, I accept the respondents' submission that if the commission proceeded when examining its jurisdiction on the basis that it was enough for the reference area to be more than trifling this was a radical misconception. At first sight it appears that this gives them a powerful case, for we find in the report that the commission calls up the idea of "something more than merely nominal." If this expression truly reflects the basis of the decision there is reason for the court to interfere. Whilst acknowledging the force of this argument, I have come to the conclusion that it gives too little weight to the reasoning of the commission as a whole . . .

[Lord Mustill examined the commission's reasoning, concluding that they had applied an interpretation of the term "substantial" which was in reality much closer to that suggested by Nourse L.J. than might have been suggested by the words which the commission had used to describe the test they applied. He continued:] There remains however the question whether, even if the commission had placed the test in broadly the right part of the spectrum of possible meanings it nevertheless failed to apply the test correctly. Here, the contest is between three methods of approach. 1. An arithmetical proportion should be struck between the reference area of the United Kingdom as a whole, as regards surface area, population and volume of the economic activity with which the reference is concerned. If the proportion(s) are too low, the area does not qualify. 2. An assessment in absolute terms of the size and importance of the area, independent of proportions 3. A mixture of the two kinds of criterion . . .

[His Lordship assessed these competing approaches, concluding:] I would prefer to state that the part must be "of such size, character and importance as to make it worth consideration for the purposes of the Act." . . .

Applying this test to the present case one will ask first whether any misdirection is established, and secondly whether the decision can be overturned on the facts. As to the first it is quite clear that the approach of the commission was in general accord with what I would propose. It is true that matters such as academic and sports activities, mentioned by the commission, are of marginal importance at the most, but I do not regard their inclusion in the list of features to which the commission paid regard as vitiating an appreciation of "substantive" which was broadly correct. On the second question the parties are at odds as to the proper function of the courts. The respondents say that the two stages of the commission's inquiry involved wholly different tasks. Once the commission reached the stage of deciding on public interest and remedies it was exercising a broad judgment whose outcome could be overturned only on the ground of irrationality. The question of jurisdiction, by contrast, is a hard-edged question. There is no room for legitimate disagreement. Either the commission had jurisdiction or it had not. The fact that it is quite hard to discover the meaning of section 64(3) makes no difference. It does have a correct meaning, and one meaning alone; and once this is ascertained a correct application of it to the facts of the case will always yield the same answer. If the commission has reached a different answer it is wrong, and the court can and must intervene.

I agree with this argument in part, but only in part. Once the criterion for a judgment has been properly understood, the fact that it was formerly part of a range of possible criteria from which it was difficult to choose and on which opinions might legitimately differ becomes a matter of history. The judgment now proceeds unequivocally on the basis of the criterion as ascertained. So far, no room for controversy. But this clear-cut approach cannot be applied to every case, for the criterion so established may itself be so imprecise that different decision-makers, each acting rationally, might reach differing conclusions when applying it to the facts of a given case. In such a case the court is entitled to substitute its own opinion for that of the person to whom the decision has been entrusted only if the decision is so aberrant that it cannot be classed as rational: *Edwards v. Bairstow* [1956] A.C. 14. The present is such a case. Even after eliminating inappropriate senses of "substantial" one is still left with a meaning broad enough to call for the exercise of judgment rather than an exact quantitative measurement. Approaching the matter in this light I am quite satisfied that there is no ground for interference by the court, since the conclusion at which the commission arrived was well within the permissible field of judgment. Indeed I would go further, and say that in my opinion it was right.

I would accordingly allow the appeal, and restore the decision of the Commissioners and the Secretary of State . . .

Lords Templeman, Goff, Lowry, and Slynn agreed with Lord Mustill. Appeal allowed.

Lord Mustill's comments are somewhat opaque. At one point in his speech he appears to suggest that the Commission was merely required to place the test 'in broadly the right part of the spectrum of possible meanings'. This implies that the *definition* of a jurisdictional statutory term may, in certain circumstances, be treated not as a hard-edged matter for the court, to which there is only one correct answer, but as a question capable of yielding a range of lawful answers, such that the decision-maker acts lawfully by choosing any of the answers within that range. However, in the penultimate paragraph of our excerpt, Lord Mustill appears to adopt a different view, suggesting that while the statutory term, being a juris-dictional one, can lawfully bear only one *definition* (*viz* that which is favoured by the reviewing court), that definition may be so vague that, in practice, its *application* may be difficult to review on a hard-edged basis. On this view, while the decision-maker in *South Yorkshire Transport* had to adopt the correct definition of the criterion 'substantial part of the UK', the reviewing court could only have upset the decision-maker's conclusion as to whether the criterion was actually met if the decision-maker had exceeded the *range* of permissible responses. It is to this matter — that is, the application of statutory criteria to the facts — that we now turn.

QUESTIONS

- How does the *South Yorkshire Transport* decision relate to the approach of the US Supreme Court in *Chevron*, discussed above at 2.2.4?
- Is the distinction which Lord Mustill appears to draw in the penultimate paragraph of our excerpt, between the definition of jurisdictional terms and their application to the facts, a helpful one?
- Is the process of judicial attribution of a fixed meaning to vague statutory terms a mean-ingful one, if (as envisaged by Lord Mustill) close judicial supervision of their application to the facts is impossible or inappropriate?

2.3 Applying Statutory Criteria to the Facts

We have seen thus far that mistakes about the applicable law are likely to constitute juris-dictional errors; reviewing courts may therefore substitute judgment concerning the mean-ing of legal terms which demarcate the decision-maker's powers. It is now necessary to consider a question which we touched on in discussing our example above in section 2.1.1, but which we have not yet considered in detail. If legislation provides that some state of affairs — for example, the making of a 'structural alteration' — must exist before a particu-lar power may be exercised, is the *existence in fact* of that state of affairs a jurisdictional matter? Whether the statutory state of affairs exists raises both questions of pure fact (*eg* what was done to the house?) and questions of judgment (*eg* does the work carried out amount to a structural alteration in the statutory sense?) Our concern here is to establish in what circumstances the state of affairs described in the statute will be regarded as a juris-dictional precondition which must exist in the court's view, such that it is able to substitute judgment in relation to these matters, and when the existence of such a state of affairs will be regarded as a matter upon which, subject only to limited judicial control, it is for the decision-maker to decide.

The following remarks of Lord Goddard CJ in *R v. Fulham, Hammersmith and Kensington Rent Tribunal, ex parte Zerek* [1951] 2 KB 1 at 6 are a useful starting point:

The law to be gathered, especially from *R* v. *Income Tax Special Commissioners* (1888) 21 Q.B.D. 313 and *Rex* v. *Lincolnshire Justices, Ex parte Brett* [1926] 2 K.B. 192 is that if a certain state of facts has to exist before an inferior tribunal have jurisdiction, they can inquire into the facts in order to decide whether or not they have jurisdiction, but cannot give themselves jurisdiction by a wrong decision upon them; and this court may, by means of proceedings for [a quashing order], inquire into the correctness of the decision. The decision as to these facts is regarded as collateral because, though the existence of jurisdiction depends on it, it is not the main question which the tribunal have to decide.

Similar sentiments were expressed in *White and Collins* v. *Minister of Health* [1939] 2 KB 838 at 855–856 in which a challenge was made to the exercise by a local authority of compulsory purchase powers which, according to the relevant legislation, could not be exercised in respect of land forming 'part of any park, garden or pleasure ground'. Drawing support from (*inter alia*) *R* v. *Bradford* [1908] 1 KB 365 and *Bunbury* v. *Fuller* (1853) 9 Ex 111, Luxmoore LJ (at 856–857) opined that 'the decision on the question whether the particular land is part of a park or not is preliminary to the exercise of the jurisdiction to make and confirm the [compulsory purchase] order . . . and is therefore open to review in this Court'. Further support for this approach can be found in our next case.

....

Khawaja v. *Secretary of State for the Home Department* [1984] AC 74
House of Lords

Section 33(1) of the Immigration Act 1971 provided that ' "entrant" means a person entering or seeking to enter the United Kingdom, and "illegal entrant" means a person unlawfully entering or seeking to enter in breach of a deportation order or of the immigration laws, and includes also a person who has so entered'. Section 26(1)(c) provided that a person would be guilty of an offence if 'he makes or causes to be made to an immigration officer or other person lawfully acting in the execution of this Act a return, statement or representation which he knows to be false or does not believe to be true'.

Khera and Khawaja, the appellants in separate appeals heard together, had entered the UK as immigrants but were subsequently detained under para 16(2) of sch 2 to the Act of 1971 (set out below in the extract from Lord Bridge's speech) pending their removal as 'illegal entrants' under s 33(1). The grounds for this were decisions and orders by immigration officers that the appellants had obtained leave to enter by deceiving immigration officers at their ports of entry as to their marital status. Khera, in an interview with British immigration authorities in India, had failed to disclose that he was married. The Home Office, in correspondence, alleged he had stated that he was unmarried and that their decision was based on this but put no evidence of the interview, by affidavit or otherwise, before the court. Khera's father, however, swore an affidavit in which he said that Khera denied having made any statement and that satisfactory communication had been prevented by language difficulties. Khawaja had travelled to the UK with a Mrs Butt, with whom he had gone through civil and Muslim ceremonies of marriage in Brussels. On arrival each presented themselves to a different immigration officer. Khawaja stated that he had come for a week to visit a cousin and Mrs Butt that she was a returning resident.

The appellants applied for judicial review, seeking, *inter alia*, quashing orders in respect of the immigration officers' orders. They failed in both the Divisional Court and the Court of Appeal, and then appealed to the House of Lords. Both the meaning of 'illegal entrant' in s 33(1) and the scope of the court's power to review the legality of a detention and proposed removal had been considered and determined by the House of Lords in *R* v. *Secretary of State for the Home Department, ex parte Zamir* [1980] AC 930. The House had then held that 'illegal entrant' was not limited to persons who entered the country clandestinely, but included also any person who obtained leave by practising fraud or deception in contravention of s 26(1)(c). It was also stated that a would-be immigrant owed 'a positive duty of candour on all material facts' to the immigration officer. The third proposition enunciated in *Zamir* concerned the scope of the court's powers of review. On this the House held that the court was limited to deciding whether there was evidence on which the immigration officer could reasonably have come to his decision. The House was invited in the present case to reconsider and not to follow its earlier decision in *Zamir*.

These extracts only deal with the scope of review, the third issue in *Zamir*. On the first two, the House held that the meaning of 'illegal entrant' adopted in *Zamir* was correct but that no 'positive duty of candour' was imposed by immigration laws.

Lord Bridge

. . . The Immigration Act 1971 provides by section 4(2):

> "The provisions of Schedule 2 to this Act shall have effect with respect to — . . . (c) the exercise by immigration officers of their powers in relation to entry into the United Kingdom, and the removal from the United Kingdom of persons refused leave to enter or entering or remaining unlawfully . . ."

Paragraphs 2 to 6 of Schedule 2 are concerned with the procedure governing the exercise of the power to grant or refuse leave to enter. The cross-heading to paragraphs 8 to 11 is: *"Removal of persons refused leave to enter and illegal immigrants."* Detailed provisions as to the giving of directions for removal are to be found primarily in paragraph 8, which empowers the immigration officer to give such directions "Where a person arriving in the United Kingdom is refused leave to enter." The vital provisions for present purposes are the following:

> "9. Where an illegal entrant is not given leave to enter or remain in the United Kingdom, an immigration officer may give any such directions in respect of him as in a case within paragraph 8 above are authorised by paragraph 8 (1).
> "16. . . . (2) A person in respect of whom directions may be given under any of paragraphs 8 to 14 above may be detained under the authority of an immigration officer pending the giving of directions and pending his removal in pursuance of any directions given."

. . . [T]he authorities from *Reg. v. Secretary of State for the Home Department, Ex parte Hussain* [1978] 1 W.L.R. 700 to *Reg. v. Secretary of State for the Home Department, Ex parte Zamir* [1980] A.C. 930 have consistently affirmed the principle that the decision of an immigration officer to detain and remove a person as an illegal entrant under these provisions can only be attacked successfully on the ground that there was no evidence on which the immigration officer could reasonably conclude that he was an illegal entrant.

It will be seen at once that this principle gives to an executive officer subject, no doubt, in reaching his conclusions of fact, to a duty to act fairly, a draconian power of arrest and expulsion based upon his own decision of fact which, if there was any evidence to support it, cannot be examined by any judicial process until after it has been acted on and then in circumstances where the person removed, being unable to attend the hearing of his appeal, has no realistic prospect of prosecuting it with success. It will be further observed that to justify the principle important words have to be read into paragraph 9 of Schedule 2 by implication. That paragraph, on the face of the language used, authorises the removal of a person who is an illegal entrant. The courts have applied it as if it authorised the removal of a person whom an immigration officer on reasonable grounds believes to be an illegal entrant. The all important question is whether such an implication can be justified . . .

In *Reg. v. Secretary of State for the Home Department, Ex parte Zamir* [1980] A.C. 930, 948–949 Lord Wilberforce said:

"The nature and process of decision conferred upon immigration officers by existing legislation is incompatible with any requirement for the establishment of precedent objective facts whose existence the court may verify.

"The immigration officer, whether at the stage of entry or at that of removal, has to consider a complex of statutory rules and non-statutory guidelines. He has to act upon documentary evidence and such other evidence as inquiries may provide. Often there will be documents whose genuineness is doubtful, statements which cannot be verified, misunderstandings as to what was said, practices and attitudes in a foreign state which have to be estimated. There is room for appreciation, even for discretion."

He proceeds to contrast the disadvantageous position of the Divisional Court as a fact-finding tribunal in the relevant field . . .

It appears to me, with every respect, that [the approaches in the earlier cases] rely upon the statutory juxtaposition of the immigration officer's power to refuse leave to enter and thereupon to order removal of the unsuccessful aspiring entrant with his power to order removal of an illegal entrant after entry as a ground for assimilating the principles by which the two powers are governed . . . Whenever a non-patrial comes from abroad he needs leave to enter the United Kingdom and the decision whether or not such leave should be granted is fairly and squarely committed to the immigration officer by the statute. This necessarily entrusts all relevant decisions of fact, as well as the application to the facts of the relevant rules and any necessary exercise of discretion, to the immigration officer. If leave to enter is refused, that decision can plainly only be challenged on the now familiar grounds on which the court has jurisdiction to review a public law decision committed by statute to an administrative authority. Following a refusal of leave to enter there can be no successful challenge to a consequential order for detention and directions for removal unless the refusal of leave to enter can itself be successfully impugned. But the detention and removal of a non-patrial resident in this country, who may or may not be a British subject, who may have been here for many years and who, on the face of it, enjoys the benefit of an express grant of leave to be here, on the ground that he is an illegal entrant, seems to me to be dependent on fundamentally different considerations. A person seeking leave to enter requires a decision in his favour which the immigration officer alone is empowered to give. The established resident who entered with express permission enjoys an existing status of which, so far as the express language of the statute goes, the immigration officer has no power whatsoever to deprive him. My Lords, we should, I submit, regard with extreme jealousy any claim by the executive to imprison a citizen without trial and allow it only if it is clearly justified by the statutory language relied on. The fact that, in the case we are considering, detention is preliminary and incidental to expulsion from the country in my view strengthens rather than weakens the case for a robust exercise of the judicial function in safeguarding the citizen's rights.

So far as I know, no case before the decisions under the Act which we are presently considering has held imprisonment without trial by executive order to be justified by anything less than the plainest statutory language, with the sole exception of the majority decision of your Lordships' House in *Liversidge v. Anderson* [1942] A.C. 206. No one needs to be reminded of the now celebrated dissenting speech of Lord Atkin in that case, nor of his withering condemnation of the process of writing into the statutory language there under consideration the words which were necessary to sustain the decision of the majority. Lord Atkin's dissent now has the approval of your Lordships' House in *Reg. v. Inland Revenue Commissioners, Ex parte Rossminster Ltd* [1980] A.C. 952. A person who has entered the United Kingdom with leave and who is detained under Schedule 2 paragraph 16 (2) pending removal as an illegal entrant on the ground that he obtained leave to enter by fraud is entitled to challenge the action taken and proposed to be taken against him both by application for habeas corpus and by application for judicial review. On the view I take, paragraph 9 of Schedule 2 must be construed as meaning no more and no less than it says. There is no room for any implication qualifying the words "illegal entrant." From this it would follow that while, prima facie, the order for detention under paragraph 16 (2) would be a sufficient return to the writ of habeas corpus, proof by the applicant that he had been granted leave to enter would shift the onus back to the immigration officer to prove that the leave had been obtained in contravention of section 26(1)(c) of the Act, in other words by fraud.

. . . I have no doubt that when a person detained and proposed to be removed as an illegal entrant enjoys the right to be in this country in pursuance of leave to enter and remain here which is valid on its face the onus lies on the immigration officer to prove the fact that the leave was obtained by fraud in contravention of section 26(1)(c) of the Act. The question about which I have felt most difficulty concerns the standard of proof required to discharge that onus. I was at first inclined to regard the judgment of Lord Parker C.J. in *Reg. v. Governor of Brixton Prison, Ex parte Ahsan* [1969] 2 Q.B. 222 as sufficient authority for the proposition that proof is required beyond reasonable doubt. But I have been persuaded by the reasoning on this point in the speech of my noble and learned friend, Lord Scarman, and by the authorities which he cites that that proposition cannot be sustained. These have led me to the conclusion that the civil standard of proof by a preponderance of probability will suffice, always provided that, in view of the gravity of the charge of fraud which has to be made out and of the consequences which will follow if it is, the court should not be satisfied with anything less than probability of a high degree. I would add that the inherent difficulties of discovering and proving the true facts in many immigration cases can afford no valid ground for lowering or relaxing the standard of proof required. If unlimited leave to enter was granted perhaps years before and the essential facts relied on to establish the fraud alleged can only be proved by documentary and affidavit evidence of past events which occurred in some remote part of the Indian sub-continent, the courts should be less, rather than more, ready to accept anything short of convincing proof. On the other hand, it must be accepted that proof to the appropriate standard can, and in the vast majority of cases will, be provided, in accordance with the established practice of the Divisional Court, by affidavit evidence alone. [On evidential matters in relation to judicial review proceedings, see below at 14.2.] I understand all your Lordships to be agreed that nothing said in the present case should be construed as a charter to alleged illegal entrants who challenge their detention and proposed removal to demand the attendance of deponents to affidavits for cross-examination. Whether to permit cross-examination will remain a matter for the court in its discretion to decide. It may be that the express discretion conferred on the court to permit cross-examination by the new procedure for judicial review under R.S.C., Ord. 53 has been too sparingly exercised when deponents could readily attend court. But however that may be, the discretion to allow cross-examination should only be exercised when justice so demands. The cases will be rare when it will be essential, in the interests of justice, to require the attendance for cross-examination of a deponent from overseas. If the alleged illegal entrant applying for habeas corpus, [a quashing order] or both, files an affidavit putting in issue the primary facts alleged against him he will himself be readily available for cross-examination, which should enable the court in the great majority of cases to decide whether or not he is a witness of truth. If he is believed, he will succeed in his application. If he is disbelieved, there will be nothing to stop the court relying on affidavit evidence, provided it is inherently credible and convincing, to prove the fraud alleged against him, even though it has not been tested by cross-examination . . .

Lord Wilberforce

. . . The third point upon which the appellants sought reconsideration of *Zamir's* case related to the scope of judicial review by the courts of decisions by the Secretary of State to remove 'illegal entrants' and to the power and duty of the courts on habeas corpus challenges to the detention of such persons. These remedies of judicial review and habeas corpus are, of course, historically quite distinct and procedurally are governed by different statutory rules, but I do not think that in the present context it is necessary to give them distinct consideration. In practice, many applicants seek both remedies. The court considers both any detention which may be in force and the order for removal: the one is normally ancillary to the other. I do not think that it would be appropriate unless unavoidable to make a distinction between the two remedies and I propose to deal with both under a common principle. Each of the present cases appears, in fact, to be of judicial review.

In *Reg. v. Secretary of State for the Home Department, Ex parte Zamir* [1980] A.C. 930 the main argument on this part of the case was that cases where it was sought to remove an "illegal entrant" were part of a category of "precedent fact" cases — where an administrative discretion exists if, but only if, some precedent fact is established to exist, and the existence of which is independently triable by a court. The best known example of this is *Eshugbayi Eleko v. Government of Nigeria* [1931] A.C. 662, where the discretionary power was exercisable only if the person affected was a native chief, so that whether he was such a chief or not was what is sometimes called a juris-dictional or collateral fact. The argument in this form was rejected in *Zamir's* case — I venture to think correctly. This rejection however in no way involves rejection of a right of judicial review of the factual element in an administrative decision. The present, as other illegal entrant cases, does involve the making of a finding of fact by the administration as can be seen by an examination of the administrative process. In fact, this falls into two parts: first, a determination by the authorities that a person is an illegal entrant; second, a discretionary decision by the Secretary of State to remove him from the country and meanwhile to detain him. Separate principles in my opinion govern these two stages. As regards the latter, review may take place upon those principles, now well familiar, which govern the review of discretionary decisions, a relevant question being whether a reasonable person, or body, could have come to that decision and the decision being upheld if the answer is positive. Review of the former stage depends upon a different formulation, namely, one appropriate as regards a determination of fact by an administrative body. If error has crept in to the decisions of the courts, which I do not think is, in fact, suggested, or into the formulation of their reasons, it has lain in the application to the first stage of language appropriate to the second, viz. in asking whether a reasonable immigration officer could have made the determination that he did. That is not, in my opinion, the correct question.

It is, I think, helpful to test the above analysis by considering what actually happens in "illegal entrant" cases. A person is found in this country in circumstances which give rise to doubt whether he is entitled to be here or not: often suspicions are provoked by an application made by him to bring in his family. So investigations are made by the Home Office, under powers which it undoubt-edly has under the Immigration Act 1971 (section 4) and Schedule 2 (paragraphs 2 and 3). Inquiry is made, of him and other witnesses, when and how he came to the United Kingdom, what docu-ments he had, what leave, if any, to enter was given. Further inquiry may have to be made in his country of origin: often this is done through the High Commission there and through the entry clearance officer from whom he may have obtained an initial clearance. Sometimes very extensive inquiries have to be made . . . The point is — and I tried to make this in *Zamir's* case — that the conclusion that a person is an illegal entrant is a conclusion of fact reached by immigration author-ities upon the basis of investigations and interviews which they have power to conduct, including interviews of the person concerned, of an extensive character, often abroad, and of documents whose authenticity has to be verified by inquiries.

Now there is no doubt that the courts have jurisdiction to review the facts on which the Home Office's conclusion was reached: there is no doubt that procedural means exist, whether under the head of habeas corpus or of judicial review, for findings of fact to be made, by the use of affidavit evidence or cross-examination upon them or oral evidence. There is no doubt that, questions of liberty and allegations of deception being involved, the court both can and should review the facts with care. The sole question is as to the nature of this review. How far can, or should, the court find the facts for itself, how far should it accept, or consider itself bound to accept, or entitled to accept, the findings of the administrative authorities? On principle one would expect that, on the one hand, the court, exercising powers of review, would not act as a court of appeal or attempt to try or retry the issue. On the other hand, since the critical conclusion of fact is one reached by an administrative authority (as opposed to a judicial body) the court would think it proper to review it in order to see whether it was properly reached, not only as a matter of procedure, but also in substance and in law . . .

[His Lordship then examined a number of the authorities and continued:] My Lords, I have ventured upon this review of some of the cases (there are many more which might have been examined) in order to show two things. First, that, whatever the theory may be, the courts have in general been willing and able to review for themselves the factual basis, on which decisions by immigration officers that persons are illegal entrants and analogous decisions are made, within the limits open to them. And the cases vividly illustrate what those limits are. They are dictated, on the one hand, by the fact that of necessity extensive fact-finding operations have to be carried out by the immigration authorities which cannot be repeated by the reviewing court; on the other hand, by the fact that these operations are carried out by administrative, not judicial, officers inevitably not wholly qualified in the process of assessing and applying evidence. Secondly, that they have not always consistently or correctly stated the basis on which such review should be made. In some instances, and this seems to be more marked in recent cases, there has been a tendency to limit the courts' power to that of ascertaining whether there was evidence on which a reasonable Secretary of State or an officer of his could have reached the decision. While there are cases where the facts are so clear that it would not make any practical difference whether this was the test or whether the court ought to appraise the evidence for itself there may be other cases, and indeed the case of Khera may be one, where a different result would follow and where the 'reasonable grounds' formula (in fact used in Khera's case) would understate the court's duty. While *Reg. v. Secretary of State for the Home Department, Ex parte Zamir* [1980] A.C. 930 fell into the former class, there were expressions used which support the 'reasonable grounds' approach which, in the light of the argument we have heard and after a further consideration of the case, require some correction.

I would therefore restate the respective functions of the immigration authorities and of the courts as follows: 1. The immigration authorities have the power and the duty to determine and to act upon the facts material for the detention as illegal entrants of persons prior to removal from the United Kingdom. 2. Any person whom the Secretary of State proposes to remove as an illegal entrant, and who is detained, may apply for a writ of habeas corpus or for judicial review. Upon such an application the Secretary of State or the immigration authorities if they seek to support the detention or removal (the burden being upon them) should depose to the grounds on which the decision to detain or remove was made, setting out essential factual evidence taken into account and exhibiting documents sufficiently fully to enable the courts to carry out their function or review. 3. The court's investigation of the facts is of a supervisory character and not by way of appeal . . . It should appraise the quality of the evidence and decide whether that justifies the conclusion reached — *eg* whether it justifies a conclusion that the applicant obtained permission to entry by fraud or deceit. An allegation that he has done so being of a serious character and involving issues of personal liberty, requires a corresponding degree of satisfaction as to the evidence. If the court is not satisfied with any part of the evidence it may remit the matter for reconsideration or itself receive further evidence. It should quash the detention order where the evidence was not such as the authorities should have relied on or where the evidence received does not justify the decision reached or, of course, for any serious procedural irregularity . . .

Lord Scarman

. . . My Lords, in most cases I would defer to a recent decision of your Lordships' House on a question of construction, even if I thought it wrong. I do not do so in this context because for reasons which I shall develop I am convinced that the *Zamir* reasoning gave insufficient weight to the important — I would say fundamental — consideration that we are here concerned with, the scope of judicial review of a power which inevitably infringes the liberty of those subjected to it.

This consideration, if it be good, outweighs, in my judgment, any difficulties in the administration of immigration control to which the application of the principle might give rise . . .

The *Zamir* decision would limit judicial review, where the executive has decided to remove someone from the country as being an illegal entrant, to 'the *Wednesbury* principle.' This principle is undoubtedly correct in cases where it is appropriate. But, as I understand the law, it cannot extend to interference with liberty unless Parliament has unequivocally enacted that it should. The principle was formulated by Lord Greene M.R. in *Associated Provincial Picture Houses Ltd. v. Wednesbury Corporation* [1948] 1 K.B. 223. The case concerned the conditions imposed upon the issue of a licence. The principle formulated was that the courts will not intervene to quash the decision of a statutory authority unless it can be shown that the authority erred in law, was guilty of a breach of natural justice or acted "unreasonably." If the authority has considered the matters which it is its duty to consider and has excluded irrelevant matters, its decision is not reviewable unless so absurd that no reasonable authority could have reached it. The principle excludes the court from substituting its own view of the facts for that of the authority.

Such exclusion of the power and duty of the courts runs counter to the development of the safeguards which our law provides for the liberty of the subject. The law has largely developed through the process of habeas corpus. But in the common law habeas corpus was itself of limited scope, though a rapid and effective remedy where it applied. It brought the gaoler and his prisoner into court; but, if the respondent's return to the writ was valid on its face, that was the end of the matter. The court could not take the case further. The great statute of 1816, Habeas Corpus Act 1816 (56 Geo. 3, c. 100), "An Act for more effectually securing the liberty of the subject" substantially extended the scope of the process. It conferred upon the judges the power in non-criminal cases to inquire into the truth of the facts contained in the return. Section 3 is the beginning of the modern jurisprudence the effect of which is to displace, unless Parliament by plain words otherwise provides, the *Wednesbury* principle in cases where liberty is infringed by an act of the executive. The section deserves quotation:

> "3 . . . in all cases provided for by this Act, although the return to any writ of habeas corpus shall be good and sufficient in law, it shall be lawful for the justice or baron before whom such writ may be returnable, to proceed to examine into the truth of the facts set forth in such return . . . and to do therein as to justice shall appertain . . ."

The court's duty is to examine into the truth of the facts set forth in the return: the section thereby contemplates the possibility of an investigation by the court so that it may satisfy itself where the truth lies. There is here a principle which the judges, faced with decisions by statutory authorities which restrict or take away liberty, have accepted as being justly met by the rule, the existence of which was recognised in *Zamir's* case though not applied, that where the exercise of executive power depends upon the precedent establishment of an objective fact, the courts will decide whether the requirement has been satisfied.

The classic dissent of Lord Atkin in *Liversidge v. Anderson* [1942] A.C. 206 is now accepted (*Reg. v. Inland Revenue Commissioners, Ex parte Rossminster Ltd* [1980] A.C. 952, 1011, 1025) as correct not only on the point of construction of regulation 18 (b) of the then emergency Regulations but in its declaration of English legal principle. Lord Atkin put it thus, at p. 245: "that in English law every imprisonment is prima facie unlawful and that it is for a person directing imprisonment to justify his act."

In an earlier Privy Council decision Lord Atkin had made the same point in the specific case of an executive decision. In *Eshugbayi Eleko v. Government of Nigeria* [1931] A.C. 662, 670, Lord Atkin said:

> "In accordance with British jurisprudence no member of the executive can interfere with the liberty or property of a British subject except on the condition that he can support the legality of his

action before a court of justice. And it is the tradition of British justice that judges should not shrink from deciding such issues in the face of the executive."

For, as Blackstone said of habeas corpus, describing it as a high prerogative writ.

"the king is at all times entitled to have an account, why the liberty of any of his subjects is restrained, wherever that restraint may be inflicted": *Commentaries*, BK. III, p. 131, 12th ed. (Christian) 1794.

There are, of course, procedural differences between habeas corpus and the modern statutory judicial review. *Reg. v. Secretary of State for the Home Department, Ex parte Zamir* [1980] A.C. 930 was a case of habeas corpus: in the instant cases the effective relief sought is [a quashing order] to quash the immigration officer's decision. But the nature of the remedy sought cannot affect the principle of the law. In both cases liberty is in issue. "Judicial review" under R.S.C., Ord. 53 and the Supreme Court Act 1981 is available only by leave of the court. The writ of habeas corpus issues as of right. But the difference arises not in the law's substance but from the nature of the remedy appropriate to the case. The writ issues as of right summoning into court the person in whose custody the subject is. It gets the custodian into court: but discharge from custody is not possible unless "the party hath a probable cause to be delivered," as Vaughan C.J. put it (in *Bushell's Case* (1670) T.J. 13, p. 132) in words quoted by Blackstone, Bk. III. This remains the law today and effectually puts habeas corpus in like case with the other form of judicial review. Whatever the process, the party seeking relief carries the initial burden of showing he has a case fit to be considered by the court. Accordingly, faced with the jealous care our law traditionally devotes to the protection of the liberty of those who are subject to its jurisdiction, I find it impossible to imply into the statute words the effect of which would be to take the provision, paragraph 9 of Schedule 2 to the Act, "out of the 'precedent fact' category" (Lord Wilberforce, *Zamir's* case at p. 948). If Parliament intends to exclude effective judicial review of the exercise of a power in restraint of liberty, it must make its meaning crystal clear.

    . . . [There is also] the problem of proof. The initial burden is upon the applicant. At what stage, if at all, is it transferred to the respondent? And, if it is transferred, what is the standard of proof he has to meet? It is clear from the passages cited from Lord Atkin's opinions in *Liversidge* v. *Anderson* [1942] AC 206 and *Eshugbayi Eleko* v. *Government of Nigeria* [1931] A.C. 662 that in cases where the exercise of executive discretion interferes with liberty or property rights he saw the burden of justifying the legality of the decision as being upon the executive. Once the applicant has shown a prima facie case, this is the law. It was so recognised by Lord Parker C.J. in *Reg. v. Governor of Brixton Prison, Ex parte Ahsan* [1969] 2 Q.B. 222, and by Lord Denning M.R. in the Court of Appeal in *Reg. v. Governor of Pentonville Prison, Ex parte Azam* [1974] A.C. 18, 32. And, I would add, it is not possible to construe section 3 of the Habeas Corpus Act 1816, as meaning anything different.

    The law is less certain as to the standard of proof. The choice is commonly thought to be between proof beyond reasonable doubt, as in criminal cases, and the civil standard of the balance of probabilities: and there is distinguished authority for the view that in habeas corpus proceedings the standard is beyond reasonable doubt, since liberty is at stake. This appears to have been the view of Lord Atkin (*Eshugbayi Eleko v. Government of Nigeria* [1931] A.C. 662, 670), and certainly was the view of Lord Parker C.J. (*Reg. v. Governor of Brixton Prison, Ex parte Ahsan* [1969] Q.B. 222). But there is a line of authority which casts doubt upon their view. The Court of Appeal has held that the standard of proof of criminal offences in civil proceedings is that of the balance of probabilities: *Hornal v. Neuberger Products Ltd* [1957] 1 Q.B. 247. As judicial review whether under the modern statutory procedure or section 3 of the Habeas Corpus Act 1816 is a civil proceeding, it would appear to be right, if *Hornal's* case was correctly decided, to apply the civil standard of proof. My Lords, I have come to the conclusion that the choice between the two standards is not one of any great moment. It is largely a matter of words. There is no need to import into this branch of the civil law the formula used for the guidance of juries in criminal cases. The civil standard as interpreted and applied by the civil courts will meet the ends of justice.

On the facts of the two cases, their Lordships (including Lords Fraser and Templeman) held that in the case of Khera the immigration officer had not proved that the appellant had obtained permission to enter by deception (there was no evidence of the particular deception before the court); his appeal was therefore allowed. However, Khawaja's appeal was dismissed because it was plain that he had deceived the immigration officer as to his marriage.

Cases like *Zerek, White and Collins*, and *Khawaja* demonstrate that circumstances clearly exist in which the existence of a state of affairs described in the statute will be treated as a jurisdictional precondition, such that the court must be satisfied as to its existence. However, while their Lordships identified strong policy reasons for such an approach in *Khawaja*, Beatson (1984) 4 *OJLS* 22 at 26 cautions that compelling reasons for judicial deference may also arise in this context:

It is generally accepted that more deference should be accorded to factual findings than to questions of law. There are three reasons for this. First, respect should be accorded to the factual findings of a body which has taken evidence or developed expertise in a given area. Secondly, reviewing courts are unable to make factual determinations in an adequate manner because even after the recent procedural reforms it appears that they will normally rely on affidavit evidence. Finally, judicial intervention in factual matters is more likely to defeat legislative intentions in allocating the implementation of a policy to an administrative body.

Beatson's first two concerns relate to the inhibitions (considered further at 14.2 below) under which reviewing courts find themselves as far as fact-finding is concerned; these concerns suggest that reviewing courts should be cautious before substituting their view of the facts for that of the original decision-maker. Beatson's third concern relates to the extent to which reviewing courts should interfere with the decision-maker's exercise of judgment on the question whether the established facts satisfy the statutory jurisdictional condition in question. Beatson observes that there is some support for the view that all inferences from primary facts — including whether those facts satisfy a legal criterion — are themselves issues of law. However, he notes that this 'analytic' approach to the fact/law distinction, if coupled with the modern view that errors of law are, in general, jurisdictional, would seriously undermine administrative autonomy. Beatson contrasts the 'analytic' approach to characterizing matters of fact and law with the 'pragmatic' approach, which holds that, within a 'zone of "reasonable" conclusions', inferences drawn from primary facts will be 'questions of fact and degree' rather than questions of law, and subject only to limited judicial review (*eg* manifestly unreasonable conclusions may be upset by the court). On this view, the extent of the 'zone of "reasonable" conclusions' — and hence the balance between administrative autonomy and judicial control — in relation to any given statutory power should be determined by considerations such as relative expertise, justiciability, and legislative intention.

This point is illustrated by the case of *R* v. *Hillingdon London Borough Council, ex parte Puhlhofer* [1986] AC 484. The question before the House of Lords was whether the claimants were homeless and hence entitled, under the Housing (Homeless Persons) Act 1977, to accommodation — a question which turned on whether they already had 'accommodation' within the meaning of the Act. Giving the only reasoned speech, Lord Brightman said (at 517):

In this situation, Parliament plainly, and wisely, placed no qualifying adjective before the word "accommodation" in . . . the Act, and none is to be implied. The word "appropriate" or "reasonable" is not to be imported . . . What is properly to be regarded as accommodation is a question of fact to be decided by the local authority. There are no rules. Clearly some places in which a person might choose or be constrained to live could not properly be regarded as accommodation at all; it would be a misuse of language to describe Diogenes as having occupied accommodation within the meaning of the Act. What the local authority have to consider, in reaching a decision whether a person is homeless for the purposes of the Act, is whether he has what can properly be described as accommodation within the ordinary meaning of that word in the English language . . .

Where the existence or non-existence of a fact is left to the judgment and discretion of a public body and that fact involves a broad spectrum ranging from the obvious to the debatable to the just conceivable, it is the duty of the court to leave the decision of that fact to the public body to whom Parliament has entrusted the decision-making power save in a case where it is obvious that the public body, consciously or unconsciously, are acting perversely.

The upshot of the reasoning adopted in *Puhlhofer* is that the statutory criterion relating to 'accommodation' was not characterized as a jurisdictional precondition: whether the claimants already had 'accommodation' was not a question which the decision-maker had to answer correctly (in the view of the court); rather, it was a matter which, subject to a requirement not to act perversely, it was for the decision-maker to determine. It follows that, in some circumstances, the determination of whether the facts satisfy a statutory criterion may be characterized as a question of fact and degree which is subject only to limited review, not substitution by the court. It should be noted that this approach bears some relationship to that adopted in *South Yorkshire Transport* (see above at 2.2.5). In that case, it will be recalled, judicial review of whether a jurisdictional statutory criterion was satisfied on the facts was limited by its ambiguity: whether the criterion was met was not a hard-edged question for the court; the decision-maker was free to apply it in any of a range of permissible ways. *Puhlhofer* and *South Yorkshire Transport* differ in that the former characterizes the statutory criterion as non-jurisdictional, whereas the latter characterizes it as jurisdictional but capable of diverse application. The judicial policy in the two cases is, however, the same — *viz* to permit judicial deference to the decision-maker's judgment on the question whether the statutory criterion is satisfied on the facts.

The difficult question, of course, remains. When will the approach adopted in *Khawaja* (according to which the court intervenes if its own view is that the statutory criterion is not met) be appropriate? And when will it instead be right to accord latitude to the decision-maker (either by holding the statutory criterion to be non-jurisdictional, as in *Puhlhofer*, or by treating the criterion as a jurisdictional matter of law, but one which is capable of diverse application, as in *South Yorkshire Transport*)? The *Khawaja* approach makes the reviewing court the ultimate judge of whether the statutory criterion is met, whereas the latter two approaches accord a zone of judgment to the decision-maker on this point. How do we know which approach to adopt? The beginnings of an answer to this question are supplied by the criticism which Hare (in Forsyth and Hare (eds), *The Golden Metwand and the Crooked Cord* (Oxford 1998) at 138) levels at the reasoning, if not the result, in *South Yorkshire Transport*:

. . . [A]rguments about where judicial deference is appropriate must be conducted in . . . terms of constitutional principle. Judicial deference may be required where a decision has policy implications which lie in the realm of executive competence but if this is the justification for judicial abstention, it is incumbent upon the courts to articulate their reasoning in terms of concepts such as justiciability rather than as an exercise in statutory construction. This will require the court to be much more explicit about the type of considerations which engage the political responsibilities of administrative agencies and should render judicial intervention more predictable.

It is, however, arguable that the House of Lords was (implicitly) acting upon such considerations in *South Yorkshire Transport*, the imprecise nature of the statutory criterion laid down by Parliament signalling the appropriate balance between judicial control and administrative autonomy *vis-à-vis* its application. Conversely, the fact that individual liberty was at stake in *Khawaja* made the more intrusive approach adopted in that case constitutionally appropriate.

Further guidance is evident elsewhere in the case law. In *Moyna* v. *Secretary of State for Work and Pensions* [2003] UKHL 44 [2003] 1 WLR 1929 at [26]–[27], Lord Hoffmann remarked that, 'It may seem rather odd to say that something is a question of fact when there is no dispute whatever over the facts and the question is whether they fall within some legal category ... [However,] the degree to which an appellate court will be willing to substitute its own judgment for that of the tribunal will vary with the nature of the question.' In particular, a broad distinction is drawn between what Sir Thomas Bingham MR, in *R* v. *Secretary of State for the Home Department, ex parte Onibiyo* [1996] QB 768 at 784–785, called 'objective precedent fact[s]' and those whose application necessarily calls for an 'exercise of judgment' by the decision-maker: while courts will treat the former as jurisdictional preconditions, about whose existence the court must be satisfied, it is more likely that the latter will be treated as matters which the decision-maker is empowered to decide, subject to much more modest judicial supervision. An example of the latter category is furnished by *Dowty Boulton Paul Ltd* v. *Wolverhampton Corporation (No 2)* [1976] Ch 13 in which it was contended (*inter alia*) that a local authority had erred by exercising powers to put certain of its land to a new use, on the ground that the statutory precondition that the land was 'not required' for the purpose for which it was originally acquired was not satisfied. Russell LJ held that the court should not make up its own mind on this matter, observing (at 26) that 'not required' meant ' "not needed in the public interest of the locality" for the original purpose', a question raising 'matters of both degree and of comparative needs, as to which there can be no question but that the local authority is better qualified than the court to judge, assuming it to be acting *bona fide* and not upon a view that no reasonable local authority could possibly take'. It is clear, therefore, that relative institutional competence is a major factor in determining the courts' approach to these 'application' questions.

QUESTIONS

- Are the courts right to be influenced by such factors in setting the standard of review in this context?
- Is the articulation of clear criteria concerning how intense such review should be possible or desirable?

2.4 Supervision of the Fact-Finding Process

We have seen that, where the court holds that a particular statutory criterion describes a state of affairs which is a jurisdictional condition, such that the court must be satisfied as to its existence, it is open to the court to examine the facts in order to decide for itself whether the condition is met.

It is convenient at this point to consider to what extent reviewing courts are able to go further than this in reviewing the fact-finding process. For example, if the court is satisfied that, on the facts, all relevant *jurisdictional conditions* are satisfied, may the court neverthe-less overturn a decision because the decision-maker has exercised its discretion subject to an erroneous understanding of relevant facts in relation to a *non-jurisdictional matter*? It is accepted that decisions made on the basis of no admissible or relevant evidence may be set aside (see, eg, *R* v. *Bedwellty Justices, ex parte Williams* [1997] AC 225 at 233); this means that a finding of fact by a decision-maker 'must be based upon some material that tends logically to show the existence of facts consistent with the finding and that the reasoning supportive of the finding, if it be disclosed, is not logically self-contradictory' (*per* Lord Diplock in *Mahon* v. *Air New Zealand Ltd* [1984] AC 808 at 821). Moreover, errors in relation to non-jurisdictional facts may lead decision-makers into other errors which are reviewable, such as the taking into account of irrelevant considerations (on which see below at 8.3). However, there has been considerable debate as to how much further courts may go (for an overview, see Jones [1990] *PL* 507). This matter was recently considered in the following case (for comment on which see Craig [2004] *PL* 788).

....

E v. *Secretary of State for the Home Department* [2004] EWCA Civ 49 [2004] QB 1044
Court of Appeal

An issue arose as to whether the Immigration Appeal Tribunal could take into account new evidence which had become available after the appellants' hearings but before the Tribunal had promulgated its decisions. The Tribunal refused to do so. The appellants appealed to the Court of Appeal. This extract is concerned only with the issue raised in the first sentence of our excerpt from the judgment.

Carnwath LJ (giving the judgment of the court)

[44] Can a decision reached on an incorrect basis of fact be challenged on an appeal limited to points of law? This apparently paradoxical question has a long history in academic discussion, but has never received a decisive answer from the courts . . .

[45] The debate received new life following the affirmative answer given by Lord Slynn in *R v Criminal Injuries Compensation Board, Ex p A* [1999] 2 AC 330 . . .

[46] One of the issues discussed in detail in argument [in *ex parte A*] was whether the decision could be quashed on the basis of a mistake, in relation to material which was or ought to have been

within the knowledge of the decision maker: see pp 333–336. Lord Slynn thought it could. He said, at pp 344–345:

> "Your Lordships have been asked to say that there is jurisdiction to quash the board's decision because that decision was reached on a material error of fact. Reference has been made to *Wade & Forsyth, Administrative Law*, 7th ed (1994), pp 316–318 in which it is said: 'Mere factual mistake has become a ground of judicial review, described as "misunderstanding or ignorance of an established and relevant fact", [*Secretary of State for Education and Science v Tameside Metropolitan Borough Council* [1977] AC 1014, 1030], or acting "upon an incorrect basis of fact" . . . This ground of review has long been familiar in French law and it has been adopted by statute in Australia. It is no less needed in this country, since decisions based upon wrong facts are a cause of injustice which the courts should be able to remedy. If a "wrong factual basis" doctrine should become established, it would apparently be a new branch of the ultra vires doctrine, analogous to finding facts based upon no evidence or acting upon a misapprehension of law.' *De Smith, Woolf & Jowell, Judicial Review of Administrative Action*, 5th ed (1995), p 288: 'The taking into account of a mistaken fact can just as easily be absorbed into a traditional legal ground of review by referring to the taking into account of an irrelevant consideration, or the failure to provide reasons that are adequate or intelligible, or the failure to base the decision on any evidence. In this limited context material error of fact has always been a recognised ground for judicial intervention.' For my part, I would accept that there is jurisdiction to quash on that ground in this case . . ."

[His Lordship noted that these comments were *obiter* (Lord Slynn decided the case on a different ground — "unfairness" — which Carnwath LJ discusses below) but that Lord Slynn had repeated his views in *R (Alconbury Developments Ltd) v. Secretary of State for the Environment, Transport and the Regions* [2003] 2 AC 295 at [53]. His Lordship then noted that differing judicial views have been expressed on this issue. He cited from Buxton LJ's judgment in *Wandsworth Borough Council v. A* [2000] 1 WLR 1246 at 1255–1256, which endorsed the view in *Puhlhofer* (see above at 2.3) that the court should not intervene on issues of fact in the absence of perversity. By way of contrast, Carnwath LJ noted the comments of Lord Scarman in *Secretary of State for Education and Science v. Tameside Metropolitan Borough Council* [1977] AC 1014 at 1030 to the effect that judicial review lies on the ground of "misunderstanding or ignorance of an established and relevant fact". After considering various other authorities and academic commentaries, his Lordship continued:]

[61] . . . [T]he editors of the current edition of *de Smith, Woolf & Jowell, Judicial Review of Administrative Action* (unlike *Wade & Forsyth, Administrative Law*) are somewhat tentative as to whether this is a separate ground of review, at para 5-094:

> "The taking into account of a mistaken fact can just as easily be absorbed into a traditional legal ground of review by referring to the taking into account of an irrelevant consideration, or the failure to provide reasons that are adequate or intelligible, or the failure to base the decision upon any evidence."

[62] We are doubtful, however, whether those traditional grounds provide an adequate explanation of the cases. We take them in turn. (i) Failure to take account of a material consideration is only a ground for setting aside a decision, if the statute expressly or impliedly requires it to be taken into account: *In re Findlay* [1985] AC 318, 333–334, per Lord Scarman . . . (ii) Reasons are no less "adequate and intelligible", because they reveal that the decision-maker fell into error; indeed that is one of the purposes of requiring reasons. (iii) Finally, it may be impossible, or at least artificial, to say that there was a failure to base the decision on *"any* evidence" . . . In most of these cases there is *some* evidential basis for the decision, even if part of the reasoning is flawed by mistake or misunderstanding.

[63] In our view, the *Criminal Injuries Compensation Board* case [1999] 2 AC 330 points the way to a separate ground of review, based on the principle of fairness. It is true that Lord Slynn distinguished between "ignorance of fact" and "unfairness" as grounds of review. However, we doubt if there is a real distinction. The decision turned, not on issues of fault or lack of fault on either side; it was sufficient that 'objectively' there was unfairness. On analysis, the "unfairness" arose from the combination of five factors: (i) an erroneous impression created by a mistake as to, or ignorance of, a relevant fact (the availability of reliable evidence to support [the claimant's] case); (ii) the fact was "established", in the sense that, if attention had been drawn to the point, the correct position could have been shown by objective and uncontentious evidence; (iii) the claimant could not fairly be held responsible for the error; (iv) although there was no duty on the [decision-maker] itself . . . to do the claimant's work of proving her case, all the participants had a shared interest in co-operating to achieve the correct result; (v) the mistaken impression played a material part in the reasoning . . .

[66] In our view, the time has now come to accept that a mistake of fact giving rise to unfairness is a separate head of challenge in an appeal on a point of law, at least in those statutory contexts where the parties share an interest in co-operating to achieve the correct result. Asylum law is undoubtedly such an area. Without seeking to lay down a precise code, the ordinary requirements for a finding of unfairness are apparent from the above analysis of the *Criminal Injuries Compensation Board* case. First, there must have been a mistake as to an existing fact, including a mistake as to the availability of evidence on a particular matter. Secondly, the fact or evidence must have been 'established', in the sense that it was uncontentious and objectively verifiable. Thirdly, the appellant (or his advisers) must not been have been responsible for the mistake. Fourthly, the mistake must have played a material (not necessarily decisive) part in the tribunal's reasoning . . .

This case establishes (at least at the level of the Court of Appeal) that, in some circumstances, a mistake of fact giving rise to unfairness will deprive the decision-maker of jurisdiction, so that it can be corrected (as in *E* itself) on appeal on a point of law and, *a priori*, via judicial review. However, the requirement that the fact in question must be 'uncontentious and verifiable' suggests that this ground of review may operate in fairly limited circumstances. Where, for instance, evidence is contested (*eg* where the tribunal reached a particular finding of fact by preferring one witness's version of events to another's) it would appear that the position adopted in *Adan* v. *Newham London Borough Council* [2001] EWCA Civ 1916 [2002] 1 WLR 2120 still holds, so that the tribunal's view must be left undisturbed by appellate (and, by analogy, reviewing) courts in the absence of '*Wednesbury* unreasonableness' (on which see below at 9.2.1).

2.5 Subjective Jurisdictional Criteria

It is not uncommon for legislation to provide that a decision-maker may do something 'if he believes' or 'if he reasonably believes' that some state of affairs exists. The first of these formulations appears to turn what would otherwise have been jurisdictional limits upon the decision-making power into an entirely subjective matter of opinion: the agency can act *if it thinks* that the jurisdictional criterion is satisfied. On this view, judicial review on jurisdictional grounds is all but eviscerated — there is nothing to review except the decision-maker's state of mind, since jurisdiction exists whenever he thinks it does.

This analysis was accepted by the Court of Appeal in *Robinson* v. *Minister of Town and*

Country Planning [1947] KB 702. The case concerned the Town and Country Planning Act 1944, s 1(1) of which provided that powers of compulsory purchase could be exercised if the Minister was 'satisfied' that redevelopment was necessary to deal satisfactorily with war damage. Lord Greene MR held at 713 that the subjective statutory language effectively precluded the court from dealing with the claimants' complaint that the compulsory purchase of their properties was not actually necessary:

... [The question] is, in my view, one of opinion and policy as to which the Minister, assuming always that he acts bona fide, is the sole judge; namely, he must be satisfied that it is requisite for the purpose of dealing satisfactorily with extensive war damage that all or some part of the land in question should be laid out afresh and redeveloped as a whole ... [T]he question is one of opinion and policy, matters which are peculiarly for the Minister himself to decide. No objective test is possible.

A very different approach — which represents the modern orthodoxy — was adopted in *Commissions of Customs and Excise* v. *Cure and Deeley Ltd* [1962] 1 QB 340. The Finance (No 2) Act 1940, s 33(1), permitted the Commissioners to 'make regulations for any matter for which provision appears to be necessary for the purpose of giving effect to the provisions of this Part of this Act and of enabling them to discharge their functions thereunder'. The Commissioners duly purported to give themselves extraordinarily wide powers, which they exercised to the detriment of the claimant. In quashing the regulation made by the Commissioners, Sachs LJ (at 366–367) said:

... I reject the view that the words "appear to them to be necessary" when used in a statute conferring powers on a competent authority, necessarily make that authority the sole judge of what are its powers as well as the sole judge of the way in which it can exercise such powers as it may have ... To my mind a court is bound before reaching a decision on the question whether a regulation is intra vires to examine the nature, objects, and scheme of the piece of legislation as a whole, and in light of that examination to consider exactly what is the area over which powers are given by the section under which the competent authority is purporting to act.

According to this view, even when the legislation uses subjective language, there will still be objective jurisdictional criteria — to be ascertained by construing the statutory scheme as whole, if necessary — which limit the decision-maker's powers.

If the statute uses the term 'reasonably' — *eg* 'if the Minister reasonably believes' — then it is even easier for the court to ensure that objective jurisdictional criteria are enforced, since here the legislation itself acknowledges that there must exist evidence which makes the decision-maker's opinion reasonable. This obvious point famously evaded the House of Lords in *Liversidge* v. *Anderson* [1942] AC 206 (a fascinating insight into which is given by Heuston (1970) 86 *LQR* 33), concerning the Secretary of State's power, under regulation 18B of the Defence (General) Regulations 1939, to order detention if he had 'reasonable cause to believe' that such action was necessary for various stated security purposes. In spite of the objective language of the statute, which at the very least seemed to require the reviewing court to insist upon some evidence as justification for the Minister's belief, the House of Lords held that this was a matter for the Minister alone. As Lord Wright put it at 268, 'He must be reasonably satisfied before he acts, but it is still his decision and not the decision of anyone else.' The conclusion of the majority was the subject of a celebrated dissenting speech by Lord Atkin. Note, in particular, the following passages from his judgment (at 227 and 245):

It is surely incapable of dispute that the words "if A has X" constitute a condition the essence of which is the existence of X and the having of it by A. If it is a condition to a right (including a power) granted to A, whenever the right comes into dispute the tribunal whatever it may be that is charged with determining the dispute must ascertain whether the condition is fulfilled. In some cases the issue is one of fact, in others of both fact and law, but in all cases the words indicate an existing something the having of which can be ascertained. And the words do not mean and cannot mean "if A thinks that he has." "If A has a broken ankle" does not mean and cannot mean "if A thinks that he has a broken ankle." "If A has a right of way" does not mean and cannot mean "if A thinks that he has a right of way." "Reasonable cause" for an action or a belief is just as much a positive fact capable of determination by a third party as is a broken ankle or a legal right. If its meaning is the subject of dispute as to legal rights, then ordinarily the reasonableness of the cause, and even the existence of any cause is in our law to be determined by the judge and not by the tribunal of fact if the functions deciding law and fact are divided . . .

I know of only one authority which might justify the . . . construction [favoured by the majority]: " 'When I use a word,' Humpty Dumpty said in rather a scornful tone, 'it means just what I choose it to mean, neither more nor less.' 'The question is,' said Alice, 'whether you can make words mean so many different things.' 'The question is,' said Humpty Dumpty, 'which is to be master — that's all.' " ("Through the Looking Glass," c. vi.) After all this long discussion the question is whether the words "If a man has" can mean "If a man thinks he has." I am of opinion that they cannot, and that the case should be decided accordingly.

Although *Liversidge* v. *Anderson* has never been overruled, it is perfectly clear that Lord Atkin's dissenting view is today regarded as the correct one for similarly-worded clauses (see, *eg*, *Nakkuda Ali* v. *Jayaratne* [1951] AC 66). The majority view, in contrast, must be seen against the backdrop of war, and of a wider mid-twentieth century judicial reticence to hold the executive to account.

2.6 Non-Compliance with Statutory Requirements

Finally, it is convenient at this point to consider in what circumstances a decision-maker's failure to comply with requirements laid down in the statute will deprive it of jurisdiction. This question assumes particular importance in the (not uncommon) situation where legislation provides that, in the course of exercising a power, the decision-maker 'shall' or 'must' carry out some procedure (*eg* serve notice, in a stated form, upon the individual concerned). If the decision-maker fails to do so, does this deprive him of jurisdiction such that his ultimate decision is invalid?

Traditionally, this question was answered by determining into which of two categories a given statutory requirement fell (see, *eg*, *Howard* v. *Boddington* (1877) 2 PD 203): if the requirement was (in today's language — the courts have not been consistent in their use of terminology) 'mandatory', non-compliance with it would render the ultimate decision invalid; contrariwise, failure to comply with a merely 'directory' requirement would not deprive the decision-maker of jurisdiction. However, doubt was cast on this approach by Lord Hailsham LC in *London and Clydeside Estates Ltd* v. *Aberdeen District Council* [1980] 1 WLR 182 at 189, who suggested that, 'It may be that what the courts are faced with is not so much a stark choice of alternatives but a spectrum of possibilities in which one compartment or description fades gradually into another.' It is now generally acknowledged that determining the effects of non-compliance is a more subtle matter than simply classifying statutory requirements as either 'mandatory' or 'directory', and that the consequences of failing to adhere to a statutory requirement may turn upon an evaluation of the likely results of treating compliance as a jurisdictional matter. This was recognized by the Court of Appeal in *R v. Immigration Appeal Tribunal, ex parte Jeyeanthan* [2000] 1 WLR 354. Lord Woolf MR (with whom Judge and May LJJ agreed) said (at 362) that

the right approach is to regard the question of whether a requirement is directory or mandatory as only at most a first step. In the majority of cases there are other questions which have to be asked which are more likely to be of greater assistance than the application of the mandatory/directory test. The questions which are likely to arise are as follows.

1. Is the statutory requirement fulfilled if there has been substantial compliance with the requirement and, if so, has there been substantial compliance in the case in issue even though there has not been strict compliance? . . .

2. Is the non-compliance capable of being waived, and if so, has it, or can it and should it be waived in this particular case? . . . I treat the grant of an extension of time for compliance as a waiver.

3. If it is not capable of being waived or is not waived then what is the consequence of the non-compliance?

Which questions arise will depend upon the facts of the case and the nature of the particular requirement. The advantage of focusing on these questions is that they should avoid the unjust and unintended consequences which can flow from an approach solely dependant on dividing requirements into mandatory ones, which oust jurisdiction, or directory, which do not. If the result of non-compliance goes to jurisdiction it will be said jurisdiction cannot be conferred where it does not otherwise exist by consent or waiver.

Applying these principles, the court concluded that the Home Secretary's failure, in seeking leave to appeal against an asylum decision, to use the form prescribed by the relevant secondary legislation did not affect the validity of the ensuing appellate proceedings. Although the court considered that the Home Secretary's failure to make a 'declaration of truth', as required by the legislation, meant that he had not substantially complied with the requirements as laid down, it concluded that this omission did not deprive the appellate tribunal of jurisdiction. Lord Woolf MR explained (at 366) that:

If in these appeals you concentrate on what the Rules intend should be the just *consequence* of non-compliance with the statutory requirements as to the contents of an application for leave to appeal I would suggest the answer to these appeals is obvious. Neither [of the asylum-seekers concerned in this case] have in any way been affected by the omission. It was as far as they were concerned a pure technicality. Other than to discipline the Secretary of State there could be no reason well after the event to treat his successful applications for leave as a nullity.

Moreover, bearing in mind that the same approach would apply to mistakes both by asylum-seekers and the Home Secretary, Judge LJ observed (at 368) that

it would be wholly unrealistic not to recognise that errors, omissions and simple oversight by individuals, many without any proper grasp of English, or any understanding of the legal processes, are inevitable. To exclude them irrevocably from the appeal process, notwithstanding an application for leave brought in time, on the basis of incurable non-compliance with the mechanics of the appeal procedure, would be entirely inconsistent with a fair and just system for dealing with their cases.

The type of approach favoured by the Court of Appeal in *Jeyeanthan* over the somewhat simplistic 'mandatory'/'directory' dichotomy was endorsed by Lord Steyn (whose speech commanded the unqualified support of Lords Cooke and Clyde) in *Attorney General's Reference (No 3 of 1999)* [2001] 2 AC 91 at 117.

2.7 Concluding Remarks

Jurisdiction is a problematic area of administrative law, owing to a combination of its conceptual complexity, the difficulty of drawing bright-line distinctions (in an area that, paradoxically, seems premised on their existence) and linguistic confusion. The following summary of conclusions must therefore be read with the foregoing discussion in mind.

The principle, at least, is clear: jurisdictional questions must be answered 'correctly', in the opinion of the reviewing court, otherwise it may substitute judgment. Isolating jurisdictional issues is more problematic.

In general, errors of law are now to be regarded as jurisdictional. This means that the interpretation of statutory provisions is generally a jurisdictional matter (*Page*). If the decision-maker attaches the wrong meaning to such a provision, the reviewing court may substitute judgment. However, three qualifications must immediately be entered. First, certain bodies — such as those applying special rules or laws (*Page*) and inferior courts (*Racal*) — may, in some circumstances, be empowered to determine conclusively certain questions of law. Secondly, there may be statutory criteria which, although regarded as jurisdictional limits on the decision-maker's powers, may be so hard to define that they are regarded as admitting of a range of meanings rather than one correct meaning, or that the reviewing court's definition, although regarded as the only correct one, is itself so imprecise that the criteria can lawfully be applied by different decision-makers in different ways (*South Yorkshire Transport*). Thirdly, there may be circumstances where a particular criterion, although laid down in statutory form, is not regarded as a jurisdictional matter at all (*Puhlhofer*); the meaning to be attributed to the statutory criterion, and whether it is met, are therefore primarily questions for the decision-maker, subject only to limited judicial review (*eg* a manifestly unreasonable interpretation might be struck down).

Where statutory criteria (appear to) require a certain state of affairs to exist, questions arise as to the extent to which the existence of such a state of affairs is a jurisdictional matter, such that the reviewing court must be satisfied as to its existence, or a matter for the decision-maker, subject only to review on grounds such as unreasonableness. We have seen that, in some circumstances, the court must itself be satisfied as to the existence of the state of affairs (*Khawaja*). However, where the process of determining whether established facts satisfy statutory criteria raises questions of policy or judgment (*Dowty*), or where the statutory criteria are themselves vague (*South Yorkshire Transport*), the reviewing court may exercise deference, intervening not on a substitutionary basis, but only if the decision-maker has reached an unreasonable conclusion. The courts are otherwise more reticent in relation to review of the fact-finding process; although the possibility of review for material error of fact has now been clearly recognized (*E*), that doctrine is qualified by the requirement mentioned in *E* that the fact in question must be 'uncontentious and verifiable'.

At the heart of this area lies a fundamental policy issue about the allocation of power between courts and decision-makers. To what extent, if any, should the reviewing court defer to the view of the decision-maker? Use of the conceptual apparatus of jurisdiction to answer this question should not obscure the fact that the real questions in this sphere are heavily policy-laden. Indeed, as we will see throughout this book, questions about how to draw the line between the powers of reviewing courts and administrative bodies form one of the principal themes in administrative law.

FURTHER RESOURCES

Allan, 'Doctrine and Theory in Administrative Law: an Elusive Quest for the Limits of Jurisdiction' [2003] *PL* 429

Beatson, 'The Scope of Judicial Review for Error of Law' (1984) 4 *OJLS* 22

Blundell, 'Material Error of Fact — Where are We Now?' [2003] *JR* 36

Craig, 'Judicial Review, Appeal and Factual Error' [2004] *PL* 788

Forsyth and Hare (eds), *The Golden Metwand and the Crooked Cord* (Oxford 1998) at 113–139 (Hare)

Gordon, 'The Relation of Facts to Jurisdiction' (1929) 45 *LQR* 458

Gordon, 'Jurisdictional Fact: An Answer' (1966) 82 *LQR* 515

Gould, '*Anisminic* and Jurisdictional Review' [1970] *PL* 358

3 THE STATUS OF UNLAWFUL ADMINISTRATIVE ACTION

3.1 Void or Voidable?

Administrative action may be unlawful for a variety of reasons. For example, the decision-maker may, as we saw in the last chapter, make a jurisdictional error of law by misinterpreting some statutory provision; it might act for an improper purpose (see ch 8) or under the (apparent) influence of bias (see ch 10); or it may act procedurally unfairly (see ch 11) or unreasonably (see ch 9). In all of these situations, the decision reached or action undertaken will be *unlawful*. But what does this mean? What is the status of such action? And what is the position of a citizen in relation to whom an unlawful decision is taken: can he ignore it, because it is unlawful, or must he obey it until or unless it is set aside by a court?

At the root of these questions lies one fundamental issue: is unlawful administrative action void or voidable? Terminology in this area is not always used consistently; however, in this chapter, we use the words 'void' and 'voidable' in the following senses (unless we indicate otherwise). If action is *voidable*, then it is to be regarded as perfectly valid unless and until it is set aside by a competent court; when it is set aside, it is quashed prospectively, meaning that it is treated as having existed until it was quashed. Therefore, if no competent person ever challenges the decision, it is for all practical purposes indistinguishable from a valid decision. However, if unlawful action is *void*, then it is invalid simply by virtue of its unlawfulness. It does not, in strict logic, need to be quashed, because as a matter of law it never existed in the first place: it is void *ab initio* (from the beginning).

3.1.1 The Practical Argument

Although the 'void or voidable?' question is of fundamental importance, English administrative law has struggled to provide a clear answer to it. This is because the question presents a difficult dilemma. For reasons which we consider below at 3.2, traditional theory suggests that unlawful administrative action should be regarded as void. However, the courts often rejected that view because of the immense practical difficulties which can result from its adoption. Most notably, it appears that if a particular act is found to be void, all subsequent acts taken in reliance upon it will also be void — a 'domino effect', whereby the failure of the first act causes all subsequent acts to fall, with potentially chaotic consequences.

Under the influence of these considerations (and others: see 3.1.2), Lord Denning concluded in *Director of Public Prosecutions* v. *Head* [1959] AC 83 that the unlawful action at stake in that case was voidable, not void. The defendant had been convicted under s 56(1)(a) of the Mental Deficiency Act 1913 of having carnal knowledge of a person who, because of her mental condition, was under the care of an institution. Although the woman with whom the defendant had had sexual relations (while she was released on licence) was under the care of such an institution, the Secretary of State had ordered her institutionalization, and later issued continuation orders in respect of her, in the absence of certificates of 'mental deficiency' which fully complied with the relevant statutory requirements. The defendant argued that this made the original institutionalization order and all subsequent continuation orders void, and that he could not therefore have committed the offence because the woman was not legally under institutional care at the relevant time. Although the conviction was in fact quashed, this particular line of argument was strongly rejected by Lord Denning at 112 (who was in the minority in expressing this view; on the majority view, see Lord Irvine's remarks in the excerpt from the *Boddington* case at 3.1.2 below):

The vital question to my mind is therefore: Was the original order absolutely void or was it only voidable? If the order had been outside the jurisdiction of the Secretary of State altogether, it would have been a nullity and void; see *The Case of the Marshalsea* (1612) 10 Co. Rep. 68b at 76a. But that is not this case. The most that appears here is that the Secretary of State — acting within his jurisdiction — exercised that jurisdiction erroneously. That makes his order voidable and not void. It is said that he made the order on no evidence or on insufficient materials. So be it. His error is a wrong exercise of a jurisdiction which he has, and not a usurpation of a jurisdiction which he has not; see *R* v. *Nat Bell Liquors Ltd* [1922] 2 A.C. 128 at 151 by Lord Sumner. If that error appears on the face of the record — as it is said to do here — it renders the order liable to be quashed . . ., but it does not make it a nullity; see *Reg.* v. *Medical Appeal Tribunal, Ex parte Gilmore* [1957] 1 Q.B. 574 at 588 by Parker LJ. Unless and until it is so quashed, it is to be regarded as good. It is, moreover, sufficient to support all the continuation orders made on the faith of it. Even if the original order should be set aside, the continuation orders would remain good: for it is a general rule that when a voidable transaction is avoided, it does not invalidate intermediate transactions which were made on the basis that it was good; see *De Reneville* v. *De Reneville* [1948] P. 100 at 111–112 by Lord Greene MR, and *Reg.* v. *Algar* [1954] 1 Q.B. 279 at 287 by Lord Goddard C.J. I would uphold therefore the contention of the Attorney-General that, whatever the position of the original order, the continuation orders were good.

Lord Denning's rejection of the argument that the original order was void was clearly influenced by his concern that reaching such a conclusion would wreak administrative chaos: if the certificates fell, then the whole superstructure of administrative actions based upon those certificates would collapse too. This is one of the central arguments against a theory which provides that unlawful administrative acts are void. (However, as we will see below at 3.3, the reality is that this 'domino effect' problem can be dealt with *while accepting the principle of voidness*.)

3.1.2 The Theoretical Argument

Lord Denning's views on voidness were also informed by his underlying theoretical perspective. He concluded that the Secretary of State had committed an error which appeared on the face of the record — an exceptional (and now practically defunct) species of error which, as we saw in ch 2, was characterized as an error *within* jurisdiction which was nevertheless reviewable. Now, it is clear (as Wade (1967) 83 *LQR* 499 at 522 recognized) that if the error in *Head* was rightly characterized as non-jurisdictional, then it was acceptable for Lord Denning to treat the decision as voidable. Today, however, the dominant view is that *any* reviewable error committed by a decision-maker will lead to an excess of 'jurisdiction' in the broad sense. Once it is recognized that jurisdiction is now the principle around which administrative law is organized, it becomes clear that all unlawful administrative action must be void. This follows because, under the contemporary, broad view of jurisdiction, unlawful administrative action is by definition outside the powers of the decision-maker: such action lacks any legal foundation, and can therefore never exist, or have existed, as a matter of law. This matter is considered in the next case (for comment on which see Forsyth [1998] *PL* 364 and Craig (1998) 114 *LQR* 535).

....

Boddington v. *British Transport Police* [1999] 2 AC 143
House of Lords

Byelaw 20 of the British Railways Board's Byelaws 1965 (made under s 67(1) of the Transport Act 1962) made it an offence to (*inter alia*) smoke on a train where 'no smoking' signs were 'exhibited in a conspicuous position'. A train operator, Network South Central, decided to prohibit smoking throughout all of its trains and displayed notices to that effect. The defendant, while in a carriage in which no smoking signs were prominently displayed, smoked a cigarette and refused to extinguish it upon being asked to do so. The defendant argued that byelaw 20 did not empower the train operator to adopt a policy of *completely* banning smoking; that its decision to post notices in every carriage was consequently *ultra vires*, and that he had therefore committed no offence because he had not smoked in a carriage in which a *valid* notice was displayed. These arguments were rejected by the stipendiary magistrate, and the defendant was convicted of an offence under byelaw 20; he appealed unsuccessfully to the Divisional Court, and thereafter to the House of Lords. The following extract is concerned only with the status of the 'no smoking' notices. Only if the notices were void, in the sense set out at the beginning of the chapter, could the defendant raise the matter by way of defence (or 'collaterally challenge' them — a term explored further at 3.4 below). For further extracts from this case, see below at 3.4.2 and 3.4.3.

Lord Irvine LC

. . . In *Director of Public Prosecutions v. Head* [1959] A.C. 83 [on which see above at 3.1.1] . . . Lord Denning, who was in the minority, was of the view that the order was valid as at the date of the alleged offence, so that the alleged offence was made out . . ., even although the order was voidable and therefore liable to be quashed . . . The majority, however, did not accept that the order was voidable rather than void, but in any event doubted that, even if it was to be characterised as voidable rather than void, a defendant could not raise the matter by way of defence. As Lord Somervell of Harrow put it, at p. 104: "Is a man to be sent to prison on the basis that an order is a good order when the court knows it would be set aside if proper proceedings were taken? I doubt it."

[After endorsing the majority view in *Head*, his Lordship continued:] In my judgment the views of the majority in [that case] have acquired still greater force in the light of the development of the basic principles of public law since [it] was decided. Lord Denning had dissented on the basis of the historic distinction between acts which were ultra vires ("outside the jurisdiction of the Secretary of State"), which he accepted were nullities and void, and errors of law on the face of the relevant record, which rendered the relevant instrument voidable rather than void. He felt able to assign the order in question to the latter category. But in 1969, the decision of your Lordships' House in *Anisminic Ltd. v. Foreign Compensation Commission* [1969] 2 A.C. 147 made obsolete the historic distinction between errors of law on the face of the record and other errors of law. It did so by extending the doctrine of ultra vires, so that any misdirection in law would render the relevant decision ultra vires and a nullity: see *Reg. v. Hull University Visitor, Ex parte Page* [1993] A.C. 682, 701–702, *per* Lord Browne-Wilkinson (with whom Lord Keith of Kinkel and Lord Griffiths agreed, at p 692), citing the speech of Lord Diplock in *O'Reilly v. Mackman* [1983] 2 A.C. 237, 278. Thus, today, the old distinction between void and voidable acts on which Lord Denning relied in *Director of Public Prosecutions v. Head* [1959] A.C. 83 no longer applies. This much is clear from the *Anisminic* case [1969] 2 A.C. 147 and these later authorities.

. . . [In *Anisminic*, Lord Reid] made it clear that all forms of public law challenge to a decision have the same effect, to render it a nullity: see especially p. 171B–F. (Also see pp 195–196, *per* Lord Pearce and p 207D–H, *per* Lord Wilberforce.) The decision of the Commission was wrong in law, and therefore a nullity, rather than a 'determination' within the protection of the ouster clause: see pp 170–171.

Thus the reservation of Lord Somervell in *Director of Public Prosecutions v. Head* [1959] A.C. 83, 104 (with which the majority allied themselves) whether the order of the Secretary of State could be described as voidable has been vindicated by subsequent developments. It is clear, in the light of *Anisminic* and the later authorities, that the Secretary of State's order in *Director of Public Prosecutions v. Head* would now certainly be regarded as a nullity (ie as void *ab initio*), even if it were to be analysed as an error of law on the face of the record. Equally, the order would be regarded as void ab initio if it had been made in bad faith, or as a result of the Secretary of State taking into account an irrelevant, or ignoring a relevant, consideration — that is, matters not appearing on the face of the record, but having to be established by evidence.

. . . In *Bugg v. Director of Public Prosecutions* [1993] Q.B. 473 the Divisional Court . . . expressed the view, at p. 493, that "except in the 'flagrant' and 'outrageous' case a statutory order, such as a byelaw, remains effective until it is quashed." Three authorities were cited which were said to support this approach: *London & Clydeside Estates Ltd v. Aberdeen District Council* [1980] 1 W.L.R. 182, 189–190 in the speech of Lord Hailsham of St Marylebone LC; *Smith v. East Elloe Rural District Council* [1956] A.C. 736, 769–770, in the speech of Lord Radcliffe and *F Hoffmann-La Roche & Co AG v. Secretary of State for Trade and Industry* [1975] A.C. 295, 366, in the speech of Lord Diplock. This approach was then elevated by the Divisional Court into a rule that byelaws which are on their face invalid or are patently unreasonable (termed "substantive" invalidity) may be called in question by way of defence in criminal proceedings, whereas byelaws which are invalid because of some defect in the procedure by which they came to be made (termed "procedural" invalidity) may not be called in question in such proceedings, so that a person might be convicted of an offence under them even if the byelaws were later quashed in other proceedings.

Strong reservations about the decision of the Divisional Court in *Bugg v. Director of Public Prosecutions* [1993] Q.B. 473 have recently been expressed by this House in *R v. Wicks* [1998] A.C. 92. I have reached the conclusion that the time has come to hold that it was wrongly decided.

I am bound to say that I do not think that the three authorities to which I have referred support the position as stated in *Bugg's* case [1993] Q.B. 473. In my judgment Lord Diplock's speech in the *F Hoffmann-La Roche* case [1995] A.C. 295, when read as a whole, makes it clear that subordinate legislation which is quashed is deprived of any legal effect at all, and that is so whether the invalidity arises from defects appearing on its face or in the procedure adopted in its promulgation. Lord Diplock himself cited, at p 366, the speech of Lord Radcliffe in *Smith v. East Elloe Rural District Council* [1956] A.C. 736, 769–770 and regarded him as saying no more about the presumption of validity than he (Lord Diplock) was saying. I agree with that view.

. . . In my judgment the reasoning of the Divisional Court in *Bugg's* case, suggesting two classes of legal invalidity of subordinate legislation, is contrary both to the *Anisminic* case and the subsequent decisions of this House to which I have referred. The *Anisminic* decision established, contrary to previous thinking that there might be error of law within jurisdiction, that there was a single category of errors of law, all of which rendered a decision ultra vires. No distinction is to be drawn between a patent (or substantive) error of law or a latent (or procedural) error of law. An ultra vires act or subordinate legislation is unlawful simpliciter and, if the presumption in favour of its legality is overcome by a litigant before a court of competent jurisdiction, is of no legal effect whatsoever.

The Divisional Court in *Bugg's* case [1993] Q.B. 473 themselves drew attention to Lord Denning's dissenting speech in *Director of Public Prosecutions v. Head* and, whilst avowing that "The distinction between orders which are void and voidable is now clearly not part of our law" identified his approach as interesting, because Lord Denning "was drawing a distinction, as we are seeking to do, between different types of invalidity:" see p 496G. However, the distinction which Lord Denning drew is one which was made redundant by the decision in the *Anisminic* case, in which all categories of unlawfulness were treated as equivalent and as having the same effect . . .

Lord Browne-Wilkinson

. . . The Lord Chancellor attaches importance to the consideration that an invalid bye-law is and always has been a nullity. The byelaw will necessarily have been found to be ultra vires; therefore it is said it is a nullity having no legal effect. I adhere to my view that the juristic basis of judicial review is the doctrine of ultra vires. But I am far from satisfied that an ultra vires act is incapable of having any legal consequence during the period between the doing of that act and the recognition of its invalidity by the court. During that period people will have regulated their lives on the basis that the act is valid. The subsequent recognition of its invalidity cannot rewrite history as to all the other matters done in the meantime in reliance on its validity. The status of an unlawful act during the period before it is quashed is a matter of great contention and of great difficulty . . .

I prefer to express no view at this stage on those difficult points . . .

Lord Slynn

. . . I consider that the result of allowing a collateral challenge in proceedings before courts of criminal jurisdiction can be reached without it being necessary in this case to say that if an act or bye-law is invalid it must be held to have been invalid from the outset for all purposes and that no lawful consequences can flow from it. This may be the logical result and will no doubt sometimes be the position but courts have had to grapple with the problem of reconciling the logical result with the reality that much have may have been done on the basis that an administrative act or a byelaw was valid. The unscrambling may produce more serious difficulties than the invalidity. The European Court of Justice has dealt with the problem by ruling that its declaration of invalidity should only operate for the benefit of the parties to the actual case or of those who had began proceedings for a declaration of invalidity before the courts' judgment. In our jurisdiction the effect of invalidity may not be relied on if limitation periods have expired or if the court in its discretion refuses relief, albeit considering that the act is invalid. These situations are of course different from those where a court has pronounced subordinate legislation or an administrative act to be unlawful or where the presumption in favour of their legality has been overruled by a court of competent jurisdiction. But even in these cases I consider that the question whether the acts or byelaws are to be treated as having at no time had any effect in law is not one which has been fully explored and is not one on which it is necessary to rule in this appeal and I prefer to express no view upon it. The cases referred to in *Wade and Forsyth, Administrative Law* 7th ed. (1997), pp. 323–324, 342–344 lead the authors to the view that nullity is relative rather than an absolute concept (p. 343) and that "void" is "meaningless in any absolute sense. Its meaning is relative:" This may all be rather imprecise but the law in this area has developed in a pragmatic way on a case by case basis . . .

Lord Steyn

. . . Leaving to one side the separate topic of judicial review of non-legal powers exercised by non statutory bodies, I see no reason to depart from the orthodox view that ultra vires is 'the central principle of administrative law' as *Wade and Forsyth, Administrative Law*, 7th ed., p. 41 described it. Lord Browne-Wilkinson observed in *Reg. v. Hull University Visitor, Ex parte Page* [1993] A.C. 682, 701:

> "The fundamental principle [of judicial review] is that the courts will intervene to ensure that the powers of public decision-making bodies are exercised lawfully. In all cases . . . this intervention . . . is based on the proposition that such powers have been conferred on the decision-maker on the underlying assumption that the powers are to be exercised only within the jurisdiction conferred, in accordance with fair procedures and, in a *Wednesbury* sense . . . reasonably. If the decision-maker exercises his powers outside the jurisdiction conferred, in a manner which is procedurally irregular or is *Wednesbury* unreasonable, he is acting ultra vires his powers and therefore unlawfully. . . ." [On '*Wednesbury* unreasonableness', see below at 9.2.1.]

This is the essential constitutional underpinning of the statute based part of our administrative law. Nevertheless, I accept the reality that an unlawful byelaw is a fact and that it may in certain circumstances have legal consequences. The best explanation that I have seen is by Dr. Forsyth who summarised the position as follows in "The Metaphysic of Nullity, Invalidity, Conceptual Reasoning and the Rule of Law," at p. 159 [on which see further below at 3.3.4]:

> "it has been argued that unlawful administrative acts are void in law. But they clearly exist in fact and they often appear to be valid; and those unaware of their invalidity may take decisions and act on the assumption that these acts are valid. When this happens the validity of these later acts depends upon the legal powers of the second actor. *The crucial issue to be determined is whether that second actor has legal power to act validly notwithstanding the invalidity of the first act.* And it is determined by a[n] analysis of the law against the background of the familiar proposition that an unlawful act is void." (Emphasis supplied.)

That seems to me a more accurate summary of the law as it has developed than the sweeping proposition in *Bugg's* case.

Lord Hoffmann

. . . I have had the advantage of reading in draft the speeches of my noble and learned friends, Lord Irvine of Lairg L.C. and Lord Steyn. For the reasons they have given I, too, would dismiss the appeal.

All of their Lordships *agreed* (as we explain below at 3.3.3) that the defendant could raise the alleged invalidity of the notices in his defence; all, therefore, appeared to subscribe to the view that unlawful administrative action is void rather than merely voidable since, if the notices had only been voidable, then they would have been valid unless or until they were quashed by a competent court. It is apparent, however, that their Lordships *disagreed* about precisely what 'voidness' means; in particular, if one holds unlawful action to be void, does it necessarily follow that it has no effect whatever, and that anything done in reliance on it must be 'unscrambled', as Lord Slynn put it? It is to these issues which we must now turn our attention.

QUESTION

- Explain how their Lordships' views as to the status of unlawful administrative action differed in *Boddington*. Which view, in your opinion, is preferable?

3.2 The Nature of Voidness

3.2.1 The Presumption of Validity

The case law concerning the status of unlawful administrative action recognizes a 'presumption of validity', according to which administrative action is presumed to be valid unless or until it is set aside by a court. The presumption played a major role in the following case.

F Hoffmann-La Roche and Co AG v. *Secretary of State for Trade and Industry* [1975] AC 295
House of Lords

The appellants marketed the drugs librium and valium. The Department of Health and Social Security, which had to meet a large part of the cost of the drugs, thought that their price was much too high. The matter was referred by the respondent to the Monopolies and Mergers Commission which in February 1973 recommended, *inter alia*, that the prices charged by the appellants for librium and valium be reduced. A few months later the Regulation of Prices (Transquilising Drugs) (No 3) Order 1973 (SI 1973/1093), which effected a compulsory price reduction by limiting the prices the appellants could charge, was made under the authority of s 10(3) of the Monopolies and Restrictive Practices (Inquiry and Control) Act 1948 and s 3(3)(a) and (d) and 4(c) of the Monopolies and Mergers Act 1965. The order came into effect on 25 June 1973 and was later approved by both Houses of Parliament, as was required by the enabling legislation if it was to remain in force for more than 28 days. On 25 June, the appellants sought a declaration that the order was *ultra vires* and invalid; three days later the respondent sought an injunction restraining the appellants from charging prices in excess of those specified in the order, and an interim injunction to prevent the higher prices from being charged pending final determination of the validity of the order. Walton J refused to grant an interim injunction, but the Court of Appeal allowed an appeal by the respondent. The appellants appealed to the House of Lords.

Lord Reid

. . . An interim injunction against a party to a litigation may cause him great loss if in the end he is successful. In the present case it is common ground that a long time — it may be years — will elapse before a decision can be given. During that period if an interim injunction is granted the appellants will only be able to make the charges permitted by the order. So if in the end the order is annulled that loss will be the difference between those charges and those which they could have made if the order had never been made. And they may not be able to recover any part of that loss from anyone. It is said that the loss might amount to £8m. The appellants' case is that justice requires that such an injunction should not be granted without an undertaking by the respondent to make good that loss to them if they are ultimately successful.

The respondent's first answer is that when an interim injunction is granted to the Crown no undertaking can be required as a condition of granting it. It is not in doubt that in an ordinary litigation the general rule has long been that no interim injunction likely to cause loss to a party will be granted unless the party seeking the injunction undertakes to make good that loss if in the end it appears that the injunction was unwarranted. He cannot be compelled to give an undertaking but if he will not give it he will not get the injunction.

But there is much authority to show that the Crown was in a different position. In general no undertaking was required of it. But whatever justification there may have been for that before 1947 I agree with your Lordships that the old rule or practice cannot be justified since the passing of the Crown Proceedings Act of that year. So if this had been a case where the Crown were asserting a proprietary right I would hold that the ordinary rule should apply and there should be no interlocutory injunction unless the Crown chose to give the usual undertaking.

But this is a case in a different and novel field. No doubt it was thought that criminal penalties were inappropriate as a means of enforcing orders of this kind, and the only method of enforcement is by injunction. Dealing with alleged breaches of the law is a function of the Crown (or of a department of the executive) entirely different in character from its function in protecting its proprietary right. It has more resemblance to the function of prosecuting those who are alleged to have committed an offence. A person who is prosecuted and found not guilty may have suffered serious loss by reason of the prosecution but in general he has no legal claim against the prosecutor. In the absence of special circumstances I see no reason why the Crown in seeking to enforce orders of this kind should have to incur legal liability to the person alleged to be in breach of the order.

It must be borne in mind that an order made under statutory authority is as much the law of the land as an Act of Parliament unless and until it has been found to be ultra vires. No doubt procedure by way of injunction is more flexible than procedure by prosecution and there may well be cases when a court ought to refuse an interim injunction or only to grant it on terms. But I think that it is for the person against whom the interim injunction is sought to show special reason why justice requires that the injunction should not be granted or should only be granted on terms.

The present case has a special feature which requires anxious consideration. As I have already indicated, the Crown has a very large financial interest in obtaining an interim injunction. The Department of Health will reap a large immediate benefit from the lower prices set out in the order at the expense of the appellants. If in the end it were decided that the order was ultra vires those prices ought never to have been enforced, the department ought never to have had that benefit and the appellants would have suffered a large loss. So why should the respondent not be required to give the undertaking which the appellants seek as a condition of getting the interim injunction?

But, on the other hand, the order which the appellants seek to annul is the law at present and if an interim injunction is refused that means that the law is not to be enforced and the appellants are to be at liberty to disregard it by charging forbidden prices. And the matter does not stop there. Doctors will continue to prescribe these drugs. Chemists will have to pay the forbidden prices if the public are to be provided with drugs which doctors think they ought to have. And chemists cannot be expected to pay the appellants' prices unless the department is willing to reimburse them. So the department will have to acquiesce in and indeed aid and abet the appellants' breaches of the law if the medical profession and the public are to get what they are entitled to.

It is true that the appellants have proposed an ingenious scheme which they would undertake to operate if an interim injunction is refused. The effect of it would be that they would continue to charge the forbidden prices but that if the order were ultimately held to be intra vires they would repay the difference between the forbidden charges which they had made and the lower charges which they ought to have made. The scheme would involve considerable practical difficulties and would probably not be fully effective, but I shall not discuss those difficulties because the serious objection would remain that the law laid down in the order is to be disregarded until the case is decided.

My Lords, if I thought that the appellants had a strong case on the merits I would try to stretch a point in their favour to protect them from obvious injustice though I would find difficulty in doing so. It is true that although we heard a good deal of argument on the merits we are not in a position to express any firm opinion as to the appellants' prospects of success. But if it is for them to show us at this stage that their case is so strong that they are entitled to some special consideration, I can say that they have completely failed to convince me that they have a strong *prima facie* case.

I would therefore dismiss this appeal.

Lord Wilberforce (dissenting)

. . . It does not, of course, follow that because there is power to impose the condition [ie to give an undertaking in damages] it ought to be imposed in this case, or similar cases. Regard must be had to the nature of the dispute and the position of the disputants. In a case such as the present, the fact that the effective plaintiff is a government department, acting in the public interest and responsible for public money, is important. The real issue is how far this difference is to be carried. The main argument relied on for preserving, in the present case, a special right for the Crown to obtain injunctions without offering an undertaking is that the Crown is "enforcing the law," and — so, I understood the argument — should not be hampered by being put on terms. Or, putting it another way, the company, being in breach of the law, is not in a position to ask for protective terms. My Lords, I am afraid that I regard this argument as fallacious. To say that the Crown is enforcing the law is a *petitio principii*, since the very issue in the action is whether what is alleged to be law (and denied to be law by the appellants) is law or not. The answer given to this is, I understand, that there is a presumption of validity until the contrary is shown. The consequence drawn from this is that unconditional obedience must be required by the court: "obey first and argue afterwards" in Lord Denning M.R.'s graphic phrase [1973] 3 W.L.R. 805, 821. I think that there is a confusion here. It is true enough that a piece of subordinate legislation is presumed to be valid against persons who have no *locus standi* to challenge it [on which see below at 15.7] — the puzzling case of *Durayappah* v. *Fernando* [1967] 2 A.C. 337 can be understood as exemplifying this. But it is quite another matter to say, and I know of no supporting authority, that such a presumption exists when the validity of the subordinate legislation is legitimately in question before a court and is challenged by a person who has *locus standi* to challenge it. Certainly no support for any such proposition is to be found in the passage, so often partially quoted, from the speech of Lord Radcliffe in *Smith* v. *East Elloe Rural District Council* [1956] A.C. 736. One has only to read what he said, at pp 769–770:

> "At one time the argument was shaped into the form of saying that an order made in bad faith was in law a nullity and that, consequently, all references to compulsory purchase orders in paragraphs 15 and 16 must be treated as references to such orders only as had been made in good faith. But this argument is in reality a play on the meaning of the word nullity. An order, even if not made in good faith, is still an act capable of legal consequences. It bears no brand of invalidity upon its forehead. Unless the necessary proceedings are taken at law to establish the cause of invalidity and to get it quashed or otherwise upset, it will remain as effective for its ostensible purpose as the most impeccable of orders."

How this can be said to support an argument that when proceedings are taken at law the impugned order must be given full legal effect against the challenger before the proceedings are decided I am unable to comprehend.

In any event the argument proves too much, for, if it were right, the court would have no discretion to refuse an injunction whatever the consequences, however irreparably disastrous, to the subject. Such rigidity of power seems to be contrary to section 45 of the Supreme Court of Judicature (Consolidation) Act 1925. Further, if one considers some of the orders which, under this same Act, can be made under section 3 the injustice of this can be easily perceived. And as an example in practice there is the case of *Post Office* v. *Estuary Radio Ltd* [1967] 1 W.L.R. 847; [1968] 2

Q.B. 740 which I discuss below, a case where an interim injunction was refused — no doubt just because to grant it would cause irreparable damage. If, then, it is said that there must always remain a residual discretion the argument vanishes: we are back on discretion.

It is said that no undertaking should be insisted on unless the effect of the appellants' eventual success were to make the order 'void *ab initio*' — the argument being that otherwise no injustice would result. Buckley L.J. ([1973] 3 W.L.R. 805, 827–828) made this the conclusion of a judgment with the rest of which I respectfully concur. This phrase 'void *ab initio*' has engendered many learned distinctions and much confused thinking — unnecessarily, in my opinion. There can be no doubt in the first place that an ultra vires act is simply void — see in confirmation *Ridge* v. *Baldwin* [1964] A.C. 40. In truth when the court says that an act of administration is voidable or void but not ab initio this is simply a reflection of a conclusion, already reached on unexpressed grounds, that the court is not willing *in casu* to give compensation or other redress to the person who establishes the nullity. Underlying the use of the phrase in the present case, and I suspect underlying most of the reasoning in the Court of Appeal, is an unwillingness to accept that a subject should be indemnified for loss sustained by invalid administrative action. It is this which requires examination rather than some supposed visible quality of the order itself.

In more developed legal systems this particular difficulty does not arise. Such systems give indemnity to persons injured by illegal acts of the administration. Consequently, where the prospective loss which may be caused by an order is pecuniary, there is no need to suspend the impugned administrative act: it can take effect (in our language an injunction can be given) and at the end of the day the subject can, if necessary, be compensated. On the other hand, if the prospective loss is not pecuniary (in our language "irreparable") the act may be suspended pending decision — in our language, interim enforcement may be refused.

There is clearly an important principle here which has not been elucidated by English law, or even brought into the open. But there are traces of it in some areas. I have referred to *Post Office* v. *Estuary Radio Ltd* [1967] 1 W.L.R. 847; [1968] 2 Q.B. 740, which arose upon a section in the Wireless Telegraphy Act 1949, similar to section 11 of the [Monopolies and Restrictive Practices (Inquiries and Control) Act 1948]. In that case the Post Office applied for an injunction and also moved for interim relief; this was refused, no doubt partly for the reason that to grant it at the interim stage would cause the defendant irreparable damage. We are not bound by the decision, but I suggest that it is based on sound principle.

Secondly, there are instances of statutes which themselves provide for the interim suspension of impugned orders. One such is the Acquisition of Land (Authorisation Procedure) Act 1946, Schedule 1, Part IV. This provides that if any person desires to question the validity of a compulsory purchase order the court may ad interim suspend the effect of the order. These are examples of at least a partial recognition in our law that the subject requires protection against action taken against him or his property under administrative orders which may turn out to be invalid. How far this principle goes need not, and cannot, be decided in the present case. But what can be said is that the combination of section 11 of the Act of 1948 with section 45 of the Supreme Court of Judicature (Consolidation) Act 1925 gives to the court a practical instrument by which injustice to private individuals, faced with possibly invalid action, may be avoided. If this is not possible in every case, it should not be rejected in a case, however special, where justice to both sides can be done.

In the present case there is the feature, special and possibly unique, that the executive, seeking to enforce the order, has itself a pecuniary interest; it is a monopoly buyer confronting a monopoly seller. It stands to make a large profit at the appellants' expense if they are right. So even if one thinks that in general there is no right of compensation for illegal action, that is not a belief which need, or should, influence the present decision. The potentiality of large loss on one side and large profit on the other are factors which are relevant to the court's discretion . . .

Lord Diplock

. . . The instant case is not one where the appellants contend that what they are threatening to do would not be a contravention of the order — as was the case in *Post Office* v. *Estuary Radio Ltd* [1967] 1 W.L.R. 847; [1968] 2 Q.B. 740. Different considerations would apply to that. Their only answer to the application for an interim injunction to enforce the order against them is that they intend to challenge its validity. It is not disputed that they have locus standi to do so, but this does not absolve them from their obligation to obey the order while the presumption in favour of its validity prevails — as it must so long as there has been no final judgment in the action to the contrary.

So in this type of law enforcement action if the only defence is an attack on the validity of the statutory instrument sought to be enforced the ordinary position of the parties as respects the grant of interim injunctions is reversed. The duty of the Crown to see that the law declared by the statutory instrument is obeyed is not suspended by the commencement of proceedings in which the validity of the instrument is challenged. Prima facie the Crown is entitled as of right to an interim injunction to enforce obedience to it. To displace this right or to fetter it by the imposition of conditions it is for the defendant to show a strong prima facie case that the statutory instrument is ultra vires.

Even where a strong prima facie case of invalidity has been shown upon the application for an interim injunction it may still be inappropriate for the court to impose as a condition of the grant of the injunction a requirement that the Crown should enter into the usual undertaking as to damages. For if the undertaking falls to be implemented, the cost of implementing it will be met from public funds raised by taxation and the interests of members of the public who are not parties to the action may be affected by it . . .

. . . I agree with the majority of your Lordships that the Secretary of State is entitled to the interim injunction that he claimed without giving any undertaking as to damages unless the appellants have succeeded in showing a strong prima facie case that the order sought to be enforced by the injunction is ultra vires. It is not for the Secretary of State to show that the appellant's case cannot possibly succeed as Walton J thought it was. It is for the appellants to show that their defence of ultra vires is likely to be successful. I agree with the majority of your Lordships that they have signally failed to do this . . .

Lords Morris and Cross delivered speeches in favour of dismissing the appeal. Appeal dismissed.

It may at first appear that adopting the presumption of validity implies that unlawful action is merely voidable. However, as the reasoning in *Hoffmann-La Roche* illustrates, this does not necessarily follow. It is perfectly possible to assume, as a working hypothesis, that administrative action is valid, while at the same time accepting that, if it is found to be unlawful, then it is void *ab initio*. Of course, this means that action which was presumed to be lawful will turn out to be void, meaning that it was *always* unlawful. This, however, presents no difficulty: the presumption of validity is necessarily an *interim* assumption about the status of the administrative action in question, and there is no incongruity in recognizing that, in some situations, that initial assumption will turn out to have been wrong. It follows that the presumption of validity can sit comfortably alongside the general principle that unlawful administrative action is void. This was recognized in clear terms by Lord Hoffmann in *R* v. *Wicks* [1998] AC 92 at 115, who said that the presumption adopted in *Hoffmann-La Roche* was 'an evidential matter at the interlocutory stage' — a 'presumption [which] existed pending a final decision by the court' and did not, therefore, imply 'the sweeping proposition that subordinate legislation must be treated for all purposes as valid until set aside'. This view was endorsed by Lords Irvine LC and Steyn in *Boddington* v. *British Transport Police* [1999] 2 AC 143 at 156 and 161, and 173–174, respectively.

The presumption of validity is relevant not only in circumstances such as those which arose in *Hoffmann-La Roche*, where interim relief was sought. Its more general significance is that when the legality of administrative action is challenged in legal proceedings, the burden of proof lies initially with the party mounting the challenge. For instance, in *Inland Revenue Commissioners* v. *Rossminster Ltd* [1980] AC 952, it was alleged that officers of the Inland Revenue had exceeded their power under s 20C(3) of the Taxes Management Act 1970 to seize, in the course of searching premises, 'any things whatsoever found there' which they had 'reasonable cause to believe may be required as evidence for the purposes of proceedings' in respect of an offence involving any form of tax fraud. Lord Diplock (at 1011) accepted that

since the act of handling a man's goods without his permission is prima facie tortious, at the trial of a civil action for trespass to goods based on the seizure and removal of things by an officer of the board in purported exercise of his powers under the subsection, the onus would be upon the officer to satisfy the court that there did in fact exist reasonable grounds that were known to him for believing that the documents he removed might be required as evidence in proceedings for some offence involving a tax fraud — not that they *would* be so required, for that the seizing officer could not know, but that they *might* be required if sufficient admissible evidence were ultimately forthcoming to support a prosecution for the offence and it were decided to prosecute.

However, the position was different in relation to a public law challenge to the exercise of the power. Having concluded that for reasons of public interest immunity the tax officers did not have to disclose the grounds of their belief, Lord Diplock (at 1013) said:

Seizure of documents by an officer of the board under section 20C(3) involves a decision by the officer as to what documents he may seize. The subsection prescribes what the state of mind of the officer must be in order to make it lawful for him to decide to seize a document: he must believe that the document may be required as evidence in criminal proceedings for some form of tax fraud and that belief must be based on reasonable grounds. The decision-making power is conferred by the statute upon the officer of the board. He is not required to give any reasons for his decision and the public interest immunity provides justification for any refusal to do so. Since he does not disclose his reasons there can be no question of setting aside his decision for error of law on the face of the record and the only ground upon which it can be attacked upon judicial review is that it was ultra vires because a condition precedent to his forming the belief which the statute prescribes, *viz* that it should be based upon reasonable grounds, was not satisfied. Where Parliament has designated a public officer as decision-maker for a particular class of decisions the High Court, acting as a reviewing court . . ., is not a court of appeal. It must proceed on the presumption omnia praesumuntur rite esse acta [all acts are presumed to be done rightly] until that presumption can be displaced by the applicant for review — upon whom the onus lies of doing so. Since no reasons have been given by the decision-maker and no unfavourable inference can be drawn for this fact because there is obvious justification for his failure to do so, the presumption that he acted intra vires can only be displaced by evidence of facts which cannot be reconciled with there having been reasonable cause for his belief that the documents might be required as evidence or alternatively which cannot be reconciled with his having held such belief at all.

It is therefore for the party seeking to challenge the administrative action to adduce evidence which calls into question its legality. Once this has been done, however, the onus shifts to the public authority which must, if its action is to survive judicial scrutiny, advance evidence which demonstrates that those actions were lawful.

QUESTION

• How do Lord Diplock's remarks in *Rossminster* relate to the approach adopted in *Khawaja* (see above at 2.3)?

3.2.2 The Principle of Legal Relativity

The presumption of validity, as set out above, is an evidential device. While it places an initial burden on claimants seeking to impugn executive action, and provides the courts with a starting point when they are considering whether to suspend administrative decisions and subordinate legislation by means of interim relief, it does not call into question the basic proposition that unlawful administrative action is void *ab initio*. In the following passage, however, Lord Diplock draws some more far-reaching conclusions from the presumption of validity.

....

F Hoffmann-La Roche and Co AG v. Secretary of State for Trade and Industry [1975] AC 295
House of Lords

For the facts, see above at 3.2.1.

Lord Diplock

. . . Under our legal system . . . the courts as the judicial arm of government do not act on their own initiative. Their jurisdiction to determine that a statutory instrument is ultra vires does not arise until its validity is challenged in proceedings inter partes either brought by one party to enforce the law declared by the instrument against another party or brought by a party whose interests are affected by the law so declared sufficiently directly to give him locus standi to initiate proceedings to challenge the validity of the instrument. Unless there is such challenge and, if there is, until it has been upheld by a judgment of the court, the validity of the statutory instrument and the legality of acts done pursuant to the law declared by it are presumed. It would, however, be inconsistent with the doctrine of ultra vires as it has been developed in English law as a means of controlling abuse of power by the executive arm of government if the judgment of a court in proceedings properly constituted that a statutory instrument was ultra vires were to have any lesser consequence in law than to render the instrument incapable of ever having had any legal effect upon the rights or duties of the parties to the proceedings (cf *Ridge v. Baldwin* [1964] A.C. 40). Although such a decision is directly binding only as between the parties to the proceedings in which it was made, the application of the doctrine of precedent has the consequence of enabling the benefit of it to accrue to all other persons whose legal rights have been interfered with in reliance on the law which the statutory instrument purported to declare . . .

My Lords, I think it leads to confusion to use such terms as "voidable," "voidable ab initio," "void" or "a nullity" as descriptive of the legal status of subordinate legislation alleged to be ultra vires for patent or for latent defects, before its validity has been pronounced on by a court of competent jurisdiction. These are concepts developed in the private law of contract which are ill-adapted to the field of public law. All that can usefully be said is that the presumption that subordinate legislation is intra vires prevails in the absence of rebuttal, and that it cannot be rebutted except by a party to legal proceedings in a court of competent jurisdiction who has locus standi to challenge the validity of the subordinate legislation in question.

All locus standi on the part of anyone to rebut the presumption of validity may be taken away completely or may be limited in point of time or otherwise by the express terms of the Act of Parliament which conferred the subordinate legislative power, though the courts lean heavily against a construction of the Act which would have this effect (cf *Anisminic Ltd.* v. *Foreign Compensation Commission* [1969] 2 A.C. 147). Such was the case, however, in the view of the majority of this House in *Smith* v. *East Elloe Rural District Council* [1956] A.C. 736, at any rate as respects invalidity on the ground of latent defects, so the compulsory purchase order sought to be challenged in the action had legal effect notwithstanding its potential invalidity. Furthermore, apart from express provision in the governing statute, locus standi to challenge the validity of subordinate legislation may be restricted, under the court's inherent power to control its own procedure, to a particular category of persons affected by the subordinate legislation, and if none of these persons chooses to challenge it the presumption of validity prevails. Such was the case in *Durayappah* v. *Fernando* [1967] 2 A.C. 337 where on an appeal from Ceylon, although the Privy Council was of opinion that an order of the Minister was ultra vires owing to a latent defect in the procedure prior to its being made, they nevertheless treated it as having legal effect because the party who sought to challenge it had, in their view, no locus standi to do so.

Lord Diplock is here advancing what Wade calls 'a general principle of legal relativity' ((1967) 83 *LQR* 499 at 512; see also (1968) 84 *LQR* 95), which holds that the proposition that unlawful administrative action is void cannot meaningfully be accepted in an absolute or abstract sense. Even if certain action is unlawful, and therefore in some sense void, it may be that no-one realizes that this is so; or that the 'wrong' person notices the unlawfulness of the action and therefore lacks standing to challenge it (see below at 15.7); or that the 'right' person notices, but is prevented by statute from seeking judicial review (see below at 15.6); or that the court, in its discretion, refuses any remedy on judicial review. In such circumstances, the action concerned is, *in a practical sense*, valid because it has not been or cannot be challenged in court. As Wade (1967) 83 *LQR* 499 at 512 puts it:

It makes no sense to speak of an act being void unless there is some person to whom the law gives a remedy. If and when that remedy is taken away, what was void must be treated as valid, being now by law unchallengeable. It is fallacious to suppose that an act can be effective in law only if it has always had some element of validity from the beginning. However destitute of legitimacy at its birth, it is legitimated when the law refuses to assist anyone who wants to bastardise it. What cannot be disputed has to be accepted.

It is important to understand that Wade is not contending that unlawful acts can *become* valid in this way; rather, he suggests that if it is impossible to challenge an act which is suspected of being unlawful, then it must be *treated as* valid. Forsyth (in Forsyth and Hare (eds), *The Golden Metwand and the Crooked Cord* (Oxford 1998) at 143) therefore writes that the effect of Wade's analysis is to characterize unlawful administrative acts as 'theoretically void, yet functionally voidable'. In light of this, does it actually matter that unlawful acts are theoretically void? The answer to this question is in the affirmative, for two reasons.

It is important, on a *theoretical* level, that we remember that unlawful acts are void. Although it is arguable that the exceptional category of review for non-jurisdictional error of law on the face of the record may survive, the dominant contemporary view is that all reviewable errors take a decision-maker beyond its powers. Such a decision is without any lawful authority and must, therefore, be void. There is an intimate and logical connection between the voidness of unlawful administrative action and the way in which administrative law is now conceptually organized around the principle of jurisdictional error. If we abandon the notion that unlawful action is void, then we implicitly undermine jurisdiction as the organizing principle.

The proposition that unlawful action is theoretically void also has important *practical* consequences. Two, in particular, should be noted. The first concerns what is known as 'collateral challenge', which is the means by which the validity in public law of acts and decisions may, instead of being challenged directly by means of judicial review, be raised incidentally or defensively in civil or criminal proceedings. We have already encountered this concept in *Boddington* v. *British Transport Police* [1999] 2 AC 143 (see 3.1.2 above), in which the defendant collaterally challenged the legality of the notice banning smoking in his railway carriage by arguing that a complete prohibition was not permitted under the relevant byelaw. The availability of collateral challenge depends upon the voidness of unlawful administrative action. If such action is merely voidable, then it is valid until quashed by the High Court on judicial review; only if it is void *ab initio* can defendants like Boddington challenge such action collaterally by contending that the unlawfulness of the decision or action in question robs it of any legal existence. The second practical consequence of holding that unlawful action is void relates to statutory provisions — known as 'ouster clauses' — which seek to exclude judicial review. We saw above at 2.2.3 that the House of Lords concluded in *Anisminic* v. *Foreign Compensation Commission* [1969] 2 AC 147 that the Commission's incorrect conclusion on a point of law made its determination void, or a 'nullity'; the determination did not therefore legally exist, and the ouster clause — forbidding the courts from interfering with the Commission's 'determinations' — did not bite.

We consider collateral challenge and ouster clauses in more detail below at 3.4 and 15.6, respectively. The important point, for the time being, is that the availability of collateral challenge and the courts' approach to ouster clauses both depend upon the voidness of unlawful administrative action. The theory of legal relativity, which emphasizes that unlawful action will often appear to be valid in a practical sense, may seem to suggest that the theoretical voidness of such action is unimportant. However, as we have seen, that is not the case. The theory of legal relativity is best regarded as an empirical observation, to the effect that theoretically void action may sometimes be treated as, or assumed to be, valid because no-one can challenge, or has challenged, it. The theory of legal relativity does not, however, undermine the fundamental proposition that in theory and in law unlawful administrative action is void.

3.3 Managing the Practical Effects of Voidness

3.3.1 The 'Domino Effect' Problem

The theory of legal relativity is concerned with the situation which arises when unlawful action is not challenged (or, more accurately, is not challenged in the right court, by a competent party, within the appropriate time limit). We now turn to a broader problem. If unlawful action *is* exposed as such, and held to be void, this risks creating serious practical problems. In particular, other administrative acts may have been committed on the strength of the original, unlawful act: for instance, many licences or grants may have been issued pursuant to an administrative policy which turns out to be unlawful. Logic seems to dictate that if the first act (in our example, the policy) is void, then all subsequent acts which were adopted in reliance upon it must also fall. Policy may, however, point in a different direction: allowing the 'domino effect' to proceed unchecked may produce chaotic, and potentially unfair (see, *eg, R v. Governor of Brockhill Prison, ex parte Evans (No 2)* [2001] 2 AC 19), consequences. How is this problem to be addressed?

3.3.2 The Void/Voidable Distinction as a Management Technique

We saw above at 3.1.1 that the practical difficulties caused by the possibility of the 'domino effect' moved Lord Denning in *Director of Public Prosecutions* v. *Head* [1959] AC 83 to reject the view that all unlawful acts are void. His approach in the next case was similar (although, as we explain below, different in one important respect).

....

R v. Paddington Valuation Officer, ex parte Peachey Property Corporation Ltd [1966] 1 QB 380
Court of Appeal

The applicant challenged a new rating valuation list — which was used to assess householders' liability to pay what is now known as 'council tax' — prepared by the Paddington Valuation Officer. Mandatory or quashing orders were sought, the ground for seeking the latter remedy being an allegation of excess of jurisdiction. The challenge was successful in the Court of Appeal, as it had been in the Divisional Court. The present excerpt is concerned only with the contrasting views of Lord Denning MR (with whom Danckwerts LJ agreed on this point) and Salmon LJ about the status of the new valuation list.

Lord Denning MR

. . . It is necessary to distinguish between two kinds of invalidity. The one kind is where the invalidity is so grave that the list is a nullity altogether. In which case there is no need for an order to quash it. It is automatically null and void without more ado. The other kind is when the invalidity does not make the list void altogether, but only voidable. In that case it stands unless and until it is set aside. In the present case the valuation list is not, and never has been, a nullity. At most the valuation officer — acting within his jurisdiction — exercised that jurisdiction erroneously. That makes the list voidable and not void. It remains good until it is set aside. "It bears no brand of invalidity upon its forehead. Unless the necessary proceedings are taken at law to establish the cause of invalidity and to get it quashed or otherwise upset, it will remain as effective for its ostensible purpose as the most impeccable of orders": see *Smith* v. *East Elloe Rural District Council* [1956] A.C. 736, 739, 770 by Lord Radcliffe. No doubt if the list is in due course avoided, certiorari must eventually go to quash it. But I see no reason why a mandamus should not issue in advance of the certiorari: compare *R* v. *Cotham etc JJ & Webb, Ex parte Williams* [1898] 1 Q.B. 802. If the existing list has been compiled on the wrong footing the court can order the valuation officer to make a new list on the right footing. (The passage of time is no bar: for Mr Blain concedes that the requirement for it to be prepared by December 31, 1962, was directory only and not mandatory.) Once the new list is made and is ready to take effect, the court can quash the old list. In that case everything done under the old list will remain good. The rates that have been demanded and paid cannot be recovered back. For it is a general rule that where a voidable transaction is avoided, it does not invalidate intermediate transactions which were made on the basis that it was good: see the cases collected in *Director of Public Prosecutions* v. *Head* [1969] A.C. 83, 111–113. By this solution, all chaos is avoided. The existing list will remain good until it is replaced by a new list: and then it will be quashed by certiorari. But I think that then it must be quashed. You cannot have two lists in being at the same time. The Divisional Court took the view that certiorari was a necessary pre-requisite to mandamus. I do not think it is a pre-requisite. Certiorari will be necessary some time, but only when the new list is ready to take effect . . .

Salmon LJ

. . . I am not altogether satisfied that there would be any power to grant mandamus and keep the 1963 valuation list in force by the simple expedient of postponing certiorari until after a new list had been prepared. No doubt it would be convenient, if possible, to follow this course, were the appeal to be allowed; indeed grave inconvenience, if not chaos, would follow if the 1956 valuation list were to be revived — which both the appellants and respondents at first agreed would be the inevitable result of allowing the appeal. It may be that mandamus can be granted without certiorari, but mandamus cannot be granted if there is a valid valuation list in being. It is not enough that the valuation officer should have prepared the list badly or even very badly. In such a case, he could not be ordered by mandamus to correct his mistakes or make a new list. In order for mandamus to lie, it must be established that he has prepared the list illegally or in bad faith, so that in effect he has not exercised his statutory function at all and that accordingly there is in reality no valid list in existence: *Reg.* v. *Cotham, etc JJ and Webb, Ex parte Williams* [1898] 1 Q.B. 802. Accordingly, it seems to me that a finding that the list is null and void is necessarily implicit in an order of mandamus.

Lord Denning MR invokes the void/voidable distinction as a management tool. By categorizing the new valuation list as marred only by an error within jurisdiction, and therefore voidable not void, he seeks to ensure that 'all chaos is avoided'. However, this approach is highly problematic for two related reasons. First, Lord Denning acknowledged in *Peachey* that (in contrast to *Head* (see above at 3.1.1)) there was no error of law on the face of the record; logically, therefore, there must either have been a jurisdictional error, which would have made the valuation list void, or no error at all, which would have precluded any judicial interference. Lord Denning's contention that the list was voidable in these circumstances was conceptually incoherent, and amounted to 'asking for the best of both worlds' as Wade (1967) 83 *LQR* 499 at 524 put it. Secondly, and of more general significance, the void/voidable distinction as a device by which to manage the consequences of unlawful administrative action would not be available today. If we accept the contemporary view that all unlawful administrative acts constitute jurisdictional errors in the broad sense, then all such acts must, as we saw above, be void. It is therefore simply not possible to obviate the 'domino effect' by categorizing unlawful acts as voidable.

The challenge, therefore, is to find a way of reconciling the modern principle that unlawful administrative action is void with the fact that administrators and individuals may well have relied upon such action. In other words, how is it possible to manage the effects of voidness so as to avoid the administrative chaos which the 'domino effect', unchecked, would wreak? In the following sections we consider two possible solutions to this problem.

3.3.3 Judicial Discretion

When it is established that administrative action is unlawful, remedies do not issue as of right, but rather at the court's discretion. Although relief is usually issued when the action in question is shown to be unlawful, it is possible for the court to refuse to issue a remedy. It follows that it would be possible for a court to acknowledge that certain administrative action was unlawful and void, but to refuse to quash it — and, by extension, subsequent action adopted on the basis of the original, void act — because to do so would cause administrative chaos. This provides the courts with a way of managing the effects of void-ness without actually denying the fundamental equation between unlawful action and void-ness. Craig, *Administrative Law* (Oxford 2003) at 698–704, believes that the careful exercise of discretion is the best way in which to deal with the effects of voidness, arguing that the transparency of this approach makes it preferable to Lord Denning's manipulation of the void/voidable distinction, which tends to conceal policy decisions behind a smokescreen of technical rhetoric. Lord Slynn, in *R* v. *Governor of Brockhill Prison, ex parte Evans (No 2)* [2001] 2 AC 19 at 26–27, also considered that 'there may be situations in which it would be desirable, and in no way unjust, that the effect of judicial rulings should be prospective or limited to certain claimants' to avoid 'unscrambling transactions perhaps long since over and doing injustice to defendants'.

However, Wade cautions against the use of judicial discretion in this way; his following remarks are applicable to any exercise of discretion in this context, irrespective of whether it is exercised openly, in the manner preferred by Craig, or covertly, by means of Lord Denning's (now outmoded) technique of manipulating the void/voidable distinction.

....

Wade, 'Unlawful Administrative Action: Void or Voidable? Part II' (1968) 84 LQR 95

. . . [D]iscretionary remedies are withheld only for recognised reasons and with the greatest cau-tion. No one would say that the trust is an insecure form of property because the only remedies are equitable and therefore discretionary. Nor would anyone say that, because *certiorari* and the declaration are discretionary remedies, the citizen cannot rely upon his long-established right to claim the protection of the court against unlawful governmental action. The principle of ultra vires has in reality never been discretionary in any substantial sense. The whole basis of civil liberty is that the acts of public authorities are white or black, lawful or unlawful, valid or void. A large area of grey, where no one could be sure of his rights, would be a dangerous innovation indeed.

. . . [I]t cannot be right for the court to confer validity, even temporarily [as in *Peachey*] on administrative action which *ex hypothesi* is unauthorised and invalid. It would be a cause for concern if the courts were to make a policy of doing this in order to save administrative inconveni-ence. For the administration can well look after its own convenience, and can obtain speedy assistance from Parliament if it creates more chaos than is tolerable. The indispensable task of the courts is to declare whether public authorities are acting lawfully or not, with complete detachment from questions of executive policy. [Lord Denning MR] himself has since said [in *Bradbury* v. *Enfield London Borough Council* [1967] 1 WLR 1311 at 1324]:

> If a local authority does not fulfil the requirements of the law, this court will see that it does fulfil them. It will not listen readily to suggestions of 'chaos' . . . Even if chaos should result, still the law must be obeyed.

. . . There is serious danger in making the *ultra vires* principle . . . discretionary. Administrative inconvenience should not be allowed to distort the law . . .

QUESTIONS

• Might Wade's concerns be met by the development of appropriate principles to guide the exercise of judicial discretion in this area?
• What principles might be appropriate, in your view?

The difficulty, of course, is that where judicial discretion is exercised so as to refuse relief, the individual concerned remains bound by the administrative act in question, even though he has demonstrated to the court that it is unlawful and void. It may seem unjust that the individual's interests are thereby subjugated to those of the wider public in order that chaos might be avoided, although an obvious way in which to alleviate the position of the individual would be through the provision of compensation — a theme upon which Lord Wilberforce expounded in his dissenting opinion in *Hoffmann-La Roche* (see above at 3.2.1).

3.3.4 The Theory of the Second Actor

Bearing in mind the criticism of the approach just described — and the fact that it may be unavailable in situations where administrative action is challenged collaterally (on which see 3.4 below) rather than directly — are there any other ways to tackle this problem?

In situations where only one administrative act is at stake, the answer would seem to be 'no': either the act is void, or it is not; and the court will either quash it, or not. In such circumstances, if the equation between voidness and quashing is to be dispensed with, then this can best be achieved by the discretionary withholding of relief. The fact that this is counterintuitive must simply be overlooked: it is the price of avoiding the undesirable consequences which would follow from quashing the void act. For example, if a trading licence is unlawfully granted, the licence is void; if the court wishes to avoid occasioning loss to the individual who has incurred expenses establishing his business on the assumption that the licence is valid, it must simply refuse to quash the void licence.

However, a more satisfactory approach has been proposed in situations concerning *series* of administrative acts, as opposed to *single* acts. Where we have such a series of acts, the central problem, as explained above, is that of the 'domino effect'. Logically, it seems that if the first act is void, all subsequent acts committed on the basis of the first act must also be void, and should therefore also fall. For instance, if regulations appear to authorize a Minister to grant licences, should all such licences be void if the regulations turn out to be void? If we adhere to the approach based upon the discretionary withholding of relief, the 'domino effect' can be avoided simply by refusing to quash any or all of the void acts (although, as noted above, such management of the 'domino effect' may be thwarted if collateral challenge, discussed below at 3.4, is available, in which case no relevant relief will be in question in relation to which discretion may be exercised). Thus the court might say that, although the regulations are unlawful, it will not quash any of the licences hitherto issued thereunder if to do so would cause chaos. On a conceptual level, however, this seems to make little sense: if the regulations are void, and do not therefore legally exist, how can the court confer *de facto* validity on licences issued thereunder? As Forsyth (in Forsyth and Hare (eds), *The Golden Metwand and the Crooked Cord* (Oxford 1998) at 144) puts it, the fundamental problem here is that 'unlawful acts which are undeniably non-existent *in law*' — such as the regulations in our example — 'do exist *in fact*. That factual existence may be perceived as legal existence; and individuals' — such as the Minister, in our example, granting licences under the void regulations — 'may understandably take decisions on that basis.'

Here, then, is the problem of the 'second actor' laid bare. Is it possible to articulate a framework within which a subsequent act may sometimes be recognized as lawful and *valid* — for example, where this is necessary to prevent the administrative chaos which would otherwise result from the unchecked 'domino effect' — without denying that the original act was *void*? Reverting to our example, might it be possible to regard licences issued before the regulations were found to be invalid as valid, while at the same time acknowledging that the regulations under which they were issued are void? The advantage of such an approach is that it would preserve theoretical orthodoxy by recognizing the voidness of the original unlawful act, while preventing its voidness from *automatically* setting in train the 'domino effect' under which all subsequent acts would fall. It is against this background that we turn to Forsyth's theory of the second actor (which was judicially approved by Lord Steyn in *Boddington* v. *British Transport Police* [1999] 2 AC 143 at 172).

....

Forsyth, ' "The Metaphysic of Nullity": Invalidity, Conceptual Reasoning and the Rule of Law'

in Forsyth and Hare (eds), *The Golden Metwand and the Crooked Cord* (Oxford 1998)

. . . The first step . . . is to investigate the ways in which undeniably void acts may have legal consequences. It is sometimes supposed that if an act is found to be void, then everything that flows from that act must also be void. The inconvenience and injustice that can readily flow from such attempted unscrambling of thoroughly scrambled eggs, is what drives some to believe that unlawful acts are not void.

But the law is not omnipotent; it cannot set everything right. Unlawful activity may (and does) have effects which cannot be rectified. Innocent third parties will have done all sorts of things that cannot be reversed or which it would be gravely unjust to reverse. For good or ill it is often impossible to return to the *status quo ante*. The law cannot wash away all signs of illegality.

Thus it is inevitable that there will be occasions on which an administrative act will be void, yet it will have legal consequences. Two important, though intimately linked, questions remain. What is the explanation for this state of affairs in terms of theory (rather than in terms of practical necessity) and how may it be determined, as a matter of law rather than judicial discretion, on what occasions void acts will have legal consequences?

The theoretical basis, it is submitted, is to be found in Hans Kelsen's Pure Theory of Law [see Kelsen (1934) 50 LQR 474]. This theory, it will be recalled, is built upon the distinction between the *Sein* (the Is) and the *Sollen* (the Ought), between the realm of things that are, ie facts or natural phenomena, and the realm of norms, including therein law. Now an administrative act, the writing of a decision letter in a planning appeal, say, is a fact. The piece of paper on which the letter is written coupled with the mental processes of the decision-maker that led up to it, are events from the realm of things that are, the *Sein*. But the meaning of that act — that certain development is permitted — is an element of the realm of norms, the *Sollen*.

Now a void act — say a decision letter written for an improper purpose — is not an act *in law* but it is and remains an act *in fact* — an event from the *Sein*. And events from the *Sein* often have an effect, directly or indirectly, in the realm of the *Sollen*. As Schiemann LJ said in *Percy* v. *Hall* [1996] 4 All ER 523 at 544, 'Manifestly in daily life the [*ultra vires* and void] enactment will have had an effect in the sense that people have regulated their conduct in light of it.' Where that conduct has legal consequences, that is, effects in the realm of the *Sollen*, those consequences flow from the legally non-existent unlawful act.

Put more precisely, the factual existence of a void act may serve as the basis for other decisions. For instance, an invalid administrative act (particular *seins* phenomenon) may, notwithstanding its non-existence in the *Sollen*, serve as the basis for another perfectly valid decision. Its factual existence, rather than its invalidity, is the cause of the subsequent act, but that act is valid since the legal existence of the first act is not a precondition for the second . . .

. . . [H]owever, [in other situations] it may be that the legal powers of the second actor depend upon the validity of the first act . . . In such cases the invalidity of the first act does involve the unravelling of later acts which rely on the first act's validity. However, the voidness of the first act does not determine whether the second act is valid. That depends upon the legal powers of the later actor. If the validity of the first act is a jurisdictional requirement for the valid exercise of the second actor's powers, then, if the first act is invalid, so is the second. Sometimes it will not be . . . and sometimes it will be . . .

The focus must thus — and this is the crucial conclusion — fall upon the second actor's legal powers . . .

Two contrasting cases are advanced by Forsyth to illustrate his argument. Both concern prosecutions (the second acts) to which earlier administrative acts (the first acts) were relevant. In the first case, *R v. Wicks* [1998] AC 92, a planning authority issued an enforcement notice, alleging that the defendant had breached planning control and requiring him to remove those parts of the building in question which exceeded a given height. The central question was whether prosecution could occur even if the enforcement notice was void. In considering this matter, Lord Hoffmann, at 117, said:

The question must depend entirely upon the construction of the statute under which the prosecution is brought. The statute may require the prosecution to prove that the act [ie the enforcement notice in this case] in question is not open to challenge on any ground available in public law . . . On the other hand, the statute may upon its true construction merely require an act which appears formally valid . . . In such a case, nothing but the formal validity of the act will be relevant . . .

Their Lordships concluded that all that was required in this case was an enforcement notice which *appeared to be valid* — that is, a notice which, on its face, complied with the requirements of the legislation under which it was issued; it would not matter if the notice was *actually void*. The second act — prosecution — could therefore take place even though the first act — the notice — was void. According to the second actor theory, this conclusion is possible because the validity of the second act depends not upon the validity or otherwise of the first, but upon the way in which we construe the second power. Here, the condition precedent to the valid exercise of the second power was something falling short of the actual validity of the first act.

Wicks may be contrasted with *Director of Public Prosecutions* v. *Head* [1959] AC 83 (see above at 3.1.1), in which the criminal liability of the defendant depended upon the validity of the order institutionalizing the alleged victim. The fact that the order was void meant that the defendant could not be successfully prosecuted for the offence. Here, then, is a situation where the second act can validly occur only if the first act is also legally valid. Once again, the crucial matter is the construction of the second power: the reason for the different outcomes in *Wicks* and *Head* is that the second power in the former case arose irrespective of the actual validity of the first act, whereas in the second case the second power arose only if the first act was actually valid.

Two points should be noted about the second actor theory. First, it elegantly reconciles the voidness of unlawful administrative action with the fact that other actors will rely upon it, thereby imbuing it with a practical effect. By focussing on the powers of the second actor, the theory confers validity upon some subsequent acts — and thereby allows the 'domino effect' to be avoided — while at the same time acknowledging the invalidity of the first act. The second actor theory is therefore helpful to the extent that it preserves theoretical orthodoxy — according to which unlawful acts must be void — while providing for the management of the consequences of voidness.

Secondly, however, it is necessary to consider how the theory works in practice. In advancing the theory, Forsyth (*op cit* at 145–146) argues that an approach based on 'conceptual reasoning' is better than one based on discretion (see above at 3.3.3), because it is preferable that the status of administrative action can be determined — and therefore predicted — by the application of fixed rules. To this end, the second actor theory lays down a clear rule which says that the validity of subsequent acts is to be determined not by the exercise of judicial discretion, but by reference to the legal definition of the second actor's powers. But how are we to decide whether or not the second actor's powers are dependent upon a valid first act? If our analysis of subsequent actors' powers is based largely upon practical considerations, such as the amount of chaos which would result if their actions had to be undone, then it might be argued that this approach is, in reality, highly discretionary: our *legal* conclusion as to whether the second actor can act irrespective of the status of the first act is simply a tissue of pseudo-conceptualism behind which lurks what is in reality a *pragmatic* conclusion about the desirability of allowing the 'domino effect' to proceed unchecked. Consider, for instance, *Percy* v. *Hall* [1997] QB 924, in which the Court of Appeal balked at the idea of holding that police constables could be liable for wrongful arrest in respect of arrests for breaches of byelaws which turned out to be *ultra vires*. Although (implicitly) consistent with the second actor theory, the conclusion reached in Simon Brown LJ's leading judgment that constables' powers of arrest should arise independently of the validity of byelaws was certainly informed by policy considerations. A similar approach is evident in Schiemann LJ's judgment at 951–952:

The policy questions which the law must address in this type of case are whether any and if so what remedy should be given to whom against whom in cases where persons have acted in reliance on what appears to be valid legislation. To approach these questions by rigidly applying to all circumstances a doctrine that the enactment which has been declared invalid was "incapable of ever having had any legal effect upon the rights or duties of the parties" seems to me, with all respect to the strong stream of authority in our law to that effect, needlessly to restrict the possible answers which policy might require.

It appears, however, that a principled approach is emerging in this context. For instance, in concluding that prosecution was possible irrespective of the actual validity of the enforcement notice in *R* v. *Wicks* [1998] AC 92, Lord Hoffmann undertook a detailed analysis of the legislative policy and history, concluding that factors thereby established, such as the need for expediency in the planning context, militated against allowing defendants in criminal proceedings to raise questions about the validity of the notices with whose breach they are charged.

The decision of *R* v. *Central London County Court, ex parte London* [1999] QB 1260 also points towards the adoption of a principled approach. An interim court order was made, the effect of which was to permit an approved social worker to make an application to hospital managers for the compulsory treatment, under s 3 of the Mental Health Act 1983, of the claimant. Such an application was duly made; the hospital managers approved it, and the claimant was subjected to compulsory treatment. The claimant challenged the legality of that treatment by attacking (on grounds which are presently unimportant) the original court order. Although Stuart-Smith LJ, with whom Robert Walker and Henry LJJ agreed, concluded that the order was valid, he went on to consider what the position would be if he were wrong on that point. If the order was void, would that automatically render the compulsory treatment unlawful, too? Stuart-Smith LJ answered this question in the negative, offering two reasons for his conclusion that the powers of the second actors — the hospital managers — arose irrespective of whether the order was legally valid. First, his Lordship relied (at 1273–1274) upon the general principle, laid down by Romer LJ in *Hadkinson* v. *Hadkinson* [1952] P 285 at 288 and approved by Lord Diplock in *Isaacs* v. *Robertson* [1985] AC 97 at 101, that, 'It is the plain and unqualified obligation of every person against, or in respect of whom, an order is made by a court of competent jurisdiction, to obey it unless and until that order is discharged.' Secondly, and more specifically, Stuart-Smith LJ placed weight upon s 6 of the Mental Health Act 1983, the gist of which is that the *existence* of an application is sufficient to justify detention under (*inter alia*) s 3, and that hospital managers are under no obligation to look behind the application (*eg* at the validity of the court order upon which the applicant's authority to make the application is founded). In light of these factors, Stuart-Smith LJ concluded that the hospital managers' powers could validly be exercised even if the first act — the court order — was invalid as a matter of law.

It follows from cases like *Wicks* and *London* that there *are* criteria which can be deployed in a principled fashion in order to assist in the construction of the second actor's powers, and that judicial decision-making in this area does not necessarily reduce to the exercise of discretion. Judges may be guided by the language of the statutory scheme, its history and policy, and by more general principles. Of course, this is not to say that discretion will not — or should not — play some role in this context. It is not improper for judges, as they seek to work out in what circumstances the second actor's powers do and do not arise, to take into account the consequences which would ensue if they concluded that those powers could be exercised only on the basis of a valid first act. Such considerations necessarily form part of the backdrop against which the legislation conferring power upon the second actor falls to be construed.

QUESTIONS

- Do you agree that the second actor theory is capable of principled application?
- What other principles may be used in order to inform our analysis of the circumstances in which the second actor's powers arise?

3.3.5 Partial Invalidity

Before leaving the subject of invalidity, it should be noted that it does not necessarily follow that because part of an administrative act is invalid, the whole is invalid. This issue typically arises in relation to delegated legislation (see generally ch 17 below), in which context the following principles were laid down by Lord Bridge in *Director of Public Prosecutions* v. *Hutchinson* [1990] 2 AC 783 at 804–811:

Taking the simplest case of a single legislative instrument containing a number of separate clauses of which one exceeds the law-maker's power, if the remaining clauses enact free-standing provisions which were intended to operate and are capable of operating independently of the offending clause, there is no reason why those clauses should not be upheld and enforced. The law-maker has validly exercised his power by making the valid clauses. The invalid clause may be disregarded as unrelated to, and having no effect upon, the operation of the valid clauses, which accordingly may be allowed to take effect without the necessity of any modification or adaptation by the court. What is involved is in truth a double test. I shall refer to the two aspects of the test as textual severability and substantial severability. A legislative instrument is textually severable if a clause, a sentence, a phrase or a single word may be disregarded, as exceeding the law-maker's power, and what remains of the text is still grammatical and coherent. A legislative instrument is substantially severable if the substance of what remains after severance is essentially unchanged in its legislative purpose, operation and effect . . .

   The test of textual severability has the great merit of simplicity and certainty. When it is satisfied the court can readily see whether the omission from the legislative text of so much as exceeds the law-maker's power leaves in place a valid text which is capable of operating and was evidently intended to operate independently of the invalid text. But I have reached the conclusion, though not without hesitation, that a rigid insistence that the test of textual severability must always be satisfied if a provision is to be upheld and enforced as partially valid will in some cases . . . have the unreasonable consequence of defeating subordinate legislation of which the substantial purpose and effect was clearly within the law-maker's power when, by some oversight or misapprehension of the scope of that power, the text, as written, had a range of application which exceeds that scope. It is important, however, that in all cases an appropriate test of substantial severability should be applied. When textual severance is possible, the test of substantial severability will be satisfied when the valid text is unaffected by, and independent of, the invalid. The law which the court may then uphold and enforce is the very law which the legislator has enacted, not a different law. But when the court must modify the text in order to achieve severance, this can only be done when the court is satisfied that it is effecting no change in the substantial purpose and effect of the impugned provision.

3.4 Collateral Challenge

3.4.1 Voidness and Collateral Challenge

The legality of administrative decisions and acts (including subordinate legislation) is often challenged directly, by means of judicial review. However, such questions of legality may also arise in other circumstances. For instance, the tenant of a council house who is sued in civil proceedings for failing to pay the rent which the council says he owes may wish to argue that the resolutions which the council adopted in order to raise his rent were *ultra vires* (see *Wandsworth London Borough Council* v. *Winder* [1985] AC 461, below at 14.3.4). Or a passenger who is prosecuted for smoking on a train may want to assert in his defence that the administrative measures purporting to prohibit smoking are *ultra vires* (as in *Boddington* v. *British Transport Police* [1999] 2 AC 143). When they make these arguments, the tenant and the passenger are mounting *collateral challenges* to the relevant administrative acts: rather than attacking those acts *directly* via judicial review proceedings, they are questioning them *indirectly*, or collaterally, in civil or criminal proceedings.

If we think further about how collateral challenge works, we will see why it is intimately connected with the idea that unlawful administrative action is void, not merely voidable. Let us take as an example the *Boddington* case, the facts of which are set out above at 3.1.2. The defendant's argument was that he could not have committed a criminal offence by falling foul of Network South Central's complete smoking ban because the train operator did not actually have the legal power necessary to institute such a ban. This reduces to the argument that the offence with which he was charged was *ultra vires*. It is obvious that the legality of the offence could be challenged by means of judicial review proceedings, and quashed if the reviewing court had found the offence to be *ultra vires*.

However, the defendant in *Boddington* — for reasons largely of convenience, as discussed at 3.4.2 — elected not to institute such proceedings. Instead, he questioned the lawfulness of the offence collaterally, raising it in his defence in the criminal proceedings which were brought against him in a magistrates' court. If unlawful administrative action is merely voidable, it remains fully valid unless and until it is set aside by a court of competent jurisdiction; however, since the magistrates' court had no power to issue a quashing order, it would have been forced to treat the allegedly unlawful administrative action or subordinate legislation as valid unless a quashing order had been issued by the Administrative Court. The legality of administrative action would therefore be open to challenge *only* directly, by means of judicial review proceedings; collateral challenge would be impossible.

The picture changes radically, however, once we acknowledge that unlawful administrative acts are void, not merely voidable. In this scenario, the availability of a quashing order is not decisive. If, as in *Boddington*, the legality of administrative action or subordinate legislation is raised collaterally, it does not matter that the court concerned has no power to issue a quashing order. In strict logic, unlawful action does not need to be quashed: it is void *ab initio*, and therefore never existed. The court's conclusion that the act in question is unlawful and void is therefore enough to dispose of the matter. Thus, in a *Boddington*-type situation, it would be open to the magistrates' court to conclude that the offence was *ultra vires* and void: non-existent and incapable of being committed. The theory of voidness and the availability of collateral challenge therefore go hand in hand.

We should, at this point, enter a caveat. It should not be inferred from the foregoing paragraph that quashing orders are redundant now that all unlawful administrative action is regarded as void. This proposition might be true in a strictly *logical* sense, but there are many *practical* reasons (considered at 13.5.1 below) why an individual may choose to seek a quashing order, rather than waiting to be prosecuted or sued and then pressing the logic of voidness through the medium of collateral challenge.

3.4.2 The Importance of Collateral Challenge

Why is the availability of collateral challenge important? Why not require anyone who wishes to challenge executive action and subordinate legislation to do so in the Administrative Court (which, presumably, is able to bring far greater expertise than, say, magistrates' courts, to such questions)? A number of reasons, based upon both the rule of law and more practical considerations, make it imperative that administrative action can be challenged collaterally. They are set out in the following extract, in which Lord Steyn takes issue with earlier decisions which sought to restrict the availability of collateral challenge.

....

Boddington v. *British Transport Police* [1999] 2 AC 143
House of Lords

For the facts, see above at 3.1.2.

Lord Steyn

. . . It is a truth generally acknowledged among lawyers that the complexity of a civil or criminal case does not depend on the level of the hierarchy of courts where it is heard. On a given day a bench of magistrates may have to decide a more difficult case than an appeal being heard by the Appellate Committee of the House of Lords . . . But in the last 10 years, in the wake of the expansion of judicial review and the resultant increase in the power of the Divisional Court, the idea has gained ascendancy that it is not part of the jurisdiction of a criminal court to determine issues regarding the validity of byelaws or administrative decisions even if the resolution of such issues could be determinative of the guilt or innocence of a defendant. Such a view was put forward by the Divisional Court in *Quietlynn* v. *Plymouth City Council* [1988] Q.B. 114 but that decision is explicable on the basis of the policy of the statute in question. In *Reg.* v. *Reading Crown Court, Ex parte Hutchinson* [1988] Q.B. 384 a differently constituted Divisional Court doubted the correctness of some of the general observations in the *Quietlynn* case. The leading decision suggestive of such a restriction on the jurisdiction of magistrates, and indeed of all criminal courts, is *Bugg* v. *Director of Public Prosecutions* [1993] Q.B. 473. In that case Woolf L.J., giving the judgment of the Divisional Court, distinguished in the context of byelaws between substantive and procedural validity and he held that while a criminal court may decide an issue as to substantive validity a question as to procedural validity is beyond its power. The decision of the Divisional Court [1997] C.O.D. 3 in the present case went significantly further. Auld L.J., sitting with Ebsworth J. and giving the reserved judgment of the Divisional Court, held that any issue of the validity of a byelaw or administrative action is beyond the jurisdiction of criminal courts . . .

The reasons [given in *Bugg* by] Woolf L.J. [for restricting collateral challenge] can be grouped under two headings. First, there are his pragmatic reasons for thinking that a criminal court is not equipped to deal with the relevant issues. Woolf L.J. said that in cases of substantive invalidity of byelaws no evidence is required whereas in cases of procedural invalidity evidence is required. The fact that evidence is required, he said, may lead to different outcomes in different courts. He said that in cases of procedural invalidity the party interested in upholding a byelaw may well not be a party to the proceedings. Secondly, Woolf L.J. relied on the developments which have taken place in judicial review over the last 25 years. The principal ground of his reasoning was that, except in "flagrant" and "outrageous" cases, a byelaw remains effective until quashed . . .

The pragmatic reasons given by Woolf L.J. need to be put in context. As Lord Hoffmann observed in *Reg.* v. *Wicks* [1998] A.C. 92, 116: "the distinction between substantive and procedural invalidity appears to cut across the distinction between grounds of invalidity which require no extrinsic evidence and those which do." An issue of substantive invalidity may involve daunting issues of fact, *eg* an issue as to unequal treatment of citizens in a pluralistic society or other forms of unreasonableness. In such a case the issues of law may also be complex. In contrast an issue of procedural invalidity of a byelaw may involve minimal evidence, e.g. simply the negative fact that an express duty to consult was breached. And the question of law may be straightforward. This aspect of the pragmatic case is not persuasive. It is true, as Woolf L.J. said, that on the evidence presented to them different magistrates' courts may come to different conclusions. But this factor proves too much: it applies equally to substantive validity. In any event, although a criminal court cannot quash byelaws the Divisional Court can on appeal on a case stated from a decision of magistrates give a ruling which will in practice be followed by other magistrates' courts. Woolf L.J. added that the party with an interest in upholding the byelaws may not be before the court. But that is also true of cases of substantive invalidity. Moreover, in a criminal case the prosecution, backed by the resources of the state, will usually put forward the case for upholding the byelaws. I therefore regard the pragmatic case in favour of a rule that magistrates may not decide issues of procedural validity, even if the distinction can be satisfactorily drawn, as questionable.

There is also a formidable difficulty of categorisation created by *Bugg's* case [1993] Q.B. 473. A distinction between substantive and procedural invalidity will often be impossible or difficult to draw. Woolf L.J. recognised that there may be cases in a grey area, e.g. cases of bad faith: p 500F. I fear that in reality the grey area covers a far greater terrain. In *Associated Provincial Picture Houses Ltd* v. *Wednesbury Corporation* [1948] 1 K.B. 223, 229, Lord Greene MR pointed out that different grounds of review 'run into one another.' A modern commentator has demonstrated the correctness of the proposition that grounds of judicial review have blurred edges and tend to overlap with comprehensive reference to leading cases: see *Fordham, Judicial Review Handbook*, 2nd ed, pp. 514–521. Thus the taking into account by a decision maker of extraneous considerations is variously treated as substantive or procedural. Moreover, even Woolf L.J.['s] categorisation of procedural invalidity is controversial. Wade and Forsyth rightly point out that contrary to normal terminology Woolf L.J. treated procedural invalidity as being not a matter of excess or abuse of power: Wade and Forsyth, *Administrative Law*, 7th ed., p. 323. Categorisation is an indispensable tool in the search for rationality and coherence in law. But the process of categorisation in accordance with *Bugg's* case which serves to carve out of the jurisdiction of criminal courts the power to decide on some issues pertinent to the guilt of a defendant, leads to a labyrinth of paths. It is nevertheless an inevitable consequence of *Bugg's* case that magistrates may have to rule on the satellite issue whether a particular challenge is substantive or procedural. That may involve hearing wide-ranging arguments. Even then there may be no clear cut answer. This is a factor militating against the pragmatic case on which Woolf L.J. relied in *Bugg's* case.

The problems of categorisation pose not only practical difficulties. As Lord Nicholls of Birkenhead explained in *Reg.* v. *Wicks* [1998] A.C. 92 they expose a fundamental problem. About the [distinction proposed] in *Bugg's* case [1993] Q.B. 473, 500, he said, at p 108:

> "On this reasoning there is not only a boundary between the two different types of invalidity. There is also an imperative need for the boundary line to be fixed and crystal clear. There can be no room for an ambiguous grey area. On this reasoning the boundary is not merely concerned with identifying the proceedings in which, as a matter of procedure, the unlawfulness issue can best be raised. Rather, the boundary can represent the difference between committing a criminal offence and not committing a criminal offence. According to this reasoning, a decision on invalidity has sharply different consequences, so far as criminality is concerned, in the two types of case. Setting aside an impugned order for procedural invalidity, as distinct from substantive invalidity, has no effect on the criminality of earliest conduct. Despite a court decision that the order was not lawfully made, the defendant is still guilty of an offence, by reason of his prior conduct. Further, it would seem to follow that in the case of procedural invalidity, the defendant could be convicted even after the order is set aside as having been made unlawfully, so long as the non-compliance occurred before the order was set aside. In cases of substantive invalidity the citizen can take the risk and disobey the order. If he does so, and the order is later held to be invalid, he will be innocent of any offence. In case of procedural invalidity, the citizen is not permitted to take this risk, however clear the irregularity may be."

I regard this reasoning as unanswerable. The rule of law requires a clear distinction to be made between what is lawful and what is unlawful. The distinction put forward in *Bugg's* case undermines this axiom of constitutional principle . . .

[Lord Steyn then turned to Woolf LJ's principled justification for restricting collateral challenge. In doing so, his Lordship expressed the views set out in the excerpt from this case above at 3.1.2, and continued:] [T]he decision in *Bugg's* case . . . contemplates that, despite the invalidity of a byelaw and the fact that consistently with *Reg.* v. *Wicks* such invalidity may in a given case afford a defence to a charge, a magistrate court may not rule on the defence. Instead the magistrates may convict a defendant under the byelaw and punish him. That is an unacceptable consequence in a democracy based on the rule of law. It is true that *Bugg's* case allows the defendant to challenge the byelaw in judicial review proceedings. The defendant may, however, be out of time before he becomes aware of the existence of the byelaw. He may lack the resources to defend his interests in two courts. He may not be able to obtain legal aid for an application for leave to apply for judicial review. Leave to apply for judicial review may be refused. At a substantive hearing his scope for demanding examination of witnesses in the Divisional Court may be restricted. He may be denied a remedy on a discretionary basis. The possibility of judicial review will, therefore, in no way compensate him for the loss of *the right* to defend himself by a defensive challenge to the byelaw in cases where the invalidity of the byelaw might afford him with a defence to the charge. My Lords, with the utmost deference to eminent judges sitting in the Divisional Court I have to say the consequences of *Bugg's* case are too austere and indeed too authoritarian to be compatible with the traditions of the common law. In *Eshugbayi Eleko* v. *Government of Nigeria* [1931] A.C. 662, a habeas corpus case, Lord Atkin observed, at p. 670, that 'no member of the executive can interfere with the liberty or property of a British subject except on condition that he can support the legality of his action before a court of justice.' There is no reason why a defendant in a criminal trial should be in a worse position. And that seems to me to reflect the true spirit of the common law . . .

Lords Irvine LC, Browne-Wilkinson, Slynn, and Hoffmann were in agreement that it was open to the defendant to challenge collaterally the smoking ban under which he was charged; however, their Lordships were also unanimous that it lay within the train operating company's powers to adopt such a ban. The defendant's appeal against conviction was therefore dismissed.

Lord Steyn's argument can be resolved into three component elements. First, he considered that it would be unworkable to try to restrict collateral challenge, along the lines suggested by Woolf LJ in *Bugg*, by attempting to distinguish between procedural and substantive errors. Secondly, it would be wrong in principle to restrict collateral challenge: in the criminal context, such restriction would permit defendants to be convicted of offences which did not, in law, exist. And, thirdly, it was naïve, for the practical reasons advanced in the closing paragraph of the extract above, to suppose that the possibility of directly challenging administrative action by means of judicial review was an adequate substitute for collateral challenge.

3.4.3 The Limits of Collateral Challenge

In spite of the importance attached to collateral challenge in *Boddington*, that case did not vouchsafe its *universal* availability: while their Lordships cast off the restrictive approach adopted in earlier cases, they recognized that there will be circumstances in which administrative action cannot be challenged collaterally. However, as Lord Irvine LC explains in the following passage, this is a conclusion which the courts will reach only with reluctance.

Boddington v. *British Transport Police* [1999] 2 AC 143
House of Lords

For the facts, see above at 3.1.2.

Lord Irvine LC

. . . [I]n every case it will be necessary to examine the particular statutory context to determine whether a court hearing a criminal or civil case has jurisdiction to rule on a defence based upon arguments of invalidity of subordinate legislation or an administrative act under it. There are situations in which Parliament may legislate to preclude such challenges being made, in the interest, for example, of promoting certainty about the legitimacy of administrative acts on which the public may have to rely.

The recent decision of this House in *Reg.* v. *Wicks* [1998] A.C. 92 is an example of a particular context in which an administrative act triggering consequences for the purposes of the criminal law was held not to be capable of challenge in criminal proceedings, but only by other proceedings. The case concerned an enforcement notice issued by a local planning authority and served on the defendant under the then current version of section 87 of the Town and Country Planning Act 1971. The notice alleged a breach of planning control by the erection of a building and required its removal above a certain height. One month was allowed for compliance. The appellant appealed against the notice to the Secretary of State, under section 174 of the Town and Country Planning Act 1990, but the appeal was dismissed. The appellant still failed to comply with the notice and the local authority issued a summons alleging a breach of section 179(1) of the Act of 1990. In the criminal proceedings which ensued, the appellant sought to defend himself on the ground that the enforcement notice had been issued ultra vires, maintaining that the local planning authority had acted in bad faith and had been motivated by irrelevant considerations. The judge ruled that these contentions should have been made in proceedings for judicial review and that they could not be gone into in the criminal proceedings. The appellant then pleaded guilty and was convicted. This House upheld his conviction. Lord Hoffmann, in the leading speech, emphasised that the ability of a defendant to criminal proceedings to challenge the validity of an act done under statutory authority depended on the construction of the statute in question. This House held that the Town and Country Planning Act 1990 contained an elaborate code including provision for appeals against notices, and that on the proper construction of section 179(1) of the Act all that was required to be proved in the criminal proceedings was that the notice issued by the local planning authority was formally valid.

The decision of the Divisional Court in *Quietlynn Ltd* v. *Plymouth City Council* [1988] 1 Q.B. 114 is justified on similar grounds: see *Reg.* v. *Wicks* [1998] A.C. 92, 117–118, per Lord Hoffmann. There, a company was operating sex shops in Plymouth under transitional provisions which allowed them to do so until their application for a licence under the scheme introduced by the Local Government (Miscellaneous Provisions) Act 1982 had been "determined." The local authority refused the application. The company was then prosecuted for trading without a licence. It sought to allege that the local authority had failed to comply with certain procedural provisions and that its application had therefore not yet been determined within the meaning of the Act. The Divisional Court held as a matter of construction that the local authority's decision was a determination, whether or not it could be challenged by judicial review. In the particular statutory context, therefore, an act which might turn out for a different purpose to be a nullity (eg so as to require the local authority to hear the application again) was nevertheless a determination for the purpose of bringing the transitional period to an end.

However, in approaching the issue of statutory construction the courts proceed from a strong appreciation that ours is a country subject to the rule of law. This means that it is well recognised to be important for the maintenance of the rule of law and the preservation of liberty that individuals affected by legal measures promulgated by executive public bodies should have a fair opportunity to challenge these measures and to vindicate their rights in court proceedings. There is a strong presumption that Parliament will not legislate to prevent individuals from doing so: "It is a principle not by any means to be whittled down that the subject's recourse to Her Majesty's courts for the determination of his rights is not to be excluded except by clear words:" *Pyx Granite Co Ltd* v. *Ministry of Housing and Local Government* [1960] A.C. 260, 286, *per* Viscount Simonds; cited by Lord Fraser of Tullybelton in *Wandsworth London Borough Council* v. *Winder* [1969] A.C. 461, 510 . . .

The particular statutory schemes in question in *Reg.* v. *Wicks* [1998] A.C. 92 and in the *Quietlynn* case [1988] 1 Q.B. 114 did justify a construction which limited the rights of the defendant to call the legality of an administrative act into question. But in my judgment it was an important feature of both cases that they were concerned with administrative acts specifically directed at the defendants, where there had been clear and ample opportunity provided by the scheme of the relevant legislation for those defendants to challenge the legality of those acts, before being charged with an offence.

By contrast, where subordinate legislation (eg statutory instruments or byelaws) is promulgated which is of a general character in the sense that it is directed to the world at large, the first time an individual may be affected by that legislation is when he is charged with an offence under it: so also where a general provision is brought into effect by an administrative act, as in this case. A smoker might have made his first journey on the line on the same train as Mr. Boddington; have found that there was no carriage free of no smoking signs and have chosen to exercise what he believed to be his right to smoke on the train. Such an individual would have had no sensible opportunity to challenge the validity of the posting of the no smoking signs throughout the train until he was charged, as Mr. Boddington was, under byelaw 20. In my judgment in such a case the strong presumption must be that Parliament did not intend to deprive the smoker of an opportunity to defend himself in the criminal proceedings by asserting the alleged unlawfulness of the decision to post no smoking notices throughout the train. I can see nothing in section 67 of the Transport Act 1962 or the byelaws which could displace that presumption. It is clear from *Wandsworth London Borough Council* v. *Winder* [1985] A.C. 461 and *Reg.* v. *Wicks* [1998] A.C. 92, 116, *per* Lord Hoffmann that the development of a statutorily based procedure for judicial review proceedings does not of itself displace the presumption.

. . . Lord Nicholls of Birkenhead noted in *Reg.* v. *Wicks*, at pp. 106–107, that there may be cases where proceedings in the Divisional Court are more suitable and convenient for challenging a byelaw or administrative decision made under it than by way of defence in criminal proceedings in the magistrates' court or the Crown Court. Nonetheless Lord Nicholls held that "the proper starting point" must be a presumption that "an accused should be able to challenge, on any ground, the lawfulness of an order the breach of which constitutes his alleged criminal offence:" see p. 106. No doubt the factors listed by Lord Nicholls [*viz* the ability of the court in question to deal with the public law issues; the importance of preventing the avoidance of the procedural safeguards inherent in judicial review [see ch 15 below]; the fact that the public body whose decision is impugned may not be a party to criminal proceedings; the risk of inconsistent decisions in various criminal proceedings each dealing with the same administrative act] may, where the statutory context permits, be taken into account when construing any particular statute to determine Parliament's intention, but they will not usually be sufficient in themselves to support a construction of a statute which would preclude the right of a defendant to raise the legality of a byelaw or administrative action taken under it as a defence in other proceedings. This is because of the strength of the presumption against a construction which would prevent an individual being able to vindicate his rights in court proceedings in which he is involved. Nor do I think it right to belittle magistrates' courts: they sometimes have to decide very difficult legal questions and generally have the assistance of a legally qualified clerk to give them guidance on the law. For example when the Human

Rights Bill now before Parliament passes into law the magistrates' courts will have to determine difficult questions of law arising from the European Convention on Human Rights. In my judgment only the clear language of a statute could take away the right of a defendant in criminal proceedings to challenge the lawfulness of a byelaw or administrative decision where his prosecution is premised on its validity . . .

Lord Irvine LC's analysis and the decisions in *Quietlynn* and *Wicks* upon which he relies demonstrate that collateral challenge may be legally prohibited by express or implied legislative provision. Forsyth [1998] *PL* 364 at 368 notes that although this may seem contrary to the ethos of *Boddington*, which clearly regards collateral challenge positively, 'that principle is, like so much else, subject to the sovereignty of Parliament'.

QUESTION

• Can you think of any circumstances in which collateral challenge, although technically possible, would be pointless? For instance, could an individual unlawfully denied a trading licence and subsequently prosecuted for trading without a licence meaningfully raise in his defence the unlawfulness of the denial of his licence?

3.5 Concluding Remarks

The notion that unlawful administrative acts are void is axiomatic: it is fundamental, in a number of ways, both to our understanding and the functioning of administrative law. In the first place, it fits squarely with the (related) ideas, advanced in chs 1 and 2, that unlawful executive action is *ultra vires* the enabling legislation (and hence lacking legal foundation *ab initio*) and thus beyond the jurisdiction of the agency. Moreover, recognizing that unlawful acts are void, not merely voidable, is central to the courts' ability to review in the face of ouster clauses (on which see further below at 15.6) and to the availability of collateral challenge, both of which phenomena are crucial to the effective maintenance of the rule of law. Of course, the theory of voidness must be reconciled with practical concerns such as the presumption of validity, the fact that it may be impossible authoritatively to impugn unlawful acts, and what we dubbed the problem of the 'domino effect'. However, as we have attempted to show in this chapter, those concerns can be addressed without questioning the fundamental principle that unlawful administrative action is void.

FURTHER RESOURCES

Craig, 'Collateral Attack, Procedural Exclusivity and Judicial Review' (1998) 114 *LQR* 535

Forsyth and Hare (eds), *The Golden Metwand and the Crooked Cord* (Oxford 1998) at 141–160 (Forsyth)

Taggart (ed), *Judicial Review of Administrative Action in the 1980s* (Auckland 1986) at 70–102 (Taggart)

Wade, 'Unlawful Administrative Action: Void or Voidable? (Part I)' (1967) 83 *LQR* 499

Wade, 'Unlawful Administrative Action: Void or Voidable? (Part II)' (1968) 84 *LQR* 95

4 DISCRETIONARY POWER: AN INTRODUCTION

Much of this book is concerned with judicial oversight of discretionary decisions — in particular, with the principles of good administration with which those wielding discretionary power are usually required to comply. However, before examining those principles in later chapters, we begin with a set of logically prior issues concerning the nature of discretionary power and the fundamental role which it has come to occupy within our system of government.

4.1 What is Discretionary Power?

In the modern administrative state, discretionary power is omnipresent. It is wielded by government officials at local and national level; by representatives of government agencies and other public bodies, and in myriad other contexts. Put simply, 'discretionary power' refers to the authority of an official or agency to make decisions within given parameters. Those parameters are typically — although, as we shall see in ch 5, not inevitably — set by legislation, as interpreted by the courts. And the matters upon which such decisions are made are almost infinite: discretionary powers play a fundamental role in contexts as diverse as planning, immigration, education, and health — and in virtually every other aspect of our lives which are subject to any form of governmental regulation or interjection. In the following passage, Galligan explores exactly what we mean when we speak of 'discretionary power'.

. . . .

Galligan, *Discretionary Powers*
(Oxford 1986)

. . . A central sense of discretionary power may be put as follows: discretion, as a way of characterizing a type of power in respect of certain courses of action, is most at home in referring to powers delegated within a system of authority to an official or set of officials, where they have some significant scope for settling the reasons and standards according to which that power is to be exercised, and for applying them in the making of specific decisions. This process of settling the reasons and standards must be taken to include not just the more obvious cases of creating standards where none are given, but also individualizing and interpreting loose standards, and assessing the relative importance of conflicting standards. Central to this sense of discretion is the idea that within a defined area of power the official must reflect upon its purposes, and then settle upon the policies and strategies for achieving them. There may be discretion in identifying and interpreting purposes; there may also be discretion as to the policies, standards, and procedures to be followed in achieving these purposes. This then is the core idea of discretion in an analytical sense; around this core, however, there are a number of other features which are characteristically present to a greater or lesser extent. Firstly, discretion occurs in a context of standards, and although in the strongest cases of discretion these standards may offer little guidance, . . . there are usually some standards guiding, constraining, and influencing the way a discretionary decision is made. Secondly, discretionary powers may be thought of as subsystems of authority within which the official has some degree of freedom and autonomy in acting as he thinks best. This means that the official has to decide to some substantial degree what the policies and standards are to be, the strategies for achieving them, and their application in specific cases, subject to whatever guidance [he] may derive from the surrounding network of constraining principles. The degree of autonomy allowed to the official varies from one context to another. Similarly, the extent to which other officials respect that autonomy and regard the initial exercise of discretion as final, also varies, although in the clearest cases of discretion the degree of finality accorded is likely to be substantial. Thirdly, there is a characteristic of discretion which is especially pertinent in the administrative context. Here the idea is that the official should not simply formulate rules of decision-making and then apply them rigorously to situations as they arise, but must maintain a special relationship between the general standard and the particular case. This is not in any sense a necessary or immanent feature of discretion, since discretion may be granted precisely for the purpose of formulating binding rules. In the administrative law context, however, it is considered to be important that the discretionary authority does not simply legislate, but maintains an attitude of reflective interaction between the policy choices made and the special features of particular cases . . .

. . . [H]ow [do] courts reach the conclusion that powers are discretionary in the sense that the standards of decision-making are to be settled with relative finality by the empowered authority [?] Various considerations bear on this conclusion, but the principal criterion is likely to be . . . whether from the terms of the delegation together with the general background it is clear that the original authority is intended by the legislature or other delegating body to have substantial control over an area of power. Often this is a matter of implication from the form the delegation takes, and the terms in which it is expressed: where little guidance is provided by way of standards, the power is likely to be considered as approaching the discretionary end of the scale; but if the standards of decision-making are laid down with any particularity, it is likely that the courts will assume general control. However. . . this need not be conclusive. There are other factors which influence the courts' attitudes in these matters: the nature and constitutional position of the authority may be significant; it is noticeable, for example, that the attitude to lower judicial authorities is often different from the attitude shown to executive ministers and other authorities of a more clearly political kind. Also, the nature of the tasks being performed may encourage different attitudes; some matters clearly are seen as within the traditional concerns of courts, while others might be regarded as involving specialized skills, or to be by nature inherently policy-based or even political. The relative importance of these factors and their relationship to each other can be determined only in the context of a particular power . . .

The cases referred to in this book provide countless examples of discretionary powers, and it would serve no useful purpose to duplicate those examples at this point. Here, instead, is just one instance of a discretionary power:

....

Immigration Act 1971

3—(5) A person who is not a British citizen is liable to deportation from the United Kingdom—

(b) if the Secretary of State deems his deportation to be conducive to the public good . . .

On its face this provision may seem straightforward; but it actually bristles with issues and difficulties which are the bread and butter of administrative law. By reference to what criteria, for instance, may the Secretary of State make decisions of this type? Can he have a policy as to how his discretion is to be exercised? Must he only consider the position of the individual concerned, or can he take into account external factors such as the UK's relations with other states? If the Secretary of State indicates to an individual — or even to the general public — how he will make decisions under this power, can he be held to such an undertaking? Must he give the person concerned a fair hearing before coming to a decision? And where, ultimately, does the balance lie between the court and the administrator (in this case, the Secretary of State) — can the court, for instance, set aside a decision simply because it thinks the Secretary of State was wrong to consider that the deportation of the person concerned would be 'conducive to the public good'?

Issues of this nature arise in relation to nearly all discretionary powers. In the following chapters, we explore these issues by examining the general principles which the courts apply when they oversee the use of discretion, and by seeking to understand what the courts are attempting to achieve as they develop the law in this area. Because public bodies (and others) now wield so much discretionary power, it is particularly important to confront these issues. Before we begin to do so, however, it is worth addressing a logically prior question: *why* do we find so much discretion in our modern system of government?

4.2 Discretion and the Administrative State

Wade and Forsyth's textbook on *Administrative Law* (Oxford 2004) begins (at 3) with the following passage:

"Until August 1914," it has been said [by Taylor, *English History, 1914–1945* (Oxford 1965) at 1], "a sensible law-abiding Englishman could pass through life and hardly notice the existence of the state, beyond the post office and the policeman." This worthy person could not, however, claim to be a very observant citizen. For by 1914 there were already abundant signs of the profound change in the conception of government which was to mark the twentieth century. The state schoolteacher, the national insurance officer, the labour exchange, the sanitary and factory inspectors, with their necessary companion the tax collector, were among the outward and visible signs of this change.

The implications of these changes are drawn out further in the following excerpt.

Sedley, 'Governments, Constitutions, and Judges'
in Richardson and Genn (eds), *Administrative Law and Government Action*
(Oxford 1994)

. . . The end of the Second World War, accurately identified by [Lord] Diplock [in *Council of Civil Service Unions* v. *Minister for the Civil Service* [1985] AC 374] as a turning point, saw the capture of the commanding heights of government by a political interest which was regarded by its opponents as inimical to the freedom of private citizens to order their own affairs . . . [E]lectoral reform had placed the command of executive government within the reach of radicals. Long before the first, nervous Labour government had taken office a career civil service was in place, owing no further debt to political patronage and bearing values and standards which, in its own mind, stood above party and class. But it was constitutionally impossible to cut the executive free of ministerial hegemony, and after 1945 departments of state were required by ministers to carry through measures restricting the activities of private citizens in favour of social welfare and economic control. Many of these ministers had, however, held office in the wartime coalition and there was no precipitate judicial reaction, much less sabotage, directed against their measures. In administrative law the courts at first barely stirred from the sleep of two generations which had descended on the Victorian judicial activists as the [career] civil service settled into running the country and the empire with professionalism and aplomb.

It is therefore much less easy to see the judicial process as one of reaction to a particular government's policies than as a response to the growth of a corporate state in which the executive, far from exercising restraint, was itself heavily interested. In this sense the post-war growth of judicial review has mimicked its earlier, mid-Victorian development in response to the first great wave of regulatory governmental institutions . . .

Thus we see that the function of the state — and the extent to which it interacts with and impacts upon the individual — had already begun to change radically by the turn of the last century, and the pace of change increased markedly following the 1939–45 war. Subject only to the attempts of the Thatcher administration in the 1980s to return to a philosophy of 'smaller' government, this expansion of the governmental function continued steadily throughout the twentieth century, and shows no sign of abating today. This is important for our purposes because discretionary power is the inevitable concomitant of an intervention-ist state; such power is one of the principal instruments by which such intervention occurs. This follows because it is clearly impossible for Parliament to make legislative provision for each and every situation which may arise in the course of the ongoing implementation of policy. Thus, while legislation may set out the general policy and establish the central principles and criteria by reference to which the policy is to be operated, the existence of discretion becomes inevitable. Decisions must be taken on the ground in individual cases; Ministers, officials, agencies, and others must therefore have discretion. Thus it is that, as the role of the state has expanded almost exponentially during the last hundred or so years, so the use of discretionary power has also exploded. As Sedley points out above, judicial review has grown in parallel, in order that adequate safeguards are applied to the expanding powers of the state.

QUESTIONS

- Should we regard the growth of judicial review as an inevitable concomitant of the expansion of discretionary power?
- Can you think of other ways in which the use of such power might be regulated?

FURTHER RESOURCES

Galligan, *Discretionary Powers* (Oxford 1990)

5 THE SCOPE OF PUBLIC LAW PRINCIPLES

5.1 Introduction

In subsequent chapters, we address the specific content of the principles of good administration that condition the exercise of many discretionary powers. We begin, however, by considering the reach of those principles. It seems intuitively right that, for instance, in exercising his powers of deportation (see above at 4.1), the Home Secretary should be required to respect public law principles of good decision-making such as fairness and rationality, as well as the human rights of the individual. But how far should the public law principles of good administration extend? What of the power to declare war? Should courts be able to scrutinize the exercise of that power for compliance with the public law principles? And what about decisions made by non-governmental bodies, but which are of public significance? Should administrative law look beyond the state, as traditionally conceived? In determining the scope of the principles of public law, should we look to who holds the power, or to the nature of the power itself? Should privatizing an activity exempt it from the norms enforced via judicial review?

When we ask whether a given power is subject to judicial review, we in fact raise two questions. ('Judicial review' is used here simply to mean judicial scrutiny for compliance with the norms of public law. Whether that scrutiny must be by means of the special 'judicial review procedure' is a distinct question that we address below at 14.2.) First, is it *amenable* in principle to judicial review? Traditionally, judicial review was essentially confined to discretionary powers granted by statute, but we will see that a new orthodoxy has now emerged, opening a wider range of powers to review. Secondly, does the exercise of the power raise *justiciable* issues? The concept of justiciability requires courts to examine the subject-matter of the power and the issues raised by its exercise — and to determine, in light of such factors, the degree to which the matter is suitable for adjudication by a court.

5.2 Statutory Powers

It is *usually* taken for granted that discretionary powers conferred by legislation are subject to judicial review. However, for two reasons, this does not *automatically* follow. First, the exercise of some functions pursuant to statutory powers or duties may be regarded as insufficiently 'public' to attract judicial review (a position which, as we consider at 5.4 below, makes certain assumptions about the function of judicial review). So, for instance, an agency's decision to contract with one tenderer rather than another may not be susceptible to review (see *Mass Energy v. Birmingham City Council* [1994] Env LR 298) unless specific factors inject a sufficient 'public element' into the decision-making process (see *R (Beer) v. Hampshire Farmers' Markets Ltd* [2003] EWCA Civ 1056 [2004] 1 WLR 233, discussed below at 5.5, and *R (Agnello) v. Hounslow London Borough Council* [2003] EWHC 3112 (Admin)).

Secondly, questions of justiciability must be confronted. This requires close judicial evaluation of the nature and subject-matter of the power, and of the appropriateness of judicial scrutiny of its exercise. Judicial reasoning in this area is therefore heavily context-dependent. From this it follows that discretionary powers cannot, and should not, be placed into two watertight categories marked 'justiciable' and 'non-justiciable', where the former are subject to the full panoply of judicial review while the latter are wholly immune from it. These are questions of degree which do not invite clear-cut answers. There exists a spectrum of justiciability ranging from powers which are completely excluded from review to powers which are subject to particularly rigorous judicial scrutiny. Between these poles, varying forms and levels of review may be appropriate: for instance, close judicial oversight of the fairness of the decision-making process may be appropriate, whereas close scrutiny of the substance of the decision might not. We explore these issues in greater detail below, as part of our discussion of prerogative powers; however, for examples of the courts grappling with these questions of justiciability in the specific context of statutory powers, see the excerpts at 9.2.2 below from *Nottinghamshire County Council* v. *Secretary of State for the Environment* [1986] AC 240 and *R (Asif Javed)* v. *Secretary of State for the Home Department* [2001] EWCA Civ 789 [2002] QB 129.

QUESTION

- The following section looks, in more detail, at how the courts approach questions of justiciability. Before reading on, consider for yourself how such matters should be approached. What principles do you think the courts should apply when deciding whether an issue is suitable for adjudication?

5.3 Prerogative Powers

5.3.1 The Nature of Prerogative Power

Munro, *Studies in Constitutional Law* (London 1999) at 256, defines the prerogative as 'comprising those [legal] attributes belonging to the Crown which derive from common law, not statute, and which still survive'. Historically, the term 'prerogative' has usually been preceded by the epithet 'royal', but constitutional convention now dictates that the vast majority of prerogative powers are, in effect, exercised by government Ministers (see further Markesinis [1973] *CLJ* 287 at 287–292). Although some constitutionalists object to the existence of the prerogative, arguing that there is no place in a modern constitution for powers which have received no democratic seal of approval (see, *eg*, Institute of Public Policy Research, *The Constitution of the United Kingdom* (London 1991) and, for discussion, Syrett

[1998] *Denning Law Journal* 111), it is important to remember that those prerogatives which remain do so because Parliament has not abolished or curtailed them. The dominant view (classically expounded by Lord Atkinson in *Attorney-General* v. *De Keyser's Royal Hotel Ltd* [1920] AC 508 at 539–540) is that the prerogative is placed in abeyance whenever legislation overlaps with it. In *R* v. *Secretary of State for the Home Department, ex parte Northumbria Police Authority* [1989] QB 26 at 44, Croom-Johnson LJ acknowledged that 'the Crown cannot act under the prerogative if to do so would be incompatible with statute'. However, in concluding in that case that no such incompatibility arose, so that the relevant prerogative and legislation could co-exist, their Lordships were clearly influenced by the fact that the former was being used for the public good, rather than (as in *De Keyser*) to attempt to undercut statutory safeguards which are beneficial to the public.

5.3.2 The Amenability of the Prerogative to Judicial Review

Although the courts traditionally refused to examine the exercise of prerogative powers, they have long been willing to adjudicate upon one aspect of the prerogative. Sir Edward Coke famously remarked in the *Case of Proclamations* (1611) 2 Co Rep 74 at 76 that 'the King hath no prerogative, but that which the law of the land allows him'. However, while welcome, such scrutiny of the prerogative was undeniably modest. Once the power in question was acknowledged to exist, such limited review left considerable scope for unchecked misuse.

Such concerns influenced the courts in a series of cases in the 1960s and 1970s (on which see Markesinis [1973] *CLJ* 287 at 292–299) which evidenced growing judicial unease at the insulation of the prerogative from administrative law's increasingly exacting standards. For instance, in *Chandler* v. *Director of Public Prosecutions* [1964] AC 763 at 810, Lord Devlin suggested that courts should be able to 'intervene to correct excess or abuse' of prerogative power. More boldly, in *Laker Airways Ltd* v. *Department of Trade* [1977] QB 643 at 705, Lord Denning MR said, 'Seeing that the prerogative is a discretionary power to be exercised for the public good, it follows that its exercise can be examined by the courts just as any other discretionary power which is vested in the executive.' Lords Devlin and Denning were not expressing majority views in *Chandler* and *Laker*; in contrast, the reviewability of the prerogative lay at the heart of the reasoning in the following case.

R v. Criminal Injuries Compensation Board, ex parte Lain [1967] 2 QB 864
Divisional Court

The Criminal Injuries Compensation Board was established by the Home Secretary under prerogative powers. The Board's terms of reference provided for *ex gratia* payments of compensation to victims of crime and, in the event of fatalities, to spouses and dependents to whom the Fatal Accidents Acts 1846–1959 applied. The compensation payable was to be assessed by reference to the normal tort principles or, where relevant, the Fatal Accidents Acts criteria. The scheme provided that deductions should be made where other payments from public funds had already been made, and that applicants dissatisfied with the decision of a single member of the Board could seek a hearing before three other members. The claimant in this case — the widow of a police officer who was the victim of a fatal shooting by a suspect — objected to the deductions made by the single member who assessed her claim. She therefore sought a hearing before three members of the Board; however, at this hearing, it was decided that further deductions should be made which had the effect of reducing the compensation to nil. When the claimant sought judicial review, the Board contended that, since it was not a body established by statute, it was not amenable to review.

Lord Parker CJ

. . . I can see no reason either in principle or in authority why a board set up as this board was set up is not a body of persons amenable to the jurisdiction of this court. True it is not set up by statute but the fact that it is set up by executive government, ie under the prerogative, does not render its acts any the less lawful. Indeed, the writ of certiorari has issued not only to courts set up by statute but to courts whose authority is derived, inter alia, from the prerogative. Once the jurisdiction is extended, as it clearly has been, to tribunals as opposed to courts, there is no reason why the remedy by way of certiorari cannot be invoked to a body of persons set up under the prerogative. Moreover the board though set up under the prerogative and not by statute had in fact the recognition of Parliament in debate and Parliament provided the money to satisfy its awards . . .

The position as I see it is that the exact limits of the ancient remedy by way of certiorari have never been and ought not to be specifically defined. They have varied from time to time being extended to meet changing conditions. At one time the writ only went to an inferior court. Later its ambit was extended to statutory tribunals determining a lis inter partes. Later again it extended to cases where there was no lis in the strict sense of the word but where immediate or subsequent rights of a citizen were affected. The only constant limits throughout were that it was performing a public duty. Private or domestic tribunals have always been outside the scope of certiorari since their authority is derived solely from contract, that is, from the agreement of the parties concerned . . .

We have as it seems to me reached the position when the ambit of certiorari can be said to cover every case in which a body of persons of a public as opposed to a purely private or domestic character has to determine matters affecting subjects provided always that it has a duty to act judicially. Looked at in this way the board in my judgment comes fairly and squarely within the jurisdiction of this court. It is, as Mr. Bridge [counsel for the defendant] said, "a servant of the Crown charged by the Crown, by executive instruction, with the duty of distributing the bounty of the Crown." It is clearly, therefore, performing public duties . . .

Diplock LJ

. . . The jurisdiction of the High Court as successor of the Court of Queen's Bench to supervise the exercise of their jurisdiction by inferior tribunals has not in the past been dependent upon the source of the tribunal's authority to decide issues submitted to its determination, except where such authority is derived solely from agreement of parties to the determination. The latter case falls within the field of private contract and thus within the ordinary civil jurisdiction of the High Court supplemented where appropriate by its statutory jurisdiction under the Arbitration Acts. The earlier history of the writ of certiorari shows that it was issued to courts whose authority was derived from the prerogative, from Royal Charter, from franchise or custom as well as from Act of Parliament. Its recent history shows that as new kinds of tribunals have been created, orders of certiorari have been extended to them too and to all persons who under authority of the Government have exercised quasi-judicial functions. True, since the victory of Parliament in the constitutional struggles of the 17th century, authority has been, generally if not invariably, conferred upon new kinds of tribunals by or under Act of Parliament and there has been no recent occasion for the High Court to exercise supervisory jurisdiction over persons whose ultimate authority to decide matters is derived from any other source. But I see no reason for holding that the ancient jurisdiction of the Court of Queen's Bench has been narrowed merely because there has been no occasion to exercise it. If new tribunals are established by acts of government, the supervisory jurisdiction of the High

Court extends to them if they possess the essential characteristics upon which the subjection of inferior tribunals to the supervisory control of the High Court is based . . .

I see no reason in principle why the fact that no authority from Parliament is required by the executive government to entitle it to decide what shall be the form of the administrative process under which compensation for crimes of violence is paid, should exempt the board from the supervisory control by the High Court over that part of its functions which are judicial in character. No authority has been cited which in my view compels us to decline jurisdiction. Certainly, applicants have an interest in the proper performance by the board of its judicial functions. And, despite Mr. Bridge's reference to the bounty of the Crown with its nostalgic echoes of Maundy Thursday, so has the public, whose money the board distributes to the tune of nearly a million pounds a year . . .

Ashworth J concurred with Lord Parker CJ and Diplock LJ that the Board was amenable to judicial review. However, all three judges agreed that the Board had not acted improperly, and the quashing order sought by the claimant was therefore not issued.

The view clearly advanced in this case is that the manner of use of prerogative power should be amenable to judicial review, and that less importance should be attached to the *source* of the power in question than to the *nature* of the powers being exercised. (Whether the judges intended to go further — extending judicial review beyond even prerogative powers — is less clear, although, as we explain below, subsequent cases have read *Lain* broadly.) The House of Lords conferred its seal of approval on this new judicial attitude to the prerogative in the so-called *GCHQ* case.

. . . .

Council of Civil Service Unions v. *Minister for the Civil Service* [1985] AC 374
House of Lords

Article 4 of the Civil Service Order in Council 1982, promulgated under prerogative power, allowed the Minister for the Civil Service to make regulations concerning civil servants' employment conditions. The Minister issued an instruction under article 4 to the effect that staff at Government Communications Headquarters (GCHQ) would no longer be permitted to belong to national trade unions. Trade union membership had been permitted since GCHQ's establishment in 1947 and there was a well-established practice of consultation at GCHQ about all important alterations to conditions of employment; however, no such consultation occurred in the instant case. The Council of Civil Service Unions and six members of staff sought judicial review, alleging a breach of the duty to act fairly and breach of legitimate expectations (on this aspect of the case see below at 7.1.3). At first instance Glidewell J concluded that the instruction was unlawful, and issued a declaratory order to that effect. The Court of Appeal, however, allowed an appeal by the Minister. The claimants appealed to the House of Lords. One of the issues which their Lordships had to confront was whether the Minister's actions were amenable to review, given that the instruction was issued under powers conferred by prerogative.

Lord Diplock

. . . Judicial review . . . provides the means by which judicial control of administrative action is exercised. The subject matter of every judicial review is a decision made by some person (or body of persons) whom I will call the "decision-maker" or else a refusal by him to make a decision.

To qualify as a subject for judicial review the decision must have consequences which affect some person (or body of persons) other than the decision-maker, although it may affect him too. It must affect such other person either: (a) by altering rights or obligations of that person which are enforceable by or against him in private law; or (b) by depriving him of some benefit or advantage which either (i) he had in the past been permitted by the decision-maker to enjoy and which he can legitimately expect to be permitted to continue to do until there has been communicated to him some rational grounds for withdrawing it on which he has been given an opportunity to comment; or (ii) he has received assurance from the decision-maker will not be withdrawn without giving him first an opportunity of advancing reasons for contending that they should not be withdrawn . . .

For a decision to be susceptible to judicial review the decision-maker must be empowered by public law (and not merely, as in arbitration, by agreement between private parties) to make decisions that, if validly made, will lead to administrative action or abstention from action by an authority endowed by law with executive powers, which have one or other of the consequences mentioned in the preceding paragraph. The ultimate source of the decision-making power is nearly always nowadays a statute or subordinate legislation made under the statute; but in the absence of any statute regulating the subject matter of the decision the source of the decision-making power may still be the common law itself, *ie*, that part of the common law that is given by lawyers the label of "the prerogative." Where this is the source of decision-making power, the power is confined to executive officers of central as distinct from local government and in constitutional practice is generally exercised by those holding ministerial rank . . .

My Lords, I intend no discourtesy to counsel when I say that, intellectual interest apart, in answering the question of law raised in this appeal, I have derived little practical assistance from learned and esoteric analyses of the precise legal nature, boundaries and historical origin of "the prerogative," or of what powers exercisable by executive officers acting on behalf of central government that are not shared by private citizens qualify for inclusion under this particular label. It does not, for instance, seem to me to matter whether today the right of the executive government that happens to be in power to dismiss without notice any member of the home civil service upon which perforce it must rely for the administration of its policies, and the correlative disability of the executive government that is in power to agree with a civil servant that his service should be on terms that did not make him subject to instant dismissal, should be ascribed to "the prerogative" or merely to a consequence of the survival, for entirely different reasons, of a rule of constitutional law whose origin is to be found in the theory that those by whom the administration of the realm is carried on do so as personal servants of the monarch who can dismiss them at will, because the King can do no wrong.

Nevertheless, whatever label may be attached to them there have unquestionably survived into the present day a residue of miscellaneous fields of law in which the executive government retains decision-making powers that are not dependent upon any statutory authority but nevertheless have consequences on the private rights or legitimate expectations of other persons which would render the decision subject to judicial review if the power of the decision-maker to make them were statutory in origin. From matters so relatively minor as the grant of pardons to condemned criminals, of honours to the good and great, of corporate personality to deserving bodies of persons, and of bounty from moneys made available to the executive government by Parliament, they extend to matters so vital to the survival and welfare of the nation as the conduct of relations with foreign states and — what lies at the heart of the present case — the defence of the realm against potential enemies . . .

My Lords, I see no reason why simply because a decision-making power is derived from a common law and not a statutory source, it should *for that reason only* be immune from judicial review . . .

Lord Fraser

. . . I . . . assume, without deciding, that . . . all powers exercised directly under the prerogative are immune from challenge in the courts. [Lord Fraser made this assumption based upon his understanding of the authorities. However, since the present case concerned the exercise of a power conferred by prerogative, rather than a direct exercise of the prerogative, Lord Fraser had to consider whether such exercises of delegated prerogative power are amenable to review.]

The second proposition [that even delegated prerogative powers are immune from review] depends for its soundness upon whether the power conferred by article 4 of the Order in Council of 1982 on the Minister for the Civil Service of "providing for . . . the conditions of service" of the Civil Service is subject to an implied obligation to act fairly . . . There is no doubt that, if the Order in Council of 1982 had been made under the authority of a statute, the power delegated to the Minister by article 4 would have been construed as being subject to an obligation to act fairly. I am unable to see why the words conferring the same powers should be construed differently merely because their source was an Order in Council made under the prerogative. It is all the more difficult in the face of article 6(4) of the Order in Council of 1982 which provides that the Interpretation Act 1978 shall apply to the Order; it would of course apply to a statutory order. There seems no sensible reason why the words should not bear the same meaning whatever the source of authority for the legislation in which they are contained. The Order in Council of 1982 was described by Sir Robert Armstrong in his first affidavit as primary legislation; that is, in my opinion, a correct description, subject to the qualification that the Order in Council, being made under the prerogative, derives its authority from the sovereign alone and not, as is more commonly the case with legislation, from the sovereign in Parliament. Legislation frequently delegates power from the legislating authority — the sovereign alone in one case, the sovereign in Parliament in the other — to some other person or body and, when that is done, the delegated powers are defined more or less closely by the legislation, in this case by article 4. But whatever their source, powers which are defined, either by reference to their object or by reference to procedure for their exercise, or in some other way, and whether the definition is expressed or implied, are in my opinion normally subject to judicial control to ensure that they are not exceeded . . .

Lord Brightman, like Lord Fraser, left open the question whether direct exercises of the prerogative could be reviewed, while accepting the possibility of review of delegated prerogative powers. Lords Scarman and Roskill, like Lord Diplock, reached the broader conclusion that, in principle, preroga-tive powers generally are subject to review. All five of their Lordships, however, concluded that, bearing in mind the national security considerations in play, the Minister had not acted unlawfully.

It is clear from Lord Diplock's speech that judicial control of the prerogative was regarded as essential to the maintenance of the rule of law. Lord Roskill took a similar view, and was anxious that the courts' ability to protect individuals against abuse of power should not be curtailed by formal source-based considerations. Whether committed under statutory or prerogative authority, '[T]he act in question is the act of the executive,' said Lord Roskill (at 417). 'To talk of that act as the act of the sovereign savours of the archaism of past centuries.'

QUESTION

- How does Lord Fraser's approach to judicial review of delegated prerogative powers relate to the *ultra vires* doctrine's rationalization of review of powers conferred by legislation (on which see above at 1.4)?

5.3.3 From Form to Substance: Justiciability as the Limiting Factor

The *GCHQ* case heralded a new judicial attitude to prerogative powers, according to which the general principles of good administration, which have long applied to statutory powers, are also applicable to exercises of the prerogative. However, notwithstanding their recognition in *GCHQ* that the prerogative is in principle amenable to review, their Lordships opined that it is not possible to review the use of *all* prerogative powers. As Lord Scarman (*op cit* at 407) put it, 'the controlling factor in determining whether the exercise of prerogative power is subject to judicial review is not its source but its subject matter'.

Council of Civil Service Unions v. *Minister for the Civil Service* [1985] AC 374
House of Lords

For the facts, see above at 5.3.2. The following extracts relate to their Lordships' deliberations on the question of justiciability.

Lord Scarman

My Lords, I would dismiss this appeal for one reason only. I am satisfied that the respondent has made out a case on the ground of national security.

Notwithstanding the criticisms which can be made of the evidence and despite the fact that the point was not raised, or, if it was, was not clearly made before the case reached the Court of Appeal, I have no doubt that the respondent refused to consult the unions before issuing her instruction of the 22 December 1983 because she feared that, if she did, union-organised disruption of the monitoring services of GCHQ could well result. I am further satisfied that the fear was one which a reasonable Minister in the circumstances in which she found herself could reasonably entertain. I am also satisfied that a reasonable Minister could reasonably consider such disruption to constitute a threat to national security. I would, therefore, deny relief to the appellants upon their application for judicial review of the instruction, the effect of which was that staff at GCHQ would no longer be permitted to belong to a national trade union.

The point of principle in the appeal is as to the duty of the court when in proceedings properly brought before it a question arises as to what is required in the interest of national security. The question may arise in ordinary litigation between private persons as to their private rights and obligations: and it can arise, as in this case, in proceedings for judicial review of a decision by a public authority. The question can take one of several forms. It may be a question of fact which Parliament has left to the court to determine: see for an example section 10 of the Contempt of Court Act 1981. It may arise for consideration as a factor in the exercise of an executive discretionary power. But, however it arises, it is a matter to be considered by the court in the circumstances and context of the case. Though there are limits dictated by law and common sense which the court must observe in dealing with the question, the court does not abdicate its judicial function. If the question arises as a matter of fact, the court requires evidence to be given. If it arises as a factor to be considered in reviewing the exercise of a discretionary power, evidence is also needed so that the court may determine whether it should intervene to correct excess or abuse of the power.

Let me give three illustrations taken from the case law of the 20th century. First, *The Zamora* [1916] 2 A.C. 77 — surely one of the more courageous of judicial decisions even in our long history. In April 1916 a question of national security came before the Judicial Committee of the Privy Council sitting in Prize. The Crown's role in the Prize Court was that of a belligerent power having by international law the right to requisition vessels or goods in the custody of its Prize Court. A neutral vessel carrying a cargo of copper (contraband) had been stopped at sea by the Royal Navy and taken to a British port. No decree of condemnation of the cargo had yet been made by the Prize Court, when the Crown intervened by summons to requisition the cargo then in the custody of the court. Lord Parker of Waddington, who delivered the judgment of the Judicial Committee, concluded, at p. 106:

> "A belligerent power has by international law the right to requisition vessels or goods in the custody of its Prize Court pending a decision of the question whether they should be condemned

or released, but such right is subject to certain limitations. First, the vessel or goods in question must be urgently required for use in connection with the defence of the realm, the prosecution of the war, or other matters involving national security. Secondly, there must be a real question to be tried, so that it would be improper to order an immediate release. And, thirdly, the right must be enforced by application to the Prize Court, which must determine judicially whether, under the particular circumstances of the case, the right is exercisable."

Discussing the first limitation, Lord Parker of Waddington observed that the judge ought, "*as a rule,*" to treat the statement of the proper officer of the Crown that the vessel or goods were urgently required for national security reasons as conclusive of the fact, and it was in this context that he delivered his famous dictum, at p. 107: "Those who are responsible for the national security must be the sole judges of what the national security requires." These words were no abdication of the judicial function, but were an indication of the evidence required by the court. In fact the evidence adduced by the Crown was not sufficient, and the court ruled that the Crown had no right to requisition. The Crown's claim was rejected "because the judge had before him no satisfactory evidence that such a right was exercisable" (p. 108). The Prize Court, therefore, treated the question as one of fact for its determination and indicated the evidence needed to establish the fact. The true significance of Lord Parker's dictum is simply that the court is in no position to substitute its opinion for the opinion of those responsible for national security. But the case is a fine illustration of the court's duty to ensure that the essential facts to which the opinion or judgment of those responsible relates are proved to the satisfaction of the court.

My second illustration is *Chandler v. Director of Public Prosecutions* [1964] A.C. 763. In this case the interest of national security came into court as a matter of fact to be established by evidence to the satisfaction of a jury in a criminal case. The appellants were convicted of conspiring to commit a breach of section 1 of the Official Secrets Act 1911, "namely, for a purpose prejudicial to the safety or interests of the state to enter a Royal Air Force station . . . at Wethersfield." There was evidence from an officer of air rank that the airfield was of importance for national security: and, as my noble and learned friend Lord Fraser of Tullybelton has pointed out, Lord Reid and Viscount Radcliffe treated his evidence as relevant to the dismissal of the appeal. Lord Devlin developed the point taken in the case on national security in a passage beginning at p. 809 which, with all respect to those who take a different view, I believe to be sound law. Having referred to the undoubted principle that all matters relating to the disposition and armament of the armed forces are left to the unfettered control of the Crown, he made three comments. First, he put the *Zamora* dictum into its true context. Secondly, he observed that, when a court is faced with the exercise of a discretionary power, inquiry is not altogether excluded: the court will intervene to correct excess or abuse. His third and, as he said, his "most significant" comment was as to the nature and effect of the principle. 'Where it operates, it limits the issue which the court has to determine; it does not exclude any evidence or argument relevant to the issue' (p. 810).

As I read the speeches in *Chandler's* case, the House accepted that the statute required the prosecution to establish by evidence that the conspiracy was to enter a prohibited place for a purpose prejudicial to the safety or interests of the state. As Parliament had left the existence of a prejudicial purpose to the decision of a jury, it was not the Crown's opinion as to the existence of prejudice to the safety or interests of the state but the jury's which mattered: hence, as Lord Devlin, at p. 811, remarked, the Crown's opinion on that was inadmissible but the Crown's evidence as to its interests was an "entirely different matter." Here, like Lord Parker in the *Zamora*, Lord Devlin was accepting that the Crown, or its responsible servants, are the best judges of what national security requires without excluding the judicial function of determining whether the interest of national security has been shown to be involved in the case.

Finally, I would refer to *Secretary of State for Defence v. Guardian Newspapers Ltd.* [1985] A.C. 339, a case arising under section 10 of the Act of 1981. As in *Chandler's* case, the interest of national security had to be considered in proceedings where it arose as a question of fact to be established to the satisfaction of a court. Though the House was divided as to the effect of the evidence, all their Lordships held that evidence was necessary so that the court could be judicially satisfied that the interest of national security required disclosure of the newspaper's source of information.

My Lords, I conclude, therefore, that where a question as to the interest of national security arises in judicial proceedings the court has to act on evidence. In some cases a judge or jury is required by law to be satisfied that the interest is proved to exist: in others, the interest is a factor to be considered in the review of the exercise of an executive discretionary power. Once the factual basis is established by evidence so that the court is satisfied that the interest of national security is a relevant factor to be considered in the determination of the case, the court will accept the opinion of the Crown or its responsible officer as to what is required to meet it, unless it is possible to show that the opinion was one which no reasonable Minister advising the Crown could in the circumstances reasonably have held. There is no abdication of the judicial function, but there is a common sense limitation recognised by the judges as to what is justiciable: and the limitation is entirely consistent with the general development of the modern case law of judicial review . . .

Lord Roskill

. . . [Having concluded that, in principle, prerogative powers may be reviewed, his Lordship continued:] But I do not think that that right of challenge can be unqualified. It must, I think, depend upon the subject matter of the prerogative power which is exercised. Many examples were given during the argument of prerogative powers which as at present advised I do not think could properly be made the subject of judicial review. Prerogative powers such as those relating to the making of treaties, the defence of the realm, the prerogative of mercy, the grant of honours, the dissolution of Parliament and the appointment of ministers as well as others are not, I think susceptible to judicial review because their nature and subject matter are such as not to be amenable to the judicial process. The courts are not the place wherein to determine whether a treaty should be concluded or the armed forces disposed in a particular manner or Parliament dissolved on one date rather than another . . .

My Lords, the conflict between private rights and the rights of the state is not novel either in our political history or in our courts. Historically, at least since 1688, the courts have sought to present a barrier to inordinate claims by the executive. But they have also been obliged to recognise that in some fields that barrier must be lowered and that on occasions, albeit with reluctance, the courts must accept that the claims of executive power must take precedence over those of the individual. One such field is that of national security. The courts have long shown themselves sensitive to the assertion by the executive that considerations of national security must preclude judicial investigation of a particular individual grievance. But even in that field the courts will not act on a mere assertion that questions of national security were involved. Evidence is required that the decision under challenge was in fact founded on those grounds. That that principle exists is I think beyond doubt. In a famous passage in *The Zamora* [1916] 2 A.C. 77 at 107 Lord Parker of Waddington, delivering the opinion of the Judicial Committee, said:

> "Those who are responsible for the national security must be the sole judges of what the national security requires. It would be obviously undesirable that such matters should be made the subject of evidence in a court of law or otherwise discussed in public."

The Judicial Committee were there asserting what I have already sought to say, namely that some matters, of which national security is one, are not amenable to the judicial process . . .

All five of their Lordships concluded that judicial review would be inappropriate, given the national security implications of the Minister's decision. It was common ground that, in situations of this kind, the court must be shown evidence establishing that national security issues are at stake. Lord Roskill considered that, once this condition is satisfied, it is inappropriate for the court to scrutinize the way in which the executive makes the relevant decision. Cases of this type therefore involve only a limited form of judicial review, in which the court's principal task is to satisfy itself that national security is genuinely in issue, rather than to examine the quality of the decision-making process itself. For further discussion of this aspect of *GCHQ*, see Forsyth (1985) 36 *NILQ* 25.

QUESTION

- Are the courts right to exercise this degree of deference when faced with decisions which involve national security?

Although reticence concerning the appropriateness of judicial review is considerable in relation to national security (on which see further *Secretary of State for the Home Department* v. *Rehman* [2001] UKHL 47 [2003] 1 AC 153; cf *A* v. *Home Secretary* [2004] UKHL 56), courts in fact grapple with questions of justiciability in a wide range of situations: see, for example, *Nottinghamshire County Council* v. *Secretary of State for the Environment* [1986] AC 240 and *R* v. *Secretary of State for the Environment, ex parte Hammersmith and Fulham London Borough Council* [1991] 1 AC 521, concerning judicial review of decisions raising national economic policy considerations, and *R (Asif Javed)* v. *Secretary of State for the Home Department* [2001] EWCA Civ 789 [2002] QB 129, in the immigration context, all of which are considered at 9.2.2 below. As far the prerogative is concerned, Lord Roskill in *GCHQ* regarded a number of such powers — including those concerning the granting of mercy and of honours, and the making of treaties — to be non-justiciable. This approach is, however, open to question. At root, the doctrine of justiciability is one of judicial self-restraint in the face of matters which are unsuitable for adjudication in the courts. It is therefore meaningless to classify particular *powers* — prerogative or otherwise — as non-justiciable; rather, the question is whether the exercise of a given power raises *issues* upon which courts are unable (or at least limited in their ability) to adjudicate. And, although the use of certain powers — *eg* the prerogative of mercy — will raise *many* issues that are unsuitable for judicial review, it does not follow that *all* of the issues thereby raised will be non-justiciable. As Allan, *Constitutional Justice: A Liberal Theory of the Rule of Law* (Oxford 2001) at 177, puts it, 'It is quite mistaken to seek to identify a field of executive power whose nature makes it unsuited to judicial review: the correct approach is always to examine the requirements of equality and procedural fairness, as they apply in the context of the decision-making process in question.' (Logically, the same should be true of the other principles of judicial review, too.) A more discriminating approach, along the lines favoured by Allan, is evident in the next case (cf *R (Abbasi)* v. *Secretary of State for Foreign and Commonwealth Affairs* [2002] EWCA Civ 1598 [2003] UKHRR 76 at [99]–[106] and *R (Campaign for Nuclear Disarmament)* v. *Prime Minister* [2002] EWHC 2777 (QB)).

....

R v. *Secretary of State for the Home Department, ex parte Bentley*
[1994] QB 349
Divisional Court

In 1952 the claimant's brother, Derek Bentley, was convicted together with Christopher Craig of the murder of a police officer. At the time the offence was committed Craig, who fired the shot, was aged 16; Bentley, who incited Craig to shoot the officer, was 19. Craig was therefore ordered to be detained at Her Majesty's pleasure. The jury recommended that the death sentence should not be applied to Bentley, but the trial judge disagreed and the Home Secretary refused to reprieve Bentley; he was therefore hanged. For many years the claimant campaigned for a posthumous pardon for her brother; in 1992 the Home Secretary reviewed the case, but ultimately refused to grant a pardon.

The Home Secretary explained his decision in the following terms: 'I have concluded that nothing has emerged from my review of this case which establishes Derek Bentley's innocence and that I therefore have no grounds for recommending a free pardon . . . In my judgment most of the concern that has arisen about this case reflects strong feelings that Derek Bentley should not have been hanged. Personally I have always agreed with that concern but I cannot now simply substitute my judgment for that of the then Home Secretary, Sir David Maxwell Fyfe . . . It has been the long established policy of successive Home Secretaries that a free pardon in relation to a conviction for an indictable offence should be granted only if the moral as well as technical innocence of the convicted person can be established. I do not believe that is the case on either point in relation to Derek Bentley.' The claimant sought judicial review of the Home Secretary's decision on the ground, *inter alia*, that the Home Secretary had misdirected himself by failing to appreciate that options other than the grant of a free pardon were open to him.

Watkins LJ

. . . It is clear . . . that one, if not the main, of the contentions made on behalf of the applicant, is that the Home Secretary misdirected himself. Therefore, it is, we think, helpful to recite parts of the affidavit of Mr. Austin Peter Wilson, an Assistant Under-Secretary of State and head of the criminal policy department in the Home Office at the present time.

In it he draws on past Home Office files, records and memoranda, as well as well known standard works including Pollock and Maitland, *The History of English Law* (1968) and Stephen, *A History of the Criminal Law of England* (1883). Constitutionally, he states, the prerogative is exercised by the sovereign on the advice of the Home Secretary in one of three ways, namely: (a) the grant of a free, ie unconditional, pardon; (b) the grant of a conditional pardon, whereby the penalty is removed, on condition that a lesser sentence is served; and (c) the remission, or partial remission, of a penalty.

The exercise of mercy by the Crown appears to have become firmly established in the middle ages, with the infringement of the King's peace emerging as the basis for criminal liability. Since major felonies were invariably capital, and pleas to self-defence had not developed, judicial procedure produced inflexible and unsatisfactory results. Use of the prerogative relieved those results . . .

[Watkins LJ then turned to the question whether the prerogative of mercy is reviewable. He reviewed the relevant authorities and reached the following conclusion:] The powers of the court cannot be ousted merely by invoking the word "prerogative." The question is simply whether the nature and subject matter of the decision is amenable to the judicial process. Are the courts qualified to deal with the matter or does the decision involve such questions of policy that they should not intrude because they are ill-equipped to do so? Looked at in this way there must be cases in which the exercise of the Royal Prerogative is reviewable, in our judgment. If, for example, it was clear that the Home Secretary had refused to pardon someone solely on the grounds of their sex, race or religion, the courts would be expected to interfere and, in our judgment, would be entitled to do so.

We conclude therefore that some aspects of the exercise of the Royal Prerogative are amenable to the judicial process. We do not think that it is necessary for us to say more than this in the instant case. It will be for other courts to decide on a case by case basis whether the matter in question is reviewable or not . . .

But is the exercise of the prerogative reviewable in the instant case? As originally framed, the applicant sought to attack the Home Secretary's application of long standing Home Office policy that a free pardon would not be granted unless he was satisfied that the person concerned was both morally and technically innocent of the crime. That disclosed an error of law, so it was argued, since it misunderstood the nature and effect of a free pardon. If that had remained the basis of the applicant's case we have considerable doubt as to whether the decision could have been reviewed on the basis contended for. We think that Mr. Richards [counsel for the defendant] was probably right in submitting that the formulation of criteria for the exercise of the prerogative by the grant of a free pardon was entirely a matter of policy which is not justiciable.

However, as the argument before us developed, it became clear that the substance of the applicant's case was that the Home Secretary failed to recognise the fact that the prerogative of mercy is capable of being exercised in many different circumstances and over a wide range and therefore failed to consider the form of pardon which might be appropriate to meet the facts of the present case. Such a failure is, we think, reviewable . . .

We can well understand the decision of the Home Secretary in so far as it constituted a response to a free (or full) pardon, but we are far from satisfied that he gave sufficient consideration to his power to grant some other form of pardon which would be suitable to the circumstances of the particular case. It is true, as the Home Secretary pointed out in the announcement of his decision, that in 1953 the then Home Secretary was working in a different climate of opinion. But, as we have already underlined, the facts of this case are very striking. There is a compelling argument that even by the standards of 1953 the then Home Secretary's decision was clearly wrong.

In these circumstances the court, though it has no power to direct the way in which the prerogative of mercy should be exercised, has some role to play. The Home Secretary's decision was directed to the grant of a free pardon. In these circumstances we do not think it would be right to make any formal order, nor is this an appropriate case for the grant of a declaration. Nevertheless, we would invite the Home Secretary to look at the matter again and to examine whether it would be just to exercise the prerogative of mercy in such a way as to give full recognition to the now generally accepted view that this young man should have been reprieved . . .

Following this judgment, the Home Secretary granted a limited pardon which, in effect, recognized that it had been inappropriate to sentence Bentley to death and that his sentence ought to have been life imprisonment.

The curious fact that no remedy was forthcoming in *Bentley* (on which see Hare [1994] *CLJ* 4) evidences a residual judicial deference in the face of some prerogative powers. This, however, is far less significant than the court's willingness to subject the matter to judicial review, and its acknowledgment, in doing so, that the use of any given power may raise both justiciable and non-justiciable matters. Similar reasoning prevailed in *Lewis v. Attorney General of Jamaica* [2001] 2 AC 50 (see further Hare [2001] *CLJ* 1) in which the Privy Council (refusing to follow its own decision in *Reckley v. Minister of Public Safety and Immigration (No 2)* [1996] AC 527) held that decisions not to grant mercy to 'death row' prisoners could be challenged on the ground that the decision-making process was flawed by procedural unfairness. As in *Bentley*, the *issues* before the court — *viz* whether the principles of natural justice had been complied with — were eminently justiciable, notwithstanding that they arose in relation to the prerogative of mercy.

Judicial willingness to distinguish between justiciable and non-justiciable *issues* in cases like *Bentley* and *Lewis*, rather than treating all exercises of given *powers* as off-limits, is to be welcomed. (Indeed, the seeds of such an approach can be found in Lord Diplock's suggestion, in *GCHQ* [1985] AC 374 at 411 itself, that the susceptibility to review of a given prerogative power cannot be stated abstractly, but must be considered in relation to the ground of complaint upon which the court is asked to adjudicate.) Nevertheless, it remains to confront the logically prior question, 'What makes an issue non-justiciable in the first place?' Harris commends the deployment of a number of criteria in undertaking this inquiry, the most significant of which are elaborated in the following excerpt.

....

Harris, 'Judicial Review, Justiciability and the Prerogative of Mercy' [2003] CLJ 631

. . . A detailed appreciation of the subject matter of the executive decision-making . . . allows determination, from the point of view of the overall constitutional structure, of whether accountability is best facilitated by the courts, left to be effected by the legislature, or not expected at all.

. . . [This] invites reflection on aspects of the current operation of the doctrine of the separation of powers. . . Positive law ensuring the independence of the judiciary is a manifestation of the doctrine of the separation of powers . . . In determining justiciability in respect of an application for judicial review, the need for the assistance of the courts' independence may be taken into account. For example, where the executive decision requires the application of human rights norms, the independence of the courts from the majority will of the people may be highly relevant to determining the constitutional appropriateness of procedural accountability being through the courts.

The independence of the courts causes their own accountability to be the least overt of the three branches of government . . . The freedom which the courts enjoy from direct political accountability is a factor in some areas of executive decision-making involving elements of policy not being considered appropriate for judicial review. Possible areas of such non-justiciability include disposition of nuclear armaments [*Chandler* v. *Director of Public Prosecutions* [1964] AC 763], national security [*ibid*], foreign relations [*R* v. *Secretary of State for Foreign and Commonwealth Affairs, ex parte Rees-Mogg* [1994] QB 552] and the distribution of scarce public resources [*R* v. *Cambridge Health Authority, ex parte B* [1995] 1 WLR 898], where society may wish review of the executive decision-making to be the responsibility of the more politically accountable legislature through ministerial responsibility.

. . . [However,] [t]he theoretical position that the courts should not review, and consequently not make policy decisions, does not correspond exactly with the practical needs of the community, or the way that the courts operate in reality. For example, the courts' development of the law of negligence has required the courts to make many policy decisions. Policy, to a greater or lesser degree, permeates most judicial decision-making. If one accepts the arguments against the courts making policy decisions, and yet acknowledges the practical necessity that the courts make some decisions with a policy element, the challenge is to formulate principles to assist in best determining those policy decisions which are capable of being justiciable and those which are not.

Finn [see 'The Justiciability of Administrative Decisions' (2002) 30 *Fed LR* 239 at 247] has commented on the need to distinguish between the decision-making of the public decision-maker being reviewed, which may be heavily policy laden, and the decision-making of the reviewing court, which need not necessarily be similarly policy laden. For example, judicial review on the natural justice ground of an alleged failure to give an applicant for a television station licence the right to be heard appropriately on its application, may not give rise to the need to consider any non-justiciable policy issues, even though the overall executive decision-making in respect of the allocation of television channels may be heavily policy laden and deserving of political, as different from judicial, accountability. The fact that an area of executive decision-making is heavily policy laden should not lead to the conclusion that particular decisions in that area are automatically non-justiciable. Political accountability through the executive and legislative branches, and judicial review through the courts, need not be mutually exclusive . . .

[A further] consideration is the suitability of the personnel, and methods of operation of the courts, to the particular decision-making which is expected of them. The necessarily limited qualities of the persons who perform the primary decision-making role in courts, namely the judges, and the procedures by which they operate, may also cause the subject matter of some disputes to be considered non-justiciable . . .

. . . [I]n some contexts, a judge's lack of expertise in relation to the subject matter of a dispute may make it difficult to achieve a quality of decision-making in which informed outside observers would have confidence. For example, if judicial review were to be sought of the exercise by the government of its prerogative power to break off diplomatic relations with a particular country, an executive argument would be likely to be made that a judge would not have the required expertise, or be capable of acquiring it during the trial, in order to decide the appropriate procedure and proportionality demanded by the executive decision. Similar concerns would be raised should judicial review be sought of the exercise of the prerogative to declare war. Both prerogatives are wide-ranging powers of the executive government which a reviewing court would find difficult to harness within concepts of legality, rationality and procedural propriety.

. . . [It is also necessary to consider the appropriateness] of the courts' processes to the determination required. Problems may flow from the fact that the courts are adversarial, participation of parties is limited, and the law of evidence may operate to constrain what is put before the court for consideration. Since the courts are not inquisitorial, they are largely dependent on the parties as to what is put before them by way of evidence and argument. The approach to evidence and argument has traditionally been conservative, with, for example, relatively little use of empirical evidence. The courts will often not have access to the breadth and depth of evidence, and spectrum of points of view, that are potentially available to the executive and legislature when they are involved in public decision-making. The executive and the legislature have the potential to listen to a wider range of people, and to bring a greater degree of direction and financial resource to the acquisition of thorough research and commentary that in many circumstances will allow better informed decision-making than can be provided by the courts. When the subject matter is policy-laden, such as in respect of the determination of issues to do with foreign affairs or the distribution of scarce resources, the courts, even if they had the requisite expertise, may not have presented to them appropriate ranges of relevant factual information to allow quality decisions to be made . . .

In the last paragraph, Harris adverts to what Fuller (1978) 92 *Harvard Law Review* 353 calls the problem of 'polycentricity'. It may be argued, however, that a finding of non-justiciability is, at best, an incomplete response to that problem, since it risks leaving citizens' rights and interests unprotected. Allison [1994] *CLJ* 367 at 382–383 therefore suggests that rights may adequately protected in a polycentric setting in one of two ways:

First, Fuller's notion of polycentricity or some such notion could be clarified to confirm the judicial restraint justified by the limits of an adversarial concept of adjudication. Other forms of social ordering would then need to be elaborated to give effect to rights which cannot adequately be given effect by adjudication. Secondly, Fuller's adversarial concept of adjudication could itself be developed to take account of the potential of judicial expertise and investigation and, so, to facilitate the satisfactory resolution of more-polycentric disputes and the judicial determination of rights.

QUESTION

- Do you agree? How might the adjudicative process be adapted so as to 'facilitate the satisfactory resolution of more-polycentric disputes'?

Two central points should be extracted from this discussion of justiciability. First, although concerns about justiciability frequently arise in relation to the prerogative, the concept applies to all forms of power which can be judicially reviewed. Secondly, reviewability is not a binary matter. It is essentially a question of degree: to *what extent* is the matter in question open to review? Justiciability-based concerns therefore inform the intensity with which courts will review administrative action; in ch 9, we explain that this assumes particular importance in relation to what is known as 'substantive review'.

5.4 *De Facto* Powers

5.4.1 The *Datafin* Case

The willingness of the courts to review prerogative, as well as statutory, powers clearly represents a breakthrough in terms of judicial vindication of the rule of law, since there is no apparent reason why citizens ought to be unprotected from abuses of power merely because of the source of the power concerned. But how far can the logic of this argument be pressed? If individuals are vulnerable to the abuse of powers which derive neither from legislation nor the prerogative, should public law protect them?

R v. Panel on Take-overs and Mergers, ex parte Datafin plc [1987] QB 815
Court of Appeal

The claimant was bidding, in competition with Norton Opax plc, to take over a company. The claimant complained to the Panel on Take-overs and Mergers that Norton Opax had acted in concert with other parties and, thus, in breach of the Code promulgated by the Panel. The Panel, however, dismissed this complaint, and the claimant sought judicial review of its decision. At first instance permission to seek judicial review was refused, on the ground that the Panel was not amenable to judicial review. When the claimant renewed its application before the Court of Appeal, the central issue for the court was therefore whether the Panel's decisions could be subject to judicial review. The nature of the Panel's powers are apparent from the excerpt, below, from the judgment of Sir John Donaldson MR.

Sir John Donaldson MR

The Panel on Take-overs and Mergers is a truly remarkable body. Perched on the 20th floor of the Stock Exchange building in the City of London, both literally and metaphorically it oversees and regulates a very important part of the United Kingdom financial market. Yet it performs this function without visible means of legal support.

The panel is an unincorporated association without legal personality and, so far as can be seen, has only about twelve members . . .

It has no statutory, prerogative or common law powers and it is not in contractual relationship with the financial market or with those who deal in that market. According to the introduction to the City Code on Take-overs and Mergers, which it promulgates: "The code has not, and does not seek to have, the force of law, but those who wish to take advantage of the facilities of the securities markets in the United Kingdom should conduct themselves in matters relating to take-overs according to the code. Those who do not so conduct themselves cannot expect to enjoy those facilities and may find that they are withheld . . ."

"Self-regulation" is an emotive term. It is also ambiguous. An individual who voluntarily regulates his life in accordance with stated principles, because he believes that this is morally right and also, perhaps, in his own long term interests, or a group of individuals who do so, are practising self-regulation. But it can mean something quite different. It can connote a system whereby a group of people, acting in concert, use their collective power to force themselves and others to comply with a code of conduct of their own devising. This is not necessarily morally wrong or contrary to the public interest, unlawful or even undesirable. But it is very different. The panel is a self-regulating body in the latter sense. Lacking any authority de jure, it exercises immense power de facto by devising, promulgating, amending and interpreting the City Code on Take-overs and Mergers, by waiving or modifying the application of the code in particular circumstances, by investigating and reporting upon alleged breaches of the code and by the application or threat of sanctions. These sanctions are no less effective because they are applied indirectly and lack a legally enforceable base . . .

As I have said, the panel is a truly remarkable body, performing its function without visible means of legal support. But the operative word is "visible," although perhaps I should have used the word "direct." Invisible or indirect support there is in abundance. Not only is a breach of the code, so found by the panel, ipso facto an act of misconduct by a member of the Stock Exchange, and the same may be true of other bodies represented on the panel, but the admission of shares to the Official List may be withheld in the event of such a breach. This is interesting and significant for listing of securities is a statutory function performed by the Stock Exchange in pursuance of the Stock Exchange (Listing) Regulations 1984 (SI 1984 No 716), enacted in implementation of EEC directives. And the matter does not stop there, because in December 1983 the Department of Trade and Industry made a statement explaining why the Licensed Dealers (Conduct of Business) Rules 1983 (SI 1983 No 585) contained no detailed provisions about take-overs. [The Master of the Rolls then went on to quote from the statement, in which the Department explained its intention to rely upon the Panel for the regulation of take-overs.]

The picture which emerges is clear. As an act of government it was decided that, in relation to take-overs, there should be a central self-regulatory body which would be supported and sustained by a periphery of statutory powers and penalties wherever non-statutory powers and penalties were insufficient or non-existent or where EEC requirements called for statutory provisions . . . The issue is thus whether the historic supervisory jurisdiction of the Queen's courts extends to such a body discharging such functions, including some which are quasi-judicial in their nature, as part of such a system.

[After referring to R v. *Criminal Injuries Compensation Board, ex parte Lain* [1967] 2 Q.B. 864 (on which see above at 5.3.2, the Master of the Rolls continued:] The Criminal Injuries Compensation Board, in the form which it then took, was an administrative novelty. Accordingly it would have been impossible to find a precedent for the exercise of the supervisory jurisdiction of the court which fitted the facts. Nevertheless the court not only asserted its jurisdiction, but further asserted that it was a jurisdiction which was adaptable thereafter. This process has since been taken further in *O'Reilly* v. *Mackman* [1983] 2 A.C. 237, 279 (*per* Lord Diplock) by deleting any requirement that the body should have a duty to act judicially; in *Council of Civil Service Unions* v. *Minister for the Civil Service* [1985] A.C. 374 by extending it to a person exercising purely prerogative power; and in *Gillick* v. *West Norfolk and Wisbech Area Health Authority* [1986] A.C. 112, where Lord Fraser of Tullybelton, at p 163F and Lord Scarman, at p 178F–H expressed the view *obiter* that judicial review would extend to guidance circulars issued by a department of state without any specific authority. In all the reports it is possible to find enumerations of factors giving rise to the jurisdiction, but it is a fatal error to regard the presence of all those factors as essential or as being exclusive of other factors. Possibly the only essential elements are what can be described as a public element, which can take many different forms, and the exclusion from the jurisdiction of bodies whose sole source of power is a consensual submission to its jurisdiction.

In fact, given its novelty, the panel fits surprisingly well into the format which this court had in mind in the *Criminal Injuries Compensation Board* case. It is without doubt performing a public duty and an important one. This is clear from the expressed willingness of the Secretary of State for Trade and Industry to limit legislation in the field of take-overs and mergers and to use the panel as the centrepiece of his regulation of that market. The rights of citizens are indirectly affected by its decisions, some, but by no means all of whom, may in a technical sense be said to have assented to this situation, eg the members of the Stock Exchange. At least in its determination of whether there has been a breach of the code, it has a duty to act judicially and it asserts that its raison d'être is to do equity between one shareholder and another. Its source of power is only partly based upon moral persuasion and the assent of institutions and their members, the bottom line being the statutory powers exercised by the Department of Trade and Industry and the Bank of England. In this context I should be very disappointed if the courts could not recognise the realities of executive power and allowed their vision to be clouded by the subtlety and sometimes complexity of the way in which it can be exerted . . .

Lloyd LJ

. . . [Counsel for the Panel, Mr Alexander, argued that, for policy reasons, the Panel should be free from the constraints of judicial review. Lloyd LJ responded to that argument in the following terms:] On the policy level, I find myself unpersuaded. Mr. Alexander made much of the word 'self-regulating.' No doubt self-regulation has many advantages. But I was unable to see why the mere fact that a body is self-regulating makes it less appropriate for judicial review. Of course there will be many self-regulating bodies which are wholly inappropriate for judicial review. The committee of an ordinary club affords an obvious example. But the reason why a club is not subject to judicial review is not just because it is self-regulating. The panel wields enormous power. It has a giant's strength. The fact that it is self-regulating, which means, presumably, that it is not subject to regulation by others, and in particular the Department of Trade and Industry, makes it not less but more appropriate that it should be subject to judicial review by the courts.

It has been said that "it is excellent to have a giant's strength, but it is tyrannous to use it like a giant." Nobody suggests that there is any present danger of the panel abusing its power. But it is at least possible to imagine circumstances in which a ruling or decision of the panel might give rise to legitimate complaint. An obvious example would be if it reached a decision in flagrant breach of the rules of natural justice. It is no answer to say that there would be a right of appeal in such a case. For a complainant has no right to appeal where the decision is that there has been no breach of the code. Yet a complainant is just as much entitled to natural justice as the company against whom the complaint is made.

Nor is it any answer that a company coming to the market must take it as it finds it. The City is not a club which one can join or not at will. In that sense, the word "self-regulation" may be misleading. The panel regulates not only itself, but all others who have no alternative but to come to the market in a case to which the code applies . . . So long as there is a possibility, however remote, of the panel abusing its great powers, then it would be wrong for the courts to abdicate responsibility. The courts must remain ready, willing and able to hear a legitimate complaint in this as in any other field of our national life. I am not persuaded that this particular field is one in which the courts do not belong, or from which they should retire, on grounds of policy. And if the courts are to remain in the field, then it is clearly better, as a matter of policy, that legal proceedings should be in the realm of public law rather than private law, not only because they are quicker, but also because the requirement of leave [on which see below at 15.2] . . . will exclude claims which are clearly unmeritorious . . .

[Lloyd LJ then turned to counsel's other principal objection to judicial review of the Panel:] On the basis of [Lord Diplock's speech in GCHQ (see above at 5.3.2)], and other cases to which Mr. Alexander referred us, he argues (i) that the sole test whether the body of persons is subject to judicial review is the source of its power, and (ii) that there has been no case where that source has been other than legislation, including subordinate legislation, or the prerogative.

I do not agree that the source of the power is the sole test whether a body is subject to judicial review, nor do I so read Lord Diplock's speech. Of course the source of the power will often, perhaps usually, be decisive. If the source of power is a statute, or subordinate legislation under a statute, then clearly the body in question will be subject to judicial review. If, at the other end of the scale, the source of power is contractual, as in the case of private arbitration, then clearly the arbitrator is not subject to judicial review: see R v. *National Joint Council for the Craft of Dental Technicians (Disputes Committee), ex parte Neate* [1953] 1 Q.B. 704.

But in between these extremes there is an area in which it is helpful to look not just at the source of the power but at the nature of the power. If the body in question is exercising public law functions, or if the exercise of its functions have public law consequences, then that may, as Mr. Lever submitted, be sufficient to bring the body within the reach of judicial review. It may be said that to refer to 'public law' in this context is to beg the question. But I do not think it does. The essential distinction, which runs through all the cases to which we referred, is between a domestic or private tribunal on the one hand and a body of persons who are under some public duty on the other . . .

Nicholls LJ agreed with Sir John Donaldson MR and Lloyd LJ that the Panel was amenable to judicial review. However, all three judges also agreed that, on the facts, the Panel had not committed any error which should be set aside on judicial review.

The importance of *Datafin* (for comment on which see Wade (1987) 103 *LQR* 323; Hilliard (1987) 50 *MLR* 372) is that it marks the first unequivocal judicial acknowledgment that the supervisory jurisdiction extends beyond the control of *legal* powers. The excerpts above raise a number of important issues which we consider in the following sections.

5.4.2 Defining the Scope of Judicial Review

Datafin suggests that the outer boundary of judicial review is traced by some concept of 'publicness': Sir John Donaldson MR said that review is possible only if a 'public element' can be found, while Lloyd LJ required the body to be 'under some public duty'. On their own, however, these labels are of little help; their true meaning can be discerned only by reference to the factual matrix in which they were deployed, four features of which stand out. First, the Panel's immense power was emphasized by the judges. Secondly, the Master of the Rolls noted that, although not established in a legal sense, the Panel enjoyed abundant 'invisible or indirect support'. Thirdly, he observed that the Panel's role within the regulatory system was attributable, to a large extent, to an 'act of government'. Finally, he considered that private law control would not be effective, but that it was 'unthinkable that . . . the panel should go on its way cocooned from the attention of the courts in defence of the citizenry'. Ultimately, the court felt that the Panel was serving an important governmental function, albeit that it happened not to be part of the structure of government in a formal or legal sense. Sir John Donaldson's suggestion that amenability turns simply on the existence of a 'public element' must therefore be viewed with some caution, since the reasoning in *Datafin* suggests a somewhat narrower approach — an impression which, as we explain below, is confirmed by subsequent cases.

5.4.3 The Limits of Review and its Underlying Rationale

Datafin raises questions about what underlying rationale should inform decisions as to the reach of the supervisory jurisdiction — which, as Bamforth [1993] *PL* 239 at 247–248 notes, is keyed into much broader questions about the purpose of judicial review itself. Although the judgments in *Datafin* do not confront this matter head-on, three possibilities arise.

Abuse of power

There are numerous references in the judgments to the considerable power wielded by the Panel; indeed, Lloyd LJ specifically mentioned the importance of correcting any abuses of such power. Dealing with the abuse of power has been presented as one of the key goals of public law in a number of cases (see, *eg, In re Preston* [1985] AC 835 at 864–865; *R v. North and East Devon Health Authority, ex parte Coughlan* [2001] QB 213 at 242–243), while Laws [1997] *PL* 455 at 464 goes as far as to assert that preventing the abuse of power is the organizing concept upon which modern public law is founded. But while judicial review undoubtedly aims to prevent or correct abuses of power, such a criterion is surely too crude to serve as the guiding principle by which to rationalize the scope of judicial review. Unless all power which is liable to abuse, including purely private power, is to be brought within the courts' supervisory jurisdiction — a conclusion that is repudiated by the judgments in *Datafin* itself — then invoking abuse of power as the organizing concept merely begs the question, 'What *type* of power?'

Governmental power

Given the emphasis placed by Sir John Donaldson on the quasi-governmental character of the Take-over Panel, might the regulation of *governmental power* provide a more intelligible organizing principle? An affirmative answer to that question is an implicit premise in the following case.

R v. Disciplinary Committee of the Jockey Club, ex parte Aga Khan [1993] 1 WLR 909
Court of Appeal

The claimant was a leading owner and breeder of racehorses. After one of his horses won a race in 1989, it was subjected to random urine testing and a prohibited substance was discovered. Although it was not alleged that the claimant was implicated, the horse was disqualified and the claimant deprived of the prize money for the race. That decision was taken by the Disciplinary Committee of the Jockey Club, the non-statutory body which regulates horse racing: all race meetings must be licensed by the Club and run according to its Rules of Racing, and all those involved in horse racing must be licensed by or registered with the Club. In 1978 the Royal Commission on Gambling described the Club as the 'supreme authority in British racing'. The claimant sought judicial review of the Club's decision. The Divisional Court, on the trial of a preliminary issue, held that the Club was not amenable to judicial review; the claimant therefore appealed to the Court of Appeal.

Sir Thomas Bingham MR

. . . The Jockey Club brings [its Rules] to bear in two main ways. First, and most importantly, it does so by contracts entered into with racecourse managements, owners, trainers and jockeys. The present case illustrates the routine practice. Thus the applicant when applying for registration as an owner (and, probably, when entering the filly for the race) and the trainer when seeking renewal of his trainer's licence each agreed to be bound in all respects by the Rules of Racing. All those seeking any licence or permit from the Jockey Club, on being registered with it, become similarly bound.

The Jockey Club cannot, of course, impose contractual conditions on those who do not seek any licence or permit from it and therefore do not enter into any contract with it. This is a class which includes members of the general public and also racecourse owners, owners, trainers and jockeys who, for whatever reason, do not choose to act under the Jockey Club rules. The Jockey Club's sanction here lies not in contract but in its domination of the market. While unrecognised meetings do occur in some parts of the country, they are insignificant. No serious racecourse management, owner, trainer or jockey can survive without the recognition or licence of the Jockey Club. There is in effect no alternative market in which those not accepted by the Jockey Club can find a place or to which racegoers may resort. Thus by means of the rules and its market domination the Jockey Club can effectively control not only those who agree to abide by its rules but also those — such as disqualified or excluded persons seeking to participate in racing activities in any capacity — who do not. For practical purposes the Jockey Club's writ runs in the British racing world, to the acknowledged benefit of British racing.

[After reviewing the authorities, the Master of the Rolls reached the following conclusion:] I have little hesitation in accepting the applicant's contention that the Jockey Club effectively regulates a significant national activity, exercising powers which affect the public and are exercised in the interest of the public. I am willing to accept that if the Jockey Club did not regulate this activity the government would probably be driven to create a public body to do so.

But the Jockey Club is not in its origin, its history, its constitution or (least of all) its membership a public body. While the grant of a royal charter was no doubt a mark of official approval, this did not in any way alter its essential nature, functions or standing. Statute provides for its representation on the Horseracing Betting Levy Board, no doubt as a body with an obvious interest in racing, but it has otherwise escaped mention in the statute book. It has not been woven into any system of governmental control of horse racing, perhaps because it has itself controlled horse racing so successfully that there has been no need for any such governmental system and such does not therefore exist. This has the result that while the Jockey Club's powers may be described as, in many ways, public they are in no sense governmental. The discretion conferred by s 31(6) of the Supreme Court Act 1981 to refuse the grant of leave or relief where the applicant has been guilty of delay which would be prejudicial to good administration can scarcely have been envisaged as applicable in a case such as this . . .

Hoffmann LJ

The Jockey Club is an exclusive private club incorporated by royal charter which controls the racing industry. It does so by tradition, widespread acceptance and the contractual consent of almost all active participants in racing to the Jockey Club's Rules of Racing and the jurisdiction of its disciplinary committee. This control gives the Jockey Club considerable power over a section of the economy which is not only important in itself but supports another important economic activity, namely horse race betting. The question in this appeal is whether the power exercised by the Jockey Club brings its decisions into the realm of public law, so that they are amenable to judicial review. In my view it does not . . .

R v. Panel on Take-overs and Mergers, ex parte Datafin plc [1987] Q.B. 815 shows that the absence of a formal public source of power, such as statute or prerogative, is not conclusive. Governmental power may be exercised *de facto* as well as *de jure*. But the power needs to be identified as governmental in nature . . . [The Take-over Panel represents] a privatisation of the business of government itself. The same has been held to be true of the Advertising Standards Authority (*R. v. Advertising Standards Authority Ltd, Ex parte Insurance Service plc* (1989) 9 Tr. L.R. 169) and the Investment Management Regulatory Organisation (IMRO) (*Bank of Scotland v. Investment Management Regulatory Organisation Ltd* 1989 S.L.T. 432). Both are private bodies established by the industry but integrated into a system of statutory regulation. There is in my judgment nothing comparable in the position of the Jockey Club. It is true that it has been incorporated by royal charter, but this seems to me simply a mark of royal favour to racing. The Jockey Club nominates three members of the Horserace Betting Levy Board, but this is to represent the disparate private interests of the racing industry, which enjoys the benefit of the levy. There is nothing to suggest that, if the Jockey Club had not voluntarily assumed the regulation of racing, the government would feel obliged or inclined to set up a statutory body for the purpose. The reactions of successive governments to the proposals of, among others, the 1978 Royal Commission on Gambling (Cmnd 7200) and the 1991 Fourth Report of the House of Commons Home Affairs Committee on the Levy on Horserace Betting suggest a determination to leave racing firmly in the private sector . . .

Farquharson LJ agreed with Sir Thomas Bingham MR and Hoffmann LJ that the disciplinary committee's decision was not amenable to judicial review.

Similar emphasis was placed on *governmental* power in *R v. Chief Rabbi of the United Hebrew Congregations of Great Britain and the Commonwealth, ex parte Wachmann* [1992] 1 WLR 1036. Holding that the Chief Rabbi's decisions are not subject to judicial review, Simon Brown J said (at 1041):

To say of decisions of a given body that they are public law decisions with public law consequences means something more than that they are decisions which may be of great interest or concern to the public or, indeed, which may have consequences for the public. To attract the court's supervisory jurisdiction there must not merely be a public but a potentially governmental interest in the decision-making power in question . . . [Reviewable non-statutory bodies operate] as an integral part of a regulatory system which, although itself non-statutory, is nevertheless supported by statutory powers and penalties clearly indicative of government concern.

This represents a less diffuse rationale than that offered by the notion of abuse of power. It also fits in with established ideas about the purpose of judicial review, which is traditionally thought of in terms of supervision of governmental authority — albeit that, post-*Datafin*, a less formalistic conception of 'government' obtains, reflecting modern developments such as the establishment of arms-length agencies, the process of contracting out, and the growth of self-regulation (on which see above at 1.5.3).

However, using governmental power as the touchstone by which to delimit judicial review is not without difficulty. First, the application of a consistent test is difficult. For instance, while Sir Thomas Bingham MR appears to suggest in *Aga Khan* that there must be some *actual* government involvement (such that the non-statutory body is somehow interwoven into more formal regulatory mechanisms), others invoke the idea of *potential* involvement either by the government (see, *eg*, the extract from Hoffmann LJ's judgment in *Aga Khan*, above) or Parliament (see, *eg*, *R v. Football Association Ltd, ex parte Football League Ltd* [1993]

2 All ER 833 at 848) by holding that the acid test of reviewability is whether, in the absence of the non-statutory body, the state would intervene to fill the gap. However, the difficulty of applying such a test is illustrated by the *Aga Khan* case. In the excerpt above, Sir Thomas Bingham MR opines that 'if the Jockey Club did not regulate this activity the government would probably be driven to create a public body to do so', yet Farquharson LJ ([1993] 1 WLR 909 at 930) reached the opposite conclusion, finding no grounds 'for supposing that, if the Jockey Club were dissolved, any governmental body would assume control of racing' — a view with which Hoffmann LJ's comments in the final paragraph of our excerpt above seem consistent. Indeed, if amenability is to turn upon what the government or Parliament might do, then we are forced to ask *which* government or *which* Parliament? The likelihood of state intervention cannot be determined in a political vacuum: it depends on the philosophy of the executive or legislature in question. On this approach, therefore, it seems that the reach of judicial review may vary according to the political colour of the government or Parliament of the day.

QUESTION

- Is this a good or a bad thing? Should judges develop their own concept of what is sufficiently 'public' to merit oversight through judicial review, or should they be influenced by the prevailing political philosophy concerning the size and role of the state?

Monopoly power

In the following passage, Woolf [1986] *PL* 220 at 224–225 sets out an alternative approach to delimiting judicial review:

The interests of the public are as capable of being adversely affected by the decisions of large corporations and large associations, be they employers or employees, and should they not be subject to challenge on *Wednesbury* grounds if that decision relates to activities which can damage the public interest? . . . Members of large companies . . . delegate to the board of the company . . . the power to make decisions which at times not only affect the company . . . but the national interest. Should it not be possible for the court to intervene if the decision has been reached without a relevant consideration being taken into account or if the decision has been taken on the basis of some irrelevant consideration in the same way as it does in the case of a public body? Powerful bodies, whether they are public bodies or not, because of their economic muscle may be in a position to take decisions which at the present time are not subject to scrutiny and which could be unfair or adversely affect the public interest.

Along with many other commentators (including Borrie [1989] *PL* 552, Beloff (1995) 58 *MLR* 143 and Forsyth [1996] *CLJ* 122), Woolf argues that control of *monopoly power* provides a coherent criterion by which to determine whether *de facto* powers should be subject to judicial review. Some judges, too, have taken the monopolistic nature of powers into account in addressing the appropriateness of judicial review: Roch J, in *R v. Disciplinary Committee of the Jockey Club, ex parte Massingberd-Mundy* [1993] 2 All ER 207 at 221, considered the existence of 'monopolistic or near monopolistic powers' to be salient to the question of amenability. But that is the exception, not the norm. In the later case of *R v. Football Association Ltd, ex parte Football League Ltd* [1993] 2 All ER 833 at 848, Rose J held that, even though the Football Association exercised 'virtually monopolistic powers', it was not amenable to judicial review. The same approach was adopted in relation to the Jockey Club in *Aga Khan*.

This reluctance to scrutinize the use of the powers of the Jockey Club, and of analogous powers, is surprising in view of *Nagle* v. *Fielden* [1966] 2 QB 633, in which the claimant challenged the Jockey Club's refusal, solely on the ground of gender, to grant her a trainer's licence. Danckwerts LJ, at 650, considered that 'the courts have the right to protect the right of a person to work when it is being prevented by the dictatorial exercise of powers by a body which holds a monopoly'. Similarly, Lord Denning MR, at 645, using language which echoes that of the public law *Wednesbury* principle (on which see below at 9.2.1), thought that, 'If [the Jockey Club] make a rule which enables them to reject his application arbitrarily or capriciously, not reasonably, that rule is bad. It is against public policy.' Against this background, it might be expected that, as Simon Brown LJ put it in *R* v. *Jockey Club, ex parte RAM Racecourses Ltd* [1993] 2 All ER 225 at 246–247, cases like *Nagle* v. *Fielden*, 'had they arisen today and not some years ago, would have found a natural home in judicial review proceedings', the implication being that such matters should now attract the application of the public law principles of good administration. However, Hoffmann LJ, in *Aga Khan* [1993] 1 WLR 909 at 932–933, did not agree, suggesting that there is 'an improvisatory air' about the approach taken in *Nagle* v. *Fielden*, which 'has probably not survived'. He opined that:

[T]he fact that the Jockey Club has power [is indisputable]. But the mere fact of power, even over a substantial area of economic activity, is not enough. In a mixed economy, power may be private as well as public. Private power may affect the public interest and the livelihoods of many individuals. But that does not subject it to the rules of public law. If control is needed, it must be found in the law of contract, the doctrine of restraint of trade, [legislation providing for the regulation of monopolies], [the relevant provisions of] the EEC Treaty and all the other instruments available in law for curbing the excesses of private power.

However, as Black (1996) 59 *MLR* 24 notes (and as Hoffmann LJ himself accepted later in his judgment), the difficulty with this argument is that while these alternative methods of legal control may be suitable in respect of commercial monopolies, there are other monopoly powers — such as those of self-regulatory bodies — to which they are not so easily applicable.

QUESTION

- Do you agree that the control of monopoly power is preferable to control of governmental power as the organizing principle by reference to which the scope of judicial review is determined?

5.4.4 Contractual Arrangements

Thus far we have seen that the courts have limited their public law jurisdiction by recourse to the criterion of governmental power. It is now necessary to address the extent to which contractual arrangements may displace the courts' willingness to review.

Notwithstanding the discouraging *dicta* set out above at 5.4.3, there are some oblique suggestions in Sir Thomas Bingham MR's judgment in *Aga Khan* [1993] 1 WLR 909 at 924 that there may be circumstances, where there is no contractual relationship between the claimant and the Jockey Club, in which the latter's decisions *can* be subjected to judicial review; Farquharson LJ (at 930) also suggested that judicial review might lie against the Club in some non-contractual settings. Similarly, Simon Brown J opined in *R v. Jockey Club, ex parte RAM Racecourses Ltd* [1993] 2 All ER 225 at 248 that the Jockey Club may be amenable to review when exercising 'quasi-licensing powers' over those with whom no contractual relationship exists — *eg* when deciding whether to allocate fixtures to a new racecourse. These *dicta* suggest that there may well be situations in which the powers of bodies such as the Jockey Club may be regarded as sufficiently 'public' or 'governmental' to attract judicial review, provided that there is no *contractual relationship* between the claimant and the defendant. Where such a relationship does exist, however, it appears that the matter is to be treated as one purely of private law (although cf on this point the decision of the Privy Council in *Mercury Energy Ltd v. Electricity Corporation of New Zealand* [1994] 1 WLR 521). This conclusion seems to follow ineluctably from the following remarks of Sir Thomas Bingham MR in the *Aga Khan* case at 924:

I would accept that those who agree to be bound by the Rules of Racing have no effective alternative to doing so if they want to take part in racing in this country. It also seems likely to me that if, instead of Rules of Racing administered by the Jockey Club, there were a statutory code administered by a public body, the rights and obligations conferred and imposed by the code would probably approximate to those conferred and imposed by the Rules of Racing. But this does not, as it seems to me, alter the fact, however anomalous it may be, that the powers which the Jockey Club exercises over those who (like the applicant) agree to be bound by the Rules of Racing derive from the agreement of the parties and give rise to private rights on which effective action for a declaration, an injunction and damages can be based without resort to judicial review. It would in my opinion be contrary to sound and long-standing principle to extend the remedy of judicial review to such a case.

The general unwillingness to permit judicial review to encroach on existing contractual relationships raises questions regarding the reality of consent. Even if one accepts that it is not public law's function to regulate relationships which are based upon consent, the courts appear to be adopting an unusually two-dimensional view of that concept. Whereas in many situations — the relationship between employer and employee being perhaps the best example — the necessity of looking beneath the surface in order to determine whether there is a real consent is well-established, the courts seem unwilling to do so in the present context. Thus, even though Farquharson LJ recognized in *Aga Khan* (at 928) that those involved in horseracing have no choice but to submit to the Jockey Club's regulation, he still felt that there was an operative consent sufficient to displace the public law jurisdiction. This approach is disputed by many writers (see, *eg*, Pannick [1992] *PL* 1 at 2–5), not least because when genuine consent is absent, this is precisely when abuse of power is most likely, and judicial protection most needed. That said, it should be noted that characterizing the matter as one of contract, rather than public, law does not necessarily leave individuals *entirely* unprotected, bearing in mind the possibility of reading in duties to act fairly and so on into contracts (on which see generally Beatson and Friedmann (eds), *Good Faith and Fault in Contract Law* (Oxford 1995), ch 10).

Whereas *Aga Khan* indicates judicial reluctance to superimpose public law controls where a contractual relationship exists between the complainant and the body, a distinct issue arises where the contractual arrangements are between a body (*eg* a company or charity) and a public authority on whose behalf the former is delivering some service. Such arrangements (which, as noted above at 1.5.3, are increasingly common) pose potentially serious problems in this context.

....

Hunt, 'Constitutionalism and the Contractualisation of Government in the United Kingdom'

in Taggart (ed), *The Province of Administrative Law* (Oxford 1997)

. . . In the United Kingdom, as in other liberal democracies, the last decade has been a period of quiet revolution in public administration. Successive governments elected on political platforms promising to "roll back the state" have presided over changes in the mode of governance which have transformed the relation between public and private. In the United Kingdom the changes began in the most obvious way in the 1980s with the relatively straightforward transfer of public corporations to the private sector. Virtually all of the main utilities (telecommunications, water, electricity, gas, rail transport) are now in private ownership, subject in each case to a specific statutory regime of regulation.

In addition to privatisation in this most obvious sense, the reinvention of government has taken a variety of other forms. Activities previously subject to close administrative controls have been deregulated, and other activities formerly carried out directly by public bodies have been "contracted out" to the private sector. Perhaps most dramatically of all, however, the techniques of public administration have been refashioned in the mould of the private commercial sector. Many of the responsibilities of central government departments have been transferred to executive agencies, whose relationship with its parent department is regulated by a Framework Document. "Internal markets" have been introduced into the provision of the most fundamental of public services such as health and education, organised around a central separation between "purchasers" and "providers" of such services. Contract has replaced command and control as the paradigm of regulation. As public lawyers we must not shrink from recognising the significance of what has happened. In short, the state has been reconceived on the model of market ordering. Such a development obviously has the most profound implications for public law . . .

The retention of the source of the power as a factor in determining amenability to judicial review, and in particular the tendency evident in *Aga Khan* to assert that a decision-maker deriving power from contract cannot be amenable to the supervisory jurisdiction, has given rise to concern about the ability of public law to respond to the contractualisation of government. For if government chooses to constitute the delivery of a particular service by way of contractual arrangements with private bodies, there must be a very real danger that courts will treat such activity as being beyond the reach of public law, and regulated by the private law of contract only. As Freedland [see [1994] *PL* 86 at 102] puts it, the fear is of a total transfer of public activity into the private sphere and thereby into the realm of private rather than public law . . .

Such fears are apparently well founded. In *R v. Servite Houses, ex parte Goldsmith* (2001) 33 HLR 369, judicial review was sought of the decision of the defendant — a charity to which Wandsworth London Borough Council had, under s 26 of the National Assistance Act 1948, contracted out the provision of accommodation in discharge of its duty under s 21 of the same — to close the home in which the claimants resided. This breached promises given by the charity that (health permitting) the claimants could remain for life. Moses J held that public law obligations, such as fidelity to the legitimate expectations (see below at 7.1) to which the 'home for life' promises had arguably given rise, could not be enforced against Servite — a conclusion that, in the absence of any contractual remedies, left the claimants without any redress. His Lordship reasoned (at 389) that, for judicial review to lie, it must be possible to 'identify sufficient statutory penetration which goes beyond the statutory regulation of the manner in which the service is provided'. This was lacking because provisions such as s 26, permitting the contracting out of service provision, have the effect of 'disentangling' the service provider from the 'statutory embrace' of the public authority. 'It follows,' said Moses J, 'that not only is the relationship between Servite and Wandsworth governed solely by the terms of the contract between them, but the relationship between Servite and the [claimants] is solely a matter of private law.'

This reasoning is criticized by Craig (2002) 118 *LQR* 551 at 564–567, who argues that there is 'nothing in the logic of contracting out' which dictates that the service provider should be free from public law obligations. Moreover, the judge's conclusion that the contracting out power divorced Servite from Wandsworth's 'statutory embrace' is counterintuitive: provisions such as s 26 have the opposite effect, says Craig, 'explicitly and directly' telling us that public functions can be performed by private parties, thereby furnishing, if anything, a *greater* degree of statutory underpinning than that which was evident in *Datafin*.

Some writers, however, question whether extending judicial review is the right response to the phenomenon of contractualization. In the following extract, Aronson doubts the viability of the whole '*Datafin* project', arguing that judicial review is not necessarily the most appropriate device by which to ensure the responsible exercise of self-regulatory powers.

....

Aronson, 'A Public Lawyer's Response to Privatisation and Outsourcing'
in Taggart (ed), *The Province of Administrative Law* (Oxford 1997)

. . . Even if the power is classified as public, the level of review which *Datafin* provides is minimal, for two reasons. First, aside from review for breach of natural justice, the court [in *Datafin*] said that its remedies would be only declaratory, and only prospective. Secondly, whilst it offered the theoretical prospect of review where the regulatory body has misinterpreted its own rules, it particularly emphasised the unlikelihood of this ever occurring, given the court's deference to the body's expertise. Lord Donaldson [in *R* v. *Panel on Take-overs and Mergers, ex parte Guinness plc* [1990] 1 QB 146 at 159–160] subsequently emphasised this vagueness about the principles of administration which *Datafin* is meant to enforce, by saying that the court should perhaps fashion an "innominate" ground of review for this sort of regulatory body, replacing "formal categorisation" with review which would be "more in the round than might otherwise be the case". Indeed, what else could he say? . . . What is the point in supervising the way a body interprets rules which it can change without legal formality? The further a regulatory regime travels from the legal paradigm, the less relevant is judicial review as an accountability device.

In addition to the problems flowing from *Datafin's* own language, it is not much of an answer to the issues raised by privatisation and outsourcing. Judicial review of a regulator (where there is one) will quell very few of the non-economic (or social justice) anxieties posed by privatisation and outsourcing, particularly where (as in *Datafin*) the regulator is free to rewrite its rules. Judicial review of the service provider (where that is different from the regulator) is subject to all of the usual defects of judicial review generally, together with some peculiar to that area. The usual defects are familiar. Judicial review can occasionally remedy individual grievances, but rarely provides systemic relief. The decisions to litigate and to maintain the litigation can be happenstantial. Judicial review proceedings often pose no real threat to the respondent, which is usually free, on its redetermination of the substantive issue, to come to the same result but in a way which is impervious to judicial criticism. And however manipulable the demarcation line may be between a decision's merits and its legality, it is a line which judicial review continues to draw, with the result that the judge's role is substantially limited. Review in the wake of privatisation and outsourcing carries the additional problem that the complainant is typically conceived as a consumer with a consumer complaint, which is not the business of judicial review . . .

Aronson goes on to argue that the new architecture of government requires us to look beyond judicial review, to other solutions such as administrative tribunals, informal regulatory devices, and, where appropriate, private law. Aronson's contribution to the debate is useful because it questions the notion that judicial review is a panacea which is to be extended as far as possible, and reminds us that questions about the scope of judicial review have a practical dimension which requires consideration of the efficacy of judicial oversight.

5.4.5 Public Law and Private Law: Should There Be a Divide?

There is a general assumption that private law and public law are fundamentally different, not only in procedural terms (on which see chs 14 and 15) but also at a substantive level. To an extent, that assumption is accurate: certain principles such as proportionality, reasonableness, legitimate expectation, and so on enjoy particular prominence in public law where they operate as controls upon the discretionary powers wielded by public sector actors. The debate about the scope of judicial review has therefore tended to focus upon the reach of these public law principles. Although, as that debate has progressed, our perception of the kinds of functions and powers which are sufficiently public to warrant the application of administrative law principles may have changed, at a more fundamental level the prevailing mindset has remained constant: the dividing line may have shifted, but the public/private distinction has remained. It is this orthodoxy which Oliver, in the following extract, seeks to question by suggesting that public law and private law are based upon shared values and that, once we recognize this, the whole enterprise of carving out different spheres of operation for public and private law becomes a meaningless and ultimately empty exercise. (Note that 'Order 53', which was the set of procedural rules governing claims for judicial review and which is referred to in the following excerpt, has now been replaced by Part 54 of the Civil Procedure Rules; on this, see below at 14.2.)

Oliver, 'Common Values in Public and Private Law and the Public/Private Divide' [1997] PL 630

In this article I shall draw on what I believe to be common underlying values in public and private law in order to explore some aspects of the public/private divide . . .

First, a few brief words about what I mean by "common underlying values in public and private law" . . . A useful place to start is with the development over the last 150 years of the law relating to what Blackstone called "the great relations" of husband and wife, parent and child and master and servant. The relationship between sovereign and subject had strong parallels with the great relations. The common law employed the concept of allegiance in marriage, employment and the sovereign–subject relationship to justify and define the authority of the more powerful party over the other and to impose duties of obedience and service on the 'subject' in the relationship. Although the concept of allegiance was not explicitly employed in the father–child relationship, the nature of that relationship was very similar to the others. In all of these relationships the strong common trend both in statutes and the common law has been to enhance the autonomy, dignity, respect, status and security of the weaker parties — which I regard as the five key values which underlie both public and private law — and to restrict the exercise of power by the more powerful parties.

In modern terms judicial review strongly reflects these key values. The requirements of legality, fairness and rationality in judicial review protect applicants from exercises of power that would be adverse to their interests — their security in the *status quo*, their status in society, their autonomy, dignity and respect. But respect for these values is not restricted to the 'great relations' and judicial review. They underlie the law of defamation and other torts, contract, property, company law and so on. For instance, defamation protects a person's social status and respect in society; negligence, assault, battery and false imprisonment protect individual autonomy and dignity; contract protects the security of the parties; and trusts protect the security of beneficiaries. There are many more examples. Hence my argument that these values span the public/private divide and permeate the law — both common law and statute . . .

I recognise that the argument that such duties may be imposed outside of judicial review undermines the public/private divide itself. That, in my view, is no bad thing. In Scotland there is no public/private divide as we know it, and the Court of Session has a supervisory jurisdiction which does not depend on whether the body or function in question is public or private. I suggest that it would be more logical and in accordance with principle if the procedural privileges attaching to Order 53 were restricted to genuinely public bodies which are directly or indirectly democratically accountable; and that the common law is moving towards imposing a spectrum or range of substantive duties of good administration or legality, fairness and rationality on powerful decision-makers, whether "public" or "private" . . .

[After considering various ways in which the common law already imposes duties of considerate decision-making, which help to enforce the five key values, Oliver continues:] But the law does not — and nor should it — impose duties of fairness and rationality on *all* exercises of private power: to do so would unduly restrict the freedom of action of private bodies and result in excessive litigation. What, then, are the criteria for determining whether such duties exist, what the content of the duties is, and what remedies should be available? First, the common law focuses on exercises of power which interfere with the five key values. It may be concerned with the *seriousness* of the impact of the decision on these values or the plaintiff in a case . . . Secondly, there are important differences between public bodies such as the Crown and local authorities, and private bodies exercising power, and these differences may affect the existence and content of the duties of considerate decision-making and the availability of remedies. The most obvious relevant difference is that private bodies are generally regarded as being entitled — within the law — to pursue their own self-regarding interests, whereas public bodies are not: they are supposed to act, within the law, in the general public interest as they see it. This consideration suggests that lighter duties — or no duties — are to be imposed in private than in public decision-making. If, in principle, a body is entitled to act selfishly, the case for imposing duties of considerate decision-making is weaker. In purely personal relationships this may mean that there is no common law duty of considerate decision-making and each party is free to act in relation to the other as he or she wishes . . .

The implications for the public/private divide as we know it are fundamental, if common law continues to develop in the ways we have considered here. The true divide should be between bodies entitled to the protection [eg short time limits, the requirement of permission and so on: see ch 15 below] of Order 53 when making decisions of a public or governmental nature and those not so entitled. The privileges afforded by Order 53 may be justified where political mechanisms are in place to check their abuse, but not in the absence of such protections. Thus central and local government and other bodies under direct or indirect political control may be entitled to rely on Order 53, but bodies such as regulators in sport should not logically be so entitled. Such bodies may nevertheless be under duties of legality, fairness and rationality. Indeed, whenever a person or body is in a position of power in relation to another, and in particular where a decision may affect the dignity, autonomy, respect, status and security of another, the question will arise whether such duties arise and what their content is. The answers to these questions will depend on a range of factors, including the extent to which the decision-maker is entitled to act self-interestedly or is under duties of altruism, the seriousness of the impact of the decision on the complainant, the degree to which the decision-maker is in a position of monopoly, the justiciability of the issue and the needs of the market. As in judicial review the content of these duties of considerate decision-making outside Order 53 will be flexible, taking into account these and other factors. When discretionary remedies are sought the court will take into account the conduct of the parties, including delay and the impact on third parties of granting a remedy. This approach, it is suggested, would be fair and rational; it would be in sympathy with the common underlying values in the law; and it would promote legal policy in favour of the control of power.

The crux of Oliver's argument (which is developed at greater length in her book *Common Values and the Public/Private Divide* (London 1999)) is that, while the standards we are entitled to expect of decision-makers vary according to the postulated criteria (monopoly, justiciability, impact, and so on), their application will not simply identify decision-makers which are *either* 'public' (hence subject to duties of considerate decision-making) *or* 'private' (so subject to no such duty). Rather, the question is one of degree: to *what extent* (if any) should the decision-maker be obligated to act considerately? Although, in practice, this approach does distinguish between bodies which we would now categorize as 'public' and 'private', the bright-line public/private distinction is replaced with a more subtle continuum.

QUESTIONS

- Do you agree with Oliver's argument?
- What difficulties might ensue if the more subtle approach which she advocates were adopted?

5.5 Section 6 of the Human Rights Act 1998

Thus far in this chapter we have been concerned with the circumstances in which defendants may be fixed with an obligation to act consistently with the general public law principles of good decision-making. It remains to confront a closely allied question: which public bodies must respect individuals' human rights arising under the European Convention on Human Rights?

......

Human Rights Act 1998

6—(1) It is unlawful for a public authority to act in a way which is incompatible with a Convention right.
  (2) Subsection (1) does not apply to an act if—
    (a) as the result of one or more provisions of primary legislation, the authority could not have acted differently; or
    (b) in the case of one or more provisions of, or made under, primary legislation which cannot be read or given effect in a way which is compatible with the Convention rights, the authority was acting so as to give effect to or enforce those provisions.
  (3) In this section 'public authority' includes—

(a) a court or tribunal, and

(b) any person certain of whose functions are functions of a public nature, but does not include either House of Parliament or a person exercising functions in connection with proceedings in Parliament.

(4) In subsection (3) "Parliament" does not include the House of Lords in its judicial capacity.

(5) In relation to a particular act, a person is not a public authority by virtue only of subsection (3)(b) if the nature of the act is private.

(6) "An act" includes a failure to act but does not include a failure to—

(a) introduce in, or lay before, Parliament a proposal for legislation; or

(b) make any primary legislation or remedial order.

Although some writers (notably Wade (2000) 116 *LQR* 217) argue for full 'horizontal effect' of the HRA, such that all defendants — public or private — would be obliged to respect Convention rights, most commentators (see, *eg*, Hunt [1998] *PL* 423 and Buxton (2000) 116 *LQR* 48) recognize that this would be inconsistent with the distinction between public authorities and others clearly envisaged by s 6. Consistently with this view, the current position is that Convention rights are directly enforceable only against public authorities. Meanwhile, private parties are bound by the ECHR only where legislation governing their relations *inter se* must be interpreted compatibly with Convention rights (under HRA s 3) or where principles of common law affecting their relationship have evolved so as to absorb Convention norms — a process which is most pronounced in relation to the tort of breach of confidence, which has developed under the influence of the Article 8 right to privacy (see Phillipson (2003) 66 *MLR* 726).

The scope of the s 6 duty to act compatibly with Convention rights is therefore crucial. Early decisions — *eg, Poplar Housing & Regeneration Community Association Ltd* v. *Donoghue* [2001] EWCA Civ 595 [2002] QB 48 and *R (Heather)* v. *Leonard Cheshire Foundation* [2002] EWCA Civ 366 [2002] 2 All ER 936 — adopted a somewhat narrow approach, borrowing from the case law on amenability to judicial review and emphasizing institutional ('what is the defendant's relationship with the state?') over functional ('is this a public function?') criteria. For instance, in the former case, the Court of Appeal, in considering the distinction between 'public' and 'private', stated (at [65]) that:

What can make an act, which would otherwise be private, public is a feature or a combination of features which impose a public character or stamp on the act. Statutory authority for what is done can at least help to mark the act as being public; so can the extent of control over the function exercised by another body which is a public authority. The more closely the acts that could be of a private nature are enmeshed in the activities of a public body, the more likely they are to be public. However, the fact that the acts are supervised by a public regulatory body does not necessarily indicate that they are of a public nature.

A rather broader approach was commended in the following case.

....

Aston Cantlow and Wilmcote with Billesley Parochial Church Council v. Wallbank [2003] UKHL 37 [2004] 1 AC 546

House of Lords

The defendants, as freehold owners of a farm constituting rectorial property, were liable to pay for all necessary repairs to the chancel of a parish church. When proceedings were brought under s 2(2) of the Chancel Repairs Act 1932, the defendants disputed their liability, arguing that the parochial church council (PCC) was obliged, by s 6 of the Human Rights Act 1998, to act compatibly with the Convention rights, and that the enforcement of chancel repair liability was inconsistent with Article 1 of Protocol 1. The PCC was successful at first instance, but the defendant successfully appealed to the Court of Appeal. The PCC then appealed to the House of Lords. The following excerpts are concerned only with the question whether the PCC constituted a public authority for s 6 purposes.

Lord Nicholls

[6] The expression 'public authority' is not defined in the Act, nor is it a recognised term of art in English law . . . So in the present case the statutory context is all important. As to that, the broad purpose sought to be achieved by section 6(1) is not in doubt. The purpose is that those bodies for whose acts the state is answerable before the European Court of Human Rights shall in future be subject to a domestic law obligation not to act incompatibly with Convention rights. If they act in breach of this legal obligation victims may henceforth obtain redress from the courts of this country. In future victims should not need to travel to Strasbourg.

[7] Conformably with this purpose, the phrase 'a public authority' in section 6(1) is essentially a reference to a body whose nature is governmental in a broad sense of that expression. It is in respect of organisations of this nature that the government is answerable under the European Convention on Human Rights. Hence, under the Human Rights Act a body of this nature is required to act compatibly with Convention rights in everything it does. The most obvious examples are government departments, local authorities, the police and the armed forces. Behind the instinctive classification of these organisations as bodies whose nature is governmental lie factors such as the possession of special powers, democratic accountability, public funding in whole or in part, an obligation to act only in the public interest, and a statutory constitution . . .

[8] A further, general point should be noted. One consequence of being a 'core' public authority, namely, an authority falling within section 6 without reference to section 6(3), is that the body in question does not itself enjoy Convention rights. It is difficult to see how a core public authority could ever claim to be a victim of an infringement of a Convention rights. A core public authority seems inherently incapable of satisfying the Convention description of a victim: 'any person, *non-governmental organisation* or group of individuals' (article 34, with emphasis added). Only victims of an unlawful act may bring proceedings under section 7 of the Human Rights Act, and the Convention description of a victim has been incorporated into the Act, by section 7(7). This feature, that a core public authority is incapable of having Convention rights of its own, is a matter to be borne in mind when considering whether or not a particular body is a core public authority. In itself this feature throws some light on how the expression 'public authority' should be understood and applied. It must always be relevant to consider whether Parliament can have intended that the body in question should have no Convention rights.

[9] In a modern developed state governmental functions extend far beyond maintenance of law and order and defence of the realm. Further, the manner in which wide ranging governmental functions are discharged varies considerably. In the interests of efficiency and economy, and for other reasons, functions of a governmental nature are frequently discharged by non-governmental bodies. Sometimes this will be a consequence of privatisation, sometimes not. One obvious example is the running of prisons by commercial organisations. Another is the discharge of regulatory functions by organisations in the private sector, for instance, the Law Society. Section 6(3)(b) gathers this type of case into the embrace of section 6 by including within the phrase 'public authority' any person whose functions include 'functions of a public nature'. This extension of the expression 'public authority' does not apply to a person if the nature of the act in question is 'private'.

[10] Again, the statute does not amplify what the expression 'public' and its counterpart 'private' mean in this context. But, here also, given the statutory context already mentioned and the repetition of the description 'public' essentially the contrast being drawn is between functions of a governmental nature and functions, or acts, which are not of that nature. I stress, however, that this is no more than a useful guide. The phrase used in the Act is public function, not governmental function.

[11] Unlike a core public authority, a 'hybrid' public authority, exercising both public functions and non-public functions, is not absolutely disabled from having Convention rights. A hybrid public authority is not a public authority in respect of an act of a private nature. Here again, as with section 6(1), this feature throws some light on the approach to be adopted when interpreting section 6(3)(b). Giving a generously wide scope to the expression 'public function' in section 6(3)(b) will further the statutory aim of promoting the observance of human rights values without depriving the bodies in question of the ability themselves to rely on Convention rights when necessary.

[12] What, then, is the touchstone to be used in deciding whether a function is public for this purpose? Clearly there is no single test of universal application. There cannot be, given the diverse nature of governmental functions and the variety of means by which these functions are discharged today. Factors to be taken into account include the extent to which in carrying out the relevant function the body is publicly funded, or is exercising statutory powers, or is taking the place of central government or local authorities, or is providing a public service.

[13] Turning to the facts in the present case, I do not think parochial church councils are 'core' public authorities. Historically the Church of England has discharged an important and influential role in the life of this country. As the established church it still has special links with central government. But the Church of England remains essentially a religious organisation. This is so even though some of the emanations of the church discharge functions which may qualify as governmental. Church schools and the conduct of marriage services are two instances. The legislative powers of the General Synod of the Church of England are another. This should not be regarded as infecting the Church of England as a whole, or its emanations in general, with the character of a governmental organisation.

[14] As to parochial church councils, their constitution and functions lend no support to the view that they should be characterised as governmental organisations or, more precisely, in the language of the statute, public authorities . . . [T]he essential role of a parochial church council is to provide a formal means, prescribed by the Church of England, whereby ex officio and elected members of the local church promote the mission of the Church and discharge financial responsibilities in respect of their own parish church, including responsibilities regarding maintenance of the fabric of the building. This smacks of a church body engaged in self-governance and promotion of its affairs. This is far removed from the type of body whose acts engage the responsibility of the state under the European Convention.

[15] I turn next to consider whether a parochial church council is a hybrid public authority. For this purpose it is not necessary to analyse each of the functions of a parochial church council and see if any of them is a public function. What matters is whether the particular act done by the plaintiff council of which complaint is made is a private act as contrasted with the discharge of a public function. The impugned act is enforcement of Mr and Mrs Wallbank's liability, as lay rectors, for the repair of the chancel of the church of St John the Baptist at Aston Cantlow. As I see it, the only respect in which there is any 'public' involvement is that parishioners have certain rights to attend church services and in respect of marriage and burial services. To that extent the state of

repair of the church building may be said to affect rights of the public. But I do not think this suffices to characterise actions taken by the parochial church council for the repair of the church as 'public'. If a parochial church council enters into a contract with a builder for the repair of the chancel arch, that could be hardly be described as a public act. Likewise when a parochial church council enforces, in accordance with the provisions of the Chancel Repairs Act 1932, a burdensome incident attached to the ownership of certain pieces of land: there is nothing particularly 'public' about this. This is no more a public act than is the enforcement of a restrictive covenant of which church land has the benefit . . .

Lord Hope

[41] The words 'public' and 'authority' in section 6(1), 'functions of a public nature' in section 6(3)(b) and 'private' in section 6(5) are, of course, important. The word 'public' suggests that there [are] some persons which may be described as authorities that are nevertheless private and not public. The word 'authority' suggests that the person has regulatory or coercive powers given to it by statute or by the common law. The combination of these two words in the single unqualified phrase 'public authority' suggests that it is the nature of the person itself, not the functions which it may perform, that is determinative. Section 6(1) does not distinguish between public and private functions. It assumes that everything that a 'core' public authority does is a public function. It applies to everything that a person does in that capacity. This suggests that some care needs to be taken to limit this category to cases where it is clear that this over-arching treatment is appropriate. The phrase 'functions of a public nature' in section 6(3), on the other hand, does not make that assumption. It requires a distinction to be drawn between functions which are public and those which are private. It has a much wider reach, and it is sensitive to the facts of each case. It is the function that the person is performing that is determinative of the question whether it is, for the purposes of that case, a 'hybrid' public authority. The question whether section 6(5) applies to a particular act depends on the nature of the act which is in question in each case . . .

[43] [After discussing the Court of Appeal's decision (see [2002] Ch 51), his Lordship observed:] [T]he width that can be given to the 'hybrid' category suggests that the purpose of the [Human Rights Act] would not be impeded if the scope to be given to the concept of a 'core' public authority were to be narrowed considerably from that indicated by the Court of Appeal . . .

[46] The reference to non-governmental organisations in article 34 [see above, para 8 of Lord Nicholls's speech] provides an important guide as to the nature of those persons who, for the purposes of s 6(1) of the Act and the remedial scheme which flows from it, are to be taken to be public authorities. Non-governmental organisations have the right of individual application to the European Court of Human Rights as victims if their Convention rights have been violated. If the [purpose of the 1998 Act is to be realised], they must be entitled to obtain a remedy for a violation of their Convention rights under section 7 in respect of acts made unlawful by section 6 . . .

[47] . . . A person who would be regarded as a non-governmental organisation within the meaning of article 34 ought not to be regarded as a 'core' public authority for the purposes of section 6. That would deprive it of the rights enjoyed by the victims of acts which are incompatible with Convention rights that are made unlawful by section 6(1) . . .

[52] The Court of Appeal left [these considerations] out of account. They looked instead for guidance to cases about the amenability of bodies to judicial review, although they recognised that they were not necessarily determinative . . . But, as Professor Oliver [[2001] PL 651] has pointed out . . ., the decided cases on the amenability of bodies to judicial review have been made for purposes which have nothing to do with the liability of the state in international law. They cannot be regarded

as determinative of a body's membership of the class of 'core' public authorities ... Nor can they be regarded as determinative of the question whether a body falls within the 'hybrid' class. That is not to say that the case law on judicial review may not provide some assistance as to what does, and what does not, constitute a 'function of a public nature' within the meaning of section 6(3)(b). It may well be helpful. But the domestic case law must be examined in the light of the jurisprudence of the Strasbourg Court as to those bodies which engage the responsibility of the State for the purposes of the Convention.

[53] At first sight there is a close link between the question whether a person is a non-governmental organisation for the purposes of article 34 and the question whether a person is a public authority against which the doctrine of the direct effect of directives operates under Community law ... [However,] [t]here is no right of individual application to the European Court of Justice in EC law. The phrase 'non-governmental organisation' has an autonomous meaning in Convention law ... [After outlining the roles of the parochial church council, his Lordship continued:]

[59] ... [N]one of these characteristics indicate that it is a governmental organisation, as that phrase is understood in the context of article 34 of the Convention. It plainly has nothing whatever to do with the process of either central or local government. It is not accountable to the general public for what it does. It receives no public funding, apart from occasional grants from English Heritage for the preservation of its historic buildings. In that respect it is in a position which is no different from that of any private individual. The statutory powers which it has been given by the Chancel Repairs Act 1932 are not exercisable against the public generally or any class or group of persons which forms part of it . . .

[61] ... There is no Act of Parliament that purports to establish it as the Church of England ... It has regulatory functions within its own sphere, but it cannot be said to be part of government. The state has not surrendered or delegated any of its functions or powers to the Church. None of the functions that the Church of England performs would have to be performed in its place by the state if the Church were to abdicate its responsibility: see *R v Chief Rabbi of the United Hebrew Congregations of Great Britain and the Commonwealth, ex parte Wachmann* [1992] 1 WLR 1036, 1042A, per Simon Brown J. The relationship which the state has with the Church of England is one of recognition, not of the devolution to it of any of the powers or functions of government . . .

[63] For these reasons I would hold that the PCC is not a 'core' public authority. As for the question whether it is a 'hybrid' public authority, I would prefer not to deal with it in the abstract. The answer must depend on the facts of each case. The issue with which your Lordships are concerned in this case relates to the functions of the PCC in the enforcement of a liability to effect repairs to the chancel ... [T]he liability of the lay-rector to repair the chancel is a burden which arises as a matter of private law from the ownership of glebe land.

[64] It is true, as Wynn-Parry J observed in *Chivers & Sons Ltd v Air Ministry* [1955] 1 Ch 585, 593, that the burden is imposed for the benefit of the parishioners. It may be said that, as the church is a historic building which is open to the public, it is in the public interest that these repairs should be carried out. It is also true that the liability to repair the chancel rests on persons who need not be members of the church and that there is, as the Court of Appeal observed [see [2002] Ch 51 at [34]], no surviving element of mutuality or mutual governance between the church and the impropriator. But none of these factors leads to the conclusion that the PCC's act in seeking to enforce the lay rector's liability on behalf of the parishioners is a public rather than a private act. The nature of the act is to be found in the nature of the obligation which the PCC is seeking to enforce. It is seeking to

enforce a civil debt. The function which it is performing has nothing to do with the responsibilities which are owed to the public by the State. I would hold that section 6(5) applies, and that in relation to this act the PCC is not for the purposes of section 6(1) a public authority.

Lords Hobhouse, Scott, and Rodger were in agreement that the PCC was not a 'core' public authority. Lords Hobhouse and Rodger further agreed that the PCC was not discharging functions of a public nature in enforcing chancel repair liability; Lord Scott, dissenting on this point, reached the contrary conclusion.

The Joint Committee on Human Rights (HL39/HC382, *The Meaning of 'Public Authority' under the Human Rights Act* (2003–04)) welcomed their Lordships' willingness in *Aston Cantlow* to balance a restrictive definition of 'core' public authorities with a wider and more flexible test for 'hybrid' bodies. Cane (2004) 120 *LQR* 41 at 45, however, is more critical, observing that their Lordships failed 'to develop what is really needed to resolve the difficulties of s 6, namely a normative theory of the reach of human rights law'.

It is, in any event, unclear to what extent *Aston Cantlow* has superseded the apparently more restrictive approach favoured by the lower courts in earlier cases. In *R (Beer)* v. *Hampshire Farmers' Markets Ltd* [2003] EWCA Civ 1056 [2004] 1 WLR 233 at [25], Dyson LJ did not regard *Aston Cantlow* as having overruled decisions such as *Donoghue* and *Heather*. In concluding that a private company, Hampshire Farmers' Markets Ltd ('HFML'), was amenable to judicial review and discharging functions of a public nature for the purposes of s 6 HRA, his Lordship accepted (at [27]) that 'it is possible to conclude that a decision by a [body which constitutes a] public authority [for s 6 purposes] is not amenable to judicial review and *vice versa*'. Nevertheless, he continued (at [29]), 'On the facts of this case, and I would suggest on the facts of most cases, the two issues march hand in hand: the answer to one provides the answer to the other.' Although attention was paid to the functions of HFML — in particular, to the fact that it was able to exclude prospective stall-holders from public markets — Dyson LJ (at [35]) refused to base his conclusion that HFML was a 'hybrid' public authority on this functional criterion alone. Instead, detailed analysis was undertaken of its relationship with Hampshire County Council, and the conclusion reached (at [40]) that:

HFML was not simply another private company that was established to run markets for profit. It was established by a local authority to take over on a non-profit basis the running of the markets that the authority had previously been running in the exercise of its statutory powers in what it considered to be the public interest.

QUESTIONS

• Was Dyson LJ right to examine the institutional status of HFML?
• Should courts, in applying s 6 HRA, draw upon administrative law cases concerning the scope of judicial review?

The Joint Committee has expressed concern at the present state of the case law, drawing particular attention to a problem which Markus [2003] *EHRLR* 92 at 97, criticizing the Court of Appeal's refusal in *Heather* to hold a contracted-out service provider subject to the HRA, describes in the following terms:

The consequence of the approach of the Court of Appeal to date is that, whether or not a person can effectively enforce their Convention rights against a provider of public services depends upon decisions made by local authorities over which a service user has little or no influence. It ignores the reality of increased reliance by local authorities upon private contractors to discharge their statutory duties and allows state bodies to avoid responsibility, deprives individuals of their ability effectively to enforce their human rights, introducing a randomness to their efficacy depending upon the arrangements in any particular geographical area.

While an expansive application of s 6 is not the only possible solution to this problem, alternatives are not without difficulty. For instance, Lord Woolf CJ's suggestion in *Heather* [2002] EWCA Civ 366 [2002] 2 All ER 936 at [34] that service providers could be placed under contractual obligations to respect Convention rights raises problems of privity (even under the Contracts (Rights of Third Parties) Act 1999 the ability of individuals to enforce terms in agency-provider contracts remains limited) and consistency (variation in contractual terms would be likely as between different contracting out authorities). Nor is reliance upon the HRA liability of the contracting out body itself a panacea. In *Heather*, the claimants' Article 8 challenge to the decision of a charitable body to close the care home in which they had been placed by their local and health authorities in exercise of statutory powers would have been sustainable *only* if the defendant (a charitable foundation) had been exercising 'functions of a public nature', since the local and health authorities — undeniably 'core' public authorities — could not themselves cause the home to remain open.

In view of these problems, the Joint Committee argued (*op cit* at [42]) that the more expansive approach of *Aston Cantlow* should be followed, and went on (at [140]) to elaborate its preferred test:

The key test of whether a function is public is whether it is one for which the government has taken responsibility in the public interest. For example, although the various activities involved in care for the sick may be performed by anyone, the State has chosen, through a comprehensive social programme, to provide healthcare to those who wish to receive healthcare from the State rather than privately. This programme is undertaken in the public interest to provide what the government considers to be an important social service. In our view, discharge of duties necessary for provision of the government programme of healthcare is a public function. Discharge of healthcare services, in itself, is not.

It followed, said the Committee (at [142]), that 'for a body to discharge a public function, it does not need to do so under direct statutory authority'. Sunkin [2004] *PL* 643 at 655–656 explains that this approach is

programmatic rather than substantive ... Focusing as it does on government programmes this approach recognises that very few services are inherently public (caring for the sick or educating children can be provided by the state or by commercial or charitable organisations) and that views about what constitutes public functions can change over time. It also recognises that the public nature of functions should not depend on the particular legal vehicle used for their performance: in particular a public function does not cease to be public simply because it has been contracted out ...

Craig (2002) 118 *LQR* 551 at 556 agrees that, 'It is difficult to see why the nature of a function should alter if it is contracted out, rather than being performed in house [*ie* by a core public authority]. If it is a public function when undertaken in house, it should equally be so when contracted out.' Against this background, consider the following extract.

....

Oliver, 'Functions of a Public Nature under the Human Rights Act'
[2004] PL 329

. . . Public authorities are bound by s. 6 HRA to respect Convention rights in all that they do, even when performing acts of a private nature. Many activities of and functions exercised by standard (or core) public authorities such as local authorities and government departments are indisputably *not* activities or functions "of a public nature". If all the functions of all core public authorities were "functions of a public nature", then there would have been no need to make the distinction in section 6 between public authorities and bodies certain of whose functions are of a public nature, for the Act could have applied quite simply to all exercises of functions of a public nature. Cleaning council offices [is] an example of an act or activity the nature of which is private. Managing car parking space would be another. Under HRA s. 6(1) standard public authorities exercising even private functions or activities are bound to respect Convention rights: the s. 6(1) duty does not depend on the classification of a function as of a public nature. However, the courts and commentators sometimes assume that the fact that a standard public authority is bound to respect Convention rights in all that it does means that all its functions are "public functions" or "functions of a public nature" when this is quite clearly not the case. In particular it is clear that not all decisions of standard public authorities are subject to judicial review.

When a standard public authority contracts or arranges informally with a private body for the latter to deliver certain services or do certain acts which the public authority itself or its employees have done in the past or might do, it follows that sometimes the activity contracted for with the private body will not be of a public nature and the private contractor will therefore not be under an obligation under s. 6 HRA to respect the Convention rights of those it deals with. An example would be where a local authority stops employing direct labour to maintain its parks and gardens and contracts the work out to self-employed gardeners or gardening contractors; or when it stops employing direct labour to clean the Town Hall and contracts with a private company for the cleaning to be done. Gardening, cleaning and managing a car park, it seems to me, are quite clearly acts the nature of which is private. If on the other hand the core public authority contracts with a private body (such as HFML in the [*Beer*] case) for the latter to exercise special statutory or common law authority, then the function will be of a public nature and the contractor will be under s. 6(3)(b) obligations.

It may of course seem unfair to the individual in receipt of services or the employee who is working for a private body rather than a public authority, that his or her Convention rights would have been respected if the activity had been done by the public authority itself and its direct labour force, but are not required to be respected by the private body to which the work is contracted out. But it was a deliberate policy in the Human Rights Act that there should be differences between the duties of public authorities and those of private bodies, unless the private body were exercising a function of a public nature, in which case the Act would have direct vertical effect . . .

QUESTIONS

- Do you agree with Oliver's analysis?
- Is the policy which she attributes to the HRA a defensible one?

Two issues should be noted in conclusion. First, Oliver is correct to point out that contracted-out service providers will *not* be bound by s 6 in respect of some functions to which s 6 does apply when they are discharged by core public authorities: the latter are bound by s 6 in all that they do, whereas the former are bound only in respect of functions of a public nature. Secondly, however, it is surely the case, on a normative level, that if something truly *is* a public function when performed in-house, then contracting-out should not render it private; as we have already seen, the contracting-out process can, in legal terms, be denied such transformative capacity provided that the test for hybrid public authorities is conceived in the programmatic terms favoured by the Joint Committee.

5.6 Concluding Remarks

Compared with the position which obtained 25 years ago, the scope of judicial review today is unrecognizable. The change is, indisputably, for the better. No longer is the prerogative regarded as a discretionary power which may be exercised without regard to the principles of good administration. Misplaced judicial deference to the 'royal' prerogative has yielded to judicial recognition that it is now, in many respects, just another executive power. Similarly, the formalism of the past has given way to a new emphasis on substance as the courts' concern with the source of the power has been eclipsed by concerns as to justiciability. These developments in relation to the prerogative are mirrored in the courts' attitude to *de facto* powers. Here, too, matters of substance, rather than form, are now to the fore as the courts strive to avoid being deceived by what Sir John Donaldson, in *Datafin*, referred to as the new subtlety and complexity of executive power. The willingness of the courts to vindicate the rule of law in these new contexts is a positive development, but there are, as we have seen, a number of difficulties which remain fully to be resolved; contractualization poses particular problems for the scope of both judicial review and s 6 HRA. Taken as a whole, however, the developments that are mapped in this chapter are to be welcomed. They evidence an increasingly mature system of administrative law which is concerned to ensure that all public power is used responsibly, and which is beginning to elevate substance over form as the new province of judicial review is mapped.

FURTHER RESOURCES

Beatson and Friedmann (eds), *Good Faith and Fault in Contract Law* (Oxford 1995), ch 10 (Beatson)

Birks (ed), *The Frontiers of Liability* (Oxford 1994), vol 1, ch 11 (Cane)

Craig, 'Contracting Out, the Human Rights Act and the Scope of Judicial Review' (2002) 118 *LQR* 551

Joint Committee on Human Rights, HL39/HC382, *The Meaning of 'Public Authority' under the Human Rights Act* (2003–04) *www.publications.parliament.uk/pa/jt200304/jtselect/jtrights/39/3902.htm*

Oliver, *Common Values and the Public/Private Divide* (London 1999)

Sunkin, 'Pushing Forward the Frontiers of Human Rights Protection: The Meaning of Public Authority under the Human Rights Act' [2004] *PL* 643

Taggart (ed), *The Province of Administrative Law* (Oxford 1997)

RETENTION OF DISCRETION

6.1 Introduction

This chapter is concerned with various principles of administrative law which require decision-makers to retain the discretion which they are granted. In general terms, the law in this area aims to ensure that decision-making occurs in accordance with the scheme envisaged by Parliament, rather than in a manner which is distorted by limitations and practices superimposed upon the discretionary power by its holder.

More specifically, the rules of administrative law which have been developed in this context serve two distinct (but related) objectives. First, they require that decision-making is carried out by the specific agency to which the discretion was, in the first place, confided; the transfer or delegation of power to other agencies is therefore, in general, prohibited. Secondly, the law seeks to ensure that the agency has at its disposal the full discretion which was granted to it, and therefore precludes behaviour — such as the adoption of rigid policies or entry into contractual arrangements — which has the effect of narrowing the discretion.

Further questions arise concerning the extent to which discretion may be limited by representations made by, or on behalf of, agencies as to how their discretionary powers will be exercised; these issues are addressed in ch 7.

6.2 Delegation of Discretionary Power

6.2.1 A Presumption Against Delegation

Discretionary power may not, in general, be delegated. This notion is sometimes expressed through the maxim *delegatus non potest delegare*, meaning that the body to which power has been delegated by Parliament may not itself delegate that power. This principle of administrative law is not, however, an immovable rule; rather, it takes effect as a presumption. When interpreting a statutory scheme the courts therefore begin by assuming that Parliament intends the power in question to be exercised only by the decision-maker specified in the legislation, and the question then becomes whether anything in the scheme rebuts that presumption, expressly or by implication.

Some legislation expressly permits discretionary powers to be delegated (see, *eg*, Local Government Act 1972, ss 101–102). However, the general policy that discretionary power should be exercised by its statutory holder means that such provisions tend to be narrowly construed. For instance, in *General Medical Council v. UK Dental Board* [1936] Ch 41, although the Dentists Act 1921 permitted the GMC to delegate functions to an executive committee, the court held that this power of delegation did not extend to disciplinary functions. This reflects the fact (also illustrated by the following case) that the courts' willingness to find statutory permission for delegation and the importance of the function in question appear to be inversely related.

....

Barnard v. National Dock Labour Board [1953] 2 QB 18
Court of Appeal

The claimants appealed from a decision of McNair J dismissing their claim for a declaration that they had been wrongfully suspended and that, as their suspension had been carried out not by the local dock labour board but by the port manager, it was unlawful.

Denning LJ

... The second matter on which the men sought the ruling of the court was the question of procedure; whether they had been lawfully suspended; and this involved a consideration of the disciplinary powers of the board. Under the Dock Workers (Regulation of Employment) Scheme, 1947, the power to suspend a man is entrusted to the local dock labour board, which is composed of equal numbers of representatives of the workers and employers. In this case the board did not themselves suspend the men; the port manager did. The local board did not have anything to do with it; they did not see the report made by the employers; they did not investigate the matter; they did not make any decision upon it themselves; they left it all to the port manager. The suspension was not brought to their notice until after the appeal tribunal had given its decision.

It was urged on us that the local board had power to delegate their functions to the port manager on the ground that the power of suspension was an administrative and not a judicial function. It was suggested that the action of the local board in suspending men was similar in character to the action of an employer in dismissing him. I do not accept this view. Under the provisions of the scheme, so far from the board being in the position of an employer, the board are put in a judicial position between the men and the employers; they are to receive reports from the employers and investigate them; they have to inquire whether the man has been guilty of misconduct, such as failing to comply with a lawful order, or failing to comply with the provisions of the scheme; and if they find against him they can suspend him without pay, or can even dismiss him summarily. In those circumstances they are exercising a judicial function just as much as the tribunals which were considered by this court in the cornporters' case, *Abbott v. Sullivan* [1952] 1 K.B. 189, and in *Lee v. Showmen's Guild of Great Britain* [1952] 2 Q.B. 329, the only difference being that those were domestic tribunals, and this is a statutory one. The board, by their procedure, recognize that before they suspend a man they must give him notice of the charge and an opportunity of making an explanation. That is entirely consonant with the view that they exercise a judicial function and not an administrative one, and we should, I think, so hold.

While an administrative function can often be delegated, a judicial function rarely can be. No judicial tribunal can delegate its functions unless it is enabled to do so expressly or by necessary implication. In *Local Government Board v. Arlidge* [1915] A.C. 120, the power to delegate was given by necessary implication; but there is nothing in this scheme authorizing the board to delegate this function, and it cannot be implied. It was suggested that it would be impracticable for the board to sit as a board to decide all these cases; but I see nothing impracticable at all; they have only to fix their quorum at two members and arrange for two members, one from each side, employers and workers, to be responsible for a week at a time: probably each pair would only have to sit on one day during their week . . .

Singleton and Romer LJJ also delivered judgments in favour of allowing the appeal. The appeal was therefore allowed.

What lies at the root of this presumption against delegation? Most straightforwardly, *parliamentary intention*: if Parliament has specified that a particular agency should take the decision, then Parliament's will must prevail. Although this follows straightforwardly from the fact that Parliament is sovereign, there are richer normative reasons why the decision should be taken by the agency chosen by Parliament. In the first place, the decision-maker designated in the legislation is likely to have been chosen because of its *institutional ability* to take decisions in the area in question, due to the expertise of its personnel, its integration into a wider decision-making structure, or its ability to gain access to relevant information and expert advice. Moreover, the designated agency is most likely to be an *accountable* decision-maker: it may well be subject to a regime of political accountability and, in any event, its role in making decisions in the relevant area will be transparent, its specification in the legislation making it readily identifiable as the responsible agency.

6.2.2 Conflicting Policies

However, while there are strong policy reasons for the existence of a presumption against delegation, these must be weighed against counterarguments which call for greater flexibility.

Willis, '*Delegatus non potest Delegare*' (1943) 21 Canadian Bar Review 257

. . . The presumption that the person named was selected because of some aptitude peculiar to himself requires the authority named in the statute to use its own peculiar aptitude and forbids it to entrust its statutory discretion to another who may be less apt than it, unless it is clear from the circumstances that some reason other than its aptitude dictated the naming of it to exercise the discretion. Because, however, the courts will readily mould the literal words of a statute to such a construction as will best achieve its object; because they will, recognizing the facts of modern government, readily imply in an authority such powers as it would normally be expected to possess; because the presumption of deliberate selection, strong when applied to the case of a principal who appoints an agent or a testator who selects a trustee, wears thin when applied to a statute which authorizes some governmental authority, sometimes with a fictitious name such as "Governor-in-Council" or "Minister of Justice", to exercise a discretion which everyone, even the legislature, knows will in fact be exercised by an unknown underling in the employ of the authority, the *prima facie* rule of *delegatus non potest delegare* will readily give way, like the principles on which it rests, to slight indications of contrary intent.

What are these indications? The *prima facie* rule is displaced, of course, by a section in the statute which expressly permits the authority entrusted with a discretion to delegate it to another. In the absence of such a provision, how does the court decide whether the rule is or is not intended to apply; how does it decide whether to read in the word 'personally' or the words 'or any person authorized by it'? The language of the statute does not, *ex hypothesi*, help it; it is driven therefore to the scope and object of the statute. Is there anything in the nature of the authority to which the discretion is entrusted, in the situation in which the discretion is to be exercised, in the object which its exercise is expected to achieve to suggest that the legislature did not intend to confine the authority to the personal exercise of its discretion? This question is answered in practice by comparing the *prima facie* rule with the known practices or the apprehended needs of the authority in doing its work; the court inquires whether the policy-scheme of the statute is such as could not easily be realized unless the policy which requires that a discretion be exercised by the authority named thereto be displaced; it weighs the presumed desire of the legislature for the judgment of the authority it has named against the presumed desire of the legislature that the process of government shall go on in its accustomed and most effective manner and where there is a conflict between the two policies, it determines which under all the circumstances is the most important . . .

As Willis indicates, the over-rigid application of the non-delegation principle is liable to compromise the efficient conduct of government — and the policy objectives underlying the non-delegation principle apply with more or less force, depending on the context. It is therefore necessary to acknowledge that demands of expediency, pragmatism, and good administration may, and sometimes do, require that decision-making is devolved. As Willis observes, one way in which the courts are able to balance these conflicting policies is by *disapplying the non-delegation principle* where the context demands. A more subtle response, however, focusses on *the nature of delegation itself*: as we will see in the following sections, there are certain practices, such as consulting outside agencies and the devolution of decision-making within government departments, which are held to be wholly acceptable practices which do not constitute delegation at all. By manipulating the concept of delegation thus, the courts are able to remove what are regarded as legitimate modes of decision-making from the reach of the non-delegation principle.

6.2.3 The Nature of Delegation

Given that delegation is *prima facie* prohibited, it is crucial to work out the location of the dividing line between practices which are considered to involve delegation and other forms of administrative conduct which are regarded as acceptable. The most straightforward cases — such as *Barnard* v. *National Dock Labour Board* [1953] 2 QB 18 (see above at 6.2.1) and *Vine* v. *National Dock Labour Board* [1957] AC 488 — are those in which the designated decision-maker purports simply to hand over its power to another agency. Such cases clearly involve delegation and therefore present little difficulty (albeit that, as seen above, the non-delegation presumption may be rebutted).

It is, however, possible for delegation to occur in more subtle ways; in such situations, the courts habitually look beyond the form of the decision-making practice, seeking instead to appreciate the reality of the situation. This can cut both ways. On the one hand, courts are alive to the fact that decision-making cannot — indeed, should not — occur within an institutional bubble. Practices such as consulting outside bodies and utilizing expertise from outside the decision-making body are to be applauded, since they tend to increase the quality of decisions, allowing the designated agency to form rounder and better-informed views. There is, however, a distinction — sometimes a fine one — between seeking guidance from an external agency and placing so much weight on its opinion that it becomes, in substance if not in form, the true decision-maker.

It follows that superficially legitimate practices may conceal arrangements that amount to delegations of power. For example, where the designated decision-maker merely ratifies decisions taken by a delegate, the courts are quick to recognize that the former's involvement is purely formal, and that the decision is in substance that of the latter. This point was taken by Denning LJ in *Barnard* [1953] 2 QB 18 at 40 (and see also *High* v. *Billings* (1903) 89 LT 550 and *Labour Relations Board of Saskatoon* v. *Spears* [1948] 1 DLR 340):

... [I]t was suggested that even if the board could not delegate their functions, at any rate they could ratify the actions of the port manager; but if the board have no power to delegate their functions to the port manager, they can have no power to ratify what he has done. The effect of ratification is to make it equal to a prior command; but just as a prior command, in the shape of a delegation, would be useless, so also is a ratification.

The courts' gaze also penetrates the surface in situations where the designated decision-maker effectively surrenders its power by making its decision contingent upon the opinion of some other agency. In this situation, too, the reality of the decision-making practice is that discretion is being exercised other than by the intended recipient: in the absence of statutory authorization, such practice constitutes unlawful delegation.

Lavender and Sons Ltd v. *Minister of Housing and Local Government* [1970] 1 WLR 1231
Queen's Bench Division

The claimant, a gravel extractor, purchased agricultural land, part of which was located in an area which, pursuant to government policy formulated on the basis of the Waters Report on sand and gravel extraction, was protected against such extraction and preserved instead for agriculture. Nevertheless, the claimant sought planning permission to extract gravel. The local planning authority consulted all interested parties including the Minster of Agriculture, who objected on agricultural grounds. The planning authority ultimately refused permission, prompting the claimant to appeal unsuccessfully to the Minister of Housing and Local Government. In explaining his decision, the Minister said that it was his policy to withhold permission in such cases 'unless the Minister of Agriculture is not opposed'; since the Minister of Agriculture had not withdrawn his objection, permission was denied. The claimant sought to have the decision of the Minister of Housing and Local Government quashed, arguing, *inter alia*, that he had unlawfully fettered his discretion by effectively giving a power of veto to the Minister of Agriculture.

Willis J

... It is common ground that the Minister must be open to persuasion that the land should not remain in the Waters reservation. How can his mind be open to persuasion, how can an applicant establish an "exceptional case" in the face of an inflexible attitude by the Minister of Agriculture? That attitude was well known before the inquiry, it was maintained during the inquiry, and presumably thereafter. The inquiry was no doubt, in a sense, into the Minister of Agriculture's objection, since, apart from that objection, it might well have been that no inquiry would have been necessary, but I do not think that the Minister after the inquiry can be said in any real sense to have given genuine consideration to whether on planning (including agricultural) grounds this land could be worked. It seems to me that by adopting and applying his stated policy he has in effect inhibited himself from exercising a proper discretion (which would of course be guided by policy considerations) in any case where the Minister of Agriculture has made and maintained an objection to mineral working in an agricultural reservation. Everything else might point to the desirability of granting permission, but by applying and acting on his stated policy I think the Minister has fettered himself in such a way that in this case it was not he who made the decision for which Parliament made him responsible. It was the decision of the Minister of Agriculture not to waive his objection which was decisive in this case, and while that might properly prove to be the decisive factor for the Minister when taking into account all material considerations, it seems to me quite wrong for a policy to be applied which in reality eliminates all the material considerations save only the consideration, when that is the case, that the Minister of Agriculture objects. That means, as I think, that the Minister has by his stated policy delegated to the Minister of Agriculture the effective decision on any appeal within the agricultural reservations where the latter objects to the working . . .

I am satisfied that the applicants should succeed. I think the Minister failed to exercise a proper or indeed any discretion by reason of the fetter which he imposed upon its exercise in acting solely in accordance with his stated policy; and further, that upon the true construction of the Minister's letter the decision to dismiss the appeal, while purporting to be that of the Minister, was in fact, and improperly, that of the Minister of Agriculture, Fisheries and Food.

An order to quash the decision of the Minister of Housing and Local Government was granted.

QUESTION

- How far, if at all, does the principle applied in *Lavender* differ from that applied in *Barnard* (see above at 6.2.1)?

6.2.4 Departmental Decision-Making in Central Government

We have already seen that the general policy that discretionary powers must be exercised by the grantee falls to be balanced against the need for efficient government and expeditious decision-making. The tension between the objectives of the non-delegation principle and these other imperatives is especially acute in relation to decision-making in central government departments, for reasons made clear in our next excerpt. As a result the courts have been persuaded, in this context, to modify their usual approach.

....

In Re Golden Chemical Products Ltd [1976] Ch 300
Chancery Division

Section 35 of the Companies Act 1967 empowered the Board of Trade, where it appeared expedient in the public interest, to present a petition for the winding up of a company. The functions of the Board of Trade were exercisable by the Secretary of State for Trade. Gill was a civil servant in the Department of Trade holding the office of Inspector of Companies. He presented a petition under s 35 in respect of Golden Chemical Products Ltd. As a preliminary issue, the court considered whether the power to present such a petition could be exercised by the Secretary of State acting through a departmental officer, rather than acting personally.

Brightman J

. . . The practice, as a general rule, is that the Inspector of Companies decides what companies shall be investigated under section 109 of the Act of 1967 and whether under section 35 it is expedient in the public interest that a company shall be wound up and whether a petition ought to be presented.

Mr. Gill's immediate superior, one of the under-secretaries, has a fairly close contact with Mr. Gill's work as Inspector of Companies and knows precisely what is going on. Mr. Gill has two chief examiners under him but they are not permitted to exercise the powers of section 35. In a very important case Mr. Gill may decide to refer the matter to the under-secretary rather than deal with it himself. Exceptionally a decision may be taken by the Secretary of State himself. But normally it is Mr. Gill, as Inspector of Companies, who operates section 35 . . . To put the matter shortly, Mr. Gill exercises the powers given to the Secretary of State by section 35 because that is the departmental practice and not because they have been delegated to him by the Secretary of State or by any other superior. I find as a fact that Mr. Gill is an officer of the Department of Trade entrusted by the Secretary of State for Trade with the power to make decisions under section 35.

Mr. Chadwick, for the Secretary of State, has formulated five propositions. (1) As a general rule a Minister is not required to exercise personally every power and discretion conferred upon him by statute. It is otherwise if there is a context in the statute which shows that the power is entrusted to the Minister personally. (2) As a general rule it is for the Minister or his appropriate officials to decide which of his officers shall exercise a particular power. (3) Unless the level at which the power is to be exercised appears from the statute, it is not for the courts to examine the level or to inquire whether a particular official entrusted with the power is the appropriate person to exercise that power. (4) As a general rule officers of a government department exercise powers incidental and appropriate to their functions. In the absence of a statutory requirement it is neither necessary nor usual for specific authority to be given orally or in writing in relation to a specific power. (5) Constitutionally there is no delegation by a Minister to his officers. When an officer exercises a power or discretion entrusted to him, constitutionally and legally that exercise is the act of the Minister.

Mr. Chadwick relies upon four cases, the earliest of which is *Carltona Ltd. v. Commissioners of Works* [1943] 2 All E.R. 560. Regulation 51(1) of the Defence (General) Regulations 1939, read with certain other enactments, provided that a competent authority, if it appeared to that authority necessary or expedient so to do, might requisition land. An assistant secretary of the Ministry of Works and Planning, which was the relevant department, signed a requisitioning notice. The notice was challenged by the proprietor of the land on the ground, among others, that the Commissioners of Works, wrongly assumed by the proprietor to be the competent authority, had not themselves personally brought their minds to bear on the exercise of the power. The argument, allowing for the necessary interpolation, was rejected. Lord Greene M.R. said, at p. 563:

> "In the administration of government in this country the functions which are given to Ministers (and constitutionally properly given to Ministers because they are constitutionally responsible) are functions so multifarious that no Minister could ever personally attend to them. To take the example of the present case no doubt there have been thousands of requisitions in this country by individual ministries. It cannot be supposed that this regulation meant that, in each case, the Minister in person should direct his mind to the matter. The duties imposed upon Ministers and the powers given to Ministers are normally exercised under the authority of the Ministers by responsible officials of the department. Public business could not be carried on if that were not the case. Constitutionally, the decision of such an official is, of course, the decision of the Minister. The Minister is responsible. It is he who must answer before Parliament for anything that his officials have done under his authority, and, if for an important matter he selected an official of such junior standing that he could not be expected competently to perform the work, the Minister would have to answer for that in Parliament. The whole system of departmental organisation and administration is based on the view that Ministers, being responsible to Parliament, will see that important duties are committed to experienced officials. If they do not do that, Parliament is the place where complaint must be made against them.
>
> In the present case the assistant secretary, a high official of the Ministry, was the person entrusted with the work of looking after this particular matter and the question, therefore, is,

relating those facts to the argument with which I am dealing, did he direct his mind to the matters to which he was bound to direct it in order to act properly under the regulation?"

The other members of the court agreed.

In the case before me, Mr. Gill, pursuant to the organisation of the Department of Trade, for which organisation the Secretary of State for Trade is responsible to Parliament, is the person who exercises the powers conferred on the Secretary of State by section 35 unless Mr. Gill decides to refer a particular matter to his superior. The *Carltona* case is authority that such a devolution of power — delegation is the wrong word — is lawful. At first blush the *Carltona* case, which has been applied in other cases, appears decisive of the preliminary issue.

[His Lordship then considered three other cases to the same effect — *Lewisham Metropolitan Borough and Town Clerk v. Roberts* [1949] 2 K.B. 608, *R v. Skinner* [1968] 2 Q.B. 700 and *R v. Holt* [1968] 1 W.L.R. 1942 — and continued:] Counsel for the company sought to breach this formidable line of authority by evolving certain counter-propositions which can be shortly paraphrased in this way. Where a power is conferred on a Minister to do an act if it appears to him expedient, the execution of that act, once it has appeared expedient to the Minister, can naturally be delegated within the department; for once the decision has been taken, the execution of the act is purely administrative. But, unless the statute conferring the power expressly or by implication otherwise provides, the initial decision-making process can be performed by someone other than the Minister if, but only if, it leads to no serious invasion of the freedom or property rights of the subject. There are, therefore, two categories of decision-making power, those which must, and those which need not, be exercised by the Minister personally. I have not formulated these propositions exactly as originally presented but I have, I hope, accurately paraphrased them so as to accord with the argument as it developed during the course of Mr. Muir Hunter's [counsel for the company] submissions. The question therefore before me, was whether the power in section 35 was such as to require the personal attention of the Minister before being exercised. He referred me first to *Liversidge v. Anderson* [1942] A.C. 206 and *Greene v. Secretary of State for Home Affairs* [1942] A.C. 284. These were cases in which the appellant sought to challenge a detention order made under the Defence (General) Regulations 1939, regulation 18B. This regulation provided that if the Secretary of State had reasonable cause to believe a person to be of hostile origin or associations, etc., he might make an order that the person be detained. It was not suggested in those cases, submitted Mr. Muir Hunter, that such a power could be exercised by a mere official of the Home Office. The appeals proceeded on the basis that the decision was taken, and was rightly taken, by the Minister personally. Mr. Muir Hunter also referred me to a large number of other cases where important issues were involved in the exercise of a statutory decision-making power and the decision was taken by the Minister personally.

. . . If there is a true distinction which must be drawn as a matter of law between powers which the Minister must exercise personally and those which can be exercised by an officer of his department, I might well come to the view that the power given by section 35 is so potentially damaging that it falls into the former category, however burdensome that may be to a Secretary of State personally. But is such a distinction to be drawn? I find no warrant for it in the authorities. In fact, the reverse. The accuracy of the breath test equipment with which *R v. Skinner* [1968] 2 Q.B. 700 was concerned was of vital importance to every motorist as indeed the judgment of the Court of Appeal recognised . . . If a motorist fails the breath test he is arrested. So if the equipment over-registers, an innocent subject is placed under arrest; if it under-registers, a potentially lethal motorist is let loose on the highway. Yet the Court of Appeal decided that although such a 'vitally important matter might well have occupied the Minister's personal attention . . . there is in principle no obligation upon the Minister to give it his personal attention': p. 709. As Mr. Chadwick pointed out, there are important cases in which the Minister will exercise a statutory discretion personally, not because it is a legal necessity but because it is a political necessity. The regulation 18B cases are examples.

I reach the conclusion that Mr. Muir Hunter's submissions have not started to breach the formidable line of authority against which they were gallantly ranged. Nor do I think that the principle which he advocates is of practical application. A distinction between a case which involves a serious invasion of the freedom or property rights of the subject, and a case which involves a similar invasion that is not serious, seems to me to be impossibly vague. I am aware that the absence of a precise demarcation line is not, as Mr. Muir Hunter reminded me, a practical impediment to telling night from day. But if Mr. Muir Hunter's principles were adopted, it seems to me that one would be groping in a perpetual twilight, except at the extremes of midnight and midday . . .

Declaration accordingly.

QUESTIONS

- Do you share Brightman J's view that statutory powers should not be divided into those which can and those which cannot be exercised by officials?
- If such division were to be undertaken, what criteria should be applied in seeking to locate a given power in one or the other category?

The 'Carltona principle', as it is known, raises a number of issues. The first concerns its relationship with the non-delegation principle. The traditional view is that the two principles can comfortably be reconciled. In his judgment above, Brightman J states that in this context we are concerned with the devolution, rather than the delegation, of power. This point was amplified by Lord Donaldson MR in R v. *Secretary of State for the Home Department, ex parte Oladehinde* [1991] 1 AC 254 at 284, who said that, when the *Carltona* principle is in play, 'The civil servant acts not as the delegate, but as the *alter ego*, of the Secretary of State. "Devolution" may be a better word [than "delegation"].' On this view, the non-delegation principle is never even engaged in *Carltona* situations, thanks to the application of the legal fiction that the Minister to whom the power is legally confided and the official who actually exercises it are one and the same person.

However, reliance upon legal fiction is rarely satisfactory: it masks the reality of the position, and inhibits attempts to rationalize and evaluate the law. A more realistic view was advanced by Lord Diplock in *Bushell* v. *Secretary of State for the Environment* [1981] AC 75 at 95. He said that, 'Discretion in making administrative decisions is conferred upon a Minister not as an individual but as the holder of an office in which he will have available to him in arriving at his decision the collective knowledge, experience and expertise of all those who serve the Crown in the department of which, for the time being, he is the political head.' Freedland [1996] *PL* 19 at 22 applauds this approach, commenting that 'rather than seeing Parliament as indulging in a fiction that Ministers will normally exercise their discretions personally, it is preferable to see the draftsman as employing a notation or code whereby the entrusting of discretion to a government department is expressed by conferring that discretion upon the Minister concerned'.

The second issue arising from *Carltona* concerns the justification for the principle. In the passage from Lord Greene's *Carltona* judgment quoted by Brightman J above, two justifications are advanced. The first concerns the *pragmatic* necessity of allowing ministerial discretion to be exercised at official level, given the vast number of powers vested in Ministers. Secondly, Lord Greene said that, in *constitutional* terms, it is acceptable for officials to exercise discretionary powers on Ministers' behalf because the former are answerable to the latter; in turn, Ministers are answerable to Parliament, through the doctrine of ministerial accountability, for the conduct of their departments. A chain of accountability therefore ensures that the exercise by officials of discretionary powers is subject to scrutiny. However, this constitutional justification for the *Carltona* doctrine is under increasing pressure. On a general level, the efficacy of the doctrine of ministerial accountability is widely questioned (see, *eg* Scott [1996] *PL* 410) in an era in which executive dominance of Parliament is more complete than ever before. More specifically, the changing architecture of government means that the lines of accountability between Ministers and officials are becoming increasingly blurred. As Freedland explains, this problem is particularly acute in relation to 'Next Steps' agencies (the role of which was explained above at 1.5.3).

....

Freedland, 'The Rule Against Delegation and the *Carltona* Doctrine in an Agency Context' [1996] PL 19

. . . The setting up of these executive agencies has proceeded on the assumption that there has been no need to seek statutory authority to make their establishment lawful and valid . . . [T]he basic constitutive act of separating off the agency within the parent department was not seen as creating or requiring the creation of a separate legal corporate entity, and was seen as lying within the inherent power of the Crown to organise the conduct of its business. Included within and inherent to that conception of the constitutional status of the new executive agencies was the view that there was no problem of unlawful or invalid delegation where a function assigned to the parent department was discharged by the agency. In particular, it seems to have been concluded that the *Carltona* principle extended to and protected the exercise by a civil servant acting within an executive agency of the department concerned, of a discretion conferred upon a Minister . . .

The parent department retains, of course, a kind of responsibility for the decision-making which occurs at agency level. But the separation of the agency as a distinct centre of decision-making means that the departmental responsibility has been turned into a secondary and essentially supervisory one. The parent department has become in effect accountable for its supervision of the agency; moreover, that departmental accountability is, in a way which mirrors that of the agency, increasingly conceived of in financial terms — the primary role of the parent department tends to become that of accounting to the Cabinet and to Parliament for the efficiency and good financial management of the departmental operation as conducted through the subsidiary agencies . . .

My argument about the non-delegation/*Carltona* doctrine [is] . . . that if its history and current state are properly understood, it becomes clear that the application of the *Carltona* doctrine was heavily contingent upon a certain structure of civil service administration which assumed and depended upon a very active notion of ministerial responsibility to Parliament. The decline of that kind of constitutional practice has meant that the application of the non-delegation/*Carltona* doctrine now requires a very specific inquiry as to whether the decision-making structure within which a particular discretion is exercised is a sufficiently integrated and coherent one to sustain the conclusion that the discretion is being exercised in a meaningful sense by the person or body and within the decision-making framework which was intended and is appropriate . . .

There have been indications (*eg* in *R* v. *Secretary of State for the Home Department, ex parte Oladehinde* [1991] 1 AC 254) that the courts are willing to apply the *Carltona* doctrine discriminatingly, such that its operation is limited to circumstances in which there is an adequate relationship of responsibility between Ministers and officials. However, it has now been established, as our next case shows, that the *Carltona* doctrine *can* apply to delegations of power to Next Steps agencies.

....

R v. *Secretary of State for Social Services, ex parte Sherwin* (1996) 32 BMLR 1
Queen's Bench Division

The Benefits Agency (which was an executive agency of the then Department for Social Security, which was responsible for making benefit payments) considered that, contrary to the view of an appeal tribunal, the claimant was not entitled to a particular benefit. The Agency therefore appealed to the Social Security Commissioner. Legislation empowered the Secretary of State to suspend payment of benefits pending appeal, provided that notice of his intention to do so was given within one month of the original award. Agency staff decided to exercise this power. The claimant contended that the power could not in law be exercised by the *Agency*; that the *Secretary of State* had failed to give the requisite notice, and that payments should therefore be made.

Latham J

. . . The *Carltona* principle entitles the Secretary of State to authorise a person of suitable seniority in his department to exercise on his behalf the discretionary power . . . [A]ny decision taken in the exercise of that power by such a person will be a decision of the Secretary of State for which the Secretary of State is constitutionally responsible and accountable to Parliament . . .

The person who exercised the power in the present case was Richard Paul Ash, who describes himself in his affidavit as follows:

> 'I have been a civil servant for a total of 21 years and am now a Higher Executive Officer . . . within the Department of Social Security . . . working at the Benefits Agency Office in Tame Valley, Birmingham where, at the time of the challenged decision I was an Assistant Manager responsible for training and appeals. In that capacity I took the decision to suspend payment of the Applicant's benefit which are challenged in these proceedings.'

. . . Prima facie, . . . the decision would appear to be an unexceptionable example of a decision taken in accordance with the *Carltona* principle. Mr Drabble, on behalf of the applicant, argues that by reason of the creation of the Benefits Agency, the position is no longer capable of being analysed in straight forward *Carltona* terms . . . One of the purposes of [the Next Steps initiative] was undoubtedly to ensure a separation between the policy functions of a department, which were to be the primary responsibility of the Secretary of State, and the operational or management functions. The extent to which the latter were to be divorced from the former in any given case was obviously intended to be determined by the framework document for the department in question. The relevant framework document setting up the Benefits Agency established it expressly as a part of the Department of Social Security. Paragraph 1.2 of the framework document is in the following terms:

> 'The Agency works within the DSS as a whole to promote economic effective and efficient coherent administration of Social Security Services. The Agency acts on behalf of and in accordance with any directions, where appropriate, of the Secretary of State for Social Security and in accordance with the framework set out in this document.'

The way in which it was to carry out its functions were set out in paras 2.1 and 3.3, which read as follows:

> 'The function of the Agency is the administration of social security benefits and other services set out in Annex A, including the handling of claims, reviews and appeals, and arranging payment. It must do this in accordance with the law and any directions from the Secretary of State . . .'

> 'The Agency acts in accordance with policy guidance issued on behalf of the Secretary of State on the administration of social security benefits and other services.'

Under the heading 'Accountability and Reporting', relations with Parliament were described in the following terms in para 4.15: 'Ministers remain accountable to Parliament for the full range of their responsibilities . . .' Mr Drabble, however, sought to persuade us that in other passages the framework document uses language which is inconsistent with the concept that a decision taken by the agency can in any real sense be described as a decision of the Secretary of State. He referred to para 4.1, which reads:

'The Secretary of State appoints a Chief Executive to manage the Agency. He delegates to him responsibility for its functions and for its performance in providing the services in section 3 above.'

He also refers to part of para 4.15 which I have already referred to. The passage reads:

'The Secretary of State will decide whether to ask the Chief Executive to write to an MP in response to a Parliamentary question about a matter delegated to the Agency under this framework document.'

He has also referred to a number of passages in which it is clear that the agency is intended to have authority to recruit staff below certain grading levels, and to have full 'delegated' powers relating to discipline and inefficiency in relation to certain grading levels. For these reasons, it is said, the agency must be regarded against the background of the [Next Steps programme generally] as an autonomous body to which the Secretary of State has purported to delegate powers in a manner which makes it impossible for a decision of a person working within the agency to be covered by the *Carltona* principle.

There may be circumstances in which an agency is established in such a way that a Minister could no longer, on any sensible analysis, be accountable to Parliament for its actions. The report of the Efficiency Unit [which gave rise to the Next Steps initiative] was alive to that potential problem. In my judgment, however, the Benefits Agency has been established in a way which does not create any such difficulty. The use of the word 'delegate' was perhaps unfortunate. But it has to be read in context. The intention was to ensure that the administration of benefits was located within a structure which, so far as possible, was a recognisable administrative entity with lines of managerial responsibility intended to make it effective. That did not affect the constitutional position when, in accordance with the guidance which I have set out above, Mr Ash exercised the Secretary of State's power [to suspend payments] . . . That power was exercised by Mr Ash as a civil servant within the Department of Social Security on the authority of the Secretary of State, in circumstances where the Secretary of State was answerable to Parliament . . .

Kennedy LJ was of the same opinion. Claim for judicial review dismissed.

QUESTION

• How, if at all, are the concerns expressed by Freedland (above) met by the judgment in *Sherwin*?

In addition to the creation of executive agencies, the performance of certain ministerial (and other) functions may now be contracted out. This point is discussed above at 1.5.3.

Finally, may the *Carltona* principle operate to legitimize the devolution of power within decision-making structures other than those of central government? The question arose in *R (Chief Constable of West Midlands Police)* v. *Birmingham Justices* [2002] EWHC 1087 (Admin) whether the Chief Constable was permitted to delegate to his officers his power under the Crime and Disorder Act 1998, s 1, to make an application for an antisocial behaviour order. In holding that he could — thereby refusing to follow *Nelms* v. *Roe* [1970] 1 WLR 4, in which the Divisional Court did not apply *Carltona* to the exercise by a superintendent of the Metropolitan Police Commissioner's powers — Sedley LJ commented (at [9]) that:

Although the *Carltona* case is frequently cited as a source of the *"alter ego"* doctrine, it can be seen that Lord Greene's reasoning is not predicated on this. It is predicated on the proposition that the departmental head is responsible for things done under his authority. The relevance of the *alter ego* doctrine is that Crown servants were at that time taken in law to hold their positions by grace and not by contract, so that the Minister was first among equals, not an employer with servants or a principal with agents. His implied power to delegate functions depended, therefore, on two things: the conferment of a power in terms which implicitly permitted their delegation and the existence of persons to whom he could delegate them without parting with ultimate responsibility.

On a broad reading, this approach liberates *Carltona* from the central government context to which it has traditionally been confined, extending it to all decision-making structures which make adequate provision for the accountability of the subordinate to the statutory holder of the power. However, the further requirement that the statute must implicitly permit delegation introduces a more orthodox note, since it has always been accepted that legislation may (by express or implied provision) authorize delegation. Although Sedley LJ's reasoning therefore appears to proceed on two different bases, it may be that a single, overarching point can be extracted from this judgment — *viz* that the courts' readiness to discover implied statutory authorization to delegate will depend, in part at least, on the extent to which the official to whom delegation is proposed can be adequately held to account by his superior.

6.3 Discretion and Policy

6.3.1 Distinguishing Policies and Rules

The *raison d'être* of discretionary power is that it permits decision-makers to respond appropriately to the demands of particular situations. However, for reasons which we explore in detail below, it is often desirable or even necessary for decision-makers to exercise their discretion in line with a policy or a set of criteria. A tension therefore arises: to what extent may administrators legitimately structure their decision-making in this way, given that the very existence of discretionary power seems to demand an individualized mode of decision-making? As Galligan [1976] *PL* 332 at 332 explains, underlying this question is a deeper one about the nature of discretion itself:

There is an idea buried deep in the hearts of various constitutional theorists and judges that "to discipline administrative discretion by rule and rote is somehow to denature it" [Smith (1945) 23 *Public Administration* 23 at 30]. According to this idea, there is something about the nature of discretionary power which requires each decision to be made according to the circumstances of the particular situation, free from the constraints of preconceived policies as to the ends and goals to be achieved by such power. The circumstances of the situation will indicate the proper decision and policy choices must remain in the background. An alternative view is to recognise that discretion entails a power in the decision-maker to make policy choices, not just to deal with the individual case, but to develop a coherent and consistent set of guidelines which seek to achieve ends and goals within the scope of powers and which determine particular decisions.

We examine, below, the underlying issues which underpin these distinct views about the relationship between discretion and policy. We begin, however, with the classic approach to this problem set out by Bankes LJ in *R v. Port of London Authority, ex parte Kynoch Ltd* [1919] 1 KB 176 at 184:

There are on the one hand cases where a tribunal in the honest exercise of its discretion has adopted a policy, and, without refusing to hear an applicant, intimates to him what its policy is, and that after hearing him it will in accordance with its policy decide against him, unless there is something exceptional in his case. I think counsel for the applicants would admit that, if the policy has been adopted for reasons which the tribunal may legitimately entertain, no objection could be taken to such a course. On the other hand there are cases where a tribunal has passed a rule, or come to a determination, not to hear any application of a particular character by whomsoever made. There is a wide distinction to be drawn between these two classes.

This analysis is useful to the extent that it highlights the basic concerns which are at stake in this context. In particular, it emphasizes that the adoption of a policy, and thus of a more structured approach to decision-making, must ultimately be reconciled with the discretionary nature of the power: hence the distinction between a policy which is flexible enough to take account of the unusual or the exceptional, and a rule which is applied so rigidly as to eviscerate any genuine discretion. However, to the extent that it implies the existence of two wholly distinct categories of case, Bankes LJ's analysis is too simplistic. It is self-evident that, between the two extremes of unstructured discretion and immovable rules, there will exist a spectrum of policies of differing degrees of rigidity. It is, as we explain below, the courts' task is to determine — taking account of such contextual factors as the nature of the decision-making function in question — whether a given policy, lying at a particular point on the continuum, is sufficiently flexible to be legitimate.

6.3.2 The Legality of Policy-Oriented Decision-Making

In light of the conflicting views of discretion considered above, it is unsurprising that the case law in this area reveals diverging opinions on the extent to which it is legitimate for administrators to overlay their discretionary powers with policy. The following case illustrates a sceptical judicial approach to policy-based decision-making.

....

Stringer v. Minister of Housing and Local Government [1970] 1 WLR 1281
Queen's Bench Division

Following informal and encouraging talks with local planning officers, the claimant sought permission to construct houses on a site in the vicinity of the Jodrell Bank radio telescope in Cheshire. In fact the local planning authority, the rural district council, and the operator of the telescope had entered into an agreement to the effect that development near to the telescope should be discouraged, in order to avoid interference with its operation. The Ministry of Housing and Local Government adopted a similar policy. The claimant's application for planning permission was refused on the ground, *inter alia*, that the proposed development would impede the effective operation of the telescope. The claimant appealed to the Minister of Housing and Local Government but, following an inquiry which found that the proposed development would be very likely to interfere with the telescope, the Minister dismissed the appeal. The claimant sought to have that decision quashed arguing, *inter alia*, that the Minister's policy was an unlawful fetter on his discretion.

Cooke J

... The Minister's anxiety that proper provision should be made for protecting the interests of the telescope is clear from many years of history. He has encouraged the definition by agreement of areas in which development is likely to interfere with the work of the telescope. He has encouraged arrangements for consultation between local authorities and the Jodrell Bank directorate about applications for planning permission in those areas. All that appears to me to be perfectly proper and in no way inconsistent with the proper performance of the Minister's quasi-judicial duties when occasion arises to perform them.

The matter, however, may be said to go further than that, because it appears that the Minister has a policy for the area around Jodrell Bank ... [I]t may be said to be a policy of discouraging development which would interfere with the efficient working of the telescope. It is not, however, as it seems to me, a policy which is intended to be pursued to the disregard of other relevant considerations. The question is whether the existence of such a policy disables the Minister from acting fairly on the consideration of an appeal.

There are obviously many matters in the field of planning legislation on which the Minister is entitled and indeed bound to have a policy ... [After considering two such cases — *Johnson and Co (Builders) Ltd* v. *Minister of Health* [1947] 2 All ER 395 and *R* v. *Port of London Authority, ex parte Kynoch Ltd* [1919] 1 KB 176 — Cooke J continued:] It seems to me that the general effect of the many relevant authorities is that a Minister charged with the duty of making individual administrative decisions in a fair and impartial manner may nevertheless have a general policy in regard to matters which are relevant to those decisions, provided that the existence of that general policy does not preclude him from fairly judging all the issues which are relevant to each individual case as it comes up for decision.

I think that in this case the Minister was entitled to have a policy in regard to Jodrell Bank, and I think that his policy is not such as to preclude him from fairly considering a planning appeal on its merits. I do not think that it precluded him from fairly considering Mr. Stringer's appeal. I do not think that the Minister has prejudged the case, or tied his own hands, or abdicated any of his functions ...

The claim to have the Minister's decision quashed was therefore dismissed.

The implications of the restrictive approach to policy seen in *Stringer* — which is not unique: for other examples, see *Merchandise Transport Ltd* v. *British Transport Commission* [1962] 2 QB 173 and *Sagnata Investments Ltd* v. *Norwich Corporation* [1971] 2 QB 614 — were explained in the following terms by Galligan, *op cit* at 349:

The principle [adopted in cases such as *Stringer*] is that a predetermined policy is only one factor among all those that may be relevant. It was thought that by regarding a predetermined policy as merely one factor, consideration of the merits in each exercise of discretion was kept to a maximum. The corollary of this principle is that where a policy functions in such a way that the only question is "should this policy apply to this situation," a sufficient consideration of other relevant factors is excluded. Such a policy was thought to function invalidly as a rule. Nowhere was this corollary expressed more forcefully than by Lord Chief Justice Hewart in *R* v. *Rotherham Licensing Justices, ex parte Chapman* [[1939] 2 All ER 710]. Licensing justices had adopted a general rule not to grant more than two occasional liquor licences to the same applicant during a certain time, but they heard and considered all applications to determine whether an exception to the rule should be made, and from time to time exceptions were made. However the Court of Appeal considered that a general rule of this kind was an invalid fetter on the justices' discretion and an abdication of their duty to hear each case on its merits.

To restrict policies in this way is to go far beyond the principle in *Kynoch*. The implications of this more restrictive approach are that not only must an authority (a) direct itself to whether in the light of the particular situation a predetermined policy ought to be altered, but also (b) must refrain from regarding a policy as anything more than one factor amongst others to take into account. In other words a policy may not become a norm which, subject only to (a), determines the outcome of particular decisions.

QUESTIONS

• Is it appropriate to adopt this restrictive view of the role of policy?
• What might be the advantages and disadvantages of such an approach?

The following case evidences a much more indulgent attitude towards policy-oriented decision-making.

British Oxygen Co Ltd v. *Minister of Technology* [1971] AC 610
House of Lords

Section 1(1) of the Industrial Development Act 1966 provided that the Board of Trade 'may make to any person carrying on a business in Great Britain a grant towards approved capital expenditure incurred by that person in providing new machinery or plant'. The Board adopted a policy of denying grants for any item of plant costing less than £25 and, in pursuance of that policy, rejected an application for a grant in respect of gas cylinders costing just under £20 each of which the claimant had, in the three years following the entry into force of the Act, purchased £4m worth. In proceedings for a declaration the court was required, *inter alia*, to determine whether the Board had properly exercised its discretion.

Lord Reid

. . . There are two general grounds on which the exercise of an unqualified discretion can be attacked. It must not be exercised in bad faith, and it must not be so unreasonably exercised as to show that there cannot have been any real or genuine exercise of the discretion. But, apart from that, if the Minister thinks that policy or good administration requires the operation of some limiting rule, I find nothing to stop him.

It was argued on the authority of *Rex v. Port of London Authority, Ex parte Kynoch Ltd.* [1919] 1 K.B. 176 that the Minister is not entitled to make a rule for himself as to how he will in future exercise his discretion. In that case Kynoch owned land adjoining the Thames and wished to construct a deep water wharf. For this they had to get the permission of the authority. Permission was refused on the ground that Parliament had charged the authority with the duty of providing such facilities. It appeared that before reaching their decision the authority had fully considered the case on its merits and in relation to the public interest. So their decision was upheld.

[After quoting the extract from Bankes LJ's judgment which is set out above at 6.3.1, Lord Reid continued:] I see nothing wrong with that. But the circumstances in which discretions are exercised vary enormously and that passage cannot be applied literally in every case. The general rule is that anyone who has to exercise a statutory discretion must not 'shut his ears to an application' (to adapt from Bankes L.J. [see [1919] 1 KB 176 at 183]). I do not think there is any great difference between a policy and a rule. There may be cases where an officer or authority ought to listen to a substantial argument reasonably presented urging a change of policy. What the authority must not do is to refuse to listen at all. But a Ministry or large authority may have had to deal already with a multitude of similar applications and then they will almost certainly have evolved a policy so precise that it could well be called a rule. There can be no objection to that, provided the authority is always willing to listen to anyone with something new to say — of course I do not mean to say that there need be an oral hearing. In the present case the respondent's officers have carefully considered all that the appellants have had to say and I have no doubt that they will continue to do so . . .

Viscount Dilhorne

. . . [T]he distinction between a policy decision and a rule may not be easy to draw. In this case it was not challenged that it was within the power of the Board to adopt a policy not to make a grant in respect of such an item. That policy might equally well be described as a rule. It was both reasonable and right that the Board should make known to those interested the policy it was going to follow. By doing so fruitless applications involving expense and expenditure of time might be avoided. The Board says that it has not refused to consider any application. It considered the appellants'. In these circumstances it is not necessary to decide in this case whether, if it had refused to consider an application on the ground that it related to an item costing less than £25, it would have acted wrongly.

I must confess that I feel some doubt whether the words used by Bankes L.J. in the passage cited above [see above at 6.3.1] are really applicable to a case of this kind. It seems somewhat pointless and a waste of time that the Board should have to consider applications which are bound as a result of its policy decision to fail. Representations could of course be made that the policy should be changed . . .

Lords Morris, Wilberforce, and Diplock agreed with Lord Reid.

The less restrictive approach to policy adopted in *British Oxygen* has been followed in many other cases, including *R v. Rochdale Metropolitan Borough Council, ex parte Cromer Ring Mill Ltd* [1982] 3 All ER 761 and *R v. Secretary of State for the Home Department, ex parte Hindley* [2001] 1 AC 410. It ascribes a generous role to policy, allowing it to become the norm upon which the decision-making process is founded, provided of course that the administrator is willing to make exceptions for unusual cases. In seeking to determine whether this residual flexibility is present, and thus capable of legitimizing the decision-maker's policy-based approach, the courts are unsurprisingly more interested in substance than in form. Consequently, even if the decision-maker claims to be willing to depart from the policy in exceptional circumstances, the court may require evidence that this actually occurs in practice and, in the absence of such evidence, may draw the inference that the policy is operated over-rigidly (see, *eg, R v. Warwickshire County Council, ex parte Collymore* [1995] ELR 217).

Although the willingness of the decision-maker to show flexibility in the face of the unusual is often the key factor *vis-à-vis* the legality of the policy, this criterion is not always determinative of the issue. For instance, in *Attorney-General ex rel Tilley* v. *Wandsworth London Borough Council* [1981] 1 WLR 854 a local authority resolved that families with young children who were intentionally homeless would not be assisted with alternative housing under the Children and Young Persons Act 1963. The Court of Appeal concluded that this policy admitted of no exceptions and was therefore over-rigid. Templeman LJ, however, went further (at 858); he was not 'persuaded that even a policy resolution hedged around with exceptions would be entirely free from attack. Dealing with children, the discretion and powers of any authority must depend entirely on the different circumstances of each child before them for consideration'. This suggests that there may be rare situations

— delineated by factors such as the subject-matter of the discretion and the legislative framework within which the discretion subsists — where the need for detailed evaluation of the merits severely reduces the role which policy may play.

Conversely, it seems that there may be situations in which it is quite legitimate to operate a policy which does not yield even in the face of exceptional circumstances. Hilson [2002] *PL* 111 at 117–120 points to a line of taxi licensing decisions — including *R* v. *Wirral Metropolitan Borough Council, ex parte Wirral Licensed Taxi Owners Association* [1983] 3 CMLR 150 and *R* v. *Hyndburn Borough Council, ex parte Rauf* (12 February 1992, unreported) — in which policies that apparently made no exceptions for unusual cases were upheld as lawful. Hilson concludes that the best rationalization of these cases is that the courts may occasionally be prepared to uphold rigid policies where the very objectives of the policy cannot be achieved if exceptions are made. That conclusion must be tempered, however, by recognition of the fact that those objectives must in the first place be lawful and, therefore, consistent with the statutory scheme (see below, ch 8), reasonable, and (where relevant) proportionate in their impact on competing rights and interests (see below, ch 9).

6.3.3 Discretion and Policy: The Underlying Issues

The foregoing section demonstrates that the courts have adopted differing views regarding the extent to which discretion may legitimately be overlaid with policy. We have seen that some of these divergences may be explained at a micro-level by reference to such factors as the content of the statutory scheme and the subject-matter and objectives of the policy. To an extent, however, the different approaches exhibited in the cases conceal an underlying disagreement as to the relative merits of, on the one hand, a flexible, highly individualized model of decision-making and, on the other hand, a more structured, policy-based approach. In the following passage, which addresses these competing models of decision-making, the footnotes are, as usual, omitted; in them, the author acknowledges reliance on Jowell [1973] *PL* 178, where you will find further discussion of these issues.

....

Hilson, 'Judicial Review, Policies and the Fettering of Discretion' [2002] PL 111

. . . In reflecting upon the non-fetter principle [that is, the principle which precludes decision-makers from eviscerating their discretion through the adoption of over-rigid policies], it is useful to think of a spectrum of administrative decision-making in routine or regular cases. At one end of the spectrum lies decision-making by rigid rules where discretion is effectively eclipsed and where there is no consideration of exceptional cases that fall outside the rules. And, at the other end of the spectrum, lies totally individualised, discretionary decision-making where rules or policies play no part at all — not even as general guides or presumptions for dealing with individual applications. There are of course advantages to both.

The advantages of exclusively rule-based decision-making are numerous. First, it ensures fairness and consistency between applicants because, in a sea of applications, like cases are more likely to be treated alike on a consistent basis with a rule as a benchmark than they are in a system of pure discretion. Secondly, adopting a rule in routine cases promotes efficiency of administration, in that decision-makers will typically be able to dispose of cases more quickly if they are following a rule. And finally, having a rule rather than discretion may be the only way to achieve officially determined aims. If, for example, a local authority believes that amusement arcades pose a threat to children and its aim is to protect them, then a rule prohibiting amusement arcades is the only way in which this aim will be achieved. Allowing discretionary exceptions would compromise the aim.

If they are made open, there are other advantages associated with rules. First, it means that individuals are able to see clearly whether they fall inside or outside the relevant rule and can thus avoid making fruitless applications. This not only saves would-be applicants time, but also reduces the workload of the administrative authority. Secondly, if the rules are open, there is a degree of accountability to the public, who will be able to subject the rules to critical scrutiny. And finally, and related to the second, is legal certainty; people know where they stand with a rule in a way that is not possible with a system of pure discretion. This enables them to plan their affairs.

The advantage of individualised decision-making in contrast, is that account is taken of all the features of an application, including any exceptional ones. This ensures that the *particular* applicant is treated justly, though, as suggested above, it is unlikely to result in fairness or consistency *as between* different applicants. Individualised decision-making may also ensure that the relevant aims are not undermined by a rigid, rule-based approach. For example, traffic police might employ a rigid rule that motorists who exceed the motorway speed limit of 70 mph by more than 7 mph will always be prosecuted. However, assuming the aim of the speed limit law is public safety, then it cannot be said that such a legalistic approach promotes the aim of the law. After all, if a person is travelling at 78 mph, but in broad daylight, on a totally clear stretch of road, public safety is not served by prosecuting. Individualised decision-making here would, of course, allow for this.

What the courts have done, in creating the non-fetter principle, is to impose a compromise between these two conflicting positions in order to try to achieve the best of both worlds. Bodies are allowed rules or policies, but they must always be prepared to consider the exceptional case. The problem is that the best of both worlds cannot be had here: where you have a compromise, you inevitably lose some of the good features from both sides . . .

QUESTIONS

- Which, if any, of the English decisions strike the 'correct' compromise?
- Is there such a thing, or does the trade-off which is called for between individualized and rule-based decision-making depend on the context?
- If so, what contextual features are relevant?

Although Hilson is correct to suggest that the courts' approach represents a compromise between, on the one hand, flexibility and, on the other, a structured, open, and consistent approach which promotes legal certainty, the modern tendency of the courts to emphasize the benefits of policy-oriented decision-making is to be welcomed. Policy is now viewed as 'an essential element in securing the coherent and consistent performance of administrative functions' (*R (Alconbury Developments Ltd)* v. *Secretary of State for the Environment, Transport and the Regions* [2001] UKHL 23 [2003] 2 AC 295 at [143] *per* Lord Clyde; see also *R (Adam)* v. *Secretary of State for the Home Department* [2004] EWCA Civ 540 at [123] *per* Carnwath LJ). Indeed, it has been suggested that, in certain contexts, the existence of a policy may be *mandatory*: in *R* v. *North West Lancashire Health Authority, ex parte A* [2000] 1 WLR 977, Auld LJ opined (at 991) that it might well be irrational — and therefore unlawful — for a health authority not to have a policy for deciding how to allocate its scarce resources by prioritizing different types of medical treatment. Moreover, the principle of legitimate expectation (see ch 7 below) is increasingly deployed to hold public bodies to their stated policies.

It is clear, therefore, that English law does not (any longer) regard policy as antithetical to the legitimate exercise of discretion — a view which fits comfortably into the broader scheme of contemporary administrative law in which considerable weight is attached to the value of legal certainty (see further Dotan (1997) 17 *OJLS* 23). It should, however, be noted that the HRA 1998 imposes a limit on the extent to which policy can condition the use of discretion. Because administrative action can now lawfully interfere with fundamental rights only to the extent necessary to advance a legitimate competing aim, it is sometimes necessary to modify or disapply policies where their application would cut down such rights. The case of *R (Daly)* v. *Secretary of State for the Home Department* [2001] UKHL 26 [2001] 2 AC 532, considered at 9.3.4 below, illustrates this point clearly.

6.4 Discretionary Power and Contractual Arrangements

Public authorities which possess discretionary powers often need to enter into contracts with outside bodies in order to function and to achieve their statutory objectives (and, as seen above at 1.5.3, it is increasingly common for the entire discharge of statutory functions to be performed by external bodies under contract). But what if a public authority enters into binding contractual arrangements which reduce or remove its ability to exercise one of its discretionary powers? Just as administrative law places restrictions upon the freedom of decision-makers to constrain their discretion by the adoption of policies — in order to ensure that discretion is exercised, rather than rules applied — so administrators are constrained in the extent to which they may tie their own hands by forming contracts which impact upon their discretionary powers. However, situations inevitably arise in which achieving the objectives which the conferral of the discretion contemplates is possible only by means of contractual arrangements which necessarily impact upon the further exercise of the discretion. The courts must therefore strike a careful balance between, on the one hand, the preservation of discretion and, on the other hand, affording public authorities that degree of freedom to enter into contracts necessary to the effective discharge of their responsibilities.

This issue was considered by the House of Lords in *Ayr Harbour Trustees* v. *Oswald* (1883) 8 App Cas 623. The Harbour Trustees exercised their statutory powers of compulsory purchase — which they held for the management and improvement of the harbour — in respect of Oswald's land, but in order to reduce the compensation payable they undertook not to use the land they acquired in a manner which would impede access from Oswald's remaining land to the harbour. Their Lordships concluded that the undertaking was invalid, Lord Blackburn (at 634) explaining his reasoning thus:

I think that where the legislature confer powers on any body to take lands compulsorily for a particular purpose, it is on the ground that the using of that land for that purpose will be for the public good. Whether that body be one which is seeking to make a profit for shareholders, or, as in the present case, a body of trustees acting solely for the public good, I think in either case the powers conferred on the body empowered to take the land compulsorily are intrusted to them, and their successors, to be used for the furtherance of that object which the legislature has thought sufficiently for the public good to justify it in intrusting them with such powers; and, consequently, that a contract purporting to bind them and their successors not to use those powers is void.

This seems to imply that the interest in preserving the administrator's discretion will always prevail over the advantages which may flow from allowing contractual arrangements to be put in place; Lord Blackburn does not appear to envisage that any kind of balance needs to be struck between these two interests. However, a different interpretation was placed upon the *Ayr Harbour* decision in *Birkdale District Electric Supply Co Ltd* v. *Corporation of Southport* [1926] AC 355. Lord Sumner said (at 371):

On examining the facts in the *Ayr Harbour* case it is plain that, in effect, the trustees did not merely propose to covenant in a manner that committed the business of the harbour to restricted lines in the future; they were to forbear, once and for all, to acquire all that the statute intended them to acquire, for, though technically they acquired the whole of the land, they were to sterilize part of their acquisition, so far as the statutory purpose of their undertaking was concerned. . . . The land itself was affected in favour of the former owner in the *Ayr* case just as a towpath is affected in favour of the owner of a dominant tenement, if he is given a personal right of walking along it. If the Ayr trustees had reduced the acquisition price by covenanting with the respondent for a perpetual right to moor his barges, free of tolls, at any wharf they might construct on the water front of the land acquired, the decision might, and I think would, have been different.

Birkdale thus moves away from the apparently extreme position of *Ayr Harbour*, rejecting the idea that contracts which impact upon the exercise of discretionary powers are inevitably void, instead adopting a more subtle test based on the compatibility of the contractual arrangements with the statutory scheme. The nature and implications of this test are usefully illustrated by the following case; although it involves the dedication of land to public use, the issue which the case raises is in principle the same as that which arises in the contractual cases.

British Transport Commission v. *Westmorland County Council* [1958] AC 126
House of Lords

In 1845 a bridge was built over a railway line in order to permit access between the parcels of land adjoining the line. Although the bridge was built only for the benefit of the owners and occupiers of the land, the public had, over a long period, also used the bridge. In 1952 the county council, in preparing a new map of the area, deemed the bridge to be a public right of way. Although it was accepted that neither the British Transport Commission nor its predecessor had actually dedicated the bridge to public use, it was argued that the public's long use of the bridge raised a presumption of dedication. The Commission countered that any such dedication would be *ultra vires* and void, because it would inhibit the exercise of its discretion under the Railways Clauses Consolidation Act 1845 to discontinue the bridge.

Viscount Simonds

. . . Any examination of this question must begin with the case of *R* v. *Inhabitants of Leake* (1833) 5 B. & Ad. 469, which has been cited in many cases, some of them in this House, and never disapproved. The decision goes to the root of the matter, and, often as they have been cited, I think I should remind your Lordships of the words of Parke J. in that case. "If," he said, "the land were vested by the Act of Parliament in commissioners, so that they were thereby bound to use it for a special purpose, incompatible with its public use as a highway, I should have thought that such trustees would have been incapable in point of law to make a dedication of it; but if such use by the public be not incompatible with the objects prescribed by the Act, then I think it clear that the commissioners have that power."

Here a principle is laid down which is supported not only by a great weight of succeeding authority but by its inherent reasonableness. For, though, on the one hand, it would be improper that commissioners or other persons having acquired land for a particular statutory purpose should preclude themselves from using it for that purpose, on the other hand, if consistently with its user for that purpose, it can be used for some other purpose also, I see no impropriety in such secondary user. If the usefulness of a parcel of land is not exhausted by its user for its statutory purpose, why should it not be used for some other purpose not incompatible with that purpose? . . .

It was . . . upon the *Ayr Harbour* case (1883) 8 App. Cas. 623 that counsel for the appellants mainly relied, suggesting, if I understood the argument, that a proper understanding of that case must lead to a decision in his favour. I think, on the contrary, that this contention is based on a radical misunderstanding of it. For it appears to me that in the *Ayr Harbour* case it was plain that the proposed agreement by the statutory body, which had acquired land for a particular purpose, that they would not use it so as to interfere with the access from other property of the vendor to the sea, was regarded as incompatible with the statutory purpose. It was in fact an example of incompatibility, not a decision to the effect that incompatibility does not supply a test. This was clearly the view of Lord Sumner in the *Birkdale* case [1926] A.C. 355 . . .

If I am right in saying that the principle of *Leake's* case must be applied here, I must next consider what is the test of incompatibility, which, as I have already said, appears to me to be the real difficulty in the case. This is a question of fact. It can be nothing else and it has been so treated, and expressly so treated, in many of the cases to which I have referred. But to say this does not completely solve the problem. For the jury or tribunal of fact must still be properly directed what is the test, and it is to this point that counsel for the appellants directed his attack. He urged that there could only be incompatibility, or, perhaps I should here say, compatibility, if it could be proved that in no conceivable circumstances could the proposed user at any future time and in any way possibly interfere with the statutory purpose for which the land was acquired . . .

My Lords, I am satisfied that this argument is misconceived . . . [T]o give to incompatibility such an extended meaning is in effect to reduce the principle to a nullity. For a jury, invited to say that in no conceivable circumstances and at no distance of time could an event possibly happen, could only fold their hands and reply that it was not for them to prophesy what an inscrutable Providence might in all the years to come disclose. I do not disguise from myself that it is difficult to formulate with precision what direction should be given to a jury. But, after all, we live in a world in which our actions are constantly guided by a consideration of reasonable probabilities of risks that can reasonably be foreseen and guarded against, and by a disregard of events of which, even if we think of them as possible, we can fairly say that they are not at all likely to happen. And it is, in my opinion, by such considerations as these, imprecise though they may be, that a tribunal of fact must be guided in determining whether a proposed user of land will interfere with the statutory purpose for which it was acquired . . .

All five of their Lordships agreed that the dedication was not incompatible with the statutory objects of the Commission, and was therefore valid.

The *Westmorland* case thus affirms that the incompatibility test is to be used in this context, and clarifies the precise nature of that test.

6.5 Concluding Remarks

We have seen in this chapter how administrative law gives effect to the important policy that decision-makers upon whom discretionary powers are conferred should retain and exercise those powers. This policy finds expression in the specific principles which limit the ability of decision-makers to delegate or transfer their powers; to narrow their discretion by adopting policies and rules, and to fetter their discretion by entering into contractual and analogous arrangements. In each of these contexts, however, other policy factors enter into play, requiring the courts to exercise sensitivity as they seek to accommodate competing imperatives. Thus the need for efficient decision-making tempers the non-delegation principle; the interests of legal certainty, consistency and transparency ameliorate the non-fettering rule in relation to policies; and the practical importance of permitting public authorities to form contractual relationships in order to realize their statutory objectives is set against the proposition that discretion should be retained rather than contracted away. While it is true, therefore, that administrative law recognizes the value of retention of discretion, the rules which have evolved in this area acknowledge that that value must be set against a wide range of competing interests.

FURTHER RESOURCES

Baldwin and Houghton, 'Circular Arguments: The Status and Legitimacy of Administrative Rules' [1986] *PL* 239

Dotan, 'Why Administrators Should be Bound by their Policies' (1997) 17 *OJLS* 23

Freedland, 'Privatising *Carltona*: Part II of the Deregulation and Contracting Out Act 1994' [1995] *PL* 21

Freedland, 'The Rule Against Delegation and the *Carltona* Doctrine in an Agency Context' [1996] *PL* 19

Galligan, 'The Nature and Function of Policy within Discretionary Power' [1976] *PL* 332

Hilson, 'Judicial Review, Policies and the Fettering of Discretion' [2002] *PL* 111

Jowell, 'Legal Control of Administrative Discretion' [1973] *PL* 178

7 LEGITIMATE EXPECTATIONS

In the previous chapter we considered how far the discretionary freedom of the decision-maker designated by statute may be constrained by delegation, entry into contractual arrangements, and the adoption of policies. This chapter concerns the extent to which a public authority's powers may be limited by representations as to how it will act. The central principle in this area of administrative law is that of legitimate expectation. We turn first to the application of that principle to lawfully created expectations, and then consider to what extent, if any, it may protect unlawfully generated expectations.

7.1 Lawfully Created Expectations

In *Council of Civil Service Unions* v. *Minister for the Civil Service* [1985] AC 374 at 408, Lord Diplock said that judicial review should lie when an individual is deprived of

some benefit or advantage which either (i) he had in the past been permitted by the decision-maker to enjoy and which he can legitimately expect to be permitted to continue to do until there has been communicated to him some rational grounds for withdrawing it on which he has been given an opportunity to comment; or (ii) he has received assurance from the decision-maker will not be withdrawn without giving him first an opportunity of advancing reasons for contending that they should not be withdrawn.

This succinct explanation of the principle of legitimate expectation is a useful starting point, but it perhaps begs more questions than it answers. When, precisely, will the individual 'legitimately' expect the conferral of the benefit? What amounts to an 'assurance'? And can legitimate expectations be protected by more than the accordance to the expectation-holder of procedurally fair treatment, which is what Lord Diplock focusses on? We address these issues below, but begin with a more fundamental question about the underlying purpose of the legitimate expectation principle.

7.1.1 Why Protect Legitimate Expectations?

At the heart of the doctrine of legitimate expectation lies a tension, familiar from the previous chapter, between the protection of administrative autonomy and the pursuit of often conflicting policy goals. Great emphasis was placed on the former in *Hughes* v.

Department of Health and Social Security [1985] AC 776. The claimants had transferred to the civil service from local authority employment in 1948 on the basis that although established civil servants could be retired at any time after reaching the age of 60, those transferring from local authorities would be allowed to continue until the age of 65 subject to continued efficiency. In 1981, however, a policy circular announced that as from 1982 employees in the claimants' grades would be retired at 61 and as from 1983 at 60. The claimants contended that they had been unfairly dismissed; the House of Lords, however, concluded that the circular had reduced the claimants' normal retiring age and that no claim for unfair dismissal was therefore possible. Lord Diplock (at 788) appeared anxious to ensure that expectations engendered by government statements should not be allowed to ossify policy:

Administrative policies may change with changing circumstances, including changes in the political complexion of governments. The liberty to make such changes is something that is inherent in our constitutional form of government. When a change in administrative policy takes place and is communicated in a departmental circular to, among others, those employees in the category whose age at which they would be compulsorily retired was stated in a previous circular to be a higher age than 60 years, any reasonable expectations that may have been aroused in them by any previous circular are destroyed and are replaced by such other reasonable expectations as to the earliest date at which they can be compelled to retire if the administrative policy announced in the new circular is applied to them.

Against considerations of this nature, however, must be set the principle of legal certainty, as Forsyth [1988] *CLJ* 238 at 239 explains:

The judicial motivation for seeking to protect [legitimate] expectations is plain: if the executive undertakes, expressly or by past practice, to behave in a particular way the subject expects that undertaking to be complied with. That is surely fundamental to good government and it would be monstrous if the executive could freely renege on its undertakings. Public trust in the government should not be left unprotected.

It is the tension between administrative autonomy and legal certainty which is the creative force that has shaped the modern concept of legitimate expectation. However, it is important at the outset to recognize that this tension should not be characterized simply as a conflict between individual and public interests. Although the principle of legal certainty captures the importance, to the individual, of being able to rely on governmental undertakings, there is also a *public* interest in legal certainty, since the community as a whole benefits from an environment in which its members are able to repose trust and confidence in their public institutions — a point which is developed in the following passage.

....

Schønberg, *Legitimate Expectations in Administrative Law* (Oxford 2000)

... [A] public authority's freedom to take action in the public interest is limited to the extent that it causes harm to particular individuals. If a public authority has induced a person to rely upon its representations or conduct, realising that such reliance was a real possibility, it is under a *prima facie* duty to act in such a way that the reliance will not be detrimental to the representee. The authority must honour the expectations created by its representation or, at least, compensate the person affected for his reliance loss ...

... In a rapidly changing and increasingly uncertain world, law is something that operators should be able to, and to a large extent do, rely on. In administrative law, the importance of certainty is increased by wide-ranging discretionary powers being vested in public authorities. Individuals cannot easily predict how discretionary powers will be exercised because the provisions conferring such powers are linguistically indeterminate and because informal working rules and other constraints, of which individuals are not normally aware, affect their exercise in practice. Representations may create expectations as to the manner of, or criteria for, their exercise. Respect for these expectations therefore makes the exercise of discretion more predictable. However, the importance of the rule of law does not stop here ... First, the rule of law presupposes formal equality. That is, like cases must be treated alike by the correct and consistent application of law. Without formal equality law becomes arbitrary and thus unpredictable and uncertain. Second, the rule of law presupposes a certain measure of constancy in the law. The law should ensure that administrative action is based on a mix of short-term exigencies and more long-term consider-ations. Individual planning becomes difficult or impossible if law and policy are changed too often and too abruptly. Moreover, frequent changes may undermine individual rights by creating uncertainty about the boundaries of those rights. The legal protection of legitimate expectations by administrative law is a way of giving expression to the requirements of predictability, formal equality, and constancy inherent in the rule of law ...

... The rule of law justification for protection of legitimate expectations has a certain "red-light" quality [see above at 1.2.1 on the meaning of this term]. However, recognition of legitimate expect-ations is not only about fairness to the individual and control of administrative power, it is also a powerful means to administrative efficacy. Administrative efficacy is an aspect of the wider notion of good administration, the enforcement of which is an important part of modern judicial review ... [A]dministrative power is more likely to be perceived as legitimate authority if exercised in a way which respects legitimate expectations. Perceived legitimate authority is more efficacious because it encourages individuals to participate in decision-making processes, to co-operate with adminis-trative initiatives, and to comply with administrative regulations. Greater compliance will in turn improve the administration's ability to solve co-ordination problems, and that may actually make its exercise of authority more legitimate. The acceptance of principles of administrative law, which require authorities to respect legitimate expectations, is therefore not merely in the interests of individuals. It is, very much, in the interest of the administration itself.

QUESTIONS

- What does Schønberg mean when he says that the 'rule of law justification . . . has a certain "red-light" quality'?
- Why does he argue that the justification for upholding legitimate expectations is wider than this?

7.1.2 Two Variables: Legitimacy and Protection

In any situation which potentially engages the legitimate expectation principle, two key criteria will inevitably be in play: that of *legitimacy*, and that of the mode of *protection* which may be extended to expectations which satisfy the first criterion. It is important to be clear about the relationship between these two variables.

The criterion of *legitimacy* is crucial: the law is concerned not simply with what indi-viduals *actually* expect in subjective terms, but only with what they are *entitled to* expect. As Lord Scarman explained in *In re Findlay* [1985] AC 318 at 338, the key question which the court must ask of the claimant is, '[W]hat was their *legitimate* expectation?' This matter is considered below at 7.1.3.

Once the court has ascertained the existence of a legitimate expectation, it must go on to consider how (if at all) it should be *protected*. If the claimant merely expects that a particular procedure will be followed before certain action is taken, then the court will generally require adherence to such a procedure (see, eg, *Attorney-General of Hong Kong v. Ng Yuen Shiu* [1983] 2 AC 629, an excerpt from which appears below at 7.1.4). Hence there can be *procedural protection* of a *procedural legitimate expectation*. However, what if the claimant's expectation was not simply that he would (say) be *consulted before* having a benefit withdrawn, but that the benefit *would not be* withdrawn? There are three principal ways in which this issue may be analysed.

First, the court may determine that, while the claimant *actually* expected the on-going conferral of the benefit (a *substantive* expectation), he was only *entitled* to expect a fair procedure (*eg*, consultation or a hearing) before the taking of the decision whether to withdraw the benefit (a *procedural legitimate* expectation). In this manner the application of the criterion of legitimacy dictates that only procedural protection is appropriate, since procedurally fair treatment is all that the claimant was legitimately entitled to expect. (The decision in *R v. Secretary of State for the Home Department, ex parte Khan* [1984] 1 WLR 1337 is arguably an example of this approach.)

Secondly, the same result would be achieved if the court held that, while the claimant was entitled to expect the on-going conferral of the benefit (a *substantive legitimate* expectation), the expectation should only be protected by requiring a fair *procedure* to be followed. This mode of analysis implies the possibility of *procedural protection* of a *substantive legitimate expectation*: it recognizes that, while the claimant was entitled to expect a substantive outcome, countervailing factors dictate that the court should only require the adoption of a fair procedure. This, in turn, reflects an underlying conclusion that the public interest in discretionary freedom, on the facts of the case, carries sufficient weight that the principle of legal certainty (which would tend to favour the substantive enforcement of the expectation) should yield.

Thirdly, and finally, the courts have recently recognized situations in which the individual expects — and is entitled to expect — a substantive outcome (a *substantive legitimate* expectation), and in which substantive protection is appropriate (so that the court requires the decision-maker to confer the benefit). This category — *substantive protection* of a *substantive legitimate expectation* — indicates judicial recognition that, in some contexts, the discretionary freedom of the decision-maker (which would favour retention of the decision-maker's ultimate substantive freedom to frustrate the expectation) must give way to the principle of legal certainty (see, *eg, R v. North and East Devon Health Authority, ex parte Coughlan* [2001] QB 213, discussed below at 7.1.5).

Thus, whenever individuals seek relief on the basis of expectations generated by public authorities, two matters are crucial. First, the court must assess what (if anything) they were legitimately entitled to expect. Secondly, the court must determine how (if at all) to protect the expectation; and, in addressing this issue, the court has to confront the relationship between the interests in discretionary freedom and legal certainty. This does not mean, however, that the issues of legitimacy and protection need be conceptualized as wholly distinct. In *R v. Ministry of Agriculture, Fisheries and Food, ex parte Hamble (Offshore) Fisheries Ltd* [1995] 2 All ER 714 at 732, Sedley J said that 'legitimate expectation is now in effect a term of art, reserved for expectations which are not only reasonable but which will be sustained by the court in the face of changes of policy'. This suggests that the expectation will only be legitimate if the court decides that it is worthy of protection; the distinct issues concerning the legitimacy of the expectation and whether (and, if so, how) it should be protected are thus presented as two sides of the same coin. Craig [1996] *CLJ* 289 at 303, however, is critical of such an approach, and argues that questions of legitimacy and protection should be kept distinct:

On the one hand, [the approach which separates legitimacy and protection] comports better with reality. To be forced to conclude that the [claimant] . . . never had any legitimate expectation . . . [just because countervailing policy factors militate against its protection] does not fit with our intuition. Our natural reaction in such a case is that there was such an expectation which has been trumped by public interest considerations . . .

On the other hand, it is conceptually clearer. There are . . . two values which are ultimately at stake in this type of case. Legal certainty is expressive of the individual's perspective; legality, as manifested through the non-fettering [or discretionary freedom] doctrine, captures the needs of the public body to develop policy. The approach favoured by Sedley J seeks to bring both of these within the phrase legitimate expectations itself: for the expectation to be legitimate it must not only be reasonable, but sustainable in the face of the need of the public body to change policy. The natural role of legitimate expectations is, however, to reflect the individual's perspective and the value of legal certainty. This is how it is employed in other contexts. It is, of course, true, as Sedley J points out, that legitimate expectations are not absolute. But this point is captured perfectly well by accepting that the public interest should allow the public body to resile from the expectation. It does not demand that the legality value should be incorporated within the phrase legitimate expectations itself.

QUESTIONS

- Contrast the notions of 'legitimacy' employed by Sedley J and Craig. Which approach do you find to be the more convincing?
- Why?

7.1.3 Legitimacy: What is the Claimant *Entitled* to Expect?

The nature and circumstances of the conduct or statement giving rise to the expectation

In the following case, the House of Lords considered the type of situations in which a legitimate expectation may arise.

Council of Civil Services Unions v. Minister for the Civil Service [1985] AC 374
House of Lords

For the facts, see above at 5.3.2. The present excerpt is concerned with whether the claimants had a legitimate expectation of consultation.

Lord Fraser

. . . Mr. Blom-Cooper [for the claimants] submitted that the Minister had a duty to consult the CCSU, on behalf of employees at GCHQ, before giving the instruction on 22 December 1983 for making an important change in their conditions of service. His main reason for so submitting was that the employees had a legitimate, or reasonable, expectation that there would be such prior consultation before any important change was made in their conditions.

It is clear that the employees did not have a legal right to prior consultation. The Order in Council confers no such right, and article 4 makes no reference at all to consultation. The Civil Service handbook (*Handbook for the new civil servant*, 1973 ed. as amended 1983) which explains the normal method of consultation through the departmental Whitley Council, does not suggest that there is any legal right to consultation; indeed it is careful to recognise that, in the operational field, considerations of urgency may make prior consultation impracticable. The Civil Service Pay and Conditions of Service Code expressly states:

> "The following terms and conditions also apply to your appointment in the Civil Service. It should be understood, however, that in consequence of the constitutional position of the Crown, the Crown has the right to change its employees' conditions of service at any time, and that they hold their appointments at the pleasure of the Crown."

But even where a person claiming some benefit or privilege has no legal right to it, as a matter of private law, he may have a legitimate expectation of receiving the benefit or privilege, and, if so, the courts will protect his expectation by judicial review as a matter of public law. This subject has been fully explained by my noble and learned friend, Lord Diplock, in *O'Reilly v. Mackman* [1983] 2 A.C. 237 and I need not repeat what he has so recently said. Legitimate, or reasonable, expectation may arise either from an express promise given on behalf of a public authority or from the existence of a regular practice which the claimant can reasonably expect to continue. Examples of the former type of expectation are *Reg. v. Liverpool Corporation, Ex parte Liverpool Taxi Fleet Operators' Association* [1972] 2 Q.B. 299 and *Attorney-General of Hong Kong v. Ng Yuen Shiu* [1983] 2 A.C. 629. (I agree with Lord Diplock's view, expressed in the speech in this appeal, that "legitimate" is to be preferred to "reasonable" in this context. I was responsible for using the word "reasonable" for the reason explained in *Ng Yuen Shiu*, but it was intended only to be exegetical of "legitimate".) An example of the latter is *Reg. v. Board of Visitors of Hull Prison, Ex parte St. Germain* [1979] Q.B. 425 approved by this House in *O'Reilly*, at p. 274D. The submission on behalf of the appellants is that the present case is of the latter type. The test of that is whether the practice of prior consultation of the staff on significant changes in their conditions of service was so well established by 1983 that it would be unfair or inconsistent with good administration for the Government to depart from the practice in this case. Legitimate expectations such as are now under consideration will always relate to a benefit or privilege to which the claimant has no right in private law, and it may even be to one which conflicts with his private law rights. In the present case the evidence shows that, ever since GCHQ began in 1947, prior consultation has been the invariable rule when conditions of service were to be significantly altered. Accordingly in my opinion if there had been no question of national security involved, the appellants would have had a legitimate expectation that the Minister would consult them before issuing the instruction of 22 December 1983 . . .

Lord Diplock

. . . To qualify as a subject for judicial review the decision must have consequences which affect some person (or body of persons) other than the decision-maker, although it may affect him too. It must affect such other person either:

(a) by altering rights or obligations of that person which are enforceable by or against him in private law; or

(b) by depriving him of some benefit or advantage which either (i) he had in the past been permitted by the decision-maker to enjoy and which he can legitimately expect to be permitted to
continue to do until there has been communicated to him some rational grounds for withdrawing it on which he has been given an opportunity to comment; or (ii) he has received assurance
from the decision-maker will not be withdrawn without giving him first an opportunity of
advancing reasons for contending that they should not be withdrawn. (I prefer to continue to
call the kind of expectation that qualifies a decision for inclusion in class (b) a "legitimate
expectation" rather than a "reasonable expectation," in order thereby to indicate that it has
consequences to which effect will be given in public law, whereas an expectation or hope that
some benefit or advantage would continue to be enjoyed, although it might well be entertained
by a "reasonable" man, would not necessarily have such consequences. The recent decision of
this House in *In re Findlay* [1985] A.C. 318 presents an example of the latter kind of expectation.
'Reasonable' furthermore bears different meanings according to whether the context in which it
is being used is that of private law or of public law. To eliminate confusion it is best avoided in
the latter.) . . .

Prima facie, therefore, civil servants employed at GCHQ who were members of national trade
unions had, at best, in December 1983, a legitimate expectation that they would continue to enjoy
the benefits of such membership and of representation by those trade unions in any consultations
and negotiations with representatives of the management of that government department as to
changes in any term of their employment. So, but again prima facie only, they were entitled, as a
matter of public law under the head of "procedural propriety," before administrative action was
taken on a decision to withdraw that benefit, to have communicated to the national trade unions by
which they had theretofore been represented the reason for such withdrawal, and for such unions
to be given an opportunity to comment on it . . .

*Notwithstanding these conclusions about the claimants' legitimate expectations, Lords Fraser,
Scarman, Diplock, Roskill, and Brightman were all of the opinion that national security considerations justified the Minister's failure to consult prior to the decision. The legality of the decision was
therefore upheld on national security grounds. Appeal dismissed.*

It is clear from this case that a legitimate expectation need not be generated by an express
statement: an established practice may lead the claimant legitimately to expect that the same
practice will be followed in the future. In the excerpt above, Lord Fraser points to cases in
which legitimate expectations have been established via both of those routes. However, while
the courts are prepared to avoid formalism by permitting a course of conduct to found
legitimate expectations, they also recognize the importance of limiting the circumstances in
which such expectations may arise. For instance, the representation — whether it is founded
on a statement or a practice — must usually, as Bingham LJ put it in *R v. Inland Revenue
Commissioners, ex parte MFK Underwriting Agencies Ltd* [1990] 1 WLR 1545 at 1569, be
'clear, unambiguous and devoid of relevant qualification'. It may also be necessary to
examine the circumstances in which the relevant statement is made. In *MFK Underwriting*,
for instance, the claimant was unable to establish a legitimate expectation arising from
representations made by the Inland Revenue — in response to questions asked of it by the
claimants — concerning how certain bonds would be taxed. Bingham LJ explained (at
1569–70) that

the taxpayer should indicate the use he intends to make of any ruling given . . . [K]nowledge that a
ruling is to be publicised in a large and important market could affect the person by whom and the
level at which a problem is considered and, indeed, whether it is appropriate to give a ruling at all
. . . The doctrine of legitimate expectation is rooted in fairness. But fairness is not a one-way street.

It imports the notion of equitableness, or fair and open dealing, to which the authority is entitled as much as the citizen.

Such judicial control of the circumstances in which a legitimate expectation may arise reflects the courts' concern to take account of both of the key factors — legal certainty and discretionary freedom — which are in play. It ensures that the public authority does not find itself bound by casual statements or by statements made on the basis of an incomplete awareness of the situation (hence safeguarding discretionary freedom), while recognizing that legal certainty will exert a stronger influence — thus favouring the designation of the expectation as legitimate — where the expectation is founded on a representation upon which it is reasonable for the individual to rely, in light of its clarity and its being issued by a public authority in full receipt of the facts.

Of course, as Bingham LJ recognized in *MFK Underwriting* (at 1569), the situation is different if the public authority itself chooses to issue a statement to the world at large: 'No doubt a statement formally published by the Inland Revenue to the world might safely be regarded as binding, subject to its terms, in any case clearly falling within them.' In this situation, the public authority chooses to promulgate the statement to the general public, and should therefore be aware of the extent to which it is likely to be relied upon. It is clear that when public authorities issue such general statements, legitimate expectations may thereby be generated. There is, therefore, no requirement that the statement be directed specifically at the individual claimant: see, *eg, Attorney-General of Hong Kong* v. *Ng Yeun Shiu* [1983] 2 AC 629, discussed below at 7.1.4.

Knowledge and reliance

Notwithstanding that the representation need not be directed towards the claimant specifically, it would seem that the claimant surely ought to *know* about the representation. Can the claimant have a legitimate expectation that he will be treated in a particular way if he was not aware of the public authority's statement or practice indicating how it intended to act?

....

Minister of State for Immigration and Ethnic Affairs v. Teoh (1995) 183 CLR 273
High Court of Australia

The respondent, a Malaysian citizen, married an Australian citizen while in Australia pursuant to a temporary entry permit. The respondent and his wife had three children. A further temporary entry permit was later issued and, before it expired, the respondent applied for a permanent entry permit. However, while that application was pending, the respondent was convicted of a number of drugs-related offences, and was sentenced to six years' imprisonment. The application for a permanent entry permit was later rejected. The respondent requested reconsideration of that decision but, following such reconsideration, the original decision was affirmed. The legality of that decision was challenged, *inter alia*, on the ground that relevant considerations had not been taken into account. On appeal to the Full Court of the Federal Court, the respondent asserted that the impact of the decision on his wife and children had not been taken into account, and that the court of first instance had erred when it reached the contrary conclusion on that point. This contention was unanimously accepted on appeal. Two of the three judges based their conclusion on the fact that Article 3.1 of the United Nations Convention on the Rights of the Child, which had been ratified by Australia, provides that 'in all actions concerning children . . . the best interests of the child shall be a primary consideration', and that ratification created a legitimate expectation that this practice would be followed in relevant cases. The Minister appealed.

Mason CJ and Deane J

. . . Junior counsel for the appellant contended that a convention ratified by Australia but not incorporated into our law could never give rise to a legitimate expectation. No persuasive reason was offered to support this far-reaching proposition. The fact that the provisions of the Convention do not form part of our law are a less than compelling reason — legitimate expectations are not equated to rules or principles of law. Moreover, ratification by Australia of an international convention is not to be dismissed as a merely platitudinous or ineffectual act, particularly when the instrument evidences internationally accepted standards to be applied by courts and administrative authorities in dealing with basic human rights affecting the family and children. Rather, ratification of a convention is a positive statement by the executive government of this country to the world and to the Australian people that the executive government and its agencies will act in accordance with the Convention. That positive statement is an adequate foundation for a legitimate expectation, absent statutory or executive indications to the contrary, that administrative decision-makers will act in conformity with the Convention and treat the best interests of the children as "a primary consideration". It is not necessary that a person seeking to set up such a legitimate expectation should be aware of the Convention or should personally entertain the expectation; it is enough that the expectation is reasonable in the sense that there are adequate materials to support it . . .

Toohey J

. . . In the present case the respondent contends for an expectation that the delegate would deal with his application in light of the criteria to be found in the Convention, particularly the principle that "the best interests of the child shall be a primary consideration". Accordingly, it was submitted, procedural fairness required that if the delegate proposed to act inconsistently with Australia's obligations under Arts 3 and 5 of the Convention, she should first have afforded the respondent the opportunity of persuading her that she should act consistently with its terms . . .

. . . Ratification of itself does not make the obligations enforceable in the courts; legislation, not executive act, is required. But the assumption of such an obligation may give rise to legitimate expectations in the minds of those who are affected by administrative decisions on which the obligation has some bearing. It is not necessary for a person in the position of the respondent to show that he was aware of the ratification of the Convention; legitimate expectation in this context does not depend upon the knowledge and state of mind of the individual concerned. The matter is to be assessed objectively, in terms of what expectation might reasonably be engendered by any undertaking that the authority in question has given, whether itself or, as in the present case, by the government of which it is a part. A subjective test is particularly inappropriate when the legitimate expectation is said to derive from something as general as the ratification of the Convention. For, by ratifying the Convention Australia has given a solemn undertaking to the world at large that it will: "in all actions concerning children, whether undertaken by public or private social welfare institutions, courts of law, administrative authorities or legislative bodies" make "the best interests of the child a primary consideration" . . .

. . . It follows that while Australia's ratification of the Convention does not go so far as to incorporate it into domestic law, it does have consequences for agencies of the executive government of the Commonwealth. It results in an expectation that those making administrative decisions in actions concerning children will take into account as a primary consideration the best interests of the children and that, if they intend not to do so, they will give the persons affected an opportunity to argue against such a course. It may be said that such a view of ratification will have undue consequences for decision-makers. But it is important to bear in mind that we are not concerned with enforceable obligations, but with legitimate expectations, and that there can be no legitimate expectation if the actions of the legislature or the executive are inconsistent with such an expectation . . .

McHugh J (dissenting)

. . . [T]he doctrine of procedural fairness is concerned with giving persons the opportunity to protect their rights, interests and reasonable expectations from the adverse effect of administrative and similar decisions. If the doctrine of legitimate expectations were now extended to matters about which the person affected has no knowledge, the term "expectation" would be a fiction so far as such persons were concerned. It is true that an expectation can only give rise to the right of procedural fairness if it is based on reasonable grounds. It must be an expectation that is objectively reasonable for a person in the position of the claimant. But that does not mean that the state of mind of the person concerned is irrelevant . . . If a person does not have an expectation that he or she will enjoy a benefit or privilege or that a particular state of affairs will continue, no disappointment or injustice is suffered by that person if that benefit or privilege is discontinued. A person cannot lose an expectation that he or she does not hold. Fairness does not require that a person be informed about something to which the person has no right or about which that person has no expectation . . .

Gaudron J agreed with Mason CJ and Deane and Toohey JJ that the appeal should be dismissed, but he based his decision on the fundamental right of the children, as Australian citizens, to have their welfare interests taken into account, rather than on the Convention. Appeal dismissed.

The comments of Mason CJ and Deane J, set out above, were quoted with approval by the Court of Appeal in *R* v. *Secretary of State for the Home Department, ex parte Ahmed and Patel* [1998] INLR 570; and Sir Louis-Blom Cooper QC (sitting as a Deputy Judge of the High Court) said, in *R* v. *Secretary of State for Wales, ex parte Emery* [1996] 4 All ER 1 at 16, that a claimant is not barred from asserting a legitimate expectation just because he was unaware of the public authority's statement or practice at the relevant time. (On appeal ([1998] 4 All ER 367) the Court of Appeal held that no legitimate expectation arose on the facts, but did not contradict the judge's statement regarding lack of knowledge.) The willingness of the Court of Appeal in *R (Abbasi)* v. *Secretary of State for Foreign and Commonwealth Affairs* [2002] EWCA Civ 1598 to recognize a legitimate expectation that the UK would consider making diplomatic representations in relation to British nationals detained overseas also suggests that knowledge is not a prerequisite, given that there was no indication that the individual concerned — a Guantanamo Bay detainee — had any knowledge of the policy statements giving rise to the expectation.

The question of knowledge, however, is a difficult one. It seems counterintuitive — even 'comical', as McHugh J put it in *Teoh* — to hold that a claimant who has been denied a particular benefit or procedure has had his legitimate expectation frustrated in circumstances where he was unaware of the statement or practice in the first place. But the position is more subtle than this. In the course of his judgment in *Emery*, Sir Louis Blom-Cooper QC endorsed the following passage from De Smith, Woolf and Jowell, *Judicial Review of Administrative Action* (London 1995) at 426:

Could an applicant claim the benefit of a representation contained in, say, a government circular which he had not seen until after the relevant decision had been made? The fact that the applicant is in the class to which the representation is directed but happens not to be aware of it should not, it is submitted, deprive him of the benefit of the representation. To do so would involve unfair discrimination between those who were and were not aware of the representation and would benefit the well-informed or well-advised. It would also encourage undesirable administrative practice by too readily relieving decision-makers of the normal consequences of their actions.

Two additional, and related, matters also throw doubt on whether knowledge should be a prerequisite. First, as we have already seen, the doctrine of legitimate expectation is concerned with what the claimant was *entitled* to expect, rather than with what he *actually* expected. Under this objective, as opposed to subjective, methodology by which the legitimate expectation is constructed, cannot factors outwith the claimant's actual knowledge be *included*, just as some factors which the claimant actually took into account may be *excluded*? The content of the legitimate expectation is an objective legal construct. It is concerned with that which the claimant was entitled to expect — and there is therefore room to argue that citizens are entitled to expect public authorities to behave in accordance with their represented practices and policies, irrespective of whether the claimant has specific knowledge thereof.

This prompts consideration of a second point, concerning the underlying basis of the legitimate expectation principle. To hold that actual knowledge on the part of the claimant should be a prerequisite is to embrace the concept of reliance as the rationale for enforcement of legitimate expectations at the expense of recognizing the other factors which are in play. In particular, as Schønberg notes (see above at 7.1.1), the legitimate expectation principle is also underpinned by the rule of law, which requires consistency and equality, and by the notion of 'good administration', which surely requires that public bodies be held to their published practices and standards. Consequently, in light of both the nature of legitimate expectations as objective legal constructs and the underlying principles which require their enforcement, there is no reason why the absence of knowledge should preclude a claim based on legitimate expectation.

If it is correct that the claimant need not personally know of the expectation, then it must follow that detrimental reliance need not be established, since it would clearly be impossible for a claimant to rely upon a representation of which he was ignorant. Indeed, in *R v. Secretary of State for Education and Employment, ex parte Begbie* [2000] 1 WLR 1115 at 1124, Peter Gibson LJ was of the view that detrimental reliance is not an absolute prerequisite; nevertheless, he acknowledged that it may be relevant:

. . . [I]t would be wrong to understate the significance of reliance in this area of the law. It is very much the exception, rather than the rule, that detrimental reliance will not be present when the court finds unfairness in the defeating of a legitimate expectation.

He endorsed the following passage from De Smith, Woolf and Jowell, *Judicial Review of Administrative Action* (London 1995) at 574:

Although detrimental reliance should not therefore be a condition precedent to the protection of a substantive legitimate expectation, it may be relevant in two situations: first, it might provide evidence of the existence or extent of an expectation. In that sense it can be a consideration to be taken into account in deciding whether a person was in fact led to believe that the authority would be bound by the representations. Second, detrimental reliance may be relevant to the decision of the authority whether to revoke a representation.

There are, however, many cases in which legitimate expectations have been held to arise in the absence of any proof of detrimental reliance (see, *eg, Attorney-General of Hong Kong* v. *Ng Yeun Shiu* [1983] 2 AC 629); more recently, in *R (Bibi)* v. *Newham London Borough Council* [2001] EWCA Civ 607 [2002] 1 WLR 237 at [26]–[32], Schiemann LJ, giving the judgment of the Court of Appeal, emphasized that reliance and detriment are not absolute prerequisites.

QUESTION

- 'The question whether an absence of knowledge on the part of the claimant should preclude an argument based on legitimate expectation ultimately turns on whether the purpose of administrative law is simply to redress wrongs occasioned to individuals or, more broadly, to secure responsible, consistent and fair government.' Comment on this statement.

The implications of the representation

The following case highlights a number of the factors which courts take into account in determining what an individual may be *entitled* to expect of a public authority. It also sheds light generally on how the courts view the question of legitimacy and its relationship with the implications of protecting the expectation.

R v. Department of Education and Employment, ex parte Begbie [2000] 1 WLR 1115
Court of Appeal

The claimant — Heather Begbie, then aged nine — was offered a place in February 1997 at an independent school which educated students up to age 18 (an 'all through' school) under the state-run assisted places scheme ('APS'), which offered financial assistance to children whose circumstances would otherwise have inhibited them from attending a fee-paying school. The Labour Party, in opposition, had indicated its intention to abolish the APS, but undertook to continue to fund children already in the scheme. After the general election in May 1997, the Education (Schools) Act 1997 was passed, abolishing the scheme. Section 2 provided that children already in primary education under the scheme would be funded only until the end of their primary education, unless the Secretary of State, in his discretion, decided that a longer period of funding should apply. The discretion was not exercised in favour of the claimant. A quashing order was sought in respect of that decision on the ground (*inter alia*) that the claimant had a legitimate expectation that, in respect of children at 'all through' schools, funding would extend beyond the end of primary education. The grounds on which the claimant relied in attempting to establish such an expectation are set out in the first paragraph of the excerpt from Peter Gibson LJ's judgment. Maurice Kay J, at first instance, had dismissed the claim; the claimant appealed to the Court of Appeal.

Peter Gibson LJ

[51] Mr. Beloff [for the claimant] argues that the statements of prominent Labour Party politicians both in opposition and in office created a legitimate expectation that Heather would enjoy the benefit of the APS until conclusion of her education at The Leys. He relies in particular in relation to the pre-election period on the letters [stating that children already in the APS would continue to be funded] of the Leader of the Opposition on 1 November 1996 to Dr. Tillson [an interested parent], on 6 December 1996 to Mrs. Treadwell [an interested grandparent], and on 27 January 1997 to Mrs. Williams [an interested parent]; Mr. Trickett's letter of 27 February 1997 [written by an MP to the parent of a child at an "all through" school under the APS, saying that funding would continue]; and the Kilfoyle letter [from the Shadow Minister for Schools, making a statement which said that funding would continue to age 13 in the case of children at schools which educated children to age

13]. And, in relation to the post-election period, the Prime Minister's "Evening Standard" article [in which he said, "No child currently at private school under the scheme or who has already got a place has lost out. They will be able to continue their education"], the Teed letter [from the Education Secretary to an interested grandparent, Mrs Teed, saying that children with places at all through schools would receive funding to age 18] and the letter of 11 March 1998 from the Secretary of State to Mrs. Begbie [saying that the undertakings previously given, regarding "all through" schools, would be met]. Mr. Beloff accepts that under the Act of 1997 the Secretary of State has a discretion and that he was entitled to formulate a policy on how the discretion would normally be exercised, but Mr. Beloff points to the fact that . . . the Secretary of State could admit further exceptions to the policy. Mr. Beloff submits that the Teed letter was a promise that those in the like circumstances to Heather would be allowed to keep their assisted places until the completion of their education, but that when the Secretary of State came to exercise his discretion in Heather's case, he reneged on that promise, consistent though that promise was with the other representations, thereby defeating legitimate expectations and that constituted an abuse of power which this court should not permit.

[52] Persuasively and skilfully though these submissions were advanced by Mr. Beloff, I am not able to accept them. No doubt statements such as those made by the Leader of the Opposition before May 1997 did give rise to an expectation that children already on the APS, from which group children at "all through" schools were not excepted, would continue to receive support in their education until it was completed, and it may be that the clear and specific statement in the Teed letter did likewise, at any rate for a time. But the question for the court is whether those statements give rise to a legitimate expectation, in the sense of an expectation which will be protected by law.

[53] I do not think that they did. As Mr. Havers Q.C., appearing with Mr. Garnham for the Crown pointed out, the starting point must be the Act of 1997. It is common ground that any expectation must yield to the terms of the statute under which the Secretary of State is required to act. S. 2(1) limits the ability of a school to provide assisted places to the circumstances provided for in subsection (2). That subsection requires a child with an assisted place who is receiving primary education to cease to hold that place at the end of the year in which the child completes his or her primary education unless discretion is exercised by the Secretary of State under para. (b). That paragraph is plainly intended to cater for the exceptional case where, having regard to particular circumstances of a particular child, it is reasonable in the eyes of the Secretary of State to make an exception for the child. As Mr. Havers submitted, if the Teed letter promise is implemented, virtually all children receiving primary education at "all through" schools would have to be allowed to keep their assisted places till the end of their secondary education. It is not in dispute that the Secretary of State is obliged to act in an even-handed manner and that if Heather were allowed to keep her assisted place, so must all others in the like circumstances. To treat the Secretary of State as bound to implement the promise in the Teed letter for all in Heather's position would plainly be outside the contemplation of the section, and contrary to what must have been intended by s. 2(2)(b).

[54] There are further difficulties in Mr. Beloff's way. His reliance on the pre-election statements founders on the fact that such statements were not made on behalf of a public authority. In *C.C.S.U. v Minister for the Civil Service* [1985] A.C. 374, Lord Fraser (at p. 401) said of legitimate expectations which may be protected by judicial review as a matter of public law:

> "Legitimate, or reasonable, expectation may arise either from an express promise given on behalf of a public authority or from the existence of a regular practice which the claimant can reasonably expect to continue."

[55] An opposition spokesman, even the Leader of the Opposition, does not speak on behalf of a

public authority. A further difficulty relates to the effect in law of a pre-election promise by politicians anxious to win the votes of electors. In *Bromley London Borough Council* v *Greater London Council* [1983] 1 A.C. 768 Lord Diplock (at p. 829) said that elected representatives must not treat themselves as irrevocably bound to carry out pre-announced policies contained in election manifestos. True it is, as Mr. Beloff pointed out, that Lord Diplock a little earlier on the same page recognised that an elected member "ought" to give considerable weight, when deciding with the other elected members whether to implement policies put forward in a manifesto, to the factor that he received the support of the electors when he fought the election on the basis of the manifesto policies. But I do not read Lord Diplock as suggesting that the obligation in the word "ought" was a legal one or giving rise to legal effects. No case has been shown to us of the court treating such a promise as of binding effect or otherwise as having legal consequences. There are good practical reasons why this should be so. As was explained on behalf of the Labour Party on 18 July 1997 in a letter to Mrs. Cutler [an interested parent]: "Only once the new Government had full access to information on APS numbers and projected spending, was it possible to present more details on our policy of phasing out the APS."

[56] It is obvious that a party in opposition will not know all the facts and ramifications of a promise until it achieves office. To hold that the pre-election promises bound a newly-elected government could well be inimical to good government. I intend no encouragement to politicians to be extravagant in their pre-election promises, but when a party elected into office fails to keep its election promises, the consequences should be political and not legal.

[57] Of the post-election statements to which Mr. Beloff points, the Prime Minister's words in the Evening Standard article must be read in their context. Most of the article was concerned with the honouring by the new government of the manifesto pledge to reduce the size of infant classes in state primary schools and the reallocation of money to achieve that. It was explained that the phasing out of the APS was funding that programme. Only in the short paragraph which I have quoted was there reference to the impact on children with existing assisted places. The words used are very general and in one sense are literally true because every child on an assisted place was allowed to continue at least for a while. But no reasonable informed reader of the article could believe that it was the announcement of a change of the policy in detailed form already promulgated. And there is Ms Mackenzie's [an APS administrator in the Department for Education and Employment] evidence that it was not so intended. Nor is there evidence of any detrimental reliance by Heather's parents on the Prime Minister's words. On the contrary, they were, very reasonably, about this time trying to obtain, through their own M.P. as well as by other means, a clear and specific statement of what the Secretary of State was intending to do about those like Heather at 'all through' schools, but the indications from government were not encouraging. Indeed one Labour M.P., Mr. Ben Bradshaw, was complaining to the Secretary of State that the government's policy was not what the Prime Minister had promised before the election.

[58] The Teed letter does contain an unambiguous representation in terms applicable to a person in Heather's position:

[59] "Where there was provision of an 'all through' school and where there has been a clear promise of a place through to the age of 18, we have agreed to honour that promise."

[60] But it was corrected some 5 weeks later by the letter from Mr. Wardle, acting on behalf of the Secretary of State, and there is no evidence that in the interim Heather's parents relied on the representation to change their position. Further there is no evidence that the Secretary of State intended to create a new category of children who would continue to keep their assisted places and

there is clear evidence from Ms Mackenzie that the Secretary of State in the Teed letter misstated by mistake what his own policy was.

[61] For my part I cannot accept that the mere fact that a clear and unequivocal statement such as that made in the Teed letter was made is enough to establish a legitimate expectation in accordance with that statement such that the expectation cannot be allowed to be defeated. All the circumstances must be considered. Where the court is satisfied that a mistake was made by the Minister or other person making the statement, the court should be slow to fix the public authority permanently with the consequences of that mistake. That is not to say that a promise made by mistake will never have legal consequences. It may be that a mistaken statement will, even if subsequently sought to be corrected, give rise to a legitimate expectation, whether in the person to whom the statement is made or in others who learnt of it, for example where there has been detrimental reliance on the statement before it was corrected. The court must be alive to the possibility of such unfairness to the individual by the public authority in its conduct as to amount to an abuse of power. But that is not this case.

[62] As for the letter of 11 March 1998 from the Secretary of State to Mrs. Begbie, while she sought to extract from it what he was saying, on her own account it left her confused (and she is plainly of high intelligence) and the Secretary of State never confirmed her understanding of the letter. He promised to return to her on it, but when belatedly there was a clear decision, that ran counter to any expectation which she had arising from that letter. In short, the letter contained no clear representation and could never reasonably have been relied on; nor was it because of Mrs. Begbie's wholly justified attempts to obtain clarification. I have to say that the way the Secretary of State dealt with the proper concerns of parents like Mrs. Begbie reflects no credit whatsoever on him. But I cannot say that his statements gave rise to a legitimate expectation, still less that there was an abuse of power . . .

Laws and Sedley LJJ agreed that the claimant had failed to establish a legitimate expectation. Appeal dismissed.

A number of factors influenced the court in reaching the conclusion that the claimant was not entitled to expect that pupils at 'all through' schools would be funded to age 18. As well as holding that this would be inconsistent with the statutory scheme — which, it was held, envisaged that APS funding should cease upon completion of primary education in all but exceptional circumstances — Peter Gibson LJ was concerned, more generally, with the consequences of permitting pre- and post-election statements to restrict the government's discretion. This suggests that, even if the criteria of legitimacy and protection are to some extent distinct, they are also to some extent related. The court denied the existence of any legitimate expectation in this case partly because the protection, or enforcement, of the claimed expectation would have impacted substantially upon the government's discretionary freedom in this context. Thus the interest in discretionary freedom trumped the principle of legal certainty so as to deny the existence of any legitimate expectation. This mode of analysis seems to bear more relation to that favoured by Sedley J in *Hamble Fisheries* than to Craig's approach (see above at 7.1.2).

7.1.4 Procedural Protection

It is uncontroversial that a court may protect an individual's expectation by requiring a fair procedure to be followed before the public authority makes the relevant decision. This mode of protection may result in the fulfilment of the claimant's legitimate expectation (if the claimant expected, or was only entitled to expect, procedural fairness); alternatively, it may be conferred in a situation where the court determines that, while the claimant reasonably expected a particular substantive outcome, competing demands based on the preservation of discretionary freedom dictate that the decision-maker, having considered the claimant's views in a procedurally fair manner, should be able to pursue a different course.

It is important to note the relationship between procedural protection of legitimate expectations and the duty to act fairly considered in ch 11. Both secure procedurally fair treatment for the individual. As we explain in ch 11, the duty to act fairly is flexible: its precise meaning turns on the context, so different situations will require different levels of fairness. The principle of legitimate expectation may well influence the precise level of fairness required in any given case — a point which Lord Denning MR recognized in *Schmidt* v. *Secretary of State for Home Affairs* [1969] 2 Ch 149 at 169. Rejecting the notion that the principles of natural justice applied only to 'judicial' as opposed to 'administrative' powers (on which see below at 11.2), Lord Denning said that

an administrative body may, in a proper case, be bound to give a person who is affected by their decision an opportunity of making representations. It all depends on whether he has some right or interest, or, I would add, some legitimate expectation, of which it would not be fair to deprive him without hearing what he has to say.

For instance, the general context (taking account of the rights or interests of the claimant liable to be affected by the decision) may indicate that the claimant is entitled only to make written representations before a decision which affects him is taken. However, if the decision-maker has undertaken to give people in the claimant's situation an oral hearing (which is a more ample form of fairness) then such a hearing must be offered. The principle of legitimate expectation (in its procedural form) and the duty to act fairly are therefore intimately connected, since the former can form a key component of the context within which the content of the latter is determined. The following case illustrates precisely this point.

....

Attorney-General of Hong Kong v. *Ng Yuen Shiu* [1983] 2 AC 629
Judicial Committee of the Privy Council

The claimant, born in China, entered Hong Kong from Macau illegally in 1967. He was removed to Macau in 1976 but, a month later, re-entered Hong Kong. By 1980, he was the part-owner of a factory in Hong Kong. For some time prior to 1980, the Hong Kong government operated a 'reached base' policy, under which illegal immigrants from China would not be removed if they managed to reach urban areas without being arrested. However, in October 1980 the government announced the termination of that policy. In response to concerns raised by illegal immigrants from Macau, a senior immigration official issued a statement saying that such immigrants 'will be treated in accordance with procedures for illegal immigrants from anywhere other than China. They will be interviewed in due course. No guarantee can be given that you may not subsequently be removed.

Each case will be treated on its merits.' A removal order was issued against the claimant without his first being given any opportunity to make representations as to why he should not be removed. The High Court refused to quash the order, but the Court of Appeal of Hong Kong granted an order prohibiting the execution of the removal order until the claimant was given the opportunity to be heard. The Attorney-General of Hong Kong appealed to the Privy Council.

Lord Fraser (giving the judgment of the Judicial Committee of the Privy Council)

. . . The argument for the Attorney-General raised two questions — one of wide general importance, the other of more limited scope. The general question, which both the High Court and the Court of Appeal decided in favour of the Attorney-General, is whether an alien who enters Hong Kong illegally has, as a general rule, a right to a hearing, conducted fairly and in accordance with the rules of natural justice, before a removal order is made against him. The narrower question is whether, assuming that the answer to the general question is in the negative, nevertheless the applicant has a right to such a hearing in the particular circumstances of this case. The Court of Appeal answered the latter question in favour of the applicant and therefore made the limited order of prohibition now under appeal. Having regard to the view which their Lordships have formed on the narrower question, it is unnecessary for them to decide the general question. They will therefore assume, without deciding, that the Court of Appeal rightly decided that there was no general right in an alien to have a hearing in accordance with the rules of natural justice before a removal order is made against him.

The narrower proposition for which the applicant contended was that a person is entitled to a fair hearing before a decision adversely affecting his interests is made by a public official or body, if he has "a legitimate expectation" of being accorded such a hearing. The phrase "legitimate expectation" in this context originated in the judgment of Lord Denning M.R. in *Schmidt v. Secretary of [State] for Home Affairs* [1969] 2 Ch. 149, 170. It is many ways an apt one to express the underlying principle, though it is somewhat lacking in precision. In *Salemi v. MacKellar (No. 2)* (1977) 137 C.L.R. 396, 404, Barwick C.J. construed the word "legitimate" in that phrase as expressing the concept of "entitlement or recognition by law." So understood, the expression (as Barwick C.J. rightly observed) "adds little, if anything, to the concept of a right." With great respect to Barwick C.J., their Lordships consider that the word "legitimate" in that expression falls to be read as meaning "reasonable." Accordingly "legitimate expectations" in this context are capable of including expectations which go beyond enforceable legal rights, provided they have some reasonable basis: see *Reg. v. Criminal Injuries Compensation Board, Ex parte Lain* [1967] 2 Q.B. 864. So it was held in *Reg. v. Board of Visitors of Hull Prison, Ex parte St. Germain (No. 2)* [1979] 1 W.L.R. 1041 that a prisoner is entitled to challenge, by judicial review, a decision by a prison board of visitors, awarding him loss of remission of sentence, although he has no legal right to remission, but only a reasonable expectation of receiving it . . .

. . . Their Lordships see no reason why the principle should not be applicable when the person who will be affected by the decision is an alien, just as much as when he is a British subject. The justification for it is primarily that, when a public authority has promised to follow a certain procedure, it is in the interest of good administration that it should act fairly and should implement its promise, so long as implementation does not interfere with its statutory duty. The principle is also justified by the further consideration that, when the promise was made, the authority must have considered that it would be assisted in discharging its duty fairly by any representations from interested parties and as a general rule that is correct.

In the opinion of their Lordships the principle that a public authority is bound by its undertakings as to the procedure it will follow, provided they do not conflict with its duty, is applicable to the undertaking given by the Government of Hong Kong to the applicant, along with other illegal immigrants from Macau, in the announcement outside the Government House on October 28, that each case would be considered on its merits. The only ground on which it was argued before the

Board that the undertaking had not been implemented was that the applicant had not been given an opportunity to put his case for an exercise of discretion, which the director undoubtedly possesses, in his favour before a decision was reached. The basis of the applicant's complaint is that, when he was interviewed by an official of the Immigration Department who recommended to the director that a removal order against him should be made, he was not able to explain the humanitarian grounds for the discretion to be exercised in his favour. In particular he had no opportunity of explaining that he was not an employee but a partner in a business which employed several workers. The evidence of the applicant, contained in an affidavit to the High Court, was that at the interview he was not allowed to say anything except to answer the questions put to him by the official who was interviewing him . . .

Their Lordships . . . are not disposed to differ from the view expressed by both the courts below, to the effect that the government's promise to the applicant has not been implemented . . .

The Privy Council substituted for the prohibiting order, issued by the Court of Appeal of Hong Kong, an order quashing the removal order, while noting that this would not prevent the issue of a fresh removal order once the claimant had been subjected to a fair procedure. Appeal dismissed.

QUESTION

- Why was it necessary, in this case, to invoke the legitimate expectation doctrine in order to secure fair treatment?

7.1.5 Substantive Protection

The substantive protection of (necessarily substantive) legitimate expectations is a more controversial matter. Procedural protection may cause delay and expense to the decision-maker, but it does not ultimately reduce the scope of its discretion: it restricts *how* it makes decisions, but not *what* decisions it is entitled to make. In contrast, substantive protection impacts upon the range of decisions open to the decision-maker: the enforcement of substantive expectations may ultimately result in the removal of the public authority's discretion in cases where the court concludes that the only lawful option is for the expectation to be satisfied. This raises difficult constitutional questions about the respective roles of courts and decision-makers, to which the courts have (at least until recently) struggled to articulate a consistent response.

Competing standards of review?

If an individual holds a substantive legitimate expectation which a decision-maker frustrates, in what circumstances should the courts intervene and compel the decision-maker to fulfil the expectation? Some cases supplied sharply contrasting answers to this question. In *R v. Ministry of Agriculture Fisheries and Food, ex parte Hamble (Offshore) Fisheries Ltd* [1995] 2 All ER 714 at 731, Sedley J said (*obiter*) that it is 'the court's duty to protect the interests of those individuals whose expectation of different treatment has a legitimacy which in fairness outtops the policy choice which threatens to frustrate it'.

A very different approach, however, was commended in the earlier case of *R v. Secretary of State for Transport, ex parte Richmond-upon-Thames London Borough Council* [1994] 1 WLR

74. Counsel argued in favour of the sort of balancing approach which later found favour with Sedley J in *Hamble Fisheries*; however, Laws J (at 94) considered that accepting such a submission

would imply that the court is to be the judge of the public interest in such cases, and thus the judge of the merits of the proposed policy change. Thus understood, Mr. Gordon's [counsel's] submission must be rejected. The court is not the judge of the merits of the decision-maker's policy. In fact, Mr. Gordon disavowed any such proposition; but if, as must be the case, the public authority in question is the judge of the issue whether "the overriding public interest" justifies a change in policy, then the submission means no more than that a reasonable public authority, having regard only to relevant considerations, will not alter its policy unless it concludes that the public will be better served by the change. But this is no more than to assert that a change in policy, like any discretionary decision by a public authority, must not transgress *Wednesbury* principles. That, however, is elementary and carries Mr. Gordon nowhere.

On this view, the court is entitled to intervene, requiring the decision-maker to satisfy the expectation, only if the original decision to frustrate the expectation is unreasonable in the *Wednesbury* sense (that is, so unreasonable that no reasonable agency would contemplate it: see below at 9.2.1). Compared with *Hamble Fisheries*, this ascribes significantly more discretionary choice to the decision-maker and gives commensurately less weight to the principle of legal certainty, since the agency, under this approach, is free to choose to frustrate the expectation so long as it remains within the relatively broad discretionary area of judgment which the *Wednesbury* doctrine supplies. This limited form of substantive protection was later endorsed by the Court of Appeal in *R v. Secretary of State for the Home Department, ex parte Hargreaves* [1997] 1 WLR 906; the *Hamble Fisheries* approach was overruled, and condemned by Hirst LJ (at 921) as a 'heresy'. (For contrasting views of *Hargreaves*, compare Forsyth [1997] *PL* 375 and Allan [1997] *CLJ* 246.)

QUESTIONS

- In principle, which approach do you consider to be preferable?
- Try to explain the different underlying visions of the relationship between judges and decision-makers which are presented by the *Hamble Fisheries* and *Hargreaves* approaches.

The Coughlan *Case*

When a differently constituted Court of Appeal revisited the question of substantive expectations in the following case, it reached a very different conclusion.

....

R v. North and East Devon Health Authority, ex parte Coughlan [2001] QB 213
Court of Appeal

The claimant was seriously injured in a road traffic accident in 1971, following which she became a long-term patient at Newcourt Hospital. In 1993 the defendant's predecessor, Exeter Health Authority, moved the claimant and several other residents to Mardon House, a new, purpose-built facility. The Newcourt residents consented to this because they had been assured that they would be able to remain at Mardon House 'for as long as they wished to stay there': it would be their 'home for life'. However, in 1998, the defendant resolved to close Mardon House, asserting that it had become 'prohibitively expensive' to run. The claimant argued (*inter alia*), successfully at first instance, that the 'home for life' promise gave rise to a substantive legitimate expectation which should be protected substantively. The Health Authority appealed.

Lord Woolf MR (giving the judgment of the court)

[55] . . . [I]t is necessary to begin by examining the court's role where what is in issue is a promise as to how it would behave in the future made by a public body when exercising a statutory function. In the past it would have been argued that the promise was to be ignored since it could not have any effect on how the public body exercised its judgment in what it thought was the public interest. Today such an argument would have no prospect of success . . .

[56] What is still the subject of some controversy is the court's role when a member of the public, as a result of a promise or other conduct, has a legitimate expectation that he will be treated in one way and the public body wishes to treat him or her in a different way. Here the starting point has to be to ask what in the circumstances the member of the public could legitimately expect. In the words of Lord Scarman in *Re Findlay* [1985] AC 318 at p 338, "But what was their *legitimate* expectation?" Where there is a dispute as to this, the dispute has to be determined by the court, as happened in *Findlay*. This can involve a detailed examination of the precise terms of the promise or representation made, the circumstances in which the promise was made and the nature of the statutory or other discretion.

[57] There are at least three possible outcomes. (a) The court may decide that the public authority is only required to bear in mind its previous policy or other representation, giving it the weight it thinks right, but no more, before deciding whether to change course. Here the court is confined to reviewing the decision on *Wednesbury* grounds. This has been held to be the effect of changes of policy in cases involving the early release of prisoners (see *Re Findlay* [1985] AC 318; *R v. Home Secretary ex parte Hargreaves* [1997] 1 WLR 906). (b) On the other hand the court may decide that the promise or practice induces a legitimate expectation of, for example, being consulted before a particular decision is taken. Here it is uncontentious that the court itself will require *the opportunity for consultation* to be given unless there is an overriding reason to resile from it (see *A-G for Hong Kong v. Ng Yuen Shiu* [1983] 2 AC 629) in which case the court will itself judge the adequacy of the reason advanced for the change of policy, taking into account what fairness requires. (c) Where the court considers that a lawful promise or practice has induced a legitimate expectation of a *benefit which is substantive*, not simply procedural, authority now establishes that here too the court will in a proper case decide whether to frustrate the expectation is so unfair that to take a new and different course will amount to an abuse of power. Here, once the legitimacy of the expectation is established, the court will have the task of weighing the requirements of fairness against any overriding interest relied upon for the change of policy.

[58] The court having decided which of the categories is appropriate, the court's role in the case of the second and third categories is different from that in the first. In the case of the first, the court is restricted to reviewing the decision on conventional grounds. The test will be rationality and whether the public body has given proper weight to the implications of not fulfilling the promise. In the case of the second category the court's task is the conventional one of determining whether the decision was procedurally fair. In the case of the third, the court has when necessary to determine whether there is a sufficient overriding interest to justify a departure from what has been previously promised.

[59] In many cases the difficult task will be to decide into which category the decision should be allotted. In what is still a developing field of law, attention will have to be given to what it is in the first category of case which limits the applicant's legitimate expectation (in Lord Scarman's words in

Re Findlay) to an expectation that whatever policy is in force at the time will be applied to him. As to the second and third categories, the difficulty of segregating the procedural from the substantive is illustrated by the line of cases arising out of decisions of justices not to commit a defendant to the Crown Court for sentence, or assurances given to a defendant by the court: here to resile from such a decision or assurance may involve the breach of legitimate expectation. (See *R v Reilly* [1985] 1 Cr. App. R (S) 273, 276; *R v Southampton Magistrates Court* [1994] Cr. App. R (S) 778, 781–2.) No attempt is made in those cases, rightly in our view, to draw the distinction. Nevertheless, most cases of an enforceable expectation of a substantive benefit (the third category) are likely in the nature of things to be cases where the expectation is confined to one person or a few people, giving the promise or representation the character of a contract. We recognise that the courts' role in relation to the third category is still controversial; but, as we hope to show, it is now clarified by authority.

[60] We consider that [counsel] are correct, as was the judge, in regarding the facts of this case as coming into the third category . . .

Having reached this conclusion, the court carried out the balancing test, concluding that the financial arguments advanced by the health authority were insufficient to justify dashing the legitimate expectation. Appeal dismissed.

Coughlan's relationship with earlier case law is somewhat strained. Lord Woolf MR sought to establish that the pre-existing jurisprudence supported the application of the balancing (as opposed to *Wednesbury*) test to category three cases. However, while a number of cases — including *R v. Secretary of State for the Home Department, ex parte Khan* [1984] 1 WLR 1337, *In re Preston* [1985] AC 835, and *R v. Inland Revenue Commissioners, ex parte MFK Underwriting Agents Ltd* [1990] 1 WLR 1545 — indicated the possibility of substantive protection of legitimate expectations, it is arguable that they left open the question whether the test to be applied was the *Wednesbury* standard, or something more exacting. Indeed, the pre-*Coughlan* case law was replete with authoritative judicial statements (see, pre-eminently, *R v. Secretary of State for the Home Department, ex parte Brind* [1991] 1 AC 696) to the effect that the *Wednesbury* principle marked the outer perimeter of substantive judicial review. And, while the House of Lords has now sanctioned recourse to the more exacting proportionality test in human rights cases (see *R (Daly)* v. *Secretary of State for the Home Department* [2001] UKHL 26 [2001] 2 AC 532), the Court of Appeal in *R (Association of British Civilian Internees: Far East Region)* v. *Secretary of State for Defence* [2003] EWCA Civ 473 [2003] QB 1397 concluded that, outside the human rights context, *Wednesbury* remains the touchstone of substantive review — a conclusion which sits uncomfortably with the approach adopted in *Coughlan*.

The intensity of the review adopted in *Coughlan* should not be underestimated. Once a case is placed within category three, it is for the court to decide 'whether the consequent frustration of the individual's expectation is so unfair as to be a misuse of the authority's power' (*Coughlan* at [82]). The application of this test in *Coughlan* itself suggests that there is a real risk, in category three cases, of the distinction between appeal and review dissolving — a concern highlighted by Sales and Steyn [2004] *PL* 564 at 591:

It is unclear from the reasoning of the court quite why the interests of the applicant should outweigh those of others to whom the health authority also had to provide services, under conditions of limited resources. The court's dismissive reference to the consequences of the health authority fulfilling the expectation as "financial only" seems, with respect, to beg this question.

Constitutionally, discretionary decisions as to the allocation of finite resources subject to many competing individual demands are generally left to bodies subject to democratic accountability and with a complete view of all the claims upon those resources, not the courts.

As well as questioning the appropriateness of the category three review conducted in *Coughlan*, it is also necessary to consider critically the manner in which cases are assigned to the different categories. In *Coughlan*, Lord Woolf suggested (at [59]) that category three situations are likely to involve an expectation which is 'confined to one person or a few people, giving the promise or representation the character of a contract'. This has been reflected in subsequent cases in which category three protection has generally been provided only in cases concerning individuals or small groups (see, eg, *R (B)* v. *Camden London Borough Council* [2001] EWHC Admin 271 (2002) 63 BMLR 154). Why is this factor considered to be of importance?

First, it was suggested in *Coughlan* (at [71]) that 'when a promise is made to a category of individuals who have the same interest, it is more likely to be considered to have binding effect than a promise which is made generally or to a diverse class, when the interests of those to whom the promise is made may differ or, indeed, may be in conflict'. Secondly, it is arguable that a higher degree of unfairness arises when a promise made to an individual or a small group is breached, because stronger expectations are likely to be engendered in such circumstances. This suggests that category three protection will not be appropriate in relation to expectations founded on general statements of policy (of which the claimant may or may not be aware); instead, as Clayton [2003] *CLJ* 93 at 103 argues, such expectations fall to be protected only on *Wednesbury* grounds. Thirdly, the restriction of high-level, category three protection to expectations engendered only in individuals or small groups may well reflect the tension which, as we have already seen, is pervasive in this area — namely the need to temper legal certainty with the preservation of discretionary freedom. Limiting the balancing approach to individual and small group cases suggests that executive autonomy will be seriously curtailed only in relation to individualized decisions and the application of policy to specific situations, leaving the administration's ability to formulate and change policy at a general level vulnerable only to the relatively deferential *Wednesbury* review which is applicable to category one cases.

QUESTION

• Does *Coughlan* adequately balance the competing demands of legal certainty and discretionary freedom?

Beyond categorization?

The implications of the *Coughlan* judgment have been explored in subsequent decisions. Of particular interest are the following comments of Laws LJ.

....

R v. Department of Education and Employment, ex parte Begbie [2000] 1 WLR 1115
Court of Appeal

For the facts, see above at 7.1.3.

Laws LJ

[77] . . . In the first of the three categories given in *Coughlan*, the test is limited to the *Wednesbury* principle . . . But in the third (where there is a legitimate expectation of a substantive benefit) the court must decide "whether to frustrate the expectation is so unfair that to take a new and different course will amount to an abuse of power" . . . However the first category may also involve deprivation of a substantive benefit. What marks the true difference between the two? . . .

[78] Fairness and reasonableness (and their contraries) are objective concepts; otherwise there would be no public law, or if there were it would be palm tree justice. But each is a spectrum, not a single point, and they shade into one another. It is now well established that the *Wednesbury* principle itself constitutes a sliding scale of review, more or less intrusive according to the nature and gravity of what is at stake . . .

[80] As it seems to me the first and third categories explained in the *Coughlan* case are not hermetically sealed. The facts of the case, viewed always in their statutory context, will steer the court to a more or less intrusive quality of review. In some cases a change of tack by a public authority, though unfair from the applicant's stance, may involve questions of general policy affecting the public at large or a significant section of it (including interests not represented before the court); here the judges may well be in no position to adjudicate save at most on a bare *Wednesbury* basis, without themselves donning the garb of policy-maker, which they cannot wear . . .

[81] In other cases the act or omission complained of may take place on a much smaller stage, with far fewer players. Here, with respect, lies the importance of the fact in the *Coughlan* case that few individuals were affected by the promise in question. The case's facts may be discrete and limited, having no implications for an innominate class of persons. There may be no wide-ranging issues of general policy, or none with multi-layered effects, upon whose merits the court is asked to embark. The court may be able to envisage clearly and with sufficient certainty what the full consequences will be of any order it makes. In such a case the court's condemnation of what is done as an abuse of power, justifiable (or rather, falling to be relieved of its character as abusive) only if an overriding public interest is shown of which the court is the judge, offers no offence to the claims of democratic power.

[82] There will of course be a multitude of cases falling within these extremes, or sharing the characteristics of one or other. The more the decision challenged lies in what may inelegantly be called the macro-political field, the less intrusive will be the court's supervision. More than this: in that field, true abuse of power is less likely to be found, since within it changes of policy, fuelled by broad conceptions of the public interest, may more readily be accepted as taking precedence over the interests of groups which enjoyed expectations generated by an earlier policy . . .

While these comments do not contradict *Coughlan*'s central conclusion that some cases will call for the high level of judicial scrutiny which the balancing test supplies, the approach proposed by Laws LJ is more subtle. *Coughlan* presupposes that the courts have two distinct modes of substantive review at their disposal, based respectively on the (highly deferential) *Wednesbury* test and the (very intensive) balancing exercise. In contrast, Laws LJ recognizes that the two tests really constitute different points on one spectrum, and that they therefore shade into one another. On this approach, the question which the court must answer is not, 'Which category should the case be put into?' but, rather, 'Exactly how intensive or deferential should the review be?' This is a more sophisticated approach which, as we will see in ch 9, reflects broader developments in the law of substantive review beyond the specific context of legitimate expectation.

Judicial reluctance to adopt the intensive review seen in *Coughlan* is also evident in the following remarks of Schiemann LJ, giving the judgment of the Court of Appeal in *R (Bibi) v. Newham London Borough Council* [2001] EWCA Civ 607 [2002] 1 WLR 237 at [40]–[43]:

The court has two functions — assessing the legality of actions by administrators and, if it finds unlawfulness on the administrators' part, deciding what relief it should give. It is in our judgment a mistake to isolate from the rest of administrative law cases those which turn on representations made by authorities. The same constitutional principles apply to the exercise by the court of each of these two functions.

The court, even where it finds that the applicant has a legitimate expectation of some benefit, will not order the authority to honour its promise where to do so would be to assume the powers of the executive. Once the court has established such an abuse it may ask the decision taker to take the legitimate expectation properly into account in the decision making process . . .

While in some cases there can be only one lawful ultimate answer to the question whether the authority should honour its promise, at any rate in cases involving a legitimate expectation of a substantive benefit, this will not invariably be the case.

Finally, it is worth noting the alternative mode of analysis favoured by Clayton [2003] *CLJ* 93 at 102–105. He argues that 'expectations' deriving from specific representations, on the one hand, and general policies, on the other, are wholly distinct creatures — so much so that the latter should not be regarded as a species of legitimate expectation doctrine:

The rationale for requiring public bodies to adhere to their policies is . . . probably best explained as an application of the principle of consistency . . . which ensures that real weight is given to the policy promulgated whilst acknowledging that a public body has a right to alter policy provided it does not act irrationally.

On this view, judicial review of departure from published *policies*, as distinct from *representations*, would lie only on the traditional *Wednesbury* basis (on which see generally below at 9.2.1).

7.1.6 Revocability of Lawful Administrative Decisions

It is convenient at this point to consider a matter which is closely allied to, but distinct from, that of the enforcement of lawfully generated *expectations as to how a body will act in the future*, by asking to what extent public bodies may revoke lawful *decisions which have already been taken*. The interests of certainty would seem to favour a general principle to the effect that such decisions are irrevocable. Such thinking seems to have appealed to the court in *In re 56 Denton Road, Twickenham* [1953] Ch 51. The War Damage Commission equivocated about the classification of the claimant's house, which had been damaged during the Second World War. At one point, the Commission classified the damage as 'not a total loss', but later changed this to 'total loss', meaning that the claimant would qualify for less compensation. Vaisey J concluded that the former classification represented a final decision by the Commission which could not be revoked, explaining (at 56–57) that

the plaintiff's counsel offered for my acceptance the following proposition: that where Parliament confers upon a body such as the War Damage Commission the duty of deciding or determining any question, the deciding or determining of which affects the rights of the subject, such decision or determination made and communicated in terms which are not expressly preliminary or provisional is final and conclusive, and cannot in the absence of express statutory power or the consent of the person or persons affected be altered or withdrawn by that body. I accept that proposition as well-founded, and applicable to the present case . . .

. . . [T]he contrary view would introduce a lamentable measure of uncertainty, and so much disturbance in the minds of those unfortunate persons who have suffered war damage that the Act cannot have contemplated the possibility of such vacillations as are claimed to be permissible in such a case as the present.

However, while lawful decisions are usually irrevocable, this is not always so: it is clear from other cases, such as *Rootkin* v. *Kent County Council* [1981] 1 WLR 1186, that in some circumstances decisions can be revoked. Akehurst [1982] *PL* 613 at 623–624 argues that it is crucial in this context to distinguish two sets of circumstances. First:

When an administrative body is empowered to determine whether an individual has a pre-existing legal right, it is performing the same type of function as a court performs. The general rule is that judgments of a court are final and cannot be revoked . . . When Parliament entrusts the task of making such a determination to an administrative body instead of a court, it is reasonable to assume that Parliament intended the decisions of such a body to enjoy the same degree of irrevocability the judgments of a court.

Secondly, however, 'different considerations apply when an administrative body is empowered to confer on an individual a benefit which he would not otherwise have possessed'. Although there is likely to be an implied discretion to revoke such decisions, the public body, in exercising such discretion, must carefully weigh the competing interests at stake, revoking the decision only if 'the public interests in favour of revocation outweigh the private interests of the beneficiary'.

7.2 Unlawfully Created Expectations

7.2.1 Introduction

We turn now to the problematic question of 'unlawfully created expectations'. We use this term to describe both expectations as to conduct which is *ultra vires* the agency concerned, and expectations as to conduct which, although *intra vires* the relevant agency, arise through representations issued by officials unauthorized to make them. As we explain below, a recent House of Lords decision has signalled a change of approach in this area. However, it remains necessary to examine the older cases in order to understand the conflicting policy interests that are in play.

7.2.2 Fairness to the Individual

The importance in this context of securing fairness for the individual appealed notably to Lord Denning. In a number of cases he sought to safeguard individuals by invoking the doctrine of estoppel, according to which, if a representation is made to an individual who then relies upon the accuracy of the statement to his detriment, it will generally be impermissible for the representor to derogate from the statement. Although the principle operates in a number of situations in private law — *eg*, it can prevent the enforcement of contractual terms which one party has led another to believe will be waived (see *Central London Property Trust Ltd* v. *High Trees House Ltd* [1947] KB 130), while the doctrine of proprietary estoppel may permit an individual who has been promised an interest in land to enforce the promise if it would be unfair to frustrate it (see *Taylors Fashions Ltd* v. *Liverpool Victoria Trustees Co Ltd* [1982] QB 133n) — we will see later that it is arguably unsuited to the public law context. Such concerns did not, however, trouble Denning J in the following case.

Robertson v. *Minister of Pensions* [1949] 1 KB 227
King's Bench Division

The War Office originally had jurisdiction over all claims in respect of disability attributable to war service. By a Royal Warrant of 1940 the jurisdiction over claims in respect of service after 3 September 1939 was transferred to the Ministry of Pensions. In 1941 the appellant, a serving officer, wrote to the War Office regarding a disability of his which had resulted from an injury in December 1939. He received a reply stating, 'Your disability has been accepted as attributable to military service.' Relying on that statement, he did not obtain an independent medical opinion on his own behalf. The Minister of Pensions later decided that the disability was not attributable to war service but to an injury sustained in 1927. On appeal from a pensions tribunal:

Denning J

. . . The assurance was given to the appellant in these explicit words: "Your disability has been accepted as attributable to military service." That was, on the face of it, an authoritative decision intended to be binding and intended to be acted on. Even if the appellant had studied the Royal Warrant in every detail there would have been nothing to lead him to suppose that the decision was not authoritative. He might well presume that the army medical board was recognized by the Minister of Pensions for the purpose of certifying his disability to be attributable to military service under the Royal Warrant of June, 1940: and that their certificate of attributability was sufficient for the purpose of the warrant.

What then is the result in law? If this was a question between subjects, a person who gave such an assurance as that contained in the War Office letter would be held bound by it unless he could show that it was made under the influence of a mistake or induced by a misrepresentation or the like. No such defence is made here. There are many cases in the books which establish that an unequivocal acceptance of liability will be enforced if it is intended to be binding, intended to be acted on, and is in fact acted on . . .

. . . Is the Minister of Pensions bound by the War Office letter? I think he is. The appellant thought, no doubt, that, as he was serving in the army, his claim to attributability would be dealt with by or through the War Office. So he wrote to the War Office. The War Office did not refer him to the Minister of Pensions. They assumed authority over the matter and assured the appellant that his disability had been accepted as attributable to military service. He was entitled to assume that they had consulted any other departments that might be concerned, such as the Ministry of Pensions, before they gave him the assurance. He was entitled to assume that the board of medical officers who examined him were recognized by the Minister of Pensions for the purpose of giving certificates as to attributability. Can it be seriously suggested that, having got that assurance, he was not entitled to rely on it? In my opinion if a government department in its dealings with a subject takes it upon itself to assume authority upon a matter with which he is concerned, he is entitled to rely upon it having the authority which it assumes. He does not know, and cannot be expected to know, the limits of its authority. The department itself is clearly bound, and as it is but an agent for the Crown, it binds the Crown also; and as the Crown is bound, so are the other departments, for they also are but agents of the Crown. The War Office letter therefore binds the Crown, and, through the Crown, it binds the Minister of Pensions. The function of the Minister of Pensions is to administer the Royal Warrant issued by the Crown, and he must so administer it as to honour all assurances given by or on behalf of the Crown.

In my opinion therefore the finding of the tribunal that the disability was not attributable to war service must be set aside . . .

Appeal allowed

A similar approach was adopted in *Lever Finance Ltd* v. *Westminster (City) London Borough Council* [1971] 1 QB 222, in which the claimant was told by a planning officer that proposed changes to a housing development were not material, and that it was therefore unnecessary to obtain further planning consent. Lord Denning MR (with whose judgment Megaw LJ agreed) reasoned (at 230) that it was not later open to the planning authority to resile from the officer's statement, given that the latter had acted with 'ostensible authority'. In the case of *Howell* v. *Falmouth Boat Construction Co Ltd* [1950] 2 KB 16 at 26, Denning LJ readily acknowledged that his approach ascribed a broad role to estoppel in public law:

The principle is this: whenever government officers, in their dealings with a subject, take on themselves to assume authority in a matter with which he is concerned, the subject is entitled to rely on their having the authority which they assume. He does not know and cannot be expected to know the limits of their authority, and he ought not to suffer if they exceed it.

QUESTIONS

- What problems might attend the adoption of Lord Denning's approach?
- Should the existence of 'ostensible authority' depend on the behaviour of the party who assumes authority, or the behaviour of the party who is actually empowered to deal with the matter?

7.2.3 Constitutionality and the Public Interest

Not everyone shared Lord Denning's enthusiasm for introducing estoppel into public law. For instance, when *Howell* went to the House of Lords, Lord Simonds strongly criticized Denning LJ's view ([1951] AC 837 at 845):

. . . I know of no such principle in our law nor was any authority for it cited. The illegality of an act is the same whether or not the actor has been misled by an assumption of authority on the part of a government officer however high or low in the hierarchy . . . The question is whether the character of an act done in face of a statutory prohibition is affected by the fact that it has been induced by a misleading assumption of authority. In my opinion the answer is clearly No. Such an answer may make more difficult the task of the citizen who is anxious to walk in the narrow way, but that does not justify a different answer being given.

Similar scepticism was evident in *Southend-on-Sea Corporation* v. *Hodgson (Wickford) Ltd* [1962] 1 QB 416, in which the Divisional Court refused to hold a public body bound by its official's unauthorized representation as to whether the claimant needed planning consent in order to put premises to a particular use. Lord Parker CJ (at 424) was persuaded that

in a case of discretion there is a duty under the statute to exercise a free and unhindered discretion. There is a long line of cases to which we have not been specifically referred which lay down that a public authority cannot by contract fetter the exercise of its discretion. Similarly, as it seems to me, an estoppel cannot be raised to prevent or hinder the exercise of the discretion.

Against this background, the Court of Appeal, in *Western Fish Products Ltd* v. *Penwith District Council* [1981] 2 All ER 204, set out a very limited approach to estoppel in public law. The claimant purchased a disused factory and began building work, believing this to be permissible on the strength of a statement made to it by a representative of the local planning authority. When the Council later required the claimant to apply for planning permission and an established use certificate, neither of which were ultimately forthcoming, the claimant asserted that the Council was estopped by its representative's assurances from disputing the claimant's right to use the land in the way it desired. Giving the judgment of the Court of Appeal, Megaw LJ concluded that, properly interpreted, the representative's statement did nothing more than confirm the right to use the land as it had previously been used, and did not amount to a representation that the claimant could use it in the proposed way without securing planning permission. However, he continued (at 217):

Even if we had been satisfied that the defendant council through their officers had represented to the plaintiffs that all they wanted to do on the . . . site could be done because of the existing uses, planning permission being required only for new buildings and structures, and that they had acted to their detriment to the knowledge of the defendant council because of their representations, their claim would still have failed.

His Lordship then proceeded to articulate a highly restrictive approach to estoppel in public law. He considered *Lever Finance Ltd* v. *Westminster (City) London Borough Council* [1971] 1 QB 222, in which, as noted above at 7.2.2, Lord Denning MR had taken a very broad view, saying (at 220–221):

In our judgment [*Lever Finance*] is not an authority for the proposition that every representation made by a planning officer within his ostensible authority binds the planning authority which employs him. For an estoppel to arise there must be some evidence justifying the person dealing with the planning officer for thinking that what the officer said would bind the planning authority. Holding an office, however senior, cannot, in our judgment, be enough by itself. In the *Lever (Finance) Ltd* case there was evidence of a widespread practice amongst planning authorities of allowing their planning officers to make immaterial modifications to the plans produced when planning permission was given. Lever (Finance) Ltd's architect presumably knew of this practice and was entitled to assume that the practice had been authorised by the planning authorities in whose areas it was followed. . . . Whether anyone dealing with a planning officer can safely assume that the officer can bind his authority by anything he says must depend on all the circumstances. In the *Lever (Finance) Ltd* case . . . [1970] 3 All ER 496, [1971] 1 QB 222 at 231 Lord Denning MR said: "Any person dealing with them [ie officers of a planning authority] is entitled to assume that all necessary resolutions have been passed." This statement was not necessary for the conclusion he had reached and purported to be an addendum. We consider it to be obiter; with all respect, it stated the law too widely.

It is clear from these remarks that *Western Fish* took a major step back from Lord Denning's broad approach to estoppel, heavily circumscribing the doctrine. As far as unauthorized representations were concerned, the lawfully designated decision-maker could be estopped by them only where the representee had good reason to believe that the representation had been issued with authority — a test which the Court of Appeal was at pains to emphasize would not be satisfied easily. This judicial reticence *vis-à-vis* estoppel in public law may be justified by two factors.

First, the *constitutional argument* holds that it is wrong, in principle, to recognize as binding decisions which are *ultra vires*. If an official issues an *ultra vires* statement which then prevents the proper decision-maker from reaching a different conclusion, the force of law is given to the official's unlawful representation. This, say Wade and Forsyth, *Administrative Law* (Oxford 2004) at 340, is fundamentally at odds with the *ultra vires* principle:

If the force of law is given to a ruling from an official merely because it is wrong, the official who has no legal power is in effect substituted for the proper authority, which is forced to accept what it considered a bad decision. To legitimate ultra vires acts in this way cannot be a sound policy, being a negation of the fundamental canons of administrative law.

QUESTIONS

- Is it necessarily 'unconstitutional' to recognize estoppel in public law?
- Is it therefore 'unconstitutional' for a court to refuse to quash unlawful administrative action because, for example, the claimant lacks standing (on which see 15.7 below) or did not issue the claim for judicial review within the relevant time limit (on which see 15.4 below)?

Secondly, in his judgment in *Western Fish, op cit* at 219, Megaw LJ alluded to the *public interest argument*:

The defendant council's officers, even when acting within the apparent scope of their authority, could not do what the [Town and Country Planning Act 1971] required the defendant council to do; and if their officers did or said anything which purported to determine in advance what the defendant council themselves would have to determine in pursuance of their statutory duties, they would not be inhibited from doing what they had to do. An estoppel cannot be raised to prevent the exercise of a statutory discretion or to prevent or excuse the performance of a statutory duty (see Spencer Bower and Turner on Estoppel by Representation (3rd Edn, 1977, p 141) and the cases there cited). The application of this principle can be illustrated on the facts of this case: under s 29 of the 1971 Act the defendant council as the planning authority had to determine applications for planning permission, and when doing so had to have regard to the provision of the development plan and 'to any other material considerations'. The plaintiffs made an application for planning permission to erect a tall chimney on the site. When considering this application the defendant council had to 'take into account any representations relating to that application' which were received by them following the publishing and posting of notices: see ss 26 and 29(2). This requirement was in the interests of the public generally. If any representations made by the defendant council's officers before the publication or posting of notices bound the council to act in a particular way, the statutory provision which gave the public opportunities of making representations would have been thwarted and the defendant council would have been dispensed from their statutory obligation of taking into account any representation made to them. The officers were appointed by the defendant council but the council's members were elected by the inhabitants of their area. Parliament by the 1971 Act entrusted the defendant council, acting through their elected members, not their officers, to perform various statutory duties. If their officers were allowed to determine that which Parliament had enacted the defendant council should determine there would be no need for elected members to consider planning applications. This cannot be. Under s 101(1) of the Local Government Act 1972 (which repealed s 4 of the 1971 Act, which re-enacted in an amended form s 64 of the Town and Country Planning Act 1968), a local authority may arrange for the discharge of any of their functions by an officer of the authority. This has to be done formally by the authority acting as such. In this case the defendant council issued standing orders authorising designated officers to perform specified functions including those arising under ss 53 and 94 of the 1971 Act. Their officers had no authority to make any other determinations under the 1971 Act. We can see no reason why Mr de Savary, acting on behalf of the plaintiffs, and having available the advice of lawyers and architects, should have assumed, if he ever did, that [the official in question] could bind the defendant council generally by anything he wrote or said.

QUESTIONS

- Should the public interest argument *always* dictate that unauthorized representations may not bind the designated decision-maker?
- Can you think of any circumstances in which the public interest argument may carry little or no weight?

7.2.4 A New Approach

The Court of Appeal's scepticism in *Western Fish* about the appropriateness of estoppel in public law is mirrored in the following judgment (for comment on which see Atrill [2003] *CLJ* 3), but a different approach is countenanced.

R v. East Sussex County Council, ex parte Reprotech (Pebsham) Ltd [2002]
UKHL 8 [2003] 1 WLR 348
House of Lords

East Sussex County Council built a waste treatment plant in 1989 which converted waste into fuel pellets; the plant was vested in ESEL, a company owned by the Council. The following year the Council and ESEL decided to sell the plant. A potential purchaser enquired whether, if they adapted the plant to generate electricity, this would be a material change of use requiring planning permission. Although the potential purchaser's legal advisors thought not, neither the interested purchaser nor ESEL sought to have this matter authoritatively determined by the Council (as planning authority) under s 64 of the Town and County Planning Act 1990 (since repealed and replaced by ss 191 and 192 of the same Act). Instead, ESEL sought — under s 73 of the Act — the variation of a condition in the original planning permission which prevented the use of power-driven machinery during certain anti-social hours. On 27 February 1991, the matter came before the Development Control Sub-Committee, which had delegated authority to deal with such matters. The County Planning Officer, in his report to the Sub-Committee, recommended that noise levels at night should not exceed certain limits. The Sub-Committee thus resolved to vary the conditions attached to the planning permission, subject to a satisfactory noise attenuation scheme. Eventually a different purchaser — Reprotech — bought the plant. Very little happened until 1998, when Reprotech took legal action in an attempt to establish that the events of 1991 gave it permission to produce electricity, subject to noise reduction. Reprotech was successful at first instance and in the Court of Appeal. The Council appealed to the House of Lords.

Lord Hoffmann

[27] ... [T]he important question ... is whether the resolution [of the Sub-Committee] counted as a determination under section 64. Such a determination is a juridical act, giving rise to legal consequences by virtue of the provisions of the statute. The nature of the required act must therefore be ascertained from the terms of the statute, including any requirements prescribed by subordinate legislation ... Whatever might be the meaning of the resolution, if it was not a determination within the meaning of the Act, it did not have the statutory consequences ...

[29] ... [A] determination is not simply a matter between the applicant and the planning authority in which they are free to agree on whatever procedure they please. It is also a matter which concerns the general public interest and which requires other planning authorities, the Secretary of State on behalf of the national interest and the public itself to be able to participate ...

[30] My Lords, it is now ten years since section 64 was repealed and I do not think there is much point in deciding which elements of the section 64 procedure might have been omitted without depriving it of the character of a statutory determination ...

[31] ... [T]he resolution of 27 February 1991 was a conditional authorisation of the planning officer to issue a new planning permission. Reprotech accepts that it did not operate as a planning permission. So far as its express terms are concerned, it has never had any legal effect. For my part, I find it impossible to see how a conditional resolution to grant planning permission which does not bind the planning authority can impliedly constitute a binding determination under section 64. In my opinion the resolution as such was not intended to have any legal effect at all. Whether a grant of planning permission would also have amounted to an implied determination need not be considered.

[32] Mr Porten QC, who appeared for the respondent, submitted that even if the resolution was not a determination under section 64, the County Council are estopped by representation or convention from denying that electricity can be generated on the site without further planning permission. I think that even if the council was a private party, there is no material upon which an estoppel can be founded. The opinion of the County Planning Officer could not reasonably have been taken as a binding representation that no planning permission was required. Planning officers are generally helpful in offering opinions on such matters but everyone knows that if a binding determination is required, a formal application must be made under what is now section 191 or 192. Nor was the committee resolution such a representation. If, as I consider, it was not a determination, it cannot have been a representation that it was. And there is no basis for finding any agreed assumption on the basis of which the parties acted. The position at the time when Reprotech bought the site and upon which the parties proceeded was that the resolution had been passed: no more and no less.

[33] In any case, I think that it is unhelpful to introduce private law concepts of estoppel into planning law. As Lord Scarman pointed out in *Newbury District Council v Secretary of State for the Environment* [1981] AC 578, 616, estoppels bind individuals on the ground that it would be unconscionable for them to deny what they have represented or agreed. But these concepts of private law should not be extended into "the public law of planning control, which binds everyone." (See also Dyson J in *R v Leicester City Council, ex parte Powergen UK Ltd* [2000] JPL 629, 637.)

[34] There is of course an analogy between a private law estoppel and the public law concept of a legitimate expectation created by a public authority, the denial of which may amount to an abuse of power: see *R v North and East Devon Health Authority, ex parte Coughlan* [2001] QB 213. But it is no more than an analogy because remedies against public authorities also have to take into account the interests of the general public which the authority exists to promote. Public law can also take into account the hierarchy of individual rights which exist under the Human Rights Act 1998, so that, for example, the individual's right to a home is accorded a high degree of protection (see *Coughlan's* case at pp 254–255) while ordinary property rights are in general far more limited by considerations of public interest . . .

[35] It is true that in early cases such as [*Wells v. Minister of Housing and Local Government* [1967] 1 WLR 1000] and *Lever Finance Ltd v Westminster (City) London Borough Council* [1971] 1 QB 222, Lord Denning MR used the language of estoppel in relation to planning law. At that time the public law concepts of abuse of power and legitimate expectation were very undeveloped and no doubt the analogy of estoppel seemed useful. In the *Western Fish* [case] the Court of Appeal tried its best to reconcile these invocations of estoppel with the general principle that a public authority cannot be estopped from exercising a statutory discretion or performing a public duty. But the results did not give universal satisfaction: see the comments of Dyson J in the *Powergen* case [2000] JPL 629, 638. It seems to me that in this area, public law has already absorbed whatever is useful from the moral values which underlie the private law concept of estoppel and the time has come for it to stand upon its own two feet.

Lord Hoffmann delivered the only reasoned speech, with which the rest of their Lordships agreed. Appeal allowed.

Lord Hoffmann's (*obiter*) comments, expressing dissatisfaction with estoppel as a tool by which to determine the effects (if any) of unlawful representations by public bodies or their officials, are unsurprising. As his Lordship observed, estoppel is a concept which was developed for the purpose of determining whether considerations of fairness should pre-clude the enforcement of private law obligations by one individual against another. The question whether unlawful representations should be enforceable in public law raises a much wider set of questions which transcend individual fairness and require attention to be paid to broader public interest considerations. Lord Hoffmann suggests that legitimate expectation is better-suited to this context, and is right to do so: we have already seen, in the context of lawful representations, that the public law doctrine of legitimate expectation is premised on the need to balance competing public and private interests. It therefore appears much better-placed than estoppel to take account of concerns about constitutionality and the public interest. Craig (1977) 93 *LQR* 398 at 420 argues that, provided an adequate mechanism exists for taking such concerns into account before deciding whether to enforce an unauthorized representation, we can — with a clear conscience — dispense with what he calls the 'jurisdictional principle' (*ie*, the rule, adopted in cases like *Western Fish*, that *ultra vires* representations are generally unenforceable):

When the basis of the jurisdictional principle is scrutinised it is found to be wanting. The objective of preventing [unlawful] extension of power by public officials is obviously correct, but the operation of the doctrine in practice is misdirected. In the rare cases of intentional extension of power it strikes at the wrong person, the innocent representee, rather than the public official. In the more common case of careless, or inadvertent, extension of power any deterrent effect upon the public officer will be minimal. The unspoken hypothesis must be that whenever, *in fact*, the powers of the body are extended any hardship to the representee must be outweighed by the harm to the public, who are the beneficiaries of the *ultra vires* principle, were estoppel allowed to operate.

> . . . [T]he complexity and diversity of situations in which representations occur does not permit of such a categorical answer. The balance of public and individual interest will produce different answers in areas as diverse as planning and licensing, social security and taxation, and even within each area. A doctrine with sufficient flexibility to recognise this diversity is needed. Whether it is introduced through the courts or through the legislature is a choice as to mechanism . . .

Precisely such a mechanism would appear to consist in the legitimate expectation doctrine. However, while it has been accepted in subsequent decisions (see, *eg, R (Wandsworth London Borough Council) v. Secretary of State for Transport, Local Government and the Regions* [2003] EWHC 622 (Admin) [2004] 1 P & CR 32 at [21], *per* Sullivan J) that *Reprotech* firmly establishes the inapplicability of estoppel in planning law — and, by extension, public law generally — the courts have not enthusiastically seized the opportunity to adopt the flexible approach favoured by Craig to the protection of unlawfully created expectations. It is true that there have been occasions on which judges appear to have countenanced a balancing test whereby the public interest in legality might be weighed against competing interests. For example, in *Henry Boot Homes Ltd v. Bassetlaw District Council* [2002] EWCA Civ 983 [2003] 1 P & CR 23 at [56], Keene LJ considered that it may be possible for a developer to enforce a legitimate expectation that the planning authority would waive planning conditions set under the statutory planning scheme; however, this would very much be the exception, not the norm:

> [Counsel] invited us to say that legitimate expectation could never operate so as to enable the developer to begin development validly and effectively in breach of condition. I am not prepared to adopt so absolute a proposition. It is possible that circumstances might arise where it was clear that there was no third party or public interest in the matter and a court might take the view that a legitimate expectation could then arise from the local planning authority's conduct or representations. But . . . one suspects that such cases will be very rare.

In order to explore more fully whether legitimate expectation theory may apply to unlawful representations — a proposition which appears counterintuitive: can *unlawfully* created expectations be *legitimate*? — it is helpful to distinguish the situations considered in the next two sections.

7.2.5 Representations Issued by Unauthorized Officials

First, consider representations relating to acts and decisions which are *intra vires* the public body but *ultra vires* the official concerned. Although some judges — *eg*, Dyson J in *R v. Leicester City Council, ex parte Powergen UK Ltd* (2000) 80 P & CR 176 at 186 — have assumed that a lack of actual authority on the part of the official making the representation conclusively precludes a legitimate expectation from arising, others have taken a rather wider approach, as the following case indicates.

....

South Buckinghamshire District Council v. *Flanagan* [2002] EWCA Civ 690
[2002] 1 WLR 2601
Court of Appeal

The local authority initiated criminal proceedings in respect of the defendants' failure to comply with enforcement notices issued under the Town and Country Planning Act 1990. The solicitor instructed to represent the council was given authority, subject to certain conditions, to discontinue the prosecutions. In fact, at the hearing, the solicitor agreed to discontinue the prosecutions *and withdraw the enforcement notices*. When the council — which had not wanted to withdraw the notices — later sought to enforce them by seeking an injunction in the county court, they were held to be estopped from doing so in light of the solicitor's (unauthorized) representation. The council successfully appealed, whereupon one of the defendants appealed, contending that the solicitor's representation gave rise to a legitimate expectation that no further enforcement of the notices would be attempted.

Keene LJ

[16] Before us Mr Lamming for the second defendant does not seek to uphold the order of the county court judge on the basis of an estoppel. He recognises that, in the light of the authorities, estoppel by representation really no longer has any part to play in planning law. That was almost the position achieved after the Court of Appeal decision in *Western Fish Products Ltd -v- Penwith District Council* [1981] 2 All ER 204, there remaining only limited circumstances where a local planning authority would be bound by such a representation. This is because planning decisions are not simply matters of private interest, confined to the developer and the local planning authority, but involve the public interest also. One is here in the realm of public law. That has now been emphasised by the House of Lords decision in *R -v- East Sussex County Council, ex parte Reprotech (Pebsham) Limited* [2002] UKHL 8, where Lord Hoffmann, with whom the other members of the House agreed, said that:

> "it is unhelpful to introduce private law concepts of estoppel into planning law." (para. 33)

Although he recognised the analogy between private law estoppel and the public law concept of a legitimate expectation created by a public authority, Lord Hoffmann pointed out that remedies against public authorities also have to take into account the interests of the general public (para 34). It is clear that the House saw the earlier cases where estoppel had been applied in planning law as an attempt to achieve justice at a time when the concepts of legitimate expectation and abuse of power had scarcely made their appearance in public law. Now that those concepts are recognised, there is no longer a place for the private law doctrine of estoppel in public law or for the attendant problems which it brings with it . . .

[18] At the outset of his submissions on this aspect of the case, Mr Lamming conceded that a legitimate expectation based on a representation allegedly made on behalf of a public body can only arise if the person making the representation as to that body's future conduct has actual or ostensible authority to make it on its behalf. That would seem to be right. Legitimate expectation involves notions of fairness and unless the person making the representation has actual or ostensible authority to speak on behalf of the public body, there is no reason why the recipient of the representation should be allowed to hold the public body to the terms of the representation. He might subjectively have acquired the expectation, but it would not be a legitimate one, that is to say it would not be one to which he was entitled.

[19] Judge Parry [in the county court] found that Mr Ikram [the solicitor] had "actual or ostensible authority" to bind the Council to withdraw the enforcement notices and not to proceed save by way

of new notices. Mr Lamming accepted, as he did before Harrison J. [on appeal from the county court], that he could not seek to rely on any actual authority possessed by Mr Ikram . . . The case for the second defendant therefore turns on the issue of whether or not Mr Ikram had the ostensible authority claimed . . .

[20] The principal contention advanced by Mr Lamming was that, by appointing Mr Ikram to represent the local planning authority in the magistrates' court proceedings, the authority had represented that he had the authority to agree to a withdrawal of not just those proceedings but the enforcement notices themselves. Such a power fell, it was said, within the usual scope of a solicitor's authority to compromise proceedings. Reliance was placed on the decision in *Waugh -v- H.B. Clifford & Sons Ltd* [1982] Ch. 374, where it was held that a solicitor retained in civil proceedings had ostensible authority to compromise the suit provided that the compromise did not involve matters collateral to the action. Matters were only to be seen as collateral if they involved some extraneous subject matter. Therefore, where proceedings had been brought against the builders/vendors of houses for defects in the houses, it was within the ostensible authority of the defendants' solicitors to agree to the repurchase of the houses at a price reflecting their value in a proper condition. In the present case it was argued that the enforcement notices and their continuing validity could not be seen as collateral to the criminal prosecutions in the magistrates' court . . .

[22] I return, therefore, to the submission based on the usual scope of a solicitor's authority to compromise proceedings. It has to be remembered that, as Harrison J. pointed out, an enforcement notice is an important public document. It runs with the land, it is registrable, and it is enforceable against any subsequent owner or occupier of the land in question, so long as it has been registered. Moreover, for an enforcement notice to take effect may require a lengthy process to be undertaken: there are rights of appeal against it to the Secretary of State, which may result in a public inquiry; there are further rights of challenge on a point of law to the courts. So an enforcement notice which has become effective, as these two notices had, is a planning instrument of some significance. It enables the local planning authority to prosecute for a breach of it, as indeed had successfully happened in the past in respect of the 1980 enforcement notice in the present case. Once such a notice has become effective, it endures in principle for an indefinite period of time, unless the local planning authority decides to exercise its statutory power under section 173A of the 1990 Act to withdraw it.

[23] It is impossible to regard it as part of the usual authority of a solicitor, appointed to prosecute for a breach of the enforcement notice, to agree to a withdrawal of the underlying notice itself. That would be an action of great significance to the local planning authority, extending far beyond the issue of the particular breach of the notice for which the prosecution has been brought. The continuing validity and force of the underlying notice are not the subject matter of those proceedings in the magistrates' court but are truly extraneous to them. It would put local planning authorities, who exercise their powers in the public interest, at the mercy of every advocate instructed to prosecute for such a breach if they were to be held bound by an agreement or representation made by that advocate as to the future validity and force of an otherwise unimpeachable enforcement notice. I find myself in full agreement with Harrison J.'s conclusion that authority to withdraw the notices themselves goes beyond what could reasonably be regarded as normally incidental to the conduct of prosecuting for a breach . . .

Keene LJ, with whom Sumner J agreed, concluded that the solicitor's lack of ostensible authority to withdraw the enforcement notices precluded any legitimate expectation that the council would not take further proceedings in respect of those notices.

The significance of this decision turns on what is meant by 'ostensible authority' (on which see generally in this context Craig (1977) 93 *LQR* 398). It is a phenomenon borrowed from the law of agency, and arises where someone or some body represents, expressly or impliedly, that the person concerned has authority to deal with certain matters on their behalf (even though he may not): hence 'ostensible', rather than 'actual', authority. It was recognized by Diplock LJ in the context of company law in *Freeman and Lockyer* v. *Buckhurst Park Properties Ltd* [1964] 2 QB 480 at 504 that unauthorized representations may bind a body with *restricted powers* only in limited circumstances:

> . . . [S]ince the conferring of actual authority upon an agent is itself an act of the corporation, the capacity to do which is regulated by its constitution, the corporation cannot be estopped from denying that it has conferred upon a particular agent authority to do acts which by its constitution, it is incapable of delegating to that particular agent.

In the public law context, this suggests that, although representations issued with ostensible authority may bind the public body (as is clearly envisaged in *Flanagan*), such authority will only arise where (i) the representation relates to conduct which the public body itself could lawfully commit, (ii) it represents (expressly or impliedly) that the official has authority over the matter in question, and (iii) he could have been so authorized.

If these criteria are met, it is then necessary to consider the status of the official's representation. It is possible to envisage circumstances in which, although an official may not have been authorized as such by the public body for whom he works, his decisions on the matter in question are nevertheless not *ultra vires*. For instance, where conditions (i) to (iii) above are met, but where an official has been instructed not to deal with the matter in question, he is clearly not 'authorized' by the public body to do so in the sense that, as a matter of employment law, he may be guilty of a disciplinary offence or breach of contract; however, by dealing with the matter in question, the official is not acting *ultra vires* in a public law sense, because these is no statutory prohibition on his doing so. A public body in such circumstances may seek to argue that the internal prohibition upon the official's dealing with the matter in question should prevent the individual from relying upon the official's conduct as something capable of binding the public authority, in which case the individual may wish to invoke a legitimate expectation — based on the public body's express or implied representation (see point (ii) above) — that the official did have authority to deal with the matter (or, to use the old language, the individual may argue that the public body is estopped from invoking the internal prohibition upon the official). However, in strict logic, it is not clear that recourse to legitimate expectation (or estoppel) is necessary in such circumstances, bearing in mind that the official's conduct is not, in the public law sense, *ultra vires*.

Even where legislation restricts the capacity of an official to act in a given matter, *eg*, by prescribing that authority must be conferred upon him *by recourse to some formal procedure*, it does not follow that failure to comply with such a statutory condition renders the official's conduct *ultra vires*. Whether this is so will turn upon whether (on the principles discussed above at 2.6) compliance with the statutory procedural requirement is a precondition upon the official's acquisition of the relevant *vires*. Although, where the public body has not conferred the relevant power upon the official in the prescribed manner, the official may (as above) be 'unauthorized' in one sense, this will not affect his *vires* in the public law sense if the statutory procedural requirement that is in play is not regarded as jurisdictional: there is, in this situation, no jurisdictional statutory prohibition on his exercising the power in question. Here, the analysis is the same as in the previous paragraph.

From these situations must be distinguished those in which there *is* some jurisdictional statutory prohibition — for example, where the relevant power could have been conferred upon the official concerned, but only by means of some statutory procedure which is regarded as a condition precedent to the acquisition of *vires* by the official. Where such a procedure is not complied with, any purported decisions of the official will be *ultra vires*. Although, in this scenario, our three conditions for ostensible authority (set out above) are met, the fact that the official's decision is *ultra vires* presents a major difficulty, since, as we have already seen (in the analogous context of estoppel), it is widely held that allowing such *ultra vires* representations to bind public bodies would be constitutionally inappropriate. However, we conclude this section by noting that, on a policy level, it is important to remember that if the courts were to recognize legitimate expectations on the basis of *ultra vires* representations of the type presently under discussion, such representations would not, without more, bind the public body concerned. Rather, the court, having recognized the legitimate expectation, would simply acquire jurisdiction to decide whether the public interest (including the public interest in the principle of legality) outweighed, on the facts, the interests of the individual.

QUESTION

• Bearing this point in mind, should the courts be willing to recognize legitimate expectations on the strength of representations which are *ultra vires* the official concerned?

7.2.6 Representations Concerning Action which is *Ultra Vires* the Agency

The courts have made it abundantly clear — see, *eg, Rowland* v. *Environment Agency* [2002] EWCA Civ 1885 [2004] 3 WLR 249 (extract below), *R (Bibi)* v. *Newnham LBC* [2001] EWCA Civ 607 [2002] 1 WLR 237 at [46], and *R (Bloggs 61)* v. *Secretary of State for the Home Department* [2003] EWCA Civ 686 [2003] 1 WLR 2724 at [39] — that the doctrine of legitimate expectation cannot operate so as to extend agencies' powers by rendering enforceable acts or decisions which are *ultra vires* the body itself.

While we will see below that there are important policy arguments which require this orthodox proposition to be re-evaluated, we focus presently on a more immediate problem. Where the ECHR is in play, domestic law's mechanical characterization of the principle of legality as a trump card which closes the door to competing arguments of fairness to the individual could fall foul of the principle of proportionality. This point is illustrated by the decision of the European Court of Human Rights in *Stretch* v. *United Kingdom* (2004) 38 EHRR 12. The applicant purchased from a local authority a 22-year lease which obliged him to erect industrial buildings and apparently conferred an option to renew for a further 21 years. When renewal negotiations had reached an advanced stage, the local authority informed the applicant that the option could not be exercised because, *inter alia*, its statutory predecessor never had legal capacity to grant such an option. This argument met with grudging acceptance in the Court of Appeal (*Stretch* v. *West Dorset District Council* (1999) 77 P & CR 342), Peter Gibson LJ noting that it seems 'unjust' that public bodies which misconstrue their powers should be able to 'take advantage of their own errors to escape from the unlawful bargains that they have made'.

The ECtHR, however, was unwilling to accept as determinative the *ultra vires* nature of the representation. Without reference to that factor, the Court held that the applicant had acquired a legitimate expectation of exercising the option; that, for the purposes of Article 1, Protocol 1 ECHR, this could be characterized as attaching to the property rights arising under the lease; and that the local authority's conduct frustrated the expectation. The legal incapacity of the public body was considered only at the final stage of the analysis:

[38] The Government have emphasised in this case the doctrine of ultra vires which provides an important safeguard against abuse of power by local or statutory authorities acting beyond the competence given to them under domestic law. The Court does not dispute the purpose or useful-ness of this doctrine which indeed reflects the notion of the rule of law underlying much of the Convention itself. It is not however persuaded that the application of the doctrine in the present case respects the principle of proportionality.

[39] The Court observes that local authorities inevitably enter into many agreements of a private law nature with ordinary citizens in the pursuance of their functions, not all of which however will concern matters of vital public concern. In the present case, the local authority entered in a lease and was unaware that its powers to do so did not include the possibility of agreeing to an option for renewal of the lease. It nonetheless obtained the agreed rent for the lease and, on exercise of the renewal of the option, had the possibility of negotiating an increase in ground rent. There is no issue that the local authority acted against the public interest in the way in which it disposed of the property under its control or that any third party interests or the pursuit of any other statutory function would have been prejudiced by giving effect to the renewal option.

This analysis — which led to the UK having to pay damages as 'just satisfaction' under Article 41 ECHR — is significant because it treats legal incapacity merely as a factor to be placed in the balance when deciding whether the legitimate expectation may lawfully be frustrated. The implications of *Stretch* for domestic law — which has traditionally treated legal incapacity in precisely the manner condemned by the ECtHR — were confronted in the next case.

....

Rowland v. *Environment Agency* [2003] EWCA Civ 1885 [2004] 3 WLR 249
Court of Appeal

In 1974, the claimant's husband purchased an estate which included Hedsor Water, a non-tidal stretch of the River Thames, believing the water to be private. This belief was founded partly on the fact that the navigation authority, assuming the stretch of river to be private, had allowed signs to be erected to that effect. However, in 2001, by which time the claimant had succeeded to the estate following the death of her husband, the navigation authority concluded that public rights of naviga-tion ('PRN') still existed in relation to Hedsor Water, and ordered the claimant to remove signs giving the contrary impression. The claimant argued that PRN did not exist over Hedsor Water or that, in the alternative, the navigation authority's conduct had given rise to a legitimate expectation that it would treat Hedsor Water as private, thereby preventing it from ordering the removal of the signs. The claimant was unsuccessful at first instance, and appealed to the Court of Appeal. All three Court of Appeal judges agreed that PRN existed over Hedsor Water and that it was beyond the powers of the navigation authority to extinguish those rights. The following excerpts are concerned only with the arguments based on legitimate expectation.

Peter Gibson LJ

[After reviewing the evidence upon which the claimant contended a legitimate expectation could be founded, his Lordship said:]

[78] . . . [S]ubject to the effect of the rule under English law that a legitimate expectation can only arise on the basis of a lawful promise or practice, I would accept that Mrs. Rowland has a legitimate expectation that she would continue to be entitled to enjoy Hedsor Water as private. However, I share Mance L.J.'s reservations about the scope and strength of that expectation in the particular circumstances (see paras. 157 and 158 of his judgment) . . .

[81] [However,] [a]s it is accepted by Mrs. Rowland there can only be a legitimate expectation founded on a lawful representation or practice, her claim to a legitimate expectation that she would continue to be entitled to enjoy Hedsor Water as private was bound to fail under English domestic law if taken alone without the Convention in the absence of any statutory basis for the extinction of PRN over Hedsor Water. I therefore turn next to the question whether the Convention has altered the position . . .

[82] Mrs. Rowland relies on Art. 8, the right to respect for private and family life, and on Art. 1 [of Protocol 1], providing for the protection of property . . .

[83] . . . [Counsel for Mrs Rowland] argued that what would be a legitimate expectation under English law, but for being ultra vires the public authority concerned, relating to specific rights connected with a specific property is a possession within the meaning of Art. 1 and so cannot be taken away or interfered with except in accordance with the requirements of Art. 1 as regards the principles of legal certainty and proportionality.

[Having considered *Stretch* v. *United Kingdom* (see above), his Lordship agreed that the expectation in the present case constituted a 'possession', and continued:]

[96] In my judgment the judge [at first instance in the present case] was right on this issue for the reasons which he gave. It was inevitable that once the Defendant was aware that it had made a mistake in allowing Hedsor Water to be treated as a private water, it, as the guardian of navigation in the Thames, should resile from its previous stance. Courts should be slow to fix a public authority permanently with the consequences of a mistake (see *Begbie* [[2000] 1 WLR 1115] at p. 1127), particularly when it would deprive the public of their rights. The Defendant had no power to fulfil the expectation of Mrs. Rowland, and it was bound to conclude that it should remove the misleading signs that Hedsor Water was private, as they were inconsistent with the continued existence of PRN over that stretch of the Thames. The rights of the public, expressly recognised by s. 1 of the [Thames Preservation Act 1885], now s. 79(1) of the [Thames Conservancy Act 1932], required nothing less. The Defendant rightly took account of the expectation of Mrs. Rowland that Hedsor Water was and would continue to be private, of the fact that Hedsor Wharf was purchased on the understanding that it was private, and of Mrs. Rowland's wish to continue to enjoy privacy. In consequence . . . it gave the assurances not to promote public use of Hedsor Water and to minimise for her the effect of removing the prohibition on the public using Hedsor Water. True it is that the details of such minimisation were not spelt out . . ., but to respond as the Defendant did. . . was in my judgment neither disproportionate nor unjustified . . .

May LJ

[99] I agree that this appeal should be dismissed for the reasons given by Peter Gibson LJ, whose account of the facts and circumstances of the appeal I gratefully adopt. I also agree with Mance LJ that it would be appropriate to grant a further declaration in the terms which he suggests. I agree with the structure of Mance LJ's reasoning which reaches his conclusion. But I would put a rather different emphasis, more favourable to Mrs Rowland, on the strength of the legitimate expectation to which in my judgment the facts give rise . . .

[100] I reach the conclusion that this appeal should be dismissed, for the reasons given by Peter Gibson and Mance LJJ, with undisguised reluctance. I say this because I regard the outcome as unjust. It is, in my view, the unjust product of a developing, but at times over complicated, body of related jurisprudence, elements of which need reconsideration. Binding authority prevents constructive reconsideration in this court. The most unusual facts and circumstances of this appeal seem to me to illustrate related problems of real importance . . .

[102] . . . English law recognises that there may be circumstances where fairness and proportionality require that a public body should not be able to resile from a representation which has resulted in a legitimate expectation in an individual or group of individuals. Unfairness may arise of the third kind identified by Lord Woolf in *R v North and East Devon Health Authority, ex parte Coughlan* [2001] QB 213 at paragraphs 57 to 58. This kind of unfairness arises where there is no overriding interest which would justify the public body in resiling from its representation. But orthodox English domestic law does not allow the individual to retain the benefit which is the subject of the legitimate expectation, however strong, if creating or maintaining that benefit is beyond the power of the public body.

[103] Such is the present case. Hedsor Water was part of the original main stream of the River Thames. From time immemorial, a public right of navigation has existed over the river. The public right of navigation now exists by statute going back to the Thames Preservation Act 1885. Successive Navigation Authorities had no power to extinguish that right. A public right of navigation cannot be extinguished by prescription, even over a period exceeding 100 . . . years. The respondents and their predecessors have acted for a period in excess of 100 years so as to give rise to the legitimate expectation on which Mrs Rowland relies. But, because the Navigation Authorities had no power to extinguish the public right of navigation over Hedsor Water, English domestic law cannot give effect to Mrs Rowland's legitimate expectation. This is unjust and illustrates a defect in the law. In my view, the just outcome of these proceedings is that Hedsor Water should remain private. English law cannot at present achieve this.

[104] So resort is had to the Human Rights Convention and jurisprudence under it. This should not be necessary. I agree that Mrs Rowland's legitimate expectation should be seen as a possession within Article 1 of the first Protocol. An intricate process of reasoning is required to reach this conclusion. But, as Peter Gibson LJ has explained in paragraph 96 of his judgment, this conclusion does not take Mrs Rowland very far. The Human Rights Convention does not enable Mrs Rowland to retain Hedsor Water as private, when to achieve this is beyond the statutory power of the respondents. They must not act so as to abuse their power, but I agree that they have not done so. Their letter of 20th February 2001 was not only considerate, but a genuine statement of the respondents' intention to moderate, so far as they were able, the effect on Mrs Rowland of their discovery that Hedsor Water is not private and cannot continue to be so . . .

[114] I have already indicated my view that the law is defective and that in consequence this court is obliged to uphold an unjust outcome. A sustained and powerful academic analysis to this end is to be found in Professor Paul Craig's *Administrative Law* . . . [See above at 7.2.4 for discussion of Craig's analysis of this point.]

[115] Professor Craig addresses and disapproves of, as I do, an unmitigated state of the law to the effect that a representation by a public authority, which the public authority has no power to make, is not binding and cannot sustain a legitimate expectation or an estoppel. The logic of the jurisdictional principle is followed through to its inexorable end. But a moment's reflection makes evident the hardship to the individual . . .

[120] [After discussing Craig's views on this issue, his Lordship concluded:] I regret that it is not, in my view, open to this court to implement Professor Craig's balancing approach. At this level, it would amount to legislation. I say nothing about whether the House of Lords could or would consider implementing it . . .

Mance LJ

[136] . . . [I]n *Bibi* [[2001] EWCA Civ 607 [2002] 1 WLR 237] (at paras. 21 and 46) this Court suggested as likely that the 'legitimacy' of any expectation depended upon whether the relevant representation was within the authority's lawful power. In *Stretch v. West Dorset CC* (11th November 1997) this Court, with no enthusiasm, applied the principle that a local authority can rely on the invalidity of its own actions (cf. *Hazell v. Hammersmith and Fulham LBC* [1992] 2 AC 1 and *Credit Suisse v. Allerdale BC* [1997] QB 306), holding invalid an option for a further 21 year term granted to the tenant under a lease for an initial 21 year term. The local authority's only relevant power was to let, and thus did not extend to granting an option. So, in the present case, Lord Lester [for the claimant] recognises that at common law, prior [to] the incorporation of the Convention on Human Rights, the Agency's lack of any power to abrogate or qualify the public's PRN, or therefore to represent that such PRN did not exist, would pose an apparently insuperable obstacle to success in an argument that the Agency by words or conduct had led Mrs Rowland to have a legitimate expectation that a PRN did exist.

[137] Since the incorporation of the Convention, Lord Lester submits, this lacuna has been closed in the context of Article 1 of the First Protocol by decisions in the European Court of Human Rights, which we should now take into account . . .

[After considering the decisions of the ECtHR in *Pine Valley Developments Ltd* v. *Ireland* (1991) 14 EHRR 319 and *Stretch* v. *United Kingdom* (2004) 38 EHRR 12, his Lordship said:]

[152] . . . [I]t can no longer be an automatic answer under English law to a case of legitimate expectation, that the Agency had no power to extinguish the PRN over Hedsor Water or to treat it as private. However, the present case differs significantly from those two cases. In *Pine Valley* and *Stretch*, the European Court was considering claims for relief against states. Those states undoubtedly had the power to pay compensation for any inability of the part of the public authority whose conduct was in issue to fulfil any legitimate expectation which it had created. Here there is before us no claim against the state, and indeed no claim for compensation against anyone. We are concerned simply and solely with a claim for declaratory relief regarding the conduct of the Agency, which can only act in accordance with its statutory mandate. That mandate involves preserving the PRN, and it is not suggested (nor could it be in the light of the public interest) that the alchemy of s. 3(1) of the Human Rights Act 1998 can affect that mandate. The Agency was therefore bound in law to adjust its attitude, as it did in December 2000, once it became apparent that the PRN had never in law been extinguished. The Court cannot grant relief which would have the effect of obliging the Agency to continue to treat Hedsor Water as private. Lord Lester's submissions recognise this. The argument is that the Agency's mandate confers on it sufficient powers and discretion for it to be able to give effect to Mrs Rowland's legitimate expectation without any need to neglect or affect that mandate. If the Agency created in Mrs Rowland an expectation which should in European Convention terms be regarded as legitimate, but which goes beyond the Agency's discretionary powers to fulfil under domestic law, that might lead to some different claim for compensation against the state. But I understood Lord Lester to accept that this would not lie against the Agency . . .

[153] The present case thus resolves itself into issues regarding the nature (including the

strength) of any expectation created by the Agency and the extent to which the Court both can and should grant relief requiring the Agency to take that expectation into account in the course of exercising its discretionary powers. For my part, I accept that the Agency's conduct conferred on Mrs Rowland a legitimate expectation to the effect, at least, that, should it transpire that Hedsor Water was not private, the Agency would, in reacting to any such discovery, take into account the previous common assumption of the Rowlands and of the Agency to the contrary and the fact that Hedsor Water has been effectively private (so far as can be judged without any serious public discontent) over many years; and would smooth the position (as far as possible consistently with its duties to preserve the PRN) for Mrs Rowland while she owns and resides at Hedsor Wharf. Considerations which can and should properly be taken into account by the Agency in that regard include the long period of Mrs Rowland's previous residence at Hedsor Wharf with her husband, during which she has foregone any opportunity of moving elsewhere, together with her wish to continue to reside there and to make it into her main English home for the rest of her life. It seems to me very likely that the expectation encouraged in Mrs Rowland would also require the Agency, at least during an initial period, to consult Mrs Rowland, particularly with regard to any steps that might be proposed following the realisation that there was still in law a PRN over Hedsor Water. Since both the Agency (which could have been expected to have a good grasp of the true position) and the Rowlands were under the like misapprehension until December 2000, I cannot regard the Rowlands' failure to investigate or appreciate the true legal position prior to that date as undermining an expectation along these lines . . .

[163] I would supplement the declarations granted [at first instance] to the Agency [that PRN existed over Hedsor Water] by a further declaration to the effect that the Agency was obliged to take into account in the exercise of its statutory functions the common assumption prior to November 2000 of the Rowlands and of the Agency to the effect that Hedsor Water was private . . .

The appeal was allowed only to the extent of granting a declaration in the terms set out in the previous paragraph.

This decision does not fundamentally challenge the orthodoxy that the courts cannot order public bodies to fulfil promises which lie beyond their powers; to that extent, *Rowland* does not embrace the balancing approach to unlawful representations favoured by Craig (see above at 7.2.4). However, it does not follow that *any* protection of unlawfully generated expectations is impossible. Where, for example, *ultra vires* decisions have already been taken in line with such expectations, the courts' remedial discretion might be exercised so as to leave such decisions intact. The situation which arose in *Rowland*, in which enforcement of an unlawful promise was sought, is more problematic, but a compromise between enforcement of *ultra vires* representations (impossible) and completely ignoring such representations (unfair, and potentially inconsistent with ECHR principles) lies in what may be termed the 'benevolent exercise of powers doctrine'. According to this approach, which enjoys particular prominence in Mance LJ's judgment, while agencies cannot be required to do the legally impossible, they *can* be required — by court order if necessary — to exercise their powers benevolently, so as to respect, as far as possible, the legitimate expectations they engendered. (So, in *Rowland*, while the navigation authority could not extinguish the PRN, it could be required to exercise its powers so as not to draw attention to the existence of the PRN.)

Two further issues require comment, beginning with the *scope* of the benevolent exercise of powers doctrine. It is clear that the Court of Appeal was moved to articulate such a doctrine in *Rowland* because a Convention right was in play, meaning that (in view of *Stretch*) the standard approach to unlawful representations would not wash. There is, however, no reason why the doctrine should be confined to cases in which legitimate expectations can be linked with Convention rights.

Secondly, what is the *content* of the benevolent exercise of powers doctrine? Just how benevolently can agencies be required (lawfully) to exercise their powers? This is an important issue which fundamentally affects the capacity of the doctrine to facilitate the striking of a meaningful balance between the public and private interests which are in play. An intriguing possibility arises in this context, the elaboration of which first requires us to consider the role of compensation in this area. Compensation in lieu of the fulfilment of unlawfully created expectations is advanced by some commentators (*eg*, Wade and Forsyth, *Administrative Law* (Oxford 2004) at 340–342) as the best means by which to reconcile the tension between public and private interests: the public interest in legality is respected (because the unauthorized representation is not enforced) while fairness to the individual will usually be achieved by the provision of monetary compensation. Others, however, voice concerns about the appropriateness of compensation. For instance, in *Rowland*, May LJ opined (at [121]) that enforcement of unlawfully generated expectations, if acceptable on a balancing test, is 'a fairer and more proportionate outcome . . . than for the public purse to compensate' the disappointed individual. A further difficulty arises, in that where breach of an expectation implies violation of a Convention right, the use of s 8 of the Human Rights Act 1998 — the obvious vehicle for a damages claim in such circumstances — would seem to be barred by s 6(2), which provides that it is not unlawful for a public authority to act in a given way when primary legislation constrains it to do so.

However, the benevolent exercise of power doctrine raises the possibility of an alternative approach to compensation (as distinct from damages). We know from the *Coughlan* case, considered above at 7.1.5, that the legitimate expectation principle does not necessarily require the individual to be given that which he expected. Rather, it places the public authority under a duty to strike a fair balance between the interests of the individual (in the fulfilment of the expectation) and of the wider community (in the pursuit of some policy objective that conflicts with the fulfilment of the individual's expectation). The ECHR principle of proportionalty also requires such a balance to be struck. Drawing upon the case of *S v. France* (1990) DR 250, it is clear that compensating an individual whose legitimate expectation is not to be fulfilled may, in some circumstances, strike the fair balance that is required, thereby avoiding a breach of the relevant Convention right (and, by extension, the *unlawful* frustration of the legitimate expectation as a matter of English law). Since s 6(1) of the Human Rights Act 1998 requires public authorities to act compatibly with the Convention rights whenever possible, it can be argued that compensation should be paid where this is necessary to strike the required fair balance, so as to avoid a breach of such rights. This, in turn, suggests that the benevolent exercise of power doctrine may be given real teeth. It is, moreover, possible to argue that this approach need not be confined to ECHR cases, since it would be open to English courts to hold in appropriate cases that the payment of compensation is a necessary component of the domestic requirement to strike a fair balance between the interests of the wider community and of the individual whose legitimate expectation the decision-maker proposes to frustrate. It clear that a requirement to pay compensation would not be appropriate in every case: the central issue here is the striking of a fair balance, and how that balance is to be struck in individual cases will depend on the circumstances, such as the relative importance of the interests of the expectation-holder and the wider community, and the options available to the decision-maker in seeking to ameliorate the position of the former. The general principle, therefore, is that the decision-maker should, in frustrating the individual's expectation, act as benevolently as is necessary to meet the fair balance requirement; the point being made here is simply that, in some cases, the degree of benevolence required may extend to the payment of compensation.

7.3 Concluding Remarks

The decline of the principle of estoppel in public law, following its Denning-induced high-water mark in the middle of the last century, stands in stark contrast to the increasing enthusiasm of courts for the protection of lawfully issued undertakings through the vehicle of legitimate expectation. In both contexts, a similar dilemma presents itself: how to resolve the tension between legal certainty (which secures fairness for the individual) and the wider interests of the community (which may require the individual's expectations to be dashed)? Yet this conundrum takes on different forms depending on the legality of the initial representation.

So far as unlawfully created expectations are concerned, the playing field is far from level. The constitutional and public interest concerns highlighted above introduce a substantial bias against the protection of the expectation induced by the representation concerned. Although some writers, notably Craig, argue that too much weight is presently attached to these concerns, the courts find them compelling — a point which remains true today, notwithstanding the shift in this context from 'estoppel' to 'legitimate expectation' analysis stimulated by the *Reprotech* decision.

In contrast, the principle of legitimate expectation has developed along quite different lines in relation to lawful representations. However, even in this context, the manner in which the competing policy interests in legal certainty and administrative autonomy should be weighed against each other raises a number of problems. This is most obviously so in relation to substantive legitimate expectations, where the protection of the individual's expectation impacts with particular force on the executive's discretionary freedom. In turn, the law of substantive expectation reflects a more general debate concerning how judges and decision-makers should relate to one another, and the extent to which judicial review may curtail the executive's freedom to formulate, apply, and change policy. It is to that wider question which we turn in the following two chapters, as we unpack the principles of reasonableness and proportionality.

FURTHER RESOURCES

Akehurst, 'Revocation of Administrative Decisions' [1982] *PL* 613

Clayton, 'Legitimate Expectations, Policy and the Principle of Consistency' [2003] *CLJ* 93

Craig, 'Representations by Public Bodies' (1977) 93 *LQR* 398

Craig, 'Substantive Legitimate Expectations in Domestic and Community Law' [1996] *CLJ* 289

Forsyth, 'The Provenance and Protection of Legitimate Expectations' [1988] *CLJ* 238

Jowell and Lester, *New Directions in Judicial Review* (London 1988) at 37–50 (Elias)

Sales and Steyn, 'Legitimate Expectations in English Public Law: An Analysis' [2004] *PL* 564

Schønberg, *Legitimate Expectations in Administrative Law* (Oxford 2000)

8 ABUSE OF DISCRETION I

8.1 Introduction

The principles considered in the two preceding chapters regulate the extent to which discretion may be restricted by making representations, entering into contracts, and so on. In this chapter and the next, we consider a further set of principles which regulate how decision-makers should behave when exercising discretion. The overarching idea running throughout the various rules developed by the courts in this field is that there is no such thing as an unfettered discretion, a proposition classically illustrated by the cases of *Anisminic Ltd* v. *Foreign Compensation Commission* [1969] 2 AC 147 (on which see below at 15.6.4) and *Padfield* v. *Minister of Agrictulture, Fisheries and Food* [1968] AC 997 (considered below at 8.3.2).

QUESTION

- Are the courts justified in refusing to countenance unfettered discretion, even if this is apparently contemplated by the statutory scheme?

Discretionary power is today regarded as an unavoidable feature of our administrative system. However, the existence of unlimited or unregulated discretion is considered anathema to the rule of law. It is unsurprising, therefore, that writers such as Allan (in Forsyth (ed), *Judicial Review and the Constitution* (Oxford 2000)) and Jowell regard the subjection of discretionary power to rule of law based constraints as a central function of administrative law.

....

Jowell, 'The Rule of Law Today'
in Jowell and Oliver (eds), *The Changing Constitution* (Oxford 2004)

... In countries with written constitutions the text itself provides the enabling features of the constitution (such as who may vote and the composition of the executive and legislature). It also provides the disabling features — normally through a Bill of Rights, which constrains government, even elected parliaments, from interfering with certain fundamental rights and freedoms (such as freedom of expression and association) which are considered necessary and integral to democracy. In Britain, the Rule of Law as an unwritten principle performs a similar disabling function ...

The practical implementation of the Rule of Law takes place primarily through judicial review of the actions of public officials. It is elaborated and given specific content when courts evaluate the exercise of discretionary powers conferred by Parliament on the executive and others exercising public functions. What have emerged as the three principal "grounds" of judicial review [as set out by Lord Diplock in *Council of Civil Service Unions v. Minister for the Civil Service* [1985] AC 374 at 410–411: see below at 9.2.1] themselves rest in large part on the Rule of Law. The first ground, that of "illegality", is designed to ensure that officials act within the scope of their lawful powers. The courts ensure that the official decisions do not stray beyond the "four corners" of a statute by failing to take into account "relevant" considerations (that is, considerations which the law requires), or by taking into account "irrelevant" considerations (that is, considerations outside the object and purpose that Parliament intended the statute to pursue). This exercise is a clear implementation of the Rule of Law, whereby the courts act as guardians of Parliament's true intent and purpose.

The second ground of review, that of 'procedural impropriety' [see chs 10–12 below], requires decision-makers to be unbiased and to grant a fair hearing to claimants before depriving them of a right or significant interest (such as an interest in livelihood or reputation) . . . [T]he right not to be condemned unheard is a central feature of the Rule of Law, which the courts presume Parliament to respect. Even where a statute is silent on that matter, the courts will insist that the "justice of the common law" (which incorporates the principle of the Rule of Law) supplies the omission of the legislature.

Over the past few years, the courts have implied a requirement of a fair hearing even where the claimant does not possess a threatened right or interest. A hearing will be required where a "legitimate expectation" [see ch 7 above] has been induced by the decision-maker. In such a case the claimant has, expressly or impliedly, been promised either a hearing or the continuation of a benefit. The courts will not sanction the disappointment of such an expectation unless the claimant is permitted to make representations on the matter. The notion of legitimate expectation is itself rooted in that aspect of the Rule of Law which requires legal certainty.

The third ground of judicial review, "irrationality" or "unreasonableness" [see ch 9 below], is more difficult to fit into the Rule of Law in so far as it governs the substance and not merely the procedure of official action . . . [I]f it is to operate as the organising principle in this context, the Rule of Law must become a substantive doctrine and not merely procedural. Our courts, through judicial review, tread warily in this area, carefully deferring to the primary decision-maker . . . [although] the courts may adopt stricter scrutiny of the decision [if it impacts upon fundamental rights] . . .

As this excerpt illustrates, many, perhaps all, of the principles applied by courts when testing the validity of purported exercises of discretion may be *related back* to the rule of law; however, that principle provides rather uncertain *guidance* in this context, bearing in mind that there is considerable disagreement (see, *eg*, Craig [1997] *PL* 467) about precisely what values the rule of law comprises. It is therefore necessary to acknowledge (see further 1.4 above) the role of *judges* in developing the principles of judicial review, albeit that they are clearly influenced by the rule of law in this regard. In the remainder of this chapter, we examine two principles of administrative law which reflect the rule of law based view that decision-makers may not enjoy unfettered discretion, and that it is the courts' role to discern and enforce appropriate limits.

8.2 Loyalty to the Statutory Scheme: The Propriety of Purpose Doctrine

8.2.1 Overlapping Principles?

The two key principles with which this chapter is concerned are those which require deci-sion-makers to act *only on the basis of factors which are legally relevant*, and which dictate that statutory powers may be used *only for the purposes for which they were created*. Taylor [1976] *CLJ* 272 at 272 writes that:

Abuse of discretion is too easily regarded as a "grab-bag" from which a ground of review can always be found to suit the conclusion sought to be reached on the merits. Judicial review is a flexible tool but each ground has a limited use. "Improper purposes" and "irrelevant factors" exist as distinct phrases because each represents a separate mode of analysis which is particularly useful in a given situation.

Taylor argues that the two principles of review serve distinct functions, and should not be used interchangeably. However, as we shall see, the courts often tend to do precisely that, not least because both modes of analysis — albeit distinguishable — can often be applied within the same factual matrix. With that point in mind, we turn to the propriety of purpose doctrine.

8.2.2 Express and Implied Purposes

It is not uncommon for legislation which confers statutory powers expressly to state the purpose or purposes for which those powers are to be used. In such situations the courts (in the absence of discovering additional, implied purposes for which the powers may legitim-ately be used) will require the decision-maker to act only for the stated purpose or purposes. It is not difficult to locate a justification for this principle. Most straightforwardly it supports the sovereignty of Parliament, ensuring that the legislature's will is executed, rather than frustrated, by requiring the powers it creates to be used for the purposes it intends. The propriety of purpose doctrine also safeguards the rule of law. One of the central strands within any conception of the rule of law is the principle of legality, which directs that the administration must be able to justify its actions by reference to some legal authority (through the existence of statutory or, much more rarely, prerogative power). The principle was explained in the following terms by Sir Thomas Bingham MR in *R* v. *Somerset County Council, ex parte Fewings* [1995] 1 WLR 1037 at 1042, a case in which the defendant council asserted an unfettered discretion to determine how its land could be used:

To the famous question asked by the owner of the vineyard ("Is it not lawful for me to do what I will with mine own?" St. Matthew, chapter 20, verse 15) the modern answer would be clear: "Yes, subject to such regulatory and other constraints as the law imposes." But if the same question were posed by a local authority the answer would be different. It would be: "No, it is not lawful for you to do anything save what the law expressly or impliedly authorises. You enjoy no unfettered discretions. There are legal limits to every power you have."

If the position were otherwise, the executive would, in practice, be free to do as it wished, and any meaningful control of its actions would be rendered impossible. The same would be true if the executive could, at whim, deploy powers granted for one purpose so as to achieve something quite different. If the executive is to be constrained by reference to the legal powers conferred upon it, then courts must be permitted to verify that those powers are not being misapplied. The operation of the propriety of purpose doctrine is illustrated by our next case (and also in *Webb* v. *Minister of Housing and Local Government* [1965] 1 WLR 755 and *Laker Airways Ltd* v. *Department of Trade* [1977] QB 643).

....

Municipal Council of Sydney v. *Campbell* [1925] AC 339
Privy Council

The facts are stated in the judgment. For a fuller statement see (1924) 24 SR (NSW) 179.

Duff J delivering the judgment of the Judicial Committee

By s. 16 of the Sydney Corporation Amendment Act, 1905, the Municipal Council of Sydney is empowered from time to time, with the approval of the Governor, to purchase or "resume" any land required for "carrying out improvements in or remodelling any portion of the city." . . . By s. 3 of an amending Act of 1906, the Council is authorized to purchase or "resume" any lands required for the opening of new public ways or for widening, enlarging or extending any public ways in the city, as well as any lands of which those required for such purposes are a part.

On March 12, 1923, the Lord Mayor prepared a minute relating to the subject of the extension of Martin Place, an important thoroughfare in the centre of Sydney, and in this minute he recommended the extension of Martin Place to Macquarie Street, and the resumption of a considerable area, which embraced property belonging to the respondents. The proposals of the Lord Mayor's minute were adopted by a resolution of the Council on June 28, and the resumption provided for by the resolution was approved by the Governor in Council.

On the application of the respondents, injunctions were granted by the Chief Judge in Equity, restraining the Council from proceeding under this resolution; and subsequently the Lord Mayor presented another minute, and on November 29 another resolution was passed by the Council, authorizing the resumption of the identical area affected by the former resolution. Again proceedings were taken before the Chief Judge in Equity, who granted injunctions restraining the Council from proceeding under the second resolution; and at the hearing of the actions these injunctions were made permanent. Admittedly, the Council had authority (under s. 3 of the amending Act of 1906) to "resume" lands for the purpose of extending Martin Place. It is also undisputed that the lands of the respondents which the Council proposes to take are not within the limits of any area which could be required for that purpose. The right to resume them is based upon the assertion that they are "required" for the purpose of remodelling and improving the city within the sense of s. 16 of the Sydney Corporation Amendment Act.

The learned Chief Judge in Equity held that in point of fact these lands were not really "required" for any such purpose, but that, as in the case of the other parts of the area affected which were not necessary for the extension of the street, the resumption proceedings were taken with the object of enabling the Council to get the benefit of any increment in the value of them arising from the extension, and thus, in some degree at all events, recouping the municipality the cost of it; and that, since the resumption of lands for such a purpose alone was indisputably not within the ambit of the authority committed to the Council, the resolutions of June and November were both invalid . . .

The legal principles governing the execution of such powers as that conferred by s. 16, in so far as presently relevant, are not at all in controversy. A body such as the Municipal Council of Sydney, authorized to take land compulsorily for specified purposes, will not be permitted to exercise its powers for different purposes, and if it attempts to do so, the Courts will interfere. As Lord Loreburn said, in *Marquess of Clanricarde v. Congested Districts Board* [79 JP 481]: "Whether it does so or not is a question of fact." Where the proceedings of the Council are attacked upon this ground, the party impeaching those proceedings must, of course, prove that the Council, though professing to exercise its powers for the statutory purpose, is in fact employing them in furtherance of some ulterior object.

Their Lordships think that the conclusion of the learned Chief Judge in Equity upon this question of fact is fully sustained by the evidence . . . [I]t is admitted that no plan of improvement or remodelling was at any time before the Council; and their Lordships think there is great force in the argument that the course of the oral discussion, as disclosed in the shorthand note produced, shows, when the events leading up to the second minute of the Lord Mayor are considered, that in November the Council was applying itself to the purpose of giving a new form to a transaction already decided upon, rather than to the consideration and determination of the question whether the lands to be taken were required for the purpose of remodelling or improvement. Their Lordships think the learned Chief Judge was right in his conclusion, that upon this question there was no real decision or determination by the Council . . .

Appeal dismissed.

Even if the enabling legislation does not specify the purposes for which discretionary power may be employed, decision-makers are still held to be constrained by the statutory scheme as a whole, and by the purposes *implicit* in that scheme, as Laws J explained in *R* v. *Somerset County Council, ex parte Fewings* [1995] 1 All ER 513 at 525:

. . . [W]here a statute does not by express words define the purposes for which the powers it confers are to be exercised, the decision-maker is bound nevertheless to ascertain and apply the aims intended, since no statute can be purposeless: and therefore unless the Act's true purpose is correctly understood the decision-maker, who is Parliament's delegate, is at risk of using powers to an end for which they were never given him. If he does so, he exceeds his authority as surely as if he transgresses the plainest statutory language.

8.2.3 The Purpose Doctrine and the Intensity of Review

There are numerous cases in which administrative action has been set aside because it contravenes implied statutory purposes; for two celebrated examples, see *Bromley London Borough Council* v. *Greater London Council* [1983] 1 AC 768 and *Congreve* v. *Home Office* [1976] QB 629. However, the judicial task of discerning implied statutory purposes from the general thrust of the legislative scheme is a difficult one — both because the scheme may be opaque, offering little guidance to the judges, and in light of the significant impact which a court's determination that a particular power is limited by an implied purpose may have on the scope of the decision-maker's discretion. These points are illustrated by our next case.

....

R v. Secretary of State for Foreign and Commonwealth Affairs, ex parte World Development Movement Ltd [1995] 1 WLR 386
Queen's Bench Division

Section 1(1) of the Overseas Development and Co-operation Act 1980 provided that, 'The Secretary of State shall have power, for the purpose of promoting the development or maintaining the economy of a country or territory outside the United Kingdom, or the welfare of its people, to furnish any person or body with assistance, whether financial, technical or of any other nature.' Purporting to act under this power, the Secretary of State approved aid and trade provision (ATP) for the construction of a hydro-electric power station on the Pergau river in Malaysia. Before final approval was given, but after the British government had informally agreed with the Malaysian government that it would contribute to the project, the Overseas Development Administration concluded that the project was economically unviable and a 'very bad buy'. The claimant, a pressure group, felt that the Secretary of State, by going ahead with the project in spite of these problems, was misusing public funds and acting unlawfully. It therefore sought judicial review. (The standing of the claimant is considered in a separate excerpt at 15.7.4.)

Rose LJ

. . . The provision of A.T.P. for a purpose known by the Government not to be "sound economic development," submitted Mr. Pleming [for the claimant], could not be within section 1 [of the Act of 1980] . . . The reason or motive [for funding the project], submitted Mr. Pleming, was political or diplomatic, namely that the Prime Minister had given an undertaking in March 1989 that Britain would provide A.T.P. support, and to go back on that word would be detrimental to the interests of Britain, British companies and British workers. Section 1, submitted Mr. Pleming, confers no power to make decisions on such a basis . . .

Mr. Richards [for the defendant] submitted that this decision was taken by the Secretary of State personally and his thinking is of decisive importance in determining the purpose for which the assistance was furnished. The Secretary of State plainly considered, from the terms of his affidavit, that the assistance was for a developmental purpose, and he also took into account additional considerations. Mr. Richards submitted further that the applicant's argument that an unsound development cannot furnish a purpose within section 1 should be rejected . . . because the word "sound" does not appear in the Act. What the statute requires is a developmental purpose within the broad terms of section 1(1), and the statutory power cannot be limited by the adoption of 'soundness' by an A.T.P. scheme or anything else . . .

For my part, I am unable to accept Mr. Richards's submission that it is the Secretary of State's thinking which is determinative of whether the purpose was within the statute and that therefore paragraph 3 of his affidavit is conclusive. Whatever the Secretary of State's intention or purpose may have been, it is, as it seems to me, a matter for the courts and not for the Secretary of State to determine whether, on the evidence before the court, the particular conduct was, or was not, within the statutory purpose.

As to the absence of the word "sound" from section 1(1), it seems to me that, if Parliament had intended to confer a power to disburse money for unsound developmental purposes, it could have been expected to say so expressly. And I am comforted in this view by the way in which the successive Ministers, guidelines, Governments and White Papers, identified by Mr. Pleming, have, over the years and without exception, construed the power as relating to economically sound development . . .

The Secretary of State is, of course, generally speaking, fully entitled, when making decisions, to take into account political and economic considerations such as the promotion of regional stability, good government, human rights and British commercial interests. In the present case, the political impossibility of withdrawing the 1989 offer has been recognised since mid-April of that year, and had there, in 1991, been a developmental promotion purpose within section 1 of the Act of 1980, it would have been entirely proper for the Secretary of State to have taken into account, also, the impact which withdrawing the 1989 offer would have had, both on the United Kingdom's credibility as a reliable friend and trading partner and on political and commercial relations with Malaysia. But for the reasons given, I am of the view, on the evidence before this court, that there was, in July 1991, no such purpose within the section. It follows that the July 1991 decision was, in my judgment, unlawful . . .

Scott Baker J delivered a short, concurring judgment. A declaration was issued to the effect that the Secretary of State's decision was unlawful.

Rose LJ's decision to read the criterion of economic soundness into the enabling provision, thereby limiting the purposes for which aid could be granted, had a major impact on the scope of the Secretary of State's power, and, allied with the court's view that the project was economically unsound, was fatal to the legality of the decision. This demonstrates the potential potency of the purpose doctrine. Once the court concludes that a statutory power may only be used to further a particular purpose, the freedom of the decision-maker is necessarily limited: unless the court is satisfied that the action undertaken by the administrator was within the purpose, it will be held unlawful. The *Pergau Dam* case — and, in particular, its use of the purpose doctrine to facilitate an intensive mode of judicial review — is roundly condemned by Irvine, *Human Rights, Constitutional Law and the Development of the English Legal System* (Oxford 2003) at 164–165:

. . . [T]he courts [in judicial review cases] have no choice but to exercise self-restraint . . . [However,] it is, perhaps, unsurprising that in this sensitive area the courts have occasionally overstepped the mark. For instance, in the *Pergau Dam* case, the issue was whether a grant of aid to help build a dam in Malaysia was "for the purpose of promoting the development" of that country within the meaning of the relevant legislation. The court held that, properly understood, this meant "sound development", and concluded that the decision to make the grant was unlawful because, in the view of the court, the grant was economically unsound. By reading an additional requirement into the statute in this way, the court took away from the executive a considerable degree of autonomy. It is this type of judicial activism which begins to blur the boundary between appeal and review, thereby undermining the constitutional foundations on which the courts' supervisory jurisdiction rests.

QUESTION

• How might the decision of the court be defended against Irvine's criticism?

It is worth noting that, if the criterion of economic soundness had been characterized by the court as a relevant consideration which the Secretary of State was obliged to take into account, rather than as part of the definition of purpose underlying the discretion, the outcome would most likely have been different since, as we shall see below, it is for the decision-maker, not the court, to determine how much weight (if any) to attach to relevant considerations. This mode of analysis tends to lead to a less intensive standard of review and, in turn, ascribes a wider discretion to the decision-maker. This demonstrates that, although the propriety of purpose and relevancy of considerations doctrines are often regarded interchangeably, they can in fact yield different styles of review and, ultimately, different results. The choice between those two approaches is therefore open to instrumental use by courts seeking to manipulate the standard and outcome of judicial review. The general failure by the judiciary explicitly to address which mode of analysis is appropriate in particular cases makes it difficult to determine whether such instrumentalism actually operates, but certainly leaves room for suspicion that, consciously or otherwise, judges pick and choose in order to produce the 'right' outcome.

8.2.4 Multiple Purposes

It is often the case that, when a public authority adopts a particular course of action pursuant to an exercise (or purported exercise) of discretion, it is motivated by more than one purpose. If all of the purposes for which the authority acts are legitimate statutory purposes, no problem arises. But what if an authority is spurred to action by a number of purposes, not all of which are legitimate? Although it has occasionally been suggested (see, eg, *Earl Fitzwilliam's Wentworth Estates Co* v. *Minister of Town and Country Planning* [1951] 1 KB 203) that the authority acts lawfully provided merely that one of its purposes is a legitimate one, the more common approach, employed in the following case, is more exacting.

....

Westminster Corporation v. *London and North Western Railway Co* [1905] AC 426
House of Lords

The Corporation had power to provide public conveniences and to construct these in, on, or under any road. It built an underground convenience in the middle of Parliament Street with access from the pavement on either side of the street. The appellant railway company owned premises opposite one of the entrances to the convenience and sought to have the conveniences removed. The company alleged that the Corporation wished to build a subway which it had no power to do. This extract is concerned only with the purposes for which the Corporation acted.

Earl of Halsbury LC

My Lords, it seems to me that the power of the local authority to erect certain public conveniences cannot be disputed. The shape, site, and extent of them are left to the discretion of the authority in question, and so far as regards the things themselves, which, under this discretion, have been erected, I do not understand that any objection can be made. The objections, so far as they assume the force of legal objections, refer to the access to them, and to the supposed motives of the local authority in the selection of the site.

Assuming the thing done to be within the discretion of the local authority, no Court has power to interfere with the mode in which it has exercised it . . .

It appears to me impossible to contend that these conveniences are not the things authorized by the Legislature. It seems to me that the provision of the statute itself contemplates that such conveniences should be made beneath public roads, and if beneath public roads some access underneath the road level must be provided; and if some access must be provided, it must be a measure simply of greater and less convenience, when the street is a wide one, whether an access should be provided at only one or at both sides of the street. That if the access is provided at both sides of the street, it is possible that people who have no desire or necessity to use the convenience will nevertheless pass through it to avoid the dangers of crossing the carriageway seems to me to form no objection to the provision itself; and I decline altogether to sit in judgment upon the discretion of the local authorities upon such materials as are before us.

I quite agree that if the power to make one kind of building was fraudulently used for the purpose of making another kind of building, the power given by the Legislature for one purpose could not be used for another . . .

Lord Macnaughten

. . . It is not enough to shew that the corporation contemplated that the public might use the subway as a means of crossing the street. That was an obvious possibility. It cannot be otherwise if you have an entrance on each side and the communication is not interrupted by a wall or a barrier of some sort. In order to make out a case of bad faith it must be shewn that the corporation constructed this subway as a means of crossing the street under colour and pretence of providing public conveniences which were not really wanted at that particular place . . .

The upshot of the approach taken by the Earl of Halsbury and Lord Macnaughten is that administrative action based upon mixed purposes will be lawful provided that the 'dominant purpose' — as Denning LJ put it in *Earl Fitzwilliam's Wentworth Estates Co* v. *Minister of Town and Country Planning* [1951] 2 KB 284 at 307 — is a legitimate one. The application of this test raises evidential difficulties, particularly if public authorities put forward legitimate purposes in order to mask other, unlawful motives for their action. The courts are, however, alert to this problem; as Lord Denning MR explained in *R* v. *Governor of Brixton Prison, ex parte Soblen* [1963] 2 QB 243 at 302, the courts will, where necessary, 'go behind' the face of the act in order to determine its true purpose. Indeed, public bodies are required to assist the reviewing court by furnishing it with relevant evidence (see below at 12.3.2), although problems may arise if evidence is withheld on grounds of public interest immunity.

8.3 Inputs into the Decision-Making Process: The Relevancy Doctrine

8.3.1 Introduction

Although it is of the essence of discretion that the decision-maker can *choose* how to resolve a particular case, it is important that he exercises judgment on the basis of germane information. The relevancy doctrine exists to this end, and was explained in the following terms by Megaw J in *Hanks* v. *Minister of Housing and Local Government* [1963] 1 QB 999 at 1020:

. . . [I]f it be shown that an authority exercising a power has taken into account as a relevant factor something which it could not properly take into account in deciding whether or not to exercise the power, then the exercise of the power, normally at least, is bad. Similarly, if the authority fails to take into account as a relevant factor something which is relevant, and which is or ought to be known to it, and which it ought to have taken into account, the exercise of the power is normally bad. I say "normally" because I can conceive that there may be cases where the factor wrongly taken into account, or omitted, is insignificant, or where the wrong taking into account, or omission, actually operated in favour of the person who later claims to be aggrieved by the decision.

By requiring decision-makers to take account of all those factors which are relevant to the matter in hand, and forbidding the consideration of irrelevant factors, the relevancy doctrine aims to uphold the quality of administrative decisions by regulating the evidence upon which they are based. Other principles of administrative law, which we consider later in the book, address the same problem in different (but complementary) ways. For instance, the principles of procedural fairness, which are addressed in ch 11, confront this issue from a pragmatic perspective; by requiring the decision-maker to listen to the views and evidence of the citizen who will be affected by the decision in question, those principles seek to ensure that the decision-maker is, in the first place, in receipt of all the relevant evidence. Meanwhile, the relevancy doctrine insists that once a fair procedure has yielded such information to the decision-maker, it must actually be taken into account when the decision is finally made. It is important, therefore, to remember that the relevancy doctrine operates not in a vacuum, but as part of a network of administrative law principles which seek to promote good decision-making. The difficulty, as we shall see, lies in determining which factors should be treated as legally relevant and legally irrelevant.

8.3.2 General Principles

The operation of the relevancy doctrine is illustrated by the following case. Note, however, that the propriety of purpose and relevancy doctrines are used somewhat interchangeably — a trait which, as we noted above, is often found in the case law.

Padfield v. *Minister of Agrictulture, Fisheries and Food* [1968] AC 997
House of Lords

Section 19(3) of the Agricultural Marketing Act 1958 provides that, 'A committee of investigation shall . . . (b) be charged with the duty, if the Minister in any case so directs, of considering, and reporting to the Minister on . . . any . . . complaint made to the Minister as to the operation of any scheme which, in the opinion of the Minister, could not be considered by a Consumers' Committee . . .' England and Wales were divided into eleven regions for the purpose of the Milk Marketing Board. Producers had to sell their milk to the Board at prices which differed from region to region to reflect the varying costs of transporting milk from the producers to the consumers. Transport costs had altered and the south-eastern region wished the differential to be altered. The constitution of the Board made it impossible for the south-eastern producers to get a majority for their proposals and they asked the Minister to appoint a committee of investigation. When the Minister refused they applied for a mandatory order directing him to refer the complaint to a committee of investigation or to deal with it according to law, *ie* on relevant considerations only, to the exclusion of irrelevant considerations. At first instance this was granted, but the Court of Appeal allowed an appeal by the Minister and the producers appealed to the House of Lords.

Lord Reid

. . . [The Minister] contends that his only duty is to consider a complaint fairly and that he is given an unfettered discretion with regard to every complaint either to refer it or not to refer it to the committee as he may think fit. The appellants contend that it is his duty to refer every genuine and substantial complaint, or alternatively that his discretion is not unfettered and that in this case he failed to exercise his discretion according to law because his refusal was caused or influenced by his having misdirected himself in law or by his having taken into account extraneous or irrelevant considerations.

In my view, the appellants' first contention goes too far. There are a number of reasons which would justify the Minister in refusing to refer a complaint. For example, he might consider it more suitable for arbitration, or he might consider that in an earlier case the committee of investigation had already rejected a substantially similar complaint, or he might think the complaint to be frivolous or vexatious. So he must have at least some measure of discretion. But is it unfettered?

It is implicit in the argument for the Minister that there are only two possible interpretations of this provision — either he must refer every complaint or he has an unfettered discretion to refuse to refer in any case. I do not think that is right. Parliament must have conferred the discretion with the intention that it should be used to promote the policy and objects of the Act; the policy and objects of the Act must be determined by construing the Act as a whole and construction is always a matter of law for the court. In a matter of this kind it is not possible to draw a hard and fast line, but if the Minister, by reason of his having misconstrued the Act or for any other reason, so uses his discretion as to thwart or run counter to the policy and objects of the Act, then our law would be very defective if persons aggrieved were not entitled to the protection of the court. So it is necessary first to construe the Act.

When these provisions were first enacted in 1931 it was unusual for Parliament to compel people to sell their commodities in a way to which they objected and it was easily foreseeable that any such scheme would cause loss to some producers. Moreover, if the operation of the scheme was put in the hands of the majority of the producers, it was obvious that they might use their power to the detriment of consumers, distributors or a minority of the producers. So it is not surprising that Parliament enacted safeguards.

The approval of Parliament shows that this scheme was thought to be in the public interest, and in so far as it necessarily involved detriment to some persons, it must have been thought to be in the public interest that they should suffer it. But in sections 19 and 20 Parliament drew a line. They provide machinery for investigating and determining whether the scheme is operating or the board is acting in a manner contrary to the public interest.

The effect of these sections is that if, but only if, the Minister and the committee of investigation concur in the view that something is being done contrary to the public interest the Minister can step in. Section 20 enables the Minister to take the initiative. Section 19 deals with complaints by individuals who are aggrieved. I need not deal with the provisions which apply to consumers. We are concerned with other persons who may be distributors or producers. If the Minister directs that a complaint by any of them shall be referred to the committee of investigation, that committee will make a report which must be published. If they report that any provision of this scheme or any act or omission of the board is contrary to the interests of the complainers *and* is not in the public interest, then the Minister is empowered to take action, but not otherwise. He may disagree with the view of the committee as to public interest, and, if he thinks that there are other public interests which outweigh the public interest that justice should be done to the complainers, he would be not only entitled but bound to refuse to take action. Whether he takes action or not, he may be criticised and held accountable in Parliament but the court cannot interfere.

I must now examine the Minister's reasons for refusing to refer the appellants' complaint to the committee . . .

The first reason which the Minister gave in his letter of March 23, 1965, was that this complaint was unsuitable for investigation because it raised wide issues. Here it appears to me that the Minister has clearly misdirected himself. Section 19 (6) contemplates the raising of issues so wide that it may be necessary for the Minister to amend a scheme or even to revoke it. Narrower issues may be suitable for arbitration but section 19 affords the only method of investigating wide issues. In my view it is plainly the intention of the Act that even the widest issues should be investigated if the complaint is genuine and substantial, as this complaint certainly is.

Then it is said that this issue should be "resolved through the arrangements available to producers and the board within the framework of the scheme itself." This re-states in a condensed form the reasons given in paragraph 4 of the letter of May 1, 1964, where it is said "the Minister owes no duty to producers in any particular region," and reference is made to the "status of the Milk Marketing Scheme as an instrument for the self-government of the industry," and to the Minister "assuming an inappropriate degree of responsibility." But, as I have already pointed out, the Act imposes on the Minister a responsibility whenever there is a relevant and substantial complaint that the board are acting in a manner inconsistent with the public interest, and that has been relevantly alleged in this case. I can find nothing in the Act to limit this responsibility or to justify the statement that the Minister owes no duty to producers in a particular region. The Minister is, I think, correct in saying that the board is an instrument for the self-government of the industry. So long as it does not act contrary to the public interest the Minister cannot interfere. But if it does act contrary to what both the committee of investigation and the Minister hold to be the public interest the Minister has a duty to act. And if a complaint relevantly alleges that the board has so acted, as this complaint does, then it appears to me that the Act does impose a duty on the Minister to have it investigated. If he does not do that he is rendering nugatory a safeguard provided by the Act and depriving complainers of a remedy which I am satisfied that Parliament intended them to have.

Paragraph 3 of the letter of May 1, 1964 [a letter written by the Ministry, explaining the considerations the Minister would take into account in deciding whether to refer the issue to a committee of investigation] refers to the possibility that, if the complaint were referred and the committee were to uphold it, the Minister "would be expected to make a statutory Order to give effect to the committee's recommendations." If this means that he is entitled to refuse to refer a complaint because, if he did so, he might later find himself in an embarrassing situation, that would plainly be a bad reason . . .

[After considering the Minister's reasons, his Lordship turned to the argument that the discretion was unfettered, and said:] I have found no authority to support the unreasonable proposition that it must be all or nothing — either no discretion at all or an unfettered discretion. Here the words "if the Minister in any case so directs" are sufficient to show that he has some discretion but they give no guide as to its nature or extent. That must be inferred from a construction of the Act read as a whole, and for the reasons I have given I would infer that the discretion is not unlimited, and that it has been used by the Minister in a manner which is not in accord with the intention of the statute which conferred it.

As the Minister's discretion has never been properly exercised according to law, I would allow this appeal. It appears to me that the case should now be remitted to the Queen's Bench Division with a direction to require the Minister to consider the complaint of the appellants according to law . . .

Lord Upjohn

. . . The Minister in exercising his powers and duties, conferred upon him by statute, can only be controlled by a prerogative writ which will only issue if he acts unlawfully. Unlawful behaviour by the Minister may be stated with sufficient accuracy for the purposes of the present appeal (and here I adopt the classification of Lord Parker C.J., in the Divisional Court): (a) by an outright refusal to consider the relevant matter, or (b) by misdirecting himself in point of law, or (c) by taking into account some wholly irrelevant or extraneous consideration, or (d) by wholly omitting to take into account a relevant consideration.

There is ample authority for these propositions which were not challenged in argument. In practice they merge into one another and ultimately it becomes a question whether for one reason or another the Minister has acted unlawfully in the sense of misdirecting himself in law, that is, not merely in respect of some point of law but by failing to observe the other headings I have mentioned.

In the circumstances of this case, which I have sufficiently detailed for this purpose, it seems to me quite clear that prima facie there seems a case for investigation by the committee of investigation. As I have said already, it seems just the type of situation for which the machinery of section 19 was set up, but that is a matter for the Minister.

He may have good reasons for refusing an investigation, he may have, indeed, good policy reasons for refusing it, though that policy must not be based on political considerations which as Farwell LJ said in *Rex* v. *Board of Education* [1910] 2 K.B. 151 at 181 are pre-eminently extraneous. So I must examine the reasons given by the Minister, including any policy upon which they may be based, to see whether he has acted unlawfully and thereby overstepped the true limits of his discretion, or, as it is frequently said in the prerogative writ cases, exceeded his jurisdiction. Unless he has done so, the court has no jurisdiction to interfere. It is not a Court of Appeal and has no jurisdiction to correct the decision of the Minister acting lawfully within his discretion, however much the court may disagree with its exercise.

[His Lordship then considered the Minister's reasons. In dealing with the argument that the discretion was 'unfettered' he said:] My Lords, I believe that the introduction of the adjective 'unfettered' and its reliance thereon as an answer to the appellants' claim is one of the fundamental matters confounding the Minister's attitude, bona fide though it be. First, the adjective nowhere appears in section 19, it is an unauthorised gloss by the Minister. Secondly, even if the section did contain that adjective I doubt if it would make any difference in law to his powers, save to emphasise what he has already, namely that acting lawfully he has a power of decision which cannot be controlled by the courts; it is unfettered. But the use of that adjective, even in an Act of Parliament, can do nothing to unfetter the control which the judiciary have over the executive, namely that in exercising their powers the latter must act lawfully and that is a matter to be determined by looking at the Act and its scope and object in conferring a discretion upon the Minister rather than by the use of adjectives . . .

Lords Hodson and Pearce delivered speeches in favour of allowing the appeal. Lord Morris delivered a speech in favour of dismissing the appeal. The appeal was therefore allowed, and the Minister was required to reconsider the matter.

As a result of the case the Minister referred the complaint to the Committee, which reported that the current prices were contrary to the interests of the south-eastern region and the public interest. However, the Minister decided not to direct the Milk Marketing Board to act on the Committee's conclusions since this could precipitate the collapse of the system for organized milk marketing, and because he had taken into account wider policy matters that were beyond the scope of the Committee's inquiry.

QUESTIONS

- Even though the Minister was obliged to take into account relevant matters and exclude irrelevant factors from consideration, the outcome in *Padfield* was ultimately unfavourable to the milk producers. Harlow [1976] *PL* 116 at 120 concludes that the judicial 'remedy had proved illusory; the same decision could be reached with only nominal deference to the court, and the waste of time and money entailed is a deterrent to future complainants'. How does this relate to the connection, postulated above at 8.3.1, between the nature of the decision-making process and the quality of its outputs?
- And what light does *Padfield* shed on the distinction between appeal and review?

One of the main difficulties which arises in this context relates to the determination of relevancy and irrelevancy. How are the courts to decide which, if any, of those categories a particular factor falls into? In pragmatic terms, a range of issues influence the courts when they deal with this matter. As Cooke J explained in *CREEDNZ* v. *Governor-General of New*

Zealand [1981] 1 NZLR 172 at 183, 'the more general and the more obviously important the consideration, the readier the court must be to hold that Parliament must have meant it to be taken into account'. The nature of the decision-making function in question is import-ant, too. For instance, in *R* v. *Secretary of State for the Home Department, ex pare Venables* [1998] AC 407, the Home Secretary, when deciding on the minimum period of detention for a child convicted of murder (a function which has since been held inconsistent with Article 5 ECHR: *Stafford* v. *United Kingdom* (2002) 35 EHRR 32), took into account public revul-sion in relation to the incident in question. The fact that the Home Secretary was exercising a sentencing power meant that he had acted improperly by considering such factors, as Lord Steyn explained at 526:

> The comparison between the position of the Home Secretary, when he fixes a tariff representing the punitive element of the sentence, and the position of a sentencing judge is correct. In fixing a tariff the Home Secretary is carrying out . . . a classic judicial function . . . Plainly a sentencing judge must ignore a newspaper campaign designed to encourage him to increase a particular sentence . . . Like a judge the Home Secretary ought not to be guided by a disposition to consult how popular a particular decision may be. The power given to him requires, above all, a detached approach. I would therefore hold that public protests about the level of a tariff to be fixed in a particular case are legally irrelevant and may not be taken into account by the Home Secretary in fixing the tariff.

The statutory scheme also plays an important part in the determination of relevancy. This point is usefully illustrated by *R* v. *Gloucestershire County Council, ex parte Barry* [1997] AC 584 and *R* v. *East Sussex County Council, ex parte Tandy* [1998] AC 714. Both cases concerned the question whether financial implications could be taken into account in determining the level of provision to make in relation to (respectively) domestic assistance for the disabled and educational services; scarcity of resources was held to be a legitimate consideration in the former case, but a prohibited consideration in the latter. The decisions were distinguished on the basis of differences between the two statutory frameworks. On the relevance of financial considerations, see also *R* v. *Chief Constable of Sussex, ex parte Inter-national Traders' Ferry Ltd* [1999] 2 AC 418 and, for discussion, Syrett [2000] 1 *Web JCLI.*

8.3.3 Relevancy, Judicial Intervention, and Executive Autonomy

An underlying tension in the relationship between the judiciary and executive may be discerned in this context. To what extent should the former, by means of the relevancy doctrine, prescribe the nature of the decision-making process and, by possible extension, its outcomes? Two particular issues arise.

The first concerns how prescriptive the courts should be in setting the parameters of the decision-making process. How willing should courts be to determine that a given factor is legally relevant, such that it *must* be taken into consideration, or legally irrelevant, such that it *must not* be? We will see below that there is a good deal to be said for judicial caution in this context, in particular for recognition of an intermediate category of factors which deci-sion-makers should be largely free to *choose* whether to consider. However, in order to demonstrate why this is important, it is first necessary to illustrate the extent to which categorizing factors as legally relevant or irrelevant may allow the courts to prescribe the premises on which decisions are taken — and perhaps (indirectly) the decisions themselves — with a high degree of specificity. This is apparent from the following case in which, by ruling certain factors to be irrelevant, the House of Lords was able to exert considerable influence over both the decision-making process and its outcome.

....

Roberts v. Hopwood [1925] AC 578
House of Lords

At a time when both the cost of living and trade union scale wage rates had been falling for some time, Poplar Borough Council resolved not to reduce its employees' wages. The Council also continued to pay male and female employees at the same rate. Section 62 of the Metropolis Management Act 1855 gave the Council power to pay employees 'such . . . wages as . . . [the Council] may think fit'. Under s 247(7) of the Public Health Act 1875 the district auditor had power to 'disallow any item of account contrary to law, and surcharge the same on the person making or authorising the illegal payment'. He calculated the amount by which the pre-1914–18 war rate should have been increased in accordance with the rise in the cost of living, added a further £1 as a margin and, after hearing representations from the councillors, reduced the figure he had been minded to disallow by £12,000. He then disallowed the remaining excess (£5,000) and surcharged those responsible. The councillors applied for a quashing order under s 247(8) of the Public Health Act 1875 (which permitted relief for errors of law and fact: *R v. Roberts* [1908] 1 KB 407). They failed in the Divisional Court but succeeded in the Court of Appeal. The district auditor appealed to the House of Lords.

Lord Buckmaster

. . . [T]he general rule applicable is that the council shall pay such wages as they may think fit, the discretion as to the reasonable nature of the wages being with them. The discretion thus imposed is a very wide one, and I agree with the principle enunciated by Lord Russell in the case of *Kruse v. Johnson* [[1898] 2 QB 91 at 99], that when such a discretion is conferred upon a local authority the Court ought to show great reluctance before they attempt to determine how, in their opinion, the discretion ought to be exercised.

Turning to what the borough council have done, the reason for their action is to be found in the affidavit sworn by Mr Scurr, Mr. Key, Mr. Lansbury and Mr. Sumner. In para. 6 of that affidavit they make the following statement: "The council and its predecessors the district board of works have always paid such a minimum wage to its employees as they have believed to be fair and reasonable without being bound by any particular external method of fixing wages, whether ascertainable by Trade Union rate, cost of living, payments by other local or national authorities or otherwise." And if the matter ended there it would be my opinion that a decision so reached could not be impeached until it were shown that it was not bona fide, and absence of bona fides is not alleged in the present proceedings. Para. 9, however, of the same affidavit puts the matter in a different form. It is there said: "9. . . . . The Council did not and does not take the view that wages paid should be exclusively related to the cost of living. They have from time to time carefully considered the question of the wages and are of the opinion, as a matter of policy, that a public authority should be a model employer and that a minimum rate of 4*l* is the least wage which ought to be paid to an adult having regard to the efficiency of their workpeople, the duty of a public authority both to the ratepayers and to its employees, the purchasing power of the wages and other considerations which are relevant to their decisions as to wages."

Now it appears that on August 31, 1921, a resolution was passed by the borough council to the effect that no reduction of wage or bonus should be made during the ensuing four months, and this was acted upon for the following twelve months. It was, I think, well within their power to fix wages for a reasonable time in advance, and there are cogent reasons why this should be done, but that decision should be made in relation to existing facts, which they appear to have ignored. In August, 1921, the cost of living had been continuously falling since November of the previous year, and it continued to fall, so that it is difficult to understand how, if the cost of living was taken into account in fixing the wages for adult workers at a minimum basis of 4*l*, the sharp decline in this important factor should have been wholly disregarded by the borough council. But the affidavit contains another statement, which I think is most serious for the council's case. It states that 4*l* a week was to be the minimum wage for adult labour, that is without the least regard to what that labour might be. It standardised men and women not according to the duties they performed, but according to the fact that they were adults. It is this that leads me to think that their action cannot be supported, and that in fact they have not determined the payment as wages, for they have eliminated the consideration both of the work to be done and of the purchasing power of the sums paid, which they themselves appear to regard as a relevant though not the dominant factor. Had they stated that they determined as a borough council to pay the same wage for the same work without regard to the sex or condition of the person who performed it, I should have found it difficult to say that that was not a proper exercise of their discretion. It was indeed argued that that is what they did, but I find it impossible to extract that from the statement contained in the affidavit. It appears to me, for the reasons I have given, that they cannot have brought into account the considerations which they say influenced them, and that they did not base their decision upon the ground that the reward for work is the value of the work reasonably and even generously measured, but that they took an arbitrary principle and fixed an arbitrary sum, which was not a real exercise of the discretion imposed upon them by the statute . . .

Lord Atkinson

. . . The council would, in my view, fail in their duty if, in administering funds which did not belong to their members alone, they put aside all [the] aids to the ascertainment of what was just and reasonable remuneration to give for the services rendered to them, and allowed themselves to be guided in preference by some eccentric principles of socialistic philanthropy, or by a feminist ambition to secure the equality of the sexes in the matter of wages in the world of labour.

It was strongly pressed in argument that the auditor believed the council acted bona fide; but what in this connection do the words "bona fide" mean? Do they mean, as apparently this gentleman thought, that no matter how excessive or illegal their scale of wages might be, they were bound to put it into force because their constituents gave them a mandate so to do, or again, do the words mean that as the payment of wages was a subject with which they had legally power to deal, the amount of their funds which they devoted to that purpose was their own concern which no auditor had jurisdiction to revise, or in reference to which he could surcharge anything? The whole system of audit to which the Legislature has subjected every municipal corporation or council is a most emphatic protest against such opinions as these . . .

[A]s wages are remuneration for services, the words "think fit" must, I think, be construed to mean "as the employer shall think fitting and proper" for the services rendered. It cannot, in my view, mean that the employer, especially an employer dealing with moneys not entirely his own, may pay to his employee wages of any amount he pleases. Still less does it mean that he can pay gratuities or gifts to his employees disguised under the name of wages . . .

What is a reasonable wage at any time must depend, of course, on the circumstances which then exist in the labour market. I do not say there must be any cheeseparing or that the datum line, as I have called it, must never be exceeded to any extent, or that employees may not be generously treated. But it does not appear to me that there is any rational proportion between the rates of wages at which the labour of these women is paid and the rates at which they would be reasonably remunerated for their services to the council . . .

Lord Sumner

. . . The respondents conceded that for wages fixed mala fide no exemption from review could be claimed and that the mere magnitude of the wages paid, relatively to the wages for which the same service was procurable, might be enough in itself to establish bad faith. This admission, I am sure, was rightly made, but it leads to two conclusions. Firstly, the final words of the section are not absolute, but are subject to an implied qualification of good faith — "as the board may bona fide think fit." Is the implication of good faith all? That is a qualification drawn from the general legal doctrine, that persons who hold public office have a legal responsibility towards those whom they represent — not merely towards those who vote for them — to the discharge of which they must honestly apply their minds. Bona fide here cannot simply mean that they are not making a profit.

The purpose, however, of the whole audit is to ensure wise and prudent administration and to recover for the council's funds money that should not have been taken out of them. If, having examined the expenditure and found clear proof of bad faith, which admittedly would open the account, the auditor further found that the councillors' evil minds had missed their mark, and the expenditure itself was right, then the expenditure itself would not be "contrary to law" and could not be disallowed. Bad faith admittedly vitiates the council's purported exercise of its discretion, but the auditor is not confined to asking, if the discretion, such as it may be, has been honestly exercised. He has to restrain expenditure within proper limits. His mission is to inquire if there is any excess over what is reasonable. I do not find any words limiting his functions merely to the case of bad faith, or obliging him to leave the ratepayers unprotected from the effects on their pockets of honest stupidity or unpractical idealism. The breach in the words "as they may think fit," which the admitted implication as to bad faith makes, is wide enough to make the necessary implication one both of honesty and of reasonableness . . .

Much was said at the Bar about the wide discretion conferred by the Local Government Acts on local authorities. In a sense this is true, but the meaning of the term needs careful examination. What has been said in cases, which lie outside the provisions as to audit altogether, is not necessarily applicable to matters, which are concerned with the expenditure of public money. There are many matters, which the Courts are indisposed to question. Though they are the ultimate judges of what is lawful and what is unlawful to borough councils, they often accept the decisions of the local authority simply because they are themselves ill equipped to weigh the merits of one solution of a practical question as against another. This, however, is not a recognition of the absolute character of the local authority's discretion, but of the limits within which it is practicable to question it. There is nothing about a borough council that corresponds to autonomy. It has great responsibilities, but the limits of its powers and of its independence are such as the law, mostly statutory, may have laid down, and there is no presumption against the accountability of the authority. Everything depends on the construction of the sections applicable. In the present case, I think that the auditor was entitled to inquire into all the items of expenditure in question, to ask whether in incurring them the council had been guided by aims and objects not open to them or had disregarded considerations by which they should have been guided, and to the extent to which they had in consequence exceeded a reasonable expenditure, it was his duty to disallow the items . . .

[After considering the facts, his Lordship said:] I think it is plain that the respondents have deliberately decided not to be guided by ordinary economic (and economical) considerations . . . I am . . . of opinion that on their own showing the respondents have exercised such discretion as the Metropolis Management Act gives to the council in the matter of wages upon principles which are not open to the council, and for objects which are beyond their powers. Their exercise of those powers was examinable by the auditor, and on the above grounds the excess expenditure was liable to be disallowed by him as contrary to law . . .

Lords Wrenbury and Carson also delivered speeches in favour of allowing the appeal. Appeal allowed.

By concluding that the council had taken into account what he considered 'eccentric principles of socialistic philanthropy' and 'a feminist ambition to secure the equality of the sexes', and by holding such considerations to be irrelevant, Lord Atkinson was able to conclude that the council's decision was unlawful. Thus the doctrine of relevancy allows potentially extensive judicial intervention in the administrative process, permitting the policy preferences of the decision-maker to be swept away if the matters upon which they are founded can be characterized by the court as irrelevant. Although judges naturally present their determinations as to relevancy in terms of statutory interpretation, it is highly likely that their own opinion of the policy issues will to some extent be in play. Indeed, in *Roberts* v. *Hopwood* itself, Lord Atkinson did not seek to disguise his disapproval of the council's progressive views on employment practice and equal treatment, opining (at 591–592) that council members were guilty of 'vanity' in attempting to appear as 'model employers', and had 'become such ardent feminists' — a term which Lord Atkinson appears to have intended pejoratively — 'as to bring about, at the expense of the ratepayers whose money they administered, sex equality in the labour market'.

While there must, of course, come a point at which decisions have to be set aside because they are founded upon irrelevant considerations — if this were not possible, then the courts would be denied an important part of their machinery for controlling arbitrary and capricious administration — there are many cases in which the question of relevancy is far from clear-cut. For instance, referring back to the facts of *Roberts* v. *Hopwood*, could it not be argued that the local authority, having discretion to pay its employees such wages as it thought fit, might legitimately have invoked ideological factors in determining their policy in that context? Is it not arguable that there may be room — and, crucially, that Parliament, in creating the discretion, might have accepted that there was such room — for a range of reasonable views on this question?

These questions, of course, go to the heart of the distinction between appeal and review, and the debate about how judges and decision-makers ought properly to relate to one another. We have already touched upon these issues (above at 1.3.1) and explore them in more detail in ch 9 below. The basic proposition, however, is straightforward — that the court's role is to review the legality of administrative decisions, not to substitute its own view for that of the decision-maker. It is on the basis of this philosophy that the doctrine of *Wednesbury* unreasonableness (see *Associated Provincial Picture Houses Ltd* v. *Wednesbury Corporation* [1948] 1 KB 223, considered below at 9.2) holds that a substantive administrative decision may be set aside only if it is so unreasonable that no reasonable authority could ever have reached it. The same philosophy, it has been argued, should inform the courts' approach to questions of relevancy and irrelevancy which, as we have seen, have potentially far-reaching consequences *vis-à-vis* the agency's autonomy. For instance Cooke J, in *Ashby* v. *Minister of Immigration* [1981] 1 NZLR 222 at 224, draws a distinction between 'obligatory considerations', which are those 'the Act expressly or impliedly requires the Minister to take account of', and 'permissible considerations', which 'can properly be taken into account but do not have to be'. On this view there exist three types of consideration: at the extremes, there are those which must be taken account of and those which must be disregarded; in between, however, is a category of factors whose relevance is for the decision-maker, rather than the court, to decide. Irvine [1996] *PL* 59 at 67 strongly approves of this approach, and of the underlying relationship between the courts and the administration which it implies:

The *Wednesbury* principle of relevance is premised upon the view that the decision-maker is in the best position . . . to determine the range of factors which bear upon his decision. The statute may expressly, or by necessary implication, provide that some factors *must*, and some *must not* be considered, but there is a margin of appreciation within which the decision-maker may decide for himself which considerations should play a part in his reasoning process. Thus, there are three categories of consideration: those that must, those that must not and those that may, in the decision-maker's discretion, be taken into account. An important part of *Wednesbury* [theory] is the recognition of this free area of optional considerations.

QUESTIONS

• Do you agree with the approach articulated by Cooke and Irvine?
• Does it pose any problems?

The second respect in which the intrusiveness of the relevancy doctrine as a principle of review falls for consideration concerns the attribution of weight to relevant factors. If the court concludes that a given factor must be taken into account — an 'obligatory consideration' — can the court go on to prescribe how seriously it is to be considered, and how much weight should be attached to it? Or is this a time for judicial control to yield to executive autonomy? Precisely this point was addressed by the House of Lords in the following case.

....

Tesco Stores Ltd v. *Secretary of State for the Environment* [1995] 1 WLR 759
House of Lords

Two supermarket chains wished to build stores, on different sites, in Witney in Oxfordshire. Both applications ultimately ended up before the Secretary of State: the Sainsbury's application (which was made by the development company Tarmac) reached the Secretary of State on appeal, while Tesco's application was called in by the Department for the Environment. At the subsequent public inquiry Tesco undertook that, if it was granted planning permission, it would fund the construction of a new relief road — a measure which, at the time, was under consideration as a possible means of reducing traffic congestion in the town — known as the West End Link (WEL). The planning inspector concluded that only one of the applications should be permitted, and recommended that Tesco's application should be granted and Tarmac's appeal dismissed. The Secretary of State, however, declined to follow those recommendations, choosing instead to allow Tarmac's appeal and dismiss Tesco's application. Tesco challenged the decision under s 288 of the Town and Country Planning Act 1990 (which provides for a form of statutory review that is substantially similar to judicial review), arguing (*inter alia*) that the Secretary of State had failed to take account of its offer to fund the WEL. Tesco succeeded at first instance, but the Court of Appeal allowed Tarmac's appeal. Tesco appealed to the House of Lords.

Lord Keith

. . . It is for the courts, if the matter is brought before them, to decide what is a relevant consideration. If the decision maker wrongly takes the view that some consideration is not relevant, and therefore has no regard to it, his decision cannot stand and he must be required to think again. But it is entirely for the decision maker to attribute to the relevant considerations such weight as he thinks fit, and the courts will not interfere unless he has acted unreasonably in the *Wednesbury* sense (*Associated Provincial Picture Houses Ltd* v. *Wednesbury Corporation* [1948] 1 K.B. 223). In assessing whether or not the Secretary of State in the instant case wrongly treated Tesco's offer of funding for the WEL as not being a material consideration in determining the competing applications for planning permission it is necessary to examine both the published policy of the Secretary of State in regard to planning obligations and the terms of his decision letter.

[After considering the relevant policy, his Lordship continued:] An offered planning obligation which has nothing to do with the proposed development, apart from the fact that it is offered by the developer, will plainly not be a material consideration and could be regarded only as an attempt to buy planning permission. If it has some connection with the proposed development which is not *de minimis*, then regard must be had to it. But the extent, if any, to which it should affect the decision is a matter entirely within the discretion of the decision maker and in exercising that discretion he is entitled to have regard to his established policy . . .

When it comes to the Secretary of State's decision letter, I am clearly of opinion that on a fair reading of it he has not disregarded Tesco's offer of funding as being immaterial. On the contrary, he has given it careful consideration. Paragraph 7 examines the effect of a new foodstore on the traffic situation in Witney, concludes that there would be a slight worsening, and agrees with the inspector that this produces some relationship between the funding of the WEL and the proposed foodstore but that the relationship is tenuous. He expresses the view that the WEL is not so closely related to any of the proposed superstores that any of them ought not to be permitted without it. He goes on to say that full funding of the WEL is not fairly and reasonably related in scale to any of the proposed developments, and further that having regard to the expected traffic and the distance between the sites and the route of the WEL it would be unreasonable to seek even a partial contribution from developers towards the cost of it. All of this seems to me, far from being a dismissal of the offer of funding as immaterial, to be a careful weighing up of its significance for the purpose of arriving at a planning decision. In paragraph 8 the Secretary of State considers whether in the event of its being reasonable to seek a partial contribution to the funding of WEL the amount of the benefit would be such as to tip the balance of the argument in favour of Tesco, and concludes that it would not. That is clearly a weighing exercise.

Upon the whole matter I am of opinion that the Secretary of State has not treated Tesco's offer of funding as immaterial, but has given it full and proper consideration, and that his decision is not open to challenge . . .

Lord Hoffmann

. . . The law has always made a clear distinction between the question of whether something is a material consideration and the weight which it should be given. The former is a question of law and the latter is a question of planning judgment, which is entirely a matter for the planning authority. Provided that the planning authority has regard to all material considerations, it is at liberty (provided that it does not lapse into *Wednesbury* irrationality) to give them whatever weight the planning authority thinks fit or no weight at all. The fact that the law regards something as a material consideration therefore involves no view about the part, if any, which it should play in the decision-making process.

This distinction between whether something is a material consideration and the weight which it should be given is only one aspect of a fundamental principle of British planning law, namely that the courts are concerned only with the legality of the decision-making process and not with the merits of the decision. If there is one principle of planning law more firmly settled than any other, it is that matters of planning judgment are within the exclusive province of the local planning authority or the Secretary of State . . .

Lords Ackner, Browne-Wilkinson, and Lloyd also agreed that Tesco's appeal should be dismissed.

Lords Keith and Hoffmann adopt substantially similar approaches. Both are agreed that the attribution of weight to relevant factors is a matter for the decision-maker, not the court, albeit that the former may not act irrationally in doing so (although cf cases to which the proportionality test is applicable: see the excerpt from the *Daly* case below at 9.3.4). However, Lord Hoffmann goes further by suggesting that it would be legitimate for the decision-maker to attach *no* weight to a relevant consideration. So, while it remains unlawful to omit to consider relevant factors, it is acceptable, at least as far as Lord Hoffmann is concerned, for decision-makers to apply their minds to such factors but to conclude that, within the specific factual matrix, no weight should be ascribed to them. Ultimately Lord Hoffmann's approach, as he readily acknowledged, ascribes quite different roles to the court and the decision-maker, and does not present the relevancy doctrine — in contrast perhaps to the decision in *Roberts* v. *Hopwood* — as a vehicle for intrusive judicial control of the decision-making process and (indirectly) its outcomes.

QUESTIONS

- Do you agree with Lord Hoffmann that the administration should be free, subject only to '*Wednesbury* irrationality', to attribute no weight to relevant considerations?
- Is this different from allowing such considerations not to be considered in the first place?

8.4 Concluding Remarks

We began this chapter with the notion that there is no such thing as an unfettered discretion, and the requirement, which derives from the rule of law, that discretionary powers must therefore be used within legally-prescribed limits. The propriety of purpose and relevancy doctrines play a central role in this context, by ensuring that discretion is exercised for the purposes for which it was conferred and that decisions are based upon relevant considerations. Together, these principles of administrative law encourage a mode of administration which is faithful to the legislative scheme set out by Parliament, and seek to prevent the use of discretionary power for extraneous reasons. They are, therefore, important mechanisms through which the goal of government limited by law may be realized.

We noted above that the courts tend to use the propriety of purpose and relevancy doctrines interchangeably. This is unsurprising, given that many factual situations can comfortably be analysed using either of the two approaches. But, by way of conclusion, we ought to consider whether there is a principled way in which the courts should decide which of the two analyses to adopt and, relatedly, whether there are any important differences between the doctrines. Taylor [1976] *CLJ* 272 argues that the proper mode of review is determined by the empowering provision. When the provision is expressed in broad terms, and gives little guidance as to how the power should be used, a purposive style of interpretation is appropriate; this naturally leads to the application of the propriety of purpose doctrine. In contrast, when the statutory scheme is more specific about the reasons for which decision-makers may act, the relevancy doctrine is apposite. This pattern does not, however, reflect the state of the authorities, and courts continue to use the two doctrines largely interchangeably.

A difference between the two modes of analysis which does emerge from the case law concerns the precise circumstances in which they trigger a finding of unlawfulness on the part of the decision-maker. We have seen that, if a decision-maker is motivated by a number of purposes, the decision will be unlawful only if the bad purpose is the dominant one. In cases which are analysed by reference to relevancy of considerations, however, a stricter test seems to apply. In *R* v. *Rochdale Metropolitan Borough Council, ex parte Cromer Ring Mill*

[1982] 3 All ER 761 at 770, Forbes J approved the following passage from De Smith's *Judicial Review of Administrative Action* (London 1980): 'If the influence of irrelevant factors is established, it does not appear to be necessary to prove that they were the sole or even the dominant influence; it seems to be enough to prove that their influence was substantial.' Thus it seems that, within some factual matrices, it may be easier for claimants to establish that a decision should be set aside on the basis of an irrelevant factor than an improper purpose, given that the test of 'substantial influence' seems easier to satisfy than that of 'dominant purpose'. On this point, see also *R v. Broadcasting Complaints Commission, ex parte Owen* [1985] QB 1153 at 1177 and *R v. Inner London Education Authority, ex parte Westminster City Council* [1986] 1 WLR 28 at 49.

FURTHER RESOURCES

Craig, 'Formal and Substantive Conceptions of the Rule of Law: An Analytical Framework' [1997] *PL* 467

Syrett, 'Of Resources, Rationality and Rights: Emerging Trends in the Judicial Review of Allocative Decisions' [2000] 1 *Web JCLI webjcli.ncl.ac.uk/2000/issue1/syrett1.html*

Taylor, 'Judicial Review of Improper Purposes and Irrelevant Considerations' [1976] *CLJ* 272

9 ABUSE OF DISCRETION II

9.1 Introduction

English administrative law has traditionally been concerned more with the *manner* in which decisions are made than with the *content* of the decisions themselves. The established grounds of review thus concentrate on such matters as the fairness of the procedure by which the decision was reached and the quality of the decision-making process. This process-oriented conception of judicial review finds its putative justification in the distinction between appeal and review (see above at 1.3.1): by confining itself to the decision-making process, the court tends to avoid interference with the merits of the decision, thereby reducing the scope for judicial usurpation of the executive's functions.

Nevertheless, the law of judicial review has never wholly eschewed examination of the outcomes of the decision-making process. We saw in ch 8 that judicial control of the decision-making process on such grounds as propriety of purpose and relevancy of considerations can influence what decisions may validly be made. Moreover, the principle of reasonableness (discussed in the following section) has long imposed a substantive, rather than a merely procedural, limitation upon the powers of decision-makers, albeit that the limit is rather modest in nature: only if the decision is seriously flawed may the court intervene on this basis. Requiring a high level of administrative fault in order to trigger substantive review significantly emasculates the courts' jurisdiction in this context. However, as this chapter explains, recent years have witnessed a number of developments in this field. The reasonableness doctrine itself has been refined so that, in some contexts at least, it now supplies a more rigorous standard of substantive review; moreover, English public law now embraces the more structured and intrusive principle of proportionality in certain spheres. It is necessary to begin, however, with the orthodox conception of reasonableness which was famously set out in the *Wednesbury* case, in order to contextualize these developments.

9.2 Reasonableness and Rationality

9.2.1 The *Wednesbury* and *GCHQ* Cases

Sedley (in Richardson and Genn (eds), *Administrative Law and Government Action* (Oxford 1994) at 38) remarks that, 'It is typical of the ahistoricism of lawyers that they treat as a landmark the *Wednesbury* case . . . in which the Master of the Rolls . . . rehearsed a number of doctrines which had been perfectly familiar to the Victorian judges.' Nevertheless, that case has become synonymous with the doctrine of reasonableness, and still forms an appropriate starting point for an exploration of the principles of substantive review which apply in English law. In the following excerpt, Lord Greene MR refers not only to the sort of substantive unreasonableness with which we are presently concerned, but also to the principles considered in the previous chapter. Because of the overlap, noted by Lord Greene, between these various grounds of review, the term '*Wednesbury* unreasonableness' is sometimes used to refer to all of them, although in this chapter we use it to refer specifically to review of the outcome of the decision-making process.

....

Associated Provincial Picture Houses Ltd. v. *Wednesbury Corporation* [1948] 1 KB 223
Court of Appeal

The defendant, which was empowered by s 1(1) of the Sunday Entertainments Act 1932 to allow cinemas to open on Sundays 'subject to such conditions as the authority think fit to impose', permitted the claimant to open its cinema provided that no children under 15 were admitted to Sunday performances. The claimant argued that the condition was *ultra vires* and accordingly sought a declaratory order.

Lord Greene MR

. . . Mr. Gallop, for the plaintiffs, argued that it was not competent for the Wednesbury Corporation to impose any such condition and he said that if they were entitled to impose a condition prohibiting the admission of children, they should at least have limited it to cases where the children were not accompanied by their parents or a guardian or some adult. His argument was that the imposition of that condition was unreasonable and that in consequence it was ultra vires the corporation. The plaintiffs' contention is based, in my opinion, on a misconception as to the effect of this Act in granting this discretionary power to local authorities. The courts must always, I think, remember this: first, we are dealing with not a judicial act, but an executive act; secondly, the conditions which, under the exercise of that executive act, may be imposed are in terms, so far as language goes, put within the discretion of the local authority without limitation. Thirdly, the statute provides no appeal from the decision of the local authority.

What, then, is the power of the courts? They can only interfere with an act of executive authority if it be shown that the authority has contravened the law. It is for those who assert that the local authority has contravened the law to establish that proposition. On the face of it, a condition of the kind imposed in this case is perfectly lawful. It is not to be assumed prima facie that responsible bodies like the local authority in this case will exceed their powers; but the court, whenever it is alleged that the local authority have contravened the law, must not substitute itself for that author- ity. It is only concerned with seeing whether or not the proposition is made good. When an executive discretion is entrusted by Parliament to a body such as the local authority in this case, what appears to be an exercise of that discretion can only be challenged in the courts in a strictly limited class of case. As I have said, it must always be remembered that the court is not a court of appeal. When discretion of this kind is granted the law recognizes certain principles upon which that discretion must be exercised, but within the four corners of those principles the discretion, in my opinion, is an absolute one and cannot be questioned in any court of law. What then are those principles? They are well understood. They are principles which the court looks to in considering any question of discretion of this kind. The exercise of such a discretion must be a real exercise of the discretion. If, in the statute conferring the discretion, there is to be found expressly or by implication matters which the authority exercising the discretion ought to have regard to, then in exercising the discretion it must have regard to those matters. Conversely, if the nature of the subject matter and the general interpretation of the Act make it clear that certain matters would not be germane to the matter in question, the authority must disregard those irrelevant collateral matters.

There have been in the cases expressions used relating to the sort of things that authorities must not do, not merely in cases under the Cinematograph Act but, generally speaking, under other cases where the powers of local authorities came to be considered. I am not sure myself whether the permissible grounds of attack cannot be defined under a single head. It has been perhaps a little bit confusing to find a series of grounds set out. Bad faith, dishonesty — those of course, stand by themselves — unreasonableness, attention given to extraneous circumstances, disregard of public policy and things like that have all been referred to, according to the facts of individual cases, as being matters which are relevant to the question. If they cannot all be confined under one head, they at any rate, I think, overlap to a very great extent. For instance, we have heard in this case a great deal about the meaning of the word "unreasonable".

It is true the discretion must be exercised reasonably. Now what does that mean? Lawyers familiar with the phraseology commonly used in relation to exercise of statutory discretions often use the word "unreasonable" in a rather comprehensive sense. It has frequently been used and is frequently used as a general description of the things that must not be done. For instance, a person entrusted with a discretion must, so to speak, direct himself properly in law. He must call his own attention to the matters which he is bound to consider. He must exclude from his consideration matters which are irrelevant to what he has to consider. If he does not obey those rules, he may truly be said, and often is said, to be acting "unreasonably." Similarly, there may be something so absurd that no sensible person could ever dream that it lay within the powers of the authority. Warrington L.J. in *Short v. Poole Corporation* [[1926] Ch 66 at 90–1] gave the example of the red- haired teacher, dismissed because she had red hair. That is unreasonable in one sense. In another sense it is taking into consideration extraneous matters. It is so unreasonable that it might almost be described as being done in bad faith; and, in fact, all these things run into one another.

In the present case, it is said by Mr. Gallop that the authority acted unreasonably in imposing this condition. It appears to me quite clear that the matter dealt with by this condition was a matter which a reasonable authority would be justified in considering when they were making up their mind what condition should be attached to the grant of this licence. Nobody, at this time of day, could say that the well-being and the physical and moral health of children is not a matter which a local authority, in exercising their powers, can properly have in mind when those questions are germane to what they have to consider. Here Mr. Gallop did not, I think, suggest that the council were directing their mind to a purely extraneous and irrelevant matter, but he based his argument on the word "unreasonable," which he treated as an independent ground for attacking the decision of the authority; but once it is conceded, as it must be conceded in this case, that the particular sub- ject-matter dealt with by this condition was one which it was competent for the authority to consider, there, in my opinion, is an end of the case. Once that is granted, Mr. Gallop is bound to say that the decision of the authority is wrong because it is unreasonable, and in saying that he is really saying that the ultimate arbiter of what is and is not reasonable is the court and not the local authority. It is just there, it seems to me, that the argument breaks down. It is clear that the local authority are entrusted by Parliament with the decision on a matter which the knowledge and experience of that authority can best be trusted to deal with. The subject-matter with which the condition deals is one relevant for its consideration. They have considered it and come to a decision upon it. It is true to say that, if a decision on a competent matter is so unreasonable that no reasonable authority could ever have come to it, then the courts can interfere. That, I think, is quite right; but to prove a case of that kind would require something overwhelming, and, in this case, the facts do not come anywhere near anything of that kind. I think Mr. Gallop in the end agreed that his proposition that the decision of the local authority can be upset if it is proved to be unreasonable, really meant that it must be proved to be unreasonable in the sense that the court considers it to be a decision that no reasonable body could have come to. It is not what the court considers unreasonable, a different thing altogether. If it is what the court considers unreasonable, the court may very well have different views to that of a local authority on matters of high public policy of this kind. Some courts might think that no children ought to be admitted on Sundays at all, some courts might think the reverse, and all over the country I have no doubt on a thing of that sort honest and sincere people hold different views. The effect of the legislation is not to set up the court as an arbiter of the correctness of one view over another. It is the local authority that are set in that position and, provided they act, as they have acted, within the four corners of their jurisdiction, this court, in my opinion, cannot interfere . . .

In the result, this appeal must be dismissed. I do not wish to repeat myself but I will summarize once again the principle applicable. The court is entitled to investigate the action of the local authority with a view to seeing whether they have taken into account matters which they ought not to take into account, or, conversely, have refused to take into account or neglected to take into account matters which they ought to take into account. Once that question is answered in favour of the local authority, it may be still possible to say that, although the local authority have kept within the four corners of the matters which they ought to consider, they have nevertheless come to a conclusion so unreasonable that no reasonable authority could ever have come to it. In such a case, again, I think the court can interfere. The power of the court to interfere in each case is not as an appellate authority to override a decision of the local authority, but as a judicial authority which is concerned, and concerned only, to see whether the local authority have contravened the law by acting in excess of the powers which Parliament has confided in them . . .

Somervell LJ and Singleton J agreed with Lord Greene MR that the local authority had not acted unlawfully. Appeal dismissed.

QUESTIONS

- Do you think that the model of substantive review set out by Lord Greene is appropriate?
- What sort of relationship between judges and decision-makers does it envisage?

It is clear that Lord Greene's central concern was to emphasize that the court's role is not to retake decisions, or to substitute its own view of the merits for that of the decision-maker — hence the rather extreme language of the *Wednesbury* test which underscores the orthodox view that the central function of the court is to review the legality, not the content, of administrative decisions. A similarly restrictive vision of substantive review was presented by Lord Diplock in his speech in *Council of Civil Service Unions* v. *Minister for the Civil Service* [1985] AC 374 at 410–411 — the '*GCHQ* case' — in which he replaced the language of 'reasonableness' with that of 'rationality':

... Judicial review has I think developed to a stage today when without reiterating any analysis of the steps by which the development has come about, one can conveniently classify under three heads the grounds upon which administrative action is subject to control by judicial review. The first ground I would call "illegality," the second "irrationality" and the third "procedural impropriety". That is not to say that further development on a case by case basis may not in course of time add further grounds. I have in mind particularly the possible adoption in the future of the principle of "proportionality" which is recognised in the administrative law of several of our fellow members of the European Economic Community; but to dispose of the instant case the three already well-established heads that I have mentioned will suffice . . .

By "irrationality" I mean what can by now be succinctly referred to as "*Wednesbury* unreasonable-ness" . . . It applies to a decision which is so outrageous in its defiance of logic or of accepted moral standards that no sensible person who had applied his mind to the question to be decided could have arrived at it. Whether a decision falls within this category is a question that judges by their training and experience should be well equipped to answer, or else there would be something badly wrong with our judicial system. To justify the court's exercise of this role, resort I think is today no longer needed to Viscount Radcliffe's ingenious explanation in *Edwards* v. *Bairstow* [1956] A.C. 14 of irrationality as a ground for a court's reversal of a decision by ascribing it to an inferred though unidentifiable mistake of law by the decision-maker. "Irrationality" by now can stand upon its own feet as an accepted ground on which a decision may be attacked by judicial review.

The restrained approach to substantive review which is commended by the *Wednesbury* and *GCHQ* rhetoric has been endorsed strongly by Irvine [1996] *PL* 59 at 60–61, who identifies three reasons for judicial self-restraint in this sphere:

First, a *constitutional imperative*: public authorities receive their powers from Parliament which intends, for good reason, that a power be exercised by the authority to which it is entrusted. This is because each and every authority has, within its field of influence, a level of knowledge and experi-ence which justifies the decision of Parliament to entrust that authority with decision-making power. Secondly, *lack of judicial expertise*: it follows that the courts are, in relative terms, ill-equipped to take decisions in place of the designated authority. This is all the more true where the decision in question is one of "policy"; and the further into the realm of policy an issue lies, the more reluctant a court should be to interfere with the authority's decision. Thirdly, the *democratic imperative*: it has long been recognised that elected public authorities, and particularly local authorities, derive their authority in part from their electoral mandate. The electoral system also operates as an important safeguard against the unreasonable exercise of public powers, since elected authorities have to submit themselves, and their decision-making records, to the verdict of the electorate at regular intervals . . .

QUESTION

- Do you find these arguments convincing? Do they support a globally restrictive approach to substantive review, or do they demand judicial self-restraint only in particular contexts (and, if so, which ones)?

Taken at face value, the passages above from *Wednesbury* and *GCHQ* — together with arguments such as those of Irvine — paint a relatively simple picture of substantive review, within which the courts scrutinize administrative decisions according to a universally defer-ential standard. However, as Jowell and Lester [1987] *PL* 368 at 372 observe, the reality is somewhat different:

. . . [The *Wednesbury* test] seeks to prevent review except in cases where the official has behaved absurdly . . . In practice, however, the courts are willing to impugn decisions that are far from absurd and are indeed often coldly rational. Were the courts only to interfere with decisions verging on the insane, a zone of immunity would be drawn around many oppressive or improper decisions that are in reality vulnerable to judicial review.

An arguably more realistic approach was advanced by Lord Cooke in *R* v. *Chief Constable of Sussex, ex parte International Traders' Ferry Ltd* [1999] 2 AC 418 at 452, who argued for a more moderate formulation of the unreasonableness test:

It seems to me unfortunate that *Wednesbury* and some *Wednesbury* phrases have become established incantations in the courts of the United Kingdom and beyond. *Associated Provincial Picture Houses Ltd. v. Wednesbury Corporation* [1948] 1 K.B. 223, an apparently briefly-considered case, might well not be decided the same way today; and the judgment of Lord Greene M.R. twice uses (at pp. 230 and 234) the tautologous formula "so unreasonable that no reasonable authority could ever have come to it". Yet judges are entirely accustomed to respecting the proper scope of administrative discretions. In my respectful opinion they do not need to be warned off the course by admonitory circumlocutions. When, in *Secretary of State for Education v. Tameside Metropolitan Borough Council* [1977] A.C. 1014, the precise meaning of "unreasonably" in an administrative context was crucial to the decision, the five speeches in the House of Lords, the three judgments in the Court of Appeal and the two judgments in the Divisional Court all succeeded in avoiding needless complexity. The simple test used throughout was whether the decision in question was one which a reasonable authority could reach. The converse was described by Lord Diplock, at p. 1064, as "conduct which no sensible authority acting with due appreciation of its responsibilities would have decided to adopt". These unexaggerated criteria give the administrator ample and rightful rein, consistently with the constitutional separation of powers.

Although this formulation is undeniably question-begging — how do we tell whether a decision is one that a 'reasonable authority' could reach? — it clearly does regularize the concept of unreasonableness by expanding its reach beyond the utterly absurd. This point was amplified by Lord Cooke in *R (Daly)* v. *Secretary of State for the Home Department* [2001] UKHL 26 [2001] 2 AC 532 at [32]:

. . . [T]he day will come when it will be more widely recognised that . . . *Wednesbury* . . . was an unfortunately retrogressive decision in English administrative law . . . in so far as it suggested that there are degrees of unreasonableness and that only a very extreme degree can bring an administrative decision within the legitimate scope of judicial invalidation. The depth of judicial review and the deference due to administrative discretion vary with the subject matter. It may well be, however, that the law can never be satisfied in any administrative field merely by a finding that the decision under review is not capricious or absurd . . .

Lord Cooke's references to the variable nature of judicial review and the related notion that, depending on the context, courts might act with more or less 'deference' in reviewing administrative decisions require further discussion. As we will see in relation to review on both *Wednesbury* and (later in the chapter) proportionality grounds, articulating a viable concept of context-sensitive judicial deference to the judgment of the executive branch is one of the most important — and perhaps difficult — challenges in administrative law today.

9.2.2 Deference and the Variable Standard of Review

Laws (in Forsyth and Hare (eds), *The Golden Metwand and the Crooked Cord* (Oxford 1998) at 186–187) writes that:

On the surface at least the test of unreasonableness or irrationality . . . is monolithic; it leaves no scope for a variable standard of review according to the subject-matter of the case . . . But in fact the courts, while broadly adhering to the monolithic language of *Wednesbury*, have to a considerable extent in recent years adopted variable standards of review [to suit the subject matter of the case before them] . . .

In some situations the courts have exhibited a willingness to intervene on substantive grounds only if the decision in question crosses an especially high threshold of unreasonableness. The courts tend to apply this principle of 'super-*Wednesbury*' review in situations where they feel that, for reasons of constitutional propriety or institutional competence, it is particularly inapposite for the judiciary to seek to assess or interfere with the content of an administrative decision (see further Jowell [1999] *PL* 448). In the following case, both of these factors were in play: the institutional competence of the court was undermined by the fact that the case raised complex issues concerning national economic policy, while the constitutional appropriateness of judicial intervention was in doubt, given that the policy had been approved by the House of Commons.

....

Nottinghamshire County Council v. *Secretary of State for the Environment* [1986] AC 240
House of Lords

A statutory and administrative scheme which aimed to reduce or restrain expenditure by local authorities was established by the Local Government, Planning and Land Act 1980 and the Local Government Finance Act 1982. Pursuant to s 60 of the 1980 Act the Secretary of State's Rate Support Grant Report (England) 1985/86 was laid before and approved by the House of Commons. If a local authority's expenditure exceeded the guidance figure in the Report, the Secretary of State was empowered by s 8(3)(c) of the 1982 Act to reduce the amount of the rate support grant made by central government to the authority. The Secretary of State used the 1984/85 budgets of local authorities and the concept of 'grant-related expenditure' (GRE) as the basis for his guidance for 1985/86. (GRE is the notional expenditure that an authority would need to incur if all authorities provided the same level of service with the same degree of efficiency at a level consistent with the government's aggregate spending plans for local government.) The 1985/86 guidance was that authorities which had budgeted to spend at or below GRE in 1984/85 could budget, in 1985/86, to spend their 1984/85 GRE plus a 3.75 per cent allowance for inflation. However, authorities which had budgeted to spend above GRE in 1984/85 could budget, in 1985/85, to spend the figure in the 1984/85 guidance plus a 3.75 per cent inflation allowance.

Nottinghamshire County Council and the City of Bradford Metropolitan Council unsuccessfully challenged the legality of the Secretary of State's guidance on two grounds. First, they argued that the Secretary of State's guidance conflicted with s 59(11A) of the 1980 Act which required that 'any guidance issued . . . be framed by reference to principles applicable to all local authorities'. The House of Lords, however, held that it was permissible to differentiate between local authorities on the basis of their past expenditure records. Secondly, the claimants contended that the defendant had acted unreasonably because the 1985/86 guidance formula was disproportionately disadvantageous to a small group of authorities whose 1984/85 guidance was below GRE and who were budgeting, in 1985/86, to spend above GRE. As the following extract shows, their Lordships also rejected this line of argument.

Lord Scarman

. . . Their second submission is that, even if the guidance complies with the words of the statute, it offends a principle of public law in that the burden which the guidance imposes on some authorities, including Nottingham and Bradford, is so disproportionately disadvantageous when compared with its effect upon others that it is a perversely unreasonable exercise of the power conferred by the statute upon the Secretary of State. The respondents rely on what has become known to lawyers as the "*Wednesbury* principles" . . .

Neither the trial judge nor the Court of Appeal accepted the second submission. But much has been made of it in the courts below and in your Lordships' House. The respondents' [that is, the local authorities'] case is that the guidance is grossly unfair, some authorities doing disproportionately well and others being hit undeservedly hard. Your Lordships have been taken through the detail and have been invited to hold that no reasonable Secretary of State could have intended consequences so disproportionate in their impact as between different local authorities. The House is invited in its judicial capacity to infer from these consequences that the Secretary of State must have abused the power conferred upon him by the Act.

The submission raises an important question as to the limits of judicial review. We are in the field of public financial administration and we are being asked to review the exercise by the Secretary of State of an administrative discretion which inevitably requires a political judgment on his part and which cannot lead to action by him against a local authority unless that action is first approved by the House of Commons.

The Secretary of State's guidance which is challenged was included in the Rate Support Grant Report for 1985–86 which was laid before and approved by the House of Commons: no payment of grant, and no reduction in the amount of grant by the Secretary of State applying a multiplier pursuant to section 59 of the Act, can be made unless covered by the report or by a supplementary report and approved by the House of Commons. I am not surprised that the trial judge and Court of Appeal declined to intervene.

My Lords, I think that the courts below were absolutely right to decline the invitation to intervene. I can understand that there may well arise a justiciable issue as to the true construction of the words of the statute and that, if the Secretary of State has issued guidance which fails to comply with the requirement of subsection (11A) of section 59 of the Act of 1980 the guidance can be quashed. But I cannot accept that it is constitutionally appropriate, save in very exceptional circumstances, for the courts to intervene on the ground of "unreasonableness" to quash guidance framed by the Secretary of State and by necessary implication approved by the House of Commons, the guidance being concerned with the limits of public expenditure by local authorities and the incidence of the tax burden as between taxpayers and ratepayers. Unless and until a statute provides otherwise, or it is established that the Secretary of State has abused his power, these are matters of political judgment for him and for the House of Commons. They are not for the judges or your Lordships' House in its judicial capacity.

For myself, I refuse in this case to examine the detail of the guidance or its consequences. My reasons are these. Such an examination by a court would be justified only if a prima facie case were to be shown for holding that the Secretary of State had acted in bad faith, or for an improper motive, or that the consequences of his guidance were so absurd that he must have taken leave of his senses. The evidence comes nowhere near establishing any of these propositions. Nobody in the case has ever suggested bad faith on the part of the Secretary of State. Nobody suggests, nor could it be suggested in the light of the evidence as to the matters he considered before reaching his decision, that he had acted for an improper motive. Nobody now suggests that the Secretary of State failed to consult local authorities in the manner required by statute. It is plain that the timetable, to which the Secretary of State in the preparation of the guidance was required by statute and compelled by circumstance to adhere, involved him necessarily in framing guidance on the basis of the past spending record of authorities. It is recognised that the Secretary of State and his advisers were well aware that there would be inequalities in the distribution of the burden between local authorities but believed that the guidance upon which he decided would by discouraging the high spending and encouraging the low spending authorities be the best course of action in the circumstances. And, as my noble and learned friend, Lord Bridge of Harwich, demonstrates, it was guidance which complied with the terms of the statute. This view of the language of the statute has inevitably a significant bearing upon the conclusion of "unreasonableness" in the *Wednesbury* sense. If, as your Lordships are holding, the guidance was based on principles applicable to all authorities, the principles would have to be either a pattern of perversity or an absurdity of such proportions that the guidance could not have been framed by a bona fide exercise of political judgment on the part of the Secretary of State. And it would be necessary to find as a fact that the House of Commons had been misled: for their approval was necessary and was obtained to the action that he proposed to take to implement the guidance.

In my judgment, therefore, the courts below acted with constitutional propriety in rejecting the so-called "*Wednesbury* unreasonableness" argument in this case . . .

"*Wednesbury* principles" is a convenient legal "shorthand" used by lawyers to refer to the classical review by Lord Greene MR in the *Wednesbury* case of the circumstances in which the courts will intervene to quash as being illegal the exercise of an administrative discretion. No question of constitutional propriety arose in the case, and the Master of the Rolls was not concerned with the constitutional limits to the exercise of judicial power in our parliamentary democracy. There is a risk, however, that the judgment of the Master of the Rolls may be treated as a complete, exhaustive, definitive statement of the law . . .

The present case raises in acute form the constitutional problem of the separation of powers between Parliament, the executive, and the courts. In this case, Parliament has enacted that an executive power is not to be exercised save with the consent and approval of one of its Houses. It is true that the framing of the guidance is for the Secretary of State alone after consultation with local authorities; but he cannot act on the guidance so as to discriminate between local authorities without reporting to, and obtaining the approval of, the House of Commons. That House has, therefore, a role and a responsibility not only at the legislative stage when the Act was passed but in the action to be taken by the Secretary of State in the exercise of the power conferred upon him by the legislation.

To sum it up, the levels of public expenditure and the incidence and distribution of taxation are matters for Parliament, and, within Parliament, especially for the House of Commons. If Parliament legislates, the courts have their interpretative role: they must, if called upon to do so, construe the statute. If a Minister exercises a power conferred on him by the legislation, the courts can investigate whether he has abused his power. But if, as in this case, effect cannot be given to the Secretary of State's determination without the consent of the House of Commons and the House of Commons has consented, it is not open to the courts to intervene unless the Minister and the House must have misconstrued the statute or the Minister has — to put it bluntly — deceived the House. The courts can properly rule that a Minister has acted unlawfully if he has erred in law as to the limits of his power even when his action has the approval of the House of Commons, itself acting not legislatively but within the limits set by a statute. But, if a statute, as in this case, requires the House of Commons to approve a Minister's decision before he can lawfully enforce it, and if the action proposed complies with the terms of the statute (as your Lordships, I understand, are convinced that it does in the present case), it is not for the judges to say that the action has such unreasonable consequences that the guidance upon which the action is based and of which the House of Commons had notice was perverse and must be set aside. For that is a question of policy for the Minister and the Commons, unless there has been bad faith or misconduct by the Minister. Where Parliament has legislated that the action to be taken by the Secretary of State must, before it is taken, be approved by the House of Commons, it is no part of the judges' role to declare that the action proposed is unfair, unless it constitutes an abuse of power in the sense which I have explained; for Parliament has enacted that one of its Houses is responsible. Judicial review is a great weapon in the hands of the judges: but the judges must observe the constitutional limits set by our parliamentary system upon their exercise of this beneficent power . . .

Lord Templeman

. . . The speech of my noble and learned friend, Lord Scarman, deals with the alternative contention by the respondent councils that the guidance issued to each of them was "unreasonable". The speech of my noble and learned friend contains a timely reminder and perceptive analysis of the principles applicable to judicial review and of the role of the courts in administrative law. The courts will not be slow to exercise the powers of judicial review in order to strike down illegality or abuse of power. The accusation of illegal conduct fails for the reasons given by my noble and learned friend, Lord Bridge of Harwich. No objective reader of the evidence filed on behalf of the department for which the Secretary of State is responsible could convict the Minister of abuse of power. The principles inspiring the 1985–86 guidance were carefully considered and evolved in the light of experience and with the obvious desire to carry out in an even-handed and equitable manner fair to all local authorities the task imposed on the Minister in the national interest of securing overall economies . . . Judicial review is not just a move in an interminable chess tournament. Although I do not blame Nottingham or Bradford for instituting these proceedings, I hope that in future local authorities will bite on the bullet and not seek to persuade the courts to absolve them from compliance with the Secretary of State's guidance. If for any particular city or for any group of cities guidance is set too low, having regard to their peculiar needs, then persuasion should be offered not to the judges, who are not qualified to listen, but to the department, the Minister, all members of parliament and ultimately to the electorate . . .

Lord Bridge delivered a speech in which he agreed with Lord Scarman. Lords Roskill and Griffiths agreed with Lord Scarman.

Two factors apparently operated to inhibit substantive review in this case: political approval of the policy and the complex nature of the economic issues involved (on which see also *R v. Secretary of State for the Environment, ex parte Hammersmith and Fulham London Borough Council* [1991] 1 AC 521). However, it is clear that, while the former may affect the intensity of judicial review, it cannot, in itself, straightforwardly remove matters from the courts' jurisdiction; this point is considered below at 17.4.3. Subsequent decisions have emphasized the latter factor as the key to understanding the *Nottinghamshire* case. Consider, for instance, the remarks of Lord Phillips MR in *R (Asif Javed) v. Secretary of State for the Home Department* [2001] EWCA Civ 789 [2002] QB 129 at [49]:

The extent to which the exercise of a statutory power is in practice open to judicial review on the ground of irrationality will depend critically on the nature and purpose of the enabling legislation. The subject matter of the legislation and the power in . . . the *Nottinghamshire* case . . . was at an extreme end of the spectrum . . . [The decision] on how to exercise the statutory power turned on political and economic considerations to be evaluated by the Minister and Parliament, whose rationality could not be measured by any yardstick available to the court. In such circumstances the statement that there was no scope for an attack on the exercise of the Secretary of State's powers on grounds of rationality in the absence of bad faith or manifest absurdity was no more than a statement of practical reality. It cannot be treated as a proposition of law applicable to any order subject to affirmative resolution . . .

This interpretation of *Nottinghamshire* points to two conclusions: that the very high level of deference to the executive in that judgment is the exception rather than the norm, and that the second *Nottinghamshire* factor — *viz* the nature of the issues raised by the exercise of the power — is key to determining the appropriate level of deference. These conclusions were affirmed by Sir Thomas Bingham MR in *R v. Ministry of Defence, ex parte Smith* [1996] QB 517 at 556 — a case, considered further below, challenging on (*inter alia*) irrationality grounds a policy (approved by both Houses of Parliament) prohibiting gays, lesbians, and bisexuals from serving in the armed forces:

It was argued for the ministry in reliance on *Reg.* v. *Secretary of State for the Environment, Ex parte Nottinghamshire County Council* [1986] A.C. 240 and *Reg.* v. *Secretary of State for the Environment, Ex parte Hammersmith and Fulham London Borough Council* [1991] 1 A.C. 521 that a test more exacting than *Wednesbury* . . . was appropriate in this case. The Divisional Court rejected this argument and so do I. The greater the policy content of a decision, and the more remote the subject matter of a decision from ordinary judicial experience, the more hesitant the court must necessarily be in holding a decision to be irrational. That is good law and, like most good law, common sense. Where decisions of a policy-laden, esoteric or security-based nature are in issue even greater caution than normal must be shown in applying the test, but the test itself is sufficiently flexible to cover all situations.

The reverse side of the deference coin is that, in some circumstances, courts are willing to evaluate the reasonableness of decisions more rigorously than usual. This point assumed particular prominence in the late 1980s and 1990s in cases concerning human rights. Most such cases would now fall to be decided under the Human Rights Act 1998, which we examine below at 9.3; it is, however, necessary to understand something of the courts' pre-HRA jurisprudence in order to contextualize the current position. An early and prominent example of this approach is supplied by the House of Lords' decision in *R v. Secretary of State for the Home Department, ex parte Brind* [1991] 1 AC 696, in which it was (unsuccessfully) contended that executive acts which effectively precluded live broadcast interviews with representatives of certain terrorist organizations were *Wednesbury* unreasonable. Their Lordships refused directly to apply Article 10 of the European Convention on Human Rights, which protects freedom of expression, on the ground that the Convention had not been incorporated into domestic law. However, Lord Bridge (at 748), building on his speech in *R v. Secretary of State for the Home Department, ex parte Bugdaycay* [1987] AC 514 at 531, did not

accept that this conclusion means that the courts are powerless to prevent the exercise by the executive of administrative discretions, even when conferred, as in the instant case, in terms which are on their face unlimited, in a way which infringes fundamental human rights. Most of the rights spelled out in terms in the Convention, including the right to freedom of expression, are less than absolute and must in some cases yield to the claims of competing public interests. Thus, article 10(2) of the Convention spells out and categorises the competing public interests by reference to which the right to freedom of expression may have to be curtailed. In exercising the power of judicial review we have neither the advantages nor the disadvantages of any comparable code to which we may refer or by which we are bound. But again, this surely does not mean that in deciding whether the Secretary of State, in the exercise of his discretion, could reasonably impose the restriction he has imposed on the broadcasting organisations, we are not perfectly entitled to start from the premise that any restriction of the right to freedom of expression requires to be justified and that nothing less than an important competing public interest will be sufficient to justify it. The primary judgment as to whether the particular competing public interest justifies the particular restriction imposed falls to be made by the Secretary of State to whom Parliament has entrusted the discretion. But we are entitled to exercise a secondary judgment by asking whether a reasonable Secretary of State, on the material before him, could reasonably make that primary judgment.

This decision marks an important stage in the development of substantive review, given its explicit acknowledgment of the possibility of a more rigorous form of review in some contexts. Indeed, by requiring the reviewing court to address (to some extent) the balance between a fundamental right and a competing public interest, Lord Bridge went some distance towards adopting the methodology which the proportionality principle embraces (on which see below at 9.3.2). However, when the Divisional Court and the Court of Appeal revisited this issue in the *Smith* case, it became clear that the *Wednesbury* doctrine, even when adapted to the human rights context, was still shot through with a judicial ethos of self-restraint which placed significant restrictions on the reviewing court.

R v. Ministry of Defence, ex parte Smith [1996] QB 517
Divisional Court and Court of Appeal

Pursuant to the policy then in force, which had been debated and supported by both Houses of Parliament and by a select committee, the claimants were dismissed from the armed forces on the sole ground that they were of homosexual orientation. The claimants challenged the decisions to dismiss them, and the policy on which those decisions were based, arguing (*inter alia*) that they were irrational. The claimants were unsuccessful in both the Divisional Court and the Court of Appeal. The present excerpts are concerned only with the standard of substantive review applied by those courts.

Sir Thomas Bingham MR (in the Court of Appeal)

. . . Mr. David Pannick, who represented three of the applicants, and whose arguments were adopted by the fourth, submitted that the court should adopt the following approach to the issue of irrationality:

"The court may not interfere with the exercise of an administrative discretion on substantive grounds save where the court is satisfied that the decision is unreasonable in the sense that it is beyond the range of responses open to a reasonable decision-maker. But in judging whether the decision-maker has exceeded this margin of appreciation the human rights context is important. The more substantial the interference with human rights, the more the court will require by way of justification before it is satisfied that the decision is reasonable in the sense outlined above."

This submission is in my judgment an accurate distillation of the principles laid down by the House of Lords in *Reg. v. Secretary of State for the Home Department, Ex parte Bugdaycay* [1987] A.C. 514 and *Reg. v. Secretary of State for the Home Department, Ex parte Brind* [1991] 1 A.C. 696 . . .

The present cases do not affect the lives or liberty of those involved. But they do concern innate qualities of a very personal kind and the decisions of which the applicants complain have had a profound effect on their careers and prospects. The applicants' rights as human beings are very much in issue. It is now accepted that this issue is justiciable. This does not of course mean that the court is thrust into the position of the primary decision-maker. It is not the constitutional role of the court to regulate the conditions of service in the armed forces of the Crown, nor has it the expertise to do so. But it has the constitutional role and duty of ensuring that the rights of citizens are not abused by the unlawful exercise of executive power. While the court must properly defer to the expertise of responsible decision-makers, it must not shrink from its fundamental duty to "do right to all manner of people" . . .

Simon Brown LJ (in the Divisional Court)

. . . I approach the case, therefore, on the conventional *Wednesbury* basis adapted to a human rights context and ask: can the Secretary of State show an important competing public interest which he could reasonably judge sufficient to justify the restriction? The primary judgment is for him. Only if his purported justification outrageously defies logic or accepted moral standards can the court, exercising its secondary judgment, properly strike it down . . .

I do not pretend to have found this an easy case. On the contrary I recall none harder. The protection of human rights is, Mr. Pannick submits, a matter with which the courts are particularly concerned and for which they have an undoubted responsibility. So they do. But they owe a duty too to remain within their constitutional bounds and not trespass beyond them. Only if it were plain beyond sensible argument that no conceivable damage could be done to the armed services as a fighting unit would it be appropriate for this court now to remove the issue entirely from the hands both of the military and of the government. If the Convention for the Protection of Human Rights and Fundamental Freedoms were part of our law and we were accordingly entitled to ask whether the policy answers a pressing social need and whether the restriction on human rights involved can be shown proportionate to its benefits, then clearly the primary judgment (subject only to a limited "margin of appreciation") would be for us and not others: the constitutional balance would shift. But that is not the position. In exercising merely a secondary judgment, this court is bound, even though adjudicating in a human rights context, to act with some reticence. Our approach must reflect, not overlook, where responsibility ultimately lies for the defence of the realm, and recognise too that Parliament is exercising a continuing supervision over this area of prerogative power.

With all these considerations in mind, I have come finally to the conclusion that, my own view of the evidence notwithstanding, the Minister's stance cannot properly be held unlawful. His suggested justification for the ban may to many seem unconvincing; to say, however, that it is outrageous in its defiance of logic is another thing. There is, I conclude, still room for two views. Similarly it is difficult to regard the policy as wholly incompatible with "accepted moral standards". There is no present uniformity of outlook on this issue: not everyone would condemn the ban on moral grounds, morally neutral though the ministry avow their own stance to be . . .

Two points should be noted about this case. First, it is of interest that some features of the factual matrix (principally the national security context) pointed towards judicial deference, while others (notably the impact of the policy on the claimants' human rights) pointed in the opposite direction. This phenomenon — which is far from unusual — calls for a more sophisticated doctrine of deference: it explodes the myth that the intensity of judicial review can be set by deciding that a particular case is 'about national security' or 'about human rights'. The form which such a doctrine of deference might take is considered below at 9.3.5 and 9.3.6. The second notable feature of *Smith* is that (as in *Brind*) the courts were only willing to go so far in restricting the decision-maker's latitude by means of an especially rigorous application of the *Wednesbury* test. It is particularly apparent from Simon Brown LJ's judgment in *Smith* that a perceived need to preserve the distinction between appeal and review — and, hence, to respect (a particular conception of) the separation of powers principle — heavily circumscribed judicial scrutiny of the policy. The claimants in *Smith* eventually took their case to the European Court of Human Rights which, as we shall below at 9.3.2, adopted a different approach.

9.3 Proportionality as a Principle of Review

In this section we compare the *Wednesbury* test with that of proportionality (on which see generally Craig in Ellis (ed), *The Principle of Proportionality in the Laws of Europe* (Oxford 1999), exploring points of difference (and, occasionally, similarity). The precise meaning of proportionality is elaborated in the remainder of this chapter but, to begin with, a working definition is called for. In *De Freitas* v. *Permanent Secretary of Ministry of Agriculture, Fisheries, Lands and Housing* [1999] 1 AC 69 at 80, Lord Clyde advanced a tripartite test — since endorsed by the House of Lords in *R (Daly)* v. *Secretary of State for the Home Department* [2001] UKHL 26 [2001] 2 AC 532 — according to which the court, in deciding whether a measure is proportionate, should ask itself

whether: (i) the legislative objective is sufficiently important to justify limiting a fundamental right; (ii) the measures designed to meet the legislative objective are rationally connected to it; and (iii) the means used to impair the right or freedom are no more than is necessary to accomplish the objective.

The proportionality test is also used in European Community law to assess the legality of Community and member state action which qualifies certain freedoms and interests recognized by Community law, as Tridimas, *The General Principles of EC Law* (Oxford 1999) at 91, explains:

. . . [I]n order to establish whether a provision of Community law is consonant with the principle of proportionality, it is necessary to establish whether the means it employs to achieve the aim correspond to the importance of the aim and whether they are necessary for its achievement. Thus, the principle comprises two tests: a test of suitability and a test of necessity. The first refers to the relationship between the means and the end. The means employed by the measure must be suitable, namely reasonably likely, to achieve its objectives. The second is one of weighing competing interests. The Court assesses the adverse consequences that the measure has on an interest worthy of legal protection and determines whether those consequences are justified in view of the importance of the objective pursued.

The perceived advantages of the proportionality test are intimately bound up with criticisms of *Wednesbury*; we begin with the latter.

9.3.1 The Methodology of *Wednesbury* Review

The reasonableness principle occupied a central place in English administrative law by setting a standard of substantive review which reflects traditional thinking about how judges and administrators should relate to one another. But the *Wednesbury* doctrine has, in recent years, been subjected to a good deal of criticism. Although numerous charges have been levelled against *Wednesbury*, the central complaints concern its *methodology* and the *substantive* level of review which it supplies.

The methodological critique is centrally concerned with transparency. It is argued that

Wednesbury review lacks this quality, because a finding of unreasonableness (or, for that matter, reasonableness) risks creating the impression of judicial decision-making by intuition since such a conclusion may be unaccompanied by any structured explanation of the judicial reasoning process which yielded it. This, to an extent, is a function of the circularity of the traditional test: if the 'unreasonable' decision is defined simply in terms of that which no reasonable decision-maker would reach, then little scope exists for the elaboration of a structured and transparent judicial decision-making process. The test, viewed in this way, naturally encourages an intuitive adjudicative method. Craig, *op cit* at 99–100, underscores this point by contrasting *Wednesbury* with the proportionality test:

Proportionality provides a more structured analysis of the kind which is often lacking under the *Wednesbury* formula . . . [Its] more structured analysis has a beneficial effect in that it requires the administration to justify its policy choice more specifically than under the traditional *Wednesbury* approach. The structure provided by the proportionality inquiry is also beneficial in relation to the courts themselves. It requires that the courts, when striking down a decision, do so on grounds which are more readily identifiable and ascertainable than is often the case under the *Wednesbury* test. This is of particular relevance given [the mismatch between the rhetoric and reality of *Wednesbury* review] . . . If it is accepted that our courts, even in cases which do not involve rights, are in reality applying *Wednesbury* more intrusively than the bare words of the test would suggest, and if it is also the case that this requires some balancing [of interests], whether explicit or implicit, then this should be as transparent as possible. The reasoning process provided by proportionality renders this more likely to occur [than the comparatively unstructured *Wednesbury* process] . . .

The transparency problem is particularly acute because of its self-evident capacity to obscure the normative foundation of substantive review. As well as understanding the structure of the courts' reasoning process, we also want to know what substantive norms the court is protecting through a finding of unreasonableness. A mere finding of 'unreasonableness' does not convey anything very particular about *why* the decision in question is objectionable, or about which values it infringes. Adherence to *Wednesbury* therefore permits the courts to vindicate (or not, as the case may be) substantive norms without necessarily identifying them explicitly, as Jowell and Lester [1987] *PL* 368 at 372 explain:

. . . [T]he *Wednesbury* test is confusing, because it is tautologous. It allows the courts to interfere with decisions that are unreasonable, and then defines an unreasonable decision as one which no reasonable authority would take . . . [This test] is unhelpful as a practical guide . . . The incantation of the word 'unreasonable' simply does not provide sufficient justification for judicial intervention. Intellectual honesty requires a further and better explanation as to *why* the act is unreasonable. The reluctance to articulate a principled justification naturally encourages suspicion that prejudice and policy considerations may be hiding underneath *Wednesbury*'s ample cloak . . .

The case of *Wheeler* v. *Leicester City Council* [1985] AC 1054 usefully illustrates the manner in which *Wednesbury* review can obscure the normative foundations of judicial decisions. The defendant authority invited a rugby club to condemn the participation of some of its players in a tour of South Africa during the apartheid era. The club refused to do so: it condemned apartheid, but considered that there were differences of opinion as to how best to break it down and that the members had individual choice as to where to play. Purporting to act under discretionary powers to regulate the use of its own land and pursuant to its general statutory duty to promote good race relations, the council passed a resolution banning the club from using its recreation ground for 12 months. In the Court of Appeal, Browne-Wilkinson LJ (whose minority conclusion was later upheld by the House of Lords) clearly articulated the normative issues at stake (at 1063–1065):

. . . [I]t is undoubtedly part of the constitution of this country that, in the absence of express legislative provision to the contrary, each individual has the right to hold and express his own views . . .

. . . Basic constitutional rights in this country such as freedom of the person and freedom of speech are based not on any express provision conferring such a right but on freedom of an individual to do what he will save to the extent that he is prevented from so doing by the law. Thus, freedom of the person depends on the fact that no one has the right lawfully to arrest the individual save in defined circumstances. The right to freedom of speech depends on the fact that no one has the right to stop the individual expressing his own views, save to the extent that those views are libellous or seditious. These fundamental freedoms therefore are not positive rights but an immunity from interference by others. Accordingly I do not consider that general words in an act of Parliament can be taken as authorising interference with these basic immunities which are the foundation of our freedom. Parliament (being sovereign) can legislate so as to do so; but it cannot be taken to have conferred such a right on others save by express words . . .

For these reasons when Parliament confers general discretionary powers on public authorities it cannot in general be taken to have contemplated that such discretions can be exercised by taking into account the lawful views of those affected by the exercise of the discretions or their willingness to express certain views. If in exercising such discretions these factors have been taken into account, the exercise of the discretion is unlawful since a legally irrelevant factor has been taken into account.

Although couched in the familiar language of irrelevant considerations, this analysis is striking for the clarity with which it identifies the values in play. It stands in sharp contrast to the following comments (at 1078–1079) of Lord Roskill (whose speech commanded the assent of three of the other judges in the House of Lords):

To my mind the crucial question is whether the conduct of the council in trying by . . . [the] questions [which they asked of the club], whether taken individually or collectively, to force acceptance by the club of their own policy (however proper that policy may be) on their own terms, as for example, by forcing them to lend their considerable prestige to a public condemnation of the tour, can be said either to be so "unreasonable" as to give rise to "*Wednesbury* unreasonableness" (*Associated Provincial Picture Houses Ltd. v. Wednesbury Corporation* [1948] 1 K.B. 223) or to be so fundamental a breach of the duty to act fairly which rests upon every local authority in matters of this kind and thus justify interference by the courts.

I do not for one moment doubt the great importance which the council attach to the presence in their midst of a 25 per cent. population of persons who are either Asian or of Afro-Caribbean origin. Nor do I doubt for one moment the sincerity of the view expressed in Mr. Soulsby's affidavit [sworn on behalf of the council] regarding the need for the council to distance itself from bodies who hold important positions and who do not actively discourage sporting contacts with South Africa. Persuasion, even powerful persuasion, is always a permissible way of seeking to obtain an objective. But in a field where other views can equally legitimately be held, persuasion, however powerful, must not be allowed to cross that line where it moves into the field of illegitimate pressure coupled with the threat of sanctions. The [council's] questions, coupled with the insistence that only affirmative answers to all four would be acceptable, are suggestive of more than powerful persuasion. The second question [did the club agree that the tour was an insult to a large proportion of the local population?] is to my mind open to particular criticism. What, in the context, is meant by "the club?" The committee? 90 playing members? 4,300 non-playing members? It by no means follows that the committee would all have agreed on an affirmative answer to the question and still less that a majority of their members, playing or non-playing, would have done so. Nor would any of these groups of members necessarily have known whether "the large proportion," whatever that phrase may mean in the context, of the Leicester population would have regarded the tour as "an insult" to them.

None of the learned judges in the courts below have felt able to hold that the action of the club was unreasonable or perverse in the *Wednesbury* sense. They do not appear to have been invited to consider whether those actions, even if not unreasonable on *Wednesbury* principles, were assailable on the grounds of procedural impropriety or unfairness by the council in the manner in which, in the light of the facts which I have outlined, they took their decision to suspend for 12 months the use by the club of the Welford Road recreation ground.

I greatly hesitate to differ from four learned judges on the *Wednesbury* issue but for myself I would have been disposed respectfully to do this and to say that the actions of the council were unreasonable in the *Wednesbury* sense . . .

QUESTIONS

- Why did Lord Roskill consider the decision to be *Wednesbury* unreasonable?
- Is his explanation adequate?

9.3.2 *Wednesbury*, Proportionality, and the Intensity of Review

Criticism of the *Wednesbury* test is not limited to its *methodological* inadequacies. At a *substantive* level, it is contended that *Wednesbury* supplies a standard of review which is too deferential. While deference may be manifestly appropriate in some situations, it is argued that where strict scrutiny is called for — paradigmatically in human rights cases — the reasonableness test is incapable of rising to the challenge. This argument is substantiated by our next case (for comment on which see Hare [2000] *CLJ* 6). As you read it, consider how the Strasbourg Court's approach differs from that of the English courts in *Smith*.

Smith v. *United Kingdom* (2000) 29 EHRR 493
European Court of Human Rights

Having failed in the domestic courts (and having been denied leave to appeal to the House of Lords) the claimants in *R* v. *Ministry of Defence, ex parte Smith* (see above at 9.2.2) took their case to the European Court of Human Rights. The Court considered (*inter alia*) whether the applicants' right to respect for private life under Article 8 ECHR had been unlawfully infringed, and whether judicial review in domestic law was an effective remedy, as required by Article 13. The Court applied the proportionality test. Having decided that the policy *interfered* with respect for the applicants' private life as recognized by Article 8(1) but that such interference served one of the *legitimate aims* as set out in Article 8(2) (*viz* the interests of national security and the prevention of disorder), the Court went on to consider whether the interference was *necessary in a democratic society*. The following excerpt illustrates the closeness with which the ECtHR examined that matter.

Judgment of the Court

[87] An interference will be considered "necessary in a democratic society" for a legitimate aim if it answers a pressing social need and, in particular, is proportionate to the legitimate aim pursued. Given the matters at issue in the present case, the Court would underline the link between the

notion of "necessity" and that of a "democratic society", the hallmarks of the latter including plural-ism, tolerance and broadmindedness.

[88] The Court recognises that it is for the national authorities to make the initial assessment of necessity, though the final evaluation as to whether the reasons cited for the interference are relevant and sufficient is one for this Court. A margin of appreciation is left open to Contracting States in the context of this assessment, which varies according to the nature of the activities restricted and of the aims pursued by the restrictions.

[89] Accordingly, when the relevant restrictions concern "a most intimate part of an individual's private life", there must exist "particularly serious reasons" before such interferences can satisfy the requirements of Article 8(2) of the Convention [*Dudgeon* v. *United Kingdom* (1982) 4 EHRR 149 at [52]]. When the core of the national security aim pursued is the operational effectiveness of the armed forces, it is accepted that each State is competent to organise its own system of military discipline and enjoys a certain margin of appreciation in this respect. The Court also considers that it is open to the State to impose restrictions on an individual's right to respect for his private life where there is a real threat to the armed forces' operational effectiveness, as the proper function-ing of an army is hardly imaginable without legal rules designed to prevent service personnel from undermining it. However, the national authorities cannot rely on such rules to frustrate the exercise by individual members of the armed forces of their right to respect for their private lives, which right applies to service personnel as it does to others within the jurisdiction of the State. Moreover, assertions as to a risk to operational effectiveness must be "substantiated by specific examples" [*Vereinigung Demokratischer Soldaten Osterreichs* v. *Austria* (1995) 20 EHRR 56 at [36] and [38]] . . .

[90] It is common ground that the sole reason for the investigations conducted and for the applicants' discharge was their sexual orientation. Concerning as it did a most intimate aspect of an individual's private life, particularly serious reasons by way of justification were required . . . [T]he Court finds the interferences to have been especially grave for the following reasons.

[The reasons highlighted by the Court included the 'exceptionally intrusive character' of the investigation process; the 'profound effect on their careers and prospects' of the applicants' dis-charges, and the 'absolute and general character of the policy', which operated 'irrespective of the individual's conduct or service record'.]

[94] Accordingly, the Court must consider whether, taking account of the margin of appreciation open to the State in matters of national security, particularly convincing and weighty reasons exist by way of justification for the interferences with the applicants' right to respect for their private lives.

[95] The core argument of the Government in support of the policy is that the presence of open or suspected homosexuals in the armed forces would have a substantial and negative effect on morale and, consequently, on the fighting power and operational effectiveness of the armed forces. The Government rely in this respect on the report of the HPAT [the Homosexuality Policy Assess-ment Team, established by the Ministry of Defence to assess the policy] . . . Although the Court acknowledges the complexity of the study undertaken by the HPAT, it entertains certain doubts as to the value of the HPAT report for present purposes. The independence of the assessment con-tained in the report is open to question given that it was completed by Ministry of Defence civil servants and service personnel . . . and given the approach to the policy outlined in the letter circulated by the Ministry of Defence in August 1995 to management levels in the armed forces [which suggested that the objective of the HPAT report was to furnish evidence for the purposes of

defending the policy against attack in the Strasbourg Court] . . . In addition, on any reading of the report and the methods used . . . only a very small proportion of the armed forces' personnel participated in the assessment. Moreover, many of the methods of assessment (including the consultation with policy-makers in the Ministry of Defence, one-to-one interviews and the focus group discussions) were not anonymous. It also appears that many of the questions in the attitude survey suggested answers in support of the policy.

[96] Even accepting that the views on the matter which were expressed to the HPAT may be considered representative, the Court finds that the perceived problems which were identified in the HPAT report as a threat to the fighting power and operational effectiveness of the armed forces were founded solely upon the negative attitudes of heterosexual personnel towards those of homosexual orientation. The Court observes, in this respect, that no moral judgment is made on homosexuality by the policy . . . It is also accepted by the Government that neither the records nor conduct of the applicants nor the physical capability, courage, dependability and skills of homosexuals in general are in any way called into question by the policy.

[97] The question for the Court is whether the above-noted negative attitudes constitute sufficient justification for the interferences at issue. The Court observes from the HPAT report that these attitudes, even if sincerely felt by those who expressed them, ranged from stereotypical expressions of hostility to those of homosexual orientation, to vague expressions of unease about the presence of homosexual colleagues. To the extent that they represent a predisposed bias on the part of a heterosexual majority against a homosexual minority, these negative attitudes cannot, of themselves, be considered by the Court to amount to sufficient justification for the interferences with the applicants' rights outlined above any more than similar negative attitudes towards those of a different race, origin or colour.

[98] The Government emphasised that the views expressed in the HPAT report served to show that any change in the policy would entail substantial damage to morale and operational effectiveness. The applicants considered these submissions to be unsubstantiated.

[99] The Court notes the lack of concrete evidence to substantiate the alleged damage to morale and fighting power that any change in the policy would entail. Thorpe L.J. in the Court of Appeal found that there was no actual or significant evidence of such damage as a result of the presence of homosexuals in the armed forces, and the Court further considers that the subsequent HPAT assessment did not, whatever its value, provide evidence of such damage in the event of the policy changing. Given the number of homosexuals dismissed between 1991 and 1996 [361], the number of homosexuals who were in the armed forces at the relevant time cannot be said to be insignificant. Even if the absence of such evidence can be explained by the consistent application of the policy, as submitted by the Government, this is insufficient to demonstrate to the Court's satisfaction that operational effectiveness problems of the nature and level alleged can be anticipated in the absence of the policy.

[100] However, in the light of the strength of feeling expressed in certain submissions to the HPAT and the special, interdependent and closely knit nature of the armed forces' environment, the Court considers it reasonable to assume that some difficulties could be anticipated as a result of any change in what is now a long-standing policy. Indeed, it would appear that the presence of women and racial minorities in the armed forces led to relational difficulties of the kind which the Government suggest admission of homosexuals would entail.

[101] The applicants submitted that a strict code of conduct applicable to all personnel would

address any potential difficulties caused by negative attitudes of heterosexuals. The Government, while not rejecting the possibility out of hand, emphasised the need for caution given the subject matter and the armed forces context of the policy . . .

[102] The Court considers it important to note, in the first place, the approach already adopted by the armed forces to deal with racial discrimination and with racial and sexual harassment and bullying . . . [Measures introduced in 1996], for example, imposed both a strict code of conduct on every soldier together with disciplinary rules to deal with any inappropriate behaviour and conduct. This dual approach was supplemented with information leaflets and training programmes, the army emphasising the need for high standards of personal conduct and for respect for others. The Government, nevertheless, underlined that it is "the knowledge or suspicion of homosexuality" which would cause the morale problems and not conduct, so that a conduct code would not solve the anticipated difficulties. However, in so far as negative attitudes to homosexuality are insuffi-cient, of themselves, to justify the policy . . ., they are equally insufficient to justify the rejection of a proposed alternative. In any event, the Government themselves recognised during the hearing that the choice between a conduct code and the maintenance of the policy lay at the heart of the judgment to be made in this case. This is also consistent with the Government's direct reliance on Section F of the HPAT's report where the anticipated problems identified as posing a risk to morale were almost exclusively problems related to behaviour and conduct. The Government maintained that homosexuality raised problems of a type and intensity that race and gender did not. However, even if it can be assumed that the integration of homosexuals would give rise to problems not encountered with the integration of women or racial minorities, the Court is not satisfied that the codes and rules which have been found to be effective in the latter case would not equally prove effective in the former. The "robust indifference" reported by the HPAT of the large number of British armed forces' personnel serving abroad with allied forces to homosexuals serving in those foreign forces, serves to confirm that the perceived problems of integration are not insuperable.

[103] The Government highlighted particular problems which might be posed by the communal accommodation arrangements in the armed forces. Detailed submissions were made during the hearing, the parties disagreeing as to the potential consequences of shared single-sex accommoda-tion and associated facilities. The Court notes that the HPAT itself concluded that separate accom-modation for homosexuals would not be warranted or wise and that substantial expenditure would not, therefore, have to be incurred in this respect. Nevertheless, the Court remains of the view that it has not been shown that the conduct codes and disciplinary rules referred to above could not adequately deal with any behavioural issues arising on the part either of homosexuals or of heterosexuals.

[104] The Government, referring to the relevant analysis in the HPAT report, further argued that no worthwhile lessons could be gleaned from the relatively recent legal changes in those foreign armed forces which now admitted homosexuals. The Court disagrees. It notes the evidence before the domestic courts to the effect that the European countries operating a blanket legal ban on homosexuals in their armed forces are now in a small minority. It considers that, even if relatively recent, the Court cannot overlook the widespread and consistently developing views and associated legal changes to the domestic laws of Contracting States on this issue.

[105] Accordingly, the Court concludes that convincing and weighty reasons have not been offered by the Government to justify the policy against homosexuals in the armed forces or, therefore, the consequent discharge of the applicants from those forces . . .

[The Court then considered whether there had been a violation of Article 13:]

[130] The Government maintained . . . that proceedings by way of judicial review afforded an effective remedy to the applicants. The applicants were able to, and did, advance the substance of the Convention arguments before the domestic courts which were, in turn, relied upon by the applicants before this Court. Any difference between the judicial review test and the test under the Convention was not central to the issues in this case and the essential reasoning of the Court of Appeal mirrored that which underpinned the Convention margin of appreciation. Both the domestic courts and the Convention organs retained a supervisory role to ensure that the State did not abuse its powers or exceed its margin of appreciation . . .

[136] The Court has found that the applicants' right to respect for their private lives was violated by the investigations conducted and by the discharge of the applicants pursuant to the policy of the Ministry of Defence against homosexuals in the armed forces. As was made clear by the High Court and the Court of Appeal in the judicial review proceedings, since the Convention did not form part of English law, questions as to whether the application of the policy violated the applicants' rights under Article 8 and, in particular, as to whether the policy had been shown by the authorities to respond to a pressing social need or to be proportionate to any legitimate aim served, were not questions to which answers could properly be offered. The sole issue before the domestic courts was whether the policy could be said to be "irrational".

[137] The test of "irrationality" applied in the present case was that explained in the judgment of Sir Thomas Bingham M.R.: a court was not entitled to interfere with the exercise of an administrative discretion on substantive grounds save where the court was satisfied that the decision was unreasonable in the sense that it was beyond the range of responses open to a reasonable decision-maker. In judging whether the decision-maker had exceeded this margin of appreciation, the human rights context was important, so that the more substantial the interference with human rights, the more the court would require by way of justification before it was satisfied that the decision was reasonable. It was, however, further emphasised that, notwithstanding any human rights context, the threshold of irrationality which an applicant was required to surmount was a high one. This is, in the view of the Court, confirmed by the judgments of the High Court and the Court of Appeal themselves. The Court notes that the main judgments in both courts commented favourably on the applicants' submissions challenging the reasons advanced by the Government in justification of the policy. Simon Brown L.J. considered that the balance of argument lay with the applicants and that their arguments in favour of a conduct-based code were powerful. Sir Thomas Bingham M.R. found that those submissions of the applicants were of "very considerable cogency" and that they fell to be considered in depth with particular reference to the potential effectiveness of a conduct-based code. Furthermore, while offering no conclusive views on the Convention issues raised by the case, Simon Brown L.J. expressed the opinion that "the days of the policy were numbered" in light of the United Kingdom's Convention obligations, and Sir Thomas Bingham M.R. observed that the investigations and the discharge of the applicants did not appear to show respect for their private lives. He considered that there might be room for argument as to whether there had been a disproportionate interference with their rights under Article 8 of the Convention. Nevertheless, both courts concluded that the policy could not be said to be beyond the range of responses open to a reasonable decision-maker and, accordingly, could not be considered to be "irrational".

[138] In such circumstances, the Court considers it clear that, even assuming that the essential complaints of the applicants before this Court were before and considered by the domestic courts, the threshold at which the High Court and the Court of Appeal could find the Ministry of Defence policy irrational was placed so high that it effectively excluded any consideration by the domestic courts of the question of whether the interference with the applicants' rights answered a pressing

social need or was proportionate to the national security and public order aims pursued, principles which lie at the heart of the Court's analysis of complaints under Article 8 of the Convention . . .

The ECtHR concluded that there had been a breach of Article 8 and, by a majority, that there had been a breach of Article 13.

QUESTIONS

• Exactly how does this decision of the ECtHR differ, in terms of the structure and intensity of the review, from the approach adopted by the English courts in *Smith*?
• Which approach is, in your view, better?

9.3.3 Towards Proportionality

The scope under proportionality for rigorous scrutiny of the putative justifications for measures which infringe human rights or other sufficiently highly-regarded interests led some judges to argue strongly *against* its adoption in English law, contending that its use would be incompatible with received perceptions of the separation of powers and the (related) distinction between appeal and review. For instance, in *R* v. *Secretary of State for the Home Department, ex parte Brind* [1991] 1 AC 696 at 766–767, Lord Lowry considered that

there is *no* authority for saying that proportionality . . . is part of the English common law and a great deal of authority the other way. This, so far as I am concerned, is not a cause for regret for several reasons: 1. The decision-makers, very often elected, are those to whom Parliament has entrusted the discretion and to interfere with that discretion beyond the limits as hitherto defined would itself be an abuse of the judges' supervisory jurisdiction. 2. The judges are not, generally speaking, equipped by training or experience, or furnished with the requisite knowledge and advice, to decide the answer to an administrative problem where the scales are evenly balanced, but they have a much better chance of reaching the right answer where the question is put in a *Wednesbury* form. The same applies if the judges' decision is appealed. 3. Stability and relative certainty would be jeopardised if the new doctrine held sway, because there is nearly always something to be said against any administrative decision and parties who felt aggrieved would be even more likely than at present to try their luck with a judicial review application both at first instance and on appeal. 4. The increase in applications for judicial review of administrative action (inevitable if the threshold of unreasonableness is lowered) will lead to the expenditure of time and money by litigants, not to speak of the prolongation of uncertainty for all concerned with the decisions in question, and the taking up of court time which could otherwise be devoted to other matters. The losers in this respect will be members of the public, for whom the courts provide a service . . .

It finally occurs to me that there can be very little room for judges to operate an independent judicial review proportionality doctrine in the space which is left between the conventional judicial review doctrine and the admittedly forbidden appellate approach. To introduce an intermediate area of deliberation for the court seems scarcely a practical idea, quite apart from the other disadvantages by which, in my opinion, such a course would be attended.

Two related premises underpin Lord Lowry's concerns. First, he advances the normative argument that the traditional *Wednesbury* approach represents the correct balance between judicial intervention and agency autonomy. Secondly, he concludes that the proportionality test strikes a different — and therefore incorrect — balance between those two factors, such that it would destroy the distinction between appeal and review. (Lord Ackner, at 762–763, shared this sentiment, opining that, 'The European [proportionality] test of "whether the 'interference' complained of corresponds to a 'pressing social need' " (*The Sunday Times* v. *United Kingdom* (1979) 2 EHRR 245, 277) must ultimately result in the question "Is the particular decision acceptable?" and this must involve a review of the merits of the decision.') We will see in the remainder of this chapter that the first premise reflects a view that is not widely shared, while the second derives from an inaccurate and incomplete understanding of the concept of proportionality.

In spite of concerns such as those voiced by Lords Ackner and Lowry in *Brind*, it is clear that even before the activation of the Human Rights Act 1998 — to which we turn shortly — English administrative law was beginning to embrace the concept of proportionality (or something like it). For instance, we noted above at 9.3 that proportionality operates as a general principle of EC law. This means (*inter alia*) that where, in cases concerning EC law, the conduct of national authorities impacts upon certain values and freedoms highly regarded by Community law, the legality of such conduct falls to be tested by reference to the proportionality doctrine. Thus, for instance, in *R* v. *Chief Constable of Sussex, ex parte International Traders' Ferry* [1999] 2 AC 418, it was necessary to determine whether a decision, taken for reasons of public policy, which had the effect of impeding exports from Britain to other member states constituted a disproportionate restriction on the free movement of goods under Article 29 EC. The House of Lords, like other British courts required to apply the proportionality test in EC cases, managed to do so without any apparent difficulty.

While proportionality has for some time been explicitly applied in cases concerning EC law, its entry into general administrative law occurred more subtly and gradually. The Divisional Court and the Court of Appeal in *Smith* (see above at 9.2.2) undertook a major revision of the *Wednesbury* test which, while not going as far as the ECtHR's application of proportionality *per se*, exhibited the essential characteristics of the latter in terms of both structured analysis and the normative demand for greater justification where important rights are in play. (See further on this point Elliott [2001] *CLJ* 301; Craig (in Ellis (ed), *The Principle of Proportionality in the Laws of Europe* (Oxford 1999) at 98–99.)

Elements of the proportionality test were evident in other cases, too. *R* v. *Secretary of State for the Home Department, ex parte Leech* [1994] QB 198 concerned a challenge to rule 33(3) of the Prison Rules 1964 (made under s 47 of the Prisons Act 1952) which conferred upon prison governors a wide discretionary power to read, examine, and censor prisoners' correspondence 'on the ground that its contents are objectionable or that it is of inordinate length'. The claimant contended that correspondence with his legal advisor about the possibility of legal proceedings was being censored. Giving the judgment of the Court of Appeal, Steyn LJ accepted that access to court is a constitutional right and that uninhibited communication with a legal advisor is an inherent part of that right; it followed (at 213–214) that

section 47(1) must be interpreted as conferring by necessary implication a power to make rules to achieve the stated objectives [*eg* establishing a framework for the regulation and management of prisons]. We are satisfied that this implied power is wide enough to comprehend rules permitting the examining and reading of correspondence passing between a prisoner and his solicitor in order to ascertain whether it is in truth bona fide correspondence between a prisoner and a solicitor and to stop letters which fail such scrutiny. But it is a rule in much wider terms that needs to be justified . . . [Counsel for the defendant's affidavit] goes no further than establishing the need for prison authorities to have the power to ascertain that purported exchanges between a prisoner and a solicitor are genuine communications between a client and solicitor, and to stop letters which fail such scrutiny. To that extent there is no dispute in this case. But there is nothing in [the] affidavit, or in counsel's arguments, which establish that objectively there is a need in the interests of the proper regulation of prisons for a rule of the width of rule 33(3).

This notion that measures affecting fundamental rights must be objectively justified was developed by Lord Steyn, as he had by then become, in *R* v. *Secretary of State for the Home Department, ex parte Simms* [2000] 2 AC 115 at 125–131 — another prisons case, this time concerning a blanket policy prohibiting prisoners from giving interviews to journalists. The legality of that policy was successfully challenged by prisoners who wished to give interviews to investigative journalists in order to contend their innocence. Lord Steyn stated:

The starting point is the right of freedom of expression. In a democracy it is the primary right: without it an effective rule of law is not possible. Nevertheless, freedom of expression is not an absolute right. Sometimes it must yield to other cogent social interests . . .

The value of free speech in a particular case must be measured in specifics. Not all types of speech have an equal value. For example, no prisoner would ever be permitted to have interviews with a journalist to publish pornographic material or to give vent to so-called hate speech. Given the purpose of a sentence of imprisonment, a prisoner can also not claim to join in a debate on the economy or on political issues by way of interviews with journalists. In these respects the prisoner's right to free speech is outweighed by deprivation of liberty by the sentence of a court, and the need for discipline and control in prisons. But the free speech at stake in the present cases is qualitatively of a very different order. The prisoners are in prison because they are presumed to have been properly convicted. They wish to challenge the safety of their convictions. In principle it is not easy to conceive of a more important function which free speech might fulfil . . .

[After considering a US case decided on similar facts, in which the court adopted a deferential approach to review, his Lordship concluded that such an approach] does not accord with the approach under English law. It is at variance with the principle that only a pressing social need can defeat freedom of expression . . . It is also inconsistent with the principle that the more substantial the interference with fundamental rights the more the court will require by way of justification before it can be satisfied that the interference is reasonable in a public law sense: *Reg.* v. *Ministry of Defence, Ex parte Smith* [1996] Q.B. 517 . . .

Declarations should be granted in both cases to the effect that the Home Secretary's current policy is unlawful, and that the governors' administrative decisions pursuant to that policy were also unlawful.

Simms and *Leech* — in common with a number of other cases, including *R* v. *Lord Saville of Newdigate, ex parte A* [2000] 1 WLR 1855, *R* v. *Secretary of State for the Home Department, ex parte Pierson* [1998] AC 539, and *R* v. *North and East Devon Health Authority, ex parte Coughlan* [2001] QB 213 — suggest that *before* the activation of the HRA English courts were willing, in limited circumstances, to engage in something akin to proportionality review, as Fordham and de la Mare [2000] *JR* 40 at 43–45 explain:

The idea [underlying the principle of legality] is simple: sources of public authorities' power should be construed as not permitting unjustified restrictions on fundamental rights, except where primary legislation deliberately authorises such restrictions . . . The most compelling application of the principle . . . is to be found in the speech of Lord Steyn . . . in *Simms* . . . As a mode of intensive domestic review, the principle of legality is a solution of breathtaking skill . . . In essence, the principle is identifying a legislatively mandated margin, whereby no power may be used to bring about an unjustified restriction of a fundamental right . . . The principle of legality seen in *Simms* hardens the *Smith* test . . . to produce a high-intensity review to match that contemplated in Strasbourg [ie ECHR] cases and Privy Council "constitutional review" cases (such as *De Freitas* [see above at 9.3]). [This is because] *Simms* uses a Strasbourg proportionality hallmark (pressing social need) . . .

QUESTIONS

- Why do Fordham and de la Mare say that *Simms* 'hardens' the *Smith* test?
- How, precisely, do the approaches adopted in the two cases differ?

9.3.4 The *Daly* Case and the Human Rights Act

Although, as we have just seen, elements of proportionality-style review were evident in English law prior to the entry into force of the HRA, that legislation acted as a catalyst for further development in this area by resolving two areas of uncertainty. First, although substantive review — at least in human rights cases — was evidently moving towards the proportionality test, many judgments were at best equivocal. Even cases like *Simms*, which appeared to embrace proportionality, did so in a somewhat qualified fashion: Lords Hobhouse and Steyn invoked both *Wednesbury* and proportionality principles, leaving a question-mark over whether proportionality had become a ground of review in its own right. Secondly, the range of rights or interests which could be protected by means of proportionality-style review was uncertain.

These issues have been clarified by the HRA — although a new set of difficulties remains to be resolved. The Act clearly establishes that domestic courts can review administrative action — and, to the extent of declaring incompatibilities under s 4, primary legislation — for compliance with the 'Convention rights' (defined by s 1 to mean Articles 2 to 12 ECHR, Articles 1 to 3 of the First Protocol, and Articles 1 and 2 of the Sixth Protocol). This follows because public authorities are now obliged to act consistently with the Convention rights (s 6) and their statutory powers must, if possible, be construed subject to the same rights (s 3). Administrative action in breach of the Convention rights can therefore be quashed as unlawful (unless such a breach is sanctioned by primary legislation (s 6(2)).

It is clear from the jurisprudence of the European Court of Human Rights, which English courts are obliged to take into account (s 2), that the concept of proportionality is inherent in many of the Convention rights, and it is therefore unsurprising that English courts have unequivocally embraced the proportionality test in relevant HRA cases. This position has been reached following some initial uncertainty (on which see Elliott [2001] *JR* 166; Blake [2002] *EHRLR* 19) stemming principally from judicial fears that unqualified adoption of proportionality would collapse the hallowed distinction between appeal and review. For instance, in *R (Mahmood)* v. *Secretary of State for the Home Department* [2001] 1 WLR 840 at [33], Laws LJ was at pains to reconcile that distinction with judicial review under the HRA:

Much of the challenge presented by the enactment of the 1998 Act consists in the search for a principled measure of scrutiny which will be loyal to the Convention rights, but loyal also to the legitimate claims of democratic power . . . The Human Rights Act 1998 does not authorise the judges to stand in the shoes of Parliament's delegates, who are decision-makers given their responsibilities by the democratic arm of the state. . . . It follows that there must be a principled distance between the court's adjudication in a case such as this and the Secretary of State's decision, based on his perception of the case's merits.

In the same case, Lord Phillips MR (at [39]) appeared to assume that such 'principled distance' could be secured only by means of some residual attachment in the human rights field to the reasonableness concept:

> . . . [T]he court can no longer uphold the decision on the general ground that there was 'substantial justification' for interference with humans rights. Interference with human rights can only be justified to the extent permitted by the Convention itself . . . When anxiously scrutinising an executive decision that interferes with human rights, the court will ask the question, applying an objective test, whether the decision-maker could reasonably have concluded that the interference was necessary to achieve one or more of the legitimate aims recognised by the Convention. When considering the test of necessity in the relevant context, the court must take into account the European jurisprudence . . .

A more satisfactory approach was adopted by the House of Lords in the following case, in which it was made clear that the proportionality test could — and should — be adopted in English law *without* requiring judges to stand in the shoes of administrators.

....

R (Daly) v. *Secretary of State for the Home Department* [2001] UKHL 26 [2001] 2 AC 532
House of Lords

All governors of closed prisons were required by the Home Secretary to operate a standard cell searching policy. Under the policy prisoners were not permitted to remain in their cells during searches, in order to prevent intimidation of those conducting the search and to stop prisoners gaining knowledge of search techniques. Prison officers were permitted to examine, but not read, legal correspondence stored in cells. The claimant, who stored such correspondence in his cell, contended that the policy requiring prisoners to be absent while their legal correspondence was examined was unlawful.

Lord Bingham

[15] It is necessary, first, to ask whether the policy infringes in a significant way Mr Daly's common law right that the confidentiality of privileged legal correspondence be maintained. He submits that it does for two related reasons: first, because knowledge that such correspondence may be looked at by prison officers in the absence of the prisoner inhibits the prisoner's willingness to communicate with his legal adviser in terms of unreserved candour; and secondly, because there must be a risk, if the prisoner is not present, that the officers will stray beyond their limited role in examining legal correspondence, particularly if, for instance, they see some name or reference familiar to them, as would be the case if the prisoner were bringing or contemplating bringing proceedings against officers in the prison. For the Home Secretary it is argued that the policy involves no infringement of a prisoner's common law right since his privileged correspondence is not read in his absence but only examined.

[16] I have no doubt that the policy infringes Mr Daly's common law right to legal professional privilege . . . In an imperfect world there will necessarily be occasions when prison officers will do more than merely examine prisoners' legal documents, and apprehension that they may do so is bound to inhibit a prisoner's willingness to communicate freely with his legal adviser.

[17] The next question is whether there can be any ground for infringing in any way a prisoner's right to maintain the confidentiality of his privileged legal correspondence. Plainly there can. Some examination may well be necessary to establish that privileged legal correspondence is what it

appears to be and is not a hiding place for illicit materials or information prejudicial to security or good order.

[18] It is then necessary to ask whether, to the extent that it infringes a prisoner's common law right to privilege, the policy can be justified as a necessary and proper response to the acknowledged need to maintain security, order and discipline in prisons and to prevent crime. Mr Daly's challenge at this point is directed to the blanket nature of the policy, applicable as it is to all prisoners of whatever category in all closed prisons in England and Wales, irrespective of a prisoner's past or present conduct and of any operational emergency or urgent intelligence. The Home Secretary's justification rests firmly on the points already mentioned: the risk of intimidation, the risk that staff may be conditioned by prisoners to relax security and the danger of disclosing searching methods.

[19] In considering these justifications, based as they are on the extensive experience of the prison service, it must be recognised that the prison population includes a core of dangerous, disruptive and manipulative prisoners, hostile to authority and ready to exploit for their own advantage any concession granted to them. Any search policy must accommodate this inescapable fact. I cannot however accept that the reasons put forward justify the policy in its present blanket form. Any prisoner who attempts to intimidate or disrupt a search of his cell, or whose past conduct shows that he is likely to do so, may properly be excluded even while his privileged correspondence is examined so as to ensure the efficacy of the search, but no justification is shown for routinely excluding all prisoners, whether intimidatory or disruptive or not, while that part of the search is conducted. [In the absence of] extraordinary conditions . . ., it is hard to regard the conditioning of staff as a problem which could not be met by employing dedicated search teams. It is not suggested that prison officers when examining legal correspondence employ any sophisticated technique which would be revealed to the prisoner if he were present, although he might no doubt be encouraged to secrete illicit materials among his legal papers if the examination were obviously very cursory. The policy cannot in my opinion be justified in its present blanket form. The infringement of prisoners' rights to maintain the confidentiality of their privileged legal correspondence is greater than is shown to be necessary to serve the legitimate public objectives already identified. I accept Mr Daly's submission on this point . . . In my opinion the policy provides for a degree of intrusion into the privileged legal correspondence of prisoners which is greater than is justified by the objectives the policy is intended to serve, and so violates the common law rights of prisoners . . .

[23] I have reached the conclusions so far expressed on an orthodox application of common law principles derived from the authorities and an orthodox domestic approach to judicial review. But the same result is achieved by reliance on the European Convention. Article 8(1) gives Mr Daly a right to respect for his correspondence. While interference with that right by a public authority may be permitted if in accordance with the law and necessary in a democratic society in the interests of national security, public safety, the prevention of disorder or crime or for protection of the rights and freedoms of others, the policy interferes with Mr Daly's exercise of his right under article 8(1) to an extent much greater than necessity requires. In this instance, therefore, the common law and the Convention yield the same result. But this need not always be so. In *Smith and Grady v United Kingdom* (1999) 29 EHRR 493, the European Court held that the orthodox domestic approach of the English courts had not given the applicants an effective remedy for the breach of their rights under article 8 of the Convention because the threshold of review had been set too high. Now, following the incorporation of the Convention by the Human Rights Act 1998 and the bringing of that Act fully into force, domestic courts must themselves form a judgment whether a Convention right has been breached (conducting such inquiry as is necessary to form that judgment) and, so far as permissible

under the Act, grant an effective remedy. On this aspect of the case, I agree with and adopt the observations of my noble and learned Lord Steyn which I have had the opportunity of reading in draft . . .

Lord Steyn

[24] My Lords, I am in complete agreement with the reasons given by Lord Bingham of Cornhill in his speech. For the reasons he gives I would also allow the appeal. Except on one narrow but important point I have nothing to add.

[25] There was written and oral argument on the question whether certain observations of Lord Phillips of Worth Matravers MR in *R (Mahmood) v Secretary of State for the Home Department* [2001] 1 WLR 840 were correct. The context was an immigration case involving a decision of the Secretary of State made before the Human Rights Act 1998 came into effect. The Master of the Rolls nevertheless approached the case as if the Act had been in force when the Secretary of State reached his decision. He explained the new approach to be adopted [see excerpt above] . . .

[26] The explanation of the Master of the Rolls in the first sentence of the cited passage requires clarification. It is couched in language reminiscent of the traditional *Wednesbury* ground of review . . . and in particular the adaptation of that test in terms of heightened scrutiny in cases involving fundamental rights as formulated in *R v Ministry of Defence, Ex p Smith* [1996] QB 517, 554E–G per Sir Thomas Bingham MR. There is a material difference between the *Wednesbury* and *Smith* grounds of review and the approach of proportionality applicable in respect of review where Convention rights are at stake.

[27] The contours of the principle of proportionality are familiar. In *de Freitas v Permanent Secretary of Ministry of Agriculture, Fisheries, Lands and Housing* [1999] 1 AC 69 the Privy Council adopted a three-stage test [see excerpt above at 9.3] . . . Clearly, these criteria are more precise and more sophisticated than the traditional grounds of review. What is the difference for the disposal of concrete cases? . . . The starting point is that there is an overlap between the traditional grounds of review and the approach of proportionality. Most cases would be decided in the same way whichever approach is adopted. But the intensity of review is somewhat greater under the proportionality approach. Making due allowance for important structural differences between various convention rights, which I do not propose to discuss, a few generalisations are perhaps permissible. I would mention three concrete differences without suggesting that my statement is exhaustive. First, the doctrine of proportionality may require the reviewing court to assess the balance which the decision maker has struck, not merely whether it is within the range of rational or reasonable decisions. Secondly, the proportionality test may go further than the traditional grounds of review inasmuch as it may require attention to be directed to the relative weight accorded to interests and considerations. Thirdly, even the heightened scrutiny test developed in *R v Ministry of Defence, ex parte Smith* [1996] QB 517, 554 is not necessarily appropriate to the protection of human rights. It will be recalled that in *Smith* the Court of Appeal reluctantly felt compelled to reject a limitation on homosexuals in the army. The challenge based on article 8 of the Convention for the Protection of Human Rights and Fundamental Freedoms (the right to respect for private and family life) foundered on the threshold required even by the anxious scrutiny test. The European Court of Human Rights came to the opposite conclusion: *Smith v United Kingdom* (1999) 29 EHRR 493 . . . [Thus] the intensity of the review, in similar cases, is guaranteed by the twin requirements that the limitation of the right was necessary in a democratic society, in the sense of meeting a pressing social need, and the question whether the interference was really proportionate to the legitimate aim being pursued.

[28] The differences in approach between the traditional grounds of review and the proportionality approach may therefore sometimes yield different results. It is therefore important that cases involving Convention rights must be analysed in the correct way. This does not mean that there has been a shift to merits review. On the contrary, as Professor Jowell [2000] PL 671, 681 has pointed out the respective roles of judges and administrators are fundamentally distinct and will remain so. To this extent the general tenor of the observations in *Mahmood* are correct. And Laws LJ rightly emphasised in *Mahmood* . . . "that the intensity of review in a public law case will depend on the subject matter in hand". That is so even in cases involving Convention rights. In law context is everything.

Lord Cooke

[29] My Lords, having had the advantage of reading in draft the speeches of my noble and learned friends, Lord Bingham of Cornhill and Lord Steyn, I am in full agreement with them. I add some brief observations on two matters, less to supplement what they have said than to underline its importance.

[30] First, while this case has arisen in a jurisdiction where the European Convention for the Protection of Human Rights and Fundamental Freedoms applies, and while the case is one in which the Convention and the common law produce the same result, it is of great importance, in my opinion, that the common law by itself is being recognised as a sufficient source of the fundamental right to confidential communication with a legal adviser for the purpose of obtaining legal advice. Thus the decision may prove to be in point in common law jurisdictions not affected by the Convention. Rights similar to those in the Convention are of course to be found in constitutional documents and other formal affirmations of rights elsewhere. The truth is, I think, that some rights are inherent and fundamental to democratic civilised society. Conventions, constitutions, bills of rights and the like respond by recognising rather than creating them.

[31] To essay any list of these fundamental, perhaps ultimately universal, rights is far beyond anything required for the purpose of deciding the present case. It is enough to take the three identified by Lord Bingham: in his words, access to a court; access to legal advice; and the right to communicate confidentially with a legal adviser under the seal of legal professional privilege. As he says authoritatively from the woolsack, such rights may be curtailed only by clear and express words, and then only to the extent reasonably necessary to meet the ends which justify the curtailment. The point that I am emphasising is that the common law goes so deep.

[32] The other matter concerns degrees of judicial review. Lord Steyn illuminates the distinctions between 'traditional' (that is to say in terms of English case law, *Wednesbury*) standards of judicial review and higher standards under the European Convention or the common law of human rights. As he indicates, often the results are the same. But the view that the standards are substantially the same appears to have received its quietus in *Smith v United Kingdom* (1999) 29 EHRR 493 and *Lustig-Prean v United Kingdom* (1999) 29 EHRR 548. [Lord Cooke then went on to make the remarks set out above at 9.2.1.]

Lords Hutton and Scott agreed with Lords Bingham, Steyn, and Cooke that the cell-searching policy was unlawful.

9.3.5 Deference

Daly's unequivocal recognition of proportionality as a principle applicable by domestic courts — marking a significant step away from the classic model of English administrative law, towards a 'culture of justification' (see Taggart (in Bamforth and Leyland (eds), *Public Law in a Multi-Layered Constitution* (Oxford 2003) at 322)) — renders it a legal landmark. However, it leaves many questions unanswered: in particular, when the proportionality test is applicable, what are the respective roles of the judge and the decision-maker under it? In other words, where does proportionality leave the distinction between appeal and review? On the one hand, as acknowledged in *Daly*, the proportionality test is capable of supplying a higher standard of scrutiny than *Wednesbury*. On the other hand, as Lord Steyn emphasized, proportionality review is not to be equated with 'merits review': judges' and administrators' roles remain 'fundamentally distinct' — a view shared by many commentators (*eg* Jowell [2000] *PL* 671 and [2003] *PL* 592; Craig (2001) 117 *LQR* 589; Atrill [2003] *PL* 41). The challenge is to develop a framework within which these twin propositions may be reconciled.

This is one of the most difficult problems in contemporary administrative law, and has stimulated considerable debate and disagreement. Although they command far from universal assent, a useful starting point is furnished by the following remarks of Lord Hope in *R v. Director of Public Prosecutions, ex parte Kebilene* [2000] 2 AC 326 at 380–381:

The doctrine of the "margin of appreciation" is a familiar part of the jurisprudence of the European Court of Human Rights. The European Court has acknowledged that, by reason of their direct and continuous contact with the vital forces of their countries, the national authorities are in principle better placed to evaluate local needs and conditions than an international court: *Buckley v. United Kingdom* (1996) 23 E.H.R.R. 101, 129, paras. 74–75. Although this means that, as the European Court explained in *Handyside v. United Kingdom* (1976) 1 E.H.R.R. 737, 753, para. 48, "the machinery of protection established by the Convention is subsidiary to the national systems safeguarding human rights," it goes hand in hand with a European supervision. The extent of this supervision will vary according to such factors as the nature of the Convention right in issue, the importance of that right for the individual and the nature of the activities involved in the case.

This doctrine is an integral part of the supervisory jurisdiction which is exercised over state conduct by the international court. By conceding a margin of appreciation to each national system, the court has recognised that the Convention, as a living system, does not need to be applied uniformly by all states but may vary in its application according to local needs and conditions. This technique is not available to the national courts when they are considering Convention issues arising within their own countries. But in the hands of the national courts also the Convention should be seen as an expression of fundamental principles rather than as a set of mere rules. The questions which the courts will have to decide in the application of these principles will involve questions of balance between competing interests and issues of proportionality.

In this area difficult choices may have to be made by the executive or the legislature between the rights of the individual and the needs of society. In some circumstances it will be appropriate for the courts to recognise that there is an area of judgment within which the judiciary will defer, on democratic grounds, to the considered opinion of the elected body or person whose act or decision is said to be incompatible with the Convention. This point is well made at p. 74, para. 3.21 of *Human Rights Law and Practice* (1999), of which Lord Lester of Herne Hill and Mr. Pannick are the general editors, where the area in which these choices may arise is conveniently and appropriately described as the "discretionary area of judgment." It will be easier for such an area of judgment to be recognised where the Convention itself requires a balance to be struck, much less so where the right is stated in terms which are unqualified. It will be easier for it to be recognised where the issues involve questions of social or economic policy, much less so where the rights are of high constitutional importance or are of a kind where the courts are especially well placed to assess the need for protection.

These comments laid to rest a debate about whether the ECtHR's 'margin of appreciation' doctrine (for an introduction to which see McBride in Ellis (ed), *The Principle of Proportionality in the Laws of Europe* (Oxford 1999)) could simply be adopted by English courts applying the HRA — a view apparently supported by Simon Brown LJ in the Divisional Court in *R* v. *Ministry of Defence, ex parte Smith* [1996] QB 517 at 541. The inappropriateness of this course lies in the fact that, as Laws [1998] *PL* 254 at 258 puts it, domestic courts (unlike the Strasbourg Court) are not 'subject to an objective inhibition generated by any cultural distance between themselves and the state organs whose decisions are impleaded before them'. Nevertheless, other factors may be present in the factual matrix which make it appropriate for national courts to defer to decision-makers' views — hence the concept of a variable 'discretionary area of judgment' endorsed by Lord Hope in the passage above which (as cases such as *Brown* v. *Stott* [2003] 1 AC 681 and *R* v. *A (No 2)* [2001] UKHL 25 [2002] 1 AC 45 show) maintains a distinction between the role of judges, on the one hand, and decision- and policy-makers, on the other. The appropriateness of that concept, and the wider question of what, if any, doctrine of deference is appropriate under the HRA, have proved highly contentious.

Before examining the debate which has ensued, it is necessary to be clear about its subject-matter. Questions of deference (sometimes referred to in domestic jurisprudence as the 'margin of discretion' or, confusingly, 'margin of appreciation') are most obviously germane to explicitly qualified rights such as those recognized by Articles 8–11 ECHR: for example, in determining whether a person's freedom of movement may be limited, how much respect should the court attach to a Home Secretary's conclusion that a restriction is 'necessary in a democratic society in the interests of . . . public order', thereby rendering it lawful under Article 9(2)?

In contrast, it may appear (see Leigh [2002] *PL* 265) that deference is irrelevant to so-called 'unqualified rights' such as the right to a fair hearing (Article 6) and the right not to be tortured (Article 3): either the right has been infringed or it has not — a matter which is surely a hard-edged question of law for the court. However, as Atrill [2003] *PL* 41 at 44 observes, the language of — and the putative distinction between — 'qualified' and 'unqualified' rights is problematic. *All* rights are 'qualified' in the sense that they are limited, albeit that the limitations upon some rights are spelled out in terms by the Convention (*eg* Article 9(2)), while the contours of others are implicit in the language which defines them. The apparently unqualified entitlement under Article 6 is implicitly qualified by the very concept of a fair hearing: as Lord Steyn recognized in *R* v. *A (No 2)* [2001] UKHL 25 [2002] 1 AC 45 at 65, the concept of fairness must be constructed, and its limits set, by reference to 'the familiar triangulation of interests of the accused, the victim and society'. Similarly, as Laws LJ observed in *R (Adam)* v. *Secretary of State for the Home Department* [2004] EWCA Civ 540 [2004] 3 WLR 561 at [66], to the extent that Article 3 imposes positive obligations on the state (*eg* to train prison officers so as to guard against prisoners subjecting one another to torture or to inhuman or degrading treatment), there exists 'some space for judgment and discretion on the part of government'. It is plain, therefore, that policy considerations are relevant to determining the scope of all rights, thus raising questions about the legitimate extent of judicial deference to the judgments of the other branches.

The nature of the concept of deference and its capacity to regulate the intensity of proportionality review are illustrated by the following case.

....

R (Farrakhan) v. *Secretary of State for the Home Department* [2002] EWCA Civ 606 [2002] QB 1391
Court of Appeal

The Home Secretary, exercising his power under s 3 of the Immigration Act 1971, refused to grant leave to enter the United Kingdom to the claimant, a United States citizen and spiritual leader of a religious, political, and social movement known as the 'Nation of Islam'. The Home Secretary, anticipating that the claimant would make inflammatory speeches which would threaten community relations and risk public disorder, invoked rule 320(6) of the Immigration Rules (made under ss 1 and 3(2) of the 1971 Act) which provides that leave to enter may be refused (*inter alia*) 'where the Secretary of State has personally directed that the exclusion of a person from the United Kingdom is conducive to the public good'. The claimant argued that the Home Secretary's decision constituted a disproportionate and hence unlawful restriction of his right of freedom of expression under Article 10 ECHR. The claimant was successful before Turner J, who held that the Home Secretary had failed to justify objectively the restriction of the claimant's rights. Sedley LJ granted the Home Secretary leave to appeal to the Court of Appeal.

Lord Phillips MR (giving the judgment of the court)

[62] Although preventing Mr Farrakhan from expressing his views was not the primary object of his exclusion, the fact remains that the Home Secretary did not wish him to address meetings in this country because he considered that such meetings might prove the occasion for disorder. To this extent, one object of his exclusion can be said to have been to prevent him exercising the right of freedom of expression in this country. In these circumstances, which are not precisely covered by the Strasbourg authorities to which we have referred, we consider that Article 10 of the Convention was in play. The Home Secretary was correct to recognise this in his decision letter, which also recognised the importance that is accorded to freedom of speech by the common law . . .

[63] The Home Secretary made it plain that he was balancing the importance of freedom of speech against the risk of disorder that might ensue if Mr Farrakhan were admitted into this country. That was an appropriate approach, for Article 10.2 recognises that the prevention of disorder is one of the legitimate aims that can justify placing restrictions on freedom of expression. Much argument before Turner J and before us was directed to the approach in such circumstances to judicial review of the Secretary of State's decision.

[64] Before the Human Rights Act 1998 came into force, the approach to judicial review in this country involved the application of the test in *Associated Provincial Picture Houses Ltd v Wednesbury Corpn* [1948] 1 KB 223. It was only appropriate for the court to overturn an administrative decision if it was one which no reasonable decision maker could have reached. Using the language of the Strasbourg jurisprudence, this test left a very wide margin of appreciation to the decision maker. Indeed, the margin was far too wide to accommodate the demands of the Convention. In deciding whether restriction of a Convention right can be justified, it is necessary to apply the doctrine of proportionality. In applying that doctrine, the width of the margin of appreciation that must be accorded to the decision maker will vary, depending upon the right that is in play and the facts of the particular case. Applying a margin of appreciation is a flexible approach; the *Wednesbury* approach is not.

[65] For this reason, in cases involving Convention rights, the courts have moved from the *Wednesbury* test towards the application of the principle of proportionality, via the stepping stone of the judgment of Sir Thomas Bingham MR in *R v Ministry of Defence, Ex p Smith* [1996] QB 517 at 554. . . .

[Lord Phillips then referred to certain passages from *Daly*, the salient parts of which appear above at 9.3.4, and continued:]

[67] When applying a test of proportionality, the margin of appreciation or discretion accorded to the decision maker is all-important, for it is only by recognising the margin of discretion that the court avoids substituting its own decision for that of the decision maker . . .

[71] Miss Carss-Frisk [for the Home Secretary] submitted that there were factors in the present case which made it appropriate to accord a particularly wide margin of discretion to the Secretary of State. We agree. We would identify these factors as follows. First and foremost is the fact that this case concerns an immigration decision. As we have pointed out, the European Court of Human Rights attaches considerable weight to the right under international law of a state to control immigration into its territory. And the weight that this carries in the present case is the greater because the Secretary of State is not motivated by the wish to prevent Mr Farrakhan from expressing his views, but by concern for public order within the United Kingdom.

[72] The second factor is the fact that the decision in question is the personal decision of the Secretary of State. Nor is it a decision that he has taken lightly. The history that we have set out at the beginning of this judgment demonstrates the very detailed consideration, involving widespread consultation, that the Secretary of State has given to his decision.

[73] The third factor is that the Secretary of State is far better placed to reach an informed decision as to the likely consequences of admitting Mr Farrakhan to this country than is the court.

[74] The fourth factor is that the Secretary of State is democratically accountable for this decision. This is underlined by the fact that s.60(9) of the [Immigration and Asylum Act 1999] precludes any right of appeal where the Secretary of State has certified that he has personally directed the exclusion of a person on the ground that this is conducive to the public good. Mr Blake submitted that the absence of a right of appeal required a particularly rigorous scrutiny under the process of judicial review. This submission appeared to us tantamount to negating the effect of s.60(9). There is no doubt that the Secretary of State's decision is subject to review, but we consider that the effect of the legislative scheme is legitimately to require the court to confer a wide margin of discretion upon the Minister.

[75] These conclusions gain support from the approach of the House of Lords to the discretion of the Secretary of State to deport a person on grounds of national security in *SSHD v Rehman* [2001] 3 WLR 877.

[76] Miss Carss-Frisk submitted that these considerations were not reflected in the judgment of Turner J., but that he had replaced his own evaluation of the relevant facts for that of the Minister. We consider that there is force in this submission.

[77] The other factor of great relevance to the test of proportionality is the very limited extent to which the right of freedom of expression of Mr Farrakhan was restricted. The reality is that it was a

particular forum which was denied to him rather than the freedom to express his views. Further-more, no restriction was placed on his disseminating information or opinions within the United Kingdom by any means of communication other than his presence within the country. In making this observation we do not ignore the fact that freedom of expression extends to receiving as well as imparting views and information and that those within this country were not able to receive these from Mr Farrakhan face to face.

[78] Sedley LJ described the grounds for excluding Mr Farrakhan as exiguous. We have already indicated that to ascertain the reasons for Mr Farrakhan's exclusion it is appropriate to have regard to all the correspondence on the subject written by or on behalf of the Secretary of State. The Home Secretary's decision had turned upon his evaluation of risk — the risk that because of his notorious opinions a visit by Mr Farrakhan to this country might provoke disorder. In evaluating that risk the Home Secretary had had regard to tensions in the Middle East current at the time of his decision. He had also had regard to the fruits of widespread consultation and to sources of informa-tion available to him that are not available to the court. He had not chosen to describe his sources of information or the purport of that information. We can see that he may have had good reason for not disclosing his sources but feel that it would have been better had he been less diffident about explaining the nature of the information and advice that he had received.

[79] We consider that the merits of this appeal are finely balanced, but have come to the conclu-sion that the Secretary of State provided sufficient explanation for a decision that turned on his personal, informed, assessment of risk to demonstrate that his decision did not involve a dis-proportionate interference with freedom of expression. The Secretary of State exercised a power expressly conferred upon him by [rule 320(6) of the Statement of Changes in Immigration Rules], whose terms are reflected in s.60(9) of the [Immigration and Asylum Act 1999]. He did so for the purpose of the prevention of disorder, which is a legitimate aim under Article 10.2 of the Conven-tion. His decision struck a proportionate balance between that aim and freedom of expression, to the extent to which that was in play on the facts of this case. This appeal will, accordingly, be allowed.

QUESTIONS

- Allan (in Dyzenhaus, *The Unity of Public Law* (Oxford 2004) at 304) comments that the scale of the deference extended by the court 'effectively eliminated the rights it had earlier purported to affirm'. Do you agree?
- How is the scrutiny afforded by application of the proportionality test in *Farrakhan* distinct from that which would obtain under the *Wednesbury* principle?

The factors militating in favour of judicial deference in *Farrakhan* are echoed by dicta of Lord Woolf CJ in *R* v. *Lambert* [2002] QB 1112 at [16], in which he considered the demo-cratic credentials of a decision-maker to be a reason for judicial deference, and *Poplar Housing and Regeneration Community Association* v. *Donoghue* [2001] EWCA Civ 595 [2002] QB 48 at [69], in which (along with democratic considerations) he argued for deference in relation to matters with 'economic and other implications . . . [that] are complex and far-reaching'. Deference has also played a particularly influential role in areas concerning dif-ficult moral issues (*eg, R (Pretty)* v. *Director of Public Prosecutions* [2001] UKHL 61 [2002] 1 AC 800) and national security (*eg, Secretary of State for the Home Department* v. *Rehman* [2001] UKHL 47 [2003] 1 AC 153; *R (Gillan)* v. *Commissioner of Police for the Metropolis* [2004] EWCA Civ 1067; cf *A* v. *Home Secretary* [2004] UKHL 56 (see Appendix below)). These may be contrasted with recent decisions concerning the right to a fair trial in criminal cases, such as, *eg*, *R* v. *A (No 2)* [2001] UKHL 25 [2002] 1 AC 45 and *R* v. *Lambert* [2001] UKHL 37 [2002] 2 AC 545; although, as noted above, the question of deference cannot be overlooked in such cases, the courts, in practice, are usually persuaded that a relatively hard-edged approach is appropriate (see further Owen (in Jowell and Cooper (eds), *Delivering Rights* (Oxford 2003) at 66)).

However, while examples such as these give a flavour of when deference may blunt proportionality review, a more thoroughgoing analytical framework is required in order to test, and ultimately guide, judicial decision-making in this area. A useful starting point is provided by *International Transport Roth GmbH* v. *Secretary of State for the Home Department* [2002] EWCA Civ 158 [2003] QB 728, concerning a challenge to a scheme operated under s 32 of the Immigration and Asylum Act 1999, making carriers liable (subject to very limited exceptions) to a fixed penalty of £2,000 for every clandestine entrant found concealed in a vehicle. It was contended, *inter alia*, that the scheme was contrary to Article 6 ECHR because it imposed disproportionate burdens on carriers: the burden was on carriers to establish blamelessness and the penalty could not be reduced to reflect different degrees of blameworthiness. This argument was accepted at first instance ((2002) 99(2) LSG 27) and a declaration of incompatibility was issued under s 4 HRA. That declaration was upheld on appeal, Simon Brown LJ holding that, even after allowing for the process of triangulation referred to above, the scheme was inconsistent with Article 6.

Laws LJ dissented. Central to his judgment was the following discussion of deference, which led him to the conclusion that it would be inappropriate for the court to rule that the scheme was an illegitimate method of pursuing the societal interest in dealing effectively with illegal immigration:

[82] In describing the tension created by the co-existence . . . of parliamentary sovereignty and fundamental or constitutional rights, the antithesis to which I drew particular attention [earlier in the judgment] was that between the vindication of such rights and the claims of primary legislation, where the two were in actual or apparent conflict. This present appeal is such a case; for the whole debate is about the effects of the relevant provisions of the 1999 Act properly construed. But there is a commoner antithesis, arising where the seeming conflict is between the protection of a fundamental right and the force of a decision made by the executive (or, it may be, contained in subordinate legislation) rather than by the primary legislature. I have used expressions such as "the democratic powers" to embrace both the legislature and the executive, as being the arms of government whose power depends, the former directly and the latter indirectly, on election by the people.

[83] Against this background, the *first* principle which I think emerges from the authorities is that greater deference is to be paid to an Act of Parliament than to a decision of the executive or subordinate measure: see in particular the . . . [judgments] of Lord Woolf [in] *Lambert* [[2002] 2 AC 545] and *Poplar* [[2002] QB 48]. Where the decision-maker is not Parliament, but a Minister or other public or governmental authority exercising power conferred by Parliament, a degree of deference will be due on democratic grounds — the decision-maker is Parliament's delegate — within the principles accorded by the cases. But where the decision-maker is Parliament itself, speaking through main legislation, the tension of which I have spoken is at its most acute. In our intermediate constitution the legislature is not subordinate to a sovereign text, as are the legislatures in "constitutional" systems. Parliament remains the sovereign legislator. It, and not a written constitution, bears the ultimate mantle of democracy in the State.

[84] The *second* principle is that there is more scope for deference "where the Convention itself requires a balance to be struck, much less so where the right is stated in terms which are

unqualified" (*per* Lord Hope in *Kebilene* [[2000] 2 AC 326 at 381] . . .). In the present case we are principally concerned with Article 6, which does not on its face require any balance to be struck: it contains no analogue of paragraph 2 in Articles 9–11, dealing with political rights. It is thus a context which militates against deference. But even here, there is no sharp edge. The right to a fair trial under EHCR Article 6(1) is certainly unqualified and cannot be abrogated. So also is the presumption of innocence (in a criminal case) arising under Article 6(2). But what is required for fairness, what is required to satisfy the presumption of innocence, may vary according to context. In relation to Article 6(2), see in particular *Salabiaku* 13 EHRR 379, in which the European Court of Human Rights held (paragraph 28) that presumptions of fact or law against the defence should be confined "within reasonable limits which take into account the importance of what is at stake and maintain the rights of the defence". Hence I think it misleading to describe Article 6 rights as "absolute", an adjective which tends to suggest that the nature of such rights is uniform, the same for every class of case (bar the distinction between civil and criminal). That is not right. The requirements of independence and impartiality are perhaps as close as one can get to uniform requirements. But even there, there may be scope for reasonable differences of view as to the conditions which have to be met. What is the degree of security of tenure that a judge must enjoy if he is to constitute a tribunal compliant with Article 6(1)? At all events, however, Article 6 is an area where the deference due to the democratic powers is limited, since the rights it guarantees are unqualified.

[85] The *third* principle is that greater deference will be due to the democratic powers where the subject-matter in hand is peculiarly within their constitutional responsibility, and less when it lies more particularly within the constitutional responsibility of the courts. The first duty of government is the defence of the realm. It is well settled that executive decisions dealing directly with matters of defence, while not immune from judicial review (that would be repugnant to the rule of law), cannot sensibly be scrutinised by the courts on grounds relating to their factual merits: see *Chandler v DPP* [1964] AC 763 at 790 per Lord Reid and 798 per Viscount Radcliffe, and the recent case of *Marchiori* [2002] EWCA Civ 03 at paragraphs 33–38 of the judgment given by myself. The first duty of the courts is the maintenance of the rule of law. That is exemplified in many ways, not least by the extremely restrictive construction always placed on no-certiorari clauses [on which see below at 15.6.3].

[86] Now this is not a case, of course, in which the courts are intruding in defence policy, or the democratic powers in the rule of law. There are no tanks on the wrong lawns. But . . . the constitutional responsibility of the democratic powers particularly includes the security of the State's borders, thus including immigration control, and that of the courts particularly includes the doing of criminal justice. If the scheme of the 1999 Act is essentially to be treated as an administrative scheme for the betterment of immigration control in a context — clandestine entrants in vehicles — acknowledged to be especially acute, the courts will accord a much greater deference to Parliament in deciding whether there is any violation of Convention rights than if it is to be regarded as a criminal statute. In the latter case, the courts are of course obliged to apply Article 6(2) and (3) as well as (1). They would do so rigorously, with much less deference to the legislature, not only in fulfilment of their duty under the HRA but also because their own constitutional responsibility makes the task a necessarily congenial one . . .

[87] The *fourth* and last principle is very closely allied to the third, and indeed may be regarded as little more than an emanation of it; but I think it makes for clarity if it is separately articulated. It is that greater or lesser deference will be due according to whether the subject matter lies more readily within the actual or potential expertise of the democratic powers or the courts. Thus, quite aside from defence, government decisions in the area of macro-economic policy will be relatively remote from judicial control: see for example *Ex p. Nottinghamshire CC* [1986] AC 240 and *Ex p.*

Hammersmith and Fulham LBC [1991] 1 AC 521. Though these were not, of course, human rights cases, like problems as to the deference due to the democratic decision-maker arise in relation to the proper intensity of judicial review in other contexts, such as were there in play. In the present case, I have no doubt that the social consequences which flow from the entry into the United Kingdom of clandestine illegal immigrants in significant numbers are far-reaching and in some respects complex. While the evidence before us gives more than a flavour of the problems, the assessment of these matters (and therefore of the pressing nature of the need for effective controls) is in my judgment obviously far more within the competence of government than the courts.

After considering the features of the scheme, Laws LJ concluded (at [109]) that

the principles which I have ventured to state relating to deference to the democratic powers are in this case particularly important. There is, surely, more than one possible or reasonable view as to the balance to be struck between the efficacy of the policy aim here, and the interests and the fair treatment of potential responsible persons . . . [T]he principles of deference (and its withholding) point to a conclusion in this case whereby the democratic powers' judgment upon the striking of the balance ought to be accepted. The first, third and fourth principles which I have described tend to yield that result. There is not sufficient substance in the bite of the second principle in the circumstances of the case to produce a contrary result. I should emphasise that if I thought there were no proper judicial controls, and/or that the scheme was criminal in nature, I would have taken a different view.

9.3.6 Democratic and Institutional Considerations

Laws LJ's judgment is to be welcomed as an attempt to articulate a principled approach to the concept of deference, and as a helpful synthesis of much of the relevant case law. It has not, however, been received uncritically. Jowell [2003] *PL* 592 at 598 acknowledges — in line with Laws LJ's fourth principle — that deference is appropriate where 'other bodies, whether Parliament, the executive or a non-departmental body containing specialist expertise, will be better equipped to decide certain questions'. However, he takes issue (*op cit* at 597) with the notion — explicit in Laws LJ's first principle, implicit in his third, and, as noted above, advanced in many other judgments — that deference should be extended to decision-makers on democratic grounds:

It is important to note that the conception of democracy which the ECHR advances fundamentally differs from that which has hitherto prevailed in the United Kingdom. The HRA may on its face be just another unentrenched statute, but its effect is to alter constitutional expectations by creating the presumption across all official decision-making that rights do and should trump convenience . . . No longer can we equate 'democratic principle' with 'majority approval'. Nor can we any longer arrogate the monopoly of legitimacy to those decisions endorsed by the electorate. The new expectations have at their heart the protection of a limited but significant catalogue of rights even against overwhelming popular will.

Even if the above paragraph is wrong . . . the courts have no need to expose their jugular whenever Parliament or its agents speak on the matter of public interest. The courts are charged by Parliament with delineating the boundaries of a rights-based democracy. In doing so, they ought not in any way to be influenced by the fact that Parliament may in the end disregard their pronouncements. Nor should they prefer the authority of Parliament or other bodies on the ground alone that they represent the popular will, or are directly or indirectly accountable to the electorate.

Hunt (in Bamforth and Leyland (eds), *Public Law in a Multi-Layered Constitution* (Oxford

2003) at 350) does not agree that considerations of democracy — or 'constitutional competence' — can so readily be dismissed, arguing that Jowell's approach

excludes from the deference inquiry important normative considerations about what the court's proper role is, by assuming that those normative questions have been settled by the HRA itself . . . But a rich conception of legality and of the rule of law should not only be able to legitimate a role for courts in enforcing legal standards on public decision-makers; it ought, at the same time, to have space for a proper role for democratic considerations, including a role for the democratic branches in the definition and furtherance of fundamental values . . .

It does not follow, however, that democratic considerations must be straightforwardly accommodated by means of deference to decisions enjoying the imprimatur of the democratic branches. An alternative approach to this problem lies in the doctrine of 'democratic dialogue', developed by Hogg and Bushell (1997) 35 *Osgoode Hall Law Review* 75 in relation to the Canadian Charter of Rights and Freedoms. They contend (*op cit* at 79) that the provision made by s 33 of the Charter for legislative override of judicial decisions striking down legislation, thereby giving legislatures the final word on human rights, opens up the possibility of 'dialogue':

Where a judicial decision is open to legislative reversal, modification, or avoidance, then it is meaningful to regard the relationship between the Court and the competent legislative body as a dialogue. In that case, the judicial decision causes a public debate in which Charter values play a more prominent role than they would if there had been no judicial decision.

Although the outcome of such debate may be the exercise of s 33 override powers, this is 'relatively unimportant because of the development of a political climate resistant to its use' (*op cit* at 83). More commonly, the legislative body will 'devise a response that is properly respectful of the Charter values that have been identified by the Court, but which accomplishes the social or economic objectives that the judicial decision has impeded' (*op cit* at 79–80). For Hogg and Bushell (*op cit* at 80), the crucial point is that, within the Charter framework, judicial decisions form part of a process of dialogue which includes the other branches, thereby 'greatly diminishing' the scope for concern about the legitimacy of judicial review.

Although Hogg and Bushell's analysis concerns judicial review of legislation in Canada, it also has resonance in relation to review of administrative action in the UK — a point noted by Clayton [2004] *PL* 33. Like its Canadian counterparts, the UK Parliament has the final word since, as a matter of domestic law, it can enact, and can refuse to amend or repeal, legislation which is incompatible with the ECHR. Consequently, if the courts strike down administrative action as being in breach of Convention rights, it remains open to Parliament to amend the legislation, conferring in unequivocal terms a statutory power to commit the action in question, in which case such action would be invulnerable to further judicial interference (ss 3(1) and (2) and 6(2), HRA). Clayton concludes (*op cit* at 47) that, 'The need to defer to Parliament or the executive becomes less compelling once it is acknowledged that the HRA envisages that the other branches of government will have a second bite at the cherry.'

We saw earlier that Hunt criticized Jowell's marginalization of concerns about the democratic (or constitutional) appropriateness of judicial intervention. Hunt (*loc cit*) develops this critique by arguing that Jowell's resultant focus on the criterion of institutional competence is also misplaced — and, more fundamentally, that the distinction between constitutional and institutional competence is itself misconceived:

Institutional constraints on judicial decision-making ought not necessarily to constrain a court to defer if it considers it to be its constitutional role to decide a particular question. Questions of institutional competence are inseparable from deeper normative questions of institutional design. Courts as institutions are designed in a particular way because of an underlying notion of their function. If, as Jowell suggests, courts now have constitutional competence to decide all questions concerning compatibility of public action with fundamental rights, they ought not to be constrained by institutional limitations: rather, institutional considerations ought to follow from the answer to the underlying normative question about the court's function. Institutional competence constraints can often be resolved, in that procedures can be changed . . . in order to accommodate what is required procedurally in order for the court to fulfil its constitutional function. [By way of example, Hunt goes on to discuss suggestions in *R* v. *Shayler* [2002] UKHL 11 [2003] 1 AC 247 that the High Court's inherent power could be used to devise a system (*eg* of special advocates) whereby it could see material too sensitive to be released to parties in order effectively to review refusals to authorise disclosure of information under the Official Secrets Act 1989.]

Hunt advances these arguments in the course of advocating a particular approach which he labels 'due deference' — a theory which he develops out of criticism of the 'spatial approach' preferred in many of the cases. Hunt traces the latter to the passage from Lord Hope's speech in *Kebilene* set out above at 9.3.5, which refers to the decision-maker's 'discretionary *area* of judgment' (emphasis added), and which is epitomized by the following remarks of Laws LJ in *Roth* at [77]:

. . . [T]he extent of any deference . . . depends in part on the nature and quality of the measure in question: more concretely, whether its content falls within the special responsibility of the executive . . . or the special responsibility of the judiciary. A paradigm of the executive's special responsibility is the security of the State's borders. A paradigm of the judiciary's special responsibility is the doing of criminal justice.

The fundamental error which, according to Hunt (*op cit* at 347), characterizes the spatial approach is the assumption that cases can be 'neatly classified into categories according to the kind of subject matter they raise, and then a particular standard of review applied to them'. The reality is more complex: for instance, 'Questions of fair trial, non-discrimination or the liberty of the individual (all matters on which courts consider themselves to have a special role) may arise in "areas" of decision-making, such as national security or social and economic policy, in which the courts have traditionally been reluctant to interfere with primary decision-makers.' Thus, although Hunt concludes that the extent of deference should be shaped by factors similar to those identified by Laws LJ in *Roth*, he argues that they should be applied in a more subtle fashion. In this sense, deference cannot simply be set at a particular level for a particular *case*; it is, instead, necessary to isolate individual *issues* or stages in the decision-making process, extending a level of deference appropriate in each instance. For example, as Jowell [2003] *PL* 592 at 598 explains, the fact that a case concerns 'national security' cannot be determinative of the appropriate level of deference. While, in determining whether there is a credible threat to national security, 'there is no reason why the courts may not concede the superior intelligence-gathering capacity of the executive to answer that question accurately', the further question whether 'free utilisation of rights of expression leave national security vulnerable' is 'one of risk assessment, which the courts may scrutinise with a somewhat higher degree of intensity than the first, purely factual, question'. There is a clear relationship between this approach and the relatively sophisticated model of justiciability (discussed above at 5.3.3) adopted in cases such as *R* v. *Secretary of State for the Home Department, ex parte Bentley* [1994] QB 349 and *Lewis* v. *Attorney General of Jamaica* [2001] 2 AC 50 and by Harris [2003] *CLJ* 631, in which the more traditional approach of treating certain discretionary powers as 'off limits' as far as judicial review is concerned is eschewed in favour a more subtle analysis of whether, and to what extent, particular grounds of review are applicable to particular aspects of the decision-making process.

It is clear, then, that although a consensus is emerging that proportionality, tempered by deference, is capable of supplying an appropriate mode of human rights review which does not collapse into full merits review, the precise contours of deference remain controversial. This is graphically illustrated by the differences of judicial opinion expressed in the following case.

....

R (ProLife Alliance) v. *BBC* [2002] EWCA Civ 297 [2003] UKHL 23 [2004] 1 AC 185
Court of Appeal and House of Lords

The claimant — a political party opposed to abortion — put up sufficient candidates to qualify for a Party Election Broadcast (PEB). It submitted to the relevant broadcasters a film which included images of mutilated aborted foetuses. Section 6(1) of the Broadcasting Act 1990 enjoins independent broadcasters to 'do all that they can to secure that . . . nothing is included in its programmes which offends against good taste or decency', and on this basis they refused to show the claimant's PEB. The BBC, which is under an essentially identical non-statutory obligation in the 'BBC Agreement', also refused to broadcast the PEB. The claimant sought judicial review, asserting that the broadcasters' decisions were incompatible with Article 10 ECHR, which protects freedom of expression, subject to Article 10(2) which allows the restriction of free speech if this is 'necessary in a democratic society' for (*inter alia*) 'the protection of the . . . rights of others'. In the Court of Appeal, having concluded that it is, in principle, possible to justify restrictions on political expression on grounds of taste and decency — so as to protect the 'rights of others' — Laws LJ went on to consider whether, within the specific factual matrix of this case, the broadcasters' decision was a lawful one.

Laws LJ

[33] . . . The English court is not a Strasbourg surrogate. The very difference between the international margin of appreciation and the municipal margin of discretion illustrates the confusion that would arise if the court so regarded itself. Our duty is to develop, by the common law's incremental method, a coherent and principled domestic law of human rights. In doing it, we are directed by the HRA (s.6) to insist on compliance by public authorities with the standards of the Convention, and to comply with them ourselves. We are given new powers and duties (HRA ss.3 and 4) to see that that is done. In all this we are to take account of the Strasbourg cases (s.2 . . .) . . .

[34] . . . Treating the ECHR text as a template for our own law runs the risk of an over-rigid approach. Travelling through the words of provisions like Article 10(2), with stops along the way to pronounce that this or that condition is met or not met, smacks to my mind of what Lord Wilberforce once condemned as the 'austerity of tabulated legalism' (see *Ministry of Home Affairs v Fisher* [1980] AC 319, 328). I accept of course that such a wintry process would be tempered by . . . the strong pragmatic philosophy of the Strasbourg court. Even so, while great respect is to be paid to the way in which the ECHR is framed, and therefore to the structure of provisions such as Article 10, I think the court's duty in confronting the claims of free speech, and the claims that may be ranged against it, in a context like that of the present case is very far distant from any exercise of textual interpretation. We are dealing here with bedrock principles. We are concerned with the protection

of free expression in the context of political debate. In the rancour and asperity of a general election this duty, owed to the people, is surely at its highest . . .

[36] . . . [A]s a matter of domestic law the courts owe a special responsibility to the public as the constitutional guardian of the freedom of political debate. This responsibility is most acute at the time and in the context of a public election, especially a general election. It has its origin in a deeper truth, which is that the courts are ultimately the trustees of our democracy's framework. I consider that this view is consonant with the common law's general recognition, apparent in recent years, of a category of fundamental or constitutional rights . . . Freedom of expression is plainly such a constitutional right, and its enjoyment by an accredited political party in an election contest must call, if anything, for especially heightened protection. We are in any case long past the point when interference with fundamental rights by public authorities can be justified by a bare demonstration of rationality or reasonableness: see *ex p Daly* . . .

[37] These considerations, with respect, give the lie to Mr Pannick's [counsel for the BBC] plea for deference to the decision-makers. If a producer were so insensitive as to authorise the inclusion of what is to be seen in the appellant's PEB video in an episode of a TV soap, the broadcasters would of course forbid its being shown and the courts would of course uphold them. That is at the extreme. There might be other more marginal situations, in which the courts would incline to defer to the broadcasters' judgment. Where the context is broadcast entertainment, I would accept without cavil that in the event of a legal challenge to a prohibition the courts should pay a very high degree of respect to the broadcasters' judgment, given the background of [the Broadcasting Act 1990, other relevant legislation, the non-statutory obligations of the BBC and the adjudications of the Broadcasting Standards Council]. Where the context is day-to-day news reporting the broadcasters' margin of discretion may be somewhat more constrained but will remain very considerable. But the *milieu* we are concerned with in this case, the cockpit of a general election, is inside the veins and arteries of the democratic process. The broadcasters' views are entitled to be respected, but their force and weight are modest at best. I emphasise this is in no sense a slur on their expertise: having looked through the evidence I am very conscious, if I may say so, of the experience and professionalism clearly possessed by Ms Sloman [the BBC's Chief Political Adviser], and her colleagues were no doubt likewise qualified. But in this context the court's constitutional responsibility to protect political speech is over-arching. It amounts to a duty which lies on the court's shoulders to decide for itself whether this censorship was justified . . .

[43] I have already made it plain that there is nothing gratuitous or sensational or untrue in the appellant's intended PEB. It is certainly graphic; and, as I have said, disturbing. But if we are to take political free speech seriously, those characteristics cannot begin to justify the censorship that was done in this case. Here the image is the message, or at least an important part of it. Certainly I would accept that the pictures do not answer the deep philosophical questions which the abortion debate generates. But they show what actually happens. I can see no answer to the claim that the appellant is entitled to show — not just tell — what happens.

[44] There may be instances, even in the context of a general election, in which political speech may justifiably be censored on grounds of taste or offensiveness. But in my judgment it would take a very extreme case, most likely involving factors, to which I have already referred, such as gratuitous sensationalism and dishonesty. It is unhelpful to try to conjure instances. On the facts of this case the broadcasters have in my judgment failed altogether to give sufficient weight to the pressing imperative of free political expression. The letter of 17th May 2001 [in which the BBC set out its objections to the broadcast] demonstrates as much. There is no recognition of the critical truth, the legal principle, that considerations of taste and decency cannot prevail over free speech by a

political party at election time save wholly exceptionally. The premise of the letter is that the appellant's message is something merely to be taken into account in judging whether the taste and decency standards are breached. That is a profoundly mistaken approach. The common law requires that the freedom of political speech to be enjoyed by an accredited party at a public election, most especially a general election, must not be interfered with save on the most pressing grounds, and such grounds will very rarely be shown by appeal to considerations of taste and decency alone . . .

[45] I am entirely clear that no such grounds are shown in the present case . . .

Jonathan Parker LJ agreed with Laws LJ. Simon Brown LJ gave a judgment agreeing with that of Laws LJ. A declaration was issued to the effect that the broadcasters' refusal to show the PEB was unlawful. The broadcasters appealed to the House of Lords.

Lord Nicholls

[16] . . . [T]he Court of Appeal in effect carried out its own balancing exercise between the requirements of freedom of political speech and the protection of the public from being unduly distressed in their own homes. That was not a legitimate exercise for the courts in this case. Parliament has decided where the balance shall be held. The latter interest prevails over the former to the extent that the offensive material ban applies without distinction to all television programmes, including party broadcasts. In the absence of a successful claim that the offensive material restriction is not compatible with the Convention rights of ProLife Alliance, it is not for the courts to find that broadcasters acted unlawfully when they did no more than give effect to the statutory and other obligations binding on them. Even in such a case the effect of section 6(2) of the Human Rights Act 1998 would have to be considered . . .

Lord Hoffmann

[49] The effect of the Court of Appeal's judgment was that instead of starting by accepting, as the judge had done, that the regulatory framework required the BBC not to screen a PEB unless it complied with generally accepted standards of taste and decency and then going on to ask whether the BBC had properly applied those standards, the Court of Appeal elided the two stages by asking whether it was consistent with freedom of speech for the BBC to apply such standards at all . . .

[51] In my opinion there are two questions to be asked. First, was Parliament entitled by section 6(1)(a) to impose on PEBs a need to comply with taste and decency standards which were meant to be taken seriously? Secondly, if it was, did the broadcasters properly apply those standards . . .

[On the first question, Lord Hoffmann concluded that Article 10 was not engaged: ProLife Alliance was merely prevented from making its point in a particular way, not denied access to television broadcasts altogether; and, in any event, 'there is no human right to use a television channel'. The real issue, therefore, was whether the requirements of taste and decency 'are a discriminatory, arbitrary or unreasonable condition for allowing a political party free access at election time to a particular public medium, namely television'. In deciding that they were not, his Lordship offered the following thoughts on deference:]

[75] My Lords, although the word "deference" is now very popular in describing the relationship between the judicial and the other branches of government, I do not think that its overtones of servility, or perhaps gracious concession, are appropriate to describe what is happening. In a society based upon the rule of law and the separation of powers, it is necessary to decide which

branch of government has in any particular instance the decision-making power and what the legal limits of that power are. That is a question of law and must therefore be decided by the courts.

[76] This means that the courts themselves often have to decide the limits of their own decision-making power. That is inevitable. But it does not mean that their allocation of decision-making power to the other branches of government is a matter of courtesy or deference. The principles upon which decision-making powers are allocated are principles of law. The courts are the independent branch of government and the legislature and executive are, directly and indirectly respectively, the elected branches of government. Independence makes the courts more suited to deciding some kinds of questions and being elected makes the legislature or executive more suited to deciding others. The allocation of these decision-making responsibilities is based upon recognised principles. The principle that the independence of the courts is necessary for a proper decision of disputed legal rights or claims of violation of human rights is a legal principle. It is reflected in article 6 of the Convention. On the other hand, the principle that majority approval is necessary for a proper decision on policy or allocation of resources is also a legal principle. Likewise, when a court decides that a decision is within the proper competence of the legislature or executive, it is not showing deference. It is deciding the law.

[77] In this particular case, the decision to make all broadcasts subject to taste and decency requirements represents Parliament's view that, as the Annan Committee [on the Future of Broadcasting: Cm 6753, 1977] put it (paragraph 16.3), "public opinion cannot be totally disregarded in the pursuit of liberty". That seems to me an entirely proper decision for Parliament as representative of the people to make. For the reasons I have given, it involves no arbitrary or unreasonable restriction on the right of free speech . . .

[78] If, as I think, Parliament was entitled to impose standards of taste and decency which were meant to be taken seriously, the next question is whether the broadcasters acted lawfully in deciding that the Alliance PEB did not comply . . .

[79] In my view the only route by which one can arrive at [the] conclusion [that the broadcasters erred in law] is that of the Court of Appeal, which is to say that the broadcasters were not entitled to apply standards of truth and decency at all. But I have already explained why I do not think that this route is legitimate. Once one accepts that the broadcasters were entitled to apply generally accepted standards, I do not see how it is possible for a court to say that they were wrong.

[80] Public opinion in these matters is often diverse, sometimes unexpected and in constant flux. Generally accepted standards on these questions are not a matter of intuition on the part of elderly male judges . . .

Lord Scott (dissenting)

[Lord Scott accepted that Article 10 was engaged. The key question, therefore, was whether the broadcasters' refusal to transmit the PEB was 'necessary in a democratic society for the protection of the right of home-owners that offensive material should not be transmitted into their homes'. He went on to restate the question thus: 'Was this a conclusion to which a reasonable decision maker, paying due regard to the Alliance's right to impart information about abortions to the electorate subject only to what was necessary in a democratic society to protect the rights of others, could have come?']

[95] In my opinion, it was not. The restrictions on the broadcasting of material offending against good taste and decency and of material offensive to public feeling were drafted so as to be capable

of application to all programmes, whether light entertainment, serious drama, historical or other documentaries, news reports, party political programmes, or whatever. But material that might be required to be rejected in one type of programme might be unexceptionable in another. The judgment of the decision maker would need to take into account the type of programme of which the material formed part as well as the audience at which the programme was directed. This was a party election broadcast directed at the electorate. He, or she, would need to apply the prescribed standard having regard to these factors and to the need that the application be compatible with the guarantees of freedom of expression contained in Article 10.

[96] The conclusion to which the broadcasters came could not, in my opinion, have been reached without a significant and fatal undervaluing of two connected features of the case: first, that the programme was to constitute a party election broadcast; second, that the only relevant criterion for a justifiable rejection on offensiveness grounds was that the rejection be necessary for the protection of the right of homeowners not to be subjected to offensive material in their own homes.

[97] The importance of the general election context of the Alliance's proposed programme cannot be overstated. We are fortunate enough to live in what is often described as, and I believe to be, a mature democracy. In a mature democracy political parties are entitled, and expected, to place their policies before the public so that the public can express its opinion on them at the polls. The constitutional importance of this entitlement and expectation is enhanced at election time.

[98] If, as here, a political party's desired election broadcast is factually accurate, not sensational-ised, and is relevant to a lawful policy on which its candidates are standing for election, I find it difficult to understand on what possible basis it could properly be rejected as being "offensive to public feeling". Voters in a mature democracy may strongly disagree with a policy being promoted by a televised party political broadcast but ought not to be offended by the fact that the policy is being promoted nor, if the promotion is factually accurate and not sensationalised, by the content of the programme. Indeed, in my opinion, the public in a mature democracy are not entitled to be offended by the broadcasting of such a programme. A refusal to transmit such a programme based upon the belief that the programme would be "offensive to very large numbers of viewers" (the [broadcasters'] letter of 17 May 2001) would not, in my opinion, be capable of being described as "necessary in a democratic society . . . for the protection of . . . rights of others". Such a refusal would, on the contrary, be positively inimical to the values of a democratic society, to which values it must be assumed that the public adhere . . .

[100] . . . [T]he decision of the BBC and the other broadcasters to refuse to transmit the Alli-ance's desired programme was, in my opinion, a decision to which no reasonable decision maker, applying the standards prescribed by paragraph 5(1)(d) of the BBC Agreement and section 6(1)(a) of the 1990 Act, and properly directing itself in accordance with article 10, could have come. I find myself in full agreement with the Court of Appeal and would dismiss this appeal.

Lord Walker

[After summarizing the case law on deference, and setting out the four principles laid down by Laws LJ in *Roth* (set out above at 9.3.5), his Lordship continued:]

[137] The second of these principles is certainly applicable in the present case and is of the greatest importance. Striking a fair balance between individual rights and the general interest of the community is inherent in the whole of the Convention: *Sporrong and Lönnroth v Sweden* (1982) 5 EHRR 35, 52, para 69. The other three points made by Laws LJ are thought-provoking but I do not

find them particularly helpful in determining this appeal, for several reasons. In this case (as in many cases raising human rights issues) responsibility for the alleged infringement of human rights cannot be laid entirely at the door of Parliament or at the door of an executive decision-maker. Responsibility for the alleged infringement is as it were spread between the two (this is a point made by Mr Andrew Geddis in an article at [2002] PL 615, 620–623). Moreover the court's (or the common law's) role as the constitutional guardian of free speech is a proposition with which many newspaper publishers might quarrel (see the observations of Lord Steyn in *Reynolds v Times Newspapers Ltd* [2001] 2 AC 127, 210–211, although in recent years your Lordships' House has fully recognised the central constitutional importance of free speech). A third difficulty is that the principles stated by Laws LJ do not allow, at any rate expressly, for the manner (which may be direct and central, or indirect and peripheral) in which Convention rights are engaged in the case before the court . . .

[139] . . . [T]he court's task is, not to substitute its own view for that of the broadcasters, but to review their decision with an intensity appropriate to all the circumstances of the case. Here the relevant factors include the following. (1) There is no challenge to the statutory (or in the case of the BBC quasi-statutory) requirement for exclusion of what I have (as shorthand) called "offensive material". That requirement is expressed in imprecise terms which call for a value judgment to be made. The challenge is to the value judgment made by the broadcasters. (2) Their remit was limited (for reasons not inimical to free speech) to a single decision either to accept or to reject the programme as presented to them. In making that decision the broadcasters were bound (in accordance with their respective codes) to have regard to the special power and pervasiveness of television. (3) Although your Lordships do not know the identities of all those involved in the decision, Ms Sloman is undoubtedly a broadcaster of great experience and high reputation. There is no reason to think that she and the others involved failed to approach their task responsibly and with a predisposition towards free speech. No doubt is cast on the good faith of any of them. (4) Free speech is particularly important in the political arena, especially at the time of a general election. That is why specific arrangements are made for PEBs, but the fact that PEBs are not immune from the general requirement to avoid offensive material is only a limited restriction on free speech, and it applies equally to all political parties. There was no arbitrary discrimination against the Alliance. (5) The effect of the decision was to deprive the Alliance of the opportunity of making a broadcast using disturbing images of the consequences of abortion. The Alliance still had (and used) the opportunity to broadcast its chosen text, and it was still at liberty to use a variety of other means of communicating its message. In that respect article 10, although engaged, was not engaged as fully as if there had been some total ban . . .

[141] I . . . see force in [the] submission that the Court of Appeal came close to overlooking the fact that PEBs are not immune from the requirement for offensive material to be excluded. I also see some force in [the] criticism that the Court of Appeal attached too much importance to the disturbing images which the Alliance wished to transmit for their shock effect. Most important of all, I think (with very great respect to the Court of Appeal) that although not avowedly engaged in a merits review, they did in fact engage in something close to that. Although my opinion has fluctuated, in the end I do not think that it has been shown that the broadcasters' decision, even if reviewed with some intensity, was wrong. I would therefore allow the appeal.

Lord Millett agreed with Lord Nicholls. Appeal allowed.

QUESTIONS

- Did Laws LJ, in the Court of Appeal, engage in (something close to) merits review?
- If so, was he wrong to do so?

The decision of the House of Lords in this case is roundly condemned by Barendt [2003] *PL* 580 at 581 (cf Geddis (2003) 66 *MLR* 885):

Passages in the speeches in the House of Lords are baffling or, to be frank, obscure. What is clear is that it misunderstood the character of the Alliance Party case. Simply put, it was that the taste and decency rule should be applied in a way compatible with freedom of political expression, exercised in this case by means of the party election broadcast . . . *Pace* Lord Hoffmann, that did not involve a claim that the statute, or the BBC Agreement, should be disregarded or not taken seriously. If he were right, we would have to conclude that any judicial decision taken under s 3 of the HRA 1998, requiring legislation to be interpreted to render it compatible with Convention rights plays fast and loose with the statute. That is clearly wrong.

The ProLife Alliance's case was merely that the broadcasters should apply the taste and decency rule compatibly with Article 10, to the extent permitted by the legislation. The legislation could comfortably have been read as leaving scope for the operation of Article 10, and hence for the sort of review of the broadcasters' discretion contemplated by the Court of Appeal and Lord Scott. It is submitted that their Lordships' error — particularly evident in the excerpt above from Lord Nicholls's speech — was to assume that Parliament had foreclosed on that possibility. The intellectual fragility of this reasoning smacks of an arbitrary and *ad hoc* approach to deference. Whether articulated or not, behind the veil of judicially-divined legislative intention must lie deeper reasons for deference; it is imperative, if that concept is to evolve into a workable and intelligible public law doctrine, that such reasons are openly stated by courts.

9.3.7 Substantive Review: The Future

Now that courts are clearly able and willing to apply the proportionality test in at least some cases, what role, if any, remains for the reasonableness test? Wade and Forsyth, *Administrative Law* (Oxford 2004) at 371, consider that *Wednesbury* 'is now in terminal decline'. Meanwhile, Craig, *Administrative Law* (Oxford 2003) at 628–635, argues that proportionality should be embraced as a general principle of judicial review, in time supplanting *Wednesbury*. This matter was considered by the Court of Appeal in *R (Association of British Civilian Internees (Far East Region))* v. *Secretary of State for Defence* [2003] EWCA Civ 473 [2003] QB 1397. Giving the judgment of the court, Dyson LJ explained:

[33] It is true that the result that follows will often be the same whether the test that is applied is proportionality or *Wednesbury* unreasonableness. This is particularly so in a case in the field of social and economic policy. But the tests are different . . . It follows that the two tests will not always yield the same results . . .

[34] . . . It seems to us that the case for [recognizing proportionality as a general principle of review in domestic law] is indeed a strong one. As Lord Slynn points out [in *R (Alconbury Developments Ltd)* v. *Secretary of State for the Environment, Transport and the Regions* [2001] UKHL 23 [2003] 2 AC 295 at [27]], trying to keep the *Wednesbury* principle and proportionality in separate compartments is unnecessary and confusing. The criteria of proportionality are more precise and sophisticated . . . It is true that sometimes proportionality may require the reviewing court to assess for itself the balance that has been struck by the decision-maker, and that may produce a different result from one that would be arrived at on an application of the *Wednesbury* test. But the strictness of the *Wednesbury* test has been relaxed in recent years even in areas which have nothing to do with fundamental rights . . . The *Wednesbury* test is moving closer to proportionality and in

some cases it is not possible to see any daylight between the two tests . . . Although we did not hear argument on the point, we have difficulty in seeing what justification there now is for retaining the *Wednesbury* test.

[35] But we consider that it is not for this court to perform its burial rites. The continuing existence of the *Wednesbury* test has been acknowledged by the House of Lords on more than one occasion. The obvious starting point is *R* v *Secretary of State for the Home Department ex p Brind* [1991] 1 AC 696 . . . [in which] all of their Lordships rejected the proportionality test in that case and applied the traditional *Wednesbury* test. In other words, they closed the door to proportionality in domestic law for the time being . . .

[37] Finally, passages in the speeches of Lord Slynn in [*R (Alconbury Developments Ltd) v Secretary of State for the Environment, Transport and the Regions* [2003] 2 AC 295, 320–321] and Lord Cooke in [*Daly* [2001] 2 AC 532, 548–549] . . . imply a recognition that the *Wednesbury* test survives, although their Lordships' clearly expressed view is that it should be laid to rest. It seems to us that this is a step which can only be taken by the House of Lords. We therefore approach the issues in the present appeal on the footing that the *Wednesbury* test does survive, and that this is the correct test to apply in a case such as the present which does not involve Community law and does not engage any question of rights under the ECHR.

This conclusion has been accepted in subsequent cases (*eg, R (Isle of Anglesey County Council)* v. *Secretary of State for Work and Pensions* [2003] EWHC 2518 (Admin); *R (Ann Summers Ltd)* v. *Jobcentre Plus* [2003] EWHC 1416 (Admin)).

Is the view advanced in the *Internees* case that *Wednesbury* review should be replaced by proportionality a convincing one? In supporting such a development, Craig (*loc cit*) contends that the inherent flexibility of proportionality means that it can, when necessary, meet the concerns of constitutional and institutional competence which underpin the deferential *Wednesbury* standard. However, conceptualized thus, does not proportionality shade into *Wednesbury*? The following passage, which deals with the role of proportionality in EU law, highlights precisely this point.

....

Tridimas, 'Proportionality in Community Law: Searching for the Appropriate Standard of Scrutiny'
in Ellis (ed), *The Principle of Proportionality in the Laws of Europe* (Oxford 1999)

. . . The principle of proportionality has exerted particular influence in the field of agricultural law. In effect, the fundamental difficulty which the Community's political institutions, and reflectively the Court, have encountered in the sphere of the common agricultural policy is how to allocate burdens in declining and oversupplied markets . . .

In relation to market regulation measures, the Court applies a loose test of proportionality. Although it is prepared to assess whether a measure is appropriate and necessary in view of all relevant circumstances and to scrutinise the way the institution concerned has exercised its discretion, where it comes to the adoption of legislative measures involving economic policy choices, it will defer to the expertise and the responsibility of the adopting institution exercising "marginal" rather than "comprehensive" review. In Case C-331/88, *Fedesa* [1990] ECR I-4023, it held that the lawfulness of the prohibition on an economic activity is subject to the condition that the prohibitory measures are appropriate and necessary in order to achieve the objectives legitimately pursued by the legislation. Where there is a choice between several appropriate measures, recourse must be had to the least onerous, and the disadvantages caused must not be disproportionate to the aims pursued. The Court qualified that principle, however, by stating:

. . . with regard to judicial review of compliance with those conditions it must be stated that in matters concerning the common agricultural policy the Community legislature has a discretionary power which corresponds to the political responsibilities given to it by [the relevant provisions of] the Treaty. Consequently, the legality of a measure adopted in that sphere can be affected only if the measure is manifestly inappropriate having regard to the objective which the competent institution is seeking to pursue.

The expression "manifestly inappropriate" delineates what the Court perceives to be the limits of its judicial function with regard to review of measures involving choices of economic policy . . . The test grants to the Community institutions ample discretion . . .

In order to determine whether a measure is necessary, the Court is receptive to argument that the same objective may be attained by less restrictive means. The case law suggests however that, in relation to policy measures, the Court does not apply the less restrictive alternative test scrupulously, relying instead on some notion of reasonableness or arbitrary conduct. In *Fedesa* it was claimed that the prohibition of certain hormones on health protection grounds was not necessary. The Court did not examine whether there were any less restrictive alternatives. It held that since the Council enjoyed discretion and had made no manifest error in considering that the prohibition was appropriate, it was also entitled to take the view that the objectives pursued could not be achieved by less onerous means . . .

QUESTION

- Does the mode of review adopted in *Fedesa* most closely resemble the *Wednesbury* or the proportionality test?

Against this background, the following comments of Laws LJ in *R (Mahmood)* v. *Secretary of State for the Home Department* [2001] 1 WLR 840 at [19] should be considered:

[I]n a case involving human rights . . . [a higher] intensity of review is generally to be followed . . . but that approach and the basic *Wednesbury* rule are by no means hermetically sealed one from the other. There is, rather, what may be called a sliding scale of review; the graver the impact of the decision in question upon the individual affected by it, the more substantial the justification that will be required. It is in the nature of the human condition that cases where, objectively, the individual is most gravely affected will be those where what we have come to call his fundamental rights are or are said to be put in jeopardy. In the present case, whether or not the Convention is under consideration, any reasonable person will at once recognise the right to family life, exemplified in the right of the parties to a genuine marriage to cohabit without any undue interference, as being in the nature of a fundamental right (I prefer the expression fundamental *freedom*) . . .

Recent cases indicate the desirability of a low, *Wednesbury* standard of review in certain contexts. For instance, the courts were unwilling in *R* v. *Secretary of State for the Environment, ex parte Spath Holme Ltd* [2001] 2 AC 349 to go beyond *Wednesbury* review of an order regulating the rent which could be charged in respect of regulated tenancies; although the order was alleged to breach Article 1 of Protocol 1 to the ECHR, the Court of Appeal held (at [64]–[67]) and the House of Lords agreed (at 395–396, *per* Lord Bingham) that striking an economically fair balance between landlords and tenants was a question of social policy for Ministers to answer, and could be set aside only if found to be perverse. Moreover, it was accepted in *R (Flash)* v. *Southwark London Borough Council* [2004] EWHC 717 (Admin) at [19] that a relaxed *Wednesbury* standard was appropriate in reviewing whether a local authority had legitimately concluded that accommodation offered to the claimant in discharge of its statutory duty was 'suitable'. Similarly, in *R (Jones)* v. *Mansfield District*

Council [2003] EWCA Civ 1408 [2004] 2 P & CR 14 at [17], Dyson LJ held that a planning authority's conclusion as to whether a proposed development was likely to have significant effects on the environment involved 'an exercise of judgment or opinion' and was therefore subject only to *Wednesbury* review. These decisions (and many others: see, *eg, R (McDonagh)* v. *Hounslow London Borough Council* [2004] EWHC 511 (Admin); *R (Peterson)* v. *First Secretary of State* [2004] EWHC 185 (Admin)) do not reluctantly perpetuate the *Wednesbury* test; they positively endorse it as an appropriate standard of review in some situations.

QUESTION

- Should proportionality replace *Wednesbury* or should courts have both at their disposal?

9.4 Concluding Remarks

One of the key foundations upon which English administrative law has been built is the distinction between review and appeal. The notion of substantive review poses a particular challenge in this context. The traditional response was to permit such review only in very limited circumstances — hence the *Wednesbury* test. However, in recent years, as a response to the growth of government and the declining ability of Parliament to hold the executive to account, the willingness of the courts to intervene has increased, culminating in acceptance (at least in some fields) of proportionality review. It is clear, though, that the courts are alive to the argument that judges and administrators should continue to serve distinct roles and, to that end, the judiciary has attempted to refashion substantive review in a manner which preserves — albeit in a more modest form — the distinction between review and appeal. In this way it is apparent that the courts are seeking to respond to changes in the legal and political environments in a manner which is sensitive to the underlying architecture of the British constitution. As we have seen, the balance between judicial protection of citizens' rights and interests and the autonomy of the other constitutional branches is dynamic; it will continue to evolve as the notion of fundamental rights becomes an increasingly embedded feature of our legal culture.

FURTHER RESOURCES

Bamforth and Leyland (eds), *Public Law in a Multi-Layered Constitution* (Oxford 2003), chs 12 (Taggart) and 13 (Hunt)

Clayton, 'Judicial Deference and Democratic Dialogue: The Legitimacy of Judicial Intervention under the Human Rights Act 1998' [2004] *PL* 33

Craig, 'The Courts, the Human Rights Act and Judicial Review' (2001) 117 *LQR* 589

Dyzenhaus (ed), *The Unity of Public Law* (Oxford 2004), ch 11 (Allan)

Ellis (ed), *The Principle of Proportionality in the Laws of Europe* (Oxford 1999)

Jowell, 'Beyond the Rule of Law: Towards Constitutional Judicial Review' [2000] *PL* 671

Tridimas, *The General Principles of EC Law* (Oxford 1999), chs 3–4

The House of Lords' decision in *A* v. *Home Secretary* [2004] UKHL 56, which is relevant to many issues considered in this chapter, was handed down after completion of the manuscript. However, an appendix has been added at the end of the book concerning that case.

10 THE RULE AGAINST BIAS

10.1 The Rule: Its Scope and Rationale

The notion of procedural fairness is a wide-ranging one, and encompasses a number of distinct principles of administrative law. We address, in chs 11 and 12, the various procedural hurdles which public authorities must clear if they are to satisfy the demands of fairness; we therefore consider such matters as the characteristics of a 'fair hearing', and the extent to which individuals must be given reasons for the conclusions at which decision-makers arrive. In this chapter, however, we are concerned with a prior question regarding not the fairness of the decision-making process (in terms of the details of the procedure which is adopted), but the nature of the decision-making body itself.

It is not difficult to identify underlying rationales for procedural fairness. It is self-evident that fairness, in some form, is a highly desirable characteristic in any system of public administration. Because it promotes full and fair consideration of the issues and evidence, procedural fairness, as Lord Steyn observed in *Raji* v. *General Medical Council* [2003] UKPC 24 [2003] 1 WLR 1052 at [13], plays 'an instrumental role in promoting just decisions'. It is normatively significant, too, because to accord fair treatment to individuals is to act in a manner which respects their dignity and value as members of the community, rather than characterizing them as the objects of an arbitrary and authoritarian governmental process. Moreover, it is important for public confidence in, and co-operation with, the administrative system that it *appears* to be fair, as well as actually being fair. We consider these underlying objectives of procedural fairness in greater detail in ch 11.

However, this chapter is concerned specifically with the rule against bias (*nemo judex in re sua*), a rule of long-standing; the crucial point, for present purposes, is that if a decision-making system is to lay claim to any degree of fairness, then the provision of unbiased tribunals and decision-makers is a pre-requisite. No amount of procedural safeguards (such as the right to legal representation or to cross-examine witnesses) is likely to deliver fairness if the tribunal is, in the first place, biased in the sense of being inherently predisposed against (or, indeed, for) the individual about whom the decision is being made. The connection between 'bias' and 'fairness' is drawn out in the following excerpt.

....

Galligan, *Due Process and Fair Procedures*
(Oxford 1996)

. . . To lack impartiality means being willing to decide a matter for reasons which are unrelated to legitimate reasons. The judge who allows his personal feelings towards a party to intrude on his deliberations, or the licensing justice who takes into account his own financial interest in the licence being refused, are both acting out of bias and have surrendered their impartiality. The personal feelings of the judge and the financial interests of the justice are reasons which should be excluded from their decisions. They are improper reasons because they are unrelated to the authoritative standards by which the cases should be decided. The judge is supposed to decide between the two parties according to the principles of civil law, while the justice should determine licensing applications according to the statutory criteria. Where there is discretion so that the judge or the justice has to settle for himself at least some of the standards to apply, it would be equally illegitimate to adopt standards based on personal feelings or financial interest. Any choice which discretion allows does not include the selection of standards based on personal feelings or financial interest.

Once the link is made between loss of impartiality and the process of reasoning which an official is required to follow, the relationship between bias and fairness can be seen. For the official who acts for improper reasons fails to apply authoritative standards correctly or to exercise discretion properly; as a consequence, the person affected is not treated in accordance with those standards and, therefore, is treated unfairly. This does not undermine the idea that reasons do not come ready-made or branded as good or bad; reasons, of course, are constructed out of a social context, guided, but not closely constricted, by given legal standards. The present argument claims merely that whatever reasons are good reasons, those displaying bias will never be amongst their number. We can now see why loss of impartiality is roundly condemned: the unseemliness of prejudice or personal interest influencing the holder of a public office is evidence of the deeper principle rather than the principle itself. We can also see that, being an attack on the idea that in any legal context there are authoritative standards to apply, the absence of impartiality is a fundamental flaw which renders the process illegitimate . . .

Galligan's explanation helpfully illuminates the connection between, on the one hand, the rule against bias and, on the other hand, the relevancy of considerations and propriety of purpose doctrines which we considered above in ch 8. All of those principles are constituted on the basis that discretion can be exercised properly only on the strength of considerations — or 'standards' — which are legitimate. Whereas the relevancy of considerations and propriety of purpose doctrines tend to focus our attention on those constraints on discretion which are explicit or implicit in the statutory scheme — and whose identification is therefore largely a matter of context — the rule against bias is concerned with a more fundamental, and more obvious, set of factors such as personal animosity and pecuniary interest, the operation of which necessarily calls into question the legitimacy of the decision-making process.

One of the objectives of the rule against bias, therefore, is to deliver a system of decision-making which, at quite a fundamental level, is *actually* fair and legitimate. However, as the following excerpt demonstrates, the rule's rationale is in fact somewhat broader — and so, as a result, is the rule itself.

....

R v. Sussex Justices, ex parte McCarthy [1924] 1 KB 256
Divisional Court of the King's Bench Division

Whitworth, the driver of a motorbike which was involved in a collision with McCarthy's motorbike, made a claim through his solicitor for damages from McCarthy. In addition, a criminal prosecution was brought for dangerous driving and McCarthy was convicted by a magistrates' court. The person who acted as the clerk to the justices on the day in question — the deputy clerk — was a partner in the firm of solicitors which was acting on Whitworth's behalf. He had retired with the justices, but, according to the justices' affidavit, he had not referred to the case during his retirement with them and he had not been consulted whilst the justices were coming to their decision.

McCarthy's solicitor stated that he (the solicitor) had been unaware of the deputy clerk's interest in the case until the justices had retired; however, he brought the matter to their attention when they returned to court. McCarthy later sought a quashing order in respect of his conviction. (On the current role and responsibilities of justices' clerks, see *Practice Note (Justices' Clerks)* [1954] 1 WLR 213 and *Practice Direction (QBD: Justices: Clerk to Court)* [2001] 1 WLR 1866.)

Lord Hewart CJ

It is clear that the deputy clerk was a member of the firm of solicitors engaged in the conduct of proceedings for damages against the applicant in respect of the same collision as that which gave rise to the charge that the justices were considering. It is said, and, no doubt, truly, that when that gentleman retired in the usual way with the justices, taking with him the notes of the evidence in case the justices might desire to consult him, the justices came to a conclusion without consulting him, and that he scrupulously abstained from referring to the case in any way. But while that is so, a long line of cases shows that it is not merely of some importance but is of fundamental importance that justice should not only be done, but should manifestly and undoubtedly be seen to be done. The question therefore is not whether in this case the deputy clerk made any observation or offered any criticism which he might not properly have made or offered; the question is whether he was so related to the case in its civil aspect as to be unfit to act as clerk to the justices in the criminal matter. The answer to that question depends not upon what actually was done but upon what might appear to be done. Nothing is to be done which creates even a suspicion that there has been an improper interference with the course of justice. Speaking for myself, I accept the statements contained in the justices' affidavit, but they show very clearly that the deputy clerk was connected with the case in a capacity which made it right that he should scrupulously abstain from referring to the matter in any way, although he retired with the justices; in other words, his one position was such that he could not, if he had been required to do so, discharge the duties which his other position involved. His twofold position was a manifest contradiction. In those circumstances I am satisfied that this conviction must be quashed, unless it can be shown that the applicant or his solicitor was aware of the point that might be taken, refrained from taking it, and took his chance of an acquittal on the facts, and then, on a conviction being recorded, decided to take the point. On the facts I am satisfied that there has been no waiver of the irregularity . . .

Lush and Sankey JJ agreed. The conviction was quashed.

Lord Hewart's directive that 'justice should not only be done, but should manifestly and undoubtedly be seen to be done' is part of the bedrock of English administrative law. It reveals a view of the rule against bias — and of the policy objectives which underpin and shape that rule — which emphasizes perception as much as reality. The purpose of the rule, on this view, is not merely to promote fairness in decision-making, but to ensure that practices which merely create an *impression* of bias are rendered unlawful. The reason for constructing the rule against bias thus is perhaps most readily apparent in relation to decision-making in a judicial context. It is clear, for instance, that public confidence in the criminal justice system depends fundamentally on the perception that criminal trials are conducted in a fair, impartial, and unbiased manner. Perception is, however, equally important in other, administrative contexts. Public trust in government — and, hence, the willingness of individuals to co-operate with public authorities in their endeavour to secure effective administration for the public good — requires a conviction on the part of the public that decision-making functions are discharged in an unbiased manner, and that applications for licences, planning permission, and so on, are determined on merit, not on grounds of status or favour.

The law in this area falls into two principal parts. We begin with cases in which the disqualification of the decision-maker is automatic, because of the directness and nature of his interest in the matter in relation to which he is asked to exercise discretion or judgment. We then turn to cases in which — in the absence of an interest of such a nature as to render disqualification automatic — the court is concerned to examine the circumstances more thoroughly, in order to determine whether there is a risk of or appearance of bias sufficient to disqualify the decision-maker.

10.2 Automatic Disqualification

10.2.1 Financial Interests

The general principle

It is a well-established proposition that, if a decision-maker has a direct financial interest in the outcome of the decision-making process, he will be automatically disqualified from taking part — and, if he takes part in spite of his interest, his decision may be set aside. In fact Jones [1999] *PL* 391 at 399 suggests that the rule

might be better thought of as a rule of automatic *disclosure*, rather than *disqualification*. The mere fact that a judge feels that he has an interest which needs to be disclosed to the parties to the litigation does not mean that he must automatically disqualify himself. It is open for him to do so, but the normal expectation would be that the decision is one for the parties (and fellow judges, if appropriate) to make. In the absence of adequate disclosure, the disqualification is retrospective, operating on appeal from the original decision.

If full disclosure is made of financial interests (or indeed any other interest that would otherwise disqualify the decision-maker on grounds of bias), it is therefore open to the relevant party to waive his right to object, provided that, as the Court of Appeal put it in *Locabail (UK) Ltd* v. *Bayfield Properties Ltd* [2000] QB 451 at 475, the waiver is 'clear and unequivocal, and made with full knowledge of all the facts relevant to the decision whether to waive or not'. (It should also be noted that the rule against bias yields in the face of both statutory authorization and necessity — that is, where no alternative decision-maker exists — although the ECtHR held in *Kingsley* v. *United Kingdom* (2002) 35 EHRR 10 (on which see further Forsyth [2001] *CLJ* 449 and Leigh [2002] *PL* 407) that the common law doctrine of necessity cannot excuse breaches of Article 6 ECHR, which we discuss below at 10.5.) We begin, however, with a classic example of the operation of the rule in circumstances in which the judge failed to disclose his financial interest — and in which, therefore, disqualification followed automatically (albeit, as Jones observes, retrospectively).

Dimes v. *The Proprietors of the Grand Junction Canal* (1852) 3 HLC 759
House of Lords

The respondent company had been involved in proceedings before Lord Cottenham LC and had been granted relief by him. Lord Cottenham, however, held shares in the company (partly on his own account, and partly as a trustee for others), and the validity of his action was in issue in this case.

Lord Campbell

No one can suppose that Lord Cottenham could be, in the remotest degree, influenced by the interests that he had in this concern; but, my Lords, it is of the last importance that the maxim that no man is to be a judge in his own cause should be held sacred. And this is not to be confined to a cause in which he is a party, but applies to a cause in which he has an interest. Since I have had the honour to be Chief Justice of the Court of Queen's Bench, we have again and again set aside proceedings in inferior tribunals because an individual, who had an interest in a cause, took a part in the decision. And it will have a most salutary influence on these tribunals when it is known that this high Court of last resort, in a case in which the Lord Chancellor of England had an interest, considered that his decree was on that account a decree not according to law, and was set aside. This will be a lesson to all inferior tribunals to take care not only that in their decrees they are not influenced by their personal interest, but to avoid the appearance of labouring under such an influence.

Lord St Leonards LC and Lord Brougham agreed that Lord Cottenham had been disqualified from acting as a judge in the proceedings in question on account of his interest.

Lord Campbell's speech begs important questions concerning the *rationale* and *scope* of this limb of the rule against bias; it is necessary to consider each in turn.

Can the automatic disqualification principle be justified?

As we observed above, the importance of securing public confidence in judicial and administrative decision-making is such that the rule against bias prohibits not only practices that are *actually* unfair, but also those which may give the *impression* of unfairness. It is unclear, however, where precisely the aspect of the bias rule presently under consideration fits into this framework. Although Lord Campbell's opening remark — that '[n]o one can suppose that Lord Cottenham could be, in the remotest degree, influenced by the interests that he had in this concern' — is questionable (see Olowofoyeku's comments in the next excerpt), the fact that he adopted that premise begs an important question: if he was satisfied that the Lord Chancellor was *not actually influenced* by his financial interest, and that *no-one could form the impression that he was so affected*, what purpose did the latter's disqualification serve?

QUESTION

- Which (if any) part of the rationale underlying the rule against bias is furthered by the decision in *Dimes*, and the principle for which it now stands?

Lord Campbell's remarks in *Dimes* notwithstanding, the thinking underlying the principle that a direct financial interest automatically disqualifies the decision-maker is that such interests are so powerful an influence that they *inevitably* create a risk of bias (actual or apprehended). However, this equation between financial interest and actual or apprehended bias can be balanced only if some rather crude, and quite possibly inaccurate, assumptions are made. The central difficulty — that the automatic disqualification rule is capable of operating on the basis of premises which are inappropriate to the specific facts of the case — follows from the very essence of the rule, which holds that a direct financial interest should disqualify the decision-maker irrespective of the context, and without the need for any detailed evaluation of the facts (beyond, that is, establishing the existence of the interest). As Olowofoyeku observes in the following passage, such an approach risks elevating expediency above a range of competing — and arguably more compelling — policy considerations. (The tests for bias, referred to in the following extract, based variously upon 'danger', 'likelihood', 'suspicion', and 'apprehension' are considered below at 10.3; for the time being, the key factor which distinguishes those tests from the automatic disqualification principle is that they require evaluation of the circumstances, and provide for disqualification only if there is a sufficient degree of likelihood that they would give rise to a perception of bias.)

......

Olowofoyeku, 'The *Nemo Judex* Rule: The Case Against Automatic Disqualification' [2000] PL 456

. . . There is nothing magical about automatic disqualification (other than expediency) which makes it better at protecting the integrity of the administration of justice than any other principle. The warning of Slade J. in *R v. Camborne Justices, ex parte Pearce* [[1955] 1 QB 41 at 51] against the erroneous impression that "it is more important that justice should appear to be done than that it should in fact be done" is salutary. Indiscriminate application of automatic disqualification, or, treating automatic disqualification as an end in itself, may well imply that such an erroneous impression is correct, and may serve to undermine the integrity of the administration of justice. For, if the purpose of the *nemo judex* rule is to preserve public confidence in the administration of justice, it may be that such confidence would be compromised rather than enhanced if the public go away feeling that justice was not done because of a "mere technicality", rather than because there was a real risk of injustice having occurred. The famous statement of Lord Denning M.R. in *Metropolitan Properties Ltd v. Lannon* [[1969] 1 QB 577 at 599] was to the effect that justice is rooted in confidence, and that confidence is destroyed when right-thinking people go away thinking that the judge was biased.

There is a corollary to this, and it is found in these words of Sackville, Finn and Kenny JJ. of the Australian Federal Court in [*Ebner v. Official Trustee in Bankruptcy* [1999] FCA 110 at [37]]:

> It would seem on the authorities (and [counsel for the applicant] said it was settled law) that a failure to disclose, say, a shareholding in a corporate party to litigation will disqualify a judge, even though the shares are worth very little and the prospect of the litigation making a difference to the price of the shares is utterly remote. If this is so, the consequence is that a judgment delivered after many days of hearing is liable to be set aside, notwithstanding that no reasonable person could suggest that there is any suspicion of judicial bias. Why is it to be assumed that the confidence of fair-minded people in the administration of justice would be shaken by the existence of a direct pecuniary interest of no tangible value, but not by the waste of resources and the delays brought about by setting aside a judgment on the ground that the judge is disqualified for having such an interest[?]

Thus, it may be that to ask whether there is any good reason in principle for limiting automatic disqualification to cases of financial interest is to ask the wrong question. [This question was prompted by the decision of the House of Lords in *R* v. *Bow Street Stipendiary Magistrate, ex parte Pinochet Ugarte (No 2)* [2000] AC 119 which, as we will see below, extended the scope of the automatic disqualification principle in English law.] It may be that a better question is whether there is any need [at all] for a rule of automatic disqualification. In *Ebner*, the Full Court of the Australian Federal Court said [at [36]] that it might be "thought somewhat anomalous that a special rule of automatic disqualification has survived for cases of direct pecuniary interest, especially in Australia where the more stringent 'reasonable suspicion' test [on which see below at 10.3.1] has been adopted". The Court referred to the statement of Lord Hewart C.J. in *R* v. *Sussex Justices, ex p. McCarthy* that justice should not only be done, but should be seen to be done as the principle underlying the Australian "reasonable suspicion" test, and queried why, if this was the case, it was necessary to have a special rule which disqualifies a judge even where an ordinary reasonable member of the public could not suspect bias on the part of the judge.

... In *Dimes* itself ... [i]t is true that Lord Campbell said that no one could suppose that Lord Cottenham could be, in the remotest degree, influenced by the interest he had in the canal company. But it has been commented [by Sackville, Finn and Kenny JJ in *Ebner, op cit*] that, "while lawyers might be prepared to accept that Lord Cottenham could not have been influenced, it is a little difficult to see why Lord Campbell was so confident that *no-one* could reasonably reach a different view". Lord Cottenham's interest of "several thousand pounds" in 1852 would probably translate to "several hundreds of thousands of pounds" today. It would be fairly open to reasonable people to suspect or apprehend that a judge might be influenced by such a substantial shareholding, *a fortiori* if the liability of the shareholders is not limited. A view that there would be a real likelihood or danger that a judge with such a stake in a litigant might be prejudiced in favour of the litigant could not be described in any way as unreasonable or fanciful, notwithstanding the judge's eminence. Therefore *Dimes* could just as easily have been decided on the basis of [a] real likelihood or danger, or reasonable apprehension, of bias ...

... [M]y conclusion is that automatic disqualification is draconian, disproportionate and unnecessary. There is nothing that can be achieved by automatic disqualification that cannot be achieved by an application of the real danger/reasonable apprehension test. On the other hand, application of the automatic disqualification rule may well lead to the disqualification of judges in situations wherein a closer inspection of the circumstances would reveal that there was never any realistic possibility of bias. While it may be expedient for judges to apply a mechanical rule, such mechanistic adjudication smacks of abdication. There may well be cases wherein it is obvious that the judgment should not be allowed to stand. Examples of such may be the ... *Dimes* [case]. Such cases can fit within the apprehended bias rule, for if, in the circumstances, reasonable people would not apprehend bias, then it cannot be said that 'it is obvious' that the judgment should not be allowed to stand ...

The scope of automatic financial disqualification

The central and pervasive problem concerning the automatic disqualification principle concerns its undiscriminating nature. It is its rigidity, and its scant regard for the broader context within which the issues arise, that are likely to cause difficulties. It is important to appreciate, however, that the principle is not quite as crude as it may first appear. In particular, there are certain financial interests which are recognized as being so remote or indirect as to fall outside the scope of automatic disqualification. The rule is sometimes stated in rather expansive terms; for instance, in *R* v. *Rand* (1866) LR 1 QB 230 at 232, Blackburn J said that 'any direct pecuniary interest, however small, in the subject of inquiry, does disqualify a person from acting as a judge in the matter'. A similarly exacting formulation was advanced in *R* v. *Camborne Justices, ex parte Pearce* [1955] 1 QB 41 at 47 by Slade J. However, a more subtle approach was recently endorsed by a Court of Appeal consisting of Lord Bingham CJ, Lord Woolf MR, and Sir Richard Scott V-C in *Locabail (UK) Ltd* v. *Bayfield Properties Ltd* [2000] QB 451 at [10]:

While the older cases speak of disqualification if the judge has an interest in the outcome of the proceedings "however small," there has in more recent authorities been acceptance of a de minimis exception: *B.T.R. Industries South Africa (Pty.) Ltd. v. Metal and Allied Workers' Union*, 1992 (3) S.A. 673, 694; *Reg. v. Inner West London Coroner, Ex parte Dallaglio* [1994] 4 All E.R. 139, 162; *Auckland Casino Ltd. v. Casino Control Authority* [1995] 1 N.Z.L.R. 142, 148. This seems to us a proper exception provided the potential effect of any decision on the judge's personal interest is so small as to be incapable of affecting his decision one way or the other; but it is important, bearing in mind the rationale of the rule, that any doubt should be resolved in favour of disqualification. In any case where the judge's interest is said to derive from the interest of a spouse, partner or other family member the link must be so close and direct as to render the interest of that other person, for all practical purposes, indistinguishable from an interest of the judge himself.

The Court of Appeal then went on to apply this more subtle view of the automatic disqualification principle to the facts of the case.

Locabail (UK) Ltd v. *Bayfield Properties Ltd* [2000] QB 451
Court of Appeal

Locabail (UK) Ltd took legal proceedings, in the latter part of 1998, against two companies which were both controlled by Mr Emmanuel, in order to enforce charges securing the payment of advances made to him. The securities consisted of property owned by the companies: Hans House, Knightsbridge, in the case of Waldorf Investment Corporation, and Hawks Hill in Surrey, in the case of Bayfield Properties Ltd. Mrs Emmanuel, however, who was (or became) a defendant in both actions, claimed, on the basis of representations made to her by her husband, and her reliance thereupon, to be the equitable owner of Hawks Hill and to have a beneficial interest in Hans House. On 27 October 1998, the judge discovered in one of the bundles a press cutting stating that the City law firm Herbert Smith was acting for Sudoexport against Mr Emmanuel and against a company (Howard Holdings Inc, a company controlled by Mr Emmanuel which had money claims against him). Previously unaware of Herbert Smith's involvement, the judge — a deputy High Court judge — immediately drew the parties' attention to the fact that he was a senior partner in the firm. Mrs Emmanuel raised no objection at the time. However, in March 1999, after the judge had rejected Mrs Emmanuel's contentions as to the beneficial ownership of the two properties, she made an application asking him to disqualify himself from further involvement in the case and to direct a rehearing before a different judge. The judge concluded that no conflict of interest arose, and refused Mrs Emmanuel's application; she therefore sought permission to appeal. Three points arose: whether the judge was automatically disqualified; if not, whether an appearance of bias arose on the facts (on which see below at 10.3), and whether Mrs Emmanuel, by inaction, had waived any right to object.

Lord Bingham of Cornhill CJ, Lord Woolf MR and Sir Richard Scott V-C

[42] [Miss Williamson, counsel for Mrs Emmanuel] submits that there was a conflict of interest between Mrs. Emmanuel and Herbert Smith's clients, Sudoexport and/or the liquidator of Howard Holdings Inc. The conflict of interest is constructed as follows: Sudoexport has money claims against Mr. Emmanuel. So does Howard Holdings Inc. in liquidation. Locabail is one of Mr. Emmanuel's creditors. If Mrs. Emmanuel's claims to equitable interests in the two properties were to succeed, there would be a reduction in the value to Locabail of its security and an increase in the

unsecured debt owing by Mr. Emmanuel to Locabail. This would be detrimental to the ability of Sudoexport and the liquidator of Howard Holdings Inc. to obtain payment of the sums owing to them by Mr. Emmanuel. The deputy judge explained the point in his judgment: "if [Mrs Emmanuel] failed, [Locabail] would be removed as a creditor in competition with Sudoexport". There is, therefore, Miss Williamson submitted, a conflict of interest between Mrs. Emmanuel and Herbert Smith's clients . . .

[47] There was an additional issue. When, on Day 8 of the hearing, the deputy judge made the disclosure recorded in the transcript, Mrs. Emmanuel could then have made an objection to the deputy judge continuing to hear the case. Or she could have asked for time to consider the position. She did neither, but allowed the hearing to continue to a conclusion. She could, after the Hawks Hill hearing had come to an end, have objected to the deputy judge hearing the Hans House appeal. She did not do so, and, without objection, he heard the appeal. Thereafter, during the three and half month delay before the reserved judgment was delivered, no bias objection was made. An inference that might be drawn is that Mrs Emmanuel wanted to await the result of the two hearings, and only made her bias objection when she knew she had lost. So the question arises whether she must be taken to have waived any bias objection.

[48] As to this, [Miss] Williamson's response was to submit, first, that the disclosure made by the deputy judge was not complete disclosure, second, that a waiver could only be effective when made by a person with full knowledge of the relevant facts and, third, that in view of Mrs. Emmanuel's incomplete knowledge of the circumstances of Herbert Smith's involvement in the litigation against her husband, she was never put to her election as to what she should do and waiver could not be raised against her.

[49] The "waiver" issue is one which, logically, falls to be considered after the bias issues have been considered . . .

[50] This is not a case in which actual bias on the part of the deputy judge is alleged. Is it a case in which the judge has a sufficient pecuniary or proprietary interest in the outcome of the trial so as to attract the automatic disqualification principle expressed in the *Dimes* case, 3 H.L.Cas. 759? If it is, then the deputy judge is automatically disqualified. If it is not, then it is a case to which the principles expressed in *Reg. v. Gough* [1993] A.C. 646 must be applied. It was suggested by Miss Williamson that this was a case to which the *Dimes* case applied. Her argument went like this. The deputy judge is a partner in Herbert Smith. Herbert Smith was acting for Sudoexport and Howard Holdings Inc. in litigation against Mr. Emmanuel. Success in achieving the maximum possible recovery from Mr. Emmanuel would enhance the goodwill of Herbert Smith and thereby tend to increase its profits. The deputy judge would share in the firm's profits. Miss Williamson suggested, also, the possibility that Herbert Smith might be acting under a conditional fee agreement with fees dependent on the level of recoveries extracted from Mr. Emmanuel. But in order to attract the *Dimes* consequence of automatic disqualification something more must, in our judgment, be present than the tenuous connection between the firm's success in an individual case on the one hand and the firm's goodwill and the level of profits on the other. And if the pecuniary or proprietary interest has to depend upon the existence of a conditional fee agreement of the unusual character suggested by Miss Williamson, there must be at least some evidence to suggest the existence of such an agreement. Here there is none. Miss Williamson's suggestion is wholly speculative and hypothetical. In our judgment this is not a case to which the *Dimes* principle of automatic disqualification applies. The *Gough* test must be applied and the court must ask itself whether 'in the circumstances of the case . . . it appears that there was a real likelihood, in the sense of a real possibility, of bias' on the part of the deputy judge: see [1993] A.C. 646, 668, per Lord Goff . . .

[The Court of Appeal then considered whether the facts gave rise to an appearance — or, using the test which was then applicable and which is discussed below, a "a real danger" — of bias, and concluded that they did not. The question of waiver was then considered.]

[68] In our judgment, Mrs. Emmanuel and her lawyers had to decide on 28 October what they wanted to do. They could have asked for time to consider the position. They could have asked the deputy judge to recuse himself and order the proceedings to be started again before another judge. They could have told the judge they had no objection to him continuing with the hearing. In the event they did nothing. In doing nothing they were treating the disclosure as being of no importance. The hearing then continued for a further seven days, judgment was reserved, the Hans House appeal was heard, judgment was reserved, and judgment in both cases was given three and half months later. During all this period Mrs. Emmanuel and her lawyers did nothing about the disclosure that had been made on 28 October. They only sprang into action and began complaining about bias after learning from the deputy judge's judgment that Mrs. Emmanuel had lost.

[69] Mrs. Emmanuel's application for permission to appeal and draft notice of appeal raise a large number of objections to the 9 March judgment expressed over several pages. We are concerned with none of these objections. They may or may not be well founded. The deputy judge may or may not have been unfair to Mrs. Emmanuel in the way in which he dealt with her evidence and that of her witnesses. These are matters which must be raised with another court on another occasion. We are concerned only with the complaint based upon an appearance of bias allegedly produced by Herbert Smith's involvement in the litigation against Mr. Emmanuel. This involvement was, in its essentials, disclosed on 28 October. It was not open to Mrs. Emmanuel to wait and see how her claims in the Locabail litigation turned out before pursuing her complaint of bias. Miss Williamson protests that on 28 October not enough was disclosed to put Mrs. Emmanuel to her election. We disagree. The essentials of the conflict of interest case that is now relied on were to be found in the press cutting. Mrs. Emmanuel wanted to have the best of both worlds. The law will not allow her to do so . . .

Permission to appeal refused.

The Court adopted a similar approach to the automatic disqualification rule in *R* v. *Bristol Betting and Gaming Licensing Committee, ex parte O'Callaghan*, which was heard with the *Locabail* case.

R v. *Bristol Betting and Gaming Licensing Committee, ex parte O'Callaghan* [2000] QB 451
Court of Appeal

The claimant was in dispute with Coral Racing Ltd over the validity of a bet which he placed and which, if valid, would have yielded a pay-out of almost £260,000. The claimant wished to attend a hearing of the Bristol Betting and Gaming Licensing Committee in May 1997 at which the renewal of Coral's permit was to be considered; he was, however, certified as medically unfit to attend and sought an adjournment. The Committee refused the adjournment, and made an award of £5,000 costs against Mr O'Callaghan. Since he was out of time for judicial review, the claimant sought an extension before Dyson J. By the time of the hearing, Coral's permit had been extended to three years; Dyson J concluded, therefore, that the only issue on which judicial review could bite was the lawfulness of the costs order and that, in light of the modest sum involved, an extension of time would not be appropriate. It then became apparent, through an article in *The Sunday Times*, that Dyson J was a director of Dyson Properties Ltd and of a related company, Gown and Mantle Ltd, which were family investment property companies whose tenants included Coral Racing Ltd. Mr O'Callaghan argued that, if Dyson J had disclosed this connection, he would have objected to his involvement in the case.

Lord Bingham of Cornhill CJ, Lord Woolf MR, and Sir Richard Scott V-C

[105] In accordance with the normal procedure adopted by the Court of Appeal when allegations are made against a judge, Dyson J. was informed of what was being relied on by Mr. O'Callaghan. By letter to this court of 28 June 1999 he confirmed that he had been a non-executive director of Dyson Properties Ltd. since the late 1980s; that it is a family property investment company, which was formed by his parents many years ago; that it holds commercial properties in the North of England; that, apart from himself, the current directors are his mother and brother; that all shares are held by members of the family (which include the judge); that he is not involved in the management of the company; that his role is limited to giving occasional advice to his brother; and that Gown and Mantle Ltd. is a wholly-owned subsidiary of Dyson Properties Ltd. (This last statement may not be entirely accurate, because it appears that the judge may also hold shares in this company). The judge adds that until he read the article in *The Sunday Times* he "was not aware that Corals was one of the company's tenants" and that the rent payable by Corals for the only shop of which it is a tenant of the company represents slightly more than four per cent. of the total rent currently receivable by the company.

[106] The Lord Chancellor gives guidance to judges on their appointment. At the time of Dyson J.'s appointment, the guidance provided that no judge should hold a *commercial directorship*. But the guide added:

> "There is, however, normally no objection to a judge holding shares in commercial companies, or taking part in the management of a family estate or farming his own land. Equally, there are some forms of non-commercial directorships which a judge may hold without objection."

[107] The current guide of October 1998 is in similar terms.

[108] It cannot be said that this is a case where the strict principle of automatic disqualification laid down in *Dimes v. Proprietors of Grand Junction Canal*, 3 H.L.Cas. 759 and *Reg. v. Bow Street Metropolitan Stipendiary Magistrate, Ex parte Pinochet Ugarte (No. 2)* [2000] 1 A.C. 119 applies. Miss Jackson [for Mr O'Callaghan] submitted that if the judicial review proceedings had continued they could have had a significant effect upon Corals and in consequence adversely affected that company's ability to meet its obligations to the Dyson family companies. We do not agree. The judicial review proceedings by the time they came before Dyson J. were only concerned with the issue of £5,000 costs. It would be absurd to suggest that recovery or non-recovery of this sum could affect Corals' ability to pay the rent of its shop in Leeds. It was suggested that the court in the judicial review proceedings could grant Mr. O'Callaghan a declaration which would be helpful in his dispute with Corals. However, we cannot see any basis for such a declaration. Once Corals' betting permits had been renewed, the judicial review proceedings could only have relevance with regard to costs. It cannot be said that the judge had anything more than a nominal and indirect interest because of his directorship and shares in the company. Such an interest does not establish a bar to the judge sitting . . .

Permission to appeal denied.

It is clear from cases such as *Locabail* and *O'Callaghan* that the automatic disqualification rule, as presently conceived, is subtle enough to ensure that not every financial interest — irrespective of how remote it may be — falls within its scope. Constructing the rule in this way goes some distance towards meeting Olowofoyeku's criticism that it is 'draconian' and 'disproportionate'. However, characterizing the rule thus is not without difficulty; the more subtly it is constructed, the more it comes to resemble a substantive evaluation of the circumstances in which the decision is made. It is clearly possible to manipulate the criterion of directness in order to ensure that only financial interests that are likely to raise a reasonable apprehension of bias fall within the rule's prohibitive scope, but this merely begs the question whether the automatic disqualification rule is necessary, given that it would appear that the underlying policy is simply to address situations which give rise to a reasonable apprehension of bias — a matter which is already covered by the apprehended bias rule which we discuss at 10.3 below. This is not to suggest that the presence of a financial interest is insignificant. It is, as a matter of fact, something which is very likely to give rise to an appearance of bias. The key point, however, is that disqualification in the face of financial interests is not an end in itself, but simply a manifestation of the wider underlying principle that judicial and administrative decision-making must not give rise to the perception of bias. It is arguable, therefore, that a single rule, based on disqualification in the face of apprehended bias, is perfectly capable of dealing with the whole range of situations which are of concern in this context — and that a single rule would better capture and reflect the policy of the law in this area.

QUESTIONS

- Do you agree?
- Should the special category of automatic disqualification remain?

10.2.2 Beyond Financial Interests: *Pinochet*

The scope of the automatic disqualification principle was clarified — in a rather surprising way — by the House of Lords in the course of the infamous *Pinochet* litigation. The events leading to the arrest of Senator Augusto Pinochet are usefully detailed in Woodhouse (ed), *The Pinochet Case: A Legal and Constitutional Analysis* (Oxford 2000), ch 1, and the remainder of that book helpfully considers the various issues arising from *Pinochet*. We are concerned here, however, specifically with the impact of the decision on the rule against bias.

....

R v. Bow Street Metropolitan Stipendiary Magistrate, ex parte Pinochet Ugarte (No 2) [2000] 1 AC 119
House of Lords

Senator Pinochet was arrested in the United Kingdom under warrants issued under s 8(1) of the Extradition Act 1989, following the issue of warrants by a Spanish court in respect of crimes against humanity which the senator was alleged to have committed, mainly in Chile. The claimant challenged the validity of the warrants, arguing that, as a former head of state, he was immune from arrest and extradition proceedings in respect of his conduct while in office. The Divisional Court accepted this argument, although the quashing of one of the warrants was stayed pending an appeal to the House of Lords by the prosecuting authorities. The appeal was successful, by a majority of three to two. In the hearing before the House of Lords, Amnesty International (AI) — a charitable organization which campaigns for respect for human rights — was granted permission to intervene, and was represented by counsel at the hearing. After the House of Lords had announced its decision, it came to light that Lord Hoffmann — one of the judges in the majority — was a director of Amnesty International Charity Ltd (AICL), a charity which was intimately related to, and undertook work on behalf of, AI in the United Kingdom. In light of this the claimant took the extraordinary step of petitioning the House of Lords to set aside its previous decision. The application was heard by a panel of five current and retired Law Lords sitting as an Appeal Committee. Lord Browne-Wilkinson, with whom the other four judges agreed, stated (at 132) that the House of Lords, "as the ultimate court of appeal, [must] have power to correct any injustice caused by an earlier order of this House". Having established this novel jurisdiction, Lord Browne-Wilkinson went on to consider whether its exercise would be appropriate.

Lord Browne-Wilkinson

. . . Senator Pinochet does not allege that Lord Hoffmann was in fact biased. The contention is that there was a real danger or reasonable apprehension or suspicion that Lord Hoffmann might have been biased, that is to say, it is alleged that there is an appearance of bias not actual bias.

The fundamental principle is that a man may not be a judge in his own cause. This principle, as developed by the courts, has two very similar but not identical implications. First it may be applied literally: if a judge is in fact a party to the litigation or has a financial or proprietary interest in its outcome then he is indeed sitting as a judge in his own cause. In that case, the mere fact that he is a party to the action or has a financial or proprietary interest in its outcome is sufficient to cause his automatic disqualification. The second application of the principle is where a judge is not a party to the suit and does not have a financial interest in its outcome, but in some other way his conduct or behaviour may give rise to a suspicion that he is not impartial, for example because of his friendship with a party. This second type of case is not strictly speaking an application of the principle that a man must not be judge in his own cause, since the judge will not normally be himself benefiting, but providing a benefit for another by failing to be impartial.

In my judgment, this case falls within the first category of case, *viz* where the judge is disqualified because he is a judge in his own cause. In such a case, once it is shown that the judge is himself a party to the cause, or has a relevant interest in its subject matter, he is disqualified without any investigation into whether there was a likelihood or suspicion of bias. The mere fact of his interest is sufficient to disqualify him unless he has made sufficient disclosure . . . I will call this "automatic disqualification".

In *Dimes v. Proprietors of Grand Junction Canal* (1852) 3 H.L.Cas 759, the then Lord Chancellor, Lord Cottenham, owned a substantial shareholding in the defendant canal which was an incorporated body. In the action the Lord Chancellor sat on appeal from the Vice-Chancellor, whose judgment in favour of the company he affirmed. There was an appeal to your Lordships' House on the grounds that the Lord Chancellor was disqualified. Their Lordships consulted the judges who advised, at p 786, that Lord Cottenham was disqualified from sitting as a judge in the cause because he had an interest in the suit. This advice was unanimously accepted by their Lordships. There was no inquiry by the court as to whether a reasonable man would consider Lord Cottenham to be biased and no inquiry as to the circumstances which led to Lord Cottenham sitting. Lord Campbell said, at p 793:

> "No one can suppose that Lord Cottenham could be, in the remotest degree, influenced by the interest he had in this concern; but, my Lords, it is of the last importance that the maxim that no man is to be a judge in his own cause should be held sacred. And that is not to be confined to a cause *in which he is a party*, but applies to a cause in which he has an interest." (Emphasis added.)

On occasion, this proposition is elided so as to omit all references to the disqualification of a judge who is a party to the suit: see, for example, *R v. Rand* (1866) L.R. 1 Q.B. 230; *R v. Gough* [1993] A.C.

646, 661. This does not mean that a judge who is a party to a suit is not disqualified just because the suit does not involve a financial interest. The authorities cited in the *Dimes* case show how the principle developed. The starting-point was the case in which a judge was indeed purporting to decide a case in which he was a party. This was held to be absolutely prohibited. That absolute prohibition was then extended to cases where, although not nominally a party, the judge had an interest in the outcome.

The importance of this point in the present case is this. Neither A.I., nor A.I.C.L., have any financial interest in the outcome of this litigation. We are here confronted, as was Lord Hoffmann, with a novel situation where the outcome of the litigation did not lead to financial benefit to anyone. The interest of A.I. in the litigation was not financial; it was its interest in achieving the trial and possible conviction of Senator Pinochet for crimes against humanity.

By seeking to intervene in this appeal and being allowed so to intervene, in practice A.I. became a party to the appeal. Therefore if, in the circumstances, it is right to treat Lord Hoffmann as being the alter ego of A.I. and therefore a judge in his own cause, then he must have been automatically disqualified on the grounds that he was a party to the appeal. Alternatively, even if it be not right to say that Lord Hoffmann was a party to the appeal as such, the question then arises whether, in non-financial litigation, anything other than a financial or proprietary interest in the outcome is sufficient automatically to disqualify a man from sitting as judge in the cause.

Are the facts such as to require Lord Hoffmann to be treated as being himself a party to this appeal? The facts are striking and unusual. One of the parties to the appeal is an unincorporated association, A.I. One of the constituent parts of that unincorporated association is A.I.C.L. A.I.C.L. was established, for tax purposes, to carry out part of the functions of A.I. — those parts which were charitable — which had previously been carried on either by A.I. itself or by A.I.L. [Amnesty International Ltd, another related registered charity]. Lord Hoffmann is a director and chairman of A.I.C.L., which is wholly controlled by A.I., since its members (who ultimately control it) are all the members of the international executive committee of A.I. A large part of the work of A.I. is, as a matter of strict law, carried on by A.I.C.L. which instructs A.I.L. to do the work on its behalf. In reality, A.I., A.I.C.L. and A.I.L. are a close-knit group carrying on the work of A.I.

However, close as these links are, I do not think it would be right to identify Lord Hoffmann personally as being a party to the appeal. He is closely linked to A.I. but he is not in fact A.I. Although this is an area in which legal technicality is particularly to be avoided, it cannot be ignored that Lord Hoffmann took no part in running A.I. Lord Hoffmann, A.I.C.L. and the executive committee of A.I. are in law separate people.

Then is this a case in which it can be said that Lord Hoffmann had an "interest" which must lead to his automatic disqualification? Hitherto only pecuniary and proprietary interests have led to automatic disqualification. But, as I have indicated, this litigation is most unusual. It is not civil litigation but criminal litigation. Most unusually, by allowing A.I. to intervene, there is a party to a criminal cause or matter who is neither prosecutor nor accused. That party, A.I., shares with the government of Spain and the C.P.S., not a financial interest but an interest to establish that there is no immunity for ex-heads of state in relation to crimes against humanity. The interest of these parties is to procure Senator Pinochet's extradition and trial a non-pecuniary interest. So far as A.I.C.L. is concerned, clause 3(c) of its memorandum provides that one of its objects is "to procure the abolition of torture, extra-judicial execution and disappearance." A.I. has, amongst other objects, the same objects. Although A.I.C.L., as a charity, cannot campaign to change the law, it is concerned by other means to procure the abolition of these crimes against humanity. In my opinion, therefore, A.I.C.L. plainly had a non-pecuniary interest, to establish that Senator Pinochet was not immune.

That being the case, the question is whether in the very unusual circumstances of this case a non-pecuniary interest to achieve a particular result is sufficient to give rise to automatic disqualification and, if so, whether the fact that A.I.C.L. had such an interest necessarily leads to the conclusion that

Lord Hoffmann, as a director of A.I.C.L., was automatically disqualified from sitting on the appeal? My Lords, in my judgment, although the cases have all dealt with automatic disqualification on the grounds of pecuniary interest, there is no good reason in principle for so limiting automatic dis-qualification. The rationale of the whole rule is that a man cannot be a judge in his own cause. In civil litigation the matters in issue will normally have an economic impact; therefore a judge is auto-matically disqualified if he stands to make a financial gain as a consequence of his own decision of the case. But if, as in the present case, the matter at issue does not relate to money or economic advantage but is concerned with the promotion of the cause, the rationale disqualifying a judge applies just as much if the judge's decision will lead to the promotion of a cause in which the judge is involved together with one of the parties. Thus in my opinion if Lord Hoffmann had been a member of A.I. he would have been automatically disqualified because of his non-pecuniary interest in establishing that Senator Pinochet was not entitled to immunity. Indeed, so much I understood to have been conceded by Mr. Duffy [for AI].

Can it make any difference that, instead of being a direct member of A.I., Lord Hoffmann is a director of A.I.C.L., that is of a company which is wholly controlled by A.I. and is carrying on much of its work? Surely not. The substance of the matter is that A.I., A.I.L. and A.I.C.L. are all various parts of an entity or movement working in different fields towards the same goals. If the absolute impartiality of the judiciary is to be maintained, there must be a rule which automatically disqualifies a judge who is involved, whether personally or as a director of a company, in promoting the same causes in the same organisation as is a party to the suit. There is no room for fine distinctions if Lord Hewart C.J.'s famous dictum is to be observed: it is "of fundamental importance that justice should not only be done, but should manifestly and undoubtedly be seen to be done:" see *Rex. v. Sussex Justices, Ex parte McCarthy* [1924] 1 K.B. 256, 259.

Since, in my judgment, the relationship between A.I., A.I.C.L. and Lord Hoffmann leads to the automatic disqualification of Lord Hoffmann to sit on the hearing of the appeal, it is unnecessary to consider the other factors which were relied on by Miss Montgomery [for the claimant], viz. the position of Lady Hoffmann as an employee of A.I. and the fact that Lord Hoffmann was involved in the recent appeal for funds for Amnesty. Those factors might have been relevant if Senator Pinochet had been required to show a real danger or reasonable suspicion of bias. But since the disqualifica-tion is automatic and does not depend in any way on an implication of bias, it is unnecessary to consider these factors. I do, however, wish to make it clear (if I have not already done so) that my decision is not that Lord Hoffmann has been guilty of bias of any kind: he was disqualified as a matter of law automatically by reason of his directorship of A.I.C.L., a company controlled by a party, A.I. . . .

It is important not to overstate what is being decided. It was suggested in argument that a decision setting aside the order of 25 November 1998 would lead to a position where judges would be unable to sit on cases involving charities in whose work they are involved. It is suggested that, because of such involvement, a judge would be disqualified. That is not correct. The facts of this present case are exceptional. The critical elements are (1) that A.I. was a party to the appeal; (2) that A.I. was joined in order to argue for a particular result; (3) the judge was a director of a charity closely allied to A.I. and sharing, in this respect, A.I.'s objects. Only in cases where a judge is taking an active role as trustee or director of a charity which is closely allied to and acting with a party to the litigation should a judge normally be concerned either to recuse himself or disclose the position to the parties. However, there may well be other exceptional cases in which the judge would be well advised to disclose a possible interest . . .

Their Lordships were unanimous that the petition should be granted, and the earlier decision of the House of Lords was therefore set aside. A panel of seven law lords, none of whom had been involved in the original appeal, was convened to reconsider the case. It concluded (by a majority of six to one) that, in respect of a small number of the charges laid against him, Senator Pinochet was not immune from extradition. The Home Secretary subsequently decided that Senator Pinochet should be extradited to Spain. Later, however, the Home Secretary concluded that Senator Pinochet was medically unfit to be tried; he therefore returned to Chile.

Lord Browne-Wilkinson was at pains, in his speech, to emphasize that — in two senses — the extension of the automatic disqualification principle in *Pinochet* was less radical than might initially appear. First, he stated that the principle, properly understood, applies (and, in theory, has always applied) to all cases in which the judge is a party, or may be treated as if a party because he has an interest — financial, proprietary, *or otherwise* — in the outcome. Secondly, Lord Browne-Wilkinson was anxious to point out that the automatic disqualification principle would, in the absence of a financial interest, operate only in the event of a rare concatenation of circumstances, such as that which arose in *Pinochet* itself.

However, each of these points on which Lord Browne-Wilkinson relies in support of the extension (or, as he would argue, clarification) of the rule in *Pinochet* is open to question. First, one of the advantages usually ascribed to the automatic disqualification principle is its efficiency: it permits the matter of disqualification to be dealt with straightforwardly, because it is triggered by particular kinds of interest — *viz* those which are financial and proprietary. We have already seen that this hard-edged approach is blunted by the courts' (understandable) willingness to examine the directness of a financial interest. But the position is now further blurred by the recognition of a new category of non-financial interests which are capable of activating the rule. This adds weight to the argument, advanced above, that the more context-sensitive the automatic disqualification rule, the more blurred the distinction between that rule and the apprehended bias rule — and, in turn, the need for the former — becomes. Secondly, it is unclear, notwithstanding Lord Browne-Wilkinson's comments, precisely how limited the circumstances are in which the *Pinochet* limb of the rule may apply. Lord Browne-Wilkinson seemed to require a combination of a strong interest on the part of the judge in some cause *and* a close relationship between the judge and a party to the case. In contrast, Lord Hutton ([2000] 1 AC 119 at 145) seemed to suggest that the rule would operate in *either* of these situations — an approach which would extend the ambit of *Pinochet* well beyond the very unusual circumstances of that case. The better view is that the automatic disqualification principle should be narrowly constructed, for the reasons advanced by the Court of Appeal in *Locabail (UK) Ltd* v. *Bayfield Properties Ltd* [2000] QB 451 at [14]:

Since any extension of the automatic disqualification rule would also, inevitably, limit the power of the judge and any reviewing court to take account of the facts and circumstances of a particular case, and would have the potential to cause delay and greatly increased cost in the final disposal of the proceedings, we would regard as undesirable any application of the present rule on automatic disqualification beyond the bounds set by existing authority, unless such extension were plainly required to give effect to the important underlying principles upon which the rule is based.

The difficulties posed by *Pinochet* are helpfully captured in the following passage by Malleson. (The extract refers to the 'real danger' test, which has since been replaced with the 'fair-minded observer' test. The differences between those tests are addressed below at 10.3.1; for the purposes of Malleson's argument, the key point is that both of those tests — unlike the automatic disqualification rule — operate only if the facts actually give rise to some perception of bias.)

....

Malleson, 'Judicial Bias and Disqualification after *Pinochet (No 2)*' (2000) 63 MLR 119

Uncertainty

By expanding the automatic disqualification [principle] . . . the House of Lords [in *Pinochet*] has increased uncertainty in relation to an aspect of disqualification which had long been settled . . . Nor can this change be justified as necessary in order to achieve justice in the light of the particular facts of the case since the same result could have been achieved within the existing rules. Despite the unusual nature of the case, the real danger test would, as Lord Woolf predicted in [*R v. Gough* [1993] AC 646 at 673] have been quite wide enough to 'produce the right answer' in the *Pinochet (No 2) case*. The nature of the relationship between Lord Hoffmann and AI as set out in the judgment was sufficiently close to allow the law lords to conclude that there was a "real danger" of bias without in any way straining the facts or their application . . . [In this way] the automatic disqualification category would have retained its limited scope . . .

Involvement of judges in public life

It was suggested in argument in court as well as by judges, lawyers and the media in response to the decision, that one consequence of setting aside the earlier decision [in *Pinochet*] would be that judges would be unable to sit on cases involving charities with which they were involved. Lord Browne-Wilkinson in his judgment clearly anticipated such concerns and rejected this view. He stressed that the facts of the present case were exceptional because first, AI was a party to the appeal, second, AI was joined in order to argue for a particular result and third, the judge was a director of a charity closely related to AI and sharing its objectives . . .

To date, such circumstances are indeed exceptional. But they are less likely to remain so in the future as the range and number of high profile human rights cases coming before the higher courts grows after the implementation of the Human Rights Act 1998. In such cases it is quite possible that charitable organisations [such] as AI, JUSTICE, Liberty, the Howard League, NACRO and others may be parties or [as Lord Browne-Wilkinson put it in *Pinochet (No 2)* [2000] 1 AC 119 at 136] be "allied to and acting with" a party to litigation or seek to be joined as interveners and be arguing for a particular result. If so, then senior judges who are directors or trustees of such organisations will be automatically disqualified from sitting. In anticipation of this development judges may decide to limit their involvement with organisations which may become parties or interveners in human rights cases. If so, this would be a serious loss both for the promotion of human rights and for the intellectual and ethical calibre of the bench.

Relationship between disclosure, waiver and disqualification

If the decision does lead to a great tendency for judges to disclose all interests which may have a bearing, however indirect, on the case, clearer rules will be needed on the relationship between disclosure, waiver and disqualification. From the *Pinochet (No 2)* judgment it is clear that disclosure followed by waiver is regarded as the principal solution to the problem of expanding the category of automatic disqualification interests. Lord Hope [[2000] 1 AC 119 at 140] relied on the judgment of Lord Buckmaster in [*Sellar* v. *Highland Railway Company* 1919 SC (HL) 19 at 21]:

> "In practice . . . the difficulty [of disqualification for bias] is one easily overcome, because, directly the fact is stated, it is common practice that counsel on each side agreed that the existence of the disqualification shall afford no objection to the prosecution of the suit, and the matter proceeds in the ordinary way . . ."

Although the judgment does not explicitly confirm that if Lord Hoffmann had disclosed his interest and there had been no objection from the parties, he could have continued to sit, this would appear to be the case. There is no suggestion in the judgment or the authorities that there are any interests which are so intimate that they cannot be waived by the parties. This position, if correct, is irreconcilable with the rationale behind the decision in *Pinochet (No 2)* as being the need to maintain public confidence in the administration of justice. It is quite possible to imagine a situation in which a judge discloses an interest which is waived by the parties in circumstances in which a reasonable observer would have regarded that justice is not being seen to be done. This might arise either because the parties have other reasons for wishing the trial to proceed before that particular judge or because counsel may be under pressure "to consent or to risk being seen as a trouble maker" [see *Commentaries on Judicial Conduct* at 74].

In Canada, the newly drafted Canadian Ethical Principles for Judges has sought to address this problem. It proposes that where a judge has a potential interest, she should make the decision as to whether or not to recuse herself without inviting the consent of counsel, perhaps in consultation with judicial colleagues. If they conclude that no "reasonable, fair minded and informed person, considering the matter, would have a reasoned suspicion of a lack of impartiality" the matter should proceed before the judge. Only if the judge remains uncertain as to whether or not that test is satisfied should she disclose the interest and invite the submissions of counsel; the purpose being not to seek permission of the parties to continue but to obtain assistance. This question of how potential bias should be identified and considered was addressed by Lord Irvine [the then Lord Chancellor] in an open letter to Lord Browne-Wilkinson written in response to the *Pinochet (No 2)* judgment. He suggested that the decision-making process should be a collective one addressed by the panel of judges before hearing each case and that responsibility for ensuring that a judge who had a conflict of interest did not sit should be that of the law lord in the chair . . .

QUESTIONS

- Was the House of Lords right, in *Pinochet*, to extend the scope of the automatic disqualification rule?
- Do any benefits follow from the approach adopted in *Pinochet* which may be set against the difficulties identified by Malleson?

For further discussion of *Pinochet* and its implications, see Jones [1999] *PL* 391; Olowo-foyeku [2000] *PL* 456; Woodhouse (ed), *The Pinochet Case: A Legal and Constitutional Analysis* (Oxford 2000); Malleson (2002) 22 *LS* 53.

10.3 The Apprehension of Bias

10.3.1 Suspicion, Likelihood, Danger: Competing Tests

The Court of Appeal commented in *Locabail (UK) Ltd* v. *Bayfield Properties Ltd* [2000] QB 451 at [16] that:

In practice, the most effective guarantee of the fundamental right [to a fair hearing by an impartial tribunal] . . . is afforded not . . . by the rules which provide for disqualification on grounds of actual bias, nor by those which provide for automatic disqualification, because automatic disqualification on grounds of personal interest is extremely rare and judges routinely take care to disqualify themselves, in advance of any hearing, in any case where a personal interest could be thought to arise. The most effective protection of the right is in practice afforded by a rule which provides for the disqualification of a judge, and the setting aside of a decision, if on examination of all the relevant circumstances the court concludes that there was a real danger (or possibility) of bias.

Disqualification on the basis of an apprehension of bias is thus distinct from the automatic disqualification principle, because the former, in contrast to the latter, requires a judgment to be made about how the particular factual situation in question is likely to be perceived. Disqualification is therefore not, on this basis, automatic — there is no inevitable presumption of bias; rather, disqualification follows only if the facts give rise to an apprehension or perception of bias.

Although the apprehended bias principle can thus be distinguished relatively straightforwardly from the automatic disqualification rule, the precise nature and content of the former is more difficult to pin down. It was for some time unclear whether the correct test to be applied was one based on a 'reasonable suspicion' or a 'real likelihood' of bias. This semantic confusion reflected disagreement about deeper issues. Through whose eyes — the court's or a reasonable person's — must the likelihood of bias be assessed? If the latter, how much knowledge of the circumstances should be imputed to the reasonable person? And what degree of likelihood is required — probability or mere possibility? Conflicting opinions were advanced in the case law over the years — see Alexis [1979] PL 143 for discussion — but, in R v. Gough [1993] AC 646, the House of Lords attempted to lay the confusion to rest. After reviewing the authorities — in particular, R v. Sussex Justices, ex parte McCarthy [1924] 1 KB 256, R v. Barnsley Licensing Justices, ex parte Barnsley and District Licensed Victuallers' Association [1960] 2 QB 167, and Metropolitan Properties Co (FGC) Ltd v. Lannon [1969] 1 QB 577 — Lord Goff (at 670) reached the following conclusion:

> I think it possible, and desirable, that the same test should be applicable in all cases of apparent bias, whether concerned with justices or members of other inferior tribunals, or with jurors, or with arbitrators. Likewise I consider that, in cases concerned with jurors, the same test should be applied by a judge to whose attention the possibility of bias on the part of a juror has been drawn in the course of a trial, and by the Court of Appeal when it considers such a question on appeal. Furthermore, I think it unnecessary, in formulating the appropriate test, to require that the court should look at the matter through the eyes of a reasonable man, because the court in cases such as these personifies the reasonable man; and in any event the court has first to ascertain the relevant circumstances from the available evidence, knowledge of which would not necessarily be available to an observer in court at the relevant time. Finally, for the avoidance of doubt, I prefer to state the test in terms of real danger rather than real likelihood, to ensure that the court is thinking in terms of possibility rather than probability of bias. Accordingly, having ascertained the relevant circumstances, the court should ask itself whether, having regard to those circumstances, there was a real danger of bias on the part of the relevant member of the tribunal in question, in the sense that he might unfairly regard (or have unfairly regarded) with favour, or disfavour, the case of a party to the issue under consideration by him . . .

The conclusion in Gough (for further discussion of which see Bing [1998] Crim LR 148) that the law should be concerned with whether there is a possibility of bias — rather than determining that bias is, on the balance of probabilities, established — is uncontroversial. The difficulty which Gough created concerned the perspective from which the determination as to a possibility of bias was to be made. By holding that the matter was to be decided by reference to the court's evaluation of the circumstances, the impression was given — notwithstanding Lord Goff's insistence that the court personifies the reasonable person —

that the test was concerned with the possibility of actual bias, rather than with how members of the public might perceive the impartiality or otherwise of the decision-maker. This, in turn, gave rise to the view that the law in this area was no longer concerned with Lord Hewart's guiding principle that justice must be seen to be done.

Thus, in *R v. Inner West London Coroner, ex parte Dallaglio* [1994] 4 All ER 139 at 151, Simon Brown LJ concluded, on the basis of *Gough*, that 'by the time the legal challenge comes to be resolved, the court is no longer concerned strictly with the appearance of bias but rather with establishing the possibility that there was actual although unconscious bias'. In the same case, Lord Bingham MR (at 161) went so far as to suggest that 'if despite the appearance of bias the court is able to examine all relevant material and satisfy itself that there was no danger of the alleged bias having in fact caused injustice, the impugned decision will be allowed to stand'. However, Rayment [1996] JR 102 at 103–104 suggests that *Gough* was, in cases such as *Dallaglio*, misunderstood, and that Lord Goff's intention, in concentrating upon the court's rather than the reasonable person's impression, was simply to ensure that the person through whose eyes the facts are assessed would, in the first place, be in receipt of the relevant facts:

The problem stems from the substitution in *Gough* of the reasonable man's impression for the impression of the court. It was not meant, I suggest, that the court should try to evaluate whether or not the original decision was [actually] unfair as a result of bias. It was simply an attempt to limit the overly sinister impression sometimes given by the reasonable man perspective. What Lord Goff could have said was that the reasonable man should be deemed to know the circumstances of the case before forming his impression. He was simplifying things by expressing the test as one to be applied directly from the court's perspective, as it would clearly know the background to a case. But he did not mean that the court should go through the evidence again to determine the danger of an actually biased result as happened in *Dallaglio*.

Nevertheless, the High Court of Australia refused to follow — and indeed strongly criticized — *Gough* in the next case.

....

Webb v. *The Queen* (1994) 181 CLR 41
High Court of Australia

The appellants were tried for murder. On the morning the judge began his summing up, a member of the jury attempted (through an intermediary) to give a bunch of flowers to the victim's mother. When the matter was drawn to the attention of the judge, he applied the real danger test as set out in *Gough*; he dismissed the application for the jury to be discharged, and both appellants were later convicted. The convictions were upheld by the Court of Criminal Appeal, whereupon the appellants appealed to the High Court of Australia.

Mason CJ and McHugh J

. . . In considering the merits of the test to be applied in a case where a juror is alleged to be biased, it is important to keep in mind that the appearance as well as the fact of impartiality is necessary to retain confidence in the administration of justice. Both the parties to the case and the general public must be satisfied that justice has not only been done but that it has been seen to be done. Of the various tests used to determine an allegation of bias, the reasonable apprehension test of bias is by far the most appropriate for protecting the appearance of impartiality. The test of "reasonable likelihood" or "real danger" of bias tends to emphasize the court's view of the facts. In that context, the trial judge's acceptance of explanations becomes of primary importance. Those two tests tend to place inadequate emphasis on the public perception of the irregular incident.

We do not think that it is possible to reconcile the decision in *Gough* with the decisions of this Court. In *Gough*, the House of Lords specifically rejected the reasonable suspicion test and the cases and judgments which had applied it in favour of a modified version of the reasonable likeli-hood test. In [*R v. Watson, ex parte Armstrong* (1976) 136 CLR 248], faced with the same conflict in the cases between the two tests, this Court preferred the reasonable suspicion or apprehension test. That test has been applied by this Court on no less than eight subsequent occasions. In the light of the decisions of this Court which hold that the reasonable apprehension or suspicion test is the correct test for determining a case of alleged bias against a judge, it is not possible to use the "real danger" test as the general test for bias without rejecting the authority of those decisions.

Moreover, nothing in the two speeches in the House of Lords in *Gough* contains any new insight that makes us think that we should re-examine a principle and a line of cases to which this Court has consistently adhered for the last eighteen years. On the contrary, there is a strong reason why we should prefer the reasoning in our own cases to that of the House of Lords. In *Gough*, the House of Lords rejected the need to take account of the public perception of an incident which raises an issue of bias except in the case of a pecuniary interest. Behind this reasoning is the assumption that public confidence in the administration of justice will be maintained because the public will accept the conclusions of the judge. But the premise on which the decisions in this Court are based is that public confidence in the administration of justice is more likely to be maintained if the Court adopts a test that reflects the reaction of the ordinary reasonable member of the public to the irregularity in question. References to the apprehension of the "lay observer" [*Vakuta v. Kelly* (1989) 167 CLR 568 at 573–574], the "fair-minded observer" [*Livesey v. New South Wales Bar Association* (1983) 151 C.L.R. 288 at 300; *Laws v. Australian Broadcasting Tribunal* (1990) 170 CLR 70 at 87], "fair-minded people" [*ibid* at 92], the "reasonable or fair-minded observer" [*Ex parte Armstrong, op cit* at 263], the "parties or the public" [*Ex parte Hoyts Corporation Pty Ltd* (1994) 119 ALR 206 at 210] and the 'reasonable person' [*Vakuta, op cit* at 576] abound in the decisions of this Court and other courts in this country. They indicate that it is the court's view of the public's view, not the court's own view, which is determinative. If public confidence in the administration of justice is to be maintained, the approach that is to be taken by fair-minded and informed members of the public cannot be ignored. Indeed, as Toohey J. pointed out in [*Vakuta v. Kelly* (1989) 167 CLR 568 at 585] in considering whether an allegation of bias on the part of a judge has been made out, the public perception of the judiciary is not advanced by attributing to a fair-minded member of the public a knowledge of the law and the judicial process which ordinary experience suggests is not the case. That does not mean that the trial judge's opinions and findings are irrelevant. The fair-minded and informed observer would place great weight on the judge's view of the facts. Indeed, in many cases the fair-minded observer would be bound to evaluate the incident in terms of the judge's findings.

A further reason for rejecting the *Gough* formulation is that, where the conduct of a juror is in issue, it will often be difficult to determine objectively whether the incident has affected or might affect the impartiality of the juror and whether directions to the jury were or will be adequate to protect the parties from the effect of the irregular incident. To place confidence in a test based on the assumption that an investigation will reveal all the facts of the incident may lead to a miscar-riage of justice. In our experience, the investigation of such incidents during the course of the trial is not exhaustive. Ordinarily, the judge simply asks the juror for an explanation. However, a juror involved in an irregular incident may feel defensive about his or her role. Understandably, the juror may seek to put the best light on the matter. Seldom, if ever, is there a detailed cross-examination of the juror by counsel or by the judge in such a case. Indeed, many counsel would consider it unwise to cross-examine the juror while the possibility existed that the trial would continue with that juror. One can never be certain, therefore, whether all the circumstances have been elicited by the trial judge. If real danger of bias was the governing criterion, the judge might reach a conclusion opposite to that which he or she might have reached if all the facts were known. The reasonable apprehension test, on the other hand, allows a margin for error in evaluating the facts as elicited. It concentrates not on whether there is a danger of bias as an objective fact, but whether a fair-minded and informed person might apprehend or suspect that bias existed.

Furthermore, if the reasonable apprehension test remains the test for alleged bias on the part of a judge, as we think it should, it is not easy to see why a different test should be applied to a juror. In criminal cases, in particular, the jury's function is of great public importance. It is certainly no less important than that of the judge sitting alone in a civil trial, a commissioner determining an industrial dispute or a member of a statutory tribunal inquiring into conduct in an industry which it supervises. The public is entitled to expect that issues tried by juries as well as judges and other public office holders should be decided by a tribunal free of prejudice and without bias . . .

It follows that the test to be applied in this country for determining whether an irregular incident involving a juror warrants or warranted the discharge of the juror or, in some cases, the jury is whether the incident is such that, notwithstanding the proposed or actual warning of the trial judge, it gives rise to a reasonable apprehension or suspicion on the part of a fair-minded and informed member of the public that the juror or jury has not discharged or will not discharge its task with impartiality . . .

Toohey, Brennan, and Deane JJ agreed with Mason CJ and McHugh J that the correct test was that of reasonable apprehension. The majority — consisting of Mason CJ, McHugh and Toohey JJ — concluded that a fair-minded observer would not have entertained a reasonable apprehension of bias on the facts, while Brennan and Deane JJ reached the opposite view. Appeal dismissed.

QUESTION

- Do you find Mason CJ and McHugh J's criticisms of the real danger test — and their reasons for preferring a test based on reasonable apprehension of bias — convincing?

10.3.2 Beyond *Gough*: The Fair-Minded and Informed Observer

In light of the difficulties caused by the *Gough* test, Lord Browne-Wilkinson, in *Pinochet (No 2)* [2000] 1 AC 119 at 136, indicated that the test may need to be reconsidered. The Court of Appeal did precisely that in *In re Medicaments and Related Classes of Goods (No 2)* [2001] 1 WLR 700. Having reviewed the authorities, Lord Phillips MR said (at [46]) that

it was possible [before *Gough*] to identify two alternative tests applied by the courts, usually in criminal proceedings, when considering whether a decision was vitiated on account of bias. (1) Did it appear to the court that there was a real danger that the judge had been biased? (2) Would an objective onlooker with knowledge of the material facts have a reasonable suspicion that the judge might have been biased?

In comparing these tests, two issues should be noted. The first concerns the *material to be taken into account* in assessing the possibility of bias. On this point, his Lordship (*op cit* at [47]) observed that

the two tests should produce the same result *unless*, when applying the first test, the court has regard to matters which do not form part of the "material facts" that fall to be taken into account when applying the second test.

This is self-evident. If, in assessing the likelihood of bias, the court takes into account *all* information available to it, then the test may collapse into one for the actual possibility of bias. In contrast, as Lord Phillips went on, at [65], to explain:

Once the reviewing court excludes from consideration matters known to it which would be outside the ken of ordinary, reasonably well informed members of the public, it seems to us that a hypothetical rather than an actual test of the likelihood of bias is being applied.

The second point concerns the *evaluation of the relevant material*. In *Medicaments*, the Court of Appeal recognized a distinction between judicial and public perceptions. Lord Phillips asked (at [67]):

What is the court to do where, although inclined to accept a statement about what the judge under review knew at any material time, it recognises the possibility of doubt and the likelihood of public scepticism? It is invidious for the reviewing court to question the word of the judge in such circumstances, but less so to say that the objective onlooker might have difficulty in accepting it.

The policy objective of preserving public confidence in the judicial and administrative machinery favours giving weight to the likely perceptions of the public — and constructing those perceptions on the basis of material available to ordinary, informed members of the public. In light of these considerations, the Court of Appeal concluded that the *Gough* test should be modified. The relevant passage from the Court's judgment is set out in the following extract from *Porter* v. *Magill* (for comment on which see Williams [2002] *CLJ* 249 and Rowbottom (2002) 118 *LQR* 364), in which the House of Lords, subject to a semantic qualification, endorsed this modification of *Gough*. Although, in *Medicaments*, the Court of Appeal was able to revise *Gough* only to the extent of its inconsistency with Article 6 ECHR (lower courts being able to revisit higher courts' decisions where this is necessary in order to give effect to Convention rights), the following case modifies the test to be applied by English courts irrespective of whether the ECHR applies. There is therefore now 'no difference between the test for bias at common law and under Article 6' (*Kataria* v. *Essex Strategic Health Authority* [2004] EWHC 641 (Admin) [2004] 3 All ER 572 at [46], *per* Stanley Burton J).

....

Porter v. *Magill* [2001] UKHL 67 [2002] 2 AC 357
House of Lords

In the mid-1980s Westminster City Council, under the leadership and deputy leadership of (respectively) Shirley Porter and David Weeks, adopted a policy of selling council houses to tenants in marginal wards in the hope that this would encourage them to vote for the Conservative Party. Legal advisors had indicated that an earlier version of the policy, under which *only* houses in marginal wards would have been offered for sale, was unlawful, and so a revised policy was implemented which permitted the sale of a larger number of homes, while still offering for sale those in the marginal wards. Opposition councillors argued that the policy would inhibit the local authority from discharging its obligations as a housing authority, and notified the auditor under s 17 of the Local Government Finance Act 1972. The auditor investigated the matter and certified, under s 20, that a number of councillors and officers, including Porter and Weeks, were guilty of wilful misconduct, by knowingly adopting and implementing a policy which was unlawful (because it deployed the power to sell council homes for an illegitimate, party political purpose). The councillors and officers were therefore liable to make good the loss of £31 million which they had caused to the council. Porter and Weeks unsuccessfully appealed against the auditor's decision to the Divisional Court. On a further appeal, however, the Court of Appeal quashed the auditor's certificates on the ground that the unlawful objectives of Porter, Weeks, and various others could not be said to have caused the losses which later occurred, because the policy had been implemented following approval by the housing committee — an event which, the Court of Appeal concluded, broke the chain of causation between the conduct of Porter, Weeks, and the other individuals concerned, and the losses. The auditor appealed to the House of Lords, which concluded that the losses could be attributed to the conduct of Porter and Weeks. However, Porter and Weeks argued that, that irrespective of the causation issue, the auditor's decision could not stand, because it was tainted by apparent bias, caused by a media conference which the auditor had held.

Lord Hope of Craighead

[100] The "reasonable likelihood" and "real danger" tests which Lord Goff described in *R v Gough* have been criticised by the High Court of Australia on the ground that they tend to emphasise the court's view of the facts and to place inadequate emphasis on the public perception of the irregular incident: *Webb v The Queen* (1994) 181 CLR 41, 50 per Mason CJ and McHugh J. There is an uneasy tension between these tests and that which was adopted in Scotland by the High Court of Justiciary in *Bradford v McLeod*, 1986 SLT 244. Following Eve J's reference in *Law v Chartered Institute of Patent Agents* [1919] 2 Ch 276 (which was not referred to in *R v Gough*), the High Court of Justiciary adopted a test which looked at the question whether there was suspicion of bias through the eyes of the reasonable man who was aware of the circumstances: see also *Millar v Dickson* 2001 SLT 988, 1002L–1003B. This approach, which has been described as "the reasonable apprehension of bias" test, is in line with that adopted in most common law jurisdictions. It is also in line with that which the Strasbourg court has adopted, which looks at the question whether there was a risk of bias objectively in the light of the circumstances which the court has identified: *Piersack v Belgium* (1982) 5 EHRR 169, 179–180, paras 30–31; *De Cubber v Belgium* (1984) 7 EHRR 236, 246, para 30; *Pullar v United Kingdom* (1996) 22 EHRR 391, 402–403, para 30. In *Hauschildt v Denmark* (1989) 12 EHRR 266, 279, para 48 the court also observed that, in considering whether there was a legitimate reason to fear that a judge lacks impartiality, the standpoint of the accused is important but not decisive: "What is decisive is whether this fear can be held objectively justified."

[101] The English courts have been reluctant, for obvious reasons, to depart from the test which Lord Goff of Chieveley so carefully formulated in *R v Gough*. In *R v Bow Street Metropolitan Stipendiary Magistrate, Ex p Pinochet Ugarte (No 2)* [2000] 1 AC 119, 136A–C Lord Browne-Wilkinson said that it was unnecessary in that case to determine whether it needed to be reviewed in the light of subsequent decisions in Canada, New Zealand and Australia. I said, at p 142F–G, that, although the tests in Scotland and England were described differently, their application was likely in practice to lead to results that were so similar as to be indistinguishable. The Court of Appeal, having examined the question whether the "real danger" test might lead to a different result from that which the informed observer would reach on the same facts, concluded in *Locabail (UK) Ltd v Bayfield Properties Ltd* [2000] QB 451, 477 that in the overwhelming majority of cases the application of the two tests would lead to the same outcome.

[102] In my opinion however it is now possible to set this debate to rest. The Court of Appeal took the opportunity in *In re Medicaments and Related Classes of Goods (No 2)* [2001] 1 WLR 700 to reconsider the whole question. Lord Phillips of Worth Matravers MR, giving the judgment of the court, observed, at p 711A–B, that the precise test to be applied when determining whether a decision should be set aside on account of bias had given rise to difficulty, reflected in judicial decisions that had appeared in conflict, and that the attempt to resolve that conflict in *R v Gough* had not commanded universal approval. At p 711B–C he said that, as the alternative test had been thought to be more closely in line with Strasbourg jurisprudence which since 2 October 2000 the English courts were required to take into account, the occasion should now be taken to review *R v*

Gough to see whether the test it lays down is, indeed, in conflict with Strasbourg jurisprudence. Having conducted that review he summarised the court's conclusions, at pp 726H–727C:

> "85 When the Strasbourg jurisprudence is taken into account, we believe that a modest adjust-ment of the test in *R v Gough* is called for, which makes it plain that it is, in effect, no different from the test applied in most of the Commonwealth and in Scotland. The court must first ascertain all the circumstances which have a bearing on the suggestion that the judge was biased. It must then ask whether those circumstances would lead a fair-minded and informed observer to conclude that there was a real possibility, or a real danger, the two being the same, that the tribunal was biased."

[103] I respectfully suggest that your Lordships should now approve the modest adjustment of the test in *R v Gough* set out in that paragraph. It expresses in clear and simple language a test which is in harmony with the objective test which the Strasbourg court applies when it is consider-ing whether the circumstances give rise to a reasonable apprehension of bias. It removes any possible conflict with the test which is now applied in most Commonwealth countries and in Scotland. I would however delete from it the reference to "a real danger". Those words no longer serve a useful purpose here, and they are not used in the jurisprudence of the Strasbourg court. The question is whether the fair-minded and informed observer, having considered the facts, would conclude that there was a real possibility that the tribunal was biased.

[104] Turning to the facts, there are two points that need to be made at the outset. The first relates to the auditor's own assertion that he was not biased. The Divisional Court said, at p 174A–B, that it had had particular regard to his reasons for declining to recuse himself in reaching its conclusion that he had an open mind and was justified in continuing with the subsequent hearings. I would agree that the reasons that he gave were relevant, but an examination of them shows that they consisted largely of assertions that he was unbiased. Looking at the matter from the stand-point of the fair-minded and informed observer, protestations of that kind are unlikely to be helpful. I think that Schiemann LJ adopted the right approach in the Court of Appeal when he said that he would give no weight to the auditor's reasons: [2000] 2 WLR 1420, 1457H. The second point relates to the emphasis which the respondents place on how the auditor's conduct appeared from the standpoint of the complainer. There is, as I have said, some support in the jurisprudence of the Strasbourg court for the proposition that the standpoint of the complainer is important. But in *Hauschildt v Denmark* (1989) 12 EHRR 266, 279, para 48 the court emphasised that what is decisive is whether any fears expressed by the complainer are objectively justified. The complainer's fears are clearly relevant at the initial stage when the court has to decide whether the complaint is one that should be investigated. But they lose their importance once the stage is reached of looking at the matter objectively.

[105] I think that it is plain, as the Divisional Court observed, at p 174B, that the auditor made an error of judgment when he decided to make his statement in public at a press conference. The main impression which this would have conveyed to the fair-minded observer was that the purpose of this exercise was to attract publicity to himself, and perhaps also to his firm. It was an exercise in self-promotion in which he should not have indulged. But it is quite another matter to conclude from this that there was a real possibility that he was biased. Schiemann LJ said, at p 1457D–E, that there was room for a casual observer to form the view after the press conference that the auditor might be biased. Nevertheless he concluded, at p 1457H, having examined the facts more closely, that there was no real danger that this was so. I would take the same view. The question is what the fair-minded and informed observer would have thought, and whether his conclusion would have been that there was real possibility of bias. The auditor's conduct must be seen in the context of the investigation which he was carrying out, which had generated a great deal of public interest. A

statement as to his progress would not have been inappropriate. His error was to make it at a press conference. This created the risk of unfair reporting, but there was nothing in the words he used to indicate that there was a real possibility that he was biased. He was at pains to point out to the press that his findings were provisional. There is no reason to doubt his word on this point, as his subsequent conduct demonstrates. I would hold, looking at the matter objectively, that a real possibility that he was biased has not been demonstrated . . .

Their Lordships unanimously supported Lord Hope's comments on the test for bias, and agreed that the auditor's decision should not be set aside. Their Lordships were also in agreement that the actions of Porter and Weeks had caused the relevant losses. Appeals allowed.

QUESTIONS

• How does the *Porter* v. *Magill* test differ from that advanced in *Gough*?
• Is the former an improvement on the latter? Why (not)?

This approach was applied by the House of Lords in *Lawal* v. *Northern Spirit Ltd* [2003] UKHL 35 [2004] 1 All ER 187, concerning the appearance of a barrister before an Employment Appeal Tribunal which included lay members who had previously sat with the barrister in his capacity as a part-time judicial member of the Tribunal. Lord Steyn noted that '[t]he small but important shift approved in *Magill* . . . has at its core the need for [what the ECtHR in *Belilos* v. *Switzerland* (1988) 10 EHRR 466 at [67] termed] "the confidence which must be inspired by the courts in a democratic society" '. Lord Steyn (at [19]) explained that the Lord Chancellor's Department (now the Department for Constitutional Affairs) had submitted that the bias challenge should fail because it proceeded on the false assumption that lay members 'are unable to differentiate between the neutral judicial function and the partisan advocacy function'. However, his Lordship felt that this argument rather missed the point: the relevant question was whether 'a fair minded and informed observer, having considered the given facts, would conclude that there was a real possibility that the tribunal was biased'. Their Lordships were unanimous that such a possibility existed. The House of Lords subsequently held in *Davidson* v. *Scottish Ministers* [2004] UKHL 34 that a judge in the Scottish Court of Session was disqualified by virtue of the fact that, in the case in question, he was called upon to interpret legislation whose meaning he had advised the House of Lords on in his former capacity as Lord Advocate. The fair-minded and informed observer, said Lord Bingham at [17], 'would conclude that there was a real possibility that [the judge], sitting judicially, would subconsciously strive to avoid reaching a conclusion which would undermine the very clear assurances he had given to Parliament [as to the effect of the legislation in question].'

These decisions appear to place English law on a footing which is once again consistent with the underlying ethos famously set out by Lord Hewart CJ in the *Sussex Justices* case. However, the extent to which the bias test has really changed remains unclear. If the *Magill* test is, in practice, to operate differently from that favoured in *Gough*, courts applying it must be sensitive to the two factors which we noted earlier: that members of the public — even reasonably informed ones — will have access to limited information concerning the circumstances of the alleged bias, and that public and judicial perceptions based on the relevant material may well diverge. In this regard, the following case, decided shortly after *Porter* v. *Magill*, is of considerable interest.

....

Taylor v. *Lawrence* [2002] EWCA Civ 90 [2003] QB 528
Court of Appeal

The judge, in a case concerning the trial of a boundary dispute, told the parties that he had been a client of the claimants' solicitors, but had not used their services for a number of years. Although none of the parties raised any objection at that time, the defendants later appealed, alleging an appearance of bias. Before the appeal was heard, it transpired that the judge and his wife had used the solicitors to amend their wills the night before he delivered his judgment; the appeal, however, was dismissed. When it later became apparent that the firm had made no charge for amending the wills, the defendants sought to have the appeal re-opened.

Lord Woolf CJ (delivering the judgment of the court)

[60] While before the *Pinochet* litigation an allegation of bias in the court was a rare event, such complaints are now becoming increasingly prevalent. In *Locabail (UK) Limited v Bayfield Properties Limited* [2000] QB 451 after hearing a number of appeals at the same time this court sought to give guidance as to the principles which should be applied. Fortunately, subsequently, in a speech of Lord Hope of Craighead in *Magill v Porter and Weeks* [2001] UKHL 67 at [99]–[104], the House of Lords has put to rest the conflicting views as to how the test in cases of apparent bias should be expressed . . . [Lord Woolf CJ set out the fair-minded observer test, and continued:]

[61] The fact that the observer has to be "fair-minded and informed" is important. The informed observer can be expected to be aware of the legal traditions and culture of this jurisdiction. Those legal traditions and that culture have played an important role in ensuring the high standards of integrity on the part of both the judiciary and the profession which happily still exist in this jurisdiction. Our experience over centuries is that this integrity is enhanced, not damaged, by the close relations that exist between the judiciary and the legal profession. Unlike some jurisdictions the judiciary here does not isolate itself from contact with the profession. Many examples of the traditionally close relationship can be given: the practice of judges and advocates lunching and dining together at the Inns of Court; the Master of the Rolls's involvement in the activities of the Law Society; the fact that it is commonplace, particularly in specialist areas of litigation and on the circuits, for the practitioners to practise together in a small number of chambers and in a small number of firms of solicitors, and for members of the judiciary to be recruited from those chambers and firms.

[62] It is also accepted that barristers from the same chambers may appear before judges who were former members of their chambers or on opposite sides in the same case. This close relationship has not prejudiced but enhanced the administration of justice. The advantages in terms of improved professional standards which can flow from these practices have been recognised and admired in other jurisdictions. Again by way of example, in the United States they have in recent years established the rapidly expanding American Inns of Court modelled on their English counterparts with the objective of improving professional standards.

[63] The informed observer will therefore be aware that in the ordinary way contacts between the judiciary and the profession should not be regarded as giving rise to a possibility of bias. On the contrary, they promote an atmosphere which is totally inimical to the existence of bias. What is true of social relationships is equally true of normal professional relationships between a judge and the lawyers he may instruct in a private capacity . . .

[72] We have not only carefully considered the "new evidence" [relating to the fact that the wills

were altered without charge] but we have also reviewed the facts as a whole, applying the now established test for bias, and having done so we do not accept that any case of apparent bias on the part of the judge is made out. We regard it as unthinkable that an informed observer would regard it as conceivable that a judge would be influenced to favour a party in litigation with whom he has no relationship merely because that party happens to be represented by a firm of solicitors who are acting for the judge in a purely personal matter in connection with a will. There is no reason to doubt the explanation for a bill not being rendered. There is no evidence that the judge knew that this was to be the case, but, even if he did, it would not alter our view . . .

[74] The judge was not required to raise his personal relations with the solicitors and it was a mistake to do so. After he had made that mistake, his subsequent conduct fuelled the Lawrences' suspicions. Regrettably the Lawrences' response to what has happened has been a wholly dis-proportionate suspicion. They are not in a position to be objective, as they cannot accept a court could decide this unfortunate litigation against them unless there was bias. The fact that their feelings are no doubt genuine cannot be allowed to dictate our conclusion. To decide that the circumstances on which they rely could give rise to a suspicion of bias would put at risk the way in which the judiciary and the legal profession conduct their relationship; a relationship which has long served the interests of justice in this country.

The substantive application was dismissed.

QUESTIONS

- Was it appropriate to impute to the fair-minded observer knowledge of how the legal profession is structured and of the relationship between judges and members of the professions?
- How, if at all, might the court's reasoning have differed had it applied the real danger, rather than the fair-minded observer, test?

The courts have shown a similar level of willingness to impute specialist knowledge to the hypothetical observer in other cases (*eg Hart* v. *Relentless Records Ltd* [2002] EWHC 1984 (Ch) [2003] FSR 36 and *Taylor* v. *Williamson* [2002] EWCA Civ 1380). Although striking a cautionary note in *Lawal, op cit* at [22] — he agreed that it was 'perhaps' the case that (as suggested in *Taylor* v. *Lawrence*) the fair-minded and informed observer would be aware of legal traditions and culture, but added that the observer 'may not be wholly uncritical' thereof — Lord Steyn was nevertheless willing to impute a considerable amount of know-ledge about the legal system to the observer. The risk, as Atrill [2003] *CLJ* 279 recognizes, is that, applied thus, the *Magill* test comes to resemble that which was adopted in *Gough*; widespread judicial ascription of specialist knowledge to the fair-minded observer risks divorcing the test from the very policy interests which it is intended to advance.

10.4 Bias, Policy, and Politics

The cases considered above largely concern the requirement that judges, or others exercising functions similar to those of judges, should be unbiased. To what extent do — and should — the same requirements apply to other decision-makers, such as those — like government Ministers and local authorities — whose position may be explicitly political? The House of Lords clearly held in *Franklin* v. *Minister of Town and Country Planning* [1948] AC 87 (an excerpt from which appears at 11.2.1) that different standards apply to political decision-makers, such that less is to be expected of them in terms of impartiality. Thus, when the Minister made a speech asserting that a new town would be built, notwithstanding that he was under a statutory duty first to hear and consider objections, his ultimate decision that the town should indeed be built was not disturbed by the court. However, in *Franklin*, the reasoning of Lord Thankerton (who gave the only reasoned speech) was heavily dependent upon the distinction between judicial and administrative functions which, until the seminal decision in *Ridge* v. *Baldwin* [1964] AC 40 (also considered below at 11.2.1), substantially circumscribed the reach of the principles of procedural fairness. The modern approach, as the following case illustrates, recognizes that individuals are entitled to a fair — and hence unbiased — decision-making process irrespective of whether the decision-maker occupies a 'judicial' or 'administrative' role.

....

R v. *Secretary of State for the Environment, ex parte Kirkstall Valley Campaign Ltd* [1996] 3 All ER 304
Queen's Bench Division

Leeds Development Corporation, acting as local planning authority, granted outline planning permission for a retail development on land owned by a rugby club. The claimant — a community group — sought to have the decision quashed, alleging that three members of the corporation, and an officer, had various interests in granting planning permission which meant that the decision was vitiated on grounds of bias. In the following extract, Sedley J refers to the *Gough* 'real danger' test as the standard applicable to judges. That has, as we saw above at 10.3.2, now been replaced by the fair-minded observer test.

Sedley J

. . . Although Mr Drabble in his submissions for the Secretary of State was content to accept . . . [the] proposition that the law on apparent bias is now to be found in unitary form in the decision of the House of Lords in *R* v *Gough* [1993] 2 All ER 724, [1993] AC 646, as developed in *R* v *Inner West London Coroner, ex p Dallaglio* [1994] 4 All ER 139, Mr Ryan [for the owner of the land concerned] has advanced a radical alternative: that non-judicial bodies such as an urban development corporation are governed by a different set of principles, to be found in a succession of cases beginning with the decision of Glidewell J in *R* v *Sevenoaks DC, ex p Terry* [1985] 3 All ER 226. If Mr Ryan is right, the question to be asked in relation to an impugned decision of a body such as the Leeds Development Corporation, is not whether on the facts now known to the court there was a real danger of bias in one or more members of the decision-making body, but whether the body as a whole can be shown to have gone beyond mere predisposition in favour of a particular course and to have predetermined it . . .

[Sedley J considered a number of authorities, some of which — including *R* v *Reading Borough Council, ex parte Quietlynn Ltd* (1986) 85 LGR 387 and *R* v *Exeter City Council, ex parte Quietlynn Ltd* (22 February 1985, unreported) — accepted a distinction, so far as the test for bias was concerned, between judicial functions and administrative and quasi-judicial functions. This distinction was recognized in order to ensure that elected representatives who took policy considerations into account would not fall foul of the rule against bias. Sedley J continued:] Today, however, following the decision in *R* v *Gough*, the same conclusion will be reached, not by drawing a line between judicial and other functions, but by deciding whether there was a real danger of bias by reference to circumstances which prominently include the particular nature and function of the body whose decision is impugned. In this way the necessary involvement of local elected councillors in matters of public controversy, and the probability that they will have taken a public stand on many of them, limits the range of attack which can properly be made upon any decision in which even a highly opinionated councillor has taken part. This is why in *R v Amber Valley DC, ex p Jackson* [1984] 3 All ER 501, [1985] 1 WLR 298 Woolf J was able to hold that although the principles of natural justice governed applications for planning permission, these principles were not violated by a decision of the majority party that it supported a particular planning application. Woolf J, without drawing any distinction between the judicial and the administrative, held ([1984] 3 All ER 501 at 509, [1985] 1 WLR 298 at 307–308):

'The rules of fairness or natural justice cannot be regarded as being rigid. They must alter in accordance with the context. Thus in the case of highways, the department can be both the promoting authority and the determining authority. When this happens, of course any reasonable man would regard the department as being predisposed towards the outcome of the inquiry. The department is under an obligation to be fair and to carefully consider the evidence given before the inquiry but the fact that it has a policy in the matter does not entitle a court to intervene. So in this case I do not consider the fact that there is a declaration of policy by the majority group can disqualify a district council from adjudicating on a planning application. It may mean that the outcome of the planning application is likely to be favourable to an applicant and therefore unfavourable to objectors. However, Parliament has seen fit to lay down that it is the local authority which have the power to make the decision . . .'

. . . Not only is there, therefore, no authority which limits the *Gough* principle to judicial or quasi-judicial proceedings; there are sound grounds of principle in modern public law for declining so to limit it. The concrete reason, which is not always given the attention it deserves, is that in the modern state the interests of individuals or of the public may be more radically affected by administrative decisions than by the decisions of courts of law and judicial tribunals. The individual who has just been tried for a minor road traffic infraction will not be much comforted by the fact that he was tried with the full safeguards of the criminal law if on returning home he finds that an administrative decision in which he had no say is going to take away his home or his job. Nothing in the years since the publication of Robson's *Justice and Administrative Law* (2nd edn, 1947) has diminished the accuracy of what Robson wrote (pp 4–5):

'. . . it is probably the fact that some functions of government are not capable of classification into legislative, executive and judicial powers. It is very difficult to discover any adequate method by which, in a highly developed country like England, judicial functions can be clearly distinguished from administrative functions. Mere names are of no avail, for, as we shall see, judges often administer, and administrators often judge. It is easy enough to take a typical example of each kind of function, and to identify it as belonging to a particular category. But that does not get us out of the difficulty, unless we can extract from it some characteristics essential to its nature. A further difficulty arises from the fact that many of the features which once belonged almost exclusively to activities that were carried on only in courts of law, are now to be observed as attaching also, to a greater or less extent, to activities carried on by other departments of government. Furthermore, what we may call the judicial attitude of mind has spread from the courts of law, wherein it originated, to many other fields, with the result that an increasingly large number of governmental activities bear the marks of both the administrative process *and* the judicial process, and cannot be distinguished by any simple test. "The changing combinations of events will beat upon the walls of ancient categories", a distinguished American judge has observed; and that is precisely what has occurred in the classification of governmental functions in England.'

. . . I hold, therefore, that the principle that a person is disqualified from participation in a decision if there is a real danger that he or she will be influenced by a pecuniary or personal interest in the outcome, is of general application in public law and is not limited to judicial or quasi-judicial bodies or proceedings.

How then will the principle apply to a body exercising town and country planning powers? In the case of an elected body the law recognises that members will take up office with publicly stated views on a variety of policy issues. In the case of an urban development corporation the Secretary of State will have had regard, in making his appointments, to 'the desirability of securing the services of people having special knowledge of the locality' (para 2(2) of Sch 26 to the [Local Government Planning and Land Act 1980]), as well as to the pro-active purpose of the corporation set out in s 136(1) 'to secure the regeneration of its area'. In both cases, where predetermination of issues or forfeiture of judgment is alleged, the court will be concerned to distinguish, within the statutory framework, legitimate prior stances or experience from illegitimate ones. But such issues will be governed by the separate line of authority on predetermination. [Earlier in his judgment, having examined relevant authorities on predetermination, Sedley J concluded that 'the decision of a body, albeit composed of disinterested individuals, will be struck down if its outcome has been predetermined whether by the adoption of an inflexible policy or by the effective surrender of the body's independent judgment'.] So far as concerns apparent bias, there can be little if any difference between an elected and an appointed planning authority. In both cases there is a constant risk that the body will have to decide matters in which a member happens to have pecuniary or personal interest. In such cases, as the Secretary of State's successive codes for urban development corporations and for local government recognise, unless it is too remote or insignificant to matter, the interest must be declared and the member concerned must not participate in the decision. The likelihood that some such conflict of interest will sooner or later arise for a member appointed to an urban development corporation pursuant to the provisions of the 1980 Act, is no more an excuse for non-observance of the principle of disqualification than it would be for a member elected to a planning authority on a platform of planning issues. The *Gough* test of bias will be uniformly applied: what will differ from case to case is the significance of the interest and its degree of proximity or remoteness to the issue to be decided and whether, if it is not so insignificant or remote as to be discounted, the disqualified member has violated his disqualification by participating in the decision.

Sedley J concluded that the claimants had not established apparent bias. Claim dismissed.

QUESTIONS

- Was Sedley J right to hold that administrative bodies are subject to the same test as judges?
- What is the significance of the fact that, in Sedley J's view, the determination of whether there is a real danger of bias — or, to use the current test, whether a fair-minded observer would reasonably apprehend bias — must be 'by reference to circumstances which prominently include the particular nature and function of the body whose decision is impugned'?

This decision must be read in light of the fact that, as is apparent from the excerpts from the *Alconbury* case below at 10.5.1 and 10.5.3, the determination of some planning matters is now (by operation of the Human Rights Act 1998) covered by Article 6 ECHR. However, this is not true of all planning cases, since Article 6 can, as we explain below at 10.5.2, apply only where the claimant's 'civil rights and obligations' are at stake. For example, in *R (Cummins)* v. *Camden London Borough Council* [2001] EWHC Admin 1116), Ouseley J stated (*obiter*) that the development of council land, including a neighbourhood football pitch, did not engage the 'civil rights and obligations' of users of the football pitch and local residents whose views from their residences would be affected by the development. When Article 6 *does* apply, further questions arise about the involvement of 'political' decision-makers; these are addressed by Lord Hoffmann in the extract at 10.5.1.

10.5 Article 6

10.5.1 Introduction: Article 6 in an Administrative Context

Issues of procedural fairness now fall for consideration under Article 6 of the European Convention on Human Rights — which is made effective in domestic law by the HRA 1998 — as well as at common law. This impacts upon both the nature and content of a fair hearing, which we consider in the following chapter, and also the need for an independent and impartial decision-maker, with which we are presently concerned. Article 6(1) of the Convention (for general discussion of which see Grosz, Beatson and Duffy, *Human Rights: The 1998 Act and the European Convention* (London 2000) at 120–129 and Gordon and Ward, *Judicial Review and the Human Rights Act* (London 2000) at 174–192) provides that:

In the determination of his civil rights and obligations or of any criminal charge against him, everyone is entitled to a fair and public hearing within a reasonable time by an independent and impartial tribunal established by law. Judgment shall be pronounced publicly but the press and public may be excluded from all or part of the trial in the interest of morals, public order or national security in a democratic society, where the interests of juveniles or the protection of the private life of the parties so require, or to the extent strictly necessary in the opinion of the court in special circumstances where publicity would prejudice the interests of justice.

Article 6(1) was originally intended to regulate the conduct only of criminal courts and civil courts in the determination of private law rights: it was explained in the dissenting opinion in *Feldbrugge* v. *The Netherlands* (1986) 8 EHRR 425 at 444 that this much is apparent from the *travaux préparatoires*. However, although some very early cases excluded public law matters from the scope of Article 6(1), the European Court of Human Rights decided in *Ringeisen* v. *Austria (No 1)* (1979–80) 1 EHRR 455 that Article 6(1) *does* apply to administrative proceedings if they are decisive of civil rights and obligations. The extension of the scope of Article 6(1) in this way is a positive development to the extent that it promotes the ideas of administrative justice and procedural fairness. However, given that Article 6(1) is — as is apparent from the text of the provision — clearly premised upon a court-based adjudicative model, its extension to the administrative context has raised a number of difficulties. In particular, the notion that administrative decisions, which often involve the formulation or application of policy, should be taken by bodies enjoying judicial-style independence poses enormous problems, both practical (our administrative system is simply not structured in that way) and of principle (are not some decisions better taken by democratically-accountable politicians than by judicial bodies?) Precisely these concerns are addressed in the following excerpt.

....

R (Alconbury Developments Ltd) v. Secretary of State for the Environment, Transport and the Regions [2001] UKHL 23 [2003] 2 AC 295
House of Lords

Alconbury Developments agreed with the Ministry of Defence that, if planning permission were granted, it would develop a disused airfield, owned by the Ministry, into a national distribution centre. Applications were made to the relevant planning authorities, but permissions were not granted; Alconbury therefore appealed. Most such appeals — although formally made to the Secretary of State — are actually determined by a planning inspector. However, under the Town and Country Planning Act 1990, sch 6, para 3(1), the Secretary of State may 'recover' an appeal: the effect of this is that the inspector simply makes a recommendation, while the decision is left to the Secretary of State. Alconbury's appeal was recovered in this way. Two groups representing local interests objected to the recovery of the appeal, contending that the Secretary of State was not an independent and impartial tribunal for Article 6(1) purposes. Alconbury therefore sought judicial review in order to clarify the position. The Divisional Court concluded that the Secretary of State did not comply with Article 6(1), and issued a declaration of incompatibility (under the Human Rights Act 1998, s 4(2)) in respect of the relevant provisions of the planning legislation. The matter then went on appeal to the House of Lords. This excerpt is concerned only with the difficulties arising from the application of Article 6(1) to administrative decision-making.

Lord Hoffmann

[69] In a democratic country, decisions as to what the general interest requires are made by democratically elected bodies or persons accountable to them. Sometimes the subject matter is such that Parliament can itself lay down general rules for enforcement by the courts. Taxation is a good example: Parliament decides on grounds of general interest what taxation is required and the rules according to which it should be levied. The application of those rules, to determine the liability of a particular person, is then a matter for independent and impartial tribunals such as the general or special commissioners or the courts. On the other hand, sometimes one cannot formulate general rules and the question of what the general interest requires has to be determined on a case by case basis. Town and country planning or road construction, in which every decision is in some respects different, are archetypal examples. In such cases Parliament may delegate the decision-making power to local democratically elected bodies or to Ministers of the Crown responsible to Parliament. In that way the democratic principle is preserved.

[70] There is no conflict between human rights and the democratic principle. Respect for human rights requires that certain basic rights of individuals should not be capable in any circumstances of being overridden by the majority, even if they think that the public interest so requires. Other rights should be capable of being overridden only in very restricted circumstances. These are rights which belong to individuals simply by virtue of their humanity, independently of any utilitarian calculation. The protection of these basic rights from majority decision requires that independent and impartial tribunals should have the power to decide whether legislation infringes them and either (as in the United States) to declare such legislation invalid or (as in the United Kingdom) to declare that it is incompatible with the governing human rights instrument. But outside these basic rights, there are many decisions which have to be made every day (for example, about the allocation of resources) in which the only fair method of decision is by some person or body accountable to the electorate.

[71] All democratic societies recognise that while there are certain basic rights which attach to the ownership of property, they are heavily qualified by considerations of the public interest. This is reflected in the terms of article 1 of Protocol 1 to the Convention . . .

[72] ... [U]nder the first paragraph, property may be taken by the state, on payment of compensation, if the public interest so requires. And, under the second paragraph, the use of property may be restricted without compensation on similar grounds. Importantly, the question of what the public interest requires for the purpose of article 1 of the First Protocol can, and in my opinion should, be determined according to the democratic principle — by elected local or central bodies or by Ministers accountable to them. There is no principle of human rights which requires such decisions to be made by independent and impartial tribunals.

[73] There is however another relevant principle which must exist in a democratic society. That is the rule of law. When Ministers or officials make decisions affecting the rights of individuals, they must do so in accordance with the law. The legality of what they do must be subject to review by independent and impartial tribunals. This is reflected in the requirement in article 1 of the First Protocol that a taking of property must be "subject to the conditions provided for by law". The principles of judicial review give effect to the rule of law. They ensure that administrative decisions will be taken rationally, in accordance with a fair procedure and within the powers conferred by Parliament. But this is not the occasion upon which to discuss the limits of judicial review. The only issue in this case is whether the Secretary of State is disqualified as a decision maker because he will give effect to policies with which, ex hypothesi, the courts will not interfere ...

[74] My Lords, these basic principles are the background to the interpretation of article 6(1) ... Apart from authority, I would have said that a decision as to what the public interest requires is not a "determination" of civil rights and obligations. It may affect civil rights and obligations but it is not, and ought not to be, a judicial act such as article 6 has in contemplation. The reason is not simply that it involves the exercise of a discretion, taking many factors into account, which does not give any person affected by the decision the right to any particular outcome. There are many such decisions made by courts (especially in family law) of which the same can be said. Such decisions may nevertheless be determinations of an individual's civil rights (such as access to his child: compare W v United Kingdom (1987) 10 EHRR 29) and should be made by independent and impartial tribunals. But a decision as to the public interest (what I shall call for short a "policy decision") is quite different from a determination of right. The administrator may have a duty, in accordance with the rule of law, to behave fairly ("quasi-judicially") in the decision-making procedure. But the decision itself is not a judicial or quasi-judicial act. It does not involve deciding between the rights or interests of particular persons. It is the exercise of a power delegated by the people as a whole to decide what the public interest requires ...

[76] In principle, therefore, and apart from authority, I would say that article 6(1) conferred the right to an independent and impartial tribunal to decide whether a policy decision by an administrator such as the Secretary of State was lawful but not to a tribunal which could substitute its own view of what the public interest required. However, section 2(1) of the Human Rights Act 1998 requires an English court, in determining a question which has arisen in connection with a Convention right, to take into account the judgments of the European Court of Human Rights ("the European court") and the opinions of the Commission. The House is not bound by the decisions of the European court and, if I thought that the Divisional Court was right to hold that they compelled a conclusion fundamentally at odds with the distribution of powers under the British constitution, I would have considerable doubt as to whether they should be followed. But in my opinion the Divisional Court misunderstood the European jurisprudence. Although the route followed by the European court has been a tortuous one and some of its statements require interpretation, I hope to demonstrate that it has never attempted to undermine the principle that policy decisions within the limits imposed by the principles of judicial review are a matter for democratically accountable institutions and not for the courts ...

[80] The seminal case [on the scope of Article 6(1)] is *Ringeisen* v *Austria (No 1)* (1971) 1 EHRR 455. This concerned an Austrian statute which required transfers of agricultural land to be approved by a District Land Transactions Commission with a right of appeal to a Regional Commission. In the absence of approval, the contract of sale was void. The purpose of the law was to keep agricultural land in the hands of farmers of small and medium holdings and the District Commission was required to refuse consent to a transfer which appeared to violate this policy. This was a classic regulatory power exercisable by an administrative body. The court nevertheless held that article 6(1) was applicable to its decision on the ground that it was "decisive" for the enforceability of the private law contract for the sale of land. Thus a decision on a question of public law by an administrative body could attract article 6(1) by virtue of its effect on private law rights. On the facts, the court held that article 6(1) had been satisfied because the Regional Commission was an independent and impartial tribunal.

[81] The full implications of *Ringeisen* were not examined by the court until some years later. It led in *König* v *Germany* 2 EHRR 170 to a sharp disagreement between those members of the court who saw it as a means of enforcing minimum standards of judicial review of administrative and domestic tribunals and those who regarded it as a potential Pandora's box and wanted to confine it as narrowly as possible. Dr König was a surgeon charged with unprofessional conduct before a specialist medical tribunal attached to the Frankfurt Administrative Court. It withdrew his right to practice and run a clinic. He appealed to an administrative Court of Appeal and there followed lengthy and complicated proceedings. His complaint to the European court under article 6(1) was that he had been denied the right to a decision "within a reasonable time". But this raised the question of whether, in principle, article 6(1) applied to disciplinary proceedings before an administrative court. By a majority, the court held that it did. On the *Ringeisen* principle, it affected private law rights such as his goodwill and his right to sell his services to members of the public.

[82] Judge Matscher delivered a powerful dissent, saying that it was unwise to try to apply the pure judicial model of article 6(1) to the decisions of administrative or domestic tribunals. They might share some characteristics with courts (eg requirements of fairness) but in other respects they were different. For example, one could not apply the imperative of a public hearing to a professional disciplinary body. A private hearing might be more in the public interest. If article 6(1) was going to be applied to administrative law, it would have to be substantially modified . . . [T]he dissent of Judge Matscher in *König's* case 2 EHRR 170 has been vindicated in the sense that the application of article 6 to administrative decisions has required substantial modification of the full judicial model . . .

QUESTIONS

• Why does Article 6(1) need to be 'substantially modified' if it is to be applied to administrative law?
• What sort of modifications might be appropriate?

We return to this judgment at 10.5.3, where we will see exactly how the 'full judicial model' is modified in the administrative context. However, before considering what Article 6(1) requires in relation to administrative decision-making, we must confront a logically prior question.

10.5.2 When does Article 6(1) Apply to Administrative Decision-Making?

When will administrative proceedings be found to be decisive of civil rights and obligations, thus triggering Article 6(1)? Here, the ECtHR has encountered considerable difficulties, largely because Article 6(1) was not originally intended to apply to administrative proceedings. The Court held in *König* v. *Federal Republic of Germany* (1979–80) 2 EHRR 170 at [88] that 'civil rights and obligations' is an autonomous European concept; the test to be applied is therefore substantive in nature, and does not turn upon the classification of the right or obligation as a matter of domestic law. In developing this autonomous concept of civil rights and obligations, the ECtHR and the (now defunct) European Commission of Human Rights have concluded that it does not extend to matters such as immigration (*Uppal* v. *United Kingdom* (1981) 3 EHRR 391), deportation (*Maaouia* v. *France* (2001) 33 EHRR 42), disputes between administrative authorities and employees who occupy 'posts involving participation in the exercise of powers conferred by public law' (*Pellegrin* v. *France* (2001) 31 EHRR 26), taxation (*Ferrazzini* v. *Italy* (2002) 34 EHRR 45), and detention on remand (*Neumeister* v. *Austria* (1979–80) 1 EHRR 91). In contrast, Article 6(1) has been held to apply to disciplinary proceedings which affect the right to pursue a profession (*König* v. *Federal Republic of Germany* (1979–80) 2 EHRR 170), expropriation of land (*Sporrong* v. *Sweden* (1983) 5 EHRR 35), and access to children (*W* v. *United Kingdom* (1988) 10 EHRR 29).

The approach of the ECtHR in this area is vague; Craig [2003] *PL* 753 at 757–758 is highly critical, commenting that it remains 'wedded to a foundational private law paradigm for the applicability of procedural rights' which obscures 'the central normative issue of which interests are sufficiently important to warrant the application of process rights'. Nevertheless, it is possible to extract some general principles. For instance, Grosz, Beatson and Duffy, *Human Rights: The 1998 Act and the European Convention* (London 2000) at 122, suggest that 'the subject-matter of the proceedings must be a *right* rather than a discretionary benefit or *ex gratia* payment, so that a person who fulfils the eligibility criteria will have an enforceable claim'; thus the greater the discretion of the administrative body, the less likely it is that its decision will be found to be decisive of civil rights and obligations. Moreover, the Court has tended to balance the public and private law features of the case, holding Article 6(1) applicable only if the latter are predominant. For instance, in *Feldbrugge* v. *The Netherlands* (1986) 8 EHRR 425 and *Deumeland* v. *Germany* (1986) 8 EHRR 448, both of which concerned entitlement to contribution-based social security benefits, the Court was prepared to hold Article 6(1) applicable. Commenting on these cases in *Runa Begum* v. *Tower Hamlets London Borough Council* [2003] UKHL 5 [2003] 2 AC 430 at [63]–[64], Lord Hoffmann explained that:

In both cases the right was created by public legislation which laid down the qualifying conditions and the rates of payment. It was an assumption by the state of responsibility for the financial security of employees and their dependants. But it had certain affinities with private insurance [since] employees paid contributions . . . [D]espite a powerful dissent from seven members of the court [in *Feldbrugge*] who said that the distinction between public and private law rights was being eroded in a way which would create great uncertainty, the majority decided that the features of private law were cumulatively predominant. It was therefore a civil right within the meaning of Article 6.

However, the case law has now developed further, and the scope of Article 6(1) has once again widened. The effect of *Salesi* v. *Italy* (1993) 26 EHRR 187 (discussed in the next extract) and the approach of the House of Lords in the following case (noted by Forsyth [2003] *CLJ* 244) suggest that Article 6(1) may now apply even when the analogy with private law rights is at best tenuous, and the administrative body's discretion substantial.

....

Runa Begum v. *Tower Hamlets London Borough Council* [2003] UKHL 5 [2003] 2 AC 430
House of Lords

Runa Begum applied to the defendant for accommodation on the ground that she was homeless. The local authority accepted that it was obliged to provide accommodation, but the accommodation which was offered was rejected by Runa Begum, who argued that it was unsuitable. An internal review was conducted under s 202 of the Housing Act 1996 by a local authority housing officer who concluded that the accommodation was suitable and that it would have been reasonable for Runa Begum to accept it. She appealed to the county court under s 204 of the 1996 Act, arguing that the defendant ought to have at least considered exercising its power to procure a review by an external agency, and that the lack of any independent scrutiny rendered the process inconsistent with Article 6(1) and, specifically, the need for an 'independent and impartial tribunal'. The county court allowed the appeal, but this decision was reversed by the Court of Appeal. Runa Begum appealed to the House of Lords, but was unsuccessful because their Lordships concluded that the possibility of appeal under s 204 compensated for the s 202 review's lack of independence and impartiality (on which see below at 10.5.3). Of present interest, however, is the fact that their Lordships assumed but did not decide — for reasons which are apparent from the extract below — that Runa Begum's civil rights and obligations were at stake in this case, and that Article 6(1) was therefore applicable.

Lord Millett

[78] The question here is whether the reviewing officer's decision that the council no longer owed its full housing duty to Runa Begum constituted a determination of her "civil rights" within the meaning of article 6(1). The European Court of Human Rights ("the Strasbourg Court") has repeatedly stated that the first step is to ascertain whether there was a *contestation* (dispute) over a "right" which can be said, at least on arguable grounds, to be recognised under national law. The dispute must be genuine and serious; it may relate not only to the actual existence of a right but also to its scope and the manner of its exercise; and the outcome of the proceedings must be directly decisive of the right in question: see, for example, *Mennitto v Italy* (2000) 34 EHRR 1122, 1129, para 23.

[79] This requirement is clearly satisfied in the present case. Once a local housing authority is satisfied that an applicant is homeless, eligible for assistance, and has a priority need, and is not satisfied that the applicant has become homeless intentionally, it is under a statutory duty to secure that accommodation is made available for his or her occupation. It is not a duty to secure the provision of accommodation if it thinks fit, which would make the outcome of the application unpredictable. It is a duty to secure the provision of accommodation in the case of any applicant who satisfies the statutory criteria. Once the duty arises, the applicant has a corresponding legal right to its performance. The housing authority has a wide discretion as to the manner in which it will perform its duty, but that is not inconsistent with the existence of a corresponding right. An applicant has a legal right, recognised by our domestic law, to have the duty performed by the local housing authority in one or other of the ways which are open to it.

[80] Runa Begum fulfilled the relevant criteria and accordingly, as the council acknowledged, it

owed her the full housing duty and she had a corresponding legal right to its performance. But it claimed that its statutory duty, and with it her corresponding right, had ceased, because it had offered her suitable accommodation and she had unreasonably refused it.

[81] Whether the accommodation which the council had offered to her and whether it was reasonable for her to occupy it depended in large measure on housing conditions prevailing in the area. The determination of the dispute therefore called for an exercise of judgment on the part of a reviewing officer with experience of such conditions. These factors made the dispute one which was eminently suitable for determination by a senior officer of the council's housing department, but they do not prevent it from involving a determination of her legal rights.

[82] Whether those rights should be classified as "civil rights" within the meaning of article 6(1) is, however, a very difficult question . . .

[86] . . . [A]rticle 6(1) was intended to be supplemented by further measures in relation to the making of administrative decisions . . .

[87] . . . [However,] [n]o such measures have been introduced, and in their absence the Strasbourg court has found it necessary to extend the scope of article 6(1) to cover some, but not all, administrative decisions. The process has been a gradual one, and may not yet be complete. Underlying the process there must, I think, have been a desire not to restrict the guarantees of a fair hearing within a reasonable time by an impartial tribunal. But the Strasbourg court has not proceeded by reference to principle or on policy grounds; instead it has adopted an incremental and to English eyes disappointingly formalistic approach, making it difficult to know where the line will finally come to be drawn . . .

[89] . . . [An important step] was taken in *Feldbrugge v The Netherlands* (1986) 8 EHRR 425 and *Deumeland v Germany* (1986) 8 EHRR 448. [After examining the decisions in these cases, discussed above, Lord Millett continued:] The decision in each case was strongly dependent on the contributory nature of the scheme and the analogy with private insurance.

[90] This is not a principled basis on which to draw the distinction between "civil rights" which are within the protection of article 6(1) and other rights which are not, and it is not surprising that the line could not be held. The meaning of "civil rights" and hence the scope of article 6(1) was extended further in *Salesi v Italy* (1993) 26 EHRR 187 and most recently in *Mennitto* (2000) 34 EHRR 1122. Both cases were concerned with non-contributory disability allowances. In *Salesi* the court referred to "the development in the law initiated by" the judgments in *Feldbrugge* and *Deumeland* and commented that the differences between social insurance and welfare assistance could not be regarded as fundamental "at the present stage of development of social security law". In these passages the Strasbourg court recognised that its jurisprudence was still developing. The decisions had the effect of extending article 6(1) to disputes in connection with non-contributory welfare schemes. In each case the critical feature which brought it within article 6(1) was that the claimant "suffered an interference with her means of subsistence and was claiming an individual, economic right flowing from specific rules laid down in a statute giving effect to the Constitution" ([26 EHRR 187 at] 199, para 19).

[91] The present case undoubtedly goes further still. It has four features which take it beyond the existing case law: (i) it is concerned with a benefit in kind; (ii) it therefore involves priority between competing claimants. There is only a finite amount of housing stock, whether it belongs to the local housing authority or is bought in; and if one applicant is allowed to remain on the unintentionally

homeless register it will be to the detriment of other homeless persons; (iii) the housing authority has a discretion as to the manner in which it will discharge its duties; and (iv) ultimately the question for determination calls for an exercise of judgment: whether the applicant has behaved reasonably in refusing an offer of accommodation, having regard to all the circumstances, and in particular housing conditions in the area.

[92] I do not suppose that the first of these is significant in itself; a right to be housed is not a right to subsistence, though it would be invidious to distinguish the two. But it leads to the others, which are significant. Runa Begum cannot be said to be claiming "an individual, economic right flowing from specific rules laid down in a statute".

[93] It is not difficult to conclude that the nature of the dispute in her case makes it inappropriate for determination by the ordinary judicial process. But it is more difficult, at least in principle, to justify withdrawing it from the protection of article 6(1). Most European states possess limited judicial control of administrative decisions; and if such decisions are outside the scope of article 6(1) then judicial control could be dispensed with altogether. The individual could be left without any right to a tribunal which was impartial or to a hearing within a reasonable time. This would be incompatible with the fundamental human right which article 6(1) was designed to secure.

[94] I am persuaded by these considerations that extending the scope of article 6(1) is a desirable end in itself, but needs to go hand in hand with moderating its requirements in the interests of efficient administration where administrative decisions are involved. In the light of the unsettled state of the jurisprudence of the Strasbourg court, therefore, I am content to assume, without deciding, that Runa Begum's claim involved a determination of her civil rights within the meaning of article 6(1) . . .

Lords Bingham, Hoffmann, and Walker also assumed, without deciding, that Article 6(1) was engaged on these facts; like Lord Millett, they considered that, if applicable, Article 6(1)'s requirements were met. Lord Hope delivered a short concurring speech.

It is apparent from this case and the developments in the European case law on which it is based that the range of administrative decisions to which Article 6(1) applies is widening significantly (albeit that limits remain: see, eg, *R (Kehoe)* v. *Secretary of State for Work and Pensions* [2004] EWCA Civ 225 [2004] 2 WLR 1481). It is noteworthy that, in *Runa Begum,* their Lordships drew a connection between the scope of Article 6(1) and the requirements which, when applicable, it imposes. Lords Bingham, Hoffmann, Walker, and Millett all preferred to await further developments in the Strasbourg case law before holding Article 6(1) applicable to situations such as that in *Runa Begum,* because they were concerned that a newly-expanded Article 6(1) should not impose unduly burdensome obligations upon administrative bodies and the courts of law responsible for hearing appeals from or reviewing the decisions of such bodies. That issue is considered in the next section.

First, however, it should be noted that it has been suggested that there exists a *common law* right to an independent and impartial tribunal. In *R (Bewry)* v. *Norwich City Council* [2001] EWHC Admin 657 [2002] HRLR 2 at [29], Moses J suggested that such a common law right is available in cases involving a 'right of review of a determination of statutory entitlement'. However, Craig, *Administrative Law* (Oxford 2003) at 474, suggests that there is no principled reason why the common law right should not be more widely available, and applicable in circumstances where Article 6 would not be. If this is so, then the implications are considerable — not least because it would render much of the case law on the scope of

Article 6 redundant; however, much clearer authority is required before we can be certain about the scope of such a right at common law.

10.5.3 What does Article 6(1) Require in the Administrative Sphere?

Article 6(1) imposes a number of obligations on the administrative decision-makers to which it applies. Some of those relate to the way in which the decision-making process is conducted, and therefore fall for consideration in ch 11. We are presently concerned with Article 6(1)'s requirements of 'independence' and 'impartiality'. Regarding the latter, the ECtHR explained in *Hauschildt* v. *Denmark* (1990) 12 EHRR 266 at 279 that:

The existence of impartiality . . . must be determined according to a subjective test, that is on the basis of the personal conviction of a particular judge in a given case, and also according to an objective test, that is ascertaining whether the judge offered guarantees sufficient to exclude any legitimate doubt in this respect.

The subjective test is concerned with actual bias, and so is rarely in issue. The objective test was described by the Court (at 279) in the following terms:

Under the objective test, it must be determined whether, quite apart from the judge's personal conduct, there are ascertainable facts which may raise doubts as to his impartiality. In this respect even appearances may be of a certain importance. What is at stake is the confidence which the courts in a democratic society must inspire in the public and above all, as far as criminal proceedings are concerned, in the accused. Accordingly, any judge in respect of whom there is a legitimate reason to fear a lack of impartiality must withdraw.

This is, unsurprisingly, very similar to the fair-minded observer test which was adopted by the English courts in *Porter* v. *Magill* (see above at 10.3.2), partly in order to render domestic law consistent with the ECHR. However, Article 6(1) goes further than the common law in an important respect. Common law bias challenges tend to focus on *personal* characteristics of the decision-maker, such as a financial interest in the outcome of the case or a pre-existing relationship with a party (although cf *Bewry*, discussed above at 10.5.2). However, Article 6(1) also permits challenges based on the *institutional* position of the decision-maker. *Prima facie*, Article 6(1) requires that decision-makers to which it applies possess the type of 'independence' and 'impartiality' associated with judicial processes. This is often not the case with administrative decision-makers, many of whom, far from being independent of the executive branch of government, are part of it and are, as a result, heavily influenced by considerations of policy.

Article 6(1) and policy-making functions

The extract from Lord Hoffmann's speech in *Alconbury* set out above at 10.5.1 highlights a number of concerns which would attend the application of Article 6(1)'s 'full judicial model' to administrators charged with making policy choices. In the next excerpt, his Lordship considers, with reference to ECtHR jurisprudence, how that model should be modified in order to take account of those concerns.

....

R (Alconbury Developments Ltd) v. Secretary of State for the Environment, Transport and the Regions [2001] UKHL 23 [2003] 2 AC 295
House of Lords

For the facts, see above at 10.5.1.

Lord Hoffmann

[84] . . . [ECtHR] cases establish that article 6(1) requires that there should be the possibility of some form of judicial review of the lawfulness of an administrative decision . . .

[86] In . . . *Albert and Le Compte v Belgium* (1983) 5 EHRR 533 . . . the court said, at paragraph 29, that although disciplinary jurisdiction could be conferred upon professional bodies which did not meet the requirements of article 6(1) (eg because they were not "established by law" or did not sit in public):

> "Nonetheless, in such circumstances the Convention calls at least for one of the two following systems: either the jurisdictional organs themselves comply with the requirements of article 6(1), or they do not so comply but are subject to subsequent control by a judicial body that has full jurisdiction and does provide the guarantees of article 6(1)."

[87] The reference to "full jurisdiction" has been frequently cited in subsequent cases and sometimes relied upon in argument as if it were authority for saying that a policy decision affecting civil rights by an administrator who does not comply with article 6(1) has to be reviewable on its merits by an independent and impartial tribunal. It was certainly so relied upon by counsel for the respondents in these appeals. But subsequent European authority shows that "full jurisdiction" does not mean full decision-making power. It means full jurisdiction to deal with the case as the nature of the decision requires.

[88] . . . [T]he leading European authority for the proposition that it is not necessary to have a review of the merits of a policy decision is *Zumtobel v Austria* (1993) 17 EHRR 116. The Zumtobel partnership objected to the compulsory purchase of their farming land to build the L52 by-pass road in the Austrian Vorarlberg. The appropriate government committee heard their objections but confirmed the order. They appealed to an administrative court, which said that the government had taken proper matters into account and that it was not entitled to substitute its decision for that of the administrative authority. They complained to the Commission and the European court that, as the administrative court could not "independently assess the merits and the facts of the case", it did not have "full jurisdiction" within the meaning of the *Albert and Le Compte* formula. The European court said, at paragraph 32, that its jurisdiction was sufficient in the circumstances of the case, "[r]egard being had to the respect which must be accorded to decisions taken by the administrative authorities on grounds of expediency and to the nature of the complaints made by the Zumtobel partnership" . . .

[123] My Lords, I must now examine the reasoning of the Divisional Court. It considered the way in which decisions are made by the Secretary of State and came to the conclusion that he was not independent or impartial. Even though the department has elaborate procedures to ensure that the decision-making process is not contaminated by reliance on facts which had not been found by the inspector or fairly put to the parties, the decision is bound to be influenced by the departmental view on policy. Mr Kingston, who appeared for the Huntingdonshire District Council, spent a good deal of time making this proposition good by examining the documents showing how the department was, at various levels, involved in the development of policy for Alconbury. But this was

entirely what I would have expected. It is the business of the Secretary of State, aided by his civil servants, to develop national planning policies and co-ordinate local policies. These policies are not airy abstractions. They are intended to be applied to actual cases. It would be absurd for the Secretary of State, in arriving at a decision in a particular case, to ignore his policies and start with a completely open mind.

[124] For these reasons, the Divisional Court said that the Secretary of State was not impartial in the manner required by article 6: "What is objectionable in terms of article 6 is that he should be the judge in his own cause where his policy is in play." (see paragraph 86). I do not disagree with the conclusion that the Secretary of State is not an independent and impartial tribunal. He does not claim to be. But the question is not whether he should be a judge in his own cause. It is whether he should be a judge at all.

[125] The Divisional Court then considered whether the requirements of article 6 were satisfied by the right to have an application for judicial review determined by a court. This was rightly described by Tuckey LJ as the crucial question. The answer he gave was that the procedure by which the Secretary of State arrived at his decision did not contain "sufficient safeguards to justify the High Court's restricted power of review". The Secretary of State, having complied with the requirements of natural justice, was "free to make his own decision" and to take account of legal and policy guidance and recommendations from within the department "which are not seen by the parties". Therefore, said Tuckey LJ, at paragraph 95:

> "In terms of article 6 the decision on the merits, which usually involves findings of fact and planning judgment, has not been determined by an independent and impartial tribunal or anyone approaching this, but by someone who is obviously not independent and impartial."

[126] There are three strands of reasoning here. First, there is the fact that the parties are not privy to the processes of decision-making which go on within the department. These contain, on the one hand, elaborate precautions to ensure that the decision-maker does not take into account any factual matters which have not been found by the inspector at the inquiry or put to the parties and, on the other hand, free communication within the department on questions of law and policy, with a view to preparing a recommendation for submission to the Secretary of State or one of the junior Ministers to whom he has delegated the decision. The latter is standard civil service procedure and takes place, as Lord Greene MR said in *B Johnson & Co (Builders) Ltd v Minister of Health* [1947] 2 All ER 395, after the Secretary of State's quasi-judicial function has been concluded and when he is acting in his capacity as an administrator making a public policy decision . . .

[127] . . . If the Secretary of State was claiming to be, in his own person, an independent and impartial tribunal, the fact that he received confidential advice and recommendations from civil servants in his department might throw some doubt upon his claim. But, since he not only admits but avers that his constitutional role is to formulate and apply government policy, the fact that both formulation and application require the advice and assistance of his civil servants is no more than one would expect.

[128] The second strand concerns the facts. These are found by the inspector and must be accepted by the Secretary of State unless he has first notified the parties and given them an opportunity to make representations in accordance with rule 17(5) of the Town and Country Planning (Inquiries Procedure) (England) Rules 2000. This is the point upon which, in my opinion, the *Bryan* case 21 EHRR 342 is authority for saying that the independent position of the inspector, together with the control of the fairness of the fact-finding procedure by the court in judicial review, is sufficient to satisfy the requirements of article 6.

[129] Finally, the third strand is that of planning judgment. In this area the principle in the *Zumtobel* case 17 EHRR 116 . . . does not require that the court should be able to substitute its decision for that of the administrative authority. Such a requirement would in my opinion not only be contrary to the jurisprudence of the European court but would also be profoundly undemocratic. The Human Rights Act 1998 was no doubt intended to strengthen the rule of law but not to inaugurate the rule of lawyers.

[130] For these reasons I respectfully disagree with the Divisional Court's conclusion that decisions by the Secretary of State in planning cases are incompatible with Convention rights . . .

Lords Slynn, Nolan, Clyde, and Hutton agreed that no breach of Article 6(1) was disclosed. The decision of the Divisional Court was therefore reversed.

The *Alconbury* decision suggests that the impact of Article 6(1) on administrative decision-making will be modest, given the capacity of judicial review to cure defects at earlier stages of the process. Poustie [2001] *EHRLR* 657 at 663 notes that:

There is nothing remarkable in this approach. It is inevitable and indeed desirable on one view of the democratic model of decision-making that administrative decisions should be made by elected representatives at local or national level. Such persons cannot be independent as they are part of the executive. Neither can they be impartial in the sense that they will be concerned with promoting and implementing their own policies. However, this does not matter as long as there is a degree of judicial control over their decision-making.

There are, however, limits to the curative principle adopted in *Alconbury*. Much must depend on the nature of the judicial review jurisdiction itself. As Lord Hoffmann's speech indicates, neither the domestic nor European case law requires the reviewing court to possess jurisdiction to re-open the merits of the decision and, if necessary, substitute judgment. Nevertheless, it is noteworthy that, in their speeches in *Alconbury*, their Lordships emphasized the breadth of the contemporary supervisory jurisdiction exercised by the English courts. For instance, Lords Slynn (at [51]) and Clyde (at [169]) drew attention to the fact that review on the ground of proportionality is now available in English law, while Lord Slynn (at [53], invoking his comments in *R* v. *Criminal Injuries Compensation Board, ex parte A* [1999] 2 AC 330 at 334–345) noted the possibility of judicial review for 'misunderstanding or ignorance of an established and relevant fact' (on which see further 2.4 above). Their Lordships' purpose, in drawing attention to the range of issues which may now be examined on judicial review, was clearly to establish its credentials for Article 6(1) purposes — a matter to which the House of Lords returned in *Runa Begum* v. *Tower Hamlets London Borough Council* [2003] UKHL 5 [2003] 2 AC 430 (discussed below).

Article 6(1) and fact-finding functions

It is important to remember that *Alconbury* concerned a challenge to the Secretary of State's role as a policy-maker. Their Lordships clearly felt that it was appropriate for Ministers to determine matters of planning policy: note Lord Hoffmann's comments above at 10.5.1, and Lord Nolan's remark (at [60]) that to hand over such functions to an 'independent and impartial body with no central electoral accountability would not only be a recipe for chaos: it would be profoundly undemocratic'. Heavily influenced by this conclusion that the Secretary of State's role was constitutionally acceptable — indeed, desirable — their Lordships held that it did not matter that the Minister was not an independent and impartial body, since the regime as a whole was Article 6-compliant by virtue of the availability of judicial review. However, a different approach applies in cases concerning fact-finding functions. The next extract demonstrates that, in such cases, much closer attention is paid to the extent of the procedural safeguards at the initial stage.

Bryan v. *United Kingdom* (1996) 21 EHRR 342
European Commission of Human Rights

Vale Royal Borough Council issued an enforcement notice under s 172 of the Town and Country Planning Act 1990 requiring the applicant to demolish buildings which had been erected without planning permission. The applicant appealed to the Secretary of State; a planning inspector was appointed, but he rejected the appeal. The applicant therefore exercised his right under s 289(1) of the 1990 Act to appeal to the High Court on a point of law. That appeal was rejected. The applicant argued before the European Commission of Human Rights that the original decision did not comply with the requirements of Article 6(1), and that the appellate jurisdiction of the High Court was incapable of curing that defect. (The Commission operated as the principal Strasbourg fact-finding organ and determined the admissibility of applications; cases could be referred to the Court for final decision if, during or after the Commission stage, a friendly settlement could not be reached. The ECHR was amended and, in 1998, the Commission was abolished and replaced by a new Court.)

Concurring opinion of Mr N Bratza

I share the view of the majority of the Commission that, on the facts of the present case, the only challenge to the enforcement notice which the applicant pursued in the High Court related to matters of planning policy and that, consistently with the Court's reasoning in the *Zumtobel* case [(1994) 17 EHRR 116], Article 6 does not in any event require that a court should have the power to substitute its view for that of the administrative authorities on matters of planning policy or "expediency" . . .

. . . I also find that there has been no violation of Article 6 in the present case on the broader ground that the powers of review of the High Court under section 289 of the 1990 Act are sufficiently wide to satisfy the requirement held by the Court to be inherent in Article 6 that the judicial body determining the applicant's civil rights and obligations should have "full jurisdiction".

It appears to me that the requirement that a court or tribunal should have "full jurisdiction" cannot be mechanically applied with the result that, in all circumstances and whatever the subject matter of the dispute, the court or tribunal must have full power to substitute its own findings of fact, and its own inferences from those facts, for that of the administrative authority concerned. Whether the power of judicial review is sufficiently wide to satisfy the requirements of Article 6 must in my view depend on a number of considerations, including the subject matter of the dispute, the nature of the decision of the administrative authorities which is in question, the procedure, if any, which exists for review of the decision by a person or body acting independently of the authority concerned and the scope of that power of review.

In my view the powers of review of the High Court, when combined with the statutory arrangements under the 1990 Act for appealing against an enforcement notice, satisfy the requirements of Article 6(1).

So far as the statutory arrangements are concerned, section 174 of the 1990 Act provides that an appeal against an enforcement notice served by a local authority may be made to the Secretary of State on grounds, inter alia, that the matters alleged in the notice do not constitute a breach of planning control. Section 175(3) of the Act provides that if an appellant or the local authority desires, the Secretary of State shall give each of them the opportunity of appearing before and being heard by a person appointed by the Secretary of State ("the inspector") and power is conferred on the inspector to determine the appeal.

In determining planning appeals inspectors act in a quasi-judicial capacity and in accordance with prescribed procedures, full powers being conferred on both parties to appear, with or without legal representation, adduce evidence, both written and oral, and make submissions of both law and fact. Further, the appeal results in a reasoned decision letter.

In paragraph 42 of the Report the Commission, while accepting that the inspector is a "tribunal" within the substantive sense of the expression as used in Article 6(1) and that such a tribunal is one "established by law", concludes that an inspector does not satisfy the requirement of independence and impartiality: it is correctly pointed out that inspectors are chosen from salaried staff of the Planning Inspectorate, which serves the Secretary of State in the furtherance of his policies, and that while the Secretary of State and his inspector are not parties to the dispute as such, the fact that those policies can be in issue on appeals means that the inspector cannot have the independence necessary for Article 6 of the Convention.

While this is true, there is equally nothing to suggest that, in finding the primary facts and in drawing conclusions and inferences from those facts, an inspector acts anything other than independently, in the sense that he is in no sense connected with the parties to the dispute or subject to their influence or control; his findings and conclusions are based exclusively on the evidence and submissions before him.

An appeal is from an inspector's decision to the High Court under Section 289 of the Act "on a point of law". As appears from the Commission's Report, this does not mean that the inspector's findings of fact or the inferences drawn by him from those facts are free from review by the Court. The Court cannot substitute its own findings of fact or its own inferences from those facts for those of the inspector. However, the Court can set aside a factual finding by an inspector if that finding is unsupported by any evidence before him. The Court can also set aside inferences drawn by the inspector from those facts if those inferences are perverse or irrational in the sense that no inspector properly directing himself could reasonably have drawn such inferences . . .

In my view this power of review of the High Court, combined with the statutory procedure for appealing against an enforcement notice, is sufficient to meet the requirement of "full jurisdiction" inherent in Article 6(1) of the Convention.

The Commission found, by majority, that the possibility of appeal to the High Court on a point of law rendered the process, taken as a whole, consistent with Article 6(1). The same conclusion was reached by the Court.

Commenting with approval on this opinion, Lord Hoffmann said in *Alconbury* [2001] UKHL 23 [2003] 2 AC 295 at [110] that its great strength was its recognition that

a tribunal may be more or less independent, depending upon the question it is being called upon to decide. On matters of policy, the inspector was no more independent than the Secretary of State himself. But this was a matter on which independence was unnecessary — indeed, on democratic principles, undesirable — and in which the power of judicial review, paying full respect to the views of the inspector or Secretary of State on questions of policy or expediency, was sufficient to satisfy article 6(1). On the other hand, in deciding the questions of primary fact or fact and degree which arose in enforcement notice appeals, the inspector was no mere bureaucrat. He was an expert tribunal acting in a quasi-judicial manner and therefore sufficiently independent to make it unnecessary that the High Court should have a broad jurisdiction to review his decisions on questions of fact.

QUESTIONS

- Do you agree that fact-finding and policy-making functions should be distinguished in this context?
- What difficulties might arise in seeking to draw such a distinction?

It follows that more judicial-style independence is required in relation to fact-finding than policy-making functions. Such independence is to be supplied pre-eminently by the sort of safeguards, operating at first instance, that were mentioned in the *Bryan* opinion. If those safeguards do not secure full compliance with the judicial model, then judicial review or appeal may compensate for this. For instance, in *Bryan* itself, the inspector's lack of institutional separation from the executive branch was 'cured' by the possibility of appeal on a point of law to the High Court. However, the greater the absence of the safeguards at first instance, the more that will be required by way of appeal or judicial review, bearing in mind the high overall degree of adherence to the judicial model that is required where fact-finding is at stake. It follows that it is perfectly possible to envisage (see, eg, *R (Q) v. Secretary of State for the Home Department* [2003] EWCA 364 [2004] QB 36) circumstances in which judicial review, with its limited scrutiny of the fact-finding process, is unable to exert sufficient curative effect for Article 6(1) purposes.

Fact-finding in relation to regulatory and welfare schemes

The current position is not quite as straightforward as the discussion thus far might suggest. The distinction between policy-making and fact-finding functions remains, with a higher degree of independence (either at first instance or by way of compensation by means of a sufficiently searching appeal or review jurisdiction) required in relation to the latter. However, distinct approaches now apply *within* the category of challenges to fact-finding functions, depending on the administrative context within which the fact-finding function in question is discharged.

....

Runa Begum v. *Tower Hamlets London Borough Council* [2003] UKHL 5 [2003] 2 AC 430
House of Lords

The facts of this case are set out in full above at 10.5.2. It will be recalled that Runa Begum complained that the a local authority's internal review, under Part VII of the Housing Act 1996, of its determination that she had unreasonably rejected an offer of accommodation failed to comply with Article 6(1), and that in rejecting her reasons for refusing the accommodation the reviewing officer had acted on the basis of mistaken facts. Their Lordships assumed, without deciding, that Article 6(1) applied in these circumstances, but as the following extract shows they concluded that the problems with the internal review could be cured by the possibility of appeal to the county court under s 204 of the 1996 Act which was able to exercise the normal judicial review jurisdiction of the High Court.

Lord Hoffmann

[41] *Bryan* was . . . a case about the application of article 6 to decisions on fact. In that respect it was distinguishable from *Alconbury*. But when one comes to consider what *Bryan* decided, it is important to notice not only what the question was (whether buildings were designed for the purposes of agriculture) but also the context in which it arose, namely, as a ground of appeal

against an enforcement notice. The inspector's decision that Bryan had acted in breach of planning control was binding upon him in any subsequent criminal proceedings for failing to comply with the notice: *R v Wicks* [1998] AC 92. This part of the appeal against the enforcement notice was closely analogous to a criminal trial and, as I noted in *Alconbury*, at pp 1416–1419, paras 89–97, used to come before the magistrates.

[42] A finding of fact in this context seems to me very different from the findings of fact which have to be made by central or local government officials in the course of carrying out regulatory functions (such as licensing or granting planning permission) or administering schemes of social welfare such as Part VII. The rule of law rightly requires that certain decisions, of which the paradigm examples are findings of breaches of the criminal law and adjudications as to private rights, should be entrusted to the judicial branch of government. This basic principle does not yield to utilitarian arguments that it would be cheaper or more efficient to have these matters decided by administrators. Nor is the possibility of an appeal sufficient to compensate for lack of independence and impartiality on the part of the primary decision maker: see *De Cubber v Belgium* (1984) 7 EHRR 236.

[43] But utilitarian considerations have their place when it comes to setting up, for example, schemes of regulation or social welfare. I said earlier that in determining the appropriate scope of judicial review of administrative action, regard must be had to democratic accountability, efficient administration and the sovereignty of Parliament. This case raises no question of democratic accountability. As Hale LJ said in *Adan's* case [2002] 1 WLR 2120, 2138, para 57:

> "The policy decisions were taken by Parliament when it enacted the 1996 Act. Individual eligibility decisions are taken in the first instance by local housing authorities but policy questions of the availability of resources or equity between the homeless and those on the waiting list for social housing are irrelevant to individual eligibility."

[44] On the other hand, efficient administration and the sovereignty of Parliament are very relevant. Parliament is entitled to take the view that it is not in the public interest that an excessive proportion of the funds available for a welfare scheme should be consumed in administration and legal disputes . . .

[46] [His Lordship cited passages from the joint dissenting opinion in *Feldbrugge* v. *The Netherlands* (1986) 8 EHRR 425 and *Matthews* v. *Eldridge* (1976) 424 US 319 in support of this view, and continued:] It therefore seems to me that it would be inappropriate to require that findings of fact for the purposes of administering the homelessness scheme in Part VII should be made by a person or body independent of the authority which has been entrusted with its administration . . .

[47] Although I do not think that the exercise of administrative functions requires a mechanism for independent findings of fact or a full appeal, it does need to be lawful and fair. It is at this point that . . . arguments . . . about the impartiality of Mrs Hayes [the local authority official] and the regulations for the conduct of reviews become relevant. To these safeguards one adds the supervisory powers of the judge on an appeal under section 204 to quash the decision for procedural impropriety or irrationality. In any case, the gap between judicial review and a full right of appeal is seldom in practice very wide. Even with a full right of appeal it is not easy for an appellate tribunal which has not itself seen the witnesses to differ from the decision-maker on questions of primary fact and, more especially relevant to this case, on questions of credibility.

[48] [Counsel] drew attention to the expanding scope of judicial review which, he said, may, in a suitable case allow a court to quash a decision on the grounds of misunderstanding or ignorance of

an established and relevant fact: see the views of Lord Slynn of Hadley in *R v Criminal Injuries Compensation Board, Ex p A* [1999] 2 AC 330, 344–345 and in the *Alconbury* case [2001] 2 WLR 1389, 1407, para 53 or, at least in cases in which Convention rights were engaged, on the ground of lack of proportionality: *R (Daly) v Secretary of State for the Home Department* [2001] 2 AC 532. He said that this should be taken into account in deciding whether the jurisdiction of the county court was adequate.

[49] I do not think that it is necessary to discuss the implications of these developments. No doubt it is open to a court exercising the review jurisdiction under section 204 to adopt a more intensive scrutiny of the rationality of the reviewing officer's conclusions of fact but this is not the occasion to enter into the question of when it should do so. When one is dealing with a welfare scheme which, in the particular case, does not engage human rights (does not, for example, require consideration of article 8) then the intensity of review must depend upon what one considers to be most consistent with the statutory scheme. In this case, Laws LJ [2002] 1 WLR 2491, 2513, para 44, said that the county court judge was entitled to subject Mrs Hayes's decision to "a close and rigorous analysis". On the other hand 17 years ago Lord Brightman, speaking for a unanimous Appellate Committee in *R v. Hillingdon London Borough Council, ex parte Puhlhofer* [1986] AC 484, 518, made it clear that their Lordships contemplated a fairly low level of judicial interventionism:

> "Parliament intended the local authority to be the judge of fact. The Act abounds with the formula when, or if, the housing authority are satisfied as to this, or that, or have reason to believe this, or that. Although the action or inaction of a local authority is clearly susceptible to judicial review where they have misconstrued the Act, or abused their powers or otherwise acted perversely, I think that great restraint should be exercised in giving leave to proceed by judicial review."

[50] All that we are concerned with in this appeal is the requirements of article 6, which I do not think mandates a more intensive approach to judicial review of questions of fact. These nuances are well within the margin of appreciation which the Convention allows to contracting states and which, in a case like this, the courts should concede to Parliament. So I do not propose to say anything about whether a review of fact going beyond conventional principles of judicial review would be either permissible or appropriate. It seems to me sufficient to say that in the case of the normal Part VII decision, engaging no human rights other than article 6, conventional judicial review such as the Strasbourg court considered in the *Bryan* case 21 EHRR 342 is sufficient.

[51] Is this view consistent with the Strasbourg jurisprudence and with *Bryan* in particular? I think it is . . .

[52] In this case the subject matter of the decision was the suitability of accommodation for occupation by Runa Begum; the kind of decision which the Strasbourg court has on several occasions called a "classic exercise of an administrative discretion". The manner in which the decision was arrived at was by the review process, at a senior level in the authority's administration and subject to rules designed to promote fair decision-making. The content of the dispute is that the authority made its decision on the basis of findings of fact which Runa Begum says were mistaken. In my opinion the Strasbourg court has accepted, on the basis of general state practice and for the reasons of good administration which I have discussed, that in such cases a limited right of review on questions of fact is sufficient . . .

[Lord Hoffmann considered the *Bryan* case further, as well as *Kingsley* v. *United Kingdom* (2001) 33 EHRR 13, and continued:]

[56] The key phrases in the judgments of the Strasbourg court which describe the cases in which a limited review of the facts is sufficient are 'specialised areas of the law' (*Bryan's* case 21 EHRR 342,

361, para 47) and 'classic exercise of administrative discretion' (*Kingsley's* case 33 EHRR 288, 302, para 53). What kind of decisions are these phrases referring to? I think that one has to take them together. The notion of a specialised area of the law should not be taken too literally. After all, I suppose carriage of goods by sea could be said to be a specialised area of the law, but no one would suggest that shipping disputes should be decided otherwise than by normal judicial methods. It seems to me that what the court had in mind was those areas of the law such as regulatory and welfare schemes in which decision-making is customarily entrusted to administrators. And when the court in *Kingsley* spoke of the classic exercise of administrative discretion, it was referring to the ultimate decision as to whether Kingsley was a fit and proper person [to hold a management position in the gaming industry] and not to the particular findings of fact which had to be made on the way to arriving at that decision. In the same way, the decision as to whether the accommodation was suitable for Runa Begum was a classic exercise of administrative discretion, even though it involved preliminary findings of fact.

[57] National traditions as to which matters are suitable for administrative decision and which require to be decided by the judicial branch of government may differ. To that extent, the Strasbourg court will no doubt allow a margin of appreciation to contracting states. The concern of the court, as it has emphasised since *Golder's* case 1 (1975) EHRR 524 is to uphold the rule of law and to insist that decisions which on generally accepted principles are appropriate only for judicial decision should be so decided. In the case of decisions appropriate for administrative decision, its concern, again founded on the rule of law, is that there should be the possibility of adequate judicial review. For this purpose, cases like *Bryan* and *Kingsley* make it clear that limitations on practical grounds on the right to a review of the findings of fact will be acceptable . . .

Lords Bingham and Millett similarly concluded that the county court's jurisdiction was adequate for Article 6(1) purposes. Lords Hope and Walker delivered only short concurring speeches.

According to Lord Hoffmann's analysis, a distinction must be drawn between fact-finding in cases concerning private rights, and those, like *Runa Begum*, involving the administration of welfare or regulatory schemes. In the former category, the requirements of independence and impartiality fall to be enforced strictly (as in *Bryan*). In the latter category, a more general requirement, that the process is 'lawful and fair', obtains. Of course, as Craig [2003] *PL* 753 at 768–770 notes, the distinction which *Runa Begum* requires us to draw, between private rights and regulatory and welfare schemes, may cause practical difficulties. It also introduces what Craig calls a 'double rights-based hurdle', in that it is now necessary to establish that both a 'civil right' (in the Article 6(1) sense) and a 'private right' (in the *Runa Begum* sense) are at stake in order to insist that Article 6 is applied with maximum vigour. This, in turn, reflects the breadth of the Article 6(1) notion of civil rights, with a core of rights that can only legitimately be adjudicated upon by means of full adherence to the judicial model, and a broader penumbra within which, as we move away from the core, adherence to that model can increasingly be displaced by utilitarian considerations.

10.6 Concluding Remarks

The absence of bias is fundamental to the notion of fairness. No amount of procedural safeguards — such as the right to be heard, to cross-examine witnesses, or to be represented by a lawyer — can yield fairness if the tribunal is, in the first place, biased. And, as we have seen, even the perception of bias is damaging to an administrative or judicial system, given the importance of ensuring public confidence in the integrity of the decision-making process. English law, on the whole, treats these matters with appropriate seriousness by recognizing the importance of ensuring the appearance — as well as the reality — of fairness. But we have also seen that these issues do not exist in a vacuum, and that other policy concerns — not least effective and efficient decision-making — make competing claims on, and ultimately help to shape, the legal rules which operate in this area. The effect given to Article 6 ECHR by the HRA has added another layer to English law in this context by increasing the scope for challenges based on the institutional position of the decision-maker. In particular, English courts, applying Article 6, are having to confront questions about the legitimacy of Parliament's allocation of decision-making functions to particular institutions which simply would not have arisen only a few years ago. In discharging this task, the courts are displaying sensitivity to democratic and other normative concerns about the locus of policy- and decision-making power. But this is, as we have seen, a difficult area, and the jurisprudence remains at an embryonic stage.

FURTHER RESOURCES

Alexis, 'Reasonableness in the Establishing of Bias' [1979] *PL* 143

Atrill, 'Who is the "Fair-Minded and Informed Observer"? Bias after *Magill*' [2003] *CLJ* 279

Craig, 'The Human Rights Act, Article 6 and Procedural Rights' [2003] *PL* 753

Galligan, *Due Process and Fair Procedures* (Oxford 1996)

Malleson, 'Safeguarding Judicial Impartiality' (2002) 22 *LS* 53

Williams, 'Bias; the Judges and the Separation of Powers' [2000] *PL* 45

Woodhouse (ed), *The Pinochet Case: A Legal and Constitutional Analysis* (Oxford 2000)

11 PROCEDURAL FAIRNESS

In this chapter we address three central issues. We begin by asking what is meant by procedural fairness. Then we address the scope of the principle — in what circumstances must decision-makers act fairly? Finally, we consider what procedural fairness means by examining the specific requirements which the doctrine imposes upon decision-makers.

11.1 The Idea of Procedural Fairness

We saw in ch 10 that if a decision-making system is to adhere to the notion of procedural fairness, then it must operate in an impartial way — hence the rule against bias. That principle is a necessary but not a sufficient condition if procedural fairness is to be realized. Although it is self-evident that the decision-maker must be impartial — meaning free from bias — the overall goals of procedural fairness can be secured only if it goes on to apply a decision-making process which is itself fair. This aspect of procedural fairness is sometimes referred to as the right to a fair hearing, and is said to be summed up by the latin maxim *audi alteram partem* — literally, 'hear the other side'. The fundamentality of this principle was underlined by Fortescue J in *R v. The Chancellor of Cambridge* (1723) 1 Stra 557, in which Dr Bentley challenged the University's decision to strip him of his degrees following alleged misconduct, without first giving him an opportunity to respond to those allegations:

I remember to have heard it observed by a very learned man upon such an occasion, that even God himself did not pass sentence upon Adam, before he was called upon to make his defence. 'Adam' (says God) 'where art thou? Has thou not eaten of the tree whereof I commanded thee that thou shouldest not eat?' And the same question was put to Eve also.

Some of the principal reasons for requiring fairness in decision-making are set out at 10.1 above. Although the importance of fair treatment may, at a general level, be uncontroversial, it is crucial to articulate *precisely* why fairness is important, since the ethos which underpins a legal system's commitment to procedural fairness necessarily plays a central role in determining the exact shape and reach of the legal rules which operate to secure such fairness. In the following passage, Galligan attempts to provide what he calls 'a general theory of fair treatment' by exploring what it is that legal rules requiring procedural fairness might seek to achieve.

Galligan, 'Procedural Fairness'

in Birks (ed), *The Frontiers of Liability* (volume one) (Oxford 1994)

. . . Consider the distribution of welfare and the case of X applying for a particular benefit. Imagine that the conditions of eligibility are clear, that X, seeking to show his entitlement, presents his case to the tribunal, and that the tribunal, after considering the claim and the relevant facts, awards the benefit. This process can be understood at two levels. At one level it is a matter of officials distributing welfare according to the criteria set by the governing statute. If the law is properly applied, those criteria are met, and the social good in distributing welfare on that basis is satisfied. Correct decisions about whether applicants are entitled to benefits means that the system is working well; mistakes mean it is not, and the social good is to that extent diminished. At this level of understanding, questions of fairness do not arise; the only concern is whether the statutory scheme is working effectively. That is important because society has decided that that is how welfare should be allocated. The role of procedures is to see that the law is applied accurately and, as a consequence, that the social good is realized. Anyone familiar with Bentham's writings will recognize here his theory of procedures [see Bentham, *A Treatise of Judicial Evidence* (London 1825)]. Bentham wrote at length about the civil and criminal trials, but his account can be transposed to other forms of decision-making. He considered accuracy of outcome, or rectitude as he called it, to be the object of the trial, subject only to considerations of delay, vexation and expense. Accurate outcomes serve the ends of utility, in particular the utility in having a stable and reliable system of civil and criminal laws. The task for rules of evidence and procedure is to produce accurate outcomes. Much of Bentham's writings was directed to the reform of those areas of English law in accordance with this view of their rightful purpose.

On this approach, the value of legal procedures is judged according to their contribution to general social goals. The object is to advance certain social goals, whether through administrative processes, or through the civil or criminal trial. The law and its processes are simply instruments for achieving some social good as determined from time to time by the law makers of the society. Each case is an instance in achieving the general goal, and a mistaken decision, whether to the benefit or the detriment of a particular person, is simply a failure to achieve the general good in that case. At this level of understanding, judgments of fairness have no place, for all that matters is whether the social good, as expressed through laws, is effectively achieved.

In order to introduce ideas of fair treatment and in particular fair procedures, we must move to a second level of understanding. For whenever pursuit of the common good involves the distribution of benefits and burdens, advantages and disadvantages to individuals (or groups), questions of fair treatment come into play. The principles of distribution are the subject-matter of fair treatment. So, whenever the state, through its officials, decides how people are to be treated, considerations of fair treatment arise. Welfare decisions can now be seen at two levels: at one, they are elements in the effective distribution of welfare, where the object is the common good; at the other, they are about the fair treatment of those persons whose cases are being considered. But fair treatment is not a kind of optional extra; it is, on the contrary, a fundamental requirement of any justifiable political and legal theory.

It is not appropriate here to attempt to provide a moral foundation for the idea that, in the distribution of advantages and disadvantages, each person should be treated fairly. It is enough to note that the principle is fundamental to liberal and democratic theory, and that it is at the foundation of western law. The underlying idea is that each person should be treated with respect. The idea of respect for each person is open-textured and wide in its reach, but in political philosophy it means at least that each person counts as an individual with interests and concerns. The notion of fair treatment is connected to respect for persons. One aspect of respect is to give a person his due, which is in turn the essential element of fair treatment. Questions of respect and, therefore, fair treatment occur in many contexts, but one of special importance is where the state has power over a person, whether in distributing benefits or imposing burdens, and must decide how that person is to be treated. The community, through its officials, has a basic duty to treat fairly those affected by its laws and legal processes . . .

In this passage Galligan helpfully identifies two distinct perspectives concerning the value of legal procedures. The first is an instrumental one: it presents legal procedures as a means to an end, the end being the effective and efficient delivery of those social goals which are set by policy-makers. The second perspective, in contrast, is non-instrumental: it requires the adoption of fair procedures because respect for the individual demands that he be treated fairly. On this view, a decision-making process which *involves* the individual — by giving him notice of the issues, allowing him to have his views taken account of and, ultimately, supplying him with reasons for the decision — characterizes him as a participant in the process of decision-making, rather than as the object of a distant and authoritarian adminis-trative regime, and in this way accords respect to him as an individual. These themes are explored further by Galligan in his book *Due Process and Fair Procedures: A Study of Administrative Procedures* (Oxford 1996) in which he concludes that the importance of procedural fairness is primarily instrumental. In the following passage, taken from a review of Galligan's book, Allan critically examines that view, concluding that it is possible — indeed desirable — to recognize *both* the instrumental *and* non-instrumental values served by procedural fairness.

. . . .

Allan, 'Procedural Fairness and the Duty of Respect' (1998) 18 OJLS 497

. . . Procedural fairness is a topic close to the heart of any lawyer who takes pride in the contribution of the rule of law to good and decent government, properly respectful of the governed. But wherein exactly lies its special importance? Do the rules of natural justice and related principles of procedural fairness serve only to guarantee that legal rules governing matters of substance are accurately applied to the appropriate cases? Or does procedural propriety have an intrinsic, non-instrumental value more directly related to the citizen's dignity? Moreover, if we acknowledge the injustice which consists in a failure to secure for people the rights which the law confers or protects, how can we justify our adoption of imperfect procedures, which we know are likely to generate mistaken decisions?

In the course of his illuminating discussion of the nature and role of procedural fairness, *Due Process and Fair Procedures*, Professor D J Galligan offers thoughtful and interesting answers to such questions. His major theme, which runs throughout the book, is that procedural fairness is fundamentally an instrumental good, in the sense that procedures should be designed to ensure accurate or appropriate outcomes. Legal processes function within a framework of values, some specific to a particular form of process and others reflecting more general moral and political ideas . . . "Dignitarian" theorists, who emphasize the intrinsic value of procedures, have failed to under-stand that treating a person in accordance with legal standards is itself an important aspect of according him respect, and accordingly they have undervalued the significance of accurate outcomes . . .

The important part played by non-outcome values — values independent of the accuracy or soundness of the substantive decision or verdict — in any complete and convincing analysis is readily acknowledged; but Laurence Tribe's suggestion, that the "rights to interchange" between citizen and official conferred by a fair hearing have intrinsic value, is typical of the dignitarian assertions which attract Galligan's scepticism. According to Tribe, such rights "express the elem-entary idea that to be a *person*, rather than a *thing*, is at least to be *consulted* about what is done with one" [*American Constitutional Law* (New York 1988) at 666]. Ronald Dworkin [*A Matter of Principle* (Oxford 1986) at 101–103] has criticized this passage as failing to explain why the absence of a hearing entails an injustice or "moral harm" which is in some sense distinct from that entailed by an inaccurate substantive decision. Galligan takes similar objection: the alleged link between respect for persons and fair procedures stands in need of explanation, which dignitarian theorists have hitherto failed to provide. The dignitarian approach may serve to remind us that non-outcome values (such as privacy and confidentiality) should not be overlooked; the rules protecting a suspect from being tricked or cajoled into confessing, for example, are based on values which are quite independent of any concern with accuracy of outcome . . . Although Galligan is right to protest against a view of procedures which belittles their instrumental value in ensuring appropriate out-comes, there are at least aspects of procedural fairness or good practice which may serve an independent function. Moreover, the whole design or character of a hearing may well reflect non-instrumental values of no less importance than those which underlie our concern for accuracy and reliability . . .

The instrumental value of procedures should not be underestimated; the accurate application of authoritative standards is, as Galligan clearly explains, an important aspect of treating someone with respect. But procedures also have *intrinsic* value in acknowledging a person's right to under-stand his treatment, and thereby to determine his response as a conscientious citizen, willing to make reasonable sacrifices for the public good. If obedience to law ideally entails a recognition of its morally obligatory character, there must be suitable opportunities to test its moral credentials. Procedures may also be thought to have intrinsic value in so far as they constitute a fair balance between the demands of accuracy and other social needs: where the moral harm entailed by erroneous decisions is reasonably assessed and fairly distributed, procedures express society's commitment to equal concern and respect for all.

Within the constraints of limited resources, the purpose of a fair hearing is to allow the individual citizen to make a genuine contribution to a decision which impinges directly on his freedom and welfare, invoking his sense of justice as much as his self-interest. The value of fair procedures finally consists in the combination of our commitment to substantive justice and our uncertainty about what that means in the circumstances of any particular case, a matter of which the person or persons most closely affected can often cast valuable light, and also, and above all, in our desire to commend the outcome to a fellow-citizen who must suffer for the common good . . .

Allan's view, according to which procedural fairness is valuable in both instrumental and non-instrumental terms, is highly persuasive. There are, nevertheless, instances when the two perspectives direct different approaches; here, a choice must be made about which underlying conception of fairness is paramount. Consider, for instance, a situation in which for some reason — perhaps because the evidence against the individual is thought to be utterly compelling — it is felt that a fair hearing 'would make no difference' (a matter which is addressed in detail below at 11.2.5). If this is so, then fair procedures appear to serve no instrumental purpose, since the 'right' result can be secured without according such treat-ment to the individual; yet it is arguable — if we embrace the view which emphasizes the intrinsic importance of fair treatment — that respect for the individual requires a fair hearing even in such circumstances.

QUESTION

- Is fairness important because it helps to secure the 'right' outcome, or does its value exist independently of this consideration?

Another response is that in some circumstances there is an instrumental value in protecting *systems* that ensure accurate results. Thus, although in a particular case a hearing might seem to offer no improvement in accuracy, permitting a decision-maker to take a short cut in such a case might lead to his doing so in other cases where, in fact, his factual assumptions were mistaken and hence the result inaccurate. A related (but distinct) point is that preserving the integrity of the system in this way helps to bolster its *perceived*, as well as its *actual*, fairness — a factor which, as noted at 10.1 above, is essential to public confidence in and co-operation with the administrative state.

11.2 The Province of Procedural Fairness

The notion of procedural fairness is ultimately fluid: it falls to be judged by reference to circumstances; more or less may be required of the decision-maker depending, for instance, upon how seriously the decision will impact upon the individual concerned. Below, at 11.3, we examine this relationship between the nature of the specific decision or administrative act and the content of the duty to act in a procedurally fair way; in the present section we address the prior — but necessarily related — issue of the province of procedural fairness. Even allowing for the flexible nature of fairness, in what circumstances do decision-makers find themselves under some obligation to act fairly? And where, precisely, is the outer perimeter of the duty to act fairly, beyond which the individual finds himself vulnerable to a mode of decision-making which is unregulated by any legal requirement of due process?

11.2.1 A Question of Function or of Impact?

The case law in this sphere evidences a number of highly significant shifts in judicial perspective. Two specific traditions may be identified, one adopting a formal approach by asking whether the power in question is 'judicial' or 'administrative' in nature, the other concentrating on the likely impact of the decision on the individual. Each approach has, at times, been dominant; the following case is a famous illustration of the latter.

....

Cooper v. The Board of Works for Wandsworth District (1863) 14 CBNS 180; 143 ER 414
Court of Common Pleas

The claimant had started to build a house without giving the required notice to the defendant district board. The board then proceeded to demolish the partially-built house without providing a hearing to the claimant. The claimant sued the defendant for trespass, arguing that a right to such a hearing ought to be implied into the relevant statutory power (s 76 of the Metropolis Local Management Act 1855).

Erle CJ

The district board here say, that no notice was given by the plaintiff of his intention to build the house in question, wherefore they demolished it. The contention on the part of the plaintiff has been, that, although the words of the statute, taken in their literal sense, without any qualification at all, would create a justification for the act which the district board has done, the powers granted by that statute are subject to a qualification which has been repeatedly recognized, that no man is to be deprived of his property without his having an opportunity of being heard. The evidence here shews that the plaintiff and the district board had not been quite on amicable terms. Be that as it may, the district board say that no notice was given, and that consequently they had a right to proceed to demolish the house without delay, and without notice to the party whose house was to be pulled down, and without giving him an opportunity of shewing any reason why the board should delay. I think that the power which is granted by the 76th section is subject to the qualification suggested. It is a power carrying with it enormous consequences. The house in question was built only to a certain extent. But the power claimed would apply to a complete house. It would apply to a house of any value, and completed to any extent; and it seems to me to be a power which may be exercised most perniciously, and that the limitation which we are going to put upon it is one which ought, according to the decided cases, to be put upon it, and one which is required by a due consideration for the public interest. I think the board ought to have given notice to the plaintiff, and to have allowed him to be heard. The default in sending notice to the board of the intention to build, is a default which may be explained. There may be a great many excuses for the apparent default. The party may have intended to conform to the law. He may have actually conformed to all the regulations which they would wish to impose, though by accident his notice may have miscarried; and, under those circumstances, if he explained how it stood, the proceeding to demolish, merely because they had ill-will against the party, is a power that the legislature never intended to confer. I cannot conceive any harm that could happen to the district board from hearing the party before they subjected him to a loss so serious as the demolition of his house; but I can conceive of a great many advantages which might arise in the way of public order, in the way of doing substantial justice, and in the way of fulfilling the purposes of the statute, by the restriction which we put upon them, that they should hear the party before they inflict upon him such a heavy loss. I fully agree that the legislature intended to give the district board very large powers indeed: but the qualification I speak of is one which has been recognized to the full extent. It has been said that the principle that no man shall be deprived of his property without an opportunity of being heard, is limited to a judicial proceeding, and that a district board ordering a house to be pulled down cannot be said to be doing a judicial act. I do not quite agree with that; neither do I undertake to rest my judgment solely upon the ground that the district board is a court exercising judicial discretion upon the point: but the law, I think, has been applied to many exercises of power which in common understanding would not be at all more a judicial proceeding than would be the act of the district board in ordering a house to be pulled down . . .

Willes, Byles, and Keating JJ agreed that there should have been a hearing.

In deciding that a right to be heard — which, as we shall see at 11.3 below, is central to any notion of procedural fairness — was implicit in the Wandsworth Board's powers, Erle CJ's focus was very clearly on questions of impact; he was centrally concerned with how the exercise of the Board's powers affected the position of the individual. The very grave implications which could follow from an exercise of the power — such as the demolition of a person's house — led Erle CJ to conclude that a duty to comply with natural justice necessarily arose. Traditionally, powers attracting such a duty were characterized as 'judicial' or 'quasi-judicial', while the term 'administrative' was used to describe a power to which no duty to comply with natural justice attached. It is important to recognize, however, that the terms 'judicial' and 'quasi-judicial' were merely used in order to signify the *conclusion* that the holder of the power was under a duty to exercise the power fairly, *as if* he were the holder of a judicial or similar office. The focus, therefore, was still on the likely *impact* of the power, since it was the question of impact which could be determinative in the categorization of the power. Thus it was quite possible to find that an *administrative* body possessed 'judicial' or 'quasi-judicial' powers if the implications of their exercise were sufficient to require adherence to principles of due process. Wade (1951) 67 *LQR* 103 at 106 explained that 'it was not the *power* which was judicial, but the procedure which the courts held must be followed before the power could be properly exercised'.

However, the courts, over time, began to lose sight of the rationale underpinning this distinction between 'judicial' and 'quasi-judicial' powers on the one hand, and 'administrative' powers on the other. They mistook the basis of the distinction, leading to the adoption of a more formal analysis which asked whether the decision-maker was discharging a 'judicial' or an 'administrative' *function*, holding that a duty to comply with natural justice applied only to the former. By shifting their analysis from questions of impact to questions of formal classification, the courts overlooked the fact that the discharge of 'administrative' functions could quite easily have a very serious impact upon the individual — a conclusion which, on an impact-oriented analysis, would activate the duty to comply with natural justice. Thus arose the fallacy that the concept of procedural fairness extended only to decision-makers exercising 'judicial' functions, in turn rendering immune from scrutiny on due process grounds whole swathes of decision-making powers which (on a formal analysis) were 'administrative' in nature. For example, the Privy Council found in *Nakkuda Ali* v. *Jayaratne* [1951] AC 66 that a trading licence could be revoked by an administrative authority without giving the licence-holder a hearing; the same conclusion was reached in *R* v. *Metropolitan Police Commissioner, ex parte Parker* [1953] 1 WLR 1150 concerning a taxi driver's licence. This approach is also evident in the following decision (on which see also above at 10.4); although it concerns the applicability of the rule against bias, rather than the availability of the procedural safeguards with which this chapter is concerned, it nevertheless powerfully illustrates a very blinkered approach to the determination of the province of procedural fairness.

....

Franklin v. *Minister of Town and Country Planning* [1948] AC 87
House of Lords

After objections had been received to the draft Stevenage New Town (Designation) Order 1946, which had been prepared by the respondent Minister under the New Towns Act 1946, a public local inquiry was held by Morris, an inspector of the Ministry of Town and Country Planning. The inspector reported to the Minister, who, having considered the report, confirmed the draft Order. The appellants — owners and occupiers of premises at Stevenage — applied to the court under s 16 of the Town and Country Planning Act 1944 for the Order to be quashed. One ground of attack was that the Minister was biased. The appellants placed particular reliance on comments regarding Stevenage that he had made at a public meeting in May 1946, two days before the empowering legislation (the New Towns Act 1946) had received its second reading in the House of Commons. Henn Collins J was in favour of quashing the Order on the ground that the Minister had not had an open mind when making his decision. He rejected the view that the Minister was acting purely administratively when making the Order and accepted that he was acting judicially or quasi-judicially in this situation. In the Court of Appeal it was assumed that *at the time of making the speech* the Minister had prejudged issues which might be raised by objectors. Nevertheless, the Minister's appeal was allowed because, in the Court of Appeal's view, the evidence did not show that the Minister had been biased when he had made the Order. There was a further appeal to the House of Lords.

Lord Thankerton

. . . In my opinion, no judicial, or quasi-judicial, duty was imposed on the respondent, and any reference to judicial duty, or bias, is irrelevant in the present case. The respondent's duties under s. 1 of the Act and sch. 1 thereto are, in my opinion, purely administrative, but the Act prescribes certain methods of or steps in, discharge of that duty. It is obvious that, before making the draft order, which must contain a definite proposal to designate the area concerned as the site of a new town, the respondent must have made elaborate inquiry into the matter and have consulted any local authorities who appear to him to be concerned, and obviously other departments of the Government, such as the Ministry of Health, would naturally require to be consulted. It would seem, accordingly, that the respondent was required to satisfy himself that it was a sound scheme before he took the serious step of issuing a draft order. It seems clear also, that the purpose of inviting objections, and, where they are not withdrawn, of having a public inquiry, to be held by someone other than the respondent, to whom that person reports, was for the further information of the respondent, in order to the final consideration of the soundness of the scheme of the designation; and it is important to note that the development of the site, after the order is made, is primarily the duty of the development corporation established under s. 2 of the Act. I am of opinion that no judicial duty is laid on the respondent in discharge of these statutory duties, and that the only question is whether he has complied with the statutory directions to appoint a person to hold the public inquiry, and to consider that person's report. On this contention of the appellants no suggestion is made that the public inquiry was not properly conducted, nor is there any criticism of the report by Mr. Morris. In such a case the only ground of challenge must be either that the respondent did not in fact consider the report and the objections, of which there is here no evidence, or that his mind was so foreclosed that he gave no genuine consideration to them, which is the case made by the appellants . . .

My Lords, I could wish that the use of the word "bias" should be confined to its proper sphere. Its proper significance, in my opinion, is to denote a departure from the standard of even-handed justice which the law requires from those who occupy judicial office, or those who are commonly regarded as holding a quasi-judicial office, such as an arbitrator. The reason for this clearly is that, having to adjudicate as between two or more parties, he must come to his adjudication with an independent mind, without any inclination or bias towards one side or other in the dispute . . . [I]n the present case, the respondent having no judicial duty, the only question is what the respondent actually did, that is, whether in fact he did genuinely consider the report and the objections . . .

Lord Thankerton concluded that, on the evidence, the Minister had not prejudged the issues and had not, therefore, acted improperly. Lords Porter, Uthwatt, Du Parcq, and Norman concurred.

Franklin epitomizes the judicial approach which determined the province of procedural fairness by reference to a narrow, formal analysis of the power, without any appreciation of the wider implications — not least the impact on individuals — of its exercise. Such cases perpetuated the fallacy that administrative decision-making was immune from the requirements of due process. Wade (1951) 67 *LQR* 103 viewed this line of case law as the product of a distorted understanding of the earlier decisions in which the terms 'judicial' (or 'quasi-judicial') and 'administrative' merely expressed a conclusion as to impact (and hence the appropriate style of procedure). However, the scaling back of procedural fairness effected by the functional dichotomy which the courts embraced must also be located within a broader context. In particular, the courts, during the early part of the twentieth century, adopted a remarkably *laissez-faire* approach when it came to scrutinizing government action, a complacency which, according to Sedley (1994) 110 *LQR* 270 at 279–284, had its roots in judicial confidence that changes to the way in which the executive operated, most notably the emergence of a modern and professional civil service, rendered the need for judicial intervention in administrative affairs less compelling.

Viewed against this background, the retreat from natural justice evidenced by cases such as *Franklin* forms only part of a wider phenomenon. By the same token, the following decision — which is widely regarded as one of the most significant landmarks in the development of our contemporary system of administrative law — must be seen not simply as a reassertion of the importance of procedural fairness, but also as fundamental to a broader renaissance in judicial oversight of the executive.

....

Ridge v. *Baldwin* [1964] AC 40
House of Lords

Ridge, the Chief Constable of Brighton, was suspended from duty after he had been arrested and charged with conspiracy to obstruct the course of justice. At his trial Ridge was acquitted; however, when sentencing two police officers from his force who were charged with him (but who were convicted), the trial judge, Donovan J, was critical of Ridge's leadership of his force. At a later date, when a corruption charge was brought against Ridge, the prosecution offered no evidence. Donovan J directed Ridge's acquittal, but made another comment concerning the leadership of the force. The watch committee met the next day (7 March 1958) and decided that Ridge should be dismissed. Section 191(4) of the Municipal Corporations Act 1882 provided that a watch committee could dismiss 'any borough constable whom they think negligent in the discharge of his duty, or otherwise unfit for the same'. Ridge was not asked to attend the meeting; he was later told that he had been summarily dismissed and was also told of certain resolutions passed at the meeting. At the request of Ridge's solicitor, the watch committee reconvened on 18 March 1958. Having received representations from Ridge's solicitor, the watch committee decided not to change its original decision. Before this second meeting Ridge gave formal notice of appeal against the original decision to the Home Secretary under the Police (Appeals) Act 1927. However, he also stated that this was without prejudice to his right to argue that the procedure adopted by the watch committee was in breach of the relevant statutory provisions and contrary to natural justice, and therefore invalid. The Home Secretary dismissed the appeal and Ridge resorted to the courts. Part of the relief sought was a declaration that the purported termination of his appointment was unlawful. Ridge's action failed before Streatfield J and his appeal was dismissed by the Court of Appeal; he appealed to the House of Lords.

Lord Reid

. . . The appellant's case is that in proceeding under the Act of 1882 the watch committee were bound to observe what are commonly called the principles of natural justice. Before attempting to reach any decision they were bound to inform him of the grounds on which they proposed to act and give him a fair opportunity of being heard in his own defence. The authorities on the applicability of the principles of natural justice are in some confusion, and so I find it necessary to examine this matter in some detail. The principle audi alteram partem goes back many centuries in our law and appears in a multitude of judgments of judges of the highest authority. In modern times opinions have sometimes been expressed to the effect that natural justice is so vague as to be practically meaningless. But I would regard these as tainted by the perennial fallacy that because something cannot be cut and dried or nicely weighed or measured therefore it does not exist . . . It appears to me that one reason why the authorities on natural justice have been found difficult to reconcile is that insufficient attention has been paid to the great difference between various kinds of cases in which it has been sought to apply the principle. What a Minister ought to do in considering objections to a scheme may be very different from what a watch committee ought to do in considering whether to dismiss a chief constable . . .

[In cases of the present type, involving dismissal from office for good cause] I find an unbroken line of authority to the effect that an officer cannot lawfully be dismissed without first telling him what is alleged against him and hearing his defence or explanation . . .

[Having cited *Bagg's Case* (1615) 11 Co Rep 93b; *R* v. *Gaskin* (1799) 8 Term Rep 209; *R* v. *Smith* (1852) 5 QB 614; *Ex parte Ramshay* (1852) 18 QB 173; *Osgood* v. *Nelson* (1872) LR 5 HL 636; *Fisher* v. *Jackson* (1891) 2 Ch 84; *Cooper* v. *Wilson* [1937] 2 KB 309, and *Hogg* v. *Scott* [1947] KB 759, his Lordship continued:] Stopping there, I would think that authority was wholly in favour of the appellant, but the respondent's argument was mainly based on what has been said in a number of fairly recent cases dealing with different subject-matter. Those cases deal with decisions by Ministers, officials and bodies of various kinds which adversely affected property rights or privileges of persons who had had no opportunity or no proper opportunity of presenting their cases before the decisions were given. And it is necessary to examine those cases for another reason. The question which was or ought to have been considered by the watch committee on March 7, 1958, was not a simple question whether or not the appellant should be dismissed. There were three possible courses open to the watch committee — reinstating the appellant as chief constable, dismissing him, or requiring him to resign. The difference between the latter two is that dismissal involved forfeiture of pension rights, whereas requiring him to resign did not. Indeed, it is now clear that the appellant's real interest in this appeal is to try to save his pension rights . . .

I would start an examination of the authorities dealing with property rights and privileges with *Cooper* v. *Wandsworth Board of Works* [(1863) 14 CBNS 180]. Where an owner had failed to give proper notice to the Board they had under an Act of 1855 authority to demolish any building he had erected and recover the cost from him. This action was brought against the board because they had used that power without giving the owner an opportunity of being heard. The board maintained that their discretion to order demolition was not a judicial discretion and that any appeal should have been to the Metropolitan Board of Works. But the court decided unanimously in favour of the owner . . .

[Lord Reid also referred to *Hopkins* v. *Smethwick Local Board of Health* (1890) 24 QBD 712; *Smith* v. *R* (1878) LR 3 App Cas 614; *De Verteuil* v. *Knaggs* [1918] AC 557, and *Spackman* v. *Plumstead District Board of Works* (1885) 10 App Cas 229, and continued:] I shall now turn to a different class of case — deprivation of membership of a professional or social body. In *Wood* v. *Woad* [(1874) LR 9 Ex 190] the committee purported to expel a member of a mutual insurance society without hearing him, and it was held that their action was void, and so he was still a member. Kelly CB said of audi alteram partem: "This rule is not confined to the conduct of strictly legal tribunals, but is applicable to every tribunal or body of persons invested with authority to adjudicate upon matters involving civil consequences to individuals." This was expressly approved by Lord Macnaghten giving the judgment of the Board in *Lapointe* v. *L'Association de Bienfaisance et de Retraite de la Police de Montréal* [[1906] AC 535] . . .

Then there are the club cases, *Fisher* v. *Keane* [(1878) 11 Ch D 353] and *Dawkins* v. *Antrobus* [(1879) 18 Ch D 615] In the former, Jessel M.R. said of the committee [at 362–363]: "They ought not, as I understand it, according to the ordinary rules by which justice should be administered by committees of clubs, or by any other body of persons who decide upon the conduct of others, to blast a man's reputation for ever — perhaps to ruin his prospects for life, without giving him an opportunity of either defending or palliating his conduct." In the latter case it was held that nothing had been done contrary to natural justice . . .

It appears to me that if the present case had arisen thirty or forty years ago the courts would have had no difficulty in deciding this issue in favour of the appellant on the authorities which I have cited. So far as I am aware none of these authorities has ever been disapproved or even doubted.

Yet the Court of Appeal have decided this issue against the appellant on more recent authorities which apparently justify that result. How has this come about?

At least three things appear to me to have contributed. In the first place there have been many cases where it has been sought to apply the principles of natural justice to the wider duties imposed on Ministers and other organs of government by modern legislation. For reasons which I shall attempt to state in a moment, it has been held that those principles have a limited application in such cases and those limitations have tended to be reflected in other decisions on matters to which in principle they do not appear to me to apply Secondly, again for reasons which I shall attempt to state, those principles have been held to have a limited application in cases arising out of war-time legislation; and again such limitations have tended to be reflected in other cases. And, thirdly, there has, I think, been a misunderstanding of the judgment of Atkin L.J. in *Rex v. Electricity Commissioners, Ex parte London Electricity Joint Committee Co.* [[1924] 1 KB 171].

In cases of the kind I have been dealing with the Board of Works or the Governor or the club committee was dealing with a single isolated case. It was not deciding, like a judge in a lawsuit, what were the rights of the person before it. But it was deciding how he should be treated — something analogous to a judge's duty in imposing a penalty. No doubt policy would play some part in the decision — but so it might when a judge is imposing a sentence. So it was easy to say that such a body is performing a quasi-judicial task in considering and deciding such a matter, and to require it to observe the essentials of all proceedings of a judicial character — the principles of natural justice.

Sometimes the functions of a Minister or department may also be of that character, and then the rules of natural justice can apply in much the same way. But more often their functions are of a very different character. If a Minister is considering whether to make a scheme for, say, an important new road, his primary concern will not be with the damage which its construction will do to the rights of individual owners of land. He will have to consider all manner of questions of public interest and, it may be, a number of alternative schemes. He cannot be prevented from attaching more importance to the fulfilment of his policy than to the fate of individual objectors, and it would be quite wrong for the courts to say that the Minister should or could act in the same kind of way as a board of works deciding whether a house should be pulled down. And there is another important difference. As explained in *Local Government Board v. Arlidge* [[1915] AC 120] a Minister cannot do everything himself. His officers will have to gather and sift all the facts, including objections by individuals, and no individual can complain if the ordinary accepted methods of carrying on public business do not give him as good protection as would be given by the principles of natural justice in a different kind of case.

We do not have a developed system of administrative law — perhaps because until fairly recently we did not need it. So it is not surprising that in dealing with new types of cases the courts have had to grope for solutions, and have found that old powers, rules and procedure are largely inapplicable to cases which they were never designed or intended to deal with. But I see nothing in that to justify our thinking that our old methods are any less applicable today than ever they were to the older types of case. And if there are any dicta in modern authorities which point in that direction, then, in my judgment, they should not be followed.

And now I must say something regarding war-time legislation. The older authorities clearly show how the courts engrafted the principles of natural justice on to a host of provisions authorising administrative interference with private rights. Parliament knew quite well that the courts had an inveterate habit of doing that and must therefore be held to have authorised them to do it unless a particular Act showed a contrary intention. And such an intention could appear as a reasonable inference as well as from express words. It seems to me to be a reasonable and almost an inevitable inference from the circumstances in which Defence Regulations were made and from their subject-matter that, at least in many cases, the intention must have been to exclude the principles of natural justice . . . I would not think that any decision that the rules of natural justice were excluded from war-time legislation should be regarded as of any great weight in dealing with a case such as this case, which is of the older type, and which involves the interpretation of an Act passed long before modern modifications of the principles of natural justice became necessary, and at a time when, as Parliament was well aware, the courts habitually applied the principles of natural justice to provisions like section 191 (4) of the Act of 1882.

The matter has been further complicated by what I believe to be a misunderstanding of a much-quoted passage in the judgment of Atkin L.J. in *Rex v. Electricity Commissioners, Ex parte London Electricity Joint Committee Co* [[1924] 1 KB 171 at 205]. He said: ". . . the operation of the writs [of prohibition and certiorari] has extended to control the proceedings of bodies which do not claim to be, and would not be recognised as, courts of justice. Wherever any body of persons having legal authority to determine questions affecting the rights of subjects, and having the duty to act judicially, act in excess of their legal authority, they are subject to the controlling jurisdiction of the King's Bench Division exercised in these writs."

A gloss was put on this by Lord Hewart C.J. in *Rex v. Legislative Committee of the Church Assembly, Ex parte Haynes-Smith* [[1928] 1 KB 411] . . . Lord Hewart said [at 415], having quoted the passage from Atkin L.J.'s judgment: ". . . It is to be observed that in the last sentence which I have quoted . . . the word is not 'or,' but 'and' . . . In order that a body may satisfy the required test it is not enough that it should have legal authority to determine questions affecting the rights of subjects; there must be superadded to that characteristic the further characteristic that the body has the duty to act judicially. The duty to act judicially is an ingredient which, if the test is to be satisfied, must be present. As these writs in the earlier days were issued only to bodies which without any harshness of construction could be called, and naturally would be called courts, so also today these writs do not issue except to bodies which act or are under the duty to act in a judicial capacity."

. . . [T]his passage . . . is typical of what has been said in several subsequent cases. If Lord Hewart meant that it is never enough that a body simply has a duty to determine what the rights of an individual should be, but that there must always be something more to impose on it a duty to act judicially before it can be found to observe the principles of natural justice, then that appears to me impossible to reconcile with the earlier authorities . . . And, as I shall try to show, it cannot be what Atkin L.J. meant.

In *Rex. v. Electricity Commissioners, Ex parte London Electricity Joint Committee Co* [[1924] 1 KB 171] . . . Bankes L.J. . . . inferred the judicial element from the nature of the power. And I think that Atkin L.J. did the same . . .

There is not a word in Atkin L.J.'s judgment to suggest disapproval of the earlier line of authority which I have cited. On the contrary, he goes further than those authorities. I have already stated my view that it is more difficult for the courts to control an exercise of power on a large scale where the treatment to be meted out to a particular individual is only one of many matters to be considered. This was a case of that kind, and, if Atkin L.J. was prepared to infer a judicial element from the nature of the power in this case, he could hardly disapprove such an inference when the power relates solely to the treatment of a particular individual.

The authority chiefly relied on by the Court of Appeal in holding that the watch committee were not bound to observe the principles of natural justice was *Nakkuda Ali v. Jayaratne* [[1951] AC 66]. In that case the Controller of Textiles in Ceylon made an order cancelling the appellant's licence to act as a dealer, and the appellant sought to have that order quashed. The controller acted under a Defence Regulation which empowered him to cancel a licence "where the controller has reasonable grounds to believe that any dealer is unfit to be allowed to continue as a dealer."

The Privy Council [at 77] regarded that as "imposing a condition that there must in fact exist such reasonable grounds, known to the controller, before he can validly exercise the power of cancellation." But according to their judgment certiorari did not lie, and no other means was suggested whereby the appellant or anyone else in his position could obtain redress even if the controller acted without a shred of evidence. It is quite true that the judgment went on, admittedly unnecessarily, to find that the controller had reasonable grounds and did observe the principles of natural justice, but the result would have been just the same if he had not. This House is not bound by decisions of the Privy Council, and for my own part nothing short of a decision of this House directly in point would induce me to accept the position that, although an enactment expressly requires an official to have reasonable grounds for his decision, our law is so defective that a subject cannot bring up such a decision for review however seriously he may be affected and however obvious it may be that the official acted in breach of his statutory obligation.

. . . [T]he crucial passage [at p 78 of the Privy Council's decision in *Nakkuda Ali* is]: "But the basis of the jurisdiction of the courts by way of certiorari has been so exhaustively analysed in recent years that individual instances are now only of importance as illustrating a general principle that is beyond dispute. That principle is most precisely stated in the words of Atkin L.J. in *Rex v. Electricity Commissioners, Ex parte London Electricity Joint Committee Co.* [[1924] 1 KB 171 at 205]" — and then follows the passage with which I have already dealt at length. And then there follows the quotation from Lord Hewart, which I have already commented on, ending with the words — "there must be superadded to that characteristic the further characteristic that the body has the duty to act judicially." And then it is pointed out [at 78]: "It is that characteristic that the controller lacks in acting under regulation 62."

Of course, if it were right to say that Lord Hewart's gloss on Atkin L.J. stated "a general principle that is beyond dispute," the rest would follow. But I have given my reasons for holding that it does no such thing, and in my judgment the older cases certainly do not "illustrate" any such general principle — they contradict it. No case older than 1911 was cited in *Nakkuda's* case on this question, and this question was only one of several difficult questions which were argued and decided. So I am forced to the conclusion that this part of the judgment in *Nakkuda's* case was given under a serious misapprehension of the effect of the older authorities and therefore cannot be regarded as authoritative.

I would sum up my opinion in this way. Between 1882 and the making of police regulations in 1920 section 191 (4) had to be applied to every kind of case. The respondents' contention is that, even where there was a doubtful question whether a constable was guilty of a particular act of misconduct, the watch committee were under no obligation to hear his defence before dismissing him. In my judgment it is abundantly clear from the authorities I have quoted that at that time the courts would have rejected any such contention. In later cases dealing with different subject-matter, opinions have been expressed in wide terms so as to appear to conflict with those earlier authorities. But learned judges who expressed those opinions generally had no power to overrule those authorities, and in any event it is a salutary rule that a judge is not to be assumed to have intended to overrule or disapprove of an authority which has not been cited to him and which he does not even mention. So I would hold that the power of dismissal in the Act of 1882 could not then have been exercised and cannot now be exercised until the watch committee have informed the constable of the grounds on which they propose to proceed and have given him a proper opportunity to present his case in defence . . .

[Lord Reid then considered the meeting of the watch committee on 18 March 1958, but concluded that it could not cure the earlier unfairness; on appeals, see below at 11.3.4.]

Lords Morris, Hodson, and Devlin also delivered speeches in favour of allowing the appeal. Lord Evershed dissented. Appeal allowed.

11.2.2 Natural Justice and Acting Fairly

The House of Lords' decision in *Ridge* v. *Baldwin* — for comment on which see De Smith (1963) 26 *MLR* 543; Goodhart (1964) 80 *LQR* 105; Bradley [1964] *CLJ* 83 — liberated natural justice from the constraints which had been imposed upon it by earlier cases, placing a renewed emphasis on the impact of administrative decisions on individuals' rights and interests.

QUESTIONS

- If the 'impact' of a decision on an individual is the touchstone in this area, how ought such impact be measured?
- Is losing one's house (*Cooper*) worse than losing one's pension (*Ridge*)?
- Is losing a social security benefit the same as losing entitlement to a pension fund to which one has contributed?

The notion of a 'duty to act judicially' was perpetuated by *Ridge*, albeit that such a duty could be inferred from the nature of the power, and hence much more readily. However, difficult questions remained. How far, post-*Ridge*, could the duty to act judicially extend? Consider the following comments of Lord Parker CJ in *In re HK (An Infant)* [1967] QB 617 at 630, a case concerning what procedural safeguards, if any, applied to immigration officers' decisions regarding permission to enter the United Kingdom:

> . . . [E]ven if an immigration officer is not in a judicial or quasi-judicial capacity, he must at any rate give the immigrant an opportunity of satisfying him of the matters in the subsection, and for that purpose let the immigrant know what his immediate impression is so that the immigrant can disabuse him. That is not, as I see it, a question of acting or being required to act judicially, but of being required to act fairly. Good administration and an honest or bona fide decision must, as it seems to me, require not merely impartiality, nor merely bringing one's mind to bear on the problem, but acting fairly; and to the limited extent that the circumstances of any particular case allow, and within the legislative framework under which the administrator is working, only to that limited extent do the so-called rules of natural justice apply, which in a case such as this is merely a duty to act fairly. I appreciate that in saying that it may be said that one is going further than is permitted on the decided cases because heretofore at any rate the decisions of the courts do seem to have drawn a strict line in these matters according to whether there is or is not a duty to act judicially or quasi judicially.

This passage is significant for two reasons. First, Lord Parker, recognizing that he was going beyond established cases, contended that the rules of natural justice could apply beyond the category of cases (itself significantly widened by *Ridge*) in which a duty to act judicially arose. Secondly, however, this was accompanied by the view that, in some cases, the requirements of natural justice extended only to a 'duty to act fairly'. Lord Parker envisaged the latter as a subset of the rules of natural justice which imposed a less onerous duty. For example, the immigration officer in *HK* itself was simply required to give the intending immigrant 'his immediate impression' so that the latter could respond — a procedure which falls some way short of the classical form of natural justice modelled on adversarial proceedings.

Although Lord Parker's approach recognized the existence of a duty to act fairly which operated beyond the confines of the duty to act judicially, it implicitly accepted a distinction between situations attracting the latter and those merely attracting the former. This led some judges, such as Lord Pearson in *Pearlberg* v. *Varty* [1972] 1 WLR 534 at 547, to continue placing considerable weight on the administrative-judicial dichotomy:

A tribunal to whom judicial or quasi-judicial functions are entrusted is held to be required to apply [natural justice] in performing those functions unless there is a provision to the contrary. But where some person or body is entrusted by Parliament with administrative or executive functions there is no presumption that compliance with the principles of natural justice is required, although, as 'Parliament is not to be presumed to act unfairly', the courts may be able in suitable cases (perhaps always) to imply an obligation to act with fairness. Fairness, however, does not necessarily require a plurality of hearings or representations and counter-representations.

Lord Pearson's reasoning differs from Lord Parker's in that the former conceives of acting fairly as distinct from compliance with natural justice, whereas the latter considered that the duties to act fairly and judicially were both (distinct) parts of natural justice. However, both *dicta* appear to accept that distinct models of procedural fairness should apply in 'judicial' and 'administrative' contexts. In that respect, they should be contrasted with Megarry V-C's more flexible use of language in *McInnes* v. *Onslow-Fane* [1978] 1 WLR 1520 at 1530:

I do not think that much help is to be obtained from discussing whether "natural justice" or "fairness" is the more appropriate term. If one accepts that "natural justice" is a flexible term which imposes different requirements in different cases, it is capable of applying appropriately to the whole range of situations indicated by terms such as "judicial," "quasi-judicial" and "administrative." Nevertheless, the further the situation is away from anything that resembles a judicial or quasi-judicial situation, and the further the question is removed from what may reasonably be called a justiciable question, the more appropriate it is to reject an expression which includes the word "justice" and to use instead terms such as "fairness," or "the duty to act fairly" . . .

On this view, our choice of language is relatively unimportant. 'Fairness' is a broad principle whose precise meaning falls to be determined in context, on a sliding-scale which does not require clear distinctions to be drawn between 'judicial', 'quasi-judicial', and 'administrative' powers. The upshot is that whether or not a 'duty to act judicially' arises, the exercise of a given decision-making power is likely to be accompanied by an obligation to respect certain procedural norms; precisely which ones depends on such factors as the importance and nature of the interests at stake.

The emergence of the duty to act fairly is to be welcomed to the extent that it enhances the requirement of fair dealing by decision-makers. However, Cane, *Administrative Law* (Oxford 2004) at 161, does not perceive it as an unqualified good, noting that, 'The notion of fairness has been used both to augment and to truncate the traditional notion of natural justice.' He goes on (*loc cit*) to argue that the courts have adopted a rather unimaginative conception of 'fairness':

If the courts viewed fairness in [a] broader way [*ie* as a means for promoting the overall fairness of decision-making processes], they might see their role as being to specify in any particular case what procedure would be most fair, whether it were an adversarial trial, an inquisitorial investigation, consultation, mediation or any other possible approach to decision-making. In fact, what the courts have actually done is to use the notion of fairness to give themselves the freedom to pick and choose from only a rather narrow menu of possibilities based on the traditional model of an adversarial trial . . . [A]s used by the courts, the notion of fairness is not a version of natural justice but an evaluative concept used to provide flexibility in applying the notion of natural justice to particular cases.

Although the flexibility inherent in the notion of fairness adopted by the courts is, for Cane, too limited, other writers, such as Mullan (1975) 25 *UTLJ* 281 at 300, welcome such flexibility as has been embraced:

. . . [T]he development of the doctrine of procedural fairness is a most desirable advance in the common law relating to judicial review of administrative action. It is desirable primarily because it allows the courts to ask what kind of procedural protections are necessary for a particular decision-making process unburdened by the traditional classification process [ie classifying a function as judicial or quasi-judicial before any procedural fairness was invoked]. In other words, it enables the asking of the real questions which the classification process has hidden artificially for many years. It recognizes that there is a very broad spectrum of decision-making functions for which varying procedural requirements are necessary and rejects the notion that such functions can be categorized satisfactorily into either one of two categories. The classification process was essentially accepted at a time when the administrative process was far less sophisticated. Its deceptive simplicity was perhaps adequate initially but it rapidly ceased to be realistic. If "fairness" enables the courts to move away from this approach much will be achieved in that an effective functional approach will have been substituted for a superficially attractive but actually inappropriate functional approach.

In contrast, other commentators have criticized the highly flexible view of procedural fairness which is now prominent in administrative law. In the following extract, it is argued that this approach — which is termed the 'activist informalist strategy' — risks both uncertainty and intervention by the judiciary in matters in which, under a traditional model of the separation of powers, they should not be involved.

....

Loughlin, 'Procedural Fairness: A Study of the Crisis in Administrative Law Theory' (1978) 28 UTLJ 215

[Having explained that the "activist informalist strategy" is one under which the courts adopt an activist approach but abandon adjudication as a model for administrative decision-making, engaging instead in a flexible supervisory role to ensure the fairness of procedures, Loughlin continues:] This approach . . . is flawed because it requires the court to engage in activities which are inconsistent with its [traditional] role . . . Under the traditional theory the courts' expertise lies in a peculiar manner of dispute resolution (adjudication). Vesting the court with a general supervisory power to inquire into the fairness of administrative procedures will lead the court into controversial areas of policy which it is required to avoid. Furthermore, due to its inherent bias in favour of adjudicative methods of dispute resolution, it may in practice . . . result in the overjudicialisation of administrative procedures . . .

   Why have the courts experienced so much difficulty in dealing with a flexible concept of requiring administrative decision-making processes to be fair? The key to the problem, I contend, lies in the failure to recognize the . . . change in the method of legal discourse and function of the courts required if the informalist approach is to be adopted . . . Mullan [(1975) 25 *UTLJ* 281 at 301] argues that "if individual decision-making functions have different characteristics then they deserve different procedural requirements". However, bearing in mind the multifarious situations involving sensitive policy issues into which administration enters, such a role will result in a tremendous expansion of the number of factors which the court must consider in looking at administrative decision-making in the context of procedural fairness. It is this potential change in the function of the court which has probably resulted in criticisms of procedural fairness in terms of certainty and predictability . . .

- Is Loughlin correct to assume that vague tests will be applied by judges to 'overjudicialise' administrative procedures?
- Does Loughlin also assume that judges are only used to applying one set of procedures to all disputes, and if so, is this assumption accurate?

11.2.3 Legitimate Expectations of Fair Treatment

The modern approach, according to which the applicability of procedural safeguards falls to be determined by reference to such factors as the impact of a given decision on the individual's rights and interests, is now augmented by the doctrine of legitimate expectation. That doctrine was considered in detail in ch 7 above, and at this point it is necessary merely to emphasize how it relates to the concept of procedural fairness. Two points should be noted.

First, the doctrine of legitimate expectation can influence the *scope* of the duty to act fairly by triggering it in circumstances in which no such duty would arise on the principles just considered. Thus the representations or conduct of a public authority may entitle an individual to fair treatment when, in the absence of such representations or conduct, he would have no enforceable procedural rights. This is classically demonstrated by the decision of the Privy Council in *Attorney-General of Hong Kong* v. *Ng Yuen Shiu* [1983] 2 AC 629, an extract from which appears above at 7.1.4.

Secondly, circumstances may arise in which an individual is entitled — by virtue, for instance, of the impact of a decision on his rights or interests — to a certain measure of procedural fairness (*eg* a right to make written representations) but can claim a higher level of procedural protection (*eg* an oral hearing) as a result of representations or conduct on the part of the decision-maker. By thus increasing the level of procedural protection to which an individual is entitled, the doctrine of legitimate expectation is capable of affecting not just the scope but also the *content* of the duty to act fairly in given circumstances.

11.2.4 Article 6: The Scope of the Right to a Fair and Public Hearing

We have noted that the common law principles of procedural fairness can be triggered either by the impact of the decision on the individual's rights or interests or by a legitimate expectation of fair treatment generated by the public body's representations or conduct. In addition, procedural safeguards may be available under Article 6 ECHR if (as explained above at 10.5.2) civil rights and obligations are at stake. We consider what Article 6 requires, when it applies, below at 11.3.

11.2.5 The Limits of Procedural Fairness

Although the general trend, identified above, is to extend the application of procedural fairness to a wider range of situations, there remain cases in which decision-makers are not subject to any obligation to act fairly. Most obviously, there exist situations in which no factor operates in the first place to trigger the duty to act fairly: if, for instance, the court concludes that the decision in question does not have any relevant impact upon the individual's rights, interests, or legitimate expectations, then no duty of fairness arises. It is also possible in principle for legislation expressly to displace the principles of procedural fairness, although the courts will only conclude with great reluctance that this was Parliament's intention (see, *eg*, *Wilkinson* v. *Barking Corporation* [1948] 1 KB 721). A further possibility is that although there may exist no *prima facie* inhibition to the applicability of the principles of procedural fairness, the wider context within which the decision-making power is exercised may raise such an obstacle. For instance, in *Council of Civil Service Unions* v. *Minister for the Civil Service* [1985] AC 374 — considered, in this regard, above at 5.3.3 — an expectation that a particular procedural safeguard (consultation) would operate was displaced by countervailing national security concerns. It will be recalled that the war-time regulation cases considered by Lord Reid in *Ridge* v. *Baldwin*, above at 11.2.1, were treated as a separate line of authority for a similar reason. Whether fair procedure, or a particular form thereof, is applicable will also depend upon construction of the statutory scheme and its purpose, a point to which we return below at 11.3.1.

It has also been said that if the provision of a hearing (or some other form of procedural fairness) 'would make no difference' — meaning that a hearing would not change the ultimate conclusion reached by the decision-maker — then no legal duty to supply a hearing arises. Such an approach was endorsed by Lord Wilberforce in *Malloch* v. *Aberdeen Corporation* [1971] 1 WLR 1578:

The appellant has first to show that his position was such that he had, in principle, a right to make representations before a decision against him was taken. But to show this is not necessarily enough, unless he can also show that if admitted to state his case he had a case of substance to make. A breach of procedure, whether called a failure of natural justice, or an essential administrative fault, cannot give him a remedy in the courts, unless behind it there is something of substance which has been lost by the failure. The court does not act in vain.

Relying on these comments, Brandon LJ opined in *Cinnamond* v. *British Airports Authority* [1980] 1 WLR 582 at 593 that 'no one can complain of not being given an opportunity to make representations if such an opportunity would have availed him nothing'.

Although this view may appear sensible, it raises a number of difficulties, usefully summarized by Bingham LJ in *R* v. *Chief Constable of Thames Valley Police, ex parte Cotton* [1990] IRLR 344 at 352. The first of these is practical in nature: if the court is to refuse to insist upon a fair procedure on this ground, then it must first be satisfied that the adoption of such a procedure would not have influenced the outcome of the decision-making process. The problem is that the court cannot know this for certain, and must instead second-guess the decision-maker by trying to work out what conclusion would have been arrived at if the evidence that a fair procedure would have elicited had been available. As Megarry J observed in *John* v. *Rees* [1970] Ch 345 at 402:

It may be that there are some who would decry the importance which the courts attach to the observance of the rules of natural justice. "When something is obvious," they may say, "why force everybody to go through the tiresome waste of time involved in framing charges and giving an opportunity to be heard? The result is obvious from the start." Those who take this view do not, I think, do themselves justice. As everybody who has anything to do with the law well knows, the path of the law is strewn with examples of open and shut cases which, somehow, were not; of unanswerable charges which, in the event, were completely answered; of inexplicable conduct which was fully explained; of fixed and unalterable determinations that, by discussion, suffered a change.

In addition to these practical difficulties, the view adopted in *Malloch* is problematic for the deeper reason that it arguably misunderstands the purpose of procedural fairness. Although the doctrine naturally seeks to ensure that all relevant evidence is presented in order that correct (or, in the context of discretionary power, rational) outcomes are secured, its importance (as we explained above at 11.1) stretches much further. First, consider the opinion of Clark [1975] *PL* 27 at 60:

The essential mission of the law in this field is to win acceptance by administrators of the principle that to hear a man before he is penalised is an integral part of the decision-making process. A measure of the importance of resisting the incipient abnegation by the courts of the firm rule that breach of audi alteram partem invalidates [the administrative decision in question], is that if it gains ground the mission of the law is doomed to fail to the detriment of all.

This suggests that one of the objectives of the law in this area is to engender a culture within the executive of fair decision-making — a view which fits with the 'green light' model, considered above at 1.2.2, one strand of which holds that administrative law should supply a template of good practice in order to improve the quality of decision-making and promote the observance of values which the legal system considers important. Clark contends that this is threatened if decision-makers are permitted to jettison the principles of procedural fairness simply because they believe that their application would make no difference. Even if, having done so, they achieve the 'right' result in an individual case, other cases are jeopardized because the administrator who escapes condemnation in such circumstances may be emboldened to cut corners in other, inappropriate, situations.

Secondly, *Malloch* attaches inadequate weight to perceptions of fairness. We have already seen in relation to bias the importance of ensuring not just a fair decision-making process, but also that citizens perceive it to be fair. The same argument can be applied in the present context: thus in *R v. Thames Magistrates' Court, ex parte Polemis* [1974] 1 WLR 1371 — a case in which it was held that the claimant had not been given reasonable opportunity to prepare his case — Lord Widgery stated at 1375–1376:

It is . . . absolutely basic to our system that justice must not only be done but must manifestly be seen to be done. If justice was so clearly not seen to be done, as on the afternoon in question here, it seems to me that it is no answer to the applicant to say: "Well, even if the case had been properly conducted, the result would have been the same." This is mixing up the doing of justice with seeing that justice is done, so I reject that argument.

Thirdly, the view advanced in *Malloch* implicitly adopts an instrumental view of procedural fairness by focussing exclusively upon the fairness of the *outcome*. In doing so, the normative value of fair treatment is overlooked. This point was touched upon by Megarry J in *John v. Rees* [1970] Ch 345 at 402 when he cautioned against underestimating 'the feelings of resentment of those who find that a decision against them has been made without their being afforded any opportunity to influence the course of events'. Such 'resentment' is engendered by the instinctive reaction that such a style of decision-making is plainly unfair; this reflects the deeper truth that to make decisions about an individual without allowing him to present his own views and feelings and to explain how the decision will impact on his life fundamentally denies his status, dignity, and autonomy. The individual is cast as some-one whose views do not deserve to be taken into account; and, on a broader canvas, the government's relationship with its citizens assumes a distinctly authoritarian character which discourages constructive discourse between individuals and public bodies.

Insisting on procedural fairness even when it would make no difference is a price that must be paid if due respect is to be accorded to the status of the individual. The notion of procedural fairness which would 'make no difference' becomes a contradiction in terms, since it rests on an exclusively outcomes-oriented view which overlooks the much wider role played by procedural fairness in an administrative state that seeks to build constructive relationships between individuals and public bodies by casting the former as participants in the process of governance. These views receive support from Bingham LJ in *R v. Chief Constable of Thames Valley Police, ex parte Cotton* [1990] IRLR 344 at 352: 'While cases may no doubt arise in which it can properly be held that denying the subject of a decision an adequate opportunity to put his case is not in all the circumstances unfair, I would expect these cases to be of great rarity.' His Lordship later admitted ([1991] *PL* 64 at 72) that, in this *dictum*, by 'expect' he meant 'hope'; it seems, therefore, that the argument that a fair hearing 'would make no difference' can still be made, but will be looked at critically.

QUESTION

- In what circumstances, if any, should the argument that a fair hearing 'would make no difference' be accepted?

The non-instrumental value of procedural protections has also been recognized by the ECtHR. For example, Article 5(4) ECHR provides that:

Everyone who is deprived of his liberty by arrest or detention shall be entitled to take proceedings by which the lawfulness of his detention shall be decided speedily by a court and his release ordered if the detention is not lawful.

In holding in *Waite* v. *United Kingdom* (2003) 36 EHRR 54 that there had been a breach of Article 5(4) when the Parole Board recalled the applicant (who was subject to a life sentence but had been released on licence) to prison without affording him an oral hearing, the ECtHR stated (at [58]–[59]) that:

The Court is not persuaded by the [UK] Government's argument which appears to be based on the speculative assumption that whatever might have occurred at an oral hearing the Board would not have exercised its power to release. Article 5(4) is first and foremost a guarantee of a fair procedure for reviewing the lawfulness of detention — an applicant is not required, as a precondition to enjoying that protection, to show that on the facts of his case he stands any particular chance of success in obtaining his release.

11.3 The Nature of Procedural Fairness

11.3.1 Fairness: A Context-Sensitive Phenomenon

We have already seen that the objectives served by the doctrine of procedural fairness are numerous, and that although its foundational function is to improve the quality of public administration by prescribing a procedural methodology which ensures that all relevant evidence is brought to the attention of the decision-maker, it can also serve to cement a relationship between the citizen and the state which is founded upon constructive discourse and to confer legal recognition upon the dignity of individuals. Just as the goals of fairness are myriad, so are the routes by which those goals may be arrived at, as Tucker LJ recognized in *Russell* v. *Duke of Norfolk* [1949] 1 All ER 109 at 117:

There are, in my view, no words which are of universal application to every kind of inquiry and every kind of domestic tribunal. The requirements of natural justice must depend on the circumstances of the case, the nature of the inquiry, the rules under which the tribunal is acting, the subject-matter that is being dealt with, and so forth. Accordingly, I do not derive much assistance from the definitions of natural justice which have been from time to time used, but, whatever standard is adopted, one essential is that the person concerned should have a reasonable opportunity to present his case.

It follows that, although an oral hearing with legal representation, cross-examination, and so on may be regarded (at least by those grounded in the tradition of adversarialism) as the paradigm of procedural fairness — epitomized by the criminal trial process — not all circumstances will call for such an elaborate approach. The way in which the requirements of fairness are influenced by context, and the allied proposition that fairness can, in some situations, be delivered without recourse to an oral hearing, are clearly illustrated by the following case.

....

Lloyd v. *McMahon* [1987] AC 625
House of Lords

Liverpool City Council failed to set a lawful rate (a forerunner of council tax) for the year 1985–1986 by the required date, causing losses to the Council in excess of £100,000. The district auditor warned councillors on a number of occasions that their failure to set a lawful rate could result in personal liability for any resultant losses. After investigating the matter — in the course of which councillors were invited to submit written representations — the auditor issued a certificate under s 20(1) of the Local Government Finance Act 1982 to the effect that the councillors were jointly and severally liable for the losses caused by their wilful misconduct. Issuing a certificate in respect of members of the local authority for sums in excess of £2,000 also carried the consequence of disqualification from office for five years. The certificate was accompanied by a statement of reasons which addressed in detail the matters raised by the councillors in their written representations. The councillors unsuccessfully appealed, under s 20(3), to the High Court and the Court of Appeal, and thereafter to the House of Lords. They alleged, *inter alia*, that the district auditor's failure to offer an oral hearing constituted a breach of procedural fairness which invalidated the s 20(1) certificate.

Lord Keith

. . . My Lords, if the district auditor had reached a decision adverse to the appellants without giving them any opportunity at all of making representations to him, there can be no doubt that his procedure would have been contrary to the rules of natural justice and that, subject to the question whether the defect was capable of being cured on appeal to the Divisional Court, the decision would fall to be quashed. In the event, written representations alone were asked for. These were duly furnished, in very considerable detail, and an oral hearing was not requested, though that could very easily have been done, and there is no reason to suppose that the request would not have been granted. None of the appellants stated, in his or her affidavit before the Divisional Court, that they had an expectation that an oral hearing, though not asked for, would be offered. The true question is whether the district auditor acted fairly in all the circumstances. It is easy to envisage cases where an oral hearing would clearly be essential in the interests of fairness, for example where an objector states that he has personal knowledge of some facts indicative of wilful misconduct on the part of a councillor. In that situation justice would demand that the councillor be given an opportunity to depone to his own version of the facts. In the present case the district auditor had arrived at his provisional view upon the basis of the contents of documents, minutes of meetings and reports submitted to the council from the auditor's department and their own officers. All these documents were appended to or referred to in the notice of 26 June sent by the district auditor to the appellants. Their response referred to other documents, which were duly considered by the district auditor, as is shown by his statement of reasons dated 6 September 1985. No facts contradictory of or supplementary to the contents of the documents were or are relied on by either side. If the appellants had attended an oral hearing they would no doubt have reiterated the sincerity of their motives from the point of view of advancing the interests of the inhabitants of Liverpool. It seems unlikely, having regard to the position adopted by their counsel on this matter before the Divisional Court, that they would have been willing to reveal or answer questions about the proceedings of their political caucus. The sincerity of the appellants' motives is not something capable of justifying or excusing failure to carry out a statutory duty, or of making reasonable what is otherwise an unreasonable delay in carrying out such a duty. In all the circumstances I am of opinion that the district auditor did not act unfairly, and that the procedure which he followed did not involve any prejudice to the appellants . . .

Lord Bridge

. . . My Lords, the so-called rules of natural justice are not engraved on tablets of stone. To use the phrase which better expresses the underlying concept, what the requirements of fairness demand when any body, domestic, administrative or judicial, has to make a decision which will affect the rights of individuals depends on the character of the decision-making body, the kind of decision it has to make and the statutory or other framework in which it operates. In particular, it is well-established that when a statute has conferred on any body the power to make decisions affecting individuals, the courts will not only require the procedure prescribed by the statute to be followed, but will readily imply so much and no more to be introduced by way of additional procedural safeguards as will ensure the attainment of fairness. It follows that the starting-point for the examination of all the appellants' submissions on this aspect of the case is the Act of 1982 . . .

So far as procedure is concerned, section 14 of the Act of 1982 provides for the issue of a code of audit practice to be approved by each House of Parliament. The code currently in force contains detailed provisions relating to objections under section 17, but none relating to the procedure to be followed when an auditor contemplates the issue of a certificate under section 20 of his own motion. The gravity of the consequences of a certificate for the person from whom the amount of a loss is certified to be due, particularly if he is a member of a local authority and the amount exceeds £2,000, are obvious enough. No one doubts that the auditor must give to such a person adequate notice of the case against him and an adequate opportunity to present to the auditor his defence to that case. I followed with interest [counsel's] carefully researched review of the history of local government audit legislation, but I did not find that it threw any light on what, in particular, is required to provide such an opportunity in the circumstances of any particular case under the statute presently in force. Still less do I attach any significance to the fact that since 1972, when provisions substantially to the like effect as those which we find in the Act of 1982 first reached the statute book, auditors have, as a matter of practice, always invited oral representations from members of local authorities before certifying the amount of any loss or deficiency as due from them. When a single individual is thought to have failed to bring a sum into account or by his wilful misconduct to have caused a loss or deficiency, it is no doubt a very appropriate practice to invite his explanation orally. But I fail to understand how that practice can constrain the courts to construe the statute as requiring an auditor proposing to act under section 20 to invite oral representations as a matter of law in every case. In this case the auditor seems to have intelligently anticipated that the Liverpool councillors who constituted the majority group would want to present a united front in their response to his notice of 26 June 1985 as they had done in their conduct of the city council's affairs during the previous year. Councillor Hamilton's letter of 19 July 1985 amply confirmed his expectation. If any councillor had wanted to put forward his own independent and individual grounds in rebuttal of the charge of wilful misconduct against himself, I have no doubt he would have done so. If any had asked to be heard orally and the auditor had refused, there would have been clear ground for a complaint of unfairness. I suppose it is conceivable that the appellants collectively might have wished to appoint a spokesman to present their case orally rather than in writing, though the case they did present, embracing as it did such a large volume of documentary material, clearly lent itself more aptly to written than oral presentation. It has never been suggested that it was unfair that the auditor did not invite the appellants to address arguments to him through solicitor or counsel. The proposition that it was, per se, in breach of the rules of natural justice not to invite oral representations in this case is quite untenable . . .

Lord Templeman agreed that the auditor's failure to offer an oral hearing did not render the process unfair. Lords Brandon and Griffiths agreed with the other three judges. Appeal dismissed.

It is clear that a number of factors informed their Lordships' view that an oral hearing was unnecessary in the circumstances. Although, as Lord Bridge noted, the consequences for councillors of a s 20(1) certificate were potentially serious — a factor which, taken on its own, would point towards a generous level of procedural protection, probably including an oral hearing — this fell to be balanced against competing considerations. Among these were the facts that the case lent itself better to written representations, given the large amount of documentary evidence upon which it turned, and that an oral hearing would have added nothing: it might have allowed the councillors to emphasize the sincerity of their motives but, as Lord Keith observed, this was irrelevant to their liability. It is also clear that Lord Keith's analysis of what fairness required was fundamentally influenced by the legislation itself. The importance statutory frameworks in this regard was underlined by Lord Reid in *Wiseman v. Borneman* [1971] AC 297 at 308:

For a long time the courts have, without objection from Parliament, supplemented procedure laid down in legislation where they have found that to be necessary for this purpose. But before this unusual kind of power is exercised it must be clear that the statutory procedure is insufficient to achieve justice and that to require additional steps would not frustrate the apparent purpose of the legislation.

Following this *dictum*, it was held in *R v. Birmingham City Council, ex parte Ferrero* [1993] 1 All ER 530 that a duty to consult should not be implied into a statutory consumer protection scheme which sought to enable the taking of prompt action in response to concerns as to the safety of products. In such cases, however, as Glidewell LJ observed in *R* v. *LAUTRO, ex parte Ross* [1993] QB 17 at 52, a lack of procedural fairness *before* the making of an urgent decision may need to be balanced by providing some sort of hearing *after* the event, in order that the issues can be considered fairly and, if necessary, the original decision revisited.

QUESTIONS

- What other factors should affect the level of procedural fairness required in a particular situation?
- Should cost be taken into account?
- Should public confidence in administrative procedures be considered?

We have already seen (note Loughlin's argument, above at 11.2.2) that the flexibility of the common law in this context can be problematic: it may cause uncertainty about what procedure is applicable in a given situation. In the following case, an attempt was made to calibrate the common law's sliding scale of fairness. Although it should not be read as establishing rigid categories to which different templates of fairness apply, it usefully indicates some of the factors which help determine where on the scale particular cases will be located.

McInnes v. *Onslow-Fane* [1978] 1 WLR 1520
Chancery Division

The claimant — who had previously held a British Board of Boxing Control promoter's licence (which lapsed in 1955), a trainer's licence, and a master of ceremonies' licence (both of which were revoked in 1973 on grounds of misconduct) — applied unsuccessfully in 1976 (not for the first time) for a BBBC boxers' manager's licence. He was given neither an oral hearing nor notice of the case against him, both of which he had requested. The claimant sought a declaration that the decision was flawed by procedural unfairness.

Megarry V-C

. . . [I]t must be considered what type of decision is in question. I do not suggest that there is any clear or exhaustive classification; but I think that at least three categories may be discerned. First, there are what may be called the forfeiture cases. In these, there is a decision which takes away some existing right or position, as where a member of an organisation is expelled or a licence is revoked. Second, at the other extreme there are what may be called the application cases. These are cases where the decision merely refuses to grant the applicant the right or position that he seeks, such as membership of the organisation, or a licence to do certain acts. Third, there is an intermediate category, which may be called the expectation cases, which differ from the application cases only in that the applicant has some legitimate expectation from what has already happened that his application will be granted. This head includes cases where an existing licence-holder applies for a renewal of his licence or a person already elected or appointed to some position seeks confirmation from some confirming authority: see, for instance, *Weinberger v. Inglis* [1919] A.C. 606; *Breen v. Amalgamated Engineering Union* [1971] 2 Q.B. 175; and see *Schmidt v. Secretary of State for Home Affairs* [1969] 2 Ch. 149, 170, 173 and *Reg. v. Barnsley Metropolitan Borough Council, Ex parte Hook* [1976] 1 W.L.R. 1052, 1058.

It seems plain that there is a substantial distinction between the forfeiture cases and the application cases. In the forfeiture cases, there is a threat to take something away for some reason: and in such cases, the right to an unbiased tribunal, the right to notice of the charges and the right to be heard in answer to the charges (which in *Ridge v. Baldwin* [1964] A.C. 40, 132, Lord Hodson said were three features of natural justice which stood out) are plainly apt. In the application cases, on the other hand, nothing is being taken away, and in all normal circumstances there are no charges, and so no requirement of an opportunity of being heard in answer to the charges. Instead, there is the far wider and less defined question of the general suitability of the applicant for membership or a licence. The distinction is well-recognised, for in general it is clear that the courts will require natural justice to be observed for expulsion from a social club, but not on an application for admission to it. The intermediate category, that of the expectation cases, may at least in some respects be regarded as being more akin to the forfeiture cases than the application cases; for although in form there is no forfeiture but merely an attempt at acquisition that fails, the legitimate expectation of a renewal of the licence or confirmation of the membership is one which raises the question of what it is that has happened to make the applicant unsuitable for the membership or licence for which he was previously thought suitable . . .

[After concluding that this was an application case rather than an expectation case — because the claimant had never before held a manager's licence — Megarry V-C commented upon the flexible nature of procedural fairness, considered various authorities, and continued:] . . . Mr. Moses [for the defendant] accepted that the board were under a duty to reach an honest conclusion without bias and not in pursuance of any capricious policy. That, I think, is right: and if the plaintiff showed that any of these requirements had not been complied with, I think the court would intervene . . . [However,] I cannot see how the obligation to be fair can be said in a case of this type to require a hearing. I do not see why the board should not be fully capable of dealing fairly with the plaintiff's application without any hearing. The case is not an expulsion case where natural justice confers the right to know the charge and to have an opportunity of meeting it at a hearing. I cannot think that there is or should be any rule that an application for a licence of this sort cannot properly be refused without giving the applicant the opportunity of a hearing, however hopeless the application, and whether it is the first or the fifth or the fiftieth application that he has made. Certainly Mr. Beloff [for the claimant] has not referred me to any authority which appears to me to give any real support to such a proposition in a case such as this. I therefore reject the contention that the board should be required to give the plaintiff a hearing or interview . . .

The claimant also failed to establish that the BBBC's refusal to give reasons for its decision (on which see ch 12 below) or notice (on which see 11.3.2 below) of the case against him constituted a breach of procedural unfairness. The court concluded that the BBBC's decision was procedurally valid, and refused to issue any declaration.

Although the claimant in *McInnes* was not entitled to an oral hearing, the BBBC was not given licence to do as it wished: it was still under a duty 'to reach an honest conclusion without bias and not in pursuance of any capricious policy'. More fundamentally, although this case is useful because it helps to calibrate the sliding scale of procedural fairness, the very sharp distinction which it draws between application and revocation cases looks overstated. For instance, in *R v. Liverpool Corporation, ex parte Liverpool Taxi Fleet Operators' Association* [1972] 2 QB 299 at 307, a taxi-licensing case, Lord Denning MR said that 'when the corporation consider applications for licences . . . they are under a duty to act fairly'. Indeed, it is not uncommon for applicants to receive a hearing in licensing cases: see, *eg, R v. Gaming Board for Great Britain, ex parte Benaim and Khaida* [1970] 2 QB 417 at 11.3.2 below. The notion that hearings are unnecessary in application cases is further qualified by *R v. Secretary of State for the Home Department, ex parte Fayed* [1998] 1 WLR 763, in which the Court of Appeal found that the Secretary of State had been wrong to refuse to hear an applicant for British citizenship. Lord Woolf MR, at 773–776, said that:

It is obvious that the refusal of their application has damaging implications for the Fayeds. This is a matter which is for them, because of their high public profile, of particular significance. The damage is the greater because it is not in dispute that they comply with the formal requirements other than that of good character the relevance of which to the refusal is not known. Apart from the damaging effect on their reputations of having their applications refused the refusals have deprived them of the benefits of citizenship. The benefits are substantial. Besides the intangible benefit of being a citizen of a country which is their and their families' home, there are the tangible benefits which include freedom from immigration control, citizenship of the European Union and the rights which accompany that citizenship — the right to vote and the right to stand in parliamentary elections. The decisions of the Minister are therefore classically ones which but for section 44(2) [of the British Nationality Act 1981, on which see below at 11.3.2] would involve an obligation on the Minister making the decision to give the Fayeds an opportunity to be heard before that decision was reached . . . The days when it used to be said that a person seeking a privilege is not entitled to be heard are long gone . . . [T]he mere fact that this is a "privilege" case did not preclude the application of the rules of natural justice.

How does this view relate to that which was advanced in *McInnes*? The language of 'hearings' can present something of an obstacle to understanding in this area. It is self-evident that, if the principles of fairness are applicable, then the decision-maker must be under a duty to gather and take into account relevant information about the individual concerned (see ch 8 above) and fairly consider it (*eg* in an unbiased fashion: see ch 10 above) in arriving at a conclusion. The real issue concerns the extent to which fairness requires the decision-maker to enter into a dialogue with the individual. It may be thought that a mere applicant (as distinct from, say, a licence-holder) should be entitled only to state his case when making the original application, and to have the information and views thereby conveyed fairly considered. The difficulty, of course, is that in application cases — just as in forfeiture cases — the decision-maker will also take into account other factors: information about the applicant's circumstances, abilities, history, and so on which are adverse to his application, as well as broader policy considerations against which the application falls to be tested. The assumption that in application (as distinct from forfeiture) cases the individual must be satisfied with stating his original case and then leaving it to the decision-maker to weigh it up against any adverse considerations is therefore questionable.

The reality is that application cases cannot be treated as a uniform category. While considerations of efficiency and economy may often necessitate the provision of limited safeguards (as recognized in *McInnes*) it will sometimes be apposite for the decision-maker to enter into a dialogue with the applicant, giving him an opportunity to comment upon the veracity and significance of information and the relevance of policy considerations which are adverse to his application. As the *Fayed* case indicates, the more important the benefit which is at stake, and the more likely is an adverse decision to reflect on the applicant's character, the more appropriate such dialogue becomes. It is clear that this dialogue need not take the form of an oral hearing: as the decision in *Lloyd* v. *McMahon* makes clear, in some circumstances it will be adequate to allow the individual to respond in writing to adverse factors which the decision-maker has identified. What is self-evident, however, is that no dialogue is possible if the decision-maker is not willing, in the first place, to reveal those adverse factors to the individual. Thus, as the following section demonstrates, the right to know the opposing case is inseparable from the right to a fair hearing.

11.3.2 The Right to Know the Opposing Case

The importance of informing the individual of the case against him — and the intimacy of the relationship between this requirement and the existence of any meaningful dialogue with the decision-maker — was classically set out by Lord Denning MR in *Kanda* v. *Government of Malaysia* [1962] AC 322 at 337, in which it was held that the dismissal of a police officer without disclosure of a report which was highly prejudicial to him was void:

> If the right to be heard is to be a real right which is worth anything, it must carry with it a right in the accused man to know the case which is made against him. He must know what evidence has been given and what statements have been made affecting him: and then he must be given a fair opportunity to correct or contradict them.

The same point was made by Lord Mustill in *R* v. *Secretary of State for the Home Department, ex parte Doody* [1994] 1 AC 531 at 560:

> Fairness will very often require that a person who may be adversely affected by the decision will have an opportunity to make representations on his own behalf either before the decision is taken with a view to producing a favourable result; or after it is taken, with a view to procuring its modification; or both . . . Since the person affected usually cannot make worthwhile representations without knowing what factors may weigh against his interests fairness will very often require that he is informed of the gist of the case which he has to answer.

There are numerous cases in which this principle has operated to render decisions void for want of fairness. For instance, in *Chief Constable of North Wales Police* v. *Evans* [1982] 1 WLR 1155 the dismissal of a probationary constable on the basis of information about his private life — that he had married his uncle's former mistress and was breaching a tenancy condition which had in fact been informally sanctioned by a council official, both of which factors were curiously thought by the police force to bring them into disrepute — was found unlawful because the allegations were never put to the constable. Similarly, when in *R* v. *Norfolk County Council, ex parte M* [1989] QB 619 the claimant's name was added to a register of known and suspected child abusers and his employer told of this registration without informing the claimant of the evidence against him and allowing him to challenge it, a quashing order was issued. The considerable importance which is attached to the right to know the opposing case is underlined by the decision of the Court of Appeal in the following case (noted by Davies [1997] *JR* 17).

....

R v. *Secretary of State for the Home Department, ex parte Fayed* [1998] 1 WLR 763
Court of Appeal

The claimants, who were born in Egypt and resident in Britain with prominent business interests, sought naturalisation under the British Nationality Act 1981. They applied in the usual way, although some months after the applications were lodged the Secretary of State issued a press statement saying that their cases were particularly difficult and sensitive. Later, he rejected their applications, refusing, in reliance on s 44(2) of the Act, to give reasons. Section 44(2) (since repealed by the Nationality, Immigration and Asylum Act 2002, s 7(1)) provided, first, that the Secretary of State 'shall not be required to assign any reason for the grant or refusal of any application under this Act the decision on which is at his discretion' and, secondly, that his decision 'shall not be subject to appeal to, or review in, any court'. The claimants, wishing to discover the reasons for their failure, sought judicial review; they were unsuccessful at first instance and appealed to the Court of Appeal. All three judges held — applying *Anisminic Ltd* v. *Foreign Compensation Commission* [1969] 2 AC 147, on which see below at 15.6.4 — that the second part of s 44(2) did not exclude their jurisdiction to review the legality of the decision. The court then had to determine the impact of the first part of s 44(2).

Lord Woolf MR

. . . [The Secretary of State's reasoning] depends alone on the argument that to comply with what would be the normal requirement to inform the Fayeds of the case which they had to meet would be inconsistent with the express prohibition contained in section 44(2) on the Secretary of State being *required to assign any reason for the grant or refusal of any application under this Act.* This prohibition it is submitted impliedly excludes the requirement to give the Fayeds and other applicants in the same position the notice which fairness dictates they need to make an application. It is contended that unless this is the situation the intention of Parliament expressed in section 44(2) would be frustrated. I cannot accept that this can possibly be the position. It is wholly inconsistent with the principles of administrative law to which I have referred [*viz* that 'any decision taken by a Minister under a discretion conferred on him by Parliament which affects a member of the public is required to be exercised in a manner which is fair' and that, when a decision is taken in breach of that requirement, an individual should have access to the courts for judicial review purposes if no other adequate remedy is available].

My reasons for this conclusion can be summarised.

A. The suggestion that notice need not be given although this would be unfair involves attributing to Parliament an intention that it has not expressly stated that a Minister should be able to act unfairly in deciding that a person lawfully in this country should be refused citizenship without the courts being able to do anything about it. This involves attributing to the protection which section 44(2) gives in relation to reasons far greater status than that to which it is entitled. English law has long attached the greatest importance to the need for fairness to be observed prior to the exercise of a statutory discretion. However English law, at least until recently, has not been so sensitive to the need for reasons to be given for a decision after it has been reached. So to exclude the need for fairness before a decision is reached because it might give an indication of what the reasons for the decision could be is to reverse the actual position. It involves frustrating the achievement of the more important objective of fairness in reaching a decision in an attempt to protect a lesser objective of possibly disclosing what will be the reasons for the decision.

B. It would be surprising if it was the implied intention of Parliament that the lack of a requirement to give reasons should have the effect of avoiding the requirement to give notice of a possible ground for refusing an application since the Minister can voluntarily both give notice and reasons if he chooses to do so. In other words, it is difficult to attach much weight to a prohibition the Minister is free to ignore. It cannot be based on an objection of principle to the giving of reasons.

C. In many situations the giving of notice of areas of concern will do no more than identify possible rather than the actual reasons. Thus as long as the Minister seeks representations for more than one area of concern the applicant in the absence of reasons will not know whether any particular area of concern played any part in the decision to refuse the application.

D. As the Minister has a discretion to give the applicant notice of an area of concern, that discretion must itself be exercised reasonably. If not to give notice would result in unfairness then the discretion can only reasonably be exercised by giving notice. It is already the practice of the Minister to inform the applicant if one of the preconditions which are discretionary bars to success are not fulfilled. If this is the practice it is by no means obvious that there is any logical reason for not taking the same course in the areas where the Secretary of State has an even wider discretion when the identity of the issues will be less ascertainable by the applicant.

E. If the Secretary of State is correct in his contention the effect of the restriction on the obligation to give reasons is far reaching indeed. In any readily identifiable situation it will totally exclude the court's power of review. It would apply, for example, if the Secretary of State was guilty of discrimination contrary to section 44(1). On an application for judicial review there is usually no discovery because discovery should be unnecessary because it is the obligation of the respondent public body in its evidence to make frank disclosure to the court of the decision-making process. (*R v Civil Service Appeal Board ex parte Cunningham* [1992] ICR 816). If it does not then usually this would be a reason for the court ordering discovery. However, if the giving of notice cannot be required, then for the same reasons it is said the respondent cannot be required to exercise the usual "cards up approach" and what is more discovery cannot be required either since this would be open to the same objection that it could result in the identification of reasons. In practice therefore what the express prohibition on an appeal and review in section 44(2) does not achieve is achieved by the exclusion of a requirement to give reasons . . .

Phillips LJ reached the same interpretation of s 44(2) as Lord Woolf MR, and the Secretary of State's decisions were therefore quashed. Kennedy LJ, dissenting, opined that Parliament had plainly intended to relieve the Secretary of State of any obligation to reveal the reasons for his decisions, and that this also relieved him 'of any duty to indicate to an applicant at any earlier stage why he is minded to refuse'.

The willingness of the majority to adopt a somewhat strained construction of s 44(2), by distinguishing between reasons (on which see ch 12) and notice in order to preserve the duty to provide the latter, underlines the intimacy of the relationship between notice and a fair hearing. Nevertheless, Lord Woolf MR recognized ([1998] 1 WLR 763 at 776–777) that the duty to give notice is limited, both in terms of when it applies and how onerous it is:

. . . [The duty to give notice] does not require the Secretary of State to do more than to identify the subject of his concern in such terms as to enable the applicant to make such submissions as he can. In some situations even to do this could involve disclosing matters which it is not in the public interest to disclose, for example, for national security or diplomatic reasons. If this is the position then the Secretary of State would be relieved from disclosure and it would suffice if he merely indicated that this was the position to the applicant who if he wished to do so could challenge the justification for the refusal before the courts. The courts are well capable of determining public interest issues of this sort in a way which balances the interests of the individual against the public interests of the state.

I appreciate there is also anxiety as to the administrative burden involved in giving notice of areas of concern. Administrative convenience cannot justify unfairness but I would emphasise that my remarks are limited to cases where an applicant would be in real difficulty in doing himself justice unless the area of concern is identified by notice. In many cases which are less complex than that of the Fayeds the issues may be obvious. If this is the position notice may well be superfluous because what the applicant needs to establish will be clear. If this is the position notice may well not be required. However, in the case of the Fayeds this is not the position because the extensive range of circumstances which could cause the Secretary of State concern mean that it is impractical for them to identify the target at which their representations should be aimed.

The circumstances in which the duty to give notice may be diluted were explored in greater detail in the following case (as well as in *In re Pergamon Press Ltd* [1971] Ch 388, in which Lord Denning MR adopted a similar approach).

R v. *Gaming Board for Great Britain, ex parte Benaim and Khaida* [1970] 2 QB 417
Court of Appeal

Under the Gaming Act 1968 a person wishing to apply to a licensing authority for a gaming licence must first apply to the Gaming Board for a certificate consenting to such an application. The claimants in this case, who sought a gaming licence in respect of Crockford's, were given a hearing but consent was refused. The Board stated that it was not obliged to give reasons for its decisions, and would not specify on which of the matters that had been discussed at the hearing it remained unsatisfied. The claimants sought a quashing order in respect of the refusal and a mandatory order to compel the Board to give sufficient information to the claimants so as to enable them to deal with the case against them.

Lord Denning MR

. . . To what extent are the board bound by the rules of natural justice? That is the root question before us. Their jurisdiction is countrywide. They have to keep under review the extent and character of gaming in Great Britain: see s. 10 (3) [of the Gaming Act 1968]. Their particular task in regard to Crockford's is to see if the applicants are fit to run a gaming club: and if so, to give a certificate of consent.

Their duty is set out in Schedule 2, para. 4 (5) and (6):

". . . (5) . . . the board shall have regard only to the question whether, in their opinion, the applicant is likely to be capable of, and diligent in, securing that the provisions of this Act and of any regulations made under it will be complied with, that gaming on those premises will be fairly and properly conducted, and that the premises will be conducted without disorder or disturbance.

"(6) For the purposes of sub-paragraph (5) . . . the board shall in particular take into consideration the character, reputation and financial standing — (a) of the applicant, and (b) of any person (other than the applicant) by whom . . . the club . . . would be managed, or for whose benefit . . . that club would be carried on, but may also take into consideration any other circumstances appearing to them to be relevant in determining whether the applicant is likely to be capable of, and diligent in, securing the matters mentioned in that sub-paragraph."

Note also that Schedule 1, paragraph 7, gives the board power to regulate their own procedure. Accordingly the board have laid down an outline procedure which they put before us. It is too long to read in full. So I will just summarise it. It says that the board will give the applicant an opportunity of making representations to the board, and will give him the best indications possible of the matters that are troubling them. Then there are these two important sentences:

"In cases where the *source or content or of this information is confidential*, the board accept that they are obliged to withhold particulars the disclosure of which would be a breach of confidence inconsistent with their statutory duty and the public interest. . . ."

"In the course of the interview the applicant will be made aware, to the greatest extent to which this is consistent with the board's statutory duty and the public interest, of the matters that are troubling the board."

Mr Quintin Hogg [counsel for the claimants] criticised that outline procedure severely. He spoke as if Crockford's were being deprived of a right of property or of a right to make a living. He read his client's affidavit saying that "Crockford's has been established for over a century and is a gaming club with a worldwide reputation for integrity and respectability," with assets and goodwill valued at

£185,000. He said that they ought not to be deprived of this business without knowing the case they had to meet. He criticised especially the way in which the board proposed to keep that confidential information. He relied on some words of mine in *Kanda v. Government of Malaya* [1962] A.C. 322, 337, when I said "that the judge or whoever has to adjudicate must not hear evidence or receive representations from one side behind the back of the other".

Mr. Hogg put his case, I think, too high. It is an error to regard Crockford's as having any right of which they are being deprived. They have not had in the past, and they have not now, any right to play these games of chance — roulette, chemin-de-fer, baccarat and the like — for their own profit. What they are really seeking is a privilege — almost, I might say, a franchise — to carry on gaming for profit, a thing never hitherto allowed in this country. It is for them to show that they are fit to be trusted with it.

If Mr. Hogg went too far on his side, I think Mr. Kidwell went too far on the other. He submitted that the Gaming Board are free to grant or refuse a certificate as they please . . . I cannot accept this view. I think the Gaming Board are bound to observe the rules of natural justice. The question is: What are those rules?

It is not possible to lay down rigid rules as to when the principles of natural justice are to apply: nor as to their scope and extent. Everything depends on the subject-matter: see what Tucker L.J. said in *Russell v. Norfolk (Duke of)* [1949] 1 All E.R. 109, 117 and Lord Upjohn in *Durayappah v. Fernando* [1967] 2 A.C. 337, 349. At one time it was said that the principles only apply to judicial proceedings and not to administrative proceedings. That heresy was scotched in *Ridge v. Baldwin* [1964] A.C. 40. At another time it was said that the principles do not apply to the grant or revocation of licences. That too is wrong. *Reg. v. Metropolitan Police Commissioner, ex parte Parker* [1953] 1 W.L.R. 1150 and *Nakkuda Ali v. Jayaratne* [1951] A.C. 66 are no longer authority for any such proposition. See what Lord Reid and Lord Hodson said about them in *Ridge v. Baldwin* [1964] A.C. 40, 77–79, 133.

So let us sheer away from those distinctions and consider the task of this Gaming Board and what they should do. The best guidance is, I think, to be found by reference to the cases of immigrants. They have no right to come in, but they have a right to be heard. The principle in that regard was well laid down by Lord Parker C.J. in *In re HK (An Infant)* [1967] 2 Q.B. 617. He said, at p. 630:

> ". . . even if an immigration officer is not in a judicial or quasi-judicial capacity, he must at any rate give the immigrant an opportunity of satisfying him of the matters in the subsection, and for that purpose let the immigrant know what his immediate impression is so that the immigrant can disabuse him. That is not, as I see it, a question of acting or being required to act judicially, but of being required to act fairly."

Those words seem to me to apply to the Gaming Board. The statute says in terms that in determining whether to grant a certificate, the board "shall have regard only" to the matters specified. It follows, I think, that the board have a duty to act fairly. They must give the applicant an opportunity of satisfying them of the matters specified in the subsection. They must let him know what their impressions are so that he can disabuse them. But I do not think that they need quote chapter and verse against him as if they were dismissing him from an office, as in *Ridge v. Baldwin* [1964] A.C. 40; or depriving him of his property, as in *Cooper v. Wandsworth Board of Works* (1863) 14 C.B.N.S. 180. After all, they are not charging him with doing anything wrong. They are simply inquiring as to his capability and diligence and are having regard to his character, reputation and financial standing. They are there to protect the public interest, to see that persons running the gaming clubs are fit to be trusted.

Seeing the evils that have led to this legislation, the board can and should investigate the credentials of those who make application to them. They can and should receive information from the police in this country or abroad who know something of them. They can, and should, receive information from any other reliable source. Much of it will be confidential. But that does not mean that the applicants are not to be given a chance of answering it. They must be given the chance, subject to this qualification: I do not think they need tell the applicant the source of their information, if that would put their informant in peril or otherwise be contrary to the public interest . . .

. . . [The] board was set up by Parliament to cope with disreputable gaming clubs and to bring them under control. By bitter experience it was learned that these clubs had a close connection with organised crime, often violent crime, with protection rackets and with strong-arm methods. If the Gaming Board were bound to disclose their sources of information, no one would 'tell' on those clubs, for fear of reprisals. Likewise with the details of the information. If the board were bound to disclose every detail, that might itself give the informer away and put him in peril. But, without disclosing every detail, I should have thought that the board ought in every case to be able to give to the applicant sufficient indication of the objections raised against him such as to enable him to answer them. That is only fair. And the board must at all costs be fair. If they are not, these courts will not hesitate to interfere.

Accepting that the board ought to do all this when they come to give their decision, the question arises, are they bound to give their reasons? I think not. Magistrates are not bound to give reasons for their decisions: see *R v. Northumberland Compensation Appeal Tribunal, Ex parte Shaw* [1952] 1 K.B. 338, at p. 352. Nor should the Gaming Board be bound. After all, the only thing that they have to give is their *opinion* as to the capability and diligence of the applicant. If they were asked by the applicant to give their reasons, they could answer quite sufficiently: "In our opinion, you are not likely to be capable of or diligent in the respects required of you." Their opinion would be an end of the matter.

Tested by those rules, applying them to this case, I think that the Gaming Board acted with complete fairness. They put before the applicants all the information which led them to doubt their suitability. They kept the sources secret, but disclosed all the information. Sir Stanley Raymond [the Chairman of the Gaming Board] said so in his affidavit: and it was not challenged to any effect. The board gave the applicants full opportunity to deal with the information. And they came to their decision. There was nothing whatever at fault with their decision of January 9, 1970. They did not give their reasons. But they were not bound to do so.

But then complaint is made as to what happened afterwards. It was said that the board did not pin-point the matters on which they thought the explanations were not satisfactory. They did not say which of the matters (a) to (e) they were not satisfied about. But I do not see anything unfair in that respect. It is not as if they were making any charges against the applicants. They were only saying they were not satisfied. They were not bound to give any reasons for their misgivings. And when they did give some reasons, they were not bound to submit to cross-examination on them . . .

Lord Wilberforce and Phillimore LJ agreed, and the appeal was dismissed.

Thus, while the giving of notice is fundamental to a fair hearing, as *Fayed* so clearly attests, the precise obligation upon the decision-maker varies according to circumstances, including the importance of the right, interest, or benefit which is at stake, as well as public interest considerations such as the need to preserve the confidentiality of sources of information. Occasionally, the material which would constitute notice, even in the limited *Benaim and Khaida* sense, may be so sensitive that disclosure to the individual party is impossible. In such circumstances, it may be necessary to consider fresh approaches to the design of the decision-making process. For instance, sensitive 'closed' material may be withheld from appellants in proceedings before the Special Immigration Appeals Commission, but a security-cleared 'special advocate' may, in such circumstances, be appointed to represent the appellant's interests (see the Special Immigration Appeals Commission Act 1997 and SI 2003/1034, Special Immigration Appeals Commission (Procedure) Rules). Whether such a system supplies procedural fairness is another matter; for a sceptical view, see Blake (2004) 154 *NLJ* 233.

Lord Denning MR in *Benaim and Khaida*, like Lord Woolf MR in *Fayed*, drew a clear distinction between the giving of notice and the giving of reasons, emphasizing that administrative law attaches much greater importance to the former which, in contrast to the latter, is often seen as a non-negotiable prerequisite of a fair hearing. Although the law on reason-giving has now moved on — we will see in ch 12 below that a duty to give reasons in now imposed in a wide range of circumstances — *Fayed* indicates that reason-giving is still seen as a less fundamental aspect of fairness than the giving of notice.

QUESTION

- Should administrative law regard the giving of notice as of more fundamental importance than the giving of reasons?

Finally, consider the restrictive approach to notice which Megarry V-C adopted in *McInnes v. Onslow Fane* [1978] 1 WLR 1520 at 1535 (for the facts, see above at 11.3.1):

Looking at the case as whole, in my judgment there is no obligation on the board to give the plaintiff even the gist of the reasons why they refused his application, or proposed to do so. This is not a case in which there has been any suggestion of the board considering any alleged dishonesty or morally culpable conduct of the plaintiff. A man free from any moral blemish may nevertheless be wholly unsuitable for a particular type of work. The refusal of the plaintiff's application by no means necessarily puts any slur on his character, nor does it deprive him of any statutory right. There is no mere narrow issue as to his character, but the wide and general issue whether it is right to grant this licence to this applicant. In such circumstances, in the absence of anything to suggest that the board have been affected by dishonesty or bias or caprice, or that there is any other impropriety, I think that the board are fully entitled to give no reasons for their decision, and to decide the application without any preliminary indication to the plaintiff of those reasons. The board are the best judges of the desirability of granting the licence, and in the absence of any impropriety the court ought not to interfere.

QUESTION

- Can this approach be reconciled with the views expressed in *Fayed* and *Benaim and Khaida* about the giving of notice?

11.3.3 Hearings: Cross-Examination, Legal Representation, and Evidence

It will, by now, be clear that the importance of context means that there exists no unitary model of the fair hearing. It follows that the extent to which fairness requires the presence of particular features such as cross-examination and legal representation varies according to the circumstances. In deciding on such matters, the courts must strike a careful balance. On the one hand, there are many circumstances in which decision-makers wish to adopt informal procedures for legitimate reasons such as expediency and economy, or simply because the nature of the issue at stake does not necessitate recourse to the classical features of the adversarial trial process. Allowing individuals to insist on cross-examination, legal representation, and so on risks the 'overjudicialisation' of such proceedings. On the other hand, there are clearly situations, as the following case illustrates, in which a formal approach is appropriate.

....

R v. *Board of Visitors of Hull Prison, ex parte St Germain (No 2)* [1979] 1 WLR 1401
Queen's Bench Division

The claimants, all of whom were inmates at Hull Prison, were charged with disciplinary offences arising from a riot. The Board of Visitors which heard the charges was empowered to make an order for loss of remission, effectively increasing the length of time served in prison. The claimants were found guilty of a number of offences. They sought judicial review, arguing that the procedure had been unfair: in particular, the chairman of the Board had refused to allow the prisoners to call certain witnesses and had admitted the hearsay evidence of witnesses who were not available to give evidence and who could not therefore be cross-examined.

Geoffrey Lane LJ (giving the judgment of the court)

. . . [Counsel for the claimants suggested] that the chairman should have no discretion to disallow the calling of a witness whose attendance is requested by the prisoner. This suggestion was largely withdrawn in the course of argument and we do not think it had any validity. Those who appear before the board of visitors on charges are, ex hypothesi, those who are serving sentences in prison. Many such offenders might well seek to render the adjudications by the board quite impossible if they had the same liberty to conduct their own defences as they would have in an ordinary criminal trial. In our judgment the chairman's discretion is necessary as part of a proper procedure for dealing with alleged offences against discipline by prisoners.

However, that discretion has to be exercised reasonably, in good faith and on proper grounds. It would clearly be wrong if, as has been alleged in one instance before us, the basis for refusal to allow a prisoner to call witnesses was that the chairman considered that there was ample evidence against the accused. It would equally be an improper exercise of the discretion if the refusal was based upon an erroneous understanding of the prisoner's defence — that an alibi did not cover the material time or day, whereas in truth and in fact it did.

A more serious question was raised as to whether the discretion could be validly exercised where it was based upon considerable administrative inconvenience being caused if the request to call a witness or witnesses was permitted. Clearly in the proper exercise of his discretion a chairman may limit the number of witnesses, either on the basis that he has good reason for considering that the total number sought to be called is an attempt by the prisoner to render the hearing of the charge virtually impracticable or where quite simply it would be quite unnecessary to call so many witnesses to establish the point at issue. But mere administrative difficulties, simpliciter, are not in our view enough. Convenience and justice are often not on speaking terms: see *per* Lord Atkin in *General Medical Council v. Spackman* [1943] A.C. 627, 638.

. . . In our view a fair chance of exculpation cannot in many cases be given without hearing the accused's witnesses, eg in a case of an alibi defence . . .

. . . [T]he right to be heard will include, in appropriate cases, the right to call evidence. It would in our judgment be wrong to attempt an exhaustive definition as to what are appropriate cases, but they must include proceedings whose function is to establish the guilt or innocence of a person charged with serious misconduct. In the instant cases, what was being considered was alleged serious disciplinary offences, which, if established, could and did result in a very substantial loss of liberty. In such a situation it would be a mockery to say that an accused had been "given a proper opportunity of presenting his case" (section 47 (2) of the Prison Act 1952) or "a full opportunity . . .

of presenting his own case" (rule 49 (2) [of the Prison Rules 1964]), if he had been denied the opportunity of calling evidence which was likely to assist in establishing the vital facts at issue.

. . . So much for the calling of witnesses. We now turn to the suggestion that hearsay evidence is not permissible in a hearing before a board of visitors. It is of course common ground that the board of visitors must base their decisions on evidence. But must such evidence be restricted to that which would be admissible in a criminal court of law? Viscount Simon L.C. in *General Medical Council v. Spackman* [1943] A.C. 627, 634, considered there was no such restriction. That was also clearly the view of the Privy Council in the *Ceylon University v. Fernando* [1960] 1 W.L.R. 223, 234. The matter was dealt with in more detail by Diplock L.J. in *Reg v. Deputy Industrial Injuries Commissioner, Ex parte Moore* [1965] 1 Q.B. 456, 488:

> "These technical rules of evidence, however, form no part of the rules of natural justice. The requirement that a person exercising quasi-judicial functions must base his decision on evidence means no more than it must be based upon material which tends logically to show the existence or non-existence of facts relevant to the issue to be determined, or to show the likelihood or unlikelihood of the occurrence of some future event the occurrence of which would be relevant. It means that he must not spin a coin or consult an astrologer, but he may take into account any material which, as a matter of reason, has some probative value in the sense mentioned above. If it is capable of having any probative value, the weight to be attached to it is a matter for the person to whom Parliament has entrusted the responsibility of deciding the issue. The supervisory jurisdiction of the High Court does not entitle it to usurp this responsibility and to substitute its own view for his." [See above at 2.3 on the current scope of the supervisory jurisdiction *vis-à-vis* the evidential basis of decisions.]

However, it is clear that the entitlement of the Board to admit hearsay evidence is subject to the overriding obligation to provide the accused with a fair hearing. Depending upon the facts of the particular case and the nature of the hearsay evidence provided to the board, the obligation to give the accused a fair chance to exculpate himself, or a fair opportunity to controvert the charge . . . may oblige the board not only to inform the accused of the hearsay evidence but also to give the accused a sufficient opportunity to deal with that evidence. Again, depending upon the nature of that evidence and the particular circumstances of the case, a sufficient opportunity to deal with the hearsay evidence may well involve the cross-examination of the witness whose evidence is initially before the board in the form of hearsay.

We again take by way of example the case in which the defence is an alibi. The prisoner contends that he was not the man identified on the roof. He, the prisoner, was at the material time elsewhere. In short the prisoner has been mistakenly identified. The evidence of identification given by way of hearsay may be of the "fleeting glance" type as exemplified by the well-known case of *Reg. v. Turnbull* [1977] Q.B. 224. The prisoner may well wish to elicit by way of questions all manner of detail, *eg* the poorness of the light, the state of confusion, the brevity of the observation, the absence of any contemporaneous record, etc., all designed to show the unreliability of the witness. To deprive him of the opportunity of cross-examination would be tantamount to depriving him of a fair hearing.

We appreciate that there may well be occasions when the burden of calling the witness whose hearsay evidence is readily available may impose a near impossible burden upon the board. However, it has not been suggested that hearsay evidence should be resorted to in the total absence of any first-hand evidence. In the instant cases hearsay evidence was only resorted to to supplement the first-hand evidence and this is the usual practice. Accordingly where a prisoner desires to dispute the hearsay evidence and for this purpose to question the witness, and where there are insuperable or very grave difficulties in arranging for his attendance, the board should refuse to admit that evidence, or, if it has already come to their notice, should expressly dismiss it from their consideration . . .

Applying these principles, the court quashed findings of guilt in relation to six of the seven claimants.

For two reasons it is unsurprising that the court took a strict view of what fairness required in this case. First, the impact of the Board's decision on the individual prisoners was potentially very serious, involving further deprivation of liberty. Secondly, because the case involved the determination of charges against the prisoners, the traditional adversarial model under which competing cases are presented and evidence is tested was of obvious relevance. A similar position obtains under Article 6(3)(d) ECHR, which requires that one 'charged with a criminal offence' (which includes certain breaches of prison rules: see *Ezeh* v. *United Kingdom* (2004) 39 EHRR 1) must be afforded the opportunity to 'examine or have examined witnesses against him'.

In other situations, cross-examination may not be necessary or appropriate. For instance, in *R* v. *Commission for Racial Equality, ex parte Cottrell and Rothon* [1980] 1 WLR 1580 the Commission for Racial Equality investigated a complaint that a firm of estate agents was acting in an unlawful and discriminatory manner. The firm was notified of the investigation and invited to make written and oral submissions, but no cross-examination of witnesses was possible. When the Commission later issued a notice under s 58(5) of the Race Relations Act 1976 requiring the firm not to commit acts of unlawful discrimination, the firm sought judicial review, contending that the process had been unfair. Lord Lane CJ, with whom Woolf J agreed, did not share that view. He said at 1587–1588:

It seems to me that there are degrees of judicial hearing, and those degrees run from the borders of pure administration to the borders of the full hearing of a criminal cause or matter in the Crown Court. It does not profit one to try to pigeon-hole the particular set of circumstances either into the administrative pigeon-hole or into the judicial pigeon-hole. Each case will inevitably differ, and one must ask oneself what is the basic nature of the proceeding which was going on here. It seems to me that, basically, this was an investigation being carried out by the commission. It is true that in the course of the investigation the commission may form a view, but it does not seem to me that that is a proceeding which requires, in the name of fairness, any right in the firm in this case to be able to cross-examine witnesses whom the commission have seen and from whom they have taken statements. I repeat the wording of section 58 (2) in emphasis of that point: 'If in the course of a formal investigation the commission become satisfied that a person is committing, . . .' and so on. It seems to me that that is so near an administrative function as to make little difference and is the type of investigation or proceeding which does not require the formalities of cross examination . . . [I]t seems to me that the decision [in the *St Germain* case] . . . was based upon facts widely differing from those in the present case. That was truly a judicial proceeding carried out by the prison visitors, and the complaint there was that there had been no opportunity to cross-examine prison officers in hotly disputed questions of identity. Speaking for myself, I derive little assistance from any dicta in that case.

This usefully illustrates the influence exerted by the courts' perception of whether the proceedings are investigative or adjudicative — although since the issue of a s 58 notice is effectively a public statement to the effect that the Commission believes that the party under investigation has committed unlawful discriminatory acts, it is not obvious that Lord Lane CJ was right to dismiss the possibility of cross-examination out of hand. Public inquiries (on which see generally ch 18 below) provide a clearer illustration of a procedure which is evidently distinct from the adjudicative model in which something akin to a charge is brought against an individual, although even here — as the contrasting speeches of Lords Diplock and Edmund-Davies demonstrate in our next extract — there is room for disagreement as to whether procedural safeguards such as cross-examination ought to apply.

....

Bushell v. *Secretary of State for the Environment* [1981] AC 75
House of Lords

A public local inquiry was held to investigate objections to two draft motorway schemes initiated by the Secretary of State under s 11 of the Highways Act 1959. The respondent objectors challenged the need for the motorways and sought to cross-examine a department witness as to the reliability of the department's method of forecasting traffic volume on the roads the motorways would be relieving. The inspector, who recommended that the schemes be made, had refused to allow this cross-examination but had permitted the objectors to call their own evidence as to the need for the motorways and the reliability of the method of forecasting. The Secretary of State accepted the inspector's recommendation. The objectors applied for the schemes to be quashed on the ground (*inter alia*) that the inspector was wrong to disallow cross-examination. The judge at first instance dismissed the application but the Court of Appeal by a majority allowed an appeal and quashed the schemes. The Secretary of State appealed to the House of Lords.

Lord Diplock

. . . The provision and improvement of a national system of routes for through traffic for which a government department and not a local authority should be the highway authority has formed a part of national transport policy since the passing of the Trunk Roads Act in 1936 . . . The construction of motorways is a lengthy and expensive process and it has been the policy of successive governments, which would in any event have been dictated by necessity, to construct the network by stages. The order in which the various portions of the network are to be constructed thus becomes as much a matter of government transport policy as the total extent and configuration of the motorway network itself. It also has the consequence that schemes . . . which the Minister proposes to make under section 11 of the Highways Act 1959 deal with comparatively short stretches in a particular locality of what, when the other stretches are completed, will be integral parts of the national network. It follows, therefore, that there will be a whole series of schemes relating to successive stretches of the national network of motorways each of which may be the subject of separate local inquiries . . .

. . . The purpose of the inquiry is to provide the Minister with as much information about [the] objections as will ensure that in reaching his decision he will have weighed the harm to local interests and private persons who may be adversely affected by the scheme against the public benefit which the scheme is likely to achieve and will not have failed to take into consideration any matters which he ought to have taken into consideration.

. . . The Highways Act 1959 being itself silent as to the procedure to be followed at the inquiry, that procedure, within such limits as are necessarily imposed by its qualifying for the description "local inquiry," must necessarily be left to the discretion of the Minister or the inspector appointed by him to hold the inquiry on his behalf, or partly to one and partly to the other. In exercising that discretion, as in exercising any other administrative function, they owe a constitutional duty to perform it fairly and honestly and to the best of their ability, as Lord Greene M.R. pointed out in his neglected but luminous analysis of the quasi-judicial and administrative functions of a Minister as confirming authority of a compulsory purchase order made by a local authority, which is to be found in *B. Johnson & Co (Builders) Ltd. v. Minister of Health* [1947] 2 All E.R. 395, 399–400 . . .

In the instant case the public inquiries into the two schemes which were for two adjoining stretches of the national motorway network were held together. There were 170 objections to the schemes which had not been withdrawn when the combined inquiry began. There were about 100 different parties who took part in it and made representations to the inspector orally or in writing in objection to or in support of the schemes. Many of these called witnesses in support of their representations. The hearing of the inquiry by the inspector took 100 working days between June 1973 and January 1974. He made his report to the Minister on June 12, 1975.

It is evident that an inquiry of this kind and magnitude is quite unlike any civil litigation and that the inspector conducting it must have a wide discretion as to the procedure to be followed in order to achieve its objectives. These are to enable him to ascertain the facts that are relevant to each of the objections, to understand the arguments for and against them and, if he feels qualified to do so, to weigh their respective merits, so that he may provide the Minister with a fair, accurate and adequate report on these matters.

Proceedings at a local inquiry at which many parties wish to make representations without incurring the expense of legal representation and cannot attend the inquiry throughout its length ought to be as informal as is consistent with achieving those objectives. To "over-judicialise" the inquiry by insisting on observance of the procedures of a court of justice which professional lawyers alone are competent to operate effectively in the interests of their clients would not be fair. It would, in my view, be quite fallacious to suppose that at an inquiry of this kind the only fair way of ascertaining matters of fact and expert opinion is by the oral testimony of witnesses who are subjected to cross-examination on behalf of parties who disagree with what they have said. Such procedure is peculiar to litigation conducted in courts that follow the common law system of procedure, it plays no part in the procedure of courts of justice under legal systems based upon the civil law, including the majority of our fellow member states of the European Community; even in our own Admiralty Court it is not availed of for the purpose of ascertaining expert opinion on questions of navigation — the judge acquires information about this by private inquiry from assessors who are not subject to cross-examination by the parties. So refusal by an inspector to allow a party to cross-examine orally at a local inquiry a person who has made statements of facts or has expressed expert opinions is not unfair per se.

Whether fairness requires an inspector to permit a person who has made statements on matters of fact or opinion, whether expert or otherwise, to be cross-examined by a party to the inquiry who wishes to dispute a particular statement must depend on all the circumstances. In the instant case, the question arises in connection with expert opinion upon a technical matter. Here the relevant circumstances in considering whether fairness requires that cross-examination should be allowed include the nature of the topic upon which the opinion is expressed, the qualifications of the maker of the statement to deal with that topic, the forensic competence of the proposed cross-examiner, and, most important, the inspector's own views as to whether the likelihood that cross-examination will enable him to make a report which will be more useful to the Minister in reaching his decision than it otherwise would be is sufficient to justify any expense and inconvenience to other parties to the inquiry which would be caused by any resulting prolongation of it.

The circumstances in which the question of cross-examination arose in the instant case were the following. Before the inquiry opened each objector had received a document containing a statement of the Minister's reasons for proposing the draft scheme . . . The second paragraph of the Minister's statement of reasons said: "The government's policy to build these new motorways" (sc. for which the two schemes provided) "will not be open to debate at the forthcoming inquiries [sic]: the Secretary of State is answerable to Parliament for this policy."

"Policy" as descriptive of departmental decisions to pursue a particular course of conduct is a protean word and much confusion in the instant case has, in my view, been caused by a failure to define the sense in which it can properly be used to describe a topic which is unsuitable to be the subject of an investigation as to its merits at an inquiry at which only persons with local interests affected by the scheme are entitled to be represented. A decision to construct a nationwide network of motorways is clearly one of government policy in the widest sense of the term. Any proposal to alter it is appropriate to be the subject of debate in Parliament, not of separate investigations in each of scores of local inquiries before individual inspectors up and down the country upon whatever material happens to be presented to them at the particular inquiry over which they preside. So much the respondents readily concede.

At the other extreme the selection of the exact line to be followed through a particular locality by a motorway designed to carry traffic between the destinations that it is intended to serve would not be described as involving government policy in the ordinary sense of that term. It affects particular local interests only and normally does not affect the interests of any wider section of the public, unless a suggested variation of the line would involve exorbitant expenditure of money raised by taxation. It is an appropriate subject for full investigation at a local inquiry and is one on which the inspector by whom the investigation is to be conducted can form a judgment on which to base a recommendation which deserves to carry weight with the Minister in reaching a final decision as to the line the motorway should follow.

Between the black and white of these two extremes, however, there is what my noble and learned friend, Lord Lane, in the course of the hearing described as a "grey area." Because of the time that must elapse between the preparation of any scheme and the completion of the stretch of motorway that it authorises, the department, in deciding in what order new stretches of the national network ought to be constructed, has adopted a uniform practice throughout the country of making a major factor in its decision the likelihood that there will be a traffic need for that particular stretch of motorway in 15 years from the date when the scheme was prepared. This is known as the "design year" of the scheme. Priorities as between one stretch of motorway and another have got to be determined somehow. Semasiologists may argue whether the adoption by the department of a uniform practice for doing this is most appropriately described as government policy or as something else. But the propriety of adopting it is clearly a matter fit to be debated in a wider forum and with the assistance of a wider range of relevant material than any investigation at an individual local inquiry is likely to provide; and in that sense at least, which is the relevant sense for present purposes, its adoption forms part of government policy.

. . . [I]f a decision to determine priorities in the construction of future stretches of the national network of motorways by reference to their respective traffic needs in a design year 15 years ahead can properly be described as government policy, as I think it can, the definition of 'traffic needs' to be used for the purposes of applying the policy, viz. traffic needs as assessed by methods described in the Red Book [*Traffic Prediction for Rural Roads (Advisory Manual On)*] and the departmental publication on the capacity of rural roads, may well be regarded as an essential element in the policy. But whether the uniform adoption of particular methods of assessment is described as policy or methodology, the merits of the methods adopted are, in my view, clearly not appropriate for investigation at individual local inquiries by an inspector whose consideration of the matter is necessarily limited by the material which happens to be presented to him at the particular inquiry which he is holding. It would be a rash inspector who based on that kind of material a positive recommendation to the Minister that the method of predicting traffic needs throughout the country should be changed and it would be an unwise minister who acted in reliance on it.

In the result — and when one is considering natural justice it is the result that matters — the objectors were allowed to voice their criticisms of the methods used to predict traffic needs for the purposes of the two schemes and to call such expert evidence as they wanted to in support of their criticisms. What they were not allowed to do was to cross-examine the department's representatives upon the reliability and statistical validity of the methods of traffic prediction described in the Red Book and applied by the department . . .

Was this unfair to the objectors? For the reasons I have already given and in full agreement with the minority judgment of Templeman L.J. in the Court of Appeal, I do not think it was . . .

Lord Edmund-Davies (dissenting)

. . . [S]eemingly unlike all previous inquiries, it followed from [the inspector's] ruling that a cardinal question in this particular inquiry was whether there existed a *need* for the contested sections of the new motorways. That topic constantly recurred during the 100 working days it lasted . . . The key witness for the department in this respect was Mr. J. A. Brooks, a traffic engineer who very favourably impressed the inspector. A proof of his evidence was produced to the Court of Appeal, and three comments may fairly be made about it. (1) It recognised the fundamental importance of establishing the need for the proposed schemes. (2) It accepted that need depended to a great extent upon traffic projections, thus foreshadowing the view of the Leitch committee (*Report of the Advisory Committee on Trunk Road Assessment*, 1977, para. 19.1) that "Traffic forecasts are of central importance in the decision to build roads." (3) For Mr. Brooks the proper starting-point for such projections was the Ministry of Transport's Advisory *Manual on Traffic Prediction for Rural Roads*, issued in 1968 and commonly known as "the Red Book." Lord Denning M.R. was, with respect, clearly right in observing, 78 L.G.R. 10, 16 that, with certain modifications which the department accepted: "The Red Book was the sheet-anchor of the department at the inquiry" . . .

The respondents sought to challenge those methods at the outset by cross-examination. They wanted an opportunity to demonstrate out of the mouths of the department witnesses themselves that the Red Book methodology was neither accurate nor reliable. But the department resisted their application to do so, submitting that the procedures adopted in the Red Book were "government policy" and so within the inspector's classification of "irrelevant matter." Most regrettably, the inspector upheld that submission and ruled that no such cross-examination could be permitted . . .

. . . It is beyond doubt that the inspector could — and should — disallow questions relating to the merits of government policy. But matters of policy are matters which involve the exercise of political judgment, and matters of fact and expertise do not become "policy" merely because a department of government relies on them. And, as the Franks committee had put it in 1957: "We see no reason why the factual basis for a departmental view should not be explained and its validity tested in cross-examination." (*Report of the Committee on Administrative Tribunals and Inquiries* (Cmnd. 218), para. 316.)

Then, if the Red Book is not "government policy," on what basis can the cross-examination of departmental witnesses relying on its methodology be properly refused? . . .

. . . The general law may, I think, be summarised in this way: (a) In holding an administrative inquiry (such as that presently being considered), the inspector was performing quasi-judicial duties. (b) He must therefore discharge them in accordance with the rules of natural justice. (c) Natural justice requires that objectors (no less than departmental representatives) be allowed to cross-examine witnesses called for the other side on all relevant matters, be they matters of fact or matters of expert opinion. (d) In the exercise of jurisdiction outside the field of criminal law, the only restrictions on cross-examination are those general and well-defined exclusionary rules which govern the admissibility of relevant evidence (as to which reference may conveniently be had to *Cross on Evidence*, 5th ed. (1979), p. 17; beyond those restrictions there is *no* discretion on the civil side to exclude cross-examination on relevant matters.

There is ample authority for the view that, as Professor H. W. R. Wade Q.C. puts it (*Administrative Law*, 4th ed (1977), p 418): ". . . it is once again quite clear that the principles of natural justice apply to administrative acts generally." And there is a massive body of accepted decisions establishing that natural justice requires that a party be given an opportunity of challenging by cross-examination witnesses called by another party on relevant issues; see, for example, *Marriott v. Minister of Health* (1935) 52 T.L.R. 63, *per* Swift J., at p 67 — compulsory purchase orders inquiry; *Errington v. Minister of Health* [1935] 1 K.B. 249, *per* Maugham L.J., at p 272 — clearance order; *Reg v. Deputy Industrial Injuries Commissioner, Ex parte Moore* [1965] 1 Q.B. 465, *per* Diplock L.J., at pp 488A, 490E–G; and *Wednesbury Corporation v. Ministry of Housing and Local Government (No 2)* [1966] 2 Q.B. 275, *per* Diplock L.J., at pp 302G–303A — local government inquiry.

Then is there any reason why those general rules should have been departed from in the present case? . . . [W]hile I am alive to the inconvenience of different inspectors arriving at different conclusions regarding different sections of a proposed trunk road, the risk of that happening cannot, in my judgment, have any bearing upon the question whether justice was done at this particular inquiry, which I have already explained was, in an important respect, unique of its kind . . . I find myself driven to the conclusion that the refusal in the instant case to permit cross-examination on what, by common agreement, was evidence of cardinal importance was indefensible and unfair and, as such, a denial of natural justice . . .

Lord Lane and Viscount Dilhorne delivered speeches in favour of allowing the appeal and Lord Fraser agreed with the speeches of the majority; the appeal was therefore allowed.

On one view, the disagreement between Lords Diplock and Edmund-Davies stems from their different perceptions of the purpose of inquiries of this nature. The former emphasized the advancement of public welfare as the primary goal and, in effect, recognized only as much 'fairness' as is possible in light of that primary goal, whereas the latter appeared to take the view that, once participation is conceded, the rules of natural justice guarantee a basic minimum of procedural safeguards stemming from the nature of the individual interests that are affected. More narrowly, Lord Diplock simply felt that it was not the function of the inquiry to investigate the reliability of the traffic forecasts used by the department, because such matters were properly regarded as policy issues; cross-examination on such matters would not, therefore, assist the inquiry in discharging its statutory functions (see also Viscount Dilhorne, [1981] AC 75 at 108–109).

Lord Diplock's approach resembles in some respects a cost-benefit analysis which asks whether the disbenefits of allowing cross-examination — such as delay and expense — would be outweighed by a likelihood that it would uncover information relevant to the inquiry or adjudication being undertaken. The appropriateness of such a balancing approach is considered, in relation to bias, by Atrill [2003] *CLJ* 279 at 284–288, and Lord Steyn recognized in *R* v. *A (No 2)* [2001] UKHL 25 [2002] 1 AC 45 at [38] that it has a role to play in relation to Article 6: note his comments on 'triangulation', considered above at 9.3.5.

The role of cost-benefit analysis in relation to administrative procedure was addressed in the following terms by Powell J in *Mathews* v. *Eldridge* (1976) 424 US 319 at 335:

. . . [I]dentification of the specific dictates of due process generally requires consideration of three distinct factors: First, the private interest that will be affected by the official action; second, the risk of an erroneous deprivation of such interest through the procedures used, and the probable value, if any, of additional or substitute procedural safeguards; and finally, the Government's interest, including the function involved and the fiscal and administrative burdens that the additional or substitute procedural requirement would entail.

This amounts to an almost mathematical analysis, within which specific weight is attached to the various recognized values in order to determine whether the provision of additional procedural safeguards, over and above those already operated by the decision-maker, would be worthwhile. However, as Mashaw (1976) 44 *U Chi LR* 28 explains, such an approach can be highly problematic. First, once this sort of cost-benefit analysis is conceded, judges are required to determine the value of factors whose worth may actually be very difficult to assess. This may involve policy determinations that judges are ill-equipped to make. Moreover, the court may need data that may be difficult to access or which may not exist. For instance, in the context of a social welfare scheme, it may be impossible for the court accurately to determine how much the provision of additional procedural safeguards would cost, not least because the expense of (for example) more sophisticated and longer hearings would have to be off-set against any savings resulting from the conferral of benefits only on deserving recipients — the number of which may (or may not) be smaller as a result of a more elaborate decision-making process. Secondly, as Mashaw, *op cit* at 48, notes, cost-benefit analysis — at least as conceived in *Matthews* v. *Eldridge* — essentially reduces to a 'utilitarian calculus' which 'views the sole purpose of procedural protections as enhancing accuracy'. This overlooks the fact that 'a lack of personal participation causes alienation and a loss of that dignity and self-respect that society properly deems independently valuable' (*op cit* at 50). Although there is no *a priori* reason why such dignitarian concerns may not be placed in the cost–benefit balance, attributing specific weight to them would be highly problematic.

QUESTIONS

- Is cost–benefit analysis an appropriate way to approach these questions?
- Can non-instrumental reasons for procedural fairness be satisfactorily accommodated within such a framework?

We turn now to consider in what circumstances fairness may require that an individual should be allowed legal representation. Although the principle of equality of arms dictates that if one side is allowed representation, then the same opportunity should be extended to the other, there is certainly no general requirement that legal representation should be permitted. Indeed, as Fenton Atkinson LJ noted in *Enderby Town Football Club Ltd* v. *Football Association Ltd* [1971] Ch 591 at 608–609, the absence of legal representation carries certain benefits in terms of speed and cost. Some circumstances, however, give rise to strong policy arguments in favour of representation, as Lord Denning MR recognized in *Pett* v. *Greyhound Racing Association Ltd* [1969] 1 QB 125 at 132:

It is not every man who has the ability to defend himself on his own. He cannot bring out the points in his own favour or the weaknesses in the other side. He may be tongue-tied or nervous, confused or wanting in intelligence. He cannot examine or cross-examine witnesses. We see it every day. A magistrate says to a man: "You can ask any questions you like"; whereupon the man immediately starts to make a speech. If justice is to be done, he ought to have the help of someone to speak for him. And who better than a lawyer who has been trained for the task? I should have thought, therefore, that when a man's reputation or livelihood is at stake, he not only has a right to speak by his own mouth. He also has a right to speak by counsel or solicitor.

The general principles which apply in this area are helpfully set out by Webster J in the following extract.

....

R v. Secretary of State for the Home Department, ex parte Tarrant [1985] QB 251
Divisional Court

The claimants were serving prison sentences and were alleged to have committed disciplinary offences: three were charged with assault or attempted assault on a prison officer, and the other two with the more serious offence of mutiny. Their cases were heard by Boards of Visitors, which were able to impose various penalties including exclusion from associated work, stoppage of earnings, cellular confinement, and loss of remission (for up to 180 days in cases of assault, and for longer in relation to mutiny). The claimants' requests for legal representation or the assistance of a friend or adviser were refused by the Boards on the ground that they were not empowered to allow such representation or assistance. In three cases the charges were found to be proved; the other two were adjourned. The claimants sought judicial review.

Webster J

[His Lordship accepted, on the authority of *Fraser* v. *Mudge* [1975] 1 W.L.R. 1132, that a prisoner has no absolute *right* to legal representation before a Board of Visitors, but concluded that such Boards have a *discretion* to allow representation. It was clear that no such discretion had been exercised in relation to any of the claimants, the assumption having been made that representation was simply not permitted. His Lordship went on to consider the principles which the Board should have applied.]

As it seems to me, the following are considerations which every board should take into account when exercising its discretion whether to allow legal representation or to allow the assistance of a friend or adviser. (The list is not, of course, intended to be comprehensive: particular cases may throw up other particular matters.)

(1) The seriousness of the charge and of the potential penalty.

(2) Whether any points of law are likely to arise. There is of course a duty to ensure that the prisoner understands the charge, a duty which is reflected in the [Home Office] Guide [on the procedure for the conduct of adjudications by boards of visitors] at p. 12, para. 11: "Ask the accused whether he understands the charge(s) and explain anything to him about which he is in any doubt." But the clerks who sit with boards are not legally qualified and there may be cases where a legal point arises with which the prisoner, without legal representation, cannot properly deal . . .

(3) The capacity of a particular prisoner to present his own case. In "Justice in Prison," a report of a committee of Justice of which Sir Brian McKenna was the chairman and which was before the court, the following passage is quoted (para. 117, p. 57) from a report by the Home Office Research Unit based on an experiment of interviewing a number of prisoners before and after adjudication of their cases:

> "Some of the prisoners were poorly educated and not very intelligent. Furthermore, a few spoke poor English and a few appeared to have psychiatric problems. Unless they are given considerable assistance, it is unrealistic to expect such men to prepare an adequate written statement or to present their case effectively." (Smith, Austin and Ditchfield, Board of Visitors Adjudications, Research Unit paper 3, Home Office 1981, p 31).

As I have said, Mr. Brown [counsel for the Boards of Visitors] does not suggest that a board has no right to admit an interpreter and there must be some cases where this is necessary. I have no doubt, moreover, that in very many cases, where assistance is necessary, the chairman of the board is capable of doing it so as to ensure the fair hearing to which the prisoner is entitled. But the standing orders, and the Guide, provide for the giving of an opportunity to a prisoner to make a written reply to the charge; and an illiterate prisoner could not make use of that opportunity without some assistance. Similarly, a board might not always be satisfied that a mentally subnormal prisoner could be assured of a full opportunity of presenting his own case merely by the assistance of the chairman of the board.

(4) Procedural difficulties. An affidavit has been sworn, in support of three of the applications, by Mr. Ivan Henry, a member of a board of visitors, a magistrate and a legal executive. He points out that a prisoner awaiting adjudication is normally kept apart from other prisoners . . . pending the adjudication and that this may inhibit the preparation of his defence. He points out that without the capacity to interview potential witnesses, prisoners are often unable to satisfy boards of visitors that it is reasonable to call a witness and that, where a prisoner asks questions through a chairman, there is frequently no effective presentation of a case or effective cross-examination or testing of

the evidence. I will consider, in more detail, the questions of calling witnesses and cross-examination later in this judgment. But in my view a board, when considering the exercise of its discretion, should take into account any special difficulties of the kind I have mentioned and should particularly bear in mind the difficulty which some prisoners might have in cross-examining a witness, particularly a witness giving evidence of an expert nature, at short notice without previously having seen that witness's evidence.

(5) The need for reasonable speed in making their adjudication, which is clearly an important consideration.

(6) The need for fairness as between prisoners and as between prisoners and prison officers.

[His Lordship then went on to apply these principles to the circumstances of the claimants. He began with Tarrant and Leyland, the two claimants charged with mutiny.] There is agreement between Mr. Brown and Mr. Collins, on behalf of Leyland, that mutiny means "an offence of collective insubordination, collective defiance or disregard of authority or refusal to obey authority": see Lord Goddard C.J. in *Reg. v. Grant* [1957] 1 W.L.R. 906, 908. At Tarrant's hearing the word was not explained to him, although at Leyland's hearing the chairman said:

> "the definition of mutiny is a concerted act of indiscipline involving more than one person relating to the overthrow or supplanting of constituted authority."

It seems to me that in most, if not all, charges of mutiny, and certainly in these two cases, questions are bound to arise as to whether collective action was intended to be collective, *ie* whether it was concerted or not, and as to the distinction between mere disobedience of a particular order on the one hand and disregard or defiance of authority on the other. In my judgment, where such questions arise or are likely to arise, no board of visitors, properly directing itself, could reasonably decide not to allow the prisoner legal representation. If this decision is to have the result that charges of mutiny will more frequently be referred to the criminal courts in some other form, I, personally, would not regard that result as a matter of regret.

The charges against Tangney and Anderson each included one charge of an assault on a prison officer under rule 51. Each of them was, therefore, exposed to the risk of "an award" of forfeiture of remission for a period not exceeding 180 days . . . For my part, I do not think that it can possibly be said that any reasonable board properly directing itself would be bound to grant legal representation or, in the case of Tangney and Anderson who applied for it, would be bound to have allowed the presence of an adviser. I would, therefore, leave the matter to be decided by any board before which it may come, if it does so . . .

A concurring judgment was delivered by Kerr LJ. Although it was not necessarily unreasonable to deny legal representation or assistance to the claimants charged with assault, the failure of the Boards to consider the possibility of allowing legal representation rendered their decision unlawful. Quashing orders were therefore issued in all five cases.

The approach of Webster J in *Tarrant* was endorsed by the House of Lords in *R v. Board of Visitors of HM Prison, The Maze, ex parte Hone* [1988] AC 379, in which it was held that two prisoners charged with assault were not entitled to legal representation. Lord Goff concluded (at 392) that

it is easy to envisage circumstances in which the rules of natural justice do not call for representation . . . as may well happen in the case of a simple assault where no question of law arises, and where the prisoner charged is capable of presenting his own case. To hold otherwise would result in wholly unnecessary delays in many cases, to the detriment of all concerned including the prisoner charged, and to wholly unnecessary waste of time and money, contrary to the public interest.

Article 6(3)(c) ECHR requires a more generous approach to the availability of legal representation in cases where an individual is 'charged with a criminal offence'. Thus, in situations where the violation of prison rules corresponds to a criminal law prohibition (*eg* assault) and the maximum award is additional days in detention, *Ezeh* v. *United Kingdom* (2004) 39 EHRR 1 now requires legal representation to be permitted. That case did not consider whether legal aid must also be afforded (it is only mandatory under Article 6 in criminal cases, and then only 'when the interests of justice so require'), but the severity of the potential punishment and financial and educational positions of many prisoners suggest that the 'interests of justice' probably do so require under Article 6(3)(c), especially where the legal issue involved is complex: *Twalib* v. *Greece* (2001) 33 EHRR 24; *Maxwell* v. *United Kingdom* (1995) 19 EHRR 97. In addition to the specific provision in Article 6(3)(c), in *Airey* v. *Ireland* (1979–80) 2 EHRR 305 the ECtHR found Ireland in breach of its obligations under Article 6(1) for failing to provide legal aid in a civil case to an impecunious woman attempting to obtain a decree of judicial separation: the complex legal issues involved, which could only be adjudicated in the High Court, the need to prove some ground for the decree (*eg* cruelty), and the emotional nature of the case meant that litigation in person was insufficient. Although a violation of Article 6(1) was found on the facts, alternative means of securing the right set out in Article 6(1), such as simplified procedures for litigants in person, were suggested by the Court.

Plainly, the mere provision of a lawyer will not always ensure that an individual receives effective procedural protection: the lawyer may, for instance, be inexperienced or incompetent. This raises two concerns. First, ineffective legal representation prevents an individual from engaging fully with the tribunal, and this engages a non-instrumental concern even where the tribunal would have acted in the same way if the individual had been better represented. This concern is not one that has featured significantly in English jurisprudence to date. Secondly, ineffective representation will often result in *other* failures in respect of the fairness of the procedure: the tribunal may reach an adverse decision in respect of the admissibility of certain evidence, for example. In cases where failures of this type lie at the door of the lawyer, courts have been reluctant to allow an individual to claim that a hearing was unfair. Thus, in *R* v. *Secretary of State for the Home Department, ex parte Al-Mehdawi* [1990] 1 AC 876, the House of Lords refused to set aside a decision adverse to the claimant merely because, through the fault of his advisers, he was unaware of and therefore unrepresented at the hearing. Lord Bridge, giving the only reasoned speech, took the view that natural justice required the decision-making body to afford an opportunity to the individual to present his case; this it had done, and it could not be said that the advisers' failure undermined the fairness of the procedure adopted by the decision-maker. Courts remain unsympathetic to such claims, although *Al-Mehdawi* was distinguished in *R (Ganidagli)* v. *Immigration Appeal Tribunal* [2001] EWHC Admin 70 [2001] INLR 479, in which it was held that there was a breach of procedural fairness where a tribunal, in breach of an agreement, went behind agreed facts in circumstances where the relevant party's lawyer could be criticized but not solely blamed for the error.

QUESTIONS

- Is the view of natural justice adopted in *Al-Mehdawi* acceptable?
- Can an individual who, through no fault of his own (but also through no fault of the decision-maker), has been unable to exercise his right to participate in the decision-making process be said to have been treated fairly?

- What problems might arise if decisions could be set aside in circumstances such as those of *Al-Mehdawi*?

11.3.4 Appeals

It is sometimes, but by no means always, the case that decisions may be appealed. This raises a number of distinct issues. First, does fairness require the possibility of appeal? The answer to this question is clearly in the negative. As Lord Denning MR explained in *Ward* v. *Bradford Corporation* (1972) 70 LGR 27 at 35, 'Natural justice does not require the provision of an appeal. So long as the party concerned has a fair hearing by a fair-minded body of men that is enough.' A right of appeal will not therefore be implied: it exists only if conferred by statute.

Secondly, if a right of appeal exists, must it be exercised before judicial review is sought? There are circumstances in which it is held that alternative remedies must be exhausted before invoking the supervisory jurisdiction, and we examine this below at 15.3 in the context of a broader discussion of restrictions on judicial review.

Thirdly, can a fair appeal cure unfairness in the original decision-making process? We have already seen (above at 10.5.3) that, where there is a breach at first instance of Article 6(1) ECHR, appeal to or review by a court of full jurisdiction may cure such a breach. As far as domestic law is concerned, the following decision (for comment on which see Elliott (1980) 43 *MLR* 66) indicates that everything turns upon the precise features of the case, such as the nature of the defect at first instance and the adequacy of the appellate body's powers.

....

Calvin v. *Carr* [1980] AC 574
Privy Council

The claimant was part owner of a horse which, though starting at short odds, only finished fourth in a race. The stewards held an inquiry and, as a result, decided to bring charges under r 135 of the Rules of Racing. The jockey was found guilty of breaching r 135(a), which required every horse to be run on its merits. The claimant was found to be a party to the breach and a disqualification of one year was imposed on him, meaning that he could not race his horses and temporarily ceased to be a member of the Australian Jockey Club. The claimant and the jockey unsuccessfully appealed to the committee of that Club. On appeal the claimant gave evidence, was legally represented, and had the opportunity to cross-examine witnesses. He subsequently challenged his disqualification and the dismissal of the appeal. At first instance Rath J found that natural justice had been breached by the stewards but that this had been cured on appeal. The claimant appealed to the Privy Council. The case was disposed of by reference to the curative effect of the appeal, on the assumption that there had been a breach of natural justice at first instance; the Judicial Committee emphasized, however, that it was arguable that no such breach had occurred.

Lord Wilberforce (delivering the judgment of the Judicial Committee)

. . . [The claimant argues] that such defects of natural justice as may have existed as regards the proceedings before the stewards, were not capable of being cured by the appeal proceedings before the committee, even though, as was not contested before this Board, these were correctly and fairly conducted. The defendants contend the contrary. This part of the argument involved consideration of a wide range of authorities of this Board, and in Australia, Canada, England and New Zealand. As regards decisions of this Board a conflict was said to exist between *Annamunthodo v. Oilfields Workers' Trade Union* [1961] A.C. 945 and *Pillai v. Singapore City Council* [1968] 1 W.L.R. 1278, each of which has been followed by other decisions . . . Other individual decisions were cited which it appears difficult to reconcile.

Although, as will appear, some of the suggested inconsistencies of decisions disappear, or at least diminish, on analysis, their Lordships recognise and indeed assert that no clear and absolute rule can be laid down on the question whether defects in natural justice appearing at an original hearing, whether administrative or quasi-judicial, can be "cured" through appeal proceedings. The situations in which this issue arises are too diverse, and the rules by which they are governed so various, that this must be so. There are, however, a number of typical situations as to which some general principle can be stated. First there are cases where the rules provide for a rehearing by the original body, or some fuller or enlarged form of it. This situation may be found in relation to social clubs. It is not difficult in such cases to reach the conclusion that the first hearing is superseded by the second, or, putting it in contractual terms, the parties are taken to have agreed to accept the decision of the hearing body, whether original or adjourned. Examples of this are *De Verteuil v. Knaggs* [1918] A.C. 557, 563; . . . and see also *Ridge v. Baldwin* [1964] A.C. 40, 79, *per* Lord Reid.

At the other extreme are cases, where, after examination of the whole hearing structure, in the context of the particular activity to which it relates (trade union membership, planning, employment, etc.) the conclusion is reached that a complainant has the right to nothing less than a fair hearing both at the original and at the appeal stage. This was the result reached by Megarry J. in *Leary v. National Union of Vehicle Builders* [1971] Ch. 34. In his judgment in that case the judge seems to have elevated the conclusion thought proper in that case into a rule of general application. In an eloquent passage he said, at p. 49:

> "If the rules and the law combine to give the member the right to a fair trial and the right of appeal, why should he be told that he ought to be satisfied with an unjust trial and a fair appeal? . . . As a general rule . . . I hold that a failure of natural justice in the trial body cannot be cured by a sufficiency of natural justice in an appellate body."

In their Lordships' opinion this is too broadly stated. It affirms a principle which may be found correct in a category of cases: these may very well include trade union cases, where movement solidarity and dislike of the rebel, or renegade, may make it difficult for appeals to be conducted in an atmosphere of detached impartiality and so make a fair trial at the first — probably branch — level an essential condition of justice. But to seek to apply it generally overlooks, in their Lordships' respectful opinion, both the existence of the first category, and the possibility that, intermediately, the conclusion to be reached, on the rules and on the contractual context, is that those who have joined in an organisation, or contract, should be taken to have agreed to accept what in the end is a fair decision, notwithstanding some initial defect.

In their Lordships' judgment such intermediate cases exist. In them it is for the court, in the light of the agreements made, and in addition having regard to the course of proceedings, to decide whether, at the end of the day, there has been a fair result, reached by fair methods, such as the parties should fairly be taken to have accepted when they joined the association. Naturally there may be instances when the defect is so flagrant, the consequences so severe, that the most perfect of appeals or re-hearings will not be sufficient to produce a just result. Many rules (including those now in question) anticipate that such a situation may arise by giving power to remit for a new hearing. There may also be cases when the appeal process is itself less than perfect: it may be vitiated by the same defect as the original proceedings: or short of that there may be doubts whether the appeal body embarked on its task without predisposition or whether it had the means to make a fair and full inquiry, for example where it has no material but a transcript of what was before the original body. In such cases it would no doubt be right to quash the original decision.

These are all matters (and no doubt there are others) which the court must consider. Whether these intermediate cases are to be regarded as exceptions from a general rule, as stated by Megarry J., or as a parallel category covered by a rule of equal status, is not in their Lordships' judgment necessary to state, or indeed a matter of great importance. What is important is the recognition that such cases exist, and that it is undesirable in many cases of domestic disputes, particularly in which an inquiry and appeal process has been established, to introduce too great a measure of formal judicialisation. While flagrant cases of injustice, including corruption or bias, must always be firmly dealt with by the courts, the tendency in their Lordships' opinion in matters of domestic disputes should be to leave these to be settled by the agreed methods without requiring the formalities of judicial processes to be introduced.

[Lord Wilberforce considered a number of Commonwealth authorities, including *Annamunthodo* v. *Oilfields Workers' Trade Union* [1961] AC 945; *Pillai* v. *Singapore City Council* [1968] 1 WLR 1278; *Denton* v. *Auckland City* [1969] NZLR 256 and *Reid* v. *Rowley* [1977] 2 NZLR 472. Although he discovered some tensions in the case law, he concluded that, on the whole, it supported their Lordships' view that no universal rule could be applied in this context. He continued:] It remains to apply the principles above stated to the facts of the present case. In the first place, their Lordships are clearly of the view that the proceedings before the committee were in the nature of an appeal, not by way of an invocation, or use, of whatever original jurisdiction the committee may have had. The nature of the appeal is laid down by section 32 of the Australian Jockey Club Act 1873, and by the rules. Under the Act, the appeal is to be in the nature of a rehearing — a technical expression which does little more than entitle the committee to review the facts as at the date when the appeal is heard (see *Builders Licensing Board (NSW)* v. *Sperway Constructions (Sydney) Pty Ltd* (1977) 51 A.L.J.R. 260, 261, *per* Mason J.) not one which automatically insulates their findings from those of the stewards. The decision is to be 'upon the real merits and justice of the case' — an injunction to avoid technicalities and the slavish following of precedents but not one which entitles the committee to brush aside defective or improper proceedings before the stewards. The section is then required to be construed as supplemental to and not in derogation of or limited by the Rules of Racing. This brings the matter of disputes and discipline clearly into the consensual field. The Rules of Racing (Local Rules 70 to 74) allow the committee to take account of evidence already taken and of additional evidence, and confer wide powers as to the disposal of appeals.

In addition to these formal requirements, a reviewing court must take account of the reality behind them. Races are run at short intervals; bets must be disposed of according to the result. Stewards are there in order to take rapid decisions as to such matters as the running of horses, being entitled to use the evidence of their eyes and their experience. As well as acting inquisitorially at the stage of deciding the result of a race, they may have to consider disciplinary action: at this point rules of natural justice become relevant. These require, at the least, that persons should be formally charged, heard in their own defence, and know the evidence against them. These essentials must always be observed but it is inevitable, and must be taken to be accepted, that there may not be time for procedural refinements. It is in order to enable decisions reached in this way to be reviewed at leisure that the appeal procedure exists. Those concerned know that they are entitled to a full hearing with opportunities to bring evidence and have it heard. But they know also that this appeal hearing is governed by the Rules of Racing, and that it remains an essentially domestic proceeding, in which experience and opinions as to what is in the interest of racing as a whole play a large part, and in which the standards are those which have come to be accepted over the history of this sporting activity. All those who partake in it have accepted the Rules of Racing, and the standards which lie behind them: they must also have accepted to be bound by the decisions of the bodies set up under those rules so long as when the process of reaching these decisions has been terminated, they can be said, by an objective observer, to have had fair treatment and consideration of their case on its merits.

In their Lordships' opinion precisely this can, indeed must, be said of the present case. The plaintiff's case has received, overall, full and fair consideration, and a decision, possibly a hard one, reached against him. There is no basis on which the court ought to interfere, and his appeal must fail . . .

Although *Calvin* v. *Carr* arose in a contractual setting, it was followed in *Lloyd* v. *McMahon* [1987] AC 625, the facts of which are set out above at 11.3.1. The latter case was disposed of on the ground that the district auditor's conduct had not been unfair, but consideration was nevertheless given to the question whether appeal (to the Divisional Court, in this instance) could cure any earlier unfairness. In the Court of Appeal, Woolf LJ — who regarded *Lloyd* v. *McMahon* as falling into the intermediate category identified in *Calvin* v. *Carr* — said at 669:

> In my view in cases such as this the question the court should ask is whether, taking into account the complainant's rights of appeal, and if those rights have been exercised what happened on the appeal, the complainant, viewing the combined proceedings as a whole, has had a fair hearing? I regard this approach as appropriate because if Parliament makes provision for an initial hearing followed by appeal then what Parliament should be presumed to intend is that the persons affected by those proceedings should be treated fairly in the proceedings as a whole. Where there are shortcomings in the initial proceedings but the appellant has in fact been dealt with fairly when the proceedings as a whole are considered, to regard the proceedings as invalid would be to condemn something as being unfair because of a flaw in a part when if the whole was considered the flaw would be sufficiently insignificant to enable the whole procedure to be regarded as unblemished. Expressing the matter slightly differently, if the whole procedure is properly regarded as being fair, then to strike that procedure down because of a flaw in part will be to apply an unduly technical approach.

A similar approach was adopted in the House of Lords by Lord Bridge. Although he felt the case turned on the construction of the particular statute, thereby making it unnecessary to examine the general principles enunciated in *Calvin* v. *Carr*, he said (at 709) that, 'It is the very amplitude of the jurisdiction which, to my mind, is all-important.' Thus, 'when the court has, as here, in fact conducted a full hearing on the merits and reached a conclusion that the issue of a certificate was justified, it would be an erroneous exercise of discretion nevertheless to quash the certificate on the ground that, before the matter reached the court, there had been some defect in the procedure followed.' In contrast, the notion that fairness is required at both stages has been endorsed in relation to criminal trials (see *R* v. *Bradford Justices, ex parte Wilkinson* [1990] 1 WLR 692 at 695, *per* Mann LJ; *R* v. *Hereford Magistrates' Court, ex parte Rowlands* [1998] QB 110 at 124, *per* Lord Bingham CJ), suggesting that the curative capacity of appeals may vary according to the nature and importance of the interests at stake. Other factors, however, may also be in play, as is shown by *R (A (A Child))* v. *Kingsmead School Governors* [2002] EWCA Civ 1822, in which it was held that a fair appeal could cure procedural defects in the defendant's decision permanently to exclude the claimant. Simon Brown LJ (at [37]) was heavily influenced by the policy implications of permitting judicial review of first instance decisions and by the position on this issue implicitly adopted in the statutory scheme:

> Plainly Parliament did not intend either hearing . . . to be unfair. But that is by no means to say that Parliament intended a pupil aggrieved by the [original] . . . decision then to invoke the courts' supervisory jurisdiction rather than proceed to appeal. It is, on the contrary, clear that Parliament intended the aggrieved pupil to seek his remedy before the [independent appeal panel]. In one sense, of course, he then obtains no redress for the earlier unfairness. But what he does obtain is a fresh and fair decision on the merits of the case by a statutory body custom-built for the purpose.

11.4 Concluding Remarks

We have seen in this chapter that the concept of procedural fairness has changed substantially in English law in recent decades. The evolution of the concept is to be traced principally to two (related) developments. In the first place, successive court decisions have significantly expanded the range of circumstances in which norms of procedural fairness are applicable: *Ridge* v. *Baldwin* liberalized the notion of being under a 'duty to act judicially', while later cases held that fairness could be required even in the absence of such a duty. Secondly, as the scope of natural justice broadened, so the obligations with which decision-makers were thereby fixed came to be conceived of in more flexible terms. These are the roots of the present-day orthodoxy — that very many administrative decision-makers are caught by the requirements of procedural fairness, but that the obligations with which they are thereby fixed are highly context-sensitive. Procedural fairness therefore can, and does, mean radically different things in different circumstances.

Although, as we have seen, these developments can be criticized — *inter alia* because the degree of flexibility may be such as to engender confusion, and in view of the courts' somewhat blinkered reliance upon a set of procedural norms drawn almost exclusively from a traditional adversarial model — they are broadly to be welcomed. It is of first importance in a democracy that, when public bodies make decisions affecting the rights, liberties, interests, or legitimate expectations of individuals, they are obliged by law to treat such individuals with respect, and as participants in, rather than as mere objects of, the administrative process. In a relationship between citizen and state thus conceived lie the seeds of a healthy polity, in which public authorities earn the trust of individuals; in which individuals are paid the respect due to them by state bodies; and in which the chances of good decisions are enhanced.

FURTHER RESOURCES

Allan, 'Procedural Fairness and the Duty of Respect' (1998) 18 *OJLS* 497

Galligan, 'Procedural Fairness' in Birks (ed), *The Frontiers of Liability* (volume one) (Oxford 1994)

Loughlin, 'Procedural Fairness: A Study of the Crisis in Administrative Law Theory' (1978) 28 *UTLJ* 215

Mashaw, 'The Supreme Court's Due Process Calculus for Administrative Adjudication in *Mathews* v. *Eldridge*: Three Factors in Search of a Theory of Value' (1976) 44 *U Chi LR* 28

Mullan, 'Fairness: The New Natural Justice' (1975) 25 *UTLJ* 281

Wade, 'The Twilight of Natural Justice?' (1951) 67 *LQR* 103

12 GIVING REASONS FOR DECISIONS

In *Stefan* v. *General Medical Council* [1999] 1 WLR 1293 at 1300, Lord Clyde noted a clear trend in English law 'towards an increased recognition of the duty upon decision-makers of many kinds to give reasons' for their decisions. Nevertheless, it remains the case that, in the oft-cited words of Lord Mustill in *R* v. *Secretary of State for the Home Department, ex parte Doody* [1994] 1 AC 531 at 564, there exists no 'general duty to give reasons' for administrative decisions. The proposition that everything depends on context therefore applies with as much force here as to the aspects of procedural fairness addressed in the two previous chapters.

12.1 Reasons, Notice, and Rationality

Before embarking on a detailed examination of the content and scope of the duty to give reasons, it is necessary briefly to distinguish that duty from other circumstances in which administrative law attaches significance to the presence or absence of some form of 'reasons'.

The first set of such circumstances has already been discussed, and need be touched upon here in passing only. We saw above at 11.3.2 that the giving of notice is considered vital to the fairness of the decision-making process: without notice of the case against the individual, the right to a hearing or to make representations is largely illusory. There is clearly a relationship between notice and reasons: as Lord Woolf MR acknowledged in *R* v. *Secretary of State for the Home Department, ex parte Fayed* [1998] 1 WLR 763 (see above at 11.3.2), requiring the giving of notice may reveal — or at least allow the claimant to deduce — the ultimate reasons for the decision.

However, this relationship notwithstanding, notice and reasons are distinct. On a practical level, notice and reasons arise at different stages in the decision-making process: notice is given *before* the decision is taken, while reasons are supplied *after* (or contemporaneously with) the decision so as to explain why it was reached. Notice is therefore inherently preliminary in nature — it indicates the case which the individual is required to answer; in contrast, reasons for the final decision express qualitative conclusions about the merits of the individual's case, and as to why the decision-maker was or was not persuaded that the claimant managed to marshal evidence and arguments sufficient to overcome the case against him. (Circumstances may, however, arise in which reasons and notice are indistinguishable: *eg* reasons for a first instance decision may also constitute notice for the purposes of a right of appeal.)

A second set of circumstances in which significance is attached to reasons — or, more specifically, their absence — should also be distinguished from the duty to give reasons with which we are concerned in this chapter. A number of *obiter dicta* in *Padfield* v. *Minister of Agriculture* [1968] AC 997 suggest that if a decision-maker fails to advance reasons in support of a decision, the court may infer that no valid reasons exist and that the decision is therefore *Wednesbury* unreasonable (see above at 9.2.1). For instance, Lord Pearce said at 1053–1054:

> I do not regard a Minister's failure or refusal to give any reasons as a sufficient exclusion of the court's surveillance. If all the prima facie reasons seem to point in favour of his taking a certain course to carry out the intentions of Parliament in respect of a power which it has given him in that regard, and he gives no reason whatever for taking a contrary course, the court may infer that he has no good reason and that he is not using the power given by Parliament to carry out its intentions.

However, this possibility of inferring irrationality in the absence of reasons is in fact of rather limited relevance to our present inquiry. First, it is clear that such an inference will be made only rarely. This point was emphasized by Lord Keith in *R* v. *Secretary of State for Trade and Industry, ex parte Lonrho plc* [1989] 1 WLR 525 at 539–540, who explained that:

> The absence of reasons for a decision where there is no duty to give them cannot of itself provide any support for the suggested irrationality of the decision. The only significance of the absence of reasons is that if all other known facts and circumstances appear to point overwhelmingly in favour of a different decision, the decision-maker, who has given no reasons, cannot complain if the court draws the inference that he had no rational reason for his decision.

Secondly, and more fundamentally, the *Padfield* approach is conceptually distinct from the duty to give reasons, because it imposes no positive obligation upon decision-makers to furnish reasons for their decisions. Toube [1997] *JR* 68 at 68–69 explains that '*Padfield* does not suggest that there is a free-standing obligation to give reasons — simply that the failure to meet a public law challenge may result in a finding of irrationality. The *Padfield* argument should [therefore] be seen as entirely distinct from the fairness-based obligation to give reasons . . .'. Taking these two points together, the most that can be said of *Padfield* is that it provides an incentive to give reasons, rather than a duty to do so.

12.2 Why Require Reasons?

12.2.1 The Virtues of Reason-Giving

Fordham [1998] *JR* 158 observes that, 'Underlying any analysis of the law on reasons is a functional question. To what ends, for what purposes, are public decision-makers (to be) required to give reasons?' In the following passage, he suggests that three dimensions underlie a fully-developed duty to give reasons. (For other explanations of the virtues of reason-giving, see Craig [1994] *CLJ* 282; JUSTICE-All Souls, *Administrative Justice: Some Necessary Reforms* (Oxford 1988); Allan (1998) 18 *OJLS* 497.)

....

Fordham, 'Reasons: The Third Dimension' [1998] JR 158

A first dimension is that the giving of reasons *serves the interests of the court* (or other tribunal) reviewing the decision. This rationale has to do with disclosure, to the court. The approach is illustrated by the comments of the Court of Appeal in *R v. Lancashire County Council, ex parte Huddleston* [1986] 2 All ER 941 at 945g and 947e, where reasons were encouraged in a spirit of co-operation by the public authority with the judicial review process.

A second dimension is that the giving of reasons *serves the interests of the person affected* by the decision. This has to do with disclosure, to the 'parties'. It is exemplified by the decision of the House of Lords in *R v. Secretary of State for the Home Department, ex parte Doody* [1994] 1 AC 531, where reasons were required because of the prisoner's basic interest in knowing why decisions affecting liberty had been taken.

The third dimension is that the giving of reasons *serves the interests of the decision-maker* in reaching the decision. This has to do not with disclosure, but discipline. The central point is simple. Consciously duty-bound to articulate their reasons, decision-makers' minds are the more focused and their substantive decision-making the better. This was recognised by the Divisional Court in *R v. Higher Education Funding Council, ex parte Institute of Dental Surgery* [1994] 1 WLR 242 at 256H (cited with approval in *R v. City of London Corporation, ex parte Matson* [1997] 1 WLR 765 (CA) at 783D and in *R v. Ministry of Defence, ex parte Murray* [1998] COD 134 (DC)), as the first of a series of factors in favour of requiring reasons, namely that 'the giving of reasons may among other things concentrate the decision-maker's mind on the right questions . . .'

Some commentators — most notably the JUSTICE-All Souls Committee (*op cit* at 70) — also point to a fourth dimension: that reason-giving enhances public confidence in decision-making 'by the knowledge that supportable reasons have to be given by those who exercise administrative power'. In any event, Fordham's analysis reveals progressively broader conceptions of the duty to give reasons, culminating in a view which sees the giving of reasons not as an optional extra which is bolted on to the end of the decision-making process, but as something which is integral to the very notion of good administration, providing an incentive to adhere to the principles of good administrative practice considered earlier in this book. Fordham goes on to argue that the way in which we view the purpose behind the giving of reasons, and in particular whether we accept all three of the dimensions which he identifies, fundamentally influences the scope of the duty and helps determine such matters as the level of detail required when giving reasons; whether they must accompany the decision or can be issued after the event; precisely when the duty arises in the first place, and the relief which is appropriate when it is breached. We explore these issues later in this chapter.

For the time being, we wish to emphasize a distinction which is latent within Fordham's analysis of the virtues of reason-giving. His first and third points highlight the capacity of reason-giving to promote the effective operation of the administrative system — in terms both of decision-making and judicial review thereof. In contrast, Fordham's second point captures a rather different aspect of the importance of reasons. The notion that those whose lives are affected by official decisions have a 'basic interest' in knowing the reasons underlying them implies a particular relationship between the government and the governed which recognizes the dignity of the latter as a participant in, rather than the object of, decision-making; on this view, reason-giving is a good in itself. This view is developed in the following passage, in which Allan (applying to reason-giving the general thesis developed in the extract which appears at 11.1 above) takes issue with the emphasis placed by Galligan,

Due Process and Fair Procedures: A Study of Administrative Procedures (Oxford 1996) (an excerpt from which also appears above at 11.1), on the instrumental benefits of due process.

....

Allan, 'Procedural Fairness and the Duty of Respect' (1998) 18 OJLS 497

. . . Although Galligan is right to protest against a view of procedures which belittles their instrumental value in ensuring appropriate outcomes, there are at least aspects of procedural fairness or good practice which may serve an independent function. Moreover, the whole design or character of a hearing may well reflect non-instrumental values of no less importance than those which underlie our concern for accuracy and reliability. The giving of reasons by officials, in particular, can readily be understood as serving a "dignitarian" function quite distinct from the arrangements for securing sound decisions. As Galligan notes, an obligation to give reasons may have a beneficial effect on the quality of the decision and in that sense contribute to fairness; but whether or not that is so in any particular case, giving reasons may be regarded as an integral part of treating a disappointed applicant with the respect which his dignity as a citizen demands. Galligan is very cautious here, sceptical of the bare claim that the giving of reasons is in itself an expression of respect; but he rightly accepts that there is value, independent of outcome, in a person being able to judge for himself whether or not an exercise of authority over him is justified. In view of the inevitable imperfections of decision-processes and the fallibility of decision-makers, the party affected is entitled to the reassurance which an expression of valid reasons, if they exist, supplies.

It is surely not hard to discern good grounds here for Laurence Tribe's suggestion [in *American Constitutional Law* (New York 1978) at 503–504] that such "rights to interchange" amount to an expression of a person's humanity, for the idea that procedures may have intrinsic value. Giving reasons expresses respect just as a refusal or failure to do so — where the failure evinces disregard for a person's opinion of the justice of his treatment — expresses contempt. As Lucas [*On Justice* (Oxford 1980) at 79–80] explains the point, a requirement to give reasons "recognizes a party's right to be disappointed by an adverse decision, and the need to assuage it". A principal purpose of the rules of natural justice, more generally, is to enable a person to *identify* with the decision-making process: by observing them we make it easier for him to accept the result, and "make it manifest to anyone disappointed at the outcome that we were solicitous of his interests and did not reach an adverse decision lightly or wantonly, but only for good reason and with evident reluctance" [*ibid*].

Tribe's reference to 'rights of interchange' suggests an important sense in which, if a fair hearing is understood to encompass the giving of reasons, it has a value quite independent of outcome. By responding to the *particular* arguments which the disappointed applicant or claimant has offered, the official attempts to persuade him of the justice of the decision in terms which acknowledge his special (even unique) position and his independence of mind. As Galligan observes, administrative decision-making generally takes place under conditions of uncertainty, complexity and incommensurability, where inquiry, argument, and deliberation are highly desirable; and the duty of respect requires that attention should be paid to the person's special case, where misjudgment is not simply a social cost but an act of injustice. The reasons given should enable a person to see that his case has been given the careful consideration which it may deserve, and thereby more readily accept the outcome as a reasonable accommodation between private and public interests.

However, there is clearly good reason for Galligan's caution. The intrinsic or non-instrumental value of reason-giving by officials depends on the sincerity with which they respond to a person's claim and examine the merits of his arguments. No reassurance is given by the statement of invalid or inadequate reasons; nor is respect shown by meeting a person's arguments, tailored to his own circumstances, with routine official responses, devised for the standard case which may be quite dissimilar. Respect is shown only when there has been a genuine effort to confront the conditions of uncertainty, complexity and incommensurability as they bear on the citizen's case; and his acceptance of the outcome as a legitimate decision is likely to depend on his being given reasons which demonstrate that such an effort has in fact been made, and the interests of justice accordingly served. To that extent, the intrinsic value of procedures is closely tied to their instrumental purpose — the former is dependent on at least moderate success in regard to the latter . . .

QUESTION

• Do you agree that reason-giving is important in itself, independent of any contribution it may make to the accuracy or correctness of the decision?

12.2.2 A General Duty to Give Reasons?

The clear virtues of reason-giving give rise to an obvious question: why does English law not recognize a general duty on the part of decision-makers to give reasons? We noted at the outset of this chapter that the starting-point of English law is that no such duty exists, albeit that certain circumstances may trigger a requirement to give reasons. The concerns which underlie the reluctance of English law to embrace a general duty were summarized in the following terms by the JUSTICE-All Souls Committee in their report, *Administrative Justice: Some Necessary Reforms* (Oxford 1988) at 70–71:

(a) Efficient administration requires free and uninhibited discussion among decision-makers, unimpeded by considerations of what can or cannot be made public subsequently.

(b) A general requirement of reasons will impose an intolerable burden on the machinery of government.

(c) Delays in the handling of business will inevitably follow and additional expense will be caused. The public at large will suffer. The benefit will not match the cost.

(d) The imposition of a general duty will have far-reaching implications for central government, local government, and for many other bodies of a public or semi-public character. Many more decisions will be opened up to the possibility of legal challenge and a further step down the road of 'judicialization' of affairs will be taken.

(e) The imposition of a [general] duty to give reasons will not necessarily mean that the true or complete reasons will be stated. Decision-makers will adapt to the new regime and acquire the art of stating sufficient by way of reasons to preclude successful challenge, but candour will not always be displayed.

The Committee did not, however, find these arguments compelling, and considered them to be outweighed by the benefits which flow from a general duty to give reasons. It concluded that the creation of a general duty should not be left to judicial development of the common law, and that legislative intervention would be preferable. The Committee was heavily influenced by section 13(1) of the Australian Administrative Decisions (Judicial Review) Act 1977 — which entitles individuals to request from the decision-maker 'a statement in writing setting out the findings on material questions of fact, referring to the evidence or other material on which those findings were based and giving reasons for the decision' — and recommended the adoption of a similar approach in English law. The Committee was particularly impressed that the Australian provision went further than a simple duty to state reasons, commenting (at 72) that the additional obligation to furnish details of the material relied upon in arriving at the decision would ensure that 'matters will be decided and justice

administered according to facts and law and not upon arbitrary or extra-legal considerations'. Such a requirement also helps to guard against the giving of standard, non-specific
reasons which bear little relation to the circumstances of the individual case — a concern
highlighted above both by Allan (at 12.2.1) and the JUSTICE-All Souls Committee (in
paragraph (e) above).

It is important to bear in mind that a *general* duty to give reasons does not amount to a
universal duty to give reasons. The starting point in a legal system which recognises a general
duty is that reasons must be given, but there will naturally be exceptional circumstances in
which reason-giving would be inappropriate. The JUSTICE-All Souls Committee (at 73)
tentatively suggested that exceptions may apply in the following areas:

(a) where the giving of reasons would be prejudicial to the interests of national security, defence, or
   international relations;

(b) where the reasons would involve disclosing material protected by legal privilege;

(c) where the reasons would disclose information made available to government in confidence (this
   heading would cover such matters as decisions as to the awarding of commercial contracts,
   licences and other privileges);

(d) where the reasons would reveal professional or trade secrets or otherwise be hurtful to the
   interests of third parties;

(e) where the decision of which reasons were sought related to the appointment to or promotion in
   any post or office or to the assignment of any specific task.

QUESTIONS

• Do these exceptions to a general duty to give reasons go too far?
• Or are there other situations in which you would wish to see administrators free from
  an obligation to justify their decisions?

In light of the conclusions of the Committee, it is interesting that its chairman, Sir Patrick
Neill, has more recently questioned the appropriateness of enacting legislation introducing a
general duty to give reasons. Writing in Forsyth and Hare (eds), *The Golden Metwand and
the Crooked Cord* (Oxford 1998), Neill concluded (at 183–184) that the time was 'not ripe'
for such a step; in reaching this view, he was influenced by two specific considerations. First,
Neill recognized, drawing upon the Australian experience, that 'it is no easy matter to draft
an Act [imposing a general duty to give reasons] and to reach a consensus on the exceptions
to the duty'. Secondly, he noted that, 'Many influences are at work supporting the movement
towards open government both as regards access to documents and information and as
regards the requirement to give reasons.' In particular, Neill pointed to the impact of the
European Convention on Human Rights and European Community Law, and the developing jurisprudence of English courts. Writing in 1998, Neill thought that these influences
'should be given another decade to mature and generate something like a general duty to
give reasons tempered by reasonable exceptions evolved empirically'. With this aspiration in
mind, we turn to consider the extent to which decision-makers are today required to give
reasons for their decisions.

12.3 The Duty to Give Reasons at Common Law

12.3.1 The Emergence of a Common Law Duty to Give Reasons

Traditionally, at common law, the requirements of natural justice did not extend to a duty to give reasons (see, *eg, McInnes* v. *Onslow-Fane* [1978] 1 WLR 1520 and the excerpt (above at 11.3.2) from *R* v. *Gaming Board for Great Britain, ex parte Benaim and Khaida* [1970] 2 QB 417). A breakthrough, however, was made in *R* v. *Civil Service Appeal Board, ex parte Cunningham* [1991] 4 All ER 310, in which the defendant, a public body established under the royal prerogative, concluded that the claimant, a prison officer, had been unfairly dismissed. However, the defendant refused to give reasons explaining how it arrived at a compensation award which, in the words of Leggatt LJ at 325, 'looks as though [it] is less than it should be'. The case is significant for its recognition of the fact that 'the duty to act fairly in this case extends to an obligation to give reasons' (*per* Leggatt LJ at 326). McCowan LJ (at 322–323) identified seven factors that militated in favour of a reason-giving duty in the circumstances:

1. There is no appeal from the Board's determination of the amount of compensation.

2. In making that determination the Board is carrying out a judicial function.

3. The Board is susceptible to judicial review.

4. . . . [T]he provision of a recommendation without reasons . . . is insufficient to achieve justice.

5. There is no statute which requires the courts to tolerate that unfairness.

6. The giving of short reasons would not frustrate the apparent purpose of the code [on civil service pay and conditions].

7. It is not a case where the giving of reasons would be harmful to the public interest.

Cunningham's recognition that the common law duty to comply with natural justice extends (in some circumstances) to a duty to give reasons was endorsed by the House of Lords in the following decision (for comment on which see Campbell [1994] *PL* 184 and Craig [1994] *CLJ* 282).

....

R v. *Secretary of State for the Home Department, ex parte Doody* [1994] 1 AC 531
House of Lords

The claimants were convicted of murder and sentenced to life imprisonment. In accordance with the then practice (since declared incompatible with Article 6(1) ECHR in *R (Anderson)* v. *Secretary of State for the Home Department* [2002] UKHL 46 [2003] 1 AC 837) the Home Secretary consulted with the trial judge and the Lord Chief Justice before determining the length of time for which the prisoners should be detained before release on licence could be considered. However, he proceeded to set periods of detention in excess of those recommended by the judiciary. The claimants sought judicial review of the Secretary of State's decisions on various grounds, one of which was his failure to give reasons for his decision.

Lord Mustill

... I ... begin by ... inquiring what requirements of fairness, germane to the present appeal, attach to the Home Secretary's [decision]. As general background to this task, I find in the more recent cases on judicial review a perceptible trend towards an insistence on greater openness, or if one prefers the contemporary jargon "transparency", in the making of administrative decisions ...

I accept without hesitation, and mention it only to avoid misunderstanding, that the law does not at present recognise a general duty to give reasons for an administrative decision. Nevertheless, it is equally beyond question that such a duty may in appropriate circumstances be implied, and I agree with the analyses by the Court of Appeal in *Reg. v. Civil Service Appeal Board, Ex parte Cunningham* [1991] 4 All E.R. 310 of the factors which will often be material to such an implication.

Turning to the present dispute I doubt the wisdom of discussing the problem in the contemporary vocabulary of "prisoner's rights," given that as a result of his own act the position of the prisoner is so forcibly distanced from that of the ordinary citizen, nor is it very helpful to say that the Home Secretary should out of simple humanity provide reasons for the prisoner, since any society which operates a penal system is bound to treat some of its citizens in a way which would, in the general, be thought inhumane. I prefer simply to assert that within the inevitable constraints imposed by the statutory framework, the general shape of the administrative regime which Ministers have lawfully built around it, and the imperatives of the public interest, the Secretary of State ought to implement the scheme as fairly as he can. The giving of reasons may be inconvenient, but I can see no ground at all why it should be against the public interest: indeed, rather the reverse. This being so, I would ask simply: Is refusal to give reasons fair? I would answer without hesitation that it is not. As soon as the jury returns its verdict the offender knows that he will be locked up for a very long time. For just how long immediately becomes the most important thing in the prisoner's life. When looking at statistics it is easy to fall into the way of thinking that there is not really very much difference between one extremely long sentence and another: and there may not be, in percentage terms. But the percentage reflects a difference of a year or years: a long time for anybody, and longer still for a prisoner. Where a defendant is convicted of, say, several armed robberies he knows that he faces a stiff sentence: he can be advised by reference to a public tariff of the range of sentences he must expect; he hears counsel address the judge on the relationship between his offences and the tariff; he will often hear the judge give an indication during exchanges with counsel of how his mind is working; and when sentence is pronounced he will always be told the reasons for it ... Contrast this with the position of the prisoner sentenced for murder. He never sees the Home Secretary; he has no dialogue with him: he cannot fathom how his mind is working. There is no true tariff, or at least no tariff exposed to public view which might give the prisoner an idea of what to expect. The announcement of his first review date arrives out of thin air, wholly without explanation. The distant oracle has spoken, and that is that.

My Lords, I am not aware that there still exists anywhere else in the penal system a procedure remotely resembling this. The beginnings of an explanation for its unique character might perhaps be found if the executive had still been putting into practice the theory that the tariff sentence for murder is confinement for life, subject only to a wholly discretionary release on licence: although even in such a case I doubt whether in the modern climate of administrative law such an entirely secret process could be justified. As I hope to have shown, however, this is no longer the practice, and can hardly be sustained any longer as the theory. I therefore simply ask, is it fair that the mandatory life prisoner should be wholly deprived of the information which all other prisoners receive as a matter of course. I am clearly of the opinion that it is not.

My Lords, I can moreover arrive at the same conclusion by a different and more familiar route, of which *Ex parte Cunningham* [1991] 4 All E.R. 310 provides a recent example. It is not, as I understand it, questioned that the decision of the Home Secretary on the penal element is susceptible to judicial review. To mount an effective attack on the decision, given no more material than the facts of the offence and the length of the penal element, the prisoner has virtually no means of ascertaining whether this is an instance where the decision-making process has gone astray. I think it important that there should be an effective means of detecting the kind of error which would entitle the court to intervene, and in practice I regard it as necessary for this purpose that the reasoning of the Home Secretary should be disclosed. If there is any difference between the penal element recommended by the judges and actually imposed by the Home Secretary, this reasoning is bound to include, either explicitly or implicitly, a reason why the Home Secretary has taken a different view. Accordingly, I consider that the respondents are entitled to an affirmative answer on the third issue . . .

Lords Keith, Lane, Templeman, and Browne-Wilkinson agreed with Lord Mustill. A quashing order was issued.

QUESTION

• Is the substance of the decision in *Doody* consistent with Lord Mustill's protestation that there is still no general duty to give reasons in English law?

Using *Doody* as a convenient starting point, it is necessary to consider the circumstances in which a duty to give reasons may arise.

12.3.2 Reasons, Appeal, and Review

Once permission has been granted for judicial review, the defendant finds itself under an obligation to disclose adequate reasons to the court in order that the legality of the decision may properly be evaluated. This point was emphasized by Sir John Donaldson MR in *R v. Lancashire County Council, ex parte Huddleston* [1986] 2 All ER 941, a case concerning a local authority's refusal to provide the claimant with a university grant. In a passage which strongly calls to mind the green light approach to administrative law examined above at 1.2.2, the Master of the Rolls said, at 945:

Counsel for the council . . . contended that it may be an undesirable practice to give full, or perhaps any, reasons to every applicant who is refused a discretionary grant, if only because this would be likely to lead to endless further arguments without giving the applicant either satisfaction or a grant. So be it. But in my judgment the position is quite different if and when the applicant can satisfy a judge of the public law court that the facts disclosed by her are sufficient to entitle her to apply for judicial review of the decision. Then it becomes the duty of the respondent to make full and fair disclosure.

Notwithstanding that the courts have for centuries exercised a limited supervisory jurisdiction by means of the prerogative writs, the wider remedy of judicial review and the evolution of what is, in effect, a specialist administrative or public law court is a post-war development. This development has created a new relationship between the courts and those who derive their authority from the public law, one of partnership based on a common aim, namely the maintenance of the highest standards of public administration.

On this analysis, once judicial review proceedings are underway the decision-maker owes a duty to the court, distinct from the individual claimant, to provide reasons for its decision. Lord Donaldson MR developed this idea further in *R* v. *Civil Service Appeal Board, ex parte Cunningham* [1991] 4 All ER 310 at 316, in which he said that 'once the public law court has concluded [at the permission stage] that there is an arguable case that the decision is unlawful, the position is transformed. The applicant may . . . not be entitled to reasons, but the court is.' Thus, as Toube [1997] *JR* 68 at 69 observes, it is the relationship between the decision-maker and the court which is central here: 'the applicant who has been [granted permission] is no more than a catalyst. The duty of full and frank disclosure, therefore, operates independently from any duty to give reasons.'

But what of the position *before* legal proceedings are commenced? The picture here is rather complex. On the one hand, the *absence* of a right of appeal may suggest that reasons should be given (see, *eg*, the remarks of McCowan LJ in the *Cunningham* case, set out above at 12.3.1). On the other hand, the *presence* of a right of appeal may point towards a duty to give reasons, since such a right is fundamentally undermined if reasons are not given at first instance (see, *eg*, *Norton Tool Co Ltd* v. *Tewson* [1973] 1 WLR 45). In the absence of reasons, the prospective appellant is ignorant as to whether good grounds for appeal exist, and therefore does not know whether exercising his right of appeal is worthwhile. (Moreover, if the right is exercised, the appellant knows nothing of the case against him, because he does not know why the original adverse decision was taken). There is therefore a strong argument in favour of giving reasons *before* appellate proceedings are launched. Against this background, Craig [1994] *CLJ* 282 at 287 writes that, 'What has always been something of a mystery is why the same reasoning should not be equally applicable to review, as opposed to appeal.' This omission was addressed by the House of Lords in *Doody*, the importance of which is explained in the following terms by Craig (*ibid* at 288–289); after citing the final paragraph from the extract from Lord Mustill's speech which appears above at 12.3.1, he writes:

Lord Mustill clearly regarded this rationale for the existence of a right to some form of reasons for the decision as an exception to the basic principle that there is no such right to reasons at common law. Yet it is difficult to see why the argument put forcefully by his Lordship would not apply in a great many cases concerning judicial review. In many such instances an "effective attack" on the decision which is being challenged will require some reasons in order to determine whether "the decision-making process has gone astray". This is particularly so given the variety of grounds on which it can be alleged that a public body acted illegally or irrationally. It may, for example, be extremely difficult to determine whether a public body really did act for improper purposes or on irrelevant considerations unless the applicant can have access to the reasons which prompted the decision. Such access may well be all the more important given that the initial decision may well have been made within the confines of "bounded rationality", in circumstances where the decision-maker possessed limited information and limited time within which to process the information. The presence of reasons may be equally important in the context of developing doctrines such as proportionality, which necessitate an inquiry into the reasons for the impugned action as part of the process of deciding whether it was or was not proportionate in the circumstances.

Craig's point is that the approach in *Doody* could logically be extended to many, if not most, situations in which an administrative decision is potentially open to judicial review: indeed he notes (*ibid* at 289) that the 'exception' set out in *Doody* 'is in danger of undermining the very generality of the original principle' that reasons are not usually required. More recently the Privy Council, in *Stefan* v. *General Medical Council* [1999] 1 WLR 1293 at 1301 (see below at 12.4.3), also countenanced the possibility that reason-giving is becoming the norm rather than the exception.

12.3.3 A 'Unitary' Test

However, *Doody* has not been subsequently interpreted in quite such an expansive manner. In the following case (noted by Allan [1994] *CLJ* 207) which was decided shortly after *Doody*, the Divisional Court attempted to synthesize the law on reason-giving, concluding that the existence (or otherwise) of a duty to give reasons is to be determined by reference to a 'unitary' test which requires consideration of a range of factors.

....

R v. *Higher Education Funding Council, ex parte Institute of Dental Surgery* [1994] 1 WLR 242
Divisional Court

The Higher Education Funding Council (HEFC) for England assessed, by using panels of academics conducting peer reviews, the quality of research produced by various institutions. The Institute of Dental Surgery was graded at point 2 (having previously been graded at point 3) on a 1–5 scale, resulting in a substantial reduction in research funding. The Institute was informed by the HEFC how the assessment had been carried out, but no reasons were given for the final decision as to grading. The Institute sought judicial review.

Sedley J (giving the judgment of the court)

. . . We readily accept Mr. Beloff's [counsel for the defendant] submission that Lord Mustill was not holding, in the final part of this passage [*viz* the first four sentences of the final paragraph of the extract from *Doody* above at 12.3.1], that reasons are called for wherever it is desired to know whether grounds for challenge exist; for to do so would be to create just such a general duty as Lord Mustill at the start of the passage was careful to exclude. Rather he was holding that in the situation of near-total ignorance and impotence in which the prisoner found himself about some-thing as vital to him as his prospects of liberty, such a duty arose. It follows nonetheless from Lord Mustill's reasoning that the "more familiar route" exemplified by *Ex parte Cunningham* [1992] I.C.R. 816 may be broader than the *Cunningham* situation alone and capable of embracing other situ-ations in which "it is important that there should be an effective means of detecting the kind of error which would entitle the court to intervene." This being so, it seems both desirable and practical to test by a common standard both the fairness of not telling a person the reasons for a decision affecting him and the desirability of exposing any grounds of legal challenge. There are, moreover, reasons of principle for a unitary test. As the judgments in *Ex parte Cunningham* show, one aspect of unfairness may be precisely the inability to know whether an error of law or of process has occurred. But since the latter is not a freestanding ground for requiring reasons (for if it were, it would apply universally), it can only be on grounds of fairness that it will arise; so that the need to know whether there has been an error of law or of process is rightly seen not as an alternative to the demands of fairness but as an aspect of them. This approach places on an even footing the multiple grounds on which the giving of reasons may in any one case be requisite. The giving of reasons may among other things concentrate the decision-maker's mind on the right questions;

demonstrate to the recipient that this is so; show that the issues have been conscientiously addressed and how the result has been reached; or alternatively alert the recipient to a justiciable flaw in the process. On the other side of the argument, it may place an undue burden on decision-makers; demand an appearance of unanimity where there is diversity; call for the articulation of sometimes inexpressible value judgments; and offer an invitation to the captious to comb the reasons for previously unsuspected grounds of challenge. It is the relationship of these and other material considerations to the nature of the particular decision which will determine whether or not fairness demands reasons.

In the light of such factors each case will come to rest between two poles, or possibly at one of them: the decision which cries out for reasons, and the decision for which reasons are entirely inapposite. Somewhere between the two poles comes the dividing line separating those cases in which the balance of factors calls for reasons from those where it does not. At present there is no sure indication of where the division comes . . . [and] this court cannot go beyond the proposition that, there being no general obligation to give reasons, there will be decisions for which fairness does not demand reasons . . .

[After considering questions of relief and reiterating the point that the interest in knowing whether the decision-making process is flawed cannot, independently of other contextual factors, generate a duty to give reasons, Sedley J, addressing the importance of the decision as a criterion relevant to the existence of a reason-giving duty, continued:] The chief benchmark of significance which we have at present in this setting is the *Doody* case . . . There the applicant knew the evidence on which he had been convicted but little else, while a considerable body of highly relevant matter had accumulated in the hands of the decision-maker and was going to affect many years of his liberty. If the Home Secretary were then to depart from the judicial view of tariff, it is not easy to think of a stronger case for the disclosure of reasons not merely to the applicant but to all mandatory life sentence prisoners, to each of whom result of the case will necessarily apply. Equally here the argument, it seems to us, must be good for all applicants, not just disappointed ones, if they want to know why they have been rated as they have been. One would like to be able to hold that for all such applicants, disappointed or not, the importance of the decision alone was enough. But to do so would generalise the duty to give reasons to a point to which this court, at least, cannot go.

We must therefore look also at the other indicia: the openness of the procedure, widely canvassed in advance and published in circular form; the voluntary submission of self-selected examples of work; the judgment of academic peers. These, it seems to us, shift the process substantially away from the pole represented by *Ex parte Doody*, not on mere grounds of dissimilarity (there will be many dissimilar cases in which reasons are nevertheless now required) but because the nature of the exercise was that it was open in all but its critical phase, and its critical phase was one in which, as Professor Davies [chief executive of the Universities Funding Council, HEFC's predecessor] deposes, "the grade awarded to a particular institution was not determined by a score against specific features." We . . . find [this] remarkable, but it is a fact and not one which Mr. Pannick [for the claimant] has been able to assault on legal grounds. In the result, the combination of openness in the run-up with the prescriptively oracular character of the critical decision makes the council's allocation of grades inapt, in our judgment, for the giving of reasons, notwithstanding the undoubted importance of the outcome to the institutions concerned.

From this case-specific conclusion, it is possible to generalise to a certain extent. The only mystery left in the process is precisely why the final grade of 2 was arrived at. As Mr. Pannick points out, the evidence is replete with answers to the question how it was arrived at, but not why. The question "why," in isolation as it can now be seen to be, is a question of academic judgment. We would hold that where what is sought to be impugned is on the evidence *no more* than an informed exercise of academic judgment, fairness alone will not require reasons to be given. This is not to say for a moment that academic decisions are beyond challenge. A mark, for example, awarded at an examiners' meeting where irrelevant and damaging personal factors have been allowed to enter into the evaluation of a candidate's written paper is something more than an informed exercise of academic judgment. Where evidence shows that something extraneous has entered into the process of academic judgment, one of two results may follow depending on the nature of the fault: either the decision will fall without more, or the court may require reasons to be given, so that the decision can either be seen to be sound or can be seen or (absent reasons) be inferred to be flawed. But purely academic judgments, in our view, will as a rule not be in the class of case exemplified, though by no means exhausted, by *Ex parte Doody*, where the nature and impact of the decision itself call for reasons as a routine aspect of procedural fairness. They will be in the *Ex parte Cunningham* [1992] I.C.R. 816 class where some trigger factor is required to show, that, in the circumstances of the particular decision, fairness calls for reasons to be given.

Is there then such a trigger factor here? The second limb of Mr. Pannick's submission is that the applicant has been confronted with a decision which, on the evidence, is inexplicable: the applicant's excellence is widely acknowledged and attested; its original rating of 2.6 would have qualified for rounding up to a 3; and the reduction to 2.4 and hence to a rating of 2 followed reconsideration in circumstances which, at the lowest, can be regarded as unsatisfactory. Mr. Beloff responds, and we agree with him, that neither intrinsically nor on the evidence is there a sufficient basis on which this court can hold the eventual rating to be so aberrant as in itself to call for an explanation. We lack precisely the expertise which would permit us to judge whether it is extraordinary or not. It may be misfortune for the applicant that the court, which in *Ex parte Cunningham* [1992] I.C.R. 816 could readily evaluate the contrast between what the board awarded and what an industrial tribunal would have awarded, cannot begin to evaluate the comparative worth of research in clinical dentistry; but it is a fact of life. The applicant's previous grading, the volume and frequency of citation of its research and the high level of peer-reviewed outside funding which it has attracted, to all of which Mr. Pannick points, may well demonstrate that the applicant has been unfortunate in the grading it has received, but such a misfortune can well occur within the four corners of a lawfully conducted evaluation . . .

In summary, then: (1) there is no general duty to give reasons for a decision, but there are classes of case where there is such a duty. (2) One such class is where the subject matter is an interest so highly regarded by the law (for example, personal liberty), that fairness requires that reasons, at least for particular decisions, be given as of right. (3) (a) Another such class is where the decision appears aberrant. Here fairness may require reasons so that the recipient may know whether the aberration is in the legal sense real (and so challengeable) or apparent; (b) it follows that this class does not include decisions which are themselves challengeable by reference only to the reasons for them. A pure exercise of academic judgment is such a decision. And (c) procedurally, the grant of leave in such cases will depend upon prima facie evidence that something has gone wrong. The respondent may then seek to demonstrate that it is not so and that the decision is an unalloyed exercise of an intrinsically unchallengeable judgment. If the respondent succeeds, the application fails. If the respondent fails, relief may take the form of an order of mandamus to give reasons, or (if a justiciable flaw has been established) other appropriate relief . . .

The claimant's challenge was rejected, and the HEFC was not required to supply reasons for its decision.

The deference of the court to questions of academic judgment assumed particular importance in this case because the court treated it as a *Cunningham*-type case: only if the decision to award a grade 2 could be characterized as 'aberrant' would the reason-giving duty be triggered, yet the court felt institutionally incompetent to determine whether the grade was extraordinary. The outcome would presumably have been different if the court had been willing to acknowledge that the enormous importance to the Institute of the grade — in terms of both its financial position and institutional morale — equated to an impact on an interest more highly regarded by law, thus making the case analogous to *Doody*. It is interesting that Sedley LJ recently suggested in *R (Wooder)* v. *Feggetter* [2002] EWCA Civ 554 [2003] QB 219 at [41] that *HEFC* 'would [not] necessarily be decided in the same way today'; Brooke LJ, at [23], agreed.

Although the summary given in the final paragraph of the *HEFC* excerpt above is helpful, too much emphasis should not be placed on the various categories of cases which Sedley J identifies; as he pointed out in *R* v. *University of Cambridge, ex parte Evans* [1998] ELR 515 at 521, those categories are not closed. Reading the *HEFC* judgment as a whole, it is clear that the court's intention was to underscore the point made by Lord Mustill in *Doody* that, ultimately, whether reasons must be given turns upon whether fairness so requires. The factors identified in the *HEFC* case are therefore best regarded as useful indicators of what fairness requires, in terms of reasons, in a given situation. This point is usefully illustrated by *R* v. *Ministry of Defence, ex parte Murray* [1998] COD 134. The reviewing court held that a Court-Martial was required to give reasons for imposing a severe sentence on an officer of good character and for rejecting his argument that his impugned behaviour was attributable (at least in part) to anti-malarial medication. It is clear that the court was influenced by both the seriousness of the matter, since the sentence imposed had the effect of ending the claimant's military career, and the (consequent) importance to the claimant of discovering whether any reviewable errors had occurred.

It is also clear that fairness may require the giving of reasons even if the interests affected by the decision are not as fundamental as liberty or livelihood, as the Court of Appeal's decision in *R* v. *City of London Corporation, ex parte Matson* [1997] 1 WLR 765 demonstrates. The claimant had been elected — through a procedure recognized as a 'local government election' by the Representation of the People Act 1983, s 191(1) — an alderman of the City of London, but the Court of Aldermen, which has a customary right to decide whether to confirm such elections, refused to do so. The claimant, concerned that the Court had been influenced by allegations of misconduct which he had attempted to rebut, sought judicial review. The Court of Appeal decided that the Court of Aldermen ought to have given reasons for its decision. As is apparent from the following extract from Neill LJ's judgment (at 776–777) the factors underlying this conclusion are varied, and as well as the fact that an important interest (*viz* reputation) was affected, the public character of the matter and the claimant's practical need to know — for purposes both of challenging the original decision and deciding whether to submit himself to election again — also weighed heavily on the court:

. . . I am persuaded that fairness and natural justice require that this decision should not be allowed to go unexplained. I have been led to this conclusion by the following considerations. (1) Mr. Matson was standing for public office and wished to serve his constituents and the City of London in that office. (2) Mr. Matson was elected by the voters at a wardmote by a substantial majority and by an electoral process recognised by section 191(1) of the Representation of the People Act 1983. (3) The second stage of the election involved a decision by the Court of Aldermen which is a court of record. (4) The decision of the court was announced in public and is a matter of public record. (5) During the course of the private interview questions were put to Mr. Matson which suggested that he had acted in an inappropriate manner. He has no means of knowing whether the court accepted his explanation. As McCowan L.J. pointed out in *Reg. v. Civil Service Appeal Board, Ex parte Cunningham* [1992] I.C.R. 816, 830H, in the absence of reasons a person in Mr. Matson's position will not know whether his submissions have been rejected or not. (6) The basis for the court's decision *may* have been that Mr. Matson lacked the necessary positive qualities for the office. On the other hand the court, or some members of it, *may* have been dissatisfied with his answers to some particular questions or as to his experience of or commitment to the City. (7) In the absence of any reasons neither Mr. Matson nor the electors can know whether he should stand again or whether, if re-elected . . ., he should supply additional information to the court. The cost and time involved in a further election is not inconsiderable. It is also to be remembered that if an alderman-elect is rejected three times in succession the Court of Aldermen is empowered to nominate and elect some other person to the office. (8) The public rejection of Mr. Matson is bound to cast a shadow on his reputation. It may be that through no fault of his he lacks those special qualities which the office of alderman demands. On the other hand his rejection may be interpreted as meaning that there is a black mark against him. (9) The giving of short reasons will not frustrate or impede the exercise by the court of its customary powers. On the contrary the articulation of short reasons will enable the court to ensure that their decisions in every case are sound and manifestly just and in the interests of the city.

A distinct point was dealt with by Swinton Thomas LJ at 783, concerning the suggestion that it would be difficult to articulate reasons for the decision:

Mr. Sullivan [counsel for the City of London] puts forward as an objection to the giving of reasons the difficulty of articulating them. He says that the reasons may be based on factual matters or an assessment of the character and personality of the alderman-elect, or a combination of the two. When objections are based on character or personality, Mr. Sullivan submits that it may be difficult to articulate the general view. It may be based on value judgments. There are 24 aldermen engaged in the process. They may have a variety of views, and there may be difficulty in expressing the view of the aldermen as a body . . . Mr. Sullivan submitted that to require the aldermen to give reasons for their decision would require them to articulate "inexpressible value judgments." I do not accept that argument. I do not believe that it would be unduly difficult or arduous for the aldermen to give a collective reason for their decision. True it is that individual members may have considered differing factors. That is likely to apply to any collective decision. There is no difficulty in articulating a factual basis for a decision. If I am right in my conclusion that the aldermen are entitled to take into account their assessment of the alderman-elect's character and personality then, equally, I do not believe that any adverse assessment involves the articulation of inexpressible value judgments. Assessments of that nature are made day in, day out, in every walk of life.

QUESTIONS

- Can the approach of Swinton Thomas LJ in *Matson* be reconciled with that of Sedley J in *HEFC* (though note the later comments of Sedley LJ mentioned above)?
- Why were the value judgments as to character in the former capable of being the subject of reasons, while the academic judgment exercised in the latter case was incapable of being reduced to reasons?

It is clear from the cases considered in this section that, in line with *Doody*, the question whether reasons must be given cannot always be answered by reference to a single criterion. Instead, a range of factors may need to be taken into account in order to determine whether fairness requires the giving of reasons. Until or unless the law recognizes a general duty to give reasons, the most the courts can do — as they have attempted to do in the cases considered above — is to identify those factors which are particularly important in deciding whether or not fairness requires the giving of reasons.

12.3.4 Reason-Giving and Legitimate Expectation

Before leaving the topic of reason-giving at common law, it is necessary briefly to address one further factor which can help to determine whether reasons must be supplied. We have already seen (above at 11.2.3) that the doctrine of legitimate expectation is capable of entitling individuals to fair treatment in circumstances where no such entitlement would otherwise arise, or alternatively of enhancing the procedural safeguards which are applicable. It is clear, therefore, that circumstances may arise in which the statements or conduct of a decision-maker may give rise to a legitimate expectation that it will furnish reasons for its decisions — a possibility acknowledged by Jowitt J in *R v. Secretary of State for Transport, ex parte Richmond-upon-Thames London Borough Council (No 4)* [1996] 1 WLR 1005 at 1020 and discussed by Craig [1994] *CLJ* 282 at 292–294.

As well as requiring reasons when an express or implied undertaking is made to the effect that reasons will be given, the principle of legitimate expectation may require reason-giving more broadly (see, *eg, R (Bibi)* v. *Newham London Borough Council* [2001] EWCA Civ 607 [2002] 1 WLR 237 at [59]). For instance, where a legitimate expectation as to substance has arisen, reasons may need to be furnished either to the individual (in circumstances where it is possible for the authority to frustrate the expectation provided, for example, that the individual has been consulted — something which can only meaningfully occur if reasons are given) or the court (if, as in *R v. North and East Devon Health Authority, ex parte Coughlan* [2001] QB 213 (see above at 7.1.5), the expectation can only be lawfully frustrated if the court is satisfied as to the necessity of such a course of action).

12.4 Statutory and Other Duties to Give Reasons

12.4.1 Introduction

In addition to the emerging common law duty, reason-giving is also required in particular contexts by a number of legislative provisions. The broadest statutory duty to give reasons is imposed by s 10 of the Tribunals and Inquiries Act 1992 which applies to the decisions of certain tribunals and certain ministerial decisions made after a statutory inquiry has been held (or in circumstances in which such an inquiry could have been required); for discussion, see below at 19.3.5. This obligation does not, however, impinge upon decision-making by other public bodies or by Ministers acting outside the context of statutory inquiries. In addition to express statutory duties to give reasons, a duty 'may arise through construction of the statutory provisions as a matter of implied intention' (*Stefan* v. *General Medical Council* [1999] 1 WLR 1293 at 1297, *per* Lord Clyde).

12.4.2 The Freedom of Information Act 2000

The Freedom of Information Act 2000 (for a detailed account of which see Birkinshaw, *Freedom of Information: The Law, the Practice and the Ideal* (London 2001), ch 6) entered fully into force in January 2005, the long delay between enactment and implementation being accounted for by the need to allow time for public authorities to ready themselves for the new culture of openness and transparency which the Act may appear to presage. Indeed, an ambitious and liberal approach to open government was originally promised shortly after the election of the Labour government in 1997 in its White Paper Cm 3818, *Your Right to Know*. However, after considerable delay — and vigorous debate within government — a draft Freedom of Information Bill was published in 1999 which disclosed rather less enthusiasm for transparency, and the resultant Act is much more conservative than the scheme originally envisaged by the White Paper.

Section 1 of the Act entitles a person who requests information from a public authority (a term which is broadly defined in sch 1) to be told whether it holds the information and, if so, to have the information communicated to him. Importantly, however, this right to information is substantially qualified by the wide range of exemptions set out in Part II. Section 2 provides that some of these exemptions are absolute (such as information supplied by, or relating to, bodies dealing with security matters; court records; and matters covered by parliamentary privilege) while other types of information (relating to such matters as defence; international relations; relations between UK national administrations; the economy; and law enforcement) are protected against disclosure only if the public interest in maintaining the exemption outweighs the public interest in disclosure. In addition to the reactive duty to disclose under s 1, public authorities are fixed by s 19 with a proactive duty to publish certain types of information.

This regime can be criticized on a number of grounds. First, the *number of exemptions* is considerable, and heavily circumscribes the right to information conferred by s 1. Secondly, the *nature of the exemptions* is contentious: many confer absolute exemption on classes of information, without regard to whether disclosure of the specific information in question would be damaging. Thirdly, even in relation to information which is exempt only if its disclosure would cause harm, the operative *test of harm* is relatively weak: it need only be shown that it is likely that prejudice (rather than, say, substantial prejudice) would be caused to the relevant interest. Fourthly, information to which the prejudice test applies can only thereby be rendered *prima facie* exempt, whereupon the s 2 balancing of interests test falls to be applied. However, Cornford [2001] 3 *Web JCLI* observes that the *s 2 public interest test* is itself highly problematic. Although it permits non-disclosure only if the public interest in maintaining the exemption outweighs the public interest in disclosure, the public interests in maintaining the exemption and in disclosure are presented as equally important; there is, therefore, no presumption in favour of disclosure under this test — a position that seems to sit uncomfortably within a 'freedom of information' regime. Fifthly, the *content of some exemptions* is controversial. In particular, ss 35 and 36 confer protection on (*inter alia*) information concerning the formulation and development of government policy and ministerial communications, and information whose disclosure would, or would be likely to, prejudice the maintenance of collective responsibility or the free and frank exchange of views within and the provision of advice to government. These provisions are felt by some writers fundamentally to contradict the spirit of a freedom of information regime by preserving the tradition of secrecy which has become the hallmark of governance in the UK.

If a public authority refuses to disclose information which has been requested, s 17 requires it to give reasons for this refusal, and the person who requested the information may ultimately complain to the Information Commissioner under s 50. If the Commissioner, having investigated the matter, finds that information has been withheld contrary to the Act, he issues a decision notice, specifying the steps to be taken by the public authority and the timeframe within which they must be taken. Where the Commissioner becomes satisfied independently of any complaint that information has been improperly withheld, he may issue an enforcement notice under s 52 requiring appropriate steps to be taken by the public body concerned. Failure to comply with a decision or enforcement notice may be referred to the High Court under s 54, and the matter can then be dealt with as if it were a contempt of court. However, the powers of the Commissioner are limited by s 53, the effect of which is to allow senior government Ministers to cancel decision or enforcement notices issued by the Commissioner in relation to government departments and public authorities designated by the Secretary of State. This power — which arises only if such a Minister is satisfied on reasonable grounds that the Act does not require disclosure of the information — effectively makes these Ministers the final judge of where the balance of public interest lies in those situations to which s 53 applies. However, reasons must be given to the complainant for s 53 decisions and there is no reason in principle why such decisions should not be amenable to judicial review. Moreover, the Information Commissioner has signalled his 'intention, on each occasion that a certificate is issued, to make a Special Report to Parliament' indicating whether he considers it 'appropriate for a certificate to have been issued' (HC669, *Annual Report* (2003–2004) at 13).

How does the Freedom of Information Act relate to the limited common law duty to give reasons for decisions? Clearly, both the Act and the duty to give reasons spring from a wider philosophy about transparency and openness in government. On a more pragmatic level, however, to what extent does the Act advance the duty to give reasons for administrative decisions? There will certainly be circumstances in which the giving of reasons will be enforceable under the Act; but those circumstances will be somewhat limited on two accounts. First, as we have seen, the ability to obtain information under the Act is heavily circumscribed by the exemptions set out in Part II. Secondly, and more fundamentally, s 1 of the Act entitles individuals to 'information': although there is nothing to suggest that reasons for a decision may not constitute 'information', ss 1(4) and 84 respectively provide that the Act only covers information which is 'held [by the public authority] at the time when the request is received' and which is 'recorded in any form'. This means that unless reasons have been formulated and recorded prior to the request for disclosure, no 'information' in the statutory sense exists. It follows that, while the Act imposes a duty (qualified by the exemptions) to disclose reasons which have been formulated and recorded, it imposes no duty to formulate or record reasons in the first place. Nevertheless, the Act will allow prospective claimants for judicial review to obtain factual information upon which administrative decisions have been based, which may allow inferences to be drawn as to likely reasons and as to whether any grounds for judicial review exist.

12.4.3 Article 6 ECHR

In considering the circumstances in which a decision-maker may be required to give reasons it is also necessary to address the impact of the European Convention on Human Rights. It is well-established that Article 6(1) requires the giving of reasons. As the European Court of Human Rights put it in *Hadjianastassiou v. Greece* (1993) 16 EHRR 219 at 237, courts must 'indicate with sufficient clarity the grounds on which they based their decision'. The general principle, therefore, is that where administrative decisions are caught by Article 6(1) (on which see above at 10.5.2), a duty to give reasons arises automatically. In *Stefan v. General Medical Council* [1999] 1 WLR 1293, a case decided shortly before the entry into force of the Human Rights Act 1998, the Privy Council suggested that the apparently clearer position under the ECHR might prompt reconsideration of domestic law in this area. Referring to the common law orthodoxy that there is no general duty to give reasons, Lord Clyde said (at 1301):

There is certainly a strong argument for the view that what were once seen as exceptions to a rule may now be becoming examples of the norm, and the cases where reasons are not required may be taking on the appearance of exceptions. But the general rule has not been departed from and their Lordships do not consider that the present case provides an appropriate opportunity to explore the possibility of such a departure. They are conscious of the possible re-appraisal of the whole position which the passing of the Human Rights Act 1998 may bring about. The provisions of article 6(1) of the Convention on Human Rights, which are now about to become directly accessible in national courts, will require closer attention to be paid to the duty to give reasons, at least in relation to those cases where a person's civil rights and obligations are being determined. But it is in the context of the application of that Act that any wide-reaching review of the position at common law should take place.

However, although a clear duty to give reasons arises *when Article 6(1) applies*, this qualification is, for two reasons, a significant one. First, we have already seen (above at 10.5.2) that the scope of Article 6(1) is itself extremely unclear, and so, therefore, is the scope of the reason-giving duty arising thereunder. Secondly, Article 6(1) applies to, and therefore imposes a duty to give reasons in, a much narrower range of administrative contexts than the common law. As Sedley LJ recognized in *R (Wooder) v. Feggetter* [2002] EWCA Civ 554 [2003] QB 219 at [46], 'the common law sets high standards of due process in non-judicial settings to which the European Court of Human Rights at Strasbourg declines to apply article 6' and in which claimants can therefore 'derive better protection from the common law than from the Convention'.

Finally, it should be noted that the duty to give reasons under Article 6(1) is qualified by the curative principle. We saw above (at 10.5.3) that such breaches of Article 6(1) as a lack of impartiality on the part of the original decision-maker may be cured by appeal to or judicial review by an independent court of full jurisdiction. In *Stefan*, at 1300, Lord Clyde affirmed that this principle extends to a failure to give reasons at first instance:

. . . [T]he existence of a right of appeal may, if it be sufficient for the purpose, enable the requirement of fairness embodied in article 6(1) to be met. The obligation on the court may remain to state reasons but a breach of the requirement of fairness embodied in article 6(1) may be obviated by the sufficiency of a right of appeal. On this approach a failure to give reasons may not be fatal to the validity of the decision.

However, this conclusion raises a curious paradox. The ECtHR recognizes that it is the giving of reasons 'which makes it possible for the accused to exercise usefully the rights of appeal' — or, by analogy, to exploit the possibility of judicial review — 'available to him' (*Hadjianastassiou v. Greece* (1993) 16 EHRR 219 at 237). Yet the application of the curative principle to a failure to give reasons has the effect of sanctioning such a failure by reference to the curative effect of an appeal which, applying the logic of the former argument, will be less valuable to the individual precisely because reasons were not disclosed at first instance. In *Stefan*, Lord Clyde (at 1300) affirmed that, the curative principle notwithstanding, 'the consideration that the reasons are useful to enable the prosecution of the right of appeal still remains valid', and thus appeared to acknowledge the problem raised by this position.

12.5 Implications of the Duty to Give Reasons

Having examined the circumstances in which a duty to give reasons arises, it remains to consider the implications which attend the imposition of such a duty. The first question which arises concerns the nature of the duty: if 'reasons' are required, what exactly does this mean? As is usual in the context of procedural fairness, much depends on the circumstances (see, *eg, Helle v. Finland* (1997) 26 EHRR 159 at 183 and *Stefan v. General Medical Council* [1999] 1 WLR 1293 at 1301 and 1304). Although relating to a specific duty arising under planning regulations, Lord Brown's remarks in *South Buckinghamshire District Council v. Porter* [2004] UKHL 33 [2004] 1 WLR 1953 at [36] are of wider significance, and usefully indicate how the content of a reason-giving duty falls to be determined:

The reasons for a decision must be intelligible and they must be adequate. They must enable the reader to understand why the matter was decided as it was and what conclusions were reached on the "principal important controversial issues" [*Hope v. Secretary of State for the Environment* (1975) 31 P&CR 120 at 123, *per* Phillips J], disclosing how any issue of law or fact was resolved. Reasons can be briefly stated, the degree of particularity required depending entirely on the nature of the issues falling for decision. The reasoning must not give rise to a substantial doubt as to whether the decision-maker erred in law, for example by misunderstanding some relevant policy or some other important matter or by failing to reach a rational decision on relevant grounds. But such adverse inference will not readily be drawn. The reasons need refer only to the main issues in the dispute, not to every material consideration. They should enable disappointed developers to assess their prospects of obtaining some alternative development permission, or, as the case may be, their unsuccessful opponents to understand how the policy or approach underlying the grant of permission may impact upon future such applications.

Although the growing *scope* of the duty to give reasons evidences an increasingly sceptical judicial view of the traditional contention that requiring reasons places an intolerable burden on decision-makers, such concerns remain potent in relation to the *content* of the duty. For instance, in *R (Asha Foundation) v. Millenium Commission* [2003] EWCA Civ 88, the defendant, in turning down the claimant's application for National Lottery funding for a museum, simply told the claimant that its application had been 'less attractive than others'.

The Court of Appeal held that nothing further was necessary, for reasons set out by Lord Woolf CJ at [29]:

When the Commission is engaged in assessing the qualities of the different applications which were before them in competition with each other, the difficulties which would be involved in giving detailed reasons become clear. First, the preference for a particular application may not be the same in the case of each commissioner. Secondly, in order to evaluate any reasons that are given for preferring one application to another, the full nature and detail of both applications has to be known. If the Commission were to be required to do what [counsel] submits was their obligation here, the Commission would have had to set out in detail each commissioner's views in relation to each of the applications and to provide the background material to Asha so that they could assess whether those conclusions were appropriate. This would be an undue burden upon any commission. It would make their task almost impossible.

A further factor which will influence the content of the duty to give reasons in a particular situation is the purpose underlying the duty. For instance, if the court locates the objective of reason-giving in the need to allow the individual to understand why the decision has been made, this may imply a quite straightforward duty to 'tell the parties in broad terms why they lost or, as the case may be, won' (*Union of Construction and Allied Trades Technicians* v. *Brain* [1981] IRLR 225 at 228, *per* Lord Donaldson MR). In contrast, as Fordham [1998] *JR* 158 at 163–164 explains, if the underlying purpose of reason-giving is viewed differently — for example, as a discipline to ensure that decision-making occurs thoroughly and lawfully — then the duty to give reasons becomes more onerous and should logically address the decision-making process as well as the conclusions reached by the agency:

. . . [I]t is surely in conducting the *reasoning* process (e.g. in identifying [relevant considerations]), and not merely in reaching the principal conclusions, that the decision-maker's mind is to be focussed. The decision-maker needs to be disciplined in addressing questions, not just arriving at answers. A word of caution though. The reality may be that the present low threshold of adequacy [of reasons] is the price of easing the passing of a more general, common law duty to give reasons. After all, a general public law obligation to articulate principal conclusions is surely not too much to ask.

QUESTION

- Do you agree that a *light* duty to give reasons is a price worth paying for a relatively *extensive* duty?

The relief which is granted for breach of a duty to give reasons should be similarly affected by the purpose underlying the duty. If reason-giving serves to inform citizens about why decisions affecting them have been made in a particular way, then a mandatory order, requiring the giving of reasons, is the remedy which would naturally lie for breach of the duty. This view was adopted by Sedley J in the *HEFC* case ([1994] 1 WLR 242 at 263). However, Fordham [1998] *JR* 158 at 160 argues that if the duty to give reasons exists to encourage a disciplined approach to decision-making, then decisions which are unaccompanied by reasons should be quashed. This follows because the provision of reasons in response to a mandatory order may merely constitute *ex post facto* rationalization which does not demonstrably ensure that the decision was taken correctly in the first place. It appears that the logic of this argument has been accepted by the courts in cases such as *R* v. *City of London Corporation, ex parte Matson* [1997] 1 WLR 765: in that case a decision was quashed for lack of reasons, not because this led to an inference of irrationality (on which see above at 12.1), but because the need for reasons constituted an independent legal requirement, breach of which invalidated the decision.

12.6 Concluding Remarks

Giving reasons for decisions should be treated as a central facet of procedural fairness in administrative law. This follows both for practical reasons — in order, for instance, that individuals may know whether it is worth appealing or seeking judicial review — and for normative reasons that spring from a conception of the relationship between the citizen and the state according to which the latter should treat the former with respect, and as a participant in the process of governance. Constructing the relationship in that manner is important not only because it recognizes the dignity of the individual, but also because it promotes a trust between citizens and public authorities that, in turn, acts as a springboard for co-operation between them. Against this background, it is heartening that, as the developing case law mapped in this chapter attests, English law now takes seriously the duty to give reasons for administrative decisions, and views with increasing scepticism the hackneyed and largely specious argument that forcing decision-makers to give reasons imposes an intolerable burden upon them. Of course, there will be some circumstances in which that argument holds water, or in which other factors point towards the inappropriateness of reason-giving. Those situations, however, are the exceptions, and it is therefore to be hoped that it is only a matter of time before English law unequivocally acknowledges a general duty to give reasons, subject to such qualifications as are necessary to accommodate the exceptional situations where reason-giving would be not be appropriate.

FURTHER RESOURCES

Birkinshaw, *Freedom of Information: The Law, the Practice and the Ideal* (London 2001)

Craig, 'The Common Law, Reasons and Administrative Justice' [1994] *CLJ* 282

Fordham, 'Reasons: The Third Dimension' [1998] *JR* 158

Forsyth and Hare (eds), *The Golden Metwand and the Crooked Cord* (Oxford 1998) at 161–184 (Neill)

Justice-All Souls Committee, *Administrative Justice: Some Necessary Reforms* (Oxford 1988), ch 3

Toube, 'Requiring Reasons at Common Law' [1997] *JR* 68

Web site of the Information Commissioner *www.informationcommissioner.gov.uk*

 REMEDIES

13.1 Introduction

Having considered, in earlier chapters, the grounds on which administrative action may be found to be unlawful, it is now necessary to address the relief which may be granted in respect of such action. We begin, in this chapter, with the remedies themselves. We then move on to consider, in chs 14 and 15 respectively, the special procedure which must usually be used in order to challenge the legality of administrative action and various restrictions faced by claimants who seek relief in respect of what is contended to be unlawful administrative action. Leaving aside, for the time being, the possibility of damages — which is addressed in ch 16 — a number of remedies need to be considered in the present context.

Supreme Court Act 1981

31—(1) An application to the High Court for one or more of the following forms of relief, namely—
    (a) a mandatory, prohibiting, or quashing order;
    (b) a declaration or injunction under subsection (2); or
    (c) an injunction under section 30 restraining a person not entitled to do so from acting in an office to which that section applies,
shall be made in accordance with rules of court by a procedure to be known as an application for judicial review.
  (2) A declaration may be made or an injunction granted under this subsection in any case where an application for judicial review, seeking that relief, has been made and the High Court considers that, having regard to—
    (a) the nature of the matters in respect of which relief may be granted by mandatory, prohibiting or quashing orders;
    (b) the nature of the persons and bodies against whom relief may be granted by such orders; and
    (c) all the circumstances of the case,
it would be just and convenient for the declaration to be made or the injunction to be granted, as the case may be.

It should be noted that new terminology (which is used throughout this book) was introduced in 2000 by the Civil Procedure Rules Part 54, r 1, and the Supreme Court Act 1981, s 31 was amended in 2004 to reflect these changes. Thus '*mandamus*' became 'mandatory order'; '*prohibition*' became 'prohibiting order', and '*certiorari*' became 'quashing order'. Meanwhile, although the phrase 'application for judicial review' — the special procedure which should generally be used to challenge the legality of administrative action (on which see ch 14 below) — is still used by the Act, the CPR (and this book) refer to the 'claim for judicial review'.

Until 1977, ordinary remedies — that is, injunctions and declarations — and prerogative remedies — mandatory, prohibiting, and quashing orders — could not be sought in the same proceedings. While the former were available in ordinary proceedings, a different procedure applied to the latter; it was therefore impossible to seek both types of relief in the same proceedings. This problem was largely resolved by the procedural reforms of 1977 (considered in detail below in ch 14) which introduced the process known as the application for judicial review — the forerunner of the modern judicial review procedure governed by CPR Part 54. That special procedure must be used if prerogative remedies are sought (CPR 54.2), while ordinary remedies are now available both in ordinary proceedings and under the judicial review procedure (CPR 54.3(1)).

13.2 Injunctions

13.2.1 The Role of Injunctions in Public Law

Injunctions are used in private law to prevent the commission of unlawful acts, while mandatory injunctions lie to compel the performance of legal duties. Injunctions serve similar functions in public law by preventing public authorities from acting *ultra vires* or, in the case of mandatory injunctions, requiring them to make those decisions or perform those acts which are legally required of them. Although there is significant overlap with the prerogative remedies — indeed in *In re M* [1994] 1 AC 377 at 415 Lord Woolf said that prohibiting and mandatory orders 'are indistinguishable in their effect from final injunctions' — there is one crucial practical difference between the ordinary and prerogative remedies: while the latter are available only in final form, injunctions can also take effect as interlocutory, or interim, relief (see Supreme Court Act 1981, s 37(1) and CPR 25.1(1)(a)). (This is now true of declarations, too: see below at 13.3.2.) Interim relief permits the court temporarily to stabilize a situation pending final adjudication — a possibility which is particularly valuable if the defendant's proposed (and allegedly unlawful) action would, if actually undertaken, render meaningless final relief (*eg* a final injunction or quashing order) granted after the commission of the act in question. For example, a court may consider granting an interim injunction to prevent the deportation of an asylum-seeker pending final determination of the legality of the decision to deport (see *In re M* [1994] AC 377, considered below at 13.2.3).

It is convenient at this point to note the role of stays of proceedings. They are usually issued in order to halt proceedings before courts or tribunals. However, there is some uncertainty as to whether they may also be issued as a form of interim relief in respect of administrative action — *eg* to halt the implementation of an administrative decision pending final determination of its legality. In *R v. Secretary of State for Education and Science, ex parte Avon County Council* [1991] 1 QB 558 at 561–562 (which the Court of Appeal considered itself bound to follow on this point in *R (H) v. Ashworth Hospital Authority* [2002] EWCA Civ 923 [2003] 1 WLR 127 at [38]) Glidewell LJ, with whom Taylor LJ and Sir George

Waller agreed, took the view that stays *can* be issued to prevent the implementation of administrative decisions, a view that was, it seems, implicitly endorsed by the House of Lords in *In re M* [1994] AC 377. However, in *Ministry of Foreign Affairs, Trade and Industry* v. *Vehicle and Supplies Ltd* [1991] 1 WLR 550, the Privy Council confined stays to proceedings before a court or tribunal. This debate assumed particular relevance when it was thought that injunctions could not be issued against Ministers of the Crown acting in their official capacity; however, now that it has been established (see below at 13.2.3) that injunctive relief does lie against Ministers, the broad role ascribed to stays in *Avon* is of less practical importance. The narrower role accorded to stays in *Vehicle and Supplies* is also consistent with the definition offered in the Glossary to the CPR.

13.2.2 The Availability of Interim Injunctions

Although interim injunctions are highly beneficial from the point of view of claimants, they are very disadvantageous to defendants, whose freedom of action they curtail and to whom inconvenience and even financial loss may be occasioned. In light of this claimants in whose favour interim injunctions are granted are normally required to undertake to compensate the defendant for any losses suffered should the claimant lose at trial, a requirement from which the Crown as claimant is no longer automatically exempt (see *Hoffmann-La Roche and Co* v. *Secretary of State for Trade and Industry* [1975] AC 295). In spite of the 'insurance' which this type of undertaking provides, the court, in exercising its discretion (see above at 3.3.3) must consider carefully whether or not interim relief is appropriate — not least because it adversely affects the defendant before any final conclusion is reached that it is acting or is proposing to act unlawfully — although this certainly does not mean that interim relief can be resisted simply because it would cause difficulties for the defendant. This much was made clear by Lord Denning MR in *Bradbury* v. *Enfield London Borough Council* [1967] 1 WLR 1311 at 1324, a case in which interim relief was granted to prevent a reorganization of schools contrary to s 13 of the Education Act 1944:

Ought an injunction to be granted against the council? It has been suggested by the chief education officer that, if an injunction is granted, chaos will supervene. All the arrangements have been made for the next term, the teachers appointed to the new comprehensive schools, the pupils allotted their places, and so forth. It would be next to impossible, he says, to reverse all these arrangements without complete chaos and damage to teachers, pupils and the public.

I must say this: If a local authority does not fulfil the requirements of the law, this court will see that it does fulfil them. It will not listen readily to suggestions of "chaos." The Department of Education and the local education authority are subject to the rule of law and must comply with it, just like everyone else. Even if chaos should result, still the law must be obeyed. But I do not think that chaos will result.

The robustness of Lord Denning's view should not, however, be taken to mean that an interim injunction will be issued irrespective of its consequences. Indeed the need for a balance to be struck between the interests of the parties lies at the heart of the 'balance of convenience' test classically expounded by Lord Diplock in *American Cyanamid Co* v. *Ethicon Ltd* [1975] AC 396 at 406:

My Lords, when an application for an interlocutory injunction to restrain a defendant from doing acts alleged to be in violation of the plaintiff's legal right is made upon contested facts, the decision whether or not to grant an interlocutory injunction has to be taken at a time when ex hypothesi the existence of the right or the violation of it, or both, is uncertain and will remain uncertain until final judgment is given in the action. It was to mitigate the risk of injustice to the plaintiff during the period before that uncertainty could be resolved that the practice arose of granting him relief by way of interlocutory injunction; but since the middle of the 19th century this has been made subject to his undertaking to pay damages to the defendant for any loss sustained by reason of the injunction if it should be held at the trial that the plaintiff had not been entitled to restrain the defendant from doing what he was threatening to do. The object of the interlocutory injunction is to protect the plaintiff against injury by violation of his right for which he could not be adequately compensated in damages recoverable in the action if the uncertainty were resolved in his favour at the trial; but the plaintiff's need for such protection must be weighed against the corresponding need of the defendant to be protected against injury resulting from his having been prevented from exercising his own legal rights for which he could not be adequately compensated under the plaintiff's undertaking in damages if the uncertainty were resolved in the defendant's favour at the trial. The court must weigh one need against another and determine where "the balance of convenience" lies.

The general structure of the balance of convenience test and its applicability in a public law context were helpfully summarized by Lord Goff in *R* v. *Secretary of State for Transport, ex parte Factortame Ltd (No 2)* [1991] 1 AC 603 at 671–672:

. . . [A] prime purpose of the guidelines established in the *Cyanamid* case was to remove a fetter which appeared to have been imposed in certain previous cases, *viz*, that a party seeking an interlocutory injunction had to establish a prima facie case for substantive relief. It is now clear that it is enough if he can show that there is a serious case to be tried. If he can establish that, then he has, so to speak, crossed the threshold; and the court can then address itself to the question whether it is just or convenient to grant an injunction.

. . . Lord Diplock approached the matter in two stages. First, he considered the relevance of the availability of an adequate remedy in damages, either to the plaintiff seeking the injunction or to the defendant in the event that an injunction is granted against him. As far as the plaintiff is concerned, the availability to him of such a remedy will normally preclude the grant to him of an interim injunction. If that is not so, then the court should consider whether, if an injunction is granted against the defendant, there will be an adequate remedy in damages available to him under the plaintiff's undertaking in damages; if so, there will be no reason on this ground to refuse to grant the plaintiff an interim injunction.

At this stage of the court's consideration of the case (which I will for convenience call the first stage) many applications for interim injunctions can well be decided. But if there is doubt as to the adequacy of either or both of the respective remedies in damages, then the court proceeds to what is usually called the balance of convenience, and for that purpose will consider all the circumstances of the case. I will call this the second stage.

In this case, the claimant sought an interim injunction to prevent the application of part of an Act of Parliament which, it was argued, was contrary to directly effective European Community law. Lord Goff did not feel that the matter could be resolved at the first stage by considering the adequacy of damages, and therefore proceeded to the second stage. In this context he felt (at 673) that 'matters of considerable weight have to be put into the balance to outweigh the desirability of enforcing, in the public interest, what is on its face the law'. He went on to note Lord Diplock's view in *F Hoffmann-La Roche and Co AG* v. *Secretary of State for Trade and Industry* [1975] AC 295 at 367 (see above at 3.2.1) that a party seeking an interim injunction in respect of secondary legislation had to 'to show a strong prima facie case that the statutory instrument is ultra vires'. Lord Goff (along with the other four judges) concluded in *Factortame* that the injunction could be granted in light of the cogency of the claimant's case and the obvious and immediate damage which would be caused if, pending determination of its compatibility with Community law, the Act in question was enforced.

Factortame (No 2) was unusual because the disapplication of *primary legislation* was involved, but our next extract demonstrates that public interest considerations also weigh heavily upon the court when interim relief is sought in respect of *administrative action*; although the next case involved an application for a stay rather than an interim injunction, the *American Cyanamid* principles were applicable.

R v. Ministry of Agriculture, Fisheries and Food, ex parte Monsanto plc [1999] QB 1161
Queen's Bench Division

Since 1974 the claimant had manufactured a leading herbicide called Roundup, the patent for which expired in 1991. In 1996 the claimant's data became available to other companies wishing to produce similar herbicides. On the basis of that data the intervener, Clayton, sought and was granted permission — known as 'me too' approval — to market its Rhizeup herbicide in the UK. The claimant sought judicial review of the approval, contending that, by virtue of article 4(1)(b) of Council Directive 91/414/EEC, the defendant had erred by relying on old data rather than examining the matter 'in the light of current scientific and technical knowledge'. As a result of other challenges by the claimant to 'me too' approvals, a preliminary reference had already been made to the European Court of Justice concerning the meaning of the relevant parts of the Directive. Since it was likely to take the ECJ some time to deal with the matter, the claimant sought a stay suspending the approval in the meantime.

Rose LJ (delivering the judgment of the court)

. . . It is common ground that this court has power to grant such relief and that it is a matter for the exercise of the court's discretion whether relief should be granted. It is also common ground that, in exercising its discretion, the court must have regard to the principles enunciated by Lord Diplock in *American Cyanamid Co. v. Ethicon Ltd.* [1975] A.C. 396, 408. But it has been a matter of contention before us as to precisely how those principles should be applied in a public law case.

. . . In our judgment, although *American Cyanamid* principles are to be applied in the present case, this must be in the context of the public law questions to which the judicial review proceedings give rise. Such proceedings are, generally speaking, intended to provide swift relief against abuse of executive power. They are neither intended for nor well suited to inhibiting commercial activity, particularly over an indefinite, substantial period of time. Monsanto's request for interim relief must, as it seems to us, be judged in that context. Plainly there is a serious question to be tried.

As to the adequacy of a remedy in damages, if Monsanto is likely to suffer loss, we accept it has no adequate remedy against Clayton or the respondents. But, in our judgment, the evidence before this court does not establish actual or likely loss. There are 35 other competitors in the market. Monsanto's own report suggests that, if prices fall, increased sales result. In the absence of any relevant figures from Monsanto we reject the suggestion that this principle is inapplicable to the United Kingdom market. Monsanto's evidence provides no detailed calculations. We are unimpressed by vague assertions about what could happen. In any event, Clayton's proffered undertaking as to ceilings would limit its involvement to a small percentage of the market. Monsanto's cross-undertaking in damages is capable of providing a remedy but we doubt whether that remedy would be adequate, because Clayton has no track record to establish likely losses and all the indications are that Clayton, whose resources are limited, would be faced by fierce resistance by Monsanto, whose resources are comparatively limitless, in seeking to establish any loss. In our judgment, therefore, Monsanto has no sustainable claim for relief based on inadequacy of damages and we doubt if damages would provide an adequate remedy for Clayton.

Turning to consider the balance of convenience, there are a number of public interest factors of relevance and significance. First, in *Reg. v. Secretary of State for Health and Norgine Ltd., Ex parte Scotia Pharmaceuticals International Ltd. (No 1)* [1997] Eu.L.R. 625, 643 Evans L.J. said that he began "with a strong presumption in favour of there being no order by way of interim relief," because such an order would have the effect of restricting free competition. We respectfully agree. Secondly, there is, in the present case, no suggested hazard to health or the environment from the use of Rhizeup and this is an important objective of the EEC Directive. Thirdly, the "me too" procedure has cost Clayton a substantial sum; and it seems to us that, if the grant of approval is in the public interest, applications should not be discouraged by the prospect that the costs thereof may be irrecoverable for a period of years if a competitor obtains interim relief: this is of particular significance when the competitor's patent and data protection have expired. Fourthly, although we attach rather less weight to this factor in the circumstances of the present case, it is in the public interest that, until set aside, the decision of a public body should be respected. This is a variant of the argument which favours maintenance of the status quo. Fifthly, the purpose of the licensing provisions is to serve the public interest, not to protect private commercial interests which are catered for by patent and data protection. That being so, we incline to the view (although it is not determinative in the present case for the reasons already given) that, even where damages are not an adequate remedy for an applicant, it may still be appropriate to refuse him interim relief in public law proceedings . . .

The application to stay the approval of Rhizeup was dismissed.

Although the court concluded that Monsanto was not likely to suffer losses as a result of the grant of 'me too' approval to Clayton, it also inclined to the view that even though damages would not have been an adequate remedy if any losses were occasioned, interim relief might still have been inappropriate. This suggests that the need for the court to address public interest issues when interim relief is sought in public law proceedings is such that, taken on its own, the inadequacy of damages will rarely, if ever, satisfy the court of the need for such relief: instead, the balance of convenience test will be applied, in which context public interest considerations will weigh heavily. For further comment on this case see Bamforth [1999] *CLJ* 1.

13.2.3 Injunctions and the Crown

Historically, the Crown could not be sued in its own courts, and coercive remedies such as injunctions therefore could not be issued against the Crown. However, as a result of statutory intervention, it *is* now possible to sue the Crown, as we explain in ch 16. Of present concern, however, is the specific question whether injunctive relief may issue against the Crown. In the public law context this question assumed considerable importance for two reasons. On a practical level, the injunction appeared to offer the only prospect of interim relief in this context (although note the possibility, considered above at 13.2.1, of issuing stays in respect of administrative action): the prerogative orders cannot take interim form and the interim declaration is a recent invention. In broader terms, the availability of coercive injunctive relief against the Crown is central to what Harlow (1994) 57 *MLR* 620 at

623 terms a 'mandatory model' of public law — a notion which Lord Templeman clearly had in mind when he said, in *In re M* [1994] 1 AC 377 at 395, that

the argument that there is no power to enforce the law by injunction or contempt proceedings against a Minister in his official capacity would, if upheld, establish the proposition that the executive obey the law as a matter of grace and not as a matter of necessity, a proposition which would reverse the result of the Civil War.

In spite of the existence of these two arguments in favour of (interim) injunctive relief in this context, it took the courts a considerable amount of time to arrive at a settled view on this point. Much of the uncertainty derived from differing interpretations of s 21 of the Crown Proceedings Act 1947. The Act was intended to liberalize proceedings against the Crown, yet s 21 was, on a number of occasions, interpreted in a restrictive manner.

Crown Proceedings Act 1947

21—(1) In any civil proceedings by or against the Crown the court shall, subject to the provisions of this Act, have power to make all such orders as it has power to make in proceedings between subjects, and otherwise to give such appropriate relief as the case may require:

Provided that:

(a) where in any proceedings against the Crown any such relief is sought as might in proceedings between subjects be granted by way of injunction or specific performance, the court shall not grant an injunction or make an order for specific performance, but may in lieu thereof make an order declaratory of the rights of the parties; and

(b) in any proceedings against the Crown for the recovery of land or other property the court shall not make an order for the recovery of the land or the delivery of the property, but may in lieu thereof make an order declaring that the plaintiff is entitled as against the Crown to the land or property or to the possession thereof.

(2) The court shall not in any civil proceedings grant any injunction or make any order against an officer of the Crown if the effect of granting the injunction or making the order would be to give any relief against the Crown which could not have been obtained in proceedings against the Crown.

The effect of s 21(1) is quite clear: injunctions may not be issued against *the Crown* in 'civil proceedings' (a term whose definition we consider below). However, s 21(2) imposes only a qualified prohibition on issuing injunctions against *officers of the Crown* (which category includes Ministers). As Lord Woolf explained in *In re M* [1994] 1 AC 377 at 412, 'That subsection is restricted in its application to situations where the effect of the grant of an injunction or an order against an officer of the Crown will be to give any relief against the Crown which could not have been obtained in proceedings against the Crown prior to the Act.' To understand the effect of s 21(2), regard must therefore be had to the position which obtained prior to the 1947 Act. After reviewing the authorities — the most significant being *Raleigh* v. *Goschen* [1898] 1 Ch 73 — Lord Woolf said at 409–410:

The position so far as civil wrongs are concerned, prior to the Act of 1947, can be summarised . . . by saying that as long as the plaintiff sued the actual wrongdoer or the person who ordered the wrongdoing he could bring an action against officials personally, in particular as to torts committed by them, and they were not able to hide behind the immunity of the Crown. This was the position even though at the time they committed the alleged tort they were acting in their official capacity. In those proceedings an injunction, including, if appropriate, an interlocutory injunction, could be granted.

In light of this, Lord Woolf concluded that the 1947 Act neither extended nor restricted the power of the courts to issue injunctions: they may not issue against the Crown; however, before 1947, they could be issued personally against officials and Ministers acting in their official capacity, and the Act did not change that position. In practical terms this means that injunctions are unavailable in civil proceedings when duties are placed on the Crown in general — because in such circumstances when a claim is made against a Minister or official they defend it in a purely representative capacity (as the nominated representative of the Crown under s 17 of the Act) — but are available when legislation places duties on named Ministers who may then be held liable for breach of their official duty.

However, in *Merricks v. Heathcoat-Amory* [1955] Ch 567 575–576, Upjohn J took the general view (subject to the possibility of 'special Acts where named persons have special duties to perform which would not be duties normally fulfilled by them in their official capacity') that when a Minister acts he does so either in a purely individual capacity (in which case the enforcement of statutory duties imposed upon him in his official capacity is beside the point) or as a representative of the Crown (in which case an injunction is prohibited by s 21 of the Crown Proceedings Act). This reasoning was endorsed by the House of Lords in *R v. Secretary of State for Transport, ex parte Factortame* [1990] 2 AC 85 — strongly criticized by Wade (1991) 107 *LQR* 4 — in which it refused to issue an interim injunction to prevent the Secretary of State for Employment from applying part of the Merchant Shipping Act 1988 pending a preliminary ruling by the European Court of Justice as to its compatibility with certain directly effective provisions of EC law. More recently, however, Lord Woolf recognized in *M* at 415 that the mistake made by Upjohn J in *Merricks* was 'to treat a duty placed upon a named Minister as being placed upon the Government as a whole', thus cloaking the Minister with Crown immunity and emasculating the jurisdiction to grant injunctions personally against Ministers acting in their official capacity.

Having established the position in relation to 'civil proceedings' under the Crown Proceedings Act 1947, the House of Lords in *M* went on to address the availability of injunctive relief in judicial review proceedings under Order 53 of the Rules of the Supreme Court (since replaced by CPR Part 54). In *R v. Secretary of State for the Home Department, ex parte Herbage* [1987] QB 872, Hodgson J had concluded that while the then-accepted *Merricks* interpretation of the Crown Proceedings Act precluded injunctive relief against Ministers and Crown officers in 'civil proceedings', the position was in any event different in relation to proceedings brought by way of a claim for judicial review. Although that view was repudiated by the House of Lords in *Factortame*, their Lordships revisited the matter in *M* (useful commentaries on which are provided by Gould [1993] *PL* 568 and Allan [1994] *CLJ* 1).

....

In re M [1994] AC 377
House of Lords

The claimant, an asylum-seeker from Zaire, was told that he would be deported on 1 May 1991. He sought permission for judicial review but was unsuccessful in both the High Court and, on 1 May 1991, the Court of Appeal. After appointing new solicitors he again sought permission in the High Court on allegedly fresh grounds. Garland J wished the claimant's deportation to be postponed, but apparently as a result of a misunderstanding the claimant was deported. Once informed of the situation overnight, the judge issued an interim mandatory injunction against the Home Secretary, Kenneth Baker, requiring him to procure the return of the claimant to the court's jurisdiction. The Home Secretary failed to do so, on the strength of legal advice to the effect that the injunction had been made without jurisdiction. Although the injunction was later discharged, the question arose whether, while the injunction had been in force, the Home Secretary had committed a contempt of court by failing to comply with it. It was therefore necessary to address the logically prior issue of the jurisdiction of the court to issue an injunction against a Minister in judicial review proceedings. At first instance, Simon Brown J concluded that s 21 precluded the issuing of an injunction in such circumstances, while the Court of Appeal held that the Home Secretary could be *personally* guilty of contempt.

Lord Woolf

. . . The language of section 23 [of the Crown Proceedings Act 1947] makes it clear that Part II of the Act does not generally apply to all proceedings which can take place in the High Court. In particular, it does not apply to the proceedings which at that time would have been brought for prerogative orders. If there is any doubt about this, that doubt is removed by the general interpretation provisions of the Act contained in section 38, section 38(2) providing:

> "In this Act, except in so far as the context otherwise requires or it is otherwise expressly provided, the following expressions have the meanings hereby respectively assigned to them, that is to say . . . 'Civil proceedings' includes proceedings in the High Court or the county court for the recovery of fines or penalties, but does not include proceedings on the Crown side of the [Queen's] Bench Division; . . ."

Proceedings for the prerogative orders were brought on the Crown side. [Such proceedings now take the form of a claim for judicial review under Part 54 of the Civil Procedure Rules, formerly the application for judicial review under Order 53 of the Rules of the Supreme Court.]

. . . Prior to the introduction of judicial review, the principal remedies which were available were certiorari, mandamus, prohibition and habeas corpus. As we are primarily concerned with the possible availability of injunction, I will focus on mandamus and prohibition since they are indistinguishable in their effect from final injunctions . . .

The prerogative remedies could not be obtained against the Crown directly as was explained by Lord Denman C.J. in *Reg. v. Powell* (1841) 1 Q.B. 352, 361:

> "both because there would be an incongruity in the Queen commanding herself to do an act, and also because the disobedience to a writ of mandamus is to be enforced by attachment."

Originally this difficulty could not be avoided by bringing the proceedings against named ministers of the Crown: *Reg. v. Lords Commissioners of the Treasury* (1872) L.R. 7 QB 387. But, where a duty was imposed by statute for the benefit of the public upon a particular Minister, so that he was under a duty to perform that duty in his official capacity, then orders of prohibition and mandamus were granted regularly against the Minister. The proceedings were brought against the Minister in his official name and according to the title of the proceedings by the Crown. The title of the proceedings would be *Reg. v. Minister, Ex parte the applicant* . . ., so that unless the Minister was treated as being distinct from the Crown the title of the proceedings would disclose the "incongruity" of the Crown suing the Crown. This did not mean that the Minister was treated as acting other than in his official capacity and the order was made against him in his official name. In accordance with this practice there have been numerous cases where prerogative orders, including orders of prohibition and mandamus, have been made against ministers . . .

[Lord Woolf set out s 31 of the Supreme Court Act 1981 (see above at 13.1) and continued:] In section 31 the jurisdiction to grant declarations and injunctions is directly linked to that which already existed in relation to the prerogative orders. The jurisdiction to award damages by contrast is restricted to those situations where damages are recoverable in an action begun by writ. It has never been suggested that a declaration is not available in proceedings against a Minister in his official capacity and if Order 53 and section 31 apply to a Minister in the case of declarations then, applying ordinary rules of construction, one would expect the position to be precisely the same in the case of injunctions. As an examination of the position prior to the introduction of judicial review indicates, because of the scope of the remedies of mandamus and prohibition the availability of injunctions against ministers would only be of any significance in situations where it would be appropriate to grant interim relief. Even here the significance of the change was reduced by the power of the court to grant a stay under Ord. 53, r. 3(10) [see now CPR Part 54, r 54.10(2).] . . .

Lord Bridge of Harwich in *Reg. v. Secretary of State for Transport, Ex parte Factortame Ltd* [1990] 2 A.C. 85 at 143 acknowledged that "the question at issue depends, first, on the true construction of section 31". Lord Bridge also accepted, at 149, that if section 31 "were to be construed in isolation" there would be "great force in the reasoning" that section 31 did enable injunctions to be granted for the first time against ministers of the Crown in judicial review proceedings. Why then did Lord Bridge come to the conclusion that an injunction could not be granted against a Minister in proceedings for judicial review?

A primary cause for Lord Bridge's taking this view was that he concluded that it would be a dramatic departure from what was the position prior to the introduction of judicial review for an injunction to be available against the Crown or a Minister of the Crown, so that the change was one which could be expected to be made only by express legislation. His conclusion was not, however, based on as comprehensive an argument of the history of both civil and prerogative proceedings as was available to your Lordships. In particular he did not have an account of the developments which had taken place in the granting of prerogative orders against ministers, which meant that in practical terms the only consequence of treating section 31 as enabling injunctions to be granted against *ministers* acting in their official capacity would be to provide an alternative in name only to the orders of prohibition and mandamus which were already available and to allow interim relief other than a stay for the first time.

A secondary cause was his reliance upon Upjohn J.'s judgment in *Merricks v. Heathcoat-Amory* [1955] Ch. 567, a judgment which as already indicated should be approached with caution. Lord Bridge was also influenced by the fact that the new Order 53 was introduced following the Law Commission's Report on Remedies in Administrative Law (1976) (Law Com. No. 73) (Cmnd. 6407) and that that report drew attention to the problem created by the lack of jurisdiction to grant interim injunctions against the Crown and recommended that the problem should be remedied by amending section 21 of the Act of 1947. The report included a draft of the legislation proposed. This proposal of the Law Commission was never implemented. Instead the decision was taken following the Law Commission's report to proceed by amendment of the Rules of the Supreme Court rather than by primary legislation. Lord Bridge in his speech [in *Factortame, op cit* at 149–150], explains why, in his view, this meant that section 31 of the Act of 1981 should be given a restricted interpretation . . . [Lord Bridge's view] deserves very careful attention coming, as it does, from a judge who is acknowledged to have made an outstanding contribution to this area of the law. Nonetheless, I do not regard it as justifying limiting the natural interpretation of section 31 so as to exclude the jurisdiction to grant injunctions, including interim injunctions, on applications for judicial review against ministers of the Crown . . .

I am, therefore, of the opinion that, the language of section 31 being unqualified in its terms, there is no warrant for restricting its application so that in respect of ministers and other officers of the Crown alone the remedy of an injunction, including an interim injunction, is not available. In my view the history of prerogative proceedings against officers of the Crown supports such a conclusion. So far as interim relief is concerned, which is the practical change which has been made, there is no justification for adopting a different approach to officers of the Crown from that adopted in relation to other respondents in the absence of clear language such as that contained in section

21(2) of the Act of 1947. The fact that in any event a stay could be granted against the Crown under Ord. 53, r. 3(10) emphasises the limits of the change in the situation which is involved. It would be most regrettable if an approach which is inconsistent with that which exists in Community law should be allowed to persist if this is not strictly necessary. The restriction provided for in section 21(2) of the Act of 1947 does, however, remain in relation to civil proceedings.

The fact that, in my view, the court should be regarded as having jurisdiction to grant interim and final injunctions against officers of the Crown does not mean that that jurisdiction should be exercised except in the most limited circumstances. In the majority of situations so far as final relief is concerned, a declaration will continue to be the appropriate remedy on an application for judicial review involving officers of the Crown. As has been the position in the past, the Crown can be relied upon to co-operate fully with such declarations. To avoid having to grant interim injunctions against officers of the Crown, I can see advantages in the courts being able to grant interim declarations . . .

Lord Woolf, with whom Lords Keith, Templeman, Griffiths, and Browne-Wilkinson agreed, went on to conclude that a contempt of court had occurred. The appeal was therefore dismissed, although the Secretary of State for Home Affairs was substituted for Kenneth Baker personally as the subject of the finding of contempt.

The *M* decision was broadly welcomed by commentators (see, *eg*, Law Com No 226, *Administrative Law: Judicial Review and Statutory Appeals* (London 1994), Part VI). There are, however, two areas in which reservation has been expressed. The first relates to enforcement. After concluding in *M* that injunctions could lie against Ministers of the Crown, Lord Woolf went on to consider (at 424–426) whether a Minister could be held to be in contempt of court:

Nolan L.J. [in the same case in the Court of Appeal: [1992] QB 270], at 311, considered that the fact that proceedings for contempt are "essentially personal and punitive" meant that it was not open to a court, as a matter of law, to make a finding of contempt against the Home Office or the Home Secretary. While contempt proceedings usually have these characteristics and contempt proceedings against a government department or a Minister in an official capacity would not be either personal or punitive (it would clearly not be appropriate to fine or sequestrate the assets of the Crown or a government department or an officer of the Crown acting in his official capacity), this does not mean that a finding of contempt against a government department or Minister would be pointless. The very fact of making such a finding would vindicate the requirements of justice. In addition an order for costs could be made to underline the significance of a contempt. A purpose of the courts' powers to make findings of contempt is to ensure that the orders of the court are obeyed. This jurisdiction is required to be coextensive with the courts' jurisdiction to make the orders which need the protection which the jurisdiction to make findings of contempt provides. In civil proceedings the court can now make orders (other than injunctions or for specific performance) against authorised government departments or the Attorney-General. On applications for judicial review orders can be made against ministers. In consequence of the developments identified already such orders must be taken not to offend the theory that the Crown can supposedly do no wrong. Equally, if such orders are made and not obeyed, the body against whom the orders were made can be found guilty of contempt without offending that theory, which would be the only justifiable impediment against making a finding of contempt.

In cases not involving a government department or a Minister the ability to *punish* for contempt may be necessary. However, as is reflected in the restrictions on execution against the Crown [see Crown Proceedings Act 1947, s 25(4)], the Crown's relationship with the courts does not depend on coercion and in the exceptional situation when a government department's conduct justifies this, a finding of contempt should suffice. In that exceptional situation, the ability of the court to make a finding of contempt is of great importance. It would demonstrate that a government department has interfered with the administration of justice. It will then be for Parliament to determine what should be the consequences of that finding. In accord with tradition the finding should not be made against the "Crown" by name but in the name of the authorised department (or the Attorney-General) or the Minister so as to accord with the body against whom the order was made. If the order was made in civil proceedings against an authorised department, the department will be held to be in contempt. On judicial review the order will be against the Minister and so normally should be any finding of contempt in respect of the order.

However, the finding under appeal is one made against Mr. Baker personally in respect of an injunction addressed to him in his official capacity as the Secretary of State for the Home Department. It was appropriate to direct the injunction to the Secretary of State in his official capacity since, as previously indicated, remedies on an application for judicial review which involve the Crown are made against the appropriate officer in his official capacity. This does not mean that it cannot be appropriate to make a finding of contempt against a Minister personally rather than against him in his official capacity provided that the contempt relates to his own default. Normally it will be more appropriate to make the order against the office which a Minister holds where the order which has been breached has been made against that office since members of the department concerned will almost certainly be involved and investigation as to the part played by individuals is likely to be at least extremely difficult, if not impossible, unless privilege is waived (as commendably happened in this case). In addition the object of the exercise is not so much to punish an individual as to vindicate the rule of law by a finding of contempt. This can be achieved equally by a declaratory finding of the court as to the contempt against the Minister as representing the department. By making the finding against the Minister in his official capacity the court will be indicating that it is the department for which the Minister is responsible which has been guilty of contempt. The Minister himself may or may not have been personally guilty of contempt. The position so far as he is personally concerned would be the equivalent of that which needs to exist for the court to give relief against the Minister in proceedings for judicial review. There would need to be default by the department for which the Minister is responsible.

Harlow (1994) 57 *MLR* 620 at 623 finds this aspect of *M* disquieting:

. . . [T]he decision does move our system of judicial review a long way towards the mandatory model for which Lord Woolf argued. A long way but not all the way because, at the end of his lengthy judgment, Lord Woolf is trapped into making a very dangerous concession . . . Without considering the alternative of committal, in principle not impossible, though complicated a little by the status of Ministers as Members of Parliament, Lord Woolf deduces that contempt proceedings are ultimately unenforceable. At the theoretical level, this admission . . . surely undercuts the fundamental premise of Lord Woolf's judgment. A mandatory model of judicial review which cannot be enforced must be a contradiction in terms.

QUESTION

• Do you agree with Harlow's criticism of *M*?

The second area of concern generated by the *M* case concerns the premise which it adopts as its starting point — that injunctions do not lie against the Crown itself, as distinct from officers of the Crown. Although Lord Woolf did not consider this impediment to be of any great significance, writers have taken issue with this view in two respects. First, Gould [1993] *PL* 568 at 577 argues that the *practical implications* of this restriction may be more important than first appears:

. . . [U]ncertainties are caused by the confusion . . . between the "Crown" and "officers of the Crown". Lord Woolf confesses to having muddied the waters by using the term 'Crown' loosely in [R v.

Licensing Authority Established under the Medicines Act 1968, ex parte Smith, Kline and French Laboratories Ltd (No 2) [1990] 1 QB 574], but he is not always consistent in his use of the terms in *M*. The clear intention, reading the judgment as a whole, is to separate remedies available against officers of the Crown, which could include injunctions, from those available against the Crown itself, which are very limited and do not include any form of coercive relief. He is of the view that the distinction between the two categories, although very important in theory, has only minimal practical effect, and notes that 'there are likely to be few situations when there will be statutory duties that place a duty on the Crown in general instead of on a named Minister'. However, in those few situations the practical significance of the distinction between a Minister and the Crown becomes very great — to the extent that the remedies available to an applicant for judicial review would be severely curtailed. Whilst it may be true now that statutes predominantly confer duties on ministers, there is nothing to prevent Parliament from adopting a form of words which confers duties directly on the Crown and using that formula more frequently than at present in order to avoid the very remedies made available in *M*.

Sedley goes further, focussing not on the practical consequences of the distinction drawn in *M* between Ministers and the Crown but on whether such a distinction is defensible in terms of *constitutional theory*.

Sedley, 'The Crown in its own Courts'
in Forsyth and Hare (eds), *The Golden Metwand and the Crooked Cord* (Oxford 1998)

. . . What . . . of the theory that the Crown can do no wrong? As a theory it hardly matters if it is now recognized in practice that the ministers and departments through whom the Crown acts are capable of doing wrong. But in theory too the proposition is flawed because it ignores the very thing that makes a democracy possible, the separation of powers. There is reality as well as symbolic force in the proposition that what the Crown in Parliament enacts is the law and in that constitutional sense right; and that what the Queen's courts hold to be the true meaning and effect of the law, whether common law or statute, is equally, in a constitutional sense, right. Neither is beyond change in the future nor beyond criticism in the present, but in both cases the Crown has constitutionally to be taken as doing no wrong if the rule of law is to be effective. In this temporary sense Parliament and the courts can each be accurately said to be a law unto themselves. But it is precisely because these are the two and the only two sovereign functions of the Crown, and because the functioning of executive government is subordinated to the approval of Parliament and the adjudication of the courts, that the Crown in its executive limb *can* in constitutional theory do wrong. It may be that the Crown as monarch is able to do no wrong, though in a constitutional monarchy there seems to be no reason why the sovereign should be — or indeed should want to be — any freer that the rest of us to break the speed limit. But there is no constitutional theory, and no need for one, which elevates ministerial authority to the status of a sovereign power in a democracy. The twentieth-century world has furnished countless reminders that it is precisely when those holding political power are able to administer the state by means of policy and discretion without regard to law or legislation that democracy founders.

The argument advanced to the Court of Appeal and the House of Lords on behalf of the Home Secretary in *M*'s case was at base a straightforward syllogism: the Crown can do no wrong and is in any case not a legal entity; it is therefore beyond the reach of the law; the Minister acting in office acts in the name and on behalf of the Crown; he too is therefore beyond the reach of the law, at least in its coercive forms. The House has not directly challenged this reasoning. It has accepted the counter-argument that the Crown is a legal entity and that its inability to do wrong is a fiction; it has held that a Minister is personally liable for wrongs albeit committed in his official capacity; but rather than go the final step of holding that the Crown can therefore properly be impleaded for wrongs done in its name by its ministers, their Lordships have concluded that the law should recognize the capacity in which the Minister has erred, but in a form which avoids impleading the Crown . . .

M v. Home Office was a powerful case on its facts, not because they were uncomplicated but because they posed a black-and-white issue: was a Minister who defied a court order answerable to the court for it, or did his status furnish him with an immunity enjoyed by the Crown? There is nothing wrong with starting from the conclusion that if the rule of law is to mean anything the latter proposition cannot be right . . . If, however, one also accepts the argument that the Crown can do no wrong, one has to find some way of prising the Minister away from the Crown without eclipsing the fact that it is in his official capacity that he has offended. This is the road their Lordships have gone down. But if one asks . . . whether it is actually the case that the Crown in its executive capacity can do no wrong, the answer is plainly No, and the whole of modern public law practice is founded upon that answer. Once this corner is turned, the way is relatively clear: the Crown's courts, applying the law laid down by Parliament and by themselves, may in a proper case hold the Crown, acting in its executive limb, to be in breach of the law without violating either the separation of powers or the status of the Crown. The status of the Crown, acknowledged by Magna Carta, the Bill of Rights, the Act of Settlement and a variety of other statutes, is that of an entity known to the law; and its horizontal division into legislative, judicial and executive functions permits ministers to be called to account politically by Parliament and legally by the courts. Once it is appreciated that these separate powers are not those of equal sovereignties within the state but that the executive, although enjoying great autonomy, is ultimately subordinated to the others, the problem of incongruity in the Crown supposedly calling itself to account melts away. In its place one sees a constitutional monarchy whose functions are so distributed that although all are carried out in the name of the Crown, their relationship to one another is the relationship demanded by one of the most fundamental of all our unwritten constitutional principles — that government is to be conducted within the law . . .

QUESTION

- Bearing in mind the arguments of Gould and Sedley, was the House of Lords right to conclude in *M* that injunctions cannot be issued against the Crown itself?

13.3 Declarations

13.3.1 The Role of Declarations in Public Law

Declarations constitute an authoritative judicial statement of a legal position but are a non-coercive form of relief. While those who act contrary to the law as spelled out in the declaration may well incur liability for the simple reason that they have breached the law so declared, no additional liability arises as a result of the existence of the declaration; this may be contrasted with the position in relation to injunctions, breach of which may ultimately result in liability for contempt of court. Declarations are a useful form of relief in a number of respects.

First, because they are non-coercive, courts may be willing to issue declarations in circumstances where an injunction, while theoretically available, might be thought inappropriate; for instance, Lord Woolf was of the opinion in *In Re M* [1994] 1 AC 377 at 423 that it would rarely be necessary to issue final injunctive relief against officers of the Crown, given the high degree of likelihood that they would co-operate fully with a declaration.

Secondly, declarations are more apt than injunctions in circumstances where the relevance of the matter under consideration is general rather than confined to the parties before the court. Relief issued in relation to primary legislation which is found to be inconsistent with directly effective EC law usefully illustrates this point. The Law Commission (Law Com No 226, *Administrative Law: Judicial Review and Statutory Appeals* (London 1994) at [6.20]) noted that

> although in *Factortame (No 2)* an interim injunction was ordered in respect of an Act of Parliament, in the case of legislation such an injunction is not entirely appropriate since it is only addressed to the law maker or those who implement or enforce it, whereas the "law" may be relied on by a wide range of third parties.

Indeed declarations were issued by the House of Lords in *R v. Secretary of State for Employment, ex parte Equal Opportunities Commission* [1995] 1 AC 1 when it was found that UK legislation was incompatible with directly effective prohibitions upon indirect gender discrimination imposed by EC law.

Thirdly, the inherent flexibility of the declaration makes it appropriate in a wide range of situations; in particular, it permits the courts to clarify the legal position in circumstances which do not yet disclose any specific public law wrong. For instance, it is clear from cases such as *Royal College of Nursing* v. *Department of Health and Social Security* [1981] 1 AC 800 and *Gillick* v. *West Norfolk and Wisbech Area Health Authority* [1986] AC 112 that declarations may be issued in relation to government circulars, to clarify whether the advice which they contain would, if followed, lead to the commission of unlawful conduct, notwithstanding that the circulars themselves did not purport to be issued pursuant to — and could not therefore be outside the scope of — any legal authority. There are, however, limits to the extent of courts' willingness to issue so-called advisory declarations, as we explain below at 15.5.

13.3.2 Interim Declarations

The House of Lords was forced to confront the availability of injunctive relief against officers of the Crown in *Factortame* and *M* because, when those cases were decided, it was the only type of relief — apart from stays, on which see above at 13.2.1 — available in interim form. As to declarations, Upjohn LJ, in *International General Electric Company of New York Ltd* v. *Commissioners of Customs and Excise* [1962] Ch 784 at 790, could 'not understand how there can be such an animal . . . as an interim declaratory order'. Similarly, in *R v. Licensing Authority Established under the Medicines Act 1968, ex parte Smith, Kline and French Laboratories Ltd (No 2)* [1990] 1 QB 574 at 601, Woolf LJ thought it 'difficult to envisage that you can have an interim declaration' (although, as the extract above at 13.2.3 shows, he later concluded in *In re M* [1994] 1 AC 377 that such a remedy would be practically useful). In the following extract the Law Commission helpfully summarizes the perceived problems associated with interim declarations, while concluding that those difficulties are not insurmountable.

....

Law Com No 226, *Administrative Law: Judicial Review and Statutory Appeals*
(London 1994)

. . . [Our] consultation paper [*Administrative Law: Judicial Review and Statutory Appeals*, Consultation Paper No 126] sought views on the relative merits of the different techniques for granting
interim relief; stays, interim injunctions and interim declarations. The last of these is at present
unknown to English law. The overall result was not conclusive. Consultees accepted that what was
needed was an effective way of preserving the status quo and a rationalisation of the different
techniques for doing so but some reservations were expressed about interim declarations. It was
said to be illogical to declare one day in interlocutory proceedings that an applicant has certain
rights and on a later day that he has not and it was suggested that interim declarations were
inconsistent with the presumption of legality [on which see above at 3.2.1] . . .

The advantages of [interim declarations] . . . are that they are not coercive, they specifically
address the interim position and are better suited to clarify the position of third parties. There is no
reason why they should not be granted on the same basis as interim injunctions. In New Zealand
there is provision for interim declaratory relief in judicial review proceedings against the Crown . . .,
and such relief is more generally available in Canada. Such declarations would refer to a right or
obligation that exists prima facie and are not therefore illogical. In making a merely interim declaration, the judge reserves his or her right and admits an obligation to re-examine the question after a
substantive hearing at the trial. In our view this consideration also meets the argument that a
declaration in an interim form may inappropriately suggest that the court has already made up its
mind as to the likely grant of final relief.

We believe that the perceived difficulties arising from the presumption of validity are met by the
fact that the burden of proof lies on the party challenging the decision. It was also commented that
it might be more difficult to deal with undertakings regarding damages by the applicant where an
interim declaration is given. We believe that where it is clear that an activity should be stopped the
principles developed in relation to injunctions could be applied or an interim injunction granted . . .

We accordingly recommend that there should be provision for . . . interim declarations . . . in
proceedings by way of judicial review . . .

The force of these arguments has now been recognized, and CPR 25.1(1)(b) permits interim
declarations to be granted. Many of the cases in which interim declarations have thus far
been sought have concerned challenges to the compatibility of primary legislation with
directly effective EC law, with interim relief being requested pending a preliminary ruling by
the European Court of Justice under Article 234 EC. In that context the courts have accepted
that the approach to interim injunctions set out by Lord Goff in *Factortame (No 2)* (see
above at 13.2.2) is also applicable to interim declarations, thus requiring a challenge to the
validity of the law in question that is, *prima facie*, so firmly based as to justify an exceptional
course being taken: *R* v. *Secretary of State for Trade and Industry, ex parte Trades Union
Congress* [2001] 1 CMLR 8 at [23], *per* Buxton LJ. Interim declarations are particularly
useful in cases where the compatibility of legislation is challenged on the ground of its
alleged incompatibility with EC law, bearing in mind that references to the European Court
of Justice under Article 234, which are often required in such cases, can take a considerable
amount of time. There are, however, few examples of interim declarations being sought or
granted in judicial review proceedings in respect of allegedly invalid *administrative* action
since, as Solomon [2001] *JR* 10 notes, in such proceedings 'it will often be the case that a
request for an expedited hearing is more appropriate than pursuing an interim remedy'.
However, in *R* v. *Independent Television Commission, ex parte TVDanmark 1 Ltd* (Queen's
Bench Division, 8 September 2000 (unreported)), in which the claimant challenged the

ITC's decision that it would be contrary to EC law to permit it to broadcast a football match to Denmark, an interim declaration was granted by Jack Beatson QC (sitting as a Deputy Judge of the High Court) to the effect that 'there was a strong *prima facie* case' — which in fact he later decided the ITC had answered: a conclusion with which the House of Lords ([2001] UKHL 42 [2001] 1 WLR 1604) agreed — 'that to grant consent to TVD's application would not breach the requirements of [the relevant EC measures]'.

13.4 Relator Proceedings

Relator proceedings are brought by the Attorney-General on behalf of a member of the public or an agency in order to obtain an injunction or declaration. One use to which such proceedings may be put is to prevent, by means of an injunction, a breach of the criminal law. However, since the effect of this is to make any subsequent breach into a contempt of court, thus potentially permitting the imposition of a sanction in excess of the statutorily prescribed maximum for the offence in question, it is generally felt, as Viscount Dilhorne made clear in his speech in *Gouriet* v. *Union of Post Office Workers* [1978] AC 435, that this course of action will be appropriate only rarely — a view affirmed (in an analogous context) by Lord Scott in *South Buckinghamshire District Council* v. *Porter* [2003] UKHL 26 [2003] 2 AC 558.

Less controversially, relator proceedings may be brought in order to obtain an injunction to prevent public authorities from acting *ultra vires* or a declaration to establish that a certain policy or decision is unlawful (see, *eg, Attorney-General ex rel Tilley* v. *Wandsworth London Borough Council* [1981] 1 WLR 854). Used in this way, the principal benefit of relator proceedings is that the individual or agency wishing to impugn the legality of administrative action need not establish standing (on which see below at 15.7). Provided that the Attorney-General lends his support to the proceedings, the relator is not required to establish that he has any personal connection with the matter of which he complains (although note that special provision is made by s 222 of the Local Government Act 1972 in respect of local authorities, according to which they may 'prosecute or defend or appear in any legal proceedings and, in the case of civil proceedings, may institute them in their own name' *without* needing to resort to relator proceedings, provided that they consider such a course of action 'expedient for the promotion or protection of the interests of the inhabitants of their area').

Clearly, the importance of relator proceedings in this regard depends in part upon the liberality of the rules on standing: the more restrictive those rules, the more important relator proceedings become as a means of escaping their strictures. Before developing this point below, it is necessary to consider the *Gouriet* case: although it concerns relator proceedings for the purpose of enforcing the criminal law by means of injunction, Lord Wilberforce's comments are of more general relevance, the sharp distinction which he draws between public and private rights being of particular interest.

Gouriet v. Union of Post Office Workers [1978] AC 435
House of Lords

Gouriet applied to the Attorney-General for his consent to act as claimant in relator proceedings for an injunction against the Union, which was alleged to be able to call on its members not to handle mail between the United Kingdom and South Africa for the week beginning 16 January 1977, as a protest against the apartheid policy then in force in South Africa. Such interference with postal communications constituted an offence under the Post Office Act 1953. The Attorney-General refused to consent and Gouriet then issued a writ in his own name. A judge in chambers refused the application on 14 January, but the Court of Appeal granted him an interim injunction the next day. At a later hearing Gouriet amended his pleadings by adding a claim for a declaration that the Attorney-General, by refusing his consent to the relator action, had wrongfully exercised his discretion. The majority of the Court of Appeal held that the courts had no jurisdiction to review the Attorney-General's decision and that Gouriet was not entitled to a permanent injunction. However, a majority also held that, in spite of the Attorney-General's refusal to give his consent, Gouriet had been entitled to claim a declaration that the Union was proposing to act unlawfully and that an interim injunction (interim declarations being unavailable at that time) could be issued pending determination of whether such a final declaration would be appropriate. Both parties appealed to the House of Lords, although Gouriet no longer claimed that the refusal of consent was wrongful or reviewable.

Lord Wilberforce

. . . There is now no longer a claim that the Attorney-General's refusal of consent to relator proceedings was improper or that it can be reviewed by the court. This issue, originally presented as one of great constitutional importance, has disappeared from the case. The importance remains, but the issue has vanished. The Attorney-General's decision is accepted as, in the courts, unassailable. The prerogatives of his office are no longer attacked. All that Mr. Gouriet now claims is that the refusal of the Attorney-General to act does not bar him from acting . . .

A relator action — a type of action which has existed from the earliest times — is one in which the Attorney-General, on the relation of individuals (who may include local authorities or companies) brings an action to assert a public right. It can properly be said to be a fundamental principle of English law that private rights can be asserted by individuals, but that public rights can only be asserted by the Attorney-General as representing the public. In terms of constitutional law, the rights of the public are vested in the Crown, and the Attorney-General enforces them as an officer of the Crown. And just as the Attorney-General has in general no power to interfere with the assertion of private rights, so in general no private person has the right of representing the public in the assertion of public rights. If he tries to do so his action can be struck out . . .

. . . [T]he Attorney-General's role has never been fictional. His position in relator actions is the same as it is in actions brought without a relator (with the sole exception that the relator is liable for costs: see *Attorney-General v. Cockermouth Local Board* (1874) L.R. 18 Eq. 172, 176, *per* Jessel M.R.). He is entitled to see and approve the statement of claim and any amendment in the pleadings, he is entitled to be consulted on discovery, the suit cannot be compromised without his approval; if the relator dies, the suit does not abate. For the proposition that his only concern is to 'filter out' vexatious and frivolous proceedings there is no authority — indeed there is no need for the Attorney-General to do what is well within the power of the court. On the contrary he has the right, and the duty, to consider the public interest generally and widely.

It was this consideration which led to the well known pronouncement of the Earl of Halsbury L.C. in 1902, for the suggestion was being made that the court could inquire whether, when the Attorney-General had consented to relator proceedings, the public had a material interest in the subject matter of the suit:

"... the initiation of the litigation, and the determination of the question whether it is a proper case for the Attorney-General to proceed in, is a matter entirely beyond the jurisdiction of this or any other court. It is a question which the law of this country has made to reside exclusively in the Attorney-General": see *London County Council v. Attorney-General* [1902] A.C. 165, *per* Earl of Halsbury L.C. at p. 169 and *per* Lord Macnaghten at p. 170.

To limit this passage to a case where the Attorney-General has given his consent (as opposed to a case where he refuses consent) goes beyond legitimate distinction: it ignores the force of the words "whether he ought to initiate litigation . . . or not": see p. 168 . . .

That it is the exclusive right of the Attorney-General to represent the public interest — even where individuals might be interested in a larger view of the matter — is not technical, not procedural, not fictional. It is constitutional . . . [I]t is also wise.

From this general consideration of the nature of relator actions, I pass to the special type of relator action with which this appeal is concerned. It is of very special character, and it is one in which the predominant position of the Attorney-General is a fortiori the general case.

This is a right, of comparatively modern use, of the Attorney-General to invoke the assistance of civil courts in aid of the *criminal law*. It is an exceptional power confined, in practice, to cases where an offence is frequently repeated in disregard of a, usually, inadequate penalty see *Attorney-General v. Harris* [1961] 1 Q.B. 74; or to cases of emergency — see *Attorney-General v. Chaudry* [1971] 1 W.L.R. 1614. It is one not without its difficulties and these may call for consideration in the future.

If Parliament has imposed a sanction (e.g., a fine of £1), without an increase in severity for repeated offences, it may seem wrong that the courts — civil courts — should think fit, by granting injunctions, breaches of which may attract unlimited sanctions, including imprisonment, to do what Parliament has not done. Moreover, where Parliament has (as here in the Post Office Act 1953) provided for trial of offences by indictment before a jury, it may seem wrong that the courts, applying a civil standard of proof, should in effect convict a subject without the prescribed trial. What would happen if, after punishment for contempt, the same man were to be prosecuted in a criminal court? That Lord Eldon L.C. was much oppressed by these difficulties is shown by the discussions in *Attorney-General v. Cleaver* (1811) 18 Ves. Jun. 210.

These and other examples which can be given show that this jurisdiction — though proved useful on occasions — is one of great delicacy and is one to be used with caution. Further, to apply to the court for an injunction at all against the threat of a criminal offence, may involve a decision of policy with which conflicting considerations may enter. Will the law best be served by preventive action? Will the grant of an injunction exacerbate the situation? (Very relevant this in industrial disputes.) Is the injunction likely to be effective or may it be futile? Will it be better to make it clear that the law will be enforced by prosecution and to appeal to the law-abiding instinct, negotiations, and moderate leadership, rather than provoke people along the road to martyrdom? All these matters — to which Devlin J. justly drew attention in *Attorney-General v. Bastow* [1957] 1 Q.B. 514, 519, and the exceptional nature of this *civil* remedy, point the matter as one essentially for the Attorney-General's preliminary discretion. Every known case, so far, has been so dealt with: in no case hitherto has it ever been suggested that an individual can act, though relator actions for public nuisance which may also involve a criminal offence, have been known for 200 years.

There are two arguments put forward for permitting individual citizens to take this action.

The first points to the private prosecution. All citizens have sufficient interest in the enforcement of the law to entitle them to take this step. Why then should this same interest not be sufficient to support preventive action by way of injunction — subject it may be, to ultimate control by the Attorney-General? At one time I was attracted by this argument. But I have reached the conclusion that I cannot accept it.

The Attorney-General's right to seek, in the civil courts, anticipatory prevention of a breach of the law, is a part or aspect of his general power to enforce, in the public interest, public rights. The distinction between public rights, which the Attorney-General can and the individual (absent special interest) cannot seek to enforce, and private rights, is fundamental in our law. To break it, as the plaintiff's counsel frankly invited us to do, is not a development of the law, but a destruction of one of its pillars. Nor, in my opinion, at least in this particular field, would removal of the distinction be desirable. More than in any other field of public rights, the decision to be taken before embarking on a claim for injunctive relief, involving as it does the interests of the public over a broad horizon, is a decision which the Attorney-General alone is suited to make: see *Attorney-General v. Bastow* [1957] 1 Q.B. 514.

This brings me to the second argument. Surely, it is said, since the whole matter is discretionary it can be left to the court. The court can prevent vexatious or frivolous, or multiple actions: the court is not obliged to grant an injunction: leave it in the court's hands. I cannot accept this either. The decisions to be made as to the public interest are not such as courts are fitted or equipped to make. The very fact, that, as the present case very well shows, decisions are of the type to attract political criticism and controversy, shows that they are outside the range of discretionary problems which the courts can resolve. Judges are equipped to find legal rights and administer, on well-known principles, discretionary remedies. These matters are widely outside those areas . . .

Viscount Dilhorne and Lords Diplock, Edmund-Davies, and Fraser also delivered speeches in favour of dismissing the appeal. Appeal dismissed.

This case raises two issues which require comment. First, their Lordships took it for granted (because the claimant did not pursue the point before them) that the Attorney-General's discretion whether to consent to relator proceedings cannot be reviewed. Since the power to consent to such proceedings is prerogative in nature, it is perhaps unsurprising that this conclusion was reached when *Gouriet* was decided in 1978 (although even then its correctness was questioned: see, *eg*, Feldman (1979) 42 *MLR* 369 at 372–373). But it is unclear whether such a conclusion can withstand more recent case law on the amenability to judicial review of prerogative powers. As we saw in ch 5 above, the effect of the House of Lords' decision in *Council of Civil Service Unions* v. *Minister for the Civil Service* [1985] AC 374 is that discretionary powers are no longer immune from judicial review merely because their source is to be found in the prerogative; rather, judicial review may lie provided that the specific issues at stake in the case are suitable for adjudication. It is, for instance, unclear why the Attorney-General's refusal to consent to relator proceedings in respect of a central government department should not lie on the ground of over-rigid policy, bearing in mind his notable reluctance to consent to proceedings against such prospective defendants.

The second point arising from *Gouriet* concerns the vision of public law, and of the individual's position in relation to it, which underpins Lord Wilberforce's speech. As far as his Lordship was concerned, the utility and importance of relator proceedings stems from the fact that 'no private person has the right of representing the public in the assertion of public rights'; only by securing the consent to relator proceedings of the Attorney-General — whose exclusive right and duty it is 'to consider the public interest generally and widely' — may an individual litigate such issues. If this conclusion is combined with the view implicit in *Gouriet* that the Attorney-General's consent is a matter of pure (unreviewable) discretion, it ascribes to individuals a highly limited capacity to use legal proceedings in order to vindicate public rights or the public interest. Such an approach is inconsistent with the argument that individuals are stakeholders in government who have a legitimate interest in ensuring that the executive respects the fundamental principles of good administration. On this view, which is now dominant, the prospective claimant's right to enforce those values transcends circumstances in which his own rights or interests are affected by unlawful action. This vision of the individual's position in respect of public law proceedings has given rise to a liberal approach to standing under CPR Part 54 which in some circumstances allows individuals to sustain judicial review claims on public interest grounds in their own names, obviating the need to resort to relator proceedings and, more generally, eschewing Lord Wilberforce's narrow view of the role of the individual in this sphere. It is true, however, that unless the law of standing becomes so liberal as to recognize an *actio popularis*, the utility of relator proceedings will remain — as will the importance of recognizing that the Attorney-General's discretion in this context is not unbounded.

13.5 Prerogative Remedies

We are concerned in this section with the three prerogative remedies mentioned in s 31(1)(a) of the Supreme Court Act 1981 (set out above at 13.1), recently renamed quashing, mandatory, and prohibiting orders. (It should also be remembered that there exists a fourth prerogative remedy, *habeas corpus*, which is used to test the legality of detention and to require the release of those unlawfully detained, but with which we shall not be dealing in this book in any detail.) It is important to note that, whereas ordinary remedies may (subject to the principle of procedural exclusivity, discussed in ch 14 below) be sought in both judicial review proceedings and ordinary proceedings, the prerogative remedies are available only if the matter is litigated by issuing a claim for judicial review under CPR Part 54. Prerogative remedies do not lie against the Crown itself, since it is the Crown which nominally issues the claim. However, it has long been accepted that prerogative remedies can be issued against officials and Ministers of the Crown.

13.5.1 Quashing Orders

Quashing orders are the most commonly sought remedy in judicial review proceedings. Their effect is to quash, with retrospective effect, administrative action which the reviewing court finds to be unlawful. The retrospectivity of the order reflects the fact that if something is *ultra vires* — which it must be if a quashing order can lie — then it is void *ab initio*, as discussed above in ch 3. This prompted Lord Denning MR in *R v. Paddington Valuation Officer, ex parte Peachey Property Corporation Ltd* [1966] 1 QB 380 at 402 to remark that, in respect of a void determination, '[T]here is no need for an order to quash it. It is automatically null and void without more ado.' This orthodoxy was reasserted by the House of Lords in *Boddington v. British Transport Police* [1999] 2 AC 143. In some situations, therefore, an individual may choose to ignore the unlawful administrative action, raising its invalidity collaterally if necessary in other proceedings rather than challenging it directly by judicial review.

Nevertheless, there remain many good reasons why a quashing order may be sought in respect of action which is thought to be void. Most obviously, the claimant may wish the court to determine authoritatively that the action in question is void, rather than simply assuming this to be the case: waiting to challenge administrative measures collaterally necessarily involves an element of risk because it may turn out (as in *Boddington* itself) that the court does not share the defendant's conviction that the measure in question is invalid. Moreover, circumstances may dictate that merely ignoring the invalid action does not advance the claimant's cause: if, for instance, a licence was sought in order to permit a given activity to be lawfully undertaken, a refusal which is *ultra vires* — because, for example, the decision not to confer a licence was preceded by an unfair procedure — does not change the fact that the individual does not possess a licence and therefore may not lawfully undertake the activity in question. In this situation, only by having the unlawful refusal quashed and requiring the decision-maker to reconsider the matter in a lawful manner may it be possible for the individual to achieve the desired outcome. It follows that, although a quashing order does not *render* unlawful administrative action invalid, because its invalidity follows *a priori* from its unlawful status, such an order is often practically important because of the need authoritatively to *establish* the unlawfulness of the action.

The court having issued a quashing order, CPR 54.19(2) provides (in substantially similar terms to the Supreme Court Act 1981, s 31(5)) that it is also open to the court to remit the matter to the decision-maker and to require it to reconsider the matter in accordance with the judgment of the court. This does not, however, permit the court to instruct the decision-maker to reach a certain conclusion, since this would eviscerate the distinction between appeal and review. Instead, the decision-maker is simply required to consider the matter again in a manner which is lawful and which avoids the errors (*eg* a breach of natural justice) identified by the court. For this reason, it is quite possible that the same decision may be reached when the matter is reconsidered. This, however, is an inevitable concomitant of the principle that reviewing courts are concerned only with the legality of administrative action. It may seem surprising, therefore, that CPR 54.19(3) provides that:

Where the court considers that there is no purpose to be served in remitting the matter to the decision-maker it may, subject to any statutory provision, take the decision itself. (Where a statutory power is given to a tribunal, person or other body it may be the case that the court cannot take the decision itself.)

This new power appears to give reviewing courts licence not merely to quash decisions but also to substitute judgment, and may therefore seem irreconcilable with the established distinction between appeal and review. The Law Commission (Law Com No 226, *Administrative Law: Judicial Review and Statutory Appeals* (London 1994) at [8.15]–[8.16]) was in general agreement with this view. It did, however, recognize that there might be cases in which a substitutionary remedy would *not* jeopardize the distinction between appeal and review. Expressing a similar opinion, Proops [2001] *JR* 216 at 218 argues that CPR 54.19(3) can — and should — be exercised in a manner sensitive to that distinction:

. . . [W]hat does it mean [in CPR 54.19(3)] to say that "there is no purpose to be served in remitting the matter"? . . . [T]he only constitutionally sound answer to this question is that the only circumstances in which "no purpose will be served in remitting the matter" are those circumstances where, on any objective view, it is clear that the original decision-maker would be compelled by the facts of the case and, further, the relevant legal principles, to decide the case in a particular way. Put another way, it is submitted that the court should exercise its power under CPR 54.19(3) only where it is clear from all the circumstances that remitting the decision would be . . . a mere formality; the judge will simply take the decision which the administrator would be required by law to take if the matter were to be remitted.

Proops's argument ultimately reduces to the proposition that CPR 54.19(3) cannot be taken to have abolished the well-established orthodoxy about the supervisory role of judicial review and to have swept away the constitutional rationale upon which that orthodoxy is based. She is therefore correct, along with Fordham [2002] *JR* 14 at 21–22, to contend for a limited interpretation of this new provision which will lead to its being used sparingly by the courts. Although there is presently little case law on 54.19(3), the interpretation urged by Proops and Fordham appears to coincide with the view of May LJ in *R (Dhadly)* v. *London Borough of Greenwich* [2001] EWCA Civ 1822 at [16] that, 'The circumstances in which r 54.19(3) applies are essentially those where there is only one substantive decision that is capable of being made and where it is a waste of time to send the thing back to the decision-making body.' Indeed this reflects the view expressed by Lord Diplock in *Cocks* v. *Thanet District Council* [1983] 2 AC 286 at 295 that, occasionally,

there will be cases where the court's decision [to quash an administrative decision] will effectively determine the issue, as for instance where on undisputed primary facts the court holds that no reasonable housing authority, correctly directing itself in law, could be satisfied that the applicant became intentionally homeless [in circumstances where establishing unintentional homelessness triggers a duty to house].

QUESTIONS

- What criteria should courts take into account in deciding whether remitting the matter to the original decision-maker would be a mere formality, thereby entitling it, in the absence of any statutory prohibition, to take the decision itself?
- For example, if a court concludes that a decision-maker has exercised its discretion so as to breach a claimant's substantive legitimate expectation of a given outcome, would it be acceptable for the court to decide the matter for itself such that the expected outcome was secured?

13.5.2 Prohibiting Orders

Whereas quashing orders set aside unlawful action which has *already been taken*, prohibiting orders preclude administrative acts *yet to be taken* which, if committed, would be unlawful. In this sense a prohibiting order is similar to an injunction, in that it anticipates and prohibits unlawful action which is yet to occur. If an administrative body undertakes action contrary to a prohibiting order then, as with an injunction, a contempt of court is committed. The circumstances in which this remedy is useful are quite limited, since it requires the claimant to know that unlawful action is planned by a public body. The type of situation in which a prohibiting order is valuable is illustrated by the case of *R* v. *Liverpool Corporation, ex parte Liverpool Taxi Fleet Operators' Association* [1972] 2 QB 299, in which the local authority resolved to increase the number of taxi licences granted, contrary to an undertaking that the total number of licences would be capped at 300 until certain proposed legislation was in force. The court considered it appropriate to issue a prohibiting order to prevent the implementation of the new policy without first hearing representations from interested persons.

13.5.3 Mandatory Orders

The role of mandatory orders is analogous to that of mandatory injunctions. Unlike prohibiting orders, which serve to *prevent* the commission of unlawful action, mandatory orders operate to *compel* public bodies to do that which is legally required of them. Mandatory orders are most obviously applicable in circumstances where legislation straightforwardly imposes a duty to do something; if the agency upon which the duty is placed fails to discharge it, then a mandatory order is appropriate to require the performance of the duty. For instance, in *Board of Education v. Rice* [1911] AC 179 the Board was required by s 7(3) of the Education Act 1902 to determine certain questions in order to resolve disputes between schools and local education authorities. The evidence established that the Board had not addressed the correct questions and had therefore failed to discharge its duty. Its decision was quashed and a mandatory order was issued, requiring the Board to look again at the matter, addressing itself to the correct questions.

Since the purpose of mandatory orders is to compel the performance of a legal *duty*, their relevance to discretionary powers — the essence of which is that the decision-maker is free to *choose* whether, rather than being duty-bound, to undertake the relevant action — may not seem obvious. It must be recalled, however, that while the decision-maker certainly has discretion over the merits, there are also duties latent within all discretionary powers. For example, a fundamental duty implicit in any discretionary power is that the recipient of such power must use it. This does not mean that the discretion must be exercised one way or the other, merely that the agency must use the power of decision conferred upon it by addressing its mind in each individual case to the question whether or not to exercise its discretion in favour of the applicant. Consequently, a decision-maker which refuses to exercise its discretion may find itself subject to a mandatory order requiring it to discharge the duty to decide which is implicit within discretionary power.

It is clear, however, from earlier chapters of this book that the latent duties under which decision-makers find themselves extend well beyond this simple duty to decide. Consequently, when a decision-maker has purported to address the question but has failed to do so consistently with the one or more of the various duties of good decision-making imposed by administrative law, a mandatory order may be issued. This point is illustrated by *Padfield v. Minister of Agriculture, Fisheries and Food* [1968] AC 997, which was considered more fully above at 8.3.2. It will be recalled that the Minister had a statutory discretion whether to refer complaints about a milk marketing scheme to a committee of investigation. The court concluded that, in refusing to refer the complaint in question to such a committee, the Minister had taken into account irrelevant considerations and/or acted for purposes contrary to those for which Parliament had conferred the power. In so concluding, the House of Lords rejected the Minister's contention that he possessed unfettered discretion, reminding him that he was under a legal duty to exercise it (*inter alia*) consistently with the objectives of the statutory scheme; a mandatory order was issued to compel the Minister to revisit the question in a manner consistent with that duty.

13.6 Concluding Remarks

In preceding chapters, we have considered the duties imposed, as a matter of public law, on decision-makers. Having established what duties are owed in a particular case, and whether they have been breached, questions of relief become crucial. We have seen in this chapter that the courts have a number of remedies at their disposal. However, a range of other issues fall for consideration. In the following two chapters, we consider the procedural context within which the legality of administrative action is challenged in court proceedings, and certain factors which restrict the availability of relief.

FURTHER RESOURCES

Civil Procedure Rules *www.dca.gov.uk/civil/procrules_fin/*

Harlow, 'Accidental Loss of an Asylum-Seeker' (1994) 57 *MLR* 620

Law Com No 226, Administrative Law: Judicial Review and Statutory Appeals (London 1994), Part VI

Lewis, *Judicial Remedies in Public Law* (London 2004), chs 6–8

Leyland and Woods (eds), *Administrative Law Facing the Future* (London 1997), ch 11 (Cane)

14 THE JUDICIAL REVIEW PROCEDURE

14.1 Introduction

Subject to the principles discussed in ch 16 below, if an individual wishes to sue a public body for breach of contract, he may simply issue a claim in the ordinary way. The same is true if the individual wishes to issue a claim in tort. These are matters of *private law*. However, what if the individual wishes to institute proceedings in respect of a *public law* matter? (We must, of course, immediately acknowledge that it is often impossible neatly to categorize cases as 'private law' or 'public law' — a matter which we consider below at 14.3.) He may, for example, wish to have a decision quashed because it was unreasonable in the *Wednesbury* sense, or taken without compliance with operative rules of natural justice. This raises two questions. First, is the prospective defendant actually subject to the public law duties to act fairly, reasonably, and so on? This falls to be determined by reference to the principles considered above in ch 5. Secondly, if the prospective defendant is subject to these public law duties, how, procedurally, may they be enforced? The general principle — which is considered in detail at 14.3, along with various exceptions to it — is that such public law matters should be litigated not by issuing a claim in the ordinary way, but through the use of a special 'judicial review procedure'.

Civil Procedure Rules, Part 54: Judicial Review and Statutory Review

1(2)   In this Section —
   (a) a 'claim for judicial review' means a claim to review the lawfulness of —
       (i)   an enactment; or
       (ii) a decision, action or failure to act in relation to the exercise of a public function.

2   The judicial review procedure must be used in a claim for judicial review where the claimant is seeking —
   (a) a mandatory order;
   (b) a prohibiting order;
   (c) a quashing order; or
   (d) an injunction under section 30 of the Supreme Court Act 1981 (restraining a person from acting in any office in which he is not entitled to act).

3(1)   The judicial review procedure may be used in a claim for judicial review where the claimant is seeking —

(a) a declaration; or

(b) an injunction . . .

It follows that a claimant wishing to argue that a defendant has contravened applicable public law principles *must* use the judicial review procedure if a prerogative remedy is sought, whereas it appears that a claimant seeking one of the ordinary remedies may *choose* whether to do so under the judicial review procedure (subject to the conditions laid down in s 31(2) of the Supreme Court Act 1981, on which see above at 13.1) or by issuing a claim in the ordinary way. This raises two issues, upon which we which focus in this chapter. First, exactly what is the judicial review procedure which claimants seeking a prerogative remedy are required to use? Secondly, to what extent may a claimant seeking to raise a public law matter avoid having to use the judicial review procedure by issuing a claim, in the ordinary way, for an injunction or declaration?

14.2 What is the Judicial Review Procedure?

14.2.1 The Origins of Today's Judicial Review Procedure

The Civil Procedure Rules were introduced, beginning in 1999, in an attempt to improve the way in which civil litigation is conducted in England and Wales. The Rules form a comprehensive code which governs such litigation; their overriding objective, according to CPR 1.1, is to enable courts to deal with cases 'justly'. It is far beyond the scope of this book to address the general content or implications of the Rules, detailed commentary on which may be found in specialist works such as Plant (ed), *Blackstone's Civil Practice* (London 2004). Instead, our interest primarily lies in the distinct procedural rules which collectively comprise the judicial review procedure. What are these rules? To what extent do they differ from those applicable to civil litigation generally? And what justifications exist for the adoption of a distinct procedural approach in this context? The answers to the first two of these questions, which are today found in the CPR, are addressed below. However, in order to understand how we have arrived at the position now set out in the Rules, and to appreciate why it has been felt by legislators that a distinct procedure is required in this area, it is first necessary to set the Rules in their historical context.

Today's judicial review procedure, the nature of which we address in the following section, shares much in common with its predecessor, which came into being as a result of reforms introduced in 1977 and finessed in 1981. Prior to those reforms, prerogative and ordinary remedies were unavailable in the same proceedings, and it was the obvious practical utility of making all remedies available in a single set of proceedings which was the driving force behind the reforms, as the following excerpt from the Law Commission report upon which the reforms were based indicates. (For further explanation of the changes wrought by the 1977–1981 reforms, see the excerpt below at 14.3.1 from Lord Diplock's speech in *O'Reilly* v. *Mackman* [1983] 2 AC 237.)

....

Law Com No 73, *Remedies in Administrative Law*
(London 1976)

. . . The unsatisfactory nature of the present position has been succinctly stated by the late Professor S A de Smith in his evidence to the Franks Committee [Cmnd 218, *Report of the Committee on Administrative Tribunals and Enquiries* (1957), Minutes of Evidence, Appendix I at 10]: —

> "Until the Legislature intervenes, therefore, we shall continue to have two sets of remedies against the usurpation or abuse of power by administrative tribunals — remedies which overlap but do not coincide, which must be sought in wholly distinct forms of proceedings, which are overlaid with technicalities and fine distinctions, but which would conjointly cover a very substantial area of the existing field of judicial control. This state of affairs bears a striking resemblance to that which obtained when English civil procedure was still bedevilled by the old forms of action."

. . . Our basic recommendation is that there should be a form of procedure to be entitled an "application for judicial review". Under cover of the application for judicial review a litigant should be able to obtain any of the prerogative orders, or, in appropriate circumstances, a declaration or an injunction. The litigant would have to specify in his application for judicial review which particular remedy or remedies he was seeking, but if he later desired to apply for a remedy for which he had not initially asked he would be able with the leave of the Court to amend his application. The vital difference, however, from the present system under Order 53 [of the Rules of the Supreme Court] would be that the litigant's choice of remedies in the Divisional Court would not be limited to the prerogative orders but would also (as mentioned above) include, in appropriate circumstances, a declaration or an injunction. Broadly speaking, the circumstances when it would appropriate to ask for a declaration or an injunction under cover of an application for judicial review would be when the case involved an issue comparable to those in respect of which an application may be made for a prerogative order — *i.e.* when an issue of public law is involved. What we are recommending is only a method whereby the different prerogative orders and the declaration and the injunction may be available to the Divisional Court in the public law field . . .

It was assumed that the implementation of many of the recommendations in the Law Commission's report would be by legislation. However, the bulk of the proposals were in fact brought into being by an amendment in 1977 to Order 53 of the Rules of the Supreme Court, this amendment coming into force in 1978 (SI 1977/1955). Order 53 was further amended in 1980 (SI 1980/2000), and the Supreme Court Act 1981 affirmed and codified certain aspects of the amendments to Order 53.

As a result of these reforms, the application for judicial review — the forerunner of today's judicial review procedure — was introduced, thus making it possible to seek prerogative and ordinary remedies in the same proceedings (*ie* the application for judicial review). Applicants for judicial review under the Order 53 had to comply with a number of conditions designed to protect public authorities against litigation which would unduly interfere with the discharge of their public functions. For instance, applicants were required to obtain the leave of the court to seek judicial review (Supreme Court Act 1981, s 31(3)) by applying *ex parte* to a Crown Office judge — that is, a judge nominated to hear public law cases (Order 53, r 3(2)); they had to avoid delay in making applications by seeking leave 'promptly and in any event within three months from the date when grounds for the application first arose' unless there was a 'good reason' for non-compliance with that requirement (Order 53, r 4(1)), and the court had a discretion to refuse to grant leave or relief on certain grounds if there was 'undue delay' in making an application (Supreme Court Act 1981, s 31(6)).

A further obstacle faced by applicants for judicial review related to the somewhat attenuated ability, or perhaps more accurately willingness, of the courts to resolve disputes of fact in judicial review cases. Under RSC Order 53 it was open to applicants to seek discovery of documents and cross-examination on affidavits, but courts were rarely minded to accede to such requests. For instance, in *R v. Secretary of State for the Environment, ex parte Islington London Borough Council* (19 July 1991, unreported), McCowan LJ said that 'unless the applicant in judicial review is in a position to assert that the evidence relied on by a Minister is false, or at least inaccurate, it is inappropriate to grant discovery in order to allow the applicant to check the accuracy of the evidence in question'. This type of approach to discovery was criticized by the Law Commission (Law Com No 226, *Administrative Law: Judicial Review and Statutory Appeal* (London 1994), Part VII), which called for a more liberal approach. Similarly, while it was possible for the courts on judicial review to permit cross-examination in order to test the veracity of evidence submitted by affidavit, Lord Diplock stated in *O'Reilly* v. *Mackman* [1983] 2 AC 237 at 282 that 'it will only be upon rare occasions that the interests of justice will require that leave be given for cross-examination of deponents on their affidavits in applications for judicial review'. Although Lord Diplock sought to justify this position by arguing that factual issues are rarely in dispute in judicial review, it is self-evident that situations will arise when cross-examination is essential: as Smith [2001] *JR* 138 at 140 puts it, 'There must be cases' — such as *R* v. *Derbyshire County Council, ex parte The Times Supplements Ltd* (1991) 3 Admin LR 241, in which Watkins LJ concluded (at 252) *after* cross-examination that councillors' evidence as to the propriety of the purpose underlying their actions 'displayed an unworthy lack of candour' — 'where insufficient extraneous evidence exists to demonstrate that a deponent is wrong, or dishonest. In such cases, what mechanism is there other than cross-examination to enable the shortcomings of an affidavit to be proved?'

As a result, many litigants opted to initiate ordinary proceedings rather than making an application for judicial review, until this means of escape from the latter was closed-off by the House of Lords in *O'Reilly* v. *Mackman* [1983] 2 AC 237. We turn to the so-called procedural dichotomy thereby established at 14.3 below; first, however, it remains to address the new judicial review procedure introduced by the CPR, and to consider the extent to which it differs from the position just described.

14.2.2 The Nature of the Judicial Review Procedure

Part 54 of the CPR entered into force on 2 October 2000 following Sir Jeffrey Bowman's *Review of the Crown Office List* (London 2000) (hereinafter 'the Bowman Report'), which advocated (with some modifications) the implementation of many of the recommendations made by the Law Commission in its 1994 review of judicial review procedure (Law Com No 226, *Administrative Law: Judicial Review and Statutory Appeals* (London 1994)) (hereinafter 'the Law Commission report'). Part 54 introduced a revised judicial review procedure. At the same time the Administrative Court was established within the Queen's Bench Division (*Practice Direction (Administrative Court: Establishment)* [2000] 1 WLR 1654) in light of Bowman's conclusion (at 19) that 'speed, certainty, efficiency, consistency and quality of decisions in public law cases can only be realised by having a dedicated office to administer cases and dedicated judicial resources to hear them'. Renaming the Crown Office List — that is, the list of Queen's Bench Division judges nominated to hear cases involving public law — the Administrative Court, said Bowman, would 'emphasise that [its] . . . main business is public and administrative law and . . . make this clear to users who are not familiar with the work at present done by the Crown Office List'.

Bowman's review was prompted by growing pressure on the Crown Office List as a result of, *inter alia*, the increasing tendency to challenge public bodies' decisions and the then imminent activation of the Human Rights Act 1998. In light of this, two of Bowman's key objectives were to reduce delays in the Crown Office List and to promote the efficient use of judicial resources, and many of his recommendations related to practical matters concerning the organization of the proposed Administrative Court. Other recommendations, which were taken up, sought to recast the language of judicial review in terms consistent with the CPR: thus (adopting the recommendation in the Law Commission report at [8.3]) the prerogative remedies have lost their Latin names (see above at 14.1), while 'applicants' have become 'claimants', respondents are now 'defendants', and 'claims' rather than 'applications' for judicial review are now issued.

But what of the judicial review procedure itself? Following Bowman's recommendations, there have been some changes in this area, but much of the old regime remains: the standing requirement (on which see 15.7 below) set out in the Supreme Court Act 1981, s 31(3) is unchanged under the new system, as is the need to issue the claim promptly and in any event within three months (CPR 54.5(1)) (discussed below at 15.4). However, while the requirement that the claimant obtains the leave — or permission, as it is now called — of the court is also still present, the nature of the permission stage is somewhat altered, and a Pre-Action Protocol has been introduced to require interaction between claimant and defendant prior to the issuing of the claim (see below at 15.2). The detail of these conditions with which intending claimants must comply under the new judicial review procedure are addressed in ch 15 below; for present purposes, it is sufficient to observe that the preconditions which restricted the availability of judicial review under the Order 53 procedure are largely replicated under the Part 54 regime.

Similarly, the notion — implicit in the courts' previous reluctance, noted above, to permit discovery and cross-examination — that the resolution of factual disputes is not usually something to be undertaken in judicial review proceedings is perpetuated under the revised procedure. (In fact, the Bowman Report (at 17) took it as read that one of the hallmarks of the work of the then Crown Office List was that it involved 'matters which can normally be decided without the need to resolve issues of fact'.) Indeed, although it is Part 54 which sets out the distinguishing features of the judicial review procedure, CPR 54.1(2)(e) provides that ' "the judicial review procedure" means the Part 8 procedure as modified by [the relevant provisions of Part 54]'. Part 8, it should be noted, applies to claims which are 'unlikely to involve a substantial dispute of fact' (CPR 8.1(2)(a)). It is clear that the new regime does little, if anything, to enhance the availability of disclosure — as discovery is now called — and cross-examination in judicial review proceedings. Thus, while disclosure is possible, it is not required unless the court specifically so orders (CPR Practice Direction 54, paragraph 12.1) and, as Cornford [2000] *Web JCLI* notes, 'it is hardly to be expected that the CPR will encourage greater disclosure of documents in judicial review, when its basic purpose is to save court time and speed up litigation'. This matter was recently considered by the Court of Appeal in *R (Quark Fishing Ltd)* v. *Secretary of State for Foreign and Commonwealth Affairs* [2002] EWCA Civ 1409, Laws LJ noting (at [50]) that while there is 'no general duty of disclosure in judicial review proceedings', public authorities are under a duty to 'assist the court with full and accurate explanations of all the facts relevant to the issue the court must decide' (on which see further above at 12.1).

Nor is cross-examination on affidavits any easier to obtain under the new system. Whereas there was a power — albeit rarely used — under Order 53 to allow cross-examination in judicial review cases, no explicit power to this effect was to be found in Part 54 in its original form, since CPR 54.16(1) rendered the power under CPR 8.6(3) to give directions requiring the attendance for cross-examination of a witness who has given written evidence inapplicable to judicial review proceedings. Smith [2001] *JR* 138 at 140 strongly criticized this apparent removal of the power to allow cross-examination, arguing that, although only occasionally necessary, cross-examination can prove invaluable in judicial review cases. In fact, it was held in *R (PG)* v. *London Borough of Ealing* [2002] EWHC 250 (Admin) that cross-examination could be allowed under other provisions of the CPR, and in any event CPR 54.16(1) has now been amended such that the power under CPR 8.6(3) is now exercisable on judicial review.

While there is no suggestion that the new procedural rules make it easier to obtain cross-examination, it appears that the Human Rights Act 1998 may demand a more liberal attitude in this regard. For instance in *R (Wilkinson)* v. *Broadmoor Hospital* [2001] EWCA Civ 1545 [2002] 1 WLR 419, in which a mental patient sought judicial review of a decision to treat him forcibly against his will, alleging that this breached his rights under Articles 2, 3, and 8 ECHR, cross-examination of doctors was held to be appropriate in order to resolve a dispute of fact. Simon Brown LJ (at [25]–[31]) was strongly influenced by the fact that the claimant's Convention rights were engaged: a relatively intensive review involving the use of proportionality was therefore appropriate, making it necessary for the court to be able to investigate and resolve the medical issues (such as whether the claimant was competent). It is also worth noting that both Simon Brown and Hale LJJ emphasized that, instead of issuing a claim for judicial review, the claimant could instead have pursued a claim in tort for assault, in which case cross-examination would have been readily available.

It follows that, with the exception of alterations to the permission stage (considered below at 15.2) and tentative indications that cross-examination may be easier to obtain in cases with a human rights dimension (a development which is, in any event, prompted by the Human Rights Act 1998, not the CPR), the judicial review procedure under Part 54 of the CPR shares much in common with its predecessor, the Order 53 application for judicial review. In particular, it is clear beyond doubt that the CPR preserve the character of the claim for judicial review as a distinct procedural model which is deliberately different from that which applies to ordinary proceedings. This reflects the conclusion reached by Bowman (at 60) that '[a] separate procedure is necessary . . . because of the special nature of judicial review and the need for speed and flexibility'. It is hardly surprising, therefore, that some claimants seek to litigate public law matters by issuing claims for injunctions or declarations in ordinary proceedings in order to escape the strictures of the judicial review procedure, thereby gaining access to more generous provision for cross-examination and disclosure and avoiding the need to obtain permission and comply with very short time limits. We consider, in the next section, the extent to which this can be done.

14.3 When Must the Judicial Review Procedure be Used?

14.3.1 Procedural Exclusivity

There was a time when the courts actively endorsed the tactic of seeking ordinary remedies instead of prerogative remedies, so as to avoid the restrictions which obtain when the latter are sought. In *Barnard* v. *National Dock Labour Board* [1953] 2 QB 18 at 41, for example, Denning LJ considered it highly desirable that litigants should adopt such a strategy in order that the capacity of the courts to enforce the law was not circumscribed by the limitations applicable to the prerogative remedies:

It is axiomatic that when a statutory tribunal sits to administer justice, it must act in accordance with the law. Parliament clearly so intended. If the tribunal does not observe the law, what is to be done? The remedy by certiorari is hedged round by limitations and may not be available. Why then should not the court intervene by declaration and injunction? If it cannot so intervene, it would mean that the tribunal could disregard the law, which is a thing no one can do in this country.

There is, however, an obvious difficulty with this view. The existence of a distinct judicial review procedure is founded upon particular policy considerations, such as the need to erect safeguards (*eg* permission and strict time limits) to prevent litigation from unduly interfering with agencies' discharge of their public functions and the desirability of swiftly resolving questions as to the legality of administrative action. Yet, if litigants have a free choice between ordinary and judicial review proceedings, they will (for the reasons considered above) usually choose the former, in turn preventing the realization of the policy objectives of the latter. The judicial review procedure is specially designed for the resolution of disputes concerning the discharge by public bodies of their public functions, and it seems to follow that the litigation of such matters should be by way of a claim for judicial review.

The House of Lords, in its landmark decision in *O'Reilly* v. *Mackman*, found the logic of this argument compelling, notwithstanding that, as we will see, its implications posed enormous practical difficulties for intending litigants. (Although Lord Diplock refers to the Order 53 procedure in his speech in *O'Reilly*, we have already seen that many of the key features of that procedure are repeated in CPR Part 54.)

....

O'Reilly v. *Mackman* [1983] 2 AC 237
House of Lords

The appellants, who were all prisoners at Hull Prison, wished to challenge decisions reached by the Prison's Board of Visitors in relation to allegations that the appellants had committed breaches of the Prison Rules 1964. It was argued that the rules of natural justice had not been complied with by the Board and the appellants sought declarations that the findings and consequent penalties were therefore null and void. They proceeded not by way of an application for judicial review under Order 53 but, instead, by ordinary proceedings begun by writ (or, in one of the four cases involved, originating summons). It was argued that the matter ought to have been pursued by means of an application for judicial review, and an application was made to strike out the statements of claim (and the originating summons) on the ground that they were an abuse of the process of the court. The application was refused by Peter Pain J at first instance but the Court of Appeal allowed an appeal by the Board. An appeal from that decision was made to the House of Lords.

Lord Diplock

. . . My Lords, it is not contested that if the allegations set out in the originating summons or statements of claim are true each of the appellants would have had a remedy obtainable by the procedure of an application for judicial review under R.S.C., Ord. 53; but to obtain that remedy, whether it took the form of an order of certiorari to quash the board's award or a declaration of its nullity, would have required the leave of the court under R.S.C., Ord. 53, r. 3 [see now CPR 54.4]. That judicial review lies against an award of the board of visitors of a prison made in the exercise of their disciplinary functions was established by the judgment of the Court of Appeal (overruling a Divisional Court) in *Reg. v. Board of Visitors of Hull Prison, Ex parte St. Germain* [1979] Q.B. 425: a decision that was, in my view, clearly right and has not been challenged in the instant appeals by the respondents.

In the *St. Germain* case, the only remedy that had been sought was certiorari to quash the decision of the board of visitors; but the alternative remedy of a declaration of nullity if the court considered it to be just and convenient would also have been available upon an application for judicial review under R.S.C., Ord. 53 after the replacement of the old rule by the new rule in 1977. In the instant cases, which were commenced after the new rule came into effect (but before the coming into force of section 31 of the Supreme Court Act 1981), certiorari would unquestionably have been the more appropriate remedy, since rule 5(4) of the Prison Rules 1964, which provides for remission of sentence up to a maximum of one-third, stipulates that the "rule shall have effect subject to any disciplinary award of forfeiture. . . ." Prison rule 56, however, expressly empowers the Secretary of State to remit a disciplinary award and, since he would presumably do so in the case of a disciplinary award that had been declared by the High Court to be a nullity, such a declaration would achieve, though less directly, the same result in practice as quashing the award by certiorari.

So no question arises as to the "jurisdiction" of the High Court to grant to each of the appellants relief by way of a declaration in the terms sought, if they succeeded in establishing the facts alleged in their respective statements of claim or originating summons and the court considered a declaration to be an appropriate remedy. All that is at issue in the instant appeal is the procedure by which such relief ought to be sought. Put in a single sentence the question for your Lordships is: whether in 1980 after R.S.C., Ord. 53 in its new form, adopted in 1977, had come into operation it was an abuse of the process of the court to apply for such declarations by using the procedure laid down in the Rules for proceedings begun by writ or by originating summons instead of using the procedure laid down by Ord. 53 for an application for judicial review of the awards of forfeiture of remission of sentence made against them by the board which the appellants are seeking to impugn?

In their respective actions, the appellants claim only declaratory relief . . . So the first thing to be noted is that the relief sought in the action is discretionary only.

It is not, and it could not be, contended that the decision of the board awarding him forfeiture of remission had infringed or threatened to infringe any right of the appellant derived from private law, whether a common law right or one created by a statute. Under the Prison Rules remission of sentence is not a matter of right but of indulgence. So far as private law is concerned all that each appellant had was a legitimate expectation, based upon his knowledge of what is the general practice, that he would be granted the maximum remission, permitted by rule 5(2) of the Prison Rules, of one third of his sentence if by that time no disciplinary award of forfeiture of remission had been made against him. So the second thing to be noted is that none of the appellants had any remedy in private law.

In public law, as distinguished from private law, however, such legitimate expectation gave to each appellant a sufficient interest to challenge the legality of the adverse disciplinary award made against him by the board on the ground that in one way or another the board in reaching its decision had acted outwith the powers conferred upon it by the legislation under which it was acting; and such grounds would include the board's failure to observe the rules of natural justice: which means no more than to act fairly towards him in carrying out their decision-making process, and I prefer so to put it.

. . . In exercising their functions under rule 51 members of the board are acting as a statutory tribunal, as contrasted with a domestic tribunal upon which powers are conferred by contract between those who agree to submit to its jurisdiction. Where the legislation which confers upon a statutory tribunal its decision-making powers also provides expressly for the procedure it shall follow in the course of reaching its decision, it is a question of construction of the relevant legislation, to be decided by the court in which the decision is challenged, whether a particular procedural provision is mandatory, so that its non-observance in the process of reaching the decision makes the decision itself a nullity, or whether it is merely directory, so that the statutory tribunal has a discretion not to comply with it if, in its opinion, the exceptional circumstances of a particular case justify departing from it. But the requirement that a person who is charged with having done something which, if proved to the satisfaction of a statutory tribunal, has consequences that will, or may, affect him adversely, should be given a fair opportunity of hearing what is alleged against him and of presenting his own case, is so fundamental to any civilised legal system that it is to be presumed that Parliament intended that a failure to observe it should render null and void any decision reached in breach of this requirement. What is alleged by the appellants other than Millbanks would amount to an infringement of the express rule 49; but even if there were no such express provision a requirement to observe it would be a necessary implication from the nature of the disciplinary functions of the board. In the absence of express provision to the contrary Parliament, whenever it provides for the creation of a statutory tribunal, must be presumed not to have intended that the tribunal should be authorised to act in contravention of one of the fundamental rules of natural justice or fairness: audi alteram partem.

In Millbanks's case, there is no express provision in the Prison Rules that the members of the board who inquire into a disciplinary offence under rule 51 must be free from personal bias against the prisoner. It is another fundamental rule of natural justice or fairness, too obvious to call for express statement of it, that a tribunal exercising functions such as those exercised by the board in the case of Millbanks should be constituted of persons who enter upon the inquiry without any pre-conceived personal bias against the prisoner. Failure to comply with this implied requirement would likewise render the decision of the tribunal a nullity. So the third thing to be noted is that each of the appellants, if he established the facts alleged in his action, was entitled to a remedy in public law which would have the effect of preventing the decision of the board from having any adverse consequences upon him.

My Lords, the power of the High Court to make declaratory judgments is conferred by what is now R.S.C., Ord. 15, r. 16. The language of the rule which was first made in 1883 has never been altered, though the numbering of the rule has from time to time been changed. It provides:

> "No action or other proceeding shall be open to objection on the ground that a merely declaratory judgment or order is sought thereby, and the court may make binding declarations of right whether or not any consequential relief is or could be claimed."

This rule . . . has been very liberally interpreted in the course of its long history, wherever it appeared to the court that the justice of the case required the grant of declaratory relief in the particular action before it. [RSC Order 15 r 16 has now been replaced by CPR 40.20, which provides that, 'The court may make binding declarations whether or not any other remedy is claimed.'] . . . Ord. 15, r. 16 says nothing as to the appropriate procedure by which declarations of different kinds ought to be sought. Nor does it draw any distinction between declarations that relate to rights and obligations under private law and those that relate to rights and obligations under public law. Indeed the appreciation of the distinction in substantive law between what is private law and what is public law has itself been a latecomer to the English legal system. It is a consequence of the development that has taken place in the last 30 years of the procedures available for judicial control of administrative action. This development started with the expansion of the grounds upon which orders of certiorari could be obtained as a result of the decision of the Court of Appeal in *Rex. v. Northumberland Compensation Appeal Tribunal, Ex parte Shaw* [1952] 1 K.B. 338; it was accelerated by the passing of the Tribunals and Inquiries Act 1958, and culminated in the substitution in 1977 of the new form of R.S.C., Ord. 53 which has since been given statutory confirmation in section 31 of the Supreme Court Act 1981.

[His Lordship then considered *Shaw*, the Tribunals and Inquiries Acts 1958 and 1971, and, in particular, s 14(1) of the latter, and continued:] . . . [Section 14(1) provides] as follows:

> "As respects England and Wales . . . any provision in an Act passed before [the commencement of this Act] that any order or determination shall not be called into question in any court, or any provision in such an Act which by similar words excludes any of the powers of the High Court, shall not have effect so as to prevent the removal of proceedings into the High Court by order of certiorari or to prejudice the powers of the High Court to make orders of mandamus: . . ."

[The 1971 Act has been repealed, but similar provision is now made by s 12(1) of the Tribunals and Inquiries Act 1992.] The subsection, it is to be observed, says nothing about any right to bring civil actions for declarations of nullity of orders or determinations of statutory bodies where an earlier Act of Parliament contains a provision that such order or determination "shall not be called into question in any court." Since actions begun by writ seeking such declarations were already coming into common use in the High Court so as to provide an alternative remedy to orders of certiorari, the section suggests a parliamentary preference in favour of making the latter remedy available rather than the former. I will defer consideration of the reasons for this preference until later.

. . . [T]he landmark decision of this House in *Anisminic Ltd. v. Foreign Compensation Commission* [1969] 2 A.C. 147, and particularly the leading speech of Lord Reid, . . . has liberated English public law from the fetters that the courts had theretofore imposed upon themselves so far as determinations of inferior courts and statutory tribunals were concerned, by drawing esoteric distinctions between errors of law committed by such tribunals that went to their jurisdiction, and errors of law committed by them within their jurisdiction. The breakthrough that the *Anisminic* case made was the recognition by the majority of this House that if a tribunal whose jurisdiction was limited by statute or subordinate legislation mistook the law applicable to the facts as it had found them, it must have asked itself the wrong question, i.e., one into which it was not empowered to inquire and so had no jurisdiction to determine. Its purported 'determination,' not being a 'determination' within the meaning of the empowering legislation, was accordingly a nullity.

Anisminic Ltd. v. Foreign Compensation Commission was an action commenced by writ for a declaration, in which a minute of the commission's reasons for their determination adverse to the plaintiff company did not appear upon the face of their determination, and had in fact been obtained only upon discovery . . . In the House of Lords the question of the propriety of suing by writ for a declaration instead of applying for certiorari and mandamus played no part in the main argument for the commission . . .

My Lords, *Anisminic Ltd. v. Foreign Compensation Commission* [1969] 2 A.C. 147 was decided by this House before the alteration was made to R.S.C., Ord. 53 in 1977 . . . The pre-1977 Order 53, like its predecessors, placed under considerable procedural disadvantage applicants who wished to challenge the lawfulness of a determination of a statutory tribunal or any other body of persons having legal authority to determine questions affecting the common law or statutory rights or obligations of other persons as individuals. It will be noted that I have broadened the much-cited description by Atkin L.J. in *Rex. v. Electricity Commissioners, Ex parte London Electricity Joint Committee Co (1920) Ltd* [1924] 1 K.B. 171, 205 of bodies of persons subject to the supervisory jurisdiction of the High Court by prerogative remedies (which in 1924 then took the form of prerogative writs of mandamus, prohibition, certiorari, and quo warranto) by excluding Atkin L.J.'s limitation of the bodies of persons to whom the prerogative writs might issue, to those "having the duty to act judicially." For the next 40 years this phrase gave rise to many attempts, with varying success, to draw subtle distinctions between decisions that were quasi-judicial and those that were administrative only. But the relevance of arguments of this kind was destroyed by the decision of this House in *Ridge v. Baldwin* [1964] A.C. 40, where again the leading speech was given by Lord Reid. Wherever any person or body of persons has authority conferred by legislation to make decisions of the kind I have described, it is amenable to the remedy of an order to quash its decision either for error of law in reaching it or for failure to act fairly towards the person who will be adversely affected by the decision by failing to observe either one or other of the two fundamental rights accorded to him by the rules of natural justice or fairness, viz. to have afforded to him a reasonable opportunity of learning what is alleged against him and of putting forward his own case in answer to it, and to the absence of personal bias against him on the part of the person by whom the decision falls to be made. In *Ridge v. Baldwin* it is interesting to observe that Lord Reid said at p. 72 "We do not have a developed system of administrative law — perhaps because until fairly recently we did not need it." By 1977 the need had continued to grow apace and this reproach to English law had been removed. We did have by then a developed system of administrative law, to the development of which Lord Reid himself, by his speeches in cases which reached this House, had made an outstanding contribution. To the landmark cases of *Ridge v. Baldwin* and *Anisminic Ltd. v. Foreign Compensation Commission* [1969] 2 A..C 147 I would add a third, *Padfield v. Minister of Agriculture, Fisheries and Food* [1968] A.C. 997, another case in which a too timid judgment of my own in the Court of Appeal was (fortunately) overruled.

Although the availability of the remedy of orders to quash a decision by certiorari had in theory been widely extended by these developments, the procedural disadvantages under which applicants for this remedy laboured remained substantially unchanged until the alteration of Order 53 in 1977. Foremost among these was the absence of any provision for discovery. In the case of a decision which did not state the reasons for it, it was not possible to challenge its validity for error of law in the reasoning by which the decision had been reached. If it had been an application for certiorari those who were the plaintiffs in the *Anisminic* case would have failed; it was only because by pursuing an action by writ for a declaration of nullity that the plaintiffs were entitled to the discovery by which the minute of the commission's reasons which showed that they had asked themselves the wrong question, was obtained. Again under Order 53 evidence was required to be on affidavit. This in itself is not an unjust disadvantage; it is a common feature of many forms of procedure in the High Court, including originating summonses; but in the absence of any express provision for cross-examination of deponents, as your Lordships who are familiar with the pre-1977 procedure will be aware, even *applications* for leave to cross-examine were virtually unknown — let alone the grant of leave itself — save in very exceptional cases of which I believe none of your Lordships has ever had actual experience. Lord Goddard C.J., whose experience was at that time unrivalled, had so stated in *Reg. v. Stokesley, Yorkshire, Justices, Ex parte Bartram* [1956] 1 W.L.R. 254, 257.

On the other hand as compared with an action for a declaration commenced by writ or originating summons, the procedure under Order 53 both before and after 1977 provided for the respondent decision-making statutory tribunal or public authority against which the remedy of certiorari was sought protection against claims which it was not in the public interest for courts of justice to entertain.

First, leave to apply for the order was required. The application for leave which was ex parte but could be, and in practice often was, adjourned in order to enable the proposed respondent to be represented, had to be supported by a statement setting out, inter alia, the grounds on which the relief was sought and by affidavits verifying the facts relied on: so that a knowingly false statement of fact would amount to the criminal offence of perjury. Such affidavit was also required to satisfy the requirement of uberrima fides, with the consequence that failure to make on oath a full and candid disclosure of material facts was of itself a ground for refusing the relief sought in the substantive application for which leave had been obtained on the strength of the affidavit. This was an important safeguard, which is preserved in the new Order 53 of 1977. The public interest in good administration requires that public authorities and third parties should not be kept in suspense as to the legal validity of a decision the authority has reached in purported exercise of decision-making powers for any longer period than is absolutely necessary in fairness to the person affected by the decision. In contrast, allegations made in a statement of claim or an indorsement of an originating summons are not on oath, so the requirement of a prior application for leave to be supported by full and candid affidavits verifying the facts relied on is an important safeguard against groundless or unmeritorious claims that a particular decision is a nullity. There was also power in the court on granting leave to impose terms as to costs or security.

Furthermore, as Order 53 was applied in practice, as soon as the application for leave had been made it provided a very speedy means, available in urgent cases within a matter of days rather than months, for determining whether a disputed decision was valid in law or not. A reduction of the period of suspense was also effected by the requirement that leave to apply for certiorari to quash a decision must be made within a limited period after the impugned decision was made, unless delay beyond that limited period was accounted for to the satisfaction of the judge. The period was six months under the pre-1977 Order 53; under the current Order 53 it is further reduced to three months.

My Lords, the exclusion of all right to discovery in application for certiorari under Order 53, particularly before the passing of the Tribunal and Inquiries Act 1958, was calculated to cause injustice to persons who had no means, if they adopted that procedure, of ascertaining whether a public body, which had made a decision adversely affecting them, had done so for reasons which were wrong in law and rendered their decision invalid. It will be within the knowledge of all of your Lordships that, at any rate from the 1950s onwards, actions for declarations of nullity of decisions affecting the rights of individuals under public law were widely entertained, in parallel to applications for certiorari to quash, as means of obtaining an effective alternative remedy. I will not weary your Lordships by reciting examples of cases where this practice received the express approval of the Court of Appeal, though I should point out that of those cases in this House in which this practice was approved, *Vine v. National Dock Labour Board* [1957] A.C. 488 and *Ridge v. Baldwin* [1964] A.C. 40 involved, as well as questions of public law, contracts of employment which gave rise to rights under private law. In *Anisminic Ltd. v. Foreign Compensation Commission* [1969] 2 A.C. 147 the procedural question was not seriously argued, while *Pyx Granite Ltd. v. Ministry of Housing and Local Government* [1960] A.C. 260, which is referred to in the notes to Order 19 appearing in the *Supreme Court Practice* (1982) as an instance of the approval by this House of the practice of suing for a declaration instead of applying for an order of certiorari, appears on analysis to have been concerned with declaring that the plaintiffs had a legal right to do what they were seeking to do without the need to obtain any decision from the Minister. Nevertheless I accept that having regard to disadvantages, particularly in relation to the absolute bar upon compelling discovery of documents by the respondent public authority to an applicant for an order of certiorari, and the almost invariable practice of refusing leave to allow cross-examination of deponents to affidavits lodged on its behalf, it could not be regarded as an abuse of the process of the court, before the amendments made to Order 53 in 1977, to proceed against the authority by an action for a declaration of nullity of the impugned decision with an injunction to prevent the authority from acting on it, instead of applying for an order of certiorari; and this despite the fact that, by adopting this course, the plaintiff evaded the safeguards imposed in the public interest against groundless, unmeritorious or tardy attacks upon the validity of decisions made by public authorities in the field of public law.

Those disadvantages, which formerly might have resulted in an applicant's being unable to obtain justice in an application for certiorari under Order 53, have all been removed by the new Order introduced in 1977. There is express provision in the new rule 8 for interlocutory applications for discovery of documents, the administration of interrogatories and the cross-examination of deponents to affidavits. Discovery of documents (which may often be a time-consuming process) is not automatic as in an action begun by writ, but otherwise Order 24 applies to it and discovery is obtainable upon application whenever, and to the extent that, the justice of the case requires [see now CPR 54.16 and Practice Direction 54, para 12, on disclosure]; similarly Order 26 applies to applications for interrogatories [see now CPR 18.1 on orders for further information]; and to applications for cross-examination of deponents to affidavits Ord. 28, r. 2(3) applies [see now CPR 8.6(3)]. This is the rule that deals with evidence in actions begun by originating summons and permits oral cross-examination on affidavit evidence wherever the justice of the case requires. It may well be that for the reasons given by Lord Denning M.R. in *George v. Secretary of State for the Environment* (1979) 77 L.G.R. 689, it will only be upon rare occasions that the interests of justice will require that leave be given for cross-examination of deponents on their affidavits in applications for judicial review. This is because of the nature of the issues that normally arise upon judicial review. The facts, except where the claim that a decision was invalid on the ground that the statutory tribunal or public authority that made the decision failed to comply with the procedure prescribed by the legislation under which it was acting or failed to observe the fundamental rules of natural justice or fairness, can seldom be a matter of relevant dispute upon an application for judicial review, since the tribunal or authority's findings of fact, as distinguished from the legal consequences of the facts that they have found, are not open to review by the court in the exercise of its supervisory powers except on the principles laid down in *Edwards v. Bairstow* [1956] A.C. 14, 36; and to allow cross-examination presents the court with a temptation, not always easily resisted, to substitute its own view of the facts for that of the decision-making body upon whom the exclusive jurisdiction to determine facts has been conferred by Parliament. Nevertheless having regard to a possible misunderstanding of what was said by Geoffrey Lane LJ in *Reg. v. Board of Visitors of Hull Prison, Ex parte St. Germain (No. 2)* [1979] 1 W.L.R 1401, 1410 your Lordships may think this an appropriate occasion on which to emphasise that whatever may have been the position before the rule was altered in 1977 in all proceedings for judicial review that have been started since that date the grant of leave to cross-examine deponents upon applications for judicial review is governed by the same principles as it is in actions begun by originating summons; it should be allowed whenever the justice of the particular case so requires.

Another handicap under which an applicant for a prerogative order under Order 53 formerly laboured (though it would not have affected the appellants in the instant cases even if they had brought their actions before the 1977 alteration to Order 53) was that a claim for damages for breach of a right in private law of the applicant resulting from an invalid decision of a public authority could not be made in an application under Order 53. Damages could only be claimed in a separate action begun by writ; whereas in an action so begun they could be claimed as additional relief as well as a declaration of nullity of the decision from which the damage claimed had flowed. Rule 7 of the new Order 53 [see now CPR 54.3(2)] permits the applicant for judicial review to include in the statement in support of his application for leave a claim for damages and empowers the court to award damages on the hearing of the application if satisfied that such damages could have been awarded to him in an action begun by him by writ at the time of the making of the application.

Finally rule 1 of the new Order 53 [see now CPR 54.3(1)] enables an application for a declaration or an injunction to be included in an application for judicial review. This was not previously the case;

only prerogative orders could be obtained in proceedings under Order 53. Declarations or injunctions were obtainable only in actions begun by writ or originating summons . . .

So Order 53 since 1977 has provided a procedure by which every type of remedy for infringement of the rights of individuals that are entitled to protection in public law can be obtained in one and the same proceeding by way of an application for judicial review, and whichever remedy is found to be the most appropriate in the light of what has emerged upon the hearing of the application, can be granted to him. If what should emerge is that his complaint is not of an infringement of any of his rights that are entitled to protection in public law, but may be an infringement of his rights in private law and thus not a proper subject for judicial review, the court has power under rule 9 (5), instead of refusing the application, to order the proceedings to continue as if they had begun by writ. There is no such converse power under the RSC to permit an action begun by writ to continue as if it were an application for judicial review; . . . nor do I see the need to amend the rules in order to create one. [However, see now CPR 30.5, discussed below at 14.3.9.]

My Lords, at the outset of this speech, I drew attention to the fact that the remedy by way of declaration of nullity of the decisions of the board was discretionary — as are all the remedies available upon judicial review. Counsel for the plaintiffs accordingly conceded that the fact that by adopting the procedure of an action begun by writ or by originating summons instead of an application for judicial review under Order 53 (from which there have now been removed all those disadvantages to applicants that had previously led the courts to countenance actions for declarations and injunctions as an alternative procedure for obtaining a remedy for infringement of the rights of the individual that are entitled to protection in public law only) the plaintiffs had thereby been able to evade those protections against groundless, unmeritorious or tardy harassment that were afforded to statutory tribunals or decision-making public authorities by Order 53, and which might have resulted in the summary, and would in any event have resulted in the speedy disposition of the application, is among the matters fit to be taken into consideration by the judge in deciding whether to exercise his discretion by refusing to grant a declaration; but, it was contended, this he may only do at the conclusion of the trial.

So to delay the judge's decision as to how to exercise his discretion would defeat the public policy that underlies the grant of those protections: viz., the need, in the interests of good administration and of third parties who may be indirectly affected by the decision, for speedy certainty as to whether it has the effect of a decision that is valid in public law. An action for a declaration or injunction need not be commenced until the very end of the limitation period; if begun by writ, discovery and interlocutory proceedings may be prolonged and the plaintiffs are not required to support their allegations by evidence on oath until the actual trial. The period of uncertainty as to the validity of a decision that has been challenged upon allegations that may eventually turn out to be baseless and unsupported by evidence on oath, may thus be strung out for a very lengthy period, as the actions of the first three appellants in the instant appeals show. Unless such an action can be struck out summarily at the outset as an abuse of the process of the court the whole purpose of the public policy to which the change in Order 53 was directed would be defeated.

My Lords, Order 53 does not expressly provide that procedure by application for judicial review shall be the exclusive procedure available by which the remedy of a declaration or injunction may be obtained for infringement of rights that are entitled to protection under public law; nor does section 31 of the Supreme Court Act 1981. There is great variation between individual cases that fall within Order 53 and the Rules Committee and subsequently the legislature were, I think, for this reason content to rely upon the express and the inherent power of the High Court, exercised upon a case to case basis, to prevent abuse of its process whatever might be the form taken by that abuse. Accordingly, I do not think that your Lordships would be wise to use this as an occasion to lay down categories of cases in which it would necessarily always be an abuse to seek in an action begun by writ or originating summons a remedy against infringement of rights of the individual that are entitled to protection in public law.

The position of applicants for judicial review has been drastically ameliorated by the new Order 53. It has removed all those disadvantages, particularly in relation to discovery, that were manifestly unfair to them and had, in many cases, made applications for prerogative orders an inadequate remedy if justice was to be done . . .

Now that those disadvantages to applicants have been removed and all remedies for infringements of rights protected by public law can be obtained upon an application for judicial review, as can also remedies for infringements of rights under private law if such infringements should also be involved, it would in my view as a general rule be contrary to public policy, and as such an abuse of the process of the court, to permit a person seeking to establish that a decision of a public authority infringed rights to which he was entitled to protection under public law to proceed by way of an ordinary action and by this means to evade the provisions of Order 53 for the protection of such authorities.

My Lords, I have described this as a general rule; for though it may normally be appropriate to apply it by the summary process of striking out the action, there may be exceptions, particularly where the invalidity of the decision arises as a collateral issue in a claim for infringement of a right of the plaintiff arising under private law, or where none of the parties objects to the adoption of the procedure by writ or originating summons. Whether there should be other exceptions should, in my view, at this stage in the development of procedural public law, be left to be decided on a case to case basis — a process that your Lordships will be continuing in the next case in which judgment is to be delivered today [*Cocks v. Thanet District Council* [1983] 2 AC 286].

In the instant cases where the only relief sought is a declaration of nullity of the decisions of a statutory tribunal, the Board of Visitors of Hull Prison, as in any other case in which a similar declaration of nullity in public law is the only relief claimed, I have no hesitation, in agreement with the Court of Appeal, in holding that to allow the actions to proceed would be an abuse of the process of the court. They are blatant attempts to avoid the protections for the defendants for which Order 53 provides.

I would dismiss these appeals.

Lords Fraser, Keith, Bridge, and Brightman agreed with Lord Diplock. Appeal dismissed.

It is noteworthy that Lord Diplock went to considerable lengths in his speech, by tracing the development of the procedural rules applicable when the prerogative orders are sought and, in particular, contrasting the positions which obtained before and after the 1977–1981 reforms, to try to justify the principle of procedural exclusivity which he articulated. This was, no doubt, due in part to the fact that, as Lord Diplock himself acknowledged, there was nothing in RSC Order 53 — just as there is nothing in CPR Part 54 now — which *required* the application for judicial review to be regarded as an exclusive procedure. The development of the exclusivity principle in *O'Reilly* therefore amounts to what Forsyth [1985] *CLJ* 415 at 422 calls 'a novel and rather cavalier use of the abuse of process jurisdiction'. However, although Lord Diplock sought to justify the exclusivity principle by reference to the fact that the 1977–1981 reforms had 'drastically ameliorated' the position of claimants, it is undeniable that those using the judicial review procedure continue to face disadvantages such as very short time limits and the reluctance, in practice, of courts to resolve factual disputes on judicial review.

QUESTION

- Do you agree with Lord Diplock's argument that the creation of the exclusivity principle was necessary to preserve the integrity of the procedure for judicial review and of the policy objectives underlying that procedure?

Once the exclusivity principle had been set out in *O'Reilly*, the courts were obliged in subsequent decisions to set about the task of deciding how to distinguish between private law issues, which could be litigated in ordinary proceedings, and public law issues, which had to be pursued by issuing (what is now called) a claim for judicial review. Unsurprisingly, this created considerable difficulties not only for the courts but also for intending litigants, who were left unsure as to which procedure they ought to use, and who risked their claims being struck out as an abuse of process if they chose the wrong procedure. This apparent elevation of form over substance led Jolowicz [1983] *CLJ* 15 at 16 (who was far from alone in criticizing *O'Reilly*: for further criticism see, *inter alios*, Wade (1985) 101 *LQR* 180; Forsyth [1985] *CLJ* 415) to comment:

It is, on the face of things, astonishing that any court, let alone the highest in the land, should spend any time at all on a question [concerning only the procedure by which relief should be sought], and it is still more astonishing that it should receive the answer given by the House of Lords. It is now well over 100 years since the original Judicature Acts were passed and it is all but 100 years since Bowen LJ felt able to say that "it is a well-established principle that the object of Courts is to decide the rights of the parties, and not to punish them for the mistakes they make in the conduct of their cases by deciding them otherwise than in accordance with their rights": *Cropper v. Smith* (1884) 26 Ch D 700 at 710. It appears that the learned Lord Justice was mistaken.

However, others (see, *eg*, the Law Commission report at [3.2]–[3.5], which did not go as far as to recommend the abolition of the exclusivity rule) have emphasized the need to balance the rule's policy objective, of giving effect to the protections afforded to public authorities by the judicial review procedure, against the interest in securing justice in individual cases. The difficulty, of course, lies in determining the extent to which the strictures of *O'Reilly* may be tempered without undermining its purpose, a tension which was adverted to by Laws J in *R v. Ministry of Agriculture Fisheries and Food ex parte Lower Burytown Farms Ltd* [1999] EuLR 129 at 137:

O'Reilly has been much discussed both in academic writing and in later judicial decisions . . . There have been two countervailing interests. On the one hand, the *O'Reilly* principle has given rise to much time-consuming and expensive debate in the courts as to what is and what is not a purely public law case, fit only for judicial review proceedings. On the other, the rule has not only provided necessary protections for bodies making decisions on the public's behalf which often affect many third parties not before the court, but in general terms has released the administration of public law from the usually inappropriate and cumbersome procedures designed for the resolution of private law disputes, enabling the courts to develop the public law jurisdiction in the swift and convenient procedural milieu of Ord 53 of the Rules of the Supreme Court.

In the years since *O'Reilly* was decided the courts have sought to balance these two considerations by articulating exceptions to the principle of procedural exclusivity while continuing to acknowledge the importance of the policy upon which it is founded. In the following sections we address the principal exceptions articulated by the courts, after which we consider to what extent, in light of these exceptions and other recent developments, a principle of procedural exclusivity can still be said to exist.

First, however, it should be noted that circumstances may arise in which claimants wish to use the judicial review procedure but are not allowed to do so. For instance, in *R v. East Berkshire Health Authority, ex parte Walsh* [1985] QB 152 a senior nursing officer sought to impugn the validity of his dismissal in judicial review proceedings. Had he secured a quashing order, he would have kept his job — the voidness of the dismissal meaning that he had never in law been dismissed — whereas, had he relied exclusively upon proceedings before an employment tribunal or for breach of contract, he may have had to settle for compensation in the event of a finding of (respectively) unfair dismissal or breach of contract. Sir John Donaldson MR, expressing a view shared by May and Purchas LJJ, considered that the claim could not be pursued by means of judicial review, explaining (at 165) that:

The ordinary employer is free to act in breach of his contracts of employment and if he does so his employee will acquire certain private law rights and remedies in damages for wrongful dismissal, compensation for unfair dismissal, an order for reinstatement or re-engagement and so on. Parliament can underpin the position of public authority employees by directly restricting the freedom of the public authority to dismiss, thus giving the employee "public law" rights and at least making him a potential candidate for administrative law remedies. Alternatively it can require the authority to contract with its employees on specified terms with a view to the employee acquiring "private law" rights under the terms of the contract of employment. If the authority fails or refuses to thus create "private law" rights for the employee, the employee will have "public law" rights to compel compliance, the remedy being mandamus requiring the authority so to contract or a declaration that the employee has those rights. If, however, the authority [as in this case] gives the employee the required contractual protection, a breach of that contract is not a matter of "public law" and gives rise to no administrative law remedies.

It follows that, in circumstances where the matter is purely one of private law, far from it being an abuse of process to issue a claim against a public authority in ordinary proceedings (see *Davy* v. *Spelthorne Borough Council* [1984] AC 262), the claim *must* be issued in such proceedings. The general question concerning the circumstances in which prospective defendants are subject to public law duties is considered in ch 5 above.

14.3.2 Waiver

Although, as we have just seen, some claimants may wish, but be unable, to use judicial review proceedings, the obverse problem is more common. It is therefore necessary to consider to what extent, post-*O'Reilly*, claimants may issue claims in ordinary proceedings where their claim relates, in whole or in part, to matters of public law. In fact, the business of articulating exceptions to the exclusivity rule began in *O'Reilly* itself. Lord Diplock considered that there would be no need to enforce the rule in circumstances where 'none of the parties objects' to the use of ordinary proceedings, a view which Lord Bridge appeared to endorse in *Gillick* v. *West Norfolk and Wisbech Area Health Authority* [1986] AC 112 at 192. This reflects the fact that the purpose of exclusivity is to protect public authorities by ensuring that the safeguards inherent in the judicial review procedure operate: if the public authority defendant does not wish to insist on those safeguards, there may seem to be no need to insist upon the use of the judicial review procedure. However it may be argued that the protections conferred by the judicial review procedure are for the benefit not merely of public authorities but also of the public itself, which has an interest in certainty as to the legal status of administrative action which the procedural restrictions — especially the short time limit — promote. On this view, a bilateral agreement between the claimant and the public authority defendant to waive the protection of the judicial review procedure should be regarded as ineffective if it is prejudicial to the interests of the wider public. It is submitted that this is the better view, since it captures the truth that while the *effect* of the procedural restrictions is to protect public authorities, the *purpose* behind this policy is to benefit not those authorities — which as public bodies have no interests of their own — but the general public. This view perhaps receives implicit support from Lord Woolf MR in *Trustees of the Dennis Rye Pension Fund* v. *Sheffield City Council* [1998] 1 WLR 840 at 849, who remarked that '[i]f the choice [of procedure] has no significant disadvantages for the parties, *the public* or the court, then it should not normally be regarded as constituting an abuse' (emphasis added).

14.3.3 Resolution of Factual Disputes

It is clear that in the *Dennis Rye* case, an excerpt from which appears below at 14.3.5, one of the factors which disposed the Court of Appeal towards allowing the use of ordinary proceedings was that factual matters were in dispute which could more easily be resolved through the use of that procedure. This approach recognizes that claimants are, in practice, disadvantaged by the judicial review procedure where factual disputes need to be resolved, Lord Diplock's contrary assertions in *O'Reilly* notwithstanding.

14.3.4 Defensive Use of Public Law Arguments

It has never been doubted that the rule of procedural exclusivity should to some extend yield in the face of collateral challenge. Indeed Lord Diplock recognized as much in his speech in *O'Reilly* v. *Mackman* [1983] 2 AC 237 at 285 itself. Moreover, in *Boddington* v. *British Transport Police* [1999] 2 AC 143, considered in detail above at 3.4, the House of Lords held that, unless the relevant legislation provides expressly or impliedly to the contrary (see, *eg, R* v. *Wicks* [1998] AC 92), the rule of law itself demands that a defendant should be able to challenge collaterally the validity of the offence with which he is charged. Procedural exclusivity thus gives way to collateral challenge in criminal proceedings.

Earlier, it had been established in *Wandsworth London Borough Council* v. *Winder* [1985] AC 461 that the same principle applies in civil proceedings. The local authority brought proceedings against one of its tenants for arrears of rent. In response, the tenant argued that the council was applying an improper rental rate to the flat, because certain resolutions which had purported to raise the applicable rent were in law invalid. The council argued that, by raising this point, the tenant was committing an abuse of process: the validity of the resolutions was clearly a public law matter, and could be raised only via judicial review. The House of Lords did not agree. Although Lord Fraser (who curiously, and it is submitted wrongly (see further Beatson (1987) 103 *LQR* 34 at 58), did not characterize this challenge as 'collateral') acknowledged the existence of sound policy reasons for the *O'Reilly* principle, he considered (at 509) that:

It would . . . be a very strange use of language to describe the respondent's behaviour in relation to this litigation as an abuse or misuse by him of the process of the court. He did not select the procedure to be adopted. He is merely seeking to defend proceedings brought against him by the appellants.

Although it is well-established that public law decisions and actions may be raised defensively, difficult questions remain about the further circumstances in which the exclusivity principle yields. In considering this matter, it is helpful to draw a broad distinction between two situations, the first concerning circumstances in which the existence of a private law right is dependent upon the exercise of some public law function, the second relating to situations in which action taken under public law powers affects private law rights which are already acknowledged to exist.

14.3.5 Private Law Rights Dependent upon Public Law

The House of Lords confronted the first of these scenarios on the same day as its decision in *O'Reilly* was handed down. *Cocks* v. *Thanet District Council* [1983] 2 AC 286 concerned a claim for (*inter alia*) a declaration to the effect that a local authority was in breach of its statutory duty under the Housing (Homeless Persons) Act 1977 to provide the claimant with permanent accommodation. Their Lordships considered that, under the statutory scheme, the individual *could* acquire enforceable private law rights to permanent accommodation, but only if the local authority first concluded (*inter alia*) that he was not intentionally homeless — an exercise of public law discretion which, under *O'Reilly*, should have been challenged by way of judicial review. This case, which appeared to indicate a judicial appetite for surgically separating public and private law for procedural purposes, needs reconsideration in light of two subsequent decisions.

O'Rourke v. *Camden London Borough Council* [1988] AC 188 concerned the duty of a local authority under s 63(1) of the Housing Act 1985 to provide temporary accommodation to the claimant if it had reason to believe that he may be homeless and have a priority need. The claimant, having been evicted from accommodation provided pursuant to s 63(1) but not rehoused pending determination of his application for permanent accommodation, argued that the council had a duty to house him, breach of which could lead to liability in damages in private law. Lord Hoffmann, who gave the only reasoned speech, rejected this contention, but in doing so departed from the reasoning of the House of Lords in *Cocks*. In particular, Lord Hoffmann felt that Lord Bridge had been wrong in *Cocks* to conclude that private law rights would arise once the local authority had made a decision in the individual's favour. Lord Hoffmann was of the view that Lord Bridge's reasoning was fatally flawed by his failure to examine whether, as a matter of statutory construction, Parliament had intended to create a duty in private law sounding in damages. Lord Hoffmann concluded that the homelessness provisions in the 1985 Act (which were the same those in the 1977 Act which were at stake in *Cocks*) were not intended to create such a duty; it followed that no private law right was or ever could have been in issue, and therefore the matter was one exclusively of public law.

The general thrust of Lord Hoffmann's speech in *O'Rourke* is to the effect that courts should reflect carefully before concluding that breaches of statutory provisions imposing duties in public law may give rise to private law rights of action. His Lordship refused to reach this conclusion in relation to the homelessness provisions because, *inter alia*, they formed part of a social welfare scheme which aimed to benefit the public generally, not just the homeless, and because the existence of the duty to provide accommodation was contingent upon the exercise of a considerable amount of discretion by the council. In light of this, Lord Hoffmann considered it unlikely that Parliament intended that errors of judgment should give rise to an obligation, enforceable in private law, to make financial reparation to disappointed individuals. However, this decision leaves open the question whether, in situations where rights enforceable in private law *are* capable of being created through the exercise of powers lying in public law, litigation in which their existence falls for determination may be undertaken by means of ordinary proceedings notwithstanding that questions of public law are necessarily involved. It was this question which occupied the Court of Appeal in our next case.

Trustees of the Dennis Rye Pension Fund v. *Sheffield City Council* [1998] 1 WLR 840
Court of Appeal

The claimants were required by the defendant local authority, by means of a repair notice under the Housing Act 1985, s 189, to carry out work on various properties so as to render them fit for human habitation. The claimants carried out the work, in respect of which they sought improvement grants under the Local Government and Housing Act 1989. The council accepted that the works concerned qualified in principle for improvement grants, thereby entitling the claimants to the payments provided that the council was satisfied that the works had been carried out to what the council regarded as a satisfactory standard. However, the council refused to make the payments, contending that the works did not meet the required standard. The claimants initiated ordinary proceedings, seeking to recover the monies which, they argued, were owed to them by the council. At first instance, before District Judge Lambert, the proceedings were struck out, *inter alia* because the decision to refuse payment was a public law matter that should have been challenged by way of judicial review. On appeal, Mance J disagreed, reinstating the claims. The council appealed to the Court of Appeal.

Lord Woolf MR

. . . Having examined the statutory provisions, I regard it as clear that in general when performing its role in relation to the making of grants the authority is performing public functions which do not give rise to private rights. This is so, even when, as here, improvement notices have been served so that the making of a grant is mandatory (section 113(1)). Even in this situation the refusal to approve an application for a grant gives rise to no right to damages and in the ordinary way the appropriate procedure will be judicial review.

. . . [However,] I would regard this as being a case where the Plaintiffs' relationship with a public body whether statutory or contractual would confer on him conditional rights to payment so that the bringing of ordinary actions to enforce those rights was not in itself an abuse of process.

In coming to that conclusion I do not feel it is necessary to go quite so far as to regard the requirement that the authority should be satisfied as being in all situations no more than in Mance J.'s words "a matter of objective, factual and technical assessment" . . . This in my view will usually, but not always, be the situation. I do accept there will be room in some cases for the authority to exercise a limited degree of judgment so that the standard which the Council is entitled to insist on before it is satisfied is not always objective. Usually the work to be carried out will need to be detailed because of the requirements of section 102 for particulars and estimates to be given prior to an application being approved. There may also be a specification (see section 118(1)). If, then, the work is carried out in accordance with what would be an implied standard, of in a good and workmanlike manner or in accordance with any specified standard, that will be the end of any ground for dissatisfaction on the part of the Council. There may on the other hand, at least theoretically, be a situation where there is no express or implied standard to which the work is to be carried out. In such a situation the Council will be entitled to set the standard and as long as they do not set a totally unreasonable requirement the work will need to be done to that standard. The standard will be only subject to a *Wednesbury* challenge.

What, in my view, is more important when considering what is the correct procedure to adopt is that in both situations any challenge to an authority's refusal to express satisfaction will depend on an examination of issues largely of fact which are more appropriately examined in the course of ordinary proceedings than on an application for judicial review. So far as the present actions are concerned there is no reason to think that when the quality of the work is examined against the particulars and estimates provided and any relevant specification, taking into account the actions of the Council's inspectors, the question of whether the Council could lawfully withhold its satisfaction will be resolved by a determination of the factual position. This is the class of issue which, if it cannot be resolved by mediation, is ideally resolved by a court with the assistance of a report from a surveyor jointly instructed by both parties. Such an approach would be infinitely more in the interests of the taxpayers of the authority, the landlord and the courts than an application for judicial review.

. . . Mr Underwood [for the Council] relies strongly on the recent decision of the House of Lords of *O'Rourke v Camden LBC* [1997] 3 WLR 86 (in which he was counsel for the authority). I, however, do not regard Lord Hoffmann's speech in that case as providing him with any support. In *O'Rourke* it was held that the Housing Act 1985 provisions as to the homeless gave rise to no private rights which would enable a private law action for damages or an injunction to be brought. In coming to this conclusion Lord Hoffmann (who gave the only reasoned speech) disapproved of Lord Bridge of Harwich's reasoning in his speech in *Cocks v Thanet DC* [[1983] 2 AC 286]. Lord Bridge had suggested there could be such a private law right which gave rise to a right to damages which only came into existence after a decision had been reached by the authority that the right existed. Lord Hoffmann [in *O'Rourke* at 93] categorised this view as "anomalous". Lord Hoffmann was not dealing with a situation involving a claim for the recovery of a sum of money which would unquestionably be due under a statute if certain conditions had or should be taken to have been met.

As Lord Hoffmann came to the conclusion that there were no private law rights at stake he did not consider the consequences of his approach on a situation where there are private law rights which would come into existence if, but only if, a statutory decision of a public body was first impugned. However his general approach suggests that the House of Lords has moved on from *Cocks*, which undesirably could cause the parties having to incur the expense of two sets of proceedings, a result which is directly opposite to that which Order 53 was intended to achieve. In the light of the decision in *O'Rourke's* Case a private right which only comes into existence in the circumstances the House of Lords imagined they were dealing with in *Cocks* is in the future going to be a rare animal indeed . . .

Well where does that leave *O'Reilly v Mackman* [1983] 2 AC 237 and what can be done to stop this constant unprofitable litigation over the divide between public and private law proceedings? What I would suggest is necessary is to begin by going back to first principles and remind oneself of the guidance which Lord Diplock gave in *O'Reilly v. Mackman*. This guidance involves recognising:

a) That remedies for protecting both private and public rights can be given in both private law proceedings and on an application for judicial review.

b) That judicial review provides, in the interest of the public, protection for public bodies which are not available in private law proceedings (namely the requirement of leave and the protection against delay). The proceedings will be heard by a High Court judge and will be managed by the Crown Office which has the necessary experience of public law proceedings to ensure that questions, such as expedition, are dealt with in a manner which is appropriate.

c) That for these reasons it is a GENERAL RULE that it is contrary to public policy 'and as such an abuse of the process of the court, to permit a person seeking to establish that a decision of a public authority infringed rights to which he was entitled to protection under public law to proceed by way of an ordinary action and by this means to evade the provisions of Order 53 for the protection of such authorities' [*per* Lord Diplock in *O'Reilly* at 285].

Having established the foundation of the general rule it seems to me that there will be a reduction in the difficulties which are apparently being *experienced* at present by practitioners and the courts, if it is remembered that:

1) If it is not clear whether judicial review or an ordinary action is the correct procedure it will be safer to make an application for judicial review than commence an ordinary action since there then should be no question of being treated as abusing the process of the court by avoiding the protection provided by judicial review. In the majority of cases it should not be necessary *for purely procedural reasons* to become involved in arid arguments as to whether the issues are correctly treated as involving public or private law or both. (For reasons of substantive law it may be necessary to consider this issue.) If judicial review is used when it should not, the court can protect its resources either by directing that the application should continue as if begun by writ or by directing it should be heard by a judge who is not nominated to hear cases in the Crown Office List. It is difficult to see how a respondent can be prejudiced by the adoption of this course and little risk that anything more damaging could happen than a refusal of leave.

(2) If a case is brought by an ordinary action and there is an application to strike out the case, the court should, at least if it is unclear whether the case should have been brought by judicial review, ask itself whether, if the case had been brought by judicial review when the action was commenced, it is clear leave would have been granted. If it would, then that is at least an indication that there has been no harm to the interests judicial review is designed to protect. In addition the court should consider by which procedure the case could be appropriately tried. If the answer is that an ordinary action is equally or more appropriate than an application for judicial review that again should be an indication the action should not be struck out . . .

. . . I hope . . . that the far from comprehensive pragmatic suggestions made above will be of some assistance. They do involve not only considering the technical questions of the distinctions between public and private rights and bodies but also looking at the practical consequences of the choice of procedure which has been made. If the choice has no significant disadvantages for the parties, the public or the court, then it should not normally be regarded as constituting an abuse. Here it is important to remember that there does not have to be an application to strike out even if it is considered that the wrong procedure has been adopted. Often the interests of justice and the parties will be better served by getting on with the action . . .

Morritt LJ agreed with Lord Woolf MR, while Pill LJ delivered a short concurring judgment in which he emphasized that the discretion of the local authority under s 117(3) as to satisfaction was extremely limited, such that the accrual of the entitlement to the grant depended essentially upon objective factors.

It is clear from this judgment that Lord Woolf was anxious to reduce litigation concerning the choice between ordinary proceedings and the judicial review procedure; indeed, he began (at 842) by lamenting the fact that although substantial judicial and financial resources had been expended, 'the courts have yet to turn their attention to the merits of the dispute'. On Lord Woolf's approach, ordinary proceedings can certainly be used to enforce private law rights whose existence is dependent upon objective factors which the court can straightforwardly assess; but even if the rights are contingent upon a discretionary decision, the limits of which are traced only by the public law *Wednesbury* principles, this does not necessarily render the use of ordinary proceedings abusive. This follows because Lord Woolf sought to move the focus of the analysis away from the rigid categorization of public and private matters, and towards more substantive questions about the appropriateness or otherwise of ordinary proceedings over judicial review. This approach is evident in the guidelines set out by Lord Woolf towards the end of our excerpt, in which he suggested that claims brought by ordinary proceedings should not be struck out if permission would have been granted had the judicial review procedure been used, and that it would be appropriate to use ordinary proceedings if the claim raised factual disputes which could not readily be resolved on judicial review. Indeed, the latter factor appears to operate in its own right — that is, without reference to whether any private law rights are at stake — as an exception to the exclusivity rule.

QUESTION

- Following *O'Rourke* and *Dennis Rye*, what is the relevance of *Cocks*?

14.3.6 Private Law Rights Affected by Public Law

What if, instead of arguing that a private law right has arisen as a result of a decision or action which lies in public law, a claimant wishes to argue that conduct lying in public law has impacted upon some private law right whose existence is not in doubt? The House of Lords had little difficulty, in the following case, in deciding that in such circumstances the use of ordinary proceedings will not constitute an abuse of process.

....

Roy v. *Kensington and Chelsea and Westminster Family Practitioner Committee* [1992] 1 AC 624
House of Lords

The claimant, a general practitioner, entered into an agreement with the defendant committee to provide medical services to the NHS. Under the relevant regulations, the committee was to make payments to doctors in accordance with the Statement of Fees and Allowances, paragraph 12.1 of which provided that a practitioner 'will be eligible for the full rate of basic practice allowance if', *inter alia*, 'he is in the opinion of the responsible committee devoting a substantial amount of time to general practice under the National Health Service'. The claimant had, between 1979 and 1987, been absent from his practice, on average, for between one-third and one-half of each year, although these absences were covered by a locum doctor. In light of this, the committee decided that the claimant was not devoting the required amount of time to general practice, and reduced his basic allowance by 20 per cent with prospective effect. The claimant challenged this decision in ordinary proceedings, seeking to impugn the decision and to recover the monies which he alleged were owed to him. The defendant successfully argued at first instance that the claimant's failure to use judicial review was an abuse of process; however, the Court of Appeal considered that a contractual relationship existed between the parties, and that ordinary proceedings were therefore appropriate. The defendant appealed to the House of Lords.

Lord Lowry

. . . [T]he Court of Appeal [1990] 1 Med. L.R. 328 . . . concluded that there was a contract for services between Dr. Roy and the committee and that it was therefore in order for Dr. Roy to sue the committee for a declaration of his rights and an order for payment. (Your Lordships have not the benefit of the Court of Appeal's view on what the position would have been assuming that no contract existed.) I cannot altogether accept the reasoning which led the members of the Court of Appeal to conclude that there was a contract, because, although there may well have been a contract for services, I am not satisfied that there was. *Reg. v. East Berkshire Health Authority, Ex parte Walsh* [1985] Q.B. 152 does not in my view provide a reliable argument in favour of saying that there was a contract in the present case and *Wadi v. Cornwall and Isles of Scilly Family Practitioner Committee* [1985] I.C.R. 492 indicates the contrary. At the same time, I would be foolish to disregard the fact that all the members of a distinguished Court of Appeal held that a contract for services existed between Dr. Roy and the committee. It shows, to say the least, that there are "contractual echoes in the relationship," as Judge White [1989] 1 Med. L.R 10, 12, put it and makes it almost inevitable that the relationship, as was said of that which arose in *Wadi's* case, gave rise to "rights and obligations" and that Dr. Roy's rights were private law rights. I would here observe that the mere fact that the Act [the National Health Service Act 1977] and the Regulations [the National Health Service (General Medical and Pharmaceutical Services) Regulations 1974] constitute a statutory scheme which lays down the doctor's "terms of service" (an expression which has contractual overtones) and creates the relationship between him and the committee, is not fatal to the idea of a contract, but that relationship did not *need* to be contractual. Moreover, the discretion which the scheme confers on the committee is not typically characteristic of a contractual relationship, and the same can be said of the appellate and supervisory role given to the Secretary of State.

But the actual or possible absence of a contract is not decisive against Dr. Roy. He has in my opinion a bundle of rights which should be regarded as his individual private law rights against the committee, arising from the statute and regulations and including the very important private law right to be paid for the work that he has done. As Judge White put it, at p. 12:

> "The rights and duties are no less real or effective for the individual practitioner. Private law rights flow from the statutory provisions and are enforceable, as such, in the courts but no contractual relations come into existence."

The judge, however, held that, *even if the doctor's rights to full payments under the scheme were contractually based*, the committee's duty was a public law duty and could be challenged only on judicial review. Mr. Collins [counsel for the defendant] admitted that, if the doctor had a *contractual* right, he could . . . vindicate it by action. But, my Lords, I go further: if Dr. Roy has any kind of *private law right*, even though not contractual, he can sue for its alleged breach.

In this case it has been suggested that Dr. Roy could have gone by judicial review, because there is no issue of fact, but that would not always hold good in a similar type of case . . . In any event, a successful application by judicial review could not lead directly, as it would in an action, to an order for payment of the full basic practice allowance. Other proceedings would be needed . . .

My Lords, whether Dr. Roy's rights were contractual or statutory, the observations made by the Court of Appeal concerning their enforcement are important . . . Nourse L.J. said, at p. 332:

> "In his argument on behalf of the committee Mr. Greening accepted that in general the contract between the committee and the practitioner gives rise to private law rights and duties. But he nevertheless submitted that the committee's duty to form an opinion under paragraph 12.1(b) of the Statement of Fees and Allowances is a public law duty which can only be enforced or controlled in proceedings for judicial review. For my part, I would reject that submission on the simple ground that the mutual rights and duties under a contract of those who are the parties to it, whether they be public bodies or private individuals, exist, and can only exist, in the field of private law. Although a public body which carries out a duty imposed on it by contract can often be said to be performing a public duty, it is not a 'public law' duty for the purposes of the classification which is in point. The duty imposed on the committee by paragraph 12.1 of the Statement of Fees and Allowances is to form an opinion as to whether the practitioner is devoting a substantial

amount of time to general practice under the National Health Service and to give a decision accordingly. If that duty is not properly discharged, the practitioner's remedies are a declaration that the decision is of no effect, an order setting it aside and, if appropriate, an injunction directing the committee to reconsider the matter and form a fresh opinion on a correct basis. It can certainly be said that these remedies are suggestive of proceedings for judicial review. But they are equally available under the law of contract and Mr Greening did not argue to the contrary. Moreover, the great majority of the rights and duties under the contract, for example the duty to pay and the right to receive the basic practice allowance once the necessary opinion has been formed, can only exist in the field of private law. If Mr Greening's argument is correct, difficult questions may arise as to whether particular rights and duties must be protected and enforced by the one procedure or the other. On practical grounds no less than on principle there is everything to be said for the view that private law applies throughout.

In order that there may be no doubt about the matter, I will add that if a practitioner wishes to question an initial decision by the committee not to accept his application to be included on their list of doctors, he must in that case take proceedings for judicial review. At that stage no contract has come into existence and the practitioner's only right is a public law right to have his application properly considered. There is the same two-stage process as there was in *Cocks v. Thanet District Council* [1983] 2 A.C. 286, albeit that there the private law rights and duties which arose at the second stage were statutory and not contractual . . ."

. . . The judgments to which I have referred effectively dispose of an argument pressed by the committee that Dr. Roy had no right to be paid a basic practice allowance until the committee had carried out their public duty of forming an opinion under paragraph 12.1(*b*), with the supposed consequence that, until that had happened, the doctor had *no private law right* which he could enforce. The answer is that Dr. Roy had a right to a fair and legally correct consideration of his claim. Failing that, his private law right has been infringed and he can sue the committee.

Mr. Collins sought to equate the committee's task under paragraph 12.1(*b*) with the council's duty in phase 1 of *Cocks v. Thanet District Council* and the committee's duty to pay with the council's duty in phase 2 . . . [However,] Mr. Cocks was simply a homeless member of the public in phase 1, whereas Dr. Roy had already an established relationship with the committee when his claim under paragraph 12.1 fell to be considered.

Dr. Roy's printed case contained detailed arguments in favour of a contract between him and the committee, but before your Lordships Mr. Lightman simply argued that the doctor had a private law right, whether contractual or statutory. With regard to *O'Reilly v. Mackman* [1983] 2 A.C. 237 he argued in the alternative. The "broad approach" was that the rule in *O'Reilly v. Mackman* did not apply generally against bringing actions to vindicate private rights in all circumstances in which those actions involved a challenge to a public law act or decision, but that it merely required the aggrieved person to proceed by judicial review only when private law rights were not at stake. The "narrow approach" assumed that the rule applied generally to *all* proceedings in which public law acts or decisions were challenged, subject to some exceptions when private law rights were involved. There was no need in *O'Reilly v. Mackman* to choose between these approaches, but it seems clear that Lord Diplock considered himself to be stating a general rule with exceptions. For my part, I much prefer the broad approach . . . It would . . ., if adopted, have the practical merit of getting rid of a procedural minefield. I shall, however, be content for the purpose of this appeal to adopt the narrow approach, which avoids the need to discuss the proper scope of the rule, a point which has not been argued before your Lordships and has hitherto been seriously discussed only by the academic writers.

. . . In conclusion, my Lords, it seems to me that, unless the procedure adopted by the moving party is ill suited to dispose of the question at issue, there is much to be said in favour of the proposition that a court having jurisdiction ought to let a case be heard rather than entertain a debate concerning the form of the proceedings . . .

Lord Bridge delivered a short concurring speech, while Lords Emslie, Griffiths, and Oliver simply agreed with Lord Lowry. Appeal dismissed.

Commenting on this case, the Law Commission (at [3.10] of its report) observed that it

does not address the difficult question of *when* a private right is created by statute; that will remain a matter of construction of individual statutes in their particular contexts. What it does is to provide guidance as to the procedural consequences of finding that such a right exists.

Addressing the former issue, Cane [1992] *PL* 193 at 197 writes:

Does *Roy* cast any light on the definition of "private law right"? Contractual and property rights are obviously private law rights, as are rights to obtain monetary awards for private law wrongs or to obtain restitution on some other basis than wrongful conduct (such as mistake of fact). The really difficult cases are those in which the right in question arises out of a statutory provision. Dr. Roy's right was such: the Court of Appeal held that there was a contract between Dr. Roy and the Committee, but the House of Lords declined to decide this issue and instead treated Dr. Roy's right as a private law statutory one. Are all statutory "rights" private law rights? Surely not! It is quite clear that not all statutory duties are actionable in private law. We know from *Cocks* v. *Thanet D.C.* that the statutory right of certain homeless persons to be housed by a local authority is a private law right [but now cf *O'Rourke*, discussed above at 14.3.5]; and we know from *Roy* that the statutory right of a registered G.P., under certain circumstances, to receive a full basic practice allowance is a private law right. But just as the courts have found it impossible to provide much guidance in general terms on the question of which statutory duties are actionable in the tort of breach of statutory duty, so it seems unlikely that much general guidance will ever be available on the question of which rights are private law rights for present purposes.

QUESTIONS

- Do you share Cane's pessimism on this point?
- Can you suggest any criteria that may provide more certain guidance in this area?

While *Roy* establishes an exception to the exclusivity principle based on the existence of 'private law rights', the House of Lords' decision in *Mercury Communications Ltd* v. *Director General of Telecommunications* [1996] 1 WLR 48 goes further. The case concerned the arrangements under which the claimant company obtained access to British Telecommunications' network for the provision of telephone services. Mercury and BT, the second defendant, sought to reach a negotiated agreement, but referred a question concerning pricing to the DGT. Mercury challenged, by way of ordinary proceedings, the DGT's determination, arguing that he had misinterpreted relevant phrases in BT's licence. Lord Slynn, giving the only reasoned speech, rejected the contention that the use of ordinary proceedings was abusive. Although no contractual or other private law issue existed between Mercury and the DGT, the latter's decision affected the private law position of the former because it impacted upon the contractual relationship between Mercury and BT. Thus it appears that the exclusivity principle gives way not only when private law rights are at stake as between the two parties to the case, but also when the defendant's decision is capable of affecting the claimant's relations in private law with others. It is also worth noting the following remarks of Lord Slynn (at 57) — effectively conceding the point made by Cane above — to the effect that the dividing line between 'public law' and 'private law' is, and is likely to remain, so ill-defined as to preclude the rigid application of the exclusivity rule:

It is of particular importance, as I see it, to retain some flexibility as the precise limits of what is called "public law" and what is called "private law" are by no means worked out. The experience of other countries seems to show that the working out of this distinction is not always an easy matter. . . . It has to be borne in mind that the overriding question is whether the proceedings constitute an abuse of the process of the court.

Lord Slynn repeated some of these remarks in *Steed* v. *Secretary of State for the Home Department* [2000] 1 WLR 1169 at 1174–1175, in which the need for a flexible approach was again emphasized.

14.3.7 Procedural Exclusivity and the Civil Procedure Rules

In its report, the Law Commission (at [3.13]–[3.14]) was satisfied that there were strong policy reasons — including 'the need for speed and certainty in administrative decision-making' — for requiring the use of what is now Part 54 'in purely public law cases'. However, it considered that

where a case involves a properly constituted private law cause of action or where it is necessary to decide whether a person should be prevented from raising a defence in such an action, on the ground that it involves an issue of public law, a more flexible procedural approach is needed to ensure that private law rights are not "trumped" by public law justifications.

Indeed, we have already seen that some flexibility was introduced through judicial development of various exceptions to the exclusivity principle. That flexibility has been further enhanced, in two respects, by the introduction of the CPR, as we explain in the following two sections.

14.3.8 A More Substantive Approach

The first point relates not to the new judicial review procedure contained in Part 54, but to the general principles underlying the CPR and, in particular, the new powers of the courts to give summary judgment. The nature and implications of these changes are apparent from the next extract. It should be noted that, at the time the following case (for comment on which see Elvin and Maurici [2000] *JR* 164; Holt [2000] *JR* 171; Hickman [2000] *JR* 178) was decided, Part 54 had not entered into force. However, the Order 53 procedure had by that time been made subject to the CPR, so that, as Jackson J commented in *Carter Commercial Developments* v. *Bedford Borough Council* [2001] EWHC Admin 669 at [28], 'the principles stated by the Court of Appeal in *Clark's* case are equally applicable now that Part 54 has come into force'.

....

Clark v. *University of Lincolnshire and Humberside* [2000] 1 WLR 1988
Court of Appeal

The claimant had been a student at the defendant institution, a university established under the Education Reform Act 1988. The student was accused of plagiarism, as a result of which she failed one of her final examinations; although the finding of plagiarism was later rescinded, a mark of zero was given for the paper concerned. The student challenged this decision by means of ordinary proceedings in which she alleged breaches of contractual rules under the university's student regulations. The defendant contended that this amounted to an abuse of process: the university was a public body and, it was argued, in the absence of a visitor [on which see the *Page* case, discussed above at 2.2.5], judicial review proceedings should have been used.

Lord Woolf MR

[26] . . . [Judicial review] proceedings now have to be initiated by use of a "claim form," maintaining the principle that all proceedings under the CPR are to be commenced in the same way . . . [Judicial review] is part of the new code of civil procedure created by the CPR. It is subject to the general overriding principles contained in Part 1.

[27] In addition, if proceedings involving public law issues are commenced by an ordinary action under Part 7 or Part 8 they are now subject to Part 24. Part 24 is important because it enables the court, either on its own motion or on the application of a party, if it considers that a claimant has no real prospect of succeeding on a claim or an issue, to give summary judgment on the claim or issue. This is a markedly different position from that which existed when *O'Reilly v Mackman* was decided. If a defendant public body or an interested person considers that a claim has no real prospect of success an application can now be made under Part 24. This restricts the inconvenience to third parties and the administration of public bodies caused by a hopeless claim . . .

[28] The distinction between proceedings under Order 53 and an ordinary claim are now limited. Under Order 53 the claimant has to obtain permission to bring the proceedings so the onus is upon him to establish he has a real prospect of success. In the case of ordinary proceedings the defendant has to establish that the proceedings do not have a real prospect of success.

[29] A university is a public body. This is not in issue on this appeal. Court proceedings would, therefore, normally be expected to be commenced under Order 53. If the university is subject to the supervision of a visitor there is little scope for those proceedings (*Page v Hull University Visitor* [1993] AC 682). Where a claim is brought against a university by one of its students, if because the university is a "new university" created by statute, it does not have a visitor, the role of the court will frequently amount to performing the reviewing role which would otherwise be performed by the visitor. The court . . . will not involve itself with issues that involve making academic judgments. Summary judgment dismissing a claim which, if it were to be entertained, would require the court to make academic judgments should be capable of being obtained in the majority of situations. Similarly, the court has now power to stay the proceedings if it came to the conclusion that . . . it would be desirable for a student to use an internal disciplinary process before coming to the court. (See CPR 1.4([2])(e))

[30] One of Lord Diplock's reasons which he gave in *O'Reilly v. Mackman* for his concern about an ordinary civil action being commenced against public bodies when a more appropriate procedure was under O.53 was the fact that in ordinary civil proceedings the claimant could defer commencing the proceedings until the last day of the limitation period. This compares unfavourably

with the requirement that, subject to the court's discretion to extend time, under O.53 proceedings have to be commenced promptly and in any event within three months. If a student could bypass this requirement to bring proceedings promptly by issuing civil proceedings based on a contract, this could have a very adverse [effect] on administration of universities . . .

[32] . . . If it is not possible to resolve the dispute internally, and there is no visitor, then the courts may have no alternative but to become involved. If they do so, the preferable procedure would usually be by way of judicial review. If, on the other hand, the proceedings are based on the contract between the student and the university then they do not have to be brought by way of judicial review.

[33] The courts today will be flexible in their approach. Already, prior to the introduction of the CPR the courts were prepared to prevent abuse of their process where there had been an inordinate delay even if the limitation period had not expired. In such a situation, the court could, in appropriate circumstances, stay subsequent proceedings. This is despite the fact that a litigant normally was regarded as having a legal right to commence proceedings at any time prior to the expiry of the limitation period. (See *Birkett v James* [1978] AC 297)

[34] The court's approach to what is an abuse of process has to be considered today in the light of the changes brought about by the CPR. Those changes include a requirement that a party to proceedings should behave reasonably both before and after they have commenced proceedings. Parties are now under an obligation to help the court further the overriding objectives which include ensuring that cases are dealt with expeditiously and fairly. (CPR 1.1(2)(d) and 1.3) They should not allow the choice of procedure to achieve procedural advantages . . .

[35] While in the past, it would not be appropriate to look at delay of a party commencing proceedings other than by judicial review within the limitation period in deciding whether the proceedings are abusive this is no longer the position. While to commence proceedings within a limitation period is not in itself an abuse, delay in commencing proceedings is a factor which can be taken into account in deciding whether the proceeding[s] are abusive. If proceedings of a type which would normally be brought by judicial review are instead brought by bringing an ordinary claim, the court in deciding whether the commencement of the proceedings is an abuse of process can take into account whether there has been unjustified delay in initiating the proceedings.

[36] When considering whether proceedings can continue the nature of the claim can be relevant. If the court is required to perform a reviewing role or what is being claimed is a discretionary remedy, whether it be a prerogative remedy or an injunction or a declaration the position is different from when the claim is for damages or a sum of money for breach of contract or a tort irrespective of the procedure adopted. Delay in bringing proceedings for a discretionary remedy has always been a factor which a court could take into account in deciding whether it should grant that remedy. Delay can now be taken into account on an application for summary judgment under CPR Part 24 if its effect means that the claim has no real prospect of success.

[37] Similarly if what is being claimed could affect the public generally the approach of the court will be stricter than if the proceedings only affect the immediate parties. It must not be forgotten that a court can extend time to bring proceedings under [Order] 53. The intention of the CPR is to harmonise procedures as far as possible and to avoid barren procedural disputes which generate satellite litigation.

[38] Where a student has, as here, a claim in contract, the court will not strike out a claim which

could more appropriately be made under Order 53 solely because of the procedure which has been adopted. It may however do so, if it comes to the conclusion that in all the circumstances, including the delay in initiating the proceedings, there has been an abuse of the process of the court under the CPR. The same approach will be adopted on an application under Part 24.

[39] The emphasis can therefore be said to have changed since *O'Reilly v Mackman*. What is likely to be important when proceedings are not brought by a student against a new university under Order 53, will not be whether the right procedure has been adopted but whether the protection provided by Order 53 has been flouted in circumstances which are inconsistent with the proceedings being able to be conducted justly in accordance with the general principles contained in Part 1. Those principles are now central to determining what is due process. A visitor is not required to entertain a complaint when there has been undue delay and a court in the absence of a visitor should exercise its jurisdiction in a similar way. The courts are far from being the ideal forum in which to resolve the great majority of disputes between a student and his or her university. The courts should be vigilant to ensure their procedures are not misused. The courts must be equally vigilant to discourage summary applications which have no real prospect of success . . .

Sedley LJ, with whom Ward LJ agreed, reached the same conclusion as Lord Woolf MR. The appeal was allowed to the extent of restoring the action.

In terms of its outcome, this decision is perhaps unremarkable. Indeed, as Sedley LJ noted at [16], the claimant in *Clark* was if anything in a stronger position than her counterpart in *Roy*: 'where in *Roy's* case a statutory relationship happened to include a contractual element, here it is a contractual relationship which happens to possess a public law dimension'. As Cornford [2000] *Web JCLI* observes, 'If the scope of the judgment is confined to litigants who have contractual rights then it breaks no new ground.' However, Lord Woolf's judgment does not seem to be thus confined, and its implications are potentially far-reaching. On Lord Woolf's view, irrespective of whether a claim concerning public law matters is begun via the judicial review procedure or by means of ordinary proceedings, the court will in substance apply the same tests. If the judicial review procedure is used, then of course the safeguards in Part 54 will apply. If, however, the claim is issued in ordinary proceedings, it is still open to the court to look at these issues: if it concludes that, had the case been brought under Part 54, it would have been rejected on, say, grounds of permission or delay, then it is open to the court to give summary judgment under Part 24. The upshot is that the procedure by which a claim is started now matters very little. According to Hickman [2000] *JR* 178 at 182:

Clark . . . means that it will be much less important whether or not proceedings are brought within Ord 53. In both cases the courts can consider whether the public body requires protection, and particularly whether there has been delay. At least the focus of argument should now shift from the precise form of the application to the more practical question of the need for protection.

This shift from form to substance is to be welcomed, and it is clearly desirable that claims should be rejected because the policy of protecting public bodies is being undermined rather than on the formal ground that the wrong procedure was used. It must be remembered, however, that it does not follow from *Clark* that the distinction between issues of public and private law has become irrelevant. It is inherent in the *Clark* approach that, even if the use of the wrong procedure is no longer fatal *per se*, categorization of the issue as public or private is still important, since if the matter is one of public law (to which none of the exceptions to *O'Reilly* applies) then *either* the claimant must use the judicial review procedure *or*, if ordinary proceedings are instead used, the court must be satisfied that the requirements of permission, promptitude, and so on would have been met had the matter been litigated by means of Part 54.

The relevance of the public/private distinction post-*Clark* is apparent from the decision in *Carter Commercial Developments* v. *Bedford Borough Council* [2001] EWHC Admin 669 in which the claimant initiated ordinary proceedings in respect of a public law issue; although the use of the wrong procedure was not determinative in itself, the court concluded that there had been a deliberate attempt to circumvent the time limits which would have applied had Part 54 been used, and on that ground the use of ordinary proceedings was found to be an abuse of process. The relevance of the public/private distinction therefore survives *Clark*: the public authorities' safeguards still apply in relation to public law matters, albeit that those safeguards are now upheld by effectively invoking them irrespective of the type of proceedings used, rather than by rigidly enforcing the procedural dichotomy of *O'Reilly* v. *Mackman*. In light of this, claimants are still best advised to litigate public law matters by means of judicial review unless one of the exceptions considered above applies; if they fail to observe this advice then the use of ordinary proceedings will not avail them if the purpose of such a strategy is simply to evade the Part 54 protections.

Finally, it should be noted that if one of the exceptions to the exclusivity principle obtains (*eg* because contractual and public law matters arise together), then, according to Sir Andrew Morritt V-C in *Phonographic Performance Ltd* v. *Department of Trade and Industry* [2004] EWHC 1795 (Ch) at [36], although, *prima face*, 'the remedies both of judicial review and of ordinary action are available', '[t]he choice of either may be an abuse of the process'. Whether this is so 'will depend on all the relevant circumstances including matters occurring before the proceedings were instituted and which remedy is in the circumstances the more appropriate'. Thus, a claimant legitimately raising a mixture of public and private law issues in ordinary proceedings will be subject to the standard limitation period for such proceedings, rather than the very short time limit for judicial review. However, even if he complies with the limitation period, he *may* still find himself guilty of an abuse of process if he fails to act promptly — although the Vice-Chancellor was anxious to emphasize that delay within the limitation period was only one factor to be taken into account, pointing to Sedley LJ's view in *Clark* at [17] that it is necessary to look at the 'entirety' of the circumstances.

14.3.9 Transfer into Part 54

The disadvantage suffered by claimants who choose the wrong procedure is ameliorated by the CPR. Transfer *out of* the judicial review procedure was possible under Order 53, and this remains the case under CPR 54.20. However, transfer *into* the judicial review procedure was not possible under Order 53 (although Lord Woolf suggested otherwise in *Trustees of the Dennis Rye Pension Fund* v. *Sheffield City Council* [1998] 1 WLR 840 at 849). The desirability of permitting such transfers was, however, widely recognized, and the Law Commission report (at [3.20]–[3.21]) proposed the amendment of Order 53 to this effect. Under the CPR, transfers into the judicial review procedure are now possible. CPR 54.20 provides that Part 30 of the Rules, which permits transfers within the High Court, 'applies to transfers *to* and from the Administrative Court' (emphasis added). Paragraph 14.2 of the Practice Direction which accompanies Part 54 goes on to explain that, 'In deciding whether a claim is suitable for transfer to the Administrative Court, the court will consider whether it raises issues of public law to which Part 54 should apply.'

QUESTION

- If the court concludes that the claimant is attempting to litigate genuinely public law issues by means of ordinary proceedings, but that the Part 54 safeguards have not been compromised, how should it decide whether to allow the ordinary proceedings to continue or to transfer the case to the Administrative Court under Part 54?

14.4 Concluding Remarks

Where does all of this leave the procedural dichotomy, articulated with such vigour by Lord Diplock in *O'Reilly* v. *Mackman* [1983] 2 AC 237? In light of *Clark* and the possibility of transfer into Part 54, the policy of upholding the safeguards for public authorities remains, but it is prosecuted by more subtle means than those envisaged in *O'Reilly*. It is true that the procedural dichotomy has now largely been eclipsed in the sense that, following *Clark*, the circumstances in which public law matters may be litigated by means of ordinary proceedings now transcend the exceptional categories considered above. However, it is also true that, although the conclusion that the matter is one of public law no longer necessarily prescribes the procedure to be used, it continues to trigger the application of the protections inherent in the judicial review procedure. The departure from the rigid technicality of *O'Reilly* and *Cocks* is to be welcomed, but it is entirely unsurprising that the public/private distinction survives, albeit in a much more subtle form: it logically *must* survive in some sense if the safeguards which Part 54 confers upon public bodies are to have any practical effect. How those safeguards work, and whether they are necessary, are different questions; we address them in the next chapter.

FURTHER RESOURCES

Beatson, ' "Public" and "Private" in English Administrative Law' (1987) 103 *LQR* 34

Bowman, *Review of the Crown Office List* (London 2000) (available in summary form at *www.dca.gov.uk/civil/bowman2000/summary2000.htm*)

Civil Procedure Rules *www.dca.gov.uk/civil/procrules_fin/*

Cornford, 'The New Rules of Procedure for Judicial Review' [2000] 5 *Web JCLI* *webjcli.ncl.ac.uk/2000/issue5/cornford5.html*

Fredman and Morris, 'The Costs of Exclusivity' [1994] *PL* 69

Law Com No 226, *Administrative Law: Judicial Review and Statutory Appeals* (London 1994), Parts II, III and VII

Lewis, *Judicial Remedies in Public Law* (London 2004), ch 3

Oliver, 'Public Law Procedures and Remedies — Do We Need Them?' [2002] *PL* 91

Supperstone and Knapman (eds), *Administrative Court Practice* (London 2002)

15 RESTRICTION OF REMEDIES

15.1 Introduction

Our concern in this chapter is with a wide range of factors that may prevent claimants from obtaining relief in respect of unlawful administrative action. Some such restrictions — *eg* statutory provisions which limit or remove the courts' jurisdiction and the courts' general reluctance to intervene in relation to hypothetical matters — can impact on claimants seeking to invoke the courts' supervisory jurisdiction irrespective of the procedure used. Others — *eg* the need to secure permission and to comply with a strict three-month time-limit — bite only when the claim is brought under CPR Part 54 (although, as we saw above at 14.3.8, where a claim has not, but ought to have been, brought under Part 54, the court may give summary judgment if the Part 54 safeguards have been flouted). In this chapter, we explain when and how these restrictions operate, and consider how they impact on intending litigants and public bodies. However, at the outset, it is worth noting that some writers question whether it is appropriate — bearing in mind the vast diversity of issues litigated by means of judicial review — to lump all such cases together by means of a common procedure with uniformly applicable safeguards. Oliver [2002] *PL* 91 at 99–100 observes that:

The Bowman Report [*Review of the Crown Office List* (London 2000)] . . . referred to "the special nature of judicial review and the need for speed and flexibility". But this report did not spell out what was special about *all* judicial review cases, or in what circumstances speed and flexibility were required to any greater extent than in private law cases where injunctions are sought. These protections in judicial review are suggestive of state prerogatives of the kind found in civil law systems, which are quite out of keeping with the common law tradition.

Thus, not only should we ask whether *particular procedural safeguards* (from the point of view of public bodies) or obstacles (from the standpoint of intending claimants) are appropriate; we also need to question the usual assumption that there should be *a uniform set of safeguards* applicable in all judicial review cases.

15.2 Permission

15.2.1 The Pre-Action Protocol

Obtaining the permission of the court marks the beginning of the judicial review process proper. However, a 'Pre-Action Protocol' (on which see further Fordham [2002] *JR* 14; Baker [2002] *JR* 69) now exists in relation to judicial review; adherence is not obligatory but, according to para 7, 'the court will normally expect all parties to have complied with it and will take into account compliance or non-compliance when giving directions for case management of proceedings or when making orders for costs'. The Protocol codifies good practice by requiring intending claimants to send a 'letter before claim' to the prospective defendant, outlining the grounds of complaint, to which the defendant is expected to reply within 14 days by means of a 'letter of response'. By encouraging interaction between the parties before the matter reaches court, this scheme seeks to promote recourse to alternative dispute resolution, such as negotiation and mediation, thereby relieving pressure on the Administrative Court.

15.2.2 Judicial Review: A Two-stage Process

If the claimant nevertheless wishes to pursue the matter litigiously, then he must secure the 'permission' (or 'leave', as it used to be known) of the court: CPR 54.4. The existence of the permission requirement necessarily means that judicial review proceedings fall into two parts, consisting of the preliminary consideration of the claim at the permission stage and, if the claim progresses, more detailed consideration at the substantive hearing. The Law Commission (Law Com No 226, *Administrative Law: Judicial Review and Statutory Appeals* (London 1994)) (hereinafter the 'Law Commission report') considered that the permission stage — or 'preliminary consideration', as they preferred to call it — was highly beneficial. First, the existence of such a 'filter' helps to ensure that only serious issues advance as far as the substantive hearing: this is advantageous from the perspective of *public bodies* — and, by extension, *the public* — since it promotes certainty and finality in decision-making by ensuring that administrative bodies are not distracted unnecessarily by the prospect of litigation (*ibid* at [3.5]–[3.6]) (but now cf below at 15.2.3 on acknowledgment of service). Secondly, the permission stage is also advantageous from the *courts'* point of view, since it allows for 'the efficient management of the caseload' (*ibid* at [5.6]), allowing them, at an early stage and without significant consumption of judicial resources, to reject cases which have little prospect of success. Thirdly, the Law Commission expressed the view — shared by, *inter alios*, Le Sueur and Sunkin [1992] *PL* 102 at 107 — that the permission stage is helpful to *claimants*, since it provides a relatively quick and inexpensive mechanism by which to obtain the opinion of the Administrative Court.

These advantages of the two-stage process notwithstanding, some commentators entertain serious doubts about its appropriateness. Wade and Forsyth, *Administrative Law* (Oxford 2004) at 657, for instance, comment that the permission requirement is wrong 'in principle' because it involves treating public authorities 'more favourably than other litigants'. Moreover, Bridges, Meszaros and Sunkin [2000] *PL* 651 at 664–666 question the practical utility of the permission stage, arguing that there is little empirical evidence to support the proposition that it is an effective case-management tool. We will see below that difficulties in applying consistent principles at the permission stage reveal further practical problems in this area.

15.2.3 Reform of the Permission Stage

The nature of the permission stage was changed significantly by the introduction of CPR Part 54 which, in this respect, was heavily influenced by the conclusions of Sir Jeffrey Bowman's *Review of the Crown Office List* (London 2000) (hereinafter the 'Bowman Report') (on which see further Cornford and Sunkin [2001] *PL* 11). One of the principal problems considered by Bowman was the increasing workload of (what is now) the Administrative Court, and the delays caused thereby. Bowman advanced a number of proposals for increasing the efficiency of the judicial review process and, more fundamentally, reducing recourse to judicial review. Two specific recommendations concerning permission were made, which were largely implemented through Part 54.

First, Bowman (at 72), building upon proposals made in the Law Commission report (at [4.4] and [5.9]–[5.12]), suggested that permission should always (in the first instance) be determined on paper. This is now largely reflected in the Practice Direction supplementing Part 54, which states (at [8.4]) that, 'The court will generally, in the first instance, consider the question of permission without a hearing.'

Whereas minimizing the use of hearings at the permission stage aids the efficient use of scarce judicial resources once permission is sought, the second important change seeks to reduce recourse to judicial review in the first place. Bowman (at 68) identified post-permission settlement as one of the underlying causes of the courts' high workload in this area. This refers to the practice of claimants using up court time by taking matters as far as obtaining permission, and then settling — often using the granting of permission as a bargaining tool — before the substantive hearing. Bowman argued that increasing early interaction between the parties was key to encouraging settlement *before* any court involvement. As well as the use of a Pre-Action Protocol, Bowman recommended — building upon the suggestion in the Law Commission report (at [4.9]–[4.11]) that judges should be able to request information on paper from defendants at the permission stage — that the permission stage should be changed from an *ex parte* procedure, involving only the claimant, to an *inter partes* procedure. Thus a claimant seeking permission is now required to file a claim form stating, *inter alia*, the question which he wants the court to decide (CPR 8.2(b)(i)) and the remedy which is sought (CPR 54.6(1)(c)). The claim form must be served on, *inter alios*, the defendant (CPR 54.7(a)), who then has an opportunity to respond by means of an acknowledgment of service (CPR 54.8). The intention is that by making the permission stage *inter partes*, prospective claimants will seek permission less readily than was the case under the *ex parte* procedure: since the claimant must now 'face' (at least on paper) the defendant at the permission stage, the obtaining of permission becomes a more onerous process, thereby reinforcing the Pre-Action Protocol's encouragement of alternative dispute resolution.

15.2.4 The Operation of the Permission Stage

On what grounds do courts decide whether to grant permission? There are a number of specific grounds on which permission may be refused, such as the claimant's absence of recourse to alternative remedies before resorting to judicial review, his failure to comply with the strict time limits which apply to judicial review, and his lack of standing. These are all considered in detail later in this chapter. In addition, the courts are concerned at the permission stage with whether the case is arguable, on which Lord Diplock offered the following guidance in *R v. Inland Revenue Commissioners, ex parte National Federation of Self-employed and Small Businesses Ltd* [1982] AC 617 at 643–644:

The whole purpose of requiring that leave should first be obtained to make the application for judicial review would be defeated if the court were to go into the matter in any depth at that stage. If, on a quick perusal of the material then available, the court thinks that it discloses what might on further consideration turn out to be an arguable case in favour of granting to the applicant the relief claimed, it ought, in the exercise of judicial discretion, to give him leave to apply for that relief.

However, asking whether the case is 'arguable' is to adopt a rather vague criterion which is difficult to apply with any consistency. These problems were highlighted by empirical research conducted by Le Sueur and Sunkin, based on decisions (arising from both oral and written applications) in two six-week sample periods in 1988 and 1989. They found, *inter alia*, a high 'error' rate: approximately 43 per cent of written applications which failed later succeeded when renewed by means of an oral application. As the following extract indicates, such problems may, at least in part, be attributable to a lack of judicial consensus as to the approach to be adopted at the permission stage.

....

Le Sueur and Sunkin, 'The Requirement of Leave' [1992] PL 102

. . . [Our research suggests] that there are two main approaches to oral hearings. For convenience, these may be labelled the "quick look" and the "good look" approaches.

Lord Diplock described the "quick look" approach in the *National Federation* case . . . [After citing the passage set out above, they continued:] For Lord Diplock, leave was a purely summary process designed to filter out the obviously unarguable applications. From this perspective, the process may be said to serve (a) the interest of efficient management, by ensuring that with a minimum investment of judge time the court lists are kept free of obviously unmeritorious cases; (b) the interests of applicants, by seeking to ensure that potentially arguable claims are not prematurely rejected; and (c) the interests of respondents, by protecting them from the need to respond to applications without any merit.

As its label suggests, the "good look" approach is a more thorough inquiry into the application. Despite Lord Diplock's fear that the whole purpose of the leave stage would be defeated if applications were given more than a "quick look", each of the actors in the leave stage may seek a careful (and costly) scrutiny . . . The court may be loath to reject complex or sensitive applications without providing a full opportunity to applicants to present their case. The interests of court administration may also be better served by a "good look" approach. The prime example is where applications are considered in the knowledge that they are representative of a large number of similar applications that are waiting in the wings. In this situation the investment of extra time on one case may be justified if it leads to a considered view that will effectively determine similar applications . . .

To judge simply by the length of hearings, it appears from [our] sample that a significant number of applications are in fact "good looks". If Lord Diplock was correct to say that anything more than a "quick perusal" would defeat the "whole objective" of the leave process, then the object of leave is being defeated in a substantial minority of cases . . .

Le Sueur and Sunkin concluded that the absence of consensus was clearly a problem, and that it should be resolved in favour of the 'quick look' approach, largely because courts are ill-equipped at the permission stage to undertake a more searching inquiry in a sufficiently rigorous manner. To this end they recommended (at 127–128) 'an express presumption in favour of granting leave', a point which was taken up in the Bowman Report which endorsed the 'quick look' model by saying (at 64–65) that 'the permission stage is [merely] intended to filter out hopeless claims' and that it should therefore be 'stated in the rules that permission should be given if the claim discloses an arguable case'. This recommendation is not, however, reflected in the CPR — an omission that Cornford [2000] *Web JCLI* laments:

What is lacking [in the CPR] is the one measure proposed by Bowman to improve the claimant's position at the permission stage. Like the old Rules, the new Rules say nothing about the criteria for the grant of permission and thus leave matters in the rather unpredictable state that they were in before.

. . . [It] can be said with some confidence . . . that the new rules governing permission increase the disadvantages of the claimant *vis-à-vis* the defendant. The proper approach to leave under the old Rules of the Supreme Court was set out by Lord Diplock in *R v Inland Revenue Commissioners, ex parte National Federation of Self-employed and Small Businesses Ltd.* [1982] AC 617 at 644 . . . The new Rules alter the character of the permission stage from a filter designed to weed out obviously unarguable cases quickly to a form of inter partes proceeding. Yet at the same time it lacks the safeguards of the claimant's interests which one would expect in a procedure designed to put the parties on an equal footing. The claimant has from the outset to go to the trouble and expense of assembling all the relevant materials and must disclose its case in full to the defendant. The defendant need do no more than give its defence in outline. In the normal course of things, the claimant will have no opportunity to rebut the allegations made by the defendant because permission will be decided on the papers. In short, whether or not judges are willing or able when applying other Parts of the CPR, to ensure that the parties are on an equal footing, the regime introduced for judicial review seems designed, in an important respect, to exclude that principle. The interests which predominate are those in saving court time, and another, not set out in the CPR's overriding objective, the importance of protecting public authorities.

QUESTION

- Do you agree that, from the claimant's perspective, the permission stage is now too onerous?

One final point should be noted, concerning appeals against refusals of permission. If, as is usually the case, the permission decision is taken without a hearing, CPR 54.12(3) permits the claimant to request that the decision be reconsidered at a hearing. If permission is refused again, then the claimant may, under CPR 52.15(1), seek permission from the Court of Appeal to appeal to that court which, under CPR 52.15(3), 'may, instead of giving permission to appeal, give permission to apply for judicial review', in which case, according to CPR 52.15(4), 'the case will proceed in the High Court unless the Court of Appeal orders otherwise'.

15.3 Exhaustion of Alternative Remedies

15.3.1 The Principle and its Rationale

It is generally accepted that, at least in principle, judicial review is a remedy of last resort, to be invoked only when other avenues have been explored; if they have not, then permission may be denied. For example, in *R v. Inland Revenue Commissioners, ex parte Preston* [1985] AC 835 at 852, Lord Scarman said that

a remedy by way of judicial review is not to be made available where an alternative remedy exists. This is a proposition of great importance. Judicial review is . . . not an appeal. Where Parliament has provided by statute appeal procedures, . . . it will only be very rarely that the courts will allow the . . . process of judicial review to be used to attack an appealable decision.

Indeed, the importance of exhausting alternative remedies is now reflected in the Pre-Action Protocol for Judicial Review, which states that:

[2] Judicial review may be used where there is no right of appeal or where all avenues of appeal have been exhausted.

[3] Where alternative procedures have not been used the judge may refuse to hear the judicial review case. However, his or her decision will depend upon the circumstances of the case and the nature of the alternative remedy. Where an alternative remedy does exist a claimant should give careful consideration as to whether it is appropriate to his or her problem before making a claim for judicial review.

The significance which is now attached to alternative dispute resolution was emphasized by Lord Woolf MR in *R (Cowl) v. Plymouth City Council* [2001] EWCA Civ 1935 [2002] 1 WLR 803 at [14] and [25]:

The courts should not permit, except for good reason, proceedings for judicial review to proceed if a significant part of the issues between the parties could be resolved outside the litigation process . . . Today sufficient should be known about alternative dispute resolution to make the failure to adopt it, in particular when public money is involved, indefensible.

We will see below that a number of exceptions to this principle have been established. First, however, what policy arguments may justify it?

....

Lewis, 'The Exhaustion of Alternative Remedies in Administrative Law' [1992] CLJ 138

. . . The courts have put forward a twofold justification of the exhaustion of remedies principle. First, [it was said in *R v. Panel on Take-overs and Mergers, ex parte Guinness plc* [1990] 1 Q.B. 146 at 177 that] if Parliament has provided an appeals procedure, it is not for the court to usurp the functions of the appellate body. The reasoning is applied also to bodies not created by statute which have their own appellate system. Secondly, the public interest dictates that judicial review should be exercised speedily, and to that end it is necessary to limit the number of cases in which judicial review is used [see the *Guinness* case at 177–178].

. . . There are further advantages in the rule. Appellate bodies may be better or equally well equipped to handle disputes of fact than a court operating the judicial review mechanisms. The courts have power in judicial review proceedings to order discovery or cross-examination. In practice, however, they rarely exercise these powers, preferring to rely on affidavit evidence or contemporaneous documentation, even in the case of disputed fact. An appellate body prepared and able to re-hear evidence and witnesses and determine questions of fact may be a better check on inadequate decisions than judicial review.

There may also be gains in expertise to be made by having recourse to alternative remedies. Where the appeal is to the court, that appeal may be to a Division of the High Court particularly familiar with the area of law in question as in tax cases, where the appeal is heard in the Chancery Division. Administrative appeal bodies may also possess relevant expertise. In tax cases, for example, the appellate body, the general or special commissioners, have wide experience of the complex and detailed tax legislation. In employment cases, the system of industrial tribunals may be better equipped to deal with industrial issues than the Divisional Court. In the event that the matter is finally brought before the courts by way of judicial review of the decision of an appellate body, the court will enjoy the advantage of a reasoned decision by those familiar with the legislation and the background issues . . .

The latter point was endorsed by Lord Woolf MR in *Cowl* at [14].

In spite of the practical advantages which appear to flow from the exhaustion principle, objections are raised against it, most prominently by Wade and Forsyth, *Administrative Law* (Oxford 2004) at 703–704:

In principle there ought to be no categorical rule requiring the exhaustion of administrative remedies before judicial review can be granted. A vital aspect of the rule of law is that illegal administrative action can be challenged in the court as soon as it is taken or threatened. There should be no need first to pursue any administrative procedure or appeal in order to see whether the action will in the end be taken or not. An administrative appeal on the merits of the case is something quite different from judicial determination of the legality of the whole matter. This is merely to restate the essential difference between review and appeal . . .

The point concerning appeal and review merits further consideration. Traditionally, they serve distinct roles, looking respectively at merits and legality: the nature of the alleged defect in the relevant administrative decision should therefore determine which is appropriate. However, Lewis [1992] *CLJ* 138 at 141–142 takes issue with this analysis:

This distinction is not in practice as watertight as at first appears. There has been a degree of convergence between appeal and review in recent years. In the area of errors of law, the overlap between appeal and review is now great. Judicial review has reached the point that almost any error of law is capable of review. There will be little difference between appeal and review in such cases. Conversely, certain errors which traditionally fall within the scope of judicial review, are also regarded as remediable on appeal. Breaches of natural justice and decisions reached on no evidence may now be corrected on appeal as well as by way of judicial review. An appellate body may therefore be able to deal not only with the merits of the case but also with errors of law and other errors rendering a decision invalid. The traditional distinction between review and appeal has been significantly eroded and does not preclude the adoption of an exhaustion of remedies rule. As many errors can now be corrected either by appeal or judicial review, the choice of which mechanism to apply must be settled by reference to other considerations.

QUESTION

• Do you agree that alternative remedies should, as a general rule, have to be used before permission to seek judicial review is granted?

15.3.2 Exceptions to the General Principle

It is clear from the terms in which he stated the exhaustion rule in *Preston* (see above at 15.3.1) that Lord Scarman envisaged that it would operate only as a general principle to which exceptions would exist. Indeed, the courts have recognized a number of circumstances in which judicial review may lie irrespective of whether other remedies have been used. It appears that the rule will not be applied if the individual concerned is able to demonstrate that his case is different from the type of case for which the appeal procedure was designed. Sir John Donaldson MR endorsed such an approach in *R v. Secretary of State for the Home Department, ex parte Swati* [1986] 1 WLR 477 at 485, in which an immigrant, having failed to appeal against a notice of refusal of leave to enter the UK, sought judicial review:

. . . [I]t is well established that in giving or refusing leave to apply for judicial review, account must be taken of alternative remedies available to the applicant. This aspect was considered by this court very recently in *R v. Chief Constable of the Merseyside Police, ex parte Calveley* [1986] 2 WLR 144 and it was held that the [supervisory] jurisdiction would not be exercised where there was an alternative remedy by way of appeal, save in exceptional circumstances. By definition, exceptional circumstances defy definition, but where Parliament provides an appeal procedure, judicial review will have no place, unless the applicant can distinguish his case from the type of case for which the appeal procedure was provided.

The applicant may have no basis for complaint at being refused leave to enter. He may have cause to complain that the immigration officer erred in her assessment of the evidence — that her credulity threshold was too high. He may have cause to complain that she misunderstood and therefore misapplied the criteria for granting leave to enter. We simply have no idea which is the case. All these matters will be open on a statutory appeal, but only the latter could form the basis for judicial review, since as Lord Brightman pointed out in *Chief Constable of the North Wales Police v. Evans* [1982] 1 WLR 1155 at 1174G, judicial review is not so much concerned with the merits of the decision as with the way in which it was reached. In a word, the applicant's case is wholly indistinguishable from the general run of cases where someone arrives in the United Kingdom and is dissatisfied because he is denied leave to enter. Accordingly, in my judgment, he should not be allowed to pursue it by way of judicial review.

Although Sir John Donaldson was correct to remark that 'exceptional circumstances defy definition', subsequent cases do at least provide some guidance. For example, it is clear that the use of a remedy by way of appeal will not be treated as a condition precedent to judicial review if the appellate body lacks the power to deal with the matter which is complained of. In *Leech v. Deputy Governor of Parkhurst Prison* [1988] AC 533, two prisoners wished to challenge deputy prison governors' findings that they were each guilty of a disciplinary offence resulting in loss of remission. A remedy existed by way of petition to the Secretary of State, who was empowered to remit the punishment but not (at that time) to quash the findings of guilt. Both claimants petitioned the Secretary of State, one successfully. However, since both wished the findings of guilt to be quashed, both sought judicial review. The question arose whether the claimants could challenge the deputy prison governors' decisions, as distinct from the Secretary of State's decisions. In deciding that they could, Lord Bridge said (at 567):

One manifest inadequacy of the remedy by petition is the absence of any power in the Secretary of State to quash the adjudication. This may seem of minor significance. If the award has been remitted, it may perhaps be of little consequence that the adjudication of guilt has not been set aside. But when the prisoner's record shows merely that the punishment awarded for an offence has been remitted by the Secretary of State, those who have to take account of the record, as for example when the prisoner's eligibility for parole is under consideration, will not know, in a case such as that of Leech, that the proceedings leading to the award were wholly invalid and it is at least possible that the record may operate to his prejudice. This is a lacuna in the rules which can readily be cured by amendment and it is very desirable that it should be. If the Secretary of State had power to quash the adjudication as well as power to remit the award, it would be difficult to suppose that the court, as a matter of discretion, would be likely to grant judicial review to a prisoner who had not petitioned the Secretary of State, save in a case of urgency where the prisoner's release was imminent but would be delayed by loss of remission ordered by the disputed award.

It is evident from these remarks that Lord Bridge considered that an alternative remedy may be rendered inadequate, such as to obviate the need to have recourse to it, not only by the limited powers of the appellate body but also by the speed with which a remedy may be issued: in urgent cases, judicial review may be appropriate given the speed with which permission may be obtained and interim relief secured. Thus the fact that, compared to judicial review, the alternative remedy in *R v. Chief Constable of the Merseyside Police, ex parte Calveley* [1986] QB 424 at 434 was 'not speedy' was apparently one of the factors which persuaded the court that the exhaustion principle should give way. Contrariwise, on the basis of the policy arguments advanced by Lewis (above at 15.3.1) the principle is more likely to be applied if the court feels that the disputed point lies within the expertise of the appellate body or if it raises disputed questions of fact which the appellate body is better placed to resolve.

15.4 Time Limits

15.4.1 Introduction

Those who wish to use the judicial review procedure must usually act very quickly.

Supreme Court Act 1981

31—(6) Where the High Court considers that there has been undue delay in making an application for judicial review, the court may refuse to grant —
    (a) leave for the making of the application; or
    (b) any relief sought on the application,
if it considers that the granting of the relief sought would be likely to cause substantial hardship to, or substantially prejudice the rights of, any person or would be detrimental to good administration.

    (7) Subsection (6) is without prejudice to any enactment or rule of court which has the effect of limiting the time within which an application for judicial review may be made.

Civil Procedure Rules, Part 54

5(1) The claim form must be filed —
    (a) promptly; and
    (b) in any event not later than 3 months after the grounds to make the claim first arose.
  (2) The time limit in this rule may not be extended by agreement between the parties.
  (3) This rule does not apply when any other enactment specifies a shorter time limit for making the claim for judicial review.

Civil Procedure Rules, Part 3

1(2) Except where these Rules provide otherwise, the court may —
    (a) extend or shorten the time for compliance with any rule, practice direction or court order (even if an application for extension is made after the time for compliance has expired) . . .

The interpretation of these provisions has caused considerable difficulties for the courts, not least because it is unclear how those contained in the Act and those found in the CPR (which largely reproduce the rules that were set down by the Rules of the Supreme Court, Ord 53, r 4) relate to one another. However, before turning to that problem, a preliminary matter should be considered. Whatever interpretative difficulties are raised by the above provisions, it is perfectly clear that they create a very narrow window of opportunity for prospective claimants, with a benchmark requirement that litigation should be initiated within three months. The justification for this very short time limit in judicial review cases is said to lie in the need for certainty in public administration: Lord Diplock considered in *O'Reilly* v. *Mackman* [1983] 2 AC 237 at 280–281 that

public authorities and third parties should not be kept in suspense as to the legal validity of a decision the authority has reached in purported exercise of decision-making powers for any longer period than is absolutely necessary in fairness to the person affected by the decision.

The Law Commission (at [5.23]–[5.26] of its report) also considered that the interests of certainty justified a general requirement that judicial review should be sought within three months of the grounds arising.

The position in relation to judicial review stands in stark contrast to that which obtains in private law. Although shorter time limits used to apply in respect of litigation against public authorities, that is no longer the case. Thus, for instance, most claims in tort against public authorities are now subject to the standard limitation period of six years under the Limitation Act 1980. Beloff (in Forsyth and Hare (eds), *The Golden Metwand and the Crooked Cord* (Oxford 1998) at 270) doubts whether a special case can convincingly be made for judicial review:

A distinction is presumably drawn between the (relatively slight) consequences to a public authority of having its funds depleted for committing a private law wrong and the (relatively significant) consequences of having its actions impeded for committing a public law wrong. And yet some of the arguments (for example, budgetary certainty) which were once relied on to justify the [shorter] private law limitation period [for public authorities] are [now] echoed in the judicial review cases.

A further difficulty concerns the generality of the strict time limit which applies to judicial review. It is self-evident that some situations will arise in which the need for certainty is paramount; but, as Oliver comments [2002] *PL* 91 at 98–99, it does not follow that this is true across the board:

Statutory limitation periods may be justifiably imposed in respect of challenges to certain orders, as is the case with compulsory purchase orders and refusals of planning permission. Short statutory time-limits could be imposed in respect of other matters where delay would materially affect the outcome of the case, as in immigration and asylum claims, for instance [on which see further below at 15.6.8]. Apart from such specific areas the disadvantages for public administration and for third parties if proceedings are brought late can be met effectively in other ways: by the exercise of the power under Part 24 [of the CPR] to give summary judgment, by the exercise of discretion in the award of remedies and by the award of costs against unsuccessful claimants.

QUESTION

- Is the general requirement that judicial review claims must be issued promptly and in any event within three months of the commission of the administrative action in question an acceptable one?

15.4.2 Interpreting the Rules

The provisions on time limits contained respectively in the Supreme Court Act 1981 and the CPR do not easily fit together, leading to considerable problems of interpretation. Authoritative guidance was, however, provided by the House of Lords in the next case. Although Lord Goff refers in his speech to RSC Ord 53, r 4, that provision is in substance identical to the rules now contained in CPR 54.5 and 3.1(2). While there is one apparent difference between the old and new rules — whereas RSC Ord 53, r 4(1), permitted time to be extended only if there was a 'good reason' for doing so, the discretion to extend time in CPR 3.1(2) is not subject to any such explicit condition — Jackson J, in *R (M)* v. *The School Organisation Committee, Oxfordshire County Council* [2001] EWHC Admin 245 at [14]–[26], appears to have proceeded on the basis that the need for a 'good reason' to extend time is implicit in CPR 3.1(2). The following remarks of Lord Goff *vis-à-vis* RSC Ord 53, r 4, are therefore equally applicable today.

....

R v. *Dairy Produce Quota Tribunal for England and Wales, ex parte Caswell* [1990] 2 AC 738
House of Lords

The claimants applied to the Dairy Produce Quota Tribunal for a wholesale milk production quota. Although disappointed by the size of the quota to which the Tribunal decided, in February 1985, they were entitled on exceptional hardship grounds, the claimants did not seek judicial review until 1987, having until then been unaware of the possibility of doing so. The claimants contended that the Tribunal had misconstrued relevant legislation, thereby calculating the quota on an incorrect basis. However, the claimants had clearly failed to act promptly and within three months, as required by the rules of court, and accepted that there had been "undue delay" within the meaning of s 31(6) of the Supreme Court Act 1981. The Tribunal argued that time should not be extended in favour of the claimants, on the ground that it had applied the same interpretation of the Regulations in other cases: if they all had to be re-opened, this would be "detrimental to good administration" in the s 31(6) sense. At first instance, it was concluded that although the Tribunal had incorrectly interpreted the Regulations, time should not be extended. The claimants appealed without success to the Court of Appeal, and then to the House of Lords. The following extract is concerned only with the interpretation of the provisions concerning time limits; their application to the facts of the case is addressed in the excerpt below at 15.4.3.

Lord Goff

. . . [T]he courts have been left with the task of giving effect to two provisions [*viz* Supreme Court Act 1981, s 31(6) and RSC Ord 53, r 4] relating to delay, which at first sight are not easy to reconcile . . . [I]n Ord 53, r. 4(1), undue delay is defined [by reference to the requirement that proceedings be commenced promptly and in any event within three months: see now CPR 54.5(1)], whereas in section 31(6) it is not . . . [R]ule 4(1) looks to the existence of good reason [a requirement which is now implicit in CPR 3.1(2): see above] for extending the specified period, whereas section 31(6) looks to certain effects of delay as grounds for refusing leave, or substantive relief, as the case may be. A further twist is provided by the fact that rule 4(1) and (2) are expressed to be without prejudice to any statutory provision which has the effect of limiting the time within which an application for judicial review may be made [see now CPR 54.5(3)]; and that section 31(6) is expressed to be without prejudice to any enactment or rule of court which had that effect. These two provisions were said by Lloyd L.J., in the Court of Appeal, to produce a *circulus inextricabilis*: [1989] 1 W.L.R. 1089, 1094F.

The relationship between Ord. 53, r. 4, and section 31(6) was considered by the Court of Appeal in *Reg. v. Stratford-on Avon District Council, Ex parte Jackson* [1985] 1 W.L.R. 1319 . . . with particular reference to the meaning of the expression "undue delay". It was there submitted that, where good reason had been held to exist for the failure to act promptly as required by Ord. 53, r. 4(1), and the time for applying for leave had therefore been extended, the effect of section 31(7) was that in such circumstances there was no power to refuse either leave to apply or substantive relief under section 31(6) on the ground of undue delay, because an extension of time under Ord. 53, r. 4, itself negatives the existence of undue delay. That submission was rejected by the Court of Appeal. Ackner L.J., who delivered the judgment of the court, said, at p 1325:

> "This is not an easy point to resolve, but we have concluded that whenever there is a failure to act promptly or within three months there is 'undue delay.' Accordingly, even though the court may be satisfied in the light of all the circumstances, including the particular position of the applicant, that there is good reason for that failure, nevertheless the delay, viewed objectively, remains 'undue delay.' The court therefore still retains a discretion to refuse to grant leave for the making of the application or the relief sought on the substantive application on the grounds of undue delay if it considers that the granting of the relief sought would be likely to cause substantial hardship to, or substantially prejudice the rights of, any person or would be detrimental to good administration."

With this conclusion, I respectfully agree. First, when section 31(6) and (7) refer to "an application for judicial review," those words must be read as referring, where appropriate, to an application for leave to apply for judicial review. Next, as I read rule 4(1), the effect of *the rule* is to limit the time within which an application for leave to apply for judicial review may be made in accordance with its terms, ie promptly and in any event within three months. The court has however power to grant leave to apply despite the fact that an application is late, if it considers that there is good reason to exercise that power; this it does by extending the period. This, as I understand it, is the reasoning upon which the Court of Appeal reached its conclusion in *Reg. v. Stratford-on-Avon District Council, Ex parte Jackson*. Furthermore, the combined effect of section 31(7) and of rule 4(1) is that there is undue delay for the purposes of section 31(6) whenever the application for leave to apply is not made promptly and in any event within three months from the relevant date.

It follows that, when an application for leave to apply is not made promptly and in any event within three months, the court may refuse leave on the ground of delay unless it considers that there is good reason for extending the period; but, even if it considers that there is such good reason, it may still refuse leave (or, where leave has been granted, substantive relief) if in its opinion the granting of the relief sought would be likely to cause hardship or prejudice (as specified in section 31(6)) or would be detrimental to good administration . . .

In this way, I believe, sensible effect can be given to these two provisions, without doing violence to the language of either. Unlike the Court of Appeal, I do not consider that rule 4(3) and section 31(7) lead to a circulus inextricabilis, because [section] 31(6) does not limit "the time within which an application for judicial review may be made" (the words used in rule 4(3)). Section 31(6) simply contains particular grounds for refusing leave or substantive relief, not referred to in rule 4(1), to which the court is bound to give effect, independently of any rule of court.

Accordingly, in the present case, the fact that the single judge had granted leave to the appellants to apply for judicial review despite the lapse (long before) of three months from the date when the ground for their application first arose, did not preclude the court from subsequently refusing substantive relief on the ground of undue delay in the exercise of its discretion under section 31(6) . . .

15.4.3 A Three-Stage Analysis

The effect of Lord Goff's interpretation of the statutory and other rules is to establish a three-stage analysis. First, it is necessary to ask whether there has been 'undue delay' in the s 31(6) sense; although this term is undefined by the statute, it is evident from CPR 54.5(1) that such delay will exist if the permission is not sought promptly and, in any event, within three months. Secondly, if there has been undue delay, the court may exercise its discretion under CPR 3.1(2) to extend time in favour of the claimant if there is a good reason for doing so. Thirdly, however, this does nothing to alter the fact that there was 'undue delay', the existence of which, according to s 31(6), triggers a judicial discretion to refuse permission or relief 'if it considers that the granting of the relief sought would be likely to cause substantial hardship to, or substantially prejudice the rights of, any person or would be detrimental to good administration'. Third-party and administrative interests recognized at stage three are therefore capable of overriding a 'good reason' for extending time which is acknowledged at stage two.

Stage one: undue delay

When does time begin to run for the purposes of assessing compliance with the stage one requirement to act promptly and, in any event, within three months? The answer, according to CPR 54.5(1), is the date on which 'the grounds to make the claim first arose' — an objective criterion which takes no account of when the claimant became aware of the grounds. Although this test is generally straightforward, difficulties can arise when the matter to which the claimant wishes to object has been the subject of more than one administrative decision.

This point is illustrated by the House of Lords' decision in *R (Burkett)* v. *Hammersmith and Fulham London Borough Council* [2002] UKHL 23 [2002] 1 WLR 1593. The claimant lived next to land in respect of which outline planning permission was sought. On

15 September 1999, the planning authority resolved to grant outline planning permission subject to, *inter alia*, the developer's entering into a satisfactory agreement under s 106 of the Town and Country Planning Act 1990 concerning the nature of the proposed development. Outline planning permission was granted on 12 May 2000. The legal issue before the House of Lords was whether time began to run on 15 September 1999 or 12 May 2000: if the former, then the claimant would be *prima facie* out of time; if the latter, then no problem regarding time limits would arise. Their Lordships concluded that, although the resolution could have been challenged, this should not (by virtue of time being deemed to have begun to run as at the date of the resolution) prevent the claimant from challenging the later grant of planning permission itself, for reasons explained by Lord Steyn (at [39]):

> As a matter of language it is possible to say in respect of a challenge to an alleged unlawful aspect of the grant of planning permission that "grounds for the application first arose" when the decision was made. The ground for challenging the resolution is that it is a decision to do an unlawful act in the future; the ground for challenging the actual grant is that an unlawful act has taken place. And the fact that the element of unlawfulness was already foreseeable at earlier stages in the planning process does not detract from this natural and obvious meaning. The context supports this interpretation. Until the actual grant of planning permission the resolution has no legal effect. It is unlawful for the developer to commence any works in reliance on the resolution. And a developer expends money on the project before planning permission is granted at his own risk. The resolution may come to nothing because of a change of circumstances. It may fall to the ground because of conditions which are not fulfilled. It may lapse because negotiations for the conclusion of a section 106 agreement break down. After the resolution is adopted the local authority may come under a duty to reconsider its decision if flaws are brought to its attention: *R v West Oxfordshire District Council, Ex parte C H Pearce Homes Ltd* (1985) 26 R.V.R. 156. Moreover, it is not in doubt that a local authority may in its discretion revoke an outline resolution. In the search for the best contextual interpretation these factors tend to suggest that the date of the resolution does not trigger the three-month time limit in respect of a challenge to the actual grant of planning permission.

It follows that although preliminary acts may be challenged — subject to the possibility, considered below at 15.5, that such challenges may be defeated on the ground of prematurity — their commission should not start the clock running such that claimants are effectively forced to challenge preliminary measures instead of 'final' measures which may well be taken more than three months later.

Two further points should be noted concerning stage one. First, acting within three months does not conclusively establish that there has been no undue delay. This follows because s 31(6) does not, as Lord Steyn put it in *Burkett* at [18], contain any 'specific time limit', and the requirements in CPR 54.5(1) to act promptly and, in any event, within three months are cumulative. Consequently, even if a claimant acts within three months, undue delay will arise if a lack of promptitude is found. This is rare but, as Lord Steyn remarked (*loc cit*), requiring claimants to act more quickly than simply within three months is 'a useful reserve power in some cases, such as where an application made well within the three month period would cause immense practical difficulties'. For instance, in *R v. Rochdale Metropolitan Borough Council, ex parte Butterworth* [2000] Ed CR 117, permission for judicial review was denied in respect of a challenge to the defendant council's decision not to allocate the claimants to their first-choice secondary schools. The claim was brought just within three months, but just after the beginning of the academic year. David Pannick QC (sitting as a Deputy Judge of the High Court) justified his finding that the claimants had not acted promptly by saying that it was imperative, in the absence of exceptional circumstances, that such decisions should be challenged before the beginning of the school year, so as to avoid disruption to the pupils concerned and to others.

Secondly, although cases like *Butterworth* demonstrate the evident utility of the discretion to deny permission, within three months, on the ground of lack of promptitude, Lords Steyn and Hope expressed concern in *Burkett* (*obiter*, at [53] and [59] respectively) that the resulting restriction on the right of access to court within a reasonable time, enshrined in Article 6(1) ECHR, may fall foul of the Convention principle of legality, which requires limitations imposed by national law on Convention rights to be formulated with sufficient certainty. However, Lord Hope concluded that this problem could be avoided provided that adequate guidance as to the application of the promptitude criterion is supplied by case law, suggesting that English judges would do well to look at the principles developed by Scottish courts in this context.

Stage two: extending time

If there has been undue delay, then the court has a discretion under CPR 3.1(2) to extend time in favour of the claimant; as noted above, it appears that the requirement in RSC Ord 53, r 4(1) of a 'good reason' for doing so is regarded as implicit in CPR 3.1(2).

Although, as we saw above at 15.2.1, the Pre-Action Protocol for Judicial Review requires intending claimants to communicate with potential defendants before seeking permission for judicial review, it appears that delay caused by compliance with the Protocol is not necessarily a good reason for extending time. This follows from the first footnote to the Protocol, which provides that:

While the court does have the discretion under Rule 3.1(2)(a) of the Civil Procedure Rules to allow a late claim, this is only used in exceptional circumstances. Compliance with the protocol alone is unlikely to be sufficient to persuade the court to allow a late claim.

However, it is clear from *R v. Rochdale Metropolitan Borough Council, ex parte Cromer Ring Mill Ltd* [1982] 3 All ER 761 that the use of alternative remedies is a good reason for extending time; it therefore seems that, while compliance with the procedural requirements of the Protocol does not itself excuse delay, time will usually be extended if such compliance produces the intended result of recourse to alternative dispute resolution. It has also been held, by Ackner LJ in *R v. Stratford-upon-Avon District Council, ex parte Jackson* [1985] 1 WLR 1319 at 1324, that obtaining legal aid is a good reason for delay. It is clear that the court's attitude to extending time will be influenced by the context. Thus, for example, in *R (M) v. The School Organisation Committee, Oxfordshire County Council* [2001] EWHC Admin 245 at [27], Jackson J concluded that no extension was appropriate in respect of a challenge to a school reorganization programme, bearing in mind that 'prolonged uncertainty is damaging to teachers, to pupils, to parents and to all the schools affected'. It is worth noting that a similar factor influenced the court in the *Butterworth* case, considered above, and could also be taken into account under s 31(6); the divisions between the three stages of the analysis should not, therefore, be taken to be watertight.

Stage three: refusal of permission or relief

Even if the court concludes, at stage two, that there is a good reason for extending time, permission (or, at the substantive hearing, relief) may be refused under s 31(6) if granting a remedy would 'be likely to cause substantial hardship to, or substantially prejudice the rights of, any person or would be detrimental to good administration'. Hardship to individuals and detriment to their rights is particularly likely if late challenges to planning decisions are permitted. For instance, in *R v. North West Leicestershire District Council, ex parte Moses* [2000] Env LR 443, permission was denied to seek judicial review of planning permission in respect of runway extensions at East Midlands Airport some years after planning consent had been granted. Simon Brown LJ had no difficulty in concluding that this would cause substantial hardship to third parties, not least the Airport which had incurred construction costs approaching £70 million. The other limb of s 31(6) — detriment to good administration — was addressed in detail in the following case.

....

R v. Dairy Produce Quota Tribunal for England and Wales, ex parte *Caswell* [1990] 2 AC 738
House of Lords

The facts are set out in the extract above at 15.4.2.

Lord Goff

. . . On the question of detriment to good administration, the judge reviewed with care the evidence before him. This consisted of an affidavit sworn by Mr. Newton, who was secretary of D.P.Q.T. [Dairy Produce Quota Tribunal] until September 1988, and two affidavits submitted by the appellants in answer to that affidavit, one sworn by Mr. May of the legal department of the National Farmers' Union, and the other by Mr. Collinson, a partner in the solicitors acting for the appellants. It appeared from the evidence that the essence of the quota system is that there is a finite amount of milk quota available, so that a quota given to one producer is not available to others. In fact, about 4,000 exceptional hardship appeals were heard by D.P.Q.T. Of these, about 600 were successful, additional quota being granted; so about 3,400 producers failed in their applications for additional quota on this ground . . . [T]he fact that judicial review was the remedy available to a milk producer aggrieved by a decision of D.P.Q.T. must have become well known at least after September 1985, when the first hearing of an application for judicial review in such a case received wide publicity in the dairy trade. Consideration was given to the possibility of other producers seeking judicial review of adverse decisions of D.P.Q.T. if the appellants' application for substantive relief was successful. It was accepted that sufficient provision had been made to deal with the appellants' claim for extra quota. But, in Mr. Newton's opinion, a small but administratively substantial number of milk producers could be encouraged to make applications for judicial review relying on the same point as the appellants, or a variation of it; and that could mean re-opening the quota for the year 1984–85, and for each succeeding year. Further allocations of quota could only be made at the expense of all other producers whose quotas would have to be reduced accordingly. Mr. Collinson, in his affidavit, questioned whether other milk producers would be likely to follow the appellants' lead and seek judicial review or whether, if they did so, they would obtain leave to apply after such a long delay.

Having reviewed the evidence, the judge expressed his conclusion on this point in the following passage in his judgment:

"It is obvious that if there are a number of applications the problem of re-opening these claims, going back now three years, is going to be very great. It arises out of events in 1985. The evidential problems are self-evident, leaving aside the question of being able fairly to deal with claims now in relation to matters in 1985. I think there is likely to be a very real problem in relation to a number of cases. I do not think the number of cases is de minimis. I have concluded that the fact that hitherto there have been only these two applications is not a matter which is of very great help in determining what the effect will be of the particular decision in this case. I have come to the clearest view that there will be a detriment to good administration if this application were granted."

The judge's conclusion, on the evidence before him, that there was likely to be a very real problem in relation to a number of cases, was a finding of fact with which I can see no reason to interfere. Once that conclusion was reached, it seems to me inevitable that to grant the relief sought in the present case would cause detriment to good administration. As Lloyd L.J. pointed out in his judgment [1989] 1 W.L.R. 1089, 1099, two things emerged from the evidence with sufficient clarity: first that, if the appellants' application for substantive relief were to be successful, there would be a significant number of further applications, and second that, if a significant number of applications were granted, then all previous years back to 1984 would have to be re-opened. These facts disclose, in my opinion, precisely the type of situation which Parliament was minded to exclude by the provision in section 31(6) relating to detriment to good administration. I do not consider that it would be wise to attempt to formulate any precise definition or description of what constitutes detriment to good administration. This is because applications for judicial review may occur in many different situations, and the need for finality may be greater in one context than in another. But it is of importance to observe that section 31(6) recognises that there is an interest in good administration independently of hardship, or prejudice to the rights of third parties, and that the harm suffered by the applicant by reason of the decision which has been impugned is a matter which can be taken into account by the court when deciding whether or not to exercise its discretion under section 31(6) to refuse the relief sought by the applicant. In asking the question whether the grant of such relief would be detrimental to good administration, the court is at that stage looking at the interest in good administration independently of matters such as these. In the present context, that interest lies essentially in a regular flow of consistent decisions, made and published with reasonable dispatch; in citizens knowing where they stand, and how they can order their affairs in the light of the relevant decision. Matters of particular importance, apart from the length of time itself, will be the extent of the effect of the relevant decision, and the impact which would be felt if it were to be re-opened. In the present case, the court was concerned with a decision to allocate part of a finite amount of quota, and with circumstances in which a re-opening of the decision would lead to other applications to re-open similar decisions which, if successful, would lead to re-opening the allocation of quota over a number of years. To me it is plain, as it was to the judge and to the Court of Appeal, that to grant the appellants the relief they sought in the present case, after such a lapse of time had occurred, would be detrimental to good administration . . .

Lords Bridge, Griffiths, Ackner, and Lowry agreed with Lord Goff. Appeal dismissed.

Beloff (in Forsyth and Hare (eds), *The Golden Metwand and the Crooked Cord* (Oxford 1998) at 279–280) highlights the contrast between *Caswell* and *Patterson* v. *Greenwich London Borough Council* (1994) 26 HLR 159, in which permission was sought to challenge a local authority's decision concerning the provision of accommodation. Although undue delay was found, it was held that granting relief would not be detrimental to good administration. Evans LJ explained (at 168) that

this case unlike *Caswell* is not one where records or books of account are closed on a regular basis, and have to be reopened if a particular past decision is revised. Rather, the provision of accommodation and the assessing of applications by homeless persons is an ongoing and continuous process . . . [T]he need to deal with such cases as they arise can properly be regarded as part of the responsibilities of good administration, and there is no evidence nor any grounds to infer that the burden will be especially or singularly great in the present case.

15.5 Prematurity and Ripeness

15.5.1 Introduction

We have already seen that, when a claimant establishes that administrative action is contrary to the principles of public law, relief does not automatically follow; rather, the court has discretion. It may therefore choose to withhold relief on the basis of, for example, the claimant's conduct or the wider public interest. (See, for instance, the argument noted at 3.3.3 above to the effect that courts might withhold relief if quashing unlawful action would wreak administrative chaos.) In this context, a further question arises concerning the types of administrative measures in respect of which the courts are prepared to issue relief. The courts' supervisory jurisdiction is most commonly exercised in relation to actions and decisions which have already been taken to the detriment of (typically, but not necessarily: see below at 15.7) the claimant, the question being whether they are lawful or not (and, if not, whether relief should be granted). There are, however, many other forms of administrative action such as government circulars, preliminary decisions which are mere staging posts *en route* to some final, legally effective decision (see, eg, *Burkett*, considered above at 15.4.3) and statements as to intended future action, to name but a few, which do not directly impact upon the rights, obligations, or interests of individuals. Should courts be willing to issue remedies in respect of such actions if they disclose an error of law or signify an intention to act unlawfully? Should courts go further, by issuing 'advisory declarations' in order to answer purely hypothetical or academic questions?

Consideration of these issues raises questions of 'prematurity' and 'ripeness': when should courts refuse to adjudicate, or refuse relief, on the ground that the claimant has moved prematurely? At what point does an issue mature into something which is ripe and appropriate for judicial review? Beatson (in Forsyth and Hare (eds), *The Golden Metwand and the Crooked Cord* (Oxford 1998) at 224–225) laments the fact that these matters receive comparatively little attention in the UK; although it is clear from the case law that these concepts exist, an articulated principled framework within which they may be understood is somewhat lacking.

15.5.2 Preliminary and Interlocutory Decisions

The context in which the concept of prematurity is most developed is that of preliminary and interlocutory decisions. Lord Steyn observed in *R (Burkett) v. Hammersmith and Fulham London Borough Council* [2002] UKHL 23 [2002] 1 WLR 1593 at [38] that:

In a context where there is a statutory procedure involving preliminary decisions leading to a final decision affecting legal rights, judicial review may lie against a preliminary decision not affecting legal rights. Town planning provides a classic case of this flexibility. Thus it is in principle possible to apply for judicial review in respect of a resolution to grant outline permission and for prohibition even in advance of it . . .

Thus, in *R v. Electricity Commissioners, ex parte London Electricity Joint Committee Company (1920) Ltd* [1924] 1 KB 171, the Attorney-General's contention that the defendant's decision could not be judicially reviewed because it could not take effect until approved by the Minister of Transport and by resolution of both Houses of Parliament was rejected by Atkin LJ at 208:

I know of no authority which compels me to hold that a proceeding cannot be . . . subject to [judicial remedies] because it is subject to confirmation or approval, even where the approval has to be that of the Houses of Parliament. The authorities are to the contrary.

In the *Electricity Commissioners* case there existed what may be called a complete, if not final, decision: a determination had been made on the issues, and a conclusion reached; in this sense, a complete decision, which would potentially have legal consequences if appropriately endorsed, existed. This situation is, however, to be distinguished from that in which a claimant seeks to intervene before any determination is made of the substantive issue which the decision-maker is empowered to decide. An example of the latter situation would be a challenge to the jurisdiction of or procedure adopted by a tribunal *before* the hearing is concluded and any decision on the issues reached. A more limited approach to judicial review applies in this context, for the policy reasons set out by McCullough J in *R v. Association of Futures Brokers and Dealers Ltd, ex parte Mordens Ltd* (1991) 3 Admin LR 254 at 263–264:

It is . . . only in the most exceptional circumstances that the court will grant judicial review of a decision taken during the course of a hearing, by a body amenable to the court's supervisory jurisdiction, before that hearing has been concluded. The practice which this court almost invariably follows is to decline to hear a challenge to an interlocutory decision until the proceedings in which it was taken have been concluded.

. . . The reasons for the general rule are obvious. To entertain challenges at the interlocutory stage would play havoc with the conduct of proceedings in courts and tribunals below. Even to make an application to this court will in most cases occasion at least some interruption to the course of those proceedings. If leave to move is given, so that a substantive hearing follows, the resulting delay will almost inevitably seriously interfere with the course of those proceedings and very likely give rise to a risk of injustice.

Not only is time wasted, relationships are upset. Once the proceedings in this court are over the hearing must resume with the tribunal once more above and between the parties, rather than alongside one and against the other, as here.

Further, to come to this court too soon is in many cases to come unnecessarily. The party aggrieved by an interlocutory decision may nevertheless be satisfied by the outcome of the proceedings. A decision which, when it was made, was thought to be wrong or likely to have a significant effect on the outcome of the proceedings may, in the end, turn out to have been right or immaterial to the result.

The difficulty lies in determining the circumstances in which this approach should be departed from. One relevant factor here is the level of impact of the preliminary decision on the remainder of the proceedings. For instance, in *R v. Secretary of State for the Environment, ex parte the Royal Borough of Kensington and Chelsea* (1987) 19 HLR 161, a public local inquiry was held in order to determine whether a local authority could compulsorily purchase certain property. The authority wished to do so because tenants living in the property complained of harassment, intimidation, and neglect on the part of the landlord; however, the inspector excluded evidence of such misconduct, ruling it irrelevant. The authority successfully sought judicial review of this decision; Taylor J concluded that the inspector had exercised his discretion unlawfully, and explained (at 173) why judicial review of a preliminary decision was, in the circumstances, appropriate:

. . . [O]ne is faced here with a most unusual case. Practically the whole and certainly the main thrust of the applicant's case at the inquiry, has by the challenged ruling been blocked as irrelevant, in my judgment, wrongly so. To decline to intervene now would not only postpone redress for a long time, and until much money has been spent, but it would stultify the presentation of the applicant's real case; the inquiry would be a barren exercise, and if it had to be repeated and reconvened, witnesses' memories would be stale and faulty.

Similarly, courts are sometimes prepared to allow challenges to the jurisdiction of a tribunal before it has reached a decision, provided that any factual information likely to be relevant to the decision as to jurisdiction has already emerged. For instance, in *R v. Broadcasting Complaints Commission, ex parte British Broadcasting Corporation* [1994] EMLR 497 the claimant had broadcast a television programme in respect of which a complaint was made to the defendant to the effect that the complainant's research had not been mentioned in the programme and that she had thereby been unfairly treated. The defendant asserted jurisdiction, notwithstanding that, according to s 150 of the Broadcasting Act 1990, the complainant had to have a 'direct interest' in the subject-matter of the allegedly unfair treatment. Before the defendant had reached a decision, the claimant sought judicial review, arguing that the statute had been misconstrued. Laws J agreed, and (at 501) replied in these terms to the defendant's assertion that judicial review had been sought prematurely:

It is . . . true . . . that a challenge to . . . jurisdiction of the kind now before the court should not be brought at least until all the relevant facts are known; if proceedings were launched before that happened, they would very likely be held to be premature. In this case, however, all the facts were made plain on the correspondence before the letter of 16 September 1992 [in which the defendant told the claimant that it considered itself to have jurisdiction]. Where that is the case, I do not consider that proceedings for judicial review concerned solely with the Commission's jurisdiction should necessarily be discouraged. I accept that in many contexts public bodies should in principle be left to carry out their functions, according to their own perceptions of their duties, without judicial interference at interim stages. But the powers of the Commission touch questions of editorial freedom; they represent a measure of supervision over free expression in the broadcasting media. That is not to say that the court should in any sense presume in favour of a restrictive approach to their interpretation, but it means that it is peculiarly important that their reach should be established, and where there exists all along a clean argument as to whether in law the Commission are entitled to entertain a complaint, it will not generally be contrary to the public interest that its merits be determined at an early stage. Certainly, there is in my judgment nothing inappropriate in these proceedings.

These comments suggest that the importance of the issue and the extent to which the legal issues can be separated from any factual disputes which are still to be resolved will influence the court's determination of whether a jurisdictional challenge is premature.

15.5.3 Advice, Guidance, Recommendations, and Views

Preliminary decisions are liable to have legal consequences in that they form part of a decision-making process which will ultimately result in a determination which has legal effects. What, however, of advice, guidance, recommendations, and views promulgated by (for instance) government departments?

....

Gillick v. *West Norfolk and Wisbech Area Health Authority* [1986] AC 112
House of Lords

The Department for Health and Social Security (DHSS) circulated guidance to area health authorities to the effect that, although the provision of contraceptive advice or treatment to children under 16 without parental consent would be unusual, such a course was open to a doctor if it was, in his clinical judgment, appropriate. The claimant sought an assurance from her area health authority that no such advice or treatment would be given, without her consent, to her daughters while under 16. No such assurance was forthcoming, the authority taking the view that, according to the circular, this was a matter for individual doctors. The claimant sought a declaration that the guidance in the circular was unlawful. This excerpt is concerned only with the courts' jurisdiction to review non-statutory guidance.

Lord Bridge

. . . Throughout the hearing of the argument in the appeal and in subsequent reflection on the questions to which it gives rise I have felt doubt and difficulty as to the basis of the jurisdiction which Mrs. Gillick invokes in her claim to a declaration against the D.H.S.S. . . . I ask myself what is the nature of the action or decision taken by the D.H.S.S. in the exercise of a power conferred upon it which entitles a court of law to intervene and declare that it has stepped beyond the proper limits of its power. I frame the question in that way because I believe that hitherto, certainly in general terms, the court's supervisory jurisdiction over the conduct of administrative authorities has been confined to ensuring that their actions or decisions were taken within the scope of the power which they purported to exercise or conversely to providing a remedy for an authority's failure to act or to decide in circumstances where some appropriate statutory action or decision was called for.

Now it is true that the Secretary of State for Health and Social Security under section 5(1)(*b*) of the National Health Service Act 1977 has a general responsibility for the provision within the National Health Service of what may be described shortly as family planning services. But only in a very loose sense could the issue of the memorandum be considered as part of the discharge of that responsibility. The memorandum itself has no statutory force whatever. It is not and does not purport to be issued in the exercise of any statutory power or in the performance of any statutory function. It is purely advisory in character and practitioners in the National Health Service are, as a matter of law, in no way bound by it.

In the light of these considerations I cannot, with all respect, agree that the memorandum is open to review on "*Wednesbury*" principles *(Associated Provincial Picture Houses Ltd. v. Wednesbury Corporation* [1948] 1 K.B. 223) on the ground that it involves an unreasonable exercise of a statutory discretion. Such a review must always begin by examining the nature of the statutory power which the administrative authority whose action is called in question has purported to exercise, and asking, in the light of that examination, what were, and what were not, relevant considerations for the authority to take into account in deciding to exercise that power. It is only against such a specific statutory background that the question whether the authority has acted unreasonably, in the *Wednesbury* sense, can properly be asked and answered. Here there is no specific statutory background by reference to which the appropriate *Wednesbury* questions could be formulated.

The issue by a department of government with administrative responsibility in a particular field of non-statutory guidance to subordinate authorities operating in the same field is a familiar feature of modern administration. The innumerable circulars issued over the years by successive departments responsible in the field of town and country planning spring to the mind as presenting a familiar example. The question whether the advice tendered in such non-statutory guidance is good or bad, reasonable or unreasonable, cannot, as a general rule, be subject to any form of judicial review. But the question arises whether there is any exception to that general rule.

Your Lordships have been referred to the House's decision in *Royal College of Nursing v. Department of Health and Social Security* [1981] A.C. 800. The background to that case was exceptional, as only becomes fully clear when one reads the judgment of Woolf J. at first instance: [1981] 1 All E.R. 545. The Royal College of Nursing ("R.C.N.") and the D.H.S.S. had received conflicting legal advice as to whether or not it was lawful, on the true construction of certain provisions of the Abortion Act 1967, for nurses to perform particular functions in the course of a novel medical procedure for the termination of pregnancy, when acting on the orders and under the general supervision of a registered medical practitioner but not necessarily in his presence. The R.C.N. had issued a memorandum and a later circular to its members to the effect that it was not lawful. The D.H.S.S. had issued a circular advising that it was lawful. The desirability of an authoritative resolution of this dispute on a pure question of law was obvious in the interests both of the nursing profession and of the public. The proceedings took the form of a claim by the R.C.N. against the D.H.S.S. for a suitable declaration and the D.H.S.S. in due course counterclaimed a declaration to the opposite effect. As Woolf J. pointed out, neither side took any point as to the jurisdiction of the court to grant a declaration. Woolf J. himself felt it necessary to raise and examine certain questions as to the locus standi of the R.C.N. to bring the proceedings and as to the propriety of their form. He answered these questions in a favourable sense to enable him to decide the disputed question of law on its merits. No technical question bearing on jurisdiction attracted any mention in the Court of Appeal or in this House. In the litigation the original conflict between the parties was reflected in a conflict of judicial opinion. On a count of judicial heads a majority of five to four favoured the R.C.N. But by a majority of three to two in your Lordships' House the D.H.S.S. carried the day and obtained the declaration they sought.

Against this background it would have been surprising indeed if the courts had declined jurisdiction. But I think it must be recognised that the decision (whether or not it was so intended) does effect a significant extension of the court's power of judicial review. We must now say that if a government department, in a field of administration in which it exercises responsibility, promulgates in a public document, albeit non-statutory in form, advice which is erroneous in law, then the court, in proceedings in appropriate form commenced by an applicant or plaintiff who possesses the necessary locus standi, has jurisdiction to correct the error of law by an appropriate declaration. Such an extended jurisdiction is no doubt a salutary and indeed a necessary one in certain circumstances, as the *Royal College of Nursing* case [1981] A.C. 800 itself well illustrates. But the occasions of a departmental non-statutory publication raising, as in that case, a clearly defined issue of law, unclouded by political, social or moral overtones, will be rare. In cases where any proposition of law implicit in a departmental advisory document is interwoven with questions of social and ethical controversy, the court should, in my opinion, exercise its jurisdiction with the utmost restraint, confine itself to deciding whether the proposition of law is erroneous and avoid either expressing ex cathedra opinions in areas of social and ethical controversy in which it has no claim to speak with authority or proferring answers to hypothetical questions of law which do not strictly arise for decision . . .

Lord Templeman agreed with Lord Bridge on this point. Lords Fraser and Scarman considered that the guidance was issued pursuant to the National Health Service Act 1977, s 5 (1)(b), and that there therefore existed an exercise of statutory power capable of judicial review. Lord Brandon expressed no view on this issue.

The effect of Lord Bridge's speech in *Gillick* and the decision in the *RCN* case to which he refers is that limited circumstances exist in which guidance may be subject to judicial review. Three points should be noted.

First, it may be that the guidance in question must have a practical impact on the parties or the public. The House of Lords was clearly influenced by this consideration in *RCN*: Lord Edmund-Davies, for instance, remarked (at 833) that 'several thousand' of the procedures in question were carried out annually, making it obviously important to clarify the legal position. Similarly, in *R v. Secretary of State for Health, ex parte Pfizer Ltd* [1999] 3 CMLR 875, a case concerning the legality of interim advice to doctors that the drug Viagra should be prescribed only in exceptional circumstances, Collins J considered (at [17]) that, 'Advice or guidance promulgated by a public authority may be the subject of judicial review if it contains an error of law. This is particularly so if it is likely to be acted upon by those it addresses'. Thus the fact that doctors were highly likely to — and, in fact, did — heed the advice was one of the factors which led to the conclusion that judicial review could lie.

Secondly, although questions arose in *RCN* and *Gillick* as to whether circulars, if followed, would result in the commission of criminal offences, it is clear that judicial review of advice can occur outwith such circumstances. For instance, the case of *R (UK Renderers Association Ltd) v. Secretary of State for the Environment, Transport and the Regions* [2001] EWHC Admin 675 [2002] Env LR 21 (upheld on appeal: [2002] EWCA Civ 749 [2003] Env LR 7) concerned a challenge to guidance issued in relation to the obligation of animal renderers under s 7(1)(a) of the Environmental Protection Act 1990 to use the 'best available techniques not entailing excessive cost' for preventing the release of prescribed substances as part of the rendering process. The claimants argued (ultimately unsuccessfully) that guidance (some of which was non-statutory in form) requiring the use of all due diligence and the taking of all reasonable steps was unlawful, on the ground that it went beyond the duty laid down in the Act. Although there was no suggestion that any unlawful conduct would result from following it, Ouseley J said (at [33]) that the 'guidance, both in its statutory and non-statutory parts, can be challenged by way of judicial review'.

Thirdly, although Lord Bridge suggested in *Gillick* (at 193–194) that courts should review advice or guidance only in relation to 'a clearly defined issue of law, unclouded by political, social or moral overtones', the *Gillick* and *RCN* decisions seem to demonstrate a judicial preparedness to intervene even if the case *does* possess such overtones. Lord Bridge's comments on this point were, however, taken at face value by Hirst LJ, holding in *R v. Secretary of State for Employment, ex parte Equal Opportunities Commission* [1993] 1 WLR 872 at 900 that the view expressed by the Secretary of State in a letter to the Equal Opportunities

Commission as to the compatibility of UK and European Union law on indirect gender discrimination was not reviewable (a conclusion later upheld by the House of Lords [1995] 1 AC 1 for reasons which are not entirely clear) because it raised matters which were 'closely interwoven with questions of social and political controversy'. Hirst LJ emphasized (at 900) that 'the extended jurisdiction applied in *Gillick* . . . is the exception rather than the rule'.

QUESTIONS

- Should courts be deterred from reviewing guidance if it raises controversial social or political questions?
- How does the position adopted in this context relate to the concept of justiciability (considered above at 5.3.3)?

15.5.4 Hypothetical Issues and Advisory Declarations

Similar problems are evident when we consider the courts' approach to hypothetical matters. To what extent should the courts exercise jurisdiction over such issues? The importance of this question is underlined in the following passage.

Laws, 'Judicial Remedies and the Constitution' (1994) 57 MLR 213

. . . There has for many years been a strong tradition in the law that the courts will only decide questions on which a live dispute turns; they will not entertain issues which they perceive as being merely hypothetical or academic. I use the word "tradition" advisedly; it is not a matter of jurisdiction, but of judicial choice. I think that the effects of this tradition are in some respects harmful to the proper development of public law, in which context it needs to be severely modified. I do not consider this theme to be one of merely peripheral importance, so as to command the attention only of specialists who might understandably find interest in any aspect of public law, however dry or marginal. It engages a question going to the very nature of the role which the judicial arm of government is to play in the State: how far should the judges act proactively, rather than merely reactively?

I should first expose a distinction which seems to me to possess some significance. It is between what may be regarded as a "hypothetical" question and what may be regarded as an "academic" question. The courts have tended to use these phrases indifferently. I do not think that they have been right to do so. We should understand an academic question to be one which does not need to be answered for any visible practical purpose at all: thus, if I were a legal antiquarian, and interested in the construction of a statute long since repealed and not replaced, I could not bring proceedings to ask the court to construe it for me, so as to satisfy my intellectual curiosity: the court will not deploy its resources so as to provide authoritative backing for one or other view being canvassed in the lecture hall or the tutorial. A hypothetical question is quite different: it is a question which may need to be answered for real practical purposes; it connotes only a situation in which the events have not yet happened which will clothe the answer to the question with immediate practical effects. . . .

Laws's observation that this issue raises fundamental questions about the judicial role is an important one. As far as public law is concerned, the willingness of the courts to review hypothetical matters reflects the extent to which the function of public law extends beyond dispute resolution to embrace the concept of expository justice. We explore these concepts below at 15.7.5, in the context of standing.

Three factors underlie the courts' traditional reluctance to review hypothetical questions. First, it is sometimes said that review of such matters is simply inconsistent with the adversarial model, which is paradigmatically concerned with the resolution of concrete issues. Consider, for instance, the following remarks of Viscount Simon LC in *Sun Life Assurance Co of Canada* v. *Jervis* [1944] AC 111 at 113:

I do not think that it would be a proper exercise of the authority which this House possesses to hear appeals if it occupies time in this case in deciding an academic question, the answer to which cannot affect the respondent in any way. If the House undertook to do so, it would not be deciding an existing lis between the parties who are before it, but would merely be expressing its view on a legal conundrum which the appellants hope to get decided in their favour without in any way affecting the position between the parties.

A second objection is that people may be affected by the decision without any opportunity of putting their arguments to the court. However, this objection only holds water if non-parties are bound by such decisions. Simon Brown LJ took it as read in *R (Campaign for Nuclear Disarmament)* v. *Prime Minister* [2002] EWHC 2777 (Admin) at [46] that advisory declarations are 'binding on all'. A different view, however, was taken by Lord Goff in *R* v. *Secretary of State for the Home Department, ex parte Wynne* [1993] 1 WLR 115 at 120. He said that if a court were to consider a hypothetical question, 'any conclusion, and the accompanying reasons, could in their turn constitute no more than *obiter dicta*, expressed without the assistance of a concrete factual situation, and would not constitute a binding precedent for the future'. Thirdly, it is sometimes said that determination of hypothetical questions is an inappropriate use of scarce judicial resources.

However, as recognized in the Law Commission report (at [8.9]–[8.14]), which recommended that explicit provision be made in legislation for the issuing of advisory declarations, provided that 'the point concerned is one of general public importance' considerable benefits may flow from judicial review of hypothetical points. In particular (but subject to the caveat which follows from Lord Goff's remarks in *Wynne*) such review may usefully increase certainty, because it enables interested parties to ascertain at an early stage whether proposed action is lawful. Thus, in *Airedale NHS Trust* v. *Bland* [1993] AC 789, a hospital was able to obtain declarations to the effect that if it terminated the life support of a patient in a persistent vegetative state, this would not amount to unlawful homicide. In this way, claimants are able to establish in advance whether a particular course of action would be lawful.

Although there are clearly advantages in allowing judicial review of some hypothetical issues, the general approach of the courts in this area is cautious, as the speech of Lord Hobhouse in *R (Pretty)* v. *Director of Public Prosecutions* [2001] UKHL 61 [2002] 1 AC 800 illustrates. The terminally ill claimant unsuccessfully challenged the defendant's refusal to assure her that her husband would not be prosecuted if he helped her to commit suicide, arguing that any such prosecution would be inconsistent with (*inter alia*) her right to life under Article 2 ECHR which, she asserted, included a right to die and to assisted suicide. The subject of the challenge was the defendant's contention that he had no legal power to guarantee immunity from prosecution in respect of events yet to occur, not least because he had no means of investigating the factual circumstances (such as the reality of the claimant's consent). In light of this, the challenge to the defendant's refusal to guarantee immunity was doomed to failure, but Lord Hobhouse considered (at [116]) whether the real issue — *viz* whether the claimant had a legal right to assisted suicide — could have been raised before the courts in some other way:

In exceptional circumstances it may be proper for a member of the public to bring proceedings against the Crown for a declaration that certain proposed conduct is lawful and name the Attorney General as the formal defendant to the claim. But that is not what occurred here and, even then, the court would have a discretion which it would normally exercise to refuse to rule upon hypothetical facts. Had the case raised by the appellant been one where it was appropriate to grant a declaration as to legality or compatibility, the court would no doubt have adopted that approach. Indeed, the judgment of the Divisional Court [see [2001] EWHC Admin 788 (2001) 63 BMLR 1] and the speeches of your Lordships on the human rights questions will no doubt provide in practice the appropriate guidance to all those concerned in this matter as to the correct understanding of the law.

These remarks conceal a curious duplicity of views. On the one hand, Lord Hobhouse seems to view in a positive light the fact that the clear substantive conclusion to which the House of Lords came (that no right to assisted suicide is implicit in the ECHR — a view shared by the European Court of Human Rights: see (2002) 35 EHRR 1) will provide guidance in the future to those in a similar position to the claimant. Yet, on the other hand, his Lordship appears to suggest that, if the case had been litigated by seeking a declaration to that effect (rather than challenging the defendant's refusal to guarantee immunity), then the court may well have refused to rule upon hypothetical facts. If the guidance supplied by the judgments is, as Lord Hobhouse suggests, of some value, it is difficult to see why it should not be available by permitting claimants to seek a declaration in such circumstances.

His caution notwithstanding, Lord Hobhouse did not rule out the possibility of judicial review of hypothetical matters, since he left open this possibility in 'exceptional circumstances'. What, then, are the circumstances in which judicial review will — or should — lie in respect of such questions? In advocating a generous approach in this area, Laws (1994) 57 *MLR* 213 at 218 identifies a number of criteria which may be relevant. As well as arguing that the courts should deploy the distinction between hypothetical and academic questions to help trace the perimeter of judicial review, he suggests that it must be possible to 'formulate the issue as to *vires* independently of the facts of any putative claim' and to find an 'effective [defendant]'. Laws's approach derives some support from the following guidance issued by the House of Lords in *R* v. *Secretary of State for the Home Department, ex parte Salem* [1999] AC 450 at 456–457, *per* Lord Slynn:

. . . [I]n a cause where there is an issue involving a public authority as to a question of public law, your Lordships have a discretion to hear the appeal, even if by the time the appeal reaches the House there is no longer a lis to be decided which will directly affect the rights and obligations of the parties inter se . . .

The discretion to hear disputes, even in the area of public law, must, however, be exercised with caution and appeals which are academic between the parties should not be heard unless there is a good reason in the public interest for doing so, as for example (but only by way of example) when a discrete point of statutory construction arises which does not involve detailed consideration of facts and where a large number of similar cases exist or are anticipated so that the issue will most likely need to be resolved in the near future.

Similar principles were applied by Lord Steyn in *R (Rusbridger)* v. *Attorney-General* [2003] UKHL 38 [2004] 1 AC 357 at [22]–[24].

QUESTIONS

- When, in your view, should courts rule on hypothetical issues? Are the courts unduly cautious in this area?
- Would you characterize their present approach in 'red' or 'green light' terms (see above at 1.2)?

15.6 Exclusion of Judicial Review

15.6.1 Introduction

Preclusive clauses, otherwise known as privative, exclusion, or ouster clauses, are statutory provisions which *prima facie* prohibit judicial review of the exercise of the discretionary powers to which they relate. As we shall see, such clauses take a variety of forms; all, however, raise the same fundamental tension between the rule of law (which strongly favours access to courts — and therefore judicial review) and the constitutional duty of the courts, under the doctrine of legislative supremacy, to give effect to the sovereign will of Parliament. Although never explicitly repudiating their loyalty to Parliament in this context, the courts pursue a clear policy of seeking to preserve judicial review in the face of preclusive provisions. This judicial attitude was recently exhibited by the Court of Appeal in *R (Sivasubramaniam)* v. *Wandsworth County Court* [2002] EWCA Civ 1738 [2003] 1 WLR 475, which had no difficulty in rejecting a submission that s 54(4) of the Access to Justice Act 1999, which precludes *appeal* against certain decisions to grant or refuse permission to appeal, implicitly prevented *judicial review* of such decisions. Lord Phillips MR said (at [43]–[44]):

Mr Sales [for the defendant] . . . [urged] us that the general presumption against ouster of judicial review should not be applied on the facts of this case. He submitted that it was clearly implicit in the provision of section 54(4) of the 1999 Act that the decision of an appeal court refusing leave to appeal was not susceptible to challenge by judicial review. The express provision that there should be no appeal from such a decision would be rendered nugatory if it could be challenged by judicial review. The object of conserving judicial resources would be frustrated if refusal of permission to appeal could be met with an application for judicial review to the High Court, which could be renewed before the Court of Appeal if unsuccessful. Section 54(4) should be read so as to treat an application for permission to claim judicial review as an appeal. Both were prohibited.

We have not been persuaded by these submissions. Nearly 50 years ago Denning LJ stated in *R v Medical Appeal Tribunal, ex parte Gilmore* [1957] 1 QB 574 at 585 that "the remedy by certiorari is never to be taken away by any statute except by the most clear and explicit words". All the authorities to which we have been referred indicate that this remains true today. The weight of authority makes it impossible to accept that the jurisdiction to subject a decision to judicial review can be removed by statutory *implication*.

This conclusion is perhaps unsurprising: preserving important constitutional rights (like access to the courts) by a mode of statutory interpretation which rejects the possibility of their curtailment by implication is a well-established methodology (see above at 1.4.3). However, we will see that, when statutory provisions appear to exclude judicial review in clear and explicit terms, this interpretative approach is pushed to — or, in the view of some commentators, beyond — its limit.

15.6.2 Finality Clauses

The courts have had little difficulty in holding that statutory provisions which provide that a decision is 'final and conclusive' do not preclude challenges to the legality of decisions by means of judicial review, as the following case shows.

....

R v. Medical Appeal Tribunal, ex parte Gilmore [1957] 1 QB 574
Court of Appeal

The claimant, who injured his left eye at work, claimed disablement benefit under the National Insurance (Industrial Injuries) Act 1946. At the time of his accident he was, as a result of an earlier accident, already injured in his left eye and almost blind in his right eye. The further injury so aggravated the condition of his left eye that he was almost totally blind. Regulations (SI 1948/1372) made under the Act stated (*inter alia*) that, in cases of injury to one of two similar organs, assessments of the extent of disablement should treat "any disability in respect of the organ . . . by reason of . . . an injury or disease received . . . before the relevant accident" (reg 2(5)) as having been incurred as a result of the loss of faculty caused by the relevant accident. A medical appeal tribunal assessed the aggravation at 20 per cent. The tribunal had before it a specialist's report setting out the facts and this was referred to in its award. The claimant applied for permission to seek judicial review in order to have the award quashed on the ground that there was a manifest error of law on the face of the record in so far as the tribunal had not taken into account the disability in the right eye. Permission was denied by the Divisional Court. There was an appeal and it was conceded that the tribunal's decision was erroneous in law. However, s 36(3) of the Act provided that any decision of a medical appeal tribunal "shall be final".

Denning LJ

. . . [I turn to] the effect of section 36 (3) . . . Do those words preclude the Court of Queen's Bench from issuing a certiorari to bring up the decision?

This is a question which we did not discuss in *Rex. v. Northumberland Compensation Appeal Tribunal, Ex parte Shaw* [[1952] 1 KB 338], because it did not there arise. It does arise here, and on looking again into the old books I find it very well settled that the remedy by certiorari is never to be taken away by any statute except by the most clear and explicit words. The word 'final' is not enough. That only means "without appeal." It does not mean "without recourse to certiorari." It makes the decision final on the facts, but not final on the law. Notwithstanding that the decision is by a statute made "final", *certiorari* can still issue for excess of jurisdiction or for error of law on the face of the record . . .

[Having discussed several authorities, he continued:] I venture therefore to use in this case the words I used in the recent case of *Taylor (formerly Kraupl) v. National Assistance Board* [[1957] P 101, [1957] 1 All ER 183] (about declarations), with suitable variations for *certiorari*: "The remedy is not excluded by the fact that the determination of the board is by statute made 'final'. Parliament only gives the impress of finality to the decisions of the tribunal on the condition that they are reached in accordance with the law."

In my opinion, therefore, notwithstanding the fact that the statute says that the decision of the medical appeal tribunal is to be final, it is open to this court to issue a certiorari to quash it for error of law on the face of the record. . . .

Parker and Romer LJJ agreed that the finality clause did not preclude judicial review for error of law.

A finality clause will not, therefore, bar judicial review of a decision, although it will prevent the decision from being challenged by appeal (on both points of fact and law: *Re Racal Communications Ltd* [1981] AC 374 at 382, *per* Lord Diplock, disagreeing with Lord Denning MR's suggestion in *Pearlman* v. *Keepers and Governors of Harrow School* [1979] QB 56 at 71 that finality clauses bar appeal only on factual issues). The underlying principle is clear; as Lord Denning MR put it in *Tehrani* v. *Rostron* [1972] 1 QB 182 at 187:

. . . [W]hen Parliament says that a decision of an inferior tribunal is to be "final", it does so on the assumption that the tribunal will observe the law. Parliament only gives the impress of "finality" to the decision on the condition that it is reached in accordance with law: and the Queen's courts will see to it that this condition is fulfilled. Accordingly if a tribunal goes wrong in law . . ., the High Court will interfere by certiorari to quash the decision.

Provided, therefore, that the supervisory jurisdiction of the High Court remains intact, in order that the legal limits of the tribunal or decision-maker's powers may be enforced, the courts are untroubled by the fact that other avenues, by which the decision might otherwise be challenged, are closed off by the finality clause.

15.6.3 'No *Certiorari*' and 'as if Enacted' Clauses

Just as the courts have experienced little difficulty in continuing to assert supervisory jurisdiction in the face of finality clauses, so they have managed to place similarly benign constructions upon a number of other types of ouster clause. For instance, Denning LJ explained in *R* v. *Medical Appeal Tribunal, ex parte Gilmore* [1957] 1 QB 574 at 586 that 'no *certiorari*' — in today's language, 'no quashing order' — clauses cannot exclude judicial review for jurisdictional error:

In contrast to the word "final" I would like to say a word about the old statutes which used in express words to take away the remedy by certiorari by saying that the decision of the tribunal "shall not be removed by certiorari". Those statutes were passed chiefly between 1680 and 1848, in the days when the courts used certiorari too freely and quashed decisions for technical defects of form. In stopping this abuse the statutes proved very beneficial, but the court never allowed those statutes to be used as a cover for wrongdoing by tribunals. If tribunals were to be at liberty to exceed their jurisdiction without any check by the courts, the rule of law would be at an end. Despite express words taking away certiorari, therefore, it was held that certiorari would still lie if some of the members of the tribunal were disqualified from acting: see *Reg. v. Cheltenham Commissioners* [(1841) 1 QB 467], where Lord Denman CJ said [at 474]: "The statute cannot affect our right and duty to [see] justice executed." So, also, if the tribunal exceeded its jurisdiction: see *Ex parte Bradlaugh* [(1878) 3 QBD 508]; or if its decision was obtained by fraud: see *Reg. v. Gillyard* [(1848) 12 QB 527], the courts would still grant certiorari.

A 'no *certiorari*' clause does not, therefore, prevent the courts from issuing (what is now referred to as) a quashing order if a jurisdictional defect can be established. Although such clauses (as opposed to finality clauses) did prevent relief from being issued in the case of errors of law which appeared on the face of the record but which did not go to jurisdiction — hence the importance in *Pearlman* v. *Keepers and Governors of Harrow School* [1979] QB 56 (see above at 2.2.4) of the claimant establishing the jurisdictional nature of the error — this problem is now unlikely to arise, given the general principle established in *R* v. *Lord President of the Privy Council, ex parte Page* [1993] AC 682 that errors of law are jurisdictional.

It is worth noting at this stage a further type of preclusive clause which, although no longer used, further reveals the courts' unwillingness to accept legislative restrictions upon their supervisory jurisdiction. An example is provided by the case of *Minister of Health* v. *The King (on the prosecution of Yaffé)* [1931] AC 494, in which the House of Lords was called upon to determine the effect of s 40(5) of the Housing Act 1925, which provided that the 'order of the Minister [to approve an improvement scheme] shall have effect as if enacted in this Act'. The apparent objective of a provision such as this is to clothe an administrative decision in the protective cloak of parliamentary sovereignty, thereby placing it beyond judicial review. That objective was not, however, secured, as Viscount Dunedin explained (at 503):

The confirmation makes the scheme speak as if it was contained in an Act of Parliament, but the Act of Parliament in which it is contained is the Act which provides for the framing of the scheme . . . If therefore the scheme, as made, conflicts with the Act, it will have to give way to the Act. The mere confirmation will not save it . . . [I]f one can find that the scheme is inconsistent with the provisions of the Act which authorizes the scheme, the scheme will be bad, and that only can be gone into by way of proceedings in *certiorari*.

15.6.4 'Shall not be Questioned' Clauses

In the next case the House of Lords was confronted with an ouster provision which appeared to exclude judicial review in very clear terms, and seemed to leave no scope for a contrary interpretation.

....

Anisminic Ltd. v. *Foreign Compensation Commission* [1969] 2 AC 147
House of Lords

For the facts and discussion of the nature of the error made by the Commission, see above at 2.2.3. These extracts are concerned with the ouster clause in the Foreign Compensation Act 1950, s 4(4), which provided that, 'The determination by the commission of any application made to them under this Act shall not be called in question in any court of law.'

Lord Reid

. . . The next argument was that, by reason of the provisions of section 4 (4) of the 1950 Act, the courts are precluded from considering whether the respondent's determination was a nullity, and therefore it must be treated as valid whether or not inquiry would disclose that it was a nullity . . .

The respondent maintains that these are plain words only capable of having one meaning. Here is a determination which is apparently valid: there is nothing on the face of the document to cast any doubt on its validity. If it is a nullity, that could only be established by raising some kind of proceedings in court. But that would be calling the determination in question, and that is expressly prohibited by the statute. The appellants maintain that that is not the meaning of the words of this provision. They say that "determination" means a real determination and does not include an apparent or purported determination which in the eyes of the law has no existence because it is a nullity. Or, putting it in another way, if you seek to show that a determination is a nullity you are not questioning the purported determination — you are maintaining that it does not exist as a determination. It is one thing to question a determination which does exist: it is quite another thing to say that there is nothing to be questioned.

Let me illustrate the matter by supposing a simple case. A statute provides that a certain order may be made by a person who holds a specified qualification or appointment, and it contains a provision, similar to section 4 (4), that such an order made by such a person shall not be called in question in any court of law. A person aggrieved by an order alleges that it is a forgery or that the person who made the order did not hold that qualification or appointment. Does such a provision require the court to treat that order as a valid order? It is a well established principle that a provision ousting the ordinary jurisdiction of the court must be construed strictly — meaning, I think, that, if such a provision is reasonably capable of having two meanings, that meaning shall be taken which preserves the ordinary jurisdiction of the court.

Statutory provisions which seek to limit the ordinary jurisdiction of the court have a long history. No case has been cited in which any other form of words limiting the jurisdiction of the court has been held to protect a nullity. If the draftsman or Parliament had intended to introduce a new kind of ouster clause so as to prevent any inquiry even as to whether the document relied on was a forgery, I would have expected to find something much more specific than the bald statement that a determination shall not be called in question in any court of law. Undoubtedly such a provision protects every determination which is not a nullity. But I do not think that it is necessary or even reasonable to construe the word "determination" as including everything which purports to be a determination but which is in fact no determination at all. And there are no degrees of nullity. There are a number of reasons why the law will hold a purported decision to be a nullity. I do not see how it could be said that such a provision protects some kinds of nullity but not others: if that were intended it would be easy to say so.

The case which gives most difficulty is *Smith v. East Elloe Rural District Council* [1956] A.C. 736 where the form of ouster clause was similar to that in the present case. But I cannot regard it as a very satisfactory case. The plaintiff was aggrieved by a compulsory purchase order. After two unsuccessful actions she tried again after six years. As this case never reached the stage of a statement of claim we do not know whether her case was that the clerk of the council had fraudulently misled the council and the Ministry, or whether it was that the council and the Ministry were parties to the fraud. The result would be quite different, in my view, for it is only if the authority which made the order had itself acted in mala fide that the order would be a nullity. I think that the case which it was intended to present must have been that the fraud was only the fraud of the clerk because almost the whole of the argument was on the question whether a time limit in the Act applied where fraud was alleged; there was no citation of the authorities on the question whether a clause ousting the jurisdiction of the court applied when nullity was in question, and there was little about this matter in the speeches. I do not therefore regard this case as a binding authority on this question . . . I have come without hesitation to the conclusion that in this case we are not prevented from inquiring whether the order of the commission was a nullity. . . .

Lord Pearce

. . . It has been argued that your Lordships should construe "determination" as meaning anything which is on its face a determination of the commission including even a purported determination which has no jurisdiction. It would seem that on such an argument the court must accept and could not even inquire whether a purported determination was a forged or inaccurate order which did not represent that which the commission had really decided. Moreover, it would mean that however far the commission ranged outside its jurisdiction or that which it was required to do, or however far it departed from natural justice its determination could not be questioned. A more reasonable and logical construction is that by "determination" Parliament meant a real determination, not a purported determination. On the assumption, however, that either meaning is a possible construction and that therefore the word "determination" is ambiguous, the latter meaning would accord with a long-established line of cases which adopted that construction . . .

In my opinion, the subsequent case of *Smith v. East Elloe Rural District Council* [1956] A.C. 736 does not compel your Lordships to decide otherwise. If it seemed to do so, I would think it necessary to reconsider the case in the light of the powerful dissenting opinions of my noble and learned friends, Lord Reid and Lord Somervell. It might possibly be said that it related to an administrative or executive decision, not a judicial decision, and somewhat different considerations might have applied; certainly none of the authorities relating to absence or excess of jurisdiction were cited to the House. I agree with Browne J [at first instance in this case: [1969] 2 AC 223] that it is not a compelling authority in the present case. . . .

Lord Wilberforce

. . . The question, what is the tribunal's proper area, is one which it has always been permissible to ask and to answer, and it must follow that examination of its extent is not precluded by a clause conferring conclusiveness, finality, or unquestionability upon its decisions. These clauses in their nature can only relate to decisions given within the field of operation entrusted to the tribunal. They may, according to the width and emphasis of their formulation, help to ascertain the extent of that field, to narrow it or to enlarge it, but unless one is to deny the statutory origin of the tribunal and of its powers, they cannot preclude examination of that extent.

It is sometimes said, the argument was presented in these terms, that the preclusive clause does not operate on decisions outside the permitted field because they are a nullity. There are dangers in the use of this word if it draws with it the difficult distinction between what is void and what is voidable, and I certainly do not wish to be taken to recognise that this distinction exists or to analyse it if it does. But it may be convenient so long as it is used to describe a decision made outside the permitted field, in other words, as a word of description rather than as in itself a touchstone.

The courts, when they decide that a "decision" is a "nullity," are not disregarding the preclusive clause. For, just as it is their duty to attribute autonomy of decision of action to the tribunal within the designated area, so, as the counterpart of this autonomy, they must ensure that the limits of that area which have been laid down are observed (see the formulation of Lord Sumner in *Rex v. Nat Bell Liquors Ltd* [1922] 2 A.C. 128, 156). In each task they are carrying out the intention of the legislature, and it would be misdescription to state it in terms of a struggle between the courts and the executive. What would be the purpose of defining by statute the limit of a tribunal's powers if, by means of a clause inserted in the instrument of definition, those limits could safely be passed?

. . . I find myself obliged to state that I cannot regard *Smith v. East Elloe Rural District Council* [1956] A.C. 736 as a reliable solvent of this appeal, or of any case where similar questions arise. The preclusive clause was indeed very similar to the present but, however inevitable the particular decision may have been, it was given on too narrow a basis to assist us here. I agree with my noble and learned friends, Lord Reid and Lord Pearce, on this matter . . .

Lords Morris and Pearson delivered speeches in which they agreed that the ouster clause would not protect a decision if a jurisdictional error could be established.

The implications of this decision are considerable. Its effect is to render 'shall not be questioned' clauses ineffective to prevent judicial review in respect of jurisdictional errors. If the decision-maker falls into such error, then its conclusion is a nullity rather than a valid determination, with the result that the ouster clause — which only prevents the questioning of such determinations — does not bite. By intervening, the court is merely ascertaining that no valid determination exists, rather than entering into the prohibited enterprise of questioning a determination which does exist. The dividing line between a nullity and a valid determination is, of course, traced by reference to the concept of jurisdictional error: whenever such an error is committed, the decision-maker steps outside of its powers and any decision it purports to reach is actually a nullity.

We saw above (at 2.2.4) that, although the *Anisminic* case laid the foundation for the emergence of a general principle that errors of law are jurisdictional, this was not confirmed until the House of Lords' decision some years later in *R* v. *Lord President of the Privy Council, ex parte Page* [1993] AC 682. Thus, when *Anisminic* was decided, errors of law on the face of the record were regarded as reviewable but non-jurisdictional forms of error of law. As a result, the interpretation accorded to the ouster clause in *Anisminic* did not entirely deprive it of effect, since it still operated to preclude review for non-jurisdictional errors. However, now that errors of law are almost inevitably jurisdictional, 'shall not be questioned' clauses will nearly always be ineffective: jurisdictional errors are reviewable notwithstanding the ouster provision, while non-jurisdictional errors are not reviewable in any event (unless the possibility of review for error of law on the face of the record survives). With or without the preclusive clause, the position as to reviewability is likely to be the same. The difficulty, therefore, is that even if *Anisminic* could originally be defended as an exercise in creative and bold interpretation, this view is difficult to sustain now that the 'interpretation' placed upon 'shall not be questioned' clauses appears to render them nugatory. This moves Wade and Forsyth, *Administrative Law* (Oxford 2004) at 719, to the conclusion that '[t]he policy of the courts thus becomes one of total disobedience to Parliament' — a view shared by, *inter alios*, Schwartz (1986) 38 *Administrative Law Review* 33 at 47–50.

QUESTIONS

- Was the House of Lords' decision in *Anisminic* an exercise in interpretation, or something more than that?
- Does it matter which of these it was?

This view of Wade and Forsyth accords, to some extent, with the extra-curial suggestion of Woolf [1995] *PL* 57 that judicial review is a constitutional fundamental which Parliament is incapable of abolishing (although he did not go as far as to argue that review may not be curtailed in specific contexts). More broadly, it reflects the opinion expressed *obiter* by Laws LJ in *International Transport Roth GmbH* v. *Secretary of State for the Home Department* [2002] EWCA Civ 158 [2003] QB 728 at [71] that 'the British system may be said to stand at an intermediate stage between parliamentary supremacy and constitutional supremacy'. On this view, the orthodox principle of automatic judicial deference to legislative enactment is gradually being qualified by means of an organic process of constitutional evolution such that higher-order principles (perhaps including that of access to justice) will eventually delimit Parliament's legislative competence (on which see further Elliott (2002) 22 *LS* 340).

These impressions are bolstered by the reaction to the recent (aborted) attempt to exclude judicial review of the decisions of the new single-tier Asylum and Immigration Tribunal (established under the Asylum and Immigration (Treatment of Claimants etc) Act 2004). A clause was inserted into what was then the Asylum and Immigration Bill which precluded 'proceedings for questioning . . . any determination' — including 'a decision about jurisdiction' — of the Tribunal on any ground, including 'lack of jurisdiction' and 'error of law' (see further Le Sueur [2004] *PL* 225). This apparently *Anisminic*-proof ouster clause was widely condemned (see, *eg*, the Constitutional Affairs Committee's *Second Report* of the 2003–2004 session (HC 211-I) at [60]–[70]). Jowell (*The Guardian*, 2 March 2004) went as far as to question the constitutionality of the proposed ouster clause, while Woolf [2004] *CLJ* 317 at 329 suggested that the clause, if enacted, 'would be so inconsistent with the spirit of mutual respect between the different arms of government that it could be the catalyst for a campaign for a written constitution'. Following sustained and intense criticism, the clause was withdrawn, and limited review of the Tribunal's decisions permitted (see below at 15.6.8).

QUESTIONS

- Should judges ignore ouster provisions?
- Is the availability of judicial review more important that judicial fidelity to Acts of Parliament?

15.6.5 Further Issues

Before leaving the subject of preclusive clauses, three further issues should be noted. First, some statutory reform has been effected in this area.

Tribunals and Inquiries Act 1992

12—(1) As respects England and Wales —
  (a) any provision in an Act passed before 1st August 1958 that any order or determination shall not be called into question in any court, or
  (b) any provision in such an Act which by similar words excludes any of the powers of the High Court,
shall not have effect so as to prevent the removal of the proceedings into the High Court by order of certiorari or to prejudice the powers of the High Court to make orders of mandamus . . .
  (3) Nothing in this section shall apply —
  (a) to any order or determination of a court of law, or
  (b) where an Act makes special provision for application to the High Court or the Court of Session within a time limited by the Act.

This provision, the origin of which lies in the Franks Committee's *Report on Administrative Tribunals and Inquiries* (Cmnd 218 at [117]), was formerly to be found in s 14 of the Tribunals and Inquiries Act 1971 and, before that, in s 11 of the Tribunals and Inquiries Act 1958: this explains the reference, in s 12(1) above, to 1 August 1958. (Section 11(3) of the 1958 Act additionally had excluded any order or determination of the Foreign Compensation Commission from the liberalizing effect of subsection (1).) The effect of s 12(1) is to preserve judicial review in the face of ouster clauses passed before the relevant date, at least when quashing and mandatory orders are sought. The omission of any reference to other remedies is curious, although in *O'Reilly* v. *Mackman* [1983] 2 AC at 278 Lord Diplock suggested that this may evidence a legislative desire to safeguard proceedings initiated via (what is now) the claim for judicial review in preference to ordinary proceedings by which injunctions and declarations might be sought. In terms of the scope of s 12(1), Dillon LJ said in *R* v. *Registrar of Companies, ex parte Central Bank of India* [1986] QB 1114 at 1182 that the matter must be approached in the context of the Act which is 'largely if not entirely concerned with the statutory tribunals listed in Schedule 1 and with decisions of Ministers reached after the holding of public inquiries'; s 12(1) does not, therefore, facilitate review of all discretionary powers to which ouster clauses are attached. The significance of the limitation upon s 12(1) imposed by subsection (3)(b) will become apparent when we consider exclusive statutory remedies at 15.6.6 below.

Secondly, we saw above (at 10.5.2) that Article 6(1) ECHR applies to the administrative process whenever civil rights and obligations fall for determination. Such determinations must be made by tribunals which are impartial and independent. Although many administrative decision-makers are not independent of the executive, this apparent infraction of Article 6(1) may be cured if provision exists for recourse to a court of 'full jurisdiction' — a characteristic which, for most purposes, is possessed by courts with powers of judicial review. An ouster clause may, however, render judicial review impossible or inadequate for Article 6(1) purposes. For instance, in *Tinnelly and Sons Ltd* v. *United Kingdom* (1999) 27 EHRR 249, a Minister issued a certificate which, according to the relevant legislation, constituted 'conclusive evidence' that it was for national security reasons that the applicants had been unsuccessful in securing a government contract. The applicants, however, contended that they had really been turned down on religious grounds. Having been unsuccessful in judicial review proceedings, they applied to the ECtHR which held (at [74]) that judicial review had inadequately safeguarded the applicants' Article 6(1) right, because the judge's 'hands were tied by the conclusive nature of the certificate and the Secretary of State's invocation of national security considerations'.

Thirdly, the existence of what are known as 'default powers' have, on occasion, been held impliedly to exclude judicial review. For example, in *Pasmore* v. *Oswaldtwistle Urban District Council* [1898] AC 387 it was held that, where legislation furnished the Local Government Board with the power to compel the performance by a local authority of its statutory duty to provide sewers, application to the Board was the only means by which the claimant could seek to have the performance of the duty enforced; the court would not issue a mandatory order. This preparedness to conclude that judicial enforcement of statutory duties can be impliedly excluded sits uncomfortably with the courts' approach to express ouster clauses, but may be explained by the Earl of Halsbury's comment (at 395) that 'it would be extremely inconvenient that each suitor in turn should be permitted to apply for a specific remedy against the body charged with the care of the health of the inhabitants of the district in respect of drainage'. In any event, it is clear that the existence default powers will not always be taken impliedly to displace judicial enforcement (see, *eg, Attorney-General ex rel McWhirter* v. *Independent Broadcasting Authority* [1973] QB 629 at 649, *per* Lord Denning MR).

15.6.6 Statutory Review

A number of statutes preclude judicial review of certain decisions, but go on to provide instead for a statutory remedy which is virtually identical to judicial review, except that the time limit is usually six weeks and there is presently no permission stage (although, in its consultation paper on *Statutory Appeals and Statutory Reviews: Proposals for Rationalising Procedures* (London 2004), the Department for Constitutional Affairs proposes that a permission stage should be introduced in this context). By virtue of s 12(3)(b) of the Tribunals and Inquiries Act 1992, s 12(1) of that Act (considered above at 15.6.5) is inapplicable to clauses which rule out standard judicial review in favour of statutory review.

Statutory review coupled with a preclusive clause is used in situations where certainty and expedition are of particular importance. For instance, legislation provides that certain public authorities may compulsorily acquire land; in such circumstances, it is imperative that the authority can be certain, before it commits public funds to the development of the land in question, about the validity of its acquisition. Adopting a model used in many other pieces of legislation, the following provision is made in respect of challenges to compulsory purchase orders.

Acquisition of Land Act 1981

23—(1) If any person aggrieved by a compulsory purchase order desires to question the validity thereof, or of any provision contained therein, on the ground that the authorisation of a compulsory purchase thereby granted is not empowered to be granted under this Act or any such enactment as is mentioned in section 1(1) of this Act, he may make an application to the High Court.

(2) If any person aggrieved by —

(a) a compulsory purchase order . . .

desires to question the validity thereof on the ground that any relevant requirement has not been complied with in relation to the order . . . he may make an application to the High Court.

(3) In subsection (2) above "relevant requirement" means —

(a) any requirement of this Act, or of any regulation under section 7(2) above, or

(b) any requirement of the Tribunals and Inquiries Act 1992 or of any rules made, or having effect as if made, under that Act.

(4) An application to the High Court under this section shall be made within six weeks —

(a) in the case of a compulsory purchase order to which the Statutory Orders (Special Procedure) Act 1945 applies (and which is not excluded by section 27 below), from the date on which the order becomes operative under that Act,

(b) in the case of a compulsory purchase order to which the said Act of 1945 does not apply, from the date on which notice of the confirmation or making of the order is first published in accordance with this Act . . .

24—(1) On an application under section 23 above the court may by interim order suspend the operation of the compulsory purchase order or any provision contained therein . . . either generally or in so far as it affects any property of the applicant, until the final determination of the proceedings.

(2) If on the application the court is satisfied that —

(a) the authorisation granted by the compulsory purchase order is not empowered to be granted under this Act or any such enactment as is mentioned in section 1(1) of this Act, or

(b) the interests of the applicant have been substantially prejudiced by any relevant requirement (as defined in section 23(3) above) not having been complied with,

the court may quash the compulsory purchase order or any provision contained therein . . . either generally or in so far as it affects any property of the applicant.

25 Subject to the preceding provisions of this Part of this Act, a compulsory purchase order . . . shall not, either before or after it has been confirmed, made or given, be questioned in any legal proceedings whatsoever.

These provisions suggest two principal conclusions: first, the order may be challenged within six weeks if it was not empowered to be granted under the legislation or if any relevant statutory requirement was not complied with; but, secondly, no other method or ground of challenge is possible.

In fact, the courts have on occasions struggled to determine the effect of schemes such as that which is contained in the 1981 Act. In the following case, their Lordships experienced difficulty with two fundamental points — *viz* the types of error which could be set aside under their statutory jurisdiction, and the question whether judicial intervention was absolutely barred upon the expiry of the six-week period. The following extract is concerned with the Acquisition of Land (Authorisation Procedure) Act 1946, a predecessor to the 1981 Act. Paragraph 15 of sch 1 to the 1946 Act is substantially similar to ss 23 and 24 of the 1981 Act, while para 16 of the former corresponds to s 25 of the latter.

Smith v. *East Elloe Rural District Council* [1956] AC 736
House of Lords

On 26 August 1948 the defendant Council made a compulsory purchase order (confirmed later that year by the Minister of Health) in relation to some land belonging to the applicant. The Council caused a house on this land to be demolished and new houses to be built by a firm of builders. The claimant issued a writ on 6 July 1954, seeking damages for trespass against the Council, a declaration that the order was made wrongfully and in bad faith, and a similar declaration in respect of its confirmation. In addition the claimant sought a declaration that Mr Pywell, the clerk to the Council, 'knowingly acted wrongfully and in bad faith in procuring the order and confirmation of the same', and also claimed damages. The writ and later proceedings were set aside because of the terms of para 16 of sch 1 to the Acquisition of Land (Authorisation Procedure) Act 1946. This decision was upheld by Havers J and the Court of Appeal. The claimant appealed to the House of Lords.

Viscount Simonds

. . . It was [argued] that, as the compulsory purchase order was challenged on the ground that it had been made and confirmed "wrongfully" and "in bad faith," paragraph 16 had no application. It was said that that paragraph, however general its language, must be construed so as not to oust the jurisdiction of the court where the good faith of the local authority or the Ministry was impugned and put in issue . . .

My Lords, I think that anyone bred in the tradition of the law is likely to regard with little sympathy legislative provisions for ousting the jurisdiction of the court, whether in order that the subject may be deprived altogether of remedy or in order that his grievance may be remitted to some other tribunal. But it is our plain duty to give the words of an Act their proper meaning and, for my part, I find it quite impossible to qualify the words of the paragraph in the manner suggested . . . What is abundantly clear is that words are used which are wide enough to cover any kind of challenge which any aggrieved person may think fit to make. I cannot think of any wider words . . .

. . . I am . . . reluctant to express a final opinion upon a matter much agitated at your Lordships' bar, whether the words "is not empowered" were apt to include a challenge not only on the ground of vires but also on the ground of bad faith or any other ground which would justify the court in setting aside a purported exercise of a statutory power. The inclination of my opinion is that they are, but I would prefer to keep the question open until it arises in a case where the answer will be decisive, as it is not here.

. . . [T]he appellant by her writ claims against the personal defendant a declaration that he knowingly acted wrongfully and in bad faith in procuring the order and its confirmation, and damages, and that is a claim which the court clearly has jurisdiction to entertain. I am far from saying that the claim has any merit. Of that I know nothing. But because the court can entertain it, I think that the Court of Appeal, to whose attention this particular aspect of the case appears not to have been called, were wrong in striking out the whole writ and I propose that their order should be varied by striking out the defendants other than Mr. Pywell . . . Against Mr. Pywell the action may proceed but upon the footing that the validity of the order cannot be questioned . . .

Lord Morton

. . . Mr. Roy Wilson, for the appellant, puts forward propositions which I summarize as follows: (1) Paragraph 15 gives no opportunity to a person aggrieved to question the validity of a compulsory purchase order on the ground that it was made or confirmed in bad faith. (2) Although, prima facie, paragraph 16 excludes the jurisdiction of the court in all cases, subject only to the provision of paragraph 15, it is inconceivable that the legislature can have intended wholly to exclude all courts from hearing and determining an allegation that such an order was made in bad faith. (3) Therefore, paragraph 16 should be read as applying only to an order or a certificate made in good faith . . .

My Lords, I accept Mr. Wilson's first proposition. I cannot construe paragraph 15 as covering a case in which all the requirements expressly laid down by statute have been observed, but the person aggrieved has discovered that in carrying out the steps laid down by statute the authority has been actuated by improper motives . . .

My Lords, having accepted Mr. Wilson's first proposition . . . I reject his second and third propositions, on the short and simple ground that the words of paragraph 16 are clear, and deprive all courts of any jurisdiction to try the issues raised by [certain] paragraphs . . . of the writ, whereby the appellant undoubtedly seeks to question the validity of the order of August 26, 1948 . . .

I would allow the writ in this action to stand only in so far as it claims relief against the respondent Pywell . . . The writ should, in my view, be set aside for want of jurisdiction in so far as it claims relief against the other respondents. The appeal should, therefore, be allowed to the extent just mentioned.

Lord Reid

. . . [I]n order to determine how far the 1946 Act has limited the jurisdiction of the courts I must see what were the grounds on which the court could give relief under the ordinary law . . . It seems to me that there were four grounds on which the courts could give relief. First, informality of procedure; where, for example, some essential step in procedure had been omitted. Secondly, ultra vires in the sense that what was authorized by the order went beyond what was authorized by the Act under which it was made. Thirdly, misuse of power in bona fide. And, fourthly, misuse of power in mala fide. In the last two classes the order is intra vires in the sense that what it authorizes to be done is within the scope of the Act under which it is made, and every essential step in procedure may have been taken: what is challenged is something which lies behind the making of the order. I separate these two classes for this reason. There have been few cases where actual bad faith has even been alleged, but in the numerous cases where misuse of power has been alleged judges have been careful to point out that no question of bad faith was involved and that bad faith stands in a class by itself.

Misuse of power covers a wide variety of cases, and I am relieved from considering at length what amounts to misuse of power in bona fide because I agree with the analysis made by Lord Greene MR in *Associated Provincial Picture Houses Ltd. v. Wednesbury Corporation* [1948] 1 K.B. 223 . . .

[Having quoted passages from this case (on which see above at 9.2.1), he continued:] I can draw no other conclusion from the form in which paragraph 15 is now enacted than that Parliament intended to exclude from the scope of this paragraph the whole class of cases referred to in the passages which I quoted. No doubt in one sense it might be said that in none of these cases is authority "empowered to be granted," but that would be a strained and unnatural reading of these words only to be accepted if there were in the Act some clear indication requiring it. But, to my mind, all the indications are the other way, and this part of the paragraph only refers to cases of ultra vires in the narrow sense in which I have used it.

If other cases of misuse of power in bona fide are excluded, can a distinction be made where mala fides is in question? As I shall explain when I come to paragraph 16, I am of opinion that cases involving mala fides are in a special position in that mere general words will not deprive the court of jurisdiction to deal with them, and, if that is so, then no question would arise under paragraph 15. But, if I am wrong about cases of mala fides being in this special position, I do not see how there can be a distinction under paragraph 15 between cases of bona fide and mala fide misuse of power. I can see nothing to indicate any intention to that effect, and if Parliament intended to treat bad faith as a special case it would be very strange to introduce the exception here. The time limit under paragraph 15 is six weeks, which is appropriate for grounds which appear from the terms of the order but not appropriate for grounds based on facts lying behind the order which may not be discoverable for some time after it is confirmed . . .

In my view, the question whether authority is empowered to be granted is intended to be capable of immediate answer: if it can depend on facts lying behind the order, then neither the Minister nor the owner could know for certain at the time of confirmation whether any order is empowered to be granted or not, because facts showing misuse of power might subsequently emerge. Accordingly, in my opinion, the appellant could not have brought her case within paragraph 15, even if she had raised it immediately after the order was confirmed.

I turn to paragraph 16 . . . In my judgment, paragraph 16 is clearly intended to exclude, and does exclude entirely, all cases of misuse of power in bona fide. But does it also exclude the small minority of cases where deliberate dishonesty, corruption or malice is involved? . . .

I think that there is still room for reason to point out that the general words in this case must be limited so as to accord with the principle, of which Parliament cannot have been ignorant, that a wrongdoer cannot rely on general words to avoid the consequences of his own dishonesty . . .

Lord Radcliffe

My Lords, I think that this appeal must fail except so far as the action against the defendant Pywell is concerned . . .

I should myself read the words of paragraph 15 (1), "on the ground that the authorization of a compulsory purchase thereby granted is not empowered to be granted under this Act," as covering any case in which the complainant sought to say that the order in question did not carry the statutory authority which it purported to. In other words, I should regard a challenge to the order on the ground that it had not been made in good faith as within the purview of paragraph 15 . . . I do not see any need to pick and choose among the different reasons which may support the plea that the authorization ostensibly granted does not carry the powers of the Act. But, even if I did not think that an order could be questioned under paragraph 15 on the ground that it had been exercised in bad faith, and I thought, therefore, that the statutory code did not allow for an order being questioned on this ground at all, I should still think that paragraph 16 concluded the matter, and that it did not leave to the courts any surviving jurisdiction . . .

At one time the argument was shaped into the form of saying that an order made in bad faith was in law a nullity and that, consequently, all references to compulsory purchase orders in paragraphs 15 and 16 must be treated as references to such orders only as had been made in good faith. But this argument is in reality a play on the meaning of the word nullity. An order, even if not made in good faith, is still an act capable of legal consequences. It bears no brand of invalidity upon its forehead. Unless the necessary proceedings are taken at law to establish the cause of invalidity and to get it quashed or otherwise upset, it will remain as effective for its ostensible purpose as the most impeccable of orders . . .

Lord Somervell

. . . The words of paragraph 15 are plainly appropriate to ultra vires in the ordinary sense. They do not in their ordinary meaning, in my opinion, cover orders which "on the face of it" are proper and within the powers of the Act, but which are challengeable on the ground of bad faith . . .

The limited right under paragraph 15, therefore, does not apply to applications based on bad faith. Pausing there, the victim of mala fides would have his ordinary right of resort to the courts. It is said, however, that paragraph 16 takes away this right. In other words, Parliament, without ever using words which would suggest that fraud was being dealt with has deprived a victim of fraud of all right of resort to the courts, while leaving the victim of a bona fide breach of a regulation with such a right. If Parliament has done this it could only be by inadvertence. The two paragraphs fall to be construed together. Mala fides being, in my opinion, clearly excluded from paragraph 15, it should not, I think, be regarded as within the general words of paragraph 16 . . .

Appeal allowed in part.

This extract discloses a variety of judicial views about the types of error which may be set aside under the statutory jurisdiction conferred by what is now the Acquisition of Land Act 1981, ss 23 and 24. Lords Morton, Reid, and Somervell concluded that review on the ground of bad faith was impossible under the statutory jurisdiction but, having reached this conclusion, the latter two judges thought that review on this ground must be untouched by the ouster clause, thereby permitting bad faith to be raised outwith the six-week statutory review period. The narrowest view was advanced by Lord Morton, who thought that challenges on the basis of bad faith were entirely excluded. Meanwhile, Viscount Simonds and Lord Radcliffe thought that bad faith *could* be raised under the statutory jurisdiction. Indeed, Lord Radcliffe's approach, which rejected any need to 'pick and choose' between different forms of error and was supported by Lord Denning MR in *Webb* v. *Minister of Housing and Local Government* [1965] 1 WLR 755 at 770 and in *R* v. *Secretary of State for the Environment, ex parte Ostler* [1977] QB 122 (considered below at 15.6.7), reflects the modern orthodoxy that all reviewable errors are species of *ultra vires*. Embracing this view means that all of the heads of review are applicable under the statutory jurisdiction, since any *ultra vires* order can be struck down on the ground that it is 'not empowered to be granted' under the enabling Act — one of the two bases upon which quashing orders may generally be issued on statutory review (see, *eg*, Acquisition of Land Act 1981, s 24(2)(a)).

The other factor which can trigger relief in these circumstances is that 'the interests of the applicant have been substantially prejudiced by any relevant requirement . . . not having been complied with' (see, *eg*, Acquisition of Land Act 1981, s 24(2)(b)). If Lord Radcliffe's broad — and, it is submitted, correct — interpretation of the phrase 'not empowered to be granted' is adopted, then one is led to ask what is added by the notion of compliance with 'any relevant requirement'. Wade and Forsyth, *Administrative Law* (Oxford 2004) at 735, suggest that this question may be answered by reference to the distinction between directory and mandatory statutory requirements (discussed above at 2.6): whereas breach of the latter renders a decision *ultra vires* (and therefore open to challenge under s 24(2)(a)), breach of the former does not and, while therefore not usually open to review, may become reviewable under s 24(2)(b) if substantial prejudice results. On this view, the grounds upon which review lies under the statutory jurisdiction are somewhat more extensive than the usual grounds for judicial review.

15.6.7 Statutory Remedies and *Anisminic*

The willingness of the majority of the judges in *East Elloe* to accept that normal supervisory jurisdiction was ousted by the statute may seem inconsistent with *Anisminic*. The relationship between those two cases was considered by the Court of Appeal in *R* v. *Secretary of State for the Environment, ex parte Ostler* [1977] QB 122, in which the claimant sought to challenge on grounds of procedural unfairness and bad faith, outwith the specified six-week period, certain orders concerned with the construction of highways; the relevant legislation provided, in the usual terms, for statutory review only. Although their Lordships were unanimous that *East Elloe* survived *Anisminic*, such that the only possibility was statutory review within six weeks, the judgments disclose some differences in the reasoning which yielded that conclusion. The centrepiece of Goff LJ's analysis (at 139) was the distinction which he drew between jurisdictional and non-jurisdictional errors:

> . . . I think there is a real distinction between the case with which the House was dealing in *Anisminic* and the case of *Smith* v. *East Elloe Rural District Council* on that ground, that in the one case the determination was a purported determination only, because the tribunal, however eminent, having misconceived the effect of the statute, acted outside its jurisdiction, and indeed without any jurisdiction at all, whereas here one is dealing with an actual decision made within jurisdiction though sought to be challenged.

From a modern perspective, this reasoning is unsatisfactory since, under the wide concept of jurisdictional error for which *Anisminic* is now seen to have laid the foundation, no distinction can be drawn between the types of errors established in *Anisminic*, on the one hand, and those alleged in *Ostler*, on the other: all are jurisdictional in nature. Another view was advanced by Lord Denning MR at 135:

> . . . [I]n the *Anisminic* case the Act ousted the jurisdiction of the court altogether. It precluded the court from entertaining any complaint at any time about the determination. Whereas in the *East Elloe* case the statutory provision has given the court jurisdiction to inquire into complaints so long as the applicant comes within six weeks. The provision is more in the nature of a limitation period than of a complete ouster.

This criterion provides a sounder basis upon which to distinguish *Anisminic* and *East Elloe*, since it reflects the underlying policy which drives the judiciary's approach to ouster clauses. That policy is, self-evidently, one of upholding the rule of law by preserving individuals' access to the courts and ensuring that administrative power is subject to principles of legality and good administration. The type of preclusive clause at stake in *Anisminic* would, if applied literally, have absolutely prevented judicial review; this provided the impetus for the robust approach of the House of Lords, in order that the rule of law might be safeguarded. In contrast, as Lord Denning MR acknowledged in *Ostler*, legislation which excludes the normal supervisory jurisdiction while providing for an alternative statutory form of review effectively imposes a limitation period rather than wholly excluding judicial review. It appears that the rule of law is not, in such circumstances, so fundamentally threatened, because review remains possible, albeit within a shorter than usual timeframe. The difficulty, however, is that — as Gravells (1978) 41 *MLR* 383 at 389 notes — a person wishing to challenge a decision may not discover and may have no means of discovering the grounds of challenge until the time limit for statutory challenge has expired. Although this is, of course, true of any time limit, the problem is particularly acute in respect of very short limits.

15.6.8 Review of Decisions by the Asylum and Immigration Tribunal

A significant proportion of the work of the Administrative Court in recent years has been accounted for by claimants seeking judicial review of decisions concerning asylum. In order to streamline the process, and in light of the government's view that some asylum-seekers sought review as a delaying tactic, a system of statutory review of the decisions of the Immigration Appeal Tribunal (IAT) on permission to appeal was introduced by s 101 of the Nationality, Immigration and Asylum Act (NIAA) 2002. This permitted review by a single High Court judge of the legality of the IAT's permission decisions, and it was held in *R (G)* v. *IAT* [2004] EWHC 588 (Admin) [2004] 3 All ER 286, that, while judicial review was not ousted as such by s 101, it was difficult to envisage any circumstances in which a claim for judicial review — instead of or in addition to statutory review — would be permitted. Statutory review occurred by reference only to written submissions and documents filed with them, and had to be sought within 14 days (cf the 'promptly and in any event within three months' requirement for judicial review, considered above at 15.4). In spite of these restrictions, the former President of the IAT, Sir Andrew Collins, giving evidence to the Constitutional Affairs Committee (see HC 211-II (2003–2004)), said that he was confident that cases were receiving sufficient judicial scrutiny.

Further significant changes in this area were made by the Aslyum and Immigration (Treatment of Claimants etc) Act (AIA) 2004 which, by amending the NIAA 2002, replaces the IAT and the adjudicators from whose decisions it heard appeals with a single-tier appellate body known as the Asylum and Immigration Tribunal (AIT). Attempts to exclude all judicial review of the AIT's decisions having been abandoned (see above at 15.6.4), s 103A of the NIAA 2002, as inserted by the AIA 2004, permits the High Court to review the AIT's decisions and, if it thinks that an error of law occurred, to order the AIT to reconsider its decision. Following such reconsideration, it is possible, under s 103B, to appeal on a point of law to the Court of Appeal. Some concern was expressed in the House of Lords debate on the Asylum and Immigration Bill about the meaning of 'error of law': Lord Ackner, for instance, wondered (HL Deb, 4 May 2004, cols 1012–1013) whether it included 'a failure to comply with the rules of natural justice'. The better view, it is submitted, was that advanced by Lord Donaldson (*ibid*, col 1006) and the Lord Chancellor (*ibid*, col 1019), that 'error of law' encompasses all of the grounds upon which judicial review would normally lie.

Like the s 101 procedure which it replaces, s 103A provides that applications may be 'determined by reference only to written submissions' (s 103A(5)). They must be made within five days of the date on which the appellant is deemed to have received notice of the AIT's decision (or 28 days if the appellant is outside the United Kingdom). The five day time limit, which was strongly criticized in debate (*op cit*, cols 1000 and 1003), raises serious questions about the extent to which statutory review in this context is a meaningful safe-guard of legality, although the position is somewhat ameliorated by the High Court's power to permit an application out of time 'where it thinks that the application could not reasonably practicably have been made within that period' (s 103A(4)(b)). Alarmingly, s 103E(8) permits the Lord Chancellor (following consultation with the Lord Chief Justice: s 103E(10)) to vary these time limits — a power which the Lord Chancellor envisaged may be exercised to 'extend *or reduce* the time limits' (*op cit*, col 999) (emphasis added).

QUESTIONS

• In the *Ostler* case (considered above at 15.6.7) Lord Denning MR said that provision for statutory review within a six-week period was 'more in the nature of a limitation period than of a complete ouster'. Is this true of the arrangements for statutory review of AIT decisions?
• If not, what should be the response of the courts?

15.7 Standing

15.7.1 Introduction

Judicial review proceedings may be initiated only by a party with standing (sometimes referred to as *locus standi*). To this end, s 31(3) of the Supreme Court Act 1981 provides that:

No application for judicial review shall be made unless the leave of the High Court has been obtained in accordance with rules of court; and the court shall not grant leave to make such an application unless it considers that the applicant has a sufficient interest in the matter to which the application relates.

The crucial issue, therefore, is whether the claimant has 'sufficient interest' in the matter; although the text of s 31(3) suggests that this is resolved at the permission stage (or, in the old language used by s 31(3), the leave stage), we will see later that in fact standing may fall for consideration at the substantive hearing, too. However, before addressing what meaning English courts have attributed to the criterion of sufficient interest, it is necessary to consider a logically prior issue: what is the purpose of — and what, therefore, is the justification for — the requirement of standing? The importance of asking this question, and of finding a satisfactory answer to it, is underlined by Schiemann [1990] *PL* 342 at 342, who explains that:

The obvious effect of locus standi rules in any legal system is to exclude some people from obtaining the assistance of the courts in declaring and enforcing the law in circumstances where others could obtain that assistance. It follows that wherever someone is thus excluded by reason of locus standi rules, the law regards it as preferable that an illegality should continue than that the person excluded should have access to the courts.

In considering what justifications might exist for rules of standing, Schiemann helpfully distinguishes between two opposing models of standing which he respectively terms 'open' and 'closed' systems: the former adopts a liberal approach to standing, with few or no restrictions on who may bring a claim, whereas there are strict standing requirements in the latter. Schiemann (*op cit* at 346–347) sees a number of advantages in an open system:

1. The chief argument in favour of a completely open system was eloquently stated by Lord

Diplock [in *R* v. *Inland Revenue Commissioners, ex parte National Federation of Self-Employed and Small Businesses Ltd* [1982] AC 617 at 644]:

> "It would, in my view, be a grave lacuna in our system of public law if a pressure group, like the federation, or even a single public-spirited taxpayer, were prevented by outdated technical rules of locus standi from bringing the matter to the attention of the court to vindicate the rule of law and get the unlawful conduct stopped."

2. It is desirable to have administrators who act according to law and who can be brought to account if they do not. The courts will not act unless set in motion by someone. The administrators will not themselves in general activate the courts since they either believe that they are acting in accordance with the law or, believing themselves to be acting illegally, will not wish this fact to be publicly proclaimed.

3. The very fact that any individual can sue the administrator will cause the latter to take greater care to act in accordance with the law.

4. Sometimes an illegal act will not affect any individual sufficiently to give him standing in a closed system.

> "Some rights are collective or diffuse in the sense that they do not belong to any individual in particular or that individuals own only an insignificant portion of them. The ancient concept of the right (or standing) to sue as the monopoly of the sole person or persons to whom the substantive right in issue 'belongs' appears hardly applicable to those rights without a holder that belong, at one and the same time, to everyone and to no one." [Cappelletti, *The Judicial Process in Comparative Perspective* (Oxford 1989) at 273]

Such a right might arguably be instanced by a right to have the town and country planning legislation properly operated so as to safeguard the open countryside or the site of a Shakespearian theatre.

5. Sometimes an illegal act will affect an individual sufficiently to give him or her standing even in a closed system but not sufficiently for him or her to bother to set the courts in motion. Thus in [*R* v. *Secretary of State for Social Services, ex parte Child Poverty Action Group* [1990] 2 QB 540 at 546], Woolf LJ observed:

> "If the applicants' contentions are correct, it is the individual claimants for supplementary benefit whose claims have been delayed who were directly affected as a result of the Secretary of State and the Chief Adjudication Officer misinterpreting their responsibilities. However, the application for judicial review has been made by the applicants because the issues raised are agreed to be important in the field of social welfare and not ones which individual claimants for supplementary benefit could be expected to raise. Furthermore, the Child Poverty Action Group and the National Association of Citizens Advice Bureaux play a prominent role in giving advice, guidance and assistance to such claimants."

However, Schiemann goes on to acknowledge (*op cit* at 348–349) that a more closed system also carries a number of benefits:

1. Being sued is a distraction from the business of governing which is the business upon which administrators are engaged. Those who are in court or drafting affidavits are not available to advise on the budget, the latest weaponry, the taking of planning decisions and so forth.

2. The possibility of being sued can cause an administrator to concentrate less on the quality of his decision and more on making it "judge proof".

3. Litigation involves various financial costs: the cost of providing courts, judges, advocates; and the cost of providing replacements for those administrators engaged in litigation. Most of these costs are borne by the public purse. The advantages of an open policy are bought at the price of less money for legal aid and so on.

4. Administration involves making decisions. Whilst such decisions are under legal attack they are in practice, if not necessarily in theory, to a greater or lesser degree in suspense. Such delay can cause substantial damage. The redevelopment of the Royal Opera House was held up for more than a year by a legally ineffective challenge brought by a local residents' group [see R v. *Westminster City Council, ex parte Monahan* [1990] QB 87]. In pure cash terms, one imagines that that will have caused substantial damage to the Royal Opera House, owners of the nearby property and others affected by the uncertainty.

5. The court provides a public platform on which the actions of the administrator can be debated. There are often those who are opposed to a particular administrative act and who will use this platform even if sure that they will lose the case. Since in our system, and in every other of which I have any knowledge, there is a regrettable waiting time before those who wish to have their disputes resolved by the courts can come before a court, one result of an open system is bound to be that this waiting time is increased.

6. "[B]ecause public law issues in general have [a] broad reach there is a problem of interest representation, of ensuring both that those interested in the suit do have a chance to make representations, and that the 'person' presenting the case adequately represents future interests." [Craig, *Administrative Law* (London 1989) at 374] The private Attorney-General in these cases is vindicating not merely his own personal concern but also the concern of many others. As a consequence both the duties of the private Attorney-General and the controlling responsibility of the court become more intense. On the one hand, the private Attorney-General cannot freely "dispose" of the collective right in issue; on the other, the judge is responsible for ensuring that the private Attorney-General's procedural behaviour is and remains throughout the proceedings, that of an adequate champion of the public cause. It is the court's function to protect the public interest as well as that of the absent members of the class whom the plaintiff represents. The court under our system is very ill-equipped to do this. One of the problems in these cases is that the effects of judicial decisions rendered in administrative law litigation often go beyond the sphere of the parties actually present in the proceedings. Some of those persons affected by the final decision have not been heard by the court. For instance, if a method of raising money is declared illegal, potential sufferers will be either those who would have benefited from the expenditure of the money thus raised or those from whom extra monies must be raised in order to make up the shortfall produced by the declaration of illegality. It may be that their views cannot adequately be weighed by the court.

QUESTIONS

- Which of the two models of standing — the 'open' and 'closed' systems — is preferable in your view?
- Why?

15.7.2 The Law Prior to the *National Federation* Case

Until comparatively recently, the law of standing was characterized by a lack of consistency. Different remedies attracted different tests, and it was even possible to discern in the case law different approaches in respect of the *same* remedy. Lord Denning MR adopted a predictably liberal view of this issue, suggesting in *R v. Greater London Council, ex parte Blackburn* [1976] 1 WLR 550 at 559 that ordinary and prerogative remedies could be granted to 'any member of the public', albeit that 'a mere busybody' would be turned away at the court's discretion. Generally speaking, however, a more restrictive approach prevailed. For example, in *Boyce v. Paddington Borough Council* [1903] 1 Ch 109, a case in which the claimant sought an injunction, Buckley J concluded (at 114) that:

A plaintiff can sue without joining the Attorney-General [see above at 13.4 on relator proceedings] in two cases: first, where the interference with the public right is such as that some private right of his is at the same time interfered with (e.g., where an obstruction is so placed in a highway that the owner of premises abutting upon the highway is specially affected by reason that the obstruction interferes with his private right to access from and to his premises to and from the highway); and, secondly, where no private right is interfered with, but the plaintiff, in respect of his public right, suffers special damage peculiar to himself from the interference with the public right.

A similar approach was adopted in *Gouriet v. Union of Post Office Workers* [1978] AC 435, a case in which a declaration was sought, the facts of which are set out at 13.4 (although Lord Diplock, at 501, took a narrower view, suggesting that a declaration could be granted *only* if private rights were at stake).

A more liberal view prevailed as far as quashing orders (and prohibiting orders, to which 'very analogous' standing rules applied according to *R v. Surrey Justices* (1870) LR 5 QB 466 at 472) were concerned. Consider, for example, Denning LJ's comments in *R v. Thames Magistrates' Court, ex parte Greenbaum* (1957) 55 LGR 129 at 132:

. . . [T]he remedy by certiorari . . . extends to any person aggrieved, and, furthermore, to any stranger. The Court of Queen's Bench, by virtue of its inherent jurisdiction over inferior tribunals, has always the right to interfere if it sees that the lower tribunal is going or has gone beyond its jurisdiction, or has acted in a way contrary to law, or appears from the record to have fallen into error in point of law: and it can so interfere, not only at the instance of a party or a person aggrieved but also at the instance of a stranger if it thinks proper. When application is made to it by a party or a person aggrieved, it will intervene (as it is said) *ex debito justitiae*, in justice to the applicant. When application is made by a stranger it considers whether the public interest demands its intervention. In either case it is a matter which rests ultimately in the discretion of the Court.

However, Denning LJ's suggestion that the court may, in its discretion, grant a quashing order in proceedings initiated by a 'stranger' did not command universal support: indeed, in *R v. Paddington Valuation Officer, ex parte Peachey Property Ltd* [1966] 1 QB 380 at 400–401 Lord Denning MR himself, with whom Danckwerts and Salmon LJJ agreed on this point, seemed to suggest that only a 'person aggrieved' could seek a quashing order. Moreover, there was disagreement as to the width of the category of aggrieved persons: Lord Denning MR took the view in *R v. Liverpool Corporation, ex parte Liverpool Taxi Fleet Operators' Association* [1972] 2 QB 299 at 308–309 that the category extended to anyone 'whose interests may be prejudicially affected by what is taking place', but in the *Greenbaum* case, *op cit* at 135, Parker LJ adopted a narrower definition based on the existence on the part of the claimant of a 'particular grievance of his own beyond some inconvenience suffered by the general public'.

A similarly uncertain picture emerges in relation to mandatory orders. A highly restrictive requirement that the claimant had to show 'a specific legal right to ask for the interference of the Court' was set out by Wright J in *R* v. *Guardians of Lewisham* [1897] 1 QB 498 at 500 and followed in many subsequent cases. In contrast, a more liberal approach was preferred by Lord Denning MR in *R* v. *Paddington Valuation Officer, ex parte Peachey Property Ltd* [1966] 1 QB 380 at 400. Speaking about both mandatory and quashing orders, he said that, 'If a ratepayer or other person finds his name included in a valuation list which is invalid, he is entitled to come to the court . . . He is not to be put off by the plea that he has suffered no damage . . .'.

15.7.3 The *National Federation* Case

Against this somewhat confusing background, and in light of the procedural reforms of 1977 which introduced the concept of 'sufficient interest' as the test for standing in claims — for both ordinary and prerogative remedies — brought under the judicial review procedure, the House of Lords took the opportunity presented in the following case to clarify matters, laying the foundation for a more straightforward and liberal approach to standing in respect of claims brought under what is now Part 54 of the Civil Procedure Rules. (When this case was decided, the sufficient interest test was found in RSC Ord 53, r 3(5), which later became r 3(7). The same test is now set out in s 31(3) of the Supreme Court Act 1981. References in the following excerpt to the leave (now 'permission') stage must be read subject to the subsequent reforms of that stage described above at 15.2.3.)

R v. *Inland Revenue Commissioners, ex parte National Federation of Self-employed and Small Businesses Ltd* [1982] AC 617
House of Lords

It was common practice among casual print workers — known informally as the 'Fleet Street Casuals' — to avoid the payment of tax in respect of casual income by falsifying information provided to the Inland Revenue. Having become aware of this practice, which had caused the loss of substantial amounts of tax, the Inland Revenue offered an amnesty: provided that the casual workers registered for tax purposes, no investigations would be made as to tax lost in certain previous years. The Revenue considered that this was the best way to regularize the situation, but the claimant — an association of small businesses and self-employed persons — argued that the Revenue had exceeded its power in granting the amnesty and sought a declaration to that effect. In the alternative, they argued that, if the Revenue did have the necessary power, reasons should have been given, that improper matters had been taken into account, that it, the Revenue, had not acted fairly as between taxpayers, and that it had failed in its duty to see that tax is duly assessed, charged, and collected; to this end, a mandatory order was sought in order to compel the assessment and collection of the tax arrears owed by the casual workers.

Lord Wilberforce

. . . In the Order which introduced the simplified remedies by way of judicial review (R.S.C., Ord. 53, dating from 1977), it is laid down (r. 3 (5)) that: "The court shall not grant leave unless it considers that the applicant has a sufficient interest in the matter to which the application relates." The issue which comes before us is presented as one related solely to the question whether the federation has the "sufficient interest" required.

In the Divisional Court, when the motion for judicial review came before it, the point as to locus standi was treated as a preliminary point. "Before we embark on the case itself," said Lord Widgery C.J., "we have to decide whether the federation has power to bring it at all." After hearing argument, the court decided that it had not. The matter went to the Court of Appeal [1980] Q.B. 407, and again argument was concentrated on the preliminary point, though it, and the judgments, did range over the merits. The Court of Appeal by majority reversed the Divisional Court and made a declaration that the applicants have a sufficient interest to apply for judicial review. On final appeal to this House, the two sides concurred in stating that the only ground for decision was whether the applicants have such sufficient interest.

I think that it is unfortunate that this course has been taken. There may be simple cases in which it can be seen at the earliest stage that the person applying for judicial review has no interest at all, or no sufficient interest to support the application: then it would be quite correct at the threshold to refuse him leave to apply. The right to do so is an important safeguard against the courts being flooded and public bodies harassed by irresponsible applications. But in other cases this will not be so. In these it will be necessary to consider the powers or the duties in law of those against whom the relief is asked, the position of the applicant in relation to those powers or duties, and to the breach of those said to have been committed. In other words, the question of sufficient interest can not, in such cases, be considered in the abstract, or as an isolated point: it must be taken together with the legal and factual context. The rule requires sufficient interest *in the matter to which the application relates*. This, in the present case, necessarily involves the whole question of the duties of the Inland Revenue and the breaches or failure of those duties of which the respondents complain.

Before proceeding to consideration of these matters, something more needs to be said about the threshold requirement of "sufficient interest." The courts in exercising the power to grant prerogative writs, or, since 1938, prerogative orders, have always reserved the right to be satisfied that the applicant had some genuine locus standi to appear before it. This they expressed in different ways. Sometimes it was said, usually in relation to certiorari, that the applicant must be a person aggrieved; or having a particular grievance (*Reg.* v. *Thames Magistrates' Court, Ex parte Greenbaum* (1957) 55 L.G.R. 129); usually in relation to mandamus, that he must have a specific legal right (*Reg.* v. *Lewisham Union Guardians* [1897] 1 Q.B 498 and *Reg.* v. *Russell, Ex parte Beaverbrook Newspapers Ltd* [1969] 1 QB 342); sometimes that he must have a sufficient interest (*R* v. *Cotham* [1898] 1 Q.B. 802, 804 (mandamus), *Ex parte Stott* [1916] 1 K.B. 7 (certiorari)). By 1977, when R.S.C. Ord. 53 was introduced, the courts, guided by Lord Parker C.J., in cases where mandamus was sought, were moving away from the *Lewisham Union* test of specific legal right, to one of sufficient interest. In *Reg.* v. *Russell* Lord Parker had tentatively adhered to the test of legal specific right but in *Reg.* v. *Customs and Excise Commissioners, Ex parte Cook* [1970] 1 W.L.R. 450 he had moved to sufficient interest. Shortly afterward the new rule (R.S.C. Ord. 53, r. 3) was drafted with these words.

R.S.C. Ord. 53 was, it is well known, introduced to simplify the procedure of applying for the relief formerly given by prerogative writ or order — so the old technical rules no longer apply. So far as the substantive law is concerned, this remained unchanged: the Administration of Justice (Miscellaneous Provisions) Act 1938 preserved the jurisdiction existing before the Act, and the same preservation is contemplated by legislation [*ie* the Supreme Court Act 1981] now pending. The Order, furthermore, did not remove the requirement to show locus standi. On the contrary, in rule 3, it stated this in the form of a threshold requirement to be found by the court. For all cases the test is expressed as one of sufficient interest in the matter to which the application relates. As to this I would state two negative propositions. First, it does not remove the whole — and vitally important — question of locus standi into the realm of pure discretion. The matter is one for decision, a mixed decision of fact and law, which the court must decide on legal principles. Secondly, the fact that the same words are used to cover all the forms of remedy allowed by the rule does not mean that the test is the same in all cases. When Lord Parker C.J. said that in cases of mandamus the test may well be stricter (sc. than in certiorari) — the *Beaverbrook Newspapers case* [1969] 1 Q.B. 342 and in *Cook's* case [1970] 1 W.L.R. 450 at 455F, "on a very strict basis," he was not stating a technical rule — which can now be discarded — but a rule of common sense, reflecting the different character of the relief asked for. It would seem obvious enough that the interest of a person seeking to compel an authority to carry out a duty is different from that of a person complaining that a judicial or administrative body has, to his detriment, exceeded its powers. Whether one calls for a stricter rule than the other may be a linguistic point: they are certainly different and we should be unwise in our enthusiasm for liberation from procedural fetters to discard reasoned authorities which illustrate this. It is hardly necessary to add that recognition of the value of guiding authorities does not mean that the process of judicial review must stand still.

In the present case we are in the area of mandamus — an alleged failure to perform a duty. It was submitted by the Lord Advocate that in such cases we should be guided by the definition of the duty, in this case statutory, and inquire whether expressly, or by implication, this definition indicates — or the contrary — that the complaining applicant is within the scope or ambit of the duty. I think that this is at least a good working rule though perhaps not an exhaustive one.

The Inland Revenue Commissioners are a statutory body. Their duties are, relevantly, defined in the Inland Revenue Regulation Act 1890 and the Taxes Management Act 1970. Section 1 of the Act of 1890 authorises the appointment of commissioners "for the collection and management of inland revenue" and confers on the commissioners "all necessary powers for carrying into execution every Act of Parliament relating to inland revenue." By section 13 the commissioners must "collect and cause to be collected every part of inland revenue and all money under their care and management and keep distinct accounts thereof."

Section 1 of the Act of 1970 provides that "Income tax . . . shall be under the care and management of the commissioners." This Act contains the very wide powers of the board and of inspectors of taxes to make assessments upon persons designated by Parliament as liable to pay income tax. With regard to casual employment, there is a procedure laid down by statutory instrument (the Income Tax (Employments) Regulations 1973 (S.I. 1973 No. 334)) by which inspectors of taxes may proceed by way of direct assessment or in accordance with any special arrangements which the Commissioners of Inland Revenue may make for the collection of the tax . . . [I]t was a "special arrangement" that the commissioners set out to make in the present case.

From this summary analysis it is clear that the Inland Revenue Commissioners are not immune from the process of judicial review. They are an administrative body with statutory duties, which the courts, in principle, can supervise. They have indeed done so — see *Reg.* v. *Income Tax Special Commissioners* (1881) 21 Q.B.D. 313, C.A. (mandamus) and *Income Tax Special Commissioners* v. *Linsleys (Established 1894) Ltd* [1958] A.C. 569, where it was not doubted that a mandamus could be issued if the facts had been right. It must follow from these cases and from principle that a taxpayer would not be excluded from seeking judicial review if he could show that the revenue had either failed in its statutory duty toward him or had been guilty of some action which was an abuse of their powers or outside their powers altogether. Such a collateral attack — as contrasted with a direct appeal on law to the courts — would no doubt be rare, but the possibility certainly exists.

The position of other taxpayers — other than the taxpayers whose assessment is in question — and their right to challenge the revenue's assessment or non-assessment of that taxpayer, must be judged according to whether, consistently with the legislation, they can be considered as having sufficient interest to complain of what has been done or omitted. I proceed thereto to examine the revenue's duties in that light.

These duties are expressed in very general terms and it is necessary to take account also of the framework of the income tax legislation. This establishes that the commissioners must assess each individual taxpayer in relation to his circumstances. Such assessments and all information regarding taxpayers' affairs are strictly confidential. There is no list or record of assessments which can be inspected by other taxpayers. Nor is there any common fund of the produce of income tax in which income taxpayers as a whole can be said to have any interest. The produce of income tax, together with that of other inland revenue taxes, is paid into the consolidated fund which is at the disposal of Parliament for any purposes that Parliament thinks fit.

The position of taxpayers is therefore very different from that of ratepayers. As explained in *Arsenal Football Club Ltd.* v. *Ende* [1979] A.C. 1, the amount of rates assessed upon ratepayers is ascertainable by the public through the valuation list. The produce of rates goes into a common fund applicable for the benefit of the ratepayers. Thus any ratepayer has an interest, direct and sufficient, in the rates levied upon other ratepayers; for this reason, his right as a "person aggrieved" to challenge assessments upon them has long been recognised and is so now in section 69 of the General Rate Act 1967. This right was given effect to in the *Arsenal* case.

The structure of the legislation relating to income tax, on the other hand, makes clear that no corresponding right is intended to be conferred upon taxpayers. Not only is there no express or implied provision in the legislation upon which such a right could be claimed, but to allow it would be subversive of the whole system, which involves that the commissioners' duties are to the Crown, and that matters relating to income tax are between the commissioners and the taxpayer concerned. No other person is given any right to make proposals about the tax payable by any individual: he cannot even inquire as to such tax. The total confidentiality of assessments and of negotiations between individuals and the revenue is a vital element in the working of the system. As a matter of general principle I would hold that one taxpayer has no sufficient interest in asking the court to investigate the tax affairs of another taxpayer or to complain that the latter has been under-assessed or over-assessed: indeed, there is a strong public interest that he should not. And this principle applies equally to groups of taxpayers: an aggregate of individuals each of whom has no interest cannot of itself have an interest.

That a case can never arise in which the acts or abstentions of the revenue can be brought before the court I am certainly not prepared to assert, nor that, in a case of sufficient gravity, the court might not be able to hold that another taxpayer or other taxpayers could challenge them. Whether this situation has been reached or not must depend upon an examination, upon evidence, of what breach of duty or illegality is alleged. Upon this, and relating it to the position of the complainant, the court has to make its decision.

[His Lordship then discussed the evidence in detail, in the course of which he said: ". . . a sense of fairness as between one taxpayer or group of taxpayers and another is an important objective, so that a sense of unfairness may be the beginning of a recognisable grievance. I say the beginning, because the income tax legislation contains a large number of anomalies which are naturally not thought to be fair by those disadvantaged." After his review of the evidence, he continued:] On the evidence as a whole, I fail to see how any court considering it as such and not confining its attention to an abstract question of locus standi could avoid reaching the conclusion that the Inland Revenue . . . were acting in this matter genuinely in the care and management of the taxes, under the powers entrusted to them. This has no resemblance to any kind of case where the court ought, at the instance of a taxpayer, to intervene. To do so would involve permitting a taxpayer or a group of taxpayers to call in question the exercise of management powers and involve the court itself in a management exercise. Judicial review under any of its headings does not extend into this area. Finally, if as I think, the case against the revenue does not, on the evidence, leave the ground, no court, in my opinion, would consider ordering discovery against the revenue in the hope of eliciting some impropriety. Looking at the matter as a whole, I am of opinion that the Divisional Court, while justified on the ex parte application in granting leave, ought, having regard to the nature of "the matter" raised, to have held that the federation had shown no sufficient interest in that matter to justify its application for relief. I would therefore allow the appeal and order that the originating motion be dismissed.

Lord Diplock

. . . I agree with my noble and learned friend that no court considering this evidence could avoid reaching the conclusion that the board and its inspector were acting solely for "good management" reasons and in the lawful exercise of the discretion which the statutes confer on them.

For my part, I should prefer to allow the appeal and dismiss the federation's application under R.S.C. Ord. 53, not upon the specific ground of no sufficient interest but upon the more general ground that it has not been shown that in the matter of which complaint was made, the treatment of the tax liabilities of the Fleet Street casuals, the board did anything that was ultra vires or unlawful. They acted in the bona fide exercise of the wide managerial discretion conferred on them by statute. Since judicial review is available only as a remedy for conduct of a public officer or authority which is ultra vires or unlawful, but not for acts done lawfully in the exercise of an administrative discretion which are complained of only as being unfair or unwise, there is a sense in which it may be said that the federation had not a sufficient interest in the matter to which their application related; but this is not a helpful statement; it would be equally true of anyone, including the Attorney-General, who sought to complain.

[Nevertheless, his Lordship went on to consider the question of the Federation's standing.]

Your Lordships can take judicial notice of the fact that the main purpose of the new Order 53 was to sweep away these procedural differences including, in particular, differences as to locus standi; to substitute for them a single simplified procedure for obtaining all forms of relief, and to leave to the court a wide discretion as to what interlocutory directions, including orders for discovery, were appropriate to the particular case.

. . . I turn first to consider what constituted locus standi to apply for one or other of the prerogative orders immediately before the new Order 53 came into force . . .

The rules as to "standing" for the purpose of applying for prerogative orders, like most of English public law, are not to be found in any statute. They were made by judges, by judges they can be changed; and so they have been over the years to meet the need to preserve the integrity of the rule of law despite changes in the social structure, methods of government and the extent to which the activities of private citizens are controlled by governmental authorities, that have been taking place continuously, sometimes slowly, sometimes swiftly, since the rules were originally propounded. Those changes have been particularly rapid since World War II. Any judicial statements on matters of public law if made before 1950 are likely to be a misleading guide to what the law is today.

In 1951, the decision of the Divisional Court in *Rex. v. Northumberland Compensation Appeal Tribunal, Ex parte Shaw* [1951] 1 Q.B. 711 resurrected error of law upon the face of the record as a ground for granting certiorari. Parliament by the Tribunals and Inquiries Act 1958 followed this up by requiring reasons to be given for many administrative decisions that had previously been cloaked in silence; and the years that followed between then and 1977 witnessed a dramatic liberalisation of access to the courts for the purpose of obtaining prerogative orders against persons and authorities exercising governmental powers. This involved a virtual abandonment of the former restrictive rules as to the locus standi of persons seeking such orders. The process of liberalisation of access to the courts and the progressive discarding of technical limitations upon locus standi is too well known to call for detailed citation of the cases by which it may be demonstrated. They are referred to and discussed in Wade, *Administrative Law*, 4th ed (1977), pp 543–546 (prohibition and certiorari) and pp 610–612 (mandamus). The author points out there that although lip-service continued to be paid to a difference in standing required to entitle an applicant to mandamus on the one hand and prohibition or certiorari on the other, in practice the courts found some way of treating the locus standi for all three remedies as being the same. A striking example of this is to be found in *Reg.* v. *Hereford Corporation, Ex parte Harrower* [1970] 1 W.L.R. 1424, where the applicants were treated as having locus standi in their capacity as ratepayers though their real interest in the matter was as electrical contractors only. For my part I need only refer to *Reg.* v. *Greater London Council, Ex parte Blackburn* [1976] 1 W.L.R. 550. In that case Mr. Blackburn who lived in London with his wife who was a ratepayer, applied successfully for an order of prohibition against the council to stop them acting in breach of their statutory duty to prevent the exhibition of pornographic films within their administrative area. Mrs. Blackburn was also a party to the application. Lord Denning M.R. and Stephenson L.J. were of opinion that both Mr. and Mrs. Blackburn had locus standi to make the application: Mr. Blackburn because he lived within the administrative area of the council and had children who might be harmed by seeing pornographic films and Mrs. Blackburn not only as a parent but also on the additional ground that she was a ratepayer. Bridge L.J. relied only on Mrs. Blackburn's status as a ratepayer; a class of persons to whom for historical reasons the court of King's Bench afforded generous access to control ultra vires activities of the public bodies to whose expenses they contributed. But now that local government franchise is not limited to ratepayers, this distinction between the two applicants strikes me as carrying technicality to the limits of absurdity having regard to the subject matter of the application in the *Blackburn* case. I agree in substance with what Lord Denning M.R. said, at p. 559, though in language more eloquent than it would be my normal style to use:

> "I regard it as a matter of high constitutional principle that if there is good ground for supposing that a government department or a public authority is transgressing the law, or is about to transgress it, in a way which offends or injures thousands of Her Majesty's subjects, then any one of those offended or injured can draw it to the attention of the courts of law and seek to have the law enforced, and the courts *in their discretion* can grant whatever remedy is appropriate." (The italics in this quotation are my own.)

The reference here is to flagrant and serious breaches of the law by persons and authorities exercising governmental functions which are continuing unchecked. To revert to technical restrictions on locus standi to prevent this that were current 30 years or more would be to reverse that progress towards a comprehensive system of administrative law that I regard as having been the greatest achievement of the English courts in my judicial lifetime.

. . . The expression that [the draftsman] used in rule 3 (5) had cropped up sporadically in judgments relating to prerogative writs and orders and consisted of ordinary English words which, on the face of them, leave the court an unfettered discretion to decide what in its own good judgment it considers to be "a sufficient interest" on the part of an applicant in the particular circumstances of the case before it. For my part I would not strain to give them any narrower meaning.

The procedure under the new Order 53 involves two stages: (1) the application for leave to apply for judicial review, and (2) if leave is granted, the hearing of the application itself. The former, or "threshold," stage is regulated by rule 3. The application for leave to apply for judicial review is made initially ex parte [cf above at 15.2.3], but may be adjourned for the persons or bodies against whom relief is sought to be represented. This did not happen in the instant case. Rule 3 (5) specifically requires the court to consider at this stage whether "it considers that the applicant has a sufficient interest in the matter to which the application relates." So this is a "threshold" question in the sense that the court must direct its mind to it and form a prima facie view about it upon the material that is available at the first stage. The prima facie view so formed, if favourable to the applicant, may alter on further consideration in the light of further evidence that may be before the court at the second stage, the hearing of the application for judicial review itself.

The need for leave to start proceedings for remedies in public law is not new. It applied previously to applications for prerogative orders, though not to civil actions for injunctions or declarations. Its purpose is to prevent the time of the court being wasted by busybodies with misguided or trivial complaints of administrative error, and to remove the uncertainty in which public officers and authorities might be left as to whether they could safely proceed with administrative action while proceedings for judicial review of it were actually pending even though misconceived . . .

My Lords, at the threshold stage, for the federation to make out a prima facie case of reasonable suspicion that the board in showing a discriminatory leniency to a substantial class of taxpayers had done so for ulterior reasons extraneous to good management, and thereby deprived the national exchequer of considerable sums of money, constituted what was in my view reason enough for the Divisional Court to consider that the federation or, for that matter, any taxpayer, had a sufficient interest to apply to have the question whether the board was acting ultra vires reviewed by the court. The whole purpose of requiring that leave should first be obtained to make the application for judicial review would be defeated if the court were to go into the matter in any depth at that stage. If, on a quick perusal of the material then available, the court thinks that it discloses what might on further consideration turn out to be an arguable case in favour of granting to the applicant the relief claimed, it ought, in the exercise of a judicial discretion, to give him leave to apply for that relief. The discretion that the court is exercising at this stage is not the same as that which it is called upon to exercise when all the evidence is in and the matter has been fully argued at the hearing of the application . . .

It would, in my view, be a grave lacuna in our system of public law if a pressure group, like the federation, or even a single public-spirited taxpayer, were prevented by outdated technical rules of locus standi from bringing the matter to the attention of the court to vindicate the rule of law and get the unlawful conduct stopped. The Attorney-General, although he occasionally applies for prerogative orders against public authorities that do not form part of central government, in practice never does so against government departments. It is not, in my view, a sufficient answer to say that judicial review of the actions of officers or departments of central government is unnecessary because they are accountable to Parliament for the way in which they carry out their functions. They are accountable to Parliament for what they do so far as regards efficiency and policy, and of that Parliament is the only judge; they are responsible to a court of justice for the lawfulness of what they do, and of that the court is the only judge. . . .

Lord Fraser

My Lords, I agree with all my noble and learned friends that this appeal should be allowed. I agree with the reasoning of Lord Wilberforce and Lord Roskill but I wish to explain my reasons in my own words.

. . . [T]he question whether the respondents have a sufficient interest to make the application at all is a separate, and logically prior, question which has to be answered affirmatively before any question on the merits arises. Refusal of the application on its merits therefore implies that the prior question has been answered affirmatively. I recognise that in some cases, perhaps in many, it may be impracticable to decide whether an applicant has a sufficient interest or not, without having evidence from both parties as to the matter to which the application relates, and that, in such cases, the court before whom the matter comes in the first instance cannot refuse leave to the applicant at the ex parte stage, under rule 3 (5). The court which grants leave at that stage will do so on the footing that it makes a provisional finding of sufficient interest, subject to revisal later on, and it is therefore not necessarily to be criticised merely because the final decision is that the applicant did not have sufficient interest. But where, after seeing the evidence of both parties, the proper conclusion is that the applicant did not have a sufficient interest to make the application, the decision ought to be made on that ground. The present appeal is, in my view, such a case and I would therefore dismiss the appeal on that ground. When it is also shown, as in this case, that the application would fail on its merits, it is desirable for that to be stated by the court which first considers the matter in order to avoid unnecessary appeals on the preliminary point.

. . . [W]hile the standard of sufficiency has been relaxed in recent years, the need to have an interest has remained and the fact that R.S.C. Ord. 53, r. 3 requires a sufficient interest undoubtedly shows that not every applicant is entitled to judicial review as of right.

The new Order 53, introduced in 1977, no doubt had the effect of removing technical and procedural differences between the prerogative orders, and of introducing a remedy by way of declaration or injunction in suitable cases, but I do not think it can have had the effect of throwing over all the older law and of leaving the grant of judicial review in the uncontrolled discretion of the court. On what principle, then, is the sufficiency of interest to be judged? All are agreed that a direct financial or legal interest is not now required, and that the requirement of a legal specific interest laid down in *Reg.* v. *Lewisham Union Guardians* [1897] 1 Q.B. 488 is no longer applicable. There is also general agreement that a mere busybody does not have a sufficient interest. The difficulty is, in between those extremes, to distinguish between the desire of the busybody to interfere in other people's affairs and the interest of the person affected by or having a reasonable concern with the matter to which the application relates. In the present case that matter is an alleged failure by the appellants to perform the duty imposed upon them by statute.

The correct approach in such a case is, in my opinion, to look at the statute under which the duty arises, and to see whether it gives any express or implied right to persons in the position of the applicant to complain of the alleged unlawful act or omission . . .

The respondents are a body with some 50,000 members, but their counsel conceded, rightly in my opinion, that if they had a sufficient interest to obtain judicial review, then any individual taxpayer, or at least any payer of income tax, must also have such an interest. I can see no justification for treating payers of income tax as having any separate interest in the matter now complained of from that of persons who pay other taxes. All taxpayers contribute to the general fund of revenue and the sense of grievance which the respondents claim to feel because of the difference between the appellants' treatment of the Fleet Street casuals and their treatment of private traders might be felt just as strongly by any honest taxpayer who pays the full amount of taxes of any kind to which he is properly liable. But if the class of persons with a sufficient interest is to include all taxpayers it must include practically every individual in the country who has his own income because there must be few individuals, however frugal their requirements, who do not pay some indirect taxes including V.A.T. It would, I think, be extravagant to suggest that every taxpayer who believes that the Inland Revenue or the Customs and Excise Commissioners are giving an unlawful preference to another taxpayer, and who feels aggrieved thereby, has a sufficient interest to obtain judicial review under R.S.C., Ord. 53. It may be that, if he was relying upon some exceptionally grave or widespread illegality, he could succeed in establishing a sufficient interest, but such cases would be very rare indeed and this is not one of them.

For these reasons I would allow the appeal on the ground that the respondents have no sufficient interest in the matters complained of.

Lord Scarman

. . . The application for judicial review was introduced by rule of court in 1977. The new R.S.C., Ord. 53 is a procedural reform of great importance in the field of public law, but it does not — indeed, cannot — either extend or diminish the substantive law. Its function is limited to ensuring "ubi jus, ibi remedium".

The new procedure is more flexible than that which it supersedes. An applicant for relief will no longer be defeated merely because he has chosen to apply for the wrong remedy. Not only has the court a complete discretion to select and grant the appropriate remedy: but it now may grant remedies which were not previously available. Rule 1 (2) enables the court to grant a declaration or injunction instead of or in addition to, a prerogative order, where to do so would be just and convenient. This is a procedural innovation of great consequence: but it neither extends nor diminishes the substantive law. For the two remedies (borrowed from the private law) are put in harness with the prerogative remedies . . .

The appeal is said by both parties to turn on the meaning to be attributed to R.S.C., Ord. 53, r. 3 (5), which has been described as the heart of the Order. It is in these terms: "The court shall not grant leave unless it considers that the applicant has a sufficient interest in the matter to which the application relates." There is, my Lords, no harm in so describing the issue, so long as it is remembered that the right to apply for a prerogative order is a matter of law, not to be modified or abridged by rule of court. The right has always been, and remains today, available only at the discretion of the High Court, which has to be exercised upon the facts of the particular case and according to principles developed by the judges. The case law, as it has developed and continues to develop in the hands of the judges, determines the nature of the interest an applicant must show to obtain leave to apply. The rule, however, presents no problems of construction. Its terms are wide enough to reflect the modern law without distorting or abridging the discretion of the judges: and it draws attention to a feature of the law, which has been overlooked in the present case. The sufficiency of the applicant's interests has to be judged in relation to the subject matter of his application. This relationship has always been of importance in the law. It is well illustrated by the history of the development of the prerogative writs, notably the difference of approach to mandamus and certiorari, and it remains a factor of importance in the exercise of the discretion today.

. . . [The Lord Advocate] submitted that, notwithstanding the language of R.S.C., Ord. 53, r. 1 (2), the court has no jurisdiction to grant to a private citizen a declaration save in respect of a private right or wrong: and he relied on the House's decision in *Gouriet* v. *Union of Post Office Workers* [1978] A.C. 435. Declaration is, of course, a remedy developed by the judges in the field of private law. *Gouriet's* case is authority for the proposition that a citizen may not issue a writ claiming a declaration or other relief against another for the redress of a public wrong unless he can persuade the Attorney-General, on his "relation," to bring the action. The case has nothing to do with the prerogative jurisdiction of the High Court; and it was decided before the introduction of the new Order 53, at a time when a declaration could not be obtained by a private citizen unless he could show (as in a claim for injunction) that a private right of his was threatened or infringed. The new Order has made the remedy available as an alternative, or an addition, to a prerogative order . . .

[Turning to the question of sufficiency of interest, his Lordship continued:] My Lords, I will not weary the House with citation of many authorities. Suffice it to refer to the judgment of Lord Parker C.J. in *Reg.* v. *Thames Magistrates' Court, ex parte Greenbaum*, (1957) 55 L.G.R. 129, a case of certiorari; and to words of Lord Wilberforce in *Gouriet* v. *Union of Post Office Workers* [1978] A.C. 435, 482, where he stated the modern position in relation to prerogative orders: "These are often applied for by individuals and the courts have allowed them liberal access under a generous conception of locus standi." The one legal principle, which is implicit in the case law and accurately reflected in the rule of court, is that in determining the sufficiency of an applicant's interest it is necessary to consider the matter to which the application relates. It is wrong in law, as I understand the cases, for the court to attempt an assessment of the sufficiency of an applicant's interest without regard to the matter of his complaint. If he fails to show, when he applies for leave, a prima facie case, or reasonable grounds for believing that there has been a failure of public duty, the court would be in error if it granted leave. The curb represented by the need for an applicant to show, when he seeks leave to apply, that he has such a case is an essential protection against abuse of legal process. It enables the court to prevent abuse by busybodies, cranks, and other mischief-makers. I do not see any further purpose served by the requirement for leave.

But, that being said, the discretion belongs to the court: and, as my noble and learned friend, Lord Diplock, has already made clear, it is the function of the judges to determine the way in which it is to be exercised. Accordingly I think that the Divisional Court was right to grant leave ex parte. Mr. Payne's affidavit of March 20, 1979, revealed a prima facie case of failure by the Inland Revenue to discharge its duty to act fairly between taxpayer and taxpayer. But by the time the application reached the Divisional Court for a hearing, inter partes, of the preliminary issue, two very full affidavits had been filed by the revenue explaining the "management" reasons for the decision not to seek to collect the unpaid tax from the Fleet Street casuals. At this stage the matters of fact and degree upon which depends the exercise of the discretion whether to allow the application to proceed or not became clear. It was now possible to form a view as to the existence or otherwise of a case meriting examination by the court. And it was abundantly plain upon the evidence that the applicant could show no such case. But the Court of Appeal, misled into thinking that, at that stage and notwithstanding the evidence available, locus standi was to be dealt with as a preliminary issue, assumed illegality (where in my judgment none was shown) and, upon that assumption, held that the applicant had sufficient interest. Were the assumption justified, which on the evidence it was not, I would agree with the reasoning of Lord Denning M.R. and Ackner L.J. I think the majority of the Court of Appeal, in formulating a test of genuine grievance reasonably asserted, were doing no more than giving effect to the general principle which Lord Mansfield C.J. had stated in the early days on the remedy. Any more stringent test would, as Wade, *Administrative Law*, 4th ed., p. 612 observes, open up "a serious gap in the system of public law."

The federation, having failed to show any grounds for believing that the revenue has failed to do its statutory duty, have not, in my view, shown an interest sufficient in law to justify any further proceedings by the court on its application. Had they shown reasonable grounds for believing that the failure to collect tax from the Fleet Street casuals was an abuse of the revenue's managerial discretion or that there was a case to that effect which merited investigation and examination by the court, I would have agreed with the Court of Appeal that they had shown a sufficient interest for the grant of leave to proceed further with their application. I would, therefore, allow the appeal.

Lord Roskill

. . . My Lords, much time was spent in the courts below and in argument before your Lordships' House with citation of well-known cases, some of now respectable antiquity in which prerogative orders or formerly prerogative writs have been allowed to issue or have been refused. With all respect to the authority of the judges by whom those cases were decided, such decisions are today of little assistance for two reasons. First, in the last 30 years — no doubt because of the growth of central and local government intervention in the affairs of the ordinary citizen since the Second World War, and the consequent increase in the number of administrative bodies charged by Parliament with the performance of public duties — the use of prerogative orders to check usurpation of power by such bodies to the disadvantage of the ordinary citizen, or to insist upon due performance by such bodies of their statutory duties and to maintain due adherence to the laws enacted by Parliament, has greatly increased. The former and stricter rules determining when such orders, or formerly the prerogative writs, might or might not issue, have been greatly relaxed. It is unnecessary in the present appeal to trace through a whole series of decisions which demonstrates that change in legal policy. The change is well known as are the decisions.

Secondly, since those cases were decided and following the change in legal policy to which I have just referred, Order 53 was introduced into the Rules of the Supreme Court in 1977 . . .

. . . Order 53 took effect on January 11, 1978, some six months after the decision of your Lordships' House in *Gouriet* v. *Union of Post Office Workers* [1978] A.C. 435, on July 26, 1977, an authority much relied upon by the learned Lord Advocate on behalf of the appellants in support of his submissions regarding the circumstances in which declarations might be granted. But *Gouriet's* case was a relator action and was not concerned with prerogative orders or judicial review, and the relevant observations of your Lordships must be read in the light of that fact and of the subsequent enactment of Order 53.

. . . [T]he court is enjoined by rule 3 (5) not to grant leave unless the applicant has a "sufficient interest" in the matter to which the application relates, plain words of limitation upon an applicant's right to relief.

In my opinion it is now clear that the solution to the present appeal must lie in the proper application of the principles now enshrined in Order 53, in the light of modern judicial policy to which I have already referred, to the facts of the present case without excessive regard to the fetters seemingly previously imposed by judicial decisions in earlier times and long before that modern policy was evolved or Order 53 was enacted.

My Lords, the all important phrase in rule 3 (5) is "sufficient interest." Learned counsel were agreed that this phrase had not been used in any previous relevant enactment. My Lords, careful review of the earlier authorities in which learned counsel for both parties engaged, reveals that many different phrases have been used in different cases to describe the required standing of a particular applicant for what is now described as judicial review before the courts would entertain his application. He might be "a party" to the relevant proceedings. He might be "a person aggrieved." He might be "a person with a particular grievance." He might be a "stranger." All those, and some other phrases, will be found in the cases. None is exhaustive or indeed definitive and indeed in this field it would be, I think, impossible to find a phrase which was exhaustive or definitive of the class of person entitled to apply for judicial review. No doubt it was for this reason that the Rules Committee of the Supreme Court in 1977 selected the phrase "sufficient interest" as one which could sufficiently embrace all classes of those who might apply, and yet permit sufficient flexibility in any particular case to determine whether or not "sufficient interest" was in fact shown . . .

Your Lordships' attention was drawn to note 14/21 to Order 53 of *The Supreme Court Practice* (1979), which your Lordships were told bore the authority of Master Sir Jack Jacob Q.C. The learned editor stated that that which was a 'sufficient interest'

" . . . appears to be a mixed question of fact and law; a question of fact and degree and the relationship between the applicant and the matter to which the application relates, having regard to all the circumstances of the case."

With this admirably concise statement, I respectfully agree.

Mr. Harvey, for the respondents, contended that not only was there jurisdiction to grant the relief sought but that his clients had a "sufficient interest" to be granted that relief because once it was accepted that the appellants were a statutory body charged with the performance of a public duty, any member of the public had a right to come to the court and complain that that duty had not been performed in some relevant respect, and that this right of that member of the public did not depend upon the precise nature of the obligation cast by the statute upon the appellants. More narrowly, Mr. Harvey argued that an individual taxpayer had as much interest in the performance by the appellants of their statutory duty as the ratepayer in the *Arsenal* case [1979] A.C. 1, and was not too remote from the appellants in seeking to insist upon performance of their duty in accordance with the law, a submission which found favour in the Court of Appeal with Ackner L.J. . . .

My Lords, Lord Denning M.R. was willing to accept the wider of these propositions founded upon what he had previously said in *Attorney-General ex rel. McWhirter* v. *Independent Broadcasting Authority* [1973] Q.B. 629, 646, and again in a revised form in *Blackburn's* case [1976] 1 W.L.R. 550, 559. He accepted that my noble and learned friend, Lord Wilberforce, had expressly disapproved the former passage in his speech in *Gouriet's* case [1978] A.C. 435, 483 but claimed that that disapproval was limited to relator actions such as *Gouriet's* case was. My Lords, with profound respect, I cannot agree. Though my noble and learned friend's disapproval was, of course, made in the context of a relator action, the view of the learned Lord Denning MR, if applied to all applications for judicial review, would extend the individual's right of application for that relief far beyond any acceptable limit, and would give a meaning so wide to a "sufficient interest" in RSC Ord 53, r 3 (5) that they would in practice cease to be, as they were clearly intended to be, words of limitation upon that right of application . . .

I . . . think that the majority of the Court of Appeal was wrong in granting the relief claimed either on the wider ground the learned Lord Denning M.R. preferred or on the narrower ground which appealed to Ackner L.J.

My Lords, I hope I yield to no one in stressing the importance that relief by way of judicial review should be freely available in whatever form may be appropriate in a particular case, and it is today especially important not to cut down by judicial decision the scope of Order 53 in creating modern procedure for applications for judicial review. I emphasise in particular that relief by way of declaration is expressly made a form of judicial review additional to or alternative to relief by way of prerogative order or injunction. The court has a general discretion which, if any, relief shall be granted and many of the old decisions restricting the circumstances in which declarations may be granted to establish legal rights seem to me to be no longer in point. On the other hand, it is equally important that the courts do not by use or misuse of the weapon of judicial review cross that clear boundary between what is administration, whether it be good or bad administration, and what is an unlawful performance of the statutory duty by a body charged with the performance of that duty . . . [T]he arguments that [the Lord Advocate] advanced on jurisdiction which I have rejected become highly relevant when the question of "sufficient interest" arises. The first question must be to inquire what is the relevant duty of the statutory body against which the order is sought, of the performance or non-performance of which complaint is sought to be made . . .

The next matter is to consider the complaint made and the relief sought. It is clear that the respondents are seeking to intervene in the affairs of individual taxpayers, the Fleet Street casual workers, and to require the appellants to assess and collect tax from them which the appellants have clearly agreed not to do. Theoretically, but one trusts only theoretically, it is possible to envisage a case when because of some grossly improper pressure or motive the appellants have failed to perform their statutory duty as respects a particular taxpayer or class of taxpayer. In such a case, which emphatically is not the present, judicial review might be available to other taxpayers. But it would require to be a most extreme case for I am clearly of the view, having regard to the nature of the appellants' statutory duty and the degree of confidentiality enjoined by statute which attaches to their performance, that in general it is not open to individual taxpayers or to a group of taxpayers to seek to interfere between the appellants and other taxpayers, whether those other taxpayers are honest or dishonest men, and that the court should, by refusing relief by way of judicial review, firmly discourage such attempted interference by other taxpayers. It follows that, in my view, taking all those matters into account, it cannot be said that the respondents had a "sufficient interest" to justify their seeking the relief claimed by way of judicial review . . .

My Lords, since preparing this speech, I have had the advantage of reading in draft the speeches of my noble and learned friends, Lord Wilberforce and Lord Fraser of Tullybelton. I am in full agreement with what both my noble and learned friends have said.

Appeal allowed.

At this stage, three points should be noted about this case. First, although it is credited with simplifying the law in this area, Lord Wilberforce said that the old case law was not irrelevant. Indeed he went as far as to suggest that the there may still be different standing tests for different remedies, singling out mandatory orders for a stricter approach — a view which Otton J appeared to share in *R* v. *HM Inspectorate of Pollution, ex parte Greenpeace (No. 2)* [1994] 4 All ER 329 at 351. However, the other judges in the *National Federation* case envisaged (some more boldly than others, it must be acknowledged) that the effect of the new 'sufficient interest' test was to introduce a uniform approach to standing in respect of all remedies. This approach has received support in subsequent cases; for instance, in *R* v. *Felixstowe Justices, ex parte Leigh* [1987] QB 582 at 597, Watkins LJ was unsympathetic to the suggestion that a stricter test applied to mandatory orders:

I do not find it necessary for the purposes of this judgment to decide, as was urged upon us by counsel for the respondents, whether or not a stricter test of sufficient interest still applies for the issue of mandamus, beyond saying that I am inclined to think it does not. The appropriate approach in this case, it seems to me, is for the court, in using what I regard as its undoubted discretion, to decide the question of sufficient interest on each application primarily within its factual context.

Secondly, although s 31(3) of the Supreme Court Act 1981 (like the rules of court considered in the *National Federation* case) appears to presuppose that the question of standing is to be determined at the permission stage, the House of Lords recognized that this matter may legitimately be readdressed at the substantive hearing. Thus, in the *National Federation* case itself, their Lordships were in agreement that it had been appropriate to grant permission, but that the *prima facie* conclusion as to standing which was reached in deciding to grant permission could legitimately be reconsidered at the substantive hearing. Reopening the question of standing at the substantive hearing is now common practice (see, *eg*, *R v. Secretary of State for the Environment, ex parte Rose Theatre Trust Co* [1990] 1 QB 504 at 519; *R v. International Stock Exchange of the United Kingdom and the Republic of Ireland Ltd, ex parte Else (1982) Ltd* [1993] QB 534 at 551).

Thirdly, the practice of reopening standing at the substantive hearing follows ineluctably from the way in which the sufficiency of a claimant's interest is, according to the *National Federation* case, to be assessed. This aspect of the decision emerges with particular clarity from Lord Wilberforce's speech, in the course of which he explained (at 630) that, in all but the most straightforward of cases, 'the question of sufficient interest can not . . . be considered in the abstract, or as an isolated point: it must be taken together with the legal and factual context'. It was these contextual factors — which included an analysis of the Inland Revenue's statutory functions and the nature and seriousness of the complaint — which ultimately led the House of Lords to conclude that the claimant had failed to establish sufficient interest. However, while the relationship between the merits of the case and the question of standing is one of the prime features of the *National Federation* case, there is some ambiguity as to precisely what this means.

QUESTIONS

- Look again at the speeches in the *National Federation* case. On the approach there adopted, does standing depend on the nature of the illegality alleged (*eg* its gravity), or on whether the alleged illegality can be established?
- Which of these alternatives do you prefer?

The implications of linking standing with merits is explored in our next extract.

....

Cane, 'Standing, Legality and the Limits of Public Law' [1981] PL 322

. . . [It used to be] assumed that standing was an issue quite separate from that of the legality of the respondent's action. Standing, it was thought, was a sort of qualification to argue the question of legality. The word "matter" in rule 3(5) [of RSC Ord 53; see now s 31(3) of the Supreme Court Act 1981] would, on this view, fall to be defined, in any particular case, without reference to whether the challenged decision or action was a breach of duty or an excess or abuse of power, that is, solely in terms of the content of the duty or power. [In the *National Federation* case] Lord Fraser of Tully-belton alone of their Lordships adopted this approach. The majority took a view which, it is suggested, contains within it the seeds of the death of standing as an independent requirement of success in an application for judicial review.

. . . There are suggestions in the judgments of Lords Diplock and Scarman that there is a direct correlation between standing and legality. Illegality generates sufficient interest; no illegality, no sufficient interest. But there are also statements which suggest that the correlation is less direct: the court should intervene at the suit of taxpayers only in cases of breach of duty or illegality which are of "sufficient gravity" [per Lord Wilberforce at 633]; or in cases of continuing "flagrant and serious breaches of the law" [per Lord Diplock at 641]; or in cases of "exceptionally grave or widespread illegality" [per Lord Fraser at 647]; or in cases of failure to perform a duty "because of some grossly improper pressure or motive" [per Lord Roskill at 662]. The structure of the reasoning can be seen very clearly in Lord Roskill's judgment. In his view, questions of the legality or other-wise of the Commissioners' decision were not relevant to the amenability of the Commissioners to judicial review, but they were relevant to the question whether the applicants had sufficient interest. Thus, the Court of Appeal went wrong, not in tying the question of standing to that of illegality, but in accepting the respondent's concession on the question of illegality instead of examining it properly.

There are perhaps two ways of interpreting this reasoning. On the first interpretation it represents a significant shift away from what might be called the "protection of the individual" view of administrative law and the function of the courts in it, to what might be called the "public interest" view of judicial review. On the former view, rules of standing play an important part in defining the role of the courts in judicial review because they determine whether the individual applicant has sufficient at stake to justify the court in listening to his complaint. On the latter view, the main question is whether the respondent body has acted properly in the sense of legally; if it has not, then there is a strong reason to allow an application to review the decision. There are two versions of the "public interest" view. The strong version favours liberalisation of access to the courts to the point where any citizen may apply for review of governmental action, success depending solely on the legality of the action and the justiciability of the issues involved. This version is spoken of as advocating an *actio popularis* or "citizen action"; it entails the abolition of standing rules as traditionally understood.

Under the qualified version, the notion of standing performs a subsidiary function. In some cases, the interest of the applicant may be so tenuous that his application can be dismissed without reference to the question of legality. In other cases the applicant's interest may be so slight that it will not be held sufficient unless he can show some gravely illegal action on the part of the respondent. In yet other cases, the applicant's interest may be sufficiently strong that he will have standing provided that he can show any illegality on the part of the respondent. This version, it might be said, enjoys the worst of all possible worlds. It requires the drawing of a distinction between different types or degrees of interest and yet it effectively destroys standing as a filter by requiring the court, in most cases, to decide all the issues before it as a single whole. It purports to liberalise access to the courts by abolishing technical differences between the standing required for various remedies, but at the same time restricts access to the successful. It lays emphasis on legality but at the same time allows only the "sufficiently interested" to raise the issue.

. . . The "new" law of standing . . ., by focusing so much on the issue of legality, has turned the question of standing very largely into a matter of fact and discretion . . .

. . . It is not impossible to have liberal rules of standing which are couched in terms of classes of applicants such as competitors or neighbours; liberality requires only that the classes be wide, not that every case be treated as a unique one to be decided on its detailed facts. . . .

QUESTIONS

- Is Cane right to criticize the relationship which the *National Federation* case establishes between legality and standing?

- Has English law adopted an approach which might, as Cane puts it, be said to enjoy 'the worst of all possible worlds'?

15.7.4 Representative Standing

Cane, *Administrative Law* (Oxford 2004) at 68, writes that 'the best test of the liberality of a regime of standing rules is how it deals with what might be called "representative standing" '. Elsewhere (see [1995] *PL* 276 at 276) he distinguishes two forms of such standing which are presently of interest: the concept of *associational standing* 'most commonly involves an unincorporated group or a corporation claiming on behalf of (the interests of) identifiable individuals who are its members or whom it claims to represent', while *public interest standing* 'involves an individual, corporation or group purporting to represent "the public interest" rather than the interests of any identified or identifiable individuals'.

The desirability of permitting associational standing may be traced to three particular policy concerns. First, by allowing one representative claimant to litigate the issue on behalf of a number of interested parties, a multiplicity of legal challenges to the same policy, or to decisions stemming from the same policy, is avoided. The resultant advantages — both to the parties and the court, in terms of saved costs and time — are obvious. Secondly, in some circumstances, a representative claimant may be better placed to argue the case than an individual party affected by the decision. This may, for instance, be the case when the representative claimant is a body which is expert in the relevant field. Thirdly, embracing the concept of associational standing may allow matters to be litigated on behalf of groups of individuals who may otherwise — by virtue of factors such as social exclusion or educational disadvantage — be unable or unlikely to have recourse to the courts. Although the question of standing was not directly confronted in *R v. Secretary of State for Social Services, ex parte Child Poverty Action Group* [1990] 2 QB 540, the desirability of permitting claims to be brought on behalf of disenfranchised groups can be seen from the judgment of Woolf LJ, who pointed out (at 546) that 'the issues raised' — concerning the provision of financial support to families on low incomes — 'are agreed to be important in the field of social welfare and not ones which individual claimants for supplementary benefit could be expected to raise'.

Because the concept of public interest standing attributes sufficient interest to litigants unconnected with the matter to which the claim relates, the factors which are said to justify it necessarily consist in different, and broader, arguments. Foremost among these is the idea that some issues are so important — for example, because they appear to disclose particularly serious illegality — that they should not go unchecked by the courts simply because no-one is peculiarly affected by the decision; this line of thinking clearly appealed to the court in *R v. Secretary of State for Foreign and Commonwealth Affairs, ex parte World Development Movement* [1995] 1 WLR 386, which we consider below. The flip-side of this approach is that when persons clearly exist who would, on normal principles, have sufficient interest to challenge a decision, the court will be less inclined to confer public interest standing upon others whose connection with the issue in question is less direct. For example, in *R (Bulger) v. Secretary of State for the Home Department* [2001] EWHC Admin 119 [2001] 3 All ER 449, the father of a boy who was murdered by two children sought to challenge the tariff period (the minimum period of imprisonment that was required for the purposes of retribution and deterrence) set by the Lord Chief Justice. The claimant was found to lack standing, for reasons explained by Rose LJ at [20]:

... [T]he threshold for standing in judicial review has generally been set by the courts at a low level. This, as it seems to me, is because of the importance in public law that someone should be able to call decision-makers to account, lest the rule of law break down and private rights be denied by public bodies . . . But in the present matter the traditional and invariable parties to criminal proceedings, namely the Crown and the defendant, are both able to, and do, challenge those judicial decisions which are susceptible to judicial review . . .

The idea underlying these comments, that it is the function of judicial review to uphold the rule of law as much as to resolve disputes between parties, is considered further below at 15.7.5.

In the context of representative standing, the liberalizing influence of the *National Federation* case — in which Lord Diplock ([1982] AC 617 at 644) went so far as to opine that, in principle, a 'single public-spirited taxpayer' could be granted standing if this was necessary to protect the public interest by vindicating the rule of law — has been keenly felt, and it can now be said with confidence that English courts recognize both associational and public interest standing. However, the progress towards this position was, perhaps inevitably, gradual, and the case of *R v. Secretary of State for the Environment, ex parte Rose Theatre Trust Co* [1990] 1 QB 504 was perceived as something of a set-back. The claimant company was formed for the purpose of preserving the remains of the Rose Theatre, and sought judicial review of the Secretary of State's refusal to list the remains under s 1 of the Ancient Monuments and Archaeological Areas Act 1979. Although permission was granted to the claimant, Schiemann J concluded at the substantive hearing that it lacked standing. He said (at 521):

It was, I think, accepted on behalf of the applicant that the company could have no greater claim to standing than the members of the campaign had before the company was made into the campaign's vehicle. In any event I so hold. It would be absurd if two people, neither of whom had standing could, by an appropriately worded memorandum, incorporate themselves into a company which thereby obtained standing.

This analysis appears to accept the possibility of associational standing, albeit that such standing was not established on the facts. The reason for that failure lies in the fact that none of the individuals for whom the company acted themselves had a sufficient interest in the subject-matter of the claim. It is in this latter point — and, in particular, in the analysis used to assess the sufficiency of the individuals' interest — that the significance of the case lies. Schiemann J appears to have assumed that the individuals — and hence the company representing them — could establish sufficient interest only by demonstrating some personal stake in the listing decision (*eg* that they were peculiarly affected by it). This overlooks the possibility that sufficient interest might instead be established by demonstrating that the importance of the matter means that its litigation is in the public interest. Thus, the rather restrictive *Rose Theatre* decision — which Otton and Sedley JJ refused to follow in *R v. HM Inspectorate of Pollution, ex parte Greenpeace (No 2)* [1994] 4 All ER 329 and *R v. Somerset County Council, ex parte Dixon* [1998] Env LR 111, respectively — seems to acknowledge the possibility that a representative claimant might be clothed with associational standing if it acts for individuals who are personally or peculiarly affected by the decision, while overlooking the possibility that such individuals might in the first place establish the sufficiency of their interest by reference purely to the public interest in litigating the matter.

Some progress towards the recognition of public interest standing was made in the *Greenpeace* case, *op cit*, in which the claimant, an internationally-renowned environmental campaign group, sought (ultimately without success) to challenge a decision about the terms on which a company, BNFL, was permitted to discharge radioactive waste from its Sellafield plant in Cumbria. In deciding that Greenpeace had sufficient interest to bring the claim, Otton J clearly embraced (at 350) the notion of associational standing:

The fact that there are 400,000 supporters in the United Kingdom carries less weight than the fact that 2,500 of them come from the Cumbria region. I would be ignoring the blindingly obvious if I were to disregard the fact that those persons are inevitably concerned about (and have a genuine perception that there is) a danger to their health and safety from any additional discharge of radioactive waste even from testing. I have no doubt that the issues raised by this application are serious and worthy of determination by this court.

However, elsewhere in his judgment, Otton J appeared to go beyond an analysis based on the idea that Greenpeace was acting for local members whose health was allegedly at risk, by observing (at 348) that the issues at stake were said to have potentially wider ramifications:

Greenpeace asserts that it represents a wider public interest. This demonstrates that the complaint is in furtherance of Greenpeace's general campaign against the use of radioactive material and the disposal of radioactive waste.

Although *Greenpeace* provides only tentative support for the existence of a doctrine of public interest standing in English law, much more certain guidance is furnished by the following decision.

....

R v. Secretary of State for Foreign and Commonwealth Affairs, ex parte World Development Movement Ltd [1995] 1 WLR 386
Queen's Bench Division

For the facts, see above at 8.2.3. This extract is concerned only with standing.

Rose LJ

. . . The affidavit of Mr. Jackson, the applicants' campaign co-ordinator, describes the applicant company. It is a non-partisan pressure group, over 20 years old and limited by guarantee. It has an associated charity which receives financial support from all the main United Kingdom development charities, the churches, the European Community and a range of other trusts. About 60 per cent. of its total income comes from members and supporters. The council of the applicants has cross-political party membership, and, indeed, historically, a Member of Parliament from each of the three main political parties has sat on the council. There are 7,000 full voting members throughout the United Kingdom with a total supporter base of some 13,000. There are 200 local groups whose supporters actively campaign through letter writing, lobbying and other democratic means to improve the quantity and quality of British aid to other countries. It conducts research and analysis in relation to aid. It is a founder member of the Independent Group on British Aid, which brings academics and campaigners together. It has pressed the British Government, the European Union, the banks and other businesses for better trade access for developing countries. It is in regular contact with the O.D.A. [the Overseas Development Administration, now the Department for International Development] and has regular meetings with the Minister of that department, and it makes written and oral submissions to a range of select committees in both Houses of Parliament. It has run all-party campaigns against aid cuts in 1987 and 1992.

Internationally, it has official consultative status with U.N.E.S.C.O. [the United Nations Educational, Scientific and Cultural Organization] and has promoted international conferences. It has brought together development groups with the O.E.C.D. [the Organisation for Economic Cooperation and Development]. It tends to attract citizens of the United Kingdom concerned about the role of the United Kingdom Government in relation to the development of countries abroad and the relief of poverty abroad.

Its supporters have a direct interest in ensuring that funds furnished by the United Kingdom are used for genuine purposes, and it seeks to ensure that disbursement of aid budgets is made where that aid is most needed. It seeks, by this application, to represent the interests of people in developing countries who might benefit from funds which otherwise might go elsewhere.

If the applicants have no standing, it is said that no person or body would ensure that powers under the Act of 1980 are exercised lawfully. For the applicants, Mr. Pleming submitted that the respondent himself, in a written statement of 2 March 1994, has expressly accepted that the matter is "clearly of public and parliamentary interest." It cannot be said that the applicants are "busybodies," "cranks" or "mischief-makers." They are a non-partisan pressure group concerned with the misuse of aid money. If there is a public law error, it is difficult to see how else it could be challenged and corrected except by such an applicant . . .

[After citing a number of authorities relied upon by the claimant, his Lordship continued:] The question of lawfulness being for the court, Mr. Pleming submitted that the court in its discretion should accept the standing of the applicants. If they cannot seek relief, he said, who can? Neither a government nor citizen of a foreign country denied aid is, in practical terms, likely to be able to bring such a challenge.

For the respondent, there is no evidential challenge to the applicants' standing. Mr. Richards made submissions on sufficiency of interest, not with a view to preventing the court from considering the substantive issue as to the validity of the decision, but because sufficiency of interest goes to the court's jurisdiction: see *per* Woolf L.J. in *Reg. v. Secretary of State for Social Services, Ex parte Child Poverty Action Group* [1990] 2 Q.B. 540, 556E–F. The applicants, Mr. Richards submitted, are at the outer limits of standing. He submitted, and indeed Mr. Pleming accepted, that neither the applicants, nor any of its individual members, have any direct personal interest in funding under the Act of 1980, but they seek to act in the interest of potential recipients of aid overseas. Mr. Richards submitted that this is too remote an interest to be sufficient, and he contrasted Greenpeace members, some of whom, as Otton J. pointed out [in the passage from page 350 of the report, set out above], were liable to be personally directly affected by radioactive discharge.

Mr. Richards accepted that the requirements of standing will vary from case to case and that the court may accord standing to someone who would not otherwise qualify, where exceptionally grave or widespread illegality is alleged . . . He referred to the speeches of both Lord Wilberforce, at p. 633B, and Lord Fraser of Tullybelton, at p. 646G, in *R v. Inland Revenue Commissioners, Ex parte National Federation of Self-Employed and Small Businesses Ltd.* [1982] A.C. 617 to the effect that a United Kingdom taxpayer's interest, which is no more than that of taxpayers in general, is insufficient to confer standing, save in an extreme case. If no United Kingdom taxpayer could raise the matter, this not being an exceptional case, the applicants, submitted Mr. Richards, cannot be in a better position.

. . . For my part, I accept that standing (albeit decided in the exercise of the court's discretion . . .) goes to jurisdiction, as Woolf L.J. said. But I find nothing in *Reg. v. Inland Revenue Commissioners, Ex parte National Federation of Self-Employed and Small Businesses Ltd.* [1982] A.C. 617 to deny standing to these applicants. The authorities referred to seem to me to indicate an increasingly liberal approach to standing on the part of the courts during the last 12 years. It is also clear from *Ex parte National Federation of Self-Employed and Small Businesses Ltd.* that standing should not be treated as a preliminary issue, but must be taken in the legal and factual context of the whole case: see *per* Lord Wilberforce, at p. 630D, Lord Fraser, at p. 645D and Lord Scarman, at p. 653F.

Furthermore, the merits of the challenge are an important, if not dominant, factor when considering standing . . .

Leaving merits aside for a moment, there seem to me to be a number of factors of significance in the present case: the importance of vindicating the rule of law, as Lord Diplock emphasised [1982] A.C. 617; the importance of the issue raised, as in Ex parte Child Poverty Action Group [1990] 2 Q.B. 540; the likely absence of any other responsible challenger, as in Ex parte Child Poverty Action Group and Ex parte Greenpeace Ltd. (No 2) [1994] 4 All E.R. 329; the nature of the breach of duty against which relief is sought (see per Lord Wilberforce, at p. 630D, in Ex parte National Federation of Self-Employed and Small Businesses Ltd.); and the prominent role of these applicants in giving advice, guidance and assistance with regard to aid: see Ex parte Child Poverty Action Group [1990] 2 Q.B. 540, 546H. All, in my judgment, point, in the present case, to the conclusion that the applicants here do have a sufficient interest in the matter to which the application relates within section 31(3) of the Supreme Court Act 1981 . . .

This decision unequivocally recognizes that standing may be conferred upon a claimant because it is in the public interest that the matters which it seeks to raise are adjudicated upon by the court, and similarly placed claimants have established standing on public interest grounds in subsequent cases (see, eg, R (Howard League for Penal Reform) v. Secretary of State for the Home Department [2002] EWHC 2497 (Admin) [2003] 1 FLR 484). The connection drawn in World Development Movement between the importance of the issue and the standing of the claimant is entirely unsurprising: it is inherent in the concept of public interest standing that sufficient interest may be generated by reference to the significance of the matter at stake, and this builds upon the contextual approach to standing favoured in the National Federation case. It appears, however, that, alongside the importance of the issue, objectively judged, the court will also address the subjective question of the claimant's motivation: in R (Feakins) v. Secretary of State for the Environment, Food and Rural Affairs [2003] EWCA Civ 1546 [2004] 1 WLR 1761 at [23], Dyson LJ considered that

if a claimant seeks to challenge a decision in which he has no private law interest, it is difficult to conceive of circumstances in which the court will accord him standing, even where there is a public interest in testing the lawfulness of the decision, if the claimant is acting out of ill-will or for some other improper purpose. It is an abuse of process to permit a claimant to bring a claim in such circumstances. If the real reason why a claimant wishes to challenge a decision in which, objectively, there is a public interest is not that he has a genuine concern about the decision, but some other reason, then that is material to the question whether he should be accorded standing.

QUESTION

- If a matter is sufficiently important to be capable of litigation on public interest grounds by a claimant with no private interest, should the subjective motivation of the claimant who actually comes forward be relevant?

Before leaving the subject of representative standing, it is necessary to consider how the extent of this concept is to be determined. As far as public interest standing is concerned, a number of limiting factors are enumerated in final paragraph of the extract above from Rose LJ's judgment in World Development Movement. Many of those factors, such as the 'importance of the issue' and the 'likely absence of any other responsible challenger', are directly or indirectly related to the overarching objective of permitting a challenge, by conferring standing on the claimant, if the public interest so requires. However, it is perhaps less easy to understand why Rose LJ attached weight to the status of the claimant, in particular its considerable expertise in the field of international development. What role does this factor play — can a lack of expertise preclude a public interest challenge and, if so, why? The expertise of claimants seeking standing on public interest grounds has been emphasized in a number of cases. For instance, in the *Howard League* case, *op cit* at [2]–[3], Munby J, in accepting that the claimant had sufficient interest, noted that its 'history and credentials need no introduction. It undoubtedly is, as it claims to be, the leading non-governmental organisation in this country concerned with penal issues and policy'. The relevance of the status and expertise of public interest claimants was explained in the following terms by Otton J in *R* v. *HM Inspectorate of Pollution, ex parte Greenpeace (No. 2)* [1994] 4 All ER 329 at 350:

BNFL rightly acknowledges the national and international standing of Greenpeace and its integrity. So must I. I have not the slightest reservation that Greenpeace is an entirely responsible and respected body with a genuine concern for the environment . . .

It seems to me that if I were to deny standing to Greenpeace those it represents might not have an effective way to bring the issues before the court. There would have to be an application either by an individual employee of BNFL or a near neighbour. In this case it is unlikely that either would be able to command the expertise which is at the disposal of Greenpeace. Consequently a less well-informed challenge might be mounted which would stretch unnecessarily the court's resources and which would not afford the court the assistance it requires in order to do justice between the parties.

QUESTION

- To what extent should courts be influenced by the status and expertise of the claimant when considering the question of public interest standing?

Turning to associational standing, it might be thought that an important limiting factor would be the relationship between the representative claimant and the constituency on behalf of which it acts. Cane [1995] *PL* 276 at 278 develops this point in the following terms:

A litigant who claims to represent the interests of identifiable individuals cannot do so convincingly unless there is a reasonably effective mechanism by which the representative can ascertain what the represented believe their interests to be. In order to be a legitimate representative, the claimant must be able to convince the court that the views put forward by it are a fair reflection of the views of the represented. In other words, the represented must have some degree of control over or some "democratic stake" (as I will call it) in the conduct of the representative. Without some such nexus between the represented and the representative, the claimant may simply be expressing a "well-informed point of view" [*Health Research Group* v. *Kennedy* (1979) 82 FRD 21]. One exception to this general principle must be recognised, however. A claimant who is the beneficiary of a statutory grant of standing to represent the interests of specific individuals may legitimately do so without consulting the represented, unless the statute requires consultation. A statutory grant of representative status [for instance, to the Equal Opportunities Commission, as recognised in *R* v. *Secretary of State for Employment, ex parte Equal Opportunities Commission* [1995] 1 AC 1] provides the legitimacy which self-appointed representatives may lack.

A strong argument in favour of recognizing the need for a democratic nexus is outlined by Miles [2000] *CLJ* 133 at 148–150 (see excerpt below at 15.7.5), who observes that, on one view, the autonomy of victims of maladministration requires that they should be able to choose whether the matter is litigated. However, we will see that this must be set against the competing view which holds that there is a general interest in good administration which may be threatened if representative claimants are barred from litigating in the place of victims who are unwilling to do so.

In fact, English courts tend not to scrutinize in any great detail the relationship between representative claimants and those for whom they supposedly speak. For instance, in *R v. Secretary of State for Social Services, ex parte Child Poverty Action Group* [1990] 2 QB 540, the claimant sought to speak on behalf of families on low incomes who were affected by the administrative arrangements being challenged. Although (for reasons that are presently unimportant) he was not required to decide the question of standing, Woolf LJ (at 547) largely took for granted the fact that the claimant could represent benefit claimants, without considering whether any sort of relationship existed between the CPAG and its constituency.

QUESTION

- Is Cane right to argue that a 'democratic nexus' must exist if standing on an associational basis is to be acknowledged?

Finally, the recommendations in the Law Commission report (at [5.16]–[5.22]) should be noted. A 'two track' system was suggested: first, standing would be enjoyed by those 'personally affected' by the decision; secondly, there should be a 'discretionary track' covering, *inter alia*, public interest challenges. Although the Law Commission agreed with consultees that factors such as the importance of the legal point, the possibility of challenge in other proceedings, the allocation of scarce judicial resources, and the concern that courts should have before them the points of view of those most directly affected may be relevant in public interest cases, it did not recommend that such criteria should be enshrined in the rules of court, preferring instead to leave judges with a 'broad discretion'.

15.7.5 The Foundations of the Law of Standing

The law of standing is shaped by, and therefore reflects, the position which a legal system adopts in relation to the nature and function of public law adjudication. These themes are explored at length and in comparative perspective by Feldman (1992) 55 *MLR* 44; in this section, however, we focus on how the standing rules currently applied in English administrative law are informed by two particular foundational issues: the way in which public law norms are conceptualized, and the function of the courts in public law cases.

First, then, how should we characterize public law norms such as the rules of natural justice and the principle that decision-makers must act in accordance with the terms and purposes of enabling legislation? Do we all have the 'right' to be treated consistently with these principles — a 'right' which, if we so desire, we might choose to waive? Or are the principles of administrative law public standards which government must not be allowed to fall short of, irrespective of whether the individual 'victim' of maladministration is minded to complain? These questions raise the distinction between individualist and communitarian characterisations of public law principles; the following excerpt explores the nature of this distinction, and explains why it has important implications for our approach to standing.

Miles, 'Standing under the Human Rights Act 1998: Theories of Rights Enforcement and the Nature of Public Law Adjudication' [2000] CLJ 133

. . . The individualist model asserts that no third party, however expert, should be able to assert the rights of competent victims in their place without their express consent to action. Individual or human rights may be viewed as akin to private law contract, tort or property rights in the sense that a form of "privity" precludes third parties from complaining about rights infringements. This position derives from a focus on the relationship between victims and rights violators which "privatises" their dispute. No *objective* interest in the conduct of the violator which could find expression in a right of a third party to bring the matter before a court is recognised, since no wrong is perpetrated except against the victim, and so only he or she is entitled to complain. And if the victim chooses not to do so, no one else can. A striking example is provided by a recent US case, *Whitmore* v. *Arkansas* [(1990) 110 S Ct 1717], where a death row inmate was denied standing to challenge the pending execution of another prisoner who had forgone his right of appeal, in part on the basis that the prisoner had voluntarily waived his rights . . .

It is inevitable that where the rights of several individuals are infringed by a similar measure, an action by one victim impugning that measure will have repercussions for the others, even where those others would rather the matter had never been raised. To that extent, the autonomy of the others, in the form of their desire that a rights violation affecting them be not complained of, is necessarily overridden. However, it is argued that where the unwanted challenge is mounted by an *ideological group*, the autonomy of the victims should preclude the action. The victim-applicant has a personal stake in the dispute giving him a moral and legal right to complain, whatever the impact of his action on other victims might be. By contrast, the (paternalistic) belief of a third party that his or her actions will help a certain class of person should not be allowed to override the wishes of those intended beneficiaries. Since it is often difficult to know whether the beneficiaries of the proposed litigation will approve of the action, it is better as a default position to bar such actions. The burden should be on the applicant to show why the case should go ahead. And on this view, in the absence of positive evidence of victim approval of the action, the applicant's paternalistic, ideological concerns are not in themselves sufficient to justify litigation.

. . . The communitarian model rejects adherence to victim autonomy as the dominant concern. This model focuses not on the specific interest of the individual victim in seeing government illegality against him or her checked, but on a broader public interest in lawful government. It is interesting to note at the outset that even some writers who argue essentially for an individualistic model of standing make an exception for cases where adherence to that view would 'prevent an issue of national interest from coming under judicial scrutiny' [Hilson and Cram (1996) 16 *LS* 1].

. . . [On the communitarian view,] [w]here a public authority has arguably breached a fundamental right or otherwise exceeded its powers, the possibility of judicial review proceedings being initiated should not be barred by the victim's refusal to seek relief. On the communitarian view, the matter is not one exclusively between victim and state, such that the victim should have the exclusive right to determine whether proceedings are brought, since the nature of the alleged illegality is not the breach of a "contract" concluded privately between those parties, but the transgression of limits on the authority's power imposed as a matter of public importance, compliance with which an individual victim should have no authority subsequently to waive. Even if the victim's consent to the impugned action of the public authority *at the time the action was taken* would have rendered that action lawful . . ., the failure to obtain *that* consent cannot be retrospectively cured by the victim's subsequent unwillingness to bring proceedings; public authorities should not be allowed to ignore legal limitations on their powers, banking on the possibility of belated waiver of compliance with those limits by the victim. The subjection of governmental power to objective controls, prescribed in advance by law, reflects a system's adherence to the concept and culture of limited government, regarded *as a matter of principle* as vitally important to society at large — not least where the limits in question ensure the observance of fundamental rights and freedoms — and not only as a matter that concerns those individuals directly affected by the exercise of governmental power. It would accordingly be inappropriate to allow victims, *via* narrow standing rules, in effect to veto litigation aimed at identifying whether government action has contravened those legal limits from proceeding. The victim's autonomy should not be afforded primacy. Hence the communitarian view recognises a collective public right, given effect by generous standing rules, to have the government held legally accountable for its actions. The only right that the victim has here is to be treated by government in accordance with the law, whether he wants such treatment or not . . .

QUESTIONS

- Which of these two views do you prefer?
- To what extent does Cane's suggested requirement (see above at 15.7.4) of a 'democratic nexus' between claimants seeking standing on associational grounds and their constituencies undermine a communitarian approach?

The fact that English law recognizes limits on standing suggests that the approach which it adopts cannot be characterized as fully communitarian in the above sense. Nevertheless, it is clear that elements of that model are to be found in the case law, as the following dictum of Sedley J in *R* v. *Somerset County Council, ex parte Dixon* [1998] Env LR 111 at 121 demonstrates:

Public law is not at base about rights, even though abuses of power may and often do invade private rights; it is about wrongs — that is to say misuses of public power; and the courts have always been alive to the fact that a person or organisation with no particular stake in the issue or outcome may, without in any sense being a mere meddler, wish and be well placed to call the attention of the court to an apparent misuse of public power. If an arguable case of such misuse can be made out on an application for leave, the court's only concern is to ensure that it is not being done for an ill motive. It is if, on a substantive hearing, the abuse of power is made out that everything relevant to the applicant's standing will be weighed up, whether with regard to the grant or simply to the form of relief.

Rules of standing also reflect a particular view about the function of public law adjudication. According to the *dispositive* justice model, the role of the courts is to resolve disputes between the parties: such a view fits with a narrow doctrine of standing which permits only the victim of maladministration to raise the matter in court. Miles, *op cit* at 153–155, distinguishes the *expository* justice model, and the wider approach to standing which it commends, in the following terms:

Under this model . . . there is no automatic reason to insist that individual victims alone be permitted to invoke the jurisdiction of the court. If the function of the court is not simply to determine disputes brought by victims but generally to expound the law, then there is no *necessary* constitutional reason (certainly not one derived from a view about the limits of the judicial function) to insist on victim standing . . . [On this view,] in so far as there is a danger that insistence on victim standing may *impede* sound exposition of the law . . ., then standing rules *should* be devised in such a way as to permit a broader range of applicants to move the court. It may be that the only acceptable standing rule in this model would be no standing rule at all, or at least a very flexible one, permitting any case to proceed if it raised a serious point which seemed to have substantive merit, despite the lack of close connection between applicant and issue.

As well as impacting upon how the law of standing is constructed, the choice between dispositive and expository models of adjudication also fundamentally informs the courts' attitude to reviewing questions which have become moot. The House of Lords' willingness to countenance judicial review in such circumstances in *R* v. *Secretary of State for the Home Department, ex parte Salem* [1999] AC 450 (see above at 15.5.4) suggests that public law adjudication in England and Wales transcends dispute resolution and is influenced, at least to some extent, by the expository model of adjudication.

15.7.6 Standing in Human Rights Cases

Article 34 of the European Convention on Human Rights provides that:

The Court may receive applications from any person, non-governmental organisation or group of individuals claiming to be the victim of a violation by one of the High Contracting Parties of the rights set forth in the Convention or the protocols thereto. The High Contracting Parties undertake not to hinder in any way the effective exercise of this right.

The use of the term 'victim' suggests an approach to standing which is very different from that which applies in English law. In particular, it implies that only those who are *actually affected* by alleged breaches of the Convention may apply to the Court. In fact, the Strasbourg jurisprudence accords a rather broader interpretation to Article 34. For example, it is accepted that an *indirect victim* of a breach of the Convention may institute proceedings: in *W* v. *United Kingdom* (1983) 32 DR 190 it was decided that a widow had standing to complain that the United Kingdom had taken inadequate steps under Article 2 to safeguard the right to life of her husband, who had been killed by terrorists. The Strasbourg case law also recognizes that *potential victims* may have standing to challenge the compatibility of national laws with the Convention. For example, in *Norris* v. *Ireland* (1991) 13 EHRR 186, the applicant wished to argue that the existence in the Republic of Ireland of legislation which criminalized gay sex constituted a breach of his Article 8 right to respect for his private life. The applicant was ultimately successful before the Court, but had first to establish that he was a victim. The Court held, at [33], that the *possibility* of prosecution was sufficient to permit the applicant to bring his case:

Admittedly, it appears that there have been no prosecutions under the Irish legislation in question during the relevant period except where minors were involved or the acts were committed in public or without consent. It may be inferred from this that, at the present time, the risk of prosecution in the applicant's case is minimal. However, there is no stated policy on the part of the prosecuting authorities not to enforce the law in this respect. A law which remains on the statute book, even though it is not enforced in a particular class of cases for a considerable time, may be applied again in such cases at any time, if for example there is a change of policy. The applicant can therefore be said to "run the risk of being directly affected" by the legislation in question.

In conceptual terms the applicant in *Norris* was *in fact* a victim, since the chilling effect of the legislation was considered to be a breach of Article 8. Nevertheless, the practical effect of this judgment is that a category of potential victims is recognized who are entitled to apply to the Strasbourg Court notwithstanding that no action has (yet) been taken which concretely interferes with or precludes the exercise of their Convention rights.

Although recognition of indirect and potential victims leads to a rather more liberal approach than that which is suggested by the bare text of Article 34, the victim requirement nevertheless substantially restricts the concept of standing which the European Court applies. It is hardly surprising, for example, that the Court concluded in *Norris*, at [30], that the victim test could not be stretched so as to 'fund an action in the nature of an *actio popularis*'. In particular, it is clear that there is little, if any, scope for arguing that a concerned citizen, a public-spirited taxpayer or an expert group can bring themselves within the test.

The absence in the Convention system of public interest standing evidences an ethos — not just in relation to standing itself, but also extending to the wider issues considered in the foregoing section — which is markedly different from that which exists in English law. This is perhaps unsurprising. The ECHR was drafted with the relationship between the citizen and the state in post-war Europe firmly in mind, and its purpose was, and remains, to protect individuals against abuses of power which undermine their basic rights. Within this context, it seems natural to characterize human rights in largely individualistic terms, and the role of the ECtHR primarily in terms of dispute resolution. It would be wrong, however, to present these conclusions in absolute terms: for instance, the Court is able under Article 37 to continue with its inquiry even if the applicant no longer wishes to pursue the matter, and showed itself willing to do so in *Tyrer* v. *United Kingdom* (1978) 2 EHRR 1 in which the practice of birching on the Isle of Mann was found inconsistent with Article 3 following the withdrawal of the applicant from the proceedings. This discloses at least a trace of the expository justice model.

Nevertheless, there are very clear differences between the English and European approaches to standing. In light of this, it may have been expected that, when the United Kingdom rendered Convention rights enforceable in national courts by means of the Human Rights Act 1998, the liberal domestic rules of standing would have been made applicable in all cases, including those concerning the ECHR. The fact that Article 34 adopts a narrower approach would have been no bar to such a solution, since it is of course always open to individual states to confer a *higher* level of protection on human rights than that which is provided for by the Convention, whether by means of defining the individual rights more broadly in national law or making more generous provision for their vindication in municipal courts. Such an approach was not, however, taken in relation to the standing test.

....

Human Rights Act 1998

7—(1) A person who claims that a public authority has acted (or proposes to act) in a way which is made unlawful by section 6(1) may —

    (a) bring proceedings against the authority under this Act in the appropriate court or tribunal, or

    (b) rely on the Convention right or rights concerned in any legal proceedings,

but only if he is (or would be) a victim of the unlawful act . . .

(3) If the proceedings are brought on an application for judicial review, the applicant is to be taken to have a sufficient interest in relation to the unlawful act only if he is, or would be, a victim of that act . . .

(7) For the purposes of this section, a person is a victim of an unlawful act only if he would be a victim for the purposes of Article 34 of the Convention if proceedings were brought in the European Court of Human Rights in respect of that act.

The effect of these provisions is that a claimant can only argue in judicial review proceedings that a public authority has acted contrary to s 6(1) of the HRA — that is, 'in a way which is incompatible with a Convention right' — if he is first able to establish that he is a 'victim' in the Article 34 sense. These arrangements, taken at face value, are problematic. It would appear that two distinct tests of standing now coexist in English public law: the liberal 'sufficient interest' test applies when a claimant wishes to allege that a public authority has acted to contrary to the established principles of administrative law (*eg* that it acted contrary to natural justice or *Wednesbury* unreasonably), while claimants seeking to establish a breach of Convention rights must bring themselves within the much narrower confines of the 'victim' criterion. From this foundational problem, two further difficulties follow. First, it seems inconsistent with a coherent system of public law to divide the law of standing in this manner, particularly in light of the fact that, as we saw above, the concept of standing is rooted in a deeper philosophy about the nature of public law norms and adjudication. Secondly, and more prosaically, this approach, if applied rigidly, would produce absurd outcomes: for instance, a pressure group — which may have sufficient interest, but would not be a victim — would be allowed to impugn administrative action on traditional grounds but not on Convention grounds.

In fact, for two reasons (considered further by Elliott [2001] *CLJ* 301 at 325–334 and Fordham [2000] *JR* 262), this problem is more apparent than real. First, there is a clear relationship between some provisions of the Convention and some long-established heads of judicial review: many of those connections have already been explored, and we refer back to our discussion (in ch 9) of the relationship between *Wednesbury* and proportionality and (in chs 10 and 11) of the influence of Article 6 on common law principles like fairness and bias. Thus we can see that certain ECHR principles are gradually being absorbed into general administrative law — for example, it will be recalled (see above at 9.3.4) that the human rights points in *R (Daly)* v. *Secretary of State for the Home Department* [2001] UKHL 26 [2001] 2 AC 532 could (according to Lord Bingham at [23]) be decided by reference exclusively to the common law, albeit that recourse to the Convention would have produced the same result. This suggests that at least some human rights arguments can be canvassed without any reliance on the 1998 Act or the Convention — and, therefore, without any need to establish victim status.

The difficulty in relying upon this process of absorption to circumvent the victim test is that its scope is uncertain: the point has certainly *not* been reached at which it may be said that the common law is shot through with all of the Convention rights to the extent that the Human Rights Act is redundant. However, even when it proves necessary to invoke the Act, it is arguable that the victim test may usually be avoided. Section 7(1) requires victim status to be established only if the claimant wishes to argue that a public authority has acted (or proposes to act) in a way which is made unlawful *by s 6(1)*. However, in the vast majority of situations, a breach of the ECHR may be established in judicial review proceedings without any reliance on s 6(1) — and, therefore, without reference to the victim test. This is the case whenever the claimant seeks to establish that a decision-maker exercising *statutory power* acted incompatibly with the Convention rights. Central to this analysis is s 3(1) of the Human Rights Act, which provides that, 'So far as it is possible to do so, primary legislation and subordinate legislation must be read and given effect in a way which is compatible with the Convention rights.' Section 3(1) therefore requires courts to read the Convention rights as limits upon statutory discretionary powers — as Feldman (in Forsyth (ed), *Judicial Review and the Constitution* (Oxford 2000), at 266) put it:

. . . [T]he Human Rights Act 1998 will generate new developments in substantive review which all have either express or clearly implied authority from Parliament . . . So far as the Convention rights open a new direction in judicial review, the path-finding judges will be able to legitimate their creativeness by referring to a sound foundation in the classical doctrine of *ultra vires*.

It is therefore arguably open to claimants to found human rights claims on s 3(1) rather than s 6(1) by contending not that the public authority has acted in a manner made unlawful by the latter, but rather that, *ab initio*, it lacked the power to act in the manner complained of because, pursuant to s 3(1), the Convention rights constitute implied statutory restrictions upon its discretionary power. The House of Lords recognized the force of this reasoning in *R (Rusbridger)* v. *Attorney-General* [2003] UKHL 38 [2004] 1 AC 357 at [21]. This analysis, however, will not avail a claimant seeking to circumvent the victim test when *non-statutory powers* are challenged on Convention grounds, since it is clear that s 3(1), which governs the interpretation of primary and subordinate legislation, can have no application in respect of such powers.

15.8 Concluding Remarks

As this chapter has demonstrated, the restrictions on obtaining relief via judicial review are many and various. Two broad themes, however, may be drawn out. First, there is a strong policy in favour of making judicial review available: witness, for instance, the liberalization of the law of standing and the courts' reluctance to allow legislative displacement of their supervisory jurisdiction. Secondly, however, there is clear recognition — evidenced by, for instance, the introduction of the Pre-Action Protocol, the reform of the permission stage, and the exhaustion of alternative remedies principle — that it is necessary to relieve pressure on the Administrative Court by encouraging the resolution of disputes otherwise than by recourse to judicial review. Taken together, these two strands reflect the contemporary view that the possibility of judicial review of government action by an independent judiciary is a crucially important constitutional longstop, but that administrative justice can, and should, also be delivered by other means. This is a matter to which we return in chs 18–20, in which we consider how administrative justice may be promoted otherwise than through court proceedings.

FURTHER RESOURCES

Andenas and Fairgreave (eds), *Judicial Review in International Perspective* (The Hague 2000), chs 19 (Wade), 20 (Beloff) and 22 (Hare)

Bamforth and Leyland (eds), *Public Law in a Multi-Layered Constitution* (Oxford 2003), ch 15 (Miles)

Bowman, *Review of the Crown Office List* (London 2000) (available in summary form at *www.dca.gov.uk/civil/bowman2000/summary2000.htm*)

Bridges, Meszaros and Sunkin, 'Regulating the Judicial Review Caseload' [2000] *PL* 651

Civil Procedure Rules *www.dca.gov.uk/civil/procrules_fin/*

Cornford and Sunkin, 'The Bowman Report, Access and the Recent Reforms of the Judicial Review Procedure' [2001] *PL* 11

DCA Consultation Paper, *Statutory Appeals and Statutory Reviews: Proposals for Rationalising Procedures* (London 2004) *www.dca.gov.uk/consult/statutory/statappeals.htm*

Feldman, 'Public Interest Litigation and Constitutional Theory in Comparative Perspective' (1992) 55 *MLR* 44

Forsyth and Hare (eds), *The Golden Metwand and the Crooked Cord* (Oxford 1998), at 221–252 (Beatson) and 267–295 (Beloff)

Law Com No 226, *Administrative Law: Judicial Review and Statutory Appeals* (London 1994), Parts IV, V, VIII and XII

Lewis, 'The Exhaustion of Alternative Remedies in Administrative Law' [1992] *CLJ* 138

Lewis, *Judicial Remedies in Public Law* (London 2004), chs 9–11

Woolf, 'The Rule of Law and a Change in Constitution' [2004] *CLJ* 317

Pre-Action Protocol *www.dca.gov.uk/civil/procrules_fin/contents/protocols/prot_jrv.htm*

16 LIABILITY OF PUBLIC AUTHORITIES AND CROWN PROCEEDINGS

16.1 General Matters

16.1.1 Introduction

This chapter will consider, *inter alia*, the liability of public authorities in Tort, Contract, and Restitution, and we shall assume a certain familiarity on the part of the reader with the general operation of at least the first two of these subjects. When a public authority is sued in such a case, the English tradition has been (in contradistinction to that found in, for example, France) for the action to be brought in the ordinary courts and for it to be resolved under the general doctrines applicable to those branches of the law: in this country there is no separate '*droit administratif*' applicable in a separate system of courts. However, this does not mean that no particular difficulties arise when public authorities are sued, and such difficulties will be the main concern of this chapter.

16.1.2 Relationship with Judicial Review

There are various aspects to the relationship between the materials in this chapter and actions directly involving the grounds of review that have been explored earlier in this book. On occasions an action for damages will boil down to a decision about one of the grounds of review: this is termed collateral challenge (see above at 3.4). A good example is provided by *Cooper* v. *Wandsworth District Board of Works* (1863) 14 CBNS 180 (see above at 11.2.1) where the trespass action raised the question of the applicability of the rules of natural justice. Although a discretionary remedy such as an injunction may be in issue in, for example, a claim in the tort of trespass or nuisance, it should be noted that where damages are sought, this will take away the court's discretion at the stage of the remedy.

A second point to note is that since 1977 it has been possible for damages, and, since

1 May 2004, for restitution and the recovery of a sum due, to be obtained in the claim for judicial review procedure (see now s 31(4) of the Supreme Court Act 1981 and CPR 54.3(2)).

Thirdly — and this is a particularly important point — the grounds of review which we have explored have involved *ultra vires* activity (subject to the question of whether there is still any life left in the doctrine of non-jurisdictional error of law on the face of the record). Whereas it is well-established that *ultra vires* activity by a public authority will not *per se* give rise to an action for damages, the concept's relevance to actions for damages is, as we shall see, more complicated.

16.1.3 The Meaning of 'the Crown' in this Context

Although references to the Crown can be to the monarch personally, we shall generally refer to it as covering the whole apparatus of central government. The Crown, in this wide sense, has legal personality as a corporation sole (but note Lord Simon's reference to it being a corporation aggregate in *Town Investments Ltd* v. *Department of the Environment* [1978] AC 359 at 400): this issue will be mentioned again when the Crown's contractual capacity is considered.

We have already paid some attention to the notion of the Crown when considering the questions of injunctive relief against the Crown and Crown servants and of the contempt jurisdiction (see 13.2.3 where *In re M* was considered). In *Town Investments Ltd* v. *Department of the Environment* [1978] AC 359 at 380–381, Lord Diplock (with the agreement of Lords Simon, Kilbrandon, and Edmund-Davies) opined that referring to executive and legislative acts as those of the 'Crown' is archaic; he preferred the term 'government', arguing that it is

appropriate to embrace both collectively and individually all of the Ministers of the Crown and parliamentary secretaries under whose direction the administrative work of government is carried on by the civil servants employed in the various government departments . . . Executive acts of government that are done by any of them are acts done by "the Crown" in the fictional sense in which that expression is now used in English public law.

As Wade and Forsyth, *Administrative Law* (Oxford, 2004) at 46, n 6, have pointed out, however, *M* distinguished between the Crown and its officers, and they are critical of contrary comments in *Town Investments*. Note also *Pearce* v. *Secretary of State for Defence* [1988] AC 755 where it was stated in the Court of Appeal that in *Town Investments* the House of Lords were not called upon to decide the meaning of the phrase 'the Crown' in the context of the Crown Proceedings Act 1947.

16.2 Tort

16.2.1 Liability in Tort Generally

Some torts (*eg* trespass: see the *Cooper* case, mentioned above) can be committed by both public and private bodies, but others (such as misfeasance in public office) can be committed only where there is some appropriate public element. Although the existence of the latter category of torts may seem to suggest that public bodies are subject to more extensive duties in this sphere, courts are on some occasions faced with an argument that the normal operation of torts in the former category should be altered in some way so as to provide greater protection for a public body.

16.2.2 The Crown's Position in Tort

Prior to 1947, the Crown could not be sued in tort, but the passing of the Crown Proceedings Act in that year altered the position.

Crown Proceedings Act 1947

2—(1) Subject to the provisions of this Act, the Crown shall be subject to all those liabilities in tort to which, if it were a person of full age and capacity, it would be subject—

    (a) in respect of torts committed by its servants or agents;

    (b) in respect of any breach of those duties which a person owes to his servants or agents at common law by reason of being their employer: and

    (c) in respect of any breach of the duties attaching at common law to the ownership, occupation, possession or control of property.

Provided that no proceedings shall lie against the Crown by virtue of paragraph (a) of this subsection in respect of any act or omission of a servant of the Crown unless the act or omission would apart from the provisions of this Act have given rise to a cause of action in tort against that sservant or agent or his estate.

(2) Where the Crown is bound by a statutory duty which is binding also upon persons other than the Crown and its officers, then, subject to the provisions of this Act, the Crown shall, in respect of a failure to comply with that duty, be subject to all those liabilities in tort (if any) to which it would be so subject if it were a private person of full age and capacity . . .

(5) No proceedings shall lie against the Crown by virtue of this section in respect of anything done or omitted to be done by any person while discharging or purporting to discharge any responsibilities of a judicial nature vested in him, or any responsibilities which he has in connection with the execution of judicial process . . .

38—(2) In this Act, except in so far as the context otherwise requires or it is otherwise expressly provided, the following expressions have the meanings hereby respectively assigned to them, that is to say—

"Agent", when used in relation to the Crown, includes an independent contractor employed by the Crown; . . .

"Officer", in relation to the Crown, includes any servant of His Majesty, and accordingly (but without prejudice to the generality of the foregoing provision) includes a Minister of the Crown [and a member of the Scottish Executive]: . . .

40—(1) Nothing in this Act shall apply to proceedings by or against, or authorise proceedings in tort to be brought against, His Majesty in His private capacity . . .

An interesting feature of the 1947 Act was highlighted as follows by Sedley LJ (delivering the Court of Appeal's judgment) in *Chagos Islanders* v. *Attorney-General* [2004] EWCA Civ 997 at [20]:

. . . [T]he 1947 Act does not work by making the state a potential tortfeasor: it works by making the Crown vicariously liable for the torts of its servants. It has only been with the enactment of the Human Rights Act 1998 that the Crown, in the form of a 'public authority', has acquired a primary liability for violating certain rights.

The 'State' can be a wider concept than the 'Crown' but Sedley LJ pointed out that at common law the *State* had no liability in tort for its servants. However, he also acknowledged that the problem does not arise if the limb of the State in question happens to have a legal corporate capacity, one example he gave being the Bank of England; nevertheless, he also pointed out that, with the exception of cases governed by the Human Rights Act 1998, the Crown is still in the pre-1947 position that in private law it can do no wrong.

QUESTION

- What is the relationship between Sedley LJ's views above and s 2(2) of the Crown Proceedings Act 1947?

16.2.3 Breach of Statutory Duty

The action for damages for breach of statutory duty is a well-recognized tort. It is a potential cause of action against private bodies upon whom a statutory duty has been imposed as well as public bodies, but is more likely to figure in a case involving the latter.

Section 2(2) of the Crown Proceedings Act 1947 (set out above at 16.2.2) deals with the Crown's liability in this tort. However, the general doctrine that the Crown is not bound by statutes unless this is a matter of express wording or necessary implication may curtail its liability, as may the requirement in s 2(2) that the statute be binding on persons other than the Crown. See generally Williams, *Crown Proceedings* (London 1948) at 47–49.

16.2.4 The Search for Legislative Intention

The key feature of the availability of a cause of action for damages for breach of statutory duty is how the courts interpret the legislative body's intention, *ie* whether they think that body intended to create a civil cause of action. On occasions the matter is simple as the intention to create or to deny this may be specifically addressed in the legislation: where this is not the case the question is no easy one. On the basis of cases such as *Ferguson v. Earl of Kinnoull* (1842) 9 Cl & Fin 251, however, it can be said that where there is a public duty of a *ministerial* character (*ie* one involving no discretion or choice), then an action will lie and the court is not concerned with statutory interpretation: see Wade and Forsyth, *Administrative Law* (Oxford 2004) at 758–760. Nevertheless, the principle does not seem to have been put to use in recent times in actions for damages for breach of statutory duty; here, the search for legislative intention has been paramount, an issue to which attention must now be turned.

X (Minors) v. *Bedfordshire County Council* [1995] 2 AC 633
House of Lords

Lord Browne-Wilkinson

My Lords, in each of these five appeals the plaintiffs by their statements of claim allege they have been injured by public authorities in the carrying out of functions imposed upon them by statute. The defendants have applied to strike out the claims on the grounds that they disclose no cause of action. In the first group of appeals (the *Bedfordshire* case and *Newham* case) the allegations are that public authorities negligently carried out, or failed to carry out, statutory duties imposed on them for the purpose of protecting children from child abuse. In the second group (the *Dorset* case, the *Hampshire* case and the *Bromley* case) the plaintiffs allege that the local authorities failed to carry out duties imposed upon them as education authorities by the Education Acts 1944 to 1981 in relation to children with special educational needs . . .

Introductory — public law and private law

The question is whether, if Parliament has imposed a statutory duty on an authority to carry out a particular function, a plaintiff who has suffered damage in consequence of the authority's performance or non-performance of that function has a right of action in damages against the authority. It is important to distinguish such actions to recover damages, based on a private law cause of action, from actions in public law to enforce the due performance of statutory duties, now brought by way of judicial review. The breach of a public law right by itself gives rise to no claim for damages. A claim for damages must be based on a private law cause of action . . .

Private law claims for damages can be classified into four different categories, viz: (A) actions for breach of statutory duty simpliciter (*ie* irrespective of carelessness); (B) actions based solely on the careless performance of a statutory duty in the absence of any other common law right of action; (C) actions based on a common law duty of care arising either from the imposition of the statutory duty or from the performance of it; (D) misfeasance in public office, i.e. the failure to exercise, or the exercise of, statutory powers either with the intention to injure the plaintiff or in the knowledge that the conduct is unlawful.

Category (D) is not in issue in this case. I will consider each of the other categories but I must make it clear that I am not attempting any general statement of the applicable law: rather I am seeking to set out a logical approach to the wide ranging arguments advanced in these appeals.

(A) *Breach of statutory duty simpliciter*

This category comprises those cases where the statement of claim alleges simply (a) the statutory duty, (b) a breach of that duty, causing (c) damage to the plaintiff. The cause of action depends neither on proof of any breach of the plaintiffs' common law rights nor on any allegation of carelessness by the defendant.

The principles applicable in determining whether such statutory cause of action exists are now well established, although the application of those principles in any particular case remains difficult.

The basic proposition is that in the ordinary case a breach of statutory duty does not, by itself, give rise to any private law cause of action. However a private law cause of action will arise if it can be shown, as a matter of construction of the statute, that the statutory duty was imposed for the protection of a limited class of the public and that Parliament intended to confer on members of that class a private right of action for breach of the duty. There is no general rule by reference to which it can be decided whether a statute does create such a right of action but there are a number of indicators. If the statute provides no other remedy for its breach and the Parliamentary intention to protect a limited class is shown, that indicates that there may be a private right of action since otherwise there is no method of securing the protection the statute was intended to confer. If the statute does provide some other means of enforcing the duty that will normally indicate that the statutory right was intended to be enforceable by those means and not by private right of action: *Cutler v. Wandsworth Stadium Ltd.* [1949] A.C. 398; *Lonrho Ltd. v. Shell Petroleum Co. Ltd. (No. 2)* [1982] A.C. 173. However, the mere existence of some other statutory remedy is not necessarily decisive. It is still possible to show that on the true construction of the statute the protected class was intended by Parliament to have a private remedy. Thus the specific duties imposed on employers in relation to factory premises are enforceable by an action for damages, notwithstanding the imposition by the statutes of criminal penalties for any breach: see *Groves v. Wimborne (Lord)* [1898] 2 Q.B. 402.

Although the question is one of statutory construction and therefore each case turns on the provisions in the relevant statute, it is significant that your Lordships were not referred to any case where it had been held that statutory provisions establishing a regulatory system or a scheme of social welfare for the benefit of the public at large had been held to give rise to a private right of action for damages for breach of statutory duty. Although regulatory or welfare legislation affecting a particular area of activity does in fact provide protection to those individuals particularly affected by that activity, the legislation is not to be treated as being passed for the benefit of those individuals but for the benefit of society in general. Thus legislation regulating the conduct of betting or prisons did not give rise to a statutory right of action vested in those adversely affected by the breach of the statutory provisions, *ie* bookmakers and prisoners: see *Cutler's* case [1949] A.C. 398; *Reg. v. Deputy Governor of Parkhurst Prison, Ex parte Hague* [1992] 1 A.C. 58. The cases where a private right of action for breach of statutory duty have been held to arise are all cases in which the statutory duty has been very limited and specific as opposed to general administrative functions imposed on public bodies and involving the exercise of administrative discretions.

(B) *The careless performance of a statutory duty — no common law duty of care*

This category comprises those cases in which the plaintiff alleges (a) the statutory duty and (b) the "negligent" breach of that duty but does not allege that the defendant was under a common law duty of care to the plaintiff. It is the use of the word "negligent" in this context which gives rise to confusion: it is sometimes used to connote mere carelessness (there being no common law duty of care) and sometimes to import the concept of a common law duty of care. In my judgment it is important in considering the authorities to distinguish between the two concepts: as will appear, in my view the careless performance of a statutory duty does not in itself give rise to any cause of action in the absence of either a statutory right of action (Category (A) above) or a common law duty of care (Category (C) . . .) . . .

Lords Jauncey, Lane, and Ackner agreed with Lord Browne-Wilkinson; Lord Nolan agreed with Lord Browne-Wilkinson on all but one point which is presently irrelevant.

The approach in X (like that adopted in *O'Rourke* v. *Camden London Borough Council* [1998] AC 188, which was discussed at 14.3.5) suggests that the claimant will experience difficulty succeeding in this tort in respect of the functions of public bodies; indeed, Stanton, Skidmore, Harris and Wright, *Statutory Torts* (London 2003) at [14-006], argued that,

'There is now virtually no chance that breach of statutory duty will have a significant role to play in this context.'

This pessimism, however, should not perhaps be taken too far. Since that view was expressed, *Cullen* v. *Chief Constable of the Royal Ulster Constabulary* [2003] UKHL 39 [2003] 1 WLR 1763 has reached the House of Lords and Lord Millett (with whose judgment Lord Rodger agreed) emphasized that, in *X*, Lord Browne-Wilkinson was dealing with regulatory or welfare legislation for the benefit of the general public and at [65] contrasted it with the situation mentioned by Lord Diplock in *Lonrho Ltd* v. *Shell Petroleum Co Ltd (No 2)* [1982] 2 AC 173 at 185:

... where upon the true construction of the Act it is apparent that the obligation or duty was imposed for the benefit or protection of a particular class of individuals, as in the case of the Factories Acts and similar legislation.

See further Lord Hutton at [44]. On the other hand, as a more restrictive matter, Lord Millett did point out in *Cullen* the further requirement in the tort that the 'breach of the duty is calculated to occasion loss of a kind for which the law normally awards damages'. (The word 'calculated' here would appear to mean 'likely' rather than its more normal everyday sense of 'intended'.)

QUESTION

- How far do you think Parliament thinks about the question of a civil action for damages when it imposes a statutory duty?

16.2.5 The Level of Liability

If the relevant intention to create a private law cause of action can be found, then potentially the claimant is in the advantageous position of suing in a tort that might involve strict liability. This is not always the position, however: all will turn on the wording of the statute, and the fault element of the duty imposed — one of the issues to keep in mind throughout this chapter — can, therefore, vary. Craig (1997) 113 *LQR* 67 at 91 suggests that the fact that strict liability would have otherwise have been imposed on the defendants in the *X* case was a factor inducing the House of Lords to reject a private law action for breach of statutory duty. We shall see (below at 16.2.7) that where the State is sued for a breach of Community law, the European Court of Justice has required a 'serious breach' to be shown before liability is established, and Craig goes on to suggest (at 92) that a test similar to that used by the European Court would have been 'an extra option'.

This idea has aroused some interest amongst the judiciary: in *Cullen, op cit,* Lords Bingham and Steyn thought that a breach of s 15 of the Northern Ireland (Emergency Provisions) Act 1987 was actionable *per se* (*ie* without proof of damage), but were inclined to hold, following the approach in the European Court of Justice, that a claimant would have to prove a serious breach before there could be an action for damages. It should be emphasized, however, that this was in a joint dissenting speech: in the absence of substantial detriment or distress, the majority thought that s 15 did not give rise to a civil cause of action.

QUESTION

- Should Craig's 'extra option' be adopted?

The relevance of discretion within a statutory duty will be further considered in the next section.

16.2.6 Relationship with *Ultra Vires*

Both *X* and *O'Rourke* refer to the existence of administrative discretion within the duty as a factor going against the inference of a parliamentary intention that breach should be actionable in damages. See further Stanton, Skidmore *et al*, *op cit* at [14-004]. Cane, *Administrative Law* (Oxford 2004) at 52, observes (albeit on what is analytically a different issue) that 'Courts are generally wary of deciding what specific actions are required by target duties. The assumption seems to be that [the] legislature intended the uncertainty inherent in such duties to be resolved by the duty-bearer, not by the court.' This sort of concern can bring in an *ultra vires* requirement before there will be liability in a case where there could be a damages action (as opposed to a case where the discretion militates against actionability in damages at all), the thinking being that courts should not attach liability to conduct lying within the bounds of the public body's discretion. See Cane's treatment (*op cit* at 286) of *Meade* v. *Haringey London Borough Council* [1970] 1 WLR 624.

16.2.7 Breach of European Community Law Obligations by the State

Breach by the State of obligations imposed upon it by EC law are generally regarded as actions in the tort of breach of statutory duty (see *Garden Cottage Foods Ltd* v. *Milk Marketing Board* [1984] AC 130 *per* Lord Diplock; *R* v. *Secretary of State for Transport, ex parte Factortame Ltd (No 7)* [2001] 1 WLR 942; cf Stanton (2004) 120 *LQR* 324 at 329–330).

The liability of the State (a term which does not necessarily mean the same as 'the Crown' — and see above at 16.2.2) in failing to implement or wrongly implementing Community law or legislating contrary to Community law rights has been developing. This is a large subject that is doubtless covered in detail in European Community law courses. However, the potential cause of action should be noted here and leading European Court of Justice cases such as *Francovich and Bonifaci* v. *Italy* [1991] ECR I-5357 and *Brasserie du Pecheur SA* v. *Germany* [1996[ECR I-1029 (on which see Craig (1997) *113 LQR* 67) are referred to in the extract below.

. . . .

R v. *Secretary of State for Transport, ex parte Factortame (No 5)* [2000] 1 AC 524
House of Lords

Lord Slynn

. . . [The] parties are, as Appellant, the Secretary of State for Transport, in effect representing the United Kingdom, and, as the Respondents, companies (or shareholders or directors of companies) and individuals who owned or managed vessels which were part of the British fishing fleet until they lost their registration on 31 March 1989 as a result of legislation, including delegated legislation, adopted in the United Kingdom. That legislation has been held by the European Court of Justice to constitute a breach of Community Law by the United Kingdom and the question on this appeal is whether the Appellant's breaches of Community Law were sufficiently serious to give rise under Community Law to a right to compensatory damages to those who can show that the breach caused them damage. Any question of causation has been left over pending a determination as to the seriousness of the breach for the purpose of Community Law.

The Divisional Court and the Court of Appeal unanimously held that the breaches were sufficiently serious for that purpose. A claim for exemplary damages, though originally made, has not been pursued before the Court of Appeal or before your Lordships' House. It is not suggested that there is any need to make a reference to the European Court under Article 177 [now Article 234] of the Treaty, the assessment of seriousness being for the national court (*Brasserie du Pecheur SA v. Federal Republic of Germany and Reg. v. Secretary of State for Transport, Ex parte Factortame Ltd. (No. 4)* (Cases C-46 and 48/93) [1996] Q.B. 404, 500, para. 58 ("Factortame III").

. . . Liability to Compensate — The Principle

My Lords in the *Fran[c]ovich* case where there had been a failure to implement a directive, the European Court said at paragraph 37 "it is a principle of Community law that the member states are obliged to make good loss and damage caused to individuals by breaches of Community law for which they can be held responsible". The court did not indicate what were the conditions for such liability or what if any defences would be available to a member state in breach of Community law obligations, save that in the case of a directive liability was conditional on there being a grant of rights to individuals by the directive, that the contents of those rights were clear, and that the loss suffered was shown to be caused by the state's breach. The further scope of the remedy was left to be worked out in subsequent cases as it has been in *Factortame III*.

The European Court has made it clear that, in deciding whether a state should be held liable, regard should be had to the principles laid down by the Court of Justice in deciding whether the Community itself would be held liable "in accordance with the general principles common to the laws of the Member States, [to] make good any damage caused by its institutions" (article 215 [now Article 288]). In *Factortame III para. 42* the Court said, "the conditions [for state liability] cannot, in the absence of particular justification, differ from those governing the liability of the Community in like circumstances. The protection of the rights which individuals derive from Community law cannot vary depending on whether a national authority or a Community authority is responsible for the damage".

The basic approach is clear. Before a member state can be held liable, a national court must find (i) that the relevant rule of Community law is one which is intended to confer rights on individuals; (ii) the breach must be sufficiently serious; (iii) there must be a direct causal link between the breach and the loss or damage complained of. That condition (i) is satisfied is rightly accepted by the Appellants; (iii) is deferred if the Respondents succeed on (ii). The question, therefore, is what constitutes being "sufficiently serious" and whether the Divisional Court and the Court of Appeal were right to hold that the breaches here were sufficiently serious. It has in this regard particularly to be borne in mind that what is attacked in the first place here is a state's decision to adopt legislation, though in the second place the respondents complain about the way in which the legislation was applied.

. . . The strict approach towards the liability of the Community in the exercise of legislative functions was due in part to the need not to hinder legislative action, "whenever the general interests of the Community requires legislative measures to be adopted which may adversely affect individual interests."

It was also in part due to the rule that the Community can only be liable where it has gravely and manifestly disregarded the limits on the exercise of its power. A national legislature may be required to achieve a particular result when it does not have a wide discretion but if it does have a wide discretion the same approach must be followed as with Community institutions.

Accordingly, [the European Court of Justice in *Factortame III* stated]:

> "55. As to the second condition, as regards to both Community liability under Article 215 [now Article 288] and Member State liability for breaches of Community law, the decisive test for finding that a breach of Community law is sufficiently serious is whether the Member State or the Community institution concerned manifestly and gravely disregarded the limits on its discretion.

> "56. The factors which the competent court may take into consideration include the clarity and precision of the rule breached; the measure of discretion left by the rule to a national or Community authorities; whether the infringement and the damage caused was intentional or involuntary; whether any error of law was excusable or inexcusable; the fact that the position taken by a Community institution may have contributed towards the omission, and the adoption or retention of national measures or practices contrary to Community law."

More recent cases show the working out of these rules. Thus in *Reg. v. H.M. Treasury, Ex parte British Telecommunications Plc.* (Case C-392–93) [1996] Q.B. 615 the Court held that where the interpretation adopted by the United Kingdom was arguable on the basis of an imprecisely worded article of the relevant directive and where there was no case law to give guidance the state was not liable in damages. In *Reg. v. Ministry of Agriculture, Fisheries and Food, Ex parte Hedley Lomas (Ireland) Ltd.* (Case C-5/94) [1997] Q.B. 139 where there was no or very little room for discretion in granting a licence that could in itself be a sufficiently serious breach. In *Dillenkofer v. Federal Republic of Germany* (Case C-178/94) [1997] Q.B. 259 it was held that a failure to implement a directive, where no or little question of legislative choice was involved, the mere infringement may constitute a sufficiently serious breach. In *Denkavit Internationaal B.V. v. Bundesamt für Finanzen* (Cases C-283/94) [1996] E.C.R. I-5063 the Court held that other member states, after discussion with the Council had adopted the same interpretation of the Directive as Germany and as there was no relevant case law of the Court it was held that the breach was not sufficiently serious.

It was also clear from the cases that it is not necessary to establish fault or negligence on the part of the member state going beyond what is relevant to show a sufficiently serious breach.

Lord Hope agreed with Lord Slynn, but added some comments of his own. Lord Nicholls agreed with Lords Slynn and Hope. Lords Hoffmann and Clyde delivered concurring speeches. Appeal dismissed.

Without entering the debate as to sovereignty, this tort would appear to require the challenged action to be *ultra vires* the State. However, note how discretion is taken account of so as to give some protection: this in turn is linked to the notion of the requirement of 'serious breach'. As indicated in the above extract, intention is not required but 'serious breach' is, and this obviously, to an extent, brings in a question of fault.

For the State's potential liability for courts, see *Köbler v. Republic Österreich* [2004] QB 848.

16.2.8 The Human Rights Act 1998: Introduction

The Human Rights Act 1998 expressly provides that damages may be awarded for a breach of s 6, and it does, therefore, constitute an actionable breach of statutory duty, although not one which Parliament has defined by reference to the traditional tort of breach of statutory duty, as some actionable duties are: see Stanton (2004) 120 *LQR* 324 at 326–328. As Parliament has specifically provided for actionability, there is no problem over divining statutory intention on this matter. Another feature to note is that it is only public authorities, as determined by s 6 of the Act (and for discussion see 5.5 above), which can be held liable; furthermore, as Sedley LJ pointed out in *Chagos Islanders* v. *Attorney-General* [2004] EWCA Civ 997 at [20], quoted in 16.2.2 above, it is a situation in which the Crown can incur a primary liability. A final point to make in this context is that in light of the wording of the HRA, whereby under s 6 it is (generally) unlawful for a public authority to contravene Convention rights, liability here will be limited to *ultra vires* activity.

We have so far avoided expressly calling this action a tort, because this has been a matter of some debate. The issue concerns the fact that s 8(3) HRA only authorizes the award of damages where the court is satisfied that such an award is necessary for there to be 'just satisfaction'. This concept, which is to be found in Art 41 of the ECHR, will be discussed below (at 16.2.11), but suffice it to say at this point that damages do not have to be awarded as an aspect of 'just satisfaction' for a breach, *ie* there is no actual right to damages on a *restitutio in integrum* basis: see Woolf (in Andenas and Fairgrieve (eds), *Judicial Review in International Perspective* (The Hague 2000) at 432); *Anufrijeva* v. *Southwark London Borough Council* [2003] EWCA Civ 1406 [2004] 2 QB 1124 at [50]. In *R (Greenfield)* v. *Secretary of State for the Home Department* [2005] UKHL 14 [2005] 1 WLR 673 the House of Lords at [19] stated that the '1998 Act is not a tort statute'.

16.2.9 The Statutory Provisions

Section 6 of the HRA and its scope has been discussed earlier (see above at 5.5). Section 7 deals with procedural matters and will be referred to below (at 16.2.12).

Human Rights Act 1998

8—(1) In relation to any act (or proposed act) of a public authority which the court finds is (or would be) unlawful, it may grant such relief or remedy, or make such order, within its powers as it considers just and appropriate.

(2) But damages may be awarded only by a court which has power to award damages, or to order the payment of compensation, in civil proceedings.

(3) No award of damages is to be made unless, taking account of all the circumstances of the case, including —
   (a) any other relief or remedy granted, or order made, in relation to the act in question (by that or any other court), and
   (b) the consequences of any decision (of that or any other court) in respect of that act,
the court is satisfied that the award is necessary to afford just satisfaction to the person in whose favour it is made.

(4) In determining —
   (a) whether to award damages, or
   (b) the amount of an award,
the court must take into account the principles applied by the European Court of Human Rights in relation to the award of compensation under Article 41 of the Convention.

(5) A public authority against which damages are awarded is to be treated — . . .
   (b) for the purposes of the Civil Liability (Contribution) Act 1978 as liable in respect of damage suffered by the person to whom the award is made.

(6) In this section —

"court" includes a tribunal;
"damages" means damages for an unlawful act of a public authority; and
"unlawful" means unlawful under section 6(1).

9—(1) Proceedings under section 7(1)(a) in respect of a judicial act may be brought only —
    (a) by exercising a right of appeal or; . . .
    (c) in such other forum as may be prescribed by rules.

(2) That does not affect any rule of law which prevents a court from being the subject of judicial review.

(3) In proceedings under this Act in respect of a judicial act done in good faith, damages may not be awarded otherwise than to compensate a person to the extent required by Article 5(5) of the Convention.

(4) An award of damages permitted by subsection (3) is to be made against the Crown; but no award may be made unless the appropriate person, if not a party to the proceedings, is joined.

(5) In this section —

"appropriate person" means the Minister responsible for the court concerned, or a person or government department nominated by him;
"court" includes a tribunal;
"judge" includes a member of a tribunal, a justice of the peace [or, in Northern Ireland, a lay magistrate] and a clerk or other officer entitled to exercise the jurisdiction of a court;
"judicial act" means a judicial act of a court and includes an act done on the instructions, or on behalf, of a judge; . . .

16.2.10 Is Fault Required?

At first sight no more would seem to be required than that a breach of a relevant provision of the ECHR has occurred. However, Fairgrieve [2001] *PL* 695 at 697–700 argues that, while for violations of fundamental provisions like Arts 2 and 3 'it may be felt that it is unnecessary to require anything over and above the elements that are required by the substantive provisions of the Convention themselves', with infractions of other rights, such as Art 6, the existence or not of fault 'may well be relevant in deciding whether the public authority should be financially responsible for the consequences of the unlawfulness . . .'. Fairgrieve suggests that this flexible approach to damages under the HRA may be facilitated by borrowing from the EC case law, under which (as seen above at 16.2.7) liability turns on whether the context-sensitive criterion of 'sufficiently serious breach' can be made out.

16.2.11 'Just Satisfaction'

The concept of 'just satisfaction' is to be found in Art 41 ECHR; in deciding whether to award damages and, if so, how much, domestic courts are required by s 8(4) HRA to pay attention to the principles which the ECtHR applies in deciding on compensation under that article of the ECHR. In 2001, the Law Commission (*Damages under the Human Rights Act 1988*, Law Com No 266) surveyed the Strasbourg jurisprudence and concluded:

3.76 It is not easy to draw clear principles from the case-law. Many points are more matters of practice or evidence than principle. Compensation may be awarded for both pecuniary and non-pecuniary loss. Non-pecuniary loss includes feelings of distress, anxiety and humiliation, and may include the loss of a relationship. The Court may reject a claim where the applicant has not established a clear causal connection between the violation of the Convention and the damage claimed, but "speculative losses" are sometimes allowed.

3.77 In many cases, usually for reasons which are not clearly defined, the court holds that a finding of a violation will itself be a sufficient just satisfaction and makes no award. Dinah Shelton [*Remedies in International Human Rights Law* (1999) p.209] suggests:

It . . . seems that the most significant factors in determining whether or not damages will be awarded are the character of the applicant, the unanimity of the Court, and the procedural or substantive nature of the right violated.

3.78 The only principle which is clearly stated in the Strasbourg case-law is that of *restitutio in integrum*. The aim of an award should be, so far as possible, to put an end to the breach and to make reparation for its consequences in such a way as to restore the situation existing before the breach. However, in applying that principle, the Court will take account of the parties' conduct "on an equitable basis", a phrase which "it has never attempted to define, or reduce to a set of principles" [Grosz, Beatson and Duffy, *Human Rights: The 1998 Act and the European Convention* (2000), p 145].

This passage should show the difficulties that may be faced by an English court dealing with a claim under s 8 HRA. The issue has been addressed in several cases since the HRA came into force: see, *eg R (Bernard)* v. *Enfield London Borough Council* [2002] EWHC 2282 (Admin) [2003] LGR 423; *R (KB)* v. *South London and South and West Region Mental Health Review Tribunal* [2003] EWHC 193 (Admin) [2004] QB 936; *Anufrijeva* v. *Southwark London Borough Council* [2003] EWCA Civ 1406 [2004] QB 1124; *R (Greenfield)* v. *Secretary of State for the Home Department* [2005] UKHL 14 [2005] 1 WLR 673. In *Anufrijeva* Lord Woolf CJ (delivering the judgment of the Court of Appeal) stressed that in this context the interests of the individual had to be balanced against the public interest and mentioned the idea of damages being a 'last resort' (referring to Scorey and Eicke, *Human Rights Damages, Principles and Practice* (looseleaf edn), para A4-040).

If damages are to be awarded, then the question of assessment arises. Lord Woolf had extra-judicially (see Andenas and Fairgrieve (eds), *Judicial Review in International Perspective* (The Hague 2000) at 434) suggested that awards should be on the low side as compared with equivalent tort damages, but this idea had not been taken up and the Court of Appeal in *Anufrijeva* had suggested (at [74]):

. . . Where . . . in a claim under the HRA, the court decides that it is appropriate to award damages, the levels of damages awarded in respect of torts as reflected in the guidelines issued by the Judicial Studies Board, the levels of awards made by the Criminal Injuries Compensation Board and by the Parliamentary Ombudsman and the Local Government Ombudsman may all provide some rough guidance where the consequences of the infringement of human rights are similar to that being considered in the comparator selected. In cases of maladministration where the consequences are not of a type which gives rise to any right to compensation under our civil law, the awards of the Ombudsman may be the only comparator.

Nevertheless, the Court also stated (at [75]) that 'a finding of a breach of a positive obligation under Article 8 [privacy and family life] to provide support will be rare, ... [that] it is unlikely that there will be any ready comparator to assist in the assessment of damages' and that damages should be modest because of limited resources. However, in *Greenfield*, although the case was concerned on its facts with Art 6, the House of Lords, speaking more generally, rejected domestic comparators for a range of reasons, and at [19] stated that courts in England and Wales 'should not aim to be significantly more or less generous than the [Strasbourg] court might be, in a case where it was willing to make an award at all'.

16.2.12 Procedural Matters

Section 7 HRA authorizes the bringing of proceedings for breach of s 6 in 'the appropriate court or tribunal' (to be laid down by rules: s 7(2) and (9)) or reliance on the Convention right in any legal proceedings. The claimant, however, has to be the 'victim' of the unlawful act (on which see above at 15.7.6). Furthermore, the time limit for bringing proceedings is one year from when the challenged act or omission occurred, but with a discretion for the court to extend it. There is also the question of the procedure by which the remedy is sought, a matter discussed in *Anufrijeva* at [79]–[81].

Any breach of s 6 HRA could be regarded as involving a private right (see Craig, *Administrative Law* (London 2003) at 800–801), but if the action is not treated as a 'true' tort (given the lack of any right to damages even if a breach is established — see above at 16.2.8), this position might be questioned. Whatever the answer to this, the Court of Appeal were concerned in *Anufrijeva* that in a case where the alleged breach of the HRA was constituted by maladministration, the costs of the action could greatly exceed the amount of damages that might be awarded. The court therefore said (at [81]) that, in future, such cases should, where possible (*ie* where the claim is not for damages alone: see CPR 54.3(2)), be brought as a claim for judicial review; even where damages were sought alone, it was thought that the action should be by means of an ordinary claim in the Administrative Court. Permission for judicial review, said the court, should not be granted if other appropriate avenues — *eg* a complaint to a relevant Ombudsman (on which see ch 20) who may be able to secure compensation for maladministration — have not been explored.

16.2.13 Misfeasance in Public Office

This is a tort which it will be seen, like a breach of s 6 HRA, requires a public element on the part of the defendant: it is a tort that is peculiar to public office. The tort was described by the Privy Council in *Dunlop* v. *Woollahra Municipal Council* [1982] AC 158 at 173 as well-established, and indeed it can be traced back to *Ashby* v. *White* (1703) 2 Ld Raym 938; 3 Ld Raym 320. The ingredients of the tort were recently considered by the House of Lords in the following case.

Three Rivers District Council v. Governor and Company of the Bank of England (No 3) [2003] 2 AC 1
House of Lords

BCCI, a deposit-taking institution licenced in the UK and supervised by the Bank of England (and later the Financial Services Authority), went into liquidation in July 1991. Until April 1990, the Bank of England had been unaware of what Lord Steyn, in his speech, called the 'fraud on a vast scale perpetrated at a senior level in BCCI' and which had been the 'principal cause of [its] collapse'. The claimants — 6,000 former depositors — sought damages from the Bank of England, alleging (inter alia) the tort of misfeasance in public office. As Lord Steyn explained, they claimed that senior officials acted in bad faith '(a) in licensing BCCI in 1979, when they knew that it was unlawful to do so; (b) in shutting their eyes to what was happening at BCCI after the licence was granted; and (c) in failing to take steps to close BCCI when the known facts cried out for action at least by the mid 80s'. On the trial of preliminary issues, it was held at first instance that (inter alia) the claim for misfeasance was unsustainable. The claimants' appeal was dismissed, whereupon they appealed to the House of Lords. This excerpt is concerned only with the misfeasance aspects of the appeal.

Lord Steyn

. . . The tort of misfeasance in public office is an exception to "the general rule that, if conduct is presumptively unlawful, a good motive will not exonerate the defendant, and that, if conduct is lawful apart from motive, a bad motive will not make him liable": Winfield and Jolowicz on Tort, 15th ed., (1998), p. 55; Bradford Corporation v. Pickles [1895] A.C. 587; Allen v. Flood [1898] A.C. 1. The rationale of the tort is that in a legal system based on the rule of law executive or administrative power "may be exercised only for the public good" and not for ulterior and improper purposes: Jones v. Swansea City Council [1990] 1 W.L.R. 54, 85F, per Nourse L.J.; a decision reversed on the facts but not on the law by the House of Lords: [1990] 1 W.L.R 1453, at 1458 . . .

The Ingredients of the tort

It is now possible to consider the ingredients of the tort. That can conveniently be done by stating the requirements of the tort in a logical sequence of numbered paragraphs.

(1) The defendant must be a public officer:

It is the office in a relatively wide sense on which everything depends. Thus a local authority exercising private-law functions as a landlord is potentially capable of being sued: Jones v. Swansea City Council. In the present case it is common ground that the Bank satisfies this requirement.

(2) The second requirement is the exercise of power as a public officer:

This ingredient is also not in issue. The conduct of the named senior officials of the Banking Supervision Department of the Bank was in the exercise of public functions. Moreover, it is not disputed that the principles of vicarious liability apply as much to misfeasance in public office as to other torts involving malice, knowledge or intention: Racz v. Home Office [1994] 2 A.C. 45.

(3) The third requirement concerns the state of mind of the defendant.

The case law reveals two different forms of liability for misfeasance in public office. First there is the case of targeted malice by a public officer i.e. conduct specifically intended to injure a person or persons. This type of case involves bad faith in the sense of the exercise of public power for an improper or ulterior motive. The second form is where a public officer acts knowing that he has no power to do the act complained of and that the act will probably injure the plaintiff. It involves bad faith inasmuch as the public officer does not have an honest belief that his act is lawful.

The distinction, and the availability of an action of the second type, was inherent in the early development of tort. A group of cases which began with *Ashby v. White* (1703), reported in 1 Smith's Leading Cases (13th ed.) 253, concerned the discretionary refusal of voting rights: see also *Drewe v. Coulton* (1787) 1 East 563n; 102 E.R. 217; *Tozer v. Child* (1857) 7 El. & Bl. 377: 119 E.R. 1286; *Cullen v. Morris* (1819) 2 Stark 577; 171 E.R. 741. In the second group of cases the defendants were judges of inferior courts, and the cases concerned liability of the judges for malicious acts within their jurisdiction: *Ackerley v. Parkinson* (1815) 3 M. & S. 411; 105 E.R. 665; *Harman v. Tappenden* (1801) 1 East 555; 102 E.R. 214; *Taylor v. Nesfield* (1854) 3 El. & Bl. 724; 118 E.R. 1312. These decisions laid the foundation of the modern tort; they established the two different forms of liability; and revealed the unifying element of conduct amounting to an abuse of power accompanied by subjective bad faith. In the most important modern case in England the existence of the two forms of the tort was analysed and affirmed: *Bourgoin S.A. v. Ministry of Agriculture, Fisheries and Food* [1986] Q.B. 716. Clarke J. followed this traditional twofold classification. He expressly held that the two forms are alternative ways in which the tort can be committed. The majority in the Court of Appeal commented on "a rather rigid distinction between the two supposed limbs of the tort" and observed that there was "the need to establish deliberate and dishonest abuse of power in every case:" [2000] 2 W.L.R. 15 at 67C–D. As a matter of classification it is certainly right to say that there are not two separate torts. On the other hand, the ingredients of the two forms of the tort cannot be exactly the same because if that were so there would be no sense in the twofold classification. Undoubtedly there are unifying features, namely the special nature of the tort, as directed against the conduct of public officers only, and the element of an abuse of public power in bad faith. But there are differences between the alternative forms of the tort and it is conducive to clarity to recognise this.

The present case is not one of targeted malice. If the action in tort is maintainable it must be in the second form of the tort. It is therefore necessary to consider the distinctive features of this form of the tort. The remainder of my judgment will be directed to this form of the tort.

The basis for the action lies in the defendant taking a decision in the knowledge that it is an excess of the powers granted to him and that it is likely to cause damage to an individual or individuals. It is, not every act beyond the powers vesting in a public officer which will ground the tort. The alternative form of liability requires an element of bad faith. This leads to what was a disputed issue. Counsel for the Bank pointed out that there was no precedent in England before the present case which held recklessness to be a sufficient state of mind to ground the tort. Counsel argued that recklessness was insufficient. The Australian High Court and the Court of Appeal of New Zealand have ruled that recklessness is sufficient: *Northern Territory v. Mengel* (1995) 69 A.J.L.R. 527; *Garrett v. Attorney-General* [1997] 2 N.Z.L.R. 332; *Rawlinson v. Rice* [1997] 2 N.Z.L.R. 651. Clarke J. lucidly explained the reason for the inclusion of recklessness [1996] 3 All E.R. 558, 581:

> "The reason why recklessness was regarded as sufficient by all members of the High Court in *Mengel* is perhaps most clearly seen in the judgment of Brennan J. It is that misfeasance consists in the purported exercise of a power otherwise than in an honest attempt to perform the relevant duty. It is that lack of honesty which makes the act an abuse of power."

The Court of Appeal accepted the correctness of this statement of principle: [2000] 2 W.L.R. 15, 61G–62A. This is an organic development, which fits into the structure of our law governing intentional torts. The policy underlying it is sound: reckless indifference to consequences is as blameworthy as deliberately seeking such consequences. It can therefore now be regarded as settled law that an act performed in reckless indifference as to the outcome is sufficient to ground the tort in its second form.

. . . [D]uring the oral hearing . . . counsel for the plaintiffs accepted that only reckless indifference in a subjective sense will be sufficient. This concession was rightly made. The plaintiff must prove that the public officer acted with a state of mind of reckless indifference to the illegality of his act: *Rawlinson v. Rice* [1997] 2 N.Z.L.R. 651. Later in this judgment I will discuss the requirement of reckless indifference in relation to the consequences of the act.

(4) Duty to the plaintiff

The question is who can sue in respect of an abuse of power by a public officer. Counsel for the Bank argued that in order to be able to claim in respect of the second form of misfeasance, there must be established "an antecedent legal right or interest" and an element of "proximity". Clarke J. did not enunciate a requirement of proximity. He observed [1996] 3 All E.R. 558, 584B:

> "If an officer deliberately does an act which he knows is unlawful and will cause economic loss to the plaintiff, I can see no reason in principle why the plaintiff should identify a legal right which is being infringed or a particular duty owed to him, beyond the right not to be damaged or injured by a deliberate abuse of power by a public officer"

The majority in the Court of Appeal held that "the notion of proximity should have a significant part to play in the tort of misfeasance, as it undoubtedly has in the tort of negligence:" [2000] 2 W.L.R. 15, 66A. Counsel for the Bank argued that both requirements are essential in order to prevent the tort from becoming an uncontrollable one. It would be unwise to make general statements on a subject which may involve many diverse situations. What can be said is that, of course, any plaintiff must have a sufficient interest to found a legal standing to sue. Subject to this qualification, principle does not require the introduction of proximity as a controlling mechanism in this corner of the law. The state of mind required to establish the tort, as already explained, as well as the special rule of remoteness hereafter discussed, keeps the tort within reasonable bounds. There is no reason why such an action cannot be brought by a particular class of persons, such as depositors at a bank, even if their precise identities were not known to the bank. The observations of Clarke J. are correct.

In agreed issue 4 the question is raised whether the Bank is capable of being liable for the tort of misfeasance in public office to plaintiffs who were potentially depositors at the time of any relevant act or omission of misfeasance by the Bank. The majority in the Court of Appeal and Auld L.J. held that this issue is unsuitable for summary determination. In my view this ruling was correct.

(5) Causation

Causation is an essential element of the plaintiffs' cause of action. It is a question of fact. The majority in the Court of Appeal and Auld L.J. held that it is unsuitable for summary determination. That is plainly correct . . .

(6) Damage and Remoteness

The claims by the plaintiffs are in respect of financial losses they suffered. These are, of course, claims for recovery of consequential economic losses. The question is when such losses are recoverable. It would have been possible, as a matter of classification, to discuss this question under paragraph 3 in which the required state of mind for this tort was examined. It is, however, convenient to consider it under the traditional heading of remoteness.

. . . The issues have been canvassed in great depth in written and oral argument. Taking into account all the matters advanced the choice before the House can be narrowed down. So far as the majority [in the Court of Appeal] was minded to adopt a stricter test than Clarke J., encapsulated in the words "knowing at the time that [the decision] *would* cause damage to the plaintiffs," they went too far. A test of knowledge or foresight that a decision *would* cause damage does not readily fit into the standard of proof generally required in the law of tort, and specifically in the case of intentional torts. Moreover, this test unnecessarily emasculates the effectiveness of the tort. The real choice is therefore between the test of knowledge that the decision would probably damage the plaintiff (as enunciated by Clarke J.) and the test of reasonable foreseeability (as contended for by counsel for the plaintiffs) . . .

Enough has been said to demonstrate the special nature of the tort, and the strict requirements governing it. This is a legally sound justification for adopting as a starting point that in both forms of the tort the intent required must be directed at the harm complained of, or at least to harm of the type suffered by the plaintiffs. This results in the rule that a plaintiff must establish not only that the defendant acted in the knowledge that the act was beyond his powers but also in the knowledge that his act would probably injure the plaintiff or person of a class of which the plaintiff was a member. In presenting a sustained argument for a rule allowing recovery of all foreseeable losses counsel for the plaintiffs argued that such a more liberal rule is necessary in a democracy as a constraint upon abuse of executive and administrative power. The force of this argument is, however, substantially reduced by the recognition that subjective recklessness on the part of a public officer in acting in excess of his powers is sufficient. Recklessness about the consequences of his act, in the sense of not caring whether the consequences happen or not, is therefore sufficient in law. This justifies the conclusion that the test adopted by Clarke J. represents a satisfactory balance between the two competing policy considerations, namely enlisting tort law to combat executive and administrative abuse of power and not allowing public officers, who must always act for the public good, to be assailed by unmeritorious actions.

It is undoubtedly right, as counsel for the plaintiffs pointed out, that the mental element required for the tort of misfeasance in public office means that it is not an effective remedy to deal with state liability for breaches of Community law: *Brasserie du Pêcheur S.A. v. Federal Republic of Germany; Reg. v. Secretary of State for Transport, Ex parte Factortame (No. 4)* Joined Cases C-46/93 and C-48/93 [1996] Q.B. 404. This consideration cannot, however, affect the decision of the House on the tort. If there is a gap it must be for Community law to fill it And our courts will loyally follow Community law.

. . . In the light of my statement of the requirements of the tort of misfeasance in public office I would adjourn this part of the appeal for further argument.

Lords Hope, Hutton, Hobhouse, and Millett delivered speeches in which they agreed with Lord Steyn's order for disposing of this appeal. Lords Hobhouse and Millett agreed with Lord Steyn's speech on the question of the misfeasance tort (and also Lord Hutton's views on that issue). When the striking out issue was further considered, the House of Lords decided that the action should not be struck out.

Various points in the *Three Rivers* case have arisen for interpretation in later cases. For example, Lord Steyn's reference (at 196) to the claimant having to establish that the 'defendant acted . . . in the knowledge that his act would probably injure the [claimant] or person of a *class* of which the [claimant] was a member' (emphasis added) was analysed in *Akenzua* v. *Secretary of State for the Home Department* [2002] EWCA Civ 1470 [2003] 1 WLR 741. Sedley LJ at [19]–[20] (with the agreement of Scott Baker and Simon Brown LJJ) took the view that the reference to such an individual or class was not a 'freestanding requirement of the tort'; rather, it followed from the 'antecedent proposition that the intent or recklessness must relate ("be directed") to the kind of harm suffered'. In Sedley LJ's opinion, it is 'an expansive rather than a restrictive element of the tort, allowing the action to be maintained even where the identities of the eventual victims are not known at the time when the tort is committed, so long as it is clear that there will be such victims'.

16.2.14 Causation and Damage

It will have been seen that Lord Steyn referred to causation as a factual issue in the *Three Rivers* case. Causation can pose a particular problem with the misfeasance tort. For example, where the claimant requires some positive exercise of power in his favour (*eg* the grant of a licence), then it may well not be clear that the wrongful denial of the licence has caused him any loss. The court may be unable to say what the result of an exercise of the power without the improper factor would have been. Another causation issue could be raised in respect of this tort — here in the situation where there has been, for example, a withdrawal of a licence — by the view in *Dunlop* v. *Woollahra Municipal Council* [1982] AC 158 at 172 (below at 16.2.17) that a person can ignore a purported exercise of power; cf above at 3.2–3.3. Despite earlier support for this view in the case law (McBride [1979] CLJ 323 at 337–340), it is submitted that it should not, and will not, be followed in English law today (and see above at 3.2–3.3).

The type of damage alleged in the *Three Rivers* case was economic loss, but it is clear that the tort also encompasses death and personal injuries and damage to property (see the *Akenzua* case). A related issue is whether damage always has to be proved or whether in any circumstances this tort is actionable *per se*. In *Watkins* v. *Secretary of State for the Home Department* [2004] EWCA Civ 966 at [67], Laws LJ opined that in cases in which constitutional (and perhaps other highly-regarded) rights are infringed, liability for misfeasance may, exceptionally, be established without proof of damage. His Lordship gave *Ashby* v. *White* (1703) 2 Ld Raym 938; 3 Ld Raym 320, where a malicious refusal of the right to vote was said to be actionable, as an example of such a case, although an obvious difficulty with Laws LJ's approach is the uncertainty as to the precise membership of the category of 'constitutional rights'.

QUESTION

• How satisfactory is the misfeasance tort in providing a remedy for someone who suffers loss as a result of *ultra vires* action by a public body?

16.2.15 The Tort of Negligence: Introduction

This common law tort with its well-known reliance upon the concept of the reasonable person has provoked much discussion over the years in relation to its application to public authority defendants — particularly where statutory *discretion* is involved. We saw in ch 9 above that the use of such discretion is rendered *ultra vires* not by unreasonableness *per se*, but only by 'total unreasonableness' — a somewhat extreme concept that does not correspond to the (generally lower) 'reasonable person' standard in negligence. Questions therefore arise as to the appropriateness of applying the latter standard to the exercise of statutory discretions, bearing in mind that the high public law unreasonableness threshold exists, in part, because of courts' perceptions of the appropriate limits of adjudication, which is linked to notions of Parliamentary mandate and relative expertise. On the other hand, it can be argued (see Craig and Fairgrieve [1999] *PL* 626 at 648–649) that the difference is not as great as might appear, given the leeway afforded to defendants in respect of breach of duty in cases of professional negligence and the way in which the *Wednesbury* unreasonableness test has been applied in practice.

QUESTION

- If proportionality takes over from *Wednesbury* as the test for review of all discretionary powers, would there still be any tension between judicial review and the tort of negligence? (Consider Hickman [2004] *CLJ* 166.)

16.2.16 Development of the Law: The Rise and Fall of *Ultra Vires*

The relationship between 'unreasonableness' in the negligence and public law senses referred to above is, in one respect, an aspect of a wider question — *viz* where the use of statutory discretion is at stake, can liability in negligence arise only if, in the first place, the public body has acted *ultra vires*? It was in cases such as *Home Office* v. *Dorset Yacht Co Ltd* [1970] AC 1004 and *Anns* v. *Merton London Borough Council* [1978] AC 728 that the House of Lords began specifically to address this issue, and establish an *ultra vires* hurdle.

Reference has already been made to *X (Minors)* v. *Bedfordshire County Council* [1995] 2 AC 633 above at 16.2.4 in the context of breach of statutory duty and the alleged facts were briefly outlined there. On the approach to the negligence issue where public authorities were sued and in the light (*inter alia*) of the House of Lords cases previously mentioned, Lord Browne-Wilkinson (whose speech, in all presently relevant respects, commanded the support of the other Law Lords) discussed cases where complaint is made of the manner of exercise of a statutory discretion (as opposed to its implementation in practice) in *X* and concluded at 737 that

in seeking to establish that a local authority is liable at common law for negligence in the exercise of a discretion conferred by statute, the first requirement is to show that the decision was outside the ambit of the discretion altogether: if it was not, a local authority cannot itself be in breach of any duty of care owed to the plaintiff.

This conclusion was intimately connected with his Lordship's view about the appropriate limits of adjudication in this sphere, as his following remarks (*op cit* at 738) — the effect of which is to establish a distinction between justiciable and non-justiciable matters — indicate:

Where Parliament has conferred a statutory discretion on a public authority, it is for that authority, not for the courts, to exercise the discretion: nothing which the authority does within the ambit of the discretion can be actionable at common law. If the decision complained of falls outside the statutory discretion, it *can* (but not necessarily will) give rise to common law liability. However, if the factors relevant to the exercise of the discretion include matters of policy, the court cannot adjudicate on such policy matters and therefore cannot reach the conclusion that the decision was outside the ambit of the statutory discretion. Therefore a common law duty of care in relation to the taking of decisions involving policy matters cannot exist.

Furthermore, even where the matter was justiciable, Lord Browne-Wilkinson would only allow the claimant to establish that the public body had gone outside its discretion by proving *Wednesbury* 'total unreasonableness', whereas we have seen above in chs 8 and 9 that there are other ways in which discretion can be exceeded. In the light of later developments this issue will not be explored further here.

Once the above thresholds had been surmounted, and in the absence of binding precedent, the familiar test laid down in *Caparo Industries plc* v. *Dickman* [1990] 2 AC 605 — requiring consideration of reasonable foreseeability, proximity, and 'fairness, justice and reasonableness' — would be applied to establish whether a duty of care existed. In the case of the implementation of a discretionary power, the court would move straight to the duty of care question without the preliminary hurdles coming in. On the distinction between manner of exercise and practical implementation see Cane, *Administrative Law* (Oxford 2004) at 276), but in either case, it was acknowledged that the statutory framework could influence the duty of care, a factor which might expand or restrict the duty concept.

In fact, in *X* — which, as will be recalled (see above at 16.2.4 for the alleged facts), concerned allegations of negligence in respect of the carrying out or failure to carry out statutory duties concerning the protection of children from abuse and the education of children with special needs — the House of Lords refused to strike out the claims on the *ultra vires* point, Lord Browne-Wilkinson recognizing a possibility of the claimants establishing that the local authorities concerned had acted outside their respective discretions (although we will see shortly that the threshold *ultra vires* requirement apparently laid down in *X* has not been applied in more recent cases). His Lordship therefore went on to apply the *Caparo* test in order to determine whether duties of care existed. We shall concentrate here on the alleged abuse cases. At this stage, his Lordship held that it would not be just or reasonable to impose a direct duty of care on a local authority in respect of children in relation to whom it had received a report of neglect or ill-treatment. Such a duty, he said, would cut across the system of statutory protection for children at risk which involved the participation of various bodies. He also noted the danger of inducing local authorities to adopt a defensive approach to their duties, and that there were statutory procedures under which grievances could be investigated. Bearing in mind the approach in *Caparo* of proceeding incrementally and by analogy to decided cases, the nearest analogies were cases in which a duty of care had been denied (*eg Hill* v. *Chief Constable of West Yorkshire* [1989] AC 53). His Lordship concluded (*op cit* at 751) that the 'courts should proceed with great care before holding liable in negligence those who have been charged by Parliament with the task of protecting society from the wrongdoings of others', opining (at 762) in one of the education cases that, if the complex machinery laid down by statute failed to confer the intended benefits, that was a matter best dealt with by an Ombudsman's investigation rather than litigation. This matter will be referred to later where we shall see that various developments have led to a different approach.

One development that should be noted at this point, however, concerns the ECHR and the use made in *X* of the *Hill* case which granted broad protection to the police on policy grounds from an action in negligence concerning the investigation of crime. The issue reached the ECtHR as a result of the litigation in *Osman* v. *Ferguson* [1993] 4 All ER 344, where it was alleged that the second claimant and his father had been shot by someone against whom the police should have previously taken action. In the Court of Appeal two of their Lordships had decided that there was a sufficiently proximate relationship, but had struck out the action under the 'fair, just and reasonable' criterion relying on the *Hill* ground for rejecting the duty of care. This striking out was held by the European Court in *Osman* v. *United Kingdom* (2000) 29 EHRR 245 to contravene Art 6 ECHR (entitlement to a hearing by a tribunal in determining a person's civil rights and obligations) in that the automatic exclusion of police liability without consideration of any countervailing policy factors was a disproportionate restriction on the right of access to the court granted by that Article.

The *Osman* case proved to be controversial in England: see, *eg* the views of Lord Browne-Wilkinson in *Barrett* v. *Enfield London Borough Council* [2001] 2 AC 550 at 558–560; Hoffman (1999) 62 *MLR* 159 at 162–164), and the position has been altered by later cases in the ECtHR. In *TP* v. *United Kingdom* (2002) 34 EHRR 42 and *Z* v. *United Kingdom* (2002) 34 EHRR 97, both of which were cases that had failed in England in the consolidated litigation in *X*, the ECtHR accepted that rejection of a case on the ground that it was not 'fair, just and reasonable' that there should be a duty of care was not a breach of Art 6: the claimant had had access to a court to argue the case before it was struck out, although as Davies (2001) 117 *LQR* 521 at 524 points out, 'courts will have to examine claimants' policy arguments "properly and fairly" (*Z* at [101]) if they are not to fall foul of Article 6'. There was another possibility for redress in these cases, however: this was if a breach of an article of the ECHR could be established (see above at 16.2.8–12). It will be seen below that this possibility had an important indirect effect on negligence liability in *D* v. *East Berkshire Community NHS Trust* [2003] EWCA Civ 1151 [2004] QB 558: see below at 16.2.6.

....

Barrett v. *Enfield London Borough Council* [2001] 2 AC 550
House of Lords

The appellant (claimant) alleged that, while still an infant, he was mistreated by his mother, and was, as a result, placed under the care of the respondent (defendant). The appellant alleged (*inter alia*) that the respondent owed (and had breached) a common law duty of care in the practical implementation of its obligations under various statutes concerning the protection and welfare of children. The common law duty was said to include a duty to act in *loco parentis* and to provide the appellant with the standard of care which could be expected of a reasonable parent. The appellant alleged that this duty had been breached by the respondent's failures (*inter alia*) to consider whether he could be placed with his half-sister on a long-term basis; have regard to his health and hygiene; find a proper home for him (he was accommodated with various foster parents and in children's homes but was not adopted); properly manage his meetings with his mother after 11 years of separation; and to provide him with appropriate psychiatric treatment. The appellant alleged that, if these breaches of duty had not occurred, then he would not 'on the balance of probabilities have left the care of the Local Authority as a young man of eighteen years with no family or attachments whatsoever, who had developed a psychiatric illness causing him to self-harm and who had been involved in criminal activities'. The Court of Appeal struck out the appellant's claim; he appealed to the House of Lords.

Lord Slynn

[Having referred to certain speeches in *Home Office* v. *Dorset Yacht Co Ltd* [1970] AC 1004 and *Anns* v. *Merton London Borough Council* [1978] AC 728, his Lordship said:] On this basis, if an authority acts wholly within its discretion — i.e. it is doing what Parliament has said it can do, even if it has to choose between several alternatives open to it — then there can be no liability in negligence. It is only if a plaintiff can show that what has been done is outside the discretion and the power, then he can go on to show the authority was negligent. But if that stage is reached, the authority is not exercising a statutory power, but purporting to do so and the statute is no defence.

This, however, does not in my view mean that if an element of discretion is involved in an act being done subject to the exercise of the overriding statutory power, common law negligence is necessarily ruled out. Acts may be done pursuant and subsequent to the exercise of a discretion where a duty of care may exist — as has often been said even knocking a nail into a piece of wood involves the exercise of some choice or discretion and yet there may be a duty of care in the way it is done. Whether there is an element of discretion to do the act is thus not a complete test leading to the result that, if there is, a claim against an authority for what it actually does or fails to do must necessarily be ruled out.

Another distinction which is sometimes drawn between decisions as to "policy" and as to "operational acts" sounds more promising. A pure policy decision where Parliament has entrusted the decision to a public authority is not something which a court would normally be expected to review in a claim in negligence. But again this is not an absolute test. Policy and operational acts are closely linked and the decision to do an operational act may easily involve and flow from a policy decision. Conversely, the policy is affected by the result of the operational act (see *Reg. v. Chief Constable of Sussex, Ex parte International Trader's Ferry Ltd.* [1998] 3 W.L.R. 1260).

Where a statutory power is given to a local authority and damage is caused by what it does pursuant to that power, the ultimate question is whether the particular issue is justiciable or whether the court should accept that it has no role to play. The two tests (discretion and policy/operational) to which I have referred are guides in deciding that question. The greater the element of policy involved, the wider the area of discretion accorded, the more likely it is that the matter is not justiciable so that no action in negligence can be brought. It is true that Lord Reid and Lord Diplock in the *Dorset Yacht* case accepted that before a claim can be brought in negligence, the plaintiffs must show that the authority is behaving so unreasonably that it is not in truth exercising the real discretion given to it. But the passage I have cited was, as I read it, obiter, since Lord Reid made it clear that the case did not concern such a claim, but rather was a claim that Borstal officers had been negligent when they had disobeyed orders given to them. Moreover, I share Lord Browne-Wilkinson's reluctance [expressed in *X v. Beds*] to introduce the concepts of administrative law into the law of negligence, as Lord Diplock appears to have done. But in any case I do not read what either Lord Reid or Lord Wilberforce in the *Anns* case (and in particular Lord Reid) said as to the need to show that there has been an abuse of power before a claim can be brought in negligence in the exercise of a statutory discretion as meaning that an action can never be brought in negligence where an act has been done pursuant to the exercise of the discretion. A claim of negligence in the taking of a decision to exercise a statutory discretion is likely to be barred, unless it is wholly unreasonable so as not to be a real exercise of the discretion, or if it involves the making of a policy decision involving the balancing of different public interests; acts done pursuant to the lawful exercise of the discretion can, however, in my view be subject to a duty of care, even if some element of discretion is involved. Thus accepting that a decision to take a child into care pursuant to a statutory power is not justiciable, it does not in my view follow that, having taken a child into care, an authority cannot be liable for what it or its employees do in relation to the child without it being shown that they have acted in excess of power. It may amount to an excess of power, but that is not in my opinion the test to be adopted: the test is whether the conditions in the *Caparo* case have been satisfied.

In *Rowling v. Takaro Properties Ltd.* [1988] A.C. 473 Lord Keith of Kinkel, said at p. 501 in giving the opinion of the Privy Council in relation to the policy/operational test:

> "They incline to the opinion, expressed in the literature, that this distinction does not provide a touchstone of liability, but rather is expressive of the need to exclude altogether those cases in which the decision under attack is of such a kind that a question whether it has been made negligently is unsuitable for judicial resolution, of which notable examples are discretionary decisions on the allocation of scarce resources or the distribution of risks: see especially the discussion in *Craig on Administrative Law* (1983), pp. 534–538. If this is right, classification of the relevant decision as a policy or planning decision in this sense may exclude liability; but a conclusion that it does not fall within that category does not, in their Lordships' opinion, mean that a duty of care will necessarily exist."

Both in deciding whether particular issues are justiciable and whether if a duty of care is owed, it has been broken, the court must have regard to the statutory context and to the nature of the tasks involved. The mere fact that something has gone wrong or that a mistake has been made, or that someone has been inefficient does not mean that there was a duty to be careful or that such duty has been broken. Much of what has to be done in this area involves the balancing of delicate and difficult factors and courts should not be too ready to find in these situations that there has been negligence by staff who largely are skilled and dedicated.

Yet although in my view the staff are entitled to rely mutatis mutandis on the principle stated in *Bolam v. Friern Hospital Management Committee* [1957] 1 W.L.R. 582, the jurisdiction to consider whether there is a duty of care in respect of their acts and whether it has been broken is there. I do not see how the interests of the child can be sufficiently protected otherwise . . .

. . . In the present case, the allegations which I have summarised are largely directed to the way in which the powers of the local authority were *exercised*. It is arguable (and that is all we are concerned with in this case at this stage) that if some of the allegations are made out, a duty of care was owed and was broken. Others involve the exercise of a discretion which the court may consider to be not justiciable — e.g. whether it was right to arrange adoption at all, though the question of whether adoption was ever considered and if not, why not, may be a matter for investigation in a claim of negligence. I do not think it right in this case to go through each allegation in detail to assess the chances of it being justiciable. The claim is of an on-going failure of duty and must be seen as a whole. I do not think that it is the right approach to look only at each detailed allegation and to ask whether that in itself could have caused the injury. That must be done but it is appropriate also to consider whether the cumulative effect of the allegations, if true, could have caused the injury.

Nor do I accept that because the court should be slow to hold that a child can sue its parents for negligent decisions in its upbringing that the same should apply necessarily to all acts of a local authority. The latter has to take decisions which parents never or rarely have to take (e.g. as to adoption or as to an appropriate foster parent or institution). In any case, in respect of some matters, parents do have an actionable duty of care.

On the basis that "X" does not conclude the present case in my view it is arguable that at least in respect of some matters alleged both individually and cumulatively a duty of care was owed and was broken . . .

Lord Hutton

. . . I do not think that the speech of Lord Browne-Wilkinson in the *Bedfordshire* case precludes a ruling in the present case that although the decisions of the defendant were within the ambit of its statutory discretion, nevertheless those decisions did not involve the balancing of the type of policy considerations which renders the decisions non-justiciable.

. . . I consider that where a plaintiff claims damages for personal injuries which he alleges have been caused by decisions negligently taken in the exercise of a statutory discretion, and provided that the decisions do not involve issues of policy which the courts are ill-equipped to adjudicate upon, it is preferable for the courts to decide the validity of the plaintiff's claim by applying directly the common law concept of negligence than by applying as a preliminary test the public law concept of *Wednesbury* unreasonableness to determine if the decision fell outside the ambit of the statutory discretion. I further consider that in each case the court's resolution of the question whether the decision or decisions taken by the defendant in exercise of the statutory discretion are unsuitable for judicial determination will require . . . a careful analysis and weighing of the relevant circumstances . . .

Lord Browne-Wilkinson delivered a speech in favour of allowing the appeal. Lords Nolan and Steyn agreed with the speeches of Lords Browne-Wilkinson, Slynn, and Hutton. Appeal allowed.

That *ultra vires* as a condition precedent to negligence claims *vis-à-vis* statutory discretions was abandoned in *Barrett* was placed beyond doubt by Lord Slynn (with whose judgment all the other Law Lords agreed) in *Phelps* v. *Hillingdon London Borough Council* [2001] 2 AC 619 at 653 where he stated:

This House decided in *Barrett v. Enfield London Borough* Council [2001] 2 A.C. 550 that the fact that acts which are claimed to be negligent are carried out within the ambit of a statutory discretion is not in itself a reason why it should be held that no claim for negligence can be brought in respect of them. It is only where what is done has involved the weighing of competing public interests or has been dictated by considerations on which Parliament could not have intended that the courts would substitute their views for the views of Ministers or officials that the courts will hold that the issue is non-justiciable on the ground that the decision was made in the exercise of a statutory discretion.

In *Barrett*, Lord Hutton acknowledged that such an approach might appear inconsistent with that of Lord Browne-Wilkinson in *X*. However, Lord Hutton said that certain *dicta* of Lord Browne-Wilkinson that could (in isolation) be taken to establish a general rule to the effect that *ultra vires* is a condition precedent had to be viewed within their particular context in the *X* case, as dealing with cases where the nature of the issues meant that the court was ill-equipped to adjudicate on matters lying within the discretion of the defendant.

Despite *Barrett* and *Phelps*, it is still possible to find in the later case law instances of an apparent reluctance totally to discard references to the need for any decision to be outside discretion before there can be liability: indeed, in *A* v. *Essex County Council* [2003] EWCA Civ 1848 [2004] 1 WLR 1881 at [48] there is reference to a particular policy decision which 'can only be challenged if it falls outside the realms of reasonableness'. Perhaps in the light of *Barrett* and *Phelps* the policy/operational distinction could have been used. More generally, see *Carty* v. *London Borough of Croydon* [2005] EWCA Civ 19.

The policy/operational distinction, which has already been mentioned (above at 16.2.16), was first specifically introduced into English law by *Anns* v. *Merton London Borough Council* [1978] AC 728 and has had a mixed reception since then. Note the discussion in *Rowling* v. *Takaro Properties Ltd* [1988] AC 583 set out above in *Barrett*. Lord Hoffmann in *Stovin* v. *Wise* was critical of the distinction, but it has received something of a boost from its treatment in *Barrett* (see above) and in *Phelps* (see, *eg* Lord Clyde [2001] 2 AC at 673–674), although it is not accepted as a conclusive or universal test.

A second factor on which *Barrett* and *Phelps* are important is the application of the *Caparo* test for establishing the existence of a duty of care. In *Barrett* the facts of the case were distinguishable from those in *X* v. *Beds*, but some of the comments in considering the question of 'fair, just and reasonable' do not sit easily alongside the approach in the earlier decision. For example, on the question of liability inducing an over-cautious approach, Lord Slynn (with whose speech Lords Nolan and Steyn agreed) approved the following view expressed by Evans LJ in the Court of Appeal in *Barrett* [1998] QB 367 at 380:

I would agree that what is said to be a "policy" consideration, namely that imposing a duty of care might lead to defensive conduct on the part of the person concerned and might require him to spend more time and resources on keeping full records or otherwise providing self-justification, if called upon to do so, should normally be a factor of little, if any, weight. If the conduct in question is of a kind which can be measured against the standards of the reasonable man, placed as the defendant was, then I do not see why the law in the public interest should not require those standards to be observed.

See too the speech of Lord Hutton [2001] 2 AC at 589 where his Lordship would not give the 'defensive approach' factor great weight in the circumstances of the *Barrett* case, and agreed (perhaps more generally and, if so, more significantly) with the last sentence quoted from Evans LJ's judgment. In *Phelps*, in which it was held that a local authority could be vicariously liable to a child for a negligent diagnosis by an educational psychologist it employed in carrying out its statutory duties in relation to education, Lord Clyde suggested (*inter alia*) that the possibility of the imposition of liability on employees of the education authority might secure high standards rather than a defensive attitude, and that alternative remedies might not be as beneficial as a negligence action.

The culmination of the comments in *Barrett* and *Phelps* on the policy factors at work in a case like *X* v. *Beds* coupled with the potential effect of courts adjudicating on Arts 3 and 8 ECHR (which could involve the sorts of enquiries that the House of Lords in *X* v. *Beds* thought were factors against it being 'fair, just and reasonable' to impose a duty of care, but which now might happen in any event), led the Court of Appeal in *D* v. *East Berkshire Community NHS Trust* [2003] EWCA Civ 1151 [2004] 2 QB 558 to the conclusion that *X* v. *Beds*, despite it being a House of Lords decision, need no longer be followed on the 'fair, just and reasonable' point. The Court of Appeal, which was dealing with three cases that involved what turned out to be incorrect allegations by the relevant professional person of sexual abuse of a child by a parent, took the view that a child (as opposed to a parent) might be owed a duty of care. We will not expand on this treatment of *D* as at the time of writing the case had been argued before the House of Lords whose judgment was awaited.

16.2.17 Particular Examples from the Administrative Law Sphere

Public authorities can, of course, be sued in a wide range of situations in the tort of negligence. At this point we will give three examples of cases in the heart of the administrative law area.

The first example is provided by *Rowling* v. *Takaro Properties Ltd* [1988] AC 473 where the Minister of Finance in New Zealand refused consent to the issue of shares in Takaro to an overseas company. Such consent was required by a statutory regulation, but, when challenged in the courts, the refusal was held to have been *ultra vires* on the ground that an irrelevant factor had been taken into account ([1975] 2 NZLR 62). The issue of the shares was part of a financial rescue scheme for Takaro and the delay caused by the legal proceedings to challenge the refusal of consent contributed in part to the main sponsors of the scheme pulling out of it. The Privy Council found that there had been no negligence, but although not deciding whether there was a duty of care, referred to various matters that were of importance on that question and which favoured no liability. Amongst these were that a negligent decision in a case like the present would only cause delay because of the availability of judicial review, that it was very unlikely that the sort of error of law involved would properly be classed as negligent, and the danger of unnecessary delay being caused by a cautious civil servant too frequently seeking a legal opinion. Cf *Lonrho plc* v. *Tebbit* [1992] 4 All ER 220.

Secondly, attention might be paid to the Privy Council's decision in *Dunlop* v. *Woollahra Municipal Council* [1982] AC 158. The defendant council had passed resolutions so as to fix a building line for the claimant's property and the number of storeys in a residential flat building on that property. In later proceedings it was established that both resolutions were invalid, the former on account of a breach of a procedural requirement governing notice to the claimant and the latter since it was *ultra vires*. The consequent negligence action was unsuccessful. In relation to the latter resolution, the Privy Council shared the trial judge's doubts as to whether there was a duty of care to see that the resolution was *intra vires*, but in any event thought there had been no breach of duty. On the position in respect of the former resolution, the Privy Council at 172 expressed the following opinion:

... [The trial judge] held that failure by a public authority to give a person an adequate hearing before deciding to exercise a statutory power in a manner which will affect him or his property, cannot by itself amount to a breach of a duty of care sounding in damages. Their Lordships agree. The effect of the failure is to render the exercise of the power void and the person complaining of the failure is in as good a position as the public authority to know that is so. He can ignore the purported exercise of the power. It is incapable of affecting his rights.

On the controversial view in the latter part of the paragraph quoted above, consider the materials above at 3.2–3.3.

The final example is *R (A) v. Secretary of State for the Home Department* [2004] EWHC 1585 (Admin) where Keith J found that a duty of care could be owed in relation to the administrative implementation of immigration decisions made in respect of the claimants. On the assumed facts they had each lost welfare benefits as a result of a mistake, in one case a letter not being sent and in the other a mistake in the terms of entry endorsed on a passport.

QUESTION

- Could any of the three examples above give rise to an action under any of the other torts previously considered in this chapter?

16.2.18 The Question of Liability for Omissions

In the tort of negligence it is in general harder to establish liability for omissions than for acts. Explanations for this situation can be found in *Stovin v. Wise* [1996] AC 923, although Lord Hoffmann did point out in that case that some of the arguments against liability for an omission do not apply where a public authority is the defendant. (On the other hand, there might be situations where it is possible to argue that a public body should not be liable for an omission even where a private individual would be liable.) In that case (the facts of which are stated, in outline, in our next excerpt) it was argued that a highway authority, in failing to exercise a statutory power, had breached a common law duty of care which, it was argued, the authority owed to the claimant. In rejecting the contention that any such duty existed, Lord Hoffmann (with whom Lords Jauncey and Goff agreed) stated (at 953) that

the minimum preconditions for basing a duty of care upon the existence of a statutory power, if it can be done at all, are, first, that it would in the circumstances have been irrational not to have exercised the power, so that there was in effect a public law duty to act, and secondly, that there are exceptional grounds for holding that the policy of the statute requires compensation to be paid to persons who suffer loss because the power was not exercised.

Against this background, we turn to the next case.

....

Gorringe v. *Calderdale Metropolitan Borough Council* [2004] 1 WLR 1057
House of Lords

Lord Hoffmann

[7] On 15 July 1996, on a country road in Yorkshire, Mrs Denise Gorringe drove her car head-on into a bus. It was hidden behind a sharp crest in the road until just before she reached the top. When she first caught sight of it, a curve on the far side may have given her the impression that it was actually on her side of the road. At any rate, she slammed on the brakes and at 50 miles an hour the wheels locked and the car skidded into the path of the bus. Mrs Gorringe suffered brain injuries severely affecting various bodily functions including speech and movement.

[8] On the face of it, the accident was her own fault. It was certainly not the fault of the bus driver. He was driving with proper care when Mrs Gorringe skidded into him. But she claims in these proceedings that it was the fault of the local authority, the Calderdale Metropolitan Borough Council. She says that the council caused the accident by failing to give her proper warning of the danger involved in driving fast when you could not see what was coming. In particular, the Council should have painted the word "SLOW" on the road surface at some point before the crest. There had been such a marking in the past, but it disappeared, probably when the road was mended seven or eight years before . . .

[His Lordship went on to reject a claim based on s 41 of the Highways Act 1980 (duty to maintain the highway) and continued:]

[17] The alternative claim is for common law negligence. Mr Wingate-Saul QC, who appeared for Mrs Gorringe, accepts that in the absence of the statutory provision to which I shall shortly refer, such a claim would be hopeless . . .

[18] . . . Mr Wingate-Saul submits that a common law duty has been created by (or "in parallel" with) section 39(2) and (3) of the Road Traffic Act 1988:

> "(2) Each local authority must prepare and carry out a programme of measures designed to promote road safety. . . .
> (3) Without prejudice to the generality of sub-section (2) above, in pursuance of their duty under that sub-section each local authority —
>> (a) must carry out studies into accidents arising out of the use of vehicles on roads . . . within their area,
>> (b) must, in the light of those studies, take such measures as appear to the authority to be appropriate to prevent such accidents, including the dissemination of information and advice relating to the use of roads, the giving of practical training to road users or any class or description of road users, the construction, improvement, maintenance or repair of roads for which they are the highway authority . . . and other measures taken in the exercise of their powers for controlling, protecting or assisting the movement of traffic on roads . . ."

[19] These provisions, with their repeated use of the word "must", impose statutory duties. But they are typical public law duties expressed in the widest and most general terms: compare section 1(1) of the National Health Service Act 1977: "It is the Secretary of State's duty to continue the promotion . . . of a comprehensive health service . . .". No one suggests that such duties are

enforceable by a private individual in an action for breach of statutory duty. They are enforceable, so far as they are justiciable at all, only in proceedings for judicial review.

[20] Nevertheless, Mr Wingate-Saul submits that section 39 casts a common law shadow and creates a duty to users of the highway to take reasonable steps to carry out the necessary studies and take the appropriate measures. At any rate, their conduct in compliance with these duties must not be such as can be described as "wholly unreasonable". The judge found that it was unreasonable for the council not to have painted a warning sign on the road and Potter LJ thought that he was entitled to come to this conclusion.

[21] The effect of statutory powers and duties on the common law liability of a highway authority was considered by this House in *Stovin v Wise* [1996] AC 923. Mrs Wise emerged from a side road and ran down Mr Stovin because she was not keeping a proper look-out. When he sued her for damages, she (or rather her insurance company) joined the Norfolk County Council as a third party because the visibility at the intersection was poor and they said that the council should have done something to improve it. The council had statutory powers which would have enabled the necessary work to be done and there was evidence that the relevant officers had decided in principle that it should be done, but they had not got round to doing it.

[22] The decision of the majority was that the council owed no private law duty to road users to do anything to improve the visibility at the intersection. "Drivers of vehicles must take the highway network as they find it." (At p. 958). The statutory power could not be converted into a common law duty. I pointed out in my speech that the council had done nothing which, apart from statute, would have attracted a common law duty of care. It had done nothing at all. The only basis on which it was a candidate for liability was that Parliament had entrusted it with general responsibility for the highways and given it the power to improve them and take other measures for the safety of their users.

[23] Since the existence of these statutory powers is the only basis upon which a common law duty was claimed to exist, it seemed to me relevant to ask whether, in conferring such powers, Parliament could be taken to have intended to create such a duty. If a statute actually imposes a duty, it is well settled that the question of whether it was intended to give rise to a private right of action depends upon the construction of the statute: see *Reg v Deputy Governor of Parkhurst Prison, Ex parte Hague* [1992] 1 AC 58, 159, 168–171. If the statute does not create a private right of action, it would be, to say the least, unusual if the mere existence of the statutory duty could generate a common law duty of care. . . .

[25] [In *O'Rourke v. Camden London Borough Council* [1998] AC 188 — see 14.3.5 above] [i]n the absence of a right to sue for breach of the statutory duty itself, it would in my opinion have been absurd to hold that the council was nevertheless under a common law duty to take reasonable care to provide accommodation for homeless persons whom it could reasonably foresee would otherwise be reduced to sleeping rough. (Compare *Stovin v Wise* at pp 952–953.) And the argument would in my opinion have been even weaker if the council, instead of being under a duty to provide accommodation, merely had a power to do so.

[26] This was the reasoning by which the majority in *Stovin v Wise* came to the conclusion that the council owed no duty to road users which could in any circumstances have required it to improve the intersection. But misunderstanding seems to have arisen because the majority judgment goes on to discuss, in the alternative, what the nature of such a duty might have been if there had been one. It suggests that it would have given rise to liability only if it would have been irrational

in a public law sense not to exercise the statutory power to do the work. And it deals with this alternative argument by concluding that, on the facts, there had been no breach even of such a duty. The suggestion that there might exceptionally be a case in which a breach of a public law duty could found a private law right of action has proved controversial and it may have been ill-advised to speculate upon such matters.

[27] The approach of the minority, in a speech by Lord Nicholls of Birkenhead, was very different. He thought that the statutory powers had invested the highway authority with general responsibilities which could in appropriate circumstances give rise to a common law duty of care. He referred to a number of circumstances which might singly or cumulatively justify the existence of a duty and he said that on the facts there had been such a duty and that the council had been in breach . . .

[32] Speaking for myself, I find it difficult to imagine a case in which a common law duty can be founded simply upon the failure (however irrational) to provide some benefit which a public authority has power (or a public law duty) to provide . . .

[33] [In a previous case (*Larner* v. *Solihull Metropolitan Borough Council* [2001] LGR 255) to which Lord Hoffmann had referred, the Court of Appeal, relying on *Stovin* v. *Wise*, had accepted that there might be exceptional circumstances where a duty of care could arise out of s 39 of the Road Traffic Act 1988. Lord Hoffmann continued:] The Court of Appeal in *Larner* . . . went on to hold that on the facts there had been no breach of duty. But the consequences of the door which it left open can be seen in the present case. The Council was obliged to give discovery of documents relating to its accident studies undertaken pursuant to section 39(3)(a), the decision-making process by which it decided what measures in the light of such studies were appropriate and the steps which had been taken to implement such measures. It was heavily criticised by the judge for the lateness and insufficiency of such discovery. The trial lasted six days, during which the Council called a number of its officers as witnesses and was criticised for not calling enough. The simple facts which I have summarised at the beginning of this speech seem to have disappeared from view in the enthusiasm for a hostile judicial inquiry into the Council's administration. If section 39 continues to provoke investigations of this nature, much of the road safety budget will be consumed in the cost of litigation.

[34] Mr Wingate-Saul said that it did not matter that the danger would have been obvious to a reasonable driver. The duties imposed upon local authorities to promote road safety were imposed in the interests of careless as well as careful drivers. Indeed, he described Mrs Gorringe as "vulnerable" because she did not know the area and compared the case with *Reeves v Commissioner of Police of the Metropolis* [2000] 1 AC 360, in which the police conceded that they owed a duty of care to a prisoner to take reasonable care to prevent him from taking his own life.

[35] Of course it is in the public interest that local authorities should take steps to promote road safety. And it would also be unwise for them to assume that all drivers will take reasonable care for their own safety or that of others. If a driver kills or injures someone else by ignoring an obvious danger, it is little consolation to the victim or his family that the other driver was wholly to blame. And even if the careless driver kills or injures only himself, the accident may have a wider impact upon his family, his economic relationships and the burden on the public services. That is why section 39 of the 1988 Act is framed as a broad public duty. In this respect there is a parallel with the duty to house the homeless discussed in *O'Rourke v Camden London Borough Council* [1998] AC 188. But the public interest in promoting road safety by taking steps to reduce the likelihood that even careless drivers will have accidents does not require a private law duty to a careless driver or

any other road user. *Reeves v Commissioner of Police of the Metropolis* was a highly exceptional case. If I may quote what I said in *Tomlinson v Congleton Borough Council* [2004] 1 AC 46, 85:

> "A duty to protect against obvious risks or self-inflicted harm exists only in cases in which there is no genuine and informed choice, as in the case of employees whose work requires them to take the risk, or some lack of capacity, such as the inability of children to recognise danger (*British Railways Board v Herrington* [1972] AC 877) or the despair of prisoners which may lead them to inflict injury on themselves (*Reeves v Commissioner of Police* [2000] 1 AC 360)."

[36] Nor does it follow that the council should be liable to compensate third parties whom careless drivers have injured. The drivers must take responsibility for the damage they cause and compulsory third party insurance is intended to ensure that they will be able to do so: compare *Stovin v Wise* at p 958 . . .

[38] My Lords, I must make it clear that this appeal is concerned only with an attempt to impose upon a local authority a common law duty to act based solely on the existence of a broad public law duty. We are not concerned with cases in which public authorities have actually done acts or entered into relationships or undertaken responsibilities which give rise to a common law duty of care. In such cases the fact that the public authority acted pursuant to a statutory power or public duty does not necessarily negative the existence of a duty. A hospital trust provides medical treatment pursuant to the public law duty in the National Health Service Act 1977, but the existence of its common law duty is based simply upon its acceptance of a professional relationship with the patient no different from that which would be accepted by a doctor in private practice. The duty rests upon a solid, orthodox common law foundation and the question is not whether it is created by the statute but whether the terms of the statute (for example, in requiring a particular thing to be done or conferring a discretion) are sufficient to exclude it. The law in this respect has been well established since *Geddis v Proprietors of the Bann Reservoir* (1878) 3 App Cas 430.

[Lord Hoffmann then explained the *Dorset Yacht* case, *Barrett*, and *Phelps* along the lines of this reasoning, and continued:]

[44] My Lords, in this case the council is not alleged to have done anything to give rise to a duty of care. The complaint is that it did nothing. Section 39 is the sole ground upon which it is alleged to have had a common law duty to act. In my opinion the statute could not have created such a duty. The action must therefore fail. For these reasons and those of my noble and learned friends Lord Scott of Foscote, Lord Rodger of Earlsferry and Lord Brown of Eaton-under-Heywood, I would dismiss the appeal.

Lord Scott

[71] . . . In my opinion, if a statutory duty does not give rise to a private right to sue for breach, the duty cannot create a duty of care that would not have been owed at common law if the statute were not there. If the policy of the statute is not consistent with the creation of a statutory liability to pay compensation for damage caused by a breach of the statutory duty, the same policy would, in my opinion, exclude the use of the statutory duty in order to create a common law duty of care that would be broken by a failure to perform the statutory duty. I would respectfully accept Lord Browne-Wilkinson's comment in *X (Minors) v Bedfordshire County Council* at page 739 that

> "the question whether there is such a common law duty and if so its ambit, must be profoundly influenced by the statutory framework within which the acts complained of were done."

But that comment cannot be applied to a case where the defendant has done nothing at all to create the duty of care and all that is relied on to create it is the existence of the statutory duty. In short, I do not accept that a common law duty of care can grow parasitically out of a statutory duty not intended to be owed to individuals.

Lords Scott, Rodger, and Brown delivered speeches in which they agreed with each other's speeches and with that of Lord Hoffmann. Lord Steyn delivered a speech in which he agreed that there was no duty of care in this case.

The basic reasoning in *Stovin* was accepted in *Gorringe*. It proceeds along the following lines. Initially it is stated, in discussing the case of statutory duties and the tort of negligence, that if Parliament is not thought to have intended to create a private cause of action for breach of statutory duty (see above at 16.2.4), then by the same policy a common law duty of care would ordinarily be excluded. However, the cogency of this idea as a basis for what follows is surely weakened once it is accepted that the search for parliamentary intent in respect of this matter is a rather artificial one; in any event the standard of liability under the statute may be strict and it does not follow that Parliament would have intended to restrict liability *in the tort of negligence* for a *negligent* breach of duty. In *Gorringe* Lord Steyn agreed with the decision concerning the lack of a duty of care in that case, but did state (in a passage (at [3]) that seems at odds with the approach of his brethren):

. . . [I]n a case founded on breach of statutory duty the central question is whether from the provisions and structure of the statute an intention can be gathered to create a private law remedy? In contradistinction in a case framed in negligence, against the background of a statutory duty or power, a basic question is whether the statute excludes a private law remedy? An assimilation of the two enquiries will sometimes produce wrong results.

In the *Stovin/Gorringe* reasoning, the next step is to put further weight on the fact that a power rather than a duty was imposed, although in *Stovin* it was acknowledged that this might be because the subject-matter precluded a duty from being sufficiently precisely stated. Again it might be asked whether in general Parliament's choice of mandatory or permissive language was really influenced by the question of common law compensation.

16.2.19 When can there be Liability?

In *Gorringe*, Lord Hoffmann (adopting a view that was mirrored by Lords Scott and Brown) sought to reconcile the approach in that case with the approach in cases such as *Barratt*. He did so by pointing out that, in *Barratt*, the local authority's alleged duty of care was founded not upon the *existence* of its relevant statutory powers, but upon the fact that it had *exercised* them in relation to the claimant by assuming parental responsibilities. In contradistinction, the (unsuccessful) argument in *Gorringe* was that the mere existence of the *statutory duty* triggered a *common law duty of care*.

Further guidance can be obtained from the recent Court of Appeal case of *Sandhar* v. *Department of Transport, Environment and the Regions* [2004] EWCA Civ 1440. This case also involved an attempt to hold a highway authority liable in negligence for an omission, the issue here relating to the question of salting of a road. In setting out the position after *Gorringe*, the Court of Appeal stated that in cases of personal or physical injury the first question would be whether (in the case of a statutory duty) there was a direct action in the tort of breach of statutory duty: this will not, of course, be a relevant question in the case of a mere statutory power. The judgment then continues (at [37]–[38]):

Although statutory duties or powers which do not give rise to a private law right of action may constitute part of the relevant factual background, the existence of those duties or powers cannot reinforce parasitically the existence of a common law duty of care in the public authority. In short, unless a statute on its proper construction provides a private law right of action or conversely unless the statute excludes it, the existence of a common law duty of care depends on unvarnished common law principles.

Personal or physical injury directly inflicted is the first building block of the law of negligence. Unless such injury is excused, it will almost always be a component of a breach of a duty of care owed by the person inflicting the injury to the person or the owner of the material object injured. For personal or physical injury which the defendant does not inflict directly or for economic loss, it is usual to look to *Caparo v Dickman* [1990] 2 AC 605 and *Henderson v Merrett Syndicates* [1995] 2 AC 145 for the unvarnished common law principles. For the reasons which I explained with reference to these cases in *Merrett v Babb* [2001] EWCA Civ 214, [2001] QB 1174 at 1192–3 (paragraph 41), reliance is an intrinsically necessary ingredient of a duty of care which appears in every formulation of a test. For the rest, it is very often a helpful guide in particular cases to ask whether the defendant is to be taken to have assumed responsibility to the claimant to guard against the loss for which damages are claimed.

(See also *Bluett* v. *Suffolk County Council* [2004] EWCA Civ 1707 where the passage above is repeated, although, by way of explanation, it is pointed out that the last sentence represents the *Henderson* principle.) The assumption of responsibility concept will, it was stated in *Sandhar*, normally require a particular relationship with an individual or individuals.

At one point in his speech in *Stovin* v. *Wise* Lord Hoffmann had raised the possibility of the fire brigade being sued, and shortly thereafter the issue reached the Court of Appeal in *Capital and Counties plc* v. *Hampshire County Council* [1997] QB 1004. Here it was decided that the brigade owed no duty of care in answering a call, nor in any failure to prevent harm at the scene of the fire. The only liability could be for causing fresh damage or increasing the risk of damage. On the other hand, in *Kent* v. *Griffiths* [2001] QB 36, distinguishing the *Capital and Counties* case, the Court of Appeal decided that the ambulance service did owe a duty of care to a person on whose behalf the ambulance had been called. In *Sandhar* it was thought that the law stated in that case was generally consistent with the law in relation to rescue organizations.

Although the approach in the recent cases has been very restrictive where omissions are concerned, it would appear from the above synthesis in *Sandhar* that it is possible to argue that, subject to the caveat in the first paragraph of the quotation from the case above, a public authority owes a duty of care even in the case of omissions whenever it is taken to have assumed responsibility. However, this phrase is so elusive in terms of its meaning that any such principle is capable of both restrictive and expansive interpretation. One linked issue to raise is the question of the scope of the concept of omission in relation to the restrictive regime of liability in negligence which prevails. Does the approach in *Stovin* (and indeed *Gorringe*) apply in the case where a public authority takes certain steps but fails to ameliorate the position? Rogers (1996) 3 *TLJ* 204 at 209 suggests that *Stovin* does, but in *Barrett* v. *Enfield Borough Council* [1999] AC 550 at 586 Lord Hutton stated that *Stovin* was only concerned with an omission to perform a statutory power and not with a case where the complaint concerned the way in which a power had been implemented. However, in a case where a public body starts to exercise a power that would have prevented harm and fails to achieve it, how hard would it be to decide that the public body has assumed a responsibility to the claimant?

It would be appropriate to end this section with a reference to the argument that has been put forward that there is no need for any special rules when public authorities are sued in negligence, and that the normal structure of the tort of negligence is capable of giving appropriate protection. Note, for example, the comment about breach of duty in professional negligence cases referred to in 16.2.15 and see, more generally, Bailey and Bowman's articles [1984] *PL* 277; [1986] *CLJ* 430; and [2000] *CLJ* 85.

QUESTION

• In the light of the materials in this section, do you agree with the view that no special protection is necessary for public authorities when sued in the tort of negligence?

16.2.20 Nuisance, *Rylands* v. *Fletcher*, and Statutory Authority

A particular area where the statutory authority defence comes up is in the sphere of nuisance and liability under the rule in *Rylands* v. *Fletcher* (1868) LR 3 HL 330.

Managers of the Metropolitan Asylum District v. *Frederick Hill, William Lund and Alfred Fripp* (1881) 6 App Cas 193
House of Lords

The respondents brought an action alleging that the appellants had caused a nuisance by building and operating near the respondents' properties a hospital for people suffering from smallpox and other infectious and contagious diseases. At the trial of the action the jury found that the hospital did constitute a nuisance and the respondents obtained judgment in their favour. In these appeal proceedings the question was whether the appellants, who had acted in accordance with the directions of the Poor Law Board (later the Local Government Board), could successfully raise the defence of statutory authority: the Metropolitan Poor Act 1867 authorized the Board to provide hospital facilities and to direct the appellants to build them. For the purposes of this appeal it was assumed that the maintenance of the hospital, irrespective of how it was run, must necessarily constitute a nuisance.

Lord Blackburn

. . . I think that the case of *The Hammersmith Railway v. Brand* [Law Rep. 4 HL 171], in your Lordships' House, settles, beyond controversy, that where the Legislature directs that a thing shall at all events be done, the doing of which, if not authorized by the Legislature, would entitle any one to an action, the right of action is taken away. It is enough to say that such was the unanimous decision of this House; but the reason briefly given by Lord *Cairns* [Law Rep. 4 HL at 215] seems indisputable. "It is a *reductio ad absurdum*" to suppose it left in the power of the person who had the cause of complaint, to obtain an injunction, and so prevent the doing of that which the Legislature intended to be done at all events. The Legislature has very often interfered with the rights of private persons, but in modern times it has generally given compensation to those injured; and if no compensation is given it affords a reason, though not a conclusive one, for thinking that the intention of the Legislature was, not that the thing should be done at all events, but only that it should be done, if it could be done, without injury to others. What was the intention of the Legislature in any particular Act is a question of the construction of the Act . . .

. . . It is clear that the burthen lies on those who seek to establish that the Legislature intended to take away the private rights of individuals, to shew that by express words, or by necessary implication, such an intention appears. There are no express words in this Act, and I think the weight of argument is rather against than in favour of such an implication . . .

Lord Watson

. . . The judgment of this House in *The Hammersmith Railway Company v. Brand* [Law Rep. 4 HL 171] determines that where Parliament has given express powers to construct certain buildings or works according to plans and specifications, upon a particular site, and for a specific purpose, the use of these works or buildings, in the manner contemplated and sanctioned by the Act, cannot, except in so far as negligent, be restrained by injunction, although such use may constitute a nuisance at common law; and that no compensation is due in respect of injury to private rights, unless the Act provides for such compensation being made. Accordingly the Respondents did not dispute that if the Appellants or the Local Government Board had been, by the *Metropolitan Poor Act*, 1867, expressly empowered to build the identical hospital which they have erected at *Hampstead*, upon the very site which it now occupies, and that with a view to its being used for the treatment of patients suffering from small-pox, the Respondents would not be entitled to the judgment which they have obtained. The Appellants do not assert that express power or authority to that effect has been given by the Act either to themselves or to the Board; but they contend that, having regard to the nature of the public duties laid upon them, and the necessities of the case, it must, on a fair construction of the Act, be held that the Legislature did intend them to exercise, and authorize them to exercise, such power and authority under the direction and control of the Poor Law Board.

I see no reason to doubt that, wherever it can be shewn to be matter of plain and necessary implication from the language of a statute, that the Legislature did intend to confer the specific powers above referred to, the result in law will be precisely the same as if these powers had been given in express terms. And I am disposed to hold that if the Legislature, without specifying either plan or site, were to prescribe by statute that a public body shall, within certain defined limits, provide hospital accommodation for a class or classes of persons labouring under infectious disease, no injunction could issue against the use of an hospital established in pursuance of the Act, provided that it were either apparent or proved to the satisfaction of the Court that the directions of the Act could not be complied with at all, without creating a nuisance. In that case, the necessary result of that which they have directed to be done must presumably have been in the view of the Legislature at the time when the Act was passed.

On the other hand, I do not think that the Legislature can be held to have sanctioned that which is a nuisance at common law, except in the case where it has authorized a certain use of a specific building in a specified position, which cannot be so used without occasioning nuisance, or in the case where the particular plan or locality not being prescribed, it has imperatively directed that a building shall be provided within a certain area and so used, it being an obvious or established fact that nuisance must be the result. In the latter case the onus of proving that the creation of a nuisance will be the inevitable result of carrying out the directions of the Legislature, lies upon the persons seeking to justify the nuisance. Their justification depends upon their making good these two propositions — in the first place, that such are the imperative orders of the Legislature; and in the second place, that they cannot possibly obey those orders without infringing private rights. If the order of the Legislature can be implemented without nuisance, they cannot, in my opinion, plead the protection of the statute; and, on the other hand, it is insufficient for their protection that what is contemplated by the statute cannot be done without nuisance, unless they are also able to shew that the Legislature has directed it to be done. Where the terms of the statute are not imperative, but permissive, when it is left to the discretion of the persons empowered to determine whether the general powers committed to them shall be put into execution or not, I think the fair inference is that the Legislature intended that discretion to be exercised in strict conformity with private rights, and did not intend to confer license to commit nuisance in any place which might be selected for the purpose . . .

His Lordship went on to dismiss the appeal. After analysing the statutory powers he rejected the defence of statutory authority, pointing out that the powers were permissive, not imperative. Appeal dismissed.

One question that can be raised in this context is whether the courts are reading too much into the words used by Parliament. With Lord Watson's speech (above) in particular in mind, Craig argues ((1980) 96 *LQR* 413 at 415) that a lot of modern legislation is

framed in permissive form for administrative reasons and contain[s] no indication of site or method because the matter is too complex or best decided upon by the public body; this tells us nothing about whether a private law action should be sustainable or not.

The defence will fail if the claimant's damage was caused by the defendant's lack of care for obviously the injury is not inevitable in that case and Parliament cannot have intended to authorize it. The view of Viscount Dunedin in *Manchester Corporation* v. *Farnworth* [1930] AC 171 at 183 is often referred to in this context (although in *Allen* v. *Gulf Oil Refining Ltd* [1981] AC at 1016 — and see Murdoch (1981) 97 *LQR* 203 at 205 — Lord Edmund-Davies took a tougher line). Viscount Dunedin's opinion was that

the criterion of inevitability is not what is theoretically possible but what is possible according to the state of scientific knowledge at the time, having also in view a certain common sense appreciation, which cannot be rigidly defined, of practical feasibility in view of situation and of expense.

The question of the precise effect of a statute on a nuisance claim can be a difficult one and in *Department of Transport* v. *North West Water Authority* [1984] AC 336 the House of Lords approved the following propositions which had been advanced (at 344) by Webster J when the case was in the High Court:

1. In the absence of negligence, a body is not liable for a nuisance which is attributable to the exercise by it of a duty imposed upon it by statute: see *Hammond v. Vestry of St. Pancras* (1874) L.R. 9 C.P. 316. 2. It is not liable in those circumstances even if by statute it is expressly made liable, or not exempted from liability, for nuisance: see *Stretton's Derby Brewery Co. v. Mayor of Derby* [1894] 1 Ch. 431, and *Smeaton v. Ilford Corporation* [1954] Ch. 450. 3. In the absence of negligence, a body is not liable for a nuisance which is attributable to the exercise by it of a power conferred by statute if, by statute, it is not expressly either made liable, or not exempted from liability, for nuisance: see *Midwood & Co. Ltd. v. Manchester Corporation* [1905] 2 K.B. 597; *Longhurst v. Metropolitan Water Board* [1948] 2 All E.R. 834; and *Dunne v. North Western Gas Board* [1964] 2 Q.B. 806. 4. A body is liable for a nuisance by it attributable to the exercise of a power conferred by statute, even without negligence, if by statute it is expressly either made liable, or not exempted from liability, for nuisance: see *Charing Cross Electricity Supply Co. v. Hydraulic Power Co.* [1914] 3 K.B. 772.

Two points should be noted. First, the references to liability in nuisance included references to liability under *Rylands* v. *Fletcher*. Secondly, a word of warning needs to be given about the use of the word 'negligence' in this passage. It was acknowledged by Webster J and the House of Lords that in this context the word has a special meaning. Lack of negligence means that the operation be conducted 'with all reasonable regard and care for the interests of other persons' *per* Lord Wilberforce in *Allen* v. *Gulf Oil Refining Ltd* [1981] AC 1001 at 1011.

16.2.21 Other Compensation Possibilities

In situations where the claimant's nuisance action has been defeated by the statutory authority defence, then there may be a claim for compensation under the Land Compensation Act
1973. Section 1 of this Act provides a right to compensation when public works cause the
value of an interest in land (see s 2) to be depreciated by physical factors (defined by s 1(2)
so as to include, *inter alia*, noise, vibration, smell, and fumes.

Complaints of the sort under consideration here may also lead to an argument that there
has been a breach by a public body of Art 8 of ECHR (privacy/family life), incorporated into
English law by the Human Rights Act 1998, and, as we have seen, under s 8 of the 1998 Act
damages may be awarded for any such breach. Of course, the 1998 Act does not allow a court
to override legislation that authorizes a breach, but the interpretative possibilities opened up
by s 3 should not be forgotten: furthermore, the claimant can still take his case to the ECtHR
against a body for which the State is responsible and in this situation the legislative authority
would not *per se* provide a defence.

16.2.22 Public Authorities and Other Aspects of the Tort of Nuisance and *Rylands* v. *Fletcher*

Another way in which statute might affect a nuisance action is if a court interprets the
relevant statute authorizing, for example, certain works as intending to change the immediate environment of the place where the alleged nuisance was suffered. The reason for this is
that in a case where the complaint relates to interference with the use and enjoyment of the
amenities of the land, as opposed to a case of physical damage, the character of the neighbourhood is taken into account. See *Allen* v. *Gulf Oil Refining Ltd* [1980] QB 156 at 172 *per*
Cumming Bruce LJ, approved in the House of Lords [1981] AC 1001.

A different situation — and one rather closer to the situation dealt with above in 16.2.20 —
is revealed by the recent case of *Marcic* v. *Thames Water Utilities Ltd* [2003] UKHL 66 [2004]
2 AC 42. Here the House of Lords refused to extend liability for sewerage to a situation
where the defendant had not created the problem but whose sewerage system was put under
pressure by more homes being connected to the system, something that the defendants were
obliged to accommodate. Although the tort of nuisance had developed to make private
parties potentially liable for failure to abate a hazard even though it was not one of the
defendant's making (*Goldman* v. *Hargrave* [1967] 1 AC 645; *Leakey* v. *National Trust for
Places of Historic Interest or Natural Beauty* [1980] QB 485), the House of Lords took the
view that any such extension of liability for the defendant public body would be inconsistent
with the statutory regime established in the Water Industry Act 1991 which contained its
own system for enforcement. This was the position even though that Act did not directly
rule out any liability for acts or omissions other than those constituting a breach of a
statutory requirement (s 18(8)).

A third issue is the extent to which public benefit or public good may adversely affect a
claimant's chances of success in a nuisance or *Rylands* v. *Fletcher* action. This is, of course,
like the other situations we have considered, not confined to cases where a public authority
is the defendant but more likely to be raised in that context. The influence of public benefit

can be felt in two distinct ways. One argument can be that the defendant was not carrying out an unreasonable user of the land given the public interest in the activity (though for the limited effect of this sort of argument, see *Winfield & Jolowicz on Tort* (London 2002), 14.8): on this view there is no liability in nuisance and hence no damages for the claimant. For there to be liability under *Rylands* v. *Fletcher* the non-natural user requirement has to be satisfied. The famous comment of Lord Moulton in *Rickards* v. *Lothian* [1913] AC 263 at 280 which referred to such a user not 'being such a use as is proper for the general benefit of the community' would appear to be potentially particularly beneficial for public authorities, but the influence of this part of Lord Moulton's views has been downgraded by recent case law in the House of Lords (*Cambridge Water Co* v. *Eastern Counties Leather plc* [1994] 2 AC 264; *Transco plc* v. *Stockport Metropolitan Borough Council* [2003] UKHL 61 [2004] 2 AC 1).

Even if the argument against liability fails (as it may well do), then the question of public benefit may re-occur at the stage of the remedy, namely that if the remedy sought is a *discretionary* one such as an injunction (as it often will be in a nuisance case) or a declaration, then it can be argued that the public interest in the activity continuing militates against its grant. For a recent example raising these sort of issues, see *Dennis* v. *Ministry of Defence* [2003] EWHC 793 (QBD) where the noise associated with training pilots, which was necessary for the defence of the realm, was held to be a nuisance despite the public benefit, but where a declaration was refused.

A final point which should briefly be noted here, as it links into a more general issue in this chapter, is that the argument that the activity of the defendant public body must be *ultra vires* before there is liability in nuisance was rejected in *Page Motors Ltd* v. *Epsom & Ewell Borough Council* (1982) 80 LGR 337, though see the comments of Cane, *Administrative Law* (Oxford 2004) at 291–292.

16.3 Contract

16.3.1 Introduction

The absence of any special body of law of public contracts means that public authorities appear to have the same freedom as the private citizen in deciding with whom to contract and on what terms. This freedom is, however, subject to restrictions imposed by (a) the *ultra vires* doctrine, (b) the laws of the European Community which apply to public contracting in the UK, and (c) specific statutes, including the Human Rights Act 1998. The contractual capacity of public bodies will be considered further below at 16.3.2.

A party to an agreement with a public authority which is not incompatible with its public duties will have 'private law' contractual rights against the authority. As a general rule this will mean that the supervisory jurisdiction by judicial review will not be available (see above at 5.4.4 and 14.3.5) — an important point given the increasing contractualization of government service delivery (discussed above at 1.5.3). See further, in this chapter, *R* v. *Lord Chancellor's Department, ex parte Nangle* [1992] 1 All ER 897, below at 16.3.8.; *McClaren* v. *Home Office* [1990] ICR 824. However, if a contract contains terms required by statute or regulations, these do raise issues of public law for which the claim for judicial review will be available. See in general Beatson (1987) 103 *LQR* 34 at 63; Ewing and Grubb (1987) 16 *ILJ* 145.

We saw above (at 5.4.4) that, even if a contract case is insufficiently 'public' for a claim for judicial review to be available, the public law principle of procedural impropriety may operate as an implied term; it is, however, unclear how far this is true of other public law principles.

16.3.2 (Basic) Contractual Capacity

The Crown has the power to contract without the need for any specific statutory authority since, as a non-statutory corporation sole, its contractual capacity does not appear to be limited. Note that it has also been called a corporation aggregate: generally on this point see Wade (in Sunkin and Payne (eds), *The Nature of the Crown* (Oxford 1999) at 23–24) where he in addition points out that Lord Woolf in *In re M* [1994] 1 AC 377 at 424 stated that the Crown could appropriately be referred to as either but Wade questions how it can be both. In certain cases the powers of individual Ministers have been defined by statute (*eg* s 1 of the Supply Powers Act 1975) or by statutory instruments made under the Ministers of the Crown Act 1975. These may limit the capacity of the Crown itself (*Cugden Rutile (No 2) Ltd v. Chalk* [1975] AC 520) or the scope of the authority possessed by Ministers and Crown agents (see below at 16.3.6). On one view of the prerogative (see Dicey, *An Introduction to the Study of the Law of the Constitution* (London 1959), ch 14 but compare Blackstone, *Commentaries,* vol 1 at 239) the Crown's power to contract could be seen as a prerogative power and this would raise the issue of control of prerogative powers which was discussed above at 5.3; if it is not seen as a prerogative power, then the type of control which was discussed at 5.4 will need to be considered.

On a procedural point, note that at one time it was recognized the Crown could be liable for breach of contract, but the only remedy was a petition of right. Legislation in 1947 changed this position.

....

Crown Proceedings Act 1947

1 Where any person has a claim against the Crown after the commencement of this Act, and, if this Act had not been passed, the claim might have been enforced, subject to the grant of His Majesty's fiat, by petition of right, or might have been enforced by a proceeding provided by any statutory provision repealed by this Act, then, subject to the provisions of this Act, the claim may be enforced as of right, and without the fiat of His Majesty, by proceedings taken against the Crown for that purpose in accordance with the provisions of this Act.

Broadly, as a result of the 1947 Act, proceedings against the Crown in contract are now similar to those applying between subjects, but there are some significant differences. As has been seen, no injunctive or specific relief may be given against the Crown in any 'civil proceedings', on which see above at 13.2.3. Other differences will be explored in this chapter, and note further s 40 of the 1947 Act which was set out above at 16.2.2.

Generally speaking, public bodies other than the Crown need statutory authority to contract, although this can be express or implied. The problems that this can cause can be shown by a case such as *Hazell* v. *Hammersmith and Fulham London Borough Council* [1992] 2 AC 1 which involved what was known as a 'swap contract'. The authority had entered into several of these contracts and would make or lose money under them depending on the movement of interest rates. The House of Lords held that the local authority had no power to enter into such swaps contracts. Large sums of money were at stake (other authorities had also entered into these sorts of contracts) but there could be no contractual action to recover money which was owed. On the possibility of restitutionary claims in this context, see 16.4 and on the pubic law aspects of the 'swaps' cases, see Bamforth (in Birks and Rose (eds), *Lessons from the Swaps Litigation* (London 2000), ch 2). Note also the invalidity of the contracts involved in *Credit Suisse* v. *Allerdale Borough Council* [1997] QB 306 and *Credit Suisse* v. *Waltham Forest London Borough Council* [1997] QB 362.

A measure of flexibility in respect of the consequences of an invalid contract is now provided by the Local Government (Contracts) Act 1997. In addition to s 1 increasing the capacity of local authorities (as defined) to contract, s 2(1) provides:

Where a local authority [as defined] has entered into a contract, the contract shall, if it is a certified contract, have effect (and be deemed always to have had effect) as if the local authority had had power to enter into it (and had exercised that power properly in entering into it).

Certification is dealt with in detail by ss 3 and 4. One particular point to note is that it must be a contract which lasts or is intended to last for five years or more and which the local authority has entered into with another for the provision of services (although assets and goods can be included with the services) in connection with the discharge of any of the authority's functions (s 4(3)), and see s 4(4) which includes certain contracts entered into by the local authority with another related to the financing of the other party to a s 4(3) contract. The Act then provides an interesting mechanism for solving some of the difficulties seen above. Under s 5 it prohibits s 2(1) from applying in a claim for judicial review (or in an audit review, as defined in s 8 of the Act) on the question whether the local authority 'had power to enter into a contract (or exercised any power properly in entering into a contract)' and makes it subject to any order or determination concerning a 'certified contract' made in such proceedings. In fact no such order or determination can affect the enforceability of a relevant discharge term (as defined) (s 6) and where it has agreed discharge terms, they are to have effect as if the local authority had had power so to agree (though this is subject to s 7(3)). In a claim for judicial review, the court can order that the contract is invalid, but even if it takes that view is not obliged to make such an order since s 5(3) lays down:

Where, on [a claim] for judicial review or an audit review relating to a certified contract entered into by a local authority, a court —

(a) is of the opinion that the local authority did not have power to enter into the contract (or exercised any power improperly in entering into it), but

(b) (having regard in particular to the likely consequences for the financial provision of the local authority and for the provision of services to the public, of a decision that the contract should not have effect) considers that the contract should have effect,

the court may determine that the contract has (and always has had) effect as if the local authority had had power to enter into it (and had exercised that power properly in entering into it).

The position where there are discharge terms has already been mentioned. Where there are no such terms which are effective between the local authority and another contractual party and the result of the order or determination in proceedings governed by s 5 is that the 'certified contract' is ineffective, s 7(2) comes into play and provides for the local authority to pay that other contractual party such sums (if any) as he would have been entitled to be paid by the local authority if the contract —

(a) had had effect until the time when the determination or order had was made, but
(b) had been terminated at that time by acceptance by him of a repudiatory breach by the local authority.

QUESTION

- Would it be better if legislation was passed giving unlimited authority to enter contracts on the part of any public body (unless expressly or impliedly prohibited by statute)?

16.3.3 Freedom to Contract

The *ultra vires* doctrine clearly has potential as a control over refusals to contract at all or only on particular terms. In principle such refusals may fall foul of the non-fettering principle or be 'unfair' in the light of an individual's legitimate expectations (above at 6.4 and 7.1 and see *Wheeler* v. *Leicester City Council* [1985] AC 1054, above at 9.3.1). In *R* v. *Lewisham LBC, ex parte Shell UK Ltd* [1988] 1 All ER 938 a council's refusal to contract with Shell UK as part of a campaign to persuade other local authorities to boycott trade with Shell UK so as to bring pressure on the Shell Group to sever its trading links with South Africa was held *ultra vires* on the ground of improper purpose under the relevant legislation. However, decisions by public authorities are not invariably susceptible to judicial review. In *R* v. *Lord Chancellor, ex parte Hibbit and Saunders* [1993] COD 326, concerning the decision of the defendant (which is, of course, a part of the Crown) not to award to the claimant a contract for reporting services in certain courts, it was held that, although there had been unfairness in the conduct of the tendering process, the decision lacked a sufficient public law element to render it amenable to judicial review. According to Waller J, the position would have been different had there been a 'statutory obligation to negotiate [the] contract in a particular way, with particular terms, and [the defendant had failed] to perform that statutory obligation', or indeed if the defendant had been acting pursuant to a particular statutory power in which an implied obligation to act fairly could have been found.

The above paragraph raises the issue of the use of the contracting power as an instrument of policy (on which see generally Arrowsmith (1995) 111 *LQR* 235). This may occur in the allocation of contracts, for example, to support certain home industries, to support regions that are underdeveloped or have a high level of unemployment by preferring tenders from companies operating in those regions, and to encourage the reorganization of an industry. Policy may also be promoted by insisting on the inclusion of certain terms in contracts, although note that if a standard term excludes or restricts liability, the Unfair Contract Terms Act 1977 will apply (and consider also the Unfair Terms in Consumer Contracts Regulations 1999).

A notable example of this use of the contracting power by government to implement a specific policy was the Labour government's attempt, between 1975 and 1978, to ensure that various non-statutory wages policies set out in 'guidelines' issued by the government were adhered to. Terms were inserted in government contracts requiring the contractor to adhere to the policies and to require a similar undertaking from any sub-contractor. Companies that broke the pay policy were placed on a 'blacklist' and were not awarded contracts thereafter. The government also sought to withhold assistance and grants under the Export Credit Guarantee scheme and the Industry Act 1972. The government had tried and failed to secure parliamentary sanction for its pay policy and these practices were accordingly criticized on constitutional grounds. Other criticism stemmed from inconsistency in the application of the 'blacklisting' policy; see further Ganz [1978] *PL* 333; Daintith (1979) 32 *CLP* 41. More broadly, between 1891 and 1983 (when it was rescinded) the Fair Wages Resolution of the House of Commons was invariably incorporated in the contracts of the government departments. *Inter alia*, this required those who contracted with the government to pay their employees wages that were not less favourable than those established for the relevant industry in the district where the work was to be carried out and to refrain from unlawful discrimination in employment.

However, public bodies are by no means unfettered in their ability to use contract as an instrument of policy. For instance, EC law imposes a number of restrictions in this area, stemming (*inter alia*) from the principles of non-discrimination enshrined in the EC Treaty; such restrictions bite, for example, if compliance with given contractual standards is liable to be more difficult for other EC, as opposed to domestic, contractors. In addition, EC law prescribes how the tendering process must be conducted in respect of certain types of contract. Moreover, s 17 of the Local Government Act 1988 imposes a general duty on local and many other public authorities to exercise their functions in relation to public works or supply contracts without reference to 'non-commercial matters'. Although exceptions do permit certain account to be taken of race relations matters (see s 18), and now (in the case of many public bodies and for certain purposes) the terms of employment used by contractors and their track-record in relation to industrial disputes (see SI 2001/909, Local Government Best Value (Exclusion of Non-Commercial Considerations) Order 2001; SI 2002/678, Local Government Best Value (Exclusion of Non-commercial Considerations) (Wales) Order 2002), s 17 is clearly a substantial curb on the use of contracting power as an instrument of policy. Note also that special provision is made in respect of Northern Ireland, bearing in mind its particular circumstances. Section 76 of the Northern Ireland Act 1998 makes it unlawful for a 'public authority carrying out functions relating to Northern Ireland to discriminate . . . against a person or class of persons on the ground of religious belief or political opinion'. As a result, it is unlawful for public authorities to discriminate on such grounds when awarding contracts. In addition, the Fair Employment and Treatment (Northern Ireland) Order 1998 prohibits discrimination in the employment context on the grounds of religious belief and political opinion, and imposes upon employers duties to record and furnish the Equality Commission for Northern Ireland with information about (*inter alia*) the community to which each employee belongs; failure to comply with this monitoring regime may result in the employer being disqualified from tendering for public authority contracts.

16.3.4 Is Parliamentary Appropriation of Funds Necessary?

....

The State of New South Wales v. *Bardolph* (1934) 52 CLR 455
High Court of Australia

Acting on the authority of the State Premier, and 'as a matter of Government policy', the New South Wales Tourist Bureau contracted for the insertion of advertisements in the claimant's newspaper, *Labor Weekly*, for a period of twelve months in the financial years 1931–32 and 1932–33. Shortly after the making of the contract there was a change of government and the new administration refused to use or to pay for any further advertising space in the newspaper. The claimant (Bardolph) continued to insert the advertisements for the remainder of the contract period and claimed £1,114 10s, the amount outstanding on the contract. The contract had not been expressly authorized by the State legislature or by any Order in Council or executive minute. The Supply and Appropriation Acts for the relevant years included the provision of sums for 'Government advertising'. This provision was for sums much larger than the amount involved in the contract.

Evatt J

. . . The suggested defence that the contract was not authorized by the Government completely fails. It is only right to add that, although raised in the pleadings, this defence was not seriously pressed at the hearing.

The main, indeed the only real defence relied upon by the State of New South Wales, was that Parliament did not make public moneys available for the express purpose of paying the plaintiff for his advertising services. The defence is, of course, quite unmeritorious, and its success might tend to establish a dangerous precedent in the future. But it raises an interesting question of law, the examination of which shows that the repudiation of subsisting agreements by a new administration can seldom be ventured upon with success . . .

[He then considered the facts in relation to the relevant grants of public money by Parliament for the period ending 30 June 1932, and concluded:] The net result is that the total supply which Parliament made available during the year for Government advertising can be reckoned as amounting to eleven-twelfths of £6,600, plus one-twelfth of £9,900, that is, £6,875 in all.

It appears from the statement prepared by Mr. Kelly, Chief Accountant at the Treasury, that if payment had been made to the plaintiff in respect of the advertisements inserted before the end of the financial year, 30th June, 1932, but not paid for, the total expenditure for the service would only have amounted to £4,595 18s, a figure considerably lower than the assumed minimum supply voted by Parliament, that is, £6,875. . . .

Before referring to what took place in the financial year 1932–1933, it is convenient to consider the legal position as it existed on and in respect of 30th June, 1932. It was argued for the State that it was a condition of the contracts with the plaintiff that all payments of money thereunder should be authorized by Act of Parliament, and it was said that no person can successfully sue the State of New South Wales in the absence of a precise or specific Parliamentary allocation of public moneys for the purpose of making payments under the contracts. It was further contended that, even in an Appropriation Act, the constitutional condition of such contracts is not fulfilled unless it can be shown that Parliament's intention was directed to the particular payment to the particular contractor. . . .

In the well-known case of *Churchward* v. *The Queen* [(1865) LR 1 QB 173], Shee J., in a passage often cited, adopted the principle that, in the case of a contract by a subject with the Crown, there should be implied a condition that the providing of funds by Parliament is a condition precedent to the Crown's liability to pay moneys which would otherwise be payable under the contract. In that case the actual promise was to pay a sum 'out of the moneys to be provided by Parliament' (see *Churchward* v. *The Queen*); so that the judgment of Shee J. went beyond the actual point necessary to determine the case. *Churchward's Case* was decided upon demurrer, the third plea alleging that 'no moneys were ever provided by Parliament for the payment to the suppliant for, *or out of which the suppliant could be paid* for the performance of the said contract, for any part of the said period subsequent to the 20th June, 1863, or for the payment to the suppliant for, and in respect of, or *out of which the suppliant could be paid* or *compensated for*, in respect of any damages sustained by the suppliant by reason of any of the breaches of the said contract committed subsequent to the said 20th of June, 1863'. (I italicize certain words.)

Further, the *Appropriation Acts* referred to in that case expressly provided that Churchward's claim was to be excluded from the large sum of money (£950,000) thereby voted for the general purposes of providing and maintaining the Post Office Packet Service. The judgment of *Shee* J. has always been accepted as determining the general constitutional principle. But it should be added that *Cockburn* C.J. said:

> "I agree that, if there had been no question as to the fund being supplied by Parliament, if the condition to pay had been absolute, or if there had been a fund applicable to the purpose, and this difficulty did not stand in the petitioner's way, and he had been throughout ready and willing to perform this contract, and had been prevented and hindered from rendering these services by the default of the Lords of the Admiralty, then he would have been in a position to enforce his right to remuneration."

It appears clear that the first part of this passage has not been acted upon by the Courts in the cases subsequently determined, and that, even where the contract to pay is in terms "absolute" and the contract fails to state that the fund has to be "supplied by Parliament," the Crown is still entitled to rely upon the implied condition mentioned by *Shee* J.

The second part of *Cockburn's* C.J. statement, that, if there is a fund 'applicable to the purpose' of meeting claims under the contract, the contractor may enforce his right to remuneration, has never, so far as I know, been questioned. Moreover, its correctness was assumed by the terms of the Crown's third plea in *Churchward's Case* which denies that moneys were ever provided by Parliament 'out of which the suppliant could be paid for the performance of the said contract.'. . . .

[He then considered *Commercial Cable Co.* v. *Government of Newfoundland* [1916] 2 AC 610 and *Auckland Harbour Board* v. *R* [1924] AC 318. The former gave no guidance as to what constitutes a sufficient expression of the legislature's discretion to grant or withhold public moneys. The latter did not] justify the theory that, where there is nothing unlawful in a contract entered into by the Crown, and that contract is authorized by responsible Ministers, and made by them in the ordinary course of administering the affairs of Government, a detailed reference to the particular contract must be found in the statutory grant in order to satisfy the constitutional condition laid down in *Churchward's Case* . . .

It has been the practice of the Government to enter into advertising contracts, the performance of which extends or may extend into more than one financial year, apart altogether from the innumerable contracts for single insertion advertisements in newspapers and periodicals. For instance, on 1st June, 1932, the Government entered into a contract with the proprietor of the *Sydney Morning Herald*, and accepted a heavy liability for advertisements covering the month of June in the financial year 1931–1932, and eleven months during the following financial year. Payments were made to the proprietor from time to time in accordance with the contract. But no reference whatever was made to this particular contract in any Act of Parliament. If the argument for the State is right, this money is recoverable back from the proprietor, although the contract has been fully performed on the part of the newspaper. Contracts of a like character were admitted in evidence in order to show the practice of the Government in relation to the Government advertising business of the State and in order to measure the precise surplus or deficiency in the Parliamentary grants for advertising. But the contracts also show that it has never been the practice for Parliament itself to consider with particularity that large number of contracts, payments under all of which are made in reliance upon the general Parliamentary grant for Government advertising. . . .

[After considering the views of Durell, *Parliamentary Grants*, pp. 21, 296, and 297, and Maitland, *Constitutional History of England*, pp. 445–6, he concluded:] [I]n the absence of some controlling statutory provision, contracts are enforceable against the Crown if *(a)* the contract is entered into in the ordinary or necessary course of Government administration, *(b)* it is authorized by the responsible Ministers of the Crown, and *(c)* the payments which the contractor is seeking to recover are covered by or referable to a parliamentary grant for the class of service to which the contract relates. In my opinion, moreover, the failure of the plaintiff to prove *(c)* does not affect the validity of the contract in the sense that the Crown is regarded as stripped of its authority or capacity to enter into the contract. Under a constitution like that of New South Wales where the legislative and executive authority is not limited by reference to subject matter, the general capacity of the Crown to enter into a contract should be regarded from the same point of view as the capacity of the King would be by the Courts of common law. No doubt the King had special powers, privileges, immunities and prerogatives. But he never seems to have been regarded as being less powerful to enter into contracts than one of his subjects. The enforcement of such contracts is to be distinguished from their inherent validity . . .

In the present case, the position as it existed on 30th June, 1932, was that *(a)* the Crown had made contracts with the plaintiff, and *(b)* moneys had been made legally available by the Supply Acts, including that of June, 1932. It is admitted that the advertising service vote, if otherwise sufficient to satisfy the rule in *Churchward's Case*, covered the service called for by the contracts with the plaintiff. On 30th June, therefore, there was *(a)* an existing contract, *(b)* a sufficient compliance with the rule in *Churchward's Case*, *(c)* a proved performance by the plaintiff of the contract on his part, *(d)* proved non-payment for this service for five weeks at £29 *12s.* 6d. per week, that is, £148 *2s.* 6d. in all.

It cannot be too strongly emphasized at all points of this case that the plaintiff's contracts were not with the Ministers individually or collectively, but with the Crown . . .

. . . The honour of the Crown demands that, subject to Parliament's having made one or more funds available, all contracts for the Crown's departments and services should be honoured. The position on 30th June, 1932, having been examined, what was the position existing on 1st July, 1932, the first day of the financial year 1932–1933? In my opinion, it was plainly this, that the plaintiff's contract with the Crown was still on foot . . . The condition that payments thereunder depended upon moneys being made legally available by Parliament still subsisted, but the contract was not inchoate or suspended but existing . . .

The only question therefore, is whether in respect to the year 1932–1933 also the condition of *Churchward's Case* was satisfied . . .

In order to secure a judgment declaring the Crown's liability, a person who has a subsisting contract with the Crown satisfies the constitutional doctrine laid down in *Churchward's Case* in respect of payments accruing during the financial year when he completes the performance of his contract if, at the time of such completion, there exists in respect of such financial year sufficient moneys in the vote for the relevant service to enable the payments in question to be lawfully made. I also think that the plaintiff is entitled to say that the constitutional doctrine was satisfied in respect of all payments falling due between 1st July, 1932, and the date of his completing his contract if, at the date of the passing of the *Appropriation Act* (8th November, 1932), enough moneys to pay him in full could have been lawfully paid or set aside to pay him from moneys then remaining from the parliamentary grant in respect of advertising. From a close consideration of the figures and evidence, I draw the inferences of fact that *(a)* on 8th November, 1932, sufficient moneys were available to pay him what was then owing to him in respect of services rendered in the year 1932–1933, and *(b)* sufficient moneys from the same grant were also available to pay him in full on 31st March, when he finally completed the performance of his contracts . . .

The above reasoning shows that the plaintiff is entitled to succeed in the argument based on *Churchward's Case*.

Judgment for the plaintiff. The State appealed to the Full Court.

Dixon J

. . . It remains to deal with the contention that the contract is unenforceable because no sufficient appropriation of moneys has been made by Parliament to answer the contract. "The general doctrine is that all obligations to pay money undertaken by the Crown are subject to the implied condition that the funds necessary to satisfy the obligation shall be appropriated by Parliament" (*New South Wales* v. *The Commonwealth [No 1]* [(1930) 44 CLR at 353]). But, in my opinion, that general doctrine does not mean that no contract exposes the Crown to a liability to suit . . . unless and until an appropriation of funds to answer the contract has been made by the Parliament concerned, or unless some statutory authorization or recognition of the contract can be found.

. . . The principles of responsible government impose upon the administration a responsibility to Parliament, or rather to the House which deals with finance, for what the Administration has done. It is a function of the Executive, not of Parliament, to make contracts on behalf of the Crown. The Crown's advisers are answerable politically to Parliament for their acts in making contracts. Parliament is considered to retain the power of enforcing the responsibility of the Administration by means of its control over the expenditure of public moneys. But the principles of responsible government do not disable the Executive from acting without the prior approval of Parliament, nor from contracting for the expenditure of moneys conditionally upon appropriation by Parliament and doing so before funds to answer the expenditure have actually been made legally available. Some confusion has been occasioned by the terms in which the conditional nature of the contracts of the Crown from time to time has been described, terms chosen rather for the sake of emphasis than of technical accuracy. But, in my opinion, the manner in which the doctrine was enunciated by *Isaacs* C.J., when he last had occasion to state it, gives a correct as well as a clear exposition of it. In *Australian Railways Union* v. *Victorian Railways Commissioners* [(1932) 46 CLR at 176], he said: "It is true that every contract with any responsible government of His Majesty, whether it be one of a mercantile character or one of service, is subject to the condition that before payment is made out of the Public Consolidated Fund Parliament must appropriate the necessary sum. But subject to that condition, unless some competent statute properly construed makes the appropriation a condition precedent, a contract by the Government otherwise within its authority is binding." Notwithstanding expressions capable of a contrary interpretation which have occasionally been used, the prior provision of funds by Parliament is not a condition preliminary to the obligation of the contract. If it were so, performance on the part of the subject could not be exacted nor could he, if he did perform, establish a disputed claim to an amount of money under his contract until actual disbursement of the money in dispute was authorised by Parliament.

[He then considered the authorities, including *Churchward* v. *R*, and continued:] [The true position there was that] the provision of funds by Parliament [was] simply . . . a contractual condition and . . . a condition which must be fulfilled before actual payment by the Crown, but not . . . a matter going to the formation, legality, or validity of the contract, and not . . . a condition precedent to suit . . .

In my opinion, it is not an answer to a suit against a State . . . upon a contract, that the moneys necessary to answer the liability have not up to the time of the suit been provided by Parliament. This does not mean that, if Parliament has by an expression of its will in a form which the Court is bound to notice, refused to provide funds for the purposes of the contract, it remains actionable . . .

That question does not arise in the present case. Indeed a ground upon which the judgment of *Evatt* J. is based is that moneys were provided by Parliament out of which the liability to the plaintiff might lawfully be discharged. I do not in any way disagree with this view, but, as I have formed a definite opinion that the contention of the Crown misconceives the doctrine upon which it is founded, I have thought it desirable to place my judgment upon the grounds I have given.

In my opinion the judgment of *Evatt* J. is right and should be affirmed.

Gavan Duffy CJ agreed with Dixon J. Rich, Starke, and McTier Nan JJ delivered judgments in favour of dismissing the appeal. Appeal dismissed.

Street, *Governmental Liability* (Cambridge, 1953) at 91–92, argues that without the necessary parliamentary appropriation the contract, although valid, is 'unenforceable' in the sense in which that word is used for contracts which do not comply with formal requirements, such as the requirement of writing formerly specified in the Statute of Frauds (see now, for example, s 2 of the Law of Property (Miscellaneous Provisions) Act 1989). Compare Turpin, *Government and Procurement Contracts* (Harlow 1989) at 93–94, who points out that in the highly unlikely event that payment was refused because it would exceed the existing appropriation, there is no reason in principle why a contractor should not be able to sue the Crown and obtain judgment. Turpin suggests that a court will normally be justified in assuming that money is or will be made available, and continues:

this inference would be rebutted only by a clear indication . . . of Parliament's unwillingness to allow payment of the contractor, or if the court were satisfied that Parliament had not voted money sufficient for this purpose and would not be asked to do so. In these remote contingencies the court would doubtless be obliged to dismiss the suit and the contract would be unenforceable against the Crown.

See further Hogg and Monahan, *Liability of the Crown* (Scarborough, Ontario 2000) at 52–54.

QUESTIONS

- In *Bardolph* did Dixon J (with whom Rich and Starke JJ agreed on this point) differ from Evatt J on the effect of a failure to appropriate?
- Whatever the relevance of parliamentary appropriation today, can and should the rule apply beyond central government?

16.3.5 The Non-Fettering Rule

This topic has already been discussed to an extent at 6.4. At that point cases such as *Ayr Harbour Trustees* v. *Oswald* (1883) 8 App Cas 623 and *Birkdale Electricity Supply Co* v. *Corporation of Southport* [1926] AC 355 were considered in relation to the question of the appropriate balance between discretionary powers and contractual arrangements. The extract below also deals with this issue, but, as a matter of convenience, has been set out in this chapter.

....

Rederiaktiebolaget Amphitrite v. *The King* [1921] 3 KB 500
King's Bench Division

During World War I the British Government operated a 'ship for ship' policy whereby neutral ships in British ports should be allowed to leave only if they were replaced by other ships of the same tonnage. The applicants, the Swedish owners of the *Amphitrite*, wrote to the British Legation in Stockholm stating that they would send the vessel to England if they were guaranteed that it would not be detained. After consulting the proper authorities, on 18 March 1918 the Legation replied: 'I am instructed to say that the S.S. *Amphitrite* will earn her own release and be given a coal cargo if she proceed to the United Kingdom with a full cargo consisting of at least 60% approved goods.' The vessel completed a round trip to Hull and the owners asked that the undertaking be renewed for another voyage. This was done, but on the second voyage she was detained and told that clearance would only be granted if the application was made through a body known as the Swedish Shipping Committee. As a result of former dealings they had had with the Germans, the applicants were disqualified from applying through the Committee and, eventually, they sold the vessel. After the war they presented a petition of right claiming damages for breach of the contract contained in the two letters.

Rowlatt J

. . . I have not to consider whether there was anything of which complaint might be made outside a Court, whether that is to say what the Government did was morally wrong or arbitrary; that would be altogether outside my province. All I have got to say is whether there was an enforceable contract, and I am of opinion that there was not. No doubt the Government can bind itself through its officers by a commercial contract, and if it does so it must perform it like anybody else or pay damages for the breach. But this was not a commercial contract; it was an arrangement whereby the Government purported to give an assurance as to what its executive action would be in the future in relation to a particular ship in the event of her coming to this country with a particular kind of cargo. And that is, to my mind, not a contract for the breach of which damages can be sued for in a Court of law. It was merely an expression of intention to act in a particular way in a certain event. My main reason for so thinking is that it is not competent for the Government to fetter its future executive action, which must necessarily be determined by the needs of the community when the question arises. It cannot by contract hamper its freedom of action in matters which concern the welfare of the State. Thus in the case of the employment of public servants, which is a less strong case than the present, it has been laid down that, except under an Act of Parliament, no one acting on behalf of the Crown has authority to employ any person except upon the terms that he is dismissible at the Crown's pleasure; the reason being that it is in the interests of the community that the Ministers for the time being advising the Crown should be able to dispense. with the services of its employees if they think it desirable. Again suppose that a man accepts an office which he is perfectly at liberty to refuse, and does so on the express terms that he is to have certain leave of absence, and that when the time arrives the leave is refused in circumstances of the greatest hardship to his family or business, as the case may be. Can it be conceived that a petition of right would lie for damages? I should think not. I am of opinion that this petition must fail and there must be judgment for the Crown.

Judgment for the Crown.

In *Robertson* v. *Minister of Pensions* [1949] 1 QB 427, Denning J stated that the doctrine of executive necessity propounded in *Amphitrite* was only *obiter* 'because the statement there was not a promise that was intended to be binding but only an expression of intention'. This does not seem convincing. However, if the *ratio* is that a contract that purports to fetter the

Crown's freedom of executive action is invalid, then the authority of the case might be thought to be affected by the fact that the case law on fettering and public authorities (see above at 6.4) was not considered.

Another problem that needs to be addressed is what real fetter there would have been on the Crown if Rowlatt J had held there was a contract, in view of the immunity of the Crown from specific performance and injunctive relief in 'civil proceedings' (see above at 13.2.3). Consider Hogg, *Liability of the Crown* (Melbourne 1971) at 139, but note Hogg and Monahan, *op cit* at 229, n 84.

Hogg and Monahan, *op cit* at 228–229

acknowledge the possibility that the Crown may feel compelled by considerations of public policy to break a contractual undertaking. If there were no doctrines of executive necessity, the ordinary law of contract would apply, and would require the Crown to negotiate with the other party for a variation or release, or to pay damages for its breach of contract. That is surely the right result. It provides compensation for the injured contractor. And it requires the public purse to bear the cost of the change of public policy.

The question of the validity of the contract is separate from the question whether the Crown or other public body is under a duty to exercise its powers consistently with the provisions of an admittedly valid contract, but as the cases, including *The Amphitrite*, have not always taken the distinction, both can conveniently be considered together. For discussion of the first in relation to public authorities other than the Crown, see above at 6.4. As far as initial validity is concerned, Rowlatt J's distinction between commercial and non-commercial contracts has been criticized (Holdsworth (1929) 45 *LQR* 166; Mitchell, *The Contracts of Public Authorities*, at 62; *Ansett Transport Industries (Operations) Pty Ltd* v. *Commonwealth of Australia* (1977) 17 *ALR* 513 at 562). It may, however, be possible to explain Rowlatt J's view that there was no contract on the ground that the only consideration moving from the Crown was the undertaking to exercise its discretion in a particular way. Even on this approach the applicability of the 'incompatibility' test used in the cases on public authorities might have saved the contract which perhaps shows that the incompatibility test espoused by those cases and the doctrine in the *Amphitrite* do not sit easily together. Are there any reasons that justify treating the Crown differently from other public authorities in this respect? See further Craig, *Administrative Law* (London, 2003) at 548–549, arguing for the incompatibility test to be applied to cases involving the Crown.

Amphitrite needs to be kept in perspective, however. Turpin, *op cit* at 90, states:

. . . [I]f the government decides that the public interest requires a government contract to be brought to an end, it will usually (in a contract for the procurement of goods or services) be able to determine the contract under the standard contractual "break" clause, rather than seek to rely on the rule of government effectiveness. In this event provision is made by the standard clause for the compensation of the contractor, in a measure less than that for contractual damages.

For examples of governmental use of the contracting power see above at 16.3.3. Note that the controls imposed by the Unfair Contract Terms Act 1977 on standard terms of business which exclude or restrict liability extend to government contracts since, by s 14, the activities of any government department are within the scope of the Act. (It will be remembered that statutes only bind the Crown by express wording or necessary implication.) Note also the Unfair Terms in Consumer Contracts Regulations 1999.

Where the Crown has made a valid contract it is necessary to consider the extent of its obligations under the contract. The question whether it is ever justifiable for the Crown to escape from an otherwise enforceable contract in the public interest is considered in the next extract.

....

Commissioners of Crown Lands v. Page [1960] 2 QB 274
Court of Appeal

The Crown had leased premises for 25 years, but eight years later, acting under the Defence (General) Regulations 1939, the Minister of Works, on behalf of the Crown, requisitioned the premises. There was no express covenant for quiet enjoyment in the lease and it was held that the implied covenant could not have been intended to 'extend to prevent the future exercise by the Crown of powers and duties imposed upon it by statute' ([1960] 2 QB at 287). The majority of the Court of Appeal reserved their opinion on what the position would have been had the covenant been express and unqualified but Devlin LJ went further.

Devlin LJ

. . . When the Crown, or any other person, is entrusted, whether by virtue of the prerogative or by statute, with discretionary powers to be exercised for the public good, it does not, when making a private contract in general terms, undertake (and it may be that it could not even with the use of specific language validly undertake) to fetter itself in the use of those powers, and in the exercise of its discretion. This principle has been accepted in a. number of authorities; it is sufficient to mention *Ayr Harbour Trustees* v. *Oswald* [(1883) 8 App Cas 623]; *Rederiaktiebolaget Amphitrite* v. *The King* [[1921] 3 KB 500]; *Board of Trade* v. *Temperley Steam Shipping Co. Ltd.* [(1926) 26 LILR 76; affirmed (1927) 27 LILR 230] and *William Cory & Sons Ltd.* v. *City of London Corporation* [[1951] 2 KB 476].

The covenant for quiet enjoyment in the present case is implied, and is not dissimilar to the contractual provision considered in the two cases last cited, which were both concerned with the implied obligation on one party to a contract not to interfere with the performance by the other party of his obligations under it. In *Board of Trade* v. *Temperley Steam Shipping Co. Ltd.*, the Board were the charterers of the defendant's ship, and it was contended that they had prevented the defendants from making their ship efficient for her service under the charterparty because one of the Board's surveyors had refused a licence to do certain repairs. In *William Cory & Sons Ltd.* v. *City of London Corporation*, the city corporation had a contract with the plaintiffs whereunder the plaintiffs undertook to remove refuse by means of lighters and barges. Some time later the city corporation passed a by-law concerning the fitment of vessels transporting refuse which it was agreed was such as to make the performance of the contract impossible. It was held by the Court of Appeal that the corporation was not in breach of the implied term.

I do not, however, rest my decision in the present case simply on the fact that the covenant for quiet enjoyment has to be implied. For reasons which I think will appear sufficiently in the next paragraph, I should reach the same conclusion if the ordinary covenant was expressed.

In some of the cases in which public authorities have been defendants, the judgments have been put on the ground that it would be ultra vires for them to bind themselves not to exercise their powers; and it has also been said that a promise to do so would be contrary to public policy. It may perhaps be difficult to apply this reasoning to the Crown, but it seems to me to be unnecessary to delve into the constitutional position. When the Crown, in dealing with one of its subjects, is dealing as if it too were a private person, and is granting leases or buying and selling as ordinary persons do, it is absurd to suppose that it is making any promise about the way in which it will conduct the affairs of the nation. No one can imagine, for example, that when the Crown makes a contract which could not be fulfilled in time of war, it is pledging itself not to declare war for so long as the contract lasts. Even if, therefore, there was an express covenant for quiet enjoyment, or an express promise by the Crown that it would not do any act which might hinder the other party to the contract in the performance of his obligations, the covenant or promise must by necessary implication be read to exclude those measures affecting the nation as a whole which the Crown takes for the public good.

. . . I need not examine the question whether, if the Crown sought to fetter its future action in express and specific terms, it could effectively do so. It is most unlikely that in a contract with the subject, it would ever make the attempt. For the purpose of this case it is unnecessary to go further than to say that in making a lease or other contract with its subjects, the Crown does not (at least in the absence of specific words) promise to refrain from exercising its general powers under a statute or under the prerogative, or to exercise them in any particular way. That does not mean that the Crown can escape from any contract which it finds disadvantageous by saying that it never promised to act otherwise than for the public good . . . Here we are dealing with an act done for a general executive purpose, and not an act done for the purpose of achieving a particular result under the contract in question . . .

16.3.6 Agency and Public Authorities' Contracts

Attorney-General for Ceylon v. *AD Silva* [1953] AC 461
Judicial Committee of the Privy Council

The Principal Collector of Customs of Ceylon, in the mistaken belief that certain steel plates belonging to the Crown which were on customs premises were unclaimed goods, obtained the permission of the Chief Secretary of Ceylon to sell them by public auction in accordance with the provisions of the Ceylon Customs Ordinance (below). The claimant, Silva, purchased the steel plates at the auction on 4 March 1947, but when the Collector refused to deliver them Silva brought an action for damages for breach of contract against the Attorney-General as the representative of the Crown. The Collector had refused to make delivery to Silva when he learned of a prior authorized sale of the steel plates to another purchaser. On 23 January 1947, the Services Disposal Board of Ceylon, which had been appointed by the Ministry of Supply in England to dispose of the steel plates, had contracted to sell them to a firm in Ceylon. The Supreme Court of Ceylon held that there had been a valid contract to sell to the claimant and awarded him substantial damages. On appeal by the Attorney-General:

Mr LMD de Silva (giving the judgment of the Judicial Committee of the Privy Council)

. . . The precise question which arises for their Lordships' decision is whether the Principal Collector of Customs had authority to enter into a contract binding on the Crown for the sale of the goods in question to the plaintiff. This question can conveniently be dealt with under two heads: had the Principal Collector actual authority to enter into a contract; if not, did he have ostensible authority to do so?

It is argued that the Principal Collector had actual authority to enter into the contract by reason of the provisions of sections 17 and 108 of the Customs Ordinance (chapter 185, Legislative Enactments of Ceylon). Section 17 makes warehouse rent payable in respect of goods left in customs warehouses . . .

. . . Section 108 authorizes the sale of goods left for more than three months in customs warehouses "to answer" the charges due thereon.

It is claimed by the plaintiff that the Customs Ordinance was binding on the Crown, that warehouse rent was due under section 17 of the Ordinance on the goods in question, and that as they had been left on the customs premises for a period longer than three months, they were liable to be sold after public advertisement under section 108. This was in fact the basis on which the Principal

Collector held the sale, and it would without doubt have been a sound basis if the property had all the time been private property. But it is argued by the Crown that, no matter what the Principal Collector thought or did, the Customs Ordinance was not binding on the Crown; that it, or at any rate the provisions in it relevant to this case, were inapplicable to property belonging to the Crown and that therefore the plaintiff's contention fails.

The first matter which arises for consideration is whether the Ordinance binds the Crown . . .

[Their Lordships, having considered the relevant legislation, concluded that the Ordinance did not bind the Crown and continued:] It has been argued that apart from the Ordinance the Principal Collector has actual authority to do what he did, and that this authority was reinforced by the letter written to him by the Chief Secretary. It is a simple and clear proposition that a public officer has not by reason of the fact that he is in the service of the Crown the right to act for and on behalf of the Crown in all matters which concern the Crown. The right to act for the Crown in any particular matter must be established by reference to statute or otherwise. It has not been shown that the Principal Collector had any authority to sell property of the Crown or to enter into a contract on its behalf for its sale: nor has it been shown that the Chief Secretary, who authorized the sale, had any such authority. His functions were defined by the Ceylon (State Council) Order in Council, 1931, and under this Order the most that can be said is that he was authorized to deal with certain Crown property under the direct administration of the Government of Ceylon. It is therefore clear that the Principal Collector of Customs had no actual authority to enter into a contract for the sale of the goods which are the subject matter of this action.

Next comes the question whether the Principal Collector of Customs had ostensible authority, such as would bind the Crown, to enter into the contract sued on. All 'ostensible' authority involves a representation by the principal as to the extent of the agent's authority. No representation by the agent as to the extent of his authority can amount to a 'holding out' by the principal. No public officer, unless he possesses some special power, can hold out on behalf of the Crown that he or some other public officer has the right to enter into a contract in respect of the property of the Crown when in fact no such right exists. Their Lordships think, therefore, that nothing done by the Principal Collector or the Chief Secretary amounted to a holding out by the Crown that the Principal Collector had the right to enter into a contract to sell the goods which are the subject-matter of this action . . .

In advertising the goods for sale the Principal Collector no doubt represented to the public that the goods were saleable. But the question is whether this act of the Principal Collector can be said to be an act of the Crown. Their Lordships have considered whether by reason of the fact that the Principal Collector had been appointed to his office under the Customs Ordinance, and was the proper officer to administer it, he must be regarded as having had ostensible authority on behalf of the Crown to represent to the public that goods advertised for sale under the Customs Ordinance were in fact saleable under that Ordinance. It is argued that, if so, although the goods were in fact not saleable under the Ordinance because they were Crown property, or property to which the sections of the Ordinance authorizing sale were not applicable, or for some other reason, the contract would be binding on the Crown and the Crown would be liable in damages as it could not fulfil it.

Their Lordships think that the Principal Collector cannot be regarded as having any such authority. He had, no doubt, authority to do acts of a particular class, namely, to enter on behalf of the Crown into sales of certain goods. But that authority was limited because it arose under certain sections of the Ordinance and only when those sections were applicable. It was said by Lord Atkinson in *Russo Chinese Bank* v. *Li Yau Sam* [[1910] AC 174 at 184]: 'If the agent be held out as having only a limited authority to do on behalf of his principal acts of a particular class, then the principal is not bound by an act done outside that authority, even though it be an act of that particular class, because, the authority being thus represented to be limited, the party prejudiced has notice, and should ascertain whether or not the act is authorized.' With that view their

Lordships respectfully agree. In that case the authority did not arise under a statute, but in their Lordships' view this fact makes no difference. If there is a difference at all it would lie in the circumstance that in a statute the limits of the authority conferred are fixed rigidly and no recourse to evidence is necessary to ascertain them. The Ordinance could no doubt have made the representation by the Principal Collector binding on the Crown, but it has not done so, and to read into it any such provision would be unduly to extend its meaning.

It may be said that it causes hardship to a purchaser at a sale under the Customs Ordinance if the burden of ascertaining whether or not the Principal Collector has authority to enter into the sale is placed upon him. This undoubtedly is true. But where, as in the case of the Customs Ordinance, the Ordinance does not dispense with that necessity, to hold otherwise would be to hold that public officers had dispensing powers because they then could by unauthorized acts nullify or extend the provisions of the Ordinance. Of the two evils this would be the greater one . . .

. . . Their Lordships will therefore humbly advise Her Majesty that the appeal be allowed . . .

It has been argued that *Silva's* case failed to take account of 'usual authority' as a distinct method of rendering a principal liable for the unauthorized acts of his agent (Treitel [1957] *PL* 321 at 337 ff), cf Craig, *Administrative Law* (London 2003) at 667, and see *Bowstead and Reynolds on Agency* (London 2001) at [3-006] for doubts as to whether usual authority is independent of implied and ostensible authority.

The position of a person who deals with a *Crown* agent acting outside the scope of his authority is exacerbated by the fact that the agent will not be personally liable on the contract (*MacBeath* v. *Haldimand* (1786) 1 TR 172) or, as other agents are, for breach of an implied warranty of authority (*Dunn* v. *MacDonald* [1897] 1 QB 401 and 555; *The Prometheus* (1949) 82 LILR 859). The doctrine of implied warranty of authority was said not to be applicable to Crown agents for reasons of public policy, *viz* that if they were not free of personal liability 'no man would accept any office of trust under Government' (*per* Ashhurst J in *MacBeath* v. *Haldimand* at 181, adopted by Charles J in *Dunn* v. *MacDonald* at 405). For criticism see Craig, *Administrative Law* (London 2003) at 155, Wade and Forsyth, *Administrative Law* (Oxford 2004) at 830, Street, *op cit* at 93.

The jurisdictional principle means that the authority of an agent cannot extend to a contract that is *ultra vires* the agent or *a fortiori* his department. Thus, in *Silva's* case, quite apart from the ordinary principles of agency, it is difficult to see how the Crown could have been bound by the contract in view of the provisions of the Customs Ordinance. For further discussion of the relationship between *ultra vires* and agency, see Craig, *op cit* at 154–155 and 665–667, and see also above 7.2 where the position concerning representations that do not involve an alleged contract is considered.

16.3.7 The Law of Crown Service

. . . .

Dunn v. *The Queen* [1896] 1 QB 116
Court of Appeal

The petitioner was appointed consular agent in the Niger Protectorate for a period of three years by Sir Claude McDonald, Her Majesty's Commissioner and Consul-General for the Protectorate. Before the end of that time the Crown dismissed him. He brought a petition of right claiming that the Crown had no right to do this and that he was therefore entitled to damages.

Lord Esher MR

In this case the petitioner was employed as a civil servant of the Crown in the public service at a certain salary, and the question has arisen with relation to his service which, in the case of *De Dohsé v. Reg.* [unreported: decided in the Court of Appeal, 2 June 1885, by Brett MR, Baggallay, and Bowen LJJ; and in the House of Lords, 25 November 1886, by Lord Halsbury LC and Lords Blackburn, Watson, and FitzGerald], I foresaw might arise . . . I said, in giving judgment in that case: "It is said that it was lawful to make such an engagement with him (the suppliant) for seven years, because the. engagement offered and proposed was not an engagement of military service, it being admitted in argument that, if the engagement was for military service as a soldier, whether as officer or private, it is contrary to public policy that any such contract should be made. Now, whether that doctrine with regard to the Crown is confined to military service or not need not be decided today, but I do not at all accept the suggestion that it is so confined. All service under the Crown itself is public service, and to my mind it is most likely that the doctrine which is said to be confined to military service applies to all public service under the Crown, because all public service under the Crown is for the public benefit." That case came before the House of Lords; and it seems to me that Lord Watson in his judgment almost in terms decides that what I thought would probably turn out to be the right view on the subject is correct. He says: "In the first place it appears to me that no concluded contract is disclosed in the statements contained in this petition of right; and in the second place I am of opinion that such a concluded contract, if it had been made, must have been held to have imported into it the condition that the Crown has the power to dismiss. Further, I am of opinion that, if any authority representing the Crown were to exclude such a power by express stipulation, that would be a violation of the public policy of the country and could not derogate from the power of the Crown." Anything more distinct and general than that there could not be. It seems to me that the rule, as laid down by the House of Lords, is in consonance with what I suggested to be the true rule in the Court of Appeal . . . It seems to me that both on authority and on principle it is clear that the petitioner is not entitled to succeed . . .

Lord Herschell

. . . I take it that persons employed as the petitioner was in the service of the Crown, except in cases where there is some statutory provision for a higher tenure of office, are ordinarily engaged on the understanding that they hold their employment at the pleasure of the Crown. So I think that there must be imported into the contract for the employment of the petitioner the term which is applicable to civil servants in general, namely, that the Crown may put an end to the employment at its pleasure. In this case there is not a tittle of evidence that, supposing it *were* possible, Sir Claude McDonald had any authority to employ the petitioner on any other terms than those which are applicable to the civil service generally. It seems to me that it is the public interest which has led to the term which I have mentioned being imported into contracts for employment in the service of the Crown. The cases cited shew that, such employment being for the good of the public, it is essential for the public good that it should be capable of being determined at the pleasure of the Crown, except in certain exceptional cases where it has been deemed to be more for the public good that some restriction should be imposed on the power of the Crown to dismiss its servants . . .

Kay LJ delivered a judgment in favour of dismissing the application. Application dismissed.

Does *Dunn* decide that the common law rule that Crown servants are dismissible at pleasure can *only be excluded by statute*, or (see Nettheim [1975] *CLJ* 253 at 271) *merely that that rule is not impliedly excluded by a contractual stipulation of a fixed term of employment with nothing more* because such a stipulation is not inconsistent with retention of the said common law power? See further Nettheim, *op cit*, but note Lord Esher's approval of Lord Watson's speech above. In *Thomas* v. *Attorney-General of Trinidad and Tobago* [1982] AC

113 at 127, the Privy Council (*obiter*) inclined strongly to the view that the common law power can be removed only by statute, while in *Council of Civil Service Unions* v. *Minister for the Civil Service* [1985] AC 374 at 409 Lord Diplock referred to the 'disability of the executive . . . to agree with a civil servant that his service should be on terms that did not make him subject to instant dismissal'. Others, however, appear to have taken the broader view. In *Reilly* v. *The King* [1934] AC 176 at 179 Lord Atkin said (*obiter*) that 'if the terms of the appointment definitely prescribe a term *and expressly provide for a power to determine "for cause"* it appears necessarily to follow that any implication of a power to dismiss at pleasure is excluded' (emphasis added). Admittedly, the terms of the appointment there were specified by statute, and it is possible that Lord Atkin's reference to 'terms' should be limited to that context; however, the view that the common law power can be contractually excluded was adopted by Denning J in *Robertson* v. *Minister of Pensions* [1949] 1 KB 227 at 231 and by Lord Goddard CJ in *Terrell* v. *Secretary of State for the Colonies* [1953] 2 QB 482 at 499–500.

Whatever the theoretical position over dismissal, there is a sharp contrast with the reality for traditionally Crown service has been one of the most secure types of employment with an extremely low rate of dismissal for misconduct or inefficiency. As Freedland writes (*The Personal Contract of Employment* (Oxford 2003) at 311), 'established civil servants had the greatest institutionally recognized expectations of job security of any major group of workers'.

16.3.8 Is there a Contract of Employment?

The question whether a civil servant has a contract of employment has been somewhat controversial over the years and it is one that, depending on the answer, brings certain legal consequences in its wake. To refer just to more recent cases, in *Council of Civil Service Unions* v. *Minister for the Civil Service* [1985] AC 374, it was said (at 419) to be common ground that there was no contractual relationship between the Crown and the staff at GCHQ. A few years later the issue arose for decision in *R* v. *Civil Service Appeal Board, ex parte Bruce* [1988] ICR 649 (affirmed [1989] ICR 171). The claimant, who had been appointed as an executive officer in the Inland Revenue in 1982, was in 1985, after due trial, not considered satisfactory and the Revenue terminated his employment. He appealed against this decision to the Civil Service Appeal Board, which, following written and oral submissions, concluded that the decision to terminate his appointment was fair. This was challenged by the claimant. In deciding that in theory the Board's decision was amenable to a claim for judicial review, which, as has been seen (above at 5.3.3) the existence of a contract may negate, May LJ stated (at 659–660):

On [the] evidence and the relevant paragraphs of the [Civil Service Pay and Conditions of Service] Code, I do not think that it is shown that prior to about 1985 the Crown intended that civil servants should have contracts of employment. Thus, in my opinion, the applicant's service with the Inland Revenue was not pursuant to any contract of employment enforceable in the Courts, but merely as an appointment on the terms of the letter [which the claimant had received] . . .

Nevertheless there is in my view nothing unconstitutional about civil servants being employed by the Crown pursuant to contracts of service, and if the Cabinet Office's re-appraisal continues on the present lines I anticipate that this is what will happen. Such a situation would in my view be wholly consistent with a modern and realistic view of the position of civil servants vis-à-vis the Crown.

In the next case extract, a different view was taken of the relevant Crown intention, but before this is set out, attention might be paid to Freedland, *The Personal Contract of Employment* (Oxford 2003) at 69–70:

... [F]rom the mid-1960s onwards, the rapid positive development of the aspect of Public Law which concerns judicial review of administrative action brought about an ironical reversal in the position of the Crown in its legal relationship with its civil servants. In the briefest summary, there were two aspects to this reversal of position. On the one hand, it became government policy from the 1980s onwards to seek to increase the efficiency of the Civil Service by means, *inter alia*, of a deliberate contractualization of the relationship between the Crown and its civil servants. On the other hand, the increased availability of judicial review to challenge dismissal from public office generally, coupled with the erosion of unrestricted Crown prerogative in the face of judicial review, meant that the Crown authorities now frequently found themselves wishing to assert that their relations with civil servants were essentially contractual and hence firmly in the sphere of private law, in order to restrict claims for judicial review in respect of discipline or dismissal of civil servants.

R v. *Lord Chancellor's Department, ex parte Nangle* [1992] 1 All ER 897
Queen's Bench Division

The claimant worked in the defendant department. Allegations that he had assaulted and sexually harassed a female colleague were upheld following an oral hearing, and he was transferred within the department, with 12 months' loss of increment. An appeal to the Permanent Secretary was dismissed, but the loss of increment was reduced to three months. The claimant sought judicial review of the decisions to uphold the complaint and to dismiss his appeal.

Stuart-Smith LJ (delivering the judgment of the court)

... Two main questions arise on this motion: (i) is the applicant employed by the Crown under a contract of service? If he is, it is accepted by Mr Tabachnik QC on his behalf that he has no remedy in public law, the case being indistinguishable from *R v East Berkshire Health Authority, ex p Walsh* [1984] 3 All ER 425. (ii) If the applicant is not employed under a contract of employment is there a sufficient public law element in the case to justify the exercise of the court's jurisdiction in judicial review?

Question 1

It is common ground between the parties that the plaintiff's employment in the department involved two of the necessary ingredients of contract, namely offer and acceptance and consideration. The point at issue is whether there was in addition an intention to enter into legal relations. It is also common ground that the Crown can enter into a contract of employment with its servants: see *Kodeeswaran v A-G of Ceylon* [1970] AC 1111 and *R v Civil Service Appeal Board, ex p Bruce* [1988] ICR 649, a case much relied upon by Mr Tabachnik.

[His Lordship then set out the second of the two paragraphs that appear above from May LJ's judgment in *Bruce*, and some of the documentation relating to Nangle's employment, including para 14 of the Civil Service Pay and Conditions of Service Code which reads as follows (and which had also been in issue in *Bruce*):

'14. For the most part, the relationship between the civil servant and the Crown remains one regulated under the prerogative and based on personal appointment. As such, a civil servant does not have a contract of employment enforceable in the courts but rather a letter of appointment, and technically the Crown still retains the right to dismiss a civil servant at pleasure. Recently, however, the legal position of civil servants has been radically changed by the growing trend for legislation to apply to the Civil Service either directly, by the provisions of the Acts themselves, or by governmental assurances that the conditions applying to civil servants will not be less favourable than those applying to other employees.'

Stuart-Smith LJ then continued:] After considering the cases of *IRC v Hambrook* [1956] 2 QB 641, the well-known dictum of Lord Atkin in *Reilly v The King* [1943] AC 176 at 180 . . . where he said that the Crown's power to dismiss its servants without notice at will 'is not inconsistent with the existence of a contract until so determined', and the decision of the Privy Council in *Kodeeswaren v A-G of Ceylon* [1970] AC 1111, May LJ in . . . *Bruce* . . . concluded that the authorities were in a confused and uncertain state. It is to be noted however that there does not appear to have been any suggestion in any of the authorities prior to *Ex p Bruce* that the reason why there was no contract between the Crown and its civil servants was due to an absence of intention to enter into legal relations; rather it was due to doubts as to the constitutional position of the Crown and its ability to bind itself in contract with its servants who were historically regarded as members of the Sovereign's household, and the belief that the ability to dismiss its servants at will was inconsistent with contract.

The first of these propositions was laid to rest in *Kodeeswaren's* case; although that case might have been decided on principles of restitution and quasi contract, it is plain that in fact it was not; it was decided that the civil servant in Ceylon had a claim in contract (see [1970] AC 1111 at 1123 per Lord Diplock). The second proposition is rebutted by the dictum of Lord Atkin to which we have referred in *Reilly's* case.

Mr Tabachnik founds his argument in the case on para 14 of the Civil Service code and the decision in *Ex p Bruce*. He also submits that the letter of appointment points in terms to an appointment rather than a contract. In our judgment the use of the word "appointment" is neutral and certainly does not negative an intention to create legal relations. Many contractual relationships of employer and employee are described as appointments.

Mr Tabachnik also relies on the attitude of the Crown in previous cases, where it is probably true to say that in the majority it has either been assumed that there was no contract or it was argued that there was none . . . But we cannot see how the Crown's attitude in other cases — which may or may not have been mistaken — can be relevant to the question whether the parties intended to create legal relations in this case.

Mr Tabachnik has also referred to a number of statutes which affect employees of the Crown, in particular: the Equal Pay Act 1970; the Industrial Relations Act 1971; the Trade Union and Labour Relations Act 1974; the Employment Protection Act 1975; the Sex Discrimination Act 1975; the Race Relations Act 1976 and the Employment Protection (Consolidation) Act 1978.

It is true that these Acts are not applied to civil servants simply by providing that the Acts shall bind the Crown. It is done in a somewhat more circumspect way. [Having referred by way of example to s 138 of the last-mentioned Act (now repealed — see below), his Lordship continued:]

For our part we do not derive any assistance from this legislation which is equally consistent with the presence or absence of a contractual relationship, though scarcely consistent with an absence of intention to create legal relations . . .

We accept that the concept of an intention to create legal relations in this context means an intention to enter into a contract legally enforceable in the courts. But the converse of the situation is that the relationship is purely voluntary or is binding in honour only . . .

Where the documents show that the parties enter into a relationship involving obligations, rights and entitlements which go both ways then prima facie the court will hold that they intend these obligations to be enforceable and not merely voluntary.

In such a business situation the onus is upon the party asserting a lack of intention to create legal relations and the onus is a heavy one: see *Edwards v Skyways Ltd* . . . [1964] 1 WLR 349 at 355 per Megaw J and *Chitty on Contracts* (26th Edition, 1989) vol 1, para 129.

With the exception of para 14 of the Civil Service code it seems to us plain beyond argument that the parties intended to create legal relations; this is consistent with the *Kodeeswaran* and [*Lam Yuk-ming* v. *A-G* [1980] HKLR 815] cases. Moreover, the earlier authorities, supported by the opinion of Lord Goddard CJ in *IRC v Hambrook* . . . do not turn on an absence of intention to create legal relations. In our judgment para 14 has to be read in context. It is to be found in a section of the code which is dealing with legislation affecting conditions of service of civil servants; it is merely part of the introduction to the legislation referred to. The purpose of the section is to describe a state of affairs as it is believed to be; not to limit or exclude rights or obligations or to restrict or exclude the enforceability of such rights or obligations. Paragraphs 11–13 merely describe the historical evolution of the Civil Service; paras 14 and 15 introduce the legislation that is thereafter referred to. The very legislation, to much of which we have earlier referred, shows that there are legal consequences of the relationship. The documentation lays down with great clarity rights, obligations and entitlements, dealing with such matters as pay, pensions, hours of attendance, holidays, sick leave, discipline and many other similar matters which are the stock in trade of a contract of employment. We cannot construe para 14 of the code as meaning that all these matters are to be voluntary only and not legally enforceable or even that such was the intention of the Crown. In our judgment it is merely descriptive of what was believed to be the position. It makes no difference that the terms are described as conditions of service as opposed to terms and conditions of contract. The relationship of employer and employee, master and servant, which plainly exists here must of its very nature be one that involves an intention to create legal relations, unless such intention is clearly excluded either expressly or by necessary implication, as it is in the religious appointments cases. In our judgment read in its proper context para 14 does not have this effect. Moreover, it seems to us that there is a fundamental inconsistency in Mr Tabachnik's argument. We find it difficult to see how the parties can have intended that their relationship should not be governed by private law, but did intend that they should be governed by public law. They either intended their relationship to have legal consequences or they did not.

For these reasons we have come to the conclusion that we should not follow the reasoning of the Divisional Court in . . . *Bruce* . . . and that the first question should be answered in favour of the respondents. This is not a matter of public law; if the applicant can establish breach of contract by failure to comply with the express or implied provision of the disciplinary code which has resulted in loss, he can sue for damages for breach of contract.

On the second question in the case, the court decided that even if there were no contract, the case lacked a sufficient public law element for a claim for judicial review to be available: see below. Application dismissed.

One of the references in *Nangle* to the application of legislation to civil servants was to s 138 of the Employment Protection (Consolidation) Act 1978: this provision has been repealed, but see now s 191 of the Employment Rights Act 1996. This makes the employee's remedies for unfair dismissal in industrial tribunals available, for the most part, to civil servants, but avoids deciding the question whether there is a contract of employment or not, the normal prerequisite of a claim. (See also the wording of s 245 of the Trade Union and Labour Relations (Consolidation) Act 1992.) In effect, the power of the Crown to dismiss at pleasure without paying compensation is now substantially limited (as it has been for a good number of years) by this statute (or its predecessors), but, as was acknowledged in *Bruce*, this does not deal with the contractual position. The unfair dismissal jurisdiction is, as is shown by *Hughes* v. *DHSS* [1985] AC 776 (see above at 7.1.1), limited, and in any case not all the statutory rights relating to employment are extended to Crown servants. In particular they are not entitled to minimum periods of notice or to redundancy payments. Although the Civil Service Pay and Conditions of Service Code is a written statement of terms and does in fact make provision for minimum periods of notice, this does not create rights but only expectations which are, as *Hughes* shows, subject to changes of policy.

If there is a contract, then in principle there should be a contractual claim for arrears of salary. However, even if no contract is held to exist, civil servants may be able to recover unpaid arrears of salary by a restitutionary claim. This may even be the case where the servant is in breach of his conditions of service: *Miles* v. *Wakefield Metropolitan District Council* [1987] AC 539.

For discussion of the development of contracts with civil servants, see Freedland [1995] *PL* 224 who suggests (*inter alia*) that 'the more the whole relationship is identified as a contractual one, the more the [prerogative power of dismissal at will] comes to seem excludable by contract'. It should be noted that many civil servants have been assigned in recent years to work in what have been termed 'Next Steps Agencies' but they remain civil servants (though for complications, see Freedland, *op cit* at 230–231).

16.3.9 Can a Claim in Judicial Review be Brought?

If in a given case there is no contract of employment, then this makes it more likely that a claim for judicial review will be available. However, note that in *Nangle* it was thought that even if (contrary to their view) there had been no contract, the case, which was involved with internal discipline and had not reached the Civil Service Appeal Board (CSAB), would have lacked a sufficient public element on its facts. On the other hand, in *Bruce* May LJ suggested that a claim for judicial review might be available in the case of a dismissal of a civil servant and any appeal to the CSAB, even if the civil servant did have a contract, a view which was in fact concurred in by the court in *Nangle* (see [1992] 1 All ER 897 at 906, and also Ewing and Grubb (1987) 16 *ILJ* 145 at 154–155).

Nangle also referred to *McClaren* v. *Home Office* [1990] ICR 824 in which Woolf LJ at 836–837 set out certain principles to be taken into account. First, 'an employee of a public body is normally in exactly the same situation as other employees', and can therefore vindicate his employment rights in a contractual claim, albeit that those rights may be circumscribed by Crown employment (*eg* because of the possibility of dismissal at will). Secondly, although judicial review normally cannot be used in respect of contractual disputes, review will lie 'where there exists some disciplinary or other body established under the prerogative or by statute to which the employer or the employee is entitled or required to refer disputes affecting their relationship', provided that that body 'has a sufficient public law element, which it almost invariably will have if the employer is the Crown, and it is not domestic or wholly informal'; even if, applying this test, judicial review is unavailable, there may be a duty upon such a body, enforceable in ordinary proceedings, to act fairly. In addition, decisions 'of general application' affecting public employees — *eg* the change in terms of employment in the *GCHQ* case (see above at 7.1.3) — may be challenged via judicial review on the usual public law grounds. It should also be noted though that in *Bruce* it was said that even if a claim for judicial review was in theory available to an individual, normally relief should be sought in industrial tribunals.

Where civil servants are able to bring claims for judicial review, the principle of legitimate expectation must be borne in mind. The *GCHQ* case (see above at 7.1.3) indicates that this may supply procedural protection not just in dismissal cases, but in relation to such matters as consultation on changes to employment terms. Furthermore, the substantive aspects of the principle of legitimate expectation may open up the possibility of arguing that, where a Crown servant has been engaged for a fixed period or on certain terms, dismissal before that or variation of those terms might be unfair and an abuse of power — although, as the *Hughes* case (see above at 7.1.1) demonstrates, it may well be that such expectations have to yield to changing circumstances and policies.

QUESTION

- Is the argument above affected by the view taken about the possibility of exclusion of the right to dismissal at pleasure discussed above at 16.3.7?

The possibility of procedural protection has been enhanced in recent years by the extension of the scope of Art 6 ECHR to a wider group of public servants: see *Pellegrin* v. *France* (2001) 31 EHRR 26, discussed by Morris [2001] *PL* 442, where the ECtHR ruled at [66] that in the context of public employment 'the only cases excluded from Article 6(1) of the ECHR are those which are raised by public servants whose duties typify the specific activities of the public service in so far as the latter is acting as the depositary of public authority responsible for protecting the general interests of the State or other public authorities.' For example, in *Devlin* v. *United Kingdom* (2002) 34 EHRR 43 at [26], the ECtHR thought that the post of an administrative assistant in the non-industrial civil service in Northern Ireland was not one that involved 'wielding a portion of the State's sovereign power', and Art 6(1) was therefore applicable.

QUESTION

- Assuming there was a choice, would you advise a civil servant that he is better off with or without a contract? (See Fredman and Morris [1988] *PL* 58.)

16.4 Restitution

16.4.1 Introduction

Broadly speaking, public bodies which have received payments or benefited by services rendered to them can be liable in the same way as private individuals under the law of restitution, a subject which has seen significant developments in recent years. Attention will be focussed here on an issue of particular importance in Administrative Law, namely the relevance of the concept of *ultra vires* and especially the development of the position concerning recovery of money paid in response to an *ultra vires* demand by a public authority. The earlier position will not be set out in the light of the seminal decision of the House of Lords in *Woolwich Building Society* v. *IRC (No 2)* [1993] AC 70.

16.4.2 The '*Woolwich* Principle'

Woolwich Building Society v. *Inland Revenue Commissioners* [1993] AC 70
House of Lords

The Woolwich Equitable Building Society had paid certain sums in tax under regulations which were later held in the courts to be *ultra vires* so far as these types of payment were concerned: see *Woolwich Equitable Building Society* v. *IRC* [1990] 1 WLR 1400. The Revenue repaid the money with interest from the date when the order of invalidity was made in the High Court, but the Woolwich claimed interest on the sums from the earlier dates on which they were actually paid. The amount in question was agreed by the parties at £6,730,000 and its recoverability depended upon whether the Woolwich had a restitutionary claim to the money from the time it was paid. This was an appeal to the House of Lords by the Crown from a decision of the Court of Appeal allowing Woolwich's claim.

Lord Goff

. . . Take any tax or duty paid by the citizen pursuant to an unlawful demand. Common justice seems to require that tax to be repaid, unless special circumstances or some principle of policy require otherwise; prima facie, the taxpayer should be entitled to repayment as of right.

. . . [Mr Glick, counsel for the Crown] asserted that, if your Lordships' House were to accept Woolwich's argument [that there is an immediate restitutionary right to the repayment of money levied under an unlawful demand], it would be impossible for us to set the appropriate limits to the application of the principle. An unbridled right to recover overpaid taxes and duties subject only to the usual six-year time bar was, he suggested, unacceptable in modern society. Some limits had to be set to such claims; and the selection of such limits, being essentially a matter of policy, was one which the legislature alone is equipped to make.

My reaction to this submission of Mr. Glick is to confess (to some extent) and yet to avoid. I agree that there appears to be a widely held view that some limit has to be placed upon the recovery of taxes paid pursuant to an ultra vires demand. I would go further and accept that the armoury of common law defences, such as those which prevent recovery of money paid under a binding compromise or to avoid a threat of litigation, may be either inapposite or inadequate for the purpose; because it is possible to envisage, especially in modern taxation law which tends to be excessively complex, circumstances in which some very substantial sum of money may be held to have been exacted ultra vires from a very large number of taxpayers. It may well therefore be necessary to have recourse to other defences, such as for example short time limits within which such claims have to be advanced . . .

In all the circumstances, I do not consider that Mr. Glick's argument, powerful though it is, is persuasive enough to deter me from recognising, in law, the force of the justice underlying Woolwich's case. Furthermore, there are particular reasons which impel me to that conclusion. The first is that this opportunity will never come again. If we do not take it now, it will be gone forever. The second is that I fear that, however compelling the principle of justice may be, it would never be sufficient to persuade a government to propose its legislative recognition by Parliament; caution, otherwise known as the Treasury, would never allow this to happen. The third is that, turning Mr. Glick's argument against him, the immediate practical impact of the recognition of the principle will be limited, for (unlike the present case) most cases will continue for the time being to be regulated by the various statutory règimes now in force. The fourth [related to timing] . . . Fifth, it is well established that, if the Crown pays money out of the consolidated fund without authority, such money is ipso facto recoverable if it can be traced: see *Auckland Harbour Board* v. *The King* [1924]

A.C. 318. It is true that the claim in such a case can be distinguished as being proprietary in nature. But the comparison with the position of the citizen, on the law as it stands at present, is most unattractive.

There is a sixth reason which favours this conclusion. I refer to the decision of the European Court of Justice, in *Amministrazione delle Finanze dello Stato v. S.p.A. San Giorgio* (Case 199/82) [1983] E.C.R. 3595, which establishes that a person who pays charges levied by a member state contrary to the rules of Community law is entitled to repayment of the charge, such right being regarded as a consequence of, and an adjunct to, the rights conferred on individuals by the Community provisions prohibiting the relevant charges: see paragraph 12 of the judgment of the court, at p. 3612. The *San Giorgio* case is also of interest for present purposes in that it accepts that Community law does not prevent a national legal system from disallowing repayment of charges where to do so would entail unjust enrichment of the recipient, in particular where the charges have been incorporated into the price of goods and so passed on to the purchaser. I only comment that, at a time when Community law is becoming increasingly important, it would be strange if the right of the citizen to recover overpaid charges were to be more restricted under domestic law than it is under European law.

I would therefore hold that money paid by a citizen to a public authority in the form of taxes or other levies paid pursuant to an ultra vires demand by the authority is prima facie recoverable by the citizen as of right. As at present advised, I incline to the opinion that this principle should extend to embrace cases in which the tax or other levy has been wrongly exacted by the public authority not because the demand was ultra vires but for other reasons, for example because the authority has misconstrued a relevant statute or regulation. It is not however necessary to decide the point in the present case, and in any event cases of this kind are generally the subject of statutory regimes which legislate for the circumstances in which money so paid either must or may be repaid. Nor do I think it necessary to consider for the purposes of the present case to what extent the common law may provide the public authority with a defence to a claim for the repayment of money so paid . . . It will be a matter for consideration whether the fact that the plaintiff has passed on the tax or levy so that the burden has fallen on another should provide a defence to his claim. Although this is contemplated by the European Court of Justice in the *San Giorgio* case, it is evident from *Air Canada v. British Columbia*, 59 D.L.R. (4th) 161 that the point is not without its difficulties; and the availability of such a defence may depend upon the nature of the tax or other levy . . .

For these reasons, I would dismiss the appeal with costs.

Lords Browne-Wilkinson and Slynn delivered speeches in favour of dismissing the appeal, the former expressly agreeing with Lord Goff's 'Woolwich principle'. Lords Keith and Jauncey delivered speeches in favour of allowing the appeal. Appeal dismissed.

16.4.3 The Scope of the '*Woolwich* Principle'

It would seem in principle that all *ultra vires* errors should fall within the *Woolwich* principle and that misconstruction of the relevant statute or regulation — a matter to which Lord Goff referred, but on which he expressed no final decision (in the penultimate paragraph of our excerpt above) — would almost always entail *ultra vires* errors in the light of the evolution of the 'error of law' concept which we charted in ch 2 above. Support was lent to this view by Sir Richard Scott V-C in *British Steel plc* v. *Customs and Excise Commissioners* [1997] 2 All ER 366 at 375–376. He said that, 'An unlawful demand for duty must, in a sense, always be an ultra vires demand.' This would be so, said his Lordship, whether 'the demand is based on ultra vires regulations, or on a mistaken view of the legal effect of valid regulations, or on a mistaken view of the facts of the case'. In all such situations, 'the taxpayer would, prima facie, become entitled, on making payment pursuant to the unlawful demand, to a common law restitutionary right to repayment', unless the legislation may be found, upon proper construction, to exclude that right.

The scope of the *Woolwich* principle would appear to be fairly wide. As Beatson (1993) 109 *LQR* 401 at 417–418 writes:

To sum up, the *Woolwich* principle clearly applies to taxes and duties levied by governmental bodies which are *ultra vires* because of the invalidity of the relevant subordinate legislation. It almost certainly applies where the *ultra vires* nature of the levy stems from an error of law or an abuse of discretion. The position of levies vitiated by procedural unfairness is less clear but, in principle, should not differ. While the House of Lords did not give explicit guidance on the range of bodies subject to the principle, it has been argued that it should apply to other public bodies whose authority to charge is subject to and limited by public law principles, and to other bodies whose authority to charge is solely the product of statute, and thus limited. While the uncertainties do not, it is submitted, undermine the coherence of the principle laid down in the case, they suggest that further statutory clarification is desirable. Additionally, considerations of policy may indicate that the principle should be limited in scope, for instance to governmental exactions or by the exclusion of the public utilities, or by the operation of prudential safeguards.

For further discussion of these latter issues see (1993) 109 *LQR* at 425–431 and more generally see the Law Commission's report, *Restitution: Mistakes of Law and Ultra Vires Public Authority Receipts and Payments* (Cm 2731, Law Com No 227, 1994 at [6.32]–[6.42]). Recently, in *Waikato Regional Airport Ltd* v. *Attorney-General (New Zealand)* [2003] UKPC 50 at [79]–[80] the Privy Council has lent support to the view that charges under statutory powers, although not a tax, are within the *Woolwich* principle. The Privy Council further stated:

Their Lordships also note (without basing their decision on it, since it was not cited or discussed in argument) that one of the cases referred to with apparent approval by Lord Goff of Chieveley in *Woolwich, South of Scotland Electricity Board v British Oxygen Company Ltd* [1959] 1 WLR 587, was a case of a public board overcharging for electricity supplies which were of commercial benefit to the recipient, but the House of Lords did not doubt that excessive charges were recoverable by the company which had paid them.

A limit to the *Woolwich* principle was found in *Norwich City Council* v. *Stringer* (2001) 33 HLR 158. In this case a landlord, to whom an overpayment of housing benefit had been wrongly paid by the local authority, sought to recover that part of the overpayment which he had in fact repaid in response to an invoice sent by the local authority. A district judge found that the local authority's claim for the money failed for lack of the necessary prior documentation. Nevertheless, the Court of Appeal rejected the landlord's restitutionary claim. *Woolwich* was distinguished on the basis that in *Stringer* there had not been 'a demand backed by coercive power of the sort which Lord Goff had in mind' (*per* Buxton LJ) and also because justice did not require the local authority to repay what on these facts would have been a windfall for the landlord.

At the time of the decision in *Woolwich*, the general position was that money paid under a mistake of law as opposed to a mistake of fact was irrecoverable (although the Woolwich was not itself mistaken in that case: it had contended throughout that the tax was invalidly demanded). There was some reference to the mistake of law issue in *Woolwich*, but the change in the law came about in *Kleinwort Benson Ltd* v. *Lincoln City Council* [1999] 2 AC 349 where the House of Lords held that there was no such general rule against recovery. If in a case that falls within the '*Woolwich* principle', the situation is also one where the payment was made by the claimant under a mistake of law, there might be an advantage in terms of the limitation period if the latter action were available (see s 32(1)(c) of the Limitation Act 1980, though note s 320 of the Finance Act 2004 affecting Inland Revenue matters). However, in *IRC* v. *Deutsche Morgan Grenfell Group plc* [2005] EWCA Civ 78 the Court of Appeal, interpreting *Woolwich*, decided that where a case fell under the principle laid down in that case, this excluded any claim on the ground of mistake of law by the claimant. Leave has been given to appeal to the House of Lords in the *Deutsche Morgan* case.

QUESTION

• If the point in the *Deutsche Morgan* case which has been outlined above is reversed by the House of Lords, how important would the '*Woolwich* principle' be?

16.4.4 Relationship with Statute

The '*Woolwich* principle' needs to be kept in perspective, for, as Lord Goff stated in *Woolwich*, most cases of wrongful payment will be covered by statutory schemes for repayment. (The provisions for repayment of tax in s 33 of the Taxes Management Act 1970 were construed in *Woolwich* as not covering the situation involved in that case because the regulation itself was *ultra vires*.) A statutory scheme may expressly or impliedly take away the common law right to restitution — a point which, as seen above at 16.4.3, Sir Richard Scott V-C acknowledged in *British Steel*. The Law Commission recommended some, but not total, rationalization of the relevant statutory taxation provisions, including the suggested application to all the statutory repayment provisions of the defence of passing on/unjust enrichment. On defences see the next section.

16.4.5 Defences

The law of restitution in general allows for various defences, reference to which can be found in the textbooks : see, *eg* Burrows, *The Law of Restitution* (London 2002), ch 15.

In the extract from *Woolwich* set out above at 16.4.2, Lord Goff touched on the question of defences in the sphere of the '*Woolwich* principle'. One point concerned limitation periods. In 2001 the Law Commission reported on the subject of limitation periods in general (*Limitation of Actions*, Law Com No 270) and in relation to restitution wanted their proposed new regime (basically three years from discovery and a ten year long stop) to apply.

Lord Goff also referred to the defence of 'passing-on' (in simple terms that the claimant managed to pass on the loss to another and therefore did not suffer detriment). In *Waikato Regional Airport Ltd* v. *Attorney-General (New Zealand)* [2003] UKPC 50 the Privy Council noted at [78] that this defence had been rejected in England in *Kleinwort Benson* v. *Birmingham City Council* [1997] QB 380 as well as in Australia, though noting that the position in Canada was different. However, they did not need to rule on the point of principle in the case in hand as the relevant factual basis had not been established. Another point referred to in *Waikato* was that Lord Goff in *Woolwich* had raised the question whether or not there ought to be a special defence for public authorities where large sums of money were at stake *ie*, the effect of disruption to public finances. The amount involved in the *Waikato* case was not such that the Privy Council had to discuss the matter to any extent, but it is worth noting that the Law Commission in 1994 (Law Com No 227 at [11.6] and [11.23]) had not favoured such a defence.

16.4.6 Claims by a Public Body

It will have been noticed that Lord Goff's fifth factor in favour of establishing the 'Woolwich principle' was the contrast if the citizen could not claim in Woolwich, with the ability of the Crown to recover, according to Auckland Harbour Board v. The King [1924] AC 318, where it had wrongly paid money out of the consolidated fund. In the Auckland Harbour case, the Privy Council stated (at 327) that any 'payment . . . made without Parliamentary authority is simply illegal and ultra vires, and may be recovered by the Government if it can . . . be traced . . . [T]o invoke analogies of what might be held in a question between subject and subject is hardly relevant.' See further Commonwealth of Australia v. Burns [1971] VR 825 where the judge would not allow a defence of estoppel to operate. This is criticized by Burrows, op cit at 422, but would seem to be in line with the approach traditionally adopted to estoppels in public law, a position which was relied upon in Burns, and also with a related case like Attorney–General for Ceylon v. Silva [1953] AC 461 which was cited in support in Burns and which was set out above at 16.3.6. (Cf the view of the Law Commission in their 1994 report on Restitution at [17.3].)

16.4.7 Procedural Matters

One procedural issue that could have posed problems for a claimant wanting to avail himself of the claim for judicial review under Part 54 concerned the extent to which the provision permitting the award of damages in CPR 54.3(2) could be used in restitution cases; but, as noted above at 16.1.2, in 2004 this provision was amended so as to allow (from 1 May 2004) a claim for judicial review to include a claim for restitution.

Another question is whether a claimant who is alleging ultra vires so as to recover, for example, taxes he has paid, has to use Part 54 or is free to bring a private law action. This 'exclusivity' issue is one that has been discussed in general terms earlier: see 14.3. It would seem to follow that on the basis that the claimant is asserting a common law right to restitution, a private law action is available (though note the comment of Lord Goff in our excerpt from Woolwich above at 16.4.2 above) but on this view and more generally see Beatson (1993) 109 LQR 1 at 4–5). The view in the text gains support from British Steel plc v. Customs and Excise Commissioners [1997] 2 All ER 336. Compare Rowe v. Vale of White Horse District Council [2003] EWHC 388 (Admin) [2003] 1 Lloyd's Rep 418 where it became apparent that the case only raised a private law issue of restitution, and Lightman J, with the consent of counsel, continued with the case as a trial of the private law matter. On the other hand, statutory appeal mechanisms or dispute resolution procedures could be taken as excluding the restitutionary right being exercised other than under the statutory mechanism provided: see Beatson (1993) 109 LQR at 421–425 and cf Autologic Holdings plc v. Inland Revenue Commissioners [2004] EWCA Civ 680 [2005] 1 WLR 52.

16.4.8 A Public Law or a Private Law Right?

A restitutionary right to recovery has been treated in this chapter as a private law right, but attention should also be paid to the view of Alder (2002) 22 *LS* 165 who, having welcomed the *prima facie* right to recovery laid down in *Woolwich*, continues at 184 as follows:

Nevertheless, there are substantial difficulties with an absolute right to recover in the sphere of public law. These are not only practical difficulties concerned with the public interest but also difficulties of principle which focus on the rule of law value that a responsible citizen should not make a payment which he believes to be unlawful. These problems could be dealt with by legislation, as was suggested in *Woolwich* itself, but there is no agreement as to what kind of principles might be appropriate. This is not surprising in as much as *Woolwich* raises issues of incommensurability between the competing values of justice to the individual, utilitarian concerns and the ideal of the rule of law.

There seems to be no advantage in attempting to deal with these problems by squeezing the *Woolwich* principle into a private law mould. In the absence of legislation it might be preferable to conceive of the Woolwich principle as embodying a public law right broadly analogous to a legitimate expectation rather than a private law right. This would enable the principle to be dealt with in the Administrative Court with its discretionary powers and would also give the citizen's claim to repayment relatively strong protection since it would be defeasible only on substantial public interest grounds. Indeed, in some respects this would be stronger than the private law principle. Existing private law grounds based on duress or mistake would still be actionable in ordinary civil proceedings against a public authority.

QUESTION

• Do you agree with Alder? Would the *Woolwich* principle be better seen as a private law or public law principle?

16.5 Remedies, Procedure, and Public Interest Immunity

16.5.1 Remedies and Procedure in General

The particular issues here to a large extent concern the Crown and the starting point is the Crown Proceedings Act 1947.

Crown Proceedings Act 1947

4—(1) Where the Crown is subject to any liability by virtue of this Part of this Act, the law relating to indemnity and contribution shall be enforceable by or against the Crown in respect of the liability to which it is so subject as if the Crown were a private person of full age and capacity . . .

(3) Without prejudice to the general effect of section one of this Act, the Law Reform (Contributory Negligence) Act, 1945 (which amends the law relating to contributory negligence) shall bind the Crown . . .

17—(1) [The Minister for the Civil Service] shall publish a list specifying the several Government departments which are authorised departments for the purposes of this Act . . . and may from time to time amend or vary the said list . . .

(2) Civil proceedings by the Crown may be instituted either by an authorised Government department in its own name, whether that department was or was not at the commencement of this Act authorised to sue, or by the Attorney General.

(3) Civil proceedings against the Crown shall be instituted against the appropriate authorised Government department, or, if none of the authorised Government departments is appropriate or the person instituting the proceedings has any reasonable doubt whether any and if so which of those departments is appropriate, against the Attorney General . . .

25—(1) Where in any civil proceedings by or against the Crown, or in any proceedings on the Crown side of the King's Bench Division, or in connection with any arbitration to which the Crown is a party, any order (including an order for costs) is made by any court in favour of any person against the Crown or against a Government department or against an officer of the Crown as such, the proper officer of the court shall, on an application in that behalf made by or on behalf of that person at any time after the expiration of twenty-one days from the date of the order or, in case the order provides for the payment of costs and the costs require to be taxed, at any time after the costs have been taxed, whichever is the later, issue to that person a certificate in the prescribed form containing particulars of the order:

Provided that, if the court so directs, a separate certificate shall be issued with respect to the costs (if any) ordered to be paid to the applicant.

(2) A copy of any certificate issued under this section may be served by the person in whose favour the order is made upon the person for the time being named in the record as the solicitor, or as the person acting as solicitor, for the Crown or for the Government department or officer concerned.

(3) If the order provides for the payment of any money by way of damages or otherwise, or of any costs, the certificate shall state the amount so payable, and the appropriate Government department shall, subject as hereinafter provided, pay to the person entitled or to his solicitor the amount appearing by the certificate to be due to him together with the interest, if any, lawfully due thereon:

Provided that the court by which any such order as aforesaid is made or any court to which an appeal against the order lies may direct that, pending an appeal or otherwise, payment of the whole of any amount so payable, or any part thereof, shall be suspended, and if the certificate has not been issued may order any such directions to be inserted therein.

(4) Save as aforesaid no execution or attachment or process in the nature thereof shall be issued out of any court for enforcing payment by the Crown of any such money or costs as aforesaid, and no person shall be individually liable under any order for the payment by the Crown, or any Government department, or any officer of the Crown as such, of any such money or costs . . .

26—(1) Subject to the provisions of this Act, any order made in favour of the Crown against any person in any civil proceedings to which the Crown is a party may be enforced in the same manner as an order made in an action between subjects, and not otherwise . . .

28—(1) Subject to and in accordance with rules of court and county court rules: —

    (a) in any civil proceedings in the High Court or a county court to which the Crown is a party, the Crown may be required by the court to make discovery of documents and produce documents for inspection; and

(b) in any such proceedings as aforesaid, the Crown may be required by the court to answer interrogatories:

Provided that this section shall be without prejudice to any rule of law which authorises or requires the withholding of any document or the refusal to answer any question on the ground that the disclosure of the document or the answering of the question would be injurious to the public interest.

Any order of the court made under the powers conferred by paragraph *(b)* of this subsection shall direct by what officer of the Crown the interrogatories are to be answered.

(2) Without prejudice to the proviso to the preceding subsection, any rules made for the purposes of this section shall be such as to secure that the existence of a document will not be disclosed if, in the opinion of a Minister of the Crown, it would be injurious to the public interest to disclose the existence thereof.

38 . . . (2) In this Act, except in so far as the context otherwise requires or it is otherwise expressly provided, the following expressions have the meanings hereby respectively assigned to them, that is to say — . . .

"Civil proceedings" includes proceedings in the High Court or the county court for the recovery of fines or penalties, but does not include proceedings on the Crown side of the King's Bench Division . . .

. . . .

SCHEDULES

. . . .

FIRST SCHEDULE PROCEEDINGS ABOLISHED BY THIS ACT

2—(1) Proceedings against His Majesty by way of petition of right . . .

One important provision of the Act concerning remedies (s 21) has already been set out and discussed: see above at 13.2.3, In relation to s 4, see further the Civil Liability (Contribution) Act 1978 (which expressly states that it binds the Crown). It should be borne in mind more generally that, as we have had occasion to state earlier in this chapter, statutes only bind the Crown if expressly so worded or as a matter of necessary implication. On s 28 of the 1947 Act, see further 16.5.3.

16.5.2 Exemplary (or Punitive) Damages

As has been seen, earlier in this section, damages are often awarded against public bodies. The position regarding exemplary damages, however, deserves some particular attention, especially in the light of the first of the three categories of case in which, in *Rookes v. Barnard* [1964] AC 1129, Lord Devlin stated such damages can be awarded. At 1226, his Lordship stated:

The first category is oppressive, arbitrary or unconstitutional action by the servants of the government. I should not extend this category ... to oppressive action by private corporations or individuals. Where one man is more powerful than another, it is inevitable that he will try to use his power to gain his ends; and if his power is much greater than the other's, he might perhaps be said to be using it oppressively. If he uses his power illegally, he must, of course, pay for his illegality in the ordinary way; but he is not to be punished simply because he is the more powerful. In the case of the government, it is different, for the servants of the government are also the servants of the people and the use of their power must always be subordinate to their duty of service.

Lord Devlin (at 1223) saw the award of exemplary damages in this category as 'restraining the arbitrary and outrageous use of executive power', and more generally (at 1226) as 'serving a useful purpose in vindicating the strength of the law'. His ruling was followed by the House of Lords when it returned to the question in *Cassell & Co Ltd* v. *Broome* [1972] AC 1027, though compare Lord Reid's view (at 1088) that the reason for the distinction between government servants and others was merely the established pattern of the pre-existing case law. *Cassell* v. *Broome* lent support to the idea that this category should be interpreted liberally so as to include local government, the police and all those 'exercising functions of a governmental character'. Nevertheless, in *Holden* v. *Chief Constable of Lancashire* [1987] QB 380, it was doubted whether the mere fact of acting without authority would thereby render a policeman's action 'unconstitutional' within Lord Devlin's category, a category that was regarded as separate from either 'oppressive' or 'arbitrary' action.

The possibilities for awarding exemplary damages have been increased recently by *Kuddus* v. *Chief Constable of Leicestershire Constabulary* [2001] UKHL 29 [2002] 2 AC 122 where the House of Lords, overruling *AB* v. *South West Water Services Ltd* [1993] QB 507, made it clear that such an award was not confined to causes of action in which they had been awarded prior to 1964 (*Rookes* v. *Barnard*). European Community law leaves the question whether exemplary damages can be awarded to national law. When this question arose in *R* v. *Secretary of State for Transport, ex parte Factortame Ltd* [1998] 1 CMLR 1353 the Divisional Court rejected such a claim on the facts involved in that case, but note the view in Stanton, Skidmore, Harris and Wright, *Statutory Torts* (London 2003) at [6-061] that *Kuddus* 'leaves open the possibility that exemplary damages may be awarded in future for a breach of statutory duty, even where the statute makes no express provision for such a remedy, if the court considers it necessary to make such an award in the event of an arbitrary, unconscionable, or unconstitutional act by a government servant. It is quite conceivable that this may be convincingly argued in an action for State liability'. Cf *Design Progressions Ltd* v. *Thurloe Properties Ltd* [2004] EWHC 324 (Ch) [2005] 1 WLR 1 (exemplary damages awarded for breach of statutory duty, but the case did not involve a claim against a public body under Lord Devlin's first category).

Turning to s 6 HRA, the ECtHR — the decisions of which s 2 HRA requires English courts to take into account — has never awarded exemplary damages (and indeed has specifically rejected the chance to do so: see Law Com No 266, *Damages under the Human Rights Act 1998* at [3.47]); there is also the point to bear in mind that the s 6 action may not be classified as a tort (see above at 16.2.8).

Kuddus left open whether there could be vicarious liability for exemplary damages as the point had not been argued, but Lord Scott expressed provisional views which were hostile to the idea, although Lord Hutton did not seem opposed to it. (Note also that in *Watkins* v. *Secretary of State for the Home Department* [2004] EWCA Civ 966 counsel for the appellant 'did not press for an award against the Home Office on [the] appeal'.) In the absence of any legislation on the matter, litigation will doubtless resolve this matter one way or the other in the future.

16.5.3 Public Interest Immunity

Section 28 of the Crown Proceedings Act 1947, above at 16.5.1, made the Crown liable to discovery of documents but aimed to preserve what used to be called 'Crown Privilege'. It was thought at that time that this power to withhold information from the court on the grounds of harm to the public interest was a part of the prerogative (although, as we shall see, this is no longer the case). Furthermore, the general view, based on *Duncan* v. *Cammell Laird & Co Ltd* [1942] AC 624, was that the Crown's view on this matter was conclusive. However, a dramatic change occurred in *Conway* v. *Rimmer* [1968] AC 910 in which the argument that s 28 of the 1947 Act had given 'statutory confirmation' to *Duncan* v. *Cammell Laird* was rejected. (For discussion of the law prior to *Conway* v. *Rimmer*, see Clark (1967) 30 MLR 489.)

....

Conway v. *Rimmer* [1968] AC 910
House of Lords

The appellant, a probationary police constable who had been acquitted on a larceny charge, brought an action for malicious prosecution against the respondent, who had been instrumental in the charge being brought. When discovery of documents was sought, immunity from production was claimed for five documents on the ground of Crown privilege, four of the five documents in question being reports on the appellant. The affidavit sworn by the Home Secretary, in which he asserted that production would harm the public interest, stated that these four documents 'fell within a class of documents comprising confidential reports by police officers to chief officers of police relating to the conduct, efficiency and fitness for employment of individual police officers under their command'. The remaining document was said to fall 'within a class of documents comprising reports by police officers to their superiors concerning investigations into the commission of crime'. The documents, Lord Reid thought, 'may be of crucial importance' to the action. In this type of claim the argument is that the authors of a particular class of documents will be less candid than they would otherwise have been, if they know the document may be disclosed at a later stage: thus the public interest is adversely affected.

A District Registrar's order in favour of production of the documents was reversed by Browne J (in chambers) in a decision upheld by the Court of Appeal. There was a further appeal to the House of Lords.

Lord Reid

[Having set out the Home Secretary's affidavit, his Lordship said:] The question whether such a statement by a Minister of the Crown should be accepted as conclusively preventing any court from ordering production of any of the documents to which it applies is one of very great importance in the administration of justice. If the commonly accepted interpretation of the decision of this House in *Duncan* v. *Cammell, Laird & Co. Ltd.* [[1942] AC 624] is to remain authoritative the question admits of only one answer — the Minister's statement is final and conclusive . . .

I have no doubt that the case of *Duncan* v. *Cammell, Laird & Co. Ltd.* was rightly decided. The plaintiff sought discovery of documents relating to the submarine *Thetis* including a contract for the hull and machinery and plans and specifications. The First Lord of the Admiralty had stated that "it would be injurious to the public interest that any of the said documents should be disclosed to any person." Any of these documents might well have given valuable information, or at least clues, to the skilled eye of an agent of a foreign power. But Lord Simon L.C. took the opportunity to deal with the whole question of the right of the Crown to prevent production of documents in a litigation. Yet a study of his speech leaves me with the strong impression that throughout he had primarily in mind cases where discovery or disclosure would involve a danger of real prejudice to the national interest. I find it difficult to believe that his speech would have been the same if the case had related, as the present case does, to discovery of routine reports on a probationer constable . . .

It is universally recognised that here there are two kinds of public interest which may clash. There is the public interest that harm shall not be done to the nation or the public service by disclosure of certain documents, and there is the public interest that the administration of justice shall not be frustrated by the withholding of documents which must be produced if justice is to be done. There are many cases where the nature of the injury which would or might be done to the nation or the public service is of so grave a character that no other interest, public or private, can be allowed to prevail over it. With regard to such cases it would be proper to say, as Lord Simon did, that to order production of the document in question would put the interest of the state in jeopardy. But there are many other cases where the possible injury to the public service is much less and there one would think that it would be proper to balance the public interests involved . . .

It is to be observed that [in *Duncan* v. *Cammell, Laird & Co. Ltd., op cit* at 642] Lord Simon referred to the practice of keeping a class of documents secret being "*necessary* [my italics] for the proper functioning of the public interest." But the certificate of the Home Secretary in the present case does not go nearly so far as that. It merely says that the production of a document of the classes to which it refers would be "injurious to the public interest": it does not say what degree of injury is to be apprehended. It may be advantageous to the functioning of the public service that reports of this kind should be kept secret — that is the view of the Home Secretary — but I would be very surprised if anyone said that that is necessary . . .

[His Lordship then referred to the Lord Chancellor's 1956 statement, which with one exception excluded from the protection of Crown privilege documents that were relevant to a defence in criminal proceedings. He continued:] That is a very wide ranging exception, for the Attorney-General stated that it applied at least to all manner of routine communications and even to prosecutions for minor offences. Thus it can no longer be said that the writer of such communications has any "certainty at the time of writing that the document would not be disclosed." So we have the curious result that 'freedom and candour of communication' is supposed not to be inhibited by knowledge of the writer that his report may be disclosed in a criminal case, but would still be supposed to be inhibited if he thought that his report might be disclosed in a civil case . . .

. . . [I]t appears to me that the present position is so unsatisfactory that this House must re-examine the whole question in light of all the authorities.

Two questions will arise: first, whether the court is to have any right to question the finality of a Minister's certificate and, secondly, if it has such a right, how and in what circumstances that right is to be exercised and made effective.

A Minister's certificate may be given on one or other of two grounds: either because it would be against the public interest to disclose the contents of the particular document or documents in question [this is known as a 'contents claim'], or because the document belongs to a class of documents which ought to be withheld, whether or not there is anything in the particular document in question disclosure of which would be against the public interest [this is known as a 'class claim']. It does not appear that any serious difficulties have arisen or are likely to arise with regard to the first class. However wide the power of the court may be held to be, cases would be very rare in which it could be proper to question the view of the responsible Minister that it would be contrary to the public interest to make public the contents of a particular document. A question might arise whether it would be possible to separate those parts of a document of which disclosure would be innocuous from those parts which ought not to be made public, but I need not pursue that question now. In the present case your Lordships are directly concerned with the second class of documents . . .

[Having surveyed the relevant authorities, he continued:] I would . . . propose that the House ought now to decide that courts have and are entitled to exercise a power and duty to hold a balance between the public interest, as expressed by a Minister, to withhold certain documents or other evidence, and the public interest in ensuring the proper administration of justice. That does not mean that a court would reject a Minister's view: full weight must be given to it in every case, and if the Minister's reasons are of a character which judicial experience is not competent to weigh, then the Minister's view must prevail. But experience has shown that reasons given for withholding whole classes of documents are often not of that character. For example a court is perfectly well able to assess the likelihood that, if the writer of a certain class of document knew that there was a chance that his report might be produced in legal proceedings, he would make a less full and candid report than he would otherwise have done.

I do not doubt that there are certain classes of documents which ought not to be disclosed whatever their content may be. Virtually everyone agrees that Cabinet minutes and the like ought not to be disclosed until such time as they are only of historical interest. But I do not think that many people would give as the reason that premature disclosure would prevent candour in the Cabinet. To my mind the most important reason is that such disclosure would create or fan ill-informed or captious public or political criticism. The business of government is difficult enough as it is, and no government could contemplate with equanimity the inner workings of the government machine being exposed to the gaze of those ready to criticise without adequate knowledge of the background and perhaps with some axe to grind. And that must, in my view, also apply to all documents concerned with policy making within departments including, it may be, minutes and the like by quite junior officials and correspondence with outside bodies. Further it may be that deliberations about a particular case require protection as much as deliberations about policy. I do not think that it is possible to limit such documents by any definition. But there seems to me to be a wide difference between such documents and routine reports. There may be special reasons for withholding some kinds of routine documents, but I think that the proper test to be applied is to ask, in the language of Lord Simon in *Duncan's* case, whether the withholding of a document because it belongs to a particular class is really "necessary for the proper functioning of the public service."

It appears to me that, if the Minister's reasons are such that a judge can properly weigh them, he must, on the other hand, consider what is the probable importance in the case before him of the documents or other evidence sought to be withheld. If he decides that on balance the documents probably ought to be produced, I think that it would generally be best that he should see them before ordering production and if he thinks that the Minister's reasons are not clearly expressed he will have to see the documents before ordering production. I can see nothing wrong in the judge seeing documents without their being shown to the parties. Lord Simon said (in *Duncan's* case) that "where the Crown is a party . . . this would amount to communicating with one party to the exclusion of the other." I do not agree. The parties see the Minister's reasons. Where a document has not been prepared for the information of the judge, it seems to me a misuse of language to say that the judge "communicates with" the holder of the document by reading it. If on reading the document he still thinks that it ought to be produced he will order its production.

But it is important that the Minister should have a right to appeal before the document is produced . . .

The documents in this case are in the possession of a police force. The position of the police is peculiar. They are not servants of the Crown and they do not take orders from the Government. But they are carrying out an essential function of Government, and various Crown rights, privileges and exemptions have been held to apply to them. Their position was explained in *Coomber* v. *Berkshire Justices* [(1883) 9 App Cas 61] and cases there cited. It has never been denied that they are entitled to Crown privilege with regard to documents, and it is essential that they should have it.

The police are carrying on an unending war with criminals many of whom are today highly intelligent. So it is essential that there should be no disclosure of anything which might give any useful information to those who organise criminal activities. And it would generally be wrong to require disclosure in a civil case of anything which might be material in a pending prosecution: but after a verdict has been given or it has been decided to take no proceedings there is not the same need for secrecy. With regard to other documents there seems to be no greater need for protection than in the case of departments of Government.

It appears to me to be most improbable that any harm would be done by disclosure of the probationary reports on the appellant or of the report from the police training centre. With regard to the report which the respondent made to his chief constable with a view to the prosecution of the appellant there could be more doubt, although no suggestion was made in argument that disclosure of its contents would be harmful now that the appellant has been acquitted. And . . . these documents may prove to be of vital importance in this litigation.

In my judgment, this appeal should be allowed and these documents ought now to be required to be produced for inspection . . .

Lord Upjohn

. . . On the one side there is the public interest to be protected; on the other side of the scales is the interest of the subject who legitimately wants production of some documents which he believes will support his own or defeat his adversary's case. Both are matters of public interest, for it is also in the public interest that justice should be done between litigating parties by production of all documents which are relevant and for which privilege cannot be claimed under me ordinary rules. They must be weighed in the balance one against the other.

Your Lordships have reviewed the earlier authorities which are many and are not easy to reconcile and I shall not discuss them again, but it seems to me that there is sufficient authority to support the view held by all of your Lordships that the claim of privilege by the Crown, while entitled to the greatest weight, is only a claim and the decision whether the court should accede to the claim lies within the discretion of the judge; and it is real discretion . . . First, with regard to the "contents" cases there is, I think, no dispute and it does not strictly arise in this case. A claim made by a Minister on the basis that the disclosure of the contents would be prejudicial to the public interest must receive the greatest weight; but even here I am of opinion that the Minister should go as far as he properly can without prejudicing the public interest in saying why the contents require protection. In such cases it would be rare indeed for the court to overrule the Minister but it has the legal power to do so, first inspecting the document itself and then, if he thinks proper to do so, ordering its production.

Secondly, the "class" cases . . .

No doubt there are many cases in which documents by their very nature fall in a class which require protection such as, only by way of example, Cabinet papers, Foreign Office dispatches, the security of the state, high level inter-departmental minutes and correspondence and documents pertaining to the general administration of the naval, military and air force services. Nearly always such documents would be the subject of privilege by reason of their contents but by their "class" in any event they qualify for privilege. So, too, high level interdepartmental communications, to take, only as an example upon establishment matters, the promotion or transfer of reasonably high level personnel in the service of the Crown. But no catalogue can reasonably be compiled. The reason for this privilege is that it would be quite wrong and entirely inimical to the proper functioning of the public service if the public were to learn of these high level communications, however innocent of prejudice to the state the actual contents of any particular document might be; that is obvious. But it has nothing whatever to do with candour or uninhibited freedom of expression; I cannot believe that any Minister or any high level military or civil servant would feel in the least degree inhibited in expressing his honest views in the course of his duty on some subject, such as even the personal qualifications and delinquencies of some colleague, by the thought that his observation might one day see the light of day. His worst fear might be libel and there he has the defence of qualified privilege like everyone else in every walk of professional, industrial and commercial life who every day has to express views on topics indistinguishable in substance from those of the servants of the Crown

So this plea of the necessity for the protection of documents written by junior servants of the Crown must depend solely on the necessity for candour . . .

. . . For my part I find it difficult to justify this when those in other walks of life which give rise to equally important matters of confidence in relation to security and personnel matters as in the public service can claim no such privilege . . .

Lords Morris, Pearce, and Hodson delivered speeches in favour of allowing the appeal. Appeal allowed.

QUESTION

• Are the courts in a better position than a Minister to balance the competing public interests? (See de Smith and Brazier, *Constitutional and Administrative Law* (London 1998) at 611.)

16.5.4 Crown Privilege Becomes Public Interest Immunity

Rogers v. *Home Secretary* [1973] AC 388
House of Lords

It is sufficient for the purposes of this extract to note that this case concerned a successful claim to immunity from production for a letter sent by an assistant chief constable to the Gaming Board. The Gaming Board was established by the Gaming Act 1968 to 'keep under review the extent, character and location of gaming facilities'. It is not a government department.

Lord Reid

. . . The ground put forward has been said to be Crown privilege. I think that that expression is wrong and may be misleading. There is no question of any privilege in the ordinary sense of the word. The real question is whether the public interest requires that the letter shall not be produced and whether that public interest is so strong as to override the ordinary right and interest of a litigant that he shall be able to lay before a court of justice all relevant evidence. A Minister of the Crown is always an appropriate and often the most appropriate person to assert this public interest, and the evidence or advice which he gives to the court is always valuable and may sometimes be indispensable. But, in my view, it must always be open to any person interested to raise the question and there may be cases where the trial judge should himself raise the question if no one else has done so. In the present case the question of public interest was raised by both the Attorney-General and the Gaming Board. In my judgment both were entitled to raise the matter. Indeed I think that in the circumstances it was the duty of the board to do as they have done . . .

The use of the term 'Crown privilege' also came in for criticism from Lords Pearson (at 406), Simon (at 406–407) and Salmon (at 412), though compare the view of Lord Scarman in *Science Research Council* v. *Nassé* [1980] AC 1028 at 1087. The preferred term is now 'public interest immunity'.

Related to the point in the extract above is the rejection by the House of Lords in *D* v. *National Society for the Prevention of Cruelty to Children* [1978] AC 171 of the idea that this immunity from production should be confined to the operations of central government departments or organs. This case concerned a civil action brought against the NSPCC, which is, of course, concerned with the welfare of children and which in particular was the only body (apart from the police and a local authority) authorized to bring care proceedings under s 1 of the Children and Young Persons Act 1969. It was held that the NSPCC could withhold the identity of a person who had made a particular allegation to them. The House of Lords did, however, proceed with some caution; an important factor in favour of the claim was the similarity of the position of the informant to that of a police informer, whose identity receives some protection from the law (though see Tapper (1978) 41 *MLR* 192). Lord Hailsham approached the case with a certain 'willingness to extend established principles by analogy and legitimate extrapolation' ([1978] AC at 226), an attitude which seems to be a fair reflection of the general line adopted in the House of Lords. On the withholding of the identity of informants, see also *Chief Constable of Greater Manchester Police* v. *McNally* [2002] 2 Cr App R 617 and on the protection of sources of information, see further *Rogers* v. *Home Secretary* [1973] AC 388 at 401, 407, and 412–413.

It would seem, therefore, that the scope of a potential claim to immunity has increased over the years; contrast the change in attitude to claims by local authorities in *Blackpool Corporation* v. *Locker* [1948] 1 KB 349 at 380 with *Re D (Infants)* [1970] 1 WLR 599. However, one stopping point was reached in *Science Research Council* v. *Nassé* [1980] AC 1028, which involved two actions by employees alleging unlawful discrimination by their employers. The employers involved in the two cases (the SRC and British Leyland) refused to disclose, in one case some confidential reports on, in the second case some confidential records of, other employees (along with certain additional material); but the House of Lords rejected the claim of public interest immunity which was raised by British Leyland. (Without going into detail, the argument against disclosure related to securing efficiency in industry and avoiding industrial unrest.) One reason for the rejection of the claim was the lack of any suitable analogy with an already accepted category.

16.5.5 Evolution of the Doctrine

As has been pointed out by Williams [1980] *CLJ* 1, until the *Burmah Oil* case, from which there is an extract below, the English cases following *Conway* v. *Rimmer* [1968] AC 910 had, with one exception (*F Hoffman La Roche & Co* v. *Department of Trade and Industry* (*The Times*, 19 April 1975)), arisen 'in contexts, such as police or customs and excise, falling outside the inner machinery of central government'. *Burmah Oil* was different.

Before the extract from *Burmah Oil* and indeed the extract after that (from *Air Canada* v. *Secretary of State for Trade* [1983] 2 AC 394) are considered, two particular factors should be mentioned here. First, as a result of various events which will be referred to in 16.5.6, the government in 1996 announced its new practice in relation to claiming public interest immunity. One point is that it will no longer make a division between class and contents claims, and this needs to be borne in mind when considering the next two extracts: however, it will be seen at 16.5.6 that class claims have not necessarily disappeared. Secondly, the two cases were decided at a time when the Rules of the Supreme Court (RSC) were in force: since then, the Civil Procedure Rules (CPR) have been introduced which, for example, refer to 'disclosure' rather than 'discovery' of documents. Nevertheless, the two cases remain of importance.

....

Burmah Oil Co Ltd v. *Governor and Company of the Bank of England* [1980] AC 1090
House of Lords

The Burmah Oil Co Ltd ('Burmah') sued the Governor and Company of the Bank of England ('the bank') in respect of the sale, by the former to the latter, of a large number of shares in the British Petroleum Co. Ltd. ('BP') at what Burmah claimed was a substantial undervalue, making the bargain unconscionable, inequitable, and unreasonable. On the instructions of the Crown, the bank objected to the production of certain documents. That objection was upheld by Foster J; following an unsuccessful appeal to the Court of Appeal on this point, Burmah appealed to the House of Lords. The Chief Secretary to the Treasury issued certificates in respect of (*inter alia*) communications between, to and from Ministers, and between, to and from senior officials of the Department of Energy, of the Treasury, and of the bank, concerning the formulation of government policy regarding the financial rescue of Burmah of which the bargain presently under consideration was a key component. Non-production of these documents, certified the Chief Secretary, was 'necessary for the proper functioning of the public service' because they all fell 'within the class of documents relating to the formulation of government policy. Such policy was decided at a very high level, involving as it did matters of major economic importance to the United Kingdom.'

Lord Wilberforce

. . . [One] argument [by Burmah] is . . . that, whatever may have been the need to protect governmental policy from disclosure at the time (1975) all is now past history: the decision has been made; the sale has gone through; Burmah has been saved from collapse. So what is the public interest in keeping up the protective screen?

I think that there are several answers to this. The first (and easiest) is that all is not past history — at least we do not know that it is. Government policy as to supporting private firms in danger of collapse: as to ownership of B.P. stock: as to the development of North Sea oil is ongoing policy; the documents are not yet for the Record Office. They are not, to use a phrase picked out of Lord Reid's speech in *Conway* v. *Rimmer* [1968] A.C. 910, 952, of purely historical interest. Secondly the grounds on which public interest immunity is claimed for this class of document are, no doubt within limits, independent of time. One such ground is the need for candour in communication between those concerned with policy making. It seems now rather fashionable to decry this, but if as a ground it may at one time have been exaggerated, it has now, in my opinion, received an excessive dose of cold water. I am certainly not prepared — against the view of the Minister — to discount the need, in the formation of such very controversial policy as that with which we are here involved, for frank and uninhibited advice from the bank to the government, from and between civil servants and between Ministers. It does not require much imagination to suppose that some of those concerned took different views as to the right policy and expressed them. The documents indeed show that they did. To remove protection from revelation in court in this case at least could well deter frank and full expression in similar cases in the future.

Another such ground is to protect from inspection by possible critics the inner working of government while forming important governmental policy. I do not believe that scepticism has invaded this, or that it is for the courts to assume the role of advocates for open government. If, as I believe, this is a valid ground for protection, it must continue to operate beyond the time span of a particular episode. Concretely, to reveal what advice was *then* sought and given and the mechanism for seeking and considering such advice, might well make the process of government more difficult *now*. On this point too I am certainly not prepared to be wiser than the Minister. So I think that the "time factor" argument must fail.

The basis for an immunity claim, then, having been laid, it is next necessary to consider whether there is any other element of public interest telling in favour of production. The interest of the proper and fair administration of justice falls under this description. It is hardly necessary to state that the mere fact that the documents are or may be "relevant" to the issues, within the extended meaning of relevance in relation to discovery, is not material. The question of privilege or immunity only arises in relation to 'relevant' documents and itself depends on other considerations, viz., whether production of these documents (admittedly relevant) is necessary for the due administration of justice. In considering how these two elements are to be weighed one against the other, the proper starting point must be the decision of this House in *Conway* v. *Rimmer* [1968] A.C. 910 . . . Of course *Conway* v. *Rimmer*, as the speeches of their Lordships show, does not profess to cover every case, nor has it frozen the law, but it does provide a solid basis for progress as regards the point now under discussion.

It may well be arguable whether, when one is faced with a claim for immunity from production on "public interest" grounds, and when the relevant public interest is shown to be of a high, or the highest, level of importance, that fact is of itself conclusive, and nothing which relates to the interest in the administration of justice can prevail against it. As Lord Pearce said in *Conway* v. *Rimmer* [1968] A.C. 910, 987: 'Obviously production would never be ordered of fairly wide classes of documents at a high level' and see *Reg.* v. *Lewes Justices, ex parte Secretary of State for the Home Department* [1973] A.C. 388, 412 *per* Lord Salmon. In the words of May J. in *Barty-King* v. *Ministry of Defence* (unreported), October 10, 1978 (concerned with internal thinking and policy at a high civil service level), it is not even necessary to bring out the scales. Mr. Silkin for the Attorney-General did not contend for any such rigorous proposition, *ie* that a high level public interest can never, in any circumstances, be outweighed. In this I think that he was in line with the middle of the road position taken by Lord Reid in *Conway* v. *Rimmer* and also with the median views of the members of the High Court of Australia in *Sankey* v. *Whitlam*, 53 A.L.J.R. 11 — see particularly the judgment of Gibbs A.C.J. I am therefore quite prepared to deal with this case on the basis that the courts may, in a suitable case, decide that a high level governmental public interest must give way to the interests of the administration of justice.

But it must be clear what this involves. A claim for public interest immunity having been made, on manifestly solid grounds, it is necessary for those who seek to overcome it to demonstrate the existence of a counteracting interest calling for disclosure of particular documents. When this is demonstrated, but only then, may the court proceed to a balancing process . . . [In] the present case . . . [t]here is not, and I firmly assert this, the slightest ground, apart from pure speculation, for supposing that there is any document in existence, among those which it is sought to withhold, or anything in a document which could outweigh the public interest claim for immunity . . .

[Having stated his reasons for this opinion more fully, he went on to the question of inspection which he thought would require "a strong positive case" to be made out.]

Lord Edmund-Davies

. . . In the face of the bank's umbrella denial of any inequality of bargaining power, the sale of B.P. stock at an undervalue, and all other forms of unconscionable conduct on their part, it could, as I think, prove a valuable reinforcement of Burmah's case if they could establish by means of some of the withheld documents that the bank had itself committed themselves to the view that the terms finally presented to Burmah were tainted by those unconscionable features of which Burmah complained.

What are the probabilities of such documentary support being in existence? Is it merely pure conjecture? If so, applying the plaintiffs' own test, production should be refused. But in my judgment, there is more to it than that . . . [I]n my judgment the existence of such documentary material is likely. And that, in my judgment, is sufficient . . .

[Having therefore moved on to consider the 'balancing exercise', he continued:] . . . [S]ince not only justice itself but also the *appearance* of justice is of considerable importance, the balancing exercise is bound to be affected to some degree where the party objecting to discovery is not a wholly detached observer of events in which it was in no way involved. It cannot realistically be thought that the government is wholly devoid of interest in the outcome of these proceedings . . .

[Lord Edmund-Davies then went on to decide that in the light of the material before the court, and especially his view (above) concerning the likelihood of documentary support for Burmah, the documents should be inspected.]

Lord Keith

. . . [I]n my opinion no definitive body of binding rules universally applicable to future cases in the field is to be gathered from the speeches delivered [in *Conway* v. *Rimmer* [1968] AC 910] and the sound development of the law now requires that it be examined afresh . . .

Lord Hodson in [*Conway* v. *Rimmer*] at p. 979 said that he did not regard the classification which places all documents under the heading either of contents or class as being wholly satisfactory. I agree with him. What really matters is the specific ground of public interest upon which the ministerial objection is based; and it scarcely needs to be said that the more clearly this ground is stated the easier will be the task of the court in weighing it against the public interest in the administration of justice. The weight of a contents claim is capable of being very readily measured. Obvious instances are documents relating to defence of the realm or relations with other states. It might be said that such documents constitute a class defined by reference to the nature of their contents. But I would prefer to regard the claim in regard to such a document as being in substance a contents claim . . .

[Having referred to Lord Upjohn's speech in *Conway* v. *Rimmer* he continued:] Claims to immunity on class grounds stand in a different category because the reasons of public interest upon which they are based may appear to some minds debatable or even nebulous. In *Duncan* v. *Cammell, Laird & Co. Ltd.* [1942] A.C. 624, Viscount Simon L.C. at p. 642 referred to cases 'where the practice of keeping a class of documents secret is necessary for the proper functioning of the public service.' These words have been seized on as convenient for inclusion in many a ministerial certificate, including the one under consideration in the present case. But they inevitably stimulate the query 'why is the concealment necessary for that purpose?' and unless it is answered there is nothing tangible to put in the balance against the public interest in the proper administration of justice.

Over a considerable period it was maintained, not without success, that the prospect of the disclosure in litigation of correspondence or other communications within government departments would inhibit a desirable degree of candour in the making of such documents, with results detrimental to the proper functioning of the public service . . . This contention must now be treated as having little weight, if any. In *Conway* v. *Rimmer* [1968] A.C. 910, Lord Morris of Borth-y-Gest, at p. 957, referred to it as being of doubtful validity. Lord Hodson, at p. 976, thought it impossible at the present day to justify the doctrine in its widest terms. Lord Pearce, at p. 986, considered that a general blanket protection of wide classes led to a complete lack of common sense. Lord Upjohn, at p. 995, expressed himself as finding it difficult to justify the doctrine 'when those in other walks of life which give rise to equally important matters of confidence in relation to security and personnel matters as in the public service can claim no such privilege.' The notion that any competent and conscientious public servant would be inhibited at all in the candour of his writings by consideration of the off-chance that they might have to be produced in a litigation is in my opinion grotesque. To represent that the possibility of it might significantly impair the public service is even more so. Nowadays the state in multifarious manifestations impinges closely upon the lives and activities of individual citizens. Where this has involved a citizen in litigation with the state or one of its agencies, the candour argument is an utterly insubstantial ground for denying him access to relevant documents. I would add that the candour doctrine stands in a different category from that aspect of public interest which in appropriate circumstances may require that the sources and nature of information confidentially tendered should be withheld from disclosure. *Reg.* v. *Lewes justices, Ex parte Secretary of State for the Home Department* [1973] A.C. 388 and *D.* v. *National Society for the Prevention of Cruelty to Children* [1978] A.C. 171 are cases in point on that matter.

I turn to what was clearly regarded in *Conway* v. *Rimmer* [1968] A.C. 910 as the really important reason for protecting from disclosure certain categories of documents on a class basis. It was thus expressed by Lord Reid . . .

[Having quoted a passage from Lord Reid's speech set out above at p 616, he continued:] Lord Hodson at p. 973 referred to classes of documents which from their very character ought to be withheld from production, such as Cabinet minutes, dispatches from ambassadors abroad and minutes of discussions between heads of departments. Lord Pearce at p. 987 said that obviously production would never be considered of fairly wide classes of documents at a high level such as Cabinet correspondence, letters or reports on appointments to office of importance and the like. Lord Upjohn spoke to similar effect at p. 993, saying that the reason for the privilege was that it would be wrong and entirely inimical to the proper functioning of the public service if the public were to learn of these high level communications, however innocent of prejudice to the state the actual contents of any particular document might be, and that this was obvious.

In my opinion, it would be going too far to lay down that no document in any particular one of the categories mentioned should never in any circumstances be ordered to be produced, and indeed I did not understand counsel for the Attorney-General to pitch his submission that high before this House. Something must turn upon the nature of the subject matter, the persons who dealt with it, and the manner in which they did so. In so far as a matter of government policy is concerned, it may be relevant to know the extent to which the policy remains unfulfilled, so that its success might be prejudiced by disclosure of the considerations which led to it. In that context the time element enters into the equation. Details of an affair which is stale and no longer of topical significance might be capable of disclosure without risk of damage to the public interest. The ministerial certificate should offer all practicable assistance on these aspects. But the nature of the litigation and the apparent importance to it of the documents in question may in extreme cases demand production even of the most sensitive communications at the highest level . . . There can be discerned in modern times a trend towards more open governmental methods than were prevalent in the past. No doubt it is for Parliament and not for courts of law to say how far that trend should go. The courts are, however, concerned with the consideration that it is in the public interest that justice should be done and should be publicly recognised as having been done. This may demand, though no doubt only in a very limited number of cases, that the inner workings of government should be exposed to public gaze, and there may be some who would regard this as likely to lead, not to captious or ill-informed criticism, but to criticism calculated to improve the nature of that working as affecting the individual citizen . . .

There are cases where consideration of the terms of the ministerial certificate and of the nature of the issues in the case before it as revealed by the pleadings, taken with the description of the document sought to be recovered, will make it clear to the court that the balance of public interest lies against disclosure. In other cases the position will be the reverse. But there may be situations where grave doubt arises, and the court feels that it cannot properly decide upon which side the balance falls without privately inspecting the documents. In my opinion the present is such a case . . . Having carefully considered all the circumstances, I have come to the conclusion that a reasonable probability exists of finding the documents in question to contain a record of the views of the responsible officials of the Bank of England expressed in such terms as to lend substantial support to the contention that the bargain eventually concluded with the appellants was unconscionable . . .

There can be no doubt that the court has power to inspect the documents privately. This was clearly laid down in *Conway* v. *Rimmer* [1968] A.C. 910. I do not consider that exercise of such power, in cases responsibly regarded by the court as doubtful, can be treated as itself detrimental to the public interest. Indeed, I am of opinion that it is calculated to promote the public interest, by adding to public confidence in the administration of justice . . . Apprehension has on occasion been expressed lest the power of inspection might be irresponsibly exercised, perhaps by one of the lower courts. As a safeguard against this, an appeal should always be available, as indicated in *Conway* v. *Rimmer* [1968] A.C. 910, *per* Lord Reid at p. 953.

For these reasons I am in agreement with the majority of your Lordships that this is a proper case for the court to requir the 10 documents in question to be made available for private inspection. I do not consider that the discretion to order or refuse production of the documents was capable of being exercised soundly and with due regard to principle in the absence of such inspection. Accordingly I see no difficulty in differing from Foster J. and the majority of the Court of Appeal.

Having inspected the documents, I agree with the majority of your Lordships, though with some hesitation, that none of them contains matter of such evidential value as to make an order for their disclosure, in all the circumstances, necessary for disposing fairly of the case.

It follows that I would dismiss the appeal.

Lord Scarman

. . . I do not . . . accept that there are any classes of document which, however harmless their contents and however strong the requirement of justice, may never be disclosed until they are only of historical interest. In this respect I think there may well be a difference between a 'class' objection and a 'contents' objection — though the residual power to inspect and to order disclosure must remain in both instances. A Cabinet minute, it is said, must be withheld from production. Documents relating to the formulation of policy at a high level are also to be withheld. But is the secrecy of the 'inner workings of the government machine' so vital a public interest that it must prevail over even the most imperative demands of justice? If the contents of a document concern the national safety, affect diplomatic relations or relate to some state secret of high importance, I can understand an affirmative answer. But if they do not (and it is not claimed in this case that they do), what is so important about secret government that it must be protected even at the price of injustice in our courts?

The reasons given for protecting the secrecy of government at the level of policy-making are two. The first is the need for candour in the advice offered to Ministers: the second is that disclosure 'would create or fan ill-informed or captious public or political criticism.' Lord Reid in *Conway* v. *Rimmer* [1968] A.C. 910, 952, thought the second 'the most important reason.' Indeed, he was inclined to discount the candour argument.

I think both reasons are factors legitimately to be put into me balance which has to be struck between the public interest in the proper functioning of the public service (i.e., the executive arm of government) and the public interest in the administration of justice. Sometimes the public service reasons will be decisive of the issue: but they should never prevent the court from weighing them against the injury which would be suffered in the administration of justice if the document was not to be disclosed. And the likely injury to the cause of justice must also be assessed and weighed. Its weight will vary according to the nature of the proceedings in which disclosure is sought, the relevance of the documents, and the degree of likelihood that the document will be of importance in the litigation. In striking the balance, the court may always, if it thinks it necessary, itself inspect the documents.

Inspection by the court is, I accept, a power to be exercised only if the court is in doubt, after considering the certificate, the issues in the case and the relevance of the documents whose disclosure is sought. Where documents are relevant (as in this case they are), I would think a pure 'class' objection would by itself seldom quieten judicial doubts — particularly if, as here, a substantial case can be made out for saying that disclosure is needed in the interest of justice . . .

Lord Salmon delivered a speech in which he favoured inspecting the documents, but, having inspected, his Lordship was in favour of dismissing the appeal. Appeal dismissed.

QUESTION

• What, if any, difference in judicial philosophy is there between Lords Wilberforce and Keith? (See Williams [1980] *CLJ* 1.)

It will have been seen that different views were expressed in *Burmah Oil* on the merits of the 'candour argument', but it is important to note that this argument was distinguished by Lord Keith in *Burmah Oil* from cases in which the source or nature of confidential information may need protection, *eg* information given to the Gaming Board or the NSPCC (see above at 16.5.4).

In relation to confidentiality more generally, it was held in *Alfred Crompton Amusement Machines Ltd* v. *Customs and Excise Commissioners (No 2)* [1974] AC 405 that confidentiality did not of itself give rise to immunity, but it was a factor to consider. In this case immunity from production was successfully sought for documents containing certain information given in confidence by third parties to the Commissioners. (Cf *Norwich Pharmacal Co* v. *Customs and Excise Commissioners* [1974] AC 133.) It was argued in *Alfred Crompton* that those who supplied the information in confidence would resent its potential disclosure to others who might in fact be their rivals in trade. This, it was said, could lead to the consequence that in future cases these people might feel tempted not to provide the information (even though there was a statutory provision requiring it to be given), and also that their relationship with the Commissioners would be prejudiced: in this way the public interest would be jeopardized. The case indeed raises the question of providing a limit on the scope of government invasion of privacy, on which see Zuckerman in Tapper (ed), *Crime, Proof and Punishment* (London 1981) at 279–280.

....

Air Canada v. *Secretary of State for Trade* [1983] 2 AC 394
House of Lords

The appellants in this action were challenging the validity of certain increases in landing charges at Heathrow Airport, and their case involved an allegation of *ultra vires* activity on the part of the Secretary of State for Trade: this in turn raised the issue of the Secretary of State's dominant purpose in doing what he had done and the factors he had taken into consideration. The Treasury Solicitor objected on the ground of public interest immunity to the production of two categories of documents (A and B) to which the appellants wished to refer. The ground of objection was similar to that in the *Burmah Oil* case, namely that the documents related to the formulation of government policy at a high level and that it was necessary to withhold them for the proper functioning of the public service. Bingham J ordered production of certain of the documents for inspection, but the Court of Appeal reversed this decision. There was an appeal to the House of Lords.

Lord Fraser

. . . I do not think that even Cabinet minutes are completely immune from disclosure in a case where, for example, the issue in a litigation involves serious misconduct by a Cabinet Minister . . . But while Cabinet documents do not have complete immunity, they are entitled to a high degree of protection against disclosure. In the present case the documents in category A do not enjoy quite the status of Cabinet minutes, but they approach that level in that they may disclose the reasons for Cabinet decisions and the process by which the decisions were reached. The reasons why such documents should not normally be disclosed until they have become of purely historical interest were considered in *Burmah Oil Co. Ltd.* v. *Governor and Company of the Bank of England* [1980] A.C. 1090 . . .

[Having set out a passage from Lord Wilberforce's speech in that case (see above), his Lordship continued:] Although Lord Wilberforce dissented from the majority as to the result in that case, I do not think that his statement of the reasons for supporting public interest immunity were in any way in conflict with the views of the majority.

In the present case, then, we have documents which are admittedly relevant to the matters in issue, in the sense explained in *Compagnie Financière et Commerciale du Pacifique* v. *Peruvian Guano Co.* (1882) 11 Q.B.D. 55, 63, *per* Brett L.J. I am willing to assume that they are, in the words of R.S.C., Ord. 24, r. 13 (1), 'necessary . . . for disposing fairly of the cause' [but note now the existence of the CPR] on the (perhaps not very rigorous) standard which would apply if this were an ordinary case in which public interest immunity had not been claimed. But it has been claimed, and the onus therefore is on the plaintiffs, as the parties seeking disclosure, to show why the documents ought to be produced for inspection by the court privately. The question of whether the court, having inspected them privately, should order them to be produced publicly is a separate question which does not arise at this stage, although as I shall seek to show in a moment it is in my opinion relevant.

. . . In an adversarial system such as exists in the United Kingdom, a party is free to withhold information that would help his case if he wishes — perhaps for reasons of delicacy or personal privacy. He cannot be compelled to disclose it against his will. It follows in my opinion that a party who seeks to compel his opponent, or an independent person, to disclose information must show that the information is likely to help his own case. It would be illogical to apply a different rule at the stage of inspection from that which applies at the stage of production. After all, the purpose of inspection by the court in many cases, including the present, would be to let the court see whether there is material in favour of disclosure which should be put in the scales to weigh against the material in favour of immunity. Inspection is with a view to the possibility of ordering production, and in my opinion inspection ought not to be ordered unless the court is persuaded that inspection is likely to satisfy it that it ought to take the further step of ordering production . . .

[Having referred to certain views in *Conway* v. *Rimmer* [1968] AC 910 on the question of inspection and to various tests in *Burmah Oil* above, his Lordship continued:] My Lords, I do not think it would be possible to state a test in a form which could be applied in all cases. Circumstances vary greatly. The weight of the public interest against disclosure will vary according to the nature of the particular documents in question; for example, it will in general be stronger where the documents are Cabinet papers than when they are at a lower level. The weight of the public interest in favour of disclosure will vary even more widely, because it depends upon the probable evidential value to the party seeking disclosure of the particular documents, in almost infinitely variable circumstances of individual cases. The most that can usefully be said is that, in order to persuade the court even to inspect documents for which public interest immunity is claimed, the party seeking disclosure ought at least to satisfy the court that the documents are very likely to contain material which would give substantial support to his contention on an issue which arises in the case, and that without them he might be 'deprived of the means of . . . proper presentation' of his case: see *Glasgow Corporation* v. *Central Land Board*, 1956 S.C. (H.L.) 1, 18, *per* Lord Radcliffe. It will be plain that that formulation has been mainly derived from the speech of my noble and learned friend, Lord Edmund-Davies, in the *Burmah Oil* case [1980] A.C. 1090, 1129, and from the opinion of McNeill J. in *Williams* v. *Home Office* [1981] 1 All E.R. 1151, 1154A. It assumes, of course, that the party seeking disclosure has already shown in his pleadings that he has a cause of action, and that he has some material to support it. Otherwise he would merely be 'fishing.'

The test is intended to be fairly strict. It ought to be so in any case where a valid claim for public interest immunity has been made . . . When the claim is a 'class' claim judges will often not be well qualified to estimate its strength, because they may not be fully aware of the importance of the class of documents to the public administration as a whole. Moreover, whether the claim is a 'class' claim or a 'contents' claim, the court will have to make its decision on whether to order production, after having inspected the documents privately, without having the assistance of argument from counsel. It should therefore, in my opinion, not be encouraged to 'take a peep' just on the off chance of finding something useful. It should inspect documents only where it has definite grounds for expecting to find material of real importance to the party seeking disclosure.

[Lord Fraser then went on to decide that the case for inspection had not been made out.]

Lord Wilberforce

. . . The appellants' claim for discovery and production rests, as it must, upon their assertion that they are necessary for the disposal fairly of the case: see R.S.C., Ord. 24, r. 13 . . .

. . . The learned judge [Bingham J] held that documents would be necessary for fairly disposing of a case or (his gloss) for the due administration of justice, if they give substantial assistance to the court in determining the facts upon which the decision in the case would depend. He considered that they were very likely to affect the outcome 'one way or the other.' The Court of Appeal, on the other hand, held that there must be a likelihood that the documents would support the case of the party seeking discovery.

On this point I agree with the Court of Appeal. In a contest purely between one litigant and another, such as the present, the task of the court is to do, and be seen to be doing, justice between the parties — a duty reflected by the word 'fairly' in the rule. There is no higher or additional duty to ascertain some independent truth. It often happens, from the imperfection of evidence, or the withholding of it, sometimes by the party in whose favour it would tell if presented, that an adjudication has to be made which is not, and is known not to be, the whole truth of the matter: yet if the decision has been in accordance with the available evidence and with the law, justice will have been fairly done. It is in aid of justice in this sense that discovery may be ordered, and it is so ordered upon the application of one of the parties who must make out his case for it. If he is not able to do so, that is an end of the matter. There is no independent power in the court to say that, nevertheless, it would like to inspect the documents, with a view to possible production, for its own assistance.

So far as authority is concerned, I do not find that the cases prior to *Burmah Oil Co. Ltd.* v. *Governor and Company of the Bank of England* [1980] A.C. 1090 support a contrary view . . . In *Burmah Oil Co. Ltd.* v. *Governor and Company of the Bank of England* [1980] A.C. 1090, the opinions referred both to the interest in the administration of justice and to the likelihood of supporting the case of the plaintiff . . . In that case, too, the present distinction sought to be made was not relevant or argued. We are therefore free to decide this case upon a common sense interpretation of the rules and upon principle. This leads, in my opinion, to the view adopted by the Court of Appeal.

The degree of likelihood (of providing support for the plaintiff's case) may be variously expressed: 'likely' was the word used by Lord Edmund-Davies in *Burmah Oil:* a 'reasonable probability' by Lord Keith of Kinkel. Both expressions must mean something beyond speculation, some concrete ground for belief which takes the case beyond a mere 'fishing' expedition. One cannot attain greater precision in stating what must be a matter of estimation. I would accept either formula.

[Lord Wilberforce then, like Lord Fraser, decided that the case for inspection had not been made out.]

Lords Edmund-Davies, Scarman, and Templeman delivered speeches in favour of dismissing the appeal (though see below).

Lord Edmund-Davies agreed with Lord Fraser's speech, although he would adopt a 'likeli-hood' test for inspection; cf Lord Fraser's reference to 'very likely' (above). A minority in *Air Canada* (Lord Scarman and Lord Templeman) would not have limited inspection to cases where production would be likely to help the case of the party seeking production: they would have allowed it when it was necessary for the fair disposal of the case. However, in the circumstances of the case, they agreed that inspection should not be carried out. Note that the majority view may prevent a party discovering a document which is fatal to his case and hence mean that litigation costs will be incurred which might otherwise have been avoided: see [1983] 2 AC at 446. Zuckerman, *Civil Procedure* (London 2003) at [18.23] argues that the 'courts have been less than enthusiastic about the *Air Canada* inspection procedure'. On the other hand, in *Balfour v. Foreign and Commonwealth Office* [1994] 1 WLR 681 at 688 the Court of Appeal expressed the view that 'once there is an actual or potential risk to national security demonstrated by an appropriate certificate the court should not exercise its right to inspect', but see Zuckerman's comments on this case (*op cit* at [18.25]). For the different stages at which inspection can take place, and on inspection in general, see Craig, *Administrative Law* (London 2003), 868–870.

QUESTION

- Does the approach in *Air Canada* give sufficient weight to the public interest in keeping government within its legal limits? (Consider Allan (1985) 101 *LQR* 200.)

16.5.6 The Questions of who should Raise the Claim and of Waiver

The traditional view has been that public interest immunity cannot be waived: it exists in the general public interest and the court should raise the matter even if the parties do not (although cf the comments of Lord Cross in *Alfred Crompton Amusement Machines Ltd v. Customs and Excise Commissioners (No 2)* [1974] AC 405 at 434). The question of public interest immunity reached the House of Lords again in the important case of *R v. Chief Constable of the West Midlands Police, ex parte Wiley* [1995] 1 AC 274 where the debate concerned whether a class claim could be made for statements made in an investigation into a complaint against the police. The House of Lords thought not (but note *Taylor v. Anderton (Police Complaints Authority intervening)* [1995] 1 WLR 447 on the position over reports from such investigations). Furthermore, although accepting Lord Hailsham's view in *D v. NSPCC* [1978] AC 171 at 230 that 'the categories of public interest are not closed', it was stated ([1995] 1 AC at 305) that the 'recognition of a new class-based public interest immunity requires clear and compelling evidence that it is necessary'. On the question of waiver, Lord Woolf (with whose speech there was broad agreement in *Wiley*) commented (at 296):

If a Secretary of State on behalf of his department as opposed to any ordinary litigant concludes that any public interest in documents being withheld from production is outweighed by the public interest in the documents being available for purposes of litigation, it is difficult to conceive that unless the documents do not relate to an area for which the Secretary of State was responsible, the court would feel it appropriate to come to any different conclusion from that of the Secretary of

State. The position would be the same if the Attorney-General was of the opinion that the documents should be disclosed. It should be remembered that the principle which was established in *Conway v. Rimmer* [1968] A.C. 910 is that it is the courts which should have the final responsibility for deciding when both a contents and a class claim to immunity should be upheld. The principle was not that it was for the courts to impose immunity where, after due consideration, no immunity was claimed by the appropriate authority. What was inherent in the reasoning of the House in that case was that because of the conflict which could exist between the two aspects of the public interest involved, the courts, which have final responsibility for upholding the rule of law, must equally have final responsibility for deciding what evidence should be available to the courts of law in order to enable them to do justice . . .

However, his Lordship (at 297) distinguished circumstances in which 'parties other than government departments are in possession of documents in respect of which public interest immunity could be claimed on a class basis' (although on such claims, see the Lord Chancellor's statement, referred to later in this section). Here, his Lordship considered that there would be

practical difficulties in allowing an individual to decide that the documents should be disclosed. The indiscriminate and, indeed, any disclosure, of documents which are the subject of a class claim to immunity can undermine that class. If the reason for the existence of the class is that those who make the statement should be assured that the statement will not be disclosed, the fact that in some cases they are disclosed undermines the assurance. The assurance can never be absolute because of the residual power of the court to order disclosure in the interest of the administration of justice. However, if the assurance is to have any value the cases where disclosure occurs have to be restricted to situations where this is necessary. Here the court may have to intervene to protect the public interest.

Having referred to some comments of Lord Simon in *R* v. *Lewes Justices, ex parte Secretary of State for the Home Department* [1973] AC 388 at 407, Lord Woolf continued (at 298):

It will be observed from that passage that when Lord Simon said that the privilege was one which could not be waived, he was referring to the situation after it had been determined that the public interest against disclosure outweighed that of disclosure in the interests of the administration of justice. When that is the determination which has been made, it is inevitable that the preservation of the document should follow so as to protect what has been held to be the dominant public interest. It is, however, unhelpful to talk of "waiver" in the different situations where the balancing of the conflicting public interests has not yet been carried out or where it has been carried out and the result requires disclosure. Although it is the practice to talk of conflicting public interests this can be misleading. The conflict is more accurately described as being between two different *aspects* of the public interest. If it is decided that the aspect of the public interest which reflects the requirements of the administration of justice outweighs the aspect of the interest which is against disclosure, then it is the public interest which requires disclosure.

His Lordship went on to say (at 299) that '[i]f the purpose of the immunity is to obtain the co-operation of an individual to the giving of a statement, I find it difficult to see how that purpose will be undermined if the maker of the statement consents to it being disclosed'.

It is clear that Lord Woolf does not believe a Minister is under a duty to claim public interest immunity and leave it to the court to decide whether, on balancing of the relevant interests, it should be produced or not. This was an important issue in the Matrix Churchill affair (see generally Leigh, [1993] *PL* 630). Three directors of a company who were charged with exporting equipment with potential military uses in contravention of the government's export guidelines wished to argue (*inter alia*) that Ministers had authorized the exports.

Public interest immunity certificates were issued and partially upheld, but the trial later collapsed amid much controversy when a Minister gave evidence that the government had been aware of the intended use of the equipment. One of the many issues arising from Matrix Churchill was the making public of legal advice to Ministers to the effect that they were duty-bound to claim public interest immunity. The effect of this, notes Woodhouse [1993] *PL* 412 at 415, was 'to depoliticise the issue and to defuse public anger over the signing of such certificates' — something she regards as an 'abdication of responsibility' that was 'politically convenient'. The Matrix Churchill affair prompted the Scott Report (HC115, *Inquiry into the Export of Defence Equipment and Dual-Use Goods to Iraq and Related Prosecutions* (1995–96)) which concluded (*inter alia*) that class claims were inappropriate in criminal cases, and that such claims should only (rarely) be sustainable in civil cases by reference to something more convincing than the so-called 'candour argument' (see also Scott [1996] *PL* 427). Thereafter the government made the following statement as to the policy it would in future adopt towards public interest immunity.

Lord Chancellor's statement in the House of Lords, 18 December 1996
HL Deb, vol 576, cols 1507–1508

My Lords, with your Lordships' leave, I should like to make a Statement on the future of public interest immunity in relation to government documents as it operates in England and Wales, in the light of the consultation following publication of the Scott Report. My right honourable and learned friend the Attorney-General is making a similar Statement in another place.

The Government are committed to the principle that there should be the maximum disclosure consistent with protecting essential public interests. Your Lordships will recall that the law which prevailed at the time of the Matrix Churchill case was further developed by the House of Lords case of ex parte Wiley in July 1994. Since that case, Ministers have had a general discretion to disclose documents without the prior approval of the court, if they consider that to be in the overall public interest. Against this background, it is the view of Sir Richard Scott that legislation on public interest immunity is neither necessary nor desirable, and the Government agree.

Public interest immunity is needed because of the potential conflict between two important public interests: the clear public interest in the administration of justice, in a criminal case the fair trial of an accused, and what is sometimes also the clear public interest in the confidentiality of certain documents or information. But your Lordships will bear in mind that the so-called immunity is subject to the ruling of the court, and that in a criminal case where government documents are in issue, the judge himself examines any such document and makes the actual decision on disclosure in the light of the facts of the case.

In their proposals for the future, the Government have had particular regard both to the recommendations of Sir Richard Scott and to the many responses received during the consultation process. The Government's conclusions represent a new approach, which is set out in a paper today being placed in the Library of both Houses.

Under this new approach, Ministers will focus directly on the damage that disclosure would cause. The former division into class and contents claims will no longer be applied. Ministers will only claim public interest immunity when it is believed that disclosure of a document would cause real damage or harm to the public interest. This new approach constitutes a change in the practice to be adopted by Ministers but fully respects existing legal principles, as developed by the courts, and is subject to the supervision of the courts. It also accords with the view expressed by the present Lord Chief Justice that, "public interest immunity should only be claimed for the bare minimum of documents for which the claim of serious harm can be seen to be clearly justified".

The Government intend that this test shall be rigorously applied before any public interest immunity claim is made for any government documents.

It is impossible in advance to describe such damage exhaustively. It may relate to the safety of an individual, such as an informant, or to a regulatory process; or it may be damage to international relations caused by the disclosure of confidential diplomatic communications. Normally it will be in the form of direct and immediate harm to, for example, the nation's economic interests or our relations with a foreign state; in some cases it may be indirect or longer-term damage, to which the disclosure of the material would contribute, as in the case of damage to a regulatory process. In any event, the nature of the harm will be clearly explained.

This new, restrictive approach will require, so far as possible, the way in which disclosure could cause real damage to the public interest to be clearly identified. Public interest immunity certificates will in future set out in greater detail than before both what the document is and what damage its disclosure would be likely to do, unless to do so would itself cause the damage which the certificate aims to prevent. This will allow even closer scrutiny of claims by the court, which is always the final arbiter.

The new emphasis on the test of serious harm means that Ministers will not, for example, claim public interest immunity to protect either internal advice or national security material merely by pointing to the general nature of the document. The only basis for claiming public interest immunity will be a belief that disclosure will cause real harm.

In relation to national security, the Government's approach takes into account the types of information which Parliament defined as sensitive in the Intelligence Services Act 1994, although as I have said a document will not attract public interest immunity simply because it falls into a pre-defined category.

Many public interest immunity claims are not the responsibility of government. Although the Government believe that their approach can be applied more widely, the paper placed in the Library only restricts government claims.

I am grateful to all those who have contributed to the debate and taken the trouble to respond to the consultation exercise in this complex area. A combination of the revised regime laid down by the House of Lords in ex parte Wiley and the Government's new approach should ensure that public interest immunity claims will be significantly less frequent in future. And I repeat that any claim in a criminal case will always in the end be subject to review by the court itself.

I believe that these factors, combined with the new test based on serious damage which I have described and which is set out more fully in the paper today being placed in each Library, provide what should prove a sensible, balanced and effective regime for the future, and I commend it to your Lordships.

For comments on the statement, see Supperstone and Coppel [1997] *PL* 211, Ganz (1997) 60 *MLR* 552. The statement is obviously important, but it must be realized that, as we saw at 16.5.4, bodies other than central government can claim public interest immunity and therefore the practice outlined in this statement might not be adopted by such bodies. To that extent class claims are unaffected. In any event, the distinction between class claims and content claims is not watertight. More fundamentally, Supperstone and Coppel, *op cit* at 212, write:

The new approach is not, however, a contents-based approach. The Government has moved away from the label of class claims but it concedes that Ministers may still apply "class reasoning" in some claims to PII [see HC Deb, vol 287, col 951]. It remains open for a Minister to argue that real damage to the public interest may be caused by the disclosure of a document not because of its contents but because it belongs to a class of documents which ought not to be disclosed. Moreover, the "candour" justification in respect of documents relating to advice to Ministers has not been disavowed. All this is not "new"; it is the same old approach minus the attachment of a label of which the judiciary are now, in any event, rightly sceptical.

QUESTIONS

- Do you share Supperstone and Coppel's concerns?
- Should the government have gone further, in your view?

16.5.7 Article 6 ECHR, the HRA, and Public Interest Immunity

Article 6's requirement of a fair trial needs to be borne in mind alongside public interest immunity. In criminal cases the ECtHR has decided in *Rowe and Davis* v. *United Kingdom* (2000) 30 EHRR 1 that the operation of public interest immunity is not necessarily in breach of Art 6, and the appropriate procedure, including the possibility of a special advocate to represent the accused's interests, has recently been laid down in *R* v. *H* [2004] UKHL 3 [2004] 2 WLR 335 (although note Part V of the Criminal Justice Act 2003, amending the Criminal Proceedings and Investigations Act 1996 which is referred to in *H*).

Of course, it would be pointless for public interest immunity to be claimed in relation to information that had been, or which could be required to be, disclosed under the Freedom of Information Act 2000. Although this may seem to imply a liberalizing influence on public interest immunity, we saw above at 12.4.2 that the Act has been criticized on account of the wide categories of information that are protected against disclosure. Of particular relevance in the present context is that (as noted at 12.4.2 above) the Act works, in part, by conferring such protection upon certain *classes* of information.

FURTHER RESOURCES

Alder, 'Restitution in Public Law: Bearing the Cost of Unlawful State Action' (2002) 22 *LS* 165

Arrowsmith, *Civil Liability and Public Authorities* (Winteringham 1992), chs 2 and 4

Craig, 'One More unto the Breach: The Community, the State and Damages Liability' (1997) 113 *LQR* 67

Fairgrieve, Andenas and Bell (eds), *Tort Liability of Public Authorities in Comparative Perspective* (London 2002), ch 4 (Fairgrieve) and ch 7 (Tridimas)

Forsyth, 'Public Interest Immunity: Recent and Future Developments' [1997] *CLJ* 51

Hickman, 'The Reasonableness Principle: Reassessing its Place in the Public Sphere' [2004] *CLJ* 166

McLean, 'The Crown in Contract and Administrative Law' (2004) 24 *OJLS* 129

Leyland and Woods (eds), *Administrative Law Facing the Future: Old Constraints and New Horizons* (London 1997), ch 14 (Tomkins)

Turpin, *Government Procurement and Contracts* (Harlow 1989), ch 4

17 DELEGATED LEGISLATION

17.1 Introduction

17.1.1 General Matters

Delegated legislation — otherwise known as secondary, subordinate, executive, or administrative legislation — is a familiar feature of the constitutional landscape in the UK. It is enacted by the *administrative* branch of government, usually under powers conferred upon it by the *legislative* branch (but occasionally under the royal prerogative). The need for such legislation is obvious. Parliament lacks (*inter alia*) the time and resources to legislate comprehensively: the conferral of law-making powers upon the executive is a long-established solution to this problem. Thus, writing in the earlier part of the last century, Chen, *Parliamentary Opinion of Delegated Legislation* (New York 1933) at 13–14, noted that in the UK the idea of 'legislative monopoly' — a notion derived from a pure conception of the separation of powers doctrine, under which only the legislature enacts legislation and to which the notion of administrative legislation is therefore anathema — has ebbed and flowed, but has 'never [been] complete':

> Before the Glorious Revolution Parliament had been "delegating legislative powers in some matters, through the old prerogative machinery, by authorizing statutory Orders in Council" [Fairlie, *Administrative Procedures in Connection with Statutory Rules and Orders in Great Britain* (Urbana 1927) at 14]. After 1688, Parliament had also found it easy and convenient "to make use of the old machinery and permit the statutory Order in Council to do what the prerogative Order in Council had been restrained from doing" [Carr, *Delegated Legislation* (Cambridge 1921) at 54]. But from the early part of the eighteenth century to the early decades of the nineteenth century, this practice was gradually abandoned. The "legislative monopoly" grew insensibly. Even the war regulations of the French Revolutionary period were embodied in Acts of Parliament. Minute details of local application were to be found in the numerous Enclosure Acts. By about 1832, this "monopoly" began to relax. Powers to issue rules and regulations were more and more frequently delegated to the executive as the volume of social legislation gradually increased. The exigencies of the [First] World War and its aftermath greatly accelerated the tendency. At the present time, many statutes, to use the metaphor of a writer in *The Times* [quoted by Stamp (1924) 2 *Journal of Public Administration* 32], "contains mere bones, and Government departments are given the power to supply any sort of flesh that they may think suitable".

The rise of delegated legislation (on which see generally Cm 4060, *Report of the Committee on Ministers' Powers* (1932)) continued apace during the latter part of the twentieth century, with particularly rapid growth — of between 50 and 100 per cent for different types of instruments — between 1981 and 1996, according to the Select Committee on Procedure (HC152, *Delegated Legislation* (1995–96) at [41]). Such legislation is now so fixed a part of public life that general concerns as to its compatibility with classical constitutional principles — not only the separation of powers, but also the rule of law and the sovereignty of Parliament — have largely been eclipsed by more specific anxieties relating to its scale and nature. For instance, the Select Committee on Procedure (*op cit* at [14]) perceived 'too great a readiness in Parliament to delegate wide legislative powers to Ministers, and no lack of enthusiasm on their part to take such powers', resulting in 'an excessive volume of delegated legislation' — a conclusion which the same Committee recently reinforced (HC48, *Delegated Legislation* (1999–2000) at [26]). Page, *Governing by Numbers* (Oxford 2001) at 25, drawing partly upon the work of Daintith and Page, *The Executive in the Constitution* (Oxford 1999), ch 8, notes that it is not just the scale, but also the nature, of delegated legislation which is changing, pointing to 'an increasing tendency for governments to use delegated legislation as a means of dealing with matters of principle and policy rather than [just] with detail'.

In light of these contemporary concerns about delegated legislation, we focus in this chapter upon the way and the context in which such legislation is made — engaging with what one commentator (Page, *op cit* at 190) has called a 'twilight zone' of obscurity — as well as the scrutiny of delegated legislation both politically and judicially.

17.1.2 Enabling Provisions

Delegated legislation takes a number of forms, and a number of different terms — rules, regulations, byelaws, Orders in Council, circulars, guidance, directions, and codes of practice — are used to describe it. The terminology can seem bewildering; however, of much greater significance than these various labels are the different sorts of provisions in primary legislation which, in the first place, confer the power to enact administrative legislation. Such provisions — sometimes called 'enabling provisions' — demarcate the extent of the administrator's legislative power: any executive legislation enacted outwith the terms of the enabling statute will be *ultra vires* and vulnerable to judicial review. (As we explain below at 17.4, the grounds of judicial review considered earlier in this book generally apply to delegated legislation, although necessarily with some differences, bearing in mind the generality of legislative measures as distinct from, say, administrative decisions concerning individual cases.)

It is therefore to the enabling provisions in primary legislation that we must look in order to understand the permitted content and nature of the resultant delegated legislation. Many such provisions are quite unremarkable, and simply confer upon the administration authority to enact secondary legislation for specific purposes laid down in the statute. A straightforward instance is provided by the Railways and Transport Safety Act 2003, s 11 of which provides (in subsection (1)) that the 'Secretary of State may make regulations in connection with the investigation of railway accidents and railway incidents', and goes on to state more precisely the ends which such regulations may serve. However, as we are about to see, some enabling provisions differ quite markedly from this run-of-the-mill example in term of the *nature* and *extent* of the power which they grant.

17.1.3 The Nature of Delegated Powers

Enabling provisions known as 'Henry VIII clauses' (in reference to that king's autocratic style) confer upon the administration a power to enact delegated legislation the effect of which is to amend or repeal primary legislation. To take a simple example, the Fireworks Act 2003 provides for (*inter alia*) the regulation of the supply of 'fireworks', a term which is defined by s 1(1). However, s 1(2) — the Henry VIII clause — states that, 'The Secretary of State may by regulations substitute a new definition of "fireworks" for the definition in subsection (1),' thereby permitting the administration to enact secondary legislation amending the parent Act.

Henry VIII clauses have attracted strong criticism from some quarters — Hewart, *The New Despotism* (London 1929) at 53, considered them 'egregious'; by permitting amendment or repeal of provisions in primary legislation, such clauses may be thought to tip the balance too far in favour of the administrative branch at the expense of Parliament.

QUESTIONS

- Is this fear of Henry VIII powers well-founded?
- How would you respond to the argument that, if the executive is thought to be misusing such powers — *eg* by using them to modify the scheme originally laid down by Parliament to an extent or in a manner that is thought to be too radical — Parliament could simply legislate to override such measures and/or withdraw the Henry VIII power in question?

Concerns about Henry VIII provisions notwithstanding, they have become a commonplace tool of modern government: as Rippon (1989) 10 *Statute Law Review* 205 observes, they are 'being used today in Act after Act on a scale that would have been absolutely unthinkable until recently'. The frequency with which Henry VIII powers are now created was of considerable concern to the House of Lords Select Committee on the Committee Work of the House, whose report in the 1991–1992 session led to the establishment of (what is now known as) the House of Lords Select Committee on Delegated Powers and Regulatory Reform (considered below at 17.3).

While most Henry VIII provisions simply empower the executive to amend or repeal the legislation containing such clauses, or statutes passed before that legislation, prospective Henry VIII clauses confer powers in respect of *later* legislation. A well-known example is s 10(2) of the Human Rights Act 1998, which allows legislation (irrespective of whether it was enacted before or after the HRA) that has been declared incompatible with the ECHR, or which, following a decision of the ECtHR, appears incompatible, to be amended by order if the Minister considers that there are 'compelling reasons' for doing so. The effectiveness of such clauses was considered in *Thoburn v. Sunderland City Council* [2002] EWHC 195 (Admin) [2003] QB 151 (for discussion of which see Barber and Young [2003] *PL* 112 at 115 and Marshall (1998) 118 *LQR* 493 at 496–499). Counsel argued that such generally-worded Henry VIII powers could not be used to enact secondary legislation that was inconsistent with provisions in later primary legislation, because such subsequent legislation would impliedly repeal the Henry VIII power to the extent that the latter had conferred *vires* to enact measures at odds with the former. This argument was rejected — and the efficacy of prospective Henry VIII powers vouchsafed — by Laws LJ who, at [50], held that, 'Generally, there is no *inconsistency* between a provision conferring a Henry VIII power to amend future legislation and the terms of any such future legislation.'

Barber and Young, *op cit* at 114, find the increasing use of prospective Henry VIII clauses disquieting, ultimately concluding that their use is only (rarely) justified by a need to empower certain institutions, such as the devolved legislatures, to defend themselves (in the name of democracy) against interference by the Westminster Parliament:

Whereas with retrospective clauses the enacting Parliament could, in theory, gauge the maximum possible extent of the power, with prospective Henry VIII clauses the enacting Parliament must put its trust entirely in the body to whom power is delegated. There is no way of assessing at the time of enactment which future statutes the power will be used against . . . Prospective Henry VIII clauses thus constitute a fetter on the power of future Parliaments, creating the risk that as yet unthought of statutes will be overturned through the exercise of delegated power.

QUESTIONS

- Do you agree?
- If (as seems inevitable) prospective Henry VIII clauses must be accepted as a feature of the modern administrative landscape, how might their misuse be guarded against?

17.1.4 The Extent of Delegated Powers

Henry VIII clauses vividly illustrate that delegated powers may transcend their classical function of simply empowering the administration to supplement statutory schemes. Just as such powers may differ in nature, so their scope may also vary dramatically. While some delegated powers are conferred in quite specific terms, others are framed much more broadly. Contrast, for instance, s 11(1) of the Railways and Transport Safety Act 2003 which, as we saw above at 17.1.3, makes quite specific provision about the nature of the secondary legislation which can be enacted under it, with s 1 of the Regulatory Reform Act 2001, which confers a power to reform legislation 'which has the effect of imposing burdens affecting persons in the carrying on of any activity' with a view to removing or reducing such burdens, or rationalizing the law. This is an extremely general and wide-ranging power, the impact of which is potentially very far-reaching. Indeed, when the Deregulation and Contracting Out Act 1994 — ss 1 to 5 and sch 1 of which were superseded by the 2001 Act — was enacted, pursuant to a government initiative (on which see Daintith and Page, *The Executive in the Constitution* (Oxford 1999) at 273–285) to reduce unnecessary regulation, the House of Lords Select Committee on Delegated Powers (HC60, *Eighth Report* (1993–1994) at [1]) commented that the Act conferred powers to make secondary legislation on a scale 'unprecedented in time of peace'.

Note should also be taken in this context of s 2(2) of the European Communities Act 1972, which permits delegated legislation to be enacted for the purposes of 'implementing any Community obligation of the United Kingdom, or enabling any such obligation to be implemented, or of enabling any rights enjoyed or to be enjoyed by the United Kingdom under or by virtue of the Treaties to be exercised'. Section 2(4) goes on to state that (subject to certain limitations in sch 2) this includes the making of any provision, of any extent, 'as might be made by Act of Parliament'. This is an extremely wide power — the effectiveness of which was confirmed in *Thoburn*, considered above — which permits secondary legislation to be made and primary legislation to be amended whenever this is necessary to give effect to new EU measures (typically pursuant to directives which require implementation at national level). Bearing in mind the considerable volume of EU measures which need implementation every year, and the wide areas of policy across which the EU's competence now extends, it is clear that s 2 confers an extraordinarily broad legislative power upon the administration.

Above, we cited s 10(2) of the HRA as an example of a Henry VIII clause; we return to it here in view of the fact that it creates a competence to enact delegated legislation notable for its scope. Not only does s 10(2) permit the amendment of legislation which has been judicially condemned as inconsistent with the ECHR; according to sch 2, para 1(1)(a) of the HRA, a s 10(2) order may also 'contain such incidental, supplemental, consequential or transitional provision as the person making it considers appropriate'. Moreover, sch 2, para 1(1)(b) provides that (except in relation to criminal liability: para 1(4)) a s 10(2) order may be made 'so as to have effect from a date earlier than that on which it is made'. In other words, legislative amendments and supplementary provisions may have retrospective effect, thereby applying to events which have already taken place. Wade (in Cambridge Centre for Public Law, *Constitutional Reform in the UK: Practice and Principles* (Oxford 1998) at 66) found these arrangements to be 'exceptionally drastic', but reluctantly concluded that they were inevitable 'as part of the mechanism for adopting an external system of law [*viz* the ECHR], and in default of new and speedy Parliamentary procedures'.

Part II of the Civil Contingencies Act 2004 cannot escape mention in the context of extensive delegated powers. The Act makes provision for emergencies, defined by s 19 as events or situations which threaten serious damage to human welfare in or the environment of part or all of the United Kingdom, or war or terrorism that threatens serious damage to the security of the UK. Section 20(1) provides that 'Her Majesty may by Order in Council make emergency regulations if satisfied that the conditions in section 21' — that it is urgently necessary to make provision to prevent, control, or mitigate an aspect or effect of an emergency that has occurred, is occurring or is about to occur — 'are satisfied'. By s 20(2), senior Ministers may make such regulations subject to the same conditions, and to the additional requirement that an Order in Council could not, without serious delay, be arranged. Emergency regulations lapse after a maximum of 30 days (s 26(1)) (but this does not prevent the making of fresh regulations (s 26(2)(a))) and after 7 days if not approved by Parliament (s 27). The range of issues which emergency regulations may cover is extraordinarily wide (s 22). In particular, they 'may make provision of any kind that could be made by Act of Parliament' (s 22(3)), including the creation of criminal offences connected with non-compliance with emergency regulations (s 22(3)(i)) and the disapplication and modification of primary legislation (s 22(3)(j)). The Joint Committee on Human Rights (HL34/HC303, *Scrutiny of Bills: Second Progress Report* (2003–04) at [1.16]) noted that the power to make emergency regulations 'potentially engages a wide range of human rights, including the right to the peaceful enjoyment of property, the right to liberty, and the right to freedom of assembly and association'. Following pressure from that Committee (among others), the Civil Contingencies Act has been drafted such that emergency regulations can be struck down under the HRA if incompatible with the Convention rights (s 30(2)) and cannot amend the HRA (s 23(5)(b)).

17.1.5 Legislative and Administrative Measures

Where does delegated *legislation* stop, and where does *administrative* action begin? It may be thought that the answer is obvious: surely legislation (delegated or otherwise) has certain fundamental characteristics — principally the laying down of rules which are of general application and which can be enforced by courts — that make it readily identifiable. On this view, anything falling short of this paradigm lacks the necessary characteristics of legislation, and is therefore merely administrative in nature. Reality, however, is more complicated; many measures now emanate from government which cannot easily be classified according to a simple legislative/administrative dichotomy. Megarry (1944) 60 *LQR* 125 at 126 used the term 'administrative quasi-legislation' to describe such measures, which — as Ganz, *Quasi-Legislation: Recent Developments in Secondary Legislation* (London 1987) at 1, notes — have been the subject of a 'population explosion' since the middle of the last century. Such measures include codes of practice and conduct, guidelines, practice statements, tax concessions, and circulars issued by government departments and other public bodies.

Whether such measures should be classified as administrative or legislative is a difficult matter, and important consequences may follow from such classification. For example, as we explain below at 17.2.2, the applicability of principles of natural justice to the exercise of a function may turn upon whether it is regarded as administrative or legislative, while the presumption against delegation (see generally above at 6.2) is applied more strictly to legislative than to administrative powers (see below at 17.4.3). In some respects, however, the category in which we place a given measure may be less important than simply ascertaining what, if any, legal effect it is capable of. A number of criteria — on which see generally Baldwin and Houghton [1986] *PL* 239 — may be applied to this end; here, we focus on two key issues.

Legal effect determined by enabling legislation

Whenever measures are adopted pursuant to primary legislation, that forms the obvious starting-point when attempting to discover the status of such measures. For example, under s 3(3)(a) of the Terrorism Act 2000, the Secretary of State is empowered to make proscription orders in respect of terrorist organizations. The effect of such an order is readily evident from other provisions in the Act: ss 11–13 make it a criminal offence to be a member of or to support such proscribed organizations, and the legal effect of s 3(1)(a) orders is therefore both substantial and clear. Similarly, the Land Registration Act 2002 provides for the making of rules on various aspects of land registration, and it is clear from the terms and scheme of the Act that the Land Registration Rules 2003 (SI 2003/1417) have legal effect in the sense that they (*inter alia*) define the legal obligations of the Land Registry and prescribe how the system operates. They therefore form an integral part of the land registration scheme, and conform to our general expectations of legislation.

Enabling legislation may, however, provide that measures adopted under statutory powers are to have only limited (or even no) legal effect. Section 38(7) of the Road Traffic Act 1988 is a case in point:

A failure on the part of a person to observe a provision of the Highway Code shall not of itself render that person liable to criminal proceedings of any kind but any such failure may in any proceedings (whether civil or criminal, and including proceedings for an offence under the [Road Traffic Offenders Act 1988, the Road Traffic (Consequential Provisions) Act 1988, this Act, the Road Traffic Regulation Act 1984], the Public Passenger Vehicles Act 1981 or sections 18 to 23 of the Transport Act 1985) be relied upon by any party to the proceedings as tending to establish or negative any liability which is in question in those proceedings.

Hence, although breaches of the Highway Code are not directly actionable, they can be taken into account in deciding (*inter alia*) whether a motorist has breached the duty of care which he owes to other road users (*Russell* v. *Smith* [2003] EWHC 2060 (Admin) (2003) 147 SJLB 1118) and whether claimants have been guilty of contributory negligence (*Froom* v. *Butcher* [1976] QB 286).

Enabling legislation may therefore confer varying levels of legal effect upon measures made under delegated powers. Sometimes, however, even though primary legislation clearly confers upon administrators the power to adopt certain measures, it is ambiguous as to their legal effect. A well-known example of this phenomenon is furnished by the Immigration Rules. Section 3(2) of the Immigration Act 1971 provides that:

The Secretary of State shall from time to time (and as soon as may be) lay before Parliament statements of the rules, or of any changes in the rules, laid down by him as to the practice to be followed in the administration of this Act for regulating the entry into and stay in the United Kingdom of persons required by this Act to have leave to enter, including any rules as to the period for which leave is to be given and the conditions to be attached in different circumstances . . .

When the status of the Immigration Rules was raised in *R* v. *Chief Immigration Officer, ex parte Bibi* [1976] 1 WLR 979 at 985, Roskill LJ said:

[Counsel] made what I hope he will forgive me calling a somewhat startling submission, namely, that the rules made by the Secretary of State under section 3 (2) of the Immigration Act 1971 were not "part of the law of this country." He said that they were but departmental circulars laying down no more than good administrative practice. With respect, I profoundly disagree. If one looks at the section which empowers the Secretary of State to make these rules one finds in section 3(2) that he shall lay before Parliament as soon as may be statements of the rules or any changes in the rules laid down by him. These rules are just as much delegated legislation as any other form of rule-making activity or delegated legislation which is empowered by Act of Parliament. Furthermore these rules are subject to a negative resolution [on which see below at 17.2.3] . . .; and it is unheard of that something which is no more than an administrative circular stating what the Home Office conceives to be good administrative practice should be subject to a negative resolution from both Houses of Parliament. These rules to my mind are just as much a part of the law of England as the Act itself.

A different view (which is now taken to be the correct one) was adopted in *R* v. *Secretary of State for Home Affairs, ex parte Hosenball* [1977] 1 WLR 766, Cumming-Bruce LJ opining (at 788) that the Rules

are a totally different kind of publication from the rules that usually come into being under the authority delegated to Ministers under Acts of Parliament; and, for my part, having scrutinised them, and observed that [they are a] curious amalgam of information and description of executive procedures, they are not in my view in any sense of themselves of legislative force.

However, while the parent Act — that is, the Immigration Act 1971 — may not have conferred 'legislative force' on the Rules *en bloc*, such force may (implicitly or otherwise) be conferred upon the Rules, or parts of them, by that Act or other legislation, as Lord Denning MR recognized in *Hosenball* at 780–781. To give just one example, it is clear that the Rules have legal effect to the extent that s 84(1)(a) of the Nationality, Immigration and Asylum Act 2002 makes it possible to appeal against an immigration decision on the ground that it was not in accordance with the Rules.

Legal effect determined by general principles of administrative law

Even if primary legislation does not confer direct legal force upon measures adopted by the administration, such measures may still acquire some legal effect through the application of general principles of law. For instance, notwithstanding the uncertainty discussed above surrounding the Immigration Rules, it is clear that the principle of legitimate expectation can be invoked in conjunction with them. As Jackson, *Immigration Law and Practice* (London 1999) at 18, explains, 'The rules are an indication of how the Secretary of State will normally exercise his statutory discretion. It is open to the Secretary of State to depart from the rules in favour of an individual, but any attempt to bypass the rules adversely to an individual would surely fail.' He concludes that, '[a]t the very least', the Rules generate a legitimate expectation 'that, while in operation, the criteria specified in them will be applied' (although, applying the principles considered in ch 7 above, it may be possible to depart from the Rules if, for instance, a hearing is given first).

Just as the Immigration Rules may acquire legal effect via general principles of administrative law, unrelated to any provision in the primary legislation under which they are made, so measures which are not in the first place made under any statutory power may also come to have legal effect. For instance, the Office of the Deputy Prime Minister publishes Planning Policy Guidance Notes — a type of circular setting out planning policy in general terms. These Notes (now being replaced with briefer Planning Policy Statements) are not issued under any statutory power, and are therefore neither strictly binding upon local planning authorities nor directly enforceable in the courts. Nevertheless, they are commonly held (see, *eg Hambleton District Council* v. *Secretary of State for the Environment* (1995) 70 P & CR 549)) to be a relevant consideration which planning authorities are obliged to take into account, departure from which they must justify by giving reasons.

17.2 The Making of Delegated Legislation

17.2.1 Publication

It is inherent in the rule of law that individuals should be governed by rules which are openly available, in order that they have the opportunity to comply with them and plan their lives accordingly. It is therefore vital that legislation — including delegated legislation — should be published. The Statutory Instruments Act 1946 requires the publication of any delegated legislation which is classified as a 'statutory instrument'. This formalistic criterion encompasses subordinate legislation made under statutory power by means of an Order in Council, as well as that which is made by a Minister of the Crown under a statutory rule-making power which is stated in the enabling provision to be exercisable by statutory instrument. (On the position in respect of rule-making powers granted before the enactment of the 1946 Act, see s 1(2).)

The publication requirement which applies to statutory instruments (subject to certain exceptions laid down in SI 1948 No 1, Statutory Instruments Regulations) is set out in the following terms by s 2(1) of the Act:

Immediately after the making of any statutory instrument, it shall be sent to the King's printer of Acts of Parliament and numbered in accordance with regulations made under this Act, and except in such cases as may be provided by any Act passed after the commencement of this Act or prescribed by regulations made under this Act, copies thereof shall as soon as possible be printed and sold by or under the authority of the King's printer of Acts of Parliament.

It appears that, although this requirement is almost always complied with, failure to do so does not render the statutory instrument invalid. This was the view of Streatfield J in *R* v. *Sheer Metalcraft Ltd* [1954] 1 QB 586 at 590, who opined that requirements as to publication are 'purely procedure for the issue of an instrument [already] validly made'. This conclusion was reached because s 3(2) of the Act provides that it is a defence to a criminal charge of contravening a statutory instrument to prove that the legislation had not been published at the date of the alleged contravention, unless it is proved that 'at that date reasonable steps had been taken for the purpose of bringing the purport of the instrument to the notice of the public, or of persons likely to be affected by it, or of the person charged'. This appears to presuppose that there are some circumstances in which a statutory instrument will be effective in spite of non-publication, and is therefore inconsistent with the view that publication is always essential to validity.

QUESTIONS

- Should non-publication render statutory instruments ineffective?
- It has been argued (by Lanham (1974) 37 *MLR* 510 and [1983] *PL* 395) that s 3(2) is merely a rather limited statutory declaration of a general rule which makes publication a prerequisite of validity. Is that a convincing argument?

It must be recalled that the 1946 Act imposes a publication requirement *only* in respect of statutory instruments, raising the prospect of non-publication of other measures, so that — in the words of Scott LJ in *Blackpool Corporation* v. *Locker* [1948] 1 KB 349 at 362 — the citizen

may remain in complete ignorance of what rights over him and his property have been secretly conferred by the Minister on some authority or other, and what residual rights have been left to himself. For practical purposes, the rule of law, of which the nation is so justly proud, breaks down . . .

However, an obligation to publish such measures may be imposed by other legislation, such as the Freedom of Information Act 2000, or by general principles of law. For example, in *Salih* v. *Secretary of State for the Home Department* [2003] EWHC 2273 (Admin), the non-publication of a policy which existed in relation to the provision of support to failed asylum-seekers under s 4 of the Immigration and Asylum Act 1999 was found to be unlawful. Stanley Burton J invoked a general constitutional principle rooted in the rule of law to the effect that legislative and analogous measures should be publicly available, explaining, at [48] and [52], that the policies of public authorities may have a significance approaching or approximating to a law, and may be equally important to the individual . . . [I]t is in general inconsistent with the constitutional imperative that statute law should be made known [on which see *R (L)* v. *Secretary of State for the Home Department* [2003] EWCA Civ 25 [2003] 1 WLR 1230] for the government to withhold information about its policy relating to the exercise of a power conferred by statute.

Assuming that Stanley Burton J was correct to apply a general principle requiring publication of the policy at stake in *Salih*, it would seem to follow ineluctably that delegated legislation not caught by the publication requirement in the Statutory Instruments Act 1946 is nevertheless, on this basis, required to be published. The policy arguments in favour of such an approach are strong.

Finally, although not concerning the publication of delegated legislation, *R (Anufrijeva)* v. *Secretary of State for the Home Department* [2003] UKHL 36 [2004] 1 AC 604 (for comment on which see Jowell [2004] *PL* 246) is worthy of note in this context. The case concerned an asylum-seeker; from the date on which her asylum claim was turned down, the Home Office treated her claim as 'having been determined' within the meaning of the relevant legislation, thereby disentitling her to further income support. However, the Home Office had not communicated its decision to the individual concerned, and the question therefore arose whether, in the absence of such communication, the claim had been 'determined' such that income support could lawfully be terminated. Their Lordships (by a majority) held that it had not. Lord Steyn, at [28]–[30], considered that the rule of law

requires that a constitutional state must accord to individuals the right to know of a decision before their rights can be adversely affected. The antithesis of such a state was described by Kafka: a state where the rights of individuals are overridden by hole in the corner decisions or knocks on doors in the early hours. That is not our system . . . In our system of law surprise is regarded as the enemy of justice.

It is strongly arguable that if general principles of constitutional law require the communication of administrative decisions, then the same principles must require the publication of legislative measures.

17.2.2 Consultation

Some statutes specifically provide for consultation in advance of the making of delegated legislation, while others do not. Two key issues therefore require discussion in this section. First, when consultation is statutorily required, what does this mean? And, secondly, if enabling legislation does not provide for consultation, may consultation nevertheless be required by general principles of administrative law? The first matter fell for consideration in the following case.

....

R v. Secretary of State for Social Services, ex parte Association of Metropolitan Authorities [1986] 1 WLR 1
Queen's Bench Division

Section 36(1) of the Social Security and Housing Benefits Act 1982 provided that before making regulations constituting the housing benefits scheme, 'the Secretary of State shall consult with organisations appearing to him to be representative of the [housing] authorities concerned'. The claimant was such an organization and on 16 November 1984 the Department of Health and Social Security, on behalf of the Secretary of State, wrote requesting its views on proposed amendments to regulations made in 1982. The letter was received on 22 November and a reply was requested by 30 November. The claimant complained of the inadequacy of the period and requested an extension of time to enable it to consult its advisers. On 4 December the Department wrote requesting the claimant's views of further proposals by 12 December. No draft of the proposed amendments was sent and a material feature — requiring local authorities to investigate whether housing benefit claimants had created joint tenancies in order to take advantage of the housing benefit scheme — was not mentioned. On 7 December a response to the first letter and on 13 December brief comments in response to the second were sent to the department. The Housing Benefits Amendment (No 4) Regulations 1984 were made on 17 December and came into operation two days later. The claimant sought, *inter alia*, a declaration that the Secretary of State had failed to fulfil his duty under s 36(1) and a quashing order in respect of the regulations because of the failure to consult.

Webster J

. . . There is no general principle to be extracted from the case law as to what kind or amount of consultation is required before delegated legislation, of which consultation is a pre-condition, can validly be made. But in any context the essence of consultation is the communication of a genuine invitation to give advice and a genuine receipt of that advice. In my view it must go without saying that to achieve consultation sufficient information must be supplied by the consulting to the consulted party to enable it to tender helpful advice. Sufficient time must be given by the consulting to the consulted party to enable it to do that, and sufficient time must be available for such advice to be considered by the consulting party. Sufficient, in that context, does not mean ample, but at least enough to enable the relevant purpose to be fulfilled. By helpful advice, in this context, I mean sufficiently informed and considered information or advice about aspects of the form or substance of the proposals, or their implications for the consulted party, being aspects material to the implementation of the proposal as to which the Secretary of State might not be fully informed or advised and as to which the party consulted might have relevant information or advice to offer.

These propositions, as it seems to me, can partly be derived from, and are wholly consistent with, the decisions and various dicta, which I need not enumerate, in *Rollo v. Minister of Town and Country Planning* [1948] 1 All E.R. 13 and *Port Louis Corporation v. Attorney-General of Mauritius* [1965] A.C. 1111 . . .

In the present case, looking at the "whole scope and purpose" of the 1982 Act, one matter which stands out is that its day-to-day administration is in the hands of local housing authorities who bear 10 per cent. of the cost of the scheme. It is common ground that in them resides the direct expertise necessary to administer schemes made under the Act on a day-to-day basis. For these reasons, if for no other, I conclude that the obligation laid on the Secretary of State to consult organisations representative of those authorities is mandatory not directory.

The last question of principle to be decided before turning to the facts is the test to be applied to the facts as I find them for the purposes of judicial review . . . [T]o what extent is it for the Secretary of State, not the court, to judge how much consultation is necessary and how long is to be given for it? The answer to that question may qualify the word "sufficient" in the requirements of consultation which I have set out above . . .

. . . [T]he first point to note is that the power to make the regulations is conferred on the Secretary of State and that his is the duty to consult. Save for those consulted, no one else is involved in the making of the regulations. Secondly, both the form or substance of new regulations and the time allowed for consulting, before making them, may well depend in whole or in part on matters of a political nature, as to the force and implications of which it would be reasonable to expect the Secretary of State, rather than the court, to be the best judge. Thirdly, issues may well be raised after the making of the regulations as to the detailed merits of one or other reason for making them, or as to the precise degree of urgency required in their making, issues which have been raised on this application. Those issues cannot be said to be wholly irrelevant to a challenge to the vires of the regulations, and Mr Beloff has not submitted that they are irrelevant; but at the same time it would seem to me to be inherently improbable that the question of the vires of the regulations should depend upon precise findings of fact on issues such as those. In my view, therefore, the court, when considering the question whether the consultation required by section 36(1) was in substance carried out, should have regard not so much to the actual facts which preceded the making of the regulations as to the material before the Secretary of State when he made the regulations, that material including facts or information as it appeared or must have appeared to him acting in good faith, and any judgments made or opinions expressed to him before the making of the regulations about those facts which appeared or could have appeared to him to be reasonable. The Department's good faith is not challenged on this application.

The effect of treating as material the facts as they appeared to the Secretary of State, and not necessarily as they were, is to give a certain flexibility to the notions of sufficiency, sufficient information, sufficient time and sufficiently informed and considered information and advice in my homespun attempt to define proper consultation. Thus, it can have the effect that what would be sufficient information or time in one case might be more or less than sufficient in another, depending on the relative degrees of urgency and the nature of the proposed regulation. There is no degree of urgency, however, which absolves the Secretary of State from the obligation to consult at all . . .

After considering the facts, his Lordship said that the urgency of the need to amend the regulations as seen by the Secretary of State and the nature of the proposed amendments did justify the department requiring that views should be expressed quickly, but did not justify requiring views within such a short time that they would be insufficiently informed or considered. Bearing in mind the fact that the claimant had no knowledge until after the regulations were made of a material feature of them, he concluded that the Secretary of State failed to fulfil his obligation to consult before making the regulations. Although a declaration to this effect was issued, no quashing order was forthcoming. In refusing to issue such an order, Webster J drew a distinction between the quashing of administrative decisions which merely affect 'the rights of one person or of a class of persons' and legislative measures 'which have become part of the public law of the land'; his Lordship was particularly influenced by the potentially chaotic consequences which might have resulted from the revocation of the regulations.

QUESTION

• Was Webster J right to refuse a quashing order in these circumstances?

If, as is often the case, enabling legislation makes no provision requiring prior consultation, then it is necessary to look to general principles of administrative law. After all, where statute fails to provide participation rights in respect of judicial or administrative decisions affecting individuals or groups, it is well-established that 'the justice of the common law will supply the omission of the legislature' (*Cooper* v. *Wandsworth Board of Works* (1863) 14 CB (NS) 180 at 194, *per* Byles J). However, as the following case demonstrates, a different approach has traditionally been adopted in relation to legislative measures.

Bates v. *Lord Hailsham of St Marylebone* [1972] 1 WLR 1373
Chancery Division

Section 56 of the Solicitors Act 1957 gave power to a committee consisting of the Lord Chancellor, the Lord Chief Justice, the Master of the Rolls, the President of the Law Society, the Chief Land Registrar, and the President of a local Law Society to make orders prescribing solicitors' remuneration in respect of non-contentious business. Section 56(3) provided that, 'Before any such order is made, the Lord Chancellor shall cause a draft thereof to be sent to the Council [of the Law Society], and the committee shall, before making the order, consider any observations in writing submitted to them by the Council within one month of the sending to them of the draft, and may then make the order, either in the form of the draft or with such alterations or additions as they may think fit.' The committee proposed to abolish scale fees for conveyancing and substitute a *quantum meruit* system. A draft order was sent to the Law Society. The claimant was a member of the British Legal Association. This body, which had 2,900 members, objected to the proposals and sought to delay the making of the order to allow further consultation with the profession. The claimant sought a declaration that any order made would be *ultra vires* unless, *inter alia*, before making the order the committee gave the British Legal Association a reasonable opportunity to make representations as to its terms.

Megarry J

. . . Mr. Nicholls relied on *Reg. v. Liverpool Corporation, Ex parte Liverpool Taxi Fleet Operators' Association* [1972] 2 Q.B. 299; and he read me some passages from the judgments of Lord Denning M.R. and Roskill L.J. It cannot often happen that words uttered by a judge in his judicial capacity will, within six months, be cited against him in his personal capacity as defendant; yet that is the position here. The case was far removed from the present case. It concerned the exercise by a city council of its powers to license hackney carriages, and a public undertaking given by the chairman of the relevant committee which the council soon proceeded to ignore. The case supports propositions relating to the duty of a body to act fairly when exercising administrative functions under a statutory power: see at pp. 307, 308 and 310. Accordingly, in deciding the policy to be applied as to the number of licences to grant, there was a duty to hear those who would be likely to be affected. It is plain that no legislation was involved: the question was one of the policy to be adopted in the exercise of a statutory power to grant licences.

In the present case, the committee in question has an entirely different function: it is legislative rather than administrative or executive. The function of the committee is to make or refuse to make a legislative instrument under delegated powers. The order, when made, will lay down the remuneration for solicitors generally; and the terms of the order will have to be considered and construed and applied in numberless cases in the future. Let me accept that in the sphere of the so-called quasi-judicial the rules of natural justice run, and that in the administrative or executive field there is a general duty of fairness. Nevertheless, these considerations do not seem to me to affect the process of legislation, whether primary or delegated. Many of those affected by delegated legislation, and affected very substantially, are never consulted in the process of enacting that legislation; and yet they have no remedy. Of course, the informal consultation of representative bodies by the legislative authority is a commonplace; but although a few statutes have specifically provided for a general process of publishing draft delegated legislation and considering objections (see, for example, the Factories Act 1961, Schedule 4), I do not know of any implied right to be consulted or make objections, or any principle upon which the courts may enjoin the legislative process at the suit of those who contend that insufficient time for consultation and consideration has been given. I accept that the fact that the order will take the form of a statutory instrument does not per se make it immune from attack, whether by injunction or otherwise; but what is important is not its form but its nature, which is plainly legislative . . .

Order accordingly.

The difficulty with *Bates* is that it is built upon precisely the distinction — between administrative and legislative functions — whose problematic nature we considered earlier. It is worth noting that that distinction has been rejected in other common law jurisdictions such as New Zealand and Australia. For instance, in *CREEDNZ Inc* v. *Governor General* [1981] 1 NZLR 172 at 189, Richard J said that 'the dividing line between "adjudication" (or "administration") on the one hand and "legislation" on the other is not easy to draw and the attempt may be an arid exercise for in the twilight area the conceptual foundations for a distinction are not self-evident'. Similarly, in *Bread Manufacturers of New South Wales* v. *Evans* (1994) 180 CLR 404, Gibbs CJ (at [14]) considered that it was inappropriate to determine the applicability of the principles of natural justice by reference to a distinction between administrative and legislative functions. Mason and Wilson JJ (at [29]) agreed that 'the application of the rules of natural justice is not to be determined merely by affixing a label to describe the character of the task which is under consideration'.

Nevertheless, in English law, the administrative/legislative distinction continues to exert influence in this context, and courts' willingness to superimpose rights of participation upon the administrative *decision-making* process (see, *eg*, *R* v. *Devon County Council, ex parte Baker* [1995] 1 All ER 73) is not mirrored in relation to administrative *legislation*. The general view is that there is no need to consult before the adoption of legislative measures, *unless* it is possible to derive a right to be consulted from the legitimate expectation doctrine (*eg* because consultation has been promised or accorded in the past, or because consistent conferral of a benefit is taken to generate a legitimate expectation of consultation before the taking of a decision not to continue to confer it). Thus, for instance, in *Leech* v. *Deputy Governor of Parkhurst Prison* [1988] AC 533 at 578, Lord Oliver spoke of a 'general common law principle which imposes a duty of procedural fairness when a public authority makes a decision *not of a legislative nature* affecting the rights, privileges and interests of individuals' (emphasis added).

The judiciary is not, however, blind to the fact that consultation in the legislative context may, at least in some circumstances, be desirable. This much is apparent from *R* v. *Secretary of State for Health, ex parte United States Tobacco International Inc* [1992] QB 353. The claimant, following encouragement from relevant government departments, built a factory in Scotland to produce oral snuff. Three years after the factory opened, the Secretary of State for Health announced his intention to ban oral snuff by making an order under s 11 of the Consumer Protection Act 1987. Although the Minister consulted the claimant (as he was required to do under s 11(5)), he failed to disclose to the claimant the scientific advice upon which his decision was based. The claimant successfully argued that this failure invalidated the consultation process, and the order was quashed. Taylor LJ concluded, at 370, that there were 'three reasons why consultation pursuant to section 11(5)(a) in the present case required a high degree of fairness and candour to be shown by the Secretary of State':

First, the history. Although the applicants cannot successfully rely on the doctrine of legitimate expectation, the fact is that they were led up the garden path. The Secretary of State must have realised once the [expert scientific committee] had recommended a ban in 1986 that if he accepted that advice, he would be executing a volte face which would seriously affect the applicants. Secondly, although the Regulations are of general application, they impinged almost exclusively on the applicants as the sole manufacturers and packagers of oral snuff in the United Kingdom. Thirdly, the effect of the Regulations was likely to be catastrophic to the applicants' business in the United Kingdom, a business in which they had been encouraged by the Government to invest substantial resources. It is well established that the claims of natural justice are particularly strong where a party is being deprived of a right previously enjoyed, especially if it involves loss of livelihood: see *McInnes v. Onslow-Fane* [1978] 1 W.L.R. 1520 and *Reg. v. Barnsley Metropolitan Borough Council, Ex parte Hook* [1976] 1 W.L.R. 1052. For these reasons it was important that the Secretary of State, when he eventually decided to propose the Regulations, should give the applicants a full opportunity to know and respond to the material and evaluations which led him to such a striking change of policy.

QUESTIONS

- Although advanced by Taylor LJ as reasons for requiring statutory consultation to be carried out *in a particular way*, might it be argued that the factors he sets out should be regarded as trigger conditions for the *existence in the first place* of a (common law) duty to consult?
- Why do you think Taylor LJ underlined the fact that these regulations 'impinged almost exclusively' upon the claimant, and was he right to do so?

It remains the case that a significant amount of secondary legislation is made without prior consultation, behind a veil of obscurity which leads Page, *Governing by Numbers* (Oxford 2001), ch 1, to call executive rule-making 'the politics of seclusion'. Should there therefore be a general requirement — imposed either by statute or common law — of consultation in this context? In the following passage, Cane is unconvinced that a higher level of participation — such as that which obtains in the US — purchases advantages which necessarily outweigh the associated costs.

....

Cane, *Administrative Law*
(Oxford 2004)

. . . The main advantages of a more formal procedure of rule-making are said to be that it gives the citizen a greater chance to participate in decision-making and that it improves the quality of the rules made. However, unless participation leads to greater satisfaction with and acceptance of the rules themselves, it is of doubtful value. If the participants object to the rules made, despite extensive involvement, and feel that participation has only 'worked' if the result they favour is reached, then participation by itself is of limited value. The [more formal] procedures used in the United States do not seem to have reduced dissatisfaction with administrative rule-making. It may be that Americans are much less happy than the British about having their lives regulated by government at all, and that this, rather than the actual content of the regulation, is the main source of the discontent. No amount of formalized procedure can overcome this problem.

As for the second alleged advantage, the concept of increased quality of rule-making is a very difficult one to pin down. If quality refers to technical matters such as drafting, participation of non-experts may not improve quality. On the other hand, consultation of those whose interests will be affected may assist the rule-maker, in designing a rule which will effectively and efficiently achieve the desired policy objectives, by providing detailed information about the circumstances in which the rule will operate. If 'quality' is really a synonym for political acceptability, then once again there may be a reason to doubt that increased popular participation will make rules more acceptable to those who dislike them.

There are considerable problems associated with more formal participatory forms of rule-making. They take a lot of time and money; and so groups with the greatest resources tend to have an advantage over less well-endowed interest groups. It is unlikely that statutory obligations to consult would overcome such inequalities in resources. Furthermore, it is not clear that hearing a wide diversity of conflicting views makes it easier to frame a rule; the result may just be that the rule finally formulated fails to satisfy many of those views. On the other hand, consultation at an early stage may at least increase levels of compliance later on and reduce the chance that those dissatis-fied with any rules made will seek actively to challenge them . . .

QUESTIONS

- Do you agree?
- How, other than by generally limiting the extent of consultation, might the problem of powerful interest groups be tackled?

Finally, it should be noted that the Cabinet Office recently issued a *Code of Practice on Written Consultation* (2004). This does not require written (or any other form of) consult-ation to be undertaken in any particular circumstances, but instead states how consultation exercises should be conducted when they are undertaken. It requires (*inter alia*) clear, concise consultation documents to be issued in good time and made widely available, and that responses are open-mindedly analysed. While these requirements are stated to have no legal force, they 'should otherwise generally be regarded as binding on UK departments and their agencies, unless Ministers conclude that exceptional circumstances require a departure' (*ibid* at 6).

17.2.3 The Role of Parliament

Since the *raison d'être* of delegated legislation is that the executive should be empowered to enact rules, liberating Parliament from the burden of legislative monopoly, it may at first seem surprising that the latter should play any role in the making of delegated legislation. Yet, while the risk of abuse of power means that the executive cannot be allowed to legislate without any sort of checks, judicial review in this sphere (discussed below at 17.4), while important, is not sufficient: it is necessary for delegated legislation to be scrutinized not just in legal, but also in political and policy, terms — a function which Parliament is better placed than the courts to discharge.

Parliament's involvement in the process of making delegated legislation varies consider-ably, depending on the terms of the enabling legislation. So-called 'affirmative instruments' must be approved by Parliament if they are to take effect (albeit that they may, depending on the terms of the enabling provision, have interim effect pending such approval). This pro-cedure, however, occupies valuable parliamentary time, and is therefore relatively uncom-mon: in the session 2002–2003, only 233 instruments were subject to this procedure. In contrast, 1,216 'negative instruments' were made: rather than requiring parliamentary *approval*, these take effect in the absence of *disapproval* or annulment (which can be expressed up to 40 days after the instrument is laid before Parliament). The annulment procedure, which is set out in s 5(1) of the Statutory Instruments Act 1946, is much more widely used because it places a far smaller burden upon parliamentary time. Indeed, secur-ing annulment of negative instruments is very difficult: individual members must attempt to find parliamentary time, and more often than not they are unsuccessful in doing so. Other delegated legislation is merely required to be laid before Parliament (in final or draft form: see ss 4(1) and 6(1) of the 1946 Act); furthermore, Page, *Governing by Numbers* (Oxford 2001) at 26, reports that 21 per cent of statutory instruments passed between 1991 and 1999 did not require any form of parliamentary approval, either because they did not have to be laid, or because no further parliamentary involvement was specified following their having been laid.

The present arrangements attracted strong criticism from the Select Committee on Procedure, which said (HC48, *Delegated Legislation* (1999–2000) at [11]):

> . . . [I]nstruments do not receive scrutiny in proportion to their merits. The current system . . . rests on the assumption that affirmative instruments are intrinsically more significant and debate-worthy than negative ones. This may be true of a majority of instruments, but it is generally acknowledged that there is a significant minority of affirmatives which deal with matters too trivial or technical to merit debate, and negatives which deal with important or sensitive matters where there is demand for a debate. This mismatch between the level of scrutiny provided for in the parent legislation and the level which is actually appropriate may arise from a variety of factors. Ministers may have up-graded procedure from negative to affirmative as a political concession during committee stage of a bill; contrariwise, the conferral of significant powers may have 'slipped through' Parliament without provision for proper scrutiny; whilst in other cases, circumstances may have changed during the years or decades since the passage of the parent legislation, rendering issues once regarded as important less so, and vice versa. Nonetheless, in the words of the Clerk of the House, 'the House is locked into a procedural approach to an instrument by provisions made sometimes many, many years before in the parent act'. As a result, the time and expertise of Members is frequently wasted in attendance at DL Committees [Standing Committees on Delegated Legislation: see below] to consider 'trivial affirmatives', often meeting for a few minutes only; whilst significant changes to the law may pass through Parliament unregarded and undebated because contained in negative instruments.

The members of the committee agreed (at [53]) with their predecessors (see HC152 (1995–96) at [1]) that the present arrangements are 'palpably unsatisfactory', making various proposals for the improvement of the system, which we consider in the following section.

17.3 Parliamentary Scrutiny

17.3.1 The Conferral of Administrative Rule-Making Powers

Pressures on parliamentary time make it difficult for detailed and systematic attention to be given to provisions in bills which relate to the conferral of rule-making powers upon the administration. In light of this, a committee of the House of Lords — now known as the Delegated Powers and Regulatory Reform Committee — was established. It scrutinizes bills, considering whether proposed grants of delegated powers are appropriate and what level of parliamentary control of the rule-making process (*eg* the negative or affirmative procedure) is desirable; special attention is paid to Henry VIII clauses, in view of the significant powers which they confer upon the executive. Although the Committee is usually presented with actual bills, it has expressed the view (HL130, *Thirty-Seventh Report* (1999–2000) at [93]) that more pre-legislative scrutiny — *ie* scrutiny of *draft* bills — would be a positive development.

The Committee (HL83, *Twenty-Sixth Report* (2000–2001) at [24]) describes its role and influence in the following terms:

> The Committee sees its role as one of advising the House; and recognises that it is for the House to decide whether or not to act on the Committee's advice. The Committee itself has no power to amend bills, but its advice has almost always been accepted by the Government and the House. Indeed this session . . ., the Government has been particularly prompt in accepting our recommendations, some of which have been far-reaching . . . [W]e are pleased to record that we have had a 100% success rate for our recommendations this session, as it means that a number of points of principle have been accepted.

Although the Royal Commission on House of Lords Reform (Cm 4534, *A House for the Future* (2000) at 45) applauded the work of the Committee, it commented that this presently tends to consist of

> resisting or restricting the grant of delegated powers. It may be that the Committee's role could evolve to include making recommendations that some provisions of Bills would be dealt with more appropriately in secondary legislation.

17.3.2 The Exercise of Administrative Rule-Making Powers

As well as scrutinizing the *conferral* of powers to enact subordinate legislation, Parliament also examines their *exercise*. Although a degree of scrutiny is possible through the affirmative and annulment procedures to which much delegated legislation is subject, a number of factors — notably the executive's dominance of Parliament, which makes disapproval or non-approval highly unlikely; the crudeness of these mechanisms, under which approval cannot usually be subject to the amendment of the legislation; and the sheer volume of delegated legislation — conspire to make these forms of control more theoretical than real. Genuine scrutiny is usually possible only through the work of committees.

17.3.3 Technical Scrutiny

Nearly all statutory instruments are scrutinized by the Joint Committee on Statutory Instruments, which was formed in 1972 to replace separate committees of the two Houses. (A separate committee of the House of Commons — the Select Committee on Statutory Instruments — still exists to scrutinize those instruments which the House of Lords plays no role in making.) The work of the Joint Committee (on which see generally Hayhurst and Wallington [1988] *PL* 547) is described in the following terms by Limon and McKay (eds),

Erskine May's Treatise on the Law, Privileges, Proceedings and Usages of Parliament (London 1997) at 591:

The Committee may draw the attention of Parliament to an instrument on any of a series of specified grounds, or any other ground not impinging on the merits of or policy behind the instrument. The particular grounds on which the Committee may act are that an instrument imposes or prescribes a charge on the public revenues or requires payments to be made for any licence or consent or other service in the courts . . .; purports to have a retrospective effect where the parent statute does not so provide; has been unjustifiably delayed in publication or being laid before Parliament; has not been notified in proper time to the Lord Chancellor [the Speaker of the House of Lords] and the Speaker [of the House of Commons] where it comes into effect before being presented to Parliament; gives rise to doubts whether it is *intra vires*, or appears to make an unusual or unexpected use of the powers conferred by the parent statute; requires elucidation as to its form ot purpose; or is defective in drafting.

Page, *Governing by Numbers* (Oxford 2001) at 161–168, concludes that the Committee enjoys a 'pervasive influence' because government officials seek to avoid condemnation by the committee, both for reasons of professional pride and because the administration is often willing to amend legislation with which the Committee is dissatisfied on *vires* grounds given the risk that a legal challenge may otherwise ensue.

17.3.4 Policy Scrutiny

While the Joint Committee may supply effective scrutiny of technical and legal matters, consideration of policy issues is outwith its remit. Lack of parliamentary time means that scrutiny of such matters is rarely possible on the floor of either House; when such scrutiny takes place, it is therefore usually by means of a standing committee. All affirmative instruments are automatically referred to such committees unless, exceptionally, the government agrees that there should be debate on the floor of the House. Meanwhile, negative instruments are only debated in standing committee if they are 'prayed against' — *ie* objected to — and if a Minister agrees to make a motion in the House to the effect that the matter should be referred to a standing committee. The matter is then referred to the committee, unless more than 20 members object, in which case the legislation must instead be debated on the floor of the House. We noted above at 17.2.3 the concern of the Select Committee on Procedure that the level of scrutiny accorded to particular statutory instruments is somewhat haphazard, depending as it does upon the distinction between affirmative and negative instruments which often bears little relation to the importance of the measure. This has led to various proposals, by the Committee and others, for reform of the way in which secondary legislation is scrutinized.

First, it has been argued that there must be a systematic way of sifting statutory instruments, to determine which are deserving of scrutiny on their merits. Building upon proposals first made by the Select Committee on Procedure (HC152, *Delegated Legislation* (1995–96)), the Royal Commission on the Reform of the House of Lords (Cm 4534, *A House for the Future* (2000) at 74) proposed the creation of a 'sifting' committee:

We believe it would strengthen Parliamentary scrutiny of Statutory Instruments if a 'sifting' mechanism could be established. This would be designed to look at the significance of every Statutory Instrument subject to Parliamentary scrutiny; call for further information from Departments where necessary; and draw attention to those Statutory Instruments which are important and those which merit further debate or consideration. Such a mechanism, perhaps in the form of a Committee, could be established by either House, or jointly, as a procedural matter. Its value would lie in focusing Parliamentary attention on those few Statutory Instruments which were of real significance. Its judgement would depend on not only the intrinsic significance of the issue concerned, but also its current political salience (which might vary over time).

This proposal was endorsed by the Procedure Committee (HC48, *Delegated Legislation* (1999–2000)) — which, in common with the Royal Commission, recommended that the Statutory Instruments Act 1946 should be amended to extend the time for praying against negative instruments from 40 to 60 days, in order to create sufficient time for scrutiny by a sifting committee and subsequent debate where appropriate. The Committee remains firmly of the view that a *joint* sifting committee should be established (see HC501, *Delegated Legislation: Proposals for a Sifting Committee* (2002–03) and HC684, *Delegated Legislation: Proposals for a Sifting Committee: The Government's Response to the Committee's First Report* (2002–03)): because most statutory instruments come before both Houses, sifting is equally desirable for both the Commons and the Lords, and a joint committee therefore represents an efficient use of resources. The Committee has also pointed out (*ibid* at [3]) that 'scrutiny of delegated legislation is an area where experience has already shown that much of the work can be undertaken by both Houses together, pooling the expertise available'. In spite of this, the government has refused to support proposals for a joint committee.

However, the House of Lords has recently established its own sifting committee, known as the Select Committee on the Merits of Statutory Instruments. According to the new Committee's terms of reference (see HL18, *Special Report: Inquiry into Methods of Working* (2003–04) at [3]), it is to consider the merits of statutory instruments

with a view to determining whether the special attention of the House should be drawn to an instrument on any of four grounds —

(a) that it is politically or legally important or gives rise to issues of public policy likely to be of interest to the House;
(b) that it is inappropriate in view of the changed circumstances since the passage of the parent Act;
(c) that it inappropriately implements EU legislation;
(d) that it imperfectly achieves its policy objectives.

The Committee (see HL73, *Special Report: The Committee's Methods of Working* (2003–04) at [48]) considers that its principal function is to 'improve debate in the House on negative instruments, both in terms of which negative instruments are debated in the House and the focus of debate on specific instruments'.

A second major reform proposal concerns the establishment of a new category of statutory instruments — so-called 'super-affirmatives'. Such instruments would be published in draft, and subject to scrutiny at that stage. In fact, regulatory reform orders, discussed below at 17.3.6, are already subject to such a procedure. However, amendments to primary legislation would be necessary to compel this approach in relation to other instruments.

17.3.5 EU Legislation

A substantial amount of delegated legislation is passed each year in order that the UK may fulfil its obligations under European Union law. Although much EU legislation is directly effective, meaning that it takes effect automatically in national legal systems, directives are not. Member states are therefore obliged to enact legislation in order to implement directives, to which end (as we saw above at 17.1.4) s 2(2) of the European Communities Act 1972 confers wide powers.

The European Scrutiny Committee of the House of Commons serves an important function by scrutinizing various documents (usually over 1,000 each year) emanating from EU institutions, including legislative proposals. The Committee refers the most important issues arising from such proposals for debate either in a European Standing Committee or, exceptionally, on the floor of the House. The House of Lords Select Committee on the European Union (largely through its seven sub-committees) performs similar functions to those of its Commons counterpart, but produces more detailed reports on a much smaller number of EU documents and proposals. The Commons and Lords committees both feel that these contrasting approaches are complementary and should be retained (see respectively HC152-xxx, *European Scrutiny in the Commons* (2001–02) at [102], and HL15, *Review of Scrutiny of European Legislation* (2002–03) at [127]).

In a recent review of the efficacy of parliamentary scrutiny of EU matters, the House of Lords Select Committee on the European Union (*ibid* at [30]) underlined the importance of its involvement 'at the earliest possible stage in the policy-making cycle. It is then that we stand the best chance of influencing policy'. Perhaps for this reason, scrutiny of EU matters in both the Commons and Lords committees focuses almost entirely upon proposals (legislative and otherwise) emanating from the EU institutions, with little specific attention to the much later stage in the cycle when the UK authorities enact delegated legislation to implement EU measures. For instance, the Commons European Scrutiny Committee considers (*op cit* at [112]) that:

It is not part of our role to monitor the transposition or implementation of EU legislation in the UK, and we would not have the time to do so. However, no other committee has this responsibility either, and much EU legislation is implemented by statutory instruments subject to the negative procedure, with the result that there may be no parliamentary scrutiny at all.

Further consideration was given to the scrutiny of secondary legislation implementing EU measures by the House of Lords Select Committee on the European Union (HL15, *Review of Scrutiny of European Legislation* (2002–03)) which reached the following conclusions (at [96]–[97]):

. . . [W]e would not wish to call on the Government to introduce more European legislation by primary rather than secondary legislation. Instead we would hope that the UK Parliament would do more to scrutinise the delegated legislation by which European law is implemented. We note that, where EU legislation is implemented by primary legislation, the full Parliamentary scrutiny process comes into play . . . Scrutiny of secondary legislation implementing EU legislation, however, is weak and needs to be strengthened.

To this end, we . . . note that the Delegated Powers and Regulatory Reform Committee does where appropriate consider, in assessing whether the delegation of power is appropriate, whether that power could be used to implement EU law. We recommend that, in addition, the scrutiny of delegated legislation implementing EU law be a key task of the House's proposed new committee on Statutory Instruments [see above on the recently-established sifting committee]. We would hope that the new committee would, wherever possible, analyse implementing instruments against concerns expressed during our own consideration of the European instrument.

One of the particular problems identified by the European committees of both Houses is that of 'gold-plating', a process whereby UK implementing legislation goes further than is actually required by EU directives with the result that British businesses are subjected to stricter regulation than their counterparts elsewhere in the EU, and therefore to competitive disadvantage. Both committees have suggested that this is a problem which could usefully be tackled by more detailed scrutiny of implementing measures.

17.3.6 Regulatory Reform Orders

Finally, it should be noted that special arrangements exist for parliamentary oversight of the extensive ministerial powers conferred by the Regulatory Reform Act 2001 (see above at 17.1.3) to amend or repeal primary legislation which imposes administrative or bureaucratic burdens. Following consultation, the Minister is required by s 6 to lay before Parliament a proposal for an order, and may not (by s 8) lay a draft order until after the expiry of a period of 60 days. During that period, the Regulatory Reform Committee of the House of Commons considers the proposal and makes a recommendation to the House either that a draft order in the terms contained in the proposal should be laid before the House, or that the proposal should be amended, or that the proposal should not be taken forward at all. The Minister then decides whether (and, if so, in what form) to lay a draft order before the House; in doing so, he must (by s 8(4)) have regard to 'any representations made during the period for Parliamentary consideration and, in particular, to any resolution or report of, or of any committee of, either House of Parliament with regard to the document'. The Committee then considers the draft order and must, within 15 sitting days, make a recommendation to the House whether the order should be approved. Scrutiny in the House of Lords is carried out by the Delegated Powers and Regulatory Reform Committee. The order can only take effect if approved by both Houses.

17.4 Judicial Scrutiny

17.4.1 Introduction

The administration's power to enact delegated legislation is constrained by the terms of the parent act (or occasionally by the extent of the royal prerogative). Thus the executive's *vires* are limited in this field just as in relation to administrative decision-making, and judicial review lies if delegated legislation is *ultra vires*. The facts that a parliamentary committee like the Joint Committee on Statutory Instruments has taken the view that a measure is *intra vires* and that delegated legislation may have received the approval of both Houses of Parliament under the affirmative procedure do not preclude judicial review (although the latter may influence the intensity of review, as we explain below). Under the separation of powers, it is the courts which bear ultimate responsibility for determining the legality of administrative action — including administrative legislation.

17.4.2 Compatibility with Primary Legislation

As with other forms of executive action, judicial review of delegated legislation frequently involves a close analysis of the enabling provisions, and other relevant Acts, in order to determine whether the subordinate provisions are *intra vires* or *ultra vires*. In some instances, the parent Act will make specific provision concerning the way in which delegated legislation is to be enacted. Non-compliance with such requirements may not render the subordinate legislation invalid: this will depend on the application of the principles set out at 2.6 above. However, the importance attached to consultation in the making of delegated legislation means that non-compliance with statutory consultation requirements is usually fatal to the validity of the legislation. For example, in *Agricultural, Horticultural and Forestry Industrial Training Board* v. *Aylesbury Mushrooms Ltd* [1972] 1 WLR 190, the Ministry of Labour created the claimant board by issuing an industrial training order under the Industrial Training Act 1964, s 1(4) of which provided that before making such an order the Minister 'shall consult' organizations and associations appearing to him to be representative of employers or employees engaged in the activities concerned. The Minister's failure to consult the Mushroom Growers' Association meant that the order could not be applied to its members. (This demonstrates that failure to comply with procedural requirements, such as consultation, need not render subordinate legislation globally invalid; it may simply render it invalid *vis-à-vis* those parties who were not consulted.) In contrast, we have already seen (above at 17.2.1) that statutory publication requirements are usually regarded as directory, such that failure to comply with them does not invalidate secondary legislation. Similarly, where the parent Act requires that delegated legislation be laid before Parliament — what constitutes laying being determined by each House: Laying of Documents (Interpretation) Act 1948 — the better view (see, *eg, Starey* v. *Graham* [1899] 1 QB 406 and, generally, Campbell [1983] *PL* 43) is that non-compliance does not affect the validity of the legislation. Where the delegated legislation takes the form of a statutory instrument, s 4(1) of the Statutory Instruments Act 1946 generally requires (subject to an exception for urgent cases) that, where the legislation is required to be laid before Parliament, 'a copy of the instrument shall be laid before each House of Parliament and . . . shall be so laid before the instrument comes into operation'. Campbell, *op cit* at 46–48, argues on the basis of the legislative history that s 4 does not make the laying of the instrument a condition precedent to its validity.

The courts' inquiry regarding the compatibility of secondary legislation with the parent Act may also take more subtle forms. For instance, *R* v. *Secretary of State for Social Security, ex parte Joint Council for the Welfare of Immigrants* [1997] 1 WLR 275 concerned regulations made under the Social Security Contributions and Benefits Act 1992, the effect of which was to preclude subsistence payments to asylum-seekers who failed to claim asylum upon arrival in the United Kingdom and to those whose claims had failed but who were in the process of exercising their right of appeal under the Asylum and Immigration Appeals Act 1993. The regulations were struck down by the Court of Appeal because, as Simon Brown LJ explained at 292, they substantially interfered with the ability of asylum-seekers to make claims and appeal against adverse decisions — actions which the 1993 Act allowed them to undertake:

Parliamentary sovereignty is not here in question: the Regulations are subordinate legislation only ... Parliament for its part has clearly demonstrated by the Act of 1993 a full commitment to the United Kingdom's ... obligations [under the Convention Relating to the Status of Refugees]. When the regulation-making power now contained in the Act of 1992 was first conferred, there was no question of asylum seekers being deprived of all benefit and thereby rendered unable to pursue their claims. Although I reject [counsel's] argument that the legislative history of this power (including, in particular, an indication to Parliament in 1986 that the Government was then intending to exercise it in continuing support of asylum seekers) itself serves to limit its present scope, the fact that asylum seekers have hitherto enjoyed benefit payments appears to me not entirely irrelevant. After all, the Act of 1993 confers on asylum seekers fuller rights than they had ever previously enjoyed, the right of appeal in particular. And yet these Regulations for some genuine asylum seekers at least must now be regarded as rendering these rights nugatory. Either that, or the Regulations necessarily contemplate for some a life so destitute that to my mind no civilised nation can tolerate it. So basic are the human rights here at issue that it cannot be necessary to resort to the European Convention on Human Rights to take note of their violation ... I would hold it unlawful to alter the benefit regime so drastically as must inevitably not merely prejudice, but on occasion defeat, the statutory right of asylum seekers to claim refugee status.

17.4.3 General Principles of Judicial Review

While the legality of secondary legislation sometimes falls to be determined, as in the *JCWI* case, by reference to the express terms of relevant primary legislation, it is often necessary for the courts to invoke wider principles of administrative law. Although we saw above that the courts are somewhat reluctant to bring general principles of fairness and participation into play in relation to rule-making, many other of the principles of judicial review which we encountered in earlier chapters are applicable here. For instance, if the administration takes into account irrelevant considerations when making delegated legislation, it is open to the court to conclude that the legislation is *ultra vires*. (Whether a quashing order would be issued is another matter, on which see above at 17.2.2.) The presumption against delegation also applies to legislative powers. Indeed, the courts are especially unwilling to conclude that the presumption has been rebutted where legislative powers are concerned: in *King-Emperor v. Benoari Lal Sarma* [1945] AC 14 at 24, Viscount Simon LC assumed, without further discussion, that a power to enact delegated legislation could not itself be delegated. Subordinate legislation made under the influence of an improper purpose is also liable to be quashed. Although, as Mason J explained in *In re Toohey; ex parte Northern Land Council* (1981) 38 ALR 439 at 484, it may be difficult as a matter of evidence to establish whether secondary legislation was in fact made under an improper influence, we have already seen (in the cases considered in ch 8 above) that the courts will, where possible, deduce purposes from objective evidence; there is no *a priori* reason why this should not occur in relation to legislative measures as well as administrative decisions.

The familiar principle of unreasonableness is also applicable to delegated legislation, although, consistently with the judicial reticence in relation to administrative action later evidenced in the *Wednesbury* case (see above at 9.2.1) itself, Lord Russell CJ was of the opinion in *Kruse v. Johnson* [1898] 2 QB 91 at 99–100 that courts should be slow to condemn byelaws on this ground:

I do not mean to say that there may not be cases in which it would be the duty of the Court to condemn by-laws ... as invalid because unreasonable. But unreasonable in what sense? If, for instance, they were found to be partial and unequal in their operation as between different classes; if they were manifestly unjust; if they disclosed bad faith; if they involved such oppressive or gratuitous interference with the rights of those subject to them as could find no justification in the minds of reasonable men, the Court might well say, "Parliament never intended to give authority to make such rules; they are unreasonable and ultra vires." But it is in this sense, and in this sense only, as I conceive, that the question of unreasonableness can properly be regarded. A by-law is not unreasonable merely because particular judges may think that it goes further than is prudent or necessary or convenient, or because it is not accompanied by a qualification or an exception which some judges may think ought to be there. Surely it is not too much to say that in matters which directly and mainly concern the people of the county, who have the right to choose those whom they think best fitted to represent them in their local government bodies, such representatives may be trusted to understand their own requirements better than judges.

A similar ethos infused the decision of the House of Lords in *Nottinghamshire County Council v. Secretary of State for the Environment* [1986] AC 240 (see above at 9.2.2). Lord Scarman was at pains to emphasize that only in the most extraordinary circumstances would the court consider reviewing the matter at stake in that case, *viz* expenditure targets for local authorities set by the Secretary of State and approved by the House of Commons. He opined (at 248) that such measures could not be struck down as unreasonable unless there was 'perversity or ... absurdity of such proportions' that the targets could not have been set by a 'bona fide exercise of political judgment on the part of the Secretary of State'.

The language used in *Kruse* v. *Johnson* and *Nottinghamshire* to describe the circumstances in which the measures in question could have been struck down as unreasonable appears extreme. Does this mean that measures — such as delegated legislation — which have received a seal of approval from Parliament (as in *Nottinghamshire*) or some other democratically-elected body (such as the local authority in *Kruse* v. *Johnson*) are peculiarly unlikely to be subject to a successful unreasonableness challenge? In seeking to answer this question, three points should be noted.

First, we have already seen (above at 9.2.1) that the language used by judges to describe the circumstances in which administrative action may be condemned as unreasonable generally tends to be somewhat extreme. The language used in the cases here under consideration must be set in that context.

Secondly, the *Nottinghamshire* case must be treated with caution. Although it appears that some weight may have been attached in that case to the fact that the measures in question had been approved by the House of Commons, subsequent case law has emphasized the particular facts of the *Nottinghamshire* decision. Thus, in *R (Asif Javed)* v. *Secretary of State for the Home Department* [2002] QB 129 [2001] EWCA Civ 789 at [48] (see above at 9.2.2) Lord Phillips attributed the extreme judicial deference exhibited in *Nottinghamshire* to the subject-matter (*viz* national economic policy) of the measures in question, not to the fact that they had received parliamentary approval.

Thirdly, the previous point notwithstanding, it does appear that, in setting the level of judicial deference in a particular case, courts may attach *some* weight to the fact that delegated legislation has been approved (actually, as in the case of affirmative instruments, or tacitly, as in the case of negative instruments) by Parliament. Having set out the approach of Lord Russell CJ in *Kruse* v. *Johnson*, Simon Brown J in *R* v. *Immigration Appeal Tribunal, ex parte Manshoora Begum* [1986] Imm AR 385 at 394 said:

... [W]here the relevant power is given, as here, to a Minister responsible to Parliament, the court is even less willing to intervene, a fortiori where, as is also the case here, the rules in question were laid before Parliament and subject to a process akin to negative resolution.

This approach does not, however, render delegated legislation invulnerable to unreasonableness review — indeed, in *Manshoora Begum* itself, a portion of the Immigration Rules was held to be unreasonable and therefore *ultra vires* the enabling provision under which it had purportedly been made.

QUESTIONS

- Look back to the discussion of deference in ch 9 above. Are the courts right to extend greater deference to legislative measures which have been democratically endorsed?
- Should the extent of judicial deference in relation to delegated legislation be informed by the adequacy of parliamentary scrutiny of such measures?

Finally, we should note a further ground of review which is of particular relevance to delegated legislation. By definition, legislation — delegated or otherwise — lays down general rules, compliance or non-compliance with which will have legal consequences. It is important, therefore, that such rules are stated clearly, in order that individuals may act accordingly. Many commentators place this requirement near the heart of the rule of law: Raz, *The Authority of Law* (Oxford 1979) at 214, writes that the law's 'meaning must be clear. An ambiguous, vague, obscure, or imprecise law is likely to mislead or confuse at least some of those who desire to be guided by it'. Some cases indicate a judicial willingness to strike down vague secondary legislation for reasons similar to those advanced by Raz. For instance, in *Kruse* v. *Johnson* [1898] 2 QB 91 at 108, Matthew J said that 'a byelaw to be valid must, among other conditions, . . . be certain, that is, it must contain adequate information as to the duties of those who are to obey'. However, more recent authority evidences a narrower approach. Approving a test laid down by Lord Denning in *Fawcett Properties Ltd* v. *Buckingham County Council* [1961] AC 636 at 677–678, Simon Brown LJ in *Percy* v. *Hall* [1997] QB 924 at 941 concluded that secondary legislation should be treated 'as valid unless so uncertain in its language as to have no ascertainable meaning, or so unclear in its effect as to be incapable of certain application in any case'. This test was preferred because it was felt that that which was advanced in *Kruse* v. *Johnson* was itself uncertain, and would, if applied literally, lead to large volumes of secondary legislation being held invalid. The court therefore recognized and accepted that, at the margins, there will often be uncertainty about precisely how a given rule applies to a particular situation, but that this should not be fatal to its validity.

17.4.4 Wider Constitutional Principles and Human Rights

As well as being open to challenge if it breaches specific statutory requirements or general principles of administrative law, delegated legislation — like other forms of administrative action — may also be rendered invalid if it conflicts with wider constitutional principles or human rights (existing at common law or under the HRA). As is apparent from the following excerpt, the courts apply a general presumption that Parliament, in enacting enabling

legislation, would not intend to empower rule-makers to contravene important constitutional princples or human rights; that general presumption is now buttressed by s 3 of the
HRA, which obliges the courts, where possible, to read all legislative provisions — including
those conferring rule-making powers — compatibly with the Convention rights.

R v. *Lord Chancellor ex parte Witham* [1998] QB 575
Divisional Court

In purported exercise of his power under s 130(1) of the Supreme Court Act 1981 to 'prescribe the
fees to be taken in the Supreme Court', the Lord Chancellor issued the Supreme Court Fees
(Amendment) Order 1996, article 3 of which repealed a provision in the Supreme Court Fees Order
1980, the effect of which had been to relieve persons in receipt of income support of the obligation
to pay court fees. As a result, the claimant — himself a recipient of income support — was
precluded by his impecuniosity from instituting proceedings for malicious falsehood and libel. He
argued that article 3 of the 1996 Order was invalid. The Human Rights Act 1998 was not in force
when this case was decided.

Laws J

. . . The common law does not generally speak in the language of constitutional rights, for the good
reason that in the absence of any sovereign text, a written constitution which is logically and legally
prior to the power of legislature, executive and judiciary alike, there is on the face of it no hierarchy
of rights such that any one of them is more entrenched by the law than any other. And if the
concept of a constitutional right is to have any meaning, it must surely sound in the protection
which the law affords to it. Where a written constitution guarantees a right, there is no conceptual
difficulty. The state authorities must give way to it, save to the extent that the constitution allows
them to deny it . . .

In the unwritten legal order of the British state, at a time when the common law continues to
accord a legislative supremacy to Parliament, the notion of a constitutional right can in my judgment inhere only in this proposition, that the right in question cannot be abrogated by the state
save by specific provision in an Act of Parliament, or by regulations whose vires in main legislation
specifically confers the power to abrogate. General words will not suffice. And any such rights will
be creatures of the common law, since their existence would not be the consequence of the
democratic political process but would be logically prior to it . . .

[Laws J considered the authorities, including *R* v. *Secretary of State for the Home Department, ex
parte Leech* [1994] QB 194 and *Raymond* v. *Honey* [1983] 1 AC 1, and continued:] It seems to me,
from all the authorities to which I have referred, that the common law has clearly given special
weight to the citizen's right of access to the courts. It has been described as a constitutional right,
though the cases do not explain what that means. In this whole argument, nothing to my mind has
been shown to displace the proposition that the executive cannot in law abrogate the right of
access to justice, unless it is specifically so permitted by Parliament; and this is the meaning of the
constitutional right. But I must explain . . . what in my view the law requires by such a permission. A
statute may give the permission expressly; in that case it would provide in terms that in defined
circumstances the citizen may not enter the court door. In *Leech* the Court of Appeal accepted, as
in its view the *ratio* of their Lordships' decision in *Raymond* vouchsafed, that it could also be done
by necessary implication. However for my part I find great difficulty in conceiving a form of words
capable of making it plain beyond doubt to the statute's reader that the provision in question
prevents him from going to court (for that is what would be required), save in a case where that is
expressly stated. The class of cases where it could be done by necessary implication is, I venture to
think, a class with no members.

. . . In my judgment the 1996 Order's effect is to bar absolutely many persons from seeking justice from the courts. Mr Richards' elegant and economical argument [for the Lord Chancellor] contains an unspoken premise. It is that the common law affords no special status whatever to the citizen's right of access to justice. He says that the statute's words are unambiguous, are amply wide enough to allow what has been done, and that there is no available *Wednesbury* complaint. That submission would be good in a context which does not touch fundamental constitutional rights. But I do not think that it can run here. Access to the courts is a constitutional right; it can only be denied by the government if it persuades Parliament to pass legislation which specifically — in effect by express provision — permits the executive to turn people away from the court door. That has not been done in this case . . .

Rose LJ agreed that the Lord Chancellor had not been authorized to prescribe fees so as to exclude those on low incomes from access to justice. A declaration was issued to the effect that article 3 of the 1996 Order was unlawful.

Although, in *R* v. *Secretary of State for the Home Department, ex parte Pierson* [1998] AC 539 at 575, Lord Browne-Wilkinson doubted whether Laws J was correct that *explicit* statutory permission was required to override constitutional rights, he agreed that, 'Such basic rights are not to be overridden by the general words of a statute since the presumption is against the impairment of such basic rights.' The notion of common law constitutional rights is not confined to access to the courts. Equivalent principles of interpretation have been applied (*inter alia*) to uphold the principle that taxes may be levied only with parliamentary consent (see *Attorney-General* v. *Wilts United Dairies Ltd* (1921) 39 TLR 781), the right of legal professional privilege (see *R (Daly)* v. *Secretary of State for the Home Department* [2001] UKHL 26 [2001] 2 AC 532), and freedom of expression (see *R* v. *Secretary of State for the Home Department, ex parte Simms* [2000] 2 AC 115).

The interpretative model under which common law rights are protected against encroachment by delegated legislation now has a statutory counterpart in the form of the HRA 1998 (for discussion of which in this context see *R (Bono)* v. *Harlow District Council* [2002] EWHC 423 (Admin) [2002] 1 WLR 2475). Section 3 obliges the courts, where possible, to read (*inter alia*) legislation that confers rule-making powers consistently with the Convention rights: those rights are therefore read into enabling provisions as implied limits upon them. It follows that ECHR-incompatible delegated legislation will generally be *ultra vires* by operation of s 3. To some extent, the advent of the HRA reduces the importance of the common law rights approach considered above. Nevertheless, it is entirely conceivable that there may be circumstances in which common law rights are more extensive than those enumerated in the Convention; for that reason, circumstances may arise in which the courts will choose to draw on the former rather than the latter. The emphasis in *Daly* on common law rights (see above at 9.3.4, noting in particular the comments of Lords Bingham and Cooke at [16] and [30] respectively) arguably lays the foundation for precisely such an approach.

17.5 Concluding Remarks

Delegated legislation is an inescapable feature of contemporary governance. The enactment of legislative rules by the administrative branch is inevitable, given the volume of regulation required by the modern state. These conclusions should not, however, disguise the fact that vigilance, in two senses, is essential in this context. First, the necessity of a degree of delegation of legislative authority should not blunt critical evaluation of the appropriateness of particular delegations; such evaluation — especially important in view of the tendency to confer increasingly broad legislative powers — is a matter for Parliament. Secondly, subordinate legislation should itself be open to critical scrutiny. The difficulty, of course, lies in the highly incomplete implementation in Britain of the separation of powers doctrine. In light of its dominance of Parliament, the administration is very strongly-placed to secure the passage of primary legislation that confers wide rule-making powers, and to survive (or even avoid meaningful) parliamentary scrutiny of delegated legislation passed under such powers. Meanwhile, the efficacy of judicial scrutiny of the legality of executive legislation is to an extent compromised by the broad nature of the enabling provisions that powerful administrations are able to procure. None of this renders political and judicial scrutiny of delegated legislation pointless; much, as we have seen in this chapter, can still be achieved: parliamentary committees are sometimes able to exert sufficient pressure to procure changes, the government's in-built majority in the House of Commons notwithstanding; and the courts do their best, where appropriate, to read enabling provisions narrowly by applying constitutional principles of interpretation and now the HRA. Nevertheless, it would be naïve to underestimate the impact in this context of the structural features of the British constitution which combine to produce a powerful executive branch which is able, through its effective control of the sovereign legislature, to confer upon itself extensive legislative powers.

FURTHER RESOURCES

Barber and Young, 'The Rise of Prospective Henry VIII Clauses and their Implications for Sovereignty' [2003] *PL* 112

Cabinet Office, *Code of Practice on Written Consultation* (2004) *www.cabinet-office.gov.uk/regulation/consultation/code.asp*

Cm 4534, *A House for the Future* (2000) *www.archive.official-documents.co.uk/document/cm45/4534/4534.htm*

Cm 4060, *Report of the Committee on Ministers' Powers* (1932)

Daintith and Page, *The Executive in the Constitution* (Oxford 1999)

Ganz, *Quasi-Legislation: Recent Developments in Secondary Legislation* (London 1987)

Leyland and Woods (eds), *Administrative Law Facing the Future: Old Constraints and New Horizons* (1997), ch 3 (Ganz)

Page, *Governing by Numbers* (Oxford 2001)

The web sites of the various parliamentary committees referred to in this chapter can be accessed via *www.parliament.uk*

 # INQUIRIES

18.1 Introduction

'Inquiries' are a familiar concept, largely because of their use in the investigation of high-profile allegations of maladministration and wrongdoing, accidents, and disasters. However, while such *ad hoc* inquiries (considered at 18.4 below) often attract the attention of the media and the public, an enormous number of inquiries is in fact undertaken each year as part of the regular decision-making process across a wide range of policy areas. Indeed, in the year 2003–2004 over 22,000 inquiries falling within the jurisdiction of the Council on Tribunals were held, according to its *Annual Report 2003/2004* (HC750 (2003–2004) at 72–73).

....

Wraith and Lamb, *Public Inquiries as an Instrument of Government*
(London 1971)

This book is about an everyday occurrence in British public administration . . . [Inquiries] vary from small routine affairs which attract a paragraph in a local newspaper to investigations at large into matters of great public importance; and they serve so many different purposes that they may seem to have little in common but the accident of a name . . .

[T]ribunals . . . tend to be linked with inquiries, but [their] purpose is fundamentally different. Public inquiries are constituted *ad hoc* to inquire into particular matters, and are for the most part concerned only to establish facts and to make recommendations. Tribunals, by contrast, have a regular or permanent existence, a defined area of jurisdiction, and the function of deciding or adjudicating in disputes . . .

. . . [I]t may be helpful to give a rough and ready classification of what public inquiries are generally about.

The largest group consists of inquiries into *appeals* against administrative decisions, usually decisions of local authorities . . . The typical appeal is against the refusal of planning permission by a local authority, and takes place every working day of the year . . .

Another group comprises inquiries into *objections*. In conduct and outward appearance, they are very like appeals, though their subject matter is less homogenous. The law offers the British citizen generous opportunities to object to anything which may affect his interests or convenience, and objections may be made to a project (such as a road, a new town or reservoir), to an administrative scheme (such as the reorganization of a water undertaking or a police force), or to the compulsory purchase of his land for public purposes.

Appeals and objections account for the overwhelming majority of public inquiries. There are, however, others, small in number and different in character, which may reconcile opposing interests, shape future policies or clear up matters of public concern. First, there are *investigations* in advance of a decision [eg whether an airport should be expanded] . . . [Then] there are those we might call *post-mortems*, for example inquiries into accidents or into matters which have been the subject of public scandal or concern . . .

It is in relation to appeals against decisions that inquiries are most commonly undertaken; and, of the 22,000 or so inquiries in the year 2003–2004 mentioned above, almost 19,000 were connected with planning appeals. Although the purpose of this chapter is to examine the nature of inquiries generally, rather than to explore specific types of inquiries in detail, it may be useful at the outset briefly to explain how inquiries arising from planning appeals work, given their widespread use.

Section 57(1) of the Town and Country Planning Act 1990 provides that 'planning permission is required for the carrying out of any development of land', where 'development' means (according to s 55(1)) 'the carrying out of building, engineering, mining or other operations in, on, over or under land, or the making of any material change in the use of any buildings or other land'. It is usually the responsibility of the local planning authority to decide planning applications under s 70 of the 1990 Act, but a right of appeal to the Secretary of State lies against such authorities' decisions in various circumstances, including outright refusal of planning permission (s 78(1)(a)). Appeals can be decided solely on the basis of written representations, but, according to s 79(2):

Before determining an appeal under section 78 the Secretary of State shall, if either the appellant or the local planning authority so wish, give each of them an opportunity of appearing before and being heard by a person appointed by the Secretary of State for the purpose.

In these circumstances, hearings are usually provided by holding a public local inquiry under s 320. Where the Secretary of State (or his officials) are to determine the appeal, an inquiry — governed by the Town and Country Planning (Inquiries Procedure) (England) Rules 2000 or the Town and Country Planning (Inquiries Procedure) (Wales) Rules 2003 — is held, the inspector makes a recommendation, and the Secretary of State, who is free to accept or reject that recommendation, then decides the appeal. This model — inquiry, followed by recommendation, followed by the taking of the ultimate decision by an accountable political figure — reflects the role which inquiries classically serve: that of gathering information and allowing people to have their say, so as to allow an informed decision to be made. However, we should note that, in the planning context, the Secretary of State now tends to determine only those appeals which raise particularly complex or sensitive issues. It is therefore common for the inspector to decide the appeal himself rather than simply making a recommendation, in which case the inquiry is governed by the Town and Country Planning Appeals (Determination by Inspectors) (Inquiries Procedure) (England) Rules 2000 and the Town and Country Planning Appeals (Determination by Inspectors) (Inquiries Procedure) (Wales) Rules 2003. We return to planning inquiries below, in order to illustrate our discussion of particular aspects of inquiries generally.

With these features of planning inquiries in mind, we turn to consider the nature and role of inquiries.

18.2 Background to the Modern Law

In his influential book *The New Despotism* (London 1929), Lord Hewart wrote (at 51):

It is sometimes enacted that, before the Minister comes to a decision, he shall hold a public inquiry, at which interested parties are entitled to adduce evidence and be heard. But that provision is no real safeguard, because the person who has the power of deciding is in no way bound by the report or the recommendations of the person who holds the inquiry, and may entirely ignore the evidence which the inquiry brought to light. He can, and in practice, sometimes does, give a decision wholly inconsistent with the report, the recommendations and the evidence, which are not published or disclosed to interested individuals. In any case, as the official [or Minister] who decides has not seen or heard the witnesses, he is as a rule quite incapable of estimating the value of their evidence. So far, therefore, as restraining the arbitrary power of the deciding official is concerned, the requirement of a public inquiry is in practice nugatory . . .

These problems arise largely because of the unusual character of inquiries. We are already familiar with the requirements that decision-makers must afford interested parties an opportunity to make representations (see ch 11 above) and take into account legally relevant information (see ch 8 above). Inquiries, however, go further, imposing as a precursor to the making of decisions an adversarial process in which competing parties present their arguments in a public forum.

QUESTION

• What principles should be used to determine whether an inquiry should be a condition precedent to the making of a decision?

As Wade and Forsyth, *Administrative Law* (Oxford 2004) at 961–962, observe, inquiries are 'a hybrid legal-and-administrative process, and for the very reason that they have been made to look as much as possible like judicial proceeding, people grumble at the fact that they fall short of it'. The question whether inquiries ought properly to be characterized as serving an administrative or a judicial role — an issue which fundamentally affects how inquiries should operate — was considered at length by the Franks Committee in its *Report of the Committee on Administrative Tribunals and Enquiries* (Cmnd 218). Having considered (with particular reference to planning inquiries) the competing administrative and judicial models — the former casting inquiries as a mere adjunct to the exercise of ministerial discretion, the latter emphasizing the adversarial nature of inquiries and the need for resultant decisions to be founded upon the evidence thereby gathered — the Committee went on:

. . . [T]hese procedures cannot be classified as purely administrative or purely judicial. They are not purely administrative because of the provision for a special procedure preliminary to the decision — a feature not to be found in the ordinary course of administration — and because this procedure . . . involves the testing of an issue, often partly in public. They are not on the other hand purely judicial, because the final decision cannot be reached by the application of rules and must allow the exercise of a wide discretion in the balancing of public and private interest. Neither view at its extreme is tenable, nor should either be emphasised at the expense of the other.

If the administrative view is dominant the public enquiry cannot play its full part in the total process, and there is a danger that the rights and interests of the individual citizens affected will not be sufficiently protected. In these cases it is idle to argue that Parliament can be relied upon to protect the citizen, save exceptionally. We agree with the following views expressed in the pamphlet entitled *The Rule of Law*: "Whatever the theoretical validity of this argument, those of us who are Members of Parliament have no hesitation in saying that it bears little relation to reality. Parliament has neither the time nor the knowledge to supervise the Minister and call him to account for his administrative decision."

If the judicial view is dominant there is a danger that people will regard the person before whom they state their case as a kind of judge provisionally deciding the matter, subject to an appeal to the Minister. This view overlooks the true nature of the proceeding, the form of which is necessitated by the fact that the Minister himself, who is responsible to Parliament for the ultimate decision, cannot conduct the enquiry in person.

The Committee's conclusion that inquiries can be characterized as neither purely judicial nor purely administrative influenced its subsequent proposals for improving inquiries. It sought to apply to inquiries the three principles of openness, fairness, and impartiality which it had already developed in relation to statutory tribunals (see ch 19 below), while recognizing (*ibid* at 61) that, in the quasi-administrative realm of inquiries, the notion of impartiality 'cannot be applied . . . without qualification'.

18.3 Statutory Inquiries Today

18.3.1 General

Many of the specific recommendations of the Franks Committee were implemented through the adoption of new administrative practices and legal rules (see further the 1963 *Annual Report of the Council on Tribunals* (London 1963), Appendix A), and its legacy is still abundantly evident. A useful starting point is furnished by the following legislation, the origins of which can be traced to the Tribunals and Inquiries Act 1958, which was enacted in the wake of the Franks Report.

Tribunals and Inquiries Act 1992

1—(1) There shall continue to be a council entitled the Council on Tribunals (in this Act referred to as "the Council") . . .

(c) to consider and report on such matters as may be referred to the Council under this Act, or as the Council may determine to be of special importance, with respect to administrative procedures involving, or which may involve, the holding by or on behalf of a Minister of a statutory inquiry, or any such procedure.

9—(1) The Lord Chancellor, after consultation with the Council, may make rules regulating the procedure to be followed in connection with statutory inquiries held by or on behalf of Ministers; and different provision may be made by any such rules in relation to different classes of such inquiries.

(2) Any rules made by the Lord Chancellor under this section shall have effect, in relation to any statutory inquiry, subject to the provisions of the enactment under which the inquiry is held, and of any rules or regulations made under that enactment.

(3) Subject to subsection (2), rules made under this section may regulate procedure in connection with matters preparatory to such statutory inquiries as are mentioned in subsection (1), and in connection with matters subsequent to such inquiries, as well as in connection with the conduct of proceedings at such inquiries.

10—(1) Subject to the provisions of this section and of section 14 [which restricts the application of the Act to certain bodies], where . . .

    (b) any Minister notifies any decision taken by him —

        (i)   after a statutory inquiry has been held by him or on his behalf, or

        (ii) in a case in which a person concerned could (whether by objecting or otherwise) have required a statutory inquiry to be so held,

it shall be the duty of the tribunal or Minister to furnish a statement, either written or oral, of the reasons for the decision if requested, on or before the giving or notification of the decision, to state the reasons.

(2) The statement referred to in subsection (1) may be refused, or the specification of the reasons restricted, on grounds of national security.

(3) A tribunal or Minister may refuse to furnish a statement under subsection (1) to a person not primarily concerned with the decision if of the opinion that to furnish it would be contrary to the interests of any person primarily concerned.

(4) Subsection (1) does not apply to any decision taken by a Minister after the holding by him or on his behalf of an inquiry or hearing which is a statutory inquiry by virtue only of an order made under section 16(2) unless the order contains a direction that this section is to apply in relation to any inquiry or hearing to which the order applies.

(5) Subsection (1) does not apply —

    (a) to decisions in respect of which any statutory provision has effect, apart from this section, as to the giving of reasons,

    (b) to decisions of a Minister in connection with the preparation, making, approval, confirmation, or concurrence in regulations, rules or byelaws, or orders or schemes of a legislative and not executive character . . .

(6) Any statement of the reasons for a decision referred to in paragraph (a) or (b) of subsection (1), whether given in pursuance of that subsection or of any other statutory provision, shall be taken to form part of the decision and accordingly to be incorporated in the record.

(7) If, after consultation with the Council, it appears to the Lord Chancellor that it is expedient that — . . .

    (b) any description of decisions of a Minister,

should be excluded from the operation of subsection (1) on the ground that the subject-matter of such decisions, or the circumstances in which they are made, make the giving of reasons unnecessary or impracticable, the Lord Chancellor may by order direct that subsection (1) shall not apply to such decisions.

(8) Where an order relating to any decisions has been made under subsection (7), the Lord Chancellor may, by a subsequent order made after consultation with the Council, revoke or vary the earlier order so that subsection (1) applies to any of those decisions.

16—(1) In this Act, except where the context otherwise requires . . .
"statutory inquiry" means —

    (a) an inquiry or hearing held or to be held in pursuance of a duty imposed by any statutory provision, or

(b) an inquiry or hearing, or an inquiry or hearing of a class, designated for the purposes of
    this section by an order under subsection (2), and

"statutory provision" means a provision contained in, or having effect under, any enactment.

(2) The Lord Chancellor may by order designate for the purposes of this section any inquiry or
hearing held or to be held in pursuance of a power conferred by any statutory provision specified or
described in the order, or any class of such inquiries or hearings.

A number of important consequences follow from the classification of an inquiry as a
'statutory inquiry' in the s 16 sense. First, in terms of supervision, statutory inquiries fall
within the purview of the Council on Tribunals, although the Council's role is purely
advisory: it can consider and report on, but has no executive power in relation to, inquiries.
Secondly, s 9 provides for the making of rules regulating statutory inquiries, although this
does not go as far as Franks suggested, since it is the Lord Chancellor, not the Council on
Tribunals, who makes such rules; the latter must simply be consulted. Section 9 and its
predecessors have supplied the platform for the implementation of many of the Franks
Committee's more specific recommendations, as we explain in the following sections.
Thirdly, it is incumbent upon Ministers to give reasons for decisions reached following a
statutory inquiry (see below at 18.3.4).

18.3.2 The Right to Know the Opposing Case

The Franks Committee (*op cit* at 62) remarked that, 'Fairness requires that those whose
individual rights and interests are likely to be adversely affected by the action proposed
should know in good time before the enquiry the case which they will have to meet.' The
following rules, which apply to inquiries held in relation to appeals against planning permission decisions and which were enacted under the power conferred by s 9 of the 1992 Act,
seek to address this issue. They are given here as an example of how the right to know the
opposing case is typically delivered in relation to inquiries.

....

Town and Country Planning (Inquiries Procedure) (England) Rules 2000

Preliminary information to be supplied by local planning authority

4—(1) The local planning authority shall, on receipt of the relevant notice, forthwith inform the
Secretary of State and the applicant in writing of the name and address of any statutory party [*ie* a
party whose views the Secretary of State is legally obliged to take into account] who has made
representations to them; and the Secretary of State shall, as soon as practicable thereafter, inform
the applicant and the local planning authority in writing of the name and address of any statutory
party who has made representations to him.

(2) This paragraph applies where —

    (a) the Secretary of State has given to the local planning authority a direction restricting the
        grant of planning permission for which application was made; or

    (b) in a case relating to listed building consent, the [Historic Buildings and Monuments]
        Commission [for England] has given a direction to the local planning authority pursuant to
        section 14 (2) of the Listed Buildings Act as to how the application is to be determined;
        or

    (c) the Secretary of State or any other Minister of the Crown or any government department,
        or any body falling within rule 11(1)(c), has expressed in writing to the local planning

authority the view that the application should not be granted either wholly or in part, or should be granted only subject to conditions; or

(d) any person consulted in pursuance of a development order has made representations to the local planning authority about the application.

(3) Where paragraph (2) applies, the local planning authority shall forthwith after the starting date inform the person concerned of the inquiry and, unless they have already done so, that person shall thereupon give the local planning authority a written statement of the reasons for making the direction, expressing the view or making the representations, as the case may be.

(4) Subject to paragraph (5), the local planning authority shall ensure that within 2 weeks of the starting date —

(a) the Secretary of State and the applicant have received a completed questionnaire and a copy of each of the documents referred to in it;

(b) any —

(i) statutory party; and

(ii) other person who made representations to the local planning authority about the application occasioning the appeal,

has been notified that an appeal has been made and of the address to which and of the period within which they may make representations to the Secretary of State . . .

Procedure where Secretary of State causes pre-inquiry meeting to be held

5—(1) The Secretary of State shall hold a pre-inquiry meeting —

(a) if he expects an inquiry to last for 8 days or more, unless he considers it is unnecessary;

(b) in respect of shorter inquiries, if it appears to him necessary.

(2) Where the Secretary of State decides to hold a pre-inquiry meeting the following provisions shall apply —

(a) the Secretary of State shall send with the relevant notice —

(i) notice of his intention to hold a pre-inquiry meeting;

(ii) a statement of the matters about which he particularly wishes to be informed for the purposes of his consideration of the application or appeal in question and where another Minister of the Crown or a government department has expressed in writing to the Secretary of State a view which is mentioned in rule 4(2)(c), the Secretary of State shall set this out in his statement;

(b) the Secretary of State shall send a copy of the statement described in the previous paragraph to the Minister or government department concerned;

(c) the local planning authority shall publish in a newspaper circulating in the locality in which the land is situated a notice of the Secretary of State's intention to hold a pre-inquiry meeting and of the statement sent in accordance with paragraph (2)(a)(ii) above; and

(d) the applicant and the local planning authority shall ensure that within 8 weeks of the starting date 2 copies of their outline statement have been received by the Secretary of State . . .

(3) The Secretary of State shall, as soon as practicable after receipt, send a copy of the local planning authority's outline statement to the applicant and a copy of the applicant's outline statement to the local planning authority.

Receipt of statements of case etc

6—(1) The local planning authority shall ensure that within —

(a) 6 weeks of the starting date, or

(b) where a pre-inquiry meeting is held pursuant to rule 5, 4 weeks of the conclusion of that pre-inquiry meeting,

2 copies of their statement of case have been received by the Secretary of State and a copy of their statement of case has been received by any statutory party . . .

(3) The applicant shall ensure that within —

    (a) in the case of an appeal or a referred application where no pre-inquiry meeting is held pursuant to rule 5, 6 weeks of the starting date, or

    (b) in any case where a pre-inquiry meeting is held pursuant to rule 5, 4 weeks of the conclusion of that pre-inquiry meeting,

2 copies of their statement of case have been received by the Secretary of State and a copy of their statement of case has been received by any statutory party.

(4) The Secretary of State shall, as soon as practicable after receipt, send a copy of the local planning authority's statement of case to the applicant and a copy of the applicant's statement of case to the local planning authority.

(5) The applicant and the local planning authority may in writing each require the other to send them a copy of any document, or of the relevant part of any document, referred to in the list of documents comprised in the party's statement of case; and any such document, or relevant part, shall be sent, as soon as practicable, to the party who required it.

(6) The Secretary of State may in writing require any other person, who has notified him of an intention or wish to appear at an inquiry, to send —

    (a) 3 copies of their statement of case to him within 4 weeks of being so required; and

    (b) a copy of their statement of case to any statutory party, and the Secretary of State shall, as soon as practicable after receipt, send a copy of each such statement of case to the local planning authority and to the applicant.

(7) The Secretary of State shall as soon as practicable —

    (a) send to a person from whom he requires a statement of case in accordance with paragraph (6) a copy of the statements of case of the applicant and the local planning authority; and

    (b) inform that person of the name and address of every person to whom his statement of case is required to be sent.

(8) The Secretary of State or the inspector may in writing require any person, who has sent to him a statement of case in accordance with this rule, to provide such further information about the matters contained in the statement of case as he may specify and may specify the time within which the information shall be received by him . . .

(12) Unless he has already done so, the Secretary of State shall within 12 weeks of the starting date send a written statement of the matters referred to in rule 5(2)(a)(ii) to —

    (a) the applicant;

    (b) the local planning authority;

    (c) any statutory party; and

    (d) any person from whom he has required a statement of case.

(13) The local planning authority shall afford to any person who so requests a reasonable opportunity to inspect and, where practicable, take copies of —

    (a) any statement of case, written comments, information or other document a copy of which has been sent to the local planning authority in accordance with this rule; and

    (b) the local planning authority's completed questionnaire and statement of case together with a copy of any document, or of the relevant part of any document, referred to in the list comprised in that statement, and any written comments, information or other documents sent by the local planning authority pursuant to this rule . . .

Date and notification of inquiry

10—(1) The date fixed by the Secretary of State for the holding of an inquiry shall be, unless he considers such a date impracticable, not later than —

    (a) Subject to paragraph (b), 22 weeks after the starting date; or

(b) in a case where a pre-inquiry meeting is held pursuant to rule 5, 8 weeks after the conclusion of that meeting.

(2) Where the Secretary of State considers it impracticable to fix a date in accordance with paragraph (1), the date fixed shall be the earliest date after the end of the relevant period mentioned in that paragraph which he considers to be practicable.

(3) Unless the Secretary of State agrees a lesser period of notice with the applicant and the local planning authority, he shall give not less than 4 weeks written notice of the date, time and place fixed by him for the holding of an inquiry to every person entitled to appear at the inquiry . . .

(4) The Secretary of State may vary the date fixed for the holding of an inquiry, whether or not the date as varied is within the relevant period mentioned in paragraph (1) . . .

(5) The Secretary of State may vary the time or place for the holding of an inquiry and shall give such notice of any variation as appears to him to be reasonable.

(6) The Secretary of State may in writing require the local planning authority to take one or more of the following steps —

　　(a) not less than 2 weeks before the date fixed for the holding of an inquiry, to publish a notice of the inquiry in one or more newspapers circulating in the locality in which the land is situated;

　　(b) to send a notice of the inquiry to such persons or classes of persons as he may specify, within such period as he may specify; or

　　(c) to post a notice of the inquiry in a conspicuous place near to the land, within such period as he may specify.

(7) Where the land is under the control of the applicant he shall —

　　(a) if so required in writing by the Secretary of State, affix a notice of the inquiry firmly to the land or to some object on or near the land, in such manner as to be readily visible to and legible by members of the public; and

　　(b) not remove the notice, or cause or permit it to be removed, for such period before the inquiry as the Secretary of State may specify.

(8) Every notice of inquiry published, sent or posted pursuant to paragraph (6), or affixed pursuant to paragraph (7), shall contain —

　　(a) a clear statement of the date, time and place of the inquiry and of the powers enabling the Secretary of State to determine the application or appeal in question;

　　(b) a written description of the land sufficient to identify approximately its location;

　　(c) a brief description of the subject matter of the application or appeal; and

　　(d) details of where and when copies of the local planning authority's completed questionnaire and any documents sent by and copied to the authority pursuant to rule 6 may be inspected.

It can be seen that these rules make detailed provision so as to ensure that the relevant parties are in receipt of one another's cases before the opening of the inquiry. Note, however, that under r 10(3), the minimum four week notice period can be waived by agreement between the applicant, the Secretary of State, and the local planning authority, to the potential detriment of third parties.

18.3.3 Participation and Procedure

We have already noted that one of the difficulties faced by inquiries is the extent to which they should fulfil — and therefore possess the characteristics of — a judicial, as distinct from an administrative, process. This issue bears clearly upon the procedure which applies at the inquiry, and particularly upon the question of participation. In the absence of rules laying down the procedure to be adopted at an inquiry, the principle of procedural fairness (see ch 11) applies, although in *Bushell* v. *Secretary of State for the Environment* [1981] AC 75 at 95 Lord Diplock cautioned against the unthinking adoption in this context of 'concepts that are appropriate to the conduct of ordinary civil litigation between private parties', preferring to state that an inquiry must be 'be fair to all those who have an interest in the decision that will follow it', but that what constitutes a fair procedure 'will depend upon the nature of its subject matter'. Usually, however, specific provision as to the procedure is made in the relevant legislation.

Town and Country Planning (Inquiries Procedure) (England) Rules 2000

Appearances at inquiry

11—(1) The persons entitled to appear at an inquiry are —
  (a) the applicant;
  (b) the local planning authority;
  (c) any of the following bodies if the land is situated in their area and they are not the local planning authority —
    (i) a county or district council;
    (ii) an enterprise zone authority designated under Schedule 32 to the Local Government, Planning and Land Act 1980;
    (iii) the Broads Authority, within the meaning of the Norfolk and Suffolk Broads Act 1988;
    (iv) a housing action trust specified in an order made under section 67(1) of the Housing Act 1988;
  (d) where the land is in an area previously designated as a new town, the Commission for the New Towns;
  (e) any statutory party [*ie* a party whose views the Secretary of State is legally obliged to take into account];
  (f) the council of the parish in which the land is situated, if that council made representations to the local planning authority in respect of the application in pursuance of a provision of a development order;
  (g) where the application was required to be notified to the Commission under section 14 of the Listed Buildings Act, the [Historic Buildings and Monuments] Commission [for England];
  (h) any other person who has sent a statement of case in accordance with rule 6(6) or who has sent an outline statement in accordance with rule 5(5).
  (2) Nothing in paragraph (1) shall prevent the inspector from permitting any other person to appear at an inquiry, and such permission shall not be unreasonably withheld.
  (3) Any person entitled or permitted to appear may do so on his own behalf or be represented by any other person.

Representatives of government departments and other authorities at inquiry

12—(1) Where —
  (a) the Secretary of State or the Commission has given a direction described in rule 4(2)(a) or (b); or
  (b) the Secretary of State or any other Minister of the Crown or any government department, or any body falling within rule 11(1)(c), has expressed a view described in rule 4(2)(c) and the local planning authority have included the terms of the expression of view in a statement sent in accordance with rule 5(2) or 6(1); or

(c) another Minister of the Crown or any government department has expressed a view described in rule 4(2)(c) and the Secretary of State has included its terms in a statement sent in accordance with rule 5(2) or 6(12),

the applicant, the local planning authority or a person entitled to appear may, not later than 4 weeks before the date of an inquiry, apply in writing to the Secretary of State for a representative of the Secretary of State or of the other Minister, department or body concerned to be made available at the inquiry.

(2) Where an application is made in accordance with paragraph (1), the Secretary of State shall make a representative available to attend the inquiry or, as the case may be, send the application to the other Minister, department or body concerned, who shall make a representative available to attend the inquiry.

(3) Any person attending an inquiry as a representative in pursuance of this rule shall state the reasons for the direction or expressed view and shall give evidence and be subject to cross-examination to the same extent as any other witness.

(4) Nothing in paragraph (3) shall require a representative of a Minister or a government department to answer any question which in the opinion of the inspector is directed to the merits of government policy.

Proofs of evidence

13—(1) Any person entitled to appear at an inquiry, who proposes to give, or to call another person to give evidence at the inquiry by reading a proof of evidence, shall —

(a) send 2 copies, in the case of the local planning authority and the applicant, or 3 copies in the case of any other person, of the proof of evidence together with any written summary, to the Secretary of State; and

(b) simultaneously send copies of these to any statutory party, and the Secretary of State shall, as soon as practicable after receipt, send a copy of each proof of evidence together with any summary to the local planning authority and the applicant . . .

(3) The proof of evidence and any summary shall be received by the Secretary of State no later than —

(a) 4 weeks before the date fixed for the holding of the inquiry, or

(b) where a timetable has been arranged pursuant to rule 8 which specifies a date by which the proof of evidence and any summary shall be received by the Secretary of State, that date.

(4) The Secretary of State shall send to the inspector, as soon as practicable after receipt, any proof of evidence together with any summary sent to him in accordance with this rule and received by him within the relevant period, if any specified in this rule.

(5) Where a written summary is provided in accordance with paragraph (1), only that summary shall be read at the inquiry, unless the inspector permits or requires otherwise.

(6) Any person, required by this rule to send copies of a proof of evidence to the Secretary of State, shall send with them the same number of copies of the whole, or the relevant part, of any document referred to in the proof of evidence, unless a copy of the document or part of the document in question is already available for inspection pursuant to rule 6(13).

(7) The local planning authority shall afford to any person who so requests a reasonable opportunity to inspect and, where practicable, take copies of any document sent to or by them in accordance with this rule.

Statement of common ground

14—(1) The local planning authority and the applicant shall —

(a) together prepare an agreed statement of common ground; and

(b) ensure that the Secretary of State receives it and that any statutory party receives a copy of it not less than 4 weeks before the date fixed for the holding of the inquiry.

(2) The local planning authority shall afford to any person who so requests, a reasonable opportunity to inspect, and where practicable, take copies of the statement of common ground sent to the Secretary of State.

Procedure at inquiry

15—(1) Except as otherwise provided in these Rules, the inspector shall determine the procedure at an inquiry.

(2) At the start of the inquiry the inspector shall identify what are, in his opinion, the main issues to be considered at the inquiry and any matters on which he requires further explanation from the persons entitled or permitted to appear.

(3) Nothing in paragraph (2) shall preclude any person entitled or permitted to appear from referring to issues which they consider relevant to the consideration of the application or appeal but which were not issues identified by the inspector pursuant to that paragraph.

(4) Unless in any particular case the inspector otherwise determines, the local planning authority shall begin and the applicant shall have the right of final reply; and the other persons entitled or permitted to appear shall be heard in such order as the inspector may determine.

(5) A person entitled to appear at an inquiry shall be entitled to call evidence and the applicant, the local planning authority and any statutory party shall be entitled to cross-examine persons giving evidence, but, subject to the foregoing and paragraphs (6) and (7), the calling of evidence and the cross-examination of persons giving evidence shall otherwise be at the discretion of the inspector.

(6) The inspector may refuse to permit the —
  (a) giving or production of evidence;
  (b) cross-examination of persons giving evidence; or
  (c) presentation of any other matter,
which he considers to be irrelevant or repetitious; but where he refuses to permit the giving of oral evidence, the person wishing to give the evidence may submit to him any evidence or other matter in writing before the close of the inquiry . . .

(8) The inspector may direct that facilities shall be afforded to any person appearing at an inquiry to take or obtain copies of documentary evidence open to public inspection.

(9) The inspector may —
  (a) require any person appearing or present at an inquiry who, in his opinion, is behaving in a disruptive manner to leave; and
  (b) refuse to permit that person to return; or
  (c) permit him to return only on such conditions as he may specify,
but any such person may submit to him any evidence or other matter in writing before the close of the inquiry.

(10) The inspector may allow any person to alter or add to a statement of case received by the Secretary of State or him under rule 6 so far as may be necessary for the purposes of the inquiry; but he shall (if necessary by adjourning the inquiry) give every other person entitled to appear who is appearing at the inquiry an adequate opportunity of considering any fresh matter or document.

(11) The inspector may proceed with an inquiry in the absence of any person entitled to appear at it.

(12) The inspector may take into account any written representation or evidence or any other document received by him from any person before an inquiry opens or during the inquiry provided that he discloses it at the inquiry.

(13) The inspector may from time to time adjourn an inquiry . . .

Site inspections

16—(1) The inspector may make an unaccompanied inspection of the land before or during an inquiry without giving notice of his intention to the persons entitled to appear at the inquiry.

(2) During an inquiry or after its close, the inspector —

(a) may inspect the land in the company of the applicant, the local planning authority and any statutory party; and

(b) shall make such an inspection if so requested by the applicant or the local planning authority before or during an inquiry . . .

These rules form a detailed code for the implementation of procedural fairness in the context of planning inquiries, and reflect many of the recommendations made by the Franks Committee. Three issues arising from these rules merit comment.

First, r 11(1), like the procedural rules governing public inquiries in many other contexts, confers a legal right to appear upon only a limited class of parties. This appears to conflict with notion of a 'public' inquiry which, as Lord Moulton observed in *Local Government Board* v. *Arlidge* [1915] AC 120 at 147–148, seems to imply unrestricted participation. In theory, procedural rules which permit only limited participation may be *ultra vires* parent Acts providing for the holding of 'public' inquiries. In practice, however, inspectors tend generously to exercise discretion such as that conferred by r 11(2) to permit the participation of parties not legally *entitled* to appear.

Secondly, while r 15(1) confers discretion upon the inspector to determine procedure at the inquiry, this discretion is of course bounded both by the rules themselves and by general principles of administrative law. It follows that discretionary power such as that conferred by r 15(6) is not unfettered: in *R* v. *Secretary of State for the Environment, ex parte the Royal Borough of Kensington and Chelsea* (1987) 19 HLR 161 at 172, Taylor J held that, although the inspector at an inquiry into proposed compulsory purchase of property was empowered by the relevant rules to determine the procedure at the inquiry, 'Totally to exclude evidence on whole issues which are, or may be, relevant is tantamount . . . to declining jurisdiction . . . [By doing so,] it follows that [the inspector] has not exercised his discretion in accordance with the law.'

Thirdly, what procedures are necessary to satisfy the requirements of fairness is fundamentally affected by the scope of the inquiry — a proposition demonstrated by the case of *Bushell* v. *Secretary of State for the Environment* [1981] AC 75. An excerpt from that case appears above at 11.3.3, where we note that contrasting judicial views about the nature and degree of fairness required in relation to the inquiry in question may be traced to divergent perceptions of public inquiries.

QUESTIONS

• Look again at the excerpts from *Bushell* above at 11.3.3. Do you prefer Lord Diplock's narrower approach to fairness in this context, or Lord Edmund-Davies's broader approach?
• Why?

18.3.4 Procedure Following the Inquiry

We saw above that Lord Hewart identified the opaqueness of the inquiry system — in particular, the non-publication of inspectors' reports and ministerial decisions which had little obvious regard to inspectors' recommendations — as one of the major reasons for dissatisfaction with it. In light of these concerns, the Franks Committee suggested that reports should be published and that Ministers should give reasons for decisions reached following inquiries.

Town and Country Planning (Inquiries Procedure) (England) Rules 2000

Procedure after inquiry

17—(1) After the close of an inquiry, the inspector shall make a report in writing to the Secretary of State which shall include his conclusions and his recommendations or his reasons for not making any recommendations . . .

Notification of decision

18—(1) The Secretary of State shall, as soon as practicable, notify his decision on an application or appeal, and his reasons for it in writing to —

   (a) all persons entitled to appear at the inquiry who did appear, and
   (b) any other person who, having appeared at the inquiry, has asked to be notified of the decision . . .

(2) Where a copy of the inspector's report is not sent with the notification of the decision, the notification shall be accompanied by a statement of his conclusion and of any recommendations made by him, and if a person entitled to be notified of the decision has not received a copy of that report, he shall be supplied with a copy of it on written application to the Secretary of State.

(3) In this rule "report" includes any assessor's report appended to the inspector's report but does not include any other documents so appended; but any person who has received a copy of the report may apply to the Secretary of State in writing, within 6 weeks of the date of the Secretary of State's decision, for an opportunity of inspecting any such documents and the Secretary of State shall afford him that opportunity.

Although these rules, like many other sets of rules governing inquiries, do not require inspectors' reports to be released to the general public, it has been general practice for some time to make such reports available, and they are now released under s 19 of the Freedom of Information Act 2000. As to reasons, s 10(1) of the Tribunals and Inquiries Act 1992 (see above at 18.3.1) requires Ministers to give reasons, on request, for decisions taken following statutory inquiries; r 18(1) goes further, requiring reasons to be given irrespective of whether they are requested. This goes some way towards meeting Lord Hewart's criticism that the effect of inquiries upon Ministers is 'in practice nugatory', since the discipline of reason-giving now forces decision-makers demonstrably to confront the evidence gathered at the inquiry and the inspector's recommendations. Exactly what constitutes adequate reasons (on which see generally above at 12.5) depends on the circumstances: the House of Lords unanimously agreed in *Save Britain's Heritage* v. *Number 1 Poultry Ltd* [1991] 1 WLR 153 that the Secretary of State's statement of reasons could be read together with the reasoning of the inspector, so that the inadequacy of the former may sometimes be cured by the sufficiency of the latter.

A further issue which requires discussion is that of extrinsic evidence. When the Minister (typically after the inquiry has closed) considers, or is invited to consider, additional evidence, difficulties arise, since parties whose interests are affected by evidence submitted outwith the inquiry do not necessarily have an opportunity to respond to it. The following rules are typical of those which seek to address this problem.

Town and Country Planning (Inquiries Procedure) (England) Rules 2000

Procedure after inquiry

17—(4) When making his decision the Secretary of State may disregard any written representations, evidence or any other document received after the close of the inquiry.

(5) If, after the close of an inquiry, the Secretary of State —

    (a) differs from the inspector on any matter of fact mentioned in, or appearing to him to be material to, a conclusion reached by the inspector; or

    (b) takes into consideration any new evidence or new matter of fact (not being a matter of government policy),

and is for that reason disposed to disagree with a recommendation made by the inspector, he shall not come to a decision which is at variance with that recommendation without first notifying the persons entitled to appear at the inquiry who appeared at it of his disagreement and the reasons for it; and affording them an opportunity of making written representations to him or (if the Secretary of State has taken into consideration any new evidence or new matter of fact, not being a matter of government policy) of asking for the reopening of the inquiry . . .

(7) The Secretary of State may, as he thinks fit, cause an inquiry to be re- opened, and he shall do so if asked by the applicant or the local planning authority in the circumstances mentioned in paragraph (5) . . .

The present procedural rules are largely the result of the criticism by the Council on Tribunals (Annual Report for 1963, Appendix A) of the 'Chalkpit inquiry' of 1961 (see *Buxton v. Minister of Housing and Local Government* [1961] 1 QB 278) in which the Minister allowed an appeal against a refusal of planning permission, notwithstanding the inspector's contrary recommendation. The latter was based on a risk of damage to adjoining land and livestock from the proposed use, yet the Minister's decision took account of evidence from another government department which suggested ways of minimizing the risk that had not been before the inquiry and upon which the objectors had had no opportunity of commenting. Although there are now rules covering this matter, the following excerpt — concerning the Town and Country Planning (Inquiries Procedure) Rules 1965, r 12(2) of which was identical in all material respects to r 17(5) of the Rules of 2000, set out above — demonstrates that their application is not without difficulty.

....

Lord Luke of Pavenham v. *Minister of Housing and Local Government* [1968] 1 QB 172
Court of Appeal

The facts are stated in Lord Denning MR's judgment.

Lord Denning MR

There is a small village in Bedfordshire called Pavenham. There used to be a mansion house there, but it has been demolished and is being replaced by other houses. On the other side of the road there is an old walled garden. It used to be the kitchen garden of the mansion house. It is about one acre in extent. It is owned by the applicant, Lord Luke, and he seeks permission to build a house there. The local planning authority refused permission for this reason:

> "The proposal would constitute an undesirable form of isolated and sporadic development outside the limits of the village of Pavenham in an area where no further development should be permitted other than that which is essential for agricultural purposes." . . .

Lord Luke appealed to the Minister under section 23 of the Town and Country Planning Act, 1962. The Minister appointed an inspector to hold an inquiry. It was held. The inspector made his report. He recommended that permission be granted. The Minister, however, disagreed with the inspector's recommendation. The Minister thought that Lord Luke's proposal was undesirable. He, therefore, confirmed the decision of the local planning authority and dismissed the appeal.

Prima facie the decision of the Minister was final: see section 23 (5) of the Act of 1962. But it was open to Lord Luke to question the Minister's decision if he could show that any of the relevant requirements [of the Act] had not been complied with: see section 179 (1) of the Act of 1962. Lord Luke did question the validity of the Minister's decision. He said that the relevant requirements had not been complied with in that the Minister had differed from the inspector on findings of fact, and that the Minister ought to have notified him (Lord Luke) of the difference and given him an opportunity of making representations to him: and had not done so. Lawton J [[1968] 1 QB 172 at 184] upheld this contention and quashed the Minister's decision. The Minister appeals to this court.

[Lord Denning then referred to r 12(2) of the 1965 Rules, and to the inspector's report and the Minister's decision letter, and continued:] Did the Minister differ from the inspector on a finding of fact? In answering this question it is essential to draw a distinction between findings of fact by the inspector and an expression of opinion by him on the planning merits. If the Minister differs from the inspector on a finding of fact, he must notify the applicant, in accordance with the rules, before coming to his decision. But if the Minister differs from the inspector on the planning merits, he can announce his decision straight away without notifying the applicant beforehand.

In the present case the inspector has divided his report into sections headed: "Findings of fact," "Inspector's conclusions" and "Recommendations." But I do not think this division is sacrosanct. We must look into them and see which of his findings are truly findings of fact and which are expressions of opinion on planning merits. All the findings which are headed "Findings of fact" numbered (1) to (12) are undoubtedly findings of fact. So also the finding (13), which states the intention of the planning authority. The inspector's "Conclusions" in paragraph (39) are partly findings of fact and partly expressions of opinion. The inspector stated a finding of fact when he said:

"The site is exceptional in that it is clearly defined by a tall and fine-looking wall and forms part of a long-established group of buildings which contribute to the attractive character of the village independent of distance."

The inspector expressed his opinion on planning merits when he said:

"A well-designed house within the walled garden would, far from harming the countryside, add to the existing charm of its setting and could not be said to create a precedent for allowing development on farmland to the north or south."

Now turning to the Minister's decision letter, the question is whether he differed from the inspector on a finding of fact. The decision letter is not happily expressed. The Minister said that he was unable to agree with the "conclusions" drawn by the inspector . . . I think the Minister's difference was only on the second sentence that "a well-designed house would," etc. He was differing from that expression of opinion by the inspector. The Minister took the view that a house would be "sporadic development" which would harm the countryside. That was a difference of opinion on a planning matter. The Minister was entitled to come to a different conclusion on such a matter without the necessity of notifying Lord Luke, or giving him an opportunity of making representations.

I must say that I have considerable sympathy with Lord Luke. The inspector's report was very much in his favour. But it must be remembered that the Minister has the responsibility for planning policy. In order to preserve our countryside he has adopted a policy of setting out an "envelope" for each village. Development is permitted within the "envelope" and not outside it. If one person is allowed to build outside, it will be difficult to refuse his neighbour. So the Minister must be strict. This is planning policy, and nothing else. The courts have no authority to interfere with the way the Minister carries it out.

I do not think the Minister was in breach of the relevant requirements. I would, therefore, allow this appeal and restore the Minister's decision.

Davies and Russell LJJ delivered judgments in favour of allowing the appeal. The appeal was therefore allowed.

As well as drawing the distinction between matters of fact and opinion for which the rules obviously call, the courts have held that the source from which evidence extrinsic to the inquiry emanates is relevant to the legitimacy of taking such information into account.

....

Bushell v. *Secretary of State for the Environment* [1981] AC 75
House of Lords

The facts are stated in the excerpt above at 11.3.3, which concerns the respondent objectors' argument that they should have been allowed to cross-examine on the reliability of departmental forecasts of traffic growth. After the inquiry had closed, the department revised its method of calculation, discovered that the capacity of existing roads was much larger than had been thought, and accordingly revised its method of forecasting. The objectors applied to have the inquiry re-opened to investigate the revised method of forecasting. The Secretary of State refused this application, saying that he would consider any further representations as to need as part of the continuous consideration of any of the department's proposals and that, if the new information led him to disagree with the inspector's recommendations, the objectors would be given an opportunity to comment on it. In his decision he said that he had taken account of the general changes in design flow standards and traffic forecasts since the inquiry and was satisfied that they did not materially affect the evidence which was the basis of the inspector's recommendation. He accepted the recommendation and made the schemes.

Lord Diplock

. . . The respondents claim that it was a denial of natural justice to them on the Minister's part not to reopen the local inquiry so as to give to objectors an opportunity of criticising these revised methods of assessment, cross-examining the department's representatives about them and advancing arguments as to the strength they added to the objectors' case . . .

My Lords, in the analysis by Lord Greene M.R. in *B Johnson & Co (Builders) Ltd.* v. *Minister of Health* [1947] 2 All E.R. 395 at 399–400 of the common case in which a Minister's functions are to confirm, modify or reject a scheme prepared and promoted by a local authority, it is pointed out that the Minister's ultimate decision is a purely administrative one. It is only at one stage in the course of arriving at his decision that there is imposed on his administrative character a character loosely described as being quasi-judicial; and that is: when he is considering the respective representations of the promoting authority and of the objectors made at the local inquiry and the report of the inspector upon them. In doing this he must act fairly as between the promoting authority and the objectors; after the inquiry has closed he must not hear one side without letting the other know; he must not accept from third parties fresh evidence which supports one side's case without giving the other side an opportunity to answer it. But when he comes to reach his decision, what he does bears little resemblance to adjudicating on a lis between the parties represented at the inquiry. Upon the substantive matter, viz., whether the scheme should be confirmed or not, there is a third party who was not represented at the inquiry, the general public as a whole whose interests it is the Minister's duty to treat as paramount. No one could reasonably suggest that as part of the decision-making process after receipt of the report the Minister ought not to consult with the officials of his department and obtain from them the best informed advice he can to enable him to form a balanced judgment on the strength of the objections and merits of the scheme in the interests of the public as a whole, or that he was bound to communicate the departmental advice that he received to the promoting authority and the objectors.

If the analogy of a lis inter partes be a false analogy even where the scheme which is the subject of the local inquiry is not a departmental scheme but one of which a public authority other than the Minister is the originator, the analogy is even farther from reflecting the essentially administrative nature of the Minister's functions when, having considered in the light of the advice of his department the objections which have been the subject of a local inquiry and the report of the inspector, he makes his decision in a case where the scheme is one that has been prepared by his own department itself and which it is for him in his capacity as head of that department to decide whether it is in the general public interest that it should be made or not. Once he has reached his decision he must be prepared to disclose his reasons for it, because the Tribunals and Inquiries Act 1971 [see now the Tribunals and Inquiries Act 1992] so requires; but he is, in my view, under no obligation to disclose to objectors and give them an opportunity of commenting on advice, expert or otherwise, which he receives from his department in the course of making up his mind. If he thinks that to do so will be helpful to him in reaching the right decision in the public interest he may, of course, do so; but if he does not think it will be helpful — and this is for him to decide — failure to do so cannot in my view be treated as a denial of natural justice to the objectors . . .

The effect of *Bushell* on this point is uncertain. Lord Diplock's view that advice given by the relevant department (unlike expert evidence from outside the department) does not have to be communicated to the objectors could undermine the progress made by the Council on Tribunals after the Chalkpit case unless a narrow view is taken of 'advice'. The authority of the case on this issue is unclear because the objectors in fact had a chance to comment on the new material and Viscount Dilhorne and Lord Lane appeared to base their conclusion on this aspect of the case on this point.

18.4 *Ad hoc* Inquiries

18.4.1 Introduction

As well serving to enhance the effectiveness of routine administrative decision-making processes, inquiries also play an important part in the investigation of actual or perceived problems such as alleged impropriety and incompetence, accidents, and disasters. The Lord Chancellor, in the course of giving evidence to the Public Administration Select Committee ('PASC') (see HC606-ii, *Government by Inquiry: Minutes of Evidence* (2003–2004)), said that the government considers it appropriate to hold such an inquiry

where you need a dispassionate, objective independent view of a set of circumstances where there is public disquiet or concern, with a view to there being a clear and definitive account of what happened, and also to make any recommendations that are required and, if necessary, to effect changes in policy.

The prominence of such inquiries as those of Sir Richard Scott into the 'arms to Iraq' affair (HC115, *Inquiry into the Export of Defence Equipment and Dual-Use Goods to Iraq and Related Prosecutions* (1995–1996); see generally Oliver [1996] PL 357), of Lord Saville into the events of Bloody Sunday (expected to report in summer 2005; see Hadfield [1999] PL 661 for discussion) and of Lord Hutton into the death of the government weapons expert Dr David Kelly (HC247, *Report of the Inquiry into the Circumstances Surrounding the Death of*

Dr David Kelly CMG (2003–2004); see Blom-Cooper and Munro [2004] *PL* 472) underline the central role of the inquiry as a method for investigating matters of public concern in an era which, according to O'Neill, *A Question of Trust* (Cambridge 2002), is characterized by a crisis of trust in public institutions.

The precise role and function of such inquiries is highly variable. In some cases, such as the Bichard Inquiry into child protection procedures following the Soham murders, very specific recommendations are made by the inquiry; indeed, when Bichard reported, he announced his intention to reconvene his Inquiry in 2005, in order to assess progress on the implementation of his recommendations. In other instances, the importance of the inquiry may be seen to lie simply in establishing what happened, and why. Speaking to the PASC (HC606-vi, *Minutes of Evidence* (2004–2005)) about his Review of Intelligence on Weapons of Mass Destruction, Lord Butler explained that his main purpose (as he saw it) was to 'tell the story':

. . . [W]e did try to give a full account of how the policy developed, how the decision came to be taken, but having given a full account of those facts, we left it to Parliament and the public to draw their conclusions about it.

The ways in which *ad hoc* inquiries are presently constituted vary dramatically: Blom-Cooper [1993] *CLP* 204 at 208 refers to 'a bewildering variety of statutory and non-statutory inquiries under ministerial or local government aegis, each one adopting different techniques suitable to the topic under scrutiny'. Many individual pieces of legislation — *eg* the Mental Health Act 1983 (see s 125) and the Transport Act 1962 (see s 90) — presently provide for the setting up of inquiries into matters arising under them, while the Tribunals of Inquiry (Evidence) Act 1921 provides a general statutory basis for establishing (upon resolution of both Houses of Parliament) an inquiry into matters of urgent public importance. However, the government considers that neither of these approaches is ideal. The Department for Constitutional Affairs noted in its paper *Effective Inquiries* (2004) ('the DCA consultation paper') at [62] that

subject-specific legislation does not cover all areas where inquiries might be needed. Recent inquiries have not always fitted easily into the range of statutory options offered by the subject-specific legislation — in some cases, because there is no legislation covering the particular subject of the inquiry, in others, because the inquiry ranges across more than one subject or Government Departmental remit.

Although the 1921 Act is not limited in this way, it is rarely used — a phenomenon that may be explained by the government's perception that it is 'intended only for the most substantial inquiries' (*ibid* at [61]) and the fact such inquiries can be established only following resolutions of both Houses of Parliament (as opposed to a simple Ministerial decision). In addition to these (actual or perceived) problems relating to the use of the 1921 Act and of specific powers in other legislation, the government argues (*ibid* at [58]) that informal, non-statutory inquiries often allow for a more flexible and 'streamlined' (and cheaper) approach. As a result, many recent prominent inquiries that could have been established on a statutory basis — *eg* Hutton (which concerned matters that might have been the subject of a 1921 Act inquiry) and Bichard (which could have been established under s 49 of the Police Act 1996) — were in fact constituted informally. Although they therefore lacked the legal powers of statutory inquiries to require the attendance of witnesses, examine them on oath, compel the production of documents, and so on, in practice this did not appear to present a problem. However, while it is beneficial if inquiries can be conducted in a spirit of co-operation, it is likely, as the government has noted (*ibid* at [65]–[67]), that there will be occasions on which that spirit is lacking; there is therefore a strong case for making legal powers available to inquiries, even if their use is only rarely required.

It is against this background that new legislation has been proposed. At the time of writing, an Inquiries Bill is before Parliament. If enacted, it will replace many existing statutory powers to hold inquiries — including the 1921 Act and certain powers in subject-specific legislation — with a general Ministerial power to establish inquiries into matters of public concern. The Bill is intended to address the problems outlined above by establishing a general (as opposed to subject-specific) power to establish inquiries, with legal powers, into matters of public concern, without any requirement (such as that which presently exists under the 1921 Act) to secure parliamentary assent. Although the possibility of informal, non-statutory inquiries would remain, it is anticipated that, under the Bill, statutory inquiries would be a more attractive proposition than at present, such that their use would increase, with a commensurate reduction in recourse to non-statutory alternatives.

Ministers presently enjoy considerable discretion concerning such matters as whether an inquiry should be held and, if so, what form it should take. The government argues (see DCA consultation paper at [17]–[18]) that this allows for appropriate flexibility. However, some writers (*eg* Steele [2004] *PL* 738 at 744–745) question whether the degree of flexibility presently enjoyed by the government in this context is too great. Looked at in one way, the possibility that Ministers could make decisions in this sphere — *eg* whether to hold an inquiry, what its terms of reference should be, and who should conduct it — under the influence of political considerations may be a cause for concern. However, it must be remembered that inquiries of the type presently under discussion form part of the *political* process; it is a function of this that Ministers, in exercising their discretion, could be influenced by such political factors as the intensity of public feeling on the matter in question, the likely political costs of (on the one hand) acceding to demands for an inquiry and (on the other hand) resisting such demands, and so on. As Sir Louis Blom-Cooper put it, speaking to the PASC (HC51-i, *Minutes of Evidence* (2004–2005)) on the subject of when public inquiries should be established, '[I]f there is a national scandal or a national disaster and public opinion will only be allayed by having an independent inquiry, then that should satisfy the criteria for setting it up. I do not think you can go further than that.' Indeed, the Department for Constitutional Affairs, as part of its consultation on inquiries, found that there was a general consensus that decisions whether to hold inquiries should be taken by Ministers (see *Effective Inquiries: Response to Consultation* (London 2004) at 7–8). There was, however, greater diversity of opinion (see *ibid* at 9–12) on such matters as inquiries' terms of reference (with some consultees advocating a duty to consult the inquiry chairman, or more widely) and the appointment of inquiry chairmen and panels (with some consultees arguing for an independent appointments body or parliamentary involvement in the appointments process).

Wide Ministerial discretion in this arena would be largely perpetuated by the Inquiries Bill. For example, the appointment of the chairman and of any other members of the inquiry panel would be a matter for the Minister, as would the setting of the terms of reference. Moreover, the relevant Minister would have a very broad discretion to terminate inquiries, as well as power to cut off funding where he believes that an inquiry is acting, or is likely to act, outwith its terms of reference. However, a number of amendments (to which the government consented) were made in the House of Lords, making consultation with the inquiry chairman a condition precedent to the exercise of many of these powers.

18.4.2 The Role of Judges in Public Inquiries

The following excerpt indicates some of the reasons why politicians may choose to hold inquiries — and why they may ask judges to preside over them.

....

Drewry, 'Judicial Inquiries and Public Reassurance' [1996] PL 368

[The author begins by quoting the following passage from an article by Marr, "Behold the Backlash, Sabres Drawn", *The Independent*, 8 June 1995]:

> "As it became clear that Parliament seemed to have been misled [over the 'arms to Iraq' affair], Mr Major [the then Prime Minister] ordered in a judge. He wanted a tough judge, for a very good reason. The administration was so lacking in authority that it was protecting itself, for the time being, with the borrowed authority of Lord Justice Scott. The tougher the judge, the stronger the shield. The judge, in return, would be given a wide remit to investigate what had gone wrong . . ."

In this notion of borrowed authority lies the main explanation for the frequent choice of senior judges . . . to chair major inquiries into political scandals, major public calamities and crises of regime-legitimacy. There are other explanations, too — in particular, a recognition of the professional expertise of judges in conducting hearings, sifting through mountains of evidence and appraising the veracity of witnesses — but the present discussion will be confined to examining the implications of the deployment by politicians of the judges' status and credibility to diffuse matters which those politicians feel they can neither safely ignore nor tackle by normal political and parliamentary methods.

British judges have often been pilloried, especially by left-wing politicians and by feminists and spokesmen for minority groups (these categories are not of course mutually exclusive) as an unrepresentative establishment clique of white middle-class males. But they are also widely recognised, even, albeit grudgingly, by some such critics, as possessing a unique combination of professional skills; and a more positive interpretation of the judges' perceived isolation from the life experiences of mere mortals is that they also display a certain lofty detachment from the rough and tumble of party politics. Herein lies the rationale of judicial inquiries . . .

The concept of "borrowed authority", mentioned earlier resonates with a widely held notion that that there is a qualitative difference, and a functional separation, between law and politics. The Harvard political scientist, Judith Shklar, suggests that this perceived separateness has an ideological basis, rooted in the concept of "legalism". Proponents of legalism, she claims, not only emphasise the inherent differences between law and politics but believe also that features of the legal process such as rule-following and the pursuit of certainty and consistency are positive ends in themselves and render law a superior commodity to politics. [Drewry then sets out the following passage from Shklar, *Legalism* (Cambridge, Mass 1964) at 111:]

> "There appears to be virtually unanimous agreement that law and politics must be kept apart as much as possible in theory no less than in practice. The divorce of law from politics is, to be sure, designed to prevent arbitrariness, and that is why there is so little argument about its necessity. However, ideologically, legalism does not stop there. Politics is regarded not only as something apart from law, but as inferior to law. Law aims at justice, while politics looks only to expediency. The former is neutral and objective, the latter the uncontrolled child of competing ideologies."

The ambivalence of our "legalistic" adherence to the separateness of law and politics is apparent in the eagerness of British politicians to exploit the apolitical credentials of the judges (and image which the judges themselves are anxious to preserve) by employing them as members and chairmen of official inquiries. In particular, whenever something happens that gives rise to a crisis of public confidence, there are calls from all sides for an independent inquiry, to be presided over by the comfortingly apolitical figure of a judge . . .

Drewry is ultimately ambivalent about the appropriateness of judicial inquiries, finding cause for reassurance in the fact that the Scott Inquiry was discomfiting to senior politicians and opened up (at least transiently) 'some of the secret places of an opaque government machine' — something which, more recently, the Hutton Inquiry notably achieved; but cause for concern, too, in the ability of crisis-beset administrations to use such inquiries to their advantage.

Whether it is appropriate to involve judges in public inquiries remains a controversial issue — although not for the government which, according to the DCA consultation paper (at [46]), believes

that it can be appropriate for judges to chair inquiries, because their experience and position make them particularly well suited to the role. The judiciary has a great deal of experience in analysing evidence, determining facts and reaching conclusions, albeit in an adversarial rather than inquisitorial context. The judiciary also has a long tradition of independence from politics, and judges are widely accepted to be free from any party political bias.

For Jowell (*The Guardian*, 3 February 2004), however, pointing to these judicial attributes rather misses the point:

It is true that judges possess special expertise in analysing evidence, assessing the credibility of witnesses, and resolving complex questions of fact. However, this skill is largely confined to the context of a particular set of circumstances, namely, those which surround the issues of guilt and liability. Did A kill B? Was X liable for damage to Y? These "yes-no" or "either-or" questions are grist to the judicial mill. And they are determined not in a vacuum, but with the guidance of principle derived from similar previous cases. Political controversies, however narrowly confined, normally involve a wider set of relevant issues than are found in the typical murder trial, and a different set of principles to those found in the law reports.

Jowell goes on to argue that the Hutton Inquiry was substantially undermined by Lord Hutton's tendency to 'confine his attentions to the cut-and-dried matters of personal liability and to avoid the wider political ramifications of his decision'. Blom-Cooper and Drewry [2004] *PL* 472 at 476 also consider that Hutton has raised fresh questions in this area:

Perhaps it might be said that the [Hutton] Report reflected absolutely Lord Hutton's qualities as a judge, meticulous and superb in the analysis of details and evidence, but more evidently questionable on matters of wider judgment . . . [T]here is . . . room to doubt whether a Law Lord's "borrowed authority" should have been lent to such an inquiry as this. When its subject-matter is considered, the Hutton Inquiry may represent the classic instance of why we should question the public's ready acceptance of asking a senior judge to hold a public inquiry.

Beatson, giving the 51st Lionel Cohen Lecture, has also expressed concern about the use of the judiciary in this context, noting various arguments to the effect that judges' involvement in inquiries may compromise their independence, actual or perceived. First, 'The involvement of a judge will not depoliticise an inherently controversial matter, and it is a mistake to raise false expectations that it will do so. Political issues cannot be resolved by the application of judicial standards and court-like procedures.' Secondly, those who are dissatisfied with the report or with the inquiry's terms of reference may seek to discredit the inquiry by criticizing the judge. Thirdly, government control over such matters as the choice of judge and determination of the inquiry's terms of reference may impact upon judicial independence. Fourthly, the existence of judicial discretion over the procedure in inquiries — a phenomenon (considered at 18.4.3 below) which contrasts with the clear procedural framework in which court proceedings occur — may lead some witnesses to feel that they were treated unfairly; such perceived deficiencies, notes Beatson, 'will follow a judge back to the Bench'. Finally, increasing recourse to judicial review of decisions taken by those chairing inquiries may be said to 'damage the perception that the judge conducting an inquiry so challenged is impartial or that the process is fair'. Although Beatson concludes that, individually, these concerns may be answered, he cautions that, cumulatively, they may have force. He therefore urges that judges should be asked to lead inquiries with a strong political flavour only where 'the matter is of vital public importance, and where there is really no alternative'. He further argues that government should not enjoy uninhibited freedom to choose the judge who is to conduct the inquiry or determine its terms of reference, suggesting that the concurrence of the head of the judiciary should be necessary with respect to the former, and that there should 'be a real opportunity for the head of the judiciary and the individual judge to have some input into the terms of reference'.

QUESTIONS

- Do you share these concerns?
- When, if ever, is it appropriate for judges to chair inquiries?

As originally drafted, the Inquiries Bill allowed the relevant Minister to appoint judges to chair inquiries after *consulting* the Senior Law Lord (in the case of a Law Lord) or the Lord Chief Justice (in the case of a High Court or circuit judge). This attracted strong criticism by, *inter alios*, Lord Woolf. In a memorandum (endorsed by the Judges Council) to the PASC, dated November 2004, he acknowledged that it would sometimes be appropriate for judges to lead inquiries, but was 'firmly of the view that the Lord Chief Justice should have to concur with any appointment to a public inquiry', bearing in mind the resource implications of judicial involvement in inquiries and the fact that some 'inquiries are of a highly politically sensitive nature' such that 'it is not appropriate for a judge to be involved'. The Bill was amended accordingly in the House of Lords, making the *consent* of the Senior Law Lord or Lord Chief Justice a condition precedent to the appointment of a judge to an inquiry. However, the government opposed this amendment, and it remains unclear, at the time of writing, how this issue will be resolved.

18.4.3 Questions of Procedure

One of the most contentious issues concerning public inquiries of the type presently under consideration is the resolution of what Blom-Cooper [1993] *CLP* 204 at 205 calls the 'tension between the purpose [of the inquiry] of eliciting the truth and the protection of the individual against whom findings of culpability may have to be made'. This issue was examined in detail in the Salmon Report (Cm 3121, *Report of the Royal Commission on Tribunals of Inquiry* (London 1966)) which recommended a number of procedural safeguards: for example, that witnesses should be given advance notice of allegations against them and the evidence on which they are based; that witnesses should have adequate opportunity to prepare their case and to be examined by their own counsel; and that they should be able to test evidence affecting them by cross-examination through counsel. By advancing these recommendations, the Salmon Report displays what Aronson and Franklin, *Review of Administrative Action* (North Ryde, NSW 1987) at 146, identify as the lawyer's instinct to 'turn to the adversary model as providing the greatest measure of procedural protection'.

However, the appropriateness of that model in relation to public inquiries has been seriously doubted. Lord Hutton, giving evidence to the PASC (HC606-i, *Government by Inquiry: Minutes of Evidence* (2003–2004)), considered that 'the Salmon principles are not to be applied inflexibly or rigidly and they have to be adapted to the circumstances of the particular inquiry'. Hutton himself chose a partly inquisitorial, partly adversarial style of procedure: witnesses were initially questioned 'neutrally' (as he put it) by counsel to the inquiry, after which some witnesses, having been given notice of 'possible criticisms', were called back to give further evidence, at which point there was cross-examination by interested parties' legal representatives.

The most prominent critic of Salmon is Sir Richard Scott. He refused to apply many of the Salmon principles to his own inquiry into the 'arms to Iraq' affair, arguing (see (1995) 111 *LQR* 596 at 598–599) that:

In an inquisitorial Inquiry there are no litigants. There are simply witnesses who have, or may have, knowledge of some of the matters under investigation. The witnesses have no "case" to promote. It is true that they may have an interest in protecting their reputations, and an interest in answering as cogently and comprehensively as possible allegations made against them. But they have no "case" in the adversarial sense. Similarly, there is no "case" against any witnesses. There may be damaging factual evidence given by others which the witness disputes. There may be opinion evidence given by others which disparages the witness. In these events the witness may need an opportunity to give his own evidence in refutation. But still he is not answering a case against himself in the adversarial sense. He is simply a witness giving his own evidence in circumstances in which he has a personal interest in being believed.

Scott's refusal to permit legal representation, cross-examination of witnesses (except by the inquiry itself), and many of the other trappings of the adversarial model was roundly condemned by Howe [1996] *PL* 445, who argued that the Scott Inquiry's ability to operate effectively and reach meaningful conclusions was thereby fundamentally undermined. The Council on Tribunals (*Advice to the Lord Chancellor on the Procedural Issues arising in the Conduct of Public Inquiries set up by Ministers* (London 1996)) has also commented that, while 'the infinite variety of circumstances that may give rise to the need for a major public inquiry make it wholly impracticable to devise a single set of model rules or guidelines', systematic restriction of classically 'adversarial' features such as legal representation may be counterproductive. Others, however, share Scott's view that adversarialism is unhelpful in this context. For instance, Blom-Cooper and Munro [2004] *PL* 472 criticize the adversarial procedure adopted at the second stage of Hutton, commenting that such a procedure is 'liable to be inimical to the aims of a process that is essentially inquisitorial'. More fundamentally, Harris [1996] *PL* 508 at 525–527 comments that underlying the discourse in this area is a

protean idea of "fairness", a concept which it may now be said underpins Anglo-Australian administrative law in the area of the hearing rule of natural justice. However, the arguments used to support a requirement of detailed "particularisation" of "allegations", or of a closer identification [by the inquiry] of "areas of concern" or of disclosure of "tentative" views or conclusions [which may be adverse to the witness are] . . . based squarely upon an *adversarial paradigm* of what [is] connoted by the idea of fairness. An alternative approach is to treat fairness as a more adaptable concept, one which will easily accommodate a shift from an adversarial model of what administrative due process requires to a situation in which what is procedurally "fair" is defined in terms of what a particular decision-making process demands . . .

. . . [T]here is encouraging evidence in Australian cases [eg *Bond* v. *Australian Broadcasting Tribunal* (1988) 84 ALR 646] decided in the context of investigative tribunals of a flexible and nuanced appreciation of what procedural fairness may mean. This approach and, it is submitted, Sir Richard Scott's report, can be seen as providing the occasion for a more general re-appraisal of the sometimes inhibiting and often inappropriate influence of the adversarial paradigm in the wider context of the administrative process. It is, in short, time for lawyers in the common law tradition to break free from the idea that there is no way of viewing fairness in the working of that process except through the prism of adversarialism . . .

QUESTION

- Harris concludes that the key objective of 'fairness' in this context is that which Lord Diplock identified in *Mahon* v. *Air New Zealand* [1954] 1 AC 808 at 821, of ensuring that witnesses are not 'left in the dark'. How should this be achieved in the context of inquiries?

The Inquiries Bill (as it exists at the time of writing) would provide inquiry chairmen with discretion as to the procedure. However, that discretion would be bounded by (*inter alia*) rules made by the Lord Chancellor (in relation to inquiries for which a UK Minister is responsible) or the relevant devolved authority (in relation to inquiries for which they are responsible). At the time of writing, no such rules have been published. However, the Lord Chancellor is expected to make a single set of rules governing all inquiries established by UK Ministers; given the diversity of inquiries to which such rules will have to apply, it is anticipated that they will be framed broadly, so as to afford discretion to inquiry chairmen to apply them in a manner appropriate to particular inquiries.

Finally, it should be noted that, while tribunals of inquiry and analogous non-statutory inquiries enjoy a good deal of discretion over the procedure which they adopt — a position which, it seems, would continue under the Inquiries Bill — it is nevertheless possible to seek judicial review of inquiries on procedural (and other) grounds, albeit that the procedural standards applied by the reviewing court will be adapted to the inquiry context. For example, in *R* v. *Lord Saville of Newdigate, ex parte A* [2000] 1 WLR 1855, soldiers who had fired live rounds on 'Bloody Sunday' and who were required to give evidence to Lord Saville's Inquiry sought judicial review of the Inquiry's general policy that, in the interests of open justice, they should be named. Lord Woolf MR, giving the judgment of the court at 1865–1866, noted that a measure of judicial deference is appropriate when courts are called on to review the decisions of 1921 Act tribunals of inquiry (although this reasoning is applicable to other types of inquiry as well):

It is accepted on all sides that the tribunal is subject to the supervisory role of the courts. The courts have to perform that role even though they are naturally loath to do anything which could in any way interfere with or complicate the extraordinarily difficult task of the tribunal. In exercising their role the courts have to bear in mind at all times that the members of the tribunal have a much greater understanding of their task than the courts. However, subject to the courts confining themselves to their well-recognised role on applications for judicial review, it is essential that they should be prepared to exercise that role regardless of the distinction of the body concerned and the sensitivity of the issues involved. The court must also bear in mind that it exercises a discretionary jurisdiction and where this is consistent with the performance of its duty it should avoid interfering with the activities of a tribunal of this nature to any greater extent than upholding the rule of law requires.

With this in mind, Lord Woolf continued (at 1867–1868):

In *In re Pergamon Press Ltd.* [1971] Ch. 388 Lord Denning M.R. said of Board of Trade inspectors that they must act fairly. He went on to indicate that inspectors have a duty to protect witnesses. He recognised, at p. 400, that inspectors "must be masters of their own procedure" but subject to the overriding requirement that "they must be fair". Although we are here concerned with a very different type of inquiry from that being considered in the *Pergamon Press* case, it can equally be said of this tribunal that while it is master of its own procedure and has considerable discretion as to what procedure it wishes to adopt, it must still be fair. Whether a decision reached in the exercise of its discretion is fair or not is ultimately one which will be determined by the courts. This is because there is an implied obligation on the tribunal to provide procedural fairness. The tribunal is not conducting adversarial litigation and there are no parties for whom it must provide safeguards. However the tribunal is under an obligation to achieve for witnesses procedures which will ensure procedural fairness: see *Lloyd v. McMahon* [1987] A.C. 625, 702–703, *per* Lord Bridge of Harwich and *Reg. v. Secretary of State for the Environment, Ex parte Hammersmith and Fulham London Borough Council* [1991] 1 A.C. 521, 598F. As to the content of the requirement of procedural fairness, this will depend upon the circumstances and in particular on the nature of the decision to be taken: see *Council of Civil Service Unions v. Minister for the Civil Service* [1985] A.C. 374, *per* Lord Diplock, at p. 411H, and *per* Lord Roskill, at p. 415A–B . . . The requirement of procedural fairness for witnesses is well recognised in the courts by allowing witnesses to give evidence behind screens. A defendant opposing the evidence being given in this way could make this a ground of complaint on appeal. At this inquiry where there are no defendants the requirement of procedural fairness surely involves an obligation to be fair to witnesses, including, for example, protecting them when necessary or giving them notice in a . . . letter of proposed findings of improper conduct.

The court concluded that the general policy of naming the soldiers in question was procedurally unfair. Judicial review of inquiries extends beyond matters of procedure: indeed, decisions made by the Bloody Sunday Inquiry itself have also been quashed on grounds such as unreasonableness (*R v. Lord Saville of Newdigate, ex parte A* [2000] 1 WLR 1855), breach of rights arising under the ECHR (*R (A) v. Lord Saville of Newdigate* [2001] EWCA Civ 2048 [2002] 1 WLR 1249), and failure to take account of relevant considerations (*R v. Lord Saville of Newdigate, ex parte B* (*The Times*, 15 April 1999). In view of the delay and disruption that can be occasioned by judicial review of inquiries, the Inquiries Bill provides that those seeking review of a decision made by a Minister in relation to an inquiry or of a member of an inquiry panel must (as well as complying with the standard time limit, on which see above at 15.4) act within 14 days of becoming aware of it.

QUESTION

- Steele [2004] *PL* 738 at 742 writes that, 'In theory, . . . [at least], public inquiries are a more effective means of achieving the goals of scandal-control, blame-attribution and lesson-learning than parliamentary investigations or litigation.' Why might this be so?

18.5 Concluding Remarks

We have seen in this chapter that 'inquiries' take a number of forms, and fulfil diverse roles within the administrative and constitutional system. The hybrid nature of many inquiries, which places them (sometimes uncomfortably) at the interface between administrative and judicial proceedings, raises a number of questions concerning how inquiries should be conducted. Straightforward answers to these questions are impossible, not least because the concept of inquiries is itself protean. We have, however, seen that the recommendations of the Franks Committee have played a major role in fashioning the contemporary approach to administrative justice in the context of inquiries. These reforms, by increasing transparency before, during and after inquiries, help to ensure — and to demonstrate — that inquiries serve a genuinely useful role in relation to the gathering of information and opinion, and that their function now transcends that which Lord Hewart attributed to them, of merely creating an *impression* of open-minded decision-makers willing to listen to others' views. As well as operating as an integral part of the administrative decision-making structure, by facilitating the taking of more informed decisions, inquiries are commonly resorted to for the purposes of investigating accidents, disasters, suspected maladministration, and so on. As we have seen, such inquiries raise difficult questions about procedure, forcing administrative lawyers to confront the fact that, while the adversarial model is traditionally viewed as the paradigm of 'fairness', the concept of due process requires considerable re-evaluation in an inquisitorial setting.

FURTHER RESOURCES

Beatson, 'Should Judges Conduct Public Inquiries?' *www.dca.gov.uk/judicial/speeches/ speechfr.htm*

Blom-Cooper, 'Public Inquiries' [1993] *CLP* 203

Department for Constitutional Affairs, consultation paper on *Effective Inquiries* *www.dca.gov.uk/consult/inquiries/index.htm*

Keeton, *Trial by Tribunal* (London 1960)

Scott, 'Procedures at Inquiries — The Duty to be Fair' (1995) 111 *LQR* 596

Steele, 'Judging Judicial Inquiries' [2004] *PL* 738

In this chapter, we have made various references to evidence taken and published by PASC during the course of its inquiry, *Government by Inquiry*. After completion of the manuscript of this book, the PASC's report was published. It has not been possible to refer to the report in this chapter, but the report—HC51-I, *Government by Inquiry* (2004–2005)—can be accessed via *www.parliament.uk/parliamentary_committees/public_administration_select_committee.cfm*. One of the central themes in the report is that Parliament should be accorded a greater role in investigating the type of matters presently covered by inquiries established by the executive. This culminated in the recommendation that 'inquiries into the conduct and actions of government should exercise their authority through the legitimacy of Parliament in the form of a Parliamentary Commission of Inquiry composed of parliamentarians and others, rather than by the exercise of the prerogative power of the Executive'. At the time of writing this postscript, a government response to the report is awaited.

STATUTORY TRIBUNALS

19.1 Introduction

19.1.1 The Growth of Tribunals

In his Review of Tribunals (*Tribunals for Users: One Service, One System* (London 2003) (hereinafter 'Leggatt' or 'the Leggatt Report')), commissioned by what was then the Lord Chancellor's Department, Sir Andrew Leggatt observed (at [1.1]) that tribunals

form the largest part of the civil justice system in England and Wales, hearing about a million cases each year. That number of cases alone makes their work of great importance to our society, since more of us bring a case before a tribunal than go to any other part of the justice system. Their collective impact is immense.

The growth of statutory tribunals mirrors the dramatic expansion of the state itself. As legislation has increasingly conferred benefits on individuals and subjected their everyday lives to growing regulation, so the scope for dispute between the individual and the state has grown. Was the Minister right to conclude that an applicant was not statutorily entitled to a particular benefit? Was a public body correct to hold that an individual was entitled to a given amount of compensation following the imposition upon him of some disadvantage? For successive generations of policy-makers, tribunals have been — and remain — the mechanism of choice for resolving disputes between the individual and the state across 'the whole range of political and social life, including social security benefits, health, education, tax, agriculture, criminal injuries compensation, immigration and asylum, rents, and parking' (Leggatt at [1.16]). (Of course, such disputes can, in principle, be resolved by means of judicial review; however, as we saw at 15.4 above, the Administrative Court rarely entertains claims for judicial review where alternative remedies, such as appeal to a tribunal, are available.)

19.1.2 Are Tribunals a Desirable Feature of the Administrative System?

Genn (1993) 56 *MLR* 393 at 393 observes that the popularity of tribunals with policy-makers can be traced to the perception that they are 'cheap, non-technical substitutes for the ordinary courts for a wide range of grievances and disputes, in which parties can initiate actions without cost or fuss'. However, these are not universally recognized as *positive* characteristics of tribunals. Abel (in Abel (ed), *The Politics of Informal Justice* (New York 1982) at 295–301) argues that tribunals offer a second-rate justice system for poorer members of society (who are more likely to be engaged in disputes with public bodies in areas, such as welfare provision, with which tribunals tend to deal). Meanwhile, Ison (in Harris and Partington (eds), *Administrative Justice in the 21st Century* (Oxford 1999)) is highly sceptical about the notion of 'administrative justice' itself, arguing (at 23) that it places undue weight on *appeals* against administrative decisions, and acts as an apologist for (what he perceives to be) the inadequacies of *first-instance* decision-making (or 'primary adjudication'):

I know of no evidence . . . to demonstrate that there is any substantial correlation between suffering and complaining [about first-instance decisions]. When decisions relate to elderly people, disabled people, single parents, small business people or immigrants, there are large numbers who suffer from erroneous decisions without filing a complaint. Indeed, the total volume of injustice is likely to be much greater among those who accept initial decisions than among those who complain or appeal. For this reason alone, thoroughness and procedural fairness are more important in primary adjudication than they are in appellate processes.

Ison is right to draw our attention to the often low take-up of grievance redress. Empirical research (see, *eg*, Cowan and Halliday, *The Appeal of Internal Review* (Oxford 2003)) suggests that take-up may be inhibited by a number of factors, including a perceived lack of independence of the grievance redress mechanism from the original decision-maker; lack of awareness of the mechanism in the first place; general perceptions of the bureaucratic system (*eg* a prospective appellant may be deterred from appealing because the original decision was handled badly, thereby giving the impression of systemic problems which would also infect any grievance redress mechanism); and the perception that pursuing the matter is likely to be a trying and time-consuming experience.

The response of policy-makers to these issues should be two-fold. In the first place, as Ison argues, the quality of first-instance decision-making should be high, in order to reduce the need to resort to such bodies as appellate tribunals: it is, after all, to everyone's advantage if the right decision can be made, and be seen to have been made, without further ado. This is recognized by the government in its recent White Paper on administrative justice (Cm 6243, *Transforming Public Services: Complaints, Redress and Tribunals* (2004) (hereinafter 'the White Paper') at [10.5]). Secondly, however, the importance of good first-instance decision-making should not obscure the fact that a good appellate structure is also valuable, not least because the latter is capable of buttressing the former. The prospect of appeal can encourage decision-makers to act properly (in order to avoid later criticism); moreover, if the relationship between decision-makers and tribunals is conceived in constructive terms, then it is possible for the latter to work with the former in order to identify and resolve systemic problems of decision-making practice at first instance (see the White Paper at [6.32]–[6.34]). It is therefore conducive to the existence of a healthy administrative system that an effective appellate structure exists — which, in turn, clearly requires the potential barriers to entry, noted in the preceding paragraph, to be addressed.

19.1.3 The Franks Report

Later in this chapter we consider how policy-makers are seeking to improve the efficacy of, and access to, the tribunals system. First, however, it is necessary to refer to the work of the Franks Committee, to which the role ascribed to tribunals in the contemporary administrative system may still be traced.

....

Cmnd 218, *Report of the Committee on Administrative Tribunals and Enquiries* (1957)

. . . Our terms of reference involve the consideration of an important part of the relationship between the individual and authority. At different times in the history of this country it has been necessary to adjust this relationship and to seek a new balance between private right and public advantage, between fair play for the individual and efficiency of administration. The balance found has varied with different governmental systems and different social patterns. Since the war the British electorate has chosen Governments which accepted general responsibilities for the provision of extended social services and for the broad management of the economy. It has consequently become desirable to consider afresh the procedures by which the rights of individual citizens can be harmonised with wider public interests.

How do disputes between the individual and authority arise in this country at the present time? In general the starting point is the enactment of legislation by Parliament. Many statutes apply detailed schemes to the whole or to large classes of the community (for example national insurance) or lay on a Minister and other authorities a general duty to provide a service (for example education or health). Such legislation is rarely sufficient in itself to achieve all its objects, and a series of decisions by administrative bodies, such as Government Departments and local authorities, is often required. For example, in a national insurance scheme decisions have to be given on claims to benefit, and in providing an educational service decisions have to be taken on the siting of new schools. Many of these decisions affect the rights of individual citizens, who may then object.

Once objection has been raised, a further decision becomes inevitable. This further decision is of a different kind: whether to confirm, cancel or vary the original decision. In reaching it account must be taken not only of the original decision but also of the objection.

These further decisions are made in various ways. Some are made in courts of law and therefore by the procedure of a court of law . . . Frequently the statutes lay down that these further decisions are to be made by a special tribunal or a Minister. For example, a contested claim to national insurance benefit has to be determined by a special tribunal, and the decision whether or not to confirm an opposed scheme for the compulsory acquisition of land by a local authority must be made by the Minister concerned. In these cases the procedure to be followed in dealing with objections to the first decision and in arriving at the further decision is laid down in the statute or in regulations made thereunder.

But over most of the field of public administration no formal procedure is provided for objecting or deciding on objections. For example, when foreign currency or a scarce commodity such as petrol or coal is rationed or allocated, there is no other body to which an individual applicant can appeal if the responsible administrative authority decides to allow him less than he has requested. Of course the aggrieved individual can always complain to the appropriate administrative authority, to his Member of Parliament, to a representative organisation or to the press. But there is no formal procedure on which he can insist.

There are therefore two broad distinctions to be made among these further decisions which we have been discussing. The first is between those decisions which follow a statutory procedure and those which do not. The second distinction is within the group of decisions subject to a statutory procedure. Some of these decisions are taken in the ordinary courts and some are taken by tribunals or by Ministers after a special procedure.

These two distinctions are essential for understanding our terms of reference. We are not instructed to consider those many cases in which no formal procedure has been prescribed. Nor are we instructed to consider decisions made in the ordinary courts. What we are instructed to consider are the cases in which the decision on objections, the further decision as we have called it, is taken by a tribunal or by a Minister after a special procedure [eg a statutory inquiry, on which see ch 18] has been followed.

. . . Although the foregoing broad analysis holds good over nearly all the field covered by our terms of reference, there are a few tribunals (for example Rent Tribunals) which determine disputes not between the individual and authority but between citizen and citizen . . .

It is noteworthy that Parliament, having decided that the decisions with which we are concerned should not be remitted to the ordinary courts, should also have decided that they should not be left to be reached in the normal course of administration. Parliament has considered it essential to lay down special procedures for them.

This must have been to promote good administration. Administration must not only be efficient in the sense that the objectives of policy are securely attained without delay. It must also satisfy the general body of citizens that it is proceeding with reasonable regard to the balance between the public interest which it promotes and the private interest which it disturbs. Parliament has, we infer, intended in relation to the subject-matter of our terms of reference that the further decisions or, as they may rightly be termed in this context, adjudications must be acceptable as having been properly made.

It is natural that Parliament should have taken this view of what constitutes good administration. In this country government rests fundamentally upon the consent of the governed. The general acceptability of these adjudications is one of the vital elements in sustaining that consent. When we regard our subject in this light, it is clear that there are certain general and closely linked characteristics which should mark these special procedures. We call these characteristics openness, fairness and impartiality.

Here we need only give brief examples of their application. Take openness. If these procedures were wholly secret, the basis of confidence and acceptability would be lacking. Next take fairness. If the objector were not allowed to state his case, there would be nothing to stop oppression. Thirdly, there is impartiality. How can the citizen be satisfied unless he feels that those who decide his case come to their decision with open minds?

To assert that openness, fairness and impartiality are essential characteristics of our subject-matter is not to say that they must be present in the same way and to the same extent in all its parts. Difference in the nature of the issue for adjudication may give good reasons for difference in the degree to which the three general characteristics should be developed and applied. Again, the method by which a Minister arrives at a decision after a hearing or enquiry cannot be the same as that by which a tribunal arrives at a decision . . . For the moment it is sufficient to point out that when Parliament sets up a tribunal to decide cases, the adjudication is placed outside the Department concerned. The members of the tribunal are neutral and impartial in relation to the policy of the Minister, except in so far as that policy is contained in the rules which the tribunal has been set up to apply . . .

At this stage another question naturally arises. On what principle has it been decided that some adjudications should be made by tribunals and some by Ministers? If from a study of the history of the subject we could discover such a principle, we should have a criterion which would be a guide for any future allocation of these decisions between tribunals and Ministers.

The search for this principle has usually involved the application of one or both of two notions, each with its antithesis. Both notions are famous and have long histories. They are the notion of what is judicial, its antithesis being what is administrative, and the notion of what is according to the rule of law, its antithesis being what is arbitrary . . .

The rule of law stands for the view that decisions should be made by the application of known principles or laws. In general such decisions will be predictable, and the citizen will know where he is. On the other hand there is what is arbitrary. A decision may be made without principle, without any rules. It is therefore unpredictable, the antithesis of a decision taken in accordance with the rule of law.

Nothing that we say diminishes the importance of these pairs of antitheses. But it must be confessed that neither pair yields a valid principle on which one can decide whether the duty of making a certain decision should be laid upon a tribunal or upon a Minister or whether the existing allocation of decisions between tribunals and Ministers is appropriate. But even if there is no such principle and we cannot explain the facts, we can at least start with them. An empirical approach may be the most useful.

Starting with the facts, we observe that the methods of adjudication by tribunals are in general not the same as those of adjudication by Ministers. All or nearly all tribunals apply rules . . . Many matters remitted to tribunals and Ministers appear to have, as it were, a natural affinity with one or other method of adjudication. Sometimes the policy of the legislation can be embodied in a system of detailed regulations. Particular decisions cannot, single case by single case, alter the Minister's policy. Where this is so, it is natural to entrust the decisions to a tribunal, if not to the courts. On the other hand it is sometimes desirable to preserve flexibility of decision in the pursuance of public policy. Then a wise expediency is the proper basis of right adjudication, and the decision must be left with a Minister.

But in other instances there seems to be no such natural affinity. For example, there seems to be no natural affinity which makes it clearly appropriate for appeals in goods vehicle licence cases to be decided by the Transport Tribunal when appeals in a number of road passenger cases are decided by the Minister.

We shall therefore respect this factual difference between tribunals and Ministers and deal separately with the two parts of the subject. When considering tribunals we shall see how far the three characteristics of openness, fairness and impartiality can be developed and applied in general and how far their development and application must be adapted to the circumstances of particular tribunals . . .

Many of the recommendations contained in the Franks Report were implemented by the Tribunals and Inquiries Act 1958 (see now the Tribunals and Inquiries Act 1992). In this chapter, we explore a number of issues concerning the role of tribunals today; their status and independence; the procedures which they adopt; the structure and organization of the tribunals system, and broader questions concerning the administration, accountability, and supervision of that system. We also examine many of the changes to the system of tribunals which are presently being planned, and the Leggatt Report, which stimulated many of the proposed changes.

19.2 The Independence of Tribunals

19.2.1 Tribunals and Government

The status of tribunals is key to their role within the system of administrative justice. A question which immediately arises is whether tribunals should be regarded as judicial or administrative bodies. It is important to confront this question at the outset because, as we will see, the response to it influences other matters, such as the relationship between tribunals and government departments, where responsibility should lie for the administration of the tribunals system, and the procedural model adopted by tribunals. The Franks Report (at [40]) approached the issue in the following terms:

Tribunals are not ordinary courts, but neither are they appendages of Government departments. Much of the official evidence . . . appeared to reflect the view that tribunals should properly be regarded as part of the machinery of administration, for which the Government must retain a close and continuing responsibility. Thus, for example, tribunals in the social service field would be regarded as adjuncts to the administration of the services themselves. We do not accept this view. We consider that tribunals should properly be regarded as machinery provided by Parliament for adjudication rather than as part of the machinery of administration.

The importance of the independence of tribunals was highlighted by the Council on Tribunals (whose role is examined below at 19.5) in its report, Cm 3744, *Tribunals: Their Organisation and Independence* (London 1997) at [2.2]:

. . . [S]ince tribunals are established to offer a form of redress, mostly in disputes between the citizen and the State, the principal hallmark of any tribunal is that it must be independent. Equally importantly, it must be perceived as such. That means that the tribunal should be enabled to reach decisions according to law without pressure either from the body or person whose decision is being appealed, or from anyone else.

Thus, while it is clearly desirable that a constructive relationship should exist between a tribunal and the government department from whose decisions it hears appeals — *eg* in order that the tribunal may identify and draw to the department's attention systemic problems with its decision-making practice — that relationship must be carefully constituted in order that independence is neither compromised nor seen to be compromised. Leggatt concluded (at [2.20]) that existing arrangements, whereby tribunals are often 'sponsored' by the departments whose work they scrutinize (that is, where the tribunal is financially dependent on the department), are problematic:

At best, such arrangements result in tribunals and their departments being, or appearing to be, common enterprises. At worst, they make the members of a tribunal feel that they have become identified with its sponsoring department, and they foster a culture in which the members feel that their prospects of more interesting work, of progression in the tribunal, and of appointments elsewhere depend on the departments against which the cases that they hear are brought.

Leggatt went on to argue (at [2.23]–[2.25]) that tribunals' independence could best be promoted by developing clear separation between the ministers and other authorities whose policies and decisions are tested by tribunals, and the minister who appoints and supports them ... The important place which tribunals now play in the modern system of administrative law would best be recognised by forming them into a coherent system to sit alongside the ordinary courts, with administrative support provided by the LCD [the Lord Chancellor's Department, which is now known as the Department for Constitutional Affairs ("DCA")].

Leggatt went on to recommend that a newly-rationalized tribunals system should be given administrative support by a new Tribunals Service, an executive agency under the auspices of (what is now) the DCA.

These recommendations have been largely accepted. The White Paper proposes a new 'tribunals system' (considered in detail at 19.4 below). It is anticipated that most tribunals presently sponsored by central government departments will migrate into this new system by 2009; as tribunals migrate, the DCA will take over responsibility for them. This is considered appropriate because the DCA does not itself make the type of decisions that are subject to appeals in tribunals, and because the Department has 'a particular mission to protect judicial independence' (White Paper at [6.14]). A new executive agency within the DCA, to be known as the Tribunals Service, should become operational in 2006. The agency, led by a Chief Executive, would provide administrative support to the tribunals which form part of the new system. The shifting of responsibility for many tribunals to the DCA and the new Tribunals Service is only one aspect of the proposals in the White Paper. The radical and far-reaching nature of those proposals will become apparent as this chapter unfolds.

19.2.2 Judicial Leadership of Tribunals

As well as addressing matters concerning the relationship between tribunals and government, those who have been concerned with promoting tribunals' independence have also turned their attention to a further range of issues concerning the organization of and appointments to tribunals. The Council on Tribunals (Cm 3744, *Tribunals: Their Organisation and Independence* (London 1997) at [2.4]) strongly recommended more widespread use of what is known as the 'presidential system', suggesting that 'the independence and integrity of a tribunals system is best served if someone from the judicial side of the tribunal is given a specific role in meeting some or all' of the pre-conditions for independence which it had identified, such as training and resource-allocation (matters which are presently often dealt with by senior tribunal and departmental administrators). In particular, the Council felt (*ibid* at [2.14]) that a senior figure from the judicial side should be concerned with 'the performance of the tribunals themselves, by ensuring that the tribunal chairmen and members carry out their judicial tasks effectively, but without in any way interfering with the exercise of their judicial discretion in individual cases' and with 'the efficient use of the judicial resources at the tribunal's disposal, through the setting of appropriate conditions and standards and monitoring of individual performance'. Ultimately, the Council concluded (at [2.19]) that 'there should be one person on the judicial side of the tribunal appointed to ... [provide] central direction'.

The White Paper (at [6.58]–[6.64]) endorses many of these views, concluding that a 'Senior President' — a judge of experience and standing equivalent to a Lord Justice of Appeal — should take responsibility for the overall direction of the new tribunals system.

Moreover, each 'jurisdiction' within the new system — that is, individual tribunals or groups of tribunals dealing with related issues — would be led by a 'President', charged with providing judicial leadership, safeguarding and developing expertise, and developing judicial training and appraisal. These proposals are likely to enhance the independence, perceived and actual, of the tribunals concerned.

19.2.3 Appointments to Tribunals

The appointment of tribunal chairmen and members is clearly crucial to tribunals' independence. The White Paper at [6.47] notes that:

The Lord Chancellor already appoints around 60% of tribunal panel members — not just legal members but, for example, medical members of the Appeals Service tribunals and the Mental Health Review Tribunal. But this leaves a number of tribunals where the Minister with responsibility for the original decision (or for the policy concerned) also appoints panel members, pays them and runs the tribunal. While those who sit in tribunals are independent of departments, and make this clear at hearings, the current arrangements mean that independence is not as manifestly clear as it should be.

In light of these concerns, change is proposed. Under the Constitutional Reform Bill (as it exists at the time of writing), certain tribunal members would be appointed by the Secretary of State for Constitutional Affairs upon the recommendation of a Judicial Appointments Commission (albeit that the Minister would have limited powers to reject a candidate selected by the Commission or require the Commission to reconsider its decision). The White Paper argues that this approach should apply to the appointment of *all* members of tribunals within the new tribunals system.

19.3 Procedure in Tribunals

19.3.1 Introduction

The procedures adopted by tribunals vary significantly, and it is impossible to summarize the various procedures here. Instead, we attempt in this section to draw out some of the key issues and themes which arise in this context. The importance of the procedures adopted by tribunals was recognized in the Franks Report at [62]–[63]:

Most of the evidence we have received concerning tribunals has placed great emphasis upon procedure, not only at the hearing itself but also before and after it. There has been general agreement on the broad essentials which the procedure, in this wider sense, should contain, for example provision for notice of the right to apply to a tribunal, notice of the case which the appellant has to meet, a reasoned decision by the tribunal and notice of any further right of appeal . . .

We agree that procedure is of the greatest importance and that it should be clearly laid down in a statute or statutory instrument. Because of the great variety of the purposes for which tribunals are established, however, we do not think it would be appropriate to rely upon either a single code or a small number of codes. We think that there is a case for greater procedural differentiation and prefer that the detailed procedure for each type of tribunal should be designed to meet its particular circumstances.

Although the Franks Committee recommended that the Council on Tribunals should draft tribunals' procedural rules, s 8 of the Tribunals and Inquiries Act 1992 merely requires the Council to be consulted. The Council expressed frustration in its *Annual Report 2001/2002* at [31] that 'some departments do not allow sufficient time for statutory consultation', urging adherence to its *Code for Consultation with the Council* (see *Annual Report 2000/2001*, Appendix E) which requires five weeks' notice in respect of routine proposals that do not raise major matters of principle, and eight weeks' notice for proposals which do raise such matters.

As well as offering its views on draft procedural rules when consulted, the Council published *Model Rules of Procedure for Tribunals* (Cm 1434) in 1991, in order to provide a blueprint in this area. However, having consulted on the draft of a revised version of that document, the Council noted in its *Annual Report 2002/2003* at 2 that:

Some commentators felt that some of the provisions, particularly those relating to evidence (for example, submission of witness statements and witness summaries) were really too prescriptive and onerous for the kinds of people, often unrepresented, who appear before certain types of tribunal. We now intend to make it clear that certain rules may not be suitable for certain tribunals. It was also evident from some of the comments that there is a need to make it clearer that the Rules are not intended to be a code to be slavishly followed.

In light of this emphasis on the need for what the Franks Committee called 'procedural differentiation', the Council published its *Guide to Drafting Tribunal Rules* in 2003, making it clear (at 3) that it was offering 'a selection of different samples of rules, inviting the reader to "pick and mix" '.

The question of independence resurfaces in relation to the making of tribunals' procedural rules. The White Paper recognizes that, where the power to make such rules is presently vested in the Minister in charge of the sponsoring department, there is a risk that the Minister may fail to strike a proper balance between the interests of the department and the user. It is therefore proposed that, as tribunals migrate into the new system, under which the DCA becomes the sponsoring department, the power to make rules in respect of such tribunals (other than employment tribunals, which are regarded as a special case) will pass to the Secretary of State for Constitutional Affairs. It is envisaged that the Secretary of State will discharge this responsibility through a procedure committee whose members will be drawn from tribunal judiciary, the Council on Tribunals, and users' representatives.

19.3.2 Formality, Representation, and the Style of Tribunal Proceedings

While it is crucial to recognize that the diversity of tribunals must be reflected at a procedural level, certain common issues arise. The first concerns the question whether tribunals should adopt formal procedural rules or instead opt for a more informal model. In relation to this dilemma, the Franks Report noted (at [64]) that:

There has been considerable emphasis, in much of the evidence we have received, upon the importance of preserving informality of atmosphere in hearings before tribunals, though it is generally conceded that in some tribunals, for example the Lands Tribunal, informality is not an overriding necessity. We endorse this view, but we are convinced that the attempt which has been made to secure informality in the general run of tribunals has in some instances been at the expense of an orderly procedure. Informality without rules of procedure may be positively inimical to right adjudication, since the proceedings may well assume an unordered character which makes it difficult, if not impossible, for the tribunal properly to sift the facts and weigh the evidence. It should here be remembered that by their very nature tribunals may well be less skilled in adjudication than courts of law. None of our witnesses would seek to make tribunals in all respects like courts of law, but there is a wide measure of agreement that in many instances their procedure could be made more orderly without impairing the desired informality of atmosphere. The object to be aimed at in most tribunals is the combination of a formal procedure with an informal atmosphere. We see no reason why this cannot be achieved. On the one hand it means a manifestly sympathetic attitude on the part of the tribunal and the absence of the trappings of a court, but on the other hand such prescription of procedure as makes the proceedings clear and orderly.

Does the adoption of a generally informal style of proceedings obviate the need for (publicly-funded) representation? At present, as far as legal representation before tribunals is concerned, s 6(6) and sch 2 of the Access to Justice Act 1999 permit the provision of legal aid in relation only to the Employment Appeal Tribunal, the Mental Health Review Tribunal, the Immigration Adjudicators and Immigration Appeal Tribunal (soon to be replaced by the Asylum and Immigration Tribunal), the Proscribed Organisations Appeal Commission, and the Special Immigration Appeals Commission. In addition, the Secretary of State has issued directions under s 6(8) permitting the funding of legal representation before the Protection of Children Act Tribunal and, in certain circumstances, the General and Special Commissioners of Income Tax and the VAT and Duties Tribunal; he may also (under s 6(8)) authorize the provision of representation before other tribunals in individual cases. Help falling short of advocacy — *eg* assistance with preparing for a tribunal case — is more readily available under the legal aid scheme, although the provision of help in individual cases depends on such factors as the financial circumstances of the party, his prospects of success, and so on. It must also be noted that assistance is sometimes available outwith the legal aid scheme, *eg* via Citizens' Advice Bureaux and the Free Representation Unit.

The White Paper does not envisage that legal aid should be made more widely available in relation to tribunal proceedings, but empirical evidence indicates that representation makes a real difference to outcomes in such proceedings. For instance, research conducted by Baldwin, Wikeley and Young in relation to social security appeals led them to the conclusion that 'expert representation [is important] in ensuring that an appellant's interests are properly protected' (see *Judging Social Security* (Oxford 1992) at 114). Moreover, Genn (1993) 56 *MLR* 393 at 400 found that:

In social security appeals tribunals [now superceded by Appeals Service tribunals], the presence of a skilled representative increased the likelihood of success from 30 to 48 per cent. In hearings before immigration adjudicators, the overall likelihood of success was increased by the presence of a representative from 20 to 38 per cent. In mental health review tribunals, the likelihood of a favourable change in conditions rose from 20 to 35 per cent as a result of representation . . .

The research indicated clearly that the presence of a representative influences the substantive outcome of hearings, irrespective of the process value that representation may provide. It also showed that the type of representation used by appellants was very important, and that specialist representatives exerted the greatest influence on the outcome of hearings.

While recognizing that there will always be certain types of case for which, and certain individuals for whom, representation is essential, the government's general position is that tribunal proceedings should be arranged such that 'individuals . . . will be able to have their case resolved with little or no support or assistance' (White Paper at [10.1]), at least at the hearing stage. This is to be achieved (*ibid* at [10.14])

by the provision of alternative approaches to dispute resolution, which do not require representation, by improved advice and assistance for the preparation of cases and by better trained and more highly skilled panel members.

This appears to presuppose that tribunals should, to some extent, depart from the adversarial model, by facilitating the presentation of individuals' cases — ensuring, for instance, that important points supporting individuals' cases are not overlooked. In fact, as Leggatt noted (at [7.4]–[7.6]), tribunals have already

developed different ways of assisting unrepresented parties, in particular when the encounter is between citizen and state, and departments are represented by an official or an advocate who is familiar with the law, the tribunal and its procedures. In these circumstances, tribunal chairmen may find it necessary to intervene in the proceedings more than might be thought proper in the courts in order to hold the balance between the parties, and enable citizens to present their cases. All the members of a tribunal must do all they can to understand the point of view, as well as the case, of the citizen. They must be alert for factual or legal aspects of the case which appellants may not bring out, adequately or at all, but which have a bearing on the possible outcomes. It may also be necessary on occasion to intervene to protect a witness or party, to avoid proceedings becoming too confrontational. The balance is a delicate one, and must not go so far on any side that the tribunal's impartiality appears to be endangered . . .

We are convinced that the tribunal approach must be an enabling one: supporting the parties in ways which give them confidence in their own abilities to participate in the process, and in the tribunal's capacity to compensate for the appellants' lack of skills or knowledge. The greatest need for that will be during hearings, which are stressful for unrepresented parties . . .

In reviewing the civil justice system generally, Lord Woolf [see *Access to Justice* (1996)] found that all parts of the system had become unnecessarily confrontational, because litigants had become used to controlling the process. Many recommendations were geared to reducing the adversarial approach, which he recognised as giving rise to unnecessary expense and delay and an inequality of arms between a powerful, wealthy litigant and a weak, under-resourced one. One of the key reforms was that the individual courts should employ better case management procedures to rebalance control between the parties and the courts, and further support the users. Clearly, the onus is even greater on tribunals, if users are to be able to make the best of their cases and present them effectively . . . [T]ribunal staff should have clearer responsibilities for explaining to users what is required to prepare a case effectively for the tribunal, and the effect and implications of any of the tribunal's interlocutory decisions.

However, the approach recommended by Leggatt is not without difficulty. For instance, Baldwin, Wikeley and Young, *op cit* at 212, found that the ability of tribunal chairmen to ameliorate the position of unrepresented appellants is severely limited. Moreover, the Council on Tribunals, in its *Response to the Consultation Paper on the Report of the Review of Tribunals by Sir Andrew Leggatt* (London 2001), expressed reservations about the appropriateness of tribunals attempting to assist unrepresented appellants, arguing that a risk could arise of compromising tribunals' independence. Instead, the Council argued for greater representation of individuals in tribunal proceedings:

The Council does not think that it is realistic to expect a situation in which most applicant users will be sufficiently capable, confident or knowledgeable to represent themselves before a tribunal. There may be particular difficulties about the case or particular difficulties for the individual. The Council does not share the view that hearings can generally take place without any help being available to an applicant user. An individual should be able to use a tribunal's services without representation if he or she so wishes. However the Council thinks it would be a mistake to assume that representation is in contradiction to a participatory kind of hearing. Representation, properly done, is often conducive to the appellant's full participation.

This thinking reflects the conclusions of Adler and Gulland, *Tribunal Users' Experiences, Perceptions and Expectations: A Literature Review* (London 2003), who noted (at 11) that most research in this area shows that 'many appellants are confused by the appeal process and have little idea of what will happen at a tribunal hearing. In some cases, they do not even realise that there will be a hearing and they are often confused by the paperwork they are sent.'

Empirical research reported on by Genn (1993) 56 *MLR* 393 also casts doubt on the proposition that the problems of unrepresented individuals may be ameliorated by recourse to such strategies as more informal proceedings. She argues that that view is based upon four misconceptions. First, she points out (at 401) that procedural straightforwardness cannot ultimately change the often complex nature of the issues which tribunals must determine:

Although most tribunal hearings are more informal and procedurally more flexible than courts, such informality has been wrongly assumed to extend to all aspects of tribunal processes. The fact that hearings are conducted across a table and that an appellant may choose whether he puts his case first are positive characteristics that should be protected and perhaps extended. However, none of the procedural informality of tribunals can overcome or alter the need for applicants to bring their cases within the regulations or statute, and prove their factual situation with evidence. Nor do informal procedures relieve tribunals from the obligation to make reasoned and consistent decisions.

Secondly, Genn notes (at 401) that procedural informality can constitute a 'trap for the unwary': relying in part on the work of Farmer, *Tribunals and Government* (London 1974) at 108–109, she observes (at 402) that:

Applicants do not succeed with cases for social security benefits because they cannot manage on their money; immigrants are not permitted to stay in the country because they want to; debtors are not permitted to avoid their debts in small claims courts because they cannot afford to pay. All must assert and establish a legal right, entitlement or defence: "the assertion of a right is a form of moral criticism: besides the expression of a demand, it involves an appeal to the authority of principle in support of one's claims" [Nonet, *Administrative Justice: Advocacy and Change in Government Agencies* (New York 1969) at 91]. This represents the "limit" of informality . . . Thus, although unrepresented appellants are free to "speak for themselves" before tribunals, and many value this freedom, it has hidden dangers . . . [D]ecision-making processes in tribunals require legally relevant and sufficient accounts. Applicants tell stories which may or may not be relevant. The result is often that they feel satisfied with the process but ultimately lose their case.

Thirdly, Genn found that appellants were less capable of presenting their cases than they themselves had expected to be. Many appellants who were interviewed as part of Genn's research, emboldened by the emphasis on informality in the information published by tribunals, made comments such as 'I'm just going to tell the truth' and 'you only need someone to speak for you if you are telling lies'. Genn found that, particularly in relation to appeals concerning social security benefits, 'many appellants seemed unprepared for the importance of law' and encountered difficulty 'in simply explaining the details of their case' (*ibid* at 407). Finally, Genn draws attention to a point which we encountered earlier — that relying on the tribunal to ameliorate the position of unrepresented appellants is fraught with difficulty — noting (at 408) that, 'Even with the best intentions, tribunals are rarely able to spend the time necessary to elicit relevant information from the undifferentiated stream in which most appellants present their stories.'

QUESTIONS

- Can the problems identified by Genn be overcome only by the provision of legal representation?
- Is the position adopted in the White Paper on this point (considered above) adequate, bearing in mind the problems raised by Genn's research?

19.3.3 Knowledge of Rights and Grounds of Appeal

In addition to the general issues concerning informality and representation just considered, it is instructive to address a number of more particular issues relating to tribunals' procedures. The concepts of natural justice and fairness are considered in detail above, in chs 10–12, but here we focus on some specific issues relating to the procedures adopted by tribunals.

First, as noted in passing at 19.1.2 above, it is self-evident that the tribunals system, as a mechanism for resolving disputes between citizens and administrative decision-makers, can only function effectively if people are aware, in the first place, of how to appeal — and, more fundamentally still, that a right of appeal exists. These matters were noted by Adler and Gulland, *op cit* at 3:

. . . [One] potential barrier that users encounter in accessing the tribunal system is knowing that they have a right of appeal (or application) in the first place. Most of the research on users' experiences looks at appellants rather than those who do not appeal . . . This means that most research is based on those who were not deterred by ignorance of their rights. Nevertheless some information can be gained from those who did appeal. There are two types of ignorance which can prevent an appellant from making an appeal — ignorance of the fact that there may be grounds for appealing against the original decision and ignorance of the procedures which need to be followed. The general conclusion, supported by much of the research evidence, is that ignorance about the grounds of appeal is often more important than ignorance of procedures, although some potential appellants may not realise that they have a right of appeal at all.

It is crucial, therefore, that the agency which makes the original adverse decision informs the individual of the possibility of appeal, as well as the potential grounds of appeal. However, Adler and Gulland identified diversity of practice in this context. For instance, it seems that there is a generally high level of awareness of appeal rights (but not necessarily understanding of specific grounds of appeal) in relation to appeals concerning such matters as social security benefits, housing benefits, and child support. These high levels of awareness are largely attributable to original decision-makers' good practice of informing individuals of their rights of appeal. In contrast, research (see Bradley, Marshall and Gath 310 (1995) *British Medical Journal* 364 and Dolan, Gibb and Coorey 10 (1999) *Journal of Forensic Psychiatry* 264) indicates that knowledge of rights of appeal against decisions to detain individuals on mental health grounds is acquired in a more *ad hoc* manner, and largely depends on whether individuals have personal experience of the system.

The White Paper acknowledges (at [10.6]–[10.10]) the need for high quality information in this area about both the reasons for original decisions and the options for challenging them. According to the White Paper, it should be the joint responsibility of departments and tribunals to explain to individuals how, and on what grounds, decisions may be challenged; however, it is also recognized that prospective appellants may value independent advice, to which end it is proposed that government should support external providers (for example in the voluntary and charitable sectors) of information about redress options.

19.3.4 Knowledge of the Case to be Met

We have already seen (above at 11.3.2) that a hearing can only be 'fair' if the individual is informed beforehand of the case against him. The Franks Report emphasized (at [71]–[72]) the importance of this aspect of natural justice in the tribunals context, observing that

> before the hearing . . . citizens should know in good time the case which they will have to meet, whether the issue to be heard by the tribunal is one between citizen and administration or between citizen and citizen. This constituent of fairness is one to which much of the evidence we have received has rightly drawn attention . . .
>
> We do not suggest that the procedure should be formalised to the extent of requiring documents in the nature of legal pleadings. What is needed is that the citizen should receive in good time beforehand a document setting out the main points of the opposing case. It should not be necessary, and indeed in view of the type of persons frequently appearing before tribunals it would in many cases be positively undesirable, to require the parties to adhere rigidly to the case previously set out, provided always that the interests of another party are not prejudiced by such flexibility.

Now, we saw in ch 12 above that public authorities are often required to give reasons for their decisions where a right of appeal exists, in order that the individual may exercise an informed judgment about whether to exercise such a right. It follows that a detailed statement of such reasons may be adequate to inform the appellant of the case against him for the purposes of fairness at the tribunal stage.

19.3.5 Reasons for Tribunals' Decisions

In the excerpt from its report at 19.1 above, the Franks Committee emphasized the importance of building a tribunals system in which the public would have confidence. The role of reason-giving (on which see generally ch 12 above) in this regard is self-evident — as Lord Phillips MR put it (albeit referring to court, rather than tribunal, decisions) in *English* v. *Emery Reimbold and Strick Ltd* [2002] EWCA Civ 605 [2003] 1 WLR 2409 at [16], 'justice will not be done if it is not apparent to the parties why one has won and the other has lost' — and it is therefore unsurprising that the Franks Committee (at [98]) was

> convinced that if tribunal proceedings are to be fair to the citizen reasons should be given to the fullest practicable extent. A decision is apt to be better if the reasons for it have to be set out in writing because the reasons are then more likely to have been properly thought out. Further, a

reasoned decision is essential in order that where there is a right of appeal [from the first instance tribunal], the applicant can assess whether he has good grounds of appeal and know the case he will have to meet if he decides to appeal.

These recommendations formed the basis of what is now s 10 of the Tribunals and Inquiries Act 1992 (which is set out above at 18.3.1). It should be noted, however, that s 10 does not impose upon all tribunals an absolute duty to give reasons. For example, the duty only applies to those tribunals listed in sch 1 to the Act, and may be displaced by provisions in other legislation (s 10(5)(a)), by national security considerations (s 10(2)), or, in certain circumstances, by order of the Lord Chancellor (s 10(7)). Moreover, the duty to give reasons does not arise automatically upon the tribunal's determination of the relevant matter: instead, reasons (written *or oral*: cf Franks' recommendation, above) need only be given 'if requested, on or before the giving or notification of the decision'. Nevertheless, it is considered best practice for tribunals to give reasons at their own initiative, irrespective of whether a request has been made. This was the view of Leggatt (at [4.8]) and is also reflected in rule 76(2)(b) and (3) of the Council on Tribunals' *Guide to Drafting Tribunal Rules* (London 2003), which provides that tribunal decisions, 'whether there has been a hearing or not, must be recorded as soon as possible in a document which' — save in the case of a decision by consent — 'must also contain a statement of the reasons . . . for the decision', and which must be sent to each party. The explanatory notes (at 143) point out that this should be the 'general rule' — implicitly recognizing that it may be inappropriate in respect of some tribunals — and go on to suggest that the standard applicable to reason-giving by tribunals is analogous to that which applies to courts' decisions (on which see Ho (2000) 20 *LS* 42). Particular emphasis is placed by the Council on the decision of the Court of Appeal in *English* v. *Emery Reimbold and Strick Ltd* [2002] EWCA Civ 605 [2003] 1 WLR 2409, which considered the duty incumbent upon judges — both at common law and under Article 6 ECHR — to give reasons for their decisions. After referring to a number of Strasbourg judgments — including *Ruiz Torija* v. *Spain* (1994) 19 EHRR 553, *Garcia Ruiz* v. *Spain* (1999) 31 EHRR 589 and *Helle* v. *Finland* (1997) 26 EHRR 159 — Lord Phillips MR concluded that:

[12] The Strasbourg court, when considering article 6, is not concerned with the merits of the decision of the domestic court that is under attack. It is concerned to see that the procedure has been fair. It requires that a judgment contains reasons that are sufficient to demonstrate that the essential issues that have been raised by the parties have been addressed by the domestic court and how those issues have been resolved. It does not seem to us that the Strasbourg jurisprudence goes further and requires a judgment to explain why one contention, or piece of evidence, has been preferred to another. The common law countries have developed a tradition of delivering judgments that detail the evidence and explain the findings in much greater detail than is to be found in the judgments of most civil law jurisdictions. We do not believe that the extent of the reasoning that the Strasbourg court requires goes any further than that which is required under our domestic law, which we are about to consider. It remains to consider, however, the nature of the judicial decisions for which reasons are required under the Strasbourg jurisprudence.

[13] All of the Strasbourg decisions to which we have so far referred were considering judgments which determined the substantive dispute between the parties. The critical issue in each case was whether the form of the judgment in question was compatible with a fair trial. Where a judicial decision affects the substantive rights of the parties we consider that the Strasbourg jurisprudence requires that the decision should be reasoned. In contrast, there are some judicial decisions where fairness does not demand that the parties should be informed of the reasoning underlying them.

Interlocutory decisions in the course of case management provide an obvious example. Further-more, the Strasbourg Commission has recognised that there are some circumstances in which the reason for the decision will be implicit from the decision itself. In such circumstances article 6 will not be infringed if the reason for the decision is not expressly spelt out by the judicial tribunal: see *X* v *Federal Republic of Germany* (1981) 25 DR 240 and *Webb* v *United Kingdom* (1997) 24 EHRR CD 73 . . .

[17] As to the adequacy of reasons, as has been said many times, this depends on the nature of the case: see for example *Flannery's* case [2000] 1 WLR 377, 382. In *Eagil Trust Co Ltd* v *Pigott-Brown* [1985] 3 All ER 119, 122 Griffiths LJ stated that there was no duty on a judge, in giving his reasons, to deal with every argument presented by counsel in support of his case:

> "When dealing with an application in chambers to strike out for want of prosecution, a judge should give his reasons in sufficient detail to show the Court of Appeal the principles on which he has acted and the reasons that have led him to his decision. They need not be elaborate. I cannot stress too strongly that there is no duty on a judge, in giving his reasons, to deal with every argument presented by counsel in support of his case. It is sufficient if what he says shows the parties and, if need be, the Court of Appeal the basis on which he has acted . . . (see Sachs LJ in *Knight* v *Clifton* [1971] Ch 700, 721)."

The courts have struggled to articulate a coherent approach to the question what effect a failure to comply with a statutory duty to give reasons has on a tribunal's decision. It has been assumed in some cases — such as *Re Poyser and Mills' Arbitration* [1964] 2 QB 467 and *Alexander Machinery (Dudley) Ltd.* v. *Crabtree* [1974] ICR 120 — that statutory require-ments to give reasons are mandatory, such that non-compliance yields an error of law. However, in other cases — including *Crake* v. *Supplementary Benefits Commission* [1982] 1 All ER 498 and *R* v. *Immigration Appeal Tribunal, ex parte Khan (Mahmud)* [1983] QB 790 — a more cautious approach to this question has been adopted. The law in this area was reviewed in the following case.

....

R v. Northamptonshire County Council ex parte Marshall [1998] COD 457
Queen's Bench Division

The Special Educational Needs Tribunal Regulations 1994, regulation 31(2) required the provision of 'a statement of the reasons (in summary form) for the tribunal's decision'. In the present case, the adequacy of the reasons given by the tribunal was challenged; while the statement of reasons was found by the court, on a statutory appeal, to be sufficient, Sedley J made the following *obiter* comments.

Sedley J

[27] I would not like to part with this case . . . without considering one question of law which would have arisen, and might now arise hereafter, on a finding favourable to an appellant. What powers does the court possess when an inferior tribunal with a duty to give reasons has failed to give any reasons or (what amounts in law to the same thing) has failed to give adequate or intelligible reasons?

[28] On judicial review, as Mr McManus accepts, authority now favours the proposition that such a failure is a free-standing ground in the court's discretion for quashing the decision as flawed: see *R.* v. *Higher Education Funding Council, ex parte Institute of Dental Surgery* [1994] 1 W.L.R. 242 at 257–8. The consequence will be that the decision must be retaken in accordance with the law.

[29] On a statutory appeal, which may well be on the identical ground, the governing authority is still the decision of a powerful Divisional Court (Lord Parker C.J., Cooke J. and Bridge J.) in *Mountview Court Properties Ltd* v. *Devlin* 21 P&CR 689, a case under s 9 and s 12 of the Tribunals and Inquiries Act 1958 [see now ss 11 and 10, respectively, of the Tribunals and Inquiries Act 1992]. At page 694, Lord Parker C.J. said:

> "What is really relied on here is, again, *Re Poyser and Mills' Arbitration* [[1964] 2 QB 467] to which I have already referred, where Megaw J. did, apparently, hold that the failure to give reasons constituted an error of law. That was in relation to an arbitration under the Agricultural Holdings Act 1948, and what Megaw J. was concerned with was an error of law on the face of the award, whereas what this court is concerned with in the present case is an appeal under section 9(1) of the Tribunals and [Inquiries] Act 1958 [see now s 11(1) of the Act of 1992], which provides that:

> > 'If any party to proceedings before any such tribunal . . . is dissatisfied in point of law with a decision of the tribunal given on or after the appointed day he may, according as rules of court may provide, either appeal therefrom to the High Court or require the tribunal to state and sign a case for the opinion of the High Court.'

> "For my part, I find it impossible to say that a failure to provide sufficient reasons of itself gives rise to the right of this court on an appeal to quash the decision of the committee. Secondly, it is to be observed that, quite apart from that, *Re Poyser and Mills' Arbitration* was really a case where, on the reasons stated, the proper inference was that there had been an error of law and that the arbitrator had misdirected himself. Of course, if the very insufficiency of the reason gives rise to a proper inference that there has been an error of law in arriving at the decision, then clearly it would be a case for quashing the decision".

[30] Bridge J., as he then was, in agreeing said:

> ". . . a failure to give reasons pursuant to the duty imposed by section 12 of the Tribunals and Inquiries Act 1958 [see now s 10 of the 1992 Act] is not *per se* a ground on which the court could properly allow an appeal under section 9, the right of appeal being conferred upon a person who is dissatisfied in point of law with a decision.

> "That language, and, indeed, any analogous language found in the statutes giving a right of appeal on a point of law, to my mind connotes that a successful appellant must demonstrate that the decision with which he is dissatisfied is itself vitiated by reason of the fact that it has been reached by an erroneous process of legal reasoning.

> "Mr Slynn concedes that there may in theory be cases where from a failure to give reasons one may legitimately infer, on a balance of probabilities, that the tribunal's process of legal reasoning may have been defective."

In *S. (A Minor)* v. *Special Educational Needs Tribunal* [1995] 1 W.L.R. 1627 Latham J. said at page 1637:

> "Of course it is not the failure to give reasons which will, of itself, justify the court allowing an appeal. That was made clear in *Mountview Court Properties* v. *Devlin* (1970) 21 P&CR 689. The failure to give intelligible reasons may well dispose the court to conclude that the tribunal must have misdirected itself or otherwise gone wrong in law. But the normal consequence, unless the case is clear, is that the matter will be remitted for rehearing and determination either by the same or a differently constituted tribunal, depending upon the circumstances of the case."

[31] This, if correct, would bring the powers of the court on a statutory appeal under [RSC] Ord

55, r 7(5) [see now CPR 52.10(2)] very close to those on judicial review where, in either case, inadequate reasons had been given. It would create a most satisfactory symmetry. But in *South Glamorgan County Council* v *L. and M.* [1996] E.L.R. 400 at page 413 Carnwath J., having cited the final part of the passage of Latham J. which I have quoted, commented:

> "If he was intending to suggest that a mere defect of reasons, not amounting to an error of law, will be sufficient by itself to empower the court, by way of final order, to remit the matter for rehearing, I would respectfully disagree. There may be rare cases where the court feels it necessary to seek additional reasons in order to dispose of the case (see *Mountview Court Properties* v. *Devlin* at p 693). However, it is only an error of law which gives the court its jurisdiction (under s 11 and Ord 55) to set aside the determination, or to order a rehearing. If no error of law is established, then the decision stands."

[32] Logically this seems to me to flow inescapably from the *Mountview* case ... What may therefore, with very great respect, deserve consideration at a higher level than this is whether the Divisional Court was right in that case to hold that to have had an adverse decision based on required reasons which, though inadequate or unintelligible — perhaps indeed because they are inadequate or unintelligible — did not disclose an error of law was not to be "dissatisfied in point of law" with a decision under what was then s 9 of the Tribunals and Inquiries Act 1958 and is now s 11 of the Tribunals and Inquiries Act 1992. So long as the *Mountview* decision stands, it seems to me as it did to Carnwath J. that remission for fuller or clearer reasons must be beyond the power of the court hearing the statutory appeal unless an error of law can be inferred, in which case remission for fuller reasons would seem to be unnecessary . . .

Woolf J reached a similar conclusion in *Crake* v. *Supplementary Benefits Commission* [1982] 1 All ER 498 at 506; however, while he regarded *Mountview* as 'the main authority to be applied', he noted that

it has to be applied in the light of the ten years which have elapsed since that case was decided. Over that period of ten years the approach of the courts with regard to the giving of reasons has been much more definite than they were at that time and courts are now much more ready to infer that because of inadequate reasons there has been an error of law, than perhaps they were prepared to at the time that the *Mountview* case was decided . . . Therefore in practice I think that there will be few cases where it will not be possible, where the reasons are inadequate, to say one way or another whether the tribunal has gone wrong in law.

QUESTIONS

- Is the law in this area satisfactory?
- Should non-compliance with a statutory requirement to give reasons be regarded as an error of law *per se*?
- Is the view that such non-compliance is not necessarily vulnerable to *appeal* on a point of law consistent with the fact that a failure to give reasons for a decision may lead to its being quashed on *judicial review*?

19.4 Appeals and the System of Tribunals

19.4.1 Towards a Tribunals System

We have already seen in this chapter that, motivated partly by concerns about the independence (actual and perceived) of tribunals, responsibility for many tribunals is in the course of being transferred from the relevant 'sponsoring departments' — *ie* the department whose work the tribunal scrutinizes — to the DCA. As part of this shift in responsibility, the Secretary of State for Constitutional Affairs, as we saw above at 19.3.1, will (along with a new procedure committee) set tribunals' procedural rules. Moreover, the Tribunals Service, a new executive agency within the DCA, will provide administrative and other support to the tribunals concerned. However, these administrative changes are only part of the story. The central plank of the reform programme is the creation of a new tribunals system which will radically change the way in which tribunals operate and relate to one another.

Leggatt found one of the defining features of the system of tribunals to be its disjointed nature (a view accepted in the White Paper at [5.14]). At the beginning of his report (at [1.3]), Leggatt observed that

the present collection of tribunals has grown up in an almost entirely haphazard way. Individual tribunals were set up, and usually administered by departments, as they developed new statutory schemes and procedures. The result is a collection of tribunals, mostly administered by departments, with wide variations of practice and approach, and almost no coherence. The current arrangements seem to us to have been developed to meet the needs and conveniences of the departments and other bodies which run tribunals, rather than the needs of the user.

Leggatt went on to note (at [3.2]–[3.3]) that the disjointedness of the tribunals system can lead to incoherence in terms of approaches, levels of administrative support, and so on:

Most tribunals are entirely self-contained, and operate separately from each other, using different practices and standards. It is obvious that the term "tribunal system" is a misnomer. Since each tribunal has evolved as a solution to a particular problem, adapted to one particular area, this lack of coherence might not matter if it could be said that decisions were of good quality, and consistent; that enough information, advice and support was available to use tribunals adequately; that the services provided were delivering what they were supposed to; and that the significant amount of money tribunals were costing was well spent. What we have learned about tribunals has convinced us that no such assurance could properly be given.

Not only does the disjointedness of the current system pose problems for tribunals; it can also be bewildering for prospective appellants. Leggatt (at [3.8]) saw rationalization and systematization as the solutions to these problems:

The overriding aim should be to present the citizen with a single, overarching structure. It would give access to all tribunals. Any citizen who wished to appeal to a tribunal would only have to submit the appeal, confident in the knowledge that one system handled all such disputes, and could be relied upon to allocate it to the right tribunal. This would be a considerable advance in clarity and simplicity for users and their advisers. The single system would enable a coherent, user-focussed approach to the provision of information which would enable tribunals to meet the claim that they operate in ways which enable citizens to participate directly in preparing and presenting their own cases.

It was therefore recommended that the present collection of separate tribunals should be replaced by a single tribunals system.

The White Paper endorses the broad thrust of Leggatt's proposals in this area. It proposes that, to begin with, the new tribunal system should encompass the ten largest central government tribunal organizations, which are collectively responsible for more than 90 per cent of tribunal cases. It is envisaged that, by 2009, other central government tribunals will have migrated into the new system. On a practical level, it is hoped that placing tribunals within a single system, under the responsibility of a single government department and supported by a single agency, will make it possible to share accommodation, administrative support facilities, and so on, and that the existence of one system will make it more straightforward for potential tribunal users to get information about how to pursue claims and, where appropriate, to take them forward.

The new system would be judicially led by a Senior President, and the system divided into different jurisdiction, each led by a President (see further above at 19.2). Jurisdictions would consist of tribunals whose work related to issues of similar subject-matter. Within this system, tribunals would retain their individual legal identities, although 'the extent to which they show a separate face to the public will depend on an assessment to be made from time to time by the organisation as a whole as to which is the most helpful approach from the point of view of the user' (White Paper at [6.38]). All members of tribunals would be appointed or transferred to a 'single judicial office', to be known as 'Tribunal Judges', while all members of the new appellate tribunal would become 'Tribunal Appellate Judges' (on which see 19.4.2 below). Judges qualified to sit in more than one jurisdiction would be able to do so, with deployment of judges to particular jurisdictions and cases a matter for the Senior President, jurisdiction Presidents, and other judicial managers. It is hoped that creating a 'single corps of tribunal judiciary' (*ibid* at [6.53]) will raise the profile and status of tribunal judicial office.

These new arrangements are perhaps best thought of in federal terms. Individual tribunals and jurisdictions will remain, but there will much greater integration and commonality than at present, in terms of judiciary, administrative arrangements, customer service interface, and so on. It is intended that the new system should have a strong overarching public identity, and that it should act as a vehicle for delivering a higher standard of administrative justice more efficiently and effectively than is possible with the existing set of disparate tribunals administered by a range of government departments.

19.4.2 Appeal from and Review of First-Tier Tribunals' Decisions

Section 11(1) of the Tribunals and Inquiries Act 1992 provides that

if any party to proceedings before any tribunal specified in [certain parts of] Schedule 1 is dissatisfied in point of law with a decision of the tribunal he may, according as rules of court may provide, either appeal from the tribunal to the High Court or require the tribunal to state and sign a case for the opinion of the High Court.

Leggatt identified a number of problems relating to the oversight of first-tier tribunals' decisions, noting (at [3.9]) that the establishment of a coherent Tribunals System would create

a clearer and simpler system for the development of the law. As things now stand, tribunals are not able to set precedents, although some of those which hear appeals from first-tier tribunals are making arrangements for designating those cases which appear to be particularly authoritative or significant. The arrangements for appealing from tribunals have developed piece-meal, and show little logic [eg some tribunals have a two-tier structure, others do not; different time limits for appealing apply in respect of different tribunals]. The relationship with the supervisory and appellate jurisdictions of the ordinary courts . . . is often confusing. We consider this a significant failing. Tribunals have developed a characteristic approach to managing hearings, and taking decisions. We think they should be charged with developing the law in a consistent way.

In view of these concerns, Leggatt proposed (at [6.10]–[6.11]) that the system for appealing against first-instance tribunals' decisions should be standardized. This proposal has been largely taken up by the White Paper. It is envisaged that, within the new tribunals system, there will be a single appellate body, whose provisional title is the Administrative Appeals Tribunal ('AAT'), dealing with appeals on points of law from first-instance citizen v. state tribunals. (In contrast, the Employment Appeal Tribunal would retain its separate identity.) Tribunal Appellate Judges would be assigned to AAT cases arising only from jurisdictions in which they were qualified. With limited exceptions, all appeals from first-instance tribunals would lie to the AAT, replacing existing arrangements both for appeal to individual second-tier tribunals (which would no longer exist: their judiciary would transfer to the AAT) and to the High Court. A further right of appeal, again on a point of law, would lie from the AAT to the Court of Appeal. Permission would be required for appeal against both first-instance and AAT decisions.

Against the background of this proposed framework, it is necessary to address two further issues. First, should decisions of the AAT be capable of setting precedent? Leggatt considered (at [6.22]) that attaching precedent-setting capacity to appellate level decisions would facilitate 'clear and consistent decision-making'. Three ways of realizing this objective were considered. First, appellate tribunals could be constituted superior courts of record, but this was rejected (at [6.23]) because (*inter alia*) it would 'undoubtedly blur the clear distinction we seek to draw between the new system and the courts'. Secondly, express statutory provisions could make all decisions of appellate tribunals binding on the first-tier tribunals. However, Leggatt noted (at [6.24]) that, while this would be an administratively straightforward solution, it would 'require users to be aware of all relevant decisions, to know what law would apply to their case', which could form 'a significant barrier to access'. Leggatt therefore recommended (at [6.26]) that it should be possible to designate particular decisions as binding:

The advantages of this are that the selectors will have before them all appealed decisions as the pool from which to select the most analytically powerful precedents. Some control over the number of precedents is also possible, to give users greater certainty. There is a theoretical disadvantage in that it allows the selectors a power that is potentially open to abuse. This could be removed by making the final adoption of precedents a collective decision. We recommend that final decisions about binding precedents should be taken by the President of the appellate tribunal concerned, subject to the approval of the Tribunals Board [a body whose creation was proposed by Leggatt, and which would have the function of directing the Tribunals System].

However, when it consulted on the Leggatt Report, the DCA found (see *Responses to the*

Consultation Paper: 'Tribunals for Users' (London 2003) at [36]) strong support for making *all* appellate decisions binding as the 'best way to resolve the inevitable range of decisions that arise where the volume of case law is very high'. This matter is not resolved by the White Paper, which simply states (at [7.20]) that 'a series of common principles with regard to precedent will be developed in partnership with the jurisdictional Presidents'.

The second issue which arises concerns what role, if any, there should be for judicial review of the decisions of first-instance tribunals and of the AAT. The general principle at present is that tribunals' decisions are amenable to judicial review, although, as we saw above at 15.4, prospective claimants are usually required to exhaust alternative remedies, such as rights of appeal, before obtaining permission to proceed with judicial review. Although any limitation upon the availability of judicial review raises important questions (see above at 15.6), the White Paper argues (at [7.27]–[7.28]) that the practical and constitutional need for judicial review in the present context will be circumscribed by the design of the new system:

Our intention is that the new [appellate] tier [of the proposed tribunal system] would be strengthened by the secondment of circuit judges and, for cases of sufficient weight, High Court Judges with the relevant expertise. The courts' traditional supervisory or appellate role would then, in most cases, be exercised by the Court of Appeal, which would be concerned only with appeals that raised an important point of principle or practice, or where some other compelling reason existed that warranted the attention of that court. Our intention is that appeals from tribunals should for the most part remain within the tribunals system and that where novel or difficult points of law are raised appeals should be to the Court of Appeal rather than the High Court.

Permission to appeal will be necessary both for an appeal from the first tier to the second tier and from an appeal from the second tier to the Court of Appeal. With this structure the only possible role for judicial review in the High Court would be on a refusal by the first and second tier to grant permission to appeal. It is this possible route to redress which has caused so much difficulty for both the Immigration Appellate Authorities and the Courts. When permission to appeal has been refused by both tiers, and provided that the tribunal appellate judiciary are of appropriate quality, as we intend that they should be, there ought not to be a need for further scrutiny of a case by the courts. However, complete exclusion of the courts from their historic supervisory role is a highly contentious constitutional proposition and so we see merit in providing as a final form of recourse a statutory review on paper by a judge of the Court of Appeal.

QUESTION

- Is limiting the availability of judicial review in this way acceptable? (Consider the general principles addressed above at 15.6, and note the form of statutory review on paper which already exists in the immigration context, as discussed above at 15.6.8.)

19.5 The Supervision and Accountability of Tribunals

The Council on Tribunals was established by the Tribunals and Inquiries Act 1958, in light of the recommendations of the Franks Report. The Council's statutory remit is now found in the following provision:

Tribunals and Inquiries Act 1992

1—(1) There shall continue to be a council entitled the Council on Tribunals . . .—

  (a) to keep under review the constitution and working of the tribunals specified in Schedule 1 (being the tribunals constituted under or for the purposes of the statutory provisions specified in that Schedule) and, from time to time, to report on their constitution and working;

  (b) to consider and report on such particular matters as may be referred to the Council under this Act with respect to tribunals other than the ordinary courts of law, whether or not specified in Schedule 1, or any such tribunal; and

  (c) to consider and report on such matters as may be referred to the Council under this Act, or as the Council may determine to be of special importance, with respect to administrative procedures involving, or which may involve, the holding by or on behalf of a Minister of a statutory inquiry, or any such procedure.

Two of the major roles fulfilled by the Council to date have been the scrutiny of draft procedural rules for tribunals (pursuant to the obligation in s 8(1) of the Tribunals and Inquiries Act 1992 (see above at 19.3.1) to consult it before making such rules) and visits to individual tribunals (which, according to the Council's web site, allow Council members to see the tribunals at work, talk to members and staff of tribunals, develop a knowledge and understanding of the problems facing tribunals and inquiries, and explain the Council's work).

However, while a positive account of the Council's role is (unsurprisingly) advanced by its former chairman, Lord Archer of Sandwell, in his contribution to Harris and Partington (eds), *Administrative Justice in the 21st Century* (Oxford 1999), others discern a number of problems in this area. Unflattering comparisons are drawn with the Australian Administrative Review Council (on which see Robertson's chapter in Harris and Partington, *op cit*) whose much wider remit allows it to play a pivotal role in the development of administrative law and adjudication generally, not just tribunals and inquiries. The present role of the Council on Tribunals can be illustrated by reference to the criticisms levelled at it — and the suggestions for change made — by the Leggatt Report, which noted (at [7.46]) that 'in default of any central direction [tribunals] have become diverse and unco-ordinated. Franks probably intended that direction to come from the Council on Tribunals. It has not.' Two central problems were identified by Leggatt. The first (at [7.47]) concerns the perceived failure of the Council to provide strategic direction:

The Council possesses a great deal of knowledge about the operation of tribunals to-day. It has made some efforts to promote policies and standards. Its Model Rules of Procedure [see now its

Guide to Drafting Tribunal Rules (London 2003)] are a major achievement. Its work on independence of tribunals and on standards of accommodation and of training deserve notice. It has also drawn attention to the importance of competence in tribunal chairmen and members. But it has not published its visit reports, nor exposed the defects they identified . . . Visitors who have given evidence to the Council have not found the experience as challenging as they should have. In focussing on the need for detailed comment on specific issues, it has given insufficient emphasis to strategic thinking about administrative justice generally or about tribunals in particular.

Secondly, Leggatt (at [7.47]–[7.48]) found that the Council was not good at publicizing its views and securing change where it had identified problems:

[The Council] has failed to gain publicity for its criticisms, for example in its Annual Reports, whether or not the failure has been due to departmental opposition . . . Because departments were under no obligation to respond to its criticisms, the Council must have felt that any good it did had to be done by stealth, rather than by confrontation, lest departments might take offence and withdraw their collaboration. With unresponsive departments, and no Select Committee to report to, it has not been giving such an account of itself as meets the demands of the twenty-first century.

While the Leggatt Report welcomed the programme for change set out by the Council in its *Annual Report 1999/2000* (in which it defines its role in more proactive terms), Leggatt (at [7.49]) set out an even bolder vision:

The Council's primary role should be to act as the hub of the wheel of administrative justice, or at any rate tribunal justice. Just as tribunals themselves cannot be expected to function properly without a Board, so the Council is needed to co-ordinate the arms of the system of administrative justice of which they are parts. The Council should monitor the development of the new Tribunals System during the first few years of its existence, and also check that the practices and procedures of Government departments are ECHR compliant. The Council should have as a primary duty the championing of the cause of users.

As well as arguing that the Council should discharge these monitoring and co-ordinating functions more energetically and pro-actively, Leggatt identified two further ways in which it felt the Council's role needed to be strengthened. First, it was argued ([at 7.51]) that there should be a 'general expectation that where the Council has made formal representations to a Government department it should receive a reasoned and constructive reply, capable of being put into the public domain'. Secondly, Leggatt noted the 'anomaly' that, while the Council must be consulted before procedural rules for tribunals are made, there is neither a requirement to consult before the enactment of primary legislation affecting tribunals nor an obligation upon Ministers to communicate to Parliament the Council's views. Leggatt recommended that, in future, 'any concerns raised by the Council should be recorded in the explanatory memoranda for Bills and Statutory Instruments, with the department's response'.

Finally, and most generally, Leggatt considered (at [7.54]) that the Council's remit should be extended beyond tribunals and inquiries, in order to reflect the fact that such mechanisms exist not in isolation, but in the context of a wider system of administrative law:

In the longer term, like the Administrative Review Council in Australia, the Council should be made responsible for upholding the system of administrative justice and keeping it under review, for monitoring developments in administrative law, and for making recommendations to the Lord Chancellor about improvements that might be made to the system. To assist users through the system, the Council should be required to ensure that the various mechanisms for redressing the grievances of members of the public work together coherently and efficiently. Joined up government demands no less.

As with many other of Leggatt's proposals, the broad thrust of his recommendations concerning the Council on Tribunals is taken up in the White Paper; under the government's proposals, many of the problems identified by Leggatt would be addressed. For instance, in order to ensure that the Council's expertise is better used by government, a code of practice is proposed, under which it would be obligatory to consult the Council on all legislation (primary and secondary) affecting tribunals; the code would also require relevant government departments to respond publicly to the Council's comments on draft legislation, and the Council's reports would be drawn to the attention of relevant select committees.

More broadly, the White Paper envisages that the Council's role will change. Some of its present functions would, under the new system, be discharged by others: for instance, its role in relation to the scrutiny of procedural rules for tribunals would be eclipsed by the creation of a procedure committee (see above at 19.3.1), while the Council's promotion of good practice through visits to individual tribunals would be less important once the Senior President and Chief Executive of the Tribunals Service were in place (who would both be charged with disseminating and encouraging best practice within the system). The government therefore envisages a substantial change in the Council's role, which would ultimately be reflected by renaming it the 'Administrative Justice Council'. The White Paper (at [11.11]–[11.12]) explains that:

What is needed for the future is a Council which can focus on improvements for the user across the whole administrative justice field, so that the new organisation, and tribunals outside the new organisation, develop and operate under the strategic oversight of an independent and authoritative body with a very wide perspective.

We therefore propose that the Council should in the longer term, while retaining its supervisory role over all types of tribunal, evolve into an advisory body for the whole administrative justice sector — an Administrative Justice Council. It would report to the Secretary of State for Constitutional Affairs who would have a parallel remit within government to take the lead on redress policy generally. We would, for instance, expect an Administrative Justice Council to make suggestions for departmental review, for proportionate dispute resolution and for the balance between the different components of the system. The Council would therefore be concerned to ensure that the relationships between the courts, tribunals, ombudsmen and other ADR routes satisfactorily reflect the needs of users. We envisage a broadbased, mixed membership under an independent Chair, bringing together user representatives and non-executive members with office holders, able to generate ideas for the future that reflect the needs of the various "constituencies" but small enough to function as a collective and active body. The Parliamentary Ombudsman is already ex officio a member of the Council on Tribunals; other officer-holder members could include the Senior President and a senior civil servant from the Cabinet Office or a major decision-making department.

It is hoped that, by recasting the Council's role in these terms, it will be able to provide the sort of strategic input — not only into tribunals, but into an integrated administrative justice system — which Leggatt found to be presently lacking.

19.6 Concluding Remarks

The changes envisaged in the recent White Paper are radical. The rationalization of tribunals through the creation of a unified tribunals system, supported by a single executive agency and overseen by the DCA, is to be welcomed on a number of counts. It should, as we have seen, enhance the independence of tribunals, underlining their status as part of the adjudicative machinery of the state, rather than administrative tools of individual government departments. The unified approach also creates an opportunity for better public understanding of and easier access to tribunals, through the creation of simple entry points into and clear pathways through the system. Of course, these benefits will not follow ineluctably; it is possible that the new system may prove administratively unwieldy and unresponsive. Nevertheless, an opportunity now exists to fashion a system which is more readily comprehensible, efficient, and user-friendly than the disjointed collection of tribunals that presently exists.

It is important to recognize, however, that the White Paper looks beyond the tribunals system, seeking to locate it within a wider administrative justice landscape. Thus the White Paper emphasizes the importance of high-quality decision-making in the first place by administrators, thereby minimizing the need to resort to grievance-redress mechanisms; of facilitating the clear presentation of individuals' cases at the initial administrative stage, in order that mistakes may be avoided; of effective complaints procedures within departments, in order that grievances can, where possible, be resolved informally; of promoting awareness of the full range of mechanisms — such as complaints to MPs and ombudsmen — for the redress of grievances; and of the need for tribunals to work with departments in order to promote good practice at the initial stage. The vision presented in the White Paper is of a joined-up system of administrative justice; its realization will be a difficult, but highly worthwhile, enterprise.

FURTHER RESOURCES

Cm 6243, *Transforming Public Services: Complaints, Redress and Tribunals* (2004): *www.dca.gov.uk/pubs/adminjust/adminjust.htm*

Harris and Partington (eds), *Administrative Justice in the 21st Century* (Oxford 1999)

Leggatt, Report of the Review of Tribunals, *Tribunals for Users: One Service, One System* (London 2001) *www.tribunals-review.org.uk*

Tribunals section of the web site of the Department for Constitutional Affairs *www.dca.gov.uk/legalsys/tribunals.htm*

Partington (ed), *The Leggatt Review of Tribunals: Academic Seminar Papers* (Bristol 2001)

Web site of the Council on Tribunals (via which Annual Reports and other Council literature referred to in this chapter are available) *www.council-on-tribunals.gov.uk*

20 OMBUDSMEN

20.1 Introduction

20.1.1 Ombudsmen in the UK

Although the origins of 'ombudsmen' can be traced to 19th century Sweden, it was not until the 1960s that the concept was embraced by the common law world. In the United Kingdom, recent years have witnessed an explosion in the use of ombudsmen for complaints-handling purposes, as the creation of such offices as the Estate Agents Ombudsman, the Funeral Ombudsman, and the Legal Services Ombudsman illustrates. While there is no legal restriction on who may be called an 'ombudsman', the web site of the British and Irish Ombudsman Association states that the term should only be used if four key criteria — the 'independence of the Ombudsman from those whom the Ombudsman has the power to investigate; effectiveness; fairness and public accountability' — are met. These criteria are advanced in an attempt to prevent the proliferation of private sector 'ombudsmen' debasing the term and the values for which it has traditionally stood.

Our concern in this chapter is with what may be called 'public sector ombudsmen'. There are various definitions of 'ombudsmen' in this context (see, *eg*, Seneviratne, *Ombudsmen: Public Services and Administrative Justice* (London 2002) at 7–10), but a useful starting point is given by Collcutt and Hourihan, *Review of the Public Sector Ombudsmen in England: A Report by the Cabinet Office* (London 2000) (hereinafter the 'Cabinet Office Review') at [1.11]:

Public sector ombudsmen in England were created by statute, are independent from the Government and are impartial in their dealings with complainants and those complained about. They exist to consider complaints by citizens that public organisations (or those acting on their behalf) have caused them injustice by maladministration . . .

Public sector Ombudsmen in England fall into three categories. (The terms 'Ombudsman' and 'Ombudsmen' are used throughout this chapter: although the legislation establishing many of the Ombudsmen refers to them as 'commissioners', that term has fallen into disuse.) The Parliamentary Ombudsman (established under the Parliamentary Commissioner Act 1967) investigates complaints of maladministration by government departments and certain public bodies; the Health Service Ombudsman (see the Health Service Commissioners Act 1993) investigates complaints concerning health care provided by both the National Health Service and private organizations, while matters relating to local government are dealt with by the Local Government Ombudsmen (established under Part II of the

Local Government Act 1974). A different system exists in Northern Ireland, where the Assembly Ombudsman for Northern Ireland (see Parliamentary Commissioner (Northern Ireland) Act 1969)) handles complaints relating to the Northern Ireland Assembly (suspended at the time of writing), while the Northern Ireland Commissioner for Complaints (see Commissioner for Complaints (Northern Ireland) Act 1969) deals with local government and health. The Scottish Parliament has opted for an integrated Scottish Public Services Ombudsman who is given jurisdiction by the Scottish Public Services Ombudsman Act 2002 over health; local government; social housing; Scottish public authorities; and (insofar as their actions concern devolved matters affecting Scotland) certain cross-border public authorities. In Wales, there are separate Ombudsmen offices covering local government; social housing; health; and the Welsh Assembly, certain Welsh public authorities and (so far as their conduct impacts upon Wales) certain other public authorities (although, as explained below at 20.5.2, it is possible for the same person to occupy all four offices). However, the Public Services Ombudsman (Wales) Bill — before Parliament at the time of writing — envisages a single Public Services Ombudsman for Wales covering all such matters. In relation to Scotland, Wales, and Northern Ireland, the Parliamentary Ombudsman remains competent to investigate maladministration in relation to non-devolved matters.

Although we refer to other Ombudsmen for the purposes of comparison where this is appropriate, we focus in this chapter on the Parliamentary Ombudsman:

Parliamentary Commissioner Act 1967

1—(1) For the purpose of conducting investigations in accordance with the following provisions of this Act there shall be appointed a Commissioner, to be known as the Parliamentary Commissioner for Administration.

(2) Her Majesty may by Letters Patent from time to time appoint a person to be the Commissioner, and any person so appointed shall (subject to subsections (3) and (3A) of this section) hold office during good behaviour.

(3) A person appointed to be the Commissioner may be relieved of office by Her Majesty at his own request, or may be removed from office by Her Majesty in consequence of Addresses from both Houses of Parliament, and shall in any case vacate office on completing the year of service in which he attains the age of sixty-five years.

(3A) Her Majesty may declare the office of Commissioner to have been vacated if satisfied that the person appointed to be the Commissioner is incapable for medical reasons —

    (a) of performing duties of his office; and

    (b) of requesting to be relieved of it.

20.1.2 The Need for and Role of Ombudsmen

Why have such elaborate and wide-ranging Ombudsmen schemes been established in the UK? It is important to recognize that the introduction of public sector Ombudsmen in the 1960s occurred in a particular legal and political context: as Bradley [1980] *CLJ* 304 at 309 puts it, 'at a time when administrative law was failing to give the individual effective protection, the creation of an Ombudsman was needed to make possible the development of a new equity, suitable for a much governed nation'. Former Parliamentary and Health Service

Ombudsman Sir Cecil Clothier [1986] *PL* 204 at 205 notes that Parliament's shortcomings were also part of the impetus for the adoption of an Ombudsman system:

Until the end of the Second World War, we had been reasonably content with a machinery for resolving disputes between citizens and the State which consisted essentially of the judges and the politicians, that is to say, Parliament and the courts. If what a government department did to an individual citizen was unlawful, the courts would take cognizance of it. If what it did was not unlawful but in some other way unconscionable, the interest of Parliament might well be aroused. Yet with the passage of time these two devices began to fail. The courts became more technical, more formal, slower and more expensive to the point at which the average citizen found it difficult to mobilize the force of law in support of his quarrel with the State. Parliament too has become preoccupied with massive and detailed legislation on the one hand and national and international policy on the other. It is not reasonable to expect such a body to devote its collective time to those problems of individuals which lack a national or international dimension. The result was that many errors in government which caused injustice and hardship went unremedied.

This passage helpfully underlines the fact that the Parliamentary Ombudsman — the first Ombudsman to be created in the UK — was conceived, as Drewry and Harlow (1990) 53 *MLR* 745 at 753 put it, as 'an adjunct to the MP's traditional and cherished role as grievance-chaser on behalf of constituents'. Richard Crossman MP, the government Minister responsible for piloting the Parliamentary Commissioner Bill through the House of Commons, appeared to share this view, stating (in the second reading debate: HC Deb, vol 734, col 49) that the Ombudsman would be a 'servant of the House'. However, Crossmann also said (*op cit*, col 44) that the Ombudsman's investigations would provide the 'cutting edge of a really impartial and really searching investigation into the workings of Whitehall'. These remarks reveal an ambivalence — shared by many others — about the Ombudsman's role. Is her function to bolster the 'grievance-chasing' role of constituency MPs, securing redress in individual cases of maladministration? Or is her concern principally with oversight of the administration at a general level, identifying problems and recommending changes?

QUESTIONS

- Which of these roles is more important, in your view?
- Why?

....

Seneviratne, *Ombudsmen: Public Services and Administrative Justice*
(London 2002)

... Two main models, or ideal types, for ombudsmen systems have been identified [by Heede, *European Ombudsman: Redress and Control at Union Level* (The Hague 2000) at 79–112]: redress and control. The primary function of a redress ombudsman is to offer and facilitate alternative dispute resolution. The control ombudsman's primary function is general supervision of state authorities, rather than the resolution of disputes. Redress model ombudsmen are created when the traditional means of redress are perceived to be insufficient. Thus, additional means are sought for the regulation of the relationship between the administration and the individual. This insufficiency could arise because the matters are not justiciable, or because of the obstacles inherent in the court process. Ombudsmen schemes adopting this model are often seen as advocates for citizens. Sometimes these ombudsmen are given powers to conduct own-initiative investigations, but this is an adjunct to their redress function. Own-initiative investigations are triggered by complaints, which draw attention to problems that need to be investigated on a large scale.

The control-type of ombudsman is fundamentally different. These schemes are created primarily to regulate the way standards are created and understood by a public authority. These ombudsmen therefore supervise the rules and the way they are interpreted. Their concern is with issues of supervision and accountability. For these ombudsmen, the ability to conduct own-initiative investigations is of major importance and complainants are informants only. Nor need there be any suspicion of a wrongful act in order for the ombudsmen to examine the functioning of the administration, as the focus is the prevention of administrative failures. The concern of these ombudsmen is the general protection of fundamental rights and individual liberties . . .

Although there is no need for the two roles to conflict, and there is clearly strong linkage between the two, decisions have to be made about which functions should take precedence. This is important because the ombudsmen have to decide whether to devote their main energies into resolving individual cases, or to tackling the systemic faults in public administration which produce such cases. Most individual ombudsman cases have limited significance. On the other hand, ombudsmen can with justification be categorised as a "deterrent to maladministration" and cumulatively their decisions "help to propagate principles of good administrative practice" [see Drewry in Leyland and Woods (eds), *Administrative Law Facing the Future: Old Constraints and New Horizons* (London 1997) at 83]. In view of this, it can be argued that ombudsmen should see their main task as seeking out systemic causes of injustice in a way courts and tribunals are ill-equipped to do. Raising standards is the most appropriate way of improving the position of the consumers of public services in general. The resolving of individual disputes, while clearly of great importance, should be one of the means to this end, rather than an end in itself . . .

Seneviratne's view that 'control' is more important than 'redress' is shared by Harlow (1978) 41 *MLR* 446 at 452, who argues that the Ombudsman's primary role 'should be that of an independent and unattached investigator, with a mandate to identify maladministration, recommend improved procedures and negotiate their implementation'. Harlow and Rawlings, *Law and Administration* (London 1997) at 423–432, develop this theme, noting a 'tension' between the 'fire-fighting' (redress) and 'fire-watching' (control) functions of the Ombudsman which has never been adequately resolved, not least because the Justice Report, *The Citizen and the Administration: The Redress of Grievances* (London 1961), which acted as the catalyst for the creation of the Parliamentary Ombudsman, did not meaningfully address the possibility of a control function.

It is clear that the present Ombudsman sees redress as central to her role. For instance, she has observed (HC847, *Annual Report 2002–2003* (2002–2003) at [2.6]) that there are now

fewer concluded statutory investigations because other — simpler and faster — means of resolving complaints short of concluding a statutory investigation are increasingly being used. The number of such cases continues to grow, thus enabling the Ombudsman to achieve the same outcome for an increasing number of complainants more quickly and cheaply than using the statutory process.

However, it does not follow that the Parliamentary Ombudsman is unconcerned with matters of control. For example, she recently reported (*ibid*, ch 3) on a large number of complaints against Jobcentre Plus, an executive agency of the Department for Work and Pensions, explaining that following her investigations the agency agreed to make various procedural changes with the objective of seeking to avoid recurrence of the problems which had prompted the complaints. Thus, in her most recent annual report (HC702, *Annual Report 2003–2004* (2003–2004) at 1), the Ombudsman stated that:

Identifying recurring themes and systemic issues that arise from complaints is a crucial part of our work. We have regularly followed up recommendations and reported on systemic issues. In addition, we are now considering issuing annual letters to the departments with which we have the most regular contact, drawing their attention to the key themes and lessons learned from the complaints we have received about them.

Moreover, according to evidence given to the Select Committee on Public Administration (HC50-i, *Minutes of Evidence* (2004–2005) at [17]), the Ombudsman — drawing upon her experience of administrative failure and the likely causes of it — is considering issuing a 'code of good administrative practice'. In this regard, it is also noteworthy that the proposed Public Services Ombudsman for Wales should have power to issue 'guidance about good administrative practice' which public bodies would be required to 'have regard to' and which would form a benchmark for any investigations by the Ombudsman.

20.1.3 Ombudsmen in a Changing Administrative Landscape

We have already observed that the Parliamentary Ombudsman was established in the late 1960s in light of concerns about the abilities of the courts and Parliament to safeguard citizens' interests *vis-à-vis* the executive. However, as the developments charted throughout this book indicate, the landscape within which public administration occurs and is regulated has changed almost beyond recognition in the intervening 40 years. We confine ourselves in this section to some of the key developments.

The supervision of administrative functions by courts has changed radically in recent decades. Individuals now resort to judicial review, and the courts execute this function, with a readiness that contrasts sharply with the more modest use and nature of judicial review at the time of the Ombudsman's creation. Nevertheless, it would be mistaken to think that the growth of judicial review renders Ombudsmen otiose. While it is true, as Bradley [1980] *CLJ* 304 at 324–329 observes, that there is an overlap between the types of complaints which may be investigated by the Ombudsman and those that can be subjected to judicial review, the two mechanisms differ markedly. First, the Ombudsman (as we explain below at 20.3) is able to investigate allegations — of rudeness, delay, and so on — which may not disclose illegality for judicial review purposes. Secondly, many of the factors which deter recourse to judicial review — in particular, cost — do not apply to the Ombudsman. Thirdly, there are, as Bradley, *op cit* at 322, notes, significant procedural factors — which we address in more detail below at 20.4 — that distinguish the Ombudsman's approach from that of the Administrative Court:

. . . [T]he Ombudsman follows an administrative, inquisitorial and private process of investigation, with full access to departmental files, full power to question civil servants and the right to expect the cooperation of the department being investigated. The adversary procedure of the courts, conducted at arm's length between the parties through legal intermediaries, could not be more different. I am in no doubt that the Ombudsman's methods enable him to get closer to reconstructing the administrative history of a citizen's case than does High Court procedure . . .

Fourthly, although it may be argued that the Parliamentary Ombudsman emphasizes 'redress' over 'control', she is, unlike the courts, sometimes able to negotiate and secure systemic changes to administrative practice. It is perhaps this ability of the Ombudsman system to address the wider picture, rather than focusing simply on individual complaints, which distinguishes it most profoundly from curial scrutiny of public administration — and which, in turn, underscores most effectively the usefulness of Ombudsmen, the increasing prominence of judicial review notwithstanding.

As we saw in ch 19, the popularity of tribunals has also grown apace in the 40 or so years since the establishment of the Parliamentary Ombudsman. However, here, too, the need for Ombudsmen to fulfil a distinctive role remains. Indeed, as we explain below at 20.3.2, the Parliamentary Commissioner Act 1967 countenances recourse to the Ombudsman only where there is no possibility of appeal to a tribunal or where it would not be reasonable to expect the individual to exercise a right of appeal. The Ombudsman is therefore intended to complement, not compete with, appellate bodies, filling gaps where the tribunal system is incomplete or inapt. Moreover, tribunals and the Ombudsman are complementary in that the matters over which they have jurisdiction are to some extent distinct, the former being empowered to examine the merits of decisions, the latter focussing on the quality of the administrative process — although it must be acknowledged (see further below at 20.3.1) that this distinction does not, indeed cannot, exist as a bright line.

The final change in the administrative landscape that falls to be considered here relates to the culture of public services. In the early 1990s the Major administration launched the Citizen's Charter, which attempted to introduce private sector management techniques for public service delivery and to posit citizens as consumers of public services by setting out their rights and the standards they were entitled to expect. Barren and Scott (1992) 55 *MLR* 526 at 526 locate the philosophical foundations of this approach in 'a blending of New Right concerns with restricting the power of bureaucracy and extending individual choice, with more widespread concerns to make government bureaucracies more responsive to the needs of users'. The 'New Right' foundations of the Citizen's Charter scheme notwithstanding, the Blair government (with some modifications, on which see Scott [1999] *PL* 595 and Drewry [2002] *PL* 9) has persisted with it. Charter Marks are awarded to public bodies — and now to commercial organizations providing services to the public on behalf of public sector organizations — which comply with good practice criteria (see the Cabinet Office's *Guide to the Charter Mark Criteria 2003* (London 2003)) including the setting and attainment of specific standards; actively engaging with customers, partners and staff, and continuously developing and improving. For present purposes, the significance of this scheme is twofold.

First, as Seneviratne, *Ombudsmen: Public Services and Administrative Justice* (London 2002) at 80, notes, 'The programme provides an opportunity to raise standards in public services, which is an aim ombudsmen would support.' In particular, the publication — pursuant to the requirement openly to set standards — by government departments and agencies of codes of practice 'will provide the ombudsman with some benchmarks against which to determine any alleged maladministration'.

Secondly, the Charter Mark scheme requires public bodies to have 'a well-publicised, easy-to-use complaints procedure, including a commitment to deal with problems fully and solve them wherever possible within a time limit' (Cabinet Office, *Guide to the Charter Mark Criteria 2003* (London 2003) at 19). This has led to a profusion of internal complaints-handling procedures, whose relationship with Ombudsmen is unclear. Seneviratne, *op cit* at 89, asks:

Is the ombudsman to be at the apex of the system, a safety valve and last resort for cases which have not been dealt with satisfactorily by the [internal] adjudicators? If so, should there be a requirement for this procedure to be exhausted before a referral to the ombudsman? . . . [However,] [t]here are problems with using the ombudsman system as a kind of vestigal appeal body. In such a role, the office may not receive sufficiently large numbers of cases to enable there to be an assessment of whether public services are performing effectively. This would reduce the ombudsman's ability to comment on and suggest improvements in administrative practice.

20.2 Bodies Subject to Investigation

The range of bodies whose conduct can be investigated by the Parliamentary Ombudsman is determined by s 4 and sch 2 of the 1967 Act.

Parliamentary Commissioner Act 1967

4—(1) Subject to the provisions of this section and to the notes contained in Schedule 2 to this Act, this Act applies to the government departments, corporations and unincorporated bodies listed in that Schedule; and references in this Act to an authority to which this Act applies are references to any such corporation or body.

(2) Her Majesty may by Order in Council amend Schedule 2 to this Act by the alteration of any entry or note, the removal of any entry or note or the insertion of any additional entry or note.

(3) An Order in Council may only insert an entry if —

(a) it relates —

(i) to a government department; or

(ii) to a corporation or body whose functions are exercised on behalf of the Crown; or

(b) it relates to a corporation or body —

(i) which is established by virtue of Her Majesty's prerogative or by an Act of Parliament or on Order in Council or order made under an Act of Parliament or which is established in any other way by a Minister of the Crown in his capacity as a Minister or by a government department;

(ii) at least half of whose revenues derive directly from money provided by Parliament, a levy authorised by an enactment, a fee or charge of any other description so authorised or more than one of those sources; and

(iii) which is wholly or partly constituted by appointment made by Her Majesty or a Minister of the Crown or government department.

(3A) No entry shall be made if the result of making it would be that the Parliamentary Commissioner could investigate action which can be investigated by the Welsh Administration Ombudsman under Schedule 9 to the Government of Wales Act 1998.

(3B) No entry shall be made in respect of —

(a) the Scottish Administration or any part of it;

(b) any Scottish public authority with mixed functions or no reserved functions within the meaning of the Scotland Act 1998; or

(c) the Scottish Parliamentary Corporate Body.

(4) No entry shall be made in respect of a corporation or body whose sole activity is, or whose main activities are, included among the activities specified in subsection (5) below.

(5) The activities mentioned in subsection (4) above are —

(a) the provision of education, or the provision of training otherwise than under the Industrial Training Act 1982;

(b) the development of curricula, the conduct of examinations or the validation of educational courses;

(c) the control of entry to any profession or the regulation of the conduct of members of any profession;

(d) the investigation of complaints by members of the public regarding the actions of any person or body, or the supervision or review of such investigations or of steps taken following them.

(6) No entry shall be made in respect of a corporation or body operating in an exclusively or predominantly commercial manner or a corporation carrying on under national ownership an industry or undertaking or part of an industry or undertaking.

(7) Any statutory instrument made by virtue of this section shall be subject to annulment in pursuance of a resolution of either House of Parliament.

(8) In this Act —

(a) any reference to a government department to which this Act applies includes a reference to any of the Ministers or officers of such a department; and

(b) any reference to an authority to which this Act applies includes a reference to any members or officers of such an authority.

Sch 2 contains a long list of bodies which can be investigated by the Ombudsman; whenever a body needs to be removed from the list, or a new one added, this may only be effected by means of an Order in Council, pursuant to the power conferred by s 4(2). This, however, is a cumbersome process; the Public Administration Select Committee (HC448, *Ombudsman Issues* (2002–2003)), among others, strongly recommends that the legislation should adopt a generic definition of the types of bodies amenable to investigation by the Ombudsman, subject to specific exceptions. In a paper entitled *Review of the Public Sector Ombudsmen in England: A Consultation Paper* (London 2000) at [2.19]–[2.20], the Cabinet Office recognized that such an approach would 'remove the need for regular amendments to the legislation as new bodies are created and existing bodies dissolved' as well as making the 'whole jurisdiction issue more transparent'. It went on to note, however, that, 'In order for this to work . . . the legislation would need to be clear as to the types of public bodies which were within jurisdiction (subject to any specified exclusion). Some types of public body are easy to define generically — *eg* government departments and agencies, NHS Trusts and local authorities. But others are not.' Notwithstanding the perceived difficulties with the present system of defining the bodies subject to the Parliamentary Ombudsman's jurisdiction, other Ombudsmen systems in the UK — including the Scottish Public Services Ombudsman and the proposed Public Services Ombudsman for Wales — adopt the same model.

20.3 Matters Subject to Investigation

Section 5 of the 1967 Act makes provision concerning the matters which may be investigated by the Ombudsman.

Parliamentary Commissioner Act 1967

5—(1) Subject to the provisions of this section, the Commissioner may investigate any action taken by or on behalf of a government department or other authority to which this Act applies, being action taken in the exercise of administrative functions of that department or authority, in any case where —

    (a) a written complaint is duly made to a member of the House of Commons by a member of the public who claims to have sustained injustice in consequence of maladministration in connection with the action so taken; and

    (b) the complaint is referred to the Commissioner, with the consent of the person who made it, by a member of that House with a request to conduct an investigation thereon.

(2) Except as hereinafter provided, the Commissioner shall not conduct an investigation under this Act in respect of any of the following matters, that is to say —

    (a) any action in respect of which the person aggrieved has or had a right of appeal, reference or review to or before a tribunal constituted by or under any enactment or by virtue of Her Majesty's prerogative;

    (b) any action in respect of which the person aggrieved has or had a remedy by way of proceedings in any court of law:

Provided that the Commissioner may conduct an investigation notwithstanding that the person aggrieved has or had such a right or remedy if satisfied that in the particular circumstances it is not reasonable to expect him to resort or have resorted to it.

(3) Without prejudice to subsection (2) of this section, the Commissioner shall not conduct an investigation under this Act in respect of any such action or matter as is described in Schedule 3 to this Act.

(4) Her Majesty may by Order in Council amend the said Schedule 3 so as to exclude from the provisions of that Schedule such actions or matters as may be described in the Order; and any statutory instrument made by virtue of this subsection shall be subject to annulment in pursuance of a resolution of either House of Parliament.

(5) In determining whether to initiate, continue or discontinue an investigation under this Act, the Commissioner shall, subject to the foregoing provisions of this section, act in accordance with his own discretion; and any question whether a complaint is duly made under this Act shall be determined by the Commissioner . . .

These provisions raise a number of issues which require further consideration.

20.3.1 'Maladministration'

Section 5(1)(a) limits the Ombudsman's investigatory powers to claims of injustice sustained in consequence of 'maladministration', while s 12(3) provides that

nothing in this Act authorises or requires the Commissioner to question the merits of a decision taken without maladministration by a government department or other authority in the exercise of a discretion vested in that department or authority.

Taken together, these provisions appear to envisage a bright-line distinction between the administrative process (which is open to investigation by the Ombudsman) and the substance or merits of decisions and policies which are the fruit of that process (which may not be investigated). This is a familiar distinction which (see chs 1 and 9 above) has classically shaped the courts' supervisory jurisdiction; but we know from that context that the line between process and merits is difficult, if not impossible, to draw cleanly. How, therefore, should 'maladministration' be defined in the Ombudsman context?

    In the second reading debate on the Parliamentary Commissioner Bill, Richard Crossman MP suggested — advancing what has since come to be known as the 'Crossman catalogue' — that had maladministration been defined in the legislation, it would have included such matters as 'bias, neglect, inattention, delay, incompetence, inaptitude, perversity, turpitude, arbitrariness and so on'. Guidance to prospective complainants on the Parliamentary and Health Service Ombudsman web site indicates that the present Ombudsman also adopts a largely process-oriented definition of maladministration:

Generally, "maladministration" means poor administration or the wrong application of rules. Some examples include: avoidable delay; faulty procedures or failing to follow correct procedures; not telling you about any rights of appeal you have; unfairness, bias or prejudice; giving advice which is misleading or inadequate; refusing to answer reasonable questions; discourtesy, and failure to apologise properly for errors; mistakes in handling your claims; not offering an adequate remedy where one is due. [However,] the Ombudsman . . . cannot investigate [*inter alia*] complaints which are about government policy or the content of legislation. Policy is for the Government to determine; and legislation is for Parliament. The Ombudsman can question discretionary decisions only if there is evidence that there has been maladministration in the way they were taken.

Harlow (1978) 41 *MLR* 446 at 453 doubts the validity of this distinction between administrative process, on the one hand, and policy and merits, on the other, but recognizes that its roots are deep:

To investigate maladministration without questioning either the policies which underlie the administrator's actions or the legal framework of those actions effectively confines the investigation to questions of procedure. Yet there is in English political theory a well recognised, if furry, boundary between the executive (administrative) functions of government and the prerogative (policy making or political) powers. Responsibility for the second is thought to be vested in the Government, answerable through the doctrine of Ministerial Responsibility to Parliament. Government and Parliament alike watch suspiciously for trespass on political territory.

In fact, the Select Committee on the Parliamentary Commissioner for Administration (now superseded by the Public Administration Select Committee), in its *Second Report* of the 1967–1968 session at [14], suggested that if the Ombudsman 'finds a decision which, judged by its effect upon the aggrieved person, appears to him to be thoroughly bad in quality, he might infer from the quality of the decision itself that there had been an element of maladministration in the taking of it and ask for its review'. Although, as Marshall [1973] *PL* 32 at 36 notes, this approach potentially cleared the way for 'a deeper scrutiny of the considerations and arguments brought to bear on administrative decisions', it has not — as is apparent from the current Ombudsman's view of maladministration, considered above — radically shifted the focus from process towards substance.

Although the elasticity of the term 'maladministration' has afforded considerable latitude to successive Ombudsmen — something which, depending on one's perspective, may engender either welcome flexibility or off-putting uncertainty — it is not *infinitely* elastic, since it is ultimately open to the courts to set its limits via judicial review. This matter was considered in a series of cases — R v. *Parliamentary Commissioner for Administration, ex parte Balchin (No 1)* [1997] JPL 917, *(No 2)* (2000) 79 P & CR 157 and *(No 3)* [2002] EWHC 1876 (Admin) — concerning planning blight caused by a decision to build a new road near to the claimants' home. In the first case, Sedley J struck down the Ombudsman's report — which concluded that no maladministration had occurred — because he had failed to consider whether the Department of Transport (as it then was) ought to have drawn the relevant local authority's attention to new statutory powers which it could have exercised to acquire the claimants' property. A fresh report by a different Ombudsman — in which it was concluded that no maladministration had occurred because the Department had not overlooked the new statutory powers — was quashed by Dyson J in the second case. He concluded (at 168) that

the finding that the [Department] did not overlook s 246(2A) [of the Highways Act 1980 — the new statutory provision in question] was at the heart of the [Ombudsman's] conclusion that there was no maladministration. It was this finding that enabled him to conclude that the decision reached by the [Department] was "within the reasonable range of responses open to them given their knowledge" and "one they were entitled to take" . . . It is not possible to say what conclusion he would have reached on the issue of maladministration if he had found that those handling the Balchins' case had overlooked s 246(2A). I think that the Commissioner was unwittingly led into error by the rather unspecific evidence of the Permanent Secretary. It is possible that . . . there were persons in the [Department] handling the Balchins' case who had not overlooked s 264(2A). But if that is so, there is no trace of them in any of the material that has been placed before me.

Most recently, Harrison J (see [2002] EWHC 1876 (Admin) at [51]) quashed the Ombudsman's third report on this matter because internal inconsistencies meant that there had been a 'failure to give adequate reasons for his decision that there was no maladministration' during a particular phase of the process. The willingness disclosed by these cases to review the Ombudsmen's decisions about whether maladministration has occurred was defended by Dyson J in *Balchin (No 2)* (2000) 79 P & CR 157 at 169, who remarked that such review involves judicial scrutiny only of the Ombudsman's reasoning process, not the substance of his decision. Yet Giddings [2000] *PL* 201 at 203 perceives problems with this approach, characterizing it as

a further move towards setting a standard of reasoning on the record for the Ombudsman which could put at risk the essential informality and accessibility of the institution. If judges require the Ombudsman to meet the decision-making standards set for courts, then what was an informal, non-judicial mechanism for complaint-handling will become a formal, judicial one — with consequent costs in time and resources which are likely to deter some potential complainants from pursuing their case.

QUESTIONS

* Is Giddens right to be concerned about judicial review of the Ombudsman?
* Should courts be more hesitant, or is it their constitutional duty to ensure that the Ombudsman — like any other public body — faithfully applies the relevant legislation?

Finally, it should be noted that s 5(1)(a) of the Parliamentary Commissioner Act 1967 limits the Ombudsman's jurisdiction to situations in which 'injustice' has resulted from maladministration. Sedley J took a broad approach in *Balchin (No 1)* [1997] JPL 917 at 926, endorsing the view of De Smith, Woolf and Jowell, *Judicial Review of Administrative Action* (London 1999) at [1.102], quoting Richard Crossman MP, that the term should cover 'not merely injury redressible in a court of law, but also "the sense of outrage aroused by unfair or incompetent administration, even where the complainant has suffered no actual loss" ' — a definition which, Sedley J noted, means that 'the defence familiar in legal proceedings, that because the outcome would have been the same in any event there has been no redressible wrong, does not run in an investigation by the [Ombudsman]'.

20.3.2 Other Modes of Redress

Section 5(2) indicates that the Ombudsman will generally not entertain complaints in relation to matters that could be the subject of appeal to a tribunal or proceedings in a court. However, the Ombudsman has discretion in this area, and may investigate if satisfied that it would not be reasonable to expect the individual to pursue such forms of redress.

This discretion is exercised differently in relation to the two modes of redress. Where the complaint could be pursued by means of appeal to a tribunal, the Ombudsman rarely investigates (see Bradley [1980] *CLJ* 304 at 317). In contrast, the Ombudsman is generally willing to investigate complaints notwithstanding the possibility that they could be pursued by means of court proceedings (typically judicial review). The development of judicial review means that, as we explained above at 20.1.3, there is now greater overlap between the matters which can raised on review and those which constitute 'maladministration' and may therefore be investigated by the Ombudsman. However, as we saw, a number of barriers to access and procedural inhibitions apply to judicial review in contrast to the Ombudsman, in light of which it is unsurprising that the Ombudsman exercises his discretion generously in this context.

It should be noted, though, that the courts can review the exercise of this discretion. In *R* v. *Commissioner for Local Administration, ex parte Croydon London Borough Council* [1989] 1 All ER 1033 at 1044, a case concerning a Local Government Ombudsman, Woolf LJ (with whom Hutchison J agreed) concluded that s 26(6)(c) of the Local Government Act 1974 (which is in identical terms to s 5(2)(b) of the Parliamentary Commissioner Act 1967) is to be construed broadly, such that the Ombudsman's involvement is generally precluded in

a situation where if the complaint was justified the person concerned might be entitled to obtain some form of remedy in respect of the subject matter of the complaint if he had commenced proceedings within the appropriate time limits. The [Ombudsman] is not concerned to consider whether in fact the proceedings would succeed. He merely has to be satisfied that the court of law is an appropriate forum for investigating the subject matter of the complaint.

Woolf LJ felt that such an approach was necessary in order to ensure that the Ombudsman system did not permit the circumvention of the procedural safeguards inherent in the claim for judicial review (on which see above at 14.2). Having said this, Woolf LJ conceded (at 1045) that the Ombudsman 'retains his discretion whether to apply the proviso' — *ie* to decide that it would be unreasonable, in the circumstances, to expect the complainant to resort to judicial review — 'and unless he exercises this discretion unlawfully the courts will not and cannot interfere with his decision'.

20.3.3 Excluded Matters

Section 5(3) precludes investigation by the Ombudsman of any matter described in sch 3. Many of the matters set out in sch 3 are unsurprising — *eg* matters certified by a Minister to affect international relations; the commencement or conduct of civil or criminal proceedings; and the grant of honours. One excluded category, however, is the source of particular controversy. Paragraph 9 of sch 3 refers to:

Action taken in matters relating to contractual or other commercial transactions, whether within the United Kingdom or elsewhere, being transactions of a government department or authority to which this Act applies or of any such authority or body as is mentioned in paragraph (a) or (b) of subsection (1) of section 6 of this Act [see below at 20.4] and not being transactions for or relating to —

    (a) the acquisition of land compulsorily or in circumstances in which it could be acquired compulsorily;

    (b) the disposal as surplus of land acquired compulsorily or in such circumstances as aforesaid.

The exclusion of contractual and commercial matters is highly significant, not least because of the increasing use of contract as an instrument of government (see generally above at 1.5.3). Two particular concerns arise. The first is described by Clothier [1986] *PL* 204 at 210–211 in the following terms:

. . . [T]here are of course many hundreds of contractors providing goods and services to government departments. Some of these are quite small concerns and may have adapted their businesses to supplying goods or services to government over many years. If they are suddenly removed from a tendering list, or without explanation omitted from an invitation to tender, they may suffer considerable hardship. They may legitimately suspect the improper influence of a competing supplier but have no way of ventilating their grievance or allaying their suspicions . . . I think that the jurisdiction of the Parliamentary [Ombudsman] should be extended into this area . . .

The second concern, relating to the increasing use of private sector organizations in the delivery of public services, was outlined in the Cabinet Office Review at [5.9]:

An increasing concern is where the line should be drawn between the public and private sector. The ombudsmen have relied on the term "on behalf of" in their legislation to allow them to handle complaints about public services which have been contracted out. For example the [Parliamentary Commissioner Act 1967, s 5(1)] says "the Commissioner may investigate any action taken by or on behalf of a government department or other authority to which this Act applies, being action taken in the exercise of administrative functions of that department or authority". Concerns have been raised about how far "behalf" can be stretched as innovative arrangements such as partnerships, franchises and local authority companies have been introduced, involving the private and voluntary sectors . . . [T]his issue is not unique to the ombudsmen and we believe should not be considered in isolation from the broader debate about what accountability arrangements need to be put in place. It does seem to us that where a service is largely publicly funded, provides a service to the public and operates within a detailed specification by a public authority to a demanding performance requirement there seems a strong case for it to be within the ombudsmen's jurisdiction.

In its response to the Cabinet Office Review, the Public Administration Select Committee (HC612, *Review of the Public Sector Ombudsmen in England* (1999–2000) at [16]) did not comment specifically on the exclusion of commercial and contractual matters, but did argue that all limits on the Ombudsman's jurisdiction should be reviewed. Its predecessor, the Select Committee on the Parliamentary Commissioner for Administration, was more forthright in its *Fourth Report* of the 1979–80 session (HC593), strongly advocating that the restriction on commercial and contractual matters should be lifted — a view which is shared by commentators such as Giddings (in giving evidence to the Public Administration Select Committee (*loc cit*)) and Seneviratne (see *Ombudsmen: Public Services and Administrative Justice* (London 2002) at 106–109 and [2000] *PL* 582 at 582–589). Not all Ombudsman systems in the UK take the same line on this matter: for example, the Public Services Ombudsman (Wales) Bill (as it exists at the time of writing) contains no restriction equivalent to that set down by para 9 of sch 3 of the 1967 Act, while the Northern Ireland Commissioner for Complaints is able to investigate local government contracts.

QUESTIONS

- How should the debate about the extent of the jurisdiction of public sector Ombudsmen relate to that concerning the scope of the public law principles enforced by the courts and of the Human Rights Act (see ch 5 above)?
- Should the same approach be taken in all these contexts? Why (not)?

20.3.4 Discretion to Investigate

The Ombudsman is not obliged to investigate matters which are within her jurisdiction: s 5(1) says that she 'may' do so. Early cases seemed to suggest that this discretion was not subject to judicial review. For instance, it is reported that in *Re Fletcher's Application* [1970] 2 All ER 527n the Court of Appeal refused to issue a mandatory order to compel the Ombudsman to initiate an investigation, and that the House of Lords subsequently refused to grant leave to appeal 'on the ground that there was no jurisdiction to order the [Ombudsman] to investigate a complaint because s 5(1) of the Parliamentary Commissioner Act 1967 conferred on him a discretion whether to investigate or not'. It would be surprising, however, if the Ombudsman's s 5(1) discretion were considered wholly immune from judicial review, given that — as we saw in ch 8 above — 'unfettered discretion' is a concept alien to English administrative law.

In fact, it has since been established that the Ombudsman's discretion whether — and, if so, how — to investigate *is* subject to supervision by the courts, at least in principle. In *R* v. *Parliamentary Commissioner for Administration, ex parte Dyer* [1994] 1 WLR 621, the claimant sought judicial review of the Ombudsman's decision to investigate only certain aspects of her complaint, but it was contended on behalf of the Ombudsman that both the drafting of the 1967 Act and the Ombudsman's accountability to (what is now) the Public Administration Select Committee rendered judicial review inappropriate. Simon Brown LJ (with whom Buckley J agreed) said (at 625) that he would

unhesitatingly reject this argument. Many in government are answerable to Parliament and yet answerable also to the supervisory jurisdiction of this court. I see nothing about the Commissioner's role or the statutory framework within which he operates so singular as to take him wholly outside the purview of judicial review.

Nevertheless, Simon Brown LJ conceded (at 626) that successful judicial review of decisions whether and, if so, how to investigate would be rare:

The intended width of these discretions is made strikingly clear by the legislature: under section 5(5), when determining whether to initiate, continue or discontinue an investigation, the Commissioner shall "act in accordance with his own discretion;" under section 7(2), "the procedure for conducting an investigation shall be such as the Commissioner considers appropriate in the circumstances of the case." Bearing in mind too that the exercise of these particular discretions inevitably involves a high degree of subjective judgment, it follows that it will always be difficult to mount an effective challenge on what may be called the conventional ground of *Wednesbury* unreasonableness.

Applying this approach, it was found that the Ombudsman had not abused his discretion; in particular, Simon Brown LJ noted (at 628) that the fact that the investigation had not resolved all of the issues raised by the claimant was far from decisive, because 'no investigation should be expected to solve all problems for all time'.

20.4 The Conduct of Investigations

It is evident from the foregoing discussion that that the Ombudsman's investigations are inquisitorial in nature, and adopt an approach which is quite distinct from court proceedings. Moreover, the Ombudsman has considerable discretion in relation to the procedure she adopts, and is not necessarily bound by the usual principles of natural justice (see, *eg, R v. Parliamentary Commissioner for Administration, ex parte Dyer* [1994] 1 WLR 621, in which it was held that natural justice did not require the Ombudsman to show a copy of his draft report to the complainant, notwithstanding that the government department concerned *had* been shown the report). In this section, we focus on a number of specific issues concerning the undertaking of investigations by the Ombudsman, to which the following provisions, along with s 5 of the 1967 Act, set out above at 20.3, are relevant.

Parliamentary Commissioner Act 1967

6—(1) A complaint under this Act may be made by any individual, or by any body of persons whether incorporated or not, not being —
   (a) a local authority or other authority or body constituted for purposes of the public service or of local government or for the purposes of carrying on under national ownership any industry or undertaking or part of an industry or undertaking;
   (b) any other authority or body within subsection (1A) below.
  (1A) An authority or body is within this subsection if —
   (a) its members are appointed by —
     (i)   Her Majesty;
     (ii) any Minister of the Crown;
     (iii) any government department;
     (iv) the Scottish Ministers;
     (v)   the First Minister; or
     (vi) the Lord Advocate, or
   (b) its revenues consist wholly or mainly of —
     (i)   money provided by Parliament; or
     (ii) sums payable out of the Scottish Consolidated Fund (directly or indirectly).
  (2) Where the person by whom a complaint might have been made under the foregoing provisions of this Act has died or is for any reason unable to act for himself, the complaint may be made by his personal representative or by a member of his family or other individual suitable to represent him; but except as aforesaid a complaint shall not be entertained under this Act unless made by the person aggrieved himself.
  (3) A complaint shall not be entertained under this Act unless it is made to a member of the House of Commons not later than twelve months from the day on which the person aggrieved first had notice of the matters alleged in the complaint; but the Commissioner may conduct an

investigation pursuant to a complaint not made within that period if he considers that there are special circumstances which make it proper to do so.

(4) [Except as provided in subsection (5) below] a complaint shall not be entertained under this Act unless the person aggrieved is resident in the United Kingdom (or, if he is dead, was so resident at the time of his death) or the complaint relates to action taken in relation to him while he was present in the United Kingdom or on an installation in a designated area within the meaning of the Continental Shelf Act 1964 or on a ship registered in the United Kingdom or an aircraft so registered, or in relation to rights or obligations which accrued or arose in the United Kingdom or on such an installation, ship or aircraft.

(5) A complaint may be entertained under this Act in circumstances not falling within subsection (4) above where —

    (a) the complaint relates to action taken in any country or territory outside the United Kingdom by an officer (not being an honorary consular officer) in the exercise of a consular function on behalf of the Government of the United Kingdom; and

    (b) the person aggrieved is a citizen of the United Kingdom and Colonies who, under section 2 of the Immigration Act 1971, has the right of abode in the United Kingdom.

7—(1) Where the Commissioner proposes to conduct an investigation pursuant to a complaint under this Act, he shall afford to the principal officer of the department or authority concerned, and to any person who is alleged in the complaint to have taken or authorised the action complained of, an opportunity to comment on any allegations contained in the complaint.

(2) Every such investigation shall be conducted in private, but except as aforesaid the procedure for conducting an investigation shall be such as the Commissioner considers appropriate in the circumstances of the case; and without prejudice to the generality of the foregoing provision the Commissioner may obtain information from such persons and in such manner, and make such inquiries, as he thinks fit, and may determine whether any person may be represented, by counsel or solicitor or otherwise, in the investigation.

(3) The Commissioner may, if he thinks fit, pay to the person by whom the complaint was made and to any other person who attends or furnishes information for the purposes of an investigation under this Act —

    (a) sums in respect of expenses properly incurred by them;

    (b) allowances by way of compensation for the loss of their time,

in accordance with such scales and subject to such conditions as may be determined by the Treasury.

(4) The conduct of an investigation under this Act shall not affect any action taken by the department or authority concerned, or any power or duty of that department or authority to take further action with respect to any matters subject to the investigation; but where the person aggrieved has been removed from the United Kingdom under any Order in force under the Aliens Restriction Acts 1914 and 1919 or under the Commonwealth Immigrants Act 1962, he shall, if the Commissioner so directs, be permitted to re-enter and remain in the United Kingdom, subject to such conditions as the Secretary of State may direct, for the purposes of the investigation.

8—(1) For the purposes of an investigation under this Act the Commissioner may require any Minister, officer or member of the department or authority concerned or any other person who in his opinion is able to furnish information or produce documents relevant to the investigation to furnish any such information or produce any such document.

(2) For the purposes of any such investigation the Commissioner shall have the same powers as the Court in respect of the attendance and examination of witnesses (including the administration of oaths or affirmations and the examination of witnesses abroad) and in respect of the production of documents.

(3) No obligation to maintain secrecy or other restriction upon the disclosure of information obtained by or furnished to persons in Her Majesty's service, whether imposed by any enactment or by any rule of law, shall apply to the disclosure of information for the purposes of an investigation under this Act; and the Crown shall not be entitled in relation to any such investigation to any such privilege in respect of the production of documents or the giving of evidence as is allowed by law in legal proceedings.

(4) No person shall be required or authorised by virtue of this Act to furnish any information or answer any question relating to proceedings of the Cabinet or of any committee of the Cabinet or to produce so much of any document as relates to such proceedings; and for the purposes of this subsection a certificate issued by the Secretary of the Cabinet with the approval of the Prime Minister and certifying that any information, question, document or part of a document so relates shall be conclusive.

(5) Subject to subsection (3) of this section, no person shall be compelled for the purposes of an investigation under this Act to give any evidence or produce any document which he could not be compelled to give or produce in civil proceedings before the Court.

9—(1) If any person without lawful excuse obstructs the Commissioner or any officer of the Commissioner in the performance of his functions under this Act, or is guilty of any act or omission in relation to any investigation under this Act which, if that investigation were a proceeding in the Court, would constitute contempt of court, the Commissioner may certify the offence to the Court . . .

10—(1) In any case where the Commissioner conducts an investigation under this Act or decides not to conduct such an investigation, he shall send to the member of the House of Commons by whom the request for investigation was made (or if he is no longer a member of that House, to such member of that House as the Commissioner thinks appropriate) a report of the results of the investigation or, as the case may be, a statement of his reasons for not conducting an investigation.

(2) In any case where the Commissioner conducts an investigation under this Act, he shall also send a report of the results of the investigation to the principal officer of the department or authority concerned and to any other person who is alleged in the relevant complaint to have taken or authorised the action complained of.

(3) If, after conducting an investigation under this Act, it appears to the Commissioner that injustice has been caused to the person aggrieved in consequence of maladministration and that the injustice has not been, or will not be, remedied, he may, if he thinks fit, lay before each House of Parliament a special report upon the case.

(4) The Commissioner shall annually lay before each House of Parliament a general report on the performance of his functions under this Act and may from time to time lay before each House of Parliament such other reports with respect to those functions as he thinks fit.

(5) For the purposes of the law of defamation, any such publication as is hereinafter mentioned shall be absolutely privileged, that is to say —
   (a) the publication of any matter by the Commissioner in making a report to either House of Parliament for the purposes of this Act;
   (b) the publication of any matter by a member of the House of Commons in communicating with the Commissioner or his officers for those purposes or by the Commissioner or his officers in communicating with such a member for those purposes;
   (c) the publication by such a member to the person by whom a complaint was made under this Act of a report or statement sent to the member in respect of the complaint in pursuance of subsection (1) of this section;
   (d) the publication by the Commissioner to such a person as is mentioned in subsection (2) of this section of a report to that person in pursuance of that subsection.

11 . . .

(2) Information obtained by the Commissioner or his officers in the course of or for the purposes of an investigation under this Act shall not be disclosed except —

    (a) for the purposes of the investigation and of any report to be made thereon under this Act;

    (b) for the purposes of any proceedings for an offence under the Official Secrets Acts 1911 to 1989 alleged to have been committed in respect of information obtained by the Commissioner or any of his officers by virtue of this Act or for an offence of perjury alleged to have been committed in the course of an investigation under this Act or for the purposes of an inquiry with a view to the taking of such proceedings; or

    (c) for the purposes of any proceedings under section 9 of this Act;

and the Commissioner and his officers shall not be called upon to give evidence in any proceedings (other than such proceedings as aforesaid) of matters coming to his or their knowledge in the course of an investigation under this Act . . .

(3) A Minister of the Crown may give notice in writing to the Commissioner, with respect to any document or information specified in the notice, or any class of documents or information so specified, that in the opinion of the Minister the disclosure of that document or information, or of documents or information of that class, would be prejudicial to the safety of the State or otherwise contrary to the public interest; and where such a notice is given nothing in this Act shall be construed as authorising or requiring the Commissioner or any officer of the Commissioner to communicate to any person or for any purpose any document or information specified in the notice, or any document or information of a class so specified.

(4) The references in this section to a Minister of the Crown include references to the Commissioners of Customs and Excise and the Commissioners of Inland Revenue.

(5) Information obtained from the Information Commissioner by virtue of section 76(1) of the Freedom of Information Act 2000 shall be treated for the purposes of subsection (2) of this section as obtained for the purposes of an investigation under this Act and, in relation to such information, the reference in paragraph (a) of that subsection to the investigation shall have effect as a reference to any investigation.

20.4.1 Own-Initiative Investigations

It is clear from s 5(1) that the Parliamentary Ombudsman — like the other UK Ombudsmen — may not investigate on her own initiative, but only upon receiving a complaint. The Cabinet Office Review (at [6.13]–[6.15]) concluded that this state of affairs was satisfactory:

It has been suggested that the ombudsmen should be given powers to be able to investigate on his own initiative — many overseas ombudsmen are able to do this (though they rarely do) and the argument for it is that it would allow problems to be addressed where no individual has complained. An own-initiative investigation could be a quicker way to tackle a perceived problem. The ombudsmen tell us that they do not feel encumbered by any lack of powers and have generally been able to investigate on the basis of a complaint where they had any concerns. They would be concerned that own-initiative investigations would alter significantly their dealings with bodies under jurisdiction. However, the ombudsmen would value an extension of their powers to allow investigation of maladministration at the request of a public authority under their jurisdiction. We believe that any power for the ombudsmen to initiate an investigation without a complaint will make them vulnerable to external pressure to examine alleged systemic weaknesses. An ombudsman's function must remain grounded in addressing injustice caused to an individual and own-initiative investigation appears inconsistent with impartiality. The landscape is crowded with bodies with regulatory and inspection bodies and keeping a clear focus on what the ombudsmen is there to do is essential if clarity is to prevail.

It is unclear why own-initiative investigations would be 'inconsistent with impartiality' since, under the present system, Ombudsmen do not mechanically investigate all complaints, instead exercising discretion in this area. Indeed, many commentators do not share the conclusion reached by the Cabinet Office Review: a number of expert observers who gave evidence to the Public Administration Select Committee considered the possibility of own-initiative investigations may well be beneficial — a view endorsed by the Committee (see HC612, *Review of the Public Sector Ombudsmen in England* (1999–2000) at [11]), along with commentators such as Harlow (1978) 41 *MLR* 446 at 453 and Seneviratne, *Ombudsmen: Public Services and Administrative Justice* (London 2002) at 125–127. It is important to remember, however, that the appropriateness of own-initiative investigations is keyed in to foundational issues about the role of Ombudsmen (see above at 20.1.2): the absence of such investigations in the UK reflects the prevailing view which emphasizes 'redress' over 'control'.

20.4.2 The MP Filter

Section 5(1) of the 1967 Act provides that the Parliamentary Ombudsman may only investigate complaints which reach him via an MP (an MP's refusal to refer to the Ombudsman apparently being immune from judicial review: *R (Murray)* v. *Parliamentary Commissioner for Administration* [2002] EWCA Civ 1472 at [17]). This is in contrast to most other countries (France being an important exception), where direct access to Ombudsmen is the norm, and to some other Ombudsmen systems in the UK: for example, members of the public can complain directly to the Health Service Ombudsman, the Scottish Public Services Ombudsman, and now — following the removal in 1988 of a requirement to route complaints via councillors — the Local Government Ombudsman; the proposed Public Services Ombudsman for Wales would also be able to receive complaints directly from the public. In fact, the 'MP filter' was originally envisaged by the Justice report which recommended the creation of an Ombudsman (*The Citizen and the Administration* (London 1961) at [157]) as a temporary measure. So why does it still exist?

On a *pragmatic* level, it is argued by some — including many MPs, as the empirical work of Drewry and Harlow (1990) 53 *MLR* 745 at 759–760 demonstrates — that the Ombudsman would be inundated without the filter; as Harlow (1978) 41 *MLR* 446 at 451 puts it, the filter 'allows the MP to settle the trivial administrative muddles', sending only the 'hard nuts' on to the Ombudsman. However, the argument that MPs are effective gatekeepers is undermined by the facts that many MPs (51 per cent, according to the Cabinet Office Review at [3.45]) automatically refer complaints to the Ombudsman when requested to do so, and that (according to the Ombudsman's *Annual Report 2003–04* (HC702, 2003–04)) of the 1,877 complaints dealt with by the Ombudsman in the year 2003–04, 43 per cent were either clearly outside jurisdiction or were found, on the basis of the papers alone, to be otherwise unsuitable for investigation (*eg* because there was no evidence of maladministration or no added value likely to be achieved for the complainant). It may be, however, that the MP filter does shield the Ombudsman in a very crude way by deterring many individuals from pursuing complaints (see further Gwyn (1982) *Pub Admin* 177 at 184–186).

On a *constitutional* level, it is sometimes argued that the MP filter is fitting because it renders the Ombudsman an adjunct of the parliamentary process, thereby reflecting the received wisdom that it is MPs who bear primary responsibility for holding the executive to account and resolving constituents' grievances against public bodies. Although such thinking was undoubtedly instrumental in the initial inclusion of the filter in the 1967 Act, it has been subjected to sustained criticism ever since — most notably by Justice (see *Our Fettered Ombudsman* (London 1977) at 16–19 and (with the All Souls Committee) *Administrative Justice: Some Necessary Reforms* (London 1988) at 88–89), and recently by the Ombudsman herself who, in evidence submitted to the Public Administration Select Committee, stated that 'in the 21st Century it really is not defensible for citizens not to have direct access to a public sector ombudsman' (HC41-i, *Minutes of Evidence* (2003–2004)). More recently, she has said that she will 'continue to press for legislative change' so as to facilitate direct access (HC702, *Annual Report 2003–2004* (2003–2004) at 4). Observing that the 'situation has . . . moved on' since the adoption of the filter, the Cabinet Office Review (at [3.43] and [3.51]) concluded that:

Modernisation of government and constitutional change have brought many means by which the citizen with a grievance can seek redress. New attitudes to customer service, organisational complaints systems including independent complaints examiners, increased use of judicial review, the Human Rights Act, Freedom of Information legislation and not least the creation of other ombudsmen, the [Health Service Ombudsman] and [the Local Government Ombudsman] — all of these provide or will provide means for an aggrieved citizen to seek redress from public authorities. The MP filter has become inconsistent and anachronistic when set in this wider context.

. . . [However, it is said that] [t]he MP filter is . . . an instrument of accountability. An individual MP is able to hold the executive to account through the [Parliamentary Ombudsman's] process — a department is required to respond to a statement of complaint and the report at the end of an investigation is provided to an MP who may wish to take action using it. We agree that in a serious case — where there is serious injustice to an individual or widespread injustice, serious maladministration, refusal by a department to remedy a clear injustice and so on — it is right that this it is publicised and steps taken to ensure redress is provided and any systemic problems addressed. The absence of the MP filter does not prevent the MP being involved . . . in lodging a complaint nor, with the agreement of the complainant, becoming involved after a complaint has been made. For example, if a decision to conduct an investigation is made the [Parliamentary Ombudsman] could, with the agreement of the complainant, contact the relevant MP. Accountability can also be maintained through general oversight and reporting mechanisms to meet concerns of individual MPs about what is happening in their constituencies.

The Public Affairs Select Committee (HC448, *Ombudsman Issues* (2002–2003) at [12]) noted that it had 'received no evidence in favour of retention of the filter other than from MPs themselves' — the Cabinet Office Review, at [3.38], found, in 1999, that 52 per cent of MPs surveyed favoured the retention of the filter, while 44 per cent preferred direct access — and recommended its abolition. The Committee added the caveat, however, that this was likely to place an increased burden on the Ombudsman, and agreed with the submission of Giddings, who had given evidence to the Committee, that the Cabinet Office Review's assumption (at [3.54]) that removing the filter would have few or no resource implications was 'optimistic, not to say naïve'. Interestingly, however, while the possibility of removing the MP filter has excited considerable debate ever since the Ombudsman was established, the present incumbent — although, as we saw above, critical of the filter — told the Select Committee (HC506-i, *Minutes of Evidence* (2002–2003) at [65]) that it is a 'minor problem' in comparison to 'the big issue, which is the constraints [in the present system] on joint working [of ombudsmen]' — an issue we examine below at 20.5.

20.4.3 Co-operation with the Ombudsman

Section 8 of the 1967 Act confers upon the Ombudsman wide-ranging powers to extract information from Ministers and officials and, as s 9 indicates, failure to co-operate with the Ombudsman may ultimately be referred to a court and dealt with as if it were contempt of court. In spite of these powers, the Ombudsman has recently encountered a less than co-operative attitude in certain quarters of government. Relations between the Ombudsman and government reached a nadir in summer 2003, when she reported (HC951, *Access to Official Information* (2002–2003)) that, in relation to investigations under the Code of Practice on Access to Government Information, she had

experienced a number of difficulties . . .; in particular a lack of knowledge among Departments about the Code and how to deal with requests made under it, unacceptable delays in responding to my Office and, in some cases, a lack of co-operation with my investigations.

Although the Information Code has now been superseded by the Freedom of Information Act 2000, and the Ombudsman's functions in this area transferred to the Information Commissioner, these difficulties are clearly of much wider significance to the Ombudsman's ability to discharge her responsibilities — a point which she underlined herself by remarking (*ibid*) that she would 'need to consider' whether she could 'properly continue' with her work if government co-operation did not improve. Following the issue of a Memorandum of Understanding, jointly with the Cabinet Office, the Ombudsman found some improvement in departmental co-operation with her over access to information, but recently noted that government obstruction in some cases continued 'to make it extremely difficult for me to carry out my responsibilities' (HC701, *Access to Official Information: Investigations Completed July 2003–June 2004* (2003–2004) at 1).

A high-profile example of lack of co-operation with the Ombudsman is provided by the long-running attempt by *The Guardian* to obtain information relating to occasions on which Ministers had reported to their respective Permanent Secretaries potential conflicts of interest under the Ministerial Code of Conduct (see HC951, *Access to Official Information* (2002–2003), investigation A16/03). Of the 17 departments contacted by *The Guardian*, 15 refused to disclose the information, citing exemptions 2 and 12 (respectively concerning internal discussion and advice, and individual privacy) of the Information Code. More than a year after the Ombudsman began to investigate the matter, the Secretary of State for Constitutional Affairs and the Minister for the Cabinet Office issued a notice under s 11(3) of the 1967 Act — a step which had never before been taken — to the effect that disclosure of the information in question would be contrary to the public interest. Although a s 11(3) notice (cf certificates under s 8(4) (set out above) concerning Cabinet proceedings) does not prohibit the Ombudsman from seeing the information in question, it prevents her from releasing it. Since the essence of the *Guardian*'s complaint was that the information should be publicly available, the s 11(3) notice precluded the Ombudsman from meaningfully taking the investigation further, as a result of which it was dropped. However, in March 2004, days before the decision to issue the s 11(3) notice was due to be judicially reviewed, the notice was withdrawn, thereby allowing the Ombudsman to resume her investigation.

20.4.4 Securing Redress

It is apparent from s 10 of the 1967 Act that the Ombudsman cannot *enforce* her recommendations *per se*: she reports and, if she finds injustice occasioned by maladministration, can recommend redress; she may, as we saw above, secure agreement from the public body concerned to make structural changes in order to obviate recurrences of the problem in question, and she may lay special reports before Parliament where it seems that injustice is unlikely to be remedied. Moreover, the Public Administration Select Committee takes an interest in the extent to which the Ombudsman's recommendations are followed, and can apply pressure — by reporting to Parliament — when they are not. Exchanges between the Ombudsman and the Committee (see, *eg*, HC506-i, *Minutes of Evidence* (2003–2004)) disclose a close working relationship, and indicate a desire on the part of the latter to support the former's work. Thus 'enforcement' of the Ombudsman's recommendations is possible, but only by indirect means. Some commentators have taken the view that these means are sufficient. For instance, Clothier [1986] *PL* 204 at 210 writes that:

Parliament wisely provided . . . that the powers of enforcement should lie with them. The threat of a report to both Houses of Parliament in a case of unremedied injustice is as good an enforcing power as any reasonable Ombudsman could wish for. In my six years of office, I was never finally denied the remedy I asked for, although occasionally I had to press a little to get it.

However, there have been occasions on which the Ombudsman's recommendations have not been fully implemented. One such (see HC951, *Access to Official Information: Investigations Completed November 2002–June 2003* (2002–2003) at 1–9) relates to a request made to a number of government departments for disclosure of information about gifts received by Ministers since 1 January 1998. Almost 16 months after the request was made, guidance was issued to all departments to the effect that the information should not be disclosed because it fell within exemption 12, which related to personal information, of the (now defunct) Information Code. The Ombudsman, having concluded that exemption 12 clearly did not apply, recommended that the information be released. Although the Cabinet Office undertook to release certain information relating to gifts received since June 2001, it refused to implement the recommendation that the requested information — relating to gifts received since 1 January 1998 — should be released. In her report (*ibid* at 9), the Ombudsman said that she was 'concerned and disappointed that the Cabinet Office feel unable to agree to my recommendation in its entirety and have refused to amend their guidance to [government departments] accordingly'.

QUESTIONS

- Should the Ombudsman's recommendations be enforceable by a court of law?
- What difficulties may arise if this course were adopted?

20.5 Problems and Reform

20.5.1 The Ombudsmen's Concerns

The Local Government, Parliamentary, and Health Service Ombudsmen presented a paper (see Cabinet Office Review, Annex A at [1]) to Ministers in October 1998 calling for a 'comprehensive review of the organisation of the public sector Ombudsmen in England'. The paper drew particular attention to two problems. First, it was noted (at [11]–[13]) that complaints 'do not necessarily relate only to the actions of a body within one ombudsman's jurisdiction'. This problem is exacerbated by 'joined-up government': the Ombudsmen noted that 'partnerships are being forged between, for example, NHS bodies and local authorities so as to achieve better assessment of the client's needs and the delivery of services to meet them' — a development which is 'welcome', but with which 'the present jurisdictions of the English Ombudsmen do not sit easily'. As a result, prospective complainants 'find it difficult to know to which Ombudsman to complain'. Secondly, it was observed (at [14]–[16]) that public understanding and awareness of the public sector Ombudsmen is poor: information provided by the separate Ombudsmen is 'fragmented' — there is not 'only "one door" to knock on', nor are the relevant forms, literature and so on common to all of the Ombudsmen. At the same time, the Ombudsmen's jurisdiction is defined by reference to such words as 'maladministration' and 'injustice' which 'are not well understood by the public'. Added to these problems are the long-running issues of delay (see below at 20.5.3) and the MP filter (see above at 20.4.2), as well as more novel problems raised by devolution (see below at 20.5.2).

20.5.2 Institutional Reform

The Ombudsmen's paper prompted the Cabinet Office Review (some aspects of which we have already referred to). The Review took seriously the Ombudsmen's concerns about their relationship with one another and with other complaints-handlers, and the difficulties posed by complaints relating to matters which cut across different Ombudsmen's jurisdictions. Indeed, the Review noted (at [2.31]) that these difficulties are thrown into especially sharp relief by problems which arise *because* of an issue's inter-agency dimension (*eg* poor communication between two bodies, each of which is subject to an investigation by a different Ombudsman), concluding (at [2.34]) that 'the present fragmented structure of public sector Ombudsmen and complaints systems [is not] able to meet the challenge of handling complaints which cross boundaries'. Taking up a suggestion made by the Ombudsmen themselves (see Cabinet Office Review, Annex A at [23]), the Review concluded (at [4.3]–[4.4]) that:

The present Commission for Local Administration provides a possible model for a future organisation. Each of the three Commissioners are Local Government Ombudsmen and have their own caseloads based on where in the England the complaint has arisen. One is Chairman and Chief Executive and is responsible for corporate functions but has no appellate role — he is not "Chief

Ombudsman". We propose that a collegiate structure, a "new Commission", could be based on a similar concept with a Chairman, possibly bearing the title Parliamentary Ombudsman, responsible for corporate matters but not with powers to overrule his fellow ombudsmen on individual cases.

At present, the ombudsmen are defined by function — central government, health service and local government — and each is confined in his or her jurisdiction to that particular function. This will be too rigid in future. All ombudsmen should be able to cover the complete jurisdiction, any functional divides being purely an administrative arrangement in the same way as areas of the country are at present with the CLA. Structural arrangements within the new organisation will need to allow for new partnerships cutting across functions but we envisage that a functional focus will predominate. This would provide advantages by maintaining expertise and engagement with the various areas of government. We see advantages in retaining specific Local Government and Health Service Ombudsman roles to underpin this focus but neither they nor their colleagues should be confined by law to particular areas of the jurisdiction. By building in this flexibility from the start we believe that the new Commission could be easily reshaped to accommodate changing government structures and it would allow other functional allocations to be made (eg an Education Ombudsman) if appropriate.

The Public Administration Select Committee was (HC162, *Review of Public Sector Ombudsmen in England* (1999–2000) at [7]), and remains (HC448, *Ombudsman Issues* (2002–2003) at [6]), strongly supportive of these recommendations, and the government indicated, by way of a written parliamentary answer (HC Deb, 20 July 2001, cols 464–465), that it would bring forward legislation to implement the Review's main recommendations. The current Parliamentary Ombudsman, however, has reservations. In a memorandum to the Select Committee (published as an annex to HC506-i, *Minutes of Evidence* (2002–2003)), she argued (at [7]–[8]) that

it is now time to shift the focus away from the creation of a single institution in "England" . . . Merging the offices of the Parliamentary [Ombudsman], the Health Service [Ombudsman] for England and the Commission for Local Administration in England, as the [Cabinet Office] Review proposed, would not, in itself, provide a comprehensive or adequate mechanism to achieve a joined-up, modern Ombudsman service. That is because my jurisdiction as [Parliamentary Ombudsman] is a United Kingdom jurisdiction. Merging the office of [Parliamentary Ombudsman] with the English Health Service and Local Government Ombudsmen does not address the fact that [the Parliamentary Ombudsman] still has a role to play in the resolution of complaints from citizens from Wales, Scotland and Northern Ireland, especially about social security, immigration or tax matters. They must still come to me as [Parliamentary Ombudsman] via a Westminster MP with such complaints. While merger might create a more seamless service for citizens in England, such reform cannot be seen as an end in itself and it would complicate the handling of complaints from those not living in England about matters not devolved to Cardiff, Belfast or Edinburgh.

The Parliamentary Ombudsman has since indicated (in evidence to the Select Committee: see HC41-i, *Minutes of Evidence* (2003–2004)) that she has 'not gone cold on the idea of the College of Ombudsmen' which the Cabinet Office Review proposed: indeed, pending possible reform, she and the Local Government Ombudsmen are already 'working together to ensure that cases which involve the jurisdiction of more than one Ombudsman are identified at the outset and investigated and reported on in a co-ordinated way' (see *ibid*, Ombudsman's memorandum at [18]). Nevertheless, she is concerned that fundamental legislative reform must be more thoroughgoing than that which the Cabinet Office Review proposed, in order that the issues caused by devolution may be adequately addressed. In the meantime, the Parliamentary and Local Government Ombudsmen are (according to a memorandum, dated 26 November 2004, submitted by the former to the Public Administration Select Committee) pressing for a regulatory reform order (on which see above at 17.3.6) to lift some of the existing restrictions on joint working.

Although reform is taking some time in relation to English and UK-wide matters, greater progress has been made elsewhere, the preferred solution being a single Ombudsman. For instance, as noted above at 20.1.1, there is now a unified Scottish Public Services Ombudsman. Although, at the time of writing, there are still four separate public sector Ombudsmen in Wales, it is now possible, following amendment of the relevant Acts of Parliament by means of delegated legislation (SI 2004/2359, The Regulatory Reform (Local Commissioner for Wales) Order 2004), for the same person to hold all four offices. Meanwhile, the Public Services Ombudsman (Wales) Bill, before Parliament at the time of writing, envisages more radical reform through the creation of a single Public Services Ombudsman for Wales. Interestingly, the Bill envisages the possibility of joint investigations by that Ombudsman and certain other Ombudsmen where the matter in question cuts across their respective jurisdictions. Given this recognition of the desirability of joint working (where appropriate), it seems likely that, in due course, other legislation will be amended to make joint investigations more widely possible.

20.5.3 Throughput

The timescale within which investigations by the Parliamentary Ombudsman are completed has, for some time, been a matter of concern. The issue was examined in detail in 1999 by the Public Administration Select Committee (HC136, *First Report* (1998–1999)) — by which time the average length of an investigation had reached 100 weeks — and by the Cabinet Office Review, which (at [2.8]) characterized 'the very long throughput times of cases investigated' as the 'principal criticism' which could be levelled at the Ombudsman.

Once a statutory investigation is launched by the issue of a statement of complaint, relevant government departments have a right under s 7(1) of the 1967 Act to respond to the allegations made by the complainant, and it appears that long throughput times are attributable in substantial part to delays in eliciting such responses — an issue to which attention is regularly drawn in the Ombudsman's annual reports (see, *eg*, HC847, *Annual Report* (2002–2003) at [1.4]). Recent years, however, have witnessed an improvement in average throughput times: although falling short of the Select Committee's target of six months (*op cit* at [9]), the figure of 41 weeks in 2002–2003 for cases in which a statutory statement of complaint was issued (see HC847, *Annual Report* (2002–2003) at [2.10]) disclosed substantial progress in this sphere. This figure had risen to 48 weeks in 2003–2004 (see HC702, *Annual Report* (2003–2004) at 33), but must be contextualised by reference to the fact that (as may be deduced from the following table) only the most complex cases are now the subject of a statutory investigation.

Cases Concluded by the Parliamentary Ombudsman, 1993 to 2003–04

	1993	1994	1995	1996	1997–98	1998–99	1999–2000	2000–01	2001–02	2002–03	2003–04
(1) Clearly outside jurisdiction	138	168	149	159	134	125	139	99	109	91	72
(2) Concluded on the papers	577	702	1077	1254	1431	916	1018	777	812	1011	738
(3A) Enquiry, positive outcome					110	90	121	313	344	425	421
(3B) Enquiry, no positive outcome								252	437	470	498
(4) Investigation but no statutory report	3	9	3	6	4	3	10	99	91	102	64
(5) Statutory report issued	208	226	245	260	376	372	313	247	195	136	84
Total cases concluded	926	1105	1474	1679	2055	1506	1601	1787	1988	2235	1877

In April 2000, new working practices were introduced and greater emphasis was placed on resolving complaints without recourse to the full statutory investigation and report procedure, where appropriate. Thus, in 2003–04, 919 cases were concluded simply by making enquiries of the department concerned; in a further 64 cases, statutory investigations were initiated but not completed (because an appropriate outcome was secured or no remedy was available). As a result, only 84 (4.5 per cent) of the 1877 concluded cases resulted in a statutory report — a sharp reduction from the 1993 figure of 22.5 per cent. The present Ombudsman, giving evidence to the Public Administration Select Committee (HC506-i, *Minutes of Evidence* (2002–2003) at [70]), commented that these changes were prompted by recognition that there was a need for 'a more diverse product range, and that the serious, heavyweight, statutory investigation should not be the core product'.

QUESTIONS

- Is this change in practice a good thing?
- How does it relate to the 'control' and 'redress' models considered above at 20.1.2?

20.6 Concluding Remarks

The role played by Ombudsmen in the modern administrative state is crucial, but altering radically. Changes in the way that public services are delivered, the growth of internal complaints-handling mechanisms, and devolution all require the role of public sector

Ombudsmen to be fundamentally re-thought. That process was begun by the Cabinet Office Review, but many issues remain to be considered. Perhaps most fundamentally, the Review gave little consideration to a question we raised towards the beginning of this chapter: are Ombudsmen principally complaints-handlers, or is their main function the improvement of administrative standards? For Thompson (2001) 64 *MLR* 459 at 465, who favours an Ombudsmen system capable not just of dispute resolution, but also of 'learning from mistakes, research and dissemination of good practice', the Review's failure to address this foundational matter is a significant one. It is also criticized by Seneviratne [2000] *PL* 582 at 591, who argues that sensible reform of the system will be possible only by relating the role of Ombudsmen to other aspects of public law, 'with the relative strengths and weaknesses of ombudsmen, courts, tribunals and other institutions being assessed'. Nevertheless, whatever its failings, the Review has at least stimulated debate about the type of Ombudsmen system which is appropriate almost 40 years on from the creation of the Parliamentary Ombudsman, underlining the need for reform in view of the radical changes which have occurred during that period.

Reform cannot come soon enough for the Public Administration Select Committee. Lamenting the government's failure to introduce legislation, the Committee (HC448, *Ombudsman Issues* (2002–2003)) recently highlighted a number of 'worrying trends' — including lack of departmental co-operation with the Ombudsman and increasing evidence of 'routine administrative failure', which was attributed to pressure on departments' running costs — which make reform, and the creation of a strong and effective Ombudsmen system fit for the 21st century, all the more urgent.

FURTHER RESOURCES

Cabinet Office, *Review of the Public Sector Ombudsmen in England: A Consultation Paper* (London 2000) *www.cabinetoffice.gov.uk/propriety_and_ethics/publications/pdf/consultation.pdf*

Cm 6243, *Transforming Public Services: Complaints, Redress and Tribunals* (2004), ch 4 *www.dca.gov.uk/pubs/adminjust/adminjust.htm*

Collcutt and Hourihan, *Review of the Public Sector Ombudsmen in England: A Report by the Cabinet Office* (London 2000) *www.cabinetoffice.gov.uk/propriety_and_ethics/publications/pdf/ombudsmenreview.pdf*

Seneviratne, *Ombudsmen: Public Services and Administrative Justice* (London 2002)

Web site of the British and Irish Ombudsman Association *www.bioa.org.uk*

Web site concerning the Charter Mark scheme *www.chartermark.gov.uk*

Web site of the Local Government Ombudsmen *www.lgo.org.uk*

Web site of the Northern Ireland Ombudsman *www.ni-ombudsman.org.uk*

Web site of the Parliamentary and Health Service Ombudsman *www.ombudsman.org.uk*

Web site of the Public Administration Select Committee *www.parliament.uk/parliamentary_committees/public_administration_select_committee.cfm*

Web site of the Scottish Public Services Ombudsman *www.scottishombudsman.org.uk*

APPENDIX

The House of Lords' decision in *A* v. *Secretary of State for the Home Department* [2004] UKHL 56 [2005] 2 WLR 87 was handed down after the relevant parts of the manuscript of this book had been submitted to the publisher. It has, however, been possible to add this appendix, outlining the decision and its relevance to matters discussed elsewhere in the book.

Background

Following the terrorist attacks in the United States on 11 September 2001, the United Kingdom Parliament enacted the Anti-terrorism, Crime and Security Act 2001 ('ATCSA'), a wide-ranging piece of legislation covering matters as diverse as terrorist property, nuclear and aviation security, and police powers. The legislation, enacted in just one month, attracted widespread criticism: Tomkins [2002] *PL* 205 at 207, for example, argues that parts of it 'seem to have very little to do with September 11', while others, 'which do seem to be closely connected, . . . contain unusually coercive powers'.

Detention without trial

It is certain provisions (now repealed) that were contained in Part IV of the Act which are of present interest. Section 21(1) empowered the Secretary of State to issue a certificate in respect of any person whose presence in the UK he reasonably believed to be a risk to national security, and whom he reasonably suspected of being a terrorist. Section 21 went on to provide that a 'terrorist', for these purposes, was a person who 'is or has been concerned in the commission, preparation or instigation of acts of international terrorism', 'is a member of or belongs to an international terrorist group' or 'has links' with a group that is 'subject to the control or influence of persons outside the United Kingdom' and which the Secretary of State 'suspects . . . is concerned in the commission, preparation or instigation of acts of international terrorism'. 'Terrorism', meanwhile, was broadly defined, as in s 1 of the Terrorism Act 2000. Although the ATCSA was not, on its face, restricted in such terms, Ministers conceded that the certification power could be exercised only in relation to those thought to be connected with Al-Qaeda.

The result of ss 22 and 23 was that grave implications attached to certification. Under s 22, it was possible to resolve to deport an individual in respect of whom a certificate had been issued — a 'suspected international terrorist' — notwithstanding that deportation could not actually occur, either for practical reasons or because it would have been inconsistent with the UK's international obligations. Of particular relevance here is the fact that deportation is contrary to Article 3 ECHR if torture or inhuman or degrading treatment is likely to occur as a result: *Chahal* v. *UK* (1996) 23 EHRR 413. Crucially, s 23 provided that suspected international terrorists who could not be deported could instead be detained under certain immigration powers — applicable only to foreign nationals — even if there was no prospect of deportation. The label 'internment' may fairly be applied to persons detained under these provisions, since incarceration was possible in the absence of their being charged with — let alone tried for or convicted of — any criminal offence. Although it was possible for such detainees voluntarily to leave the UK, this was largely (but not, as we will see below, entirely) academic; as Lord Nicholls put it in *A* (at [81]):

> Their prison, it is said, has only three walls. But their freedom [to leave the UK] is more theoretical than real. This is demonstrated by the continuing presence in [HMP] Belmarsh of most of those detained. They prefer to stay in prison rather than face the prospect of ill treatment in any country willing to admit them.

Although, by s 21(8), decisions to issue s 21 certificates could not be judicially reviewed, s 25 allowed appeals against such decisions to the Special Immigration Appeals Commission ('SIAC'), a judicial body established under the Special Immigration Appeals Commission Act 1997. SIAC could cancel a certificate if it considered that there were no reasonable grounds justifying the Secretary of State's suspicion that the individual concerned was an international terrorist or his belief that the individual's presence in the UK posed a risk to national security. SIAC upheld only one such appeal, in the case of *M* v. *Secretary of State for the Home Department* (8 March 2004) (upheld by the Court of Appeal: [2004] EWCA Civ 324 [2004] 2 All ER 863). Periodic reviews of the operation of the detention provisions, required by s 28, were carried out by Lord Carlile. In January 2004 he found himself 'entirely satisfied that the criteria [for certification] were met [in respect of all the detainees], and would have been very surprised if certification had not taken place' (a conclusion with which, as we have seen, SIAC did not agree in relation to 'M'); he found himself similarly satisfied that the criteria were met in relation to those detained when he reported in February 2005. In addition, a comprehensive review of the ATCSA was carried out by a committee of Privy Councillors (as required by s 122); the committee reported in December 2003 (HC100, *Anti-terrorism, Crime and Security Act 2001 Review: Report* (2003–2004)), strongly condemning (*inter alia*) the Part IV detention provisions. Those provisions had to be renewed annually by an order issued under s 29(2) and approved by Parliament, although they have now (as explained below) been repealed.

....

The ECHR

Part IV of the ATCSA was clearly incompatible with Article 5 ECHR, which provides that '[e]veryone has the right to liberty and security of person' and that '[n]o one shall be deprived of his liberty' save in certain defined situations. According to Article 5(1)(f), one of those situations is 'the lawful arrest or detention of a person . . . against whom action is being taken with a view to deportation', but individuals detained under Part IV of the ATCSA did not fall into this category, given that they could not be deported. The UK therefore sought to derogate from the ECHR, as is provided for by Article 15(1):

> In time of war or other public emergency threatening the life of the nation any High Contracting Party may take measures derogating from its obligations under this Convention to the extent strictly required by the exigencies of the situation, provided such measures are not inconsistent with its other obligations under international law.

Whether these criteria for derogation were met was central to the *A* case. The question was one which their Lordships could address for the following reason. Section 1(2) of the Human Rights Act 1998 provides that the 'Convention rights' — that is, certain of the rights laid down in the ECHR, including Article 5 — are to 'have effect for the purposes of this Act' subject to (*inter alia*) 'any designated derogation'. Section 14(1) goes on to explain that 'designated derogation' means (*inter alia*) 'any derogation by the United Kingdom from an Article of the Convention, or of any protocol to the Convention, which is designated for the purposes of this Act in an order made by the Secretary of State'. As well as notifying the Secretary General of the Council of Europe of the derogating measures — ie Part IV of the ATCSA — and the reasons for them, the Secretary of State, in purported exercise of his power under s 14(1), made the Human Rights Act 1998 (Designated Derogation) Order 2001 (SI 2001/3644). However, as Baroness Hale explained in *A* at [225] (although cf Lord Scott at [151]–[152]):

Such an order would not be within his powers if it provided for a derogation which was not allowed by the Convention. Section 30(2) and (5) of the [ATCSA] allow the detainees to challenge this derogation from their article 5(1) rights in proceedings before SIAC and in an appeal from SIAC's decision. Thus it is that we have power to consider the validity of the Derogation Order made by the Secretary of State and to quash it if it is invalid.

If the derogation order was quashed, this would render Article 5(1) an operative 'Convention right' for present purposes, and the undoubted incompatibility with that right of the detention regime would allow their Lordships to issue a declaration of incompatibility under s 4 HRA in respect of Part IV of the ATCSA. Therefore, a central question in the case was the validity (which fell to be tested by reference to Article 15 ECHR) of the derogation order, since the quashing of that secondary legislation was a condition precedent to the issuing of a declaration that Part IV was incompatible with Article 5.

In addition, in view of the fact that Part IV could apply only to foreign nationals, it was argued that it was incompatible with Article 14 ECHR, which provides that:

The enjoyment of the rights and freedoms set forth in this Convention shall be secured without discrimination on any ground such as sex, race, colour, language, religion, political or other opinion, national or social origin, association with a national minority, property, birth or other status.

Article 14 was an operative 'Convention right' irrespective of the validity of the derogation order, since there had been no attempt to derogate from it, and the question, on this point, was simply whether Part IV was incompatible with Article 14.

....

Was there a 'public emergency threatening the life of the nation'?

By a majority, the House of Lords (like the Court of Appeal: [2002] EWCA Civ 1502 [2004] QB 335) did not disturb the conclusion of SIAC — reached on the basis of both 'open' (publicly available) material and 'closed' material containing sensitive information — that the view that there was a 'public emergency threatening the life of the nation' was justified on the evidence.

In considering how this question should be addressed, Lord Bingham placed considerable weight on the ECtHR decision in *Lawless* v. *Ireland (No 3)* (1961) 1 EHRR 15 — a case concerned with what Lord Bingham (at [17]) called 'very low-level IRA terrorist activity in Ireland and Northern Ireland between 1954 and 1957' — and on decisions such as *Ireland* v. *United Kingdom* (1978) 2 EHRR 25 and *Brannigan and McBride* v. *United Kingdom* (1993) 17 EHRR 539 in which the ECtHR emphasised that states should be accorded a 'wide margin of appreciation' in this context. He concluded (at [28]):

If . . . it was open to the Irish Government in *Lawless* to conclude that there was a public emergency threatening the life of the Irish nation, the British Government could scarcely be faulted for reaching that conclusion in the much more dangerous situation which arose after 11 September.

As well as relying on the empirical fact of the ECtHR's deferential attitude in this area, Lord Bingham (at [29]) considered such deference to be normatively desirable:

. . . I would accept that great weight should be given to the Home Secretary, his colleagues and Parliament on this question, because they were called on to exercise a pre-eminently political judgment. It involved making a factual prediction of what various people around the world might or might not do, and when (if at all) they might do it, and what the consequences might be if they did. Any prediction about the future behaviour of human beings (as opposed to the phases of the moon or high water at London Bridge) is necessarily problematical. Reasonable and informed minds may differ, and a judgment is not shown to be wrong or unreasonable because that which is thought likely to happen does not happen. It would have been irresponsible not to err, if at all, on the side of safety. As will become apparent, I do not accept the full breadth of the Attorney General's argument on what is generally called the deference owed by the courts to the political authorities. It is perhaps preferable to approach this question as one of demarcation of functions or what Liberty in its written case called "relative institutional competence". The more purely political (in a broad or narrow sense) a question is, the more appropriate it will be for political resolution and the less likely it is to be an appropriate matter for judicial decision. The smaller, therefore, will be the potential role of the court. It is the function of political and not judicial bodies to resolve political questions. Conversely, the greater the legal content of any issue, the greater the potential role of the court, because under our constitution and subject to the sovereign power of Parliament it is the function of the courts and not of political bodies to resolve legal questions. The present question seems to me to be very much at the political end of the spectrum: see *Secretary of State for the Home Department v Rehman* [2001] UKHL 47, [2003] 1 AC 153, para 62, per Lord Hoffmann.

Seven of the other eight judges were prepared to accept that there was a 'public emergency', some more enthusiastically than others. Like Lord Bingham, Baroness Hale drew a fairly sharp distinction between the matter presently under consideration (whether there was a 'public emergency') and the other question raised by Article 15 (whether the measures adopted were 'strictly required by the exigencies of the situation'). She was clear (at [226]) that, 'If a Government were to declare a public emergency where patently there was no such thing, it would be the duty of the court to say so.' The present situation, however, was different:

The attacks launched on the United States on [11 September 2001] were clearly intended to threaten the life of that nation. SIAC were satisfied that the open and closed material before them justified the conclusion that there was also a public emergency threatening the life of this nation. I, for one, would not feel qualified or even inclined to disagree.

However, not all of the judges were willing to concede the 'public emergency' point quite this readily, or to conceive of the courts' role in such narrow terms (at least on these facts). Lord Scott, for instance, accepted (at [154]) that there was a 'public emergency' only with great reluctance — and even then, only after some notably trenchant criticism of the government's recent record:

The Secretary of State is unfortunate in the timing of the judicial examination in these proceedings of the 'public emergency' that he postulates. It is certainly true that the judiciary must in general defer to the executive's assessment of what constitutes a threat to national security or to 'the life of the nation'. But judicial memories are no shorter than those of the public and the public have not forgotten the faulty intelligence assessments on the basis of which United Kingdom forces were sent to take part, and are still taking part, in the hostilities in Iraq. For my part I do not doubt that there is a terrorist threat to this country and I do not doubt that great vigilance is necessary, not only on the part of the security forces but also on the part of individual members of the public, to guard against terrorist attacks. But I do have very great doubt whether the 'public emergency' is one that justifies the description of 'threatening the life of the nation'. Nonetheless, I would, for my part, be prepared to allow the Secretary of State the benefit of the doubt on this point and accept that the threshold criterion of article 15 is satisfied.

Meanwhile, Lord Hope (at [107]) accepted that 'the executive and the legislature are to be accorded a wide margin of discretion in matters relating to national security', but said that 'the width of the margin depends on the context' and that 'any interference with the right to liberty must be accorded the fullest and most anxious scrutiny'. Consequently, while conceding (at [116]) that 'the questions whether there is an emergency and whether it threatens the life of the nation are pre-eminently for the executive and for Parliament', he considered that judges should nevertheless subject to 'very close analysis' the government's contentions as to the nature of any emergency, and the measures necessary to deal with it. Thus, while Lord Hope accepted (at [119]) that a 'public emergency' existed, it was 'constituted by the threat that [terrorist] attacks will be carried out' *in the future*; although that was sufficient to amount to a 'current state of emergency', it was an emergency 'on a different level . . . from that which would undoubtedly ensue if the threats were ever to materialise'. This analysis of the 'emergency' point fed directly into Lord Hope's approach to the question whether detention without trial was 'strictly necessary' since, as his Lordship put it (at [116]), 'One cannot say what the exigencies of the situation require without having clearly in mind what it is that constitutes the emergency.'

Lord Hoffmann was alone in concluding that there was no 'public emergency' in the Article 15 sense. Only three years earlier in *Secretary of State for the Home Department* v. *Rehman* [2001] UKHL 47 [2003] 1 AC 153 at [62], Lord Hoffmann had opined that the events of 11 September 2001 were

a reminder that in matters of national security, the cost of failure can be high. This seems to me to underline the need for the judicial arm of government to respect the decisions of ministers of the Crown on the question of whether support for terrorist activities in a foreign country constitutes a threat to national security. It is not only that the executive has access to special information and expertise in these matters. It is also that such decisions, with serious potential results for the community, require a legitimacy which can be conferred only by entrusting them to persons responsible to the community through the democratic process. If the people are to accept the consequences of such decisions, they must be made by persons whom the people have elected and whom they can remove.

His approach was strikingly different in *A*. Lord Hoffmann started from the premise (at [86]) that detention without trial is 'antithetical to the instincts and traditions of the people of the United Kingdom'. Unlike Lord Bingham, Lord Hoffmann (at [92]) thought the wide margin of appreciation extended by the ECtHR in cases like *Lawless* irrelevant: sitting as a *national* court, the House of Lords' task was to 'decide the matter for ourselves'. His Lordship considered (at [91]) that the 'nation', in Article 15, is to be regarded as 'a social organism', such that the 'life of the nation is not coterminous with the lives of its people'. Noting, by way of recent example, that the 'Spanish people have not said that what happened in Madrid, hideous crime as it was, threatened the life of their nation', Lord Hoffmann concluded (at [96]) that, 'Terrorist violence, serious as it is, does not threaten our institutions of government or our existence as a civil community.' Instead, he said (at [97]):

The real threat to the life of the nation, in the sense of a people living in accordance with its traditional laws and political values, comes not from terrorism but from laws such as these. That is the true measure of what terrorism may achieve. It is for Parliament to decide whether to give the terrorists such a victory.

Were the measures 'strictly required by the exigencies of the situation'?

Although, as we have seen, some judges, such as Lord Bingham and Baroness Hale, were willing to temper with a good measure of deference their consideration of the executive's conclusions as to the existence of a 'public emergency', the proportionality question (*ie* whether the measures were 'strictly required') was approached quite differently. For example, Lord Bingham, responding to the Attorney-General's submission that judges should be slow to question Parliament's preferred approach in this sphere, agreed (at [39]) that 'any decision made by a representative democratic body must of course command respect', but said that 'the degree of respect will be conditioned by the nature of the decision'. It followed, said Lord Bingham (at [42]), that:

The Attorney General is fully entitled to insist on the proper limits of judicial authority, but he is wrong to stigmatise judicial decision-making as in some way undemocratic. It is particularly inappropriate in a case such as the present in which Parliament has expressly legislated in section 6 of the [HRA] to render unlawful any act of a public authority, including a court, incompatible with a Convention right, has required courts (in section 2) to take account of relevant Strasbourg jurisprudence, has (in section 3) required courts, so far as possible, to give effect to Convention rights and has conferred [via s 30 of the ATCSA] a right of appeal on derogation issues. The effect is not, of course, to override the sovereign legislative authority of the Queen in Parliament, since if primary legislation is declared to be incompatible the validity of the legislation is unaffected (section 4(6)) and the remedy lies with the appropriate minister (section 10), who is answerable to Parliament. The 1998 Act gives the courts a very specific, wholly democratic, mandate.

One of the most striking features of the majority's approach to the proportionality question was its unwillingness to concede a high degree of deference merely because of the national security context. Thus, Lord Nicholls observed (at [81]) that:

The subject matter of the legislation is the needs of national security. This subject matter dictates that, in the ordinary course, substantial latitude should be accorded to the legislature. But the human right in question, the right to individual liberty, is one of the most fundamental of human rights.

Similarly, Lord Rodger (at [176]) considered that, 'Due deference does not mean abasement before [the] views [of the government and Parliament], even in matters relating to national security.' Against this background, of the eight judges who had to consider whether the measures adopted in Part IV of the ATCSA were 'strictly required' (Lord Hoffmann, in light of his conclusion on the 'public emergency' question, did not need — and preferred not — to consider this issue), all but one (Lord Walker) considered that they were not. Three aspects of their Lordships' reasoning should be noted.

First, and perhaps most significantly, the detention regime, as we have seen, applied only to foreign nationals. This proved fatal to the scheme's compatibility with the ECHR. All of the majority judges who addressed the proportionality question were in agreement on this point. It is, in fact, a strikingly simple one, and was expressed succinctly by Baroness Hale who, having noted the absence of any power to detain British nationals, observed (at [231]) that:

The conclusion has to be that it is not necessary to lock up the nationals. Other ways must have been found to contain the threat which they present. And if it is not necessary to lock up the nationals it cannot be necessary to lock up the foreigners. It is not strictly required by the exigencies of the situation.

Secondly, as explained above, it was, at least theoretically, possible for those detained under Part IV to leave the UK voluntarily (although, as Lord Nicholls noted (see above), this was rarely a realistic, let alone attractive option, for the detainees). One of the detainees, however, who was able to go to France, did so. Lord Bingham (at [33]) observed that

allowing a suspected international terrorist to leave our shores and depart to another country, perhaps a country as close as France, there to pursue his criminal designs, is hard to reconcile with a belief in his capacity to inflict serious injury to the people and interests of this country.

Similarly, Baroness Hale (at [230]) pointed out that

the very fact that it is a prison with only three walls also casts doubt upon whether it is 'strictly required by the exigencies of the situation'. What sense does it make to consider a person such a threat to the life of the nation that he must be locked up without trial, but allow him to leave, as has happened, for France where he was released almost immediately?

Thirdly, doubt was also cast on whether the detention regime was 'strictly required' by the failure of the government to 'show that monitoring arrangements or movement restrictions less severe than incarceration in prison would not suffice' (*per* Lord Scott at [155]). As Lord Bingham put it (at [35]), when SIAC granted bail to detainee 'G' (see *G* v. *Secretary of State for the Home Department* (20 May 2004)), it did so

on condition (among other things) that he wear an electronic monitoring tag at all times; that he remain at his premises at all times; that he telephone a named security company five times each day at specified times; that he permit the company to install monitoring equipment at his premises; that he limit entry to his premises to his family, his solicitor, his medical attendants and other approved persons; that he make no contact with any other person; that he have on his premises no computer equipment, mobile telephone or other electronic communications device; that he cancel the existing telephone link to his premises; and that he install a dedicated telephone link permitting contact only with the security company. The appellants suggested that conditions of this kind, strictly enforced, would effectively inhibit terrorist activity. It is hard to see why this would not be so.

As noted above, Lord Walker was the sole dissentient. Unlike the majority, his Lordship considered (at [209]) that deference should play a major role not only in relation to the 'public emergency' question, but also at the proportionality stage of the analysis:

When this country is faced, as it is, with imminent threats from enemies who make use of secrecy, deception and surprise, the need for anti-terrorist measures to be 'strictly necessary' must be interpreted in accordance with the precautionary principle recognised by the Strasbourg Court in *Ireland v United Kingdom*.

Adopting this approach, Lord Walker was satisfied (as the Court of Appeal had been) that Part IV was 'strictly required'.

Article 14 ECHR

There had, as explained above, been no attempt to derogate from Article 14. Although not a freestanding equality clause, Article 14 prohibits discrimination on various grounds — including nationality: see, *eg, Gaygusuz* v. *Austria* (1997) 23 EHRR 364 — in relation to the enjoyment of the other rights set out in the Convention. The argument in *A* was that the Part IV regime's restriction of foreign but not British nationals' Article 5 rights breached Article 14. This argument met with success before SIAC, but not in the Court of Appeal. We have already seen that, in the House of Lords, the differential treatment of foreigners and nationals was felt, by the majority, fundamentally to undermine the assertion that detention of the former was 'strictly required' for the purposes of Article 15. The majority was also of the view that Article 14 itself was violated by Part IV.

The central issue was whether any difference in treatment between those in the position of the detainees and the relevant 'comparator' group could be objectively justified. The choice of comparator was therefore essential, as Lord Bingham (at [52]) explained:

The Attorney General submitted that the position of the appellants should be compared with that of non-UK nationals who represented a threat to the security of the UK but who could be removed to their own or to safe third countries. The relevant difference between them and the appellants was that the appellants could not be removed. A difference of treatment of the two groups was accordingly justified and it was reasonable and necessary to detain the appellants. By contrast, the appellants' chosen comparators were suspected international terrorists who were UK nationals. The appellants pointed out that they shared with this group the important characteristics (a) of being suspected international terrorists and (b) of being irremovable from the United Kingdom. Since these were the relevant characteristics for purposes of the comparison, it was unlawfully discriminatory to detain non-UK nationals while leaving UK nationals at large.

It was the appellants' view which prevailed in the House of Lords, since, as Lord Bingham put it (at [54]), 'The comparison contended for by the Attorney General might be reasonable and justified in an immigration context, but cannot in my opinion be so in a security context, since the threat presented by suspected international terrorists did not depend on their nationality or immigration status.' Once this question as to the comparator had been resolved, Lord Bingham (like the other judges in the majority) was led to the conclusion (at [68]) that, 'What cannot be justified here is the decision to detain one group of suspected international terrorists, defined by nationality or immigration status, and not another. To do so was a violation of Article 14.'

Concluding remarks

The House of Lords' decision in *A* is highly significant on at least two levels. First, although, as Lord Scott observed (at [142]), 'It has not been suggested, nor could it be suggested, that the [ATCSA] is otherwise than an effective enactment made by a sovereign legislature,' the declaration of incompatibility issued by their Lordships has not been without impact. While Lord Scott was right that the 'import of such a declaration is political not legal', its political implications have been considerable. As a result of the decision in *A*, the detention without trial provisions in the ATCSA have been repealed. Amid notable controversy, Parliament enacted the Prevention of Terrorism Act 2005 which provides for a range of controls to be imposed on suspected (British and foreign) terrorists.

Secondly, and of particular relevance to administrative law, *A* represents a break with tradition in relation to national security cases, and, as a result, constitutes an important milestone in the development of human rights review and the associated doctrine of 'deference'. As the remarks of Lord Hoffmann in *Rehman*, cited above, indicate, judicial review of decisions concerning national security matters has traditionally been reticent, to say the least. What is striking about *A* is their Lordships' willingness to adopt a nuanced approach to deference, the national security context notwithstanding. In particular, the majority's adoption of a deferential attitude to the 'public emergency' question but a more interventionist approach at the proportionality stage indicates clear judicial recognition at the highest level that cases are not, so far as deference is concerned, monolithic. This, in turn, reflects the sort of arguments advanced by writers such as Jowell and Hunt (see above at 9.3.6), who urged the courts to recognise that the level of deference should be set not at a uniform level for a *case*, but at a level appropriate to each of the *issues* arising in the case.

Against this background, it is unsurprising that, while most of their Lordships considered themselves ill-equipped to subject to rigorous scrutiny the government's view that there was a 'public emergency', bearing in mind that this view depended on, *inter alia*, the interpretation of intelligence material and the making of predictions on the basis thereof, they did not find themselves under an equivalent inhibition when it came to determining whether the measures adopted were 'strictly required'. Their Lordships were well equipped to recognise the flaws in the Part IV scheme, and to recognise that the 'prison with three walls' argument and the non-detention of British nationals seriously undermined the government's contention that detention of certain foreign nationals was 'strictly required'. These, the two most important strands in their Lordships' reasoning, allowed them to arrive at their conclusion that Part IV did not pass muster under Article 15 by recourse to what amounted essentially to logical analysis. In this situation, the established reasons for deference to the judgment of the political branches — such as institutional competence and democratic concerns — did not bite with any decisive force: the House did not need to evaluate any finely balanced 'pros' and 'cons' since, as Lord Hope (at [132]) recognised, the differential treatment of nationals and non-nationals rendered the scheme so flawed as to make it 'irrational'.

In light of this, their Lordships did not need to examine closely what is often the central question in a proportionality analysis — *viz* whether the objective could have been achieved by means less restrictive of the right in question. For example, while Lord Bingham (see above) thought it was 'hard to see' why less restrictive measures, such as close monitoring, would not 'effectively inhibit terrorist activity', he (like the other judges) did not need to come to a firm view on this point. Yet, in many senses, it is this question which, if asked by the court, engages the doctrine of deference — or at least the concerns underlying it — most directly, since it is here that the 'merits' of the case become hardest to avoid. To what extent are judges qualified to decide on what constitutes the 'least restrictive' method by which to reduce (or minimise: which of these it should be is itself a policy question) the risk posed by terrorism? Although it is not suggested that politicians are somehow uniquely able to answer questions such as this, it is undeniable that they raise policy-laden issues of risk–benefit assessment which courts are not necessarily well placed to determine. It is for precisely this reason that the courts have developed the notion of deference, recognising that it is sometimes inappropriate for judges to decide for themselves what constitutes the least restrictive — and only lawful — response to a problem, instead leaving open to the decision-maker a (confined) range of tolerably proportionate responses. (For recent clear judicial discussion of this point, see *R (Clays Lane Housing Co-operative Ltd)* v. *The Housing Corporation* [2004]

INDEX